Behavior in Organizations

Understanding and Managing the Human Side of Work

Eighth Edition

■ **JERALD GREENBERG**
The Ohio State University

■ **ROBERT A. BARON**
Rensselaer Polytechnic Institute

Prentice Hall

Pearson Education International

Editor-in-Chief: Jeff Shelstad
Senior Managing Editor (Editorial): Jennifer Glennon
Assistant Editor: Jessica Sabloff
Editorial Assistant: Kelly Wendrychowicz
Media Project Manager: Michele Faranda
Senior Marketing Manager: Shannon Moore
Marketing Assistant: Christine Genneken
Managing Editor (Production): Judy Leale
Production Editor: Virginia Somma
Production Assistant: Joe DeProspero
Permissions Supervisor: Suzanne Grappi
Associate Director, Manufacturing: Vincent Scelta
Production Manager: Arnold Vila
Design Manager: Maria Lange
Art Director: Kevin Kall
Interior Design: Karen Quigley
Cover Design: Karen Quigley
Cover Illustration: Artville
Illustrator (Interior): Rainbow Graphics
Manager, Print Production: Christy Mahon
Composition: Rainbow Graphics
Full-Service Project Management: Linda Begley/Rainbow Graphics
Printer/Binder: Quebecor Taunton

Credits and acknowledgments borrowed from other sources and reproduced, with permission, in this textbook appear on pages 637–660, 673.

Pearson Education LTD.
Pearson Education Australia PTY, Limited
Pearson Education Singapore, Pte. Ltd
Pearson Education North Asia Ltd
Pearson Education, Canada, Ltd
Pearson Educación de Mexico, S.A. de C.V.
Pearson Education–Japan
Pearson Education Malaysia, Pte. Ltd
Pearson Education Upper Saddle River, New Jersey

10 9 8 7 6 5 4 3 2
ISBN 0-13-111592-8

Beha... ...ations

Understand... ...Side of Work

To Pepper, Scooter, Sparky, Roach, Gourmet—and of course,
the Best Giraffe in the whole Serengeti.
J.G.

To Rebecca, who has truly brought sunshine into my life.
R.A.B.

PART I: INTRODUCTION TO ORGANIZATIONAL BEHAVIOR 1
1. The Field of Organizational Behavior 1

PART II: BASIC HUMAN PROCESSES 37
2. Perception and Learning: Understanding and Adapting to the Work Environment 37
3. Individual Differences: Personality and Abilities 79
4. Emotions and Stress on the Job 113

PART III: THE INDIVIDUAL IN THE ORGANIZATION 145
5. Work-Related Attitudes: Feelings About Jobs, Organizations, and People 145
6. Motivation in Organizations 188
7. Career Dynamics 227

PART IV: GROUP DYNAMICS 271
8. Group Processes and Work Teams 271
9. Communication in Organizations 316
10. Decision Making in Organizations 357
11. Interpersonal Behavior: Working with and Against Others 403

PART V: INFLUENCING OTHERS 436
12. Influence, Power, and Politics in Organizations 436
13. Leadership in Organizations 469
14. Organizational Culture, Creativity, and Innovation 513

PART VI: ORGANIZATIONAL PROCESSES 547
15. Organizational Structure and Design 547
16. Managing Organizational Change: Strategic Planning and Organizational Development 586

APPENDIX
I. Theory and Research: Tools for Learning About Behavior in Organizations 623

Notes 637
Glossary 661
Photo Credits 673
Company Index 675
Name Index 679
Subject Index 681

Preface xxi
Acknowledgments xxvii

PART I: INTRODUCTION TO ORGANIZATIONAL BEHAVIOR 1

Chapter 1: The Field of Organizational Behavior 1

■ **PREVIEW CASE: PHARMACIA: WHERE PEOPLE ARE THE PRESCRIPTION FOR SUCCESS 1**

Organizational Behavior: Its Basic Nature 3
What Is the Field of Organizational Behavior All About? 4 ■ Why Is It Important to Know About OB? 6

What Are the Field's Fundamental Assumptions? 8
OB Recognizes the Dynamic Nature of Organizations 8 ■ OB Assumes There Is No "One Best" Approach 9

OB Then and Now: A Capsule History 9
The Early Days: Scientific Management and the Hawthorne Studies 9 ■ Classical Organizational Theory 10 ■ Late Twentieth Century: Organizational Behavior as a Social Science 12 ■ OB Today: The Infotech Age 12

OB Responds to the Rise of Globalization and Diversity 13
International Business and the Global Economy 13 ■ The Shifting Demographics of the Workforce: Trends Toward Diversity 17

OB Responds to Advances in Technology 19
Leaner Organizations: Downsizing and Outsourcing 20 ■ The Virtual Corporation: A Network of Temporary Organizations 22 ■ Telecommuting: Going to Work Without Leaving Home 22

OB Responds to People's Changing Expectations 23
In Search of Flexibility: Responding to Needs of Employees 23 ■ The Quality Revolution 27 ■ Corporate Social Responsibility: The (Sometimes) Ethical Organization 28

Summary and Review of Learning Objectives 31
Points to Ponder 32
Developing OB Skills 33
Case in Point: There's No Business Like Shoyu Business 35

■ *Special Sections*
OB IN A DIVERSE WORLD: Iceland Unplugged—and Thriving 14
BEST PRACTICES: Employee Support Policies 18

OB IN AN E-WORLD: *Making Telecommuting Work* 24
HOW TO DO IT: *Conducting an Ethics Audit* 30

PART II: BASIC HUMAN PROCESSES 37

Chapter 2: Perception and Learning: Understanding and Adapting to the Work Environment 37

■ PREVIEW CASE: PREPARING SALES REPS FOR THE "REAL WHIRLED" 37

Social Perception and Social Identity: Understanding Others and Ourselves 38
Social Perception: What Are Others Like? 39 ■ Social Identity Theory:
Who Are You? 40

The Attribution Process: Judging the Causes of Others' Behavior 41
Making Correspondent Inferences: Using Acts to Judge Dispositions 41 ■ Causal
Attribution of Responsibility: Answering the Question "Why?" 42

The Imperfect Nature of Social Perception 43
Stereotypes: Fitting Others into Categories 44 ■ Perceptual Biases: Systematic Errors
in Perceiving Others 46 ■ Self-Fulfilling Prophecies: The Pygmalion Effect and the
Golem Effect 48

Perceiving Others: Organizational Applications 50
Performance Appraisal: Formal Judgments About Job Performance 50 ■ Impression
Management in the Employment Interview: Looking Good to Prospective Employers
52 ■ Corporate Image: Impression Management by Organizations 53

Learning: Adapting to the World Around Us 55
Operant Conditioning: Learning Through Rewards and Punishments 56 ■
Observational Learning: Learning by Imitating Others 59

Applications of Learning in Organizations 60
Training: Learning and Developing Job Skills 61 ■ Innovative Reward Systems: Going
Beyond Merit Pay 64 ■ Organizational Behavior Management: Positively Reinforcing
Desirable Organizational Behaviors 66 ■ Discipline: Eliminating Undesirable
Organizational Behaviors 67 ■ Knowledge Management: Sharing What Is Known 70

Summary and Review of Learning Objectives 72
Points to Ponder 74
Developing OB Skills 75
Case in Point: Finding a Safe Way to Smile at Safeway 77

■ *Special Sections*
HOW TO DO IT: *Overcoming Bias in Social Perception 49*
OB IN A DIVERSE WORLD: *Performance Evaluations: Comparing the United States
and Japan 52*
OB IN AN E-WORLD: *E-Training: Booming—But Beware 64*
BEST PRACTICES: *Using 360-Degree Feedback: Three Profiles 68*

Chapter 3: Individual Differences: Personality and Abilities 79

■ PREVIEW CASE: THE LIFE OF THE PARTY? 79

Personality: What It Is and How It Is Measured 81
Defining Personality 81 ■ The Role of Personality in Organizational Behavior 81 ■
How Do We Measure Personality? 83

Key Work-Related Aspects of Personality 85
The Big Five Dimensions of Personality: Our Most Fundamental Traits 85 ■ Positive and Negative Affectivity: Tendencies Toward Feeling Good or Bad 87 ■ Two Aspects of the Self: Self-Efficacy and Self-Monitoring 88

Additional Work-Related Aspects of Personality 92
Machiavellianism: Using Others to Get Ahead 92 ■ The Type A Behavior Pattern: Being in a Hurry—and Irritable—Can Be Costly to Your Health 94 ■ Achievement Motivation: The Quest for Excellence 95 ■ Morning Persons and Evening Persons: "Oh, How I Hate to Get Up in the . . ." 98

Abilities: Having What It Takes 100
Intellectual Abilities: Various Forms of Intelligence 100 ■ Physical Abilities 105

Summary and Review of Learning Objectives 106
Points to Ponder 107
Developing OB Skills 109
Case in Point: Nancy's Quiche: Where People Skills Really Matter 111

■ *Special Sections*
BEST PRACTICES: Increasing Self-Efficacy Among Employees 90
OB IN A DIVERSE WORLD: Achievement Motivation and Economic Growth 98
HOW TO DO IT: Coping with the "Graveyard Shift" 99
OB IN AN E-WORLD: Are Face-to-Face Meetings Obsolete? For Some Purposes and Some People, the Answer is "Yes" 102

Chapter 4: Emotions and Stress on the Job 113

■ PREVIEW CASE: SEPH BARNARD: AN ENTREPRENEUR "TIRED AND TRUE" 113

Emotions and Mood in Organizations 114
The Basic Nature of Emotions 115 ■ The Basic Nature of Mood 116 ■ Emotions, Mood, and Job Performance 117

Managing Emotions in Organizations 118
Emotional Dissonance and Emotional Labor 118 ■ Organizational Compassion: Managing Emotion in Times of Trauma 119

Stress in Organizations 121
What Is Stress? 121 ■ Causes of Stress in the Workplace 122 ■ Major Effects of Organizational Stress 128

Reducing Stress: What Can Be Done? 131
Organizational Resources for Managing Stress 131 ■ How Can You Manage Your Own Stress? 132 ■ Putting It All Together: Three Major Approaches to Reducing Stress 136

Summary and Review of Learning Objectives 138
Points to Ponder 139
Developing OB Skills 140
Case in Point: Parenthood and Dot-Coms: A Recipe for Stress 142

Video Case: Stress 144

■ *Special Sections*
OB IN AN E-WORLD: Using "Emoticons" to Express Emotions in E-Mail: Do Those Smiley Faces Make Any Difference? 116
HOW TO DO IT: Coping with the Emotional Fallout of Terrorism: How Can Companies Help? 120
OB IN A DIVERSE WORLD: Who's More Stressed Out: Men or Women? 132
BEST PRACTICES: Fighting the Battle Against Stress 134

Chapter 5: Work-Related Attitudes: Feelings About Jobs, Organizations, and People 145

■ PREVIEW CASE: "ISLAM 101": BASIC TRAINING AT FORD AFTER SEPTEMBER 11 145

Attitudes: What Are They? 147
Three Essential Components of Attitudes 147 ■ Basic Definitions 148

Job Satisfaction: Attitudes Toward One's Job 148
Are People Generally Satisfied with Their Jobs? 148 ■ Measuring Job Satisfaction: Assessing Reactions to Work 151 ■ Theories of Job Satisfaction 153

Consequences of Job Dissatisfaction 156
Absenteeism 156 ■ Turnover 156 ■ Task Performance: Are Happy Workers Productive Workers? 158 ■ Guidelines for Promoting Job Satisfaction 159

Organizational Commitment: Feelings of Attachment Toward Organizations 160
Varieties of Organizational Commitment 161 ■ Why Strive for a Committed Workforce? 163 ■ Approaches to Developing Organizational Commitment 164

Prejudice: Negative Attitudes Toward Others 168
Prejudice Versus Discrimination: A Key Distinction 168 ■ The Reality of Diversity and the Problems of Prejudice 169

Everyone Can Be a Victim of Prejudice 169
Prejudice Based on Age 170 ■ Prejudice Based on Physical Condition 170 ■ Prejudice Against Women 171 ■ Prejudice Based on Sexual Orientation 172 ■ Prejudice Based on Race and National Origin 173 ■ Prejudice Based on Religion 173

Managing a Diverse Workforce: Current Practices 175
Do Companies Care About Diversity? 175 ■ What Are Today's Companies Doing About Diversity? 175 ■ Varieties of Diversity Management Programs 177 ■ Diversity Management Is Generally Effective 180

> *Summary and Review of Learning Objectives 181*
> *Points to Ponder 183*
> *Developing OB Skills 184*
> *Case in Point: Texaco Yesterday Versus Today: Now, Only the Oil Is Crude 186*

> ■ *Special Sections*
> *OB IN A DIVERSE WORLD: Absenteeism: Same Behavior, Different Meaning in Different Countries 164*
> *OB IN AN E-WORLD: Gripe Sites: Where Dissatisfied Workers Go to Cyber-Vent and Good Managers Go to Learn 166*
> *BEST PRACTICES: The Very Best at Diversity: Pacific Enterprises 178*
> *HOW TO DO IT: Avoiding Pitfalls in Diversity Management 180*

Chapter 6: Motivation in Organizations 188

■ PREVIEW CASE: PAULA LAWLOR: NOT YOUR ORDINARY CEO 188

Motivation in Organizations: Its Basic Nature 190
Components of Motivation 190 ■ Three Key Points About Motivation 191

Motivating by Meeting Needs 192
Maslow's Need Hierarchy Theory 192 ■ Alderfer's ERG Theory 194 ■ Managerial Applications of Need Theories 195

Motivating by Setting Goals 196

Goal-Setting Theory 196 ■ Managers' Guidelines for Setting Effective Performance
Goals 197

Motivating by Being Fair: Organizational Justice 200
Distributive Justice: Equity Theory 201 ■ Procedural Justice: Making Decisions Fairly
204 ■ Interactional Justice 205 ■ Organizational Justice: Some Motivational Tips for
Managers 205

Motivating by Altering Expectations 207
Basic Elements of Expectancy Theory 207 ■ Managerial Applications of Expectancy
Theory 209

Motivating by Structuring Jobs to Make Them Interesting 212
Job Enlargement and Job Enrichment 213 ■ The Job Characteristics Model 214 ■
Techniques for Designing Jobs That Motivate: Some Managerial Guidelines 218

   Summary and Review of Learning Objectives 219
   Points to Ponder 221
   Developing OB Skills 221
   Case in Point: Wal-Mart: Everyday Motivated Employees 224

Video Case: Motivating Employees 226

   ■ *Special Sections*
   BEST PRACTICES: Meeting Needs in High Style 198
   OB IN A DIVERSE WORLD: Why Do Americans Work Longer Hours
      Than Germans? 210
   OB IN AN E-WORLD: Incentive Stock Options at Dot-Coms: Then and Now 214
   HOW TO DO IT: Making Autonomy Work 218

Chapter 7: Career Dynamics 227

■ PREVIEW CASE: FOR TODAY'S M.B.A.'S, JOB CHOICE IS DOT-COMPLICATED 227

The Basic Nature of Careers 228
What Is a Career? 228 ■ Today's Careers Are Not What They Used to Be 230 ■ Types
of Careers 233 ■ Career Stages 236

Making Career Choices 237
Holland's Theory of Vocational Choice 237 ■ Career Anchors 240 ■ Job
Opportunities 241

Organizational Socialization: Learning the Ropes 241
Anticipatory Socialization: Avoiding Entry Shock with Realistic Job Previews 241 ■
The Encounter Stage 244 ■ The Metamorphosis Stage 244

Mentoring: Socializing People Individually 245
Development of the Mentoring Process 245 ■ Benefits and Costs of Mentoring 246 ■
Mentoring Members of Diverse Groups 248

Challenges in Established Careers 248
Confronting the Career Plateau 249 ■ Making Career Changes 250 ■ Planning for
Succession and Retirement 253

Personal Challenges and Strategies for Career Management 256
Job Rotation 256 ■ Entrepreneurship: Should You Start Your Own Business? 257 ■
Starting a Home-Based Business 259 ■ The Glass Ceiling: A Career Challenge for
Women 261 ■ Dealing with the Dual Career 262 ■ Hiring a Career Coach 264

   Summary and Review of Learning Objectives 264
   Points to Ponder 266
   Developing OB Skills 266
   Case in Point: Toal's Career Takes Its Toll 269

■ *Special Sections*
OB IN A DIVERSE WORLD: Lifetime Employment: Why It Exists—and Still Works—in
*   Japan 232*
OB IN AN E-WORLD: Making Connections in Cyberspace: Online Networking 252
HOW TO DO IT: Tips on Finding a New Job 254
BEST PRACTICES: Helping Entrepreneurs Make It B.I.G. 260

PART IV: GROUP DYNAMICS 271

Chapter 8: Group Processes and Work Teams 271

■ **PREVIEW CASE: PEOPLE POWER AT CONSOLIDATED DIESEL 271**

Groups at Work: Their Basic Nature 273
What Is a Group? A Working Definition 273 ■ Types of Groups 274 ■ Why Do People
Join Groups? 275 ■ How Groups Are Formed 277

The Structural Dynamics of Work Groups 279
Roles: The Hats We Wear 279 ■ Norms: A Group's Unspoken Rules 280 ■ Status: The
Prestige of Group Membership 281 ■ Cohesiveness: Getting the Team Spirit 283

Individual Performance in Groups 284
Social Facilitation: Working in the Presence of Others 284 ■ Social Loafing: "Free
Riding" When Working with Others 287

Teams: Special Kinds of Groups 291
Defining Teams and Distinguishing Teams from Groups 291 ■ Types of Teams 293 ■
Creating Teams: A Four-Stage Process 299

Effective Team Performance 300
How Successful Are Teams? A Look at the Evidence 300 ■ Potential Obstacles to
Success: Why Some Teams Fail 302

How to Develop Successful Teams 303
Provide Training in Team Skills 303 ■ Compensate Team Performance 305 ■ Provide
Support 305 ■ Communicate the Urgency of the Team's Mission 307 ■ Promote
Cooperation Within and Between Teams 308 ■ Select Team Members Based on Their
Skills or Potential Skills 308 ■ A Cautionary Note: Developing Successful Teams
Requires Patience 308

Summary and Review of Learning Objectives 309
Points to Ponder 310
Developing OB Skills 311
Case in Point: A Team Approach to Selling at Cutler-Hammer 313

Video Case: Work Groups 315

■ *Special Sections*
OB IN A DIVERSE WORLD: Performance in Culturally Diverse Groups 290
HOW TO DO IT: Learning from High-Performance Teams 294
BEST PRACTICES: SEI Investments: Where Total Teamwork Rules 298
OB IN AN E-WORLD: Extreme Team Building: A Metaphor for the Internet
*   Economy 306*

Chapter 9: Communication in Organizations 316

■ **PREVIEW CASE: US WEST: INFORMATION SHARING IN REAL TIME 316**

Communication: Its Basic Nature 318
Communication: A Working Definition and Description of the Process 318

The Fundamental Role of Communication in Organizations 320

Verbal Communication: Sharing Messages with Words 321
Traditional Verbal Media Vary in Richness 322 ■ Computer-Mediated
Communication 323 ■ Matching the Medium to the Message 324

Nonverbal Communication: Communicating Without Words 325
Style of Dress: Communicating by Appearance 326 ■ Time: The Waiting Game 327 ■
The Use of Space: What Does It Say About You? 328

Individual Differences in Communication 329
Personal Communication Style 329 ■ Gender Differences in Communication: Do
Women and Men Communicate Differently? 331 ■ Cross-Cultural Differences in
Communication 332

Formal and Informal Communication in Organizations 332
Formal Communication: Up, Down, and Across the Organizational Chart 333 ■
Informal Communication Networks: Behind the Organizational Chart 336 ■
Communicating Inside Versus Outside the Organization 339

Improving Your Communication Skills 340
Use Simple, Clear Language 341 ■ Become an Active, Attentive Listener 341 ■
Gauge the Flow of Information: Avoiding Overload 343 ■ Give and Receive Feedback:
Opening Channels of Communication 345 ■ Be a Supportive Communicator:
Enhancing Relationships 347 ■ Use Inspirational Communication Tactics 348

Summary and Review of Learning Objectives 350
Points to Ponder 352
Developing OB Skills 353
*Case in Point: Physician Sales & Service: Where Keeping Up with Policies Is More
Fun Than Any Policy Manual 355*

■ *Special Sections*
OB IN AN E-WORLD: The Spam Problem: Costlier Than You May Think 320
*OB IN A DIVERSE WORLD: "Hola and Hello": Welcome to StarMedia's
Trilingual Webcast 324*
OB IN A DIVERSE WORLD: Promoting Cross-Cultural Communication 334
*HOW TO DO IT: Communicating the Ultimate Organizational Bad News: "You're
Fired!" 336*
BEST PRACTICES: Mistake of the Month 348

Chapter 10: Decision Making in Organizations 357

■ PREVIEW CASE: THE ENRON–ARTHUR ANDERSEN SCANDAL: DECISION
MAKING GONE AWRY 357

The Nature of Decision Making 359
A General, Analytical Model of the Decision-Making Process 359 ■ The Broad
Spectrum of Organizational Decisions 361

Factors Affecting Decisions in Organizations 365
Decision Style: Individual Differences in Decision Making 365 ■ Group Influences: A
Matter of Trade-Offs 368 ■ Organizational Barriers to Effective Decisions 369 ■
Cultural Differences in Decision Making 370 ■ Time Pressure: Making Decisions in
Emergencies 371

How Are Individual Decisions Made? 373
The Rational-Economic Model: In Search of the Ideal Decision 373 ■ The
Administrative Model: The Limits of Human Rationality 373 ■ Image Theory: An
Intuitive Approach to Decision Making 374

Imperfections in Individual Decisions 375
Framing Effects 376 ■ Reliance on Heuristics 378

The Inherently Biased Nature of Individual Decisions 378
Bias Toward Implicit Favorites 379 ■ Hindsight Bias 379 ■ Person Sensitivity Bias 380 ■ Escalation of Commitment Bias 381

Group Decisions: Do Too Many Cooks Spoil the Broth? 383
When Are Groups Superior to Individuals? 383 ■ When Are Individuals Superior to Groups? 385

Traditional Techniques for Improving the Effectiveness of Decisions 385
Techniques for Improving Individual Decision Making 386 ■ Techniques for Enhancing Group Decisions 389

Computer-Based Approaches to Promoting Effective Decisions 393
Electronic Meetings 393 ■ Computer-Assisted Communication 393 ■ Group Decision Support Systems 395

> *Summary and Review of Learning Objectives 396*
> *Points to Ponder 397*
> *Developing OB Skills 398*
> *Case in Point: Keeping the New Orleans Saints Marching Down the Field 401*

> ■ *Special Sections*
> *BEST PRACTICES: Naval Officers Use Decision Support Systems to Make Combat Decisions 362*
> *OB IN AN E-WORLD: Adaptive Agents as Decision Aids 366*
> *HOW TO DO IT: Strategies for Avoiding Groupthink 370*
> *OB IN A DIVERSE WORLD: Are U.S. Businesses Overly Concerned About Ethical Decisions? 388*

Chapter 11: Interpersonal Behavior: Working With and Against Others 403

■ **PREVIEW CASE: A VENTI CUP OF TRUST BREWS AT STARBUCKS** 403

The Dynamics of Interpersonal Relationships 405
Psychological Contracts: Our Expectations of Others 405 ■ The Importance of Trust in Relationships 406

Prosocial Behavior: Helping Others 408
Organizational Citizenship Behavior: Above and Beyond Job Requirements 409 ■ Whistle-Blowing: Helping Through Dissent 410

Cooperation: Providing Mutual Assistance 412
Pure Competition Occurs Rarely 412 ■ Determinants of Cooperation 413 ■ Cooperation Between Organizations 414

Conflict: The Inevitable Result of Incompatible Interests 416
Causes of Conflict 416 ■ Consequences of Conflict: Both Negative and Positive 417

Managing Organizational Conflict 419
Negotiating Win-Win Solutions 419 ■ Alternative Dispute Resolution 420

Deviant Organizational Behavior 422
Varieties of Deviant Behavior 423 ■ Workplace Aggression: Physical or Verbal Abuse and Bullying 424 ■ Employee Theft 429

> *Summary and Review of Learning Objectives 430*
> *Points to Ponder 431*
> *Developing OB Skills 432*
> *Case in Point: The True Story of George, the "Paraillegal" 434*

■ *Special Sections*
HOW TO DO IT: Being an Effective Whistle-Blower 413
BEST PRACTICES: Integrative Agreements as Solutions to Organizational Conflicts 422
OB IN A DIVERSE WORLD: Negotiating Tactics in the United States, Germany, and Japan 424
OB IN AN E-WORLD: Cyberloafing: Deviant Behavior Goes High Tech 426

PART V: INFLUENCING OTHERS 436

Chapter 12: Influence, Power, and Politics in Organizations 436

■ PREVIEW CASE: THE MAN WHO SWALLOWED CHRYSLER 436

Social Influence: A Basic Organizational Process 438
Social Influence, Power, and Politics: Their Basic Nature 438 ■ Tactics of Social Influence: Getting to "Yes" 439 ■ Other Tactics of Influence 441

Individual Power: A Basis for Influence 443
Position Power: Influence That Comes with the Office 443 ■ Personal Power: Influence That Comes from the Individual 445 ■ Power: How Is It Used? 447 ■ Empowerment: The Shifting Bases of Power in Today's Organizations 448 ■ Employees' Reactions to Empowerment: Always Positive? 449

Group or Subunit Power: Structural Determinants 450
The Resource Dependency Model: Controlling Critical Resources 451 ■ The Strategic Contingencies Model: Power Through Dependence 453

Organizational Politics: Power in Action 454
The Antecedents of Politics: Why and When It Occurs 455 ■ Political Tactics: What Forms Do They Take? 457 ■ Organizational Politics: Its Effects 458

The Ethics of Organizational Politics 459
What, If Anything, Is Unethical About Organizational Politics? 459 ■ Assessing the Ethics of Political Behavior 461

Summary and Review of Learning Objectives 463
Points to Ponder 464
Developing OB Skills 465
Case in Point: The Smith Brothers: A Low-Key Approach to Gaining—and Keeping—Organizational Power 468

■ *Special Sections*
OB IN AN E-WORLD: Download Time: Is It Always a Negative for Companies Doing E-Business? 440
HOW TO DO IT: Protecting Yourself from Unwanted Influence 442
BEST PRACTICES: Joe Torre: The Yankees' Power Hitter without a Bat 446
OB IN A DIVERSE WORLD: Empowerment in Low Power Distance and High Power Distance Cultures 450

Chapter 13: Leadership in Organizations 469

■ PREVIEW CASE: URBAN BOX OFFICE LOSES ITS LEADER, THEN THE BUSINESS 469

The Nature of Leadership 470
Leadership: A Working Definition 470 ■ Leaders Versus Managers: A Key Distinction—At Least in Theory 471

The Trait Approach to Leadership: Having the Right Stuff 472
The Great Person Theory 473 ▪ What Are the Characteristics of Great Leaders? 473

Leadership Behavior: What Do Leaders Do? 474
Participative Versus Autocratic Leadership Behaviors 475 ▪ Person-Oriented Versus Production-Oriented Leaders 477 ▪ Developing Successful Leadership Behavior: Grid Training 478

Leaders and Followers 479
The Leader–Member Exchange (LMX) Model: The Importance of Being in the "In-Group" 480 ▪ The Challenge of Leading Work Teams 481 ▪ The Attribution Approach: Leaders' Explanations of Followers' Behavior 484

Change-Oriented Leadership: Future Visions 485
Charismatic Leadership: That "Something Special" 486 ▪ Transformational Leadership: Beyond Charisma 488

Contingency Theories of Leader Effectiveness 490
LPC Contingency Theory: Matching Leaders and Tasks 491 ▪ Situational Leadership Theory: Adjusting Leadership Style to the Situation 493 ▪ Path-Goal Theory: Leaders as Guides to Valued Goals 494 ▪ Normative Decision Theory: The Right Time for Employee Participation 495 ▪ Substitutes for Leadership: When Leaders Are Superfluous 500

Leadership Development: Bringing Out the Leader Within You 502
360-Degree Feedback 503 ▪ Networking 504 ▪ Executive Coaching 504 ▪ Mentoring 506 ▪ Job Assignments 506 ▪ Action Learning 507

Summary and Review of Learning Objectives 507
Points to Ponder 509
Developing OB Skills 509
Case in Point: Chan Suh: Not Your Typical Advertising Executive—Yet 512

▪ *Special Sections*
HOW TO DO IT: Boosting Cultural Intelligence 475
BEST PRACTICES: Coaching: From Locker Room to Boardroom 496
OB IN AN E-WORLD: Leading in the Digital Age 502
OB IN A DIVERSE WORLD: Guanxi: Social Networking in China 504

Chapter 14: Organizational Culture, Creativity, and Innovation 513

▪ PREVIEW CASE: SULLIVAN PARK: WHERE CORNING INVENTS THE FUTURE 513

The Basic Nature of Organizational Culture 515
Organizational Culture: A Definition and Core Characteristics 515 ▪ Cultures Within Organizations: One or Many? 518 ▪ The Role of Culture in Organizations 518

Identifying Organizational Cultures: The Double S Cube 518
Two Underlying Dimensions of Organizational Culture 519 ▪ Four Organizational Cultures 520 ▪ Interpreting Organizational Culture 521

Creating and Sustaining Organizational Culture 522
How Is Organizational Culture Created? 522 ▪ Tools for Transmitting Culture 523

Organizational Culture: Its Consequences and Capacity to Change 526
The Effects of Organizational Culture 526 ▪ Why and How Does Organizational Culture Change? 528

Creativity in Individuals and Teams 529
Components of Individual and Team Creativity 530 ▪ A Model of the Creative Process 532

Promoting Creativity in Organizations 533
Training People to Be Creative 533 ■ Developing Creative Work Environments 533

The Process of Innovation 536
Components of Innovation: Basic Building Blocks 536 ■ Stages of the Organizational
Innovation Process 538

Summary and Review of Learning Objectives 540
Points to Ponder 542
Developing OB Skills 543
Case in Point: IDEO: Where Silliness Is Taken Seriously 545

■ *Special Sections*
*OB IN AN E-WORLD: Today, High-Tech Start-Ups Fill the Spirit Rather Than the
    Bank Account 516*
HOW TO DO IT: Boosting Creativity by Making Jobs Intrinsically Interesting 534
*OB IN A DIVERSE WORLD: Where in the World Is Entrepreneurial Creativity
    Promoted? 536*
BEST PRACTICES: How Effective Companies Inspire Innovation 540

PART VI: ORGANIZATIONAL PROCESSES 547

Chapter 15: Organizational Structure and Design 547

■ PREVIEW CASE: VF CORP. SEWS TOGETHER ITS OPERATIONS 547

Organizational Structure: The Basic Dimensions of Organizations 548
Hierarchy of Authority: Up and Down the Organizational Ladder 550 ■ Division of
Labor: Carving Up the Jobs 551 ■ Span of Control: Breadth of Responsibility 552
Line Versus Staff Positions: Decision Makers Versus Advisors 553 ■ Decentralization:
Delegating Power Downward 554

Departmentalization: Ways of Structuring Organizations 555
Functional Organizations: Departmentalization by Task 555 ■ Product Organizations:
Departmentalization by Type of Output 556 ■ Matrix Organizations:
Departmentalization by Both Function and Product 558

Organizational Design: Coordinating the Structural Elements of Organizations 560
Classical and Neoclassical Approaches: The Quest for the One Best Design 561 ■ The
Contingency Approach: Design According to Environmental Conditions 562 ■
Mintzberg's Framework: Five Organizational Forms 566 ■ The Boundaryless
Organization: A New Corporate Architecture 568

Interorganizational Designs: Going Beyond the Single Organization 572
Conglomerates: Diversified "Megacorporations" 573 ■ Strategic Alliances: Joining
Forces for Mutual Benefit 574

Summary and Review of Learning Objectives 578
Points to Ponder 580
Developing OB Skills 581
*Case in Point: Ameritech and Random House Join Forces on Emerging
    Technology 583*

Video Case: Organizational Structure 585

■ *Special Sections*
HOW TO DO IT: Designing High-Tech Organizations with Flexibility in Mind 559
BEST PRACTICES: Horizontal Organizations: Structuring by Process 562
OB IN AN E-WORLD: When Should an Organization Go Virtual? 572
OB IN A DIVERSE WORLD: Joint Ventures in China: Beware of Obstacles 576

Chapter 16: Managing Organizational Change: Strategic Planning and Organizational Development 586

■ PREVIEW CASE: MAKING CHANGE AT THE U.S. MINT 586

The Prevalence of Change in Organizations 588
The Message Is Clear: Change or Disappear! 588 ■ Change Is a Global Phenomenon 590

The Nature of the Change Process 590
Targets: What Is Changed? 590 ■ Forces Behind Unplanned Organizational Change 593

Strategic Planning: Deliberate Change 595
Basic Assumptions About Strategic Planning 595 ■ About What Do Companies Make Strategic Plans? 596 ■ The 10 Steps of the Strategic Planning Process 598

Resistance to Change: Maintaining the Status Quo 601
Individual Barriers to Change 601 ■ Organizational Barriers to Change 602 ■ Readiness for Change: When Will Organizational Change Occur? 603 ■ How Can Resistance to Organizational Change Be Overcome? 604

Organizational Development Interventions: Implementing Planned Change 607
Management by Objectives: Clarifying Organizational Goals 607 ■ Survey Feedback: Inducing Change by Sharing Information 609 ■ Appreciative Inquiry 610 Action Labs 611 ■ Quality of Work Life Programs: Humanizing the Workplace 612

Critical Questions About Organizational Development 613
The Effectiveness of Organizational Development: Does It Really Work? 613 ■ Is Organizational Development Dependent on National Culture? 614 ■ Is Organizational Development Inherently Unethical? 616

Summary and Review of Learning Objectives 617
Points to Ponder 618
Developing OB Skills 619
Case in Point: GM Is Driven to Change—And the Chevrolet SSR Is the Vehicle 621

Video Case: Organizational Change 622

■ *Special Sections*
OB IN A DIVERSE WORLD: Strategic Values: More American Than Universal 602
HOW TO DO IT: Making Changes Stick: Tips from Three Established Organizations 608
OB IN AN E-WORLD: Using Online Competitive Intelligence for Organizational Change 610
BEST PRACTICES: Simulating Organizational Change 614

Appendix I: Theory and Research: Tools for Learning About Behavior in Organizations 623

Notes 637
Glossary 661
Photo Credits 673
Company Index 675
Name Index 679
Subject Index 681

ORGANIZATIONAL BEHAVIOR: THE ULTIMATE REALITY SHOW

Three years ago, when the previous edition of this book was published, Enron and WorldCom were successful and highly acclaimed companies; involvement in a dot-com was an assured path to riches, and September 11 was just a date on the calendar. Today, that's all changed. In a very short time, it's become a different world, especially the business world. Companies that once moved "from bricks to clicks" today are returning to bricks, but are keeping the clicks as well. Many organizations that downsized in a sagging economy subsequently rehired employees, only to downsize once more. And, workplaces that used to be considered safe havens from the uncertainties of a sometimes evil world, today are considered far more vulnerable than ever.

To be sure, in preparing the eighth edition of *Behavior in Organizations,* we have taken careful notice of today's ethical scandals, the always shifting—and sometimes troubled—economy, and underlying concerns about terrorism that reside in our consciousness. Then again, doing otherwise would be impossible. As chroniclers of the world of work and organizations, we cannot help but come across these themes. These issues, and many others, are on the minds of the students we teach in the classroom (undergraduates, MBA candidates, and doctoral students), the workers we train on the job (ranging from minimum-wage laborers to top CEOs), and the officials from the companies to whom we provide consulting services (from start-ups to *Fortune* 500 firms). Whatever is on their minds also is on ours. And, these concerns get translated into coverage in this book.

For the most part, what everyone wants is relevance. "Theories and research are important," our students acknowledge, so long as they offer insight into what's happening in individual's heads, what's going on in work teams, and how people are interacting with their organizations. "Tell me something I need to know," they clamor; so we listen, and we deliver. And, if those plaques acknowledging our teaching and scholarship that line the walls of our offices mean anything, we have been delivering precisely what's needed in an effective manner for more than 60 years combined. In preparing this book, our mission was to capture this relevance in a form that could enlighten our target audience—college students who desire to learn about the complexities of human behavior in organizations.

Fortunately, we are in a good position to appreciate these complexities. When not plying our trade in the classroom or the executive suite, we can be found conducting research that contributes to the scholarly contributions that are the foundation of our field. Indeed, this is our fundamental task as professors who work in universities at which scholarship is not only valued, but demanded. And, we are proud of the body of knowledge our field's research has generated—not just our own work, but also the research of our many colleagues in the field. After all, without such scholarly contributions, we would have no basis for knowing—let alone, teaching—anything about behavior in organizations that went beyond mere speculation based on personal experience. Of course, as a field, organizational behavior (OB) is firmly grounded in science—and these scientific underpinnings also are highlighted in this book. Indeed, this has been a hallmark of *Behavior in Organizations* throughout the quarter-century of its life. The hundreds of professors who have adopted earlier editions of this book throughout the years, and the thousands of students who have read it, have valued our research-based approach. These individuals, our core constituency, surely will be pleased to find that this orientation has been retained in this edition of the text.

Thus far, we have referred to this book as practical in orientation and also research-based. Indeed, we have taken extensive steps to ensure that it is the best of these seemingly disparate worlds. This is not a contradiction. Rather, this duality echoes the fundamental orientation of the field of OB. It is based on theory and research, but it is not pure, "ivory tower" research. It is work that offers key insights into the world of work. Because the field of OB is a blend of research, theory, and practical application, so too, quite deliberately, is this book.

We think of organizational behavior as an ever-shifting terrain—and, our job is to map that terrain for current travelers. It is a scientific field that chronicles the ongoing nature of real organizations and the behavior of those individuals and teams that work within them. As economic, technological and social conditions change, so too does the field. Some topics grow in popularity as others wane. Issues and problems that at one time may have seemed so important now may seem outdated. And of course, as advances in research and theory occur, new insight is provided about phenomena that shape the course of managerial practice.

Because the field of OB is constantly adjusting to reality, we think of it—and this book—as "the ultimate reality show." As in the TV show, *Survivor*, only the most adaptable individuals and teams in the workplace can be expected to make it to tomorrow. And, as in the TV show, *Big Brother*, relationships with other people also hold the key to success at work. Finally, just as winners in these television programs stand to receive large sums of money and are likely to enjoy the experience of playing the game, so too do employers and employees benefit financially and personally when they have mastered OB. Unlike these so-called "reality" shows, with their carefully scripted scenarios and meticulously chosen casts, however, behavior in organizations *is* reality. Its effects are ongoing and profound. And this is why we consider it to be "the ultimate" in reality, and why we put so much care into preparing this book.

A CAREFULLY BALANCED APPROACH TO THE FIELD

We think of this book's coverage as offering a carefully balanced approach to OB. Some competing textbooks focus a great deal on one topic or another. Others invest all their intellectual capital in a particular conceptual or pedagogical approach. These presentations are then justified as selling points. We do not do take this approach. Although such books are unique, their uniqueness comes at a cost: Skewed approaches do not reflect what today's field of OB is really like. To us, characterizing the field as it is, is crucial—and, a responsibility we don't take lightly. For this reason, we focus on representing OB as the balanced, integrated field it is.

To illustrate this point, let's consider how our balanced approach comes across in three major respects—topic coverage, mix of theory and practice, and pedagogical focus.

Topic Coverage: Old and New

You would not have a serious OB book without paying attention to Weber's concept of bureaucracy, Maslow's need hierarchy theory, and dozens of other classic theories and studies. Such works are to be found on these pages. Competing for space are an equal number of more contemporary approaches to OB that also have received our attention. Consider, for example, just a few of the many new topics covered in this book.

- Ethics audits (Chapter 1)
- Corporate social responsibility (Chapter 1)
- E-training (Chapter 2)

- Chief Knowledge Officer (Chapter 2)
- Successful intelligence (Chapter 3)
- Emoticons (Chapter 4)
- Organizational compassion (Chapter 4)
- Religious intolerance (Chapter 5)
- Cyber-venting (Chapter 5)
- Incentive stock option plans (Chapter 6)
- Online networking (Chapter 7)
- Business incubators (Chapter 7)
- High performance teams (Chapter 8)
- Law of telecosm (Chapter 8)
- Cross-cultural communication (Chapter 9)
- Computer-mediated communication (Chapter 9)
- Adaptive agents (Chapter 10)
- Person sensitivity bias (Chapter 10)
- Workplace bullying (Chapter 11)
- Cyberloafing (Chapter 11)
- Download time (Chapter 12)
- Executive coaching (Chapter 13)
- Action learning (Chapter 13)
- Entrepreneurial creativity (Chapter 14)
- Spinoffs (Chapter 15)
- Networked incubators (Chapter 15)
- Action labs (Chapter 16)
- Appreciative inquiry (Chapter 16)
- Online surveys (Appendix I)

Theory? Research? Practice? Yes, Yes, and Yes!

In an old TV commercial, two people are found arguing whether the product in question is a candy mint or a breath mint. Shortly into the debate (albeit not quick enough for our tastes), we are spared by someone who proposes a resolution: "Stop," she says, "You're both right." We are reminded of this drama whenever we hear similar discussions about OB. To those who wish to argue that "OB is a theoretical field" or that "OB is an applied field," we issue the same admonishment: "Stop, you're both right."

Indeed, our image of the field of OB is that it is an applied science—that is, science undertaken with practical applications in mind. Those of us who are involved in OB think of ourselves as scientist-practitioners. We conduct "pure" scientific research for purposes of understanding fundamental individual, group, and organizational processes. We then put this knowledge to use in organizations. And, based on what we learn, we then go back to the drawing board, revising our underlying theories as dictated, and conduct more research. This leads to more application, and so the cycle continues. This, we believe makes the field of OB so special, so unique, and so important.

We have gone out of our way in this book to capture this process of moving from theory, to research, to application, back to theory. This is a broad and dynamic approach, making it difficult to capture, but we believe we have done so—at least, wherever the various pieces of the puzzle are identifiable. For example, in Chapter 2 we cover both theories of learning and how these theories are involved in such organizational practices as training and organizational behavior modification. We designed parallels between theory and practice in Chapter 5, where we consider theories of job satisfaction and organizational commitment, as well as ways these approaches may be applied to improving these important organizational attitudes. And, we do the same in Chapter 6, where we highlight the practical implications of each of the theories of motivation we discuss.

More than simply indicating how various theories *may be* applied, we identify precisely how they *are being* applied in today's organizations. So, for example, in Chapter 7, we not only describe the mentorship process, but precisely the forms it is taking today.

Similarly, our discussion of diversity management programs in Chapter 5 not only analyzes the various forms such programs take, but brings these abstractions to life by identifying exactly what certain companies are doing by way of diversity management. These are just a few examples. We systematically discuss actual organizational practices throughout this book. Our reasons for doing so are straightforward: It not only brings the theoretical material to life, but it also illustrates the simple truth that the practice of OB is crucial in today's organizations. To talk only about theory, or research, or practical application (potential or actual), would be misleading. Because the field of OB is all these things. So too have we incorporated all of these elements into this book.

Pedagogical Focus: Knowledge and Skills

Educators tell us that there is a fundamental distinction between teaching people about something—providing *knowledge*—and showing them how to do something—developing their *skills*. In the field of OB, this distinction becomes blurred. After all, to fully appreciate how to do something you have to have the requisite knowledge. For this reason, we pay attention in this book to both knowledge and skills.

As an illustration, consider how the two orientations come together in Chapter 14. We not only describe how the process of creativity works, but we also provide tools for developing one's own creativity. The same duality also may be seen in Chapter 9. In the course of describing organizational communication we discuss the process of listening. Then, to help readers become effective listeners, we present an exercise designed to promote active listening skills. By doing this—not only in these two examples, but throughout the book—we intend to enable readers to understand OB, and also to help them practice it in their own lives.

Taken together, our coverage of classic and cutting-edge topics, our attention to the blend between theory, research, and practice, and our dual emphasis on knowledge and skills reflects what we consider a balanced and realistic orientation to OB. This is the essence of the field as it exists today, and this book, as we present it to you here.

NEW CHAPTERS AND SPECIAL FEATURES

In the course of revising this book we made many changes. Some of these came in the process of seeking that balance to which we just referred, and others were necessitated by our commitment to advancing the latest advances in the field. Many of the changes we made are subtle, referring only to how a topic was framed relative to others. A good many other changes are more noticeable, and involve the shifting of major topics into new places and the addition of brand new topics. Doing this required the creation of several new chapters and the addition of new features.

New and Newly Organized Chapters

Readers who are already familiar with this book will immediately note some new and newly organized chapters. Some examples:

- Chapter 4, "Emotions and Stress on the Job." This chapter brings together new material on two rapidly developing topics in the field of OB. Conceptual advances in the area of emotions and affect are paired with important practical applications regarding stress management to provide valuable personal guidance for readers. Here, the emphasis is on both how to manage others as well as the more basic issue of managing oneself.
- Chapter 11, "Interpersonal Behavior: Working With and Against Others." By highlighting both the positive and negative sides of human nature, this chapter juxtaposes two opposing themes in the field of OB. It provides an opportunity to expand our coverage of the growing literature on deviant behavior in organizations, and to contrast it with a more established literature on helping and cooperating with others.

Newly expanded material on the psychological contract and trust further reflect recent conceptual advances in these areas.

■ Chapter 7, "Career Dynamics." Given the importance of developing and managing careers to readers, we now devote an entire chapter to this topic. Classic research on making career choices is paired with current thinking on frequently changing careers. Practical advice is given about how to use the Internet for informal networking and to facilitate job hunting.

New Special Features

A new feature of this book is designed to make it easier than ever for readers to access material of special applied interest. In addition to many in-text examples, each chapter also contains a section entitled **"Best Practices."** These sections provide a close-up look at OB in practice—extended examples of current organizational practices that illustrate key concepts from the book. This brings the material to life and makes it more relevant to students. Some examples include:

■ "The Best at Diversity: Pacific Enterprises" (Chapter 5)
■ "SEI Investments: Where Total Teamwork Rules" (Chapter 8)
■ "Naval Officers Use Decision Support Systems to Make Combat Decisions" (Chapter 10)
■ "Coaching: From Locker Room to Boardroom" (Chapter 13)
■ "How Effective Companies Inspire Innovation" (Chapter 14)
■ "Simulating Organizational Change" (Chapter 16)

Another applied feature of the book is more hands-on in nature. Special sections called, **"How to Do It,"** present several concrete tips for readers to follow when attempting to carry out some practice related to the field of OB. Examples include the following.

■ "Conducting an Ethics Audit" (Chapter 1)
■ "Coping with the Emotional Fallout of Terrorism: How Can Companies Help?" (Chapter 4)
■ "Avoiding Pitfalls in Diversity Management" (Chapter 5)
■ "Being an Effective Whistle-Blower" (Chapter 11)
■ "Boosting Cultural Intelligence" (Chapter 13)
■ "Making Changes Stick: Tips from Three Established Organizations" (Chapter 16)

A third new feature of this book is designed to help readers understand how the field of OB influences and is influenced by rapid advances in information technology. These special sections, called, **"OB in an E-World,"** highlight one of the most potent sources for organizational change today. Some examples are as follows.

■ "Making Telecommuting Work" (Chapter 1)
■ "E-Training: Booming, but Beware" (Chapter 2)
■ "Using "Emoticons" to Express Emotions in E-Mail: Do Those Smiley Faces Make Any Difference?" (Chapter 4)
■ "Making Connections in Cyberspace: Online Networking" (Chapter 7)
■ "The Spam Problem: Costlier Than You May Think" (Chapter 9)
■ "When Should an Organization Go Virtual?" (Chapter 15)
■ "Using Online Competitive Intelligence for Organizational Change" (Chapter 16)

A fourth new feature included in this book is entitled **"OB in A Diverse World."** The material in these special sections highlights two critical features of today's workplace: the global and international nature of organizations, and the high level of racial and ethnic diversity found in organizations. The emphasis is on how OB practices differ in various nations and for various ethnic groups within the North American workplace. Here are just a few selected examples:

■ "Performance Evaluations: Comparing the United States and Japan" (Chapter 2)
■ "Why Do Americans Work Longer Hours Than Germans?" (Chapter 6)
■ "Performance in Culturally Diverse Groups" (Chapter 8)

- "'Hola and Hello': Welcome to StarMedia's Trilingual Webcast" (Chapter 9)
- "Are U.S. Businesses Overly Concerned About Ethical Decisions?" (Chapter 10)
- "Negotiating Tactics in the United States, Germany, and Japan" (Chapter 11)
- "*Guanxi:* Social Networking in China" (Chapter 13)

New End-of-Chapter Pedagogical Features

At the end of each chapter, two groups of pedagogical features may be found. The first, named **"Points to Ponder,"** includes three types of questions:

- **Questions for Review.** These are questions designed to help students determine the extent to which they picked up the major points contained in each chapter.
- **Experiential Questions.** These are questions that get students to understand various OB phenomena by thinking about how various experiences in their work lives.
- **Questions to Analyze.** The questions in this category are designed to help readers think about the interconnections between various OB phenomena and/or how they may be applied.

The second category of pedagogical features found at the end of each chapter is referred to as **"Experiencing Organizational Behavior."** This includes the following four types of experiential exercises.

- **Individual Exercise.** Students can complete these exercises on their own to gain some insight into various OB phenomena.
- **Group Exercise.** By working in small groups, students completing these exercises will be able to experience an important OB phenomenon or concept. The experience itself also will help them develop team-building skills.
- **Web Surfing Exercises.** Each chapter contains two exercises that require students to look for various types of OB-related information on the Internet. Each of these exercises gives students an opportunity to expand upon material they read in the chapter.
- **Practicing OB.** This exercise is applications-based. It describes a hypothetical problem situation and challenges the reader to explain how various OB practices can be applied to solving it.

RETURN OF YOUR FAVORITE SPECIAL FEATURES

Fans of the previous edition of this book needn't worry about the whereabouts of the book's most popular special features. These are back, and better than ever. These include the following:

- **Cases.** Each chapter contains two cases, the many of which are completely new or updated. One at the beginning of the chapter, **Preview Case,** is designed to set-up the material that follows by putting it in the context of a real organizational event. The chapter-end case, **Case in Point,** is designed to review the material already covered and to bring that material to life. Specific tie-ins are made by use of discussion questions appearing after each **"Case in Point"** feature.
- **Talking Graphics.** All data presented in graphs come complete with labeled boxes literally pointing at the major idea it contains. Between the highly descriptive in-text material, the detailed captions, and these talking graphics, students will continue to find this book approachable and easy to understand.

UPDATED SUPPLEMENTS PACKAGE

Instructors adopting this book have available a wide array of ancillary materials designed to help them teach their courses. Likewise, students using this book have access to many useful tools to help them use this book more effectively. These supplements are designed specifically for this book and are carefully coordinated with its content and features.

- **Instructor's Manual.** Contains a variety of useful features for instructors using this book in their classes. Among these are learning objectives; chapter outlines with case summaries; chapter summaries; and suggested answers to all "Points to Ponder" and "Case in Point" questions. The Instructor's Manual also includes a video guide for the "On Location at Student Advantage" video series.
- **Test Item File.** Contains 100 items per chapter, including multiple-choice, true/false, and essay questions.
- **PowerPoint Slides.** Included on the Instructor's Resource CD-ROM, as well as on the Web site for the text, the PowerPoint presentation includes more than 300 slides that highlight fundamental concepts and integrate key graphs, figures, and illustrations from the text.
- **Instructor's Resource CD-ROM.** This all-in-one multimedia product is an invaluable asset for professors who prefer to work with electronic files rather than traditional print supplements. This CD-ROM contains the Instructor's Resource Manual, PowerPoint Slides, and the Test Item File.
- **Custom Web Site (http://www.prenhall.com/greenberg).** Faculty can access and download all supplements (Instructor's Manual, PowerPoint Slides, and Test Item File) online.
- **On Location at Student Advantage Video Series.** Video segments filmed at Studentadvantage.com, a real student resource company, cover such key topics as, organizational change, groups, stress, organizational structure, and motivation. Summaries of these video cases and discussion questions appear in the text.
- **Internet Study Guide.** A Web site for this book (www.prehall.com/greenberg) contains a variety of useful exercises to help students assess their mastery of the material covered in this book. Specifically, for each chapter, there are multiple-choice questions, true/false questions, and Internet exercises.

FINALLY—AND MOST IMPORTANTLY—ACKNOWLEDGMENTS

Writing is a solitary task. However, turning millions of bytes of information stored on a handful of plastic disks into a book is a magical process that requires an army of talented folks. In preparing this text, we have been fortunate enough to be assisted by many dedicated and talented people. Although we cannot possibly thank all of them here, we wish to express our appreciation to those whose help has been most valuable.

First, our sincere thanks to our colleagues who read and commented on various portions of the manuscript for this and earlier editions of this book. Their suggestions were invaluable, and helped us in many ways. These include:

Royce L. Abrahamson, Southwest Texas State University
Rabi S. Bhagat, Memphis State University
Ralph R. Braithwaite, University of Hartford
Stephen C. Buschardt, University of Southern Mississippi
Dawn Carlson, University of Utah
M. Suzzanne Clinton, Cameron University
Roy A. Cook, Fort Lewis College
Cynthis Cordes, State University of New York at Binghamton
Janice Feldbauer Austin Community College
Patricia Feltes, Southwest Missouri State University
Olene L. Fuller, San Jacinto College North
Richard Grover, University of Southern Maine
Courtney Hunt, University of Delaware
Ralph Katerberg, University of Cincinnati
Paul N. Keaton, University of Wisconsin at LaCrosse
Mary Kernan, University of Delaware
Daniel Levi, California Polytechnic State University
Jeffrey Lewis, Pitzer College
Rodney Lim, Tulane University
Charles W. Mattox, Jr., St. Mary's University

James McElroy, Iowa State University
Richard McKinney, Southern Illinois University
Linda Morable, Richland College
Paula Morrow, Iowa State University
Audry Murrell, University of Pittsburgh
David Olsen, California State University-Bakersfield
William D. Patzig, James Madison University
Shirley Rickert, Indiana University—Purdue University at Fort Wayne
David W. Roach, Arkansas Tech University
Dr. Meshack M. Sagini Langston University
Terri A. Scandura, University of Miami, Coral Gables
Holly Schroth University of California Berkely
Marc Siegall, California State University, Chico
Taggart Smith, Purdue University
Patrick C. Stubbleine, Indiana University—Purdue University at Fort Wayne
Paul Sweeney, Marquette University
Craig A. Tunwall, Ph.D. SUNY Empire State College
Carol Watson, Rider University
Philip A. Weatherford, Embry-Riddle Aeronautical University
Richard M. Weiss, University of Delaware

Second, we wish to express our appreciation to our editor, Jennifer Glennon, who saw us through this project. And, of course, we would be remiss in not thanking Jerome Grant, Jeff Shelstad, and Shannon Moore key members of the PH team, for their steadfast support of this book.

Third, our sincere thanks go out to Prentice Hall's top-notch production team for making this book so beautiful—Virginia Somma, production editor; Kevin Kall, senior designer; Suzanne Grappi, permissions coordinator; Mary Ann Price, photo researcher; and Linda Begley of Rainbow Graphics. Their diligence and skill with matters of design, permissions, and illustrations—not to mention constant refinements—helped us immeasurably throughout the process of preparing this work. It was a pleasure to work with such kind and understanding professionals, and we are greatly indebted to them for their contributions.

Finally, Jerald Greenberg wishes to acknowledge the helpful research assistance of Brian Dineen and Marie-Èlené Roberge whose contributions helped considerably in writing this book. He also thanks the family of the late Irving Abramowitz for their generous endowment to the Ohio State University, which provided invaluable support during the writing of this book.

To all these truly outstanding people, and to many others too, our warm personal regards.

In Conclusion: An Invitation for Feedback

Looking back, we honestly can say that we have spared no effort in preparing a book that reflects the current character of the field of OB regarding both scientific inquiry and practical application. Of course, whether and to what extent we have reached this goal, however, can only be judged by you, our colleagues and students. So, as always, we sincerely invite your input. Feel free to e-mail us or to leave a message at our publisher's Web site (http://www.prenhall.com).

Please let us know what you like about the book and what features need improvement. Such feedback is always welcomed, and it will not fall on deaf ears. We promise faithfully to take your comments and suggestions to heart and to incorporate them into the next edition of this book.

Jerald Greenberg
greenberg.1@osu.edu

Robert A. Baron
baronr@rpi.edu

The Field of Organizational Behavior

■ PREVIEW CASE
PHARMACIA: WHERE PEOPLE ARE THE PRESCRIPTION FOR SUCCESS

On April 3, 2000, the huge chemical bioengineering division of Monsanto merged with the multinational drug giant, Pharmacia & Upjohn (P&U), to create the Pharmacia Corporation—one of the world's fastest-growing pharmaceutical companies, with 59,000 employees in 60 countries. Prospects for the newly enlarged business were excellent, as Monsanto's top-selling arthritis drugs and contraceptives, combined with P&U's successes in antibiotics, all but ensured Pharmacia's dominance in the prescription drug business. Despite drug industry analysts' confidence in Pharmacia's success, Fred Hassan, the company's CEO, knew that a healthy bottom line was not automatic. Based on his 25 years of experience in the pharmaceutical industry, he realized that the key to success was the company's people. After all, he reasoned, for the new company to prosper, it had to keep on board the talented people who were responsible for success in the first place.

> For the new company to prosper, it had to keep on board the talented people who were responsible for success in the first place.

Hassan learned the hard way that this was easier said than done. When he became P&U's CEO in 1997, he took the reins of a newly merged company that until then was two multinational drug companies—Pharmacia AB, a Swedish company, and the Upjohn Co., based in Kalamazoo, Michigan. Further complicating things, P&U was completing the takeover of the Italian pharmaceutical company, Farmitalia. P&U's financial picture was bleak, and morale was low, threatening to harm the company even further. Through several heart-to-heart discussions with his associates, Hassan learned that the core of the problem was that the employees were highly anxious about what the future had in store for them. After all, mergers bring ambiguity, and employees who don't fully understand their company's goals—and even whether or not they will be keeping their jobs—can hardly be expected to be happy and productive.

To promote trust and acceptance within the workforce, Hassan met with the company's key personnel in Milan, Stockholm, and Kalamazoo, where he listened carefully to people's gripes and fears and took careful notes on everything he heard. The biggest problem, he discovered, had to do with culture clashes. Americans, for example, complained at having to work in Italian offices where people smoked, whereas Europeans complained about the Americans' arrogance and poor language skills. As a result, employees from each country worked together but routinely ignored their overseas colleagues. At this very time, when most CEOs would be inclined to focus exclusively on balance sheets, Hassan recognized the importance of focusing eye-to-eye with the very people who were responsible for those numbers.

Although a clash between national cultures was not the issue when Monsanto joined P&U, Hassan recognized that insecurities were sure to run high following the merger. Losing the top people would surely be a recipe for disaster. So, he came up with a "Hate-to-Lose List," naming 100 valued employees at P&U and a like number at Monsanto. He then focused his efforts on reassuring these individuals that they were going to be a valuable part of the new company and that their jobs were safe. The pressures for financial success at the new Pharmacia Corporation are intense, Hassan admits, but the key to success, he acknowledges, is the behavior and attitudes of its people—the one resource he manages most carefully. According to the company's Web site, Pharmacia's goal is to become "the best managed company in the industry." Given Hassan's approach, it seems well on its way to achieving this lofty ambition.

W hat image comes to mind when you think of a huge pharmaceutical company like Pharmacia? Most likely, it's a huge building with miles of offices, laboratories containing the latest high-tech instruments, and a sprawling factory floor decked out with aisles of complicated-looking equipment. Although such facilities certainly are important when it comes to housing where work is done, what's missing from the picture is the one most important ingredient of organizations themselves—*people*. This idea was not lost on Fred Hassan as he faced several huge mergers during the past few years. He carefully listened to his employees' concerns, he noted their low morale, he acknowledged their fears about the future, and he recognized the national differences that kept them from working together. More importantly, he did something to address these issues. In short, he recognized the importance of the human side of work, which happens to be the topic of this book. Indeed, this case highlights several key aspects of human behavior in organizations that will be fully explained in the chapters that follow.

Hassan is clearly aware of a key fact: No matter how good a company's product or service may be, and no matter how far its equipment pushes the cutting edge of technology, there can be no company without people—from the founder to the loyal employees, it's all about people (see Figure 1.1). In fact, if you've ever ran or managed a business, you know that "people problems" can bring an organization down very rapidly. Hence, it makes sense to realize that "the human side of work" (not coincidentally, part of the subtitle of this book) is a critical element in the effective functioning—and basic existence—of organizations. It is this people-centered orientation that is taken in *organizational behavior* (*OB*)—the field specializing in the study of human behavior in organizations.

OB scientists and practitioners study and attempt to solve problems by using knowledge derived from research in the *behavioral sciences,* such as psychology and

FIGURE 1.1
Patagonia Recognizes the Importance of People
Dave Abeloe works at the Reno, Nevada, distribution center for Patagonia, a company that manufactures rugged, good-looking adventure clothing and equipment. Company officials are convinced that Patagonia's success, even throughout turbulent economic times, may be attributed not to its technically sophisticated manufacturing processes but to something far more fundamental—its outstanding relationship with its employees.

sociology. In other words, the field of OB is firmly rooted in science. It relies on research to derive valuable information about organizations and the complex processes operating within them. Such knowledge is used as the basis for helping to solve a wide range of organizational problems. For example, what can be done to make people more productive and more satisfied on their jobs? When and how should people be organized into teams? How should jobs and organizations be designed so that people best adapt to changes in the environment? These are just a few of the many important questions that are addressed by the field of organizational behavior.

As you read this text, it will become very clear that OB specialists have attempted to learn about a large variety of issues involving people in organizations. In fact, over the past few decades, OB has developed into a field so diverse that its scientists have examined just about every conceivable aspect of behavior in organizations.[1] The fruits of this labor already have been enjoyed by people interested in making organizations not only more productive but also more pleasant for those working in them.

In the remainder of this chapter we will give you the background information you will need to understand the scope of OB and its importance. With this in mind, this first chapter is designed to introduce you formally to the field of OB by focusing on its history and its fundamental characteristics. We will begin by formally defining OB, describing exactly what it is and what it seeks to accomplish. Following this, we will summarize the history of the field, tracing its roots from its origins to its emergence as a modern science. Then, in the final sections of the chapter, we will discuss the wide variety of factors that make the field of OB the vibrant, ever-changing field it is today. After this, we will be ready to face the primary goal of this book: to enhance your understanding of the human side of work by giving you a comprehensive overview of the field of organizational behavior.

ORGANIZATIONAL BEHAVIOR: ITS BASIC NATURE

As the phrase implies, OB deals with organizations. Although you already know from experience what an organization is, a formal definition would help avoid ambiguity. An **organization** is a structured social system consisting of groups and individuals working together to meet some agreed-upon objectives. In other words, organizations consist of people who, alone and together in work groups, strive to attain common goals. Although this definition is rather abstract, it is sure to take on more meaning as you continue reading this book. We say this with confidence because the field of OB is concerned with organizations of all types, whether large or small in size, public or private in

organization

A structured social system consisting of groups and individuals working together to meet some agreed-upon objectives.

ownership (i.e., whether or not shares of stock are sold), and whether they exist to earn a profit or to enhance the public good (i.e., *nonprofit organizations,* such as charities and civic groups). Regardless of the specific goals sought, the structured social units working together toward them may be considered organizations.

To launch our journey through the world of OB, we will answer two key questions that you are likely to have on your mind: (1) What is the field of organizational behavior all about? (2) Why is it important to know about OB?

What Is the Field of Organizational Behavior All About?

organizational behavior
The field that seeks increased knowledge of all aspects of behavior in organizational settings through the use of the scientific method.

As we have been alluding, the field of **organizational behavior** deals with human behavior in organizations. Formally defined, organizational behavior is the multidisciplinary field that seeks knowledge of behavior in organizational settings by systematically studying individual, group, and organizational processes. This knowledge is used both by scientists interested in understanding human behavior and by practitioners interested in enhancing organizational effectiveness and individual well-being. In this book we will highlight both these purposes, focusing on how scientific knowledge has been—or may be—used for these practical purposes.

Our definition of OB highlights four central characteristics of the field. First, OB is firmly grounded in the scientific method. Second, OB studies individuals, groups, and organizations. Third, OB is interdisciplinary in nature. And fourth, OB is used as the basis for enhancing organizational effectiveness and individual well-being. We will now take a closer look at these four characteristics of the field.

OB applies the scientific method to practical managerial problems. In our definition of OB, we refer to seeking knowledge and to studying behavioral processes. This should not be surprising since, as we noted earlier, OB knowledge is based on the **behavioral sciences.** These are fields such as psychology and sociology that seek knowledge of human behavior and society through the use of the scientific method. Although not as sophisticated as many scientific fields, such as physics or chemistry—nor as mature as them—OB's orientation is still scientific in nature. Thus, like other scientific fields, OB seeks to develop a base of knowledge by using an empirical, research-based approach. That is, it is based on systematic observation and measurement of the behavior or phenomenon of interest. As we will describe in the Appendix, organizational research is neither easy nor foolproof. Yet, it is widely agreed that the scientific method is the best way to learn about behavior in organizations. For this reason, the scientific orientation should be acknowledged as a hallmark of the field of OB.

behavioral sciences
Fields such as psychology and sociology that seek knowledge of human behavior and society through the use of the scientific method.

As they seek to improve organizational functioning and the quality of life of people working in organizations, managers rely heavily on knowledge derived from OB research. For example, researchers have shed light on such practical questions as:

- How can goals be set to enhance people's job performance?
- How may jobs be designed so as to enhance employees' feelings of satisfaction?
- Under what conditions do individuals make better decisions than groups?
- What can be done to improve the quality of organizational communication?
- What steps can be taken to alleviate work-related stress?
- How can leaders enhance the effectiveness of their teams?

Throughout this book we will describe scientific research and theory bearing on the answers to these and dozens of other practical questions. It is safe to say that the scientific and applied facets of OB not only coexist but also complement each other. Indeed, just as knowledge about the properties of physics may be put to use by engineers, and engineering data can be used to test theories of basic physics, so too are knowledge and practical applications closely intertwined in the field of OB.

OB focuses on three levels of analysis: Individuals, groups, and organizations. To best appreciate behavior in organizations, OB specialists cannot focus exclusively on individuals acting alone. After all, in organizational settings people frequently work together in groups and teams. Furthermore, people—alone and in groups—both influence and are influenced by their work environments. Considering this, it should not be surprising to learn that the field of OB focuses on three distinct levels of analysis—*individuals, groups,* and *organizations* (see Figure 1.2).

The field of OB recognizes that all three levels of analysis must be considered to fully comprehend the complex dynamics of behavior in organizations. Careful attention to all three levels of analysis is a central theme in modern OB and will be fully reflected throughout this text. For example, we will be describing how OB specialists are concerned with individual perceptions, attitudes, and motives. We also will be describing how people communicate with each other and coordinate their activities between themselves in work groups. Finally, we will examine organizations as a whole—the way they are structured and operate in their environments and the effects of their operations on the individuals and groups within them.

OB is multidisciplinary in nature. When you consider the broad range of issues and approaches taken by the field of OB, it is easy to appreciate the fact that the field is multidisciplinary in nature. By this, we mean that it draws on a wide variety of social science disciplines. Rather than studying a topic from only one particular perspective, the field of OB is likely to consider a wide variety of approaches. These range from the highly individual-oriented approach of psychology, through the more group-oriented approach of sociology, to issues in organizational quality studied by management scientists.

For a summary of some of the key fields from which the field of OB draws, see Table 1.1. If, as you read this book, you recognize some particular theory or approach as familiar, chances are good that you already learned something about it in another class. What makes OB so special is that it combines these various orientations together into a single—very broad and very exciting—field.

OB seeks to improve organizational effectiveness and the quality of life at work. In the early part of the twentieth century, as railroads opened up the western portion of the United States and the nation's population rapidly grew (it doubled from 1880 to 1920!), the demand for manufactured products was great. New manufacturing plants were built, attracting waves of new immigrants in search of a living wage and laborers lured off farms by the employment prospects factory work offered. These men and women found that factories were gigantic, noisy, hot, and highly regimented—in short, brutal places in which to work. Bosses demanded more and more of their employees and treated them like disposable machines, replacing those who quit or who died from accidents with others who waited outside the factory gates.

Clearly, the managers of a century ago held very negative views of employees. They assumed that people were basically lazy and irresponsible and treated them with disrespect. This very negativistic approach, which has been with us for many years, reflects

FIGURE 1.2
The Three Levels of Analysis Used in Organizational Behavior
To fully understand behavior in organizations, we must consider three levels of analysis: processes occurring within *individuals, groups,* and *organizations.*

Group Processes
(e.g., communication)

Individual Processes
(e.g., work attitudes)

Organizational
Processes
(e.g., structure)

TABLE 1.1   THE MULTIDISCIPLINARY ROOTS OF OB

Specialists in OB derive knowledge from a wide variety of social science disciplines to create a unique, multi-disciplinary field. Some of the most important parent disciplines are listed here, along with some of the OB topics to which they are related (and the chapters in this book in which they are discussed).

DISCIPLINE	RELEVANT OB TOPICS
Psychology	Perception and learning (Chapter 2); personality (Chapter 3); emotion and stress (Chapter 4); attitudes (Chapter 5); motivation (Chapter 6); decision making (Chapter 10); creativity (Chapter 14)
Sociology	Group dynamics (Chapter 8); socialization (Chapter 8); communication (Chapter 9)
Anthropology	Organizational culture (Chapter 14); leadership (Chapter 13)
Political science	Interpersonal conflict (Chapter 11); organizational power (Chapter 12)
Economics	Decision making (Chapter 10); negotiation (Chapter 11); organizational power (Chapter 12)
Management science	Technology (Chapter 16); organizational quality and change (Chapter 16)

Theory X

A traditional philosophy of management suggesting that most people are lazy and irresponsible and will work hard only when forced to do so.

Theory Y

A philosophy of management suggesting that under the right circumstances people are fully capable of working productively and accepting responsibility for their work.

the traditional view of management called the **Theory** X orientation. This philosophy of management assumes that people are basically lazy, dislike work, need direction, and will work hard only when they are pushed into performing.

Today, however, if you asked corporate officials to describe their views of human nature, you'd probably find some more optimistic beliefs. Although some of today's managers still think that people are basically lazy, most would argue that the vast majority of people are capable of working hard under the right conditions. If employees are recognized for their efforts (such as by being fairly paid) and are given an opportunity to succeed (such as by being well trained), they may be expected to put forth considerable effort without being pushed. Management's job, then, is to create those conditions that make people want to perform as desired.

The approach that assumes that people are not intrinsically lazy and that they are willing to work hard when the right conditions prevail is known as the **Theory Y** orientation. This philosophy assumes that people have a psychological need to work and seek achievement and responsibility. In contrast to the Theory X philosophy of management, which essentially demonstrates distrust for people on the job, the Theory Y approach is strongly associated with improving the quality of people's work lives (for a summary of the differences, see Figure 1.3).

The Theory Y perspective prevails within the field of organizational behavior today. It assumes that people are highly responsive to their work environments and that the ways they are treated will influence the ways they will act. In fact, OB scientist are very interested in learning exactly what conditions will lead people to behave most positively—that is, what makes work both productive for organizations and enjoyable for the people working in them. (Do your own assumptions about people at work more closely match a Theory X or Theory Y perspective? To find out, complete the Individual Exercise at the end of this chapter.)

Why Is It Important to Know About OB?

Have you ever had a job where people don't get along, nobody knows what to do, everyone is goofing off, and your boss is—well, putting it politely, unpleasant? We can't imagine that you liked working in that company at all. Now think of another position in which everyone is friendly, knowledgeable, hardworking, and very pleasant. Obviously, that's more to your liking. Such a situation is one in which you are likely to be interested

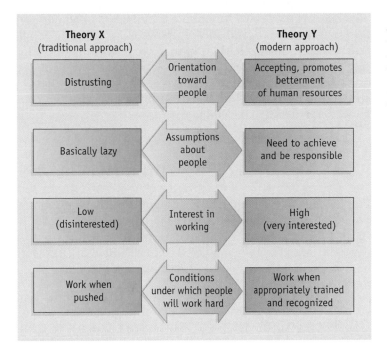

FIGURE 1.3
Theory X Versus Theory Y: A Summary
The traditional *Theory X* orientation toward people is far more negativistic than the more contemporary *Theory Y* approach, which is widely accepted today. Some of the key differences between these management philosophies are summarized here.

Theory X (traditional approach)		Theory Y (modern approach)
Distrusting	Orientation toward people	Accepting, promotes betterment of human resources
Basically lazy	Assumptions about people	Need to achieve and be responsible
Low (disinterested)	Interest in working	High (very interested)
Work when pushed	Conditions under which people will work hard	Work when appropriately trained and recognized

in going to work, doing your best, and taking pride in what you do. What lies at the heart of these differences are all issues that are of great concern to OB scientists and practitioners—and ones that we will cover in this book.

"Okay," you may be asking yourself, "in some companies things are nice and smooth, but in others, relationships are rocky—does it really matter?" As you will see throughout this book, the answer is a resounding *yes!* For now, here are just a few highlights of specific ways in which OB matters to people and the organizations in which they work.

- Companies whose managers accurately appraise the work of their subordinates enjoy lower costs and higher productivity than those that handle their appraisals less accurately.[2]
- People who are satisfied with the way they are treated on their jobs are generally more pleasant to their coworkers and bosses and are less likely to quit than those who are dissatisfied with the way others treat them.[3]
- People who are carefully trained to work together in teams tend to be happier and more productive than those who are simply thrown together without any definite organizational support.[4]
- Employees who believe they have been treated unfairly on the job are more likely to steal from their employers and to reject the policies of their organizations than those who believe they have been fairly treated.[5]
- People who are mistreated by their supervisors on the job have more mental and physical illnesses than those who are treated with kindness, dignity, and respect.[6]
- Organizations that treat employees well with respect to pay/benefits, opportunities, job security, friendliness, fairness, and pride in the company are on average twice as profitable as the Standard & Poor's 500 companies.[7]
- Companies that offer good employee benefits and that have friendly conditions are more profitable than those that are less people oriented.[8]

By now, you might be asking yourself: Why, if OB is so important, is there no one person in charge of it in an organization? After all, companies tend to have officials who are responsible for other basic areas, such as finance, accounting, marketing, and production. Why not OB? If you've never heard of a vice president of OB or a manager of organizational behavior, it's because organizations do not have any such formal posts. So then, back to the question: Who is responsible for organizational behavior? In a sense, the answer is everyone! Although OB is a separate area of study, it cuts across all areas of organizational functioning. Managers in all departments have to know such things as how to motivate their employees, how to keep people satisfied with their jobs, how to communicate fairly, how to make teams function effectively, and how to design jobs most effectively. In short, dealing with people at work is everybody's responsibility on the job. So, no matter what job you do in a company, knowing something about OB is sure to help you do it better. This is precisely why it's so vitally important for you to know the material in this book.

WHAT ARE THE FIELD'S FUNDAMENTAL ASSUMPTIONS?

The field of OB is guided by two straightforward assumptions—fundamental ideas that are widely accepted by everyone who does scientific research on OB or who puts these findings into practice in organizations. First, OB recognizes that organizations are dynamic and always changing. Second, the field of OB assumes there is no one single best way to behave in organizations and that different approaches are called for in different situations.

OB Recognizes the Dynamic Nature of Organizations

Although OB scientists and practitioners are interested in the behavior of people, they also are concerned about the nature of organizations themselves. Under what conditions will organizations change? How are organizations structured? How do organizations interact with their environments? These and related questions are of major interest to specialists in OB.

open systems

Self-sustaining systems that transform input from the external environment into output, which the system then returns to the environment.

OB scientists recognize that organizations are not static but are dynamic and everchanging entities. In other words, they recognize that organizations are **open systems**—that is, self-sustaining entities that use energy to transform resources from the environment (such as raw materials) into some form of output (e.g., a finished product).[9] Figure 1.4 summarizes some of the key properties of open systems.

As this diagram illustrates, organizations receive input from their environments and continuously transform it into output. This output gets transformed back into input, and the cyclical operation continues. Consider, for example, how organizations may tap the human resources of the community by hiring and training people to do jobs. These individuals may work to provide a product in exchange for wages. They then spend these wages, putting money back into the community, allowing more people to afford the company's products. This, in turn, creates the need for still more employees,

FIGURE 1.4

Organizations as Open Systems
The *open systems approach* is characteristic of modern-day thinking in the field of OB. It assumes that organizations are self-sustaining—that is, that they transform inputs to outputs in a continuous fashion.
(*Source:* Based on suggestions by Katz & Kahn, 1978; see Note 9.)

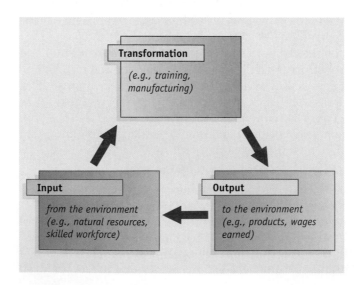

and so on. If you think about it this way, it's easy to realize that organizations are dynamic and constantly changing.

The dynamic nature of organizations can be likened to the operations of the human body. As people breathe, they take in oxygen and transform it into carbon dioxide. This, in turn, sustains the life of green plants, which in turn, emit oxygen for people to breathe. The continuous nature of the open system characterizes not only human life but the existence of organizations as well.

OB Assumes There Is No "One Best" Approach

What's the most effective way to motivate people? What style of leadership works best? Should groups of individuals be used to make important organizational decisions? Although these questions are quite reasonable, there is a basic problem with all of them. Namely, they all assume that there is a simple, unitary answer—that is, one best way to motivate, to lead, and to make decisions.

Specialists in the field of OB today agree that there is no one best approach when it comes to such complex phenomena. To assume otherwise is not only overly simplistic and naive but, as you will see, grossly inaccurate. When it comes to studying human behavior in organizations, there are no simple answers. For this reason, OB scholars embrace a **contingency approach**—an orientation that recognizes that behavior in work settings is the complex result of many interacting forces. This orientation is a hallmark of modern OB. Consider, for example, how an individual's personal characteristics (e.g., personal attitudes and beliefs) in conjunction with situational factors (e.g., an organization's climate, relations between coworkers) all may work together when it comes to influencing how a particular individual is likely to behave on the job.

With this in mind, explaining OB phenomena often requires saying, "it depends." As our knowledge of work-related behavior becomes increasingly complex, it is difficult to give "straight answers." Rather, it is usually necessary to say that people will do certain things "under some conditions" or "when all other factors are equal." Such phrases provide a clear indication that the contingency approach is being used. In other words, a certain behavior occurs "contingent upon" the existence of certain conditions—hence, the name. Not surprisingly, you will come across several contingency approaches to OB in this book.

contingency approach
A perspective suggesting that organizational behavior is affected by a large number of interacting factors. How someone will behave is said to be contingent upon many different variables at once.

OB THEN AND NOW: A CAPSULE HISTORY

Today we take for granted the importance of understanding the functioning of organizations and the behavior of people at work. However, it was only 100 years ago that people first became interested in studying behavior in organizations and only during the last 50 years that it gained widespread acceptance.[10] To enable you to appreciate how the relatively young field of OB got to where it is today, we now will outline its history and describe some of the most influential forces in its development.

The Early Days: Scientific Management and the Hawthorne Studies

The first attempts to study behavior in organizations came out of a desire by industrial efficiency experts to improve workers' productivity. Their central question was straightforward: What could be done to get people to do more work in less time? This question was posed in a period of rapid industrialization and technological change in the United States. As engineers attempted to make machines more efficient, it was a natural extension of their efforts to work on the human side of the equation—making people more productive, too.

Among the earliest pioneers in this area was Frederick Winslow Taylor, an engineer who noticed the inefficient practices of the employees in the steel mill in which he

time-and-motion study

A type of applied research designed to classify and streamline the individual movements needed to perform jobs with the intent of finding "the one best way" to perform them.

scientific management

An early approach to management and organizational behavior emphasizing the importance of designing jobs as efficiently as possible.

human relations movement

A perspective on organizational behavior that rejects the primarily economic orientation of scientific management and recognizes, instead, the importance of social processes in work settings.

Hawthorne studies

The earliest systematic research in the field of OB, this work was performed to determine how the design of work environments affected performance.

worked and attempted to change them.[11] This led Taylor to study the individual movements of laborers performing different jobs, searching for ways to perform them that resulted in the fewest wasted movements. Research of this type was referred to as **time-and-motion studies.** In 1911, Taylor advanced the concept of **scientific management,** which not only identified ways to design manual labor jobs more efficiently but also emphasized carefully selecting and training people to perform them. Although we take these ideas for granted today, Taylor is acknowledged to be the first person to carefully study human behavior at work.[12]

Inspired by the prospects of scientific management, other work experts advanced the idea that social factors operating in the workplace are an important determinant of how effectively people work. At the forefront of this effort was Elton W. Mayo, an organizational scientist and consultant widely regarded as the founder of what is called the **human relations movement.**[13] This approach emphasized that the social conditions existing in organizations—the way employees are treated by management and the relationships they have with each other—influence job performance.[14]

This orientation was developed in the first studies of organizational behavior known as the **Hawthorne studies.** Begun in 1927 at the Western Electric's Hawthorne Works near Chicago, Mayo and his associates were interested in determining, among other things, how to design work environments in ways that increased performance. With this objective in mind, they systematically altered key aspects of the work environment (e.g., illumination, the length of rest pauses, the duration of the workday and workweek) to see their effects on work performance. What they found was baffling: Productivity improved following almost every change in working conditions.[15] In fact, performance remained extremely high even when conditions were returned to the way they were before the study began. However, workers didn't always improve their performance. In another set of studies, workers sometimes restricted their output deliberately. Not only did they stop working long before quitting time, but in interviews, they also admitted that they easily could have done more if they desired.

What accounts for these fascinating findings? Mayo recognized that the answer resided in the fact that how effectively people work depends not only on the physical characteristics of the working conditions but also on the social conditions encountered. In the first set of studies, in which productivity rose in all conditions, people simply were responding favorably to the special attention they received. Knowing they were being studied made them feel special and motivated them to do their best. Hence, it was these social factors more than the physical factors that had such profound effects on job performance. The same explanation applies to the case in which people restricted their performance. Here employees feared that because they were being studied, the company eventually was going to raise the amount of work they were expected to do each day. So to guard against the imposition of unreasonable standards (and, hopefully, to keep their jobs!), the workers agreed among themselves to keep output low. In other words, informal rules were established about what constituted acceptable levels of job performance. These social forces at work in this setting proved to be much more potent determinants of job performance than the physical factors studied.

This conclusion, based on the surprising findings of the Hawthorne studies, is important because it ushered in a whole new way of thinking about behavior at work. It suggests that to understand behavior on the job we must fully appreciate people's attitudes and the processes by which they communicate with each other. This way of thinking, so fundamental to modern OB, may be traced back to Elton Mayo's pioneering Hawthorne studies.

Classical Organizational Theory

classical organizational theory

An early approach to the study of management that focused on the most efficient way of structuring organizations.

During the same time that proponents of scientific management got people to begin thinking about the interrelationships between people and their jobs, another approach to managing people emerged. This perspective, known as **classical organizational the-**

ory, focused on the efficient structuring of overall organizations. The idea was that there is an ideal way to efficiently organize work in all organizations—much as proponents of scientific management searched for the ideal way to perform particular jobs.

One of the most influential classical organizational theorists was Henri Fayol, a French industrialist who pioneered various ideas about how organizations should be structured. For example, Fayol advocated that there should be a **division of labor,** the practice of dividing work into specialized tasks that enable people to specialize in what they do best. He also argued that in any organization it always should be clear to whom each worker is responsible—that is, which managers have authority over them. Although many of these ideas are regarded to be simplistic today, they were considered quite pioneering some 80 years ago.

Another well-known classical organizational theorist is the German sociologist, Max Weber.[16] Among other things, Weber is well known for proposing a form of organizational structure known as the **bureaucracy**—a form of organization in which a set of rules is applied that keep higher-ranking organizational officials in charge of lower-ranking workers, who fulfill the duties assigned to them. As the description suggests, bureaucracies are organizations that carefully differentiate between those who give the orders and those who carry them out. A fan of bureaucracies, Henry Ford openly endorsed "the reduction of the necessity for thought on the part of the worker."[17] Making this possible are rules such as those summarized in Table 1.2.

Given your own experiences with bureaucracies, you're probably not surprised to hear that this particular organizational form has not proven to be the perfect way to organize all work. Weber's universal view of bureaucratic structure contrasts with the more modern approaches to organizational design (see Chapter 15) that claim that different forms of organizational structure may be more or less appropriate under different situations. (This is the contingency approach we described earlier.) Also, because bureaucracies draw sharp lines between the people who make decisions (managers) and those who carry them out (workers), they are not particularly popular today. After all, contemporary employees prefer to have more equal opportunities to make decisions than bureaucracies permit. Still, contemporary OB owes a great deal to Weber for his many pioneering ideas.

division of labor
The practice of dividing work into specialized tasks that enable people to specialize in what they do best.

bureaucracy
An organizational design developed by Max Weber that attempts to make organizations operate efficiently by having a clear hierarchy of authority in which people are required to perform well-defined jobs.

TABLE 1.2 CHARACTERISTICS OF AN IDEAL BUREAUCRACY

According to Max Weber, bureaucracies are the ideal organizational form. To function effectively, bureaucracies must possess the characteristics identified here.

CHARACTERISTIC	DESCRIPTION
Formal rules and regulations	Written guidelines are used to control all employees' behaviors.
Impersonal treatment	Favoritism is to be avoided, and all work relationships are to be based on objective standards.
Division of labor	All duties are divided into specialized tasks and are performed by individuals with the appropriate skills.
Hierarchical structure	Positions are ranked by authority level in clear fashion from lower-level to upper-level ones.
Authority structure	The making of decisions is determined by one's position in the hierarchy; higher-ranking people have authority over those in lower-ranking positions.
Lifelong career commitment	Employment is viewed as a permanent, lifelong obligation on the part of the organization and its employees.
Rationality	The organization is committed to achieving its ends (e.g., profitability) in the most efficient manner possible.

Late Twentieth Century: Organizational Behavior as a Social Science

Based on contributions noted thus far, the realization that behavior in work settings is shaped by a wide range of individual, group, and organizational factors set the stage for the emergence of the science of organizational behavior. By the 1940s, doctoral degrees were awarded in OB and the first textbooks were published.[18] By the late 1950s and early 1960s, OB was clearly a going concern. By the 1970s, active programs of research were going on—investigations into such key processes as motivation and leadership, and the impact of organizational structure.[19]

Unfortunately—but not unexpectedly for a new field—the development of scientific investigations into managerial and organizational issues was uneven and unsystematic in the middle part of the twentieth century. In response to this state of affairs, the Ford Foundation sponsored a project in which economists carefully analyzed the nature of business education in the United States. They published their findings in 1959, in what became a very influential work known as the *Gordon and Howell report.*[20] In this work, it was recommended that the study of management pay greater attention to basic academic disciplines, especially the social sciences. This advice had an enormous influence on business school curricula during the 1960s and promoted the development of the field of organizational behavior. After all, it is a field that draws heavily on the basic social science disciplines recommended for incorporation into business curricula in this report.

Stimulated by this work, the field of OB rapidly grew into one that borrowed heavily from other disciplines. In fact, the field of OB as we know it today may be characterized as a hybrid science that draws from many social science fields. For example, as we noted in Table 1.1, studies of personality, learning, and perception draw on psychology. Similarly, the study of group dynamics and leadership relies heavily on sociology. The topic of organizational communication networks, obviously, draws on research in the field of communication. Power and politics are studied by political scientists. Anthropologists study cross-cultural themes. And OB scientists look to the field of management science to understand ways to manage quality in organizations. By the time the twentieth century drew to a close, OB clearly was a multidisciplinary field that was making important contributions to both science and practice.

OB Today: The Infotech Age

A century ago, when scientists first became aware of the importance of managing people, their primary challenge involved getting individuals to work efficiently, and they did so by treating people like the machines with which they worked—pushing them as hard as possible, sometimes until they broke down. Then, as we became more aware of the importance of the human element in the workplace, it became fashionable to treat people in a more humane fashion. Today, in what has been called *the infotech age,* computer technology has made it possible to eliminate vast amounts of grunt work that laborers used to have to perform (see Figure 1.5). Much boring, monotonous, and dangerous physical labor has been eliminated by computer technology, and this has changed considerably the way people work.

Modern technology also has changed the way managers operate. Traditionally, low-level workers gathered information and fed it to higher-level workers, who carefully analyzed it all and made decisions for lower-level workers to carry out. Today, however, easy access to information in computer databases has made it possible for almost any worker to gather the facts needed to make his or her own decisions. And, although some managers still make decisions on behalf of their workers, today we are likely to see employees making many of their own decisions with the aid of information stored on computers. Because managers no longer have to be highly involved in their subordinates' work, they are free to concentrate on the big picture and to come up with innovative ways to improve the whole organization.

At the same time, the best managers have learned that they can use this opportunity, as one observer said, "to tap employees' most essential humanity, their ability to create,

FIGURE 1.5
Work in Today's Infotech Age
Computer technology has eliminated the drudgery of many traditional jobs. Just ask these monks.
(*Source:* Reprinted with permission of Cartoonbank.com)

judge, imagine, and build relationships."[21] It is this focus that characterizes today's organizations—hence, the field of OB. Today, people are likely to care at least as much about the work they do as the money they make. They are likely to be deeply concerned about what their organization stands for and the extent that they can make meaningful contributions to it. In short, contemporary OB recognizes that people care more than ever about the interpersonal side of work—recognition, relationships, and social interaction.

Despite the fact that technology has advanced, changing the way employees work, people themselves have not changed. All of us are human, and just because we work differently than before, we should not discard the things about the behavior of people we have learned over the years.[22] Twenty-first-century OB scientists are busily at work cultivating that humanity by doing things that make it possible to do work that is more challenging, meaningful, and interesting to them than ever before. Although this focus is not entirely unique to the twenty-first century, it's safe to say that its keen emphasis is indeed a key characteristic of modern OB.

To fully appreciate the nature of OB as a contemporary field, it is important to recognize its connection to the various economic, social, and cultural trends and forces that shape today's society. Specifically, these include three prominent trends: (1) the rise of global businesses with culturally diverse workforces, (2) rapid advances in technology, and (3) the rising expectations of people in general. We will discuss these forces in the three remaining sections of this chapter.

OB RESPONDS TO THE RISE OF GLOBALIZATION AND DIVERSITY

When your grandfather went to work, chances are good that he faced a world of work that was quite different than the kind that exists today. For one, the company he worked for was likely to be headquartered in the United States and faced competition from other U.S.-based organizations. He also was unlikely to find many women on the job—at least, not in high-ranking positions—nor were there as many African Americans, Hispanics, and Asians working along with him. And, when he reached 65, in all likelihood, he retired. As we will describe here, this picture has all but disappeared. Today's organizations are global in nature, and are populated by women and people of color, not to mention individuals who are working well into what would have once been considered "retirement years." All of this, as we will note, has important implications for OB.

International Business and the Global Economy

To fully understand behavior in organizations we must appreciate the fact that today's organizations operate within an economic system that is truly international in scope.[23]

There's no mistaking the fact that advances in technology have made globalization a reality. After all, high-tech devices make it easier than ever for people to communicate with one another regardless of where they may be located in the world. As a case in point, consider Iceland—a country in which, over the years, physical isolation and rugged terrain made communication difficult or impossible. Today, however, the advent of wireless telecommunications technology has turned things around. In fact, this country of only 279,000 inhabitants is the most computer-savvy and Internet-using population in the world today.[25] With 75.8 percent of its residents using cellular phones, Iceland currently ranks first among the world's nations with respect to the adoption of mobile phones. It also ranks third internationally in per capita connections to the Internet.

These distinctions reflect more than Icelanders' interest in keeping in touch with friends and relatives in places where land lines are difficult to install. It also reflects their interest in diversifying the country's economic base. Nearly 70 percent of Iceland's income comes from the fishing industry, and in a country with

globalization
The process of interconnecting the world's people with respect to the cultural, economic, political, technological, and environmental aspects of their lives.

The nations of the world are not isolated from one another economically; what happens in one country has effects on other countries. For example, when terrorists struck the United States on September 11, 2001, it sent ripples throughout the economic markets of the world for many months. This tendency for countries to be influenced by one another is known as **globalization**—the process of interconnecting the world's people with respect to the cultural, economic, political, technological, and environmental aspects of their lives.[24] The trend toward globalization, which has been widespread in recent years, has been fueled by three major forces. First, technology has drastically lowered the cost of transportation and communication, thereby enhancing opportunities for international commerce (for an example, see the OB in a Diverse World section above). Second, laws restricting trade generally have become liberalized throughout the world (e.g., in the United States and other heavily industrialized countries, free trade policies have been advocated). Third, developing nations have sought to expand their economies by promoting exports and opening their doors to foreign companies seeking investments.

multinational enterprises (MNEs)
Organizations that have significant operations spread throughout various nations but are headquartered in a single country.

If international trade is the major driver of globalization, then the primary vehicles are **multinational enterprises** (MNEs)—organizations that have significant operations spread throughout various nations but are headquartered in a single country. General Electric (GE) is an example of an MNE. It employs 313,000 people in companies located throughout the world. Yet, they all draw resources from company headquarters in Fairfield, Connecticut (see Figure 1.6). They also adhere to the same strategy—to insist on excellence for customers in all endeavors. As you might imagine, the rise of MNEs has resulted in large numbers of people, known as **expatriates,** who are citizens of one country living and working in another country. For example, at Matsushita Electric, the large Japan-based MNE, over half of the employees live and work in other countries.[26]

expatriates
People who are citizens of one country but who are living and working in another country.

culture
The set of values, customs, and beliefs that people have in common with other members of a social unit (e.g., a nation).

While working abroad, people are exposed to different **cultures**—the set of values, customs, and beliefs that people have in common with other members of a social unit (e.g., a nation).[27] And, when people are faced with new culture, it is not unusual for them to become confused and disoriented—a phenomenon known as **culture shock.**[28] People also experience culture shock when they return to their native cultures after spending time away from home—a process of readjustment known as **repatriation.** In general, the phenomenon of culture shock results from people's recognition of the fact

culture shock
The tendency for people to become confused and disoriented as they attempt to adjust to a new culture.

only limited natural resources, technology provides useful ways to move in new directions. In general, Icelanders are highly educated and literate and enjoy technical innovation. They are also very well trained in technology (ranking fifth worldwide in the availability of technical skills) and have a strong entrepreneurial spirit. Given these human resources, it is not surprising that Iceland's move to a high-tech economy has proven successful. The software business is booming and, although the information technology industry currently accounts for only 5 percent of Iceland's national profits, this figure is expected to double in only a few years. Also thriving is the development of e-commerce (i.e., business conducted over the Web). Despite the country's isolated location, the technically competent people of Iceland are making it a Mecca of European high tech.

Not surprisingly, foreign companies have been investing in Iceland's booming high-tech businesses. In fact, the largest telecommunications company, TAL, although an Icelandic company, has majority ownership by the American company, World Wide International. As a result, Iceland has become a far wealthier and more active member of the international global community than ever before. And this has led Iceland to become the nation with the highest employment rate in the world (97.3 percent). This stimulates the economy, which leads Icelanders to become even wealthier. If this keeps up, you soon will be seeing "Product of Iceland" labels on more than just packages of frozen fish and records by Björk.

that others may be different from them in ways that they never imagined, and this takes some getting used to.

Scientists have observed that the process of adjusting to a foreign culture generally follows a U-shaped curve (see Figure 1.7).[29] That is, at first, people are optimistic and excited about learning a new culture. This usually lasts about a month or so. Then, for the next several months, they become frustrated and confused as they struggle to learn the new culture (i.e., culture shock occurs). Finally, after about six months, people adjust to their new cultures and become more accepting of them and satisfied with them. These observations imply that feelings of culture shock are inevitable. Although some degree of frustration may be expected when you first enter a new country, the more time you spend learning its ways, the better you will come to understand and accept your new surroundings.[30]

repatriation
The process of readjusting to one's own culture after spending time away from it.

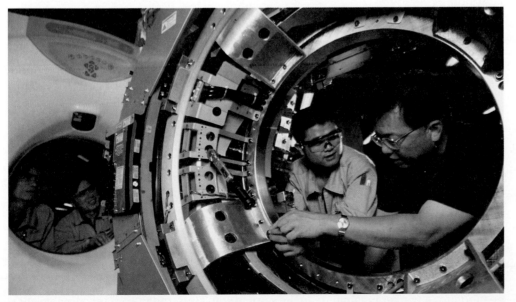

FIGURE 1.6

GE: A Multinational Enterprise
With offices and factories located in over 100 countries, GE is a good example of a multinational enterprise. This fact comes as no surprise to Chih Chen, the manager of GE's manufacturing plant in Beijing, China, shown here (right) inspecting a medical-imaging machine assembled at his facility. This is just one of four Asian locations that manufactures medical equipment designed at GE's Medical Systems located in Milwaukee and sold throughout the world.

FIGURE 1.7

Adjusting to Foreign Culture: The General Stages

People's adjustment to new cultures generally follows the U-shaped curve illustrated here. After an initial period of excitement, *culture shock* often sets in. Then, after this period of adjustment (about six months), the more time spent in the new culture, the better it is accepted.

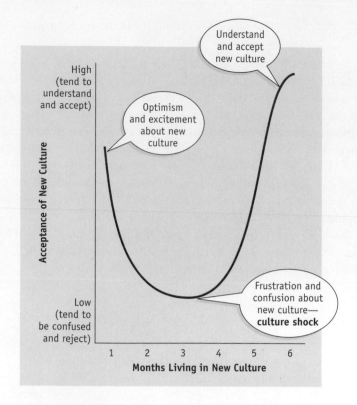

In general, culture shock results from the tendency for people to be highly *parochial* in their assumptions about others, taking a narrow view of the world by believing that there is one best way of doing things. They also tend to be highly *ethnocentric*, believing that their way of doing things is the best way. For example, Americans tend to be highly parochial by speaking only English (whereas most Europeans speak several languages) and ethnocentric by believing that everyone else in the world should learn their language. As we just explained, over time, exposure to other cultures teaches people that there may be many different ways of doing the same thing (making them less parochial) and that these may be equally good, if not better (making them less ethnocentric). Although these biases may have been reasonable for Americans 50 years ago when the United States was the world's dominant economic power (producing three-quarters of its wealth), such views would be extremely costly today. Indeed, because the world's economy is global in nature, highly parochial and ethnocentric views cannot be tolerated.

Analogously, highly narrow and biased views about the management of people in organizations may severely limit our understanding about behavior in organizations. During the 1950s and 1960s, management scholars tended to overlook the importance of cultural differences in organizations. They made two key assumptions: (1) that principles of good management are universal, and (2) that the best management practices are ones that work well in the United States.[31] This highly inflexible approach is known as the **convergence hypothesis.** Such a biased orientation reflects the fact that the study of behavior in organizations first emerged at a time in which the United States was the world's predominant economic power.

With the ever-growing global economy, it has become clear that an American-oriented approach may be highly misleading when it comes to understanding organizational practices that work best in various countries. In fact, there may be many possible ways to manage effectively, and these will depend greatly on the individual culture in which people live. This alternative approach, which is widely accepted today, is known as the **divergence hypothesis.** Following this orientation, understanding the behavior of people at work requires carefully appreciating the cultural context within which they operate. For example, whereas American cultural norms suggest that it would not be inappropriate for an employee to question his or her superior, it would be taboo for a worker in Japan to do the same thing. Thus, today's organizational schol-

convergence hypothesis

A biased approach to the study of management, which assumes that principles of good management are universal, and that ones that work well in the United States will apply equally well in other nations.

divergence hypothesis

The approach to the study of management that recognizes that knowing how to manage most effectively requires clear understanding of the culture in which people work.

ars are becoming increasingly sensitive to the ways in which culture influences organizational behavior.

The Shifting Demographics of the Workforce: Trends Toward Diversity

Thus far, we have been discussing cultural differences between people from companies in different nations. However, widespread cultural differences also may be found *within* organizations. A broad range of people from both sexes, different races, ethnic groups, nationalities, and ages can be found throughout U.S. organizations, and as summarized in Figure 1.8, their proportions have been changing.[32] Modern organizations are doing many things to accommodate—and capitalize on—growing levels of diversity within the workforce.

More women are in the workforce than ever before. In the 1950s, the "typical American family" was characterized by a man who went to work and his wife, who stayed at home and watched the children. Although this profile still may be found, it is far from common. In fact, over half of all women are employed outside the home, and just under half of all people in the workplace (46.2 percent) are women—and these figures have been rising steadily over the years (see Figure 1.8).[33] This trend stems from not only economic necessity but also from the growing social acceptance of women working outside the home. As women, who traditionally have worked inside the home, have moved to working outside the home, companies have found it beneficial—or even necessary, in some cases—to make accommodations that help make this possible. For a look at some of the most popular practices in this regard, see the Best Practices section that follows.

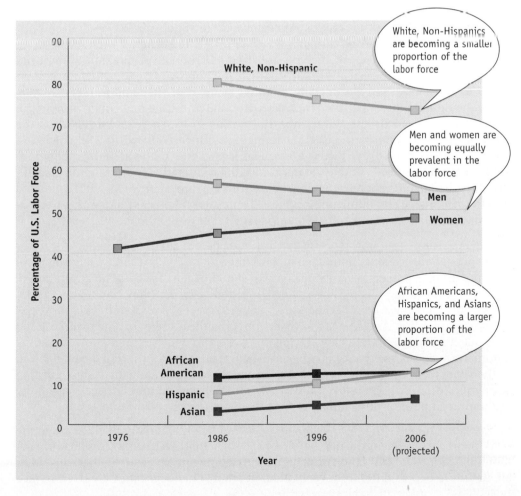

FIGURE 1.8

Women and Minorities in the Workplace: Their Numbers Are Rising
Statistics have shown that the relative percentage of whites in the U.S. workforce, although currently highest, is dropping. However, the relative percentage of women, African Americans, Hispanics, and Asians is rising. As this trend continues, the term *minority* group promises to lose its meaning.
(*Source:* Based on data reported by Lerman & Schmidt, 2002; see Note 32.)

BEST PRACTICES
EMPLOYEE SUPPORT POLICIES

With increasing frequency, companies are taking proactive steps to help employees meet their personal needs and family obligations. In so doing, they make it possible for employees to satisfy the demands imposed by their nonwork lives. And this allows companies to draw on the talents of a diverse group of prospective employees who otherwise might not be able to lend their talents to the organization. Three practices have proven especially useful in this regard.

■ **Child-care facilities.** These are sites at or near company locations where parents can leave their children while they are working. America West, for example, believes so strongly in the importance of providing child care that it offers these services 24 hours a day. The company even maintained these benefits while it was going through bankruptcy proceedings in 1991.[34]

■ **Elder-care facilities.** Just as companies are making facilities available to employees for taking care of their children, they are, with increasing frequency, making facilities available for the care of their elderly relatives, such as parents and grandparents.[35] For example, Lancaster Laboratories (in Lancaster, Pennsylvania) provides a place where its employees can bring adult family members who are in need of care during working hours.[36] The *St. Petersburg Times* advises its employees about ways to help meet the problems of elderly family members.[37] Given projections that multigenerational families will become increasingly commonplace in the next

---

child-care facilities
Sites at or near company locations where parents can leave their children while they are working.

elder-care facilities
Facilities at which employees at work can leave elderly relatives for whom they are responsible (such as parents and grandparents).

baby boom generation
The generation of children born in the economic boom period following World War II.

Racial and ethnic diversity is reality. As recently as the middle of the twentieth century, the workplace was composed primarily of white males. Today, however, the balance of men and women in the workplace is almost equal, and the proportion of minority group members has grown so rapidly that white people are a considerably smaller majority (see Figure 1.8). Specifically, although white non-Hispanic workers are currently the dominant group, their proportion dropped from 79.8 percent in 1986 to 75.3 percent in 1996 and is expected to drop still further to 72.7 percent by 2006.[42] At the same time, there will be increases in the numbers of African Americans, Hispanics, and Asians in the workforce (see Figure 1.8)—in large part due to liberal immigration policies. Beginning in 1990, members of minority groups entered the workforce at a greater rate than the majority, thereby making them even more prevalent. In fact, it is estimated that by 2050, racial and ethnic minorities will comprise 47 percent of the U.S. population, making obsolete the current term *minority*.[43]

People are living—and working—longer than ever before. In the years after World War II, the peacetime economy flourished in the United States. With it came a large increase in population as soldiers returned from the war and began families. The generation of children born during this period is widely referred to as the **baby boom generation.** Today, the first of these baby boomers are turning 55 and are considered "older workers" by labor economists. And, only a few years from now, the number of older people in the workplace will swell dramatically. Living in a period in which retirement is no longer automatic at age 65, aged baby boomers will comprise a growing part of the population in the years to come. In fact, people over 85 years old are already the fastest-growing segment of the U.S. population.[44] Clearly, this trend has profound implications on the traditional patterns of work and retirement that have developed over the years.

Implications for OB. That more women, people of color, and older workers are in the workforce than ever before is not merely an idle sociological curiosity. It also has important implications for OB—and ones that we will examine more closely in this book. After all, the more people differ from each other, the more challenges they are likely to face few decades, experts expect elder-care facilities to grow in popularity.

- **Personal support policies.** These are widely varied practices that help employees meet the demands of their family lives, freeing them to concentrate on their work. For example, the SAS Institute (Cary, North Carolina) not only offers its employees free, on-site Montessori child care but also nutritious take-home dinners. Wilton Connor Packaging (Charlotte, North Carolina) provides even more unusual forms of support, such as an on-site laundry, high school equivalency classes, door-to-door transportation, and a children's clothing swap center.[38]

Although these practices may be expensive, the organizations that use them generally are convinced that they are in several respects wise investments. First, they help retain highly valued employees—not only keeping them from competitors but also saving the costs of having to replace them. In fact, officials at AT&T found that the average cost of letting new parents take up to a year of unpaid parental leave was only 32 percent of an employee's annual salary, compared with the 150 percent cost of replacing that person permanently.[39]

Second, by alleviating the distractions of having to worry about nonwork issues, employees are free to concentrate on their jobs and to be their most creative. Research has found that people who use the support systems their employers provide are not only more active in team problem-solving activities but also are almost twice as likely to submit useful suggestions for improvement. Commenting on such findings, Ellen Galinsky, co-president of the Families & Work Institute, said, "There's a cost to *not* providing work and family assistance."[40]

A third benefit—and an important one, at that—is that such policies help attract the most qualified human resources, giving companies that use them a competitive edge over those that do not.[41]

when interacting with one another. How these play out is likely to be seen on the job in important ways. For example, as we will describe, differences in age, gender, and ethnic group membership are likely to bring with them differences in communication style that must be addressed for organizations to function effectively (see Chapter 10). It also is the case that people at different stages of their lives are likely to be motivated by different things (see Chapter 6) and to be satisfied with different aspects of their jobs (see Chapter 5). And, as people adjust to a wider diversity in the workplace, issues about their norms and values (see Chapter 8) are likely to come up, as well as their willingness to accept others who are different from themselves (see Chapter 5). This can have important implications for potential conflict in the workplace (see Chapter 12) and their career choices (see Chapter 7), which may be expected to influence their capacity to work effectively as members of the same work teams (see Chapter 9).

personal support policies
Widely varied practices that help employees meet the demands of their family lives, freeing them to concentrate on their work.

OB RESPONDS TO ADVANCES IN TECHNOLOGY

Since the industrial revolution, people performed carefully prescribed sets of tasks—known as *jobs*—within large networks of people who answered to those above them in hierarchical arrangements known as *organizations*. This picture, although highly simplistic, does a good job of characterizing the working arrangements that most people had during much of the twentieth century. However, today, in the twenty-first century, the essential nature of jobs and organizations as we have known them is changing. Although many factors are responsible for such change, experts agree that the major catalyst is rapidly advancing computer technology, especially the use of the Internet and wireless technology (see Figure 1.9).[45] As you might imagine, this state of affairs has important implications for organizations—and, hence, the field of OB. After all, as more work is shifted to digital brains, some work that was once performed by human brains becomes obsolete. At the same time, new opportunities arise as people scurry to find

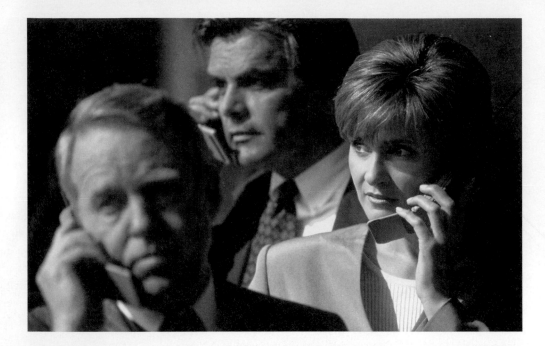

their footing amidst the shifting terrain of the high-tech revolution. The implications of this for OB are considerable. We will now consider some of the most prominent trends in the world of work that have been identified in recent years. These involve how work is organized and performed, as well as the need for flexibility.

Leaner Organizations: Downsizing and Outsourcing

Technology has made it possible for fewer people to do more work than ever before. Automation, the process of replacing people with machines, is not new, of course; it has gone on, slowly and steadily, for centuries. Today, however, because it is not large mechanical devices but the manipulation of digital data that is responsible for how people work, scientists have referred to the *informating* of the workplace.

informate

The process by which workers manipulate objects by "inserting data" between themselves and those objects.

The term **informate** describes the process by which workers manipulate objects by "inserting data" between themselves and those objects.[46] When jobs are informated, information technology is used to change a formerly physical task into one that involves manipulating a sequence of digital commands. So, for example, a modern factory worker can move around large sheets of steel by pressing a few buttons on a keypad. Likewise, with the right programming, an order entered into a salesperson's laptop computer can trigger a chain of events involving everything associated with the job: placing an order for supplies, manufacturing the product to exact specifications, delivering the final product, sending out an invoice, and even crediting the proper commission to the salesperson's payroll check.

Unlike the gradual process of automation, today's technology—and the process of informating—is occurring so rapidly that the very nature of work is changing as fast as we can keep up. With this, many jobs are disappearing, leaving organizations (at least the most successful ones!) smaller than before.[47] Product manufacturing also has been informated. At GE's Faunc Automation plant in Charlottesville, Virginia, for example, circuitboards are manufactured by half as many employees as required before informating the facility.[48] Not only blue-collar, manual labor jobs are being eliminated but also white-collar, mental labor jobs are disappearing as well. In many places, middle managers are no longer needed to make decisions that can now be made by computers. It's little wonder that middle managers, although only 10 percent of the workforce, comprise 20 percent of recent layoffs.

downsizing

The process of adjusting downward the number of employees needed to work in newly designed organizations (also known as *rightsizing*).

Indeed, organizations have been rapidly reducing the number of employees needed to operate effectively—a process known as **downsizing**.[49] Typically, this involves more than just laying off people in a move to save money. It is directed at adjusting the number of employees needed to work in newly designed organizations and is, therefore, also known as **rightsizing**.[50] Whatever you call it, the bottom line is clear. Many organizations need fewer people to operate today than in the past—sometimes far fewer. The statistics tell a sobering tale. From January 1997 through December 1999, 3.3 million American workers found their jobs eliminated.[51] Since 2000, the most job losses have occurred in Internet-based ("dot-com") companies, retail stores, the auto industry, and media (e.g., publishing and advertising). Downsizings are not a unique manifestation of current economic trends. During the past decade, some degree of downsizing has occurred in about half of all companies—especially in the middle-management and supervisory ranks (to see who's most likely and least likely to get laid off, see Table 1.3).[52] Experts agree that rapid changes in technology have been largely responsible for much of this.

rightsizing
See *downsizing*.

Another way organizations are restructuring is by completely eliminating those parts of themselves that focus on noncore sectors of the business (i.e., tasks that are peripheral to the organization) and hiring outside firms to perform these functions instead—a practice known as **outsourcing**.[53] By outsourcing secondary activities an organization can focus on what it does best, its key capability—what is known as its **core competency.** Companies like ServiceMaster, which provides janitorial services, and ADP, which provides payroll processing services, make it possible for their client organizations to concentrate on the business functions most central to their missions. So, for example, by outsourcing its maintenance work or its payroll processing, a manufacturing company may grow smaller and focus its resources on what it does best—manufacturing.

outsourcing
The process of eliminating those parts of organizations that focus on noncore sectors of the business (i.e., tasks that are peripheral to the organization) and hiring outside firms to perform these functions instead.

core competency
An organization's key capability, what it does best.

Some critics fear that outsourcing represents a "hollowing out" of companies—a reduction of functions that weakens organizations by making them more dependent on others.[54] Others counter that outsourcing makes sense when the work that is outsourced is not highly critical to competitive success (e.g., janitorial services), or when it is so highly critical that it can succeed only by seeking outside assistance.[55] For example, it is widespread practice for companies selling personal computers today to outsource the manufacturing of various components (e.g., hard drives, CD-ROMs, and chips) to other companies.[56] Although this practice may sound atypical compared to what occurs in most manufacturing companies, it isn't. In fact, one industry analyst has

TABLE 1.3   ARE YOU LIKELY TO BECOME A VICTIM OF DOWNSIZING?

Based on prevailing patterns of downsizing, some people are more vulnerable to getting laid off, whereas others are generally safer. Here are some rough guidelines for assessing your own vulnerability to downsizing.

YOU ARE VULNERABLE TO GETTING LAID OFF IF . . .	YOU ARE MORE IMMUNE FROM LAYOFFS IF . . .
You are paid over $150,000.	You have a good relationship with your boss.
You are inflexible and unwilling to transfer to a new job or to another city.	You have a midrange salary.
You work in retail, automotive, or manufacturing businesses.	You generate revenue for the company
You are a top executive of a division that is not performing up to expectations.	You have expertise in a technical field
You lack computer skills.	You have demonstrated willingness to work long hours whenever necessary
You do not have good leadership skills.	You are willing to relocate to another city or to transfer to another position in the company

(*Source:* Based on suggestions by McGinn & Naughton, 2001; see Note 52.)

estimated that 30 percent of the largest American industrial firms outsource over half their manufacturing.[57]

The Virtual Corporation: A Network of Temporary Organizations

virtual corporation
A highly flexible, temporary organization formed by a group of companies that join forces to exploit a specific opportunity.

As more and more companies are outsourcing various organizational functions and are paring down to their core competencies, they might not be able to perform all the tasks required to complete a project. However, they certainly can perform their own highly specialized part of it very well. Now, if you put together several organizations whose competencies complement each other and have them work together on a special project, you'd have a very strong group of collaborators. This is the idea behind an organizational arrangement that is growing in popularity—the **virtual corporation.** A virtual corporation is a highly flexible, temporary organization formed by a group of companies that join forces to exploit a specific opportunity.[58]

For example, various companies often come together to work on special projects in the entertainment industry (e.g., to produce a motion picture) and in the field of construction (e.g., to build a shopping center). After all, technologies are changing so rapidly and skills are becoming so specialized these days that no one company can do everything by itself. And so, they join forces temporarily to form virtual corporations—not permanent organizations but temporary ones without their own offices or organizational charts. Although virtual corporations are not yet common, experts expect them to grow in popularity in the years ahead.[59] As one consultant described the virtual corporation, "It's not just a good idea; it's inevitable."[60]

Telecommuting: Going to Work Without Leaving Home

telecommuting (teleworking)
The practice of using communications technology so as to enable work to be performed from remote locations, such as the home.

In recent years, the practice of **telecommuting** (also known as **teleworking**) has been growing in popularity. This is the practice of using communications technology so as to enable work to be performed from remote locations, such as the home. Telecommuting—which is used at such companies as JCPenney and Pacific Bell—makes it possible for employees to avoid the hassle of daily commuting.[61] It also allows companies to comply with governmental regulations (e.g., the Federal Clean Air Act of 1990) requiring them to reduce the number of trips made by their employees.

Statistics indicate that telecommuting is in full swing today.[62] In fact, as of 2001, 28.8 million American workers (one in five) engaged in some form of telework, representing a 17 percent increase from 2000. Not surprisingly, according to an official of the International Teleworkers Association and Council, "Telework has evolved beyond the pioneering telecommuters of the '80s," and "it appears to be entering the mainstream of today's workforce."

The typical telecommuter works at least one full day away from the traditional office—most from the road or from home, with smaller numbers working at special telework centers (offices in different locations that telecoworkers from different companies can rent as needed) or satellite offices (small facilities operated by the company for use by its own employees). Most teleworkers use some combination of these facilities. Most teleworkers are employees of very small companies (that cannot afford permanent facilities) or very large companies (that easily can afford having some employees work off-site).

Given its technological advantage, it's probably not too surprising that IBM has been one of the first companies to use telecommuting (see Figure 1.10). Although IBM's midwestern division is headquartered in Chicago, few of its 4,000 employees (including salespeople and customer service technicians) show up more than once or twice a week. Instead, they have "gone mobile," using the company's ThinkPad computers, fax modems, e-mail, and cellular phones to do their work from remote locations. In just a few years, the company has slashed its real estate space by 55 percent and cut the number of fixed computer terminals required, and does a better job of satisfying its cus-

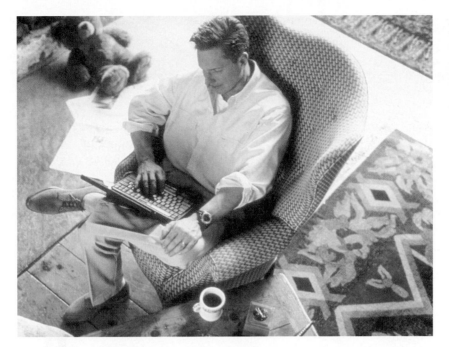

FIGURE 1.10
Telecommuting in Action: Is This Man at Work?
Employees at IBM's midwestern division use their portable computers to do their work from remote locations. As technology makes it easier and less expensive to telecommute, a growing number of companies have been adopting this trend.

tomers' needs. And, at the same time, telecommuting has done well for IBM employees: 83 percent report not wanting to return to a traditional office environment.

Reports from companies such as Great Plains Software, The Traveler's Insurance Co., U.S. West Communications, and the NPD Group have all reported similar benefits with respect to savings in office expenses, gains in productivity, and satisfaction among employees.[63] Most telecommuters like the arrangement, reporting that it gives them the kind of flexibility they need to balance work and family matters. Not surprisingly, the vast majority of telecommuters are highly committed to their companies and plan on staying at their companies.

Despite these benefits, as you might imagine, telecommuting is not for everyone; it also has its limitations.[64] It works best on jobs that require concentration, have well-defined beginning and end points, are easily portable, call for minimal amounts of special equipment, and can be done with little supervision.[65] Fortunately, at least some aspects of most sales and professional jobs meet these standards. Even so, making telecommuting work requires careful adjustments in the way work is done. (For a closer look at these considerations, see the OB in an E-World section that follows.) Also, many people just don't have the kind of self-discipline needed to get work done without direct supervision. To see if you are the kind of person who is likely to succeed at telecommuting, see the Individual Exercise at the end of this chapter (see pages 33–34).

OB RESPONDS TO PEOPLE'S CHANGING EXPECTATIONS

OB scientists do not work in a vacuum. Instead, they are highly responsive to people's changing expectations concerning various aspects of work. This is the case with respect to (1) the flexibility employees expect from employers, (2) the quality consumers demand from the products they buy, and (3) the socially responsible behavior people in general expect from the companies with which they do business. We now will discuss each of these forces and their impact on modern OB.

In Search of Flexibility: Responding to Needs of Employees

Earlier we mentioned that organizations are doing many different things to accommodate workers from two-income families, single-parent households, and people taking

OB IN AN E-WORLD
MAKING TELECOMMUTING WORK

What happens when people who might ordinarily come into contact with each other on their jobs no longer have that social contact? Several things may happen. For example, when employees do not see each other on a regular basis, it is difficult to build the team spirit that is needed to establish quality goods and services in some organizations. As a result, telecommuting does not lend itself to all jobs. It works best for jobs that involve information handling, significant amounts of automation, and relatively little face-to-face contact. Sales representatives, computer programmers, word processing technicians, insurance agents, and securities traders are all good candidates for telecommuting.

This is not to say that all such individuals performing these jobs should be issued a laptop and sent packing. Good candidates for telecommuting must have the emotional maturity and self-discipline to work without direct supervision. To assist those who have difficulty adjusting to telecommuting, IBM carefully monitors the work of its telecommuters and offers counseling to those who appear to be having trouble.

To function effectively, workers who telecommute must be thoroughly trained in the use of the technologies that are required for them to do their work off-site, as well as the proper conditions for working safely (e.g., avoiding physical problems

care of elderly relatives. Often what's most needed is not a formal program, but greater flexibility. The diversity of lifestyles demands a diversity of working arrangements. Some organizations have proven to be so flexible that they even accommodate employees taking care of their dogs (see Figure 1.11). Although Fido might not be a common sight in today's offices (even if, as some say, business has "gone to the dogs"), several practices have gained in popularity in recent years that provide the flexibility today's workers need.

Flexible hours. If you take a look around your workplace, you'll find people at different stages of their lives. Some are single and just getting started in their careers, others may be raising families, and still others may have tried retirement but have chosen to return to work. These different individuals are likely to require different working hours. This

FIGURE 1.11
Fido-Friendly Flexibility
Although dogs might not be a common sight in offices, some companies are allowing their employees to share their workspaces with their pets. Because Brenda Wrigley's employer, Syracuse University, is flexible about allowing her to bring her 7-year-old golden retriever, Missy, to the office, Wrigley is relieved of the responsibility of having to arrange for "dogsitting" while at work. The benefits to morale are considerable. Just ask Missy, whose name appears alongside Wrigley's on the office door.

resulting from staring into video terminals for hours on end and from overusing wrist muscles). They also must be trained in ways to function independently, such as how to manage their time effectively, and how to avoid interference from their families while working. IBM does this, focusing not only on the technical aspects of working with computers at home but also doing so in ways that are safe and effective.

IBM also faces the issue of establishing fair wages for telecommuters. For workers who are paid by the amount of work produced, such as the number of insurance claims processed, this is not a problem. Clear criteria for measuring performance (e.g., specific quantity and quality goals) are enormously helpful when paying telecommuters. However, for salaried employees doing jobs for which clear performance criteria are difficult to come by, policies need to be established regarding what telecommuters should do say, when they complete their work in less than the allotted time. At the office, they would pitch in and help others, but away from the office, they may be tempted to goof off. The key task is to resolve all potentially thorny policy issues regarding pay and performance expectations *before* employees begin telecommuting—and ensuring that they are clearly understood and accepted.

Clearly, telecommuting has its limits, but it also has a special place in today's world of work. Given that technology is making it increasingly easier and less expensive for people to telecommute (and traffic congestion is making it increasingly difficult for them to do otherwise), companies would be wise to consider the points outlined here and to respond accordingly.

has led contemporary organizations to put programs into place that allow for flexibility. One popular way of doing this is by implementing what are known as **flextime programs**—policies that give employees some discretion over when they can arrive and leave work, thereby making it easier to adapt their work schedules to the demands of their personal lives.

Typically, flextime programs require employees to work a common core of hours, such as 9:00 A.M. to 12 noon and 1:00 P.M. to 3:00 P.M. Scheduling the remaining hours, within certain spans (such as 6:00 to 9:00 A.M. and 3:00 to 6:00 P.M.), is then left up to the employees themselves. Generally, such programs have been well received and have been linked to improvements in performance and job satisfaction, as well as drops in employee turnover and absenteeism.[66] In recent years companies such as Pacific Bell and Duke Power Company have found that flexible work scheduling has helped their employees meet the demands of juggling their work and family lives.[67]

flextime programs
Policies that give employees some discretion over when they can arrive and leave work, thereby making it easier to adapt their work schedules to the demands of their personal lives.

The contingent workforce: "Permanent temporary" employees. Recognizing that not all jobs are required to be performed all the time, many organizations are eliminating permanent jobs and hiring people to perform them whenever required. Such individuals comprise what has been referred to as the **contingent workforce**—people hired by organizations temporarily to work as needed for finite periods of time.[68] This practice serves not only the needs of companies that cannot afford to have full-time employees in part-time positions but also the needs of individuals who are interested in working only occasionally. The contingent workforce includes not only the traditional part-time employees, such as department store Santas, but also freelancers (i.e., independent contractors who are self-employed), on-call workers (i.e., people who are called into work only when needed), and workers provided by temporary help agencies. According to the Bureau of Labor Statistics, contingent workers comprise only about 4 percent of the total workforce, most of whom are young (under 25) and poorly educated (high school dropouts). As shown in Figure 1.12, the specific jobs contingent workers do are most frequently in clerical fields.[69] Such highly flexible arrangements make it possible for organizations to grow or shrink as needed and to have access to experts with specialized knowledge when these are required.

contingent workforce
People hired by organizations temporarily to work as needed for finite periods of time.

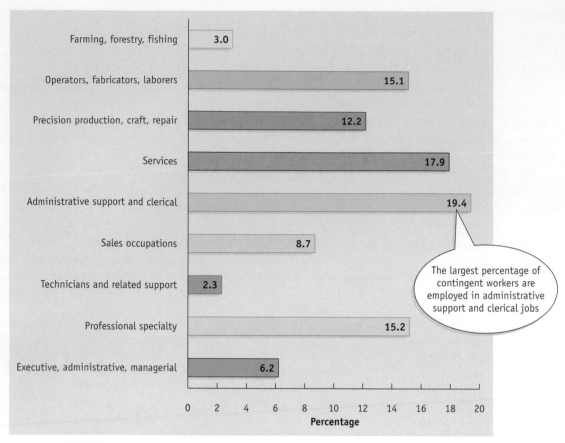

FIGURE 1.12
Contingent Workers: What Kinds of Jobs Do They Do?
As summarized here, contingent workers perform a wide variety of jobs. Most of these jobs are in service businesses and in administrative support and clerical positions.
(*Source:* Based on data from the Bureau of Labor Statistics, 2001; see Note 67.)

The trend toward corporate restructuring has caused many companies to keep their staff sizes so small that they must frequently draw on the services of Manpower, or any other of the nation's 7,000 temporary-employment firms.[70] As a result, many professionals are working on a part-time or freelance basis. For example, about 43 percent of new attorneys leave their first job within three years because they are being asked to work long hours that interfere with the time spent with their families. Growing numbers of lawyers choose to work permanently on a part-time basis.[71] This comes at a cost, however. As you might imagine, people who work half time earn less than those who work full time—but considerably less than half as much. For example, according to the Institute for Women's Policy Research, managers who earn $3,200 per month working full time can expect to earn as little as $800 to $1,200 per month working half time.[72]

Compressed workweeks. Instead of working five days of eight hours each, growing numbers of people are enjoying working **compressed workweeks**—the practice of working fewer days each week but longer hours each day (e.g., four 10-hour days). The popular practice among fire fighters of being on-duty for 24 hours and then off-duty for 48 hours is a good example of the compressed workweek. Shell Canada has found that compressed workweek schedules have helped it make more efficient use of its manufacturing plant in Sarnia, Ontario. The Royal Bank of Canada, headquartered in Montreal, has found that compressed workweek options greatly help its recruitment efforts by offering prospective employees the choice of schedules based on either compressed workweeks (four 9.5-hour days) or standard five-day workweeks.[73]

Job sharing. **Job sharing** is a form of regular part-time work in which pairs of employees assume the duties of a single job, splitting its responsibilities, salary, and benefits in

compressed workweeks
The practice of working fewer days each week but longer hours each day (e.g., four 10-hour days).

job sharing
A form of regular part-time work in which pairs of employees assume the duties of a single job, splitting its responsibilities, salary, and benefits in proportion to the time worked.

proportion to the time worked. Job sharing is rapidly growing in popularity as people enjoy the kind of work that full-time jobs allow but require the flexibility of part-time work. Often job sharing arrangements are temporary.

At Xerox, for example, several sets of employees share jobs, including two female employees who once were sales rivals but who joined forces to share one job when they each faced the need to reduce their working hours so they could devote time to their new families.[74] Pella (the Iowa-based manufacturer of windows) has found job sharing to be successful in reducing absenteeism among its production workers and clerical employees.[75]

Voluntary reduced work time (V-time) programs. Programs known as **voluntary reduced work time (V-time) programs** allow employees to reduce the amount of time they work by a certain amount (typically 10 or 20 percent), with a proportional reduction in pay. Over the past few years, these programs have become popular in various state agencies in the United States. For example, various employees of the New York State government have enjoyed having professional careers but with hours that make it possible for them to also meet their family obligations. Not only does the state benefit from the money saved, but the employees also enjoy the extra time they gain for nonwork pursuits.

voluntary reduced work time (V-time) programs
Programs that allow employees to reduce the amount of time they work by a certain amount (typically 10 or 20 percent), with a proportional reduction in pay.

The Quality Revolution

For many years, people complained but could do little when the goods they purchased fell apart, or the service they received was second-rate. After all, if everything in the market is shoddy, there are few alternatives. Then, Japanese companies such as Toyota and Nissan entered the American auto market. Their cars generally were more reliable, less expensive, and better designed than the offerings from Ford, General Motors, and Chrysler—companies that had become complacent about offering value to their customers. When Japanese automakers began capturing the American auto market in record numbers, American companies were forced to rethink their strategies—and to change their ways.

Today's companies operate quite differently than the American auto companies of decades past. For them, the watchword is not "getting by" but "making things better," what has been referred to as *the quality revolution*. The best organizations are ones that strive to deliver better goods and services at lower prices than ever before. Those that do so flourish, and those that do not tend to fade away.

One of the most popular approaches to establishing quality is known as **total quality management (TQM)**—an organizational strategy of commitment to improving customer satisfaction by developing techniques to carefully manage output quality. TQM is not so much a special technique as a well-ingrained set of corporate values—a way of life demonstrating a strong commitment to improving quality in everything that is done.

total quality management (TQM)
An organizational strategy of commitment to improving customer satisfaction by developing techniques to carefully manage output quality.

According to W. Edwards Deming, the best-known advocate of TQM, successful TQM requires that everyone in the organization—from the lowest-level employee to the CEO—must be fully committed to making whatever innovations are necessary to improve quality. This involves both carefully measuring quality (through elaborate statistical procedures) and taking whatever steps are necessary to improve it. Typically, this requires continuously improving the manufacturing process in ways that make it possible for higher quality to result.

For example, when Toyota engineers developed the highly regarded luxury sedan from its Lexus division, the LS 400, it purchased competing cars from Mercedes and BMW, disassembled them, examined the parts, and developed ways of building an even better car. This process of comparing one's own products or services with the best from others is known as **benchmarking.** Spending some $500 million in this process, Toyota was clearly dedicated to creating a superior product. And, given the recognition that Lexus continues to receive for its high quality, it appears as if Toyota's TQM efforts have paid off.

benchmarking
The process of comparing one's own products or services with the best from others.

Another key ingredient of TQM is incorporating concern for quality into all aspects of organizational culture (a concept we will discuss more fully in Chapter 13).[76] At Rubbermaid, for example, concern for quality is not only emphasized in the company's manufacturing process but also in its concern for cost, service, speed, and innovation. To assure that it is meeting quality standards, many companies conduct **quality control audits**—careful examinations of how well it is meeting its standards. For example, companies such as Pepsi Cola and FedEx regularly interview their clients to find out what problems they may be having. These responses are then taken very seriously in making whatever improvements are necessary to avoid them in the future.

Some companies have been so very successful at achieving high quality in all respects that they have been honored for their accomplishments by being given the **Malcom Baldrige Quality Award.** This annual award recognizes American companies—both large and small and in both service and manufacturing—that practice effective quality management and make significant improvements in the quality of their goods and services.[77] The major goal of the award is to promote quality achievement by recognizing those companies that deliver continually improving value to customers while maximizing their overall productivity and effectiveness. To ensure that all companies can benefit from the winner's experiences, winning companies are expected to share their successful quality strategies with other American firms. This has been done in the form of personal presentations, books, and cases presented on videotape.[78] Indeed, companies that have won over the years, such as various divisions of IBM and TRW, have set high-quality standards to which other companies aspire.[79]

Corporate Social Responsibility: The (Sometimes) Ethical Organization

The history of American business is riddled with sordid tales of magnates who would go to any lengths in their quest for success, destroying in the process not only the country's natural resources and the public's trust but also the hopes and dreams of millions of people. For example, tales abound of how John D. Rockefeller, founder of Standard Oil, regularly bribed politicians and stepped all over people in his quest to monopolize the oil industry.

We do not mean to imply that unsavory business practices are only a relic of the past. Indeed, they tend to be all too common today. For example, as 2001 came to a close, the business world was shocked by allegations of financial misdeeds among officers of Enron, who made over $1 billion in allegedly illegal stock trades before driving the once giant energy company into bankruptcy.[80] Only a few years earlier, accusations of fraudulent practices in its auto-repair business tarnished the reputation of the venerable retailing giant, Sears.[81] And, despite efforts to stop the practice, many garments continue to be made by people working long hours for low wages in unsafe and uncomfortable factories known as **sweatshops** (see Figure 1.13).

Clearly, human greed has not faded from the business scene. However, something *has* changed—namely, the public's acceptance of unethical behavior on the part of organizations. Consider this statement by a leading expert on business ethics.

> Ethical standards, whether formal or informal, have changed tremendously in the last century. Boldly stated, no one can make the case that ethical standards have fallen in the latter decades of the twentieth century. The reverse is true. Standards are considerably higher. Business-people themselves, as well as the public, expect more sensitive behavior in the conduct of economic enterprise. The issue is not just having the standards, however. It is living up to them.[82]

To the extent that people are increasingly intolerant of unethical business activity, it makes sense for the field of OB to examine the factors that encourage unethical practices. Even more importantly, we need to develop strategies for promoting the ethical conduct of employees and socially responsible behavior among organizations.

What is corporate social responsibility? The term **corporate social responsibility** is used to describe business decision making linked to ethical values, compliance with legal requirements, and respect for individuals, the community at large, and the environment. It involves operating a business in a manner that meets or exceeds the ethical,

FIGURE 1.13

Sweatshops: An All-Too-Common Practice
Sweatshops represent one of the most prevalent forms of socially irresponsible (not to mention abusive and illegal) behavior by companies today—a fact that has not been lost on these highly vocal members of labor unions. These angry protesters are standing across from a Gap store in New York City to bring attention to that company's alleged use of sweatshops.

legal, and public expectations that society has of business. Some examples of exemplary corporate social responsibility are as follows:

- *Natura Cosmeticos:* This Brazilian company promotes and supports local human rights initiatives (e.g., it does not use child labor), it promotes education, and it encourages its employees to volunteer for nonprofit organizations in their community.
- *Starbucks Coffee Co.:* Offering more than just a good cup of coffee, Starbucks has programs that benefit employees (e.g., retirement plans for even part-time workers), communities (e.g., promoting local charities), and the environment (e.g., developing reusable cups) (see Figure 1.14).
- *The Co-operative Bank:* One of the most innovative banks in the United Kingdom, the Co-operative Bank refrains from making socially irresponsible investments (e.g., it will not finance weapons deals, the fur trade, and companies involved in animal testing).

FIGURE 1.14

Starbucks: Where Social Responsibility Is Always Brewing
Many consider Starbucks a model of what a socially responsible company should be like. In addition to granting generous stock options, retirement plans, and full benefits to its 35,000 employees (even those who work part-time), Starbucks is dedicated to treating its employees with dignity and respect and to contributing positively to the communities in which it operates. To ensure that this happens, Starbucks has a special division of corporate social responsibility.

It is important to note that corporate social responsibility is not merely a collection of isolated practices or occasional gestures, nor does it involve initiatives motivated by marketing or public relations benefits. Instead, corporate social responsibility is a comprehensive set of policies, practices, and programs that are integrated throughout business operations and decision-making processes that are supported and rewarded by top management. Importantly, social responsibility involves more than simply making a few charitable donations. It must be a commitment to doing what's best for people and the community (as is the case with the three companies spotlighted here).

Why should companies care about ethical behavior? Obviously, companies *should* do things to promote ethical behavior among employees simply because they are morally correct. All too often, however, forces deter people from always doing the right thing. As you know, pressure to meet "the bottom line" sometimes encourages people to do whatever it takes to make money, even if it leads them to behave unethically. For example, some unscrupulous stockbrokers have been known to boost their own sales commissions by encouraging clients to make investments they know are questionable. Corporate leaders need to be concerned about this, if not for moral reasons, then for the simple business reason that good ethics will pay off in the long run. Indeed, although the stockbroker in our example may make money in the short term by his actions, he is sure to lose business in the long run as knowledge of his behavior spreads. In general, *good ethics is good business.* These benefits take several forms, including the following:[83]

- *Improved financial performance:* Companies that make a clear commitment to ethics outperform those that make no such commitment on standard measures of financial success.
- *Reduced operating costs:* Many efforts to reduce waste and to save energy designed to protect the natural environment also help save money.
- *Enhanced corporate reputation:* Many customers are loyal to companies that demonstrate their commitment to social causes. For example, Ben & Jerry's Homemade and The Body Shop are two companies that have benefited by promoting the socially responsible things they do for the community, courting customers who share their values.
- *Increased ability to attract and retain employees:* People generally like working at companies of which they can be proud and that treat them well. When talented employees are difficult to find, socially responsible companies have an easier job in getting people to work for them—and in keeping them.

ethics officers

Individuals (usually at the vice presidential level) who oversee the ethics of a company's operations.

code of ethics

A document describing what an organization stands for and the general rules of conduct it expects of its employees (e.g., to avoid conflicts of interest, to be honest, etc.).

Promoting ethical behavior. Companies that take social responsibility seriously do several things to ensure the ethical behavior of everyone in the company. For example, they have **ethics officers,** individuals (usually at the vice president level) who oversee the ethics of a company's operations. A socially responsible company also has a **code of ethics**—a document describing what an organization stands for and the general rules of conduct it expects of its employees (e.g., to avoid conflicts of interest, to be honest, etc.).[84] Almost all large companies have codes of ethics in place. For them to work and to be more than just "window dressing," however, codes of ethics must be used in conjunction with training programs that reinforce the company's values.[85] Finally, just as companies regularly audit their books to check on irregularities in their finances, they regularly should assess the moral-

CONDUCTING AN ETHICS AUDIT

An ethics audit can reveal a lot about a company's commitment to ethics. To recognize these benefits, it's crucial to conduct ethics audits in an appropriate manner. The following guidelines will help.[86]

1. Make sure that top executives, such as the CEO, are committed to the ethics audit and appoint a committee to guide it.

2. Create a diverse team of employees to write questions regarding the company's ethical performance. These should focus on existing practices (e.g., do people regularly pad their expense accounts).

3. Carefully analyze official documents, such as ethical mission statements and codes of ethics for clarity and thoroughness.

4. Ask people why they think unethical behaviors have occurred.

5. Compare your company's ethical practices to those of other companies in the same industry.

6. Write a formal report summarizing these findings and present it to all concerned parties.

Conducting an ethics audit can be a very difficult experience because it forces everyone to take a hard look at the company and their own behavior. It is not "a warm and fuzzy" experience. In fact, it can reveal some rather unpleasant things about the company's practices and the values of those who are in charge. However, it is a necessary tool for assessing any company's underlying commitment to ethical behavior.

ity of their employees' behavior so as to identify irregularities in this realm as well. Such assessments are known as **ethics audits.** These require actively investigating and documenting incidents of dubious ethical value; discussing them in an open, honest fashion; and developing a concrete plan to avoid such actions in the future.

ethics audit
The process of actively investigating and documenting incidents of dubious ethical value within a company.

SUMMARY AND REVIEW OF LEARNING OBJECTIVES

1. Define the concepts of organization and organizational behavior (OB).
An organization is a structured social system consisting of groups and individuals working together to meet some agreed-upon objectives. Organizational behavior is the field that seeks knowledge of behavior in organizational settings by systematically studying individual, group, and organizational processes.

2. Describe the field of organizational behavior's commitment to the scientific method and the three levels of analysis it uses.
The field of OB seeks to develop a base of knowledge about behavior in organizations by using an empirical, research-based approach. As such, it is based on systematic observation and measurement of the behavior or phenomenon of interest. The field of OB uses three levels of analysis: individuals, work groups, and entire organizations—all relying on the scientific method.

3. Trace the historical developments and schools of thought leading up to the field of organizational behavior today.
The earliest approaches to organizational behavior relied on scientific management, an approach that essentially treated people like machines, emphasizing what it took to get the most out of them. For example, this approach relied on time-and-motion study, a type of applied research designed to find the most efficient way for people to perform their jobs. As this approach grew unpopular, it was supplanted by the human relations movement, which emphasized the importance of noneconomic, social forces in the workplace—an approach that remains popular to this day. Such factors were demonstrated in the Hawthorne studies, the first large-scale research project conducted in a work organization that demonstrated the importance of social forces in determining productivity. In contrast with scientific management's orientation toward organizing the work of individuals, proponents of classical organizational theory developed ways of efficiently structuring the way work is done. Weber's concept of bureaucracy is a prime example of this approach. Contemporary OB is characterized not by one best approach to management, but by systematic scientific research inspired from several social science disciplines. It takes a contingency approach to OB, recognizing that behavior may be influenced by a variety of different forces at once, thereby rejecting the idea that there is any single most effective approach to managing behavior in organizations.

4. Identify the fundamental assumptions of the field of organizational behavior.
The field of OB assumes (1) that organizations can be made more productive while also improving the quality of people's work life, (2) that there is no one best approach to studying behavior in organizations, and (3) that organizations are dynamic and ever changing.

5. Describe how the field of OB today is being shaped by the global economy, increasing racial and ethnic diversity in the workforce, and advances in technology.
The world's economy is becoming increasingly global, a trend that is affecting the field of OB in several distinct ways. For example, organizations are expanding overseas, requiring people to live and work in different countries, requiring considerable adjustment. As this occurs, much of what we thought we knew about managing people is

proven to be limited by the culture in which that knowledge was developed (U.S. culture, in most cases). Racial and ethnic diversity in the workplace is in large part the result of shifting patterns of immigration that have brought more foreign nationals into the workforce. It also is the result of changes in social values and the economy that have made the presence of women common in today's workplace. Also, thanks to modern medicine, people are living longer and retiring from work later than ever before. Because technology has made it possible for fewer people to do more work, many organizations have been growing smaller through downsizing. Furthermore, as technology becomes increasingly specialized, organizations have found it useful to hire other companies to do nonessential aspects of their operations that they once performed themselves—a process known as outsourcing.

6. Explain how rising expectations about quality and socially responsible behavior have influenced the field of OB.

Today's consumers are demanding high-quality products and services, a trend that is encouraging companies to develop ways of meeting these demands—thereby remaining in existence and possibly staying ahead of competitors. The popular policy of continuously improving products and services, referred to as total quality management (TQM), is a response to this trend. The public at large also appears to be growing tired of accounts of unethical practices both by individuals and by companies as a whole. As a result, many companies are adopting policies that enhance the ethical nature of their behavior (e.g., conducting ethics audits and developing codes of ethics). Such practices have been shown to have a positive influence on the bottom line.

POINTS TO PONDER

Questions for Review

1. How can the field or organizational behavior contribute to both the effective functioning of organization *and* to the well-being of individuals? Are these goals inconsistent? Why or why not?
2. What is the contingency approach, and why is it so popular in the field of OB today?
3. Explain how the field of organizational behavior stands to benefit by taking a global perspective. What would you say are the major challenges associated with such a perspective?
4. How has the growing quest for quality products and services affected the nature of work?

Experiential Questions

1. Think about a person with whom you may have worked who happens to be very different from you, such as someone of the opposite sex who also is a member of a different racial group and/or a different country. In what ways was this experience challenging for you? In what ways did these differences prove to be beneficial? What insight do you believe the field of OB can give you with respect to this experience?
2. How has your own life, and the lives of your own family members, changed because of flexible, new working arrangements that have become popular in recent years?
3. Describe some work situation in which you found yourself torn between behaving in an ethical and an unethical manner. What forces pulled you in each direction? What did you finally do? What might have led you to behave differently?

Questions to Analyze

1. Although only some people in an organization need to know about marketing or accounting or production, almost everyone benefits by knowing about organiza-

tional behavior. Do you agree with this statement? If not, why not? If so, exactly how can knowing OB help you in your own work?

2. The practice of engineering is constantly evolving, but the basic rules of physics on which it rests remain relatively unchanged. Do you think the same relationship exists between technology and OB? In other words, do the things that have made organizations and individuals successful in yesterday's low-tech era remain relevant today, or are they changing along with technology?

3. Although many employees enjoy the flexibility of working lots of part-time jobs or working for a series of employers on a temporary basis, it comes at a cost: Such employees often make low wages, have little security, and cannot count on having fringe benefits. How do you think this trend affects organizations? How are companies helped and how are they harmed by this trend? Do you think this trend has any adverse effects on a company's products?

DEVELOPING OB SKILLS

INDIVIDUAL EXERCISE

Is Telecommuting Right for You?

When some people hear about telecommuting, the first thing they think is that it's an opportunity to goof off. Or, even if they're well intentioned, they may recognize that without the discipline of having to be at a certain place at a certain time, they'd never get anything done. If so, then telecommuting wouldn't be right for them. How about you? Are you a good candidate for a job that involves telecommuting? This exercise will help you find out.

Directions
Read and think about each of the following statements. Then, being as honest as possible, indicate the extent to which each one describes you by using the following scale. Write your answers on the line next to each statement.

- 1 = Doesn't describe me at all
- 2 = Describes me a little
- 3 = Describes me moderately well
- 4 = Describes me very well
- 5 = Describes me perfectly

_____ 1. I am able to set and meet my own deadlines.
_____ 2. I am very focused and get things done even when no one is watching me.
_____ 3. I generally do an effective job of managing my time.
_____ 4. When I'm doing something important, I tend not to be distracted by other things.
_____ 5. I am comfortable working alone.
_____ 6. I generally know when it's time to stop working for the day.
_____ 7. I am well-versed in my company's procedures and policies.
_____ 8. I know how to support my coworkers even when I'm not around.
_____ 9. I don't mind being flexible about my work schedule.
_____ 10. I generally communicate well with others with whom I work.

Scoring and Intepretation
Add the numbers corresponding to your responses. These will range from 10 to 50. Higher scores reflect greater readiness for telecommuting. Scores below 15 suggest that you are not yet ready for telecommuting. Scores over 35 suggest that you are adequately prepared for a job involving telecommuting. Scores from 15 to 35 suggest that you are not yet ready but that you have the potential to become a telecommuter once you have developed the skills reflected by these statements.

1. Did your score suggest that you are likely to succeed as a telecommuter? How does this assessment compare with your own personal experiences in this regard?
2. What skills does this exercise suggest are important for telecommuters to have? Based on what you know about telework, what additional skills do you think this exercise should have included?
3. How can you go about developing the skills it takes to be an effective telecommuter?

GROUP EXERCISE

Common Sense About Behavior in Organizations: Putting It to the Test

Even if you already have a good intuitive sense about behavior in organizations, some of what you think may be inconsistent with established research findings (many of which are noted in this book). So that you don't have to rely on your own judgments (which may be idiosyncratic), working with others in this exercise will give you a good sense of what our collective common sense has to say about behavior in organizations. You just may be enlightened.

Directions

Divide the class into groups of about five. Then within these groups discuss the following statements, reaching a consensus as to whether each is true or false. Spend approximately 30 minutes on the entire discussion.

1. People who are satisfied with one job tend to be satisfied with other jobs, too.
2. Because "two heads are better than one," groups make better decisions than individuals.
3. The best leaders always act the same, regardless of the situations they face.
4. Specific goals make people nervous; people work better when asked to do their best.
5. People get bored easily, leading them to welcome organizational change.
6. Money is the best motivator.
7. Today's organizations are more rigidly structured than ever before.
8. People generally shy away from challenges on the job.
9. Using multiple channels of communication (e.g., written and spoken) tends to add confusion.
10. Conflict in organizations is always highly disruptive.

Scoring

Give your group one point for each item you scored as follows: 1 = True, 2 = False, 3 = False, 4 = False, 5 = False, 6 = False, 7 = False, 8 = False, 9 = False, and 10 = False. (Should you have questions about the answers, information bearing on them appears in this book as follows: 1 = Chapter 5, 2 = Chapter 9, 3 = Chapter 12, 4 = Chapter 4, 5 = Chapter 16, 6 = Chapter 4, 7 = Chapter 14, 8 = Chapter 4, 9 = Chapter 8, 10 = Chapter 10.)

Questions for Discussion

1. How well did your group do? Were you stumped on a few?
2. Comparing your experiences to those of other groups, did you find that there were some questions that proved trickier than others (i.e., ones in which the scientific findings were more counterintuitive)? If you did poorly, don't be frustrated. These statements are a bit simplistic and need to be qualified to be fully understood. Have your instructor explain the statements that the class found most challenging.
3. Did this exercise give you a better understanding of the sometimes surprising (and complex) nature of behavior in organizations?

WEB SURFING EXERCISE

Family-Friendly Companies

Over the years, several companies have been selected by magazines such as *Fortune* and *Working Mother* as being family-friendly places in which to work. Among these are SAS Institute (www.sas.com), Bristol-Myers Squibb Co. (www.bms.com), Citigroup (www.citigroup.com), and IBM (www.ibm.com). Visit the Web sites of each of these companies.

1. Briefly describe the family-friendly policies of each company.
2. Describe how these companies' policies are similar to each other or different from each other.
3. Of all the policies about which you read, which particular one do you think would be most attractive to you? Why?

Corporate Social Responsibility

In various countries throughout the world, groups have been formed that define standards for socially responsible behavior. Among these are the following: The Global Reporting Initiative (www.globalreporting.org), The Council on Economic Priorities Accredidation Agency (www.cepaa.org), the Caux Round Table (www.cauxroundtable.org), and the Keidenren Charter for Good Corporate Behavior (www.keidanren.or.jp). Visit each organization's Web site.

1. Describe the basic mission or objectives of each group.
2. In what ways are these organizations similar and different from one another?
3. In general, do you believe these organizations will be effective or ineffective in meeting their objectives? Explain why.

PRACTICING OB

Moving to Santiago

Your U.S.-based company is setting up a new division in Chile, requiring three top executives to move to Santiago for several years. Given the lengthy stay, they will be moving their families along with them and setting up new households.

1. What problems would you anticipate these executives will have as they adjust to their new surroundings?
2. What specific measures could be taken to help these individuals avoid the symptoms of culture shock that are likely to arise?
3. What difficulties might these individuals have when they return to their own country at the end of their assignments? What could be done to minimize these problems?

CASE IN POINT

There's No Business Like Shoyu Business

How many companies can you think of that have been in continuous operation since 1630? Pass? Okay, then, how about companies that have manufacturing plants in both urban Tokyo and rural Wisconsin? Not getting any easier? Here's the final hint: It manufactures the world's oldest condiment from fermented soy beans and wheat. Give up? It's Kikkoman—one of Japan's oldest and largest companies, known worldwide for its soy sauce (called *shoyu* in Japanese).

Kikkoman soy sauce holds a commanding 50 percent share of the market for Oriental bottle sauces in North America and 30 percent in Japan. To meet worldwide demand (it is sold in 100 countries around the world), production has increased tenfold in the past 20 years. In 1997 alone, Kikkoman produced and sold some 116 million gallons of the ebony-colored liquid. That's really an enormous quantity when you consider that soy sauce isn't gulped like a soft drink but sprinkled sparingly onto foods to help bring out their natural flavors. Another fact that makes this statistic so impressive is that Kikkoman makes its soy sauce using a method dating back to the seventeenth century, requiring several months of brewing time before it is ready.

Although it relies on traditional, natural ingredients (including a proprietary microorganism to create a culture called *koji*) instead of chemical substitutes used by competitors, Kikkoman is far from ancient in its manufacturing processes. Its state-of-the-art manufacturing plants in Walworth, Wisconsin, and a brand new one in the Netherlands use the most modern technology available. In fact, outside of the soy sauce business, Kikkoman is regarded as a world leader in genetic engineering, biotechnology, and biochemistry. In fact, using cell fusion technology, Kikkoman has developed an entirely new species of citrus fruit—hardly what you'd think of from a company pushing 400 years old.

Actually, there are several ways in which Kikkoman is unusual. To begin, its founder is a woman—incredibly rare for the 1600s. Also, unlike most Japanese companies, which produce goods that originated in the United States (such as autos and electronic goods), Kikkoman has turned its uniquely Japanese product into a staple found in kitchens around the world. Still, the company adheres to the strongly held Japanese tradition of being loyal to employees, an ideal that most Western companies have abandoned. In fact, Kikkoman's commitment to treating individual workers like family permeates all aspects of the company's operations. Interestingly, it was Kikkoman's adherence to the honored Asian traditions of harmony and loyalty that made it an attractive partner for U.S.-based companies, such as Xerox, expanding into the Japanese and Chinese markets. Today, in large part because of such partnerships, Kikkoman is considered one of the key players in the world of international business.

Despite its long, international reach, Kikkoman is faithful to the countries in which it does business. In the Walworth, Wisconsin, plant, for example, the only items—including both ingredients (mostly soy, wheat, salt, and water) and equipment—that are not procured locally are the specialized items needed to make soy sauce. Kikkoman has been a generous contributor to the local community, not only in terms of expanding its tax base but also in making contributions to everything from 4-H projects to college scholarships for high school students.

It is obvious that Kikkoman, with roots going back to feudal Japan but also poised on the cutting edge of biotechnology, has taken more than its share of risks over the years. As the ancient Japanese saying goes, "A frog in the well does not know the ocean." Clearly, Kikkoman has long left the well and continues to explore many different oceans.

Critical Thinking Questions

1. What does this case illustrate about the global nature of business today?
2. What challenges do you think Japanese employees of Kikkoman would face while working in rural Wisconsin?
3. What did Kikkoman do that demonstrated a high degree of social responsibility, and how do you think the company benefited as a result?

Perception and Learning: Understanding and Adapting to the Work Environment

2

LEARNING OBJECTIVES

After reading this chapter, you should be able to:

1. Distinguish between the concepts of social perception and social identity.
2. Explain how the attribution process works and describe the various sources of bias in social perception.
3. Understand how the process of social perception operates in the context of performance appraisals, employment interviews, and the cultivation of corporate images.
4. Define learning and describe the two types most applicable to OB: operant conditioning and observational learning.
5. Describe how principles of learning are involved in organizational training and innovative reward systems.
6. Compare the way organizations use reward in organizational behavior management programs, how they can use punishment most effectively when administering discipline, and how they can manage knowledge effectively.

■ PREVIEW CASE
PREPARING SALES REPS FOR THE "REAL WHIRLED"

What do you get when you put eight young people in their twenties together in a beach house for two months during the summer? The answer is not the latest reality-based TV show, but the basis for what home appliance giant Whirlpool claims is one of its most effective sales tools. Dubbed "Real Whirled," after the MTV show *Real World* that inspired it, its goal is straightforward: to get sales reps to know the company's products by giving them personal experiences with these appliances as consumers.

Indeed, the six women and two men who lived together in a small house in St. Joseph, Michigan, washed their clothes, prepared their meals, and cleaned their house using only Whirlpool products, and spent the rest of their time talking to each other about what they learned. After leaving the house, they then passed along their newfound wisdom to salespeople at Whirlpool retailers, who in turn shared these experiences with prospective customers and frequently turned them into actual customers.

Although the residents didn't confront judgments from national TV viewers, they faced the scrutiny of a much more demanding audience—hungry executives from company headquarters in nearby Benton Harbor, who dropped by for meals. Serving undercooked chicken or wearing dirty clothes made residents not only look incompetent to their bosses but also left them unsatisfied and uncomfortable in their daily lives. To avoid this fate, they carefully studied the features of the appliances they used and taught each other various tips and tricks they learned along the way.

If you inquire about a Whirlpool microwave oven at Home Depot or Sears, the salesperson is very likely to tell you how you can use it to prepare Dan's delicious blueberry crisp, and how he came about developing it that summer in the beach house.

Until his Real Whirled experience, for example, Dan Fitzgerald, a 26-year-old college grad and new hire, hardly knew how to cook for himself, let alone how to make a blueberry crisp in the microwave. Today, however, if you inquire about a Whirlpool microwave oven at Home Depot or Sears, the salesperson is very likely to tell you how you can use it to prepare Dan's delicious blueberry crisp, and how he came about developing it that summer in the beach house.

Stories such as these are precisely what Whirlpool's former director of sales operations, Josh Gitlin, claims makes the Real Whirled experience so valuable. Before reps were able to talk firsthand about their experiences with Whirlpool appliances, all they could do was share statistics touting their quality. But numbers only go so far when it comes to telling why one should buy a particular appliance. A more compelling story comes from recreating a consumer's problem and showing him or her how to use a product to solve it. This is precisely what those eight residents learned that summer—and precisely what makes today's Whirlpool sales reps so professional and effective. As Gitlin put it, "I don't know how we survived before this program."

Do you think you would enjoy going through an experience like Real Whirled? Whether or not you personally would be comfortable with such an intensive encounter, it's clear that Whirlpool officials are pleased with the program's success. From an OB perspective, there are two reasons why its effectiveness is not particularly surprising. First, it's clear that the session was an effective way of getting the sales reps to learn what they needed to know about the products they sell. And *learning*, as you might imagine, is a vital process when it comes to getting people to perform effectively on the job. Second, it is apparent that the eight participants were interested in developing their new cooking and cleaning skills so as to avoid suggesting to their housemates and their bosses that they were not particularly adept at these things. Selling household appliances for a living, it was important for them to convince others that they knew all about using these products. In other words, they were concerned about the way other people perceived them, which is a key part of the process known as *social perception*.

Because social perception and learning are so fundamental to the way people behave in organizations, we devote this chapter to describing these topics in detail. Specifically, we begin by discussing the various processes that are responsible for social perception and the specific ways they operate in organizations. Then we move on to the topic of learning. Here, too, we cover both the basic principles that are responsible for successful learning followed by specific applications of these principles on the job. After reading this chapter, you will come away with a good understanding of some of the basic psychological processes that contributed to the success of the Real Whirled program—processes that are helpful to understand to be successful yourself.

SOCIAL PERCEPTION AND SOCIAL IDENTITY: UNDERSTANDING OTHERS AND OURSELVES

Obviously, when it comes to forming opinions, there is a subtle, yet powerful, process going on—a process people use to judge and understand the people and things with which they come into contact. This process, known as *social perception*, will be described here. Then, after focusing on how we come to make judgments of others, we will examine the other side of the coin—namely, how we come to develop identities of ourselves. As you read about these phenomena, you will learn about processes that are so basic that you probably never thought about them before. As you will see, a great deal of insight can be derived by making explicit these important processes that we generally take for granted.

Social Perception: What Are Others Like?

Suppose you meet your new boss. You know her general reputation as a manager, you see the way she looks, hear the words she says, and read the memos she writes. In no time at all, you're trying to figure her out. Will she be easy to work with? Will she like you? Will she do a good job for the company? On the basis of whatever information you have available to you, even if it's very little, you will try to understand her and how you will be affected by her (see Figure 2.1). Put differently, you will attempt to combine the various things you learn about her into a meaningful picture. This is the process known as **social perception**—the process of combining, integrating, and interpreting information about others to gain an accurate understanding of them.

The social perception process is so automatic that we are almost never aware that it's happening. Yet, it goes on all the time in organizations. Indeed, other people—whether they're bosses, coworkers, subordinates, family, or friends—can have a profound effect on us. To understand the people around us—to figure out who they are and why they do what they do—may be very helpful. After all, you wouldn't want to ask your boss for a raise when you believe he or she is in a bad mood! Clearly, social perception is very important in organizations, which is why we will examine it so carefully in this chapter.[1]

Specifically, we will explore various aspects of the social perception process in the sections that follow. To begin, we will describe the **attribution** process—that is, the way people come to judge the underlying causes of others' behavior. Then, we will note various imperfections of this process, errors and sources of bias that contribute to inaccurate judgments of others—as well as ways of overcoming them. Finally, we will highlight specific ways in which the attribution process is used in organizations. Before getting to this, however, we first turn attention to an even more basic matter—coming to understand who we are ourselves.

social perception
The process of combining, integrating, and interpreting information about others to gain an accurate understanding of them.

attribution
The process through which individuals attempt to determine the causes behind others' behavior.

FIGURE 2.1
Meeting New People: An Opportunity for Social Perception
Meeting new people presents many opportunities to combine, integrate, and interpret a great deal of information about them—the process of *social perception*.

Social Identity Theory: Who Are You?

How would you answer if someone asked, "Who are you?" There are many things you could say. For example, you could focus on individual characteristics, such as your appearance, your personality, and your special skills and interests—that is, your **personal identity.** You also could answer in terms of the various groups to which you belong, saying, for example, that you are a student in a particular organizational behavior class, an employee of a certain company, or a citizen of a certain country—that is, your **social identity.** The conceptualization known as **social identity theory** recognizes that the way we perceive others and ourselves is based on both our unique characteristics (i.e., personal identity) and our membership in various groups (i.e., social identity).[2] For an overview of this approach, see Figure 2.2.

Social identity theory claims that the way we identify ourselves is likely to be based on our uniqueness in a group. Say, for example, that you are the only business major in an English class. In this situation, you will be likely to identify yourself as "the business major," and so too will others come to recognize you as such. In other words, that will become your identity in this particular situation. Because we belong to many groups, we are likely to have several unique aspects of ourselves to use as the basis for establishing our identities (e.g., you may be the only left-handed person, the only one to have graduated college, or even the only one to have committed a crime).

How do we know which particular bases for defining our personal identities people will choose? Given the natural desire to perceive ourselves positively and to get others to see us positively as well, we are likely to identify ourselves with groups we believe to be perceived positively by others. We know, for example, that people in highly regarded professions, such as doctors, are more inclined to identify themselves with their professions than those who have lower-status jobs.[3] Likewise, people tend to identify themselves with winning sports teams by wearing the colors and logos of those teams. In fact, the tendency to wear clothing that identifies oneself as a fan of a certain team depends on how successful that team has been: The better a team has performed, the more likely its fans are to sport apparel that publicly identifies them with that team.[4]

In addition to explaining how we perceive ourselves, social identity theory also explains how we come to perceive others. Specifically, the theory explains that we focus on the differences between ourselves and other individuals as well as members of other groups (see the lower portion of Figure 2.2). In so doing, we tend to simplify things by

personal identity
The characteristics that define a particular individual.

social identity
Who a person is, as defined in terms of his or her membership in various social groups.

social identity theory
A conceptualization recognizing that the way we perceive others and ourselves is based on both our unique characteristics (see *personal identity*) and our membership in various groups (see *social identity*).

FIGURE 2.2

Social Identity Theory: An Overview
According to *social identity theory,* people identify themselves in terms of their individual characteristics and their memberships in various groups. They then compare themselves to other individuals and groups to help define who they are, both to themselves and others.

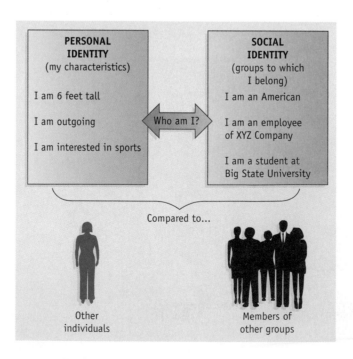

assuming that people in different groups share certain qualities that make them different from ourselves—even if they really are not so different after all.

Not only do we perceive others as different from ourselves, but we also perceive the differences in negative ways. This is particularly so when we are competing against them (see Chapter 12). Take athletic competitions, for example. If you ever have heard the negative things that students from one college or university say about those from other schools that they are competing against in various sports, then you know quite well the phenomenon we are describing here. Although such perceptions tend to be exaggerations—and inaccurate as a result—most of us stick with these perceptions, nevertheless. The reason why is simple. Making such categorizations helps bring order to the world. After all, distinguishing between "the good guys" and "the bad guys" makes otherwise complex judgments quite simple. And, after all, bringing simplicity to a complex world is what social perception is all about.

THE ATTRIBUTION PROCESS: JUDGING THE CAUSES OF OTHERS' BEHAVIOR

A question we often ask about others is "why?" Why did Tonya not return my call? Why did John goof up the order? Why did the company president make the policy she did? When we ask such questions, we are attempting to get at two different types of information: (1) what someone is really like (i.e., what traits and characteristics he or she possesses) and (2) what made the person behave as he or she did (i.e., what accounted for his or her actions). As we will see, people attempt to answer these questions in different ways.[5]

Making Correspondent Inferences: Using Acts to Judge Dispositions

Situations frequently arise in organizations in which we want to know what someone is like. Is your opponent a tough negotiator? Are your coworkers prone to be punctual? The more you know about what people are like, the better equipped you are to know what to expect and how to deal with them. How, precisely, do we go about identifying another's traits?

Generally speaking, the answer is that we learn about others by observing their behavior and then inferring their traits from this information. The judgments we make about what someone is like based on what we have observed about him or her are known as **correspondent inferences**.[6] Simply put, correspondent inferences are judgments about people's dispositions, traits, and characteristics, that correspond to what we have observed of their actions (see Figure 2.3).

correspondent inferences
Judgments about people's dispositions, traits, and characteristics, that correspond to what we have observed of their actions.

Challenges in judging others accurately. At first blush, it would appear to be a simple matter to infer what people are like based on their behavior. A person with a disorganized desk may be perceived as being sloppy. Someone who slips on the shop floor may be considered clumsy. Such judgments might be accurate, but not necessarily! After all, the messy desk actually may be the result of a coworker's rummaging through it to find an

FIGURE 2.3
Correspondent Inferences: Judging Dispositions Based on Behavior
One of the ways in which we come to judge what others are like is by making inferences about them that follow from what we have observed of their behavior. Such judgments, known as *correspondent inferences,* are frequently misleading. How might the inference summarized here be inaccurate?

important report. Similarly, the person who slipped could have encountered oily conditions under which anyone, even the most coordinated individual, would have fallen. In other words, it is important to recognize that the judgments we make about someone may be inaccurate because there are *many possible causes of his or her behavior.* People's underlying characteristics certainly may play a large role in determining what they do, but as we will explain in the next section, it also is possible for behavior to be shaped by external forces. (In our examples, these external factors would be the coworker's actions and the slippery floor.) For this reason, correspondent inferences may not always be accurate.

Correspondent inferences also might not be accurate because *people on the job tend to conceal some of their traits*—especially those likely to be viewed as negative. So, for example, a sloppy individual may work hard in public to appear to be organized. Likewise, the unprincipled person may talk a good show about the importance of being ethical. In other words, people often do their best to disguise some of their basic traits. In summary, because behavior is complex and has many different causes, and because people sometimes purposely disguise their true characteristics, forming correspondent inferences is a risky business.

Making accurate inferences about others. Despite such difficulties, we can use several techniques to help make more accurate correspondent inferences.

First, we can focus on others' behavior in situations in which they do not *have to* behave in a pleasant or socially acceptable manner. For example, anyone would behave in a courteous manner toward the president of the company, so when people do so, we don't learn too much about them. However, only those who are *really* courteous would be expected to behave politely toward someone of much lower rank—that is, someone toward whom they don't have to behave politely. In other words, someone who is polite toward the company president but condescending toward a secretary is probably really arrogant. The way people behave in situations in which a certain behavior is not clearly expected of them may reveal a great deal about their basic traits and motives.

Similarly, we can learn a great deal about someone by *focusing on behavior for which there appears to be only a single logical explanation.* For example, imagine finding out that your friend accepts a new job. Upon questioning him, you learn that the position is very high paying, involves interesting work, and is in a desirable location. What have you learned about what's important to your friend? Not too much. After all, any of these are good reasons to consider taking a position. Now imagine finding out that the work is very dangerous and that the job is in an undesirable location but that it pays very well. In this case, you're more prone to learn something about your friend— namely, that he highly values money. Clearly, the opportunity to make accurate correspondent inferences about people is far greater in situations in which there is only one plausible explanation for their behavior.

Causal Attribution of Responsibility: Answering the Question "Why?"

Imagine finding out that your boss just fired one of your fellow employees. Naturally, you'd ask yourself, "Why did he do that?" Was it because your coworker violated the company's code of conduct? Or was it because the boss is a cruel and heartless person? These two answers to the question "why?" represent two major classes of explanations for the causes of someone's behavior:

internal causes of behavior
Explanations based on actions for which the individual is responsible.

external causes of behavior
Explanations based on situations over which the individual has no control.

- **Internal causes of behavior**—explanations based on actions for which the individual is responsible.
- **External causes of behavior**—explanations based on situations over which the individual has no control.

In our example, the internal cause would be the person's violation of the rules, and the external cause would be the boss's cruel and arbitrary behavior.

Generally speaking, it is very important to be able to determine whether an internal or an external cause is responsible for someone's behavior. Knowing why something happened to someone else might better help you prepare for what might happen to you. For example, in this case, if you believe that your colleague was fired because of something for which she was responsible herself, such as violating a company rule, then you might not feel as vulnerable as you would if you thought she was fired because of the arbitrary, spiteful nature of your boss. In the latter case, you might decide to take some precautionary actions, to do something to protect yourself from your boss, such as staying on his good side, or even giving up and finding a new job—before you are forced to do so.

Kelley's theory of causal attribution. When it comes to social perception, the question of interest to social scientists is: How do people go about judging whether someone's actions were caused by internal or external factors? An answer to this question is provided by **Kelley's theory of causal attribution.** According to this conceptualization, we base our judgments of internal and external causality on observations we make with respect to three types of information.[7] These are as follows:

- **Consensus**—the extent to which other people behave in the same manner as the person whom we're judging. If others do behave similarly, consensus is considered high; if they do not, consensus is considered low.
- **Consistency**—the extent to which the person we're judging acts the same way at other times. If the person does act the same way at other times, consistency is high; if he or she does not, then consistency is low.
- **Distinctiveness**—the extent to which a person behaves in the same manner in other contexts. If he or she behaves the same way in other situations, distinctiveness is low; if he or she behaves differently, distinctiveness is high.

According to the theory, after collecting this information, we combine what we have learned to make our attributions of causality. Here's how. If we learn that other people act like this one (consensus is high), this person behaves in the same manner at other times (consistency is high), and that this person does not act in the same manner in other situations (distinctiveness is high), we are likely to conclude that this person's behavior stemmed from *external* causes. In contrast, imagine learning that other people do not act like this one (consensus is low), this person behaves in the same manner at other times (consistency is high), and that this person acts in the same manner in other situations (distinctiveness is low). In this case, we will probably conclude that this person's behavior stemmed from *internal* causes.

An example. Because this explanation is highly abstract, let's consider an example that helps illustrate how the process works. Imagine that you're at a business lunch with several of your company's sales representatives when the sales manager makes some critical remarks about the restaurant's food and service. Further imagine that no one else in your party acts this way (consensus is low), you have heard her say the same things during other visits to the restaurant (consistency is high), and that you have seen her acting critically in other settings, such as the regional sales meeting (distinctiveness is low). What would you conclude in this situation? Probably that she is a "picky" person, someone who is difficult to please. In other words, her behavior stems from internal causes.

Now imagine the same setting but with different observations. Suppose that several other members of your group also complain about the restaurant (consensus is high), that you have seen this person complain in the same restaurant at other times (consistency is high), but that you have never seen her complain about anything else before (distinctiveness is high). By contrast, in this case, you probably would conclude that the restaurant really *is* inferior. In this case, the sales manager's behavior stems from external causes. For a summary of these contrasting conclusions, see Figure 2.4.

THE IMPERFECT NATURE OF SOCIAL PERCEPTION

Computers may analyze information in an accurate, unbiased, tireless fashion, but the same cannot be said about human beings. We are far from perfect when it comes to

Kelley's theory of causal attribution
The approach suggesting that people will believe others' actions to be caused by internal or external factors based on three types of information: *consensus, consistency,* and *distinctiveness.*

consensus
In *Kelley's theory of causal attribution,* information regarding the extent to which other people behave in the same manner as the person being judged.

consistency
In *Kelley's theory of causal attribution,* information regarding the extent to which the person being judged acts the same way at other times.

distinctiveness
In *Kelley's theory of causal attribution,* information regarding the extent to which a person behaves in the same manner in other contexts.

FIGURE 2.4
Kelley's Theory of Causal Attribution: A Summary
In determining whether others' behavior stems mainly from internal or external causes, we focus on the three types of information illustrated here.

gathering information about others and then making judgments about them. In fact, it is more likely to be the rule rather than the exception that our judgments of others will be imperfect. After all, we are not exactly unbiased in the judgments we make. As you might imagine, this can lead to serious problems for individuals and the organizations in which they work. In this section, we will explore this state of affairs in some detail. We will begin by describing how everyone relies on stereotypes, which are likely to be inaccurate. Next, we will explain the various systematic biases that come into play when judging others. Finally, we will explain how one type of bias can have a profound effect on job performance. Throughout this section, of course, we also will identify various things you can do to overcome these problems.

Stereotypes: Fitting Others into Categories

What comes to mind when you think about people who wear glasses? Are they studious? Eggheads? Although there is no evidence of such a connection, it is interesting to note that for many people such an image lingers in their minds. Of course, this is only one example. You probably can think of many other commonly held beliefs about the characteristics of people belonging to specific groups. Such statements usually take the form: "People from group *X* possess characteristic *Y*." In most cases, the characteristics described tend to be negative. Assumptions of this type are referred to as **stereotypes**—beliefs that members of specific groups tend to share similar traits and behaviors.

Deep down inside many of us know, of course, that not all people belonging to a specific group posses the negative characteristics with which we associate them. In other words, most of us accept that the stereotypes we use are at least partially inaccurate. After all, not *all X*'s are *Y*; there are exceptions (maybe even quite a few!). If so, then why are stereotypes so prevalent? Why do we use them?

Why do we rely on stereotypes? To a great extent, the answer resides in the fact that people tend to do as little cognitive work as possible when it comes to thinking about others.[8] That is, we tend to rely on mental shortcuts. If assigning people to groups allows us to assume that we know what they are like and how they may act, then we can save the tedious work of learning about them as individuals. After all, we come into contact with so many people that it's impractical, if not impossible, to learn everything about them we need to know. So, we rely on readily available information—such as someone's age, race, gender, or job type—as the basis for organizing our perceptions in a coherent way.

So, for example, if you believe that members of group *X* (those who wear glasses, for example) tend to possess trait *Y* (studiousness, in this case), then simply observing that

stereotypes
Beliefs that all members of specific groups share similar traits and are prone to behave the same way.

someone falls into category *X* becomes the basis for your believing that he or she possesses *Y*. To the extent that the stereotype applies in this case, then the perception will be accurate. However, such mental shortcuts often lead us to make inaccurate judgments about people. This is the price we pay for using stereotypes.

The dangers of using stereotypes in organizations. The problem with stereotypes, of course, is that they lead us to judge people prematurely—without the benefit of learning more about them than just the categories into which they fit. Still, we all rely on stereotypes at least sometimes; their temptation is far too great to resist.

It is easy to imagine how the use of stereotypes can have a powerful effect on the kinds of judgments people make in organizations. For example, if a personnel officer believes that members of certain groups are lazy, then he purposely may avoid hiring or promoting individuals who belong to those groups. The personnel officer may firmly believe that he is using good judgment—gathering all the necessary information and listening to the candidate carefully. Still, without being aware of it, the stereotypes he holds may influence the way he judges certain individuals. The result, of course, is that the fate of the individual in question is sealed in advance—not necessarily because of anything he or she may have done or said, but by the mere fact that he or she belongs to a certain group. In other words, even people who might not intend to act in a bigoted fashion still may be influenced by the stereotypes they hold.

In some cases, stereotyping can be very costly to its victims—literally. A recent study by the National Bureau of Economic Research conducted over a 10-year period found that white women who were overweight by an average of 65 pounds earned hourly wages that were, on average, 7 percent lower than their nonoverweight counterparts (see Figure 2.5).[9] As the scientists noted, that's like losing the pay boost that would have been earned by a year of education or three years of work experience. Interestingly, both overweight and nonoverweight women held the same kinds of jobs and had the same levels of experience, suggesting that the lower pay of obese women reflects society's negative stereotypes toward them. It's fascinating to note that the same effects of weight on pay were *not* found among African American women. Although there may be several possible explanations for this racial difference, greater acceptance of different body types and fewer negative stereotypes about obese women among African Americans appear to be key factors.

It's important to acknowledge that the effects of stereotyping others are not always as profound. Referring to accountants as "bean counters" and professors as "absent minded" are observations that also reflect stereotypes—ones that appear to be only mildly negative. Still, it must be cautioned that by holding stereotypes of people in vari-

FIGURE 2.5

Thinner Paychecks for Obese Women: Negative Effects of Stereotypes
Because negative stereotypes about individuals who are overweight are wide spread, obese white women tend to be paid less than their average-weight counterparts, although they generally hold comparable positions. This effect does not exist among African American women, largely because such negative stereotypes are less prevalent within the African American community.

ous groups you run the risks of promoting unfair discrimination (Chapter 5), causing miscommunication (Chapter 10), and generating interpersonal conflict (Chapter 12).

Perceptual Biases: Systematic Errors in Perceiving Others

Researchers have noted that there are several systematic biases that interfere with making completely accurate judgments of others. These reflect systematic biases in the ways we think about others in general. Collectively, these biases are referred to as **perceptual biases.** We will consider five such biases—the *fundamental attribution error,* the *halo effect,* the *similar-to-me effect, selective perception,* and the *first-impression error.*

The fundamental attribution error. Despite what Kelley's theory may imply, people are *not* equally predisposed to reach judgments regarding internal and external causality. Rather, they are more likely to explain others' actions (particularly negative ones) in terms of internal causes rather than external causes. In other words, we are prone to assume that others' behavior is due to the way they are—their traits and dispositions (e.g., "she's just that kind of person"). So, for example, we are more likely to assume that someone who shows up for work late does so because she is lazy rather than because she got caught in traffic. This perceptual bias is so strong that it has been referred to as the **fundamental attribution error.**[10]

This particular bias stems from the fact that it is far simpler to explain someone's actions in terms of his or her traits than to recognize the complex pattern of situational factors that may have affected his or her actions. As you might imagine, this tendency can be quite damaging in organizations. Specifically, it leads us to prematurely assume that people are responsible for the negative things that happen to them (e.g., "he wrecked the company car because he is careless") without considering external alternatives, ones that may be less damning (e.g., "another driver hit the car"). And this can lead to inaccurate judgments about people.

The halo effect: Keeping perceptions consistent. Have you ever heard someone say something like, "She's very smart, so she also must be hardworking"? Or, "He's not too bright, so I guess he's lazy"? If so, then you are already aware of a common perceptual bias known as the **halo effect.**[11] Once we form a positive impression of someone, we tend to view the things that person does in favorable terms—even things about which we have no knowledge. Similarly, a generally negative impression of someone is likely to be associated with negative evaluations of that person's behavior. Both of these tendencies are referred to as halo effects (even the negative case, despite the fact that the word *halo* has positive connotations).

In organizations, the halo effect often occurs when superiors rate subordinates using a formal performance appraisal form. In this context (described more fully later in this chapter), a manager evaluating one of his or her employees highly on some dimension may assume that an individual who is so good at this particular thing also must be good at other things. The manager would then be likely to evaluate that person highly on other dimensions (see Figure 2.6). Put differently, the halo effect may be responsible for finding high correlations between the ratings given to people on various dimensions. When this occurs, the resulting evaluations are lacking in accuracy, and the quality of the resulting evaluations is compromised.

The similar-to-me effect: "If you're like me, you must be pretty good." Another common type of perceptual bias involves the tendency for people to perceive more favorably others who are like themselves than those who are dissimilar. This tendency, known as the **similar-to-me effect,** constitutes a potential source of bias when it comes to judging other people. In fact, research has shown that when superiors rate their subordinates, the more similar the parties are, the higher the rating the superior tends to give.[12] This tendency applies with respect to several different dimensions of similarity, such as similarity of work values and habits, similarity of beliefs about the way things should be at work, and similarity with respect to demographic variables (such as age, race, gender, and work experience).

perceptual biases

Predispositions that people have to misperceive others in various ways. Types include the *fundamental attribution error,* the *halo effect,* the *similar-to-me-effect,* the *selective perception,* and *first-impression error.*

fundamental attribution error

The tendency to attribute others' actions to internal causes (e.g., their traits) while largely ignoring external factors that also may have influenced behavior.

halo effect

The tendency for our overall impressions of others to affect objective evaluations of their specific traits; perceiving high correlations between characteristics that may be unrelated.

similar-to-me effect

The tendency for people to perceive in a positive light others who are believed to be similar to themselves in any of several different ways.

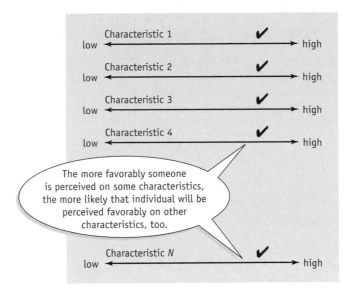

FIGURE 2.6
The Halo Effect: A Demonstration
One manifestation of the halo effect is the tendency for people rating others to give either consistently high ratings (if the individual is generally perceived in a positive manner) or low ratings (if the individual is generally perceived in a negative manner). Because each rating dimension is not considered independently, inaccurate evaluations may result.

This effect appears to be partly the result of the tendency for people to be able to empathize and relate better to similar others and to be more lenient toward them. However, it also appears that subordinates tend to be more trusting and confident in supervisors whom they perceive as similar to themselves than those perceived as dissimilar.[13] As a result, they may have a more positive relationship with such individuals, and this may lead superiors to judge similar subordinates more favorably.

Selective perception: Focusing on some things while ignoring others. Another perceptual bias known as **selective perception** refers to the tendency for individuals to focus on certain aspects of the environment while ignoring others.[14] Insofar as we operate in complex environments in which there are many stimuli that demand our attention, it makes sense that we tend to be selective, narrowing our perceptual fields. This constitutes a bias insofar as it limits our attention to some stimuli while heightening our attention to other stimuli.

As you might imagine, this process occurs in organizations. In fact, research has shown that top executives asked to indicate the functions of their organizations that contribute most strongly to the organizations' effectiveness tend to cite functional areas that matched their backgrounds.[15] For example, executives whose backgrounds were in sales and marketing perceived changes in a company's line of products and services as being most important. Similarly, those who worked previously in research and development focused more on product designs than on other issues in their perceptions of the business environment. In other words, executives tend to be affected by selective perception. That is, they give greatest attention to those aspects of the business environment that match their background experiences. Keeping this tendency in mind, it is easy to understand why different people may perceive the same situations very differently.

First-impression error: Confirming one's expectations. Often the way we judge someone is not based solely on how well that person performs now but rather on our initial judgments of that individual—that is, our *first impressions*. To the extent that our initial impressions guide our subsequent impressions, we have been victimized by **first-impression error.**

As you might imagine, this error can be especially problematic in organizations in which accurately judging others' performance is a crucial managerial task. When a subordinate's performance has improved, that needs to be recognized, but to the extent that current evaluations are based on poor first impressions, recognizing such improvement is unlikely. Likewise, inaccurate assessments of performance will result when initially good performers leave positive impressions that linger on even when confronted with evidence suggesting that one's performance has dropped (for a summary, see Figure 2.7).

selective perception
The tendency to focus on some aspects of the environment while ignoring others.

first-impression error
The tendency to base our judgments of others on our earlier impressions of them.

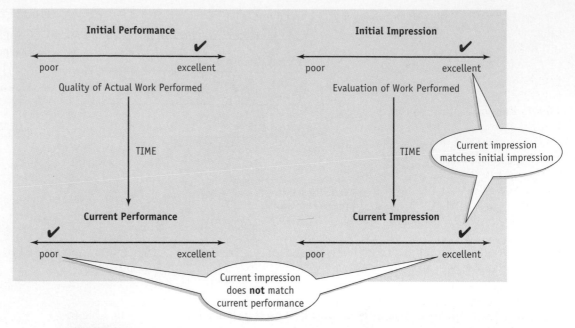

FIGURE 2.7
First-Impression Error: A Summary
When a *first-impression error* is made, the way we evaluate someone is more highly influenced by our initial impressions of that person than by his or her current performance. In this example, someone who was initially perceived as performing well continues to be rated highly despite a downturn in performance.

Research suggests that first-impression error may take very subtle forms.[16] For example, in one study, corporate interviewers evaluated prospective job applicants by viewing the application blanks and test scores of prospective employees. The more highly interviewers judged the applicants based on these two criteria alone, the more positively the applicants were treated during the interview process. In fact, candidates who made initially positive impressions were treated more positively during the interview (e.g., they were spoken to in a more pleasant interpersonal style). Thus, instead of using the interviews to gather additional unbiased information, as you would expect (and hope!), the recruiters appeared to use the interviews simply to confirm the first impressions they already developed on the basis of the test scores and application blanks. This study provides clear evidence of the first-impression error in action.

Self-Fulfilling Prophecies: The Pygmalion Effect and the Golem Effect

In case it isn't already apparent just how important perceptions are in the workplace, consider the fact that the way we perceive others actually can dictate how effectively people will work. Put differently, perceptions can influence reality! This is the idea behind what is known as the **self-fulfilling prophecy**—the tendency for someone's expectations about another to cause that individual to behave in a manner consistent with those expectations.

Self-fulfilling prophecies can take both positive and negative forms. In the positive case, holding high expectations of another tends to improve that individual's performance. This is known as the **Pygmalion effect.** This effect was demonstrated in a study of Israeli soldiers who were taking a combat command course.[17] The four instructors who taught the course were told that certain trainees had high potential for success, whereas the others had either normal potential or an unknown amount of potential. In reality, the trainees identified as belonging to each of these categories were assigned to that condition at random. Despite this, trainees who were believed to have high potential were found at the end of the training session to be more successful (e.g., they had

self-fulfilling prophecy
The tendency for someone's expectations about another to cause that person to behave in a manner consistent with those expectations. This can be either positive (see the *Pygmalion effect*) or negative (see the *Golem effect*) in nature.

Pygmalion effect
A positive instance of the *self-fulfilling prophecy,* in which people holding high expectations of another tend to improve that individual's performance.

higher test scores). This demonstrates the Pygmalion effect: Trainees who were expected to do well actually did well.

Researchers also have found that the self-fulfilling prophecy works in the negative direction—that is, low expectations of success lead to poor performance. This is known as the **Golem effect.** Illustrating the Golem effect, researchers have found that paratroopers whose instructors expected them to perform poorly in their training class did, in fact, perform worse than those about whom instructors had no advance expectations.[18] Clearly, this effect can be quite devastating, but fortunately it can be overcome.

A recent study compared the performance of female military recruits enrolled in a special training program for Israeli soldiers whose limited schooling and mental test scores put them at risk for failure in the military.[19] Platoon leaders in the experimental group were told, "You will be training recruits whose average ability is significantly higher than usual for special recruits" and that "you can expect better than average achievement from the recruits in your platoon." Leaders of the control group were not given any such information, and their recruits showed the Golem effect. However, no such effect was found in the experimental group, suggesting that even those who are expected to perform poorly can be kept from doing so by being led to believe that success is possible.

Why do both positive and negative self-fulfilling prophecies occur? Research into the underlying processes responsible for self-fulfilling prophecies suggest that both types of self-fulfilling prophecies operate according to the four steps summarized in Figure 2.8.[20]

OVERCOMING BIAS IN SOCIAL PERCEPTION

Biases in social perception are inevitable. Fortunately, there are things we can do to reduce their impact. Here are several guidelines to follow to help you perceive others more accurately in the workplace.

- *Do not overlook the external causes of others' behavior.* The fundamental attribution error leads us to discount the possibility that people's poor performance may be due to conditions beyond their control. To combat this, ask yourself if anyone else may have performed just as poorly under the same conditions. If the answer is yes, then you should not automatically assume that the poor performer is to blame.
- *Identify your stereotypes.* We all rely on stereotypes, but if you try to become more aware of them, you will be able to catch yourself using them—and doing this may stop you from making inaccurate decisions.
- *Evaluate people based on objective factors.* The more objective the information you use to judge others, the less your judgments will be subjected to perceptual distortion. So, whenever possible, judge work performance more on quantifiable measures of quantity (e.g., sales volume) and quality (e.g., error rate) than on personal judgments.
- *Avoid making rash judgments.* It is human nature to jump to conclusions about people, but when you can, take the time to get to know people better before judging them. What you learn may make a big difference in your opinion.

We realize that many of these tactics are far easier to say than to do. However, to the extent that we conscientiously try to apply these suggestions to our everyday interactions with others in the workplace, we stand a good chance of perceiving people more accurately.

FIGURE 2.8
The Self-Fulfilling Prophecy: A Summary
The processes underlying the self-fulfilling prophecy are summarized here. As indicated, its effects may produce positive effects (known as the Pygmalion effect) or negative effects (known as the Golem effect).

The lesson to be learned from research on self-fulfilling prophecies is very clear: Managers should take concrete steps to promote the Pygmalion effect and to discourage the Golem effect. When leaders display enthusiasm toward people and express optimism about each person's potential, such positive expectations become contagious and spread throughout the organization. As a case in point, consider the great enthusiasm and support that Gordon Bethune showed toward employees of Continental airlines in 1995 when he took over as that bankrupt company's CEO.[21] It would have been easy for him to be unsupportive and to show his disappointment with the workforce, but he did just the opposite. Only a few years after Bethune was at the helm, the airline turned around to become one of the most successful carriers in the sky today. Although the changes he made to the airline's systems and equipment helped, these things alone would not have been enough if the employees had felt like failures. Indeed, Bethune's acceptance and enthusiasm toward members of Continental's workforce contributed greatly to giving the encouragement needed to bring the airline "from worst to first."

PERCEIVING OTHERS: ORGANIZATIONAL APPLICATIONS

perception
The process through which people select, organize, and interpret information.

Thus far, we have identified some of the basic processes of social perception and have alluded to ways in which they are involved in organizational behavior. Now in this section we will make these connections more explicit. Specifically, we will describe the role of **perception** in three organizational activities: *employee performance appraisal,* the *employment interview,* and the organization's development of its *corporate image.*

Performance Appraisal: Formal Judgments About Job Performance

performance appraisal
The process of evaluating employees on various work-related dimensions.

One of the most obvious instances in which social perception occurs is when someone formally evaluates the job performance of another. This process, known as **performance appraisal,** may be defined as the process of evaluating the work of others on various work-related dimensions. Typically, performance appraisals are conducted on an annual or semiannual basis, usually for purposes of determining raises, promotions, and training needs.[22] When properly conducted, performance appraisals provide valuable feedback that point the way toward improving job performance (see Figure 2.9).

An inherently biased process. Ideally, this process should be completely rational, leading to unbiased and objective judgments about exactly how well each employee performed, and how he or she should be treated. However, based on what we have said about perception thus far, you're probably not surprised to learn that the performance evaluation process is far from objective. Indeed, people have a limited capacity to process, store, and retrieve information, making them prone to bias when it comes to evaluating others.[23]

Several such biases have been observed by researchers. For example, it has been found that people's ratings of others' performance depends on the extent to which that performance is consistent with their initial expectations. Researchers in one study, for example, asked bank managers to indicate how well they expected their newest tellers to perform their jobs.[24] Then, four months later they were asked to rate the tellers' actual job performance. It was found that managers gave higher ratings to those tellers whose performance matched their earlier expectations than to those who did either better or worse than predicted. These effects are unsettling insofar as they suggest that the improved performance of some employees may go unrecognized—or, worse yet, be downgraded! Of course, to the extent that human resource management decisions are made on the basis of several sources of information, besides judgments by a single superior, it is unlikely that such biased judgments may go uncorrected. Nonetheless, these findings clearly underscore a key point: Perceptions are based not only on the

FIGURE 2.9
Performance Appraisal: A Potentially Valuable Source of Feedback
The performance appraisal process enables employees to make the kind of adjustments needed to improve their job performance. Fortunately, most workers who solicit information about how well they're doing find their supervisors to be far more receptive than the one shown here. (Copyright Ted Goff 2002.)

"You were doing just fine until you came in here and bothered me by asking how you were doing."

characteristics of the person being perceived, but on the characteristics of the perceiver as well.

This conclusion is supported by research showing several different attribution biases in evaluations of job performance. Consider, for example, research illustrating how the similar-to-me effect operates in a performance appraisal situation. Research conducted at a bank, for example, has shown that the more tellers do things to cultivate positive impressions on their superiors (e.g., do favors for them, agree with their opinions), the more those superiors view those tellers as being similar to themselves. And the more similar they are believed to be, the more highly the superiors evaluated their work.[25]

As you might imagine, employees often attempt to make themselves look good to superiors by offering explanations of their work that focus on the internal reasons underlying their good performance and the external reasons underlying their poor performance. Indeed, two equally good performers are unlikely to receive the same performance ratings when different attributions are made about the underlying causes of their performance. Managers tend to give higher ratings to individuals whose poor performance is attributed to factors outside the individual's control (e.g., someone who is trying hard but is too inexperienced to succeed) than to those whose poor performance they attribute to internal factors (e.g., those who are believed to be capable but who are just lazy and holding back). In other words, our evaluations of others' performance are qualified by the nature of the attributions we make about that performance.

Findings such as these illustrate our point that organizational performance evaluations are far from the unbiased, rational procedures one would hope to find. Instead, they represent a complex mix of perceptual biases—effects that must be appreciated and well understood if we are to have any chance of ultimately improving the accuracy of the performance evaluation process. As you will see in the OB in a Diverse World section that follows, cultural differences in the performance appraisal process complicate things further.

OB IN A DIVERSE WORLD
PERFORMANCE EVALUATIONS: COMPARING THE UNITED STATES AND JAPAN

Beyond individual biases that make the process of evaluating work performance inherently imprecise, widespread cultural differences also are likely to make a big difference when it comes to performance appraisal. In other words, the way people tend to evaluate others' work is likely to be influenced by the nations from which they come.[26] This shouldn't be too surprising if you consider that people from various countries differ with respect to several key variables involved in the performance appraisal process, such as how willing they are to be direct with others and how sensitive they are to differences in status. This point is illustrated clearly by comparing U.S. and Japanese companies with respect to the performance appraisal practices they use.

Although direct supervisors are likely to conduct appraisals in both countries, the ways they go about doing so are very different in several key respects. For example, the American worker's job performance typically is appraised annually. However, in Japan, judgments of how effectively a worker is developing on the job usually occur monthly. Then, an overall evaluation of performance effectiveness is given only after a long time has passed—usually 12 years—making it possible for a highly meaningful assessment to occur. Although this may make little sense in the

Impression Management in the Employment Interview: Looking Good to Prospective Employers

impression management
Efforts by individuals to improve how they appear to others.

The desire to make a favorable impression on others is universal. In one way or another, we all do things to attempt to control how other people see us, often attempting to get them to think of us in the best light possible. This process is known as **impression management**.[30] Generally, individuals devote considerable attention to the impressions they create in the eyes of others—especially when these others are important, such as prospective employers.

The impressions prospective employers form of us may be based on subtle behaviors, such as how we dress and speak, or more elaborate acts, such as announcing our accomplishments (see Figure 2.10).[31] They may be the result of calculated efforts to get others to think of us in a certain way or be the passive, unintended effects of our actions.

When it comes to the employment interview, for example, there are several things job candidates commonly do to enhance the impressions they make. In a recent study researchers audiotaped the interviews between college students looking for jobs and representatives of companies that posted openings at the campus job placement center.[32] The various statements made by the candidates were categorized with respect to the impression management techniques they used. Several tactics were commonly observed. Table 2.1 lists these specific tactics, gives an example of each, and shows the percentage of candidates who used these techniques. Interestingly, the most common technique was *self-promotion*, that is, flatly asserting that one has desirable characteristics. In this case, candidates commonly described themselves as being hardworking, interpersonally skilled, goal oriented, and effective leaders.

Importantly, the study also found that candidates used these impression management techniques with great success. The more they relied on these tactics, the more positively they were viewed by the interviewer along several important dimensions (e.g., fit with the organization). This study not only confirms that job candidates do indeed rely on impression management techniques during job interviews but also that these cultivate the positive impressions desired. With this in mind, the job interview may be seen as an ongoing effort on behalf of candidates to present themselves favor-

United States, where long-term commitments to companies are atypical, this approach is possible in Japan, where employees and companies tend to be highly loyal to each other, and where loyalty is rewarded by lifetime employment and regular promotion.[27]

The United States and Japan differ as well in terms of precisely how performance appraisals are conducted. In the United States, companies almost always rely on an official form to provide a precise written record of a supervisor's evaluation. In Japan, however, such directness would be considered inappropriate, and comments about performance are handled orally in a very subtle manner. In keeping with their bluntness, Americans generally are not reluctant to rebut (or, at least, to ask questions about) the judgments made about them. However, very few Japanese employees would consider challenging their supervisors so overtly, politely accepting their supervisors' judgments.

Finally, in the United States, it is almost always the individual worker who is evaluated. In Japan, however, the group or work team tends to be judged as a whole. This reflects the fact that Japanese society generally values collective efforts—people pitching in to work together is what matters most. Americans, by contrast, tend to be far more concerned about their individual performance and their individual rewards.[28]

Although you may find these differences to be interesting curiosities, Americans doing business in Japan and Japanese doing business in the United States recognize the importance of such differences. Indeed, the willingness of American managers from General Motors and Japanese managers from Toyota to understand what it takes to appraise one another's work is considered a key determinant of the long-term success of the ongoing business partnerships between these two automotive giants.[29]

ably and for interviewers to try to see through those attempts to judge candidates accurately. As the evidence suggests, this task may not be as simple as it seems.

Corporate Image: Impression Management by Organizations

Not only individuals but also entire organizations desire to cultivate positive impressions. These impressions are known as **corporate image**.[33] As you might imagine, the impression an organization makes on people can have a considerable effect on the way these individuals relate to it. Extending our discussion of the job recruitment setting, not only do individual candidates want to make good impressions on prospective employers but employers also want their job offers to be accepted by the best candidates.

corporate image
The impressions that people have of an organization.

FIGURE 2.10

Dressing For Success Requires Dressing for the Job
It's important for employees to make favorable impressions on others by wearing the clothing expected of them on the job. For many today, this consists of "business casual" attire. At most small, high-tech companies, for example, where casual dress (sometimes, very casual) is standard, an employee would look out of place showing up in a formal business suit. Likewise, a tee shirt and jeans would make an unfavorable impression in the executive suite, where the classic business suit remains standard attire. The most positive impressions may be made by dressing in the manner considered appropriate for the job.

TABLE 2.1 HOW DO JOB APPLICANTS GO ABOUT PRESENTING THEMSELVES FAVORABLY?

Researchers have systematically recorded and categorized what job applicants say to present themselves favorably to recruiters interviewing them. Here is a list of techniques found during one recent study along with the frequencies with which they were used. Descriptions and examples of each technique are given as well.

IMPRESSION MANAGEMENT TECHNIQUE	DESCRIPTION	FREQUENCY USING TECHNIQUE(%)
Self-promotion	Directly describing oneself in a positive manner for the situation at hand (e.g., "I am a hard worker").	100
Personal stories	Describing past events that make oneself look good (e.g., "In my old job, I worked late anytime it was needed").	96
Opinion conformity	Expressing beliefs that are assumed to be held by the target (e.g., agreeing with something the interviewer says).	54
Entitlements	Claiming responsibility for successful past events (e.g., "I was responsible for the 90 percent sales increase that resulted").	50
Other enhancement	Making statements that flatter, praise, or compliment the target (e.g., "I am very impressed with your company's growth in recent years").	46
Enhancements	Claiming that a positive event was more positive than it really was (e.g., "Not only did our department improve, it was the best in the entire company").	42
Overcoming obstacles	Describing how one succeeded despite obstacles that should have lowered performance (e.g., "I managed to get a 3.8 average although I worked two part-time jobs").	33
Justifications	Accepting responsibility for one's poor performance but denying the negative implications of it (e.g., "Our team didn't win a lot, but it's just how you play the game that really matters").	17
Excuses	Denying responsibility for one's actions (e.g., "I didn't complete the application form because the placement center ran out of them").	13

(*Source:* Based on information in Stevens & Kristof, 1995; see Note 32.)

Research has shown that a company's image is strongly related to people's interest in seeking employment with it.[34] Specifically, it has been found that the more favorable a company's reputation is considered to be (based on a *Fortune* magazine survey), the more interested prospective employees are in working there. (For a list of some of the most admired companies identified in a recent *Fortune* survey, see Table 2.2.[35]) This is important insofar as organizations must recruit the best prospective employees to perform at high levels. Given this important point, it seems worthwhile to consider exactly what factors contribute to a corporate image.

One thing that influences a company's image is the amount of information people have about it from *recruitment ads*. In general, longer ads are associated with more positive images. This may not only be because of what is said in the ad itself but, also the mere length of the ad itself. Specifically, because recruitment ads emphasize the benefits of employment with a firm, longer ads describe more benefits than shorter ones, thereby creating even stronger positive images. Moreover, to the extent that people believe that longer ads reflect a company's commitment to obtaining good employees (by their willingness to invest in a large ad), they may be more impressed with a company as a prospective place to work.

Another mechanism that an organization uses to promote its corporate image is its *annual report*—a company's official statement to its stockholders on its activities during the previous year and its current financial state. These booklets contain such things as letters from CEOs and descriptions of projects and future plans—in short, information that helps shape the image of the company in the minds of both employees and stockholders.

TABLE 2.2 AMERICA'S MOST ADMIRED COMPANIES

According to a recent survey by *Fortune* magazine, the following companies are the most admired ones in the United States. Positive corporate images are important insofar as they help attract qualified job candidates.

RANK	COMPANY	PRINCIPLE PRODUCT OR SERVICE
1	General Electric	Broadcasting, electric appliances
2	Southwest Airlines	Air transportation
3	Wal-Mart Stores	Variety retail
4	Microsoft	Computer software
5	Berkshire Hathaway	Investments
6	Home Depot	Hardware and home goods retail
7	Johnson & Johnson	Beauty care products
8	FedEx	Package delivery service
9	Citigroup	Banking services
10	Intel	Computer chips

(*Source: Fortune,* 2002; see Note 35.)

Traditionally, annual reports have been strikingly beautiful, glossy booklets with elaborate photography and glitzy images, trappings of success designed to instill confidence in the minds of investors. In recent years, however, many companies –St. Paul Companies, Avery Dennison, and General Dynamics, among them—have spared such expenses, issuing bare-bones annual reports.[36] The reason: to promote an image of austerity. As today's investors are looking for value, companies are going out of their way to cultivate the impression that they're not wasting money. Looking *too* successful by squandering money on elaborate annual reports may raise questions about where the profits are going.

So, whether these publications are elaborate or just plain vanilla, annual reports are designed to cultivate "the right" corporate image—whatever that may be. Clearly, just like individuals, organizations also stand to benefit by making positive impressions on others and work hard at doing so.

LEARNING: ADAPTING TO THE WORLD AROUND US

Thus far in this chapter we have focused on perception, one of the basic human psychological processes involved in explaining behavior in organizations. However, another process is equally important—*learning*. After all, learning is involved in a broad spectrum of organizational behaviors, ranging from developing new vocational skills, through changing the way people do their jobs, to managing employees in ways that foster the greatest productivity. Not surprisingly, the more a company fosters an environment in which employees are able to learn, the more productive and profitable that organization is likely to be.[37] Naturally, scientists in the field of OB are extremely interested in understanding the process of learning—both how it occurs and how it may be applied to the effective functioning of organizations.

Before we turn our attention to these matters, we should first explain exactly what we mean by learning. Specifically, we define **learning** as a relatively permanent change in behavior occurring as a result of experience.[38] Despite its simplicity, several aspects of this definition bear further explanation. First, learning requires that some kind of

learning
A relatively permanent change in behavior occurring as a result of experience.

change occurs. Second, this change must be more than just temporary. Finally, it must be the result of experience—that is, continued contact with the world around us. Given this definition, we cannot say that short-lived performance changes on the job, such as those due to illness or fatigue, are the result of learning. Like so many concepts in the social sciences, learning is a difficult concept for scientists to understand because it cannot be directly observed. Instead, it must be inferred on the basis of relatively permanent changes in behavior.

Although scientists recognize that there are several different kinds of learning, we will examine two that are most likely to occur in organizations. These are *operant conditioning* and *observational learning*.

Operant Conditioning: Learning Through Rewards and Punishments

Imagine you are a chef working at a catering company where you are planning a special menu for a fussy client. If your dinner menu is accepted and the meal is a hit, the company stands a good chance of picking up a huge new account. You work hard at doing the best job possible and present your culinary creation to the skeptical client. Now, how does the story end? If the client loves your meal, your grateful boss gives you a huge raise and a promotion. However, if the client hates it, your boss asks you to turn in your chef's hat. Regardless of which of these outcomes occurs, one thing is certain: Whatever you did in this situation, you will be sure to do it again if it was successful and to avoid doing again if it failed.

This situation nicely illustrates an important principle of **operant conditioning** (also known as **instrumental conditioning**)—namely, that our behavior produces consequences and that how we behave in the future will depend on what those consequences are. If our actions have had pleasant effects, then we will be likely to repeat them in the future. If, however, our actions have unpleasant effects, we are less likely to repeat them in the future. This phenomenon, known as the **law of effect,** is fundamental to operant conditioning. Our knowledge of this phenomenon comes from the work of the famous social scientist B. F. Skinner.[39] Skinner's pioneering research has shown us that it is through the connections between our actions and their consequences that we learn to behave in certain ways. We summarize this process in Figure 2.11.

Reinforcement contingencies. Operant conditioning is based on the idea that behavior is learned because of the pleasurable outcomes that we associate with it. In organizations, for example, people usually find it pleasant and desirable to receive monetary bonuses, paid vacations, and various forms of recognition. The process by which people learn to perform acts leading to such desirable outcomes is known as **positive reinforcement.** Whatever behavior led to the positive outcomes is likely to occur again, thereby strengthening that behavior. For a reward to serve as a positive reinforcer, it must be made contingent on the specific behavior sought. So, for example, if a sales representative is given a bonus after landing a huge account, that bonus will only reinforce the per-

---

operant conditioning

The form of learning in which people associate the consequences of their actions with the actions themselves. Behaviors with positive consequences are acquired; behaviors with negative consequences tend to be eliminated.

instrumental conditioning

See *operant conditioning*.

law of effect

The tendency for behaviors leading to desirable consequences to be strengthened and those leading to undesirable consequences to be weakened.

positive reinforcement

The process by which people learn to perform behaviors that lead to the presentation of desired outcomes.

FIGURE 2.11

The Operant Conditioning Process: An Overview

The basic premise of *operant conditioning* is that people learn by connecting the consequences of their behavior with the behavior itself. In this example, the manager's praise increases the subordinate's tendency to perform the job properly in the future. Learning occurs by providing the appropriate antecedents and consequences.

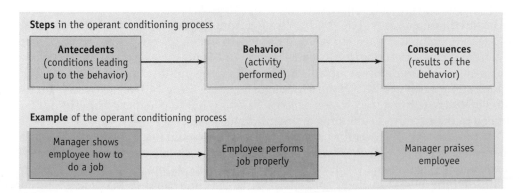

son's actions *if* he or she associates it with the landing of the account. When this occurs, the individual will be more inclined in the future to do whatever helped get the account.

Sometimes we also learn to perform acts because they permit us to avoid undesirable consequences. Unpleasant events, such as reprimands, rejection, probation, and termination, are some of the consequences faced for certain negative actions in the workplace. The process by which people learn to perform acts leading to the avoidance of such undesirable consequences is known as **negative reinforcement,** or **avoidance.** Whatever response led to the termination of these undesirable events is likely to occur again, thereby strengthening that response. For example, you may stay late at the office one evening to revise a sales presentation because you believe that the boss will "chew you out" if it's not ready in the morning. You have learned how to avoid this type of aversive situation, and you behave accordingly.

Thus far, we have identified responses that are strengthened—because they lead either to positive consequences or to the termination of negative consequences. However, the connection between a behavior and its consequences is not always strengthened; such links also may be weakened. This is what happens in the case of **punishment.** Punishment involves presenting an undesirable or aversive consequence in response to an unwanted behavior. A behavior accompanied by an undesirable outcome is less likely to recur if the person associates the negative consequences with the behavior. For example, if you are chastised by your boss for taking excessively long coffee breaks, you may be considered punished for this action. As a result, you will be less likely to take long breaks again in the future.

The link between a behavior and its consequences also may be weakened by withholding reward—a process known as **extinction.** When a response that was once rewarded is no longer rewarded, it tends to weaken and eventually die out— or be *extinguished.* Let's consider an example. Suppose for many months you brought boxes of donuts to your weekly staff meetings. Your colleagues always thanked you as they gobbled them down. You were positively reinforced by their approval, so you continued bringing the donuts. Now, after several months of eating donuts, your colleagues have begun dieting. So, although tempting, your donuts go uneaten. After several months of no longer being praised for your generosity, you will be unlikely to continue bringing donuts. Your once rewarded behavior will die out; it will be extinguished.

The various relationships between a person's behavior and the consequences resulting from it—*positive reinforcement, negative reinforcement, punishment,* and *extinction*—are known collectively as **contingencies of reinforcement.** They represent the conditions under which rewards and punishments will be either given or taken away. The four contingencies we discussed are summarized in Table 2.3. As we will see

negative reinforcement
The process by which people learn to perform acts that lead to the removal of undesired events.

avoidance
See *negative reinforcement.*

punishment
Decreasing undesirable behavior by following it with undesirable consequences.

extinction
The process through which responses that are no longer reinforced tend to gradually diminish in strength.

contingencies of reinforcement
The various relationships between one's behavior and the consequences of that behavior —positive reinforcement, negative reinforcement, punishment, and extinction.

TABLE 2.3   CONTINGENCIES OF REINFORCEMENT: A SUMMARY

The four contingencies of reinforcement may be distinguished by the presentation or withdrawal of a pleasant or an unpleasant stimulus. Positively or negatively reinforced behaviors are strengthened, whereas punished or extinguished behaviors are weakened.

STIMULUS PRESENTED OR WITHDRAWN	DESIRABILITY OF STIMULUS	NAME OF CONTINGENCY	STRENGTH OF RESPONSE	EXAMPLE
Presented	Pleasant	Positive reinforcement	Increases	Praise from a supervisor encourages continuing the praised behavior.
	Unpleasant	Punishment	Decreases	Criticism from a supervisor discourages enacting the punished behavior.
Withdrawn	Pleasant	Extinction	Decreases	Failing to praise a helpful act reduces the odds of helping in the future.
	Unpleasant	Negative reinforcement	Increases	Future criticism is avoided by doing whatever the supervisor wants.

later in this chapter, administering these contingencies can be an effective tool for managing behavior in organizations.

Schedules of reinforcement: Patterns of administering rewards Thus far, our discussion of whether a reward will be presented or withdrawn has assumed that the presentation or withdrawal will follow each occurrence of behavior. However, it is not always practical (or, as we will see, advisable) to do this. It is important as well to consider exactly *when* behavior will be reinforced. The rules governing the timing and frequency of reinforcement are known as **schedules of reinforcement.**

Rewarding *every* desired response made is called **continuous reinforcement.** Unlike animals performing tricks in a circus, people on the job are rarely reinforced continuously. Instead, organizational rewards tend to be administered following **partial reinforcement** (also known as **intermittent reinforcement**) schedules. That is, rewards are administered intermittently, with some desired responses reinforced and others not. Four varieties of partial reinforcement schedules have direct application to organizations.[40]

- **Fixed interval schedules** are those in which reinforcement is administered the first time the desired behavior occurs after a specific amount of time has passed. For example, the practice of issuing paychecks each Friday at 3:00 P.M. is an example of a fixed interval schedule insofar as the rewards are administered at regular times. Fixed interval schedules are not especially effective in maintaining desired behavior. For example, employees who know that their boss will pass by their desks every day at 11:30 A.M. will make sure they are working hard at that time. However, without the boss around to praise them, they may take an early lunch or otherwise not work as hard because they know that they will not be positively reinforced for their efforts or punished for not working.

- **Variable interval schedules** are those in which a variable amount of time (based on some average amount) must elapse between administering reinforcements. For example, a bank auditor may make surprise visits to branch offices an average of once every six weeks (e.g., visits may be four weeks apart one time, and eight weeks apart another time). The auditor may be said to be using a variable interval schedule. Because the bank managers cannot tell exactly when their branch may be audited, they cannot afford to slack off. Another inspection may be closer than they think! Not surprisingly, variable interval schedules generally are more effective than fixed interval schedules.

- **Fixed ratio schedules** are those in which reinforcement is administered the first time the desired behavior occurs after a specified number of such actions have been performed. For example, suppose members of a sales staff know that they will receive a bonus for each $1,000 worth of goods they sell. Immediately after receiving the first reward, performance may slack off. But as their sales begin to approach $2,000, the next level at which reward is expected, performance will once again improve.

- **Variable ratio schedules** are those in which a variable number of desired responses (based on some average amount) must elapse between the administration of reinforcements. People playing slot machines provide a good example. Most of the time when people put a coin into the slot they lose. But, after some unknown number of plays, the machine will pay off. Because gamblers can never tell which pull of the handle will win the jackpot, they are likely to keep on playing for a long time. As you might imagine, variable ratio schedules tend to be more effective than fixed ratio schedules.

The various schedules of reinforcement we described here have a number of important similarities and differences. We have summarized these in Figure 2.12. As you review this diagram, it is important to keep in mind that these schedules represent "pure" forms. Used in practice, several different reinforcement schedules may be combined, making complex new schedules. Still, whether they operate separately or in conjunction with one another, it is important to recognize the strong influences that schedules of reinforcement can have on people's behavior in organizations.

---

schedules of reinforcement
Rules governing the timing and frequency of the administration of reinforcement.

continuous reinforcement
A schedule of reinforcement in which all desired behaviors are reinforced.

partial reinforcement
A schedule of reinforcement in which only some desired behaviors are reinforced. Types include fixed interval, variable interval, fixed ratio, and variable ratio.

intermittent reinforcement
See *partial reinforcement*.

fixed interval schedules
Schedules of reinforcement in which a fixed period of time must elapse between the administration of reinforcements.

variable interval schedules
Schedules of reinforcement in which a variable period of time (based on some average) must elapse between the administration of reinforcements.

fixed ratio schedules
Schedules of reinforcement in which a fixed number of responses must occur between the administration of reinforcements.

variable ratio schedules
Schedules of reinforcement in which a variable number of responses (based on some average) must occur between the administration of reinforcements.

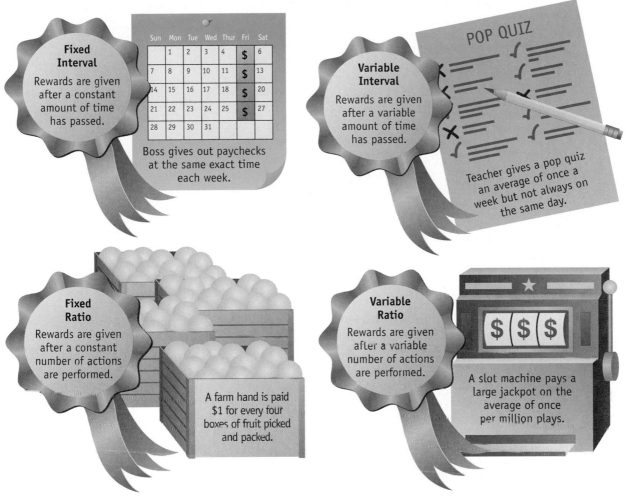

FIGURE 2.12
Schedules of Reinforcement: A Summary
The four schedules of reinforcement summarized here represent different ways of administering reward intermittently.

Observational Learning: Learning by Imitating Others

Although operant conditioning is based on the idea that we engage in behaviors for which we are directly reinforced, many of the things we learn on the job are *not* directly reinforced. Suppose, for example, on your new job you see one of your fellow sales representatives developing a potentially valuable sales lead by joining a local civic organization. Soon thereafter, talking to people around the office, you find that yet another one of your colleagues has picked up a lucrative lead from a civic group to which he belongs. Chances are, after observing this several times, you too will eventually make the connection between joining such groups and getting sales leads. Although you may not have made useful contacts from such groups yourself, you would come to expect these leads to pan out on the basis of what you have observed from others. This is an example of a kind of learning known as **observational learning** or **modeling**.[41] It occurs when someone acquires new knowledge *vicariously*—that is, by observing what happens to others. The person whose behavior is imitated is referred to as the *model*.

Steps in the observational learning process. For people to learn by observing models, several processes must occur (for a summary of these, see Figure 2.13).

1. The learner must pay careful *attention* to the model; the greater the attention, the more effective the learning will be. To facilitate learning, models sometimes call

observational learning
The form of learning in which people acquire new behaviors by systematically observing the rewards and punishments given to others.

modeling
See *observational learning.*

FIGURE 2.13

Observational Learning: An Overview
The process of observational learning requires that an observer pay attention to and remember a model's behavior. By observing what the model did and rehearsing those actions, the observer may learn to imitate the model, but only if the observer is motivated to do so (i.e., if the model was rewarded for behaving as observed).

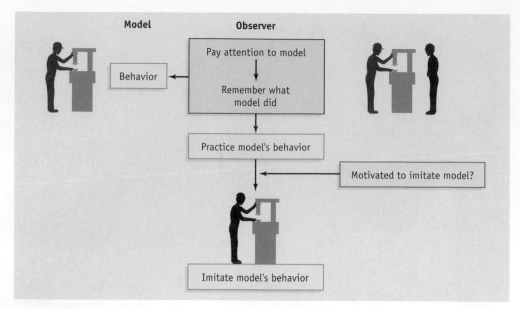

attention to themselves. This is what happens when supervisors admonish their subordinates to "pay close attention" to what they're doing.

2. People must have good *retention* of the model's behavior. It helps to be able to develop a verbal description or a mental image of someone's actions in order to remember them. After all, we cannot learn from observing behavior we cannot remember.

3. There must be some *behavioral reproduction* of the model's behavior. Unless people are capable of doing exactly what the models do, they will not be able to learn from observing them. Naturally, this ability may be limited at first but improve with practice.

4. Finally, people must have some *motivation* to learn from the model. Of course, we don't emulate every behavior we see. Instead, we focus on those we have some reason or incentive to match—such as actions for which others are rewarded.

Examples of observational learning in organizations. A great deal of what is learned about how to behave in organizations can be explained as the result of the process of observational learning.[42] For example, observational learning is a key part of many formal job instruction training programs.[43] As we will explain in the next section, when trainees are given a chance to observe experts doing their jobs and an opportunity to practice the desired skills followed by feedback on their work, they tend to learn new job skills quite effectively.

Observational learning also occurs in a very informal, uncalculated manner. For example, people who experience the norms and traditions of their organizations and who subsequently incorporate these into their own behavior may be recognized as having learned through observation. Indeed, people tend to learn the culture of their organizations (a topic that we will discuss in Chapter 14) through observational learning.

It is important to note that people learn not only what to do by observing others but also what *not* to do. Specifically, research has shown that people observing their coworkers getting punished for behaving inappropriately on the job tend to refrain from engaging in those same actions themselves.[44] As you might imagine, this is a very effective way for people to learn how to behave—without ever experiencing any displeasure themselves.

APPLICATIONS OF LEARNING IN ORGANIZATIONS

The principles of learning we have discussed thus far are used in organizations in many different ways. We will now discuss five systematic approaches to incorporating the various principles of learning in organizations: *training, innovative reward systems, organizational behavior management, discipline,* and *knowledge management.*

Training: Learning and Developing Job Skills

Probably the most obvious use to which principles of learning may be applied in organizations is **training**—the process through which people systematically acquire and improve the skills and knowledge needed to better their job performance. Just as students learn basic educational skills in the classroom, employees must learn job skills. Training is used not only to prepare new employees to meet the challenges of the jobs they will face but also to upgrade and refine the skills of existing employees. In fact, it has been estimated that American companies spend about $66 billion on training annually.[45]

training
The process of systematically teaching employees to acquire and improve job-related skills and knowledge.

Varieties of training. Training takes many forms. Some training is quite informal in nature, consisting of having experienced employees take new employees under their wings to show them how to do the job in question. Training also may involve formal **classroom training** in which instructors describe various requirements of the job and provide tips on how to meet them. Typically, people learning new skills in the classroom are given an opportunity to practice these skills in either a simulated work setting or on the job itself.

classroom training
Formal training in which instructors describe various job requirements and provide tips on how to meet them.

Consider, for example, how people are trained as account representatives at the collection agency, OSI. The account reps are the individuals who call consumers to arrange payment on seriously delinquent accounts. The reps receive four days of intensive classroom training, covering things such as approaches to take in getting people to pay, procedures to follow for sending payment, payment programs available to the consumer, and the laws that bill collectors are required to follow. This classroom training is supplemented by making simulated practice calls in which the budding reps get to practice their new skills. Following this training, they are allowed to make actual calls, but these are closely monitored by experienced personnel who stand ready to guide the trainee as needed.

Growing in popularity today are formal **apprenticeship programs,** in which classroom training is systematically combined with on-the-job instruction over a long period (often several years in the case of skilled tradespeople, such as carpenters, electricians, and masons). Recognizing the importance of such programs in developing human resources, the U.S. federal government has invested hundreds of millions of dollars in apprenticeship programs, encouraging training partnerships between government and private industry.[46] Apprenticeship programs often are designed and regulated by professional trade associations. The American Culinary Federation, for example, has a program that certifies apprentice chefs, who are required to complete a specific course of study and to demonstrate specific competencies while working in restaurant kitchens over a three-year period.

apprenticeship programs
Formal training programs involving both on-the-job and classroom training usually over a long period; often used for training people in the skilled trades.

Today, given the increasing globalization of the workplace, it is not surprising that companies are sending their employees to work abroad. A growing number of companies are discovering that employees are more likely to succeed in their overseas assignments when they have been thoroughly trained in the culture of the country in which they will be living. Sure, it helps to know the language of the host country, but that's just the beginning. If you've ever lived in another country, or even visited one, for that matter, then you can appreciate how vital it would be to understand fully the culture of the people in any country in which you are doing business. With this in mind, many companies have been investing in **cross-cultural training** (CCT), a systematic way of preparing employees to live and work in another country.[47] Actually, CCT is not a single method but a variety of specific training techniques that have proven effective. For a summary of some of the most effective CCT methods, see Table 2.4.

cross-cultural training (CCT)
A systematic way of preparing employees to live and work in another country.

Another popular form of training is **executive training programs**—sessions in which companies systematically attempt to develop the skills of their top leaders, such as how to use computer software, or more general skills, such as how to get along with

executive training programs
Sessions in which companies systematically attempt to develop their top leaders, either in specific skills or general managerial skills.

TABLE 2.4 SUMMARY OF TECHNIQUES USED IN CROSS-CULTURAL TRAINING (CCT)

People working overseas often are trained for their assignments using one or more of the techniques described here.

Cultural briefings	Explain the major aspects of the host country culture, including customs, traditions, everyday behaviors.
Area briefings	Explain the history, geography, economy, politics, and other general information about the host country and region.
Cases	Portray a real-life situation in business or personal life to illustrate some aspect of living or working in the host culture.
Role playing	Allows the trainee to act out a situation that he or she might face in living or working in the host country.
Culture assimilator	Provides a written set of situations that the trainee might encounter in living or working in the host country. Trainee selects from a set of responses to the situation and is given feedback as to whether it is appropriate and why.
Field experiences	Provide an opportunity for the trainee to go to the host country or another unfamiliar culture to experience living and working for a short time.

(*Source: International Organizational Behavior* by Francesco & Gold, © 1998. Reprinted by permission of Prentice-Hall, Inc., Upper Saddle River, NJ.)

others.[48] This is accomplished either by bringing in outside experts to train personnel in-house or by sending them to specialized programs conducted by private consulting firms or by colleges and universities.[49] Taking advantage of today's high-tech opportunities, many companies are finding that it's both convenient and effective to offer executive training online. (For a closer look at this practice, see the OB in an E-World section on page 64).

Many companies (e.g., Apple Computer, the Tennessee Valley Authority, and Sprint, to name only a few) are so serious about training that they have developed their own **corporate universities**—facilities devoted to handling a company's training needs on a full-time basis.[50] There are so many of these, in fact, that by 2010 there will be more corporate universities than traditional ones, according to one estimate.[51] Established in 1927 and still going strong, the first corporate university is the "General Motors Institute," which trains employees on almost every skill required by GM's tens of thousands of worldwide employees. Among the best-known facilities is McDonald's "Hamburger University," in which McDonald's franchisees learn and/or polish the skills needed to successfully operate a McDonald's restaurant. Like several other companies, such as Saturn and Motorola (see Figure 2.14), McDonald's has its own campus with full-time instructors. However, most corporate universities are less elaborate programs run by either the human resources department or a few top executives. Even very small Internet start-ups can have their own corporate universities by using any of a growing number of firms that provide this service. Although the curricula vary widely, most corporate universities emphasize leadership development (which we address in Chapters 13 and 16).

It is important to note that most organizational training is not as formal as the approaches we have been describing. Still, training is involved in everyday job instruction in which employees simply are told about the job, shown how to do it, and allowed to practice as a more experienced coworker watches and offers suggestions. Informal though it may be, this too is training, and it requires every bit as much attention to the principles of learning for it to be successful as more formal methods.

As you might imagine, no one approach to training is ideal. Some techniques are better suited to learning certain skills than are others because they incorporate more principles of learning than others. Not surprisingly, the best training programs often use

corporate universities

Centers devoted to handling a company's training needs on a full-time basis.

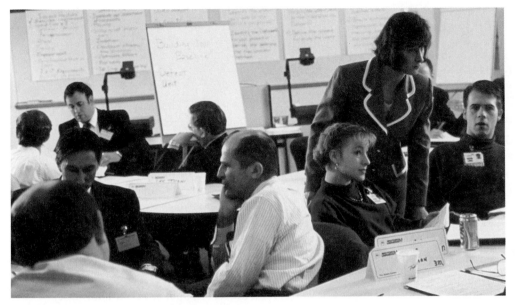

FIGURE 2.14
Training Is a Continuing Process at Motorola
The high-tech giant, Motorola, is a firm believer in the value of ongoing training as a key to the company's competitiveness in the rapidly advancing field of wireless technology. Established in 1981, "Motorola University" is a broad-based corporate training facility headquartered in Schaumburg, Illinois. At this facility, and at various satellite locations through-out the world, Motorola trains thousands of its own employees and those of its clients—including the suppliers shown here learning the latest techniques for ensuring high-quality manufacturing. Today, online learning has vastly extended Motorola University's reach, accounting for about half of all the students trained.

many different approaches, thereby assuring that several different learning principles are incorporated into training.[57]

Keys to effective training. If you recall some of the ways you learned various skills, such as how to study, drive, or use a computer, you probably can appreciate some of the principles that help make training effective. Four major principles are most relevant.

- **Participation.** People not only learn more quickly but also retain the skills longer when they have actively participated in the learning process. This applies to the learning of both motor tasks as well as cognitive skills. For example, when learning to swim, there's no substitute for actually getting in the water and moving your arms and legs. In the classroom, students who listen attentively to lectures, think about the material, and get involved in discussions tend to learn more effectively than those who just sit passively.

- **Repetition.** If you know the old adage "Practice makes perfect," you are already aware of the benefits of repetition on learning. Perhaps you learned the multiplication table, or a poem, or a foreign language phrase by going over it repeatedly. Indeed, mentally "rehearsing" such cognitive tasks has been shown to increase our effectiveness at performing them.[58] Scientists have established not only the benefits of repetition on learning but also have shown that these effects are even greater when practice is spread out over time than when it is lumped together. After all, when practice periods are too long, learning can suffer from fatigue, whereas learning a little bit at a time allows the material to sink in.

- **Transfer of training.** As you might imagine, for training to be most effective, what is learned during training sessions must be applied to the job. In general, the more closely a training program matches the demands and conditions faced on a job, the more effective that training will be. A good example is the elaborate simulation devices used to train pilots and astronauts. By closely simulating actual job conditions and equipment, the skills practiced are expected to transfer to the job.[59]

- **Feedback.** It is extremely difficult for learning to occur in the absence of feedback—that is, knowledge of the results of one's actions. Feedback provides information about the effectiveness of one's training, indicating improvements that need to be made.[60] For example, it is critical for people being trained as word processing operators to know exactly how many words they correctly entered per minute if they are to be able to gauge their improvement.

One type of feedback that has become popular in recent years is known as **360-degree feedback**—the process of using multiple sources from around the organization to evaluate the work of a single individual. This goes beyond simply collecting feedback

participation
Active involvement in the process of learning; more active participation leads to more effective learning.

repetition
The process of repeatedly performing a task so that it may be learned.

transfer of training
The degree to which the skills learned during training sessions may be applied to performance of one's job.

feedback
Knowledge of the results of one's behavior.

360-degree feedback
The practice of collecting performance feedback from multiple sources at a variety of organizational levels.

OB IN AN E-WORLD
E-TRAINING: BOOMING—BUT BEWARE

Training based on disseminating information online (e.g., through the Internet or a company's internal intranet network), known as **e-training**, is booming. Although only $2.2 billion was spent on online training in 2000, representing a meager slice of the total $66 billion corporate training pie, this figure has grown to about $11 billion today.[52] Online training is so popular, in fact, that savvy investment companies (e.g., Chase Capital and Merrill Lynch) have been funneling tens of millions of dollars into companies such as Ninth House and Global Learning Systems, which provide multimedia employee training.[53] Currently, over 5,000 companies offer all or some of their employee training online.[54] Given this popularity, it is important to consider the effectiveness of online training. In a word, the answer is "mixed." Many swear by it, but e-training is not without some bugs.

Compared to traditional, classroom-based corporate training programs, the primary benefits of online training are (1) the flexibility it offers trainees, (2) speed and efficiency, and (3) reduced cost. Karen Calise, who designs and lays out encyclopedia pages, swears by the flexibility offered by the online courses in design she has taken through Sessions.edu. Although she misses hanging out with classmates like she did when she took a classroom-based course in Web design, this single mom is willing to give up the socializing in favor of the "24/7 flexibility" the online training offers. She is so sold on online training that she says, "I don't want to ever step foot in a classroom again."[55]

The speed and efficiency of online training make it a favorite of many company officials. At Cisco Systems, Tom Kelly, vice president of worldwide training, relies on Internet-based tools to bring 4,000 sales reps up-to-date on the company's latest prod-

---

e-training

Training based on disseminating information online, such as through the Internet or a company's internal intranet.

from superiors, as is customary, and extends to gathering feedback from other sources, such as one's peers, direct reports (i.e., immediate subordinates), customers, and even oneself (see Figure 2.15).[61] Many companies—including General Electric, AT&T, Monsanto, Florida Power and Light, DuPont, Westinghouse, Motorola, Fidelity Bank, FedEx, Nabisco, and Warner-Lambert—have used 360-degree feedback to give more complete performance information to their employees, greatly improving not only their own work but overall corporate productivity as well.[62] To get a feel for how some companies are using this technique, see the Best Practices section on page 68.

In sum, these four principles—*participation, repetition, transfer of training,* and *feedback*—are key to the effectiveness of any training program. The most effective training programs are those that incorporate as many of these principles as possible.

Innovative Reward Systems: Going Beyond Merit Pay

When we talk about using reward in organizations, we tend mostly to focus on pay and fringe benefits that are based on standards such as merit (i.e., how well one performs) or seniority (i.e., how long one has remained on the job). In recent years, however, organizations have begun using approaches that are far more innovative. Because these are based on various principles of learning, it makes sense to identify them here.

Skill-based pay. Traditionally, employees are paid on the basis of the jobs they perform; some jobs are paid more than others. In **skill-based pay,** however, people are paid based on the number of different skills they have learned—skills that may, at least eventually, prove useful to their organizations. Under a skill-based pay system, for an employee to get a raise, he or she must demonstrate ability to perform a new skill relevant to performing one or more jobs. This is in contrast to traditional pay systems in which raises are given on the basis of meritorious performance of a job or seniority in the company.

---

skill-based pay

An innovative reward system in which people are paid based on the number of different skills they have learned relevant to performing one or more jobs in the organization.

ucts every two months.[56] Doing such training in the classroom would be useless because many of Cisco's high-tech products would be outdated before most of the sales force was sufficiently trained to sell them.

Many training professionals like online training because it can be a great money saver. The A. W. Chesterton Co., which makes complex and highly specialized pumps and hydraulic systems, used to have to fly its reps from all around the world to Boston each year for four weeks of classroom training. The bill was enormous, without even considering all the time away from customers. Today, most of the company's training is done online with only two weeks devoted to training in person, saving the company hundreds of thousands of dollars a year.

Although beneficial in many respects, e-training is far from perfect. One problem that many companies are facing is that it is very costly for them to produce self-paced, online training materials (about six to eight times more expensive than traditional learning materials), which drastically cuts into any short-term savings that may result. Probably the most serious limitation is that many workers are uncomfortable with it. Even the most computer-savvy employee may find it deceptively easy to click ahead, thinking they know material that they really don't know that well. Others simply miss the social aspect of learning, the one-on-one experience they have in the classroom with their peers and the trainer (which, for some, may be a distraction). Indeed, some experts agree that one advantage of the traditional classroom experience is that it brought people together out of the office, a benefit that the more impersonal experience of sitting in front of a computer screen simply cannot offer.

Although we wouldn't be surprised to see more and more e-training in the future, we suspect that the inherent benefits of in-person training by a knowledgeable and caring human being will not permit traditional training to disappear altogether. Online technology may best be considered an adjunct to the total training package—a single tool rather than a replacement for the traditional, in-person training experience.

At the toy maker Lego Systems, for example, employees are paid on the basis of how effectively they have demonstrated competence in each of three areas that were found to exist in abundance among the top performers. These are technical skills, team achievement skills, and personal skills.[65] Although such a system may seem strange, at least at first, it actually has several important advantages.[66] Specifically, skill-based pay systems encourage the development of key skills that help the company grow and develop. And, because of the variety of skills involved, employees stand to be more highly motivated to perform their jobs (as we will see in Chapter 6). Because skill-based pay is a relatively new approach to compensation, its effectiveness hasn't been fully tested. However, preliminary reports have suggested that it may be very promising.[67]

Team-based rewards. Traditional compensation systems, as we noted, focus on individual performance. However, a growing number of companies emphasize the performance of entire teams rather than individual employees (a trend that we will describe more fully in Chapter 8).[68] In such cases, it may be potentially disruptive to reward people solely for their own individual performance while ignoring their team's accomplishments. After all, it is a basic principle of learning that people will perform behaviors that are positively reinforced. Therefore, rewarding behaviors that contribute to group success today will encourage further contributions to group success tomorrow. This is the idea behind what is called **team-based rewards.**

It is only natural for employees at all levels to have concerns about team-based reward systems. After all, most Westerners grow up learning to value the importance of individual achievement. In fact, they tend to be afraid of having "freeloaders" on their team who don't do their fair share but who receive the same pay as everyone else (see Chapter 8). Not surprisingly, many companies that have introduced team-based rewards use them in conjunction with traditional, individual-based pay (e.g., this approach is used at a Unisys office in Bismarck, North Dakota, and at Trigon Blue Cross-

team-based rewards
Innovative reward systems in which employees are paid on the basis of their team's performance.

FIGURE 2.15

360-Degree Feedback: An Overview
Many companies rely on *360-degree feedback* to provide valuable insight into how performance may be improved. As summarized here, this technique involves collecting performance feedback from multiple sources.

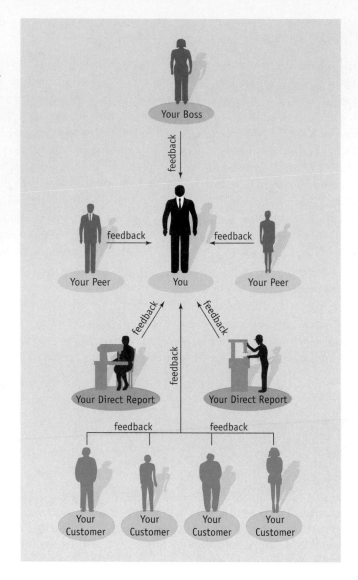

Blue Shield of Virginia).[69] Although these companies have been pleased with the results of their team-based reward systems, we caution that most companies are still experimenting with such systems. Until systematic studies are done evaluating the effectiveness of team-based reward systems over a long period of time, it is difficult to offer definitive recommendations about when and how such systems should be implemented.[70] Still, given the growth of teams in the workplace (see Chapter 8), it's clear that team-based reward systems represent one of the most important and promising innovations in reward systems.

Organizational Behavior Management: Positively Reinforcing Desirable Organizational Behaviors

Earlier, in describing operant conditioning, we noted that the consequences of our behavior determine whether we repeat it or abandon it. Behaviors that are rewarded tend to be strengthened and repeated in the future. With this in mind, it is possible to administer rewards selectively to help reinforce behaviors that we wish to be repeated in the future. This is the basic principle behind *organizational behavior management* (also known as *organizational behavior modification*). **Organizational behavior management** (or **OB Mod,** for short) may be defined as the systematic application of positive reinforcement principles in organizational settings for the purpose of raising the incidence of desirable organizational behaviors.[71]

organizational behavior management
The practice of altering behavior in organizations by systematically administering rewards.

organizational behavior modification (OB Mod)
See *organizational behavior management.*

Organizational behavior management programs have been used successfully to stimulate a variety of behaviors in many different organizations.[72] For example, a particularly interesting and effective program has been used in recent years at Diamond International, the Palmer, Massachusetts, company of 325 employees that manufactures Styrofoam egg cartons. In response to sluggish productivity, a simple but elegant reinforcement was put into place. Any employee working for a full year without an industrial accident is given 20 points. Perfect attendance is given 25 points. Once a year, the points are totaled. When employees reach 100 points, they get a blue nylon jacket with the company's logo on it and a patch identifying their membership in the "100 Club." Those earning still more points receive extra awards. For example, at 500 points, employees can select any of a number of small household appliances. These inexpensive prizes go a long way toward symbolizing to employees the company's appreciation for their good work.

This program has helped improve productivity dramatically at Diamond International. Since the OB Mod program began, output has improved 16.5 percent, quality-related errors have dropped 40 percent, grievances have decreased 72 percent, and time lost due to accidents has been lowered by 43.7 percent. The result of all of this has been over $1 million in gross financial benefits for the company—and a much happier workforce. Needless to say, this has been a very simple and effective organizational behavior management program. Although not all such programs are equally successful, evidence suggests that they are generally quite beneficial. For example, highly successful OB Mod programs have been used at such companies as General Electric, Weyerhauser, and General Mills.

Discipline: Eliminating Undesirable Organizational Behaviors

Just as organizations systematically use rewards to encourage desirable behavior, they also use punishment to discourage undesirable behavior. Problems such as absenteeism, lateness, theft, and substance abuse cost companies vast sums of money. Many companies attempt to manage such situations by using **discipline**—the systematic administration of punishment.

By administering an unpleasant outcome (e.g., suspension without pay) in response to an undesirable behavior (e.g., excessive tardiness), companies seek to minimize that behavior. In one form or another, using discipline is a relatively common practice. Survey research has shown, in fact, that 83 percent of companies use some form of discipline, or at least the threat of discipline, in response to undesirable behaviors.[73] But, as you might imagine, disciplinary actions taken in organizations vary greatly. At one extreme, they may be very formal, such as written warnings that become part of the employee's permanent record. At the other extreme, they may be informal and low key, such as friendly reminders and off-the-record discussions between supervisors and their problem subordinates.

In a survey, nursing supervisors were asked to list the disciplinary actions they most used and to rank them with respect to their severity.[74] The results, summarized in Figure 2.16, reveal that a broad spectrum of disciplinary measures are used, ranging from very lenient to very harsh. Although this represents the responses of a limited sample, we suspect that these results are fairly typical of what would be found across a wide variety of jobs.

Disciplinary practices in organizations. One very common practice involves using punishment *progressively*—that is, starting mildly and then increasing in severity with each successive infraction. This is the idea behind **progressive discipline**—the practice of basing punishment on the frequency and severity of the infraction.[75]

Let's consider an example of how progressive discipline might work for a common problem such as chronic absenteeism or tardiness. First, the supervisor may give the employee an informal oral warning. Then, if the problem persists, there would be an official meeting with the supervisor, during which time a formal warning would be

discipline
The process of systematically administering punishment.

progressive discipline
The practice of gradually increasing the severity of punishments for employees who exhibit unacceptable job behavior.

BEST PRACTICES
USING 360-DEGREE FEEDBACK: THREE PROFILES

If you think about it, the practice of giving questionnaires to various people in an organization to assess how large groups of them feel about each other can serve many purposes. Not only might the survey findings be used to help assess job performance, but they also can be used for many other purposes as well. For example, 360-degree feedback can be used to systematically assess training needs, to determine new products and services desired by customers, to gauge team members' reactions to each other, and to learn about a variety of potential human resource problems.[63] To better understand these and other uses of this popular tool, we will now consider three specific examples of 360-degree feedback in action.[64]

■ *Promoting change at the Landmark Stock Exchange.* The Landmark Stock Exchange is one of several smaller stock exchanges that operate in the United States. Eclipsed by the giant exchanges, such as the New York Stock Exchange and NASDAQ, Landmark has been striving to become the best marketplace in the world by providing faster and more accurate movement of stock than its well-known competitors. Meeting this objective requires a willingness to go along with rapid change and innovation. To see how it was doing in this regard, Landmark implemented a 360-degree feedback program that provided employees with feedback in such key areas as consulting others, inspiring others, team building, and networking. This feedback was then used as the basis for

issued. The next offense would result in a formal written warning that becomes part of the employee's personnel record. Subsequent offenses would lead to suspension without pay. And finally, if all this failed, the employee would be terminated. In the case of more serious offenses—such as gambling, for example—some of the preliminary steps would be dropped, and a formal written warning would be given. For the most serious

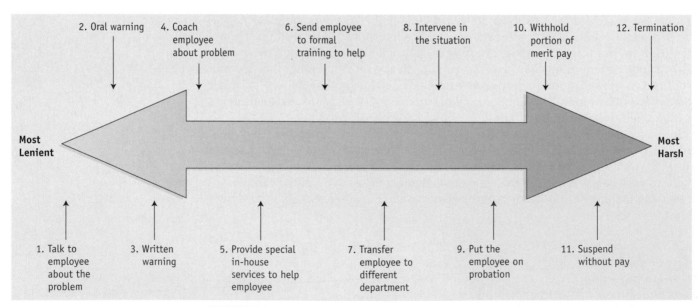

FIGURE 2.16
A Continuum of Disciplinary Measures
Ranked from mildest to most severe, these are the most commonly used disciplinary tactics used by nursing supervisors.
(*Source:* Based on findings reported by Trahan & Steiner, 1994; see Note 74.)

providing systematic training in ways to change any behaviors found lacking.

- *Developing leaders at Leher McGovern Bovis.* Leher McGovern Bovis (LMB) was responsible for the renovation and restoration of such New York City landmarks as the Statue of Liberty and Grand Central Terminal. LMB is unique in the construction industry in the attention it pays to developing its employees' leadership skills, preparing them for senior positions in the company. Company officials implemented a 360-degree feedback program that helped identify people's readiness for advancement to leadership positions within the company and the best candidates for management training. The 360-degree feedback program helped reduce turnover among project managers from 12 percent down to only 2 percent.

- *Identifying training and selection requirements at Northwestern Mutual Life Insurance Company.* To meet growing competition, Northwestern Mutual Life (NML) restructured its offices, which required them to identify many new managers. The company used a 360-degree feedback program to assess the potential of individual agents to be promoted to these new managerial positions. Also, by systematically noting shortcomings, they used this information to identify the most-needed forms of management training. NLM's 360-degree feedback program has made the task of selecting and training managers more effective than ever.

As these examples illustrate, 360-degree feedback can be a very successful tool to help meet a wide variety of organizational objectives. For this reason, it continues to be very popular and may be expected to remain in widespread use in the future.

offenses, such as stealing or intentionally damaging company property, officials would move immediately to the most severe step, immediate dismissal.

Companies with the most effective disciplinary programs tend to *make the contingencies clear,* for example, by publicizing punishment rules in the company handbook. When this is done, employees know exactly what kind of behaviors the company will not tolerate, often minimizing the need to actually use discipline at all.

It probably comes as no surprise to you that supervisors do not always punish all inappropriate behaviors they encounter.[76] A key reason for this is that supervisors may feel constrained by limitations imposed by labor unions or by their own lack of formal authority. Also, in the absence of a clear company policy about how to use discipline, individuals may fear strong negative emotional reactions from the punished individual, if not also revenge and retaliation. As a result, many supervisors may turn the other way and simply do nothing when employees behave inappropriately. Although doing nothing may be easy in the long run, ignoring chronic problems is a way of informally approving of them, leading to increasingly serious problems in the future.

With this in mind, companies with the best disciplinary programs make it a practice to *take immediate action.* At Honda of America, for example, human resource specialist Tim Garrett notes that the company pays very close attention to all infractions of the rules, including ones "that other companies wouldn't think of paying attention to," adding, "if there's a problem, we'll pay attention to it right away."[77]

Keys to using punishment effectively. Obviously, it isn't easy to know exactly when and how to administer punishment, and how it can be done in a way that is considered fair and reasonable. Fortunately, research and theory have pointed to some effective principles that may be followed to maximize the effectiveness of discipline in organizations.[78] We summarize these in Table 2.5. If, after going through this list, you are thinking that it is truly difficult to properly administer rewards and punishments in organizations, you have reached the same conclusion as experts in the field of organizational behavior. Indeed, one of the key skills that make some managers so effective is their ability to influence others by properly administering rewards and punishments.

TABLE 2.5 TIPS FOR USING DISCIPLINE EFFECTIVELY

Disciplining employees is not as easy as it looks. It can be full of pitfalls, and most people don't know how to do it appropriately. The suggestions on this list represent some useful guidelines to follow in making your own disciplinary efforts as effective as possible. When reviewing these suggestions, be sure to think about the explanations for each one and how the suggestion is illustrated by the example.

SUGGESTION	EXPLANATION	EXAMPLE: *BOB IS OFTEN LATE TO WORK, SO THE MANAGER SHOULD...*
Deliver punishment immediately after the undesirable response occurs.	The less time that passes between the occurrence of an undesirable behavior and the administration of a negative consequence, the more strongly people will make the connection between them.	Talk to him about it immediately after he arrives.
Give moderate levels of punishment— nothing too high or too low.	If the consequences for performing an undesirable action are not very severe, then it is unlikely to operate as a punishment. If they are too severe, people are likely to protest.	Avoid being too lenient (e.g., by rolling his or her eyes) or too harsh (e.g., firing Bob if he is only a minute or two late).
Punish the undesirable behavior, not the person.	Punishment should be impersonal in nature and focus on an individual's actions rather than his or her personality.	Refrain from calling Bob "lazy" but explain the problems that result (e.g., customers cannot reach him) when he is not at his desk on time.
Use punishment consistently across occasions.	If you sometimes fail to punish a wrongdoing, you may send the message that you sometimes can get away with breaking the rules.	"Write up" Bob each and every time he is late.
Punish everyone equally for the same infraction.	If some people are punished while others are not, you will be accused of favoritism and will be considered unfair.	"Write up" all employees whenever they are late, just as is done with Bob.
Clearly communicate the reasons for the punishment given.	Making clear exactly what behaviors lead to what disciplinary actions makes punishment more effective.	Explain to Bob that his punishment is "nothing personal" but is based on his lateness.
Do not follow punishment with noncontingent rewards.	Sometimes people attempt to minimize the pain of punishment by doing something nice to make up for it. This may make everyone feel better, but it reinforces the undesirable behavior.	Resist the temptation to let Bob go home early (with pay) to "think about the problem."

Knowledge Management: Sharing What Is Known

Thus far, our discussion of learning has focused on individuals. One by one, employees learn what they need to know and develop areas of expertise that are called on when needed to perform a certain job. However, there are occasions in which somebody in an organization requires special expertise but doesn't know how to find it within the company. When this occurs, the company may waste time and money by "reinventing the wheel," developing expertise that already exists (if they only knew where to find it!). In other cases, if the necessary expertise is not tapped or new expertise is not developed, then either something will get done improperly or it will not get done at all.

Acknowledging this situation, in recent years many companies have instituted what is known as *knowledge management* programs. **Knowledge management** is defined as the process of gathering, organizing, and sharing a company's information and knowledge assets. Typically, knowledge management programs involve using technology to establish repository databases and retrieval systems. These are ways of using computers to sort through and identify the areas of expertise represented in the company—that is, its **intellectual capital.** But don't misunderstand: Knowledge management relies on human skills for success. Computers merely organize what those skills are and where in the company they may be found. One-third of all companies and 80 percent of large multinational enterprises (see Chapter 1) already have a knowledge management system in place, and most others expect to implement one in the near future.[79]

knowledge management
The process of gathering, organizing, and sharing a company's information and knowledge assets.

intellectual capital
Areas of expertise represented by the employees within a company.

Knowledge management has been in use at British Petroleum (BP), where an employee-driven database available on the company's intranet contains information about the expertise of some 10,000 employees, making it a simple task to determine "who knows what."[80] They also employ **knowledge managers**—individuals who are specifically charged with organizing the wealth of corporate knowledge represented by its people and ensuring that this information gets used effectively. In growing numbers of companies, people responsible for knowledge management hold senior executive positions known as **chief knowledge officer (CKO).** Knowledge managers at BP actively seek out and summarize the lessons learned in various business units and distill the main points over the intranet. Harnessing knowledge in this way has led to considerable savings in the cost of construction and increased efficiency in the drilling of oilfields. As a general guide to what knowledge managers (including CKOs) do, see Table 2.6.

Knowledge management also has helped Siemens, the European conglomerate that makes everything from power plants to X-ray machines. With almost a half-million workers around the world, Siemens employees have a lot of knowledge, but most of it goes to waste because people in different parts of the company don't even know that certain types of expertise exist. To help, company officials developed "ShareNet," an online database that helps Siemens employees find instantly the advice they need from others within the company.[81] Using this vast resource, Siemens has generated some $122 million in extra sales, making it an outstanding investment in view of the only $7.8 million it cost to get the system going. Highly impressive results of implementing knowledge management programs also have been reported at IBM. Using "Eureka," a database compiled by Xerox technicians, has made it possible for that company's service representatives to slash in half the average amount of time required to repair one of its copy machines. Another database of corporate expertise has made it possible for IBM consultants to reduce the average time it takes to prepare a proposal from 200 hours down to 30 hours, boosting sales dramatically. Such impressive results have made knowledge management efforts popular, despite the fact that they are neither inexpensive to create nor easy to manage. (For another success story, see Figure 2.17).

In closing, it's important to note that simply having a knowledge management program does not ensure success. Employees also must use it, but too often they don't. Organizational experts Jeffrey Pfeffer and Robert Sutton have described this state of affairs as the **knowing–doing gap**—the tendency for employees to refrain from using the knowledge that's available to them in the company, leading to poor performance.[82] Although there are many possible reasons for not using a knowledge management system, the most dominant is the tendency for employees to be afraid of expressing their

knowledge managers
Individuals who are responsible for organizing the wealth of corporate knowledge represented by its people and ensuring that this information gets used effectively.

chief knowledge officer (CKO)
A senior-level executive who is responsible for knowledge management within his or her company. (See *knowledge management.*)

knowing–doing gap
The tendency for employees to refrain from using the knowledge that's available to them in their company, leading to poor performance.

TABLE 2.6   KNOWLEDGE MANAGERS: WHAT DO THEY DO?

In contemporary organizations, it is widely recognized that not only financial resources but also human resources are essential to success. With this in mind, individuals referred to as *knowledge managers* are often made responsible for managing and ensuring proper use of the knowledge that a company's employees have. In some companies, such individuals hold senior executive positions known as *chief knowledge officer (CKO).* Although the work of knowledge managers differs between companies, these individuals generally have the primary responsibilities listed here.

- Explain the company's knowledge management efforts to everyone from board member to low-level employee.
- Secure funding for knowledge management projects.
- Promote job flexibility within the company, making it possible for people with good ideas to execute them readily.
- Develop, maintain, and promote use of an online database of ideas that is readily accessible to all.
- Discourage keeping information and ideas within a single division; encouraging all ideas, research findings, and experiences to be shared with others.

(*Source:* Based on information reported by Gross, 2000; see Note 79.)

FIGURE 2.17

A Whiter Shade of Paper: Knowledge Management to the Rescue
Leif Christensen, president of Manistique Papers in Michigan's upper peninsula, was having a problem at his paper recycling plant: The peroxide he was using to remove ink wasn't getting the paper bright enough for his customers. Searching for help, he turned to the company's chemical supplier, Buckman Labs. The situation was then posted on Buckman's Internet discussion group, which reached the company's experts in specialty chemicals around the world. Only 48 hours later a solution was posted from Buckman reps in Finland and Belgium. Apparently, a rare bacteria was breaking down the peroxide, and an antidote was provided. Without Buckman's knowledge management program, a solution to the problem would have taken far longer—if one was ever found at all.

ideas (for fear of giving people in other parts of the company an advantage over them) or of seeking ideas from others (for fear of admitting that they don't know something). Obviously, for knowledge management to be effective, people in the company have to be willing to both donate and receive information. To ensure that their company's vast knowledge resources are put to use, executives at Siemens have put various incentives in place (such as free trips) to encourage the company's many experts to add their expertise to the database and to encourage employees to use others' expertise contained in the database. Given the success of the company's ShareNet system, it's apparent that the knowing–doing gap may not be found at Siemens. In fact, on the heels of its success, similar systems are being introduced in the company's telecom unit (for sales reps) and its vast research and development unit (for engineers).

SUMMARY AND REVIEW OF LEARNING OBJECTIVES

1. Distinguish between the concepts of social perception and social identity.
Social perception is the process through which people select, organize, and interpret the information around them as it pertains to other people. According to social identity theory, the way we perceive others and ourselves is based on both our own unique characteristics (known as personal identity) and our membership in various groups (known as social identity).

2. Explain how the attribution process works and describe the various sources of bias in social perception.
The process of attribution involves judging the underlying reasons for people's behavior. Some of our judgments are based on inferences made on the basis of observing others' behavior. These judgments, known as correspondent inferences, are often inaccurate. Our search for explanations about the causes of others' behavior leads us to make either judgments of internal causality (the individual is responsible for his or her own actions) or external causality (someone or something else is responsible). Kelley's theory of causal attribution explains that such judgments will be based on three types of information: consensus (whether others act in a similar manner), consistency (whether the individual previously acted this way in the same situation), and distinctiveness (whether this person acted similarly in different situations). Several types of systematic errors, known as perceptual biases, limit the accuracy of social perception. These

include the fundamental attribution error (the tendency to attribute others' actions to internal causes), the halo effect (the tendency to perceive others in either consistently positive or negative terms), the similar-to-me effect (the tendency to perceive similar others in a favorable light), first-impression error (the tendency for initial impressions to guide subsequent ones), and selective perception (the tendency for people to focus on only certain aspects of the environment). Perceptual inaccuracies also result from the tendency for people to rely on the use of stereotypes (the judgments of others based on the categories to which they belong). Perceptual biases can result in self-fulfilling prophecies (the tendency for someone's expectations about another to cause that individual to behave in a manner consistent with those expectations). These can be positive in nature, such as when expecting someone's performance to be good actually makes it so (known as the Pygmalion effect). They also can be negative, such as when someone's performance is bad because it was expected to be bad (known as the Golem effect).

3. Understand how the process of social perception operates in the context of performance appraisals, employment interviews, and the cultivation of corporate images.
Biased judgments about others sometimes occur during the process of performance appraisal. In this context, people judge as superior those individuals whose performance matches their expectations. They also view people positively when their good performance is attributed to internal sources and when their poor performance is attributed to external sources. People are generally interested in getting others to perceive them favorably, and their efforts in this regard are referred to as impression management. This process is particularly important in employment interviews, although it sometimes interferes with the accuracy of information presented about individuals or companies. An organization's overall impression on people, its corporate image, is a determinant of its ability to attract qualified job applicants.

4. Define learning and describe the two types most applicable to OB: operant conditioning and observational learning.
Learning refers to relatively permanent changes in behavior occurring as a result of experience. In organizations, learning generally takes the form of operant conditioning and observational learning. In operant conditioning, individuals learn to behave certain ways based on the consequences of their actions. Stimuli that increase the probability of the behaviors preceding it are known as reinforcers. Reinforcement may be either positive, if it is based on the presentation of a desirable outcome, or negative, if it is based on the withdrawal of an unwanted outcome. The probability of certain responses can be decreased if an unpleasant outcome results (punishment) or if a pleasant outcome is withdrawn (extinction). Observational learning involves learning by modeling the behavior of others. By paying attention to and rehearsing the behavior of others, we can learn vicariously, that is, through the model's experiences.

5. Describe how principles of learning are involved in organizational training and innovative reward systems.
Learning is directly involved in efforts to teach people to acquire new job skills in the process known as training. Training is most effective when people can participate actively in the learning process, repeat the desired behaviors, receive feedback on their performance, and learn under conditions closely resembling those found on the job. Today companies are experimenting with innovative reward systems that include skill-based pay (i.e., paying people for the various skills they have demonstrated on the job) and team-based rewards (i.e., paying people for their contributions to team performance).

6. Compare the way organizations use reward in organizational behavior management programs, how they can use punishment most effectively when administering discipline, and how they can manage knowledge effectively.
Organizational behavior management is a systematic attempt to apply principles of reinforcement to the workplace to improve organizational functioning. Reinforcing

desired behaviors can improve organizational functioning greatly. In contrast to applications of reinforcement, discipline is the systematic application of punishments to minimize undesirable organizational behaviors. Discipline is most effective when punishment is applied immediately after the undesirable activity, moderately severe, focused on the activity rather than the individual, applied consistently over time and for all employees, clearly explained and communicated, and not weakened by the use of inadvertent rewards. Many of today's companies have knowledge management programs, which allow them to gather, organize, and share all the knowledge and expertise of its employees (referred to as human capital). Individuals known as knowledge managers often are responsible for knowledge management efforts.

POINTS TO PONDER

Questions for Review

1. What is social perception and how is it applicable to the field of OB?
2. How do people come to make judgments about what others are like (known as the attribution process)?
3. In what ways is the attribution process biased, and what can be done about it?
4. How do operant conditioning and observational learning operate in the workplace?
5. What are the fundamental principles of learning and how are they involved in organizations?
6. What should be done to ensure that efforts to punish employees are as effective as possible?

Experiential Questions

1. Think of a time when you made judgments about a new coworker as you got to know him or her. In what ways were these judgments biased? As you got to know this person better, did you change your mind? What lesson can you learn about reaching judgments about people prematurely?
2. As a manager, it's important not to judge employees based on your expectations. If you do, the Pygmalion effect or the Golem effect may occur. Think back to a situation on the job or at school in which either you or your supervisor/teacher had expectations that led to one of these self-fulfilling prophecies. Exactly what happened? How was everyone involved affected, both positively and negatively? What could have been done to avoid this problem?
3. Think about any work-related training programs in which you may have been involved. In what ways were these efforts successful? What might have been done to make them even more effective?

Questions to Analyze

1. The attribution process is inherently inaccurate and subject to bias. In view of this, what chance do you think managers have of making accurate assessments of their subordinates' job performance? What could be done to combat these limitations thereby making these important assessments more accurate?
2. E-training is very popular today. What specific advice would you give anyone launching a corporate e-training program who wants to make it as effective as possible? Do you think e-training ever can be as effective as in-person training? In what ways might it be even more effective than in-person training?
3. Overall, do you think that managers will be able to more effectively change their subordinates' performance by using reward or by using punishment? However you answer, what specific steps would you take to make these efforts most effective? Explain your recommendations.

INDIVIDUAL EXERCISE

Identifying Occupational Stereotypes

Although we usually reserve our concern over stereotypes to women and members of racial and ethnic minorities, the simple truth is that people can hold stereotypes toward members of just about *any* group. And, in organizations, people are likely to hold stereotypes about others based on a variable whose importance cannot be down-played—the occupational groups to which they belong. What we expect of people and the way we treat them are likely to be affected by stereotypes about their professions. This exercise will help you better understand this phenomenon.

Directions

Using the following scale, rate the each of the following occupational groups with respect to how much of each characteristic people in these groups tend to show.

1 = not at all
2 = a slight amount
3 = a moderate amount
4 = a great amount
5 = an extreme amount

Accountants	*Professors*	*Lawyers*
___interesting	___interesting	___interesting
___generous	___generous	___generous
___intelligent	___intelligent	___intelligent
___conservative	___conservative	___conservative
___shy	___shy	___shy
___ambitious	___ambitious	___ambitious

Clergy	*Physicians*	*Plumbers*
___interesting	___interesting	___interesting
___generous	___generous	___generous
___intelligent	___intelligent	___intelligent
___conservative	___conservative	___conservative
___shy	___shy	___shy
___ambitious	___ambitious	___ambitious

Questions for Discussion

1. Did your ratings of the various groups differ? If so, which were perceived most positively and which were perceived most negatively?
2. On what characteristics, if any, did you find no differences with respect to the various groups? What do you think this means?
3. To what extent did your ratings agree with those of others? In other words, was there general agreement about the stereotypical nature of people in various occupational groups?
4. To what extent were your responses based on specific people you know? How did knowledge, or lack of knowledge, of members of the various occupational groups influence your ratings?
5. Do you believe that by becoming aware of these stereotypes you will perpetuate them in the future or refrain from behaving in accord with them? Explain.

Role Play: Conducting a Disciplinary Interview

Knowing how to discipline employees who behave inappropriately is an important managerial skill. The trick is to change the bad behavior into good behavior permanently, getting people to accept their mistakes and understand how to correct them. As you might imagine, this is often far more difficult than it sounds. After all, people are generally reluctant to admit their errors and may have developed bad work habits that must be overcome. In addition, they tend to resist being chastised and don't like listening to criticism. With this in mind, disciplining others represents quite a challenge for managers, making it a skill worth developing.

Directions

1. Select four students from the class and divide them into two pairs. One person from each pair should read only the role sheet for Andy F., machine operator, and the other person from each pair should read only the role sheet for Barry B., his supervisor. Send both pairs outside the room until called upon.
2. Members of the class will serve as observers and should read both role sheets.
3. Call in the first pair of role players and ask them to spend about 10 to 15 minutes playing their roles—that is, acting as they would if they were the characters about whom they just read in the role sheets. They should feel free to assume any additional facts not described in these sheets.
4. Members of the class should observe the role play, taking careful notes. The class should *not* get involved in what the actors are saying but pay close attention to it.
5. Repeat steps 3 and 4 with the second pair of role players.

Role Sheets

Andy F., Machine Operator
You have worked at Acme Manufacturing for six years and have had a good record. Because you do your job so well, you sometimes take liberties and horse around with your buddies. For example, one Friday afternoon you were caught dancing around the shop floor when a good song came on the radio. Barry B., your supervisor, called you on the carpet for leaving your station. You think he has it in for you and is trying to run you off the job. Although you were acting silly, you are convinced that it doesn't matter since you were getting your job done. Now he has called you in to see him to discuss the situation.

Barry B., Supervisor
After several years of experience in other shops, you were hired by Acme Manufacturing to be its new shop supervisor, a job you've had for only four months. Things have gone well during that time, but you've been having trouble with one machine operator, Andy F. Andy seems to do an acceptable job but is not giving it his all. Part of the problem is that he goofs around a lot. You have spoken to him about this informally a few times on the floor but to no avail. One Friday afternoon you caught him away from his station, dancing around the shop floor. Not only wasn't he doing his own job, but he was also distracting the others. You have just called Andy in to see you to discuss the situation.

Questions for Discussion

1. Did the supervisor, Barry B., define the problem in a nonthreatening way?
2. Did both parties listen to each other, or did they shut each other out, merely explaining their own sides of the story?
3. Did Barry B. suggest specific things that Andy F. could do to improve? Were the specific punishments associated with future bad acts spelled out explicitly?
4. Were the discussions impersonal in nature, or did the parties focus on each other's personalities?

5. Considering all these questions, which supervisor would you say did a better job of administering discipline? What could be done to improve the way each supervisor conducted the disciplinary meeting?

WEB SURFING EXERCISE

Corporate Image

Visit the Web sites of any three companies in which you have an interest or curiosity. Study these by reading about the company itself, its products, and its executives or other employees.

1. Based on this experience, what were your impressions of each company? What factors contributed to these impressions?
2. How do these impressions compare to what you may have believed about the company before you examined its Web site? Do you think your impressions based on the Web site will contribute to any new impressions you may develop?
3. Based on what you read, do you think you might be interested in working for that company someday? What particular information lead to these impressions?

E-Training

There are currently over 5,000 corporate training companies that offer their services online. Some of the most dominant ones are Cognitive Arts, DigitalThink, DeVry, ExecuTrain, Global Knowledge Network, Learning Tree, MindLeaders, Netg, Provant, SkillSoft, SmartForce, and SMGnet. As you might expect, these differ from one another in important ways. To get a sense of what they are like, visit the Web sites of any four of these companies and answer the following questions. Their Web addresses consist of the name of the company (without any spaces) preceded by "www" and followed by ".com".

1. What are each company's major areas of expertise?
2. Who are some of each company's largest clients?
3. What image of each company is connoted by its Web site?

PRACTICING OB

Managing People Who Are Goofing Off

Employees at a corporate call center have not been spending enough time at their cubicles answering phones, as required. Instead, they've been walking throughout the facility, talking to each other about personal matters. In other words, they're socializing and goofing off instead of working. Important calls have gone unanswered and customer service problems have arisen as a result.

1. What attributions would you be prone to make about these employees, and how might these be related to the performance evaluations you give them?
2. What types of errors would you be prone to make while making these judgments, and what might you do to overcome them so that you can make more accurate judgments?
3. How might you use training, innovative reward systems, organizational behavior management programs, and discipline to address the problem?

CASE IN POINT

Finding a Safe Way to Smile at Safeway

Any training course on the essentials of customer service will advise you always to smile at customers and to make eye contact with them. In fact, it seems so obvious as to not need repeating. Little would you imagine, therefore, that doing precisely this would actually cause problems for some supermarket clerks! Nonetheless, a dozen employees at a Safeway store in California recently claimed that their eye contact and smiles have elicited unwanted attention from shoppers who have mistaken these friendly gestures as acts of flirting. Some clerks have had to resort to hiding in the store to escape customers who were hungry for services that weren't for sale. A produce clerk at one northern California store was even followed to her car and propositioned by a supermarket shopper who got the wrong idea.

The root of the problem, argue the 12 clerks who filed grievances with their union in summer 1998, is Safeway's "Superior Service" policy, which explicitly requires them to smile at customers and to maintain three seconds of eye contact with each one. It also expects clerks to anticipate customers' needs, to help them find items for which they're looking, and to call them by name if paying by check or credit card.

This policy was in place for five years before Safeway officials started enforcing it by using undercover shoppers to spot violators, who were then sent letters warning them of the negative evaluations and disciplinary measures (even firing!) that could result from failing to comply. Soon thereafter, the incidents of customer harassment began. The union is seeking a modified policy that gives workers some discretion in the matter, allowing them to choose whether or not to maintain eye contact or to refuse to carry a customer's bags to his car at night.

From its headquarters in Pleasanton, California, Safeway officials are quick to acknowledge that although some customers get out of hand, this is not the result of their policy. They add that not one of the store's 150,000 employees ever have been fired for failing to be friendly. However, 100 have been sent to a day-long remedial training class on friendliness, what they call "Smile School." Says Safeway spokesperson Debra Lambert, "This is not about discipline. It's about treating customers well and training employees to do that." Think about this when you complain about that surly clerk who doesn't even look up to acknowledge you the next time you're in your local supermarket looking for laundry detergent.

Critical Thinking Questions

1. How, specifically, is the process of attribution illustrated in this case?
2. What do you suppose is being done to help train people to be more friendly toward customers? In other words, what would you imagine goes on in Safeway's "Smile School"?
3. What do you think of the practice of sending undercover shoppers to stores to spot violators of the customer service policy? In your opinion, is it ethical?
4. Describe what you believe might be the progressive discipline steps outlined in the warning letter sent to unfriendly Safeway clerks.

Individual Differences: Personality and Abilities

3

LEARNING OBJECTIVES

After reading this chapter, you should be able to:
1. Define personality and describe its role in the study of organizational behavior.
2. Identify the big five dimensions of personality and describe what is meant by positive and negative affectivity.
3. Describe the Type A and Type B behavior patterns and describe the nature of Machiavellianism.
4. Define achievement motivation (or need for achievement) and describe the difference between learning, performance, and avoidance goal orientations.
5. Describe the differences between morning and evening persons and the relevance of this individual difference to on-the-job behavior.
6. Define cognitive intelligence, practical intelligence, emotional intelligence, and successful intelligence.

■ PREVIEW CASE
THE LIFE OF THE PARTY?

What's your image of the CEO of a company that earned $32.5 million in operating profits on almost $130 million in revenues during the last 12 months—a company that outsells its nearest rivals by almost three to one? Probably, the picture you bring to mind is one of a fairly reserved person dressed in a dark business suit, someone with a sober, cautious approach to life—and to doing business. But think again: That image would be dead wrong where Jeff Taylor, the CEO of Monster.com, the leading job-search Web site firm, is concerned. Far from being reserved, Taylor is a youthful-appearing 40-year-old who is fond of such activities as leading his employees in competition-bashing (and off-color) songs at the company's annual meetings, where he also dances up a storm and hugs everyone in sight. Although he is married and the father of three, he parties late into the night with his employees, and not always in a highly restrained manner. As he puts it, "If somebody wants to dance funky and close, I'll dance funky and close."

> "Leaders must make work fun. The best combination for our company is a work-hard, play-hard atmosphere."

Recently, Taylor accepted a challenge from Richard Branson, chairman of Virgin Group Ltd., to go water skiing behind the company's blimp. (Monster.Com and Virgin Group Ltd. both own blimps, which they use for promotional purposes.) Taylor won hands down, skiing an amazing 3.3 miles versus Branson's 1.5 miles. So, to put it mildly, "reserved" is definitely *not* the right adjective to describe this particular CEO. As his Vice President for Sales, Peter Blacklow, puts it, "Jeff has a high fun quotient." And as Taylor himself remarks, "Leaders must make work fun. The best combination for our company is a work-hard, play-hard atmosphere."

What do the employees of Monster.com think of their CEO? Most seem to love him. As one puts it, "He's a great people person and he enjoys playing hard as much as working hard." Given Monster.com's success at a time when many other dot-com companies are falling by the wayside, it is just possible that Taylor's approach may be the right one—at least for him and in this particular industry.

As Jeff Taylor proves, all CEOs are not alike—far from it. But you already knew that, because your own life has certainly taught you that people differ in many ways. Some are reserved, whereas others are outgoing; some are trusting, whereas others are suspicious; some seek status and power, whereas others have no desire to be in charge. The list is practically endless because people do indeed differ along many different dimensions. And such *individual differences* are important: They are often (although not always) reflected in people's behavior, and, of course, the ways in which people behave or act exert strong effects on their relations with others, the course of their careers, and many other work-related issues. But you also know that individual differences are not the only factor that shapes our behavior. The situations in which we find ourselves are important, too. For instance, even fun-loving people act in a sober, reserved way at serious meetings, and people who are mild-mannered and easygoing do lose their tempers on occasion—such as when they are provoked beyond endurance! In other words, *situational constraints* sometimes prevent individuals from acting in the ways they normally do—ways consistent with their own preferences or inclinations.

Although people differ along a great many dimensions, researchers who have studied such differences often divide them into two major categories: *personality* and *abilities*. We'll define both of these terms in more detail later, but for now, we will simply note that personality refers to the traits and characteristics that make individuals unique as individuals, whereas abilities refer to the capacities they possess (or acquire) for performing various tasks.

Do the traits shown by Jeff Taylor make him an effective CEO for Monster.com? Judging from the company's success, they do. But let's hold off on this question until a little later in this chapter where we will consider in more detail the effects of having a friendly, extroverted personality on success in a wide range of business settings.

Because OB scientists believe that individual differences are important, such differences long have been a topic of research in our field. To provide you with an overview of the key findings of this work, we will proceed as follows. First, we'll focus on *personality,* offering a more formal and complete definition of this concept, plus an examination of its potential role in organizational behavior. Next, we'll consider the question of how personality and other individual differences can be measured. Since traits and abilities are not physical quantities that can be measured directly, this turns out to be a tricky task—but one, we're happy to report, that can be accomplished effectively. After examining these measurement methods, we'll turn to several specific aspects of personality—ones that have been found to have important effects on organizational processes. Finally, we'll examine several important *abilities*—mental and physical capacities to perform various tasks and the role of such abilities in work-related behavior.

PERSONALITY: WHAT IT IS AND HOW IT IS MEASURED

"Personality is the glitter that sends your little gleam across the footlights and the orchestra pit into that big black space where the audience is." (Mae West, 1975)

That's an interesting observation and does, in a sense, capture the essence of personality: It is, in many ways, what makes us each of us unique—what sets us apart from others. But as we'll now see, there is more to this concept, too; and since understanding the nature of personality is crucial to appreciating its potential role in organizational behavior, let's take a closer look at just what it involves.

Defining Personality

If we learn anything from our experiences with other people, it is this: They are all, in some ways, *unique*—they all possess a distinct pattern of traits and characteristics not fully duplicated in any other person. Moreover, this pattern of traits tends to be stable over time. Thus, if you know someone who is optimistic, confident, and friendly today, the chances are good that he or she also showed these same traits in the past and will continue to show them in the future. Together, these two features form the basis for a useful working definition of **personality**—the unique and relatively stable pattern of behavior, thoughts, and emotions shown by individuals.[1]

Just how stable are various aspects of personality—or individual differences—in general? Recent evidence suggests that they are quite stable.[2] For instance, consider job satisfaction, a topic we'll examine in Chapter 5. Growing evidence confirms what informal observation suggests: Some people tend to be satisfied no matter what the conditions are where they work, whereas others tend to be dissatisfied. This doesn't imply that job satisfaction can't be changed or that it is not affected by working conditions—far from it. But it does suggest that because of important individual differences, some people carry with them, from situation to situation, strong tendencies to be satisfied or dissatisfied with their jobs or organizations.

Need another example? Consider Jeff Taylor, the CEO of Monster.com whom we just described in the Preview Case. He is described by most people as being extraverted and expressive—he expresses his inner feelings openly. To the extent he possesses this trait (and he certainly appears to do so!), we would expect that he would show such behavior not just at parties and sales meetings but in other settings, too—for instance, when interacting with his family and even, perhaps, when negotiating with customers. In the latter context, for instance, he might express his reactions to offers from the other side both openly and strongly rather than holding them inside (see Figure 3.1). But please note: As we'll soon see, personality does not always shape overt behavior. Sometimes situational constraints prevent individuals from behaving in the ways they would prefer to behave and in ways that accurately reflect their personalities. But when such constraints are lacking, personality does affect our behavior and this, in turn, can have important implications for organizational behavior.

personality
The unique and relatively stable patterns of behavior, thoughts, and emotions shown by individuals.

The Role of Personality in Organizational Behavior

The point mentioned previously about situations is an important one, so let's clarify it now. Yes, people possess stable traits and characteristics that predispose them to behave in certain ways. But sometimes, they cannot express these tendencies in their overt behavior because the situations in which they find themselves prevent them from doing so or strongly suggest that other kinds of behavior are more useful or appropriate. For instance, consider someone who has a very quick temper. Normally, she reacts to being irritated by others with an emotional explosion. But suppose that the job market is poor and that she needs her job very badly. Furthermore, imagine that she is annoyed by the CEO of the company. Will she explode? Probably not; the constraints against doing so are so strong that the person in question probably will do her best to conceal

FIGURE 3.1

Personality Matters!
By nature, some individuals are highly expressive, and tend to show their feelings openly. Others, however, are inclined to hold their feelings inside. Such differences are likely to be seen in many ways on the job.

her anger. Similarly, let's consider Jeff Taylor, CEO of Monster.com, once again. Clearly, he has a strong tendency to express himself openly. But suppose that one day he were invited to a dinner at the White House, with the President and First Lady. Do you think he would be more reserved in this situation than in his own company? Perhaps; and, again, it would be because of the situation in which he found himself and the powerful effects it exerts on behavior.

Interestingly, because the impact of situational variables is so strong, some social scientists once rejected the notion of personality altogether, arguing instead that how we behave is determined mainly by the external conditions we face.[3] But today, most experts believe that stable personality traits *do* exist and that these lead people to behave consistently over time and in different settings. In fact, most experts in the field of organizational behavior believe that *both* the person and the situation play a role in determining behavior in organizations. In other words, behavior usually is the result of both characteristics of an individual (his or her knowledge, abilities, skills, and personality) and the nature of the situation (see Figure 3.2). This approach, known as the **interactionist perspective,** is the prevailing one today.[4]

interactionist perspective
The view that behavior is a result of a complex interplay between personality and situational factors.

FIGURE 3.2

The Interactionist Perspective
According to the *interactionist perspective,* behavior usually is determined by a complex interplay between individual differences and a host of situational factors.

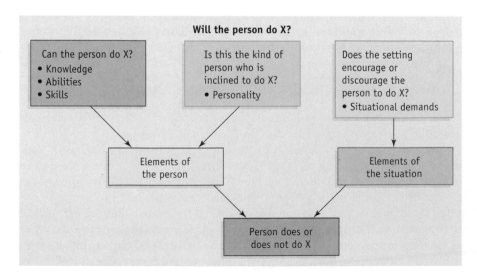

Another important implication of the interactionist approach is that some people may be better suited to certain jobs than others. This notion is referred to as **person–job fit,** formally defined as the extent to which the traits and abilities of individuals match the requirements of the jobs they must perform.[5] Indeed, a large body of evidence indicates that the more closely individuals' personalities, traits, and abilities match those required by a given job, the more productive and satisfied they tend to be (for a more detailed discussion of career success, see Chapter 7).[6]

One more point: Although various aspects of personality do indeed affect behavior in work settings, in many cases they do not exert these effects directly. Rather, stable personality traits affect more temporary states and it is *these* that actually affect overt behavior and performance. For example, consider two people: One is almost always in a good mood and the other is almost always in a bad mood. In general, the first person outperforms the second on many tasks. Why? Simply because he or she is in a good mood rather than a bad mood and moods affect task performance? Perhaps. But research findings suggest that the happy person may tend to do better on many tasks because this person also has higher confidence in his or her ability to perform well, and it is this factor rather than simply being in a good mood that produces improved performance. In contrast, the person who is usually in a bad mood may become anxious, and anxiety, as you know from your own experience, can often interfere with good performance.[7] The main point is simply this: Various aspects of personality do affect task performance and other aspects of behavior in work settings, but they do not always produce such effects in a direct manner. Rather, they often operate indirectly, affecting performance through their effects on other task-specific factors.

person–job fit
The extent to which individuals possess the traits and competencies required to perform specific jobs.

How Do We Measure Personality?

Physical traits such as height and weight can be measured readily by means of simple tools. Various aspects of personality, however, cannot be assessed quite so simply. There are no rulers and no thermometers that we can put to the task. How, then, can we quantify differences between individuals with respect to their various personality characteristics? Several methods exist for accomplishing this task. In this section, we'll describe the two that are most important and will then consider some of the essential requirements of all procedures for measuring individual differences.

Objective tests: Indicating on paper and pencil who we are. Have you ever completed a questionnaire in which you are asked to indicate whether each of a set of statements is true or false about yourself, the extent to which you agree or disagree with various sentences, or which of a pair of named activities you prefer? If so, chances are good that you have completed what is known as an **objective test**—a paper-and-pencil inventory in which people are asked to respond to a series of questions designed to measure one or more aspects of their personality. Objective tests are the most widely used method of measuring both personality and mental abilities (such as intelligence). (For some examples of objective tests of personality, see the Developing OB Skills section at the end of this chapter.)

objective tests
Questionnaires and inventories designed to measure various aspects of personality.

People's answers to the questions on objective tests are scored by means of special scoring keys. The score obtained by a specific person is then compared with those obtained by hundreds or even thousands of other people who have taken the test previously. In this way, an individual's relative standing on the trait or ability being measured can be determined. People's scores can then be used to predict various aspects of behavior, as we will see throughout this chapter. These tests are considered "objective" because they can be scored directly, simply by counting responses that fall into various categories and comparing them to others' scores.

Reliability and validity: Essential requirements of personality tests. Imagine that you weigh yourself on your bathroom scale every day. One day the weight reads "150 pounds." The next day it reads "140 pounds." Although you may be happy with the result, you probably would suspect that something is wrong: You could not possibly

reliability
The extent to which a test yields consistent scores on various occasions.

validity
The extent to which a test actually measures what it claims to measure.

have lost 10 pounds in a single day. Instead, it is much more likely that there is something wrong with the scale: It is not recording your weight consistently. More formally, we would say that the scale is not measuring your weight in a *reliable* manner. Clearly, if we are to have confidence in something we measure—people's weights, their personalities, or anything else—we must be able to measure it reliably. The **reliability** of a measure refers to the extent to which it is stable and consistent over time.

As you might imagine, a measure of personality must have a high degree of reliability in order to be useful. Only those tests that show high degrees of reliability are used in research in the field of OB. After all, tests that do not yield reliable results tell us little—or, even worse, they may be misleading.

In addition to being reliable, a test also must be *valid*—it must really measure what it claims to measure. Perhaps an example will help. Have you ever seen a device such as the one in Figure 3.3? It claims to measure your "sex appeal." In fact, though, it does not. The liquid moves and a score appears, but it is certainly not related to your "sex appeal"—or anything else about you, for that matter. In this example, the measure obtained is low in **validity**—it does not really measure what it claims to measure.

It is very important to establish the validity of any tests of personality we use because if they are low in validity, then they are essentially useless. After all, they are not measuring what we want to measure or what they claim to measure. How do we assess a test's validity? In actual practice, the process is a complex one, requiring many systematic steps and sophisticated statistical procedures. In essence, though, a test's validity is established by demonstrating that scores on it are related to other aspects of behavior that are already known to reflect the trait being measured. In other words, a test of a personality trait is valid to the extent that what it measures is closely related to the "true" measure of that trait, as assessed by other established tests. For instance, a test of sales ability would be valid to the extent that successful salespersons score high on it, whereas those who are unsuccessful score low.

At this point, we should note that all of the traits and abilities considered in this chapter are measured by tests known to be both reliable and valid. Thus, you can be confident that the findings we discuss are, in fact, related to important aspects of personality—ones that have significant implications for various forms of organizational behavior.

FIGURE 3.3
Validity: Why It's Important
The device shown here has no validity: It does not really measure sex appeal, which it claims to measure. Similarly, to be useful, a personality test must measure what it purports to measure. This means that the scores it produces must be related to "true" measures of the characteristic in question.

To conclude, personality is an important determinant of behavior in organizations, but, as we have repeatedly noted, it is only one of several factors that may be involved. Moreover, measuring personality is a task that presents several difficult challenges. Still, to fully understand behavior in organizations, it is important to recognize and acknowledge differences in people's personalities. With this in mind, we will now turn our attention to the important task of examining those aspects of personality that are most influential when it comes to organizational behavior.

KEY WORK-RELATED ASPECTS OF PERSONALITY

Now that we have defined personality and described how it is measured, we will consider several aspects of it that have been found to be closely linked to important aspects of organizational behavior. In this first section, we'll consider ones that many researchers agree are especially basic or important. Then, in succeeding sections, we'll consider several additional aspects that are not considered to be as basic but that also have important implications for behavior in work settings.

The Big Five Dimensions of Personality: Our Most Fundamental Traits

How many different words can you think of that describe others' personalities? Would you believe *17,953?* That's the number of personality-related works found in a search of an English language dictionary in a study conducted over 60 years ago.[8] Even after combining words with similar meanings, the list still contained fully 171 distinct traits. Does this mean that we must consider a huge number of traits to fully understand the role of personality in organizational behavior?

Fortunately, the answer appears to be "no." A growing body of evidence points to the conclusion that, in fact, there may be only five key dimensions to consider. Because these same five dimensions have emerged in so many different studies conducted in so many different ways, they are referred to as the **big five dimensions of personality.**[9] These are five basic aspects of personality that are assumed to underlie many specific traits. Specifically, these are as follows:

big five dimensions of personality
Five basic dimensions of personality that are assumed to underlie many specific traits.

- *Conscientiousness:* The extent to which individuals are hardworking, organized, dependable, and persevering (high conscientiousness) versus lazy, disorganized, and unreliable (low conscientiousness).
- *Extraversion:* The degree to which individuals are gregarious, assertive, and sociable (high extraversion) versus being reserved, timid, and quiet (low extraversion, or introversion).
- *Agreeableness:* The extent to which individuals are cooperative and warm (highly agreeable) versus cold and belligerent (highly disagreeable).
- *Emotional Stability:* The degree to which individuals are insecure, anxious, depressed, and emotional (emotionally unstable) versus calm, self-confident, and secure (emotionally stable).
- *Openness to Experience:* The extent to which individuals are creative, curious, and cultured (open to experience) versus practical and with narrow interests (closed to experience).

Scientists measure these personality dimensions as they do most others—by using objective measures (as described earlier) in which the people whose personalities are being assessed answer various questions about themselves using paper-and-pencil tests. You can learn a great deal about a personality characteristic by examining some of the items used to measure it. With this in mind, Table 3.1 shows some sample items similar to those used to assess individuals' standing on each of the big five dimensions of personality. By completing these items, you stand to gain some insight into where *you* stand with respect to these important traits.

TABLE 3.1   THE BIG FIVE DIMENSIONS OF PERSONALITY

The items listed here are similar to ones used to measure each of the *big five dimensions of personality*. Answering them may give you some insight into these key aspects of your personality.

Directions: Indicate the extent to which you agree or disagree with each item by entering a number in the space beside it. Enter 5 if you agree strongly with the item, 4 if you agree, 3 if you neither agree nor disagree, 2 if you disagree, and 1 if you disagree strongly.

Conscientiousness:

_____ I keep my room neat and clean.

_____ People generally find me to be extremely reliable.

Extraversion:

_____ I like lots of excitement in my life.

_____ I usually am very cheerful.

Agreeableness:

_____ I generally am quite courteous to other people.

_____ People never think I am cold and sly.

Emotional Stability:

_____ I often worry about things that are out of my control.

_____ I usually feel sad or "down."

Openness to Experience:

_____ I have a lot of curiosity.

_____ I enjoy the challenge of change.

Scoring: Add your scores for each item. Higher scores reflect greater degrees of the personality characteristic being measured.

How important are the big five dimensions of personality? Research suggests that the answer is "very!" First, several of the big five dimensions are related to work performance.[10] This is true across many different occupational groups (e.g., professionals, police, managers, salespersons, skilled laborers) and several kinds of performance measures (e.g., ratings of individuals' performance by managers or others, performance during training programs, personnel records). In general, *conscientiousness* shows the strongest association with task performance: The higher individuals are on this dimension, the higher their performance.[11] However, emotional stability, too, is related to task performance, although not as strongly or consistently; again, the more emotionally stable individuals are, the better their task performance.[12]

Other dimensions of the big five also are linked to task performance but in more specific ways. For instance, agreeableness is positively related to the interpersonal aspects of work (e.g., getting along well with others). And for some occupations—ones requiring individuals to interact with many other people during the course of the day (e.g., managers and police officers, sales)—extraversion is positively related to performance. It is especially noteworthy that individuals' standing on several of the big five dimensions of personality is related to performance of the teams to which they belong. Specifically, research has found that the higher the average scores of team members on conscientiousness, agreeableness, extraversion, and emotional stability, the higher was their teams' performance (as rated by managers).[13] Overall, it appears that the big five dimensions are indeed a key determinant of job performance.

In addition, these basic aspects of personality are linked to other important organizational processes. For instance, they provide a useful framework for understanding job applicants and for choosing the best ones for various jobs (i.e., for maximizing person–job fit).[14] And recent evidence suggests that openness to experience and conscientiousness are related to creativity and innovation, although in opposite ways. Openness to experience seems to facilitate such behavior, whereas conscientiousness can reduce it.[15] Interestingly, however, such effects occur only under specific conditions. In other words, openness to experience facilitates creativity and innovation (see Chapter 14) only when such behavior is encouraged by the organization (e.g., job holders are allowed to work on tasks that permit them to be creative). Similarly, conscientiousness tends to reduce creativity and innovation when conditions encourage this kind of outcome (e.g., when supervisors closely monitor employees' behavior). This is a clear illustration of the interactionist perspective we emphasized earlier: Behavior in work settings is a joint product of both individual characteristics (e.g., the big five dimensions) *and* the situations in which people work. Despite such complexities, the overall conclusion seems clear: The big five dimensions of personality are highly relevant to several important aspects of organizational behavior.

Positive and Negative Affectivity: Tendencies Toward Feeling Good or Bad

It is a basic fact of life that our moods fluctuate rapidly—and sometimes greatly—throughout the day (see Chapter 4). An e-mail message containing good news may leave us smiling, whereas an unpleasant conversation with a coworker may leave us feeling gloomy. Such temporary feelings are known as *mood states* and are likely to affect anyone at any time. However, mood states are only part of the total picture when considering the way we feel at work.

In addition, people also differ with respect to more stable tendencies to experience positive or negative feelings.[16] As personal experience suggests, some people tend to be "up" most of the time, whereas others tend to be more subdued or even depressed—and these tendencies are apparent in a wide range of contexts. In other words, at any given moment people's moods or *affective states* are based both on temporary conditions (i.e., mood states) and relatively stable differences in people's lasting dispositions to experience positive or negative feelings (i.e., stable traits).

These differences in people's predispositions toward positive and negative moods can be viewed as an important aspect of their personalities. In fact, such differences are related to the ways they approach events and experiences in their lives—and on their jobs. Specifically, individuals who are high in the trait of **positive affectivity** tend to have an overall sense of well-being, see people and events in a positive light, and tend to experience positive emotional states. In contrast, those high in the trait of **negative affectivity** tend to hold negative views of themselves and others, interpret ambiguous situations in a negative manner, and frequently experience negative emotional states (see Figure 3.4).[17]

positive affectivity
The tendency to experience positive moods and feelings in a wide range of settings and under many different conditions.

negative affectivity
The tendency to experience negative moods in a wide range of settings and under many different conditions.

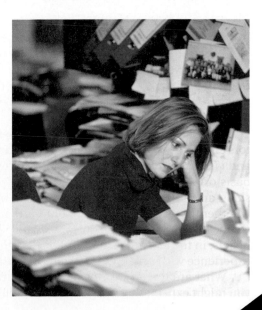

FIGURE 3.4
Positive and Negative Affectivity: An Important Personality Trait
Although anyone might be happy or sad at any given time, some people—those possessing the trait of *positive affectivity*—tend to see things in a positive way and have an overall sense of well-being, whereas others—those possessing the trait of *negative affectivity*—tend to hold negative views of people and situations.

Do people who are high in positive affectivity behave differently than those high in negative affectivity when it comes to organizational behavior? Research findings suggest that they do. For example, in one study researchers assessed the positive and negative affectivity of people who also participated in a series of exercises simulating business decision making.[18] Several different measures of performance on this important task were gathered—accuracy (the number of decisions that were correct), rankings of overall performance by other students, and managerial potential (ratings by experts of the degree to which participants could succeed as a manager). The results were clear: On each of these measures, people with high levels of positive affectivity were superior to those with high levels of negative affectivity.

Research also indicates that affectivity influences not only individual performance, but the performance of work teams as well. For example, it has been found that work groups that have a positive affective tone (those in which the average level of positive affectivity is high) function more effectively than groups that have a negative affective tone (those in which the average level of negative affectivity is high).[19]

Finally, we should note that negative affectivity appears to be related to workplace aggression and other forms of dysfunctional (i.e., counterproductive) behavior at work (see Chapter 11).[20] The link does not appear to be a simple one: Persons high in negative affectivity are not always more aggressive at work than other persons. But this may be because they are engaging in passive, hidden acts of aggression rather than overt ones; and in addition, they may be more likely to serve as targets of aggression from others in their organizations because of their surface passivity.[21] Overall, negative affectivity may not only be unpleasant to the persons who experience it: It also may contribute to an unpleasant—and unproductive—work environment.

Two Aspects of the Self: Self-Efficacy and Self-Monitoring

Suppose that two individuals are assigned the same task by their supervisor. One is confident of her ability to carry it out successfully, whereas the other has some serious doubts. Which person is more likely to succeed? The first person may be said to be higher in a personality characteristic known as **self-efficacy**—the belief in one's own capacity to execute courses of action required to reach specific levels of performance.[22] Simply put, self-efficacy refers to individuals' confidence in their capacity to perform a specific task.[23] Judgments of self-efficacy consist of three basic components.[24]

- *magnitude*—the level at which an individual believes she or he can perform.
- *strength*— the person's confidence that she or he can perform at that level.
- *generality*—the extent to which self-efficacy in one situation or for one task extends to other situations and other tasks.

When considered in the context of any given task, self-efficacy is not, strictly speaking, an aspect of personality.[25] However, people also seem to acquire general expectations about their abilities to mobilize the motivation, cognitive resources, and strategies needed to exert control over the events in their lives.[26] Such generalized beliefs about their task-related capabilities are stable over time, and these can be viewed as an important aspect of personality. Such beliefs, known as **general self-efficacy,** have been found ˅ect actual performance at work.[27]

˅ow do beliefs about self-efficacy develop? Evidence indicates that two major factors ˅ involved: *direct experience*—feedback from performing similar tasks in the past, ˅*rious experience*—observations of others' performance on these tasks.[28] On the ˅ information from these sources, people reach initial conclusions about the ˅d abilities required to succeed on the task—whether they possess these, ˅here are factors or conditions that may interfere with their performance, and ˅ether, these conclusions shape people's current beliefs of self-efficacy. These ˅rn, are then adjusted in the light of new information—for example, further ˅vith actually performing the task.

˅ the effects of such generalized beliefs about one's self-efficacy? First, as ˅ect, such judgments can influence strongly many critical aspects of orga-

self-efficacy

Individuals' beliefs concerning their ability to perform specific tasks successfully.

nizational behavior. For example, people who expect to do well—who believe they "have what it takes"—often really *do* succeed. At the very least, they do better than individuals who are more skeptical about their ability to perform adequately.[29] This makes sense if you think about it. After all, when we feel optimistic about our capacity to succeed, we are willing to intensify our efforts and to persist in the face of long odds and setbacks. However, when we feel we don't stand much of a chance, we are unlikely to rise to the occasion and simply give up. Not surprisingly, people who are higher in self-efficacy also tend to be happier with their work and with their lives in general.[30]

Self-efficacy also plays a role in *entrepreneurship* and in encouraging innovation within existing organizations.[31] Recent findings indicate that teams of corporate entrepreneurs who are high in self-efficacy are more successful in obtaining corporate funding for new projects than teams that are low in self-efficacy.[32] Why? Because teams high in self-efficacy, who believe in their own ability to turn their idea for an innovation into a successful product, are more persuasive than teams lower in self-efficacy—and this increases their chances of gaining the financial support they seek.

Fortunately, generalized self-efficacy, unlike several other aspects of personality, can be changed. In other words, people who, on the basis of life experiences, have reached the conclusion that they are not very competent or effective, can, in fact, learn to see themselves and their abilities in a more positive light under certain conditions. Furthermore, such changes can have dramatic effects on people's lives.

Demonstrating this, a team of researchers helped raise the self-efficacy of a group of unemployed Israeli vocational workers in two ways—first, by teaching them how to search for jobs more effectively (e.g., how to present their skills to prospective employers) and, second, by sharing the stories of others who successfully found jobs.[33] (In other words, they received both the direct experiences and vicarious experiences to which we referred earlier.) This occurred as part of a series of intensive workshops conducted over 2½ weeks in which the unemployed workers were given critical feedback designed to help them carefully hone their skills as job seekers, thereby boosting their beliefs about their capacities to achieve success on this important task. Shortly thereafter, their feelings of self-efficacy were boosted dramatically, and these translated into success: People whose self-efficacy was low before training developed higher feelings of self-efficacy during training, and importantly these individuals proved to be as successful in finding jobs as those who had high levels of self-efficacy to begin with (see Figure 3.5).

These findings are important for several reasons. First, they suggest that a fundamental aspect of people's personality can be changed in a way that can have beneficial effects on their well-being (and society's well-being, too). From a practical perspective, this means that concrete steps can be taken to help unemployed people become reemployed.

FIGURE 3.5

Self-Efficacy, Job Loss, and the Chances of Getting Another Job
When individuals lose their jobs, their self-efficacy often suffers. Training in job-search skills, however, can restore lost confidence and this, in turn, can increase the chances that such persons will find another job.

When people believe that they can do a job, and do it well, the chances that they really *can* often increase. Why? Because heightened feelings of self-efficacy (belief in one's ability to accomplish a specific task) have important benefits. They increase both motivation and persistence ("Why give up? I know I can make it!") and encourage individuals to set challenging goals ("I know I can do this well"). So, encouraging high levels of self-efficacy among employees is well worthwhile. How can companies reach this objective? Here are some concrete tips.

1. *Give constructive—not destructive—feedback.* If you think about it, there is only one rational reason to give people feedback on their work: to help them improve. Other motives certainly exist (e.g., some managers give employees' negative feedback to "put them in their place" or to "even the score"), but they are *not* rational and are counterproductive from the point

of view of increasing self-efficacy. On the other hand, constructive feedback that focuses on how employees can improve their performance can add to self-efficacy because it helps reassure the recipients that they *can* get there—that they have or can soon acquire the skills or strategies necessary for success.

One company that focuses on delivering *only* constructive feedback to employees is CHP, an HMO located in the Northeast. At CHP, managers are specifically trained to recognize that "feedback" is synonymous with "helping." They attend workshops in which they practice giving their subordinates feedback *only* when it can help them improve and *only* to reach this goal. The result? After this program was instituted, turnover dropped more than 30 percent and employee satisfaction rose significantly.

2. *Expose employees to models of good performance—and success.* How do people learn to do their jobs effectively? From direct

Systematic training in self-efficacy appears to be an effective means of helping persons who suffer from low self-efficacy take more control over their lives—in short, helping them to help themselves. Can organizations do anything to encourage self-efficacy among their employees? Absolutely. For some tips on how this goal can be reached please see the Best Practices section above.

Self-monitoring: Self-image versus private reality. Imagine that you are a first-level supervisor. Will you behave differently when interacting with your subordinates than with your boss or with your boss's boss? Interestingly, different people are likely to answer this question in contrasting ways. Some know that they can readily change their behavior to match each situation they encounter and strive to make the best possible impression on others. As a result, they adopt one style when dealing with their subordinates and another—perhaps, more respectful—when dealing with their boss. In contrast, other individuals are less willing to change their personal style in this manner. With them, "what you see is what you get" across a wide range of contexts. Such persons are unlikely to behave differently toward members of different groups with whom they come into contact.

This aspect of personality, known as *self-monitoring*, has been found to have important implications for organizational behavior.[34] Formally, **self-monitoring** may be defined as the tendency for people to change the way they behave to suit the situation in which they are acting. As this definition suggests, high self-monitors may be expected to have a distinct edge in situations in which making an impression on others is important (recall our discussion of *impression management* in Chapter 2). Because they are willing to change their behavior to suit the situations they face, people who are high self-monitors are inclined to do whatever it takes to generate positive reactions from others. And this, as you might imagine, can lead to important differences between high and low self-monitors with respect to such important factors as task performance, career success, and the quality of their relationships with others.

self-monitoring
A personality trait involving the extent to which individuals adapt their behavior to the demands of specific situations so as to make good impressions on others.

practice, of course; but in addition, they learn many skills and strategies from others. And the more of these they possess, the more likely they are to perform well—and so, to experience increased self-efficacy. Companies that adopt carefully planned mentoring programs—programs in which inexperienced employees work closely with successful, experienced ones—can help build self-efficacy among their employees (see Chapter 7).

The university where one of us works has adopted such a program for junior faculty. Each new faculty member is assigned a more senior faculty member—and, importantly, a successful one—by her or his department chair or dean. These faculty mentors are not there to look over the shoulders of new faculty; rather, their role is to give their junior colleagues advice on their careers and on how the system works. The program has been very successful: Junior faculty members report that it has helped them "get up to speed" very quickly and saved them countless disappointments. There is no direct evidence that the program builds self-efficacy, but informal discussions with the faculty members involved suggest that this is indeed one of the benefits.

3. *Seek continuous improvement.* Another technique for enhancing self-efficacy involves the quest for continuous improvement. GE's "Six Sigma" program, for instance, rests on the basic idea that "we can do it better—always!" The term *six sigma* refers to outstanding performance far above average (*sigma* is a statistical term relating to the normal distribution, and six sigma units above the mean is considered very far above it). Although some employees find this approach daunting at first, meetings and workshops soon convince them that they are part of a truly superb organization that simply will not settle for "average." The result? Employees come to view themselves as superior, and both self-efficacy and performance benefit.

Through these and related steps companies can boost self-efficacy among their employees. The underlying reason may be expressed by paraphrasing the British novelist, Aldous Huxley: "Those who believe that they are competent are generally those who achieve."

Self-monitoring and work performance. Do people who differ with respect to self-monitoring also differ with respect to how they well they perform their jobs? The simple answer is "yes"—at least for certain kind of jobs. Specifically, high self-monitors tend to do better than low self-monitors in jobs requiring what are known as *boundary-spanning* activities. These are tasks that involve communicating and interacting with people from contrasting professional or occupational groups (see Chapter 9). For example, the chairperson of an academic department in your college or university may play the role of boundary spanner. This individual interacts not only with faculty members but also with administrators and may be considered a member of both groups. In other words, he or she "spans the boundary" between the two groups.

Since successful boundary spanners are required to adjust their actions to the expectations and styles of each group (faculty members and administrators, such as deans, in this case), high self-monitors are particularly well equipped to interact with both groups, and they tend to do so successfully.[35] Low self-monitors, in contrast, are more poorly equipped to perform boundary-spanning roles and are generally not as adept at handling them. Given how important boundary-spanning roles can be in most organizations, it makes good sense to consider assigning people high in self-monitoring to such positions.

Self-monitoring and career success. As you might imagine, self-monitoring has an important impact on one's career success (see Chapter 7). Specifically, high self-monitors tend to obtain more promotions than low self-monitors, especially when these promotions involve movement from one company to another.[36]

Why is this so? A likely answer is that high self-monitors' greater willingness to adapt their behavior to the situations they encounter and to act in ways that please others helps them to get over the all-important first round of promotion contests.[37] High self-

FIGURE 3.6

High Self-Monitoring: A Mixed Bag
People who are high in *self-monitoring* behave in ways that are aimed at pleasing others. When these actions are perceived as being positive (a sign of empathy), they tend to form close relationships with others and get promoted. However, when these same actions are perceived negatively (e.g., being "phony"), they tend to form only shallow relationships with others and tend to be held back in their careers.

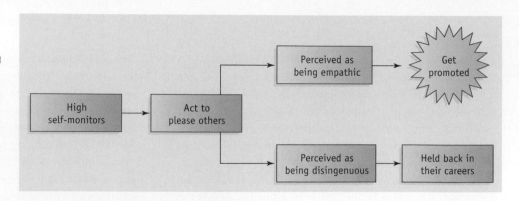

monitors seem to approach various situations by asking, "What kind of person does this situation require, and how can I best be that person?" In contrast, low self-monitors ask, "How can I best be *me* in this situation?" The result is that high self-monitors make a better impression on others, giving them the edge in getting early promotions. Once they do, they are on the road to success, and their careers often prosper.

Another reason behind the success of many high self-monitors is their ability to empathize with others—to be able to "walk in their shoes," or to "see the world through their eyes." As a case in point, several observers attribute the outstanding success of Orit Gadiesh, head of Bain & Co., a highly successful management consulting firm, to her tendency to engage in self-monitoring.[38] Although Gadiesh is often noticed first for her flamboyant personal style (marked in part by her multihued hairdo), it is her ability to look at things from others' perspectives that truly impresses her clients. Says James Morgan, CEO of Philip Morris USA, "Orit has that talent for making you feel you're the most important person in the room. She bleeds your blood." It is this high degree of *empathy*—a characteristic commonly found among high self-monitors—that keeps her clients impressed and coming back for more.

Interpersonal relationships: The potential liability of self-monitoring. Before you conclude that being high in self-monitoring is a true blessing when it comes to one's working life, we must caution that there also is a downside to this trait. Namely, because high self-monitors are so changeable, they have been referred to as "social chameleons"—that is, people who risk being viewed as unreliable, inconsistent, or even manipulative.[39] Given such perceptions, it is not surprising that high self-monitors tend to form less stable and shallower personal relationships with others than low self-monitors.[40]

Also, because high self-monitors tend to change their behavior across situations, they generally seek different friends for different settings. In contrast, low self-monitors remain much the same, and, as a result, they form fewer—but deeper—relationships. In short, self-monitoring, like most other dimensions of personality, has complex effects, and any assessment of the relative costs and benefits of being high or low on this dimension must take careful account of such complexity. For a summary of the positive and negative aspects of high self-monitoring, see Figure 3.6.

ADDITIONAL WORK-RELATED ASPECTS OF PERSONALITY

Although many experts on personality consider the dimensions we have considered so far to be among the most important, they are not the only ones with implications for organizational behavior. Here we'll examine some of the others that have been found to be important.

Machiavellianism: Using Others to Get Ahead

In 1513, the Italian philosopher Niccolo Machiavelli published a book entitled *The Prince*. In it, he outlined a ruthless strategy for seizing and holding political power. The essence of his approach was *expediency:* Do whatever is required to get ahead of another. Among the guiding principles he recommended were the following:

- Never show humility; arrogance is far more effective when dealing with others.
- Morality and ethics are for the weak; powerful people feel free to lie, cheat, and deceive whenever it suits their purpose.
- It is much better to be feared than loved.

In short, Machiavelli urged those who desired power to adopt an approach based totally on expedience or usefulness. Let others be swayed by friendship, loyalty, or beliefs about decency and fair play; a truly successful leader, he suggested, should always be above those factors. He or she should be willing to do *whatever it takes to win.*

Clearly (and fortunately!), the vast majority of people with whom we interact don't adopt Machiavelli's philosophy. But some do seem to embrace many of these principles. This fact led researchers to propose that acceptance of this ruthless creed reflects yet another dimension of personality—one known, appropriately, as **Machiavellianism.** Persons high on this dimension (high Machs) accept Machiavelli's suggestions and seek to manipulate others in a ruthless manner.[41] In contrast, persons low on this dimension (low Machs) reject this approach and *do* care about fair play, loyalty, and other principles Machiavelli rejected. Machiavellianism is measured by means of a brief questionnaire called the *Mach Scale.* Items similar to ones on the Mach Scale are shown in Table 3.2.

Machiavellianism
A personality trait involving willingness to manipulate others for one's own purposes.

The characteristics of high Machs. What are persons who score high in the Machiavelllanism scale like? Recent research suggests that they are very much like individuals described by psychologists as being *psychopaths.*[42] Such persons are glib and charming, lie easily, have no qualms about manipulating or conning others, have little remorse or guilt over harming others, and are callous and show little empathy toward others. In addition, they also tend to be impulsive, irresponsible, and prone to feeling bored. If this description sounds to you like the "con artists" we often read about in the news, you are correct: Recent evidence suggests that persons scoring high in Machiavellianism show precisely these characteristics.[43]

TABLE 3.2   MEASURING MACHIAVELLIANISM

The items listed here are similar to those included in one of the most widely used measures of Machiavellianism. One's score on this scale reflects the willingness to manipulate others in order to get ahead

Directions: In the space next to each item, enter a number that characterizes your own feelings about that statement. If you disagree strongly, enter 1; if you disagree, enter 2; if you neither agree nor disagree, enter 3; if you agree, enter 4; if you strongly agree, enter 5.

____1. The best way to handle people is telling them what they want to hear.

____2. When you ask someone to do something for you, it is best to give the real reasons for wanting it rather than giving reasons that might carry more weight.

____3. Anyone who completely trusts anyone else is asking for trouble.

____4. It is hard to get ahead without cutting corners and bending the rules.

____5. It is safest to assume that all people have a vicious streak—and that it will come out when given a chance.

____6. It is never right to lie to someone else.

____7. Most people are basically good and kind.

____8. Most people work hard only when they are forced to do so.

Scoring: Add your responses to items 1, 3, 4, 5, and 8. To this number add the sum of 2, 6, and 7, after scoring them in reverse (so, if you responded with a 5, add 1 point; if you responded with a 4, add 2 points; if you responded with a 3, add 3 points; if you responded with a 2, add 4 points; and if you responded with a 1, add 5 points). Then, add your scores. The higher your score, the more Machiavellian you tend to be.

Given that they may be backstabbers, being able to spot high Machs is especially important on the job. What specific tactics should you watch for as a sign that someone is a high Mach? Among other things, high Machs may be expected to do the following:

1. Neglect to share important information (e.g., claim to "forget" to tell you about key meetings and assignments).
2. Find subtle ways of making you look bad to management (e.g., damn you with faint praise).
3. Fail to meet their obligations (e.g., not hold up their end on joint projects, thereby causing you to look bad).
4. Spread false rumors about you (e.g., make up things about you that embarrass you in front of others).

In other words, high Machiavellians are definitely not team players; their only concern is themselves and their own well-being. So if an organization acquires a large number of such persons, watch out: Lots of potentially dangerous political activity is likely to follow. (We'll examine organizational politics in more detail in Chapter 12.)

Machiavellianism and success. If high Machs are willing to do whatever it takes to succeed, you might expect that they would tend to be successful. However, this is not always so. How well they do tends to be associated with two important factors—the kind of jobs they have and the nature of the organizations in which they work.

For example, research has shown that Machiavellianism is not closely related to success in the kinds of jobs in which people operate with a great deal of autonomy. These are jobs—such as salesperson, marketing executive, and university professor—in which employees have a great deal of freedom to act as they wish, giving them good opportunities to free themselves from the high Machs' clutches (or to avoid interacting with them altogether!).[44] For much the same reason, high Machs tend to be much more successful in organizations that are *loosely structured* (i.e., ones in which there are few established rules) than those that are *tightly structured* (i.e., ones in which rules regarding expected behavior are clear and explicit).[45] The reasoning is simple: When rules are vague and unclear, it is far easier for high Machs to "do their own thing," whereas when they are bound by strict rules, high Machs are far more limited in what they can do.

The Type A Behavior Pattern: Being in a Hurry— and Irritable—Can Be Costly to Your Health

Think about the people you know. Can you name one who always seems to be in a hurry, is extremely competitive, and is often irritable? Now try to name one who shows the opposite pattern—someone who is usually relaxed, not very competitive, and easygoing. The people you have in mind represent extremes on one key dimension of personality: The first person demonstrates what is known as the **Type A behavior pattern;** the second represents the **Type B behavior pattern.**[46] People in the first group—classified as Type A—show high levels of competitiveness, irritability, and time urgency; they are always in a hurry. In contrast, people classified as Type B show the opposite pattern: They are much calmer and laid back.

As you might guess, Type A and Type B individuals tend to behave in very different ways on the job.[47] These differences fall into three categories—those involving personal health, task performance, and relations with others.[48] Because we will examine the impact of the Type A behavior pattern on health in connection with our discussion of stress in Chapter 4, we will focus here on the Type A behavior pattern's connections to task performance and to interpersonal relations.

Type As and task performance. First, do Type As and Type Bs differ with respect to job performance? Given their high level of competitiveness, it seems reasonable to expect that Type As will work harder at various tasks than Type Bs—and, as a result, will perform at higher levels. In fact, however, the situation turns out to be more complex than this. Type As *do* tend to work faster on many tasks than Type Bs, even when no pressure

Type A behavior pattern
A pattern of behavior involving high levels of competitiveness, time urgency, and irritability.

Type B behavior pattern
A pattern of behavior characterized by a casual, laid-back style; the opposite of the Type A behavior pattern.

or deadline is involved. Similarly, Type As are able to get more done in the presence of distractions,[49] and they tend to seek more difficult and challenging work than Type Bs.[50]

It would be misleading, though, to assume that Type As are always superior to Type Bs. Indeed, Type As frequently perform poorly on certain kinds of tasks, including those requiring patience or careful judgment. They are simply in too much of a hurry to complete such work effectively.[51]

Consistent with this idea, surveys reveal that most top executives are Type Bs rather than Type As.[52] Several factors probably contribute to this pattern. First, it is possible that Type As simply don't last long enough to rise to the highest management levels (as we will see in Chapter 4, the health risks of their "always-in-a-hurry" lifestyle are too great!). Second, the irritability or hostility often shown by Type As may have negative effects on their careers, preventing them from rising to the top of their organizations. In fact, Type As do appear to have very "short fuses"—they often become angry and behave aggressively in situations that others may be inclined simply to ignore.[53] Finally, their impatience is often incompatible with the deliberate, carefully considered decisions required of top-level managers.

A good example of a top executive who appears to be Type B is Jack Smith, the long-time former CEO of General Motors. Smith is described by those who know him as someone who remains calm in almost all situations and who rarely loses his temper. And although he certainly works hard to assure GM's success, he is *not* in a hurry, and he doesn't like to make waves. In fact, he has been criticized by outsiders for showing too much loyalty to subordinates, treating them with "kid gloves" even when they fail at important tasks. Similarly, he has remained above the fray, refusing to take vigorous action to stop costly squabbling between GM's various divisions. Of course, it is Jack Smith who saved GM from what seemed like certain bankruptcy in the early 1990s, so it is clear that his calm, "one-step-at-a-time" approach *can* work quite well. Indeed, the fact that a majority of top executives appear to be Type Bs suggests that this kind of approach may often be more effective than the irritable, perfection-seeking, always-in-a-hurry style shown by Type As.

In sum, neither pattern—Type A nor Type B—has an overall edge when it comes to task performance. Although Type As may excel on tasks involving time pressure or solitary work, Type Bs have the advantage when it comes to tasks involving complex judgments and accuracy as opposed to speed. So, the question of whether Type As or Type Bs make more productive employees boils down to the issue of person–job fit, which we discussed earlier in this chapter: Productivity is enhanced when people perform the kinds of jobs that are "right" for them.

Type As and interpersonal relations. A key aspect of success on many kinds of jobs involves getting along with others. As your intuition may suggest, the more relaxed style of Type Bs would make them better suited to those kinds of jobs in which interpersonal skills are important.

Indeed, this prediction has been confirmed by research findings. Because of their impatience and irritability, Type As tend to annoy their coworkers. Moreover, they also are more likely to lose their tempers and to lash out at others. As a result, Type As tend to become involved in more conflicts at work than Type Bs.[54] In fact, recent evidence suggests that Type As also may be more likely than Type Bs to engage in various forms of aggressive and counterproductive behavior (such as saying negative things about coworkers and the company itself), an important form of behavior that we will examine more closely in Chapter 11.

In conclusion, although Type As often seem to be "cyclones of activity" and may move large volumes of work across their desks very quickly, there is definitely a downside to this pattern, both for the Type As themselves and for their coworkers and organizations.

Achievement Motivation: The Quest for Excellence

Can you recall the person in your high school class who was named "most likely to succeed"? If so, you probably are thinking of someone who was truly competitive, an individual who wanted to win in every situation—or, at least, in all the important ones. As you think about it, you are acknowledging an important difference between people—the tendency for some individuals to be more concerned than others about coming out on top and achieving success. This is a key personality variable known as **achievement motivation** (also known as **need for achievement**)—the strength of an individual's desire to excel, to succeed at difficult tasks and to do them better than others.

Need achievement and attraction to difficult tasks. One of the most interesting differences between high- and low-need achievers involves their pattern of preferences for tasks of varying difficulty. As we will note later, these differences may have profound effects on managerial success.

Because high need achievers so strongly desire success, they tend to steer away from performing certain kinds of tasks—those that are very easy and those that are very difficult. After all, especially simple tasks are not challenging enough to allow them to feel that they have achieved anything, and especially difficult ones are certain to result in failure, an unacceptable outcome. Not surprisingly, high-need achievers are most strongly attracted to tasks that are moderately challenging, thereby preferring tasks of intermediate difficulty.[55]

In contrast, the opposite pattern occurs among people who are low in achievement motivation. That is, they much prefer very easy and very difficult tasks to ones that are moderately difficult. The reasoning is simple. People low in achievement motivation like to perform easy tasks because success is virtually certain, not threatening the way they perceive themselves. At the same time, because failure is certain on difficult tasks, it can be dismissed readily as not indicative of anything unflattering about themselves. Failure on a moderately difficult tasks, however, may be the basis for making unflattering attributions about oneself (see Chapter 2), so low need achievers may shy away from such tasks. Although these differences between high need achievers and low need achievers are interesting by themselves, their real value becomes most evident when considering the role they play on people's success as managers.

Are high-need achievers successful managers? We have described people high in achievement motivation as having a highly task-oriented outlook. They are strongly concerned with getting things done, which encourages them to work hard and to strive for success. But do they always succeed, especially in managerial positions? As in the case of so many other questions in the field of OB, the answer is not straightforward.

Given their intense desire to excel, it seems reasonable to expect that people high in achievement motivation will attain greater success in their careers than others. This is true to a limited extent. Research has shown that people high in achievement motivation tend to gain promotions more rapidly than those who are low in achievement motivation, at least early in their careers.[56] Their interest in attaining success "jump starts" their careers. However, as their careers progress, their unwillingness to tackle difficult challenges becomes a problem that interferes with their success.

Moreover, they tend to be so highly focused on their own success that they sometimes refrain from delegating authority to others, thereby failing to give subordinates the tools they need to make the best possible decisions on behalf of their organizations. Research has shown that CEOs who are high in achievement motivation tend to keep organizational power in the hands of just a few people, failing to empower their team members as needed, which often proves to be an ineffective strategy for management.[57]

At the same time, people high in achievement motivation have an important advantage—the fact that they have a strong desire for feedback regarding their performance. In other words, because they so greatly want to succeed, they have a strong interest in knowing just how well they are doing so they can adjust their goals accordingly (see Chapter 6). Not surprisingly, people who are high in need achievement have a strong preference for merit-based pay systems (i.e., those in which pay is based on performance) because these systems recognize people's individual achievements. At the same time, they tend to dislike seniority-based pay systems (i.e., those in which pay is based on how long one has worked in the company) because these fail to take into account differences between people's job-based achievements (besides merely staying on the job, that is).[58]

Achievement motivation and goal orientation: Do people differ in the kind of success they seek? So far, our discussion has implied that the desire to excel or achieve is an important dimension along which people differ, and this is certainly true. But individuals also differ with respect to the *kind* of success they want to attain. Recent findings indicate, in fact, that people can have any one of three contrasting *goal orientations* when performing various tasks.[59] First, they may wish to perform well because they like a challenge and the opportunity to learn new skills (this is known as a *learning goal orientation*). Second, they may want to do well in order to show others how competent they are—to gain their approval (this is known as a *performance goal orientation*). And, finally, they may want to do well—to achieve—to avoid appearing incompetent and receiving negative evaluations from others (this is known as an *avoidance goal orientation*).[60] (See Figure 3.7 for an overview of these three goal orientations.)

The existence of these three different goal orientations (reasons for wanting to do well in various tasks) has important implications for performance in work settings. For instance, a learning goal orientation is strongly related to general self-efficacy—people's estimate of their ability to perform successfully in a wide variety of challenging situations (see page 88).[61] The higher their learning goal orientation, the greater their general self-efficacy. Since self-efficacy, in turn, exerts strong effects on performance, it is clear that a learning orientation can be advantageous with respect to performing many jobs. Similarly, research findings indicate that a learning goal orientation may be helpful from the point of view of benefiting from on-the-job feedback: People high in this orientation want to receive feedback and pay careful attention to it, since it will help them to learn. In contrast, neither a performance goal orientation nor an avoidance goal orientation seems to confer similar benefits.[62] So overall, organizations should strive to select people who have a learning goal orientation or to encourage such an orientation among their employees. How can this be attained? In part by giving employees an opportunity to acquire new skills on their jobs and by rewarding them for doing so—not just for being competent at what they already know. For instance, United Technologies seeks to encourage a learning goal orientation among its employees by encouraging them to take advanced courses in their specialty—or in management. Indeed, United Technologies, as well as many other companies, actually covers the entire cost of an M.B.A. for individuals they consider to be on the "fast track" for success in their careers.

A learning goal orientation also may be more common among entrepreneurs than other persons. This may help explain why some highly successful entrepreneurs, who

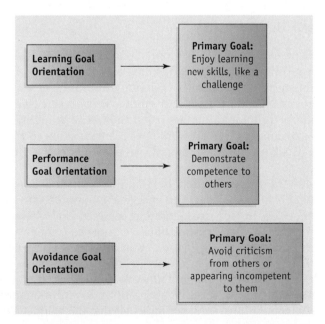

FIGURE 3.7

Learning, Performance, and Avoidance Goal Orientations
Individuals differ with respect to their *goal orientations*—in a sense, the kind of success or achievement they seek. Individuals who adopt a learning orientation seek achievement because they like a challenge and enjoy learning new skills. Persons who adopt a performance orientation seek success or achievement mainly to demonstrate their competence to others. Those who adopt an avoidance orientation want to succeed in order to avoid criticism from others or to avoid appearing incompetent.

Economists have demonstrated that a wide variety of factors—including the price and availability of natural resources, labor costs, and government policies that encourage or discourage growth—contribute to national differences in economic growth and development. However, these factors do not tell the whole story. Indeed, there is also an important individual difference factor involved as well—national differences in achievement motivation.

Although achievement motivation, strictly speaking, relates to individuals, considerable evidence suggests that it also varies across different cultures, too. What's more, these differences are related to important economic variables.

This point is illustrated dramatically in a classic study in which researchers analyzed children's stories from 22 different cultures with respect to the degree to which they contained themes of achievement motivation (e.g., the story "The Little Engine That Could," which is read by millions of children in the United States, reflects a great deal of achievement motivation).[63] The investigators then related the levels of achievement motivation indicated by these stories to key measures of economic

---

have already earned more money than they will ever need, sell their successful companies in order to start new ones. For instance, consider Mukesh Chatter, an entrepreneur who, in 1999, sold the company he had founded to Lucent Technologies for $1 billion. Within a year, he decided to start yet another company. When asked why, he replied: "Because what I really love is starting something new, learning things I didn't know before, and making things happen." That sounds very much like a learning goal orientation to us!

Achievement motivation clearly influences the success of individuals—of that there can be no doubt. But does it also contribute to the economic well-being of entire societies? For information suggesting that it does, please see the OB in a Diverse World section above.

Morning Persons and Evening Persons: "Oh, How I Hate to Get Up in the . . ."

At present, about 20 percent of people in the U.S. labor force work at night or on rotating shifts.[66] This figure has increased in recent years and, given that more and more business are choosing to operate around the clock, it is likely to continue its upward course.[67] Unfortunately, this trend can be costly given that the health and well-being of many individuals suffers when they work at night.[68] Yet, as you probably know from experience, there are some people who seem to thrive on "the graveyard shift" and actually prefer it. (In fact, if you are up late at night reading this, you may be one of them!)

The suggestion that there may be individual differences in the times of day at which people feel most alert and energetic is supported by evidence showing that such differences do, in fact, exist, and that these are stable over time. Specifically, it appears that most people fall into one of two categories—either they are **morning persons,** who feel most energetic early in the day, or they are **evening persons,** who feel most energetic at night.

Presumably, evening persons would find the task of adapting to night work less stressful than morning persons and would, consequently do better work when exposed to such conditions. Evidence indicates that this is indeed the case. For example, consider an

morning persons
Individuals who feel most energetic and alert early in the day.

evening persons
Individuals who feel most energetic and alert late in the day.

development (e.g., per capita income and per capita electrical production). Their findings were impressive: The greater the emphasis placed on achievement in the children's stories in various nations, the more rapid was the economic growth in these nations as the children grew up!

Interestingly, these findings are not just a fluke; similar results have been reported repeatedly.[64] For example, a massive study involving more than 12,000 participants in 41 different countries has confirmed the idea that national differences in achievement motivation can be quite real and that they are related to differences in economic growth.[65] Specifically, it was found that various attitudes toward work, such as competitiveness, were different across countries, and that those countries whose citizens were most competitive tended to be those that had higher rates of economic growth.

But how, you may be wondering, can this be so? How can achievement motivation, which is a characteristic of individuals, influence economic activity? Perhaps the answer lies in the following fact: In the final analysis, economic trends are the reflection of actions by large numbers of individuals. To the extent that this is so, it is not really very surprising that factors such as achievement motivation might well play a role in shaping the destiny of national economies. The economic whole, after all, is indeed the sum of its parts—and these "parts" consist of thinking, feeling, behaving human beings!

interesting study involving a population with which most readers will be familiar—college students. The students participating in this research project were asked to keep diaries in which they reported the times each day when they slept and when they studied.[69] In addition, information was obtained from university records concerning the students' class schedules and their academic performance. All participants also completed a brief questionnaire designed to measure the tendency to be a morning or evening person.

Results revealed intriguing differences between participants who were classified as being high in the tendency to be a morning person or high in the tendency to be an evening person. As might be expected, morning persons reported sleeping primarily at night and studying in the morning, whereas evening persons reported the opposite pattern. Similarly, class schedules for the two groups also indicated interesting differences: Students classified as morning persons tended to schedule their classes earlier in the day than those classified as evening students. Perhaps most interesting of all, morning students did better in their early classes than they did in their later ones, whereas the opposite was true for students who were classified as being evening persons (see Figure 3.8).

These findings and those of many other studies suggest that individual differences in preferences for various times of day are not only real, but also that they are very important when it comes to job performance.[70] Ideally, only individuals who are at their best late in the day should be assigned to night work. The results of following such a policy might well be better performance, better health, and fewer accidents for employees—outcomes beneficial to both individual workers and their organizations.

COPING WITH THE "GRAVEYARD SHIFT"

Everyone is a morning person or a night person to some degree. This fact can have serious effects when we are required, by our jobs, to work at times when we feel less alert. For instance, 24-hour grocery stores, round-the-clock production, and many other changes in the way businesses operate require a growing number of persons to work the "graveyard shift" (midnight to 8:00 AM)—a time when many of us are at low ebb physically and in terms of their alertness. What can you do to lessen the misery—and danger—of working on such a shift if you have to do it? Here are some tips:

- Adjust your schedule so that you get enough hours of sleep. Although it is tempting to stay up during the day, don't do it; you really do need your rest!
- Make the room in which you sleep as dark and soundproof as possible. Light interferes with the normal sleep mechanisms, and will make it harder for you to get the rest you need.
- Try to change your schedule on the weekend as little as possible. If you revert to staying up late on Friday and Saturday nights, you will find it harder to go to sleep in the afternoon on Sunday when you must return to work.
- Avoid changing your shift unless you have to. It is hard enough to adjust to one change; several can pose a very serious health hazard. So avoid swing shifts if at all possible.

FIGURE 3.8

Time of Day and Academic Performance
Students who felt most alert and energetic early in the day (known as *morning persons*) did better in early classes than in late classes. In contrast, students who felt most alert and energetic late in the day (known as *evening persons*) did better in late classes than in early classes. (*Source:* Based on data from Guthrie, Ash, & Bandapudi, 1995; see Note 66.)

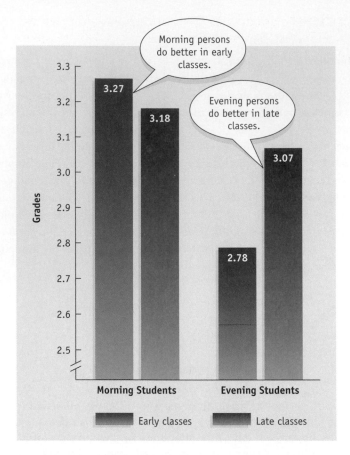

ABILITIES: HAVING WHAT IT TAKES

"To do easily what is difficult for others is the mark of talent. To do what is impossible for talent is the mark of genius." Henri-Frédéric Amiel (1856)

abilities
Mental and physical capacities to perform various tasks.

As this quotation suggests, human beings differ greatly with respect to their **abilities**—the capacity to perform various tasks.[71] For example, no matter how hard we might have tried, neither of the authors of this book could ever have made it as a professional basketball player. We are simply not tall enough to succeed! However, we have other abilities—at least, so we like to believe—including ones that some famous athletes may not possess. As you can readily guess, people differ with respect to a very large number of abilities. Among these, though, abilities falling into two major groups are most relevant to behavior in work settings—*intellectual abilities,* which involve the capacity to perform various cognitive tasks, and *physical abilities,* which refer to the capacity to perform various physical actions.

Intellectual Abilities: Various Forms of Intelligence

cognitive intelligence
The ability to understand complex ideas, to adapt effectively to the environment, to learn from experience, to engage in various forms of reasoning, and to overcome obstacles by careful thought.

information processing
Cognitive effort involving the combination, integration, and use of complex information.

Traditionally, when people speak about someone's intelligence, they are referring to a specific kind of ability that psychologists term **cognitive intelligence.** This refers to the ability to understand complex ideas, to adapt effectively to the environment, to learn from experience, to engage in various forms of reasoning, and to overcome obstacles by careful thought.[72] As you know from popular discussions about *IQ tests,* people have this type of intelligence to varying degrees. You also probably realize that different jobs place contrasting demands on people with respect to the amount of cognitive intelligence needed to succeed. Success in some jobs, such as top executive positions, requires high levels of **information processing**—cognitive effort involving the combination, integration, and use of complex information. In contrast, other jobs are far less demanding with respect to such abilities; they are largely routine and do not require careful thought or analysis of information.

Although this approach has been around for over 100 years, it is widely recognized today that cognitive intelligence is only one aspect of human intelligence. Experts on this topic generally agree that intelligence is not a single, unitary ability; rather, it involves a group of different kinds of abilities.[73] Although several different forms of intelligence have been identified (including the cognitive or analytical intelligence measured by traditional IQ tests), three others forms have been found to be more closely linked to various forms of behavior in organizations. One of these is *practical intelligence,* what we commonly call "street smarts." People with high amounts of practical intelligence are adept at solving the problems of everyday life. Another form of intelligence, known as *emotional intelligence,* refers to people's abilities to be sensitive to their own and others' emotions. Both of these forms of intelligence play an important role in various forms of organizational behavior, and for this reason, we will describe them in detail. After we consider these topics, we'll also briefly discuss a third type of intelligence known as *successful intelligence*—the kind that may be most useful to entrepreneurs.[74]

Practical intelligence: Solving the problems of everyday life effectively. Let's begin with an example of practical intelligence in operation. In Tallahassee, Florida, the city provides trash containers to all residents. For many years, sanitation workers would retrieve containers of refuse from citizens' backyards, bring them to the truck, empty them, and then return the containers to their original locations. This system continued until one day a newly hired employee considered this situation and realized that the amount of work involved could be cut almost in half through one simple but ingenious change. Can you guess the solution he devised? It was deceptively simple. After emptying each trash can, it would be brought to the next yard instead of being returned to its original location. There, it would replace the full container that would then be carried to the truck. Since all trash cans were identical, it made no difference to each resident which trash can they received back. However, this simple step saved one entire trip to each backyard for the trash collectors. The employee who came up with this scheme appears to have a great deal of what is called **practical intelligence**—the ability to devise effective ways of getting things done. Growing evidence suggests that practical intelligence is indeed different from the kind of intelligence measured by IQ tests and that it is especially important in business settings.[75]

How, precisely, do people with high amounts of practical intelligence go about solving problems? The secret to their success resides in what is known as **tacit knowledge**—that is, knowledge about how to get things done. In contrast with formal academic knowledge, which, as you know, often involves memorizing definitions, formulas, and other information, tacit knowledge is far more practical in nature. Specifically, tacit knowledge has three major characteristics.

practical intelligence
Adeptness at solving the practical problems of everyday life.

tacit knowledge
Knowledge about how to get things done.

1. Tacit knowledge is *action oriented.* It involves "knowing how" to do something, as opposed to "knowing that" something is the case. For example, skilled athletes can perform amazing feats on the playing field although they may not be able to put into words *how* they perform those actions.
2. Tacit knowledge *allows individuals to achieve goals they personally value.* As such, it is practically useful, focusing on knowledge that is relevant to them—a concern voiced by any student ever heard complaining about academic course content, saying "This stuff is not relevant; I can't use it for anything in my life!"
3. Tacit knowledge usually *is acquired without direct help from others.* In fact, such knowledge is often acquired on one's own, largely because it is often unspoken. As such, people must recognize it, and its value, for themselves. For instance, although no one may ever tell an employee that getting help from a more senior person will aid his or her career, he or she may both recognize this fact and act on it.

How can we measure practical intelligence and the tacit knowledge on which it is based? The most popular—and useful—approach involves the following steps. First,

OB IN AN E-WORLD
ARE FACE-TO-FACE MEETINGS OBSOLETE? FOR SOME PURPOSES AND SOME PEOPLE, THE ANSWER IS "YES"

In recent years, many companies have begun to ask: "Do we really need so many face-to-face meetings?" In other words, is it really necessary for employees to fly to distant cities for business meetings? Or can such meetings be held electronically without any major loss—and with the obvious benefits of reduced costs and increased safety? Although there is no simple answer to this question, many companies have reached the conclusion—at least tentatively—that travel is out and videoconferencing is in.

For example, executives at Masimo, a medical-technology company in Irvine, California, decided on September 12, 2001 that they would invest in teleconferencing equipment.[80] As Brad Lanagdale, Masimo's chief financial officer, put it, "The day after the World Trade Center we said, 'Let's do it.'" He adds: "Personally, I think there's been far too much traveling around the country for 30-minute meetings."

And many other executives agree with him. But this does not mean that face-to-face meetings are doomed. As noted by Ray

people known to be highly successful in a given job are asked to describe critical incidents they have encountered in their work. Then, they are asked to describe how they solved these problems and—more importantly—to describe the ways they went about solving these problems that differ from those used by less successful people in their field. On the basis of their answers, test questions for practical intelligence are devised. These questions are then used to measure such intelligence in other groups of people.

For example, questions to assess practical intelligence among managers might ask individuals taking the test to rate the quality of various options for handling situations managers often face—for instance, devising a strategy to counteract a competitor or deciding which of several companies should be awarded a contract. The closer the answers of people taking the test come to the strategies preferred by highly successful managers, the higher their practical intelligence. Research using such measures of practical intelligence indicate that it is often closely related to success in business settings—much more closely, in fact, than tests of cognitive intelligence.[76]

In sum, growing evidence suggests that there is indeed more to intelligence than the verbal, mathematical, and reasoning abilities that often are associated with academic success. Practical intelligence, too, is important and contributes to success in many areas of life.

Emotional intelligence: Managing the feeling side of life effectively. A second kind of intelligence that can often play an important role in behavior in organizations is known as **emotional intelligence** (or **EQ**). According to Daniel Goleman, author of several bestselling books on this topic, emotional intelligence refers to a cluster of abilities relating to the emotional or "feeling" side of life.[77] Specifically, emotional intelligence involves several major components. The key ones are as follows.

emotional intelligence (EQ)

A cluster of skills relating to the emotional side of life (e.g., the ability to recognize and regulate one's own emotions, to influence those of others, and to self-motivate).

1. *The ability to recognize and regulate our own emotions.* People with high EQs are able to recognize that they may be growing angry but manage to hold their tempers in check, nevertheless.
2. *The ability to recognize and influence others' emotions.* Those with high EQs possess the ability to gauge the degree to which other people are interested in what they have to say and have the capacity to make others enthusiastic about their ideas.

Ozzie, an expert on groupware programs and founder of Groove Networks, face-to-face meetings are still valuable under certain circumstances—in particular, when such tasks of managing conflicts or delicate negotiations are concerned. In other words, videoconferencing and other forms of electronic communication may work well for factual, productivity-related tasks, but may not be a good substitute for direct face-to-face contact when emotions are concerned.

And, of course, it is precisely in such contexts that people who are high in emotional intelligence have an important edge. Because they are adept at managing their own emotions and influencing the emotions of others, they often "shine" in face-to-face interactions, where they can put such skills to use. So, for example, if we asked highly successful salespersons, who are often very high in these aspects of emotional intelligence, whether they would be willing to try to work with customers through electronic means, we're confident that most would reply "no way!" They know very well that their particular skills and abilities are most useful when they can deal with potential customers "in the flesh."

This suggests that videoconferencing may not be readily and enthusiastically embraced by all employees—and that it may not be suitable for all companies. As is often the case, it offers a mixed assortment of benefits and costs, and each person—and organization—must weigh these carefully in the balance before deciding whether or not electronic meetings are justified.

3. *Self-motivation.* Individuals with high amounts of emotional intelligence are able to motivate themselves to work long and hard on various tasks and resist the temptation to quit or give up.
4. *The ability to form effective long-term relationships with others.* Those with high EQs have demonstrated the capacity to keep lots of different relationships going over long periods of time, often despite many life changes. As part of this, they tend to be proficient in such skills as being able to coordinate efforts with people, capable of negotiating solutions to complex interpersonal problems, and are good at getting others to like and trust them.

Is emotional intelligence valuable in organizational settings? Growing evidence indicates that it is. For example, research has found that several aspects of emotional intelligence (e.g., accuracy in "reading" others) are highly related to entrepreneurs' financial success.[78] Likewise, other findings indicate that scientists who are adept at accurately "reading others" and who, partly because of this ability, tend to be liked by their colleagues are more productive than scientists who are lower in this aspect of emotional intelligence. So overall, being high in various aspects of emotional intelligence can be helpful to one's career and to organizational success. Recognizing this fact, some organizations, such as the U.S. Air Force, are considering candidates' emotional intelligence when making key placement decisions.[79] Still other organizations, such as Hong Kong Telecom, are even training employees in ways of boosting their emotional intelligence. Although emotional intelligence is a new concept, it clearly holds a great deal of promise when it comes to understanding behavior in organizations. (Is there any connection between emotional intelligence and the growing tendency of companies to hold meetings electronically rather than face-to-face? Perhaps so. For a discussion of this issue, see the OB in an E-World section above.)

Successful intelligence: Adding creativity to the mix. That entrepreneurs play a major role in generating wealth for their societies, as well as themselves, is clear. In fact, in the United States, the new jobs created by start-up companies more than made up for the large cuts in number of employees made by large, existing companies during the 1980s and 1990s. And this, in turn, contributed substantially to the prosperity enjoyed by

American society during those decades.[81] But what sets entrepreneurs—and especially, successful ones—apart from other persons?

Although we don't yet have a firm or final answer to these questions, some experts contend that part of the answer lies in what is known as **successful intelligence**—intelligence that represents a good balance between cognitive intelligence (IQ), practical intelligence, and creative intelligence. Creative intelligence, in turn, involves the ability to think flexibly and to be ahead of the pack. As we will describe in Chapter 14, creative thinkers see alternative ways of defining and solving problems and these are the kind of people who recognize opportunities others often overlook.[82] Accordingly, this is an essential ingredient in entrepreneurial success.

Why do entrepreneurs need successful intelligence to be effective? Because any one or even two of the varieties of intelligence we have discussed will not be enough. Creative intelligence allows would-be entrepreneurs to come up with new ideas—but they also need analytical intelligence to evaluate these ideas and decide whether they are any good, and practical intelligence to be able to turn the ideas into actual businesses. To this, we would add that they also need some aspects of emotional intelligence to generate enthusiasm for their ideas among others, to make a good impression on them, and so on. Recent evidence suggests that such abilities—sometimes known as *social competence* (the ability to interact effectively with others)—is indeed closely related to entrepreneurs' success.[83] Specifically, entrepreneurs who are especially adept at perceiving others' emotions accurately and at expressing their own emotions clearly earned significantly higher income from their businesses than entrepreneurs who were lower on these skills.

It appears that part of the answer to the question: "Why are some entrepreneurs more successful than others?" does indeed involve social competence, which can be viewed as an important aspect of successful intelligence. We should add that social competence is important in many other business contexts, too—from making a good impression on others in job interviews (see Chapter 2) to closing deals during negotiations (see Chapter 11). And as suggested by the cartoon in Figure 3.9, people who are lacking such skills tend to experience less positive outcomes in many areas of life!

successful intelligence
Intelligence that represents a good balance between cognitive intelligence (IQ), practical intelligence, and creative intelligence.

FIGURE 3.9

The Costs of Poor Social Skills
The man in this cartoon is demonstrating what most of us would describe as very poor social skills. What will he experience as a result of these poor skills? Nothing very positive, we're sure!
(*Source:* Reprinted with permission of Cartoonbank.com. *The New Yorker* Collection.)

"It's better than my mother's cooking but not as good as my first wife's."

Other cognitive abilities. Although various types of intelligence are important, as we have noted, they are not the only types of cognitive abilities that matter when it comes to behavior in organizations. There also are several more specific aspects of cognitive functioning that are related to job performance. Among these are the following:

- *Perceptual speed:* The ability to quickly recognize similarities and differences in visual stimuli (e.g., a designer recognizing irregular patterns in a fabric).
- *Number aptitude:* The ability to work with numbers in a quick and accurate manner (e.g., an accountant spotting an error in a financial report).
- *Spatial visualization:* The ability to imagine how various objects will look when rotated or moved in space (e.g., an architect planning a change in a building design).

Obviously, it is essential to match people to those jobs that best suit their abilities. Air traffic controllers must have good perceptual speed, comptrollers need good number aptitude, and engineers must be adept at spatial visualization. People who find that they lack the basic abilities to carry out their jobs usually recognize this early in their careers (if not on their own, then because others, often insensitively, point it out to them) and shift their careers in the direction of jobs that better match the abilities they do have (see Chapter 7).

Physical Abilities

When we speak of **physical abilities** we are referring to people's capacities to engage in the physical tasks required to perform a job. Although different jobs require different physical abilities, there are several types of physical abilities that are common to a wide variety of jobs. These include the following:

physical abilities
People's capacities to engage in the physical tasks required to perform a job.

- *Strength:* The capacity to exert physical force against various objects.
- *Flexibility:* The capacity to move one's body in an agile manner.
- *Stamina:* The capacity to endure physical activity over prolonged periods.
- *Speed:* The ability to move quickly.

If we were to consider all the jobs that people perform, it might be possible to identify those that require primarily intellectual abilities and those that require primarily physical abilities. For example, being a chemist in a research laboratory of a large company involves mainly intellectual abilities, whereas being a construction worker involves mainly physical abilities. In fact, though, almost all jobs require *both* cognitive and physical abilities for success. For example, one of us knows a woman who works as a DNA analyst for the state police. Her job is complex and requires many cognitive abilities. But she also must transfer fluids from one container to another over and over again—a job that becomes quite tiring and that requires considerable physical stamina. Similarly, consider a bricklayer who works in landscape construction. Although this job certainly requires physical abilities, it also requires a lot of careful thought—for example, in laying out decorative patterns in brick walks (see Figure 3.10).

This blending of cognitive and physical abilities also is required by many other jobs, so it is important for companies to consider this fact to protect the health and well-being of their employees. For example, administrative assistants and office workers of all types often must sit in specific postures, enter alpha-numeric characters at a computer keyboard, and/or stoop over files for hours at a stretch. Despite the fact that considerable flexibility is needed for such jobs, training in this important area is only rarely provided. Not surprisingly, research has shown that engaging in such tasks over prolonged periods can have adverse effects on health (especially when done improperly).[84] As recognition of this fact has grown, many companies have adopted procedures designed to promote the health and well-being of employees performing physical tasks. One clear example of such efforts is provided by the U.S. Postal Service (USPS), which has redesigned the leather mailbags used by letter carriers.

The design of these bags hasn't changed much in centuries, and this is unfortunate, because letter carriers throughout the world report that their mailbags are a cause of considerable discomfort. These bags are designed to carry heavy loads—a minimum of

FIGURE 3.10

Most Jobs Require a Mix of Cognitive and Physical Abilities
People working in research laboratories rely on many cognitive skills—but they also must perform a number of physical tasks that can be quite tiring (left photo). Similarly, bricklayers use many physical abilities, but they must also plan complex, decorative layouts, which involves cognitive abilities (right photo).

35 pounds and often much more. And because they rest on one shoulder, they also cause a large number of muscle and back injuries.[85]

This fact has led the USPS to fund research focused on the task of designing a better mailbag—one that is less likely to cause back strain and other injuries to Postal Service employees. With this in mind, the USPS conducted a study comparing two new and improved designs to the traditional mailbag.[86] One of the new designs involved having the mailbag supported at the waist by a belt. The other mailbag had two pouches and was supported by both shoulders. The three designs (the original design and the two new ones) were compared by measuring muscle fatigue among male volunteers both before and after using each mailbag for an hour.

The results were clear: Although all three bags produced some fatigue, the standard bag produced significantly *more* fatigue than the other two designs. The conclusion? The standard mailbag can definitely be improved. As a result, the USPS is currently considering a change to the improved designs. And it seems likely that if this shift is actually made the incidence of back strain and back injuries among employees will drop dramatically. Whether or not the change is implemented is up to the USPS, of course. However, we cannot resist the temptation to point out that this is a compelling illustration of how the findings of careful research can be used to make useful recommendations about company policy—and to improve outcomes that are important to employees, including their job satisfaction, performance, and health.

SUMMARY AND REVIEW OF LEARNING OBJECTIVES

1. Define personality and describe its role in the study of organizational behavior.
Personality is the unique and relatively stable pattern of behavior, thoughts, and emotions shown by individuals. Along with abilities (the capacity to perform various tasks) and various situational factors, personality determines behavior in organizations. This idea is reflected by the interactionist perspective that is widely accepted in the field of organizational behavior today.

2. Identify the big five dimensions of personality and describe what is meant by positive and negative affectivity.
The big five dimensions of personality are conscientiousness, extraversion, agreeableness, emotional stability, and openness to experience. Two of these dimensions, consci-

entiousness and emotional stability, have been found to be good predictors of success in many different jobs. Positive and negative affectivity refer to stable tendencies for people to experience positive or negative moods at work, respectively.

3. Describe the Type A and Type B behavior patterns and describe the nature of Machiavellianism.

People showing the Type A behavior pattern are highly competitive, irritable, and always in a hurry. Such persons tend to perform better than those with the opposite pattern—Type B—on tasks requiring speed. However, they may perform less well than Type Bs on tasks requiring considered judgment. People who adopt a manipulative approach to their relations with others are described as being high in Machiavellianism (known as high Machs). They are not influenced by considerations of loyalty, friendship, or ethics. Instead, they simply do whatever is needed to get their way.

4. Define achievement motivation (or need for achievement) and describe the difference between learning, performance, and avoidance goal orientations.

Achievement motivation (or need for achievement) refers to the strength of an individual's desire to excel—to succeed at difficult tasks and to do them better than others. A learning goal orientation involves the desire to succeed in order to master new skills. A performance goal orientation involves the desire to succeed in order to demonstrate one's competence to others. An avoidance goal orientation involves the desire to succeed to avoid criticism from others or appearing to be incompetent.

5. Describe the difference between morning and evening persons and the relevance of this individual difference to on-the-job behavior.

Morning persons are individuals who feel most energetic early in the day. Evening persons are those who feel most energetic at night. People tend to do their best work during that portion of the day that they prefer and when they are most energetic.

6. Define cognitive intelligence, practical intelligence, emotional intelligence, and successful intelligence.

Cognitive intelligence is the ability to understand complex ideas, to adapt effectively to the environment, to learn from experience, to engage in various forms of reasoning, and to overcome obstacles by careful thought. It is what we traditionally have in mind when we refer to intelligence. However, other forms of intelligence have been recognized as well, and these play important roles in organizational functioning. These are practical intelligence, which is the ability to come up with effective ways of getting things done, and emotional intelligence, which is a cluster of abilities relating to the emotional or "feeling" side of life. An additional kind of intelligence, successful intelligence, involves a combination of creative intelligence, analytical intelligence, practical intelligence, and some aspects of emotional intelligence.

POINTS TO PONDER

Questions for Review

1. Why might two individuals whose personalities are very similar behave differently in a given situation?
2. How does a close person–job fit contribute to good performance?

3. What is the difference between being in a good mood and having the characteristic of positive affectivity?
4. If you had to choose someone for the job of accountant, would you prefer an individual who is high in conscientiousness, high in openness to experience, or high in extraversion? Suppose that you were hiring someone to perform a job that required very fast performance. Would you prefer to hire a Type A or Type B person? Why?
5. How does having low self-efficacy interfere with task performance?
6. Why are persons high in self-monitoring so effective in boundary-spanning positions? Can you think of jobs that they would *not* do very well?
7. If you suspect that someone with whom you are dealing is high in Machiavellianism, what steps should you take to protect yourself from this person?
8. Would you prefer to hire employees who are high in learning goal orientation or performance goal orientation? Why?
9. Suppose that you are a morning person—you feel most alert and energetic early in the day. What steps can you take to make this characteristic a plus for your personal productivity?
10. Successful entrepreneurs are often persons who did not excel in school. Can you explain why this might be so?
11. What is practical intelligence? How does it differ from emotional intelligence?

Experiential Questions

1. Have you ever worked for an organization that selected future employees by means of psychological tests? If so, do you think the tests made sense—for instance, did they really measure what they were supposed to measure?
2. Have you ever known someone you considered to be high in extraversion? If so, what kind of jobs do you think they would perform best? Worst?
3. Where do you think you stand with respect to self-efficacy? Are you fairly confident that you can accomplish most tasks you set out to do? Or do you have doubts about your ability to succeed in many situations?
4. Have you ever encountered someone who was very high in cognitive intelligence (the kind that IQ tests measure) but low in practical intelligence? How could you tell?

Questions to Analyze

1. Although behavior in work settings usually is influenced both by the traits people possess and the situations in which they work, we often tend to assume that traits are more important—that people behave as they do because they are "that kind of person." Do you think this tendency can lead to serious errors in terms of understanding others—errors that can prove costly to organizations? How?
2. Some employees never complain and seem to be satisfied with their jobs, no matter what these jobs involve. Others, in contrast, complain frequently and seem to be dissatisfied with any job they hold. Do you think such persons differ in terms of negative and positive affectivity?
3. Organizations fail for a lot of reasons—many of them economic. But suppose an organization collected a sizable number of employees who were high in Machiavellianism and many who were Type A. Do you think this "mix" of people might adversely affect the organization's performance?
4. Suppose you had to choose—you could be high in cognitive intelligence, emotional intelligence, *or* practical intelligence. On which of these dimensions would you want to be highest? Why?

INDIVIDUAL EXERCISE

Measuring Your Own Self-Monitoring

As you read about the personality characteristic of self-monitoring, did you suspect that you are high or low on this trait? In other words, are you someone who is, in a sense, capable of being a very different person in different situations? If so, then you may be a high self-monitor. To see where you stand on this important dimension, complete and score this questionnaire by following the directions.

Directions

For each of the following statements, indicate whether it is true (or mostly true) or false (or mostly false) about yourself. If a statement is true (or mostly true) enter the letter *T* in the blank space to the left of it. If it is false (or mostly false), enter the letter *F.*

_____ 1. It is difficult for me to imitate the actions of other people.

_____ 2. My behavior usually reflects my true feelings, attitude, or beliefs.

_____ 3. At parties and social gatherings, I always try to say and do things others will like.

_____ 4. I can give a speech on almost any topic—even ones about which I know very little.

_____ 5. I would probably make a very poor actor.

_____ 6. Sometimes I put on a show to impress or entertain people.

_____ 7. I find it difficult to argue for ideas in which I don't believe.

_____ 8. In different situations and with different people I often act in very different ways.

_____ 9. I would not change my attitudes or my actions in order to please other people or win their approval.

_____ 10. Sometimes other people think I am experiencing stronger emotions than I really am.

_____ 11. I am not especially good at making other people like me.

_____ 12. If I have a strong reason for doing so, I can look others in the eye and lie with a straight face.

_____ 13. I make up my own mind about movies, books, or music; I don't rely on the advice of my friends in these respects.

_____ 14. At a party, I usually let others keep the jokes and stories going.

_____ 15. I'm not always the person I seem to be.

Scoring

1. To obtain your score, use the following key. Give yourself one point for each of your answers that agrees with the key:
   1. F, 2. F, 3. T, 4. T, 5. F, 6. T, 7. F, 8. T, 9. F, 10. T, 11. F, 12. T, 13. F, 14. F, 15. T
2. Add the number of items you answered according to the key.
3. If your total was 8 or higher, your are probably high in self-monitoring. If it was 4 or lower, you are relatively low on this dimension.

Questions for Discussion

1. How did you score? How did this compare to others in your class?
2. Is being a high self-monitor always a "plus"? Or can you think of situations in which being high on this trait might have a negative impact on one's career or job performance?
3. Suppose you were hiring employees for each of the following jobs. Would you prefer people who are high or low in self-monitoring for each of these positions? (a) salesperson (b) engineer (c) accountant (d) human resources manager

GROUP EXERCISE

Machiavellianism in Action: The $10 Game

People who are high in Machiavellianism (high Machs) often come out ahead in dealing with others because they are true pragmatists. That is, they tend to be willing to do or say whatever it takes to win or to get their way. Several questionnaires exist for measuring Machiavellianism as a personality trait. However, tendencies in this direction also can be observed in many face-to-face situations. The following exercise offers one useful means for observing individual differences with respect to Machiavellianism.

Directions

1. The class is divided into groups of three.
2. The three people in each group are handed a sheet with the following instructions. Imagine that I have placed a stack of ten $1 bills on the table in front of you. This money will belong to *any two of you* who can decide how to divide it.
3. Groups are allowed up to 10 minutes to reach a decision on this task.
4. Each group is then asked whether they reached a decision and, if so, what it was. In each group, it probably will be found that two people agreed on how to divide the money, leaving the third "out in the cold."

Questions for Discussion

1. How did the two-person groups form? Was there a particular person in each group who was largely responsible for the formation of the winning coalition?
2. Why did the third person get left out of the agreement? What did this person say or do—or fail to say or do—that led to his or her being omitted from the two-person coalition that divided the money?
3. Do you think that actions in this situation are related to Machiavellianism? How? In other words, what particular things did anyone do that you took as an indicator of being a high Mach?
4. How can people low in Machiavellianism protect themselves from being left "out in the cold" in such situations?

WEB SURFING EXERCISE

Person–Job Fit

Go to the Web site of any large organization and search for information relating to its hiring practices. Try to find information on the specific skills, abilities, and traits the company is seeking in its employees.

1. Is such information available?
2. Are any of the skills, abilities, or traits mentioned related to the ones discussed in this chapter?
3. If so, do you think the company is seeking an appropriate mix of personal characteristics in employees? (This may depend on its business and the industry in which it operates.)

The Big Five Dimensions of Personality

Use any major search engine to search for sites dealing with the big five dimensions of personality. Then, after you locate these sites, refine your search to look for information about their relationships to behavior in work settings.

1. From what kinds of sources did you find "hits"? Were they from educational institutions, consulting firms, or other sources?

2. Did any of these sites include actual tests that you could take? If so, was the site sponsored by a company selling personality assessment services?
3. Did you find any sites relating the big five dimensions to organizational behavior? If so, what kind of information did they contain? For instance, which dimensions of the big five were mentioned most? What kinds of work behavior were associated with them?

PRACTICING OB

The Good Idea That Failed

An entrepreneur has a very good idea for a new product; there is nothing like it on the market, and all his friends think it can't miss. Yet, he seems unable to find the financing he needs to get started, despite the fact that the economy is strong and many venture capitalists are looking for projects to fund. Many venture capitalists have expressed considerable interest in his business plan, but after interviewing him, they indicate that they do not want to be involved. He is starting to get discouraged and may soon give up the entire project.

1. Why do you think he is unable to get financing for his idea—is it something about him, something about the idea, something about the economy?
2. If you think it is something about him that is causing his difficulties, what precisely is it? (Hint: Is he lacking in motivation? Some kind of intelligence? Does he possess the wrong pattern of personality traits?)
3. If you believe that his problems stem from something about him as a person, can this "something" (whatever it is) be changed?

CASE IN POINT

Nancy's Quiche: Where People Skills Really Matter

Nancy Mueller was viewed by her friends as a good all-around cook, but her specialty was the little snacks people love to eat during cocktail hours. Her miniature quiches, especially, were always a hit. After listening to people praise these snacks for years, Nancy began to wonder: "Maybe there's a market for them." She looked around and literally tasted the competition stocked by local groceries, and concluded that she was really on to something. So she set up shop in her own kitchen and began baking "Nancy's Quiches." After baking several hundred, she boxed them, loaded them into the family station wagon, and set off to find her customers. At first, she reports, local stores were reluctant to try her products; after all, they already had national brands in their freezer sections, so why take a chance on her small, unknown company? But—and this is an important point—Nancy was persistent and also persuasive. "I got them to taste my quiches," she says, and then, "most would realize that they were much better than what the stores were currently selling." Customers, too, quickly caught on, and sales took off.

The rest is history—happy history. Nancy moved her operation to a small store, then to a larger one, next to a small factory, and finally to a large plant, equipped with all the latest high-tech systems for food preparation and baking. Currently, her company has 300 employees and produces 50 tons of product per day. It is the largest processor and marketer of frozen quiche products in the world. To what does she attribute her tremendous success? Ms. Mueller's answer is a single word: passion. By this she means strong belief in one's products and ideas. As she puts it: "You've got to know deep down in your heart that it will work—that you have a great product and a great idea." And in her view, people skills, too, are vital. "Getting along with people is absolutely crucial—

the most important skills a manager or entrepreneur can have. If I didn't like people and communicate with them well, I wouldn't have been able to hire the people I wanted, attract the customers I needed, or do anything else that was important to running, and growing, my business."

Nancy was chosen as the "Entrepreneur of the Year" at the university where one of us works, and she impressed everyone she met as being a warm, friendly, outgoing, and very likeable person—someone who can, indeed, get along well with others in many different respects. In fact, everyone who met her had the same reaction: "I'd buy a quiche—or anything else—from her anytime!" Recently, Nancy sold her company to a very large corporation for a figure around $500 million. So, do people skills matter? In a sense, Nancy Mueller is the charming, impressive proof that they do!

Critical Thinking Questions

1. Nancy Mueller is certainly high in emotional intelligence and practical intelligence. Do you think she is high in successful intelligence, too?
2. Suppose Nancy Mueller did not possess such great "people skills." Do you think her company still would have been a success? Why or why not?
3. If you had the choice to be high in one kind of intelligence—cognitive, emotional, practical, or successful—which would you prefer? Why? Which is more important to the work you currently do or that you expect to be doing in the future?

Emotions and Stress on the Job

4

LEARNING OBJECTIVES

After reading this chapter, you should be able to:
1. Distinguish between emotions and moods.
2. Describe the effects of emotions and moods on behavior in organizations.
3. Describe ways that people manage their emotions in organizations.
4. Identify the major causes and consequences of stress.
5. Identify various organizational resources for managing stress.
6. Identify various ways that we can manage our own stress as individuals.

■ PREVIEW CASE
SEPH BARNARD: AN ENTREPRENEUR "TIRED AND TRUE"

If you need an occasional blank cassette tape for your personal camcorder, audio tape deck, or VCR, you probably pick it up at your nearest discount store or supermarket. But where do radio and TV stations and professional video production companies shop for the miles and miles of high-quality tape they use? For about a decade, many have been purchasing such products from Tape Resources, Inc., the Virginia Beach, Virginia–based supplier of audio and video tape to the industry.

Although this company now has 13 full-time employees and does $5.3 million in annual sales, it wasn't always thriving. In fact, when Seph Barnard, the president of the company, first bought it in 1993, the firm was in deep financial trouble. Tape Resources needed Barnard's full-time attention, and he proved he was up to the task of turning it around. Acknowledging that "the thing that gives me enjoyment in life is the challenge," Barnard transformed the company into one of the 500 fastest-growing companies in the United States.

The company's strategy is straightforward: It doesn't compete with larger companies on price but instead, offers great service—free, same-day shipping of any of the 250 brands and lengths of blank tapes and disks kept in stock. To ensure high-quality customer service, Barnard kept close tabs on all business operations himself. Not content to rest on the company's success, he worked tirelessly on everything from sending out checks and examining invoices to even assembling the shelves in the company's warehouse. If there was something to be done, he did it. With 18-hour days and no vacations, the company consumed his life. And there

> **If there was something to be done, he did it. With 18-hour days and no vacations, the company consumed his life.**

was no escaping it when he got home, either. Barnard's wife, Dawn-Marie, was in charge of Tape Resources' human resources department. Barnard characterized himself as being "really focused." To say the least! You might even say he was driven—if not obsessed—with success.

Unfortunately, Barnard's relentless schedule took its toll on him. He never had a moment's rest. Even while eating dinner, he'd be mulling things over in his mind. He had no hobbies and virtually no social life. No matter where he was physically, mentally he was at work. Exhausted, he became remote—so much so that he began working at home, where Dawn-Marie often fielded his phone calls. Things needed to change, and they did one day when Barnard received a letter from a prominent investment-banking firm indicating that a large office supply company was interested in buying his business.

This could have been "the out" that many would have taken in this situation—especially considering the $2 million it would have put in Barnard's pocket. But he didn't take it. Although selling the company would have solved some of his personal worries, it probably would have meant destroying much of what he worked so hard to create. He couldn't bring himself to do this. Instead, he chose to hand over the reins of the company to David Durovy, the company's sales manager, and he empowered the other employees to make their own decisions. This freed Barnard to take a sabbatical. He'll travel for six months or so, and come back to Virginia Beach refreshed and renewed. What will he do when he comes back? He plans to check in on Tape Resources only occasionally. "I'm starting to recognize there's a time to hand a company over and stand back," he says, acknowledging that this time has come. What then? Barnard freely admits that he'll probably do what he really likes most—start up another company (or two, or three)!

Clearly, many things about Seph Barnard stand out as special. One of his most unique qualities is his capacity to express his emotions toward other things and people—whether showing his feelings toward Tape Resources as an entity or the loyal employees who have stuck with him over the years. The nature of people's feelings, as reflected in their *emotions* and *mood,* is of vital importance in our everyday lives on the job. As such, it is one of the two major topics covered in this chapter.

This case also reveals something else about Barnard that is crucial: He worked so hard that he gave up everything else in his life, which he knew wasn't healthy. After a few years of this, he decided not to sell the company but to change his role in it, leaving daily operations in the hands of his sales manager and decision making in the hands of the employees themselves. This was Seph Barnard's way of keeping his sanity in the face of the high level of stress that pervaded his daily life. Given its relevance to personality and emotions, *stress* is the second major topic we will consider in this chapter.

We begin this chapter with an overview of emotions and mood in organizations, describing their basic nature and the important role they play. Building on this, we will move on to the very practical topic of managing emotions in organizations. Then, in the final two major sections, we will describe the nature of stress, especially as it affects us on the job, focusing closely on specific steps that can be taken to minimize its often harmful effects.

EMOTIONS AND MOOD IN ORGANIZATIONS

If you think about any work experiences you have had, it's easy to recognize how our everyday feelings—emotions and moods—play an important role in how we think and act. If emotions and moods seem like they may be trivial, it's simply because their effects are so widespread that we take them for granted. However, their impact on the way we work can be considerable.[1] Consider, for example, the following.

- It was a beautiful, sunny day—the kind that inspired Mark to come up with lots of new ideas for his clients.
- Janet was so upset about not making any progress on her sales report that she left her desk and went to the gym to work out.
- It was a special day for Kim. She was so pleased that Michael agreed to marry her that she made her way through her delivery route in half the usual time—and with a lively spring in her step.

Not only do scientists acknowledge that people's feelings at any given time are important but they also recognize that two different kinds of feelings are involved—*emotions* and *mood*. Although you certainly have experienced different emotional states and different moods in your life, and have seen them in others, you shouldn't assume that you know exactly how they influence behavior in organizations. As you will see, each of these states is far more complex than you might imagine.

The Basic Nature of Emotions

By definition, **emotions** are overt reactions that express feelings about events. You get angry when a colleague takes advantage of you. You become sad when your best friend leaves to take a new job. And you become afraid of what the future holds when a larger firm merges with the company in which you've worked for 15 years. These are all examples of emotional reactions. Despite their obvious differences, all emotions share four key properties.

emotions
Overt reactions that express feelings about events.

1. *Emotions always have an object.* Something or someone triggers emotions. For example, you may recognize that your boss made you angry when he falsely accused you of making a mistake or that your boyfriend surprised you with an engagement ring. In each case, there is someone who caused your emotional reaction.
2. *There are six major categories of emotions.* People do not have an infinite (or even a very large) number of different emotions. Rather, research has shown that all emotions fall into the following six major categories: anger, fear, joy, love, sadness, and surprise. These also have associated with them the various subcategories shown in Figure 4.1.[2]
3. *Expression of major emotions is universal.* People throughout the world generally portray the same emotions by using the same facial expressions. In fact, even people living in remote parts of the world tend to express the same emotions in the same manner.[3] As a result, we can do a pretty good job of recognizing the emotional states of others if we pay attention to their facial expressions.
4. *Culture determines how and when people express emotions.* Although people throughout the world generally express their emotions in the same manner, informal standards govern the degree to which it is acceptable for them to do so.[4] These expectations are known as **display rules.** For example, Italian cultural norms accept public displays of emotion (e.g., hugging good-bye at the airport or yelling at one

FIGURE 4.1
Major Categories of Emotion and Associated Subcategories
Scientists have found it useful to categorize people's emotions into the six major categories (and associated subcategories) identified here.
(*Source:* Based on information reported by Weiss & Cropanzano, 1996; see Note 2.)

Anger	Fear	Joy	Love	Sadness	Surprise
• Disgust	• Alarm	• Cheerfulness	• Affection	• Disappointment	[No subcategories]
• Envy	• Anxiety	• Contentment	• Longing	• Neglect	
• Exasperation		• Enthrallment	• Lust	• Sadness	
• Irritation		• Optimism		• Shame	
• Rage		• Pride		• Suffering	
• Torment		• Relief		• Sympathy	
		• Zest			

OB IN AN E-WORLD

USING "EMOTICONS" TO EXPRESS EMOTIONS IN E-MAIL: DO THOSE SMILEY FACES MAKE ANY DIFFERENCE?

Today, e-mail is one of the most common forms of communication, and some predict that it will even surpass face-to-face communication in popularity in the near future. As useful and as indispensable as e-mail has become, people sometimes find it frustrating to try to express their emotions in an e-mail message. After all, traditional e-mail is limited to alphanumeric characters and lacks the nonverbal information that makes face-to-face communication so rich (see Chapter 9). After all, although you can change the tone of your voice or make a face to express how you feel about something, it's harder to do this using only a keyboard.

In recent years, however, people have, rather ingeniously, developed simple graphic representations of facial expressions

to express emotions. Known as **emoticons,** short for "emotional icons," these are created by typing characters such as commas, hyphens, and parentheses, which are viewed by tilting one's head to the left (treating left as top). The most common emoticons are as follows:

:-) smile

:-(frown

;-) wink

People generally use emoticons to qualify their emotions in important ways, such as to communicate sarcasm. For example, the presence of the smiley face in the message, "he's really smart

---

emoticons

Simple graphic representations of facial expressions created by typing characters such as commas, hyphens, and parentheses used to express emotions.

display rules

Cultural norms about the appropriate ways to express emotions.

mood

An unfocused, relatively mild feeling that exists as background to our daily experiences.

another in public) whereas cultural norms frown on such public displays in Great Britain, encouraging people there to "tone down" their emotional displays. (Expressing emotions is particularly challenging when communicating online. However, as you will see in the OB in an E-World section above, people have developed ingenious ways to overcome this inherent limitation.)

The Basic Nature of Mood

In contrast to emotions, which are highly specific and intense, we also have feelings that are more diffuse in scope, which are known as *moods*. Scientists define **mood** as an unfocused, relatively mild feeling that exists as background to our daily experiences. Whereas we are sure to recognize the emotions we are feeling, moods are more subtle and difficult to detect. For example, you may say that you are in a good mood or a bad mood, but this isn't as focused as saying that you are experiencing a certain emotion, such as anger or sadness.

Moods, as we all know, fluctuate rapidly, sometimes widely, during the course of a day. Whereas favorable feedback from our bosses may make us feel good, harsh criticism may put us in a bad mood. Such temporary shifts in feeling *states*—short-term differences in the way we feel—are only partly responsible for the mood that we demonstrate. Superimposed over these passing conditions are also more stable personality *traits*—consistent differences between our predispositions toward experiencing positive or negative affect, as we discussed in Chapter 3. Mood, in other words, is a combination of both who we are because of our personalities and because of the conditions we face.[7]

Not surprisingly, then, the moods we experience can be based on our individual experiences (e.g., receiving a raise), as well as the general characteristics of our work groups or organizations (e.g., the extent to which they are upbeat, energetic, and enthusiastic). For example, the importance of having fun at work is emphasized at such companies as Southwest Airlines and Ben and Jerry's Homemade Ice Cream.[8] No wonder people working for these companies are generally in a good mood. Being in a good

:-)" may be used to connote that the person in question is really not so smart at all.

Are these common emoticons really effective in qualifying messages as intended? Recent research has revealed that emoticons do *not* always qualify the meanings of written messages as the sender desires.[5] For example, a negative message accompanied by a wink or a frown is not seen as being any more sarcastic or negative in tone than the words by themselves. For example, the study found that sending the message, "That class was awful ;-)" was perceived to be as sarcastic as, "That class was awful." Likewise, saying, "That class was awful :-(" was perceived as negatively as, "That class was awful." In the case of positive statements, the effects were interesting. Saying, "That class was great :-)" suggested that the speaker was happier than saying, "that class was great," but it did not send the message that the class was any better. In other words, emoticons don't always have the effects that the communicator intended. One possible reason for this is that emoticons tend to be overused. As a result, their impact has diminished over time.

Additional research has shown some interesting sex differences in the use of emoticons.[6] In general, women use emoticons more frequently than men. However, when men are communicating with women, they use emoticons more frequently than they do when they are communicating with other men. This is in keeping with research showing that in general men feel more comfortable expressing their emotions to women than to other men. Interestingly, men and women use emoticons differently. Whereas women use emoticons to be humorous, men use them to be teasing and sarcastic. Yeah, right ;-).

In conclusion, you should be careful using emoticons because they don't always do a good job of getting your message across. In fact, using emoticons is more likely to send a message about the gender of the communicator than it is to qualify the emotional meaning of the message itself.

mood is nice, of course, but does it have any effect on job performance? We now will address this question.

Emotions, Mood, and Job Performance

Research has found that emotions and mood play an important role on the job insofar as they influence job performance.[9] Will you work at your best when you are in a highly emotional state? Probably not. Someone who is excited because she is about to go on vacation or attend an exciting sporting event the next day might not be focusing on the job as completely as she otherwise might when in a less emotional state.

The negative impact of emotional states is even greater in the case of negative emotions (see Figure 4.2). Consider, for example, an employee who is unhappy and upset because he received an unsatisfactory performance rating. This individual may be expected to be so distraught that he will lose the capacity to pay attention and become distracted from his work. Not only is this likely to impede task performance, but it also is likely to interfere with the potentially useful feedback that this individual might receive from the supervisor giving the evaluation. For this reason, managers should not even try to get messages across to people who are upset. In the case of the poorly performing employee, it may be best to wait until another time when the employee can be better focused to help him learn ways of improving.

It probably comes as no surprise that differences in people's characteristic levels of mood also play an important role in organizational behavior. For example, research has found that people showing high positive affectivity do a better job of making decisions than those showing high negative affectivity (recall our discussion of positive and negative affectivity in Chapter 3). Specifically, they made decisions that were more accurate, more important to the group's effectiveness, and were rated by experts as having greater managerial potential.

Research also has shown that our moods influence the way we behave on the job in several important respects. First, researchers have shown that mood is related to mem-

FIGURE 4.2
Emotional Barriers to Selling Life Insurance
Life insurance is a $21 billion a year business for American Express, but selling policies brings unique emotional challenges. Not only don't customers like to talk about their own demise, but also they generally distrust life insurance salespeople. For many years, American Express salespeople generally disliked selling life insurance policies because consumers' reactions made them feel uncomfortable. To overcome these problems, the company trained salespeople to become more aware of their emotions. This, in turn, helped them cope more effectively with their feelings, which, in turn, boosted sales.

mood congruence

The tendency to recall positive things when you are in a good mood and to recall negative things when you are in a bad mood.

ory. Specifically, we know that being in a positive mood helps people recall positive things and being in a negative mood helps people recall negative things.[10] This idea is known as **mood congruence.** For example, if you go to work while you're in a good mood, chances are that this will help you remember those things on the job that also put you in a good mood, such as the friendly relationships you have with your coworkers. Likewise, if you are in a bad mood, you are likely to recall negative things associated with work, such as a recent fight with your boss.

Mood also biases the way we evaluate people and things. For example, people report greater satisfaction with their jobs while they are in a good mood than while they are in a bad mood.[11] Being in a good mood also leads people to judge others' work more positively. The practical advice is clear: Make sure your boss is in a good mood before he or she conducts your annual performance evaluation. It just may make a difference!

Finally, it is important to note that mood strongly affects the extent to which people help each other, cooperate with each other, and refrain from behaving aggressively (forms of behavior we will discuss in more detail in Chapter 11). People who are in a good mood also tend to be more generous and are inclined to help their fellow workers who may need their assistance. So, if you need help with an important project on the job, it may be in your best interest to approach someone who is in a good mood. People who are in a good mood also are inclined to work carefully with others to resolve conflicts with them, whereas people in a bad mood are likely to keep those conflicts brewing. As a result, if someone is in a bad mood, this might not be the best time to sit down with her to discuss ways of settling an argument she is having with you. Let it rest for now—or, better yet, help put that person in a good mood before approaching this issue. With this in mind we now turn our attention to the matter of managing emotions.

MANAGING EMOTIONS IN ORGANIZATIONS

As we discussed in Chapter 3 when describing *emotional intelligence,* emotions are important on the job insofar as people who are good at "reading" and understanding emotions in others, and who are able to regulate their own emotions, tend to have an edge when it comes to dealing with others.[12] As we will now describe, this is only one possible way in which people manage their emotions in organizations.

Emotional Dissonance and Emotional Labor

Imagine that you are flight attendant for a major airline. After a long flight with rude passengers, you finally reach your destination. You feel tired and annoyed, but you do not have the option of expressing how you really feel. You don't even have the luxury of acting neutrally and expressing nothing at all. Instead, you are expected to act peppy and cheerful, smile and thank the passengers for choosing the airline, and cheerfully say good-bye (more like "b'bye") to them as they exit the plane. The conflict between the emotion you feel (anger) and the emotion you are required to express (happiness) may take its toll on your well-being. This example illustrates a kind of situation that is all too typical—one in which you are required to display emotions on the job that are inconsistent with how you actually feel. This phenomenon, known as **emotional dissonance,** can be a significant source of work-related stress (the major topic that we will discuss later in this chapter).[13] Emotional dissonance is likely to occur in situations in which there are strong expectations regarding the emotions you are expected to display by virtue of your job requirements. Our flight attendant example illustrates this point. The same applies to salesclerks, bank tellers, tour guides, and just about anyone who provides services to the public at large.

emotional dissonance
Inconsistencies between the emotions we feel and the emotions we express.

When emotional dissonance occurs, people often have to try very hard to ensure that they display the appropriate emotions. The psychological effort involved in doing this is referred to as **emotional labor.** If you ever find yourself "biting your tongue"— that is, holding back from saying what you want to say—you are expending a great deal of emotional labor.

emotional labor
The psychological effort involved in holding back one's true emotions.

One of the biggest challenges that people face in an effort to avoid emotional dissonance (and expending the emotional labor associated with it) occurs whenever they find themselves dealing with diverse groups of others. This was the case, for example, in Salt Lake City when the Winter Olympics was held there in 2002. Most hotel clerks and taxi drivers in this inland city were not used to interacting with people from foreign countries. This often left them feeling frustrated, grumpy, and irritated when they faced the challenges of interacting with others who had different customs or who did not speak their language (see Figure 4.3). However, it was important for them to present themselves in a favorable manner so as to create a positive impression of their city, state, and country. To avoid emotional dissonance while also providing the best possible service, many of the area's service providers received special training in advance of the games.[14]

Organizational Compassion: Managing Emotion in Times of Trauma

Emotions clearly are very important whenever some sort of tragedy occurs that affects a company. This may happen, for example, when a beloved leader passes away, such as

FIGURE 4.3

Interacting with Foreigners: An Emotional Challenge of Olympic Proportions
Service workers from Salt Lake City had to work hard at controlling their emotions when facing the frustrations of interacting with foreign visitors to their area for the 2002 Winter Olympics. Although the emotional labor spent may have been considerable, the effort was necessary to promote a positive image of their city, state, and country.

when Dave Thomas, founder of Wendy's, died in 2001. A natural disaster might cause the closing of businesses, such as when the 1994 earthquake that struck Northridge, California, forced the temporary closing of two Macy's stores. A financial scandal, such as what happened at Enron in 2002, might knock a once mighty company into oblivion. And, of course, we cannot forget how the horrific tragedies of September 11, 2001, led to the destruction of hundreds of businesses and the disruption of thousands more in New York City. In these and other such disasters, the emotions of everyone in the workplace run high as employees at all levels struggle collectively to deal with the trauma.

Although little, if anything, can be done to avoid certain disasters, fortunately, there is something that leaders and managers can do to help everyone involved return to business as usual.[15] Specifically, company officials should create an environment in which people can express their emotions and in which they can do something to alleviate their own and others' suffering. In other words, they should express **organizational compassion.**

organizational compassion
Steps taken by organizational officials to alleviate the suffering of its employees or others.

To illustrate what we mean, let's compare the reactions of officials from two different companies to the devastation that followed when terrorist planes destroyed the World Trade Center. On September 11, 2001, Edmond English, the president of TJX, a company that lost seven employees on one of the planes that struck one of the towers, showed incredible compassion. As soon as information became available, he gathered his staff together to confirm that their colleagues were among the victims. The very day of the attacks he brought in grief counselors to help the employees. He chartered planes to bring the victims' relatives to company headquarters (near Boston) and greeted each family member in person. And he also told the workers that they could take time off as needed. Most did not. Instead, they opted to come to work and help each other through the trauma. The steps that Mr. English took enabled TJX employees to express their emotions and to alleviate their own and their colleagues' suffering. As a result, the company got back to normal relatively quickly. Because people were able to bring their pain to the office, rather than being forced to ignore or suppress it, they were able to get back to work.

By contrast, let's consider what occurred at a publishing company close to ground zero, whose officers opted to conduct business as usual. They held regularly scheduled meetings and provided little or no support for those seeking to express their emotions. Terrified and confused employees showed up, but they couldn't concentrate on their work, as you might imagine. Even more seriously, the message that the company sent about its lack of compassion during these trying times took its toll on the loyalty of the employees. After all, who would want to work for a company that shows such callous disregard for their emotional well-being? Obviously, organizational compassion is important.

Experts recommend that organization leaders carefully assess the extent to which they demonstrate compassion in times of need. To help guide such efforts, they recommend considering the factors described in Figure 4.4. Specifically, compassionate reactions should (1) cover a broad scope of activities,

HOW TO DO IT

COPING WITH THE EMOTIONAL FALLOUT OF TERRORISM: HOW CAN COMPANIES HELP?

In the aftermath of the September 11, 2001 terrorist strikes on the United States, millions of Americans who once felt safe at work suddenly felt vulnerable. Not only did they grieve for the thousands who died in the attacks, but they also experienced fear of future attacks—both from further airplane strikes and from deadly anthrax spores. Given the emotional fallout, companies found it necessary to cope in ways that they may never have considered earlier. According to Dr. Steven E. Hyman, former director of the National Institutes of Mental Health, there are several things companies can do to help.[16]

1. *Leaders should provide accurate information.* It is not always clear what to do, but whatever is being done to promote workplace safety should be communicated clearly to all.

2. *Encourage social interaction.* During periods of emotional stress, one of the most effective ways to cope is by interacting with others. Social networks provide comfort and support, reducing anxiety and depression. When disaster strikes, company social events should not be canceled—they should be held because they are useful mechanisms for fostering social support.

3. *Health services should be promoted.* It's easy for people to become ill when their emotions are running high. As such, the company should encourage employees to take care of themselves, taking full advantage of the medical, counseling, and health club services that may be available.

4. *Try to return to normalcy.* We all like having our routines, and these are shattered during times of trauma. To help return to normal, it is useful to try to get back to "business as usual." This is not to ignore the emotions that people feel because these need to be acknowledged. Still, it's useful to regain the security of one's regular routine.

Although we all hope that it never again will be necessary to respond to another terrorist attack, these suggestions are useful for responding to any type of traumatic situation that may occur (e.g., a natural disaster, such as a tornado or hurricane).

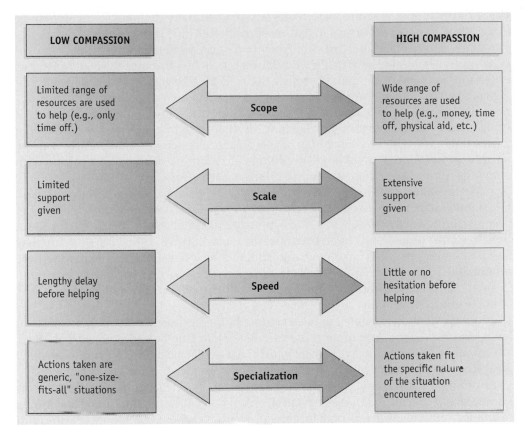

FIGURE 4.4

The Four S's of Organizational Compassion
To be as compassionate as possible, organizational officials should pay attention to the four dimensions identified here. Greater scope, more generous scale, more rapid speed, and greater specialization of response are indications of an organization's compassion competence. This is important insofar as it helps employees heal emotionally when times are tough. For example, an organization would show compassion when it (1) treats an ill employee by doing lots of things to help, such as sending flowers, delivering meals, providing financial support, helping with child care, and so on (broad scope); (2) does these things generously, such as providing the amount of help needed as opposed to only limited amounts (extensive scale); (3) acts quickly, such as by leaping into action to provide help right away (rapid speed); and (4) specializes its action, such as by catering to the unique needs of this particular sick individual instead of offering a fixed, standard package of benefits (greater specialization). (*Source:* Based on suggestions by Dutton et al., 2002; see Note 15.)

(2) be extensive in scale, (3) occur rapidly without hesitation, and (4) be highly specialized to fit the situation.

STRESS IN ORGANIZATIONS

Stress is an all too common part of life today, something few individuals can avoid. In fact, a nationwide survey conducted by a large life insurance company showed that nearly 46 percent of American workers believe their jobs are highly stressful.[17] For 27 percent, work was the single greatest source of stress in their lives. And growing evidence suggests that high levels of stress adversely affect physical health, psychological well-being, and many aspects of task performance.[18] Such evidence makes a strong case for understanding organizational stress. In this section of the chapter, we will review the major causes and effects of stress. Then, in the final section, we will describe various ways of effectively managing stress so as to reduce its negative impact. Before doing this, however, we will define stress more carefully and distinguish it from other concepts to which it is related.

What Is Stress?

What do each of the following situations have in common?

- You are fired the day before you become eligible to receive your retirement pension.
- You find out that your company is about to eliminate your department.
- Your boss tells you that you will not be getting a raise this year.
- Your spouse is diagnosed with a serious illness.

The answer, besides that they are all awful situations, is that each situation involves external events (i.e., ones beyond your own control) that create extreme demands on

stressor

Any demand, either physical or psychological in nature, encountered during the course of living.

stress

The pattern of emotional states and physiological reactions occurring in response to demands from within or outside an organization. (See *stressor.*)

cognitive appraisal

A judgment about the stressfulness of a situation, based on the extent to which someone perceives a stressor as threatening and capable of coping with its demands.

strain

Deviations from normal states of human functioning resulting from prolonged exposure to stressful events.

you. Stimuli of this type are known as **stressors,** formally defined as any demands, either physical or psychological in nature, encountered during the course of living.

When people encounter stressors, their bodies (in particular, sympathetic nervous systems and endocrine systems) are mobilized into action through elevated heart rate, blood pressure, and respiration.[19] Arousal rises quickly to high levels, and many physiological changes take place. If the stressors persist, the body's resources eventually may become depleted, at which point people's ability to cope (at least physically) decreases sharply, and severe biological damage may result. It is these patterns of responses that we have in mind when we talk about stress. Specifically, scientists define **stress** as the pattern of emotional states and physiological reactions occurring in response to demands from within or outside organizations (i.e., stressors).

The mechanisms by which stressors lead to stress reactions are not direct and mechanical in nature. Specifically, stress involves people's **cognitive appraisal** of the potential stressors they face—that is, their judgment about the stressfulness of a situation. In simple terms, for stress to occur people must perceive (1) that the situation they face is somehow threatening to them and (2) that they will be unable to cope with these potential dangers or demands—that the situation, in essence, is beyond their control. In short, stress does not simply shape people's thoughts; it also derives from them and is strongly affected by them.

To the extent that people appraise various situations as stressors, they are likely to have stress reactions. And often these can have damaging behavioral, psychological, and/or medical effects. Indeed, physiological and psychological stress reactions can be so great that eventually they take their toll on the body and mind, resulting in such maladies as insomnia, cardiovascular disease, and depression. Such reactions are referred to as **strain,** which may be defined as deviations from normal states of human functioning resulting from prolonged exposure to stressful events. Reactions commonly take the form of physical ailments, emotional problems, and impaired job performance. For a summary of the relationship between stressors, stress, and strain, please refer to Figure 4.5. (As you probably have seen in dealing with different people in your own life, some individuals are far tougher than others. That is, they have the mental toughness to focus their minds and manage their emotions under stressful conditions.[20] To see how well you and your fellow team members fare in this regard, complete the Group Exercise on pages 140–141.)

Causes of Stress in the Workplace

Stress is caused by many different factors. For example, stress is caused by personal factors such as problems with family members, financial problems, and illness. Stress also is caused by societal factors, such as concerns over crime, terrorism, and downturns in the economy. However, in this book, we are concerned mostly with job-related stress. What causes stress in work settings? Unfortunately, as you will see, the list is quite long; many different factors play a role in creating stress in the workplace.

Occupational demands. Some jobs, such as firefighter, senior executive, and surgeon, expose the people who hold them to high levels of stress. Others, such as purchasing

FIGURE 4.5

Stressors, Stress, and Strain: Recognizing the Distinctions

Stimuli known as *stressors* (which are both physical and psychological in nature) lead to stress reactions when they are *cognitively appraised* as being threatening and beyond one's control. The deviations from normal states resulting from stress are known as *strain*. Both physical and emotional ailments as well as impaired job performance result from strain.

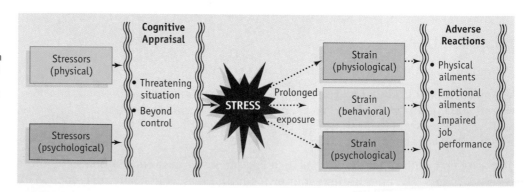

agent, broadcast technician, and actuary do not. This basic fact—that some jobs are much more stressful than others—has been confirmed by the results of a survey involving more than 130 different occupations.[21] For a listing of some of the most stressful jobs, see Table 4.1.

What, precisely, makes some jobs more stressful than others? Research has shown that several features of jobs determine the levels of stress they generate. Specifically, people experience greater stress the more their jobs require

- Making decisions
- Constantly monitoring devices or materials
- Repeatedly exchanging information with others
- Working in unpleasant physical conditions
- Performing unstructured rather than structured tasks

The greater the extent to which a job possesses these characteristics, the higher the level of stress that job produces among individuals holding it. Nurses and long-distance bus drivers perform jobs that match this profile—and, not surprisingly, people doing these jobs tend to show many of the adverse signs of stress. This is not to imply that people do not experience stress in every job. In fact, as you can see from Figure 4.6, many different causes of stress can be found in different types of jobs.[22]

Conflict between work and nonwork. If you've ever known anyone who has had to face the demands of working while at the same time trying to raise a family, or if you are doing so yourself, you probably are well aware of how difficult this situation can be. Not only must you confront the usual pressures to spend time at work and concentrate on what you're doing, but you also must pay attention to the demands placed on you by members of your family (e.g., to spend time with them). When people confront such

TABLE 4.1 WHAT JOBS ARE MOST—AND LEAST—STRESSFUL?

Using a variety of standards, scientists rated 250 different jobs regarding how stressful they are. Shown here are the rankings and stress scores for selected occupations. (Higher scores reflect greater levels of stress encountered.)

RANK SCORE	STRESS SCORE	RANK SCORE	STRESS SCORE
1. U.S. president	176.6	47. Auto salesperson	56.3
2. Firefighter	110.9	50. College professor	54.2
3. Senior executive	108.6	60. School principal	51.7
6. Surgeon	99.5	103. Market research analyst	42.1
10. Air traffic controller	83.1	104. Personnel recruiter	41.8
12. Public relations executive	78.5	113. Hospital administrator	39.6
16. Advertising account executive	74.6	119. Economist	38.7
17. Real estate agent	73.1	122. Mechanical engineer	38.3
20. Stockbroker	71.7	124. Chiropractor	37.9
22. Pilot	68.7	132. Technical writer	36.5
25. Architect	66.9	149. Retail salesperson	34.9
31. Lawyer	64.3	173. Accountant	31.1
33. General physician	64.0	193. Purchasing agent	28.9
35. Insurance agent	63.3	229. Broadcast technician	24.2
42. Advertising salesperson	59.9	245. Actuary	20.2

(*Source*: Reprinted by permission of the *Wall Street Journal*; © 1997 Dow Jones & Company, Inc. All rights reserved worldwide.)

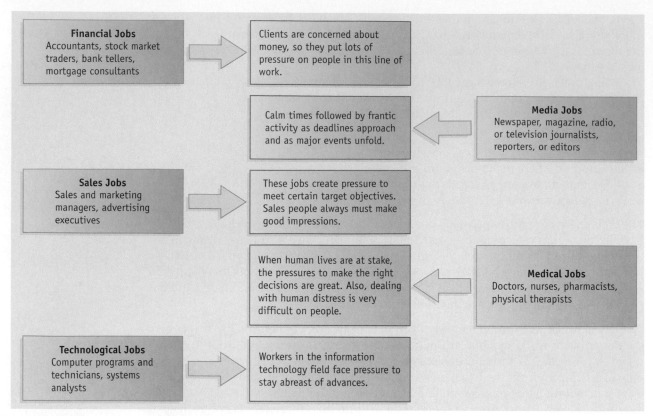

FIGURE 4.6

All Jobs Have Their Own Unique Stressors
Although some jobs are generally more stressful than others, all jobs have associated with them some unique stressors. Some of the most common ones are summarized here.

role conflict
Incompatibilities between the various sets of obligations people face.

role juggling
The need to switch back and forth between the demands of work and family.

role ambiguity
Uncertainty about what one is expected to do on a job.

incompatibilities in the various sets of obligations they have, they are said to experience **role conflict** (we will discuss various types of role conflict in Chapter 8). As you might expect, when we experience conflicts between our work and nonwork lives, something has to give. Not surprisingly, the more time people devote to their jobs, the more events in their nonwork lives (e.g., personal errands) adversely affect their jobs (e.g., not being able to get the job done on time).

The stressful nature of role conflicts is particularly apparent among one group whose members are often expected to switch back and forth rapidly between the demands of work and family—a source of stress known as **role juggling.** This is an especially potent source of stress among one very large segment of the population—parents (see Figure 4.7). Indeed, the more working mothers and fathers are forced to juggle the various roles in their lives, the less fulfilling they find those roles to be, and the more stress they suffer in their lives.[23] For an example of conflict between work and family obligations, see the Case in Point section at the end of this chapter (p. 142).

Role ambiguity: Stress from uncertainty. Even if individuals are able to avoid the stress associated with role conflict, they still may encounter an even more common source of job-related stress: **role ambiguity.** This occurs when people are uncertain about several aspects of their jobs (e.g., the scope of their responsibilities, what's expected of them, and how to divide their time between various duties). Most people dislike such uncertainty and find it quite stressful, but it is difficult to avoid. In fact, role ambiguity is quite common: 35 to 60 percent of employees surveyed report experiencing it to some degree.[24] Clearly, managers who are interested in promoting a stress-free workplace should go out of their way to help employees understand precisely what they are expected to do. As obvious as this may sound, such advice is ignored all too frequently in actual practice.

Overload and underload. When the phrase "work-related stress" is mentioned, most people envision scenes in which employees are asked to do more work than they possi-

FIGURE 4.7
Working at Home: One Solution to Stress Caused by Work–Family Conflict
A few years ago, Shannon Entin founded FitnessLink, a health and fitness Web site, as a part-time business from her home in Lambertville, New Jersey. Shortly there-after, around the time her son Logan was born, the company began to take off. To maintain a balance between her work and family life, Shannon and husband Paul quit their full-time jobs and run the company out of their home office.

bly can handle. Such an image is indeed quite legitimate, for such *overload* is an important cause of stress in many work settings. In fact, in today's business environment, where many companies are trimming staff size (the phenomenon known as *downsizing*, which we will discuss in Chapter 16), fewer employees are required to do more work than ever before. A distinction needs to be made, however, between **quantitative overload**—the belief that one is required to do more work than possibly can be completed in a specific period; and **qualitative overload**—the belief that one lacks the required skills or abilities to perform a given job.

Today, as you know, overload is a problem when it comes to the management of information. Because we live in an information age, a period in which information is not only essential but also widely available, we are faced with more information than ever before. And with this comes pressure to store and process all that information in our heads as we strive to keep up with it all. This is known as **information anxiety.** As shown in Figure 4.8, information anxiety takes a variety of different forms.[25]

quantitative overload
The belief that one is required to do more work than possibly can be completed in a specific period.

qualitative overload
The belief that one lacks the required skills or abilities to perform a given job.

information anxiety
Pressure to store and process a great deal of information in our heads and to keep up constantly with gathering it.

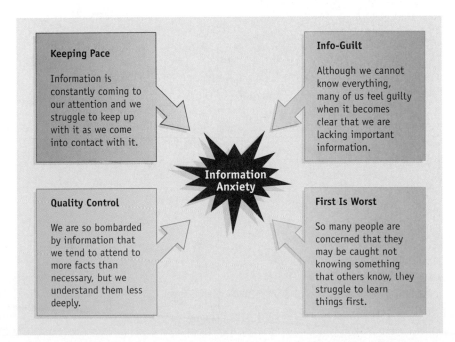

FIGURE 4.8
Information Anxiety: A Modern-Day Stressor
The glut of information with which people today come into contact can be a significant source of overload. As summarized here, this problem takes a variety of different forms.

Keeping Pace
Information is constantly coming to our attention and we struggle to keep up with it as we come into contact with it.

Info-Guilt
Although we cannot know everything, many of us feel guilty when it becomes clear that we are lacking important information.

Information Anxiety

Quality Control
We are so bombarded by information that we tend to attend to more facts than necessary, but we understand them less deeply.

First Is Worst
So many people are concerned that they may be caught not knowing something that others know, they struggle to learn things first.

Overload is only part of the total picture when it comes to stress. Although being asked to do too much can be stressful, so also can being asked to do too little. In fact, there seems to be considerable truth in the following statement: "The hardest job in the world is doing nothing—you can't take a break." *Underload* leads to boredom and monotony. Since these reactions are quite unpleasant, underload, too, can be stressful. Again, there is a distinction between the *quantitative* and *qualitative* aspects. **Quantitative underload** refers to the boredom that results when employees have so little to do that they find themselves sitting around doing nothing much of the time. In contrast, **qualitative underload** refers to the lack of mental stimulation that accompanies many routine, repetitive jobs. Both quantitative and qualitative overload and underload are unpleasant, and researchers have linked them to high levels of stress. For a summary of how the concepts of overload and underload relate to stress, see Figure 4.9.

Responsibility for others: A heavy burden. By virtue of differences in their jobs, some people (such as managers and supervisors) tend to deal more with people than others. And people, as you probably suspect, can be a major source of stress. In general, individuals who are responsible for other people experience higher levels of stress than those who have no such responsibility. Such individuals are more likely to report feelings of tension and anxiety and are more likely to show overt symptoms of stress, such as ulcers or hypertension, than their counterparts in nonsupervisory positions.

This probably isn't too surprising if you think about it. After all, managers are often caught between the need to satisfy their staff members (e.g., giving them raises) while simultaneously meeting the demands of their own superiors (e.g., maintaining budgets). They also are often faced with meeting a wide variety of demands and responsibilities that often weigh heavily on them (see Figure 4.10). Not surprisingly, many managers think of stress as a normal, everyday part of their jobs.

Importantly, managers who deal with people ineffectively—such as those who communicate poorly and who treat people unfairly—add stress to the lives of the people they supervise. As you surely know from your own experiences, a poor manager can

quantitative underload
The boredom that results when employees have so little to do that they find themselves sitting around doing nothing much of the time.

qualitative underload
The lack of mental stimulation that accompanies many routine, repetitive jobs.

FIGURE 4.9
Overload and Underload: Important Sources of Stress
As summarized here, stress can stem from both overload and underload—each of which takes both quantitative and qualitative forms.

The belief that one is expected to do more than is possible

Quantitative Overload

The belief that one lacks the required skills or abilities

Qualitative Overload

Having too little work to do

Quantitative Underload

Lack of mental stimulation from the job

Qualitative Underload

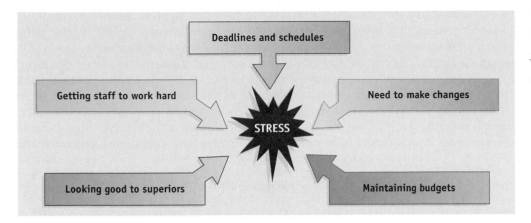

FIGURE 4.10
Manager: A Particularly Stressful Job
Being responsible for others makes the job of managers especially stressful. Some of the major stressors affecting managers are identified here.

be quite a significant source of stress. That said, it is clear that knowing and effectively practicing what you have learned about OB in this book can help alleviate stress among others in the workplace.

Lack of social support: The costs of isolation. According to an old saying, "misery loves company." With respect to stress, this statement implies that if we have to face stressful conditions, it's better to do so along with others (and with their support) rather than alone. Does this strategy actually work? In general, the answer is "yes." Research has shown that when individuals believe they have the friendship and support of others at work—that is, when they have **social support**—their ability to resist the adverse effects of stress increases. For example, a recent study found that police officers who felt they could talk to their colleagues about their reactions to a traumatic event (such as a shooting) experienced less stressful reactions than those who lacked such support.[26] Clearly, social support can be an important buffer against the effects of stress.[27]

social support
The friendship and support of others, which help minimize reactions to stress.

Social support can come from many different sources. One of these is cultural norms (e.g., caring for the elderly is valued among the Japanese, thereby reducing the social isolation many elderly people otherwise experience). Another source of social support is social institutions (e.g., counseling from the church or school officials, help from the Red Cross). And, of course, probably the most important and valuable source of support comes from one's own friends and family members. Various sources help in several different ways.[28] These are as follows:

- *Boosting self-esteem*—Others can help make us feel better about ourselves.
- *Sharing information*—Talking to other people can help us learn about ways of coping with problems and give us a new perspective on things.
- *Providing diversion*—Spending time with others can be a friendly diversion from life's stressors, taking your mind off them.
- *Giving needed resources*—Time spent with others can result in their helping by giving you money, advice, or other recourses needed to alleviate stress.

As we have shown here, not only does misery love company, but also company can help alleviate misery. This is something worth remembering the next time you feel stressed. Remember, don't go it alone. Friends can help, so seek them out.

Sexual harassment: A pervasive problem in work settings. There can be no doubt that one particularly troublesome source of stress in today's workplace is **sexual harassment**—unwanted contact or communication of a sexual nature, usually against women. The stressful effects of sexual harassment stem from both the direct affront to the victim's personal dignity and the harasser's interference with the victim's capacity to do the job. After all, it's certainly difficult to pay attention to what you're doing on your job when you have to concentrate on ways to ward off someone's unwanted attentions! Not surprisingly, sexual harassment has caused some people to experience many severe symptoms of illness, including various forms of physical illness, and voluntary turnover.[29]

sexual harassment
Unwanted contact or communication of a sexual nature, usually against women.

Unfortunately, this particular source of work-related stress is shockingly common. Indeed, when asked in a *New York Times*/CBS News poll whether they had ever been the object of sexual advances, propositions, or unwanted sexual discussions from men who supervise them, fully 30 percent of the women surveyed answered "yes." And this is not a one-sided perception: When asked if they had ever said or done something at work that could be construed by a female colleague as harassment, fully 50 percent of the men polled indicated that they had done so.[30] The good news is that many companies are training employees in ways to avoid sexual harassment, and such efforts are helping people become aware of ways they are behaving that may be considered inappropriate.

Major Effects of Organizational Stress

By now, we're sure you are probably convinced that stress stems from many sources and that it exerts important effects on the people who experience it. What may not yet be apparent, though, is just how powerful and far-reaching such effects can be. In fact, so widespread are the detrimental effects of stress (i.e., strain) that it has been estimated that its annual costs exceed 10 percent of the U.S. gross national product![31] For some other alarming statistics about stress, see Table 4.2.[32]

Stress and task performance. The most current evidence available suggests that stress exerts mainly negative effects on task performance. In other words, performance can be disrupted even by relatively low levels of stress: The greater the stress people encounter on the job; the more adversely affected their job performance tends to be.[33]

As tempting as it may be to accept this idea, it does not always apply. For example, some individuals seem to "rise to the occasion" and turn in exceptional performances at times of high stress. This may result from the fact that they are truly expert in the tasks being performed, making them so confident in what they are doing that they appraise a potentially stressful situation as a challenge rather than a threat. People also differ widely with respect to the impact of stress on task performance. Whereas some people

---

TABLE 4.2 SOME ALARMING STATISTICS ABOUT STRESS TODAY

Recent statistics tell a sobering story about the effects of stress today. In general, people are aware of the effects of stress in their lives but are still doing things that promote stress, creating dramatic costs in the workplace.

People feel the effects of stress:

- 36 percent feel used up at the end of the workday.
- 28 percent work so hard they do not have time or energy to spend with their families.
- 26 percent feel emotionally drained by their work.

People are aware that they may be contributing to their own stress levels:

- 83 percent of people would prefer to have a $10,000 per year raise than an extra hour per day at home.
- 71 percent of people are unwilling to make trade-offs between home and work.
- 49 percent of people indicate that they are not in control of how many hours they work.

Stress is costly:

- Unscheduled absences due to stress have tripled from 1995 to 1999 and cost companies $602 per year for each employee.
- Among the industrialized nations, Americans work more but produce less than those in many other countries, making the cost of labor highly inefficient.
- On average, companies spend a quarter of their after-tax profits on medical bills.
- In the United States, stress-related problems are linked to half of all premature deaths.
- In Norway, sickness at work costs 10 percent of the gross national product.

(*Sources:* Based on data reported by Niemann, 1999, Wah, 2000; see Note 32; and Heller & Hindle, 1998; see Note 22.)

seem to thrive on stress, finding it exhilarating and improving their performance, others seek to avoid high levels of stress, finding it upsetting and a source of interference with job performance.

Stress as a source of desk rage. A particularly unsettling manifestation of stress on the job that has become all too prevalent in recent years is known as **desk rage**—the lashing out at others in response to stressful encounters on the job. Just as angered drivers have been known to express their negative reactions to others in dangerous ways (commonly referred to as *road rage*), so too have office workers been known to behave violently toward others when stressed out by long hours and difficult working conditions. What makes desk rage so frightening is how extremely widespread it is and, as a recent survey indicates, the many different forms it takes (see Figure 4.11).[34]

desk rage

Lashing out at others in response to stressful encounters on the job.

Burnout: Stress and psychological adjustment. Most jobs involve some degree of stress. Yet, somehow, the people performing them manage to cope. That is, they continue to function despite their daily encounters with various stressors. Others, however, are not so fortunate, and over time find themselves worn down by chronic levels of stress.[35] Such people are often described as suffering from **burnout**—a syndrome of emotional, physical, and mental exhaustion coupled with feelings of low self-esteem or low self-efficacy, resulting from prolonged exposure to intense stress, and the strain reactions following from them (see Figure 4.12).

burnout

A syndrome of emotional, physical, and mental exhaustion coupled with feelings of low self-esteem or low self-efficacy, resulting from prolonged exposure to intense stress, and the strain reactions following from them.

Fortunately, some of the signs of burnout are clear, if you know what to look for. The distinct characteristics of burnout are as follows.

1. *Physical exhaustion.* Victims of burnout have low energy and feel tired much of the time. In addition, they report many symptoms of physical strain such as frequent headaches, nausea, poor sleep, and changes in eating habits (e.g., loss of appetite).
2. *Emotional exhaustion.* Depression, feelings of helplessness, and feelings of being trapped in one's job are all part of burnout.
3. *Depersonalization.* People suffering from burnout often demonstrate a pattern of attitudinal exhaustion known as **depersonalization.** Specifically, they become cynical about others, tend to treat others as objects rather than as people, and hold negative attitudes toward them. In addition, they tend to derogate themselves, their jobs, their organizations, and even life in general. To put it simply,

depersonalization

A pattern of behavior occurring in burnout marked by becoming cynical toward others, treating others as objects, and holding negative attitudes toward others.

Percentage of Respondents

- Witnessed yelling or other verbal abuse: 42
- Yelled at co-workers: 29
- Cried over work-related issues: 23
- Saw someone purposely damage company equipment: 14
- Saw physical violence: 10
- Hit a co-worker: 2

FIGURE 4.11
Common Forms of Desk Rage
Adults completing a survey were asked to indicate the negative signs of stress they either experienced directly or witnessed in the workplace. As summarized here, their responses indicated that *desk rage* took many different forms.
(*Source:* Based on data collected by Integra Reality Resources, reported in *Business Week,* November 2, 2000; see Note 34.)

FIGURE 4.12

Major Components of Burnout
As shown, *burnout* results from exposure to intense and prolonged work-related stress. It consists of three major components: *emotional exhaustion, depersonalization,* and *reduced feelings of personal accomplishment.*

they come to view the world around them through dark gray rather than rose-colored glasses.

4. *Feelings of low personal accomplishment.* People suffering from burnout conclude that they haven't been able to accomplish much in the past and assume that they probably won't succeed in the future.

Stress and health: The silent killer. How strong is the link between stress and personal health? The answer, say medical experts, is "very strong, indeed." In other words, physiological strain reactions can be quite severe. In fact, some authorities estimate that stress plays a role in anywhere from 50 to 70 percent of all forms of physical illness.[36] Moreover, included in these figures are some of the most serious and life-threatening ailments known to medical science. A list of some of the more common ones is shown in Table 4.3. Even the most cursory look at this list must leave you with the conclusion that the health-related effects of stress are not only quite widespread but also extremely serious.

TABLE 4.3   HEALTH-RELATED CONSEQUENCES OF STRESS

Stress causes a variety of different health problems, including medical, behavioral, and psychological problems. Listed here are some of the major consequences within each category.

MEDICAL CONSEQUENCES	BEHAVIORAL CONSEQUENCES	PSYCHOLOGICAL CONSEQUENCES
Heart disease and stroke	Smoking	Family conflict
Backache and arthritis	Drug and alcohol abuse	Sleep disturbances
Ulcers	Accident proneness	Sexual dysfunction
Headaches	Violence	Depression
Cancer	Appetite disorders	
Diabetes		
Cirrhosis of the liver		
Lung disease		

(*Source:* Based on material reported by Quick & Tetrick, 2002; see Note 36.)

REDUCING STRESS: WHAT CAN BE DONE?

Stress stems from so many different factors and conditions that to eliminate it entirely from our lives is impossible. However, there still are many things that companies can do to reduce the intensity of stress on employees and to minimize its harmful effects. There also are things we can do as individuals to reduce stress on our own. In this section of the chapter we will consider both organizational and individual tactics for reducing stress.

Organizational Resources for Managing Stress

Fortunately, several good strategies exist for attaining these goals.[38] To ensure that these tactics are followed, many companies have introduced systematic programs designed to help employees reduce and/or prevent stress. The underlying assumption of these programs is that by minimizing employees' adverse reactions to stress, they will be healthier, less likely to be absent, and, consequently, more productive on the job—which, in turn, has beneficial effects on the bottom line.

Employee assistance programs. A recent survey of major companies found that nearly two-thirds have **employee assistance programs (EAPs)** in place.[39] These are plans that provide employees with assistance for various personal problems (e.g., substance abuse, career planning, and financial and legal problems). The Metropolitan Life Insurance Company (MetLife), for example, has one of the most extensive EAPs in use today. It offers toll-free telephone consultation for employees who wish to talk about their problems, as well as on-site access to medical and psychological professionals. As is always the case in such programs, anonymity is important. Employees seeking help are assured that nobody in their company will be able to learn that they have sought the services of the EAP.

> **employee assistance programs (EAPs)**
> Plans that provide employees with assistance for various personal problems (e.g., substance abuse, career planning, and financial and legal problems).

One way for employees to access counseling assistance that is growing in popularity is known as **e-therapy** (or **cybertherapy**). This involves having employees with psychological problems communicate with trained counselors by way of e-mail, using what has been called "the virtual couch." Because of the great flexibility in scheduling that this service provides, along with ready access to professionals with a wide variety of specialties, e-therapy is becoming a popular service for EAPs to provide.

> **e-therapy**
> The process by which people with psychological problems communicate with trained counselors via e-mail.
>
> **cybertherapy**
> See *e-therapy.*

Wellness programs. About 56 percent of today's larger companies have **wellness programs.** These involve training employees in a variety of things they can do to promote healthy lifestyles. Wellness programs usually consist of workshops in which employees can learn many things to reduce stress and maintain their health. Exercise, nutrition, and weight-management counseling are among the most popular areas covered. Companies that have used such programs have found that they pay off handsomely. For example, at its industrial sites that offer wellness programs, DuPont has found that absenteeism is less than half of what it is at sites that do not offer such programs. Companies such as The Travelers Corporation and the Union Pacific Railroad have enjoyed consistently high returns for each dollar they invest in employee wellness.

> **wellness programs**
> Company-wide programs in which employees receive training regarding things they can do to promote healthy lifestyles.

Absence control programs. Acknowledging that employees sometimes need to take time off the job to relieve stress, a few companies are offering **absence control programs**—procedures that give employees flexibility in when they will be taking time off work. Typically, employees take time off work when they are suffering problems caused by stress, but absence control programs allow employees to take time off *before* these problems develop (hopefully, requiring less time off).[40] Importantly, they recognize that such absences are important and should not be considered grounds for discipline. For example, some companies offer employees a predetermined number of days known as a "paid-leave bank," from which they can draw for any reason without having to call in sick. In a variation of this, the clothing retailer Eddie Bauer offers what it calls "balance days"—that is, days employees can take off to help juggle their work and personal

> **absence control programs**
> Procedures that give employees flexibility with respect to when they can take time off work.

OB IN A DIVERSE WORLD
WHO'S MORE STRESSED OUT: MEN OR WOMEN?

Although life can be tough on anybody, it seems that women generally face more stressors than men. After all, women are more likely than men to carry the primary responsibility for raising children at home while also facing responsibilities on the job. Women also are more likely than men to be victims of sexual harassment on the job. And women are more likely than men to confront discriminatory practices that keep them from advancing as rapidly on the job. All of these are significant sources of stress, suggesting that stress may take more of a toll on working women than working men.

A few years ago, a comprehensive survey was conducted to address this question by comparing the stressors faced by men and women in the workplace.[37] Some 900 employees representing 28 different companies were surveyed. Stress was measured by way of a sophisticated questionnaire that assessed various causes and effects of stress. The researchers did, in fact, find that women face more stressors and are more adversely affected by them than men.

These differences took many forms. First, compared to men, women reported facing significantly greater amounts of stress

---

demands. Whenever possible, the company asks for advance notice before granting balance days so that the employee's work group can plan accordingly and not be left unexpectedly shorthanded.

stress management programs
Systematic efforts to train employees in a variety of techniques that they can use to become less adversely affected by stress.

Stress management programs. Systematic efforts known as **stress management programs** involve training employees in a variety of techniques (e.g., meditation and relaxation) that they can use to become less adversely affected by stress. (We describe many of these techniques later.) These are used by about a quarter of all large companies. Among them is the Equitable Life Insurance Company. Its "Emotional Health Program" offers training in a variety of ways that employees can learn to relax, including napping. Although some managers might not like the idea of seeing their employees asleep on the job, others recognize that brief naps can, in fact, help their employees recharge and combat the negative effects of stress. This isn't even the most unusual approach that companies are taking to combat the effects of stress among employees. For a look at some of the most novel approaches that today's companies are taking to win the war against stress, see the Best Practices section that follows.

How Can You Manage Your Own Stress?

Even if your own company does not have a formal program in place to manage stress, there still are several things you can do by yourself to help control the stress in your life. We will now describe several such tactics.

Manage your time. As we noted earlier, overload is a common source of stress. Avoiding overload is made possible by taking control over how you spend your time. This isn't always easy, of course, when the phone is always ringing and people are stopping by to talk to you. However, people who don't manage their time effectively find themselves easily overwhelmed, falling behind, not getting important things done, and having to work longer hours as a result. Not surprisingly, **time management,** the practice of taking control over how you spend time, is a valuable managerial skill. Some of the most effective time management practices are as follows:

time management
The practice of taking control over how you spend time.

- *Prioritize your activities.* Distinguish between tasks that are urgent (ones that must be performed right away) and important (ones that must be done but can wait).

from many different sources. Specifically, they encountered more changes and greater pressure to perform well on the job. They also coped less effectively with those stressors. For example, they managed their time less efficiently and were less likely to take direct action about these situations. However, women did do a better job than men of coping with the stressors they faced by taking care of themselves (e.g., maintaining healthy habits) and by seeking social support (e.g., talking to friends about their problems). Despite this, however, women still coped less effectively overall, leading them to suffer more physical symptoms (e.g., elevated blood pressure), behavioral symptoms (e.g., sleeplessness), and emotional symptoms (e.g., anxiety and depression).

It is interesting to note that the triggers of stress reactions in women and men are different. Women show more symptoms of physical distress if the jobs they face are chaotic or demanding. For men, however, symptoms of stress are more likely to result when they face ambiguous demands about what to do or when they work in a highly competitive atmosphere.

These findings call attention to the importance of taking steps to alleviate the stressors faced by women in the workplace. Although men face many of the same stressors, women are more inclined to suffer problems because of them, suggesting the importance of including women in corporate stress management programs.

When determining how to spend your time, assign the greatest priority to tasks that are both important and urgent, a lower priority to tasks that are important but less urgent, and the lowest priority to tasks that are neither important nor urgent (see Figure 4.13).

- *Allocate your time realistically.* When planning, accurately assess how much time needs to be spent on each of the various tasks you perform.
- *Take control of your time.* Make a "to do" list and carefully keep track of what you have to accomplish. Unless an urgent situation comes up, stay focused and don't allow others to derail you. The more you allow other people to interfere with your time, the less you will have accomplished at the end of the day.

We realize, of course, that these suggestions might not be easy to follow at first. However, with a little practice, they can become part of the way you work. As you find them helping you become more successful, they are likely to become routine. And, as they help you relieve stress in your life and even avoid it altogether, you can expect these practices to become some of your most effective work habits.

FIGURE 4.13

Assigning Priorities: An Effective Stress Management Technique
Managing time is an effective way of minimizing stress. One of the most important considerations when managing time is *assigning priorities* to the tasks you are performing. In doing so, it is useful to distinguish between tasks that are routine (which should be given the lowest priority), tasks that are important but not urgent (which should be given intermediate priority), and tasks that are important and urgent (which should be given the highest priority).

BEST PRACTICES
FIGHTING THE BATTLE AGAINST STRESS

Although many companies are doing things to help their employees reduce the effects of stress, some are being particularly creative.[41] Given how successful they've been, it is worthwhile to know about some of these novel practices.

You've heard of teachers taking sabbaticals—time off so they can recharge and/or learn new skills. What you might not know is that growing numbers of companies are offering sabbaticals to their employees as well. Take Arrow Electronics, for example, the Melville, New York, company specializing in distributing electronic components and computer products to industrial and commercial customers. After working for seven years, employees are allowed to take a 10-week paid sabbatical during which they can do whatever they want. Company officials claim that the 1,400

employees who have taken advantage of this benefit return to their jobs refreshed and with greater appreciation for their work.

A quite different approach has been in use at Burmah Castrol, the multinational distributor of specialty lubricants and chemicals to businesses based in the United Kingdom. Here Tony Yardley-Jones serves as "Chief Medical Advisor," a post requiring him to provide strategic vision and advice on matters of occupational health. For example, when many of the company's top executives were asked to do more work in less time, they began showing signs of stress-related illness. To alleviate these problems, Yardley-Jones conducted workshops in which employees were trained in various biomedical techniques that helped them recognize signs of stress (e.g., adrenaline rushes and increased heartbeat) and showed them how to control these reactions by

Eat a healthy diet and be physically fit. Growing evidence indicates that reduced intake of salt and saturated fats and increased consumption of fiber- and vitamin-rich fruits and vegetables are steps that can greatly increase the body's ability to cope with the physiological effects of stress.[42] Regular exercise also helps. People who exercise regularly obtain many benefits closely related to resistance of the adverse effects of stress (see Figure 4.14). For example, fitness reduces both the incidence of cardiovascular illness and the death rate from such diseases. Similarly, physical fitness lowers blood pressure, an important factor in many aspects of personal health.

With this in mind, it is not surprising that growing numbers of companies are taking steps to ensure that their employees engage in regular exercise. Will Smith, III, for example, the CEO of Denver-based Ensicon, a provider of technical consultants to bio-

FIGURE 4.14

Exercise: An Effective Stress Reduction Technique
Although most people might not want to follow this dog's specific advice regarding how to exercise, he does have the right idea: Exercise can help reduce stress.
(© 1998 Randy Glasbergen www.glasbergen.com)

"Hold the sock tight in your mouth, then race from room to room as fast as you can—it's the greatest stress management technique ever!"

using various concentration techniques (i.e., "mind over matter").

Other companies take a far simpler approach. They help manage stress on a one-by-one basis by having employees look for signs that their colleagues may be suffering the adverse effects of stress. For example, in the restaurant business, where very long hours are the rule, employees of Hard Rock Café International are encouraged to do whatever it takes to help their fellow employees avoid stress.

Case in point: When the wife of the general manager of the Hard Rock in San Diego went into labor the same time as the restaurant's opening night, executives told him to join his wife instead of staying for the festivities. Although his presence was critical to the event, execs realized that people are the company's top asset, and they released him from his obligations so he could be with his wife (and his newborn son!) at this important time in their lives. This program appears to be working: Hard Rock has one of the lowest turnover rates in the restaurant industry today—about half the national average.

As you might imagine, stress can be particularly acute for entrepreneurs who run their own small businesses. After all, they are expected to be everywhere at once. This was the problem faced by Cynthia Guiang, who cofounded the Townsend Agency, an advertising and public relations firm in San Diego. A few years after founding the business, she had her first two children, making time together with the family necessary but difficult to find. Rather boldly, she started saying something that many entrepreneurs learn only after it's too late—"no."

Now, at the end of the day, she simply leaves her work behind and goes home rather than staying long hours at the office. Instead of causing the business to crumble, as she feared, her improved mood created such harmony in her life that it caused her to be far more kind and supportive of people than she used to be, encouraging her associates to work at peak performance. Taking steps to reduce the stress in her life not only promoted her own health but the health of her company's bottom line as well.

medical and engineering companies, recognizes that his 30 corporate staffers are likely to experience high amounts of stress as they struggle to keep up with the long hours they face.[43] To keep them healthy and focused on the job, he offers them 90-minute lunch hours and pays their initiation to a local health club. And, if they keep exercising for a year, he also pays half their dues.

Relax and meditate. When you think of successful executives at work, what picture comes to mind? Most of us would probably conjure up an image of someone on three phones at once, surrounded by important papers in a whirlwind of activity. Probably the farthest thing from your mind would be the image of someone resting calmly in a serene setting. Yet, for a growing number of today's employees, this picture is quite common.

What's going on in these companies is designed to help people become more productive, not in the traditional, stress-inducing way, but by helping them cope more effectively with stress. One technique used in this regard is **meditation**, the process of learning to clear one's mind of external thoughts, often by repeating a single syllable (known as a *mantra*) over and over again. Those who follow this systematic way of relaxing claim that it helps a great deal in relieving the many sources of stress in their lives.

meditation
The process of learning to clear one's mind of external thoughts, often by repeating a single syllable (known as a *mantra*) over and over again.

Get a good night's sleep. Interestingly, one of the most effective ways to alleviate stress-related problems is one of the simplest—if you can do it. We're talking about good old-fashioned *sleep*. We all need a certain amount of sleep to allow our bodies to recharge and function effectively. Eight hours per day is average, although some need more and others can function just fine on less. Although a restful night's sleep can help people ward off the harmful effects of stress, the problem for many is that they are so stressed that they cannot get to sleep. In recent years, as employees at many high-tech companies find themselves expected to work around the clock to meet intense competition, the problem of *insomnia* has reached epidemic proportions.[44] According to the National Institutes of Health, **insomnia** is the experience of inadequate or poor-quality sleep. It is characterized by such symptoms as difficulty getting to sleep, difficulty main-

insomnia
The experience of inadequate and poor-quality sleep.

taining sleep, or waking up too early. Depending on how long the symptoms last, it can be classified as either transient (up to three weeks in duration), intermittent (on and off), or chronic (lasting over three weeks).[45]

In any of these cases, the results are the same—being tired and unprepared to expend the needed energy, focus, and concentration at work. This not only leads to poor performance, but it also makes us more poorly equipped to handle the stressful situations we may encounter. As a result, even more stress is likely to occur. Obviously, something needs to be done to break this cycle of stress and sleeplessness (see Figure 4.15). One effective means of doing this is to take steps to get a good night's sleep. For some suggestions in this regard, see Table 4.4.

Avoid inappropriate self-talk. This involves telling ourselves over and over how horrible and unbearable it will be if we fail, if we are not perfect, or if everyone we meet does not like us. Such thoughts seem ludicrous when spelled out in the pages of a book, but the fact is that most people entertain them at least occasionally. Unfortunately, such thoughts can add to personal levels of stress, as individuals *awfulize* or *catastrophize* in their own minds the horrors of not being successful, perfect, or loved. Fortunately, such thinking can be readily modified. For many people merely recognizing that they have implicitly accepted such irrational and self-defeating beliefs is sufficient to produce beneficial change and increased resistance to stress.

Control your reactions. When faced with stressful events, people often protect themselves from the rising tide of anxiety by adopting actions that are *incompatible* with such feelings. For example, instead of allowing our speech to become increasingly rapid and intense as we become upset, we can consciously modulate this aspect of our behavior. A reduction in arousal and tension may result. People who practice this skill report great success. In other words, practice acting calmly, and you just may find yourself getting calmer.

When confronted with rising tension, people may find it useful to consciously choose to insert a brief period of delay known as a **time-out.** This can involve taking a short break, going to the nearest restroom to splash cold water on your face, or any other action that yields a few moments of breathing space. Such actions interrupt the cycle of ever-rising tension that accompanies stress and can help to restore equilibrium and the feeling of being at least partly in control of ongoing events.

Putting It All Together: Three Major Approaches to Reducing Stress

By now, you probably have reached the conclusion that reducing stress is difficult and, of course, this is correct. The challenge stems not only from the wide number of different factors involved but also from a lack of certainty about what it means to reduce stress. Do we eliminate stressors altogether? Do we take steps to try to minimize the

time-out
A brief delay in activities designed to reduce mounting tension.

FIGURE 4.15
**Sleeplessness and Stress:
A Vicious Cycle**
People who are experiencing stress tend to find it difficult to sleep (a condition known as insomnia). This causes them to be tired and to work poorly as a result. This, in turn, leads to more stress. One of the easiest ways to break this cycle is to get more restful sleep.

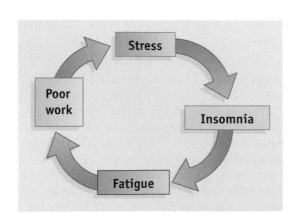

TABLE 4.4 GETTING INTO THE GOOD SLEEP HABIT

If you're thinking that it's unnecessary to learn how to get a good, restful sleep, you may be one of the fortunate people who manage to do so. For millions of people who suffer from stress, however, getting to sleep and staying asleep isn't so easy. Here are some tips for getting a satisfying sleep.

SUGGESTION	EXPLANATION
Schedule your sleep.	You have to set aside a certain time of day to sleep and stick to it. As your body gets used to the routine, it will be easier to get to sleep and to stay asleep.
Don't go to bed after strenuous activity.	You need to get ready for sleep by relaxing, so create a psychological and physiological "buffer zone" by reading or watching television before going to bed. Don't try to get to sleep immediately after exercising or doing work.
Avoid stimulants before bedtime.	Nicotine and caffeine are stimulants, so don't smoke or drink coffee before going to bed. Spicy or heavy foods also will keep you up as your body works to digest them, so avoid them as the evening progresses.
Don't eat or work in bed.	You should associate your bed only with sleeping. If you eat in bed or bring work to bed, you are likely to have other less restful associations with it that may interfere with sleep.
Clear your mind.	If you are restless and thinking about things, get out of bed and do something else until you are tired and are ready to clear your mind.

(*Source*: Based on suggestions from the American Academy of Sleep Medicine, 2002; see Note 39.)

effects of stress? Or do we simply treat the symptoms of stress medically and psychologically? As you will see in this section, all three approaches have some value.

Primary prevention. Probably the most direct way to reduce stress is to attempt to eliminate stressors from one's life. This approach is known as **primary prevention.** A primary prevention strategy would involve, for example, relocating a company's offices from a congested city to a more pleasant, rural community. Although this might alleviate some sources of stress, it might create others, such as forcing people to move or to face long commutes. And, of course, it's likely to be prohibitively expensive for a company to relocate. Besides, primary prevention involves eliminating sources of stress and this is almost never practical. After all, there are always sources of stress in our lives, and eliminating some is likely to uncover others. In other words, although primary prevention tactics may be most effective, they are also the least practical.

primary prevention
A category of stress prevention techniques aimed at eliminating stressors from people's lives.

Secondary prevention. Acknowledging the difficulty of primary prevention efforts, many experts recognize that stress is inevitable but that its effects can be minimized. This is known as **secondary prevention.** For example, companies that provide access to sports facilities are taking steps to help employees stay healthy, which strengthens their immune systems, making them less susceptible to stress-related illness. Health and fitness facilities also provide opportunities for people to talk to one another, providing the social support that can be so very helpful when it comes to alleviating the symptoms of stress.

secondary prevention
A category of stress prevention techniques aimed at minimizing the effects of stress in people's lives.

Tertiary prevention. Finally, reducing stress often results in simply treating its symptoms, which may well be serious. If stressors cannot be removed from our lives (through primary prevention efforts) or if steps cannot be taken to minimize their problems (through secondary prevention efforts), we are then left with only one alternative—treating the symptoms of the problems that result (e.g., high blood pressure or depression). Such efforts are referred to as **tertiary prevention** techniques. Company-wide

tertiary prevention
A category of stress prevention techniques aimed at treating stress-related symptoms.

FIGURE 4.16

Three Major Stress Prevention and Reduction Approaches
Efforts to prevent or reduce stress fall into the three major categories summarized here: *primary prevention* (attempting to eliminate stressors), *secondary prevention* (doing things to avoid stress-related problems), and *tertiary prevention* (treating symptoms caused by stressors).

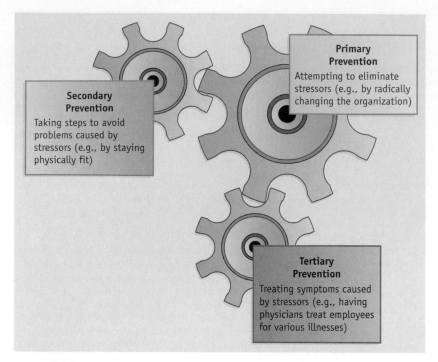

Secondary Prevention
Taking steps to avoid problems caused by stressors (e.g., by staying physically fit)

Primary Prevention
Attempting to eliminate stressors (e.g., by radically changing the organization)

Tertiary Prevention
Treating symptoms caused by stressors (e.g., having physicians treat employees for various illnesses)

programs that help employees stop smoking fall into the category of tertiary prevention. So, too, do EAP programs, mentioned on page 131 (which may provide counseling for such stress-related problems as drug abuse). Medical insurance also can be considered as a means of tertiary prevention. For a summary of the differences between primary, secondary, and tertiary prevention techniques, see Figure 4.16.

SUMMARY AND REVIEW OF LEARNING OBJECTIVES

1. Distinguish between emotions and moods.
Whereas emotions are overt reactions that express people's feelings about a specific event, moods are more general. Specifically, moods are unfocused, relatively mild feelings that exist as background to our daily experiences.

2. Describe the effects of emotions and moods on behavior in organizations.
Emotions affect behavior in organizations in various ways. For example, negative emotions tend to interfere with job performance. This is largely because people who are upset tend to neither listen to nor understand the performance feedback they receive. People also are more likely to help others when they are in good moods than when they are in bad moods.

3. Describe ways that people manage their emotions in organizations.
One way people manage their emotions is by keeping their negative feelings to themselves. Rather than offending another with their actual negative feelings, people may engage in the emotional labor of disguising their true feelings. The inconsistency between the emotions people express and the emotions they feel is known as emotional dissonance. People in organizations also manage their emotions by displaying compassion for others when needed. This is especially important during major crises and emergencies.

4. Identify the major causes and consequences of stress.

Stress is caused by many different factors, including occupational demands, conflicts between the work and nonwork aspects of people's lives (i.e., role conflict), not knowing what is expected on the job (i.e., role ambiguity), overload and underload, having responsibility for other people, not having social support, and experiencing sexual harassment. In general, stress adversely affects task performance and leads to desk rage, burnout (physical, mental, and emotional exhaustion), and a wide range of medical and psychological problems.

5. Identify various organizational resources for managing stress.

To help reduce employees' stress, companies are doing such things as using employee assistance programs (which, with growing popularity, are likely to include e-therapy, also called cybertherapy), wellness programs, absence control programs, and stress management programs.

6. Identify various ways that we can manage our own stress as individuals.

As individuals, we can control the stress we face in our lives by following good time management techniques, eating a healthy diet and being physically fit, relaxing and meditating, avoiding inappropriate self-talk, and taking control over our reactions. These activities fall into three categories: primary prevention (which seeks to eliminate stressors), secondary prevention (which seeks to avoid stress-related problems), and tertiary prevention (which involves treating stress-related symptoms).

POINTS TO PONDER

Questions for Review

1. What are emotions and moods, and how do they influence people's behavior in organizations?
2. What are emoticons, and what role do they play in communicating by e-mails?
3. What advice would you give to a company interested in managing employees' emotions in times of trauma?
4. What are the differences between stressors, stress, and strain?
5. What are the primary causes and consequences of stress on the job?
6. What steps can be taken to minimize the potentially harmful effects of stress on the job?

Experiential Questions

1. Think of a time when it was necessary for you to express compassion on the job in response to a traumatic situation. What were the circumstances? What did you do that was effective? What steps might you take to become even more effective the next time it is necessary to express compassion on the job?
2. What was the most stressful situation you ever encountered on the job? What were the stressors, and how did you react, both physically and psychologically? What role did social support play in helping you manage this stress?
3. What experiences have you had using stress management techniques—either formally or informally? For example, do you meditate? Do you find that physical exercise helps you relieve stress? Does talking to others help at all? Of the various techniques described in this chapter, which one do you think you would find most beneficial?

Questions to Analyze

1. We all experience emotions, but some people disguise their true feelings better than others. Do you think this is a helpful or harmful thing to do? Under what con-

ditions do you think it would be most useful to express your true feelings? Likewise, when do you think it would be best to keep your feelings to yourself?

2. Social support can be a very helpful means to reduce stress. However, do you think it's wise to seek social support on the job, where you stand to make yourself vulnerable by talking about your work-related stressors (e.g., by showing your weaknesses, or by speaking negatively about your bosses)? Or do you think that only your coworkers are in a good position to understand your work-related stressors, suggesting that you should talk to them about the work-related stress you are experiencing?

3. Stress management programs generally work well, but they are not always as effective as hoped. What problems and limitations do you believe may interfere with the effectiveness of stress management programs? How can these problems and limitations be overcome?

DEVELOPING OB SKILLS

INDIVIDUAL EXERCISE

Assessing Your Emotional Intelligence

As shown in this chapter and in Chapter 3, emotional intelligence—the capacity to read other's emotions—is important. Several different techniques are used to assess emotional intelligence. Completing this exercise will get you a good feel for what emotional intelligence is and how it is measured. Two different kinds are presented in this exercise.

Directions

Complete the emotional intelligence tests found online at iVillage, a site specializing in giving health-related advice (quiz.ivillage.com/health/tests/eqtest2.htm), and at The Hay Group, a well-respected consulting firm (ei.haygroup.com/default.asp).

Questions for Discussion

1. What different assumptions about the basic nature of emotional intelligence are reflected by these two tests?
2. What did these tests reveal about your own emotional intelligence? Were these revelations different for each test? If so, which was more surprising to you and which revealed things about you that you already knew?
3. Based on these tests, how do you think you can raise your own emotional intelligence?

GROUP EXERCISE

Are You Tough Enough to Endure Stress?

A test known as the Attentional and Interpersonal Style (TAIS) inventory has been used in recent years to identify the extent to which a person can stay focused and keep his or her emotions under control—the core elements of performing well under high-pressure conditions (see Note 20). Completing this exercise (which is based on questions similar to those actually used by such groups as Olympic athletes and U.S. Navy Seals) will help you understand your own strengths and limitations in this regard. And, by discussing these scores with your teammates, you will come away with a good feel for the extent to which those with whom you work differ along this dimension as well.

Directions

1. Gather in groups of three or four people who know each other fairly well. If you are part of an intact group, such as a work team, or a team of students working on a class project, meet with your fellow group members.

2. Individually complete the following questionnaire by responding to each question as follows: "never," "rarely," "sometimes," "frequently," or "always."

_____ 1. When time is running out on an important project, I am the person who should be called on to take control of the group.

_____ 2. When listening to a piece of music, I can pick out a specific voice or instrument.

_____ 3. The people who know me think of me as being "serious."

_____ 4. It is important to me to get a job completely right in every detail, even if it means being late.

_____ 5. When approaching a busy intersection, I easily get confused.

_____ 6. Just by looking at someone, I can figure out what he or she is like.

_____ 7. I am comfortable arguing with people.

_____ 8. At a cocktail party, I have no difficulty keeping track of several different conversations at once.

3. Discuss your answers with everyone else in your group. Item by item, consider what each person's response to each question indicates about his or her ability to focus.

Questions for Discussion

1. Which questions were easiest to interpret? Which were most difficult?
2. How did each individual's responses compare with the way you would assess his or her ability to focus under stress?
3. For what jobs is the ability to concentrate under stress particularly important? For what jobs is it not especially important? How important is this ability for the work you do?

WEB SURFING EXERCISE

Emoticons

In addition to the commonly used happy, sad, and winking emoticons described in this chapter, clever computer users have developed a wide array of emoticons to express just about every conceivable thought (and several that are inconceivable). You can find many interesting examples at the following sites.

www.computeruser.com/resources/dictionary/emoticons.html
www.cknow.com/ckinfo/emoticons.htm
www.netlingo.com/smiley.cfm
www.pb.org/emoticon.html
www.windweaver.com/emoticon.htm
www.won.nl/dsp/usr/mvketel/Internet/emoticon.html

After visiting these sites, answer the following questions about them.

1. Do you think some of the more unusual emoticons are useful for expressing emotion in everyday online communication, or do you think they are merely ways of expressing one's cleverness? Explain your answer.
2. Which of these emoticons, if any, do you think you will use now that you know about them? How do you think they will be useful in communicating your emotions?
3. What kind of unintentional message do you think you may be sending about yourself by using emoticons? Do you think you may appear silly or frivolous by using them? Explain.

Stress Management

Several associations and private companies are dedicated to reducing stress. Some examples include the American Institute of Stress (www.stress.org), the International Stress Management Association (www.imsa.org.uk), the Institute for Stress

Management (www.hyperstress.com), and the Center for Stress Management (www.managingstress.com). Visit these Web sites and answer the following questions.

1. How do the approaches of each of these associations or companies differ from one another?
2. What unique services or suggestions are offered by each one?
3. Of the various approaches described in these sites, which ones do you most prefer and which do you least prefer? Explain the basis for these preferences.

PRACTICING OB

Stressed-Out Employees Are Resigning

As the managing director of a large e-tail sales company, you are becoming alarmed about the growing level of turnover your company has been experiencing lately. It already has passed the industry average, and you are concerned about the company's capacity to staff the call center and the warehouse during the busy holiday period. In conducting exit interviews, you learned that the employees who are leaving generally like their work and the pay they are receiving. However, they are displeased with the way their managers are treating them, and this is creating stress in their lives. They are quitting so they can take less stressful positions in other companies. Answer the following questions based on material in this chapter.

1. Assuming that the employees' emotions and moods are negative, what problems would you expect to find in the way they are working?
2. How should the company's supervisors behave differently to get their subordinates to experience less stress on the job (or, at least, get them to react less negatively)?
3. What could the individual employees do to help manage their own stress more effectively?

CASE IN POINT

Parenthood and Dot-Coms: A Recipe for Stress

What do you get when you combine a job that requires an insane schedule with the demands of parenthood? The answer is *stress*—and lots of it. Just ask Melissa Lloyd, the only senior female executive at Hotlinks, a small Internet start-up in Mountain View, California, that provides online bookmarking and search services. When she worked at Procter & Gamble, she could have taken advantage of the company's liberal benefits, such as maternity leave, flextime, and job-sharing. But, as vice president of marketing for a 25-person company, these are not options. In the highly competitive and fast-moving world of the Internet, Hotlinks could afford neither giving up a key executive nor providing expensive day care facilities. The stubborn conflict between growing a company and growing a family forced Melissa to make some tough decisions.

Acknowledging that her family came first, Melissa decided to take 12 weeks of unpaid leave (as covered by California law) and then return to work for 8- or 9-hour days instead of her usual 10- or 11-hour days. Others take a different route. According to Tuck Richards, an Internet consultant, many employees of high-tech start-up firms arrange for people such as friends, relatives, and professional nannies to take care of their families while they return to work as soon as physically possible. It's not that these individuals are unconcerned about their families. Rather, they are gambling that they will be able to make up for the present absence from their families by making it big and retiring in only a few years.

During the boom days of the Internet, only a few years ago in the late 1990s, hopes of making it rich led many to choose work ahead of their families. Back then, talk of family-friendly policies was limited because employees knew they were expected to stay at the office no matter long it took to get things done. Today, however, with Internet success stories the exception rather than the rule, it's more common for parents working at dot-coms to do what Melissa did by putting their families first.

Although the breakneck pace of Internet start-ups has slowed down, employees of such firms are still expected to put in long hours. And doing so still interferes with child-rearing, which remains a problem given that most of the employees of Internet companies are of child-rearing age. Generous benefits still aren't available, but today's start-up firms have developed several useful ways of adapting. In general, this means working smarter than ever before.

At some companies, such as Scient, the San Francisco–based e-commerce service provider, this takes the form of giving employees the flexibility to work whatever hours are best for them, even if it means leaving work to attend to family responsibilities and then returning to the office later in the day. Employees at Autobytel.com, the e-commerce car dealership, go out of their way to be incredibly nimble with their scheduling, such as by doing things at odd times of day. And the company's culture is such that this is accepted.

Breakaway Solutions, the Boston-based Internet consulting company, has found a good way of dealing with the problem: It arranged for consultants to cut their travel time by 200 to 600 percent by opening smaller offices across the country. Although this isn't exactly cheap, Breakaway enjoys a 97 percent retention rate, which is almost unheard of in that industry. Its efforts at making it possible to have both a work life and a family life are the key.

Critical Thinking Questions

1. What stresses do you think employees are likely to face as they struggle with making decisions that pit their jobs against their families?
2. Although it is costly for small companies to have family-friendly policies like big companies, do you think that the savings resulting from retaining good employees and reducing their stress levels may offset these expenses?
3. In addition to the several solutions identified here, what else do you think could be done to avoid the "either-or" decision that Melissa Lloyd faced?

Stress

When Student Advantage (SA) was first formed, most of the employees were single and in their twenties. Working long hours was not a problem for them. Today, however, many SA employees are older and have families at home. As a result, they suffer conflicts between the pressures of the job, with its long hours, and the need to spend time at home with their spouses and children. To address this issue, SA managers are empowered to make decisions about giving employees time off the job, giving them the flexibility needed to balance work and family life.

The tight deadlines and the constantly changing conditions (e.g., rapid growth and the need to adjust to a more highly structured workplace) are two serious sources of stress at SA. However, maintaining a fun workplace where everyone is treated like family is key to helping everyone deal with the stressors they face. To maintain this, the company hires prospective employees based not only on their technical qualifications, but on their approachability as individuals. Although adverse reactions to stressors at SA are few, those who have difficulty coping have access to an employee assistance program (EAP) that puts them in touch with professionals who can help them deal with the stressors they face.

Questions for Discussion

1. What kinds of role conflicts are experienced at SA? How does the role juggling that follows from this lead to stress?
2. How does the problem of overload contribute to stress at SA? What particular form of overload is most likely to occur?
3. In what ways does social support alleviate stress among employees at SA?
4. What specific indications would you look for at SA to suggest that workers are having adverse reactions to stress (e.g., mental, physical, organizational)?
5. What specific steps could be taken to reduce the adverse effects of stressors experienced at SA?

Work-Related Attitudes: Feelings About Jobs, Organizations, and People

LEARNING OBJECTIVES

After reading this chapter, you should be able to:

1. Define attitudes and describe their basic components.
2. Describe the concept of job satisfaction and summarize two major theories of job satisfaction.
3. Explain the major consequences of job dissatisfaction and ways of overcoming them.
4. Describe the concept of organizational commitment, the major consequences of low levels of organizational commitment, and how to overcome them.
5. Distinguish between prejudice and discrimination, and identify various victims of prejudice in organizations.
6. Describe some of the steps being taken by organizations today to manage diversity in the workforce and their effectiveness.

■ PREVIEW CASE
"ISLAM 101": BASIC TRAINING AT FORD AFTER SEPTEMBER 11

Under normal circumstances, it would not be necessary for employees of a large automotive manufacturing company to have any special knowledge of the Islamic world and the Muslim religion. But in the wake of the September 11, 2001, terrorist attacks, circumstances were anything but normal. This was especially the case at Ford Motor Company; headquartered in Dearborn, Michigan, which, as home to many Muslim immigrants from Middle Eastern countries, is one of the largest Arab-American communities in the United States.

Suspicions toward Ford's many Muslim employees grew, as did tensions that promised to threaten harmony in the workforce unless something was done. To neutralize these fears, a grass-roots group of Middle Eastern workers was formed. Within days of the terrorist attack, they organized a fund-raising concert to aid the families of the victims. This helped people grieve together, making them feel better, but it did little to promote understanding of the Muslim world, which now was beginning to be the focus of ridicule by many of Ford's non-Islamic employees.

Recognizing that something had to be done, Mona Abdalall, who heads Ford's Interfaith Network (a group that represents seven different religious groups within the company), came up with a simple but elegant solution. She held an "Islam 101" meeting, designed to help people understand what Islam is all about. A high-ranking Muslim spiritual leader was brought in for the occasion, who reassured those gathered that the Koran (the Muslim bible) forbids killing in all forms. The terrorists, he explained, were radicals, who misinterpreted their religion and were not at all like the millions of other peace-loving Muslims in the world.

When, to everyone's surprise, over 500 people showed up at this meeting, Abdalall, a 17-year employee at Ford, scheduled smaller, more intimate meetings of 60. Only several months later did interest in these sessions begin to wane. Although a few non-Muslims remained skeptical, the vast majority left the sessions with a better understanding of Islamic culture and the Muslim religion—an understanding that appears to be breeding tolerance and acceptance during a particularly difficult period.

According to Samia Barnat, a manufacturing engineer who is Muslim, the results of these sessions are immediately noticeable. The year before the meetings, for example, coworkers used to offer her food during Ramadan, the month-long holiday, not realizing that Muslims fast during the days. Now, as more people have learned about her religious beliefs and customs, she feels better accepted.

Amidst the evil of the September 11, 2001 terrorist attacks, it has been reassuring to find good. Americans have a renewed sense of patriotism, and people throughout the world have developed greater sensitivity to one another and have grown intolerant of hatred and bigotry. As regrettable as it was that it took an unspeakable tragedy to bring this about, Ford surely is fortunate to find that a new spirit of personal inquisitiveness and acceptance has developed in Dearborn. Instead of being ignorant about Islamic people—or, worse yet, harboring suspicions about them—Ford employees now have a greater understanding of this culture than ever before. This, in turn, has eased tensions and makes it easier for people of various races and religions to work together in harmony. As a result, Ford now can draw on its valuable human capital to improve business. And this, in turn, will keep employees feeling good about working for the giant automaker, thereby keeping them on the job.

Obviously, such feelings can have a strong impact on the way we behave in organizations. Indeed, such feelings—*attitudes* as they are called—represent an important part of people's lives, particularly on the job. Not only may our attitudes toward our jobs or organizations—referred to as *work-related attitudes*—have profound effects on the way we perform but also on the quality of life we experience while at work. We will carefully examine these effects in this chapter.

Specifically, we will begin by describing the general nature of attitudes. With this background behind us, we will take a closer look at several specific types of work-related attitudes. We'll start with *job satisfaction*—essentially, people's positive or negative feelings about their jobs.[1] We will describe some of the major factors contributing to feelings of satisfaction and dissatisfaction with one's work and then consider the consequences of such reactions on organizational behavior.

Building on this, we will turn to another important work-related attitude—*organizational commitment.* This has to do with people's feelings about the organizations for which they work—the degree to which they identify with the organizations that employ them (much as patriotism reflects commitment to one's country).[2] Finally, we will turn to a special type of attitude with which you are likely to be all too familiar and that was involved in what occurred at Ford—namely, *prejudice.* This involves negative views about others who fall into certain categories, such as women and ethnic minorities, to mention just a few.[3] As we will see, such attitudes can have a seriously disruptive impact on the lives of individuals and the effective functioning of the organizations in which they are employed.

ATTITUDES: WHAT ARE THEY?

If we asked you how you feel about your job, we'd probably find you to be very opinionated. You might say, for example, that you really like it and think it's very interesting. Or perhaps you may complain about it bitterly and feel bored out of your mind. Maybe you'd hold views that are more complex, liking some things (e.g., "my boss is great") but disliking others (e.g., "the pay is terrible").

Three Essential Components of Attitudes

Regardless of exactly how you might feel, the attitudes you express may be recognized as consisting of three major components: an *evaluative component,* a *cognitive component,* and a *behavioral component.*[4] Because these represent the basic building blocks of our definition of attitudes, it will be useful for us to take a closer look at them (see Figure 5.1).

We have suggested that attitudes have a great deal to do with how we feel about something. Indeed, this aspect of an attitude, its **evaluative component,** refers to our liking or disliking of any particular person, item, or event (what might be called the *attitude object,* or the focus of our attitude). You may, for example, feel positively or negatively toward your boss, the sculpture in the lobby, or the fact that your company just landed a large contract.

Attitudes involve more than feelings; they also involve knowledge— that is, what you believe to be the case about an attitude object. For example, you might believe that one of your coworkers is paid much more than you, or that your supervisor doesn't know too much about the job. These beliefs, whether they're completely accurate or totally false, comprise the **cognitive component** of attitudes.

As you might imagine, the things you believe about something (e.g., "my boss is embezzling company funds") and the way you feel about it (e.g., "I can't stand working for him") may have some effect on the way you are predisposed to behave (e.g., "I'm going to look for a new job"). In other words, attitudes also have a **behavioral component**—a predisposition to act in a certain way. It is important to note that such a predisposition may *not* actually be predictive of one's behavior. For example, although you may be interested in taking a new job, you might not actually take one if a better position isn't available or if there are other aspects of the job you like enough to compensate for the negative feelings. In other words, your intention to behave a certain way may or may not dictate how you actually will behave.

evaluative component (of attitudes)
Liking or disliking of any particular person, item, or event.

cognitive component (of attitudes)
The things we believe about an attitude object, whether they are true or false.

behavioral component (of attitudes)
Predisposition to behave in a way consistent with our beliefs and feelings about an attitude object.

FIGURE 5.1
Three Basic Components of Attitudes
Attitudes are composed of the three fundamental components shown here: the *evaluative* component, the *cognitive* component, and the *behavioral* component.

Basic Definitions

attitudes
Relatively stable clusters of feelings, beliefs, and behavioral intentions toward specific objects, people, or institutions.

Combining these various components, we can define **attitudes** as relatively stable clusters of feelings, beliefs, and behavioral predispositions (i.e., intentions toward some specific object). By including the phrase "relatively stable" in the definition, we are referring to something that is not fleeting and that, once formed, tends to persist. Indeed, as we will explain throughout this chapter (and also in Chapter 16), changing attitudes may require considerable effort.

work-related attitudes
Attitudes relating to any aspect of work or work settings.

When we speak about **work-related attitudes,** we are talking about those lasting feelings, beliefs, and behavioral tendencies toward various aspects of the job itself, the setting in which the work is conducted, and/or the people involved. As you will discover as you read this chapter, work-related attitudes are associated with many important aspects of organizational behavior, including job performance, absence from work, and voluntary turnover.

Now that we have identified the basic nature of attitudes, we are prepared to turn our attention to specific work-related attitudes. We will begin by describing a very fundamental work-related attitude—*job satisfaction,* or attitudes toward one's job.

JOB SATISFACTION: ATTITUDES TOWARD ONE'S JOB

If you were to ask people about their jobs, you likely would find that they have strong opinions about how they feel (e.g., "I really dislike what I do"), what they believe (e.g., "we provide important services to the community"), and how they intend to behave (e.g., "I am going to look for a new position"). When you consider that people spend roughly one-third of their lives at work, and that what we do to earn a living represents a central aspect of how we think of ourselves as individuals, such strong feelings should not be surprising.

The various attitudes people hold toward their jobs are referred to as *job satisfaction,* one of the most widely studied work-related attitudes and the topic we now will consider. Formally, we define **job satisfaction** as individuals' positive or negative attitudes toward their jobs.[5]

job satisfaction
Positive or negative attitudes held by individuals toward their jobs.

In taking a closer look at job satisfaction, we will address several major issues. For example, we will consider how job satisfaction is measured, which is a key issue involved in assessing this concept. We also will describe various theories of job satisfaction as systematic attempts to address how the process of job satisfaction works. Following this, we will review the major factors that are responsible for making people satisfied or dissatisfied with their jobs. Then, finally, we will consider the principal effects of job satisfaction on various aspects of organizational behavior. Before considering these topics, however, we will begin by addressing a very basic question: Are people generally satisfied with their jobs?

Are People Generally Satisfied with Their Jobs?

If you were to make assumptions about people's general levels of job satisfaction from stories you read in the newspaper about disgruntled workers going on strike or even killing their supervisors, you probably would think that people are generally very dissatisfied with their jobs.[6] However, these are just extreme examples. For the most part, evidence suggests that the vast majority of people actually are quite satisfied with their jobs. However, there are huge differences in job satisfaction between people from different countries.[7] As summarized in Figure 5.2, the percentage of workers reporting that they are very satisfied was considerably higher in the world's industrialized nations than in those countries whose companies are undergoing the transition from communism.

Despite this optimistic picture, it has become clear that overall levels of satisfaction have begun dropping off sharply in the early part of the twenty-first century. In general, it appears that malaise has been setting in as the economy has taken a turn for the

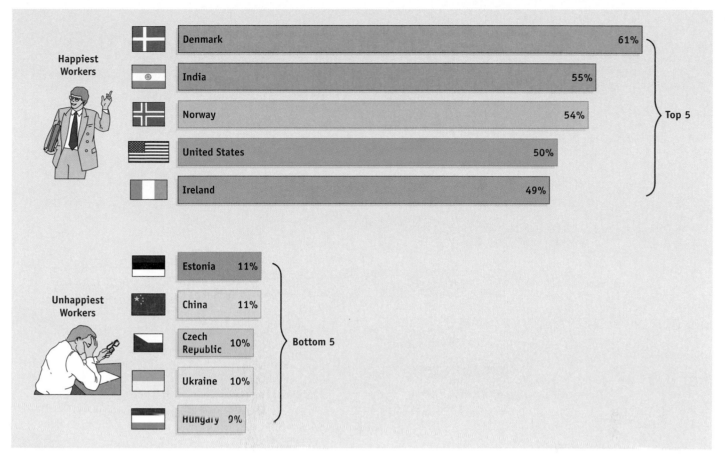

FIGURE 5.2
Are Workers Satisfied? It Depends on Where They Live
In a recent survey, 9,300 adults from 39 countries were asked how satisfied they were with their jobs. As shown here, workers from more advanced countries (where conditions are generally very good) were more satisfied than those from newly developing economies (where conditions can be very poor).
(*Source:* Based on Boyle, 2001; see Note 7.)

worse.[8] As many people lose jobs they've held for a long time, those who remain feel understandably insecure about their futures and find themselves having to work harder than ever before to pick up the slack that remains. Although the drop cuts across all age groups, it was most pronounced among people from 45 to 54—individuals who are most vulnerable to losing their jobs because they are well paid and who are so highly experienced that they are expected to pitch in when labor gaps occur in their companies. As you might imagine, this is only part of the picture. Recent survey research reveals that a wide variety of factors has contributed to lowered levels of morale in recent years (see Figure 5.3).[9]

Certain groups of people are more satisfied with their jobs than others. As you might imagine, the complete picture is more complex; not everyone doing every type of job is equally satisfied. There exist certain groups for whom specific patterns of job satisfaction or dissatisfaction have been clearly established. So, then, who tends to be most satisfied with their jobs? Here are some key findings.

- White-collar personnel (e.g., managerial and professional people) tend to be more satisfied than blue-collar personnel (e.g., physical laborers, factory workers).[10]
- Older people are generally more satisfied with their jobs than younger people. Interestingly, satisfaction does not increase at an even pace. People become more satisfied with their jobs in their thirties (as they become more successful), level off in their forties (as they become disenchanted), and become more satisfied again in their late fifties (as they resign themselves to their lot in life).[11]

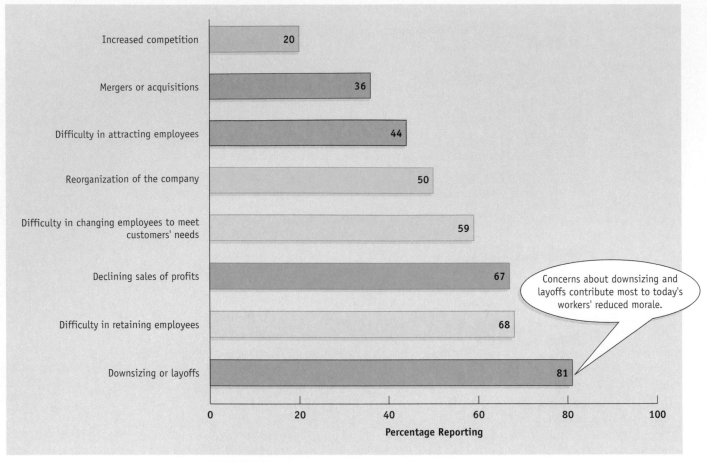

FIGURE 5.3
Lowered Morale in Tough Economic Times: Many Causes
Recent survey research has shown that many different factors contribute to people's general dissatisfaction with their jobs. As summarized here, downsizing or layoffs represented the greatest source of concern among today's workers.
(*Source:* Based on data reported by the Gallop Organization and the Carlson Marketing Group, 2002; see Note 9.)

- People who are more experienced on their jobs are more highly satisfied than those who are less experienced.[12] This shouldn't be too surprising since people who are highly dissatisfied with their jobs may be expected to find new jobs when they can. Moreover, the longer someone stays on a job, the more strongly that person has to rationalize his or her tenure by perceiving the job in a positive light.
- Women and members of minority groups tend to be more dissatisfied with their jobs than men and members of majority groups. This appears to be due to the tendency for victims of employment discrimination (a topic we will discuss later in this chapter) to be channeled into lower-level jobs and positions with limited opportunities for advancement.[13]

Some individuals are always more satisfied with their jobs than others: Job satisfaction as a personal disposition. Not only may certain groups of people be more satisfied with their jobs than others, but also it appears that some individuals are likely to be either consistently satisfied or dissatisfied with their jobs. This is the basic idea behind the **dispositional model of job satisfaction.** The main idea is that job satisfaction is a relatively stable disposition of an individual—that is, a characteristic that stays with people across situations. According to this conceptualization, people who like whatever jobs they're doing at one point in time are expected to like the jobs they're doing at another point in time, even if they're doing different jobs.

This is exactly what researchers have found. Consider, for example, a fascinating study of over 5,000 men who changed jobs between 1969 and 1971.[14] In this investiga-

dispositional model of job satisfaction

The conceptualization proposing that job satisfaction is a relatively stable disposition of an individual—that is, a characteristic that stays with people across situations.

tion, expressions of job satisfaction were relatively stable. In other words, despite the fact that they had different jobs, men who were satisfied or dissatisfied in 1969 tended to be equally satisfied or dissatisfied in 1971. More recent research has found that these effects last even longer—10 years in one study. Specifically, the more people reported feeling satisfied and involved with their jobs at one time, the more they also felt this same way 10 years later, even though lots of things may have changed. (For a general overview of these effects, see Figure 5.4.) Such findings provide good support for the dispositional model of job satisfaction, leading us to conclude quite simply that some people tend to be more satisfied than others with whatever jobs they have.

Measuring Job Satisfaction: Assessing Reactions to Work

Although people have many different attitudes toward various aspects of their jobs, these are not as easy to assess as you might think. Not only can't you directly observe an attitude, but also, as we noted, you cannot accurately infer its existence on the basis of people's behavior. So, for the most part, we have to rely on what people tell us to determine their attitudes. However, people are generally not entirely open about their attitudes and keep much of what they feel to themselves. Moreover, sometimes our attitudes are so complex that it's difficult to express them in any coherent fashion—even if we are willing to do so.

In view of these challenges, social scientists have worked hard over the years to develop instruments designed to systematically measure job satisfaction.[15] Several useful techniques have been developed, including *rating scales* or *questionnaires, critical incidents,* and *interviews.*

Rating scales and questionnaires. The most common approach to measuring job satisfaction involves the use of questionnaires in which highly specialized rating scales are completed. Using this method, people answer questions allowing them to report their reactions to their jobs. Several different scales have been developed for this purpose, and these vary greatly in form and scope (see Table 5.1).

One of the most popular instruments is the **Job Descriptive Index (JDI),** a questionnaire in which people indicate whether or not each of several adjectives describes a particular aspect of their work.[16] Questions on the JDI deal with five distinct aspects of jobs: the work itself, pay, promotional opportunities, supervision, and people (coworkers).

Job Descriptive Index (JDI)
A rating scale for assessing job satisfaction. Individuals respond to this questionnaire by indicating whether or not various adjectives describe aspects of their work.

FIGURE 5.4
The Dispositional Model of Job Satisfaction: General Findings
Results supporting the *dispositional model of job satisfaction* generally take the form summarized here: Some people are consistently more satisfied with their jobs than others, even when they have held different positions over long periods of time.

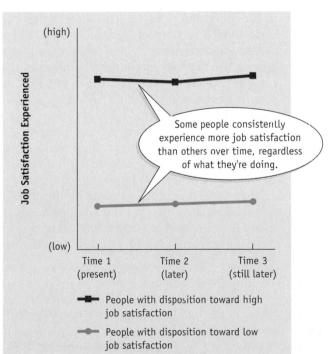

TABLE 5.1 MEASURES OF JOB SATISFACTION: SOME WIDELY USED SCALES

The items shown here are similar to those used in three popular measures of job satisfaction.

JOB DESCRIPTIVE INDEX (JDI)	MINNESOTA SATISFACTION QUESTIONNAIRE (MSQ)	PAY SATISFACTION QUESTIONNAIRE (PSQ)
Enter "Yes," "No," or "?" for each description or word below as it applies to the particular aspect of your job identified.	Using the following scale, indicate the extent to which you are satisfied with each aspect of your present job. Enter one number next to each aspect.	Using the following scale, indicate the extent to which you are satisfied with each aspect of present pay. Enter one number next to each aspect.
Work itself: ___Routine ___Satisfactory ___Good	1 = Extremely dissatisfied 2 = Not satisfied 3 = Neither satisfied nor dissatisfied 4 = Satisfied 5 = Extremely satisfied	1 = Extremely dissatisfied 2 = Not satisfied 3 = Neither satisfied nor dissatisfied 4 = Satisfied 5 = Extremely satisfied
Promotions: ___Dead-end job ___Few promotions ___Good opportunity for promotion	___Utilization of your abilities ___Authority ___Company policies and practices ___Independence ___Supervision–human relations	Satisfaction with pay level: ___My current pay ___Size of my salary Satisfaction with raises: ___Typical raises ___How raises are determined

(*Sources:* Based on items from the JDL, MSQ, and PSQ; see Notes 17, 18, and 19.)

Minnesota Satisfaction Questionnaire (MSQ)

A rating scale for assessing job satisfaction in which people indicate the extent to which they are satisfied with various aspects of their jobs.

Pay Satisfaction Questionnaire (PSQ)

A questionnaire designed to assess employees' level of satisfaction with various aspects of their pay (e.g., its overall level, raises, benefits).

critical incidents technique

A procedure for measuring job satisfaction in which employees describe incidents relating to their work that they find especially satisfying or dissatisfying.

Recent research has shown that the JDI is a highly effective measure of job satisfaction insofar as it is both reliable and valid—two vital criteria for judging psychological tests that we described in Chapter 3.[17]

Another widely used measure is the **Minnesota Satisfaction Questionnaire (MSQ),** which uses a different approach.[18] People completing this scale rate the extent to which they are satisfied or dissatisfied with various aspects of their jobs (e.g., their pay and chances for advancement). Higher scores reflect higher degrees of job satisfaction.

Although the JDI and the MSQ measure many different aspects of job satisfaction, other scales focus more narrowly on specific facets of satisfaction. For example, as its name suggests, the **Pay Satisfaction Questionnaire (PSQ)** is concerned with attitudes toward various aspects of pay.[19] The PSQ provides valid measures of such critical aspects as satisfaction with pay level, pay raises, fringe benefits, and the structure and administration of the pay system.[20]

An important advantage of these and other rating scales is that they can be completed quickly and efficiently by large numbers of people. Another benefit is that when the same questionnaire already has been administered to many thousands of individuals, average scores for people in many kinds of jobs and many types of organizations are available. This makes it possible to compare the scores of people in a given company with these averages, providing measures of *relative* satisfaction. This may not only be useful information for scientists interested in studying job satisfaction but also for companies interested in learning about trends in the feelings of its employees.

Critical incidents. A second procedure for assessing job satisfaction is the **critical incidents technique.** Here individuals describe events relating to their work that they find especially satisfying or dissatisfying. Their replies are then examined to uncover underlying themes. For example, if many employees mentioned on-the-job situations in which they were treated rudely by their supervisors or if employees praised supervisors for the sensitivity they showed in a difficult period, this would suggest that supervisory style plays an important role in their job satisfaction.

Interviews. A third procedure for assessing job satisfaction involves carefully interviewing employees in face-to-face sessions. By questioning people in person about their attitudes, it is often possible to explore them more deeply than by using highly structured questionnaires. By carefully posing questions to employees and systematically recording their answers, it is possible to learn about the causes of various work-related attitudes. For example, one team of researchers relied on face-to-face meetings with employees to learn their feelings about their company's recent bankruptcy filing.[21] The highly personal approach to data collection was particularly effective in gathering reactions to such a complex and difficult situation.

Theories of Job Satisfaction

What makes some people more satisfied with their jobs than others? What underlying processes account for people's feelings of job satisfaction? Insight into these important questions is provided by various theories of job satisfaction. We will describe two of the most influential approaches—*two-factor theory* and *value theory*.

Two-factor theory. Think about some things that may have happened on your job that made you feel especially satisfied or dissatisfied. What were these events? (This is an example of the description of the *critical incidents technique* described previously.) Over 30 years ago an organizational scientist posed this question to more than 200 accountants and engineers and carefully analyzed their responses.[22] What that scientist found was somewhat surprising: Different factors accounted for job satisfaction and dissatisfaction.

Although you might expect that certain factors lead to satisfaction when they are present and dissatisfaction when they are absent, this was *not* the case. **Two-factor theory** suggests that job satisfaction and dissatisfaction stem from different sources (see Figure 5.5). In particular, dissatisfaction was associated with conditions surrounding the jobs (e.g., working conditions, pay, security, quality of supervision, and relations with others) rather than the work itself. Because these factors prevent negative reac-

two-factor theory
A theory of job satisfaction suggesting that satisfaction and dissatisfaction stem from different groups of variables (*motivators* and *hygiene factors,* respectively).

FIGURE 5.5
Two-Factor Theory: A Summary
According to the *two-factor theory,* job satisfaction is caused by a set of factors referred to as *motivators,* whereas job dissatisfaction is caused by a different set of factors, known as *hygiene factors.*

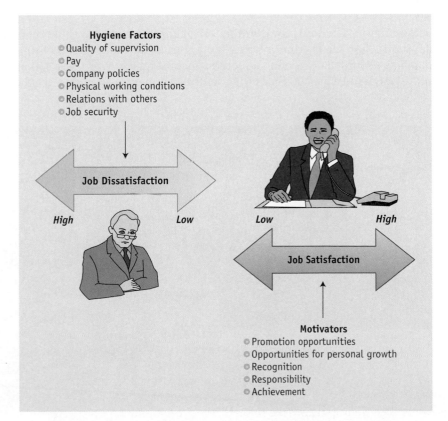

tions, they are referred to as *hygiene* (or *maintenance*) *factors*. By contrast, satisfaction was derived from factors associated with the work itself or to outcomes directly resulting from it, such as the nature of the jobs, achievement in the work, promotion opportunities, and chances for personal growth and recognition. Because such factors are associated with high levels of job satisfaction, they are called *motivators*.

Research testing two-factor theory has yielded mixed results. Some studies have found that job satisfaction and dissatisfaction were based on different factors and that these are in keeping with the distinct motivators and hygiene factors suggested by the theory.[23] Other studies, however, have found that aspects of work labeled as hygiene factors and motivators exerted strong effects on both satisfaction and dissatisfaction, thereby casting doubt on two-factor theory.[24] In view of such equivocal evidence, we must label two-factor theory as an intriguing but unverified framework for understanding job satisfaction.

Still, two-factor theory has important implications for managing organizations. Specifically, managers would be well advised to focus their attention on factors known to promote job satisfaction, such as opportunities for personal growth. Indeed, many of today's companies have realized that satisfaction within their workforces is enhanced when they provide opportunities for their employees to develop their repertoire of professional skills on the job. For example, front-line service workers at Marriott Hotels, known as "guest services associates," are hired to perform a variety of tasks, including checking guests in and out, carrying their bags, and so on (see Figure 5.6).[25] Instead of doing just one job, this approach enables Marriott employees to call on and develop many of their talents, thereby adding to their level of job satisfaction.

Two-factor theory also implies that steps should be taken to create conditions that help avoid dissatisfaction—and it specifies the kinds of variables required to do so (i.e., hygiene factors). For example, creating pleasant working conditions may be quite helpful in getting people to avoid being dissatisfied with their jobs. Specifically, research has shown that dissatisfaction is great under conditions that are highly overcrowded, dark, and noisy and that have extreme temperatures and poor air quality.[26] These factors that are associated with the conditions under which work is performed but not directly linked to the work itself contribute much to the levels of job dissatisfaction encountered.

value theory (of job satisfaction)
A theory suggesting that job satisfaction depends primarily on the match between the outcomes individuals value in their jobs and their perceptions about the availability of such outcomes.

Value theory. A second important theory of job satisfaction is **value theory**.[27] This conceptualization claims that job satisfaction exists to the extent that the job outcomes (such as rewards) an individual receives matches those outcomes that are desired. The more people receive outcomes they value, the more satisfied they will be; the less they

FIGURE 5.6
Opportunities for Personal Growth Promote Job Satisfaction at Marriott Hotels
The two-factor theory of job satisfaction recognizes that employees will be satisfied with jobs that offer opportunities for them to grow and develop. With this in mind, "guest services associates" at Marriott Hotels are given an opportunity to perform a wide variety of jobs. Not only does this help them develop new job skills, but also it keeps them from getting bored.

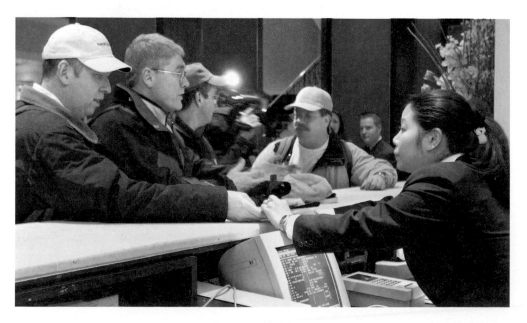

receive outcomes they value, the less satisfied they will be. Value theory focuses on *any* outcomes that people value, regardless of what they are. The key to satisfaction in this approach is the *discrepancy* between those aspects of the job one has and those one wants; the greater the discrepancy, the less people are satisfied.

Research provides good support for value theory. Using a questionnaire, one team of investigators measured how much of various job facets—such as freedom to work one's own way, learning opportunities, promotion opportunities, and pay level—a diverse group of workers wanted and how much they felt they already had.[28] They also measured how satisfied the respondents were with each of these facets and how important each facet was to them. As shown in Figure 5.7, an interesting trend emerged: Those aspects of the job about which respondents experienced the greatest discrepancies were the ones with which they were most dissatisfied, and those with which they experienced the smallest discrepancies were the ones with which they were most satisfied. Interestingly, the researchers also found that this relationship was greater among individuals who placed a high amount of satisfaction on a particular facet of the job. In other words, the more important a particular facet of the job was believed to be, the less satisfied people were when they failed to get as much of this facet as they wanted.

An interesting implication of value theory is that it calls attention to the aspects of the job that need to be changed for job satisfaction to result. Specifically, the theory suggests that these aspects might not be the same ones for all people but might be any valued aspects of the job about which people perceive serious discrepancies. By emphasizing values, this theory suggests that job satisfaction may be derived from many factors. Thus, an effective way to satisfy employees would be to find out what they want and, to the extent possible, give it to them.

Believe it or not, this is sometimes easier said than done. In fact, organizations sometimes go through great pains to find out how to satisfy their employees. With this in mind, a growing number of companies, particularly big ones, have been systematically surveying their employees. For example, FedEx has been so interested in tracking

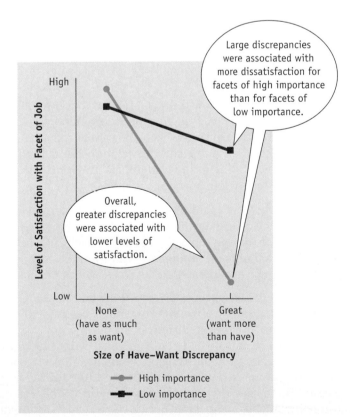

FIGURE 5.7

Job Satisfaction: The Result of Getting What We Want
Research has shown that the larger the discrepancy that exists between what people have and what they want with respect to various facets of their jobs (e.g., pay, learning opportunities), the more dissatisfied they are with their jobs. This relationship is greater among those who place a great deal of importance on that facet than among those who consider it less important.
(*Source:* Adapted from McFarlin & Rice, 1992; see Note 28.)

the attitudes of its employees that it has started using a fully automated online survey. The company relies on information gained from surveys of its U.S.-based employees as the key to identifying sources of dissatisfaction among them.

CONSEQUENCES OF JOB DISSATISFACTION

People talk a great deal about the importance of building employee satisfaction, assuming that morale is critical to the functioning of organizations. As we will see, although job satisfaction does indeed influence organizations, its impact is not always as strong as one might expect. Thus, we might ask: What are the consequences of job dissatisfaction? Our summary will focus on two main variables—employee withdrawal (i.e., absenteeism and turnover) and job performance.

Absenteeism

When employees are dissatisfied with their jobs, they try to find ways of reducing their exposure to them. That is, they stay away from their jobs—a phenomenon known as **employee withdrawal.** Two main forms of employee withdrawal are absenteeism and voluntary turnover.[29] By not showing up to work and/or by quitting to take a new job, people may be expressing their dissatisfaction with their jobs or attempting to escape from the unpleasant aspects of them they may be experiencing. Although voluntary turnover is permanent and absenteeism is a short-term reaction, both are popular but problematic ways of withdrawing from dissatisfying jobs.

employee withdrawal
Actions such as chronic absenteeism and voluntary turnover (i.e., quitting one's job) that enable employees to escape from adverse organization situations.

Research has shown that the less people are satisfied with their jobs, the more likely they are to be absent.[30] The strength of this relationship, however, is only modest. The reason is that dissatisfaction with one's job is likely to be just one of many factors influencing people's decisions to report or not report to work. For example, even someone who really dislikes her job may not be absent if she believes her presence is necessary to complete an important project. However, another employee might dislike his job so much that he will "play hooky" without showing any concern over how the company will be affected. Thus, although it's not a perfectly reliable reaction to job dissatisfaction, absenteeism is one of its most important consequences.

Turnover

Another costly form of withdrawal related to job satisfaction is *voluntary turnover*—quitting one's job. As you might expect, in general, the lower people's levels of satisfaction with their jobs, the more likely they are to consider resigning and actually to do so. As in the case of absenteeism, this relationship is modest, and for similar reasons.[31] Many factors relating to the individuals, their jobs, and economic conditions shape decisions to move from one job to another.

Turnover is costly. Organizations are highly concerned about withdrawal insofar as it is generally very costly. As shown in Table 5.2, the expenses involved in selecting and training employees to replace those who have resigned can be considerable—ranging from 70 to 200 percent of the employee's annual compensation.[32] Even unscheduled absences can be expensive—averaging as high as $757 per employee, by one estimate.[33]

In high-tech fields, where salaries are high and skills are scarce, the expenses of replacing employees can be astronomical. For example, in 2000, Synopsys, a Mountain View, California–based software firm was losing 35 employees per month—which, at about $100,000 per replacement, led not only to a serious brain drain but a financial one, too. To turn around the hemorrhaging, company officials focused 30 percent of their time on employee retention, and they began interviewing employees to find out what it would take to keep them satisfied and on the payroll. Although this attention detracted from ongoing business, it was necessary to keep the company afloat.

TABLE 5.2 REPLACING EXECUTIVES IS COSTLY: DO THE MATH

The editors of *Working Woman* magazine computed that it costs $64,000 to conduct a national search to replace a midlevel executive at a large company in an urban market. Although the actual numbers will vary, depending on factors such as the nature of the job, the industry, and the location, it's clear that the costs of replacing a high-ranking official can be considerable. Here's how they came up with the figure.

CATEGORY	EXPENDITURE
Fees for national search firms	$10,000
Lost customers or accounts	8,000
Local and national newspaper ads	8,000
Moving expenses for new, out-of-town hire	7,000
Signing bonus for new hire	6,000
Training for new employee	6,000
Interview expenses (including travel)	4,000
Time of managers spent reviewing candidates	4,000
Overtime expenses due to extra workload	4,000
Loss of employees looking for new jobs	3,000
Work put on hold, projects set aside	2,000
Time lost due to lowered morale, complaining	2,000
TOTAL	***$64,000***

(*Source:* Information reported by *Working Woman*, 2000; see Note 34.)

The unfolding model of voluntary turnover. As you might imagine, the decision to quit one's job is not taken lightly; people consider a variety of different factors before making such an important decision. These have been described in a recently proposed conceptualization known as the **unfolding model of voluntary turnover,** which is summarized in Figure 5.8.[34] According to this conceptualization, whether or not someone quits a job is said to depend on the way two key factors unfold. These are as follows:

unfolding model of voluntary turnover

A conceptualization that explains the cognitive processes through which people make decisions about quitting or staying on their jobs.

■ *Shock to the system*—An attention-getting event that gets employees to think about their jobs (e.g., merger with another company).
■ *Decision frames*—A set of internalized rules and images regarding how to interpret something that has occurred (e.g., "based on what I know from the past, is there an obvious response?").

As shown in Figure 5.8, the unfolding model of voluntary turnover recognizes that four possible *decision paths* can result. Trace these paths through the diagram as you read about each.

1. In *decision path 1* (shown in red), a shock to the system occurs that matches an existing decision frame. So, for example, suppose your company loses a large account. This unusual occurrence constitutes a shock to your system. You think about what occurred and assess what it means. If it has been your experience (directly or through others) that when accounts are lost, jobs are lost, you automatically will decide to quit. This doesn't take much consideration. Likewise, it's an easy decision for you if you reach the conclusion that lost accounts don't really mean anything, so you decide to stay.

2. In *decision path 2* (shown in blue), a shock to the system also occurs, but in this case it fails to match a decision frame, and there is no specific job alternative. For example, suppose a leveraged buyout occurs (i.e., your company was taken over by another). This comes as a shock, but it's not exactly clear to you what it means. In

FIGURE 5.8

The Unfolding Model of Voluntary Turnover

According to the *unfolding model of voluntary turnover,* people make decisions about staying or leaving their current jobs based on a complex set of cognitive processes. The major considerations are whether or not there is a shock to the system (i.e., if something occurs that makes you consider leaving) and your decision frame (i.e., the things you believe). The various decision paths are summarized here.
(*Source:* Based on suggestions by Mitchell & Lee, 2001; see Note 32.)

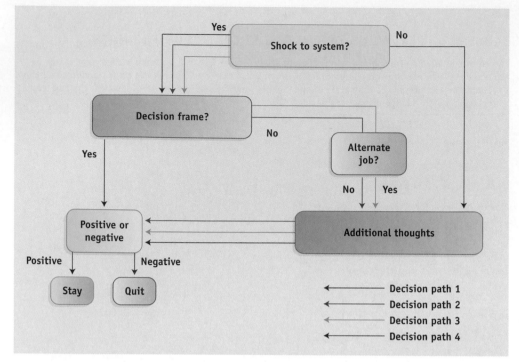

such a case, you might assess how you feel about your organization. If upon further reflection you decide you like it, you probably will stay, especially since there is no alternative. If, however, this gets you to think about how bad the job is, you might decide to leave anyway, even without another job to fall back on. In either case, it's not immediately obvious to you what to do because you lack a decision frame, so you are forced to give the matter a lot of thought.

3. In *decision path 3* (shown in green), a shock to the system occurs and it fails to match a decision frame, but here there is a specific job alternative available. For example, suppose there's a leveraged buyout. Again, this comes as a shock, and you find it difficult to interpret because it does not match any existing decision frames. However, in this case, because there's an alternate job available, you compare your present job to this possible new one. If you think the future will be better by staying, you will be likely to do so. However, if you are so dissatisfied with your present job that you think the new one will be better, you will be inclined to leave. This, too, will be a difficult decision, although it's made easier by the presence of an alternative.

4. Finally, in *decision path 4* (shown in black), there is no shock to the system (e.g., no lost account and no leveraged buyout). As a result, no decision frame is considered, leaving you unlikely to consider leaving in the first place. Under such circumstances, if you're feeling dissatisfied, you may be inclined to quit if other conditions are right, but otherwise you probably would be unwilling to bother doing so, leading you to stay. In either case, it may take a while for you to make the decision since no shock to the system has occurred.

Clearly, the unfolding model is quite complex. However, despite this complexity and the fact that the conceptualization is new to the field of OB, it has received strong research support.[35] Accordingly, the unfolding model may be considered a valuable approach to understanding the relationship between job satisfaction and turnover.

Task Performance: Are Happy Workers Productive Workers?

Many people believe that happy workers are productive workers. But is this really the case? In other words, *is* job satisfaction, in fact, directly linked to task performance or organizational productivity? Research suggests that the relationship is positive but not especially strong. In fact, after reviewing hundreds of studies on this topic, it has been found that the mean correlation between job satisfaction and performance is extremely modest (only 0.17, which, as explained in Appendix I, is quite small).[36] Why does job satisfaction have such a limited relationship to performance? There are several explanations.

First, in many work settings, there is little room for large changes in performance. Some jobs are structured so that the people holding them *must* maintain at least some minimum level of performance just to remain at their jobs. For others, there may be very little leeway for exceeding minimum standards. Thus, the range of possible performance in many jobs is highly restricted. Moreover, for many employees, the rate at which they work is closely linked to the work of others or the speed at which various machines operate. As such, their performance may have such little room to fluctuate that it may not be highly responsive to changes in their attitudes.

Second, job satisfaction and performance actually may not be directly linked. Rather, any apparent relationship between them may stem from the fact that both are related to a third factor—receipt of various rewards. Some scientists have suggested that the relationship works as follows.[37] Past levels of performance lead to the receipt of both extrinsic rewards (e.g., pay, promotions) and intrinsic rewards (e.g., feelings of accomplishment). If employees judge these to be fair, they eventually may recognize a link between their performance and these outcomes. This, in turn, may have two effects. First, it may encourage high levels of effort and, thus, good performance. Second, it may lead to high levels of job satisfaction. In short, high productivity and high satisfaction may both stem from the same conditions. These two factors themselves, however, may not be directly linked. For these and other reasons, job satisfaction may not be directly related to performance in many contexts.

Although job performance might not be affected adversely by dissatisfaction, the concept of job satisfaction is very important. Naturally, as working people, we all want to be satisfied with our jobs. Not only does satisfaction keep us from withdrawing from our jobs, but it also makes them more pleasant and enjoyable. And this, of course, is an important end in itself.

Guidelines for Promoting Job Satisfaction

In view of the negative consequences of dissatisfaction, it makes sense to consider ways of raising satisfaction and preventing dissatisfaction on the job. Based on what scientists know about this, here are several suggestions.

1. *Make jobs fun.* People are more satisfied with jobs they enjoy doing than those that are dull and boring. Although some jobs are intrinsically boring, it's possible to infuse some level of fun into almost any job. Some creative techniques that have been used include passing bouquets of flowers from one person's desk to another's every half hour and taking fun pictures of others on the job and posting them on the bulletin board.[38] For some more interesting examples of things companies can do to make the workplace fun, see Table 5.3.

2. *Pay people fairly.* People who believe that their organizations' pay systems are inherently unfair tend to be dissatisfied with their jobs. This not only applies to salary and hourly pay but also to fringe benefits (as we will describe in Chapter 6). Consistent with value theory, they feel fairly paid and when people are given opportunities to select the fringe benefits they most desire, their job satisfaction tends to rise.

3. *Match people to jobs that fit their interests.* The more people find that they are able to fulfill their interests while on the job, the more satisfied they will be with those jobs. With this in mind, companies such as Coca-Cola and the Walt Disney Company offer individualized counseling to employees so that their personal and professional interests can be identified and matched.

4. *Avoid boring, repetitive jobs.* Most people tend to find little satisfaction in performing highly boring, repetitive jobs. In keeping with two-factor theory, people are far more satisfied with jobs that allow them to achieve success by freely taking control over how they are going to do things. (We will describe this idea more thoroughly when discussing motivation in Chapter 6.)

TABLE 5.3   HAVING FUN AT WORK: SOME EXAMPLES

Companies that take steps to help their employees have fun at work tend to have employees who are highly satisfied with their jobs. Here are a few examples of particularly unusual things that some companies are doing.

Capitol One	An annual investment of $320 per employee is made on a "fun budget." This has been used for such activities as white-water rafting.
CDW Computer Centers	Once a month workers get Krispy Kreme doughnuts. And every Wednesday during the summer months they also get Dairy Queen treats.
Snapple	The company built a makeshift miniature golf course in its corporate head-quarters out of everyday materials found in the office.
Berkeley Systems	A corkscrew slide was built so workers could have fun as they glide quickly down to lower floors.
Pixar Studios	A "funhouse" was built in which people can work while surrounded by toys. Employees needing to go somewhere in the building ride scooters to their destinations.
Pacific Power and Electric	"Frisbee Memo Day" is held, in which formal memos and messages are delivered to people in the office by attaching them to Frisbees and throwing them to their intended recipient.

(*Sources:* Based on material reported in Note 38.)

Although promoting job satisfaction is worthwhile all the time, it is especially important during tough economic times—when confidence and morale are eroding and uncertainty about the future abounds. Moreover, maintaining job satisfaction during tough times is made especially challenging by the fact that managers are likely to be on edge themselves. With this in mind, it is worthwhile to pay close attention to the preceding suggestions under such occasions. In addition, it also is advisable to take certain special steps to promote job satisfaction when times are tough and people are likely to feel most at risk for losing their jobs.[39] Some useful suggestions in this regard are summarized in Table 5.4.

In conclusion, there is good news for managers interested in promoting satisfaction (and avoiding dissatisfaction) among employees. Although it might not always be easy to make a special effort to promote job satisfaction, especially amidst the hectic pace of everyday work, the effort promises to be well worthwhile.

ORGANIZATIONAL COMMITMENT: FEELINGS OF ATTACHMENT TOWARD ORGANIZATIONS

organizational commitment
The extent to which an individual identifies and is involved with his or her organization and/or is unwilling to leave it.

Thus far, our discussion has centered on people's attitudes toward their jobs. However, to fully understand work-related attitudes we also must focus on people's attitudes toward the organizations in which they work—that is, their **organizational commitment.** The concept of organizational commitment is concerned with the degree to which people are involved with their organizations and are interested in remaining within them.[40]

This important attitude may be completely unrelated to job satisfaction. For example, a nurse may really like the kind of work she does but dislike the hospital in which she works, leading her to seek a similar job elsewhere. By the same token, a waiter may have positive feelings about the restaurant in which he works but may dislike waiting on tables. These complexities illustrate the importance of studying organizational commitment. Our presentation of this topic will begin by examining the different dimensions of

TABLE 5.4 BUILDING JOB SATISFACTION IN TOUGH TIMES: SOME SUGGESTIONS

Whenever there's a downturn in the economy, people understandably become worried about their financial well-being. Because maintaining job security is critical, insecure but talented workers are likely to "jump ship," taking other jobs while they can. To avoid the mass exodus that's likely to result, managers can benefit by taking the following steps.

SUGGESTION	COMMENT OR EXPLANATION
Be open and honest about the company's financial situation.	Instead of hiding the facts, employees deserve to understand the nature of the challenges the company is facing. When they do, they may be more willing to pitch in and help. If they suspect you are keeping things from them, they will leave for sure.
Spend time with your best workers, helping them develop their careers.	When times are tough, it's the best workers who have the greatest opportunities to find other jobs, although these are the very people who are needed the most. By spending time with such individuals, it is possible to help them understand their role in helping to turn the company around.
Break assignments into manageable chunks.	With an uncertain future, people may be concerned about making very long-range plans for the company. Dividing projects into smaller time frames (e.g., three to six months) makes it possible for them to enjoy a sense of accomplishment, promoting satisfaction.
Pay people what they're worth.	Fair pay is vital to keeping any employee satisfied. However, it's even more crucial to pay people what they're worth when times are tough. Should they begin to believe they are worth considerably more outside the company, they will be motivated to look for employment elsewhere.

(*Source:* Based on suggestions by Rochman, 2001; see Note 39.)

organizational commitment. We will then review the impact of organizational commitment on organizational functioning and conclude by presenting ways of enhancing commitment.

Varieties of Organizational Commitment

Being committed to an organization is not only a matter of "yes or no" or even "how much." Distinctions also can be made with respect to "what kind" of commitment. Specifically, scientists have distinguished among three distinct forms of commitment, which we will review here (see summary in Figure 5.9).[41] These are significant insofar as their importance has been established in research conducted in countries throughout the world.[42]

Continuance commitment. Have you ever stayed on a job because you just don't want to bother to find a new one? If so, you are already familiar with the concept of **continuance commitment.** This refers to the strength of a person's desire to remain working for an organization due to his or her belief that it may be costly to leave. The longer people remain in their organizations, the more they stand to lose what they have invested in the organization over the years (e.g., retirement plans, close friendships). Many people are committed to staying on their jobs simply because they are unwilling to risk losing these things. Such individuals may be said to have a high degree of continuance commitment. Not surprisingly, research has found that people are less likely to leave jobs when fewer alternatives are present than when there are many other jobs to be found.[43]

Signs suggest that continuance commitment is not as high today as it used to be. Traditionally, people sought jobs that would offer them lifetime employment. Many

continuance commitment
The strength of a person's desire to continue working for an organization because he or she needs to do so and cannot afford to leave.

FIGURE 5.9

Organizational Commitment:
Three Types
Organizational commitment consists of
the three facets shown here: *continuance*
commitment, normative commitment, and
affective commitment.

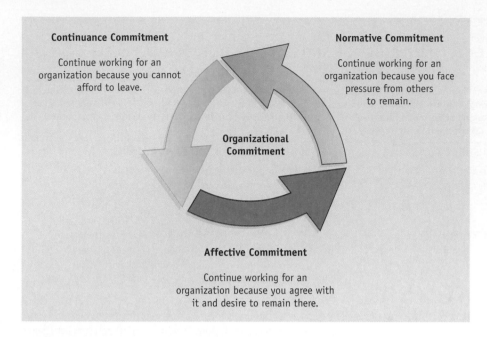

employees would stay on their jobs their whole working lives, starting at the bottom and
working their way up to the top. But today, that scenario is not readily found; the unspoken pact of job security in exchange for loyalty has all but faded from the organizational
scene. In the words of a young project manager working at a New Jersey location of
Prudential, "If the economy picked up, I'd consider a job elsewhere much sooner than
before. I wouldn't bat an eye."[44] This expression of the willingness to leave one's job
reflects a low degree of continuance commitment. The statistics in Table 5.5 tell the
story in striking terms.[45]

affective commitment

The strength of a person's desire to work
for an organization because he or she
agrees with its underlying goals and
values.

Affective commitment. A second type of organizational commitment is **affective com-**
mitment—the strength of people's desires to continue working for an organization
because they agree with its underlying goals and values. People feeling high degrees of
affective commitment desire to remain in their organizations because they endorse
what the organization stands for and are willing to help it in its mission.

TABLE 5.5   IS LOYALTY DEAD? LOOK AT THE NUMBERS

Recent statistics paint a bleak picture of the state of loyalty in the American workplace. As noted here,
today's workers are not reluctant to move on to "greener pastures."

Size matters: Loyalty to small companies is greater.

- Almost 80 percent of people working in small organizations (those with fewer than 1,000 employees)
  feel very loyal to their companies, whereas under 50 percent of people working in large organizations
  (more than 10,000 employees) feel the same.

Americans are mobile: Job-hopping is not uncommon.

- In 2001, one in ten American workers changed their employers: 6 percent took jobs at other companies,
  3 percent retired, and 1 percent became self-employed.
- U.S. corporations lose about half their employees every four to five years.

Money talks: People are chasing higher salaries.

- Forty-four percent of technical workers admitted that they would be lured to a new job by a pay raise of
  20 percent or less above their current salary.

(Sources: Based on data reported in Note 45.)

Sometimes, particularly when an organization is undergoing change, employees may wonder whether their personal values continue to be in line with those of the organization in which they continue to work. When this happens, they may question whether they still belong and, if they believe not, they may resign.

A few years ago, Ryder Truck Company successfully avoided losing employees on this basis by publicly reaffirming its corporate values. Ryder was facing a situation in which the company was not only expanding beyond its core truck leasing business but also facing changes due to deregulation (e.g., routes, tariffs, taxes). To help guide employees through the tumultuous time, chief executive Tony Burns went out of his way to reinforce the company's core values—support, trust, respect, and striving. He spread the message far and wide throughout the company, using videotaped interviews, articles in the company magazine, plaques, posters, and even laminated wallet-size cards carrying the message of the company's core values. Along with other Ryder officials, Burns is convinced that reiterating the company's values was responsible for the high level of affective commitment that the company enjoyed during this turbulent period.

Normative commitment. A third type of organizational commitment is **normative commitment.** This refers to employee's feelings of obligation to stay with the organization because of pressures from others. People who have high degrees of normative commitment are greatly concerned about what others would think of them for leaving. They are reluctant to disappoint their employers and are concerned that their fellow employees may think poorly of them for resigning.

Normative commitment, like the other two forms of commitment, is typically assessed using a paper-and-pencil questionnaire. (To see what questions measuring organizational commitment look like and to assess your own degree of organizational commitment, see the Individual Exercise on page 184.)

normative commitment
The strength of a person's desire to continue working for an organization because he or she feels obligations from others to remain there.

Why Strive for a Committed Workforce?

As you might imagine, people who feel deeply committed to their organizations behave differently than those who do not. Specifically, several key aspects of work behavior have been linked to organizational commitment.

Committed employees are less likely to withdraw. The more highly committed employees are to their organizations, the less likely they are to resign and to be absent (what we referred to as employee withdrawal in the context of job satisfaction). Being committed leads people to stay on their jobs and to show up when they are supposed to. (Although high rates of absenteeism may be signs of low organizational commitment, it is likely that people's willingness to be absent from work may be based in part on their national background. For a look at this possibility, see the OB in a Diverse World section on page 164.)

This phenomenon has been demonstrated in a large-scale survey in which dropout rates among U.S. Air Force cadets were traced over the four years required to get a degree. The more strongly committed to the service the cadets were upon entering the program, the less likely they were to drop out.[46] The finding that commitment levels could predict behavior so far into the future is a good indication of the importance of organizational commitment as a work-related attitude.

Committed employees are willing to make sacrifices for the organization. Beyond remaining in their organizations, those who are highly committed to them demonstrate a great willingness to share and make the sacrifices required for the organization to thrive. This is particularly important in today's high-tech world, where dot-com workers are expected to put in very long hours.

So, how can company officials enhance commitment to stimulate people to make sacrifices? One approach is by making sacrifices themselves—and this is precisely what several of today's top corporate officers have been doing.[49] For example, in 2001 the co-CEO of the investment firm Charles Schwab, David Pottruck, slashed his own pay in

OB IN A DIVERSE WORLD
ABSENTEEISM: SAME BEHAVIOR, DIFFERENT MEANING IN DIFFERENT COUNTRIES

It is easy to understand why people who are uncommitted to their jobs may want to stay away from them, potentially resulting in high rates of absenteeism. However, the degree to which people actually express their low commitment by staying away from their jobs appears to depend on the cultures from which they come. This idea was tested recently in an interesting study in which large groups of employees from Canada and the People's Republic of China were surveyed about their attitudes toward being absent from work.[47]

In general, Chinese managers paid far greater attention to matters of absenteeism than their Canadian counterparts. For the most part, absence was very strongly discouraged—so much so that even an uncommitted Chinese worker would be unlikely to stay home from work. In keeping with this, the Chinese frowned on absence based on illness, whereas the Canadians

half. Carly Fiorina, CEO of Hewlett-Packard, passed up her $650,000 semiannual bonus, and Cisco Systems' CEO, John Chambers, donated his entire salary back to the company, which enabled three employees on the layoff list to keep their jobs. The idea is simple: Employees are encouraged to make sacrifices when they witness their own bosses making sacrifices.

These examples should not be taken as an indication that only highly magnanimous gestures result from commitment. In fact, even small acts of helping others are likely to occur among people who are highly committed to their organizations. This makes sense if you consider that it would take people who are highly committed to their organizations to be willing to make the investment needed to give of themselves for the good of the company. Not surprisingly, research has found that regular, full-time employees are both more committed to their organizations and more likely to pitch in and help others than contingent employees (i.e., those who have no ongoing employment relationship and who are called into work only when needed).[50] After all, employees whose employers are not committed to them have little reason to feel committed in return—or to demonstrate that commitment by doing the little things that make life at work more pleasant.

In view of these benefits of organizational commitment, it makes sense for organizations to take the steps necessary to enhance commitment among its employees. We will now describe various ways of doing so.

Approaches to Developing Organizational Commitment

Some determinants of organizational commitment fall outside of managers' spheres of control, giving them few opportunities to enhance these feelings. For example, commitment tends to be lower when the economy is such that employment opportunities are plentiful. An abundance of job options surely lowers continuance commitment, and there's not too much a company can do about it. However, although managers cannot control the external economy, they can do several things to make employees want to stay working for the company—that is, to enhance affective commitment.

Make jobs interesting and give people responsibility. People tend to be highly committed to their organizations to the extent that they have a good chance to take control over the way they do their jobs and are recognized for making important contributions. As we will discuss in Chapter 6, giving people interesting work to do and giving them

164 PART III: THE INDIVIDUAL IN THE ORGANIZATION

generally accepted illness as a valid excuse for being out of work. This is in keeping with the idea that in Chinese culture a person of good character is expected to maintain self-control and that taking time off work due to illness would be an indication of lack of control.[48]

There was an interesting exception to this general tendency for the Chinese to frown on absenteeism. Specifically, compared to the Canadians, the Chinese were more likely to take time off work to deal with personal or domestic issues. There are two reasons for this. First, unlike their Canadian counterparts, the Chinese are not paid when they do not go to work. As such, they are not receiving pay for work they didn't do, avoiding the potential guilt of overpayment inequity (see Chapter 6). Furthermore, during the time of the study, it first became possible in China for citizens to own private homes. Recognizing this, employers generally considered it acceptable for employees to take time off work to attend to household maintenance.

These findings underscore a key point: Whereas lack of commitment may encourage absenteeism (promoting an attitude in favor of it), this alone may not dictate whether or not someone actually will be absent. Determining this, as indicated here, requires an understanding of the values regarding absenteeism operating within an employee's culture.

responsibility over that work is an effective way of motivating people known as *job enrichment*.

This approach worked well for the Ford Motor Company. In the early 1980s, Ford confronted a crisis of organizational commitment in the face of budget cuts, layoffs, plant closings, lowered product quality, and other threats. In the words of Ernest J. Savoie, the director of Ford's Employee Development Office:

> The only solution for Ford, we determined was a total transformation of our company . . . to accomplish it, we had to earn the commitment of all Ford people. And to acquire that commitment, we had to change the way we managed people.[51]

With this in mind, Ford instituted its *Employee Involvement* program, a systematic way of involving employees in many aspects of corporate decision making. Employees not only got to perform a wide variety of tasks but also enjoyed considerable autonomy in doing them (e.g., freedom to schedule work and to stop the assembly line if needed). By 1985, Ford employees were more committed to their jobs—so much so, in fact, that the acrimony that usually resulted at contract renewal time had all but vanished. Although employee involvement may not be the cure for all commitment ills, it clearly was highly effective in this case.

Align the interests of the company with those of the employees. Whenever making something good for the company also makes something good for its employees, those employees are likely to be highly committed to those companies. Many companies do this directly by introducing **profit-sharing plans**—that is, incentive plans in which employees receive bonuses in proportion to the company's profitability. Such plans often are quite effective in enhancing organizational commitment, especially when they are perceived to be administered fairly.

profit-sharing plans
Incentive plans in which employees receive bonuses in proportion to the company's profitability.

For example, Prince Corporation, the Holland, Michigan, auto parts manufacturer, gives its employees yearly bonuses based on several indices: the company's overall profitability, the employee's unit's profitability, and his or her individual performance. Similarly, workers at Allied Plywood Corporation (a wholesaler of building materials in Alexandria, Virginia) receive cash bonuses based on company profits, but these are distributed monthly as well as yearly. The monthly bonuses are the same size for all, whereas the annual bonuses are given in proportion to each employee's individual contributions to total profit, days worked, and performance. These plans are good examples of some of the things companies are doing to enhance commitment. Although the plans differ, their underlying rationale is the same: By letting employees share in the

The picture of workers hanging around the water cooler and complaining about their bosses and the company is a time-worn image. Today, however, growing numbers of workers have a new place to go to gripe about what's on their minds—the Internet. To the worker, the main advantage of doing one's griping online—a practice dubbed *cyberventing*—is anonymity. Unlike griping at the water cooler, nobody needs to know who made a comment posted online. In that way, it's like a message scrawled onto the bathroom wall. To company officials, there's an advantage as well: The messages are all there in one place to be digested—that is, *if* they can be stomached.

Kyle Shannon, the cofounder of Agency.com learned this the hard way. One day he logged onto Vault.com, a career guidance Web site at which people can post public messages. What he found shocked him.[52] People who said they were his employees complained about such things as seeing people cry at work regularly and the incompetence of some key employees. After Shannon regained his composure, he posted his own response. He acknowledged the company's "growing pains" and apologized to workers who were dissatisfied. He also vowed to take their complaints seriously. In fact, he took them so seriously that shortly thereafter he started his own discussion forum and invited his company's employees to contribute. As they unloaded, relationships between people in the office improved dramatically. After dismissing a few meaningless complaints, he took very seriously the problems he learned about and worked hard to improve things. The feedback he got was invaluable. Instead of seeing droves of unhappy people demonstrate their lack of commitment to the company by resigning, Agency.com employees worked harder and felt better about the company than ever.

In part, this worked because Shannon had an opportunity to learn about problems and to take steps to solve them. It also worked because Shannon sent the message that he cared about

company's profitability, they are more likely to see their own interests as consistent with those of their company. And, when these interests are aligned, commitment is high.

Enthusiastically recruit new employees whose values closely match those of the organization. Recruiting new employees is important not only insofar as it provides opportunities to find people whose values match those of the organization but also because of the dynamics of the recruitment process itself (see Figure 5.10). Specifically, the more an organization invests in someone by working hard to lure him or her to the company, the more that individual is likely to return the same investment of energy by expressing commitment toward the organization. In other words, companies that show their employees they care enough to work hard to attract them are likely to find those individuals strongly committed to the company.

Listen to your employees. In many ways, the easiest way to enhance commitment is also the most effective and the least expensive—simply listening to employees. As tempting as it may be to ignore employees who gripe about things, behind the griping and moaning may be some very serious problems and some very useful suggestions for solving them. Addressing the problems that are identified can be a useful way of building commitment—but, of course, you first have to make the investment of opening yourself to what they have to say. Besides, the mere act of listening to employees shows them that you care about what they have to say. And employees tend to be more committed to companies whose officials demonstrate that they care about them than those that do not send this same message. Although most of the whining and complaining that employees do is done in person, these days many people are voicing their complaints online. And, as described in the OB in an E-World section above, such complaints can be an invaluable tool for enhancing commitment.

his employees, and his commitment to them enhanced their commitment to his company. Shannon was smart, but it's easy to imagine how someone might get so upset as to ruin the great opportunities gripe sites offer to enhance commitment. In fact, making a few mistakes can even start a feud that makes things worse. To avoid such problems, management expert Bob Rosner has made the following suggestions that are worth following.[53]

- *Pick up on misinformation and set the record straight.* Many times employees are upset about things that are just inaccurate, such as false rumors. Without being defensive, explain things like they are.
- *Don't take it personally.* Workers need to vent, and you may be the victim. However, it's not likely that it's you they don't like. Rather, it's likely to be some situation that can be fixed. Besides, even if they don't like you personally, don't let it get to you. Nobody is loved by everyone.
- *Encourage people to contact you directly.* Instead of hiding behind the computer screen, it helps to give people your name and contact number. They appreciate it when you are approachable, and it shows you care.
- *Hold a "town meeting" on the matter at hand.* Chances are good that if one person voices a complaint, many people are thinking the same thing. Rather than put one person on the spot, hold a company-wide (or department-wide) meeting to clear the air.
- *Provide an anonymous forum for complaints.* The problem with the Internet is that it's open to everyone, including people in front of whom you would rather not hang your "dirty laundry" (e.g., competitors and prospective customers). Setting up an internal network, an intranet, would be preferable.

According to Rosner, getting people to complain about their companies is a good sign, an indication that they really care about them. After all, they wouldn't bother complaining about a company that didn't matter to them. Although this may be difficult to keep in mind when people are complaining about your company, it appears that doing so can yield useful benefits in terms of enhanced commitment.

"You're just the man we're looking for. Come around to this side of the desk, and I'll gather up my things and get the heck out of here."

FIGURE 5.10

The Recruiting Process: An Important Determinant of Organizational Commitment
The way we are treated by company officials during the recruiting process sends strong messages about the extent to which the company is interested in us. This interest, in turn, influences our own commitment toward the company. Unfortunately, although the job candidate shown here can have the job, he's unlikely to be very committed to it—if he even were to consider it at all.
(*Source:* ©The New Yorker Collection 1992, Leo Cullum, cartoonbank.com. All rights reserved.)

In conclusion, it is useful to think of organizational commitment as an attitude that may be influenced by managerial actions. Not only might people be selected who are predisposed to be committed to the organization, but also various measures can be taken to enhance commitment in the face of indications that it is suffering.

PREJUDICE: NEGATIVE ATTITUDES TOWARD OTHERS

"Don't jump to conclusions." That's advice we often hear. But, when it comes to forming attitudes toward others, it is often ignored. Instead, people frequently *do* jump to conclusions about others—and on the basis of very limited information. If you have ever made a judgment about someone else on the basis of his or her ethnic background, age, gender, sexual orientation, or physical condition, then you are well aware of this tendency. As we discussed in conjunction with the topic of *stereotypes* (see Chapter 2), such judgments are frequently negative in nature.

Prejudice Versus Discrimination: A Key Distinction

prejudice

Negative attitudes toward the members of specific groups, based solely on the fact that they are members of those groups (e.g., age, race, sexual orientation).

A negative attitude we hold toward another based on his or her membership in a particular groups is referred to as **prejudice.**[54] Not only might people holding prejudicial attitudes have negative beliefs and feelings, but also these may predispose people to behave in ways consistent with these attitudes. For example, it would not be surprising to find that an employment interviewer who holds negative stereotypes toward members of a certain minority group evaluates negatively a candidate belonging to that group and is disinterested in hiring such an individual.

discrimination

The behavior consistent with a prejudicial attitude; the act of treating someone negatively because of his or her membership in a specific group.

Then, if this prejudicial attitude actually leads the interviewer to not hire the candidate, this may be said to be an act of **discrimination.** That is, the interviewer acted consistently with his or her negative attitude by not giving the candidate a fair chance and treating different people in different ways. The key thing to keep in mind is this: Prejudice is a negative attitude, whereas discrimination is the behavior that follows from it (the behavioral expression of that attitude). For a summary of this idea, see Figure 5.11.

FIGURE 5.11

Prejudice Versus Discrimination: A Key Distinction

Prejudice is an attitude and, as such, consists of the three basic components of attitudes. *Discrimination* refers to behavior based on that attitude. The example presented here illustrates this important distinction.

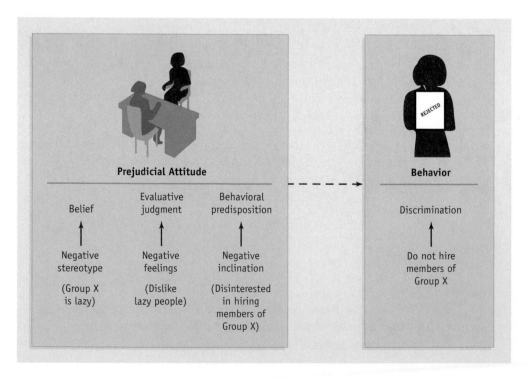

The Reality of Diversity and the Problems of Prejudice

One of the reasons why organizational leaders must be concerned about prejudicial attitudes in the workplace is that such views cannot be tolerated in today's workplace, where ethnic and cultural diversity is the rule (see Chapter 1).

The reality of diversity. There can be no mistaking the fact that the United States is an ethnically diverse nation—and that it is getting increasingly more so. For example, it has been estimated that by the year 2040 half of the U.S. population will be composed of people of African, Latin, Native American, and/or Asian descent. In addition, women— who for many years only infrequently worked outside the home—are currently filling 65 percent of all new jobs, and in just a few years about half of the civilian workforce will be composed of females.[55] For some companies, diversity is already a reality. For example, at the Solectron Corporation, a computer assembly company in Milpitas, California, 30 nationalities can be found speaking 40 different languages and dialects among the company's 3,200 employees.[56]

Interestingly, as this picture of the highly diverse American workforce unfolds, equally real are the unfortunate facts that prejudice against various groups still exists and that these prejudices are likely to have serious consequences. Before describing the nature of such prejudicial attitudes, we first will outline some of the general problems that they create.

Problems stemming from prejudice in the workplace. First, prejudice can be a *source of serious friction or conflict* between people. Although a highly diverse workforce can potentially bring the advantage of differing opinions and perspectives, this may turn into a disadvantage among individuals who hold prejudicial attitudes. Indeed, if one's group membership causes an underlying current of distrust, then the conflict that results may be disruptive to the organization as people fail to cooperate with each other to get their jobs done. In extreme cases, the discriminatory actions that follow from prejudicial attitudes culminate in legal action—be it employees charging their employer with unfair discrimination[57] or customers charging companies with discriminatory actions.[58]

Second, prejudice may have *adverse effects on the careers of people who are the targets of such attitudes.* Affected individuals may encounter various forms of discrimination—some very subtle, but others quite overt—with respect to hiring, promotion, and pay. For example, as we will detail later in this chapter, although there are more women in the workforce who are doing higher-level work than ever before, they remain highly underrepresented in the upper echelons of organizations.[59] Because the discrimination is quite real but not openly admitted, it is frequently referred to as the **glass ceiling**— that is, a barrier that cannot be seen.

Third, we cannot overlook the devastating psychological impact of prejudice on victims of discrimination. Not only is the victim penalized but so, too, are others who share the same background—what has been called **covictimization**.[60] To the extent that talented individuals are passed over because of their membership in certain groups, individuals suffer an affront to their self-esteem that can be quite harmful. This, of course, is in addition to the loss to the organization of overlooking talented individuals simply because they are not white males. In today's highly competitive global economy, this is a mistake that no company can afford to make.

glass ceiling
An invisible barrier to job advancement caused by prejudicial attitudes toward some groups, such as women.

covictimization
The negative psychological impact suffered by individuals who share the same background as direct victims of discrimination.

EVERYONE CAN BE A VICTIM OF PREJUDICE

If there is any one truly "equal opportunity" for people in today's workplace, it is that we *all* stand a chance of being the victim of prejudice. Unfortunate as it may be, there are many different "groupisms"—that is, prejudices based on membership in certain groups—and no one is immune.[61]

Prejudice Based on Age

As people are living longer and the birth rate is holding steady, the median age of Americans is rising all the time. Despite this trend—often referred to as the "graying of America"—prejudice against older people is all too common. Although U.S. laws (e.g., the Age Discrimination in Employment Act) have done much to counter employment discrimination against older workers, prejudices continue to exist.[62] Part of the problem resides in stereotypes that older workers are too set in their ways to train and that they will tend to be sick or accident-prone. As in the case of many attitudes, these prejudices are not founded on accurate information. In fact, survey findings paint just the opposite picture: A Yankelovich poll of 400 companies found that older workers are considered very good or excellent, especially in such critical areas as punctuality, commitment to quality, and practical knowledge.

It is not just older workers who find themselves victims of prejudice, but younger ones as well. For them, part of the problem is that as the average age of the workforce advances (from an average of 29 in 1976 to 39 today), there develops a gap in expectations between the more experienced older workers who are in charge and the younger employees just entering the workforce.[63] Specifically, compared to older workers, who grew up in a different time, today's under-thirty employees view the world differently. They are more prone to question the way things are done, to not see the government as an ally, and to not expect loyalty. They are likely to consider self-development to be their main interest and they are willing to learn whatever skills are necessary to make them marketable. These differing perspectives may lead older employees, who are likely to be their superiors, to feel uncomfortable with their younger colleagues.

Prejudice Based on Physical Condition

There are currently some 43 million Americans with disabilities, 14.6 million of whom are of working age, between 16 and 65. However, only about 30 percent of these individuals are working—and among these, most work only part time or irregularly. Clearly, there exist barriers that are keeping millions of potentially productive people from gainful employment. The most formidable barriers are not physical ones but are attitudinal. Most people who are not physically challenged don't know how to treat those who are, nor do they know what to expect from such individuals. Experts advise that people with disabilities don't want to be pitied but want to be respected for the skills and commitment to work they bring to their jobs. That is, they wish to be recognized as whole people who just happen to have a disabling condition rather than a special class of "handicapped people."

Legal remedies have been enacted to help break down these barriers. For example, in the early 1990s, legislation known as the Americans with Disabilities Act (ADA) was enacted in the United States to protect the rights of people with physical and mental disabilities. Its rationale is straightforward: Simply because an employee is limited in some way does not mean that accommodations cannot be made to help that individual perform his or her job (see Figure 5.12).[64] Companies that do not comply are subject to legal damages, and recent violators have paid dearly. However, probably the most important reason to refrain from discriminating against people with disabilities is not simply to avoid fines but to tap into a pool of people who are capable of making valuable contributions if given an opportunity.

Although you would expect that the ADA has helped people with disabilities, as intended, recent research reveals that the percentage of disabled adults in the workforce has *dropped* by one-third since the law came into effect in 1992.[65] This is especially surprising since the demand for workers rose considerably during this period. Some economists have argued that the ADA backfired because the cost of accommodating disabled workers (and risking lawsuits if fired) has dissuaded many employers from hiring people with disabilities. Still others have argued that the U.S. Social Security Administration now pays out so much more than it did before in disability payments that there's little incentive for some people with physical disabilities to work at all. However, other economists counter that all of this is misleading. The real reason for

FIGURE 5.12
Accommodating People with Physical Handicaps: Capitalizing on Human Resources
To comply with the Americans with Disabilities Act, companies are finding simple ways of accommodating employees who have physical disabilities. Doing so not only avoids discrimination but also enables companies to take full advantage of their human resources. The Gap store in New York at which Freddy Laboy works has benefited from making simple accommodations for his disability.

these statistics, they argue, is that fewer working people than ever consider themselves "work disabled," thereby throwing off the statistics.

Whatever the reason, one key point is clear: Although conditions are still far from perfect with respect to the hiring of workers with physical disabilities, companies that have done so have benefited from these new members of their workforce.[66] Several good examples can be found in today's workplace.[67] For example, through its "Able to Work" program, Microsoft actively recruits people with disabilities. Johnson & Johnson tailor-makes work assignments for its employees with physical disabilities. Companies such as Honeywell and Catepillar use many high-tech innovations to assist their disabled employees. These examples and countless others represent the many successful efforts that have been put into place to accommodate people with disabilities, which enable them to become productive employees.

Prejudice Against Women

There can be no mistaking the widespread—and ever growing—presence of women in today's workforce. Although almost half of all American workers are women, only about one large company in nine is headed by a woman.[68] Is this likely to change? At the CEO level, the figures are worse: 82 percent of executives completing a recent *Business Week*/Harris poll indicated that it was not likely that their company would have a female CEO in the next 10 years. Thus, it appears that "women populate corporations, but they rarely run them."[69] In fact, of the 825 companies surveyed, fewer than 1 percent had a woman as CEO.[70] For some additional recent data on the percentage of women holding top organizational positions, see Figure 5.13.[71] Equality for women in the workplace is improving, although it is a slow victory, to be sure.

Why is this the case? Although sufficient time may not have passed to allow more women to work their way into the top echelons of organizations, there appear to be more formidable barriers. Most notably, it is clear that powerful *sex role stereotypes* persist with narrow-minded beliefs about the kinds of tasks for which women are most appropriately suited. For example, 8 percent of the respondents to the *Business Week*/Harris poll indicated that females are not aggressive or determined enough to make it to the top. Although this number is small, it provides good evidence of the persistence of a nagging—and highly limiting—stereotype. The existence of this problem has led growing numbers of women to venture out on their own. In fact, twice as many women than men are starting their own small businesses.

As more women advance up the ranks, they may be expected to hire other women, potentially breaking the pattern of discrimination that has been so prevalent for many

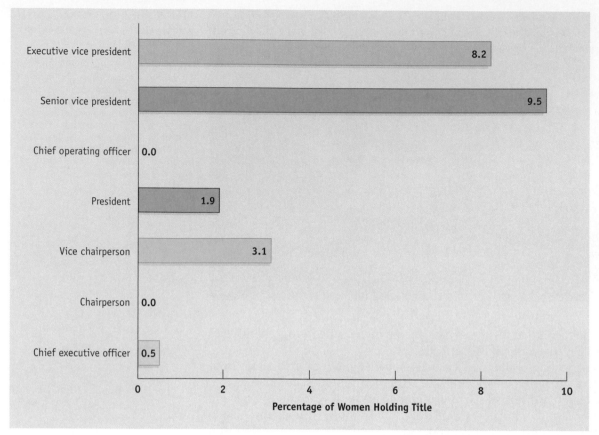

FIGURE 5.13
Women Are Still Not Prevalent at the Top of the Corporate Ladder
Although women and men are almost equally represented in today's workforce, very few women have worked their way up to the top positions in large organizations. This graph summarizes the percentage of women holding various corporate titles according to a recent survey.
(*Source:* Catalyst, 2000; see Note 71.)

years. In fact, this trend already appears to have begun in some industries, such as California's luxury wine business.[72] A specific example of this can be seen at Charles Schwab, the large brokerage firm, where the founder's daughter, Carrie Schwab Pomerantz, is a high-ranking official. At this firm, 36 percent of the executives are women, the most on Wall Street, whereas only 11 percent may be found at at such competitors as Morgan Stanley Dean Witter and Paine Webber.[73]

Prejudice Based on Sexual Orientation

Unlike people with physical disabilities who are protected from discrimination by federal law, no such protection exists (yet, at least!) for another group whose members are frequently victims of prejudice—gay men and lesbian women. (However, several states and over 100 municipal laws have been enacted to protect the rights of gays and lesbians in the workplace.) Unfortunately, although more people than ever are tolerant of nontraditional sexual orientations, antihomosexual prejudice still exists in the workplace.[74] Indeed, about two-thirds of CEOs from major companies admit their reluctance to put a homosexual on a top management committee. Not surprisingly, without the law to protect them and widespread prejudices against them, many gays and lesbians are reluctant to openly make their sexual orientations known.

Fears of being "discovered" and exposed as a homosexual represent a considerable source of stress among such individuals. For example, a gay vice president of a large office-equipment manufacturer admitted in a magazine interview that he'd like to become the company's CEO but fears that his chances would be ruined if his sexual orientation were to become known. If the pressure of going through working life with a disguised identity is disruptive, imagine the cumulative effect of such efforts on organizations in which several employees are homosexual. Such misdirection of energy can become quite a serious threat to productivity. In the words of consultant Mark Kaplan, "gay and lesbian employees use a lot of time and stress trying to conceal a big part of their identity."[75] To work in an organization with a homophobic culture and to have to endure jokes slurring gays and lesbians can easily distract even the most highly focused employees.

To help avoid these problems—and out of respect for diverse sexual orientations—many organizations have adopted internal fair employment policies that include sexual orientation. In addition, some companies are actively working to prohibit discrimination on the basis of sexual orientation. Extending this idea, still other companies are now extending fringe benefits, which traditionally have been offered exclusively to opposite-sex partners, to same-sex domestic partners as well. For example, companies such as Ben and Jerry's Homemade, Inc. (in Waterbury, Vermont), MCA, Inc. (in Universal City, California), and Beth Israel Medical Center (in New York) extend fringe benefits to their employees' partners regardless of whether they are of the same sex or the opposite sex. Clearly, although some companies are passively discouraging diversity with respect to sexual orientation, others encourage it, much to their own—and their employees'—advantages.

Prejudice Based on Race and National Origin

The history of the United States is marked by struggles over acceptance of people of various racial and ethnic groups. Although the American workplace is now more racially diverse than ever, it is clear that prejudice lingers on (see Figure 5.14).[76]

Not only do members of various minority groups believe they are the victims of prejudice and discrimination, but they also are taking action. For example, the number of complaints of discrimination based on national origin filed at the Equal Employment Opportunity Commission (EEOC) has been increasing steadily in recent years. The numbers are even more extreme with respect to complaints based on race. These more than doubled in the decade from 1991 to 2001.[77] Moreover, discrimination victims have been winning such cases. For example, in 1993 the Supreme Court of the state of Washington upheld a $389,000 judgment against a Seattle bank brought by a Cambodian American employee fired because of his accent.

Outside the courtroom, companies that discriminate pay in other ways as well—notably in lost talent and productivity. According to EEOC Commissioner Joy Cherian, employees who feel victimized "may not take the initiative to introduce inventions and other innovations," adding, "every day, American employers are losing millions of dollars because these talents are frozen."[78] Some companies are taking concrete steps to help minimize these problems. For example, AT&T Bell Labs in Murray Hill, New Jersey, is working with managers to find ways of helping the company's many ethnic minority employees get promoted more rapidly. Similarly, Hughes Aircraft Company of Los Angeles has been assigning mentors to minority group employees to help teach them about the company's culture and the skills needed to succeed. Although both examples are only modest steps, they represent very encouraging trends intended to help reduce a long-standing problem.

Prejudice Based on Religion

As illustrated by our Preview Case, religious prejudice can be a serious problem. Although freedom of religion is the law of the land, it's sad but true that many Americans are made to feel uneasy because of their religious beliefs. In extreme cases, people have suffered through acts of **religious intolerance,** defined as actions taken against a person or group that follows a different faith. Such acts might take many forms, ranging from subtle, yet painful, ridicule to physical attacks on people and vandalism in places of worship.

religious intolerance
Actions taken against a person or group that follows a different faith (e.g., personal ridicule, vandalism).

FIGURE 5.14

Does Racial Discrimination Exist? It Depends on Whom You Ask
A survey of American workers shows that racial discrimination is believed to be prevalent in many forms. Its main victims, African Americans, tend to be more aware of discrimination than those who are least affected by it, white Americans.
(*Source:* Based on data reported by Fernandez & Barr, 1993; see Note 76.)

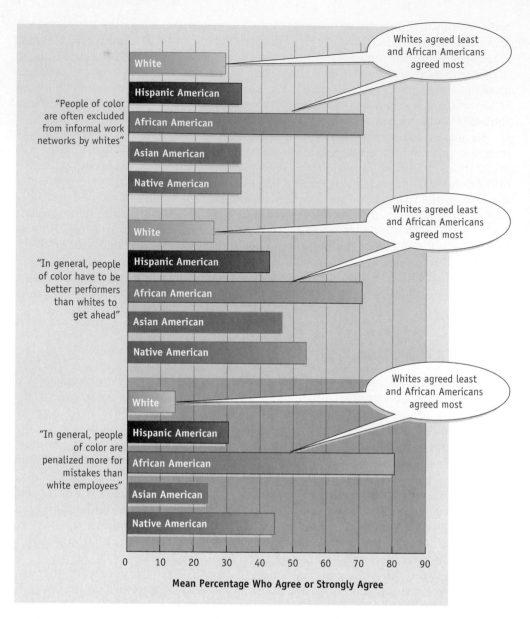

A recent survey of a broad cross section of Americans has shown that religious bias is a reality of the U.S. workplace.[79] It also is a serious concern for management, given that almost half of those who reported religious discrimination indicated that their performance was adversely affected. Equally disturbing was the finding that 45 percent of employees considered quitting because of religious discrimination. Whereas Christians and Jews were least likely to be victims of discrimination, Buddhists, Hindus, and Muslims were most likely to experience religious bias. Of these various groups, Muslims expected to receive—and actually experienced—more bias than the others.

Things are improving, however. Ironically, this appears to be a result of the September 11 terrorist attacks. A survey found that the percentage of Americans holding favorable views of Muslims rose from 45 percent several months before the attacks to 59 percent after the attacks.[80] Apparently, Americans have become better educated about the Muslim religion as the many peace-loving members of this community have taken great pains to distance themselves from the horrific acts of a few extremists. And, of course, Ford (see Preview Case) and other companies have gone out of their way to ensure that religious intolerance does not occur.

Despite such efforts, it appears that company officials don't always know how to handle religious discrimination. Less than a quarter of the people who experience religious discrimination report it to their bosses. Generally, this is because they either don't know where to go in the company to express their concerns or because they feel that nothing would happen if they did. In fact, only 40 percent of companies provide any materials describing their policies on religious bias. In general, then, it appears that issues of religious prejudice remain largely ignored in many companies. Given the extent of the problem, coupled with the success that companies such as Ford have had in turning it around, we suspect that efforts to stem the tide of religious discrimination will become more commonplace in the years ahead.

MANAGING A DIVERSE WORKFORCE: CURRENT PRACTICES

Having established that prejudices abound and that these may be harmful in the workplace, a question arises as to precisely what organizations are doing about this state of affairs. To begin answering this question, it is important to get a sense of the importance of diversity issues in today's organizations.

Do Companies Care About Diversity?

With this in mind, we must ask if companies care about diversity. Specifically, is it of concern to them, and if so, why? We will address these issues here.

Are matters of diversity on today's corporate agendas? A few years ago the American Society for Training and Development surveyed a sample of *Fortune* 1000 companies regarding their stance on diversity issues. The results suggest that diversity management was *not* at the top of their agenda. Only 11 percent reported that it was a high priority, but most—33 percent—indicated that they were only beginning to look at it. In fact, a quarter of the companies surveyed indicated that they weren't doing anything at all.[81]

However, an encouraging sign is that the trend is clearly toward more activity, not less. Additional survey results found that 55 percent of employees believe that their company's management has become more strongly supportive of diversity programs over the past two years. Only 4 percent indicated a decrease in attention to diversity management efforts.[82] In fact, 91 percent indicated that their company's senior management considers the treatment of people to be the "make-or-break corporate resource" of the day.[83] So, to answer the question raised at the beginning of this section—yes, concern about diversity issues is rapidly growing.

Why do companies engage in diversity management efforts? If you're a skeptic, you may believe that companies pay attention to diversity management so as to respond to government pressure. However, surveys have shown that this was identified as a contributing factor by only 29 percent of the respondents.[84] By contrast, the same survey found that the two major reasons are:

- Senior managers' awareness of the importance of diversity management programs (identified as a contributing factor by 95 percent of the respondents).
- Recognition of the need to attract and retain a skilled workforce (identified as a contributing factor by 90 percent of the respondents).

Clearly, today's managers are firm believers in the value of having a diverse workforce.

What Are Today's Companies Doing About Diversity?

It's one thing to identify prejudicial attitudes and quite another to eliminate them. Two major approaches have been taken toward doing precisely this—*affirmative action laws* and *diversity management programs*.

Affirmative action laws. Traditionally, in the United States, **affirmative action laws** have been used to promote the ethical treatment of women and members of minority groups in organizations. Derived from civil rights initiatives of the 1960s, these gener-

affirmative action laws
Legislation designed to give employment opportunities to groups that have been underrepresented in the workforce, such as women and members of minority groups.

ally involve efforts to give employment opportunities to groups of individuals who traditionally have been disadvantaged. The rationale is quite reasonable: By encouraging the hiring of women and minority group members into positions in which they traditionally have been underrepresented, more people will be exposed to them, forcing them to see that their negative stereotypes were misguided. Then, as these stereotypes begin to crumble, prejudice will be reduced, along with the discrimination on which it is based.

After some 40 years of experience with affirmative action programs, it is clear that there have been major gains in the opportunities that have become available to women and minority groups. Yet, they are not always well accepted.[85] Not surprisingly, several myths about affirmative action programs have developed over the years.[86] For a summary of these and the facts that refute them, see Table 5.6.

Diversity management programs. However, many of today's organizations are interested in going beyond affirmative action by not just hiring a wider variety of different people but also by creating an atmosphere in which diverse groups can flourish. They are not merely trying to obey the law or attempting to be socially responsible, but also they recognize that diversity is a business issue. As one consultant put it, "A corporation's success will increasingly be determined by its managers' ability to naturally tap the full potential of a diverse workforce."[87] Or, in the words of Virginia Clarke, a top recruiter for an executive search firm, "There is a strong business case [for diversity] now . . . A third of all Americans belong to minority groups . . . [so] a diverse workplace isn't a luxury, it's a necessity."[88]

It is with this goal in mind that many organizations are adapting **diversity management programs**—efforts to celebrate diversity by creating supportive, not just neutral, work environments for women and minorities (see Figure 5.15).[89] Simply put, the underlying philosophy of diversity management programs is that cracking the glass ceiling requires that women and minorities are not just tolerated but also valued.[90] In

diversity management programs
Programs in which employees are taught to celebrate the differences between people and in which organizations create supportive work environments for women and minorities.

TABLE 5.6   AFFIRMATIVE ACTION: MYTH VERSUS FACT

Throughout the years, various myths about the ineffectiveness of affirmative action programs have become popular. However, as summarized here, these don't square with the facts.

MYTH	FACT
Affirmative action has not led to increased representation of women and minorities in the workplace.	Gains have been substantial. Affirmative action programs have helped 5 million minority group members and 6 million white and minority women rise to higher positions.
Affirmative action programs reduce the self-esteem of women and racial minorities.	The opposite is true. By providing women and minority group members opportunities to succeed, their self-esteem actually increases.
Affirmative action will cause white workers to lose jobs.	Even if every unemployed African American worker (2 million) replaced a white worker (100 million), hardly any whites would be affected at all.
Affirmative action plans bring unqualified people into the workplace.	Affirmative action programs specify that only qualified women and minority group members be hired.
The public no longer supports affirmative action programs.	This is overstated. Eighty percent of Americans currently believe that some sort of affirmative action is a good idea.
Although affirmative action programs may have been useful in the 1960s, they are less beneficial today.	The playing field is still far from level. For every dollar earned by men, women earn 74 cents, African American women earn 63 cents, and Hispanic women earn only 57 cents.

(*Source:* Based on information from Polus, 1996; see Note 86.)

FIGURE 5.15

Coke Learns a Lesson About the Importance of Diversity
Following a recent lawsuit in which African American employees alleged that Coke was discriminating against members of racial minorities, the company took great pains to reinvent itself by becoming more diversity friendly. Company vice president, Carl Ware, was put in charge of this effort. His suggestion to tie managers' compensation (including his own) to the attainment of diversity goals was put into place immediately.

this section of the chapter we will identify various types of diversity management programs and then describe some examples of successful diversity management efforts.

What are companies doing to foster diversity in the workforce? A large-scale survey by the Society for Human Resource Management and the Commerce Clearing House has found that several diversity management practices are widespread.[91] These include:

- Promoting policies that discourage sexual harassment (93 percent of organizations surveyed).
- Providing physical access for employees with physical disabilities (76 percent).
- Offering flexible work schedules (66 percent).
- Allowing days off for religious holidays that may not be officially recognized (58 percent).
- Offering parental leaves (57 percent).

However, this same survey found what organizations did *not* do in the way of following up on their diversity efforts. Among companies that conduct some type of diversity training only 30 percent gather any type of formal data to see if it is working. Still fewer, only 20 percent formally reward managers for their efforts to promote diversity in the workplace.

The bottom line is clear: Although there's a lot of talk about diversity in today's organizations, there is generally more talk than action. Still, there are encouraging signs of improvement on the horizon. Given the growing awareness of the importance of diversity management activities, we suspect that more and more companies will be attempting to enhance their competitiveness in the marketplace by capitalizing on the diversity of their workforces. (For a close-up look at what one particular company is doing in this regard, see the Best Practices section on page 178.) With this in mind, we will now summarize some of the specific tactics used to manage diversity in the workplace.

Varieties of Diversity Management Programs

In general, diversity management programs fall into two categories: *awareness-based diversity training* and *skill-based diversity training* (see Figure 5.16).[95]

Awareness-based diversity training. Specifically, **awareness-based diversity training** is designed to raise people's awareness of diversity issues in the workplace and to get them to recognize the underlying assumptions they make about people. It is a very basic orientation, a starting point—one that takes a cognitive approach. Typically, it involves teaching people about the business necessity of valuing diversity and makes them sen-

awareness-based diversity training
A type of diversity management program designed to make people more aware of diversity issues in the workplace and to get them to recognize the underlying assumptions they make about people.

BEST PRACTICES
THE VERY BEST AT DIVERSITY: PACIFIC ENTERPRISES

Although most companies express commitment to having a diverse workforce and make some effort at promoting diversity, a few have gone to great lengths to show how serious they are about being truly inclusive when it comes to hiring, promoting, and retaining members of minority groups. It was precisely with the goal of identifying such exemplary organizations that *Fortune* magazine conducted a study evaluating the largest U.S.-based companies with respect to their commitment to racial and ethnic diversity—the "diversity elite."[92] Among the various categories in which companies were scored were representation by minority group members (especially in top-paid, key executive positions and on boards of directors) and the variety of diversity management programs in force.

Making the top 25 were such highly recognizable corporate icons as BankAmerica, Marriott, Pitney Bowes, Allstate, FedEx, Du Pont, Xerox, Anheuser-Busch, and Nike—all of which have been very active in promoting diversity within their ranks. Heading the list, however, was a less well-known company—Pacific Enterprises

(PE), the Los Angeles–based energy-services holding company whose Southern California Gas Co. is the largest natural-gas utility in the United States. This $2.8-billion-a-year company, along with BankAmerica, is unusual in that it made virtually all of its corporate contributions to organizations that benefit minorities.

What really vaulted PE to the top spot in the diversity elite was its tremendous successes in retaining minority employees and promoting them to top positions. In fact, a quarter of all of PE's board members, a third of its corporate officials and managers, and over half of its workforce of 7,100 are members of racial and ethnic minorities. The fact that these numbers are higher than those of any other company surveyed (and considerably higher than the national averages for all companies) reflects PE's strategy of providing excellent service by having employees who are similar to its customers. And, given what PE's treasurer, Dennis Arriola, refers to as the company's "smorgasbord of customers," it is no surprise that PE goes out of its way to maintain a "smorgasbord of employees" to serve them.[93]

FIGURE 5.16

Diversity Management: Two Major Approaches to Training
Skills-based diversity training builds on the approach taken by *awareness-based diversity training*. However, both approaches strive toward achieving the same goals. (*Source:* Adapted from material in Carnevale & Stone, 1995; see Note 81.)

As has been the case for most companies today, in an era in which companies are starving for talented employees, keeping these individuals on the payroll has been an ongoing challenge for Pacific Enterprises. In the company's arsenal of tactics for winning the retention battle has been an especially potent weapon known as the Readiness for Management (RFM) program—a systematic effort at training and promoting minority employees before they are lured away by other companies. The RFM program allows employees to nominate themselves for the managerial fast track by giving them a series of self-assessment tests to determine the areas in which they most need to improve their managerial skills and then guides them in developing these skills.

Over the years, the RFM program has identified some of PE's most talented minority employees who otherwise might have been overlooked as prospects for management positions. This program has helped Pacific Enterprises retain its large base of minority employees by convincing them that PE is a great company in which to work. Patricia Wallace is a good case in point. An African American graduate of the RFM program, she has worked her way up from an entry-level position to manager of the company's call centers. Although she admits to having "gotten restless from time to time," Wallace readily acknowledges the company's commitment to continuous learning, and she has remained at PE because, as she puts it, "working here is probably as good as it gets."[94] Although Wallace probably didn't realize it when she spoke those words, the *Fortune* study bears out her observation.

To demonstrate to employees just how good they have it at PE, the company does something quite unusual: It actively encourages them to explore jobs elsewhere! In fact, PE goes so far as to teach its people the skills of résumé writing and interviewing that would make them more attractive to the competition. Yet, even when flirting with other companies, most PE employees have followed Patricia Wallace's lead, electing to stay put. The more they look around, the better they appreciate the quality of life they enjoy at PE. We suspect that few other companies would be as secure as Pacific Enterprises when it comes to tolerating their employees' notions of resigning, let alone encouraging them to leave by showing them the door. Then again, no other company ranks number one on the list of the diversity elite.

sitive to their own cultural assumptions and biases. This may involve using various experiential exercises that help people view others as individuals as opposed to stereotyped members of groups.

Skills-based diversity training. Building on the awareness approach is **skills-based diversity training.** This orientation is designed to develop people's skills with respect to managing diversity. As such, it goes beyond raising awareness to developing the tools needed to interact effectively with others. There are four main tools involved in this process.[96] These include:

skills-based diversity training
An approach to diversity management that goes beyond *awareness-based diversity training* and is designed to develop people's skills with respect to managing diversity.

- *Cross-cultural understanding*—Understanding the cultural differences responsible for why coworkers behave differently on the job.
- *Intercultural communication*—Learning to ensure that verbal and nonverbal barriers to communication across cultures are overcome.
- *Facilitation skills*—Training in how to help others alleviate misunderstanding that may result from cultural differences.
- *Flexibility and adaptability*—Cultivating the ability to patiently take new and different approaches when dealing with others who are different.

Both approaches to diversity training have the same long-term goals: They strive to make interaction between diverse groups of people easier and more effective. Then, once people are paying attention to each other, the road is paved for morale to improve, for productivity to be enhanced, and for people to be able to focus their creative energies.

AVOIDING PITFALLS IN DIVERSITY MANAGEMENT

Although most companies have been pleased with the ways their diversity management efforts have promoted harmony between employees, some have encountered problems. In the most serious cases, diversity management efforts have backfired, leaving race and gender divisions even greater than prior to the intervention.[97] Fortunately, several of the problems can be identified in advance.

1. *Focus on a range of differences between people—not stereotypes.* Thinking of people in stereotypical ways can create barriers that interfere with looking at people as individuals. So, instead of looking at the *average* differences between people (which may reinforce stereotypes), experts recommend that managing diversity demands accepting a *range* of differences between people, a range that promises to become even greater in the years ahead.[98]

2. *Managers should not treat someone as special because he or she is a member of a certain group.* Group membership is not as important as having unique skills or abilities. To the extent that managers are trained to seek, recognize, and develop the talents of their employees regardless of the groups to which they belong, they will help break down the barriers that made diversity training necessary in the first place.[99]

3. *Managing diversity requires total managerial support.* Perhaps the main key to the effectiveness of diversity management is complete managerial support. Indeed, you cannot do something as complex as celebrate diversity with a one-time effort. Successful diversity management requires sustained attention to diversity in all organizational activities.[100] Without completely supporting diversity activities, organizations are bound to be disappointed with their efforts.

Given that diversity management programs can be effective in helping organizations tap the rich pool of talent found in a highly diverse workforce, care should be taken to avoid these potential pitfalls.

Diversity Management Is Generally Effective

With all of these benefits in hand, organizations are positioned to attain their ultimate goal—to improve their economic position in the marketplace. Does this, in fact, happen? In other words, are diversity management efforts effective? Do highly diverse companies have a competitive advantage over less diverse companies? In a word, "yes."

The evidence: Diversity is good business. Recent evidence paints a very positive picture of the ultimate effectiveness of diversity management efforts. Researchers reasoned that when companies effectively use their human resources they can lower their costs and thereby perform better than their competition.[101] To test this notion they compared two groups of companies from 1986 through 1992. One group was composed of organizations that received awards from the U.S. Department of Labor for their exemplary efforts at managing diversity. The other group was composed of companies that had settled large claims against them for employment discrimination.

To compare the performance of these organizations, the researchers relied on a key index of economic success—stock returns. Their findings were striking: Companies that made special efforts to use their diverse human resources were considerably more profitable than those that discriminated against their employees. The researchers explain that the organizations that capitalize on the diversity of their workforces are better able to attract and maintain the talented people needed for organizations to thrive. Clearly, managing diversity makes sense not only because it is the right way to treat people, but also because it is good business! With this in mind, it is not surprising to find that so many different companies have a wide variety of programs in place to celebrate diversity (see Table 5.7).[102]

Guidelines for ensuring success. Given that growing numbers of companies are recognizing the benefits of having a racially and ethnically diverse workforce, it pays to consider the things that have made diversity management effective.[103] Based on the experiences of many companies over the years, it's clear that several steps must be taken to make diversity management work. The key ones are as follows:

1. *Actively pursue the best people.* Instead of waiting for talented minority candidates to come to them, the most diversity-friendly companies go out of their way to find these prospective employees. For example, they recruit from historically black colleges and universities, and they contact Hispanic labor organizations.

2. *Make sure that people are accepted and fit in.* Getting a diverse group of people in the door is one thing, but helping them develop into good employees who feel welcome is quite another. The trick is to emphasize cooperation and teamwork between all employees by getting them to work together (we will examine these topics more closely in Chapters 8 and 11).

3. *Educate everyone.* It's not good enough for only some people in the company to value diversity. To be most effective, everyone needs to fully understand the impor-

TABLE 5.7 DIVERSITY MANAGEMENT: SOME CURRENT PRACTICES

Many of today's companies are taking proactive steps to celebrate the diverse backgrounds of their employees. Summarized here are just a few illustrative practices.

COMPANY	NAME OF PROGRAM	DESCRIPTION
Pitney Bowes	Pitney Bowes Celebrates Diversity Around the World	Held a week-long outreach program consisting of over 100 events in which employees, customers, and community neighbors in 40 states and 11 countries recognized everyone else's ethnic backgrounds
DaimlerChrysler	Minority Dealer Program	Actively develops dealerships owned by members of the ethnic communities the company serves
Tellabs	You've Got ConneXions	Offers lavish rewards to employees for referring talented members of ethnic minorities
AT&T	Gay and Lesbian Awareness Week	Designates one week in which gay and lesbian issues are discussed and celebrated
Pace Food	Bilingual Operations	Presents all staff meetings and company publications in both English and Spanish
DuPont Corp.	Committee to Achieve Cultural Diversity	Holds focus groups that lead to career development programs for minority group members

(*Source:* Based on information from Gingold, 2000; see Note 102.)

tance of having a diverse workforce. As such, diversity management efforts should be aimed at everyone.

4. *Assess how you're doing.* Managing diversity, like any important goal, involves keeping careful track of progress. Only when you closely monitor who you're hiring and how well they're doing can you take the steps needed to improve. In other words, don't just institute a program and let it go. You also have to measure its effectiveness and improve it as needed.

5. *Pay attention to details.* When managing diversity, no effort is too small. For example, you should be sensitive to cultural differences in style of dress and food preferences. After all, you don't have much of a chance of feeling welcome if the company cafeteria doesn't serve any food you'd like to eat.

6. *Plan for the future.* Some of the most diversity-conscious companies are not just doing things to promote diversity today but also ensuring that they will have a diverse workforce tomorrow. IBM, for example, has taken steps to ensure that it will be able to hire qualified women engineers by investing in a summer science program for middle school girls.

In conclusion, diversity management can be a highly successful way to promote equality in the workplace. This, in turn, helps attract pools of talented workers who might have been overlooked and helps companies better serve their ethnically diverse customers. However, success is not automatic. It pays to follow these six suggestions when seeking to enhance diversity in a systematic fashion.

SUMMARY AND REVIEW OF LEARNING OBJECTIVES

1. Define attitudes and describe their basic components.
Attitudes are the stable clusters of feelings, beliefs, and behavioral tendencies directed toward some aspect of the external world. Work-related attitudes involve such reactions toward various aspects of work settings or the people in them. All attitudes consist of a cognitive component (what you believe), an evaluative component (how you feel), and a behavioral component (the tendency to behave in a certain way).

2. Describe the concept of job satisfaction and summarize two major theories of job satisfaction.

Job satisfaction involves positive or negative attitudes toward one's work. According to the two-factor theory, job satisfaction and dissatisfaction stem from different factors. Specifically, it claims that factors leading to job satisfaction stem from factors associated with the work itself (known as motivators) and that factors leading to job dissatisfaction are associated with the conditions surrounding jobs (e.g., the work environment). Value theory suggests that job satisfaction reflects the apparent match between the outcomes individuals desire from their jobs (what they *value*) and what they believe they are actually receiving.

3. Explain the major consequences of job dissatisfaction and ways of overcoming them.

When people are dissatisfied with their jobs, they tend to withdraw. That is, they are frequently absent and are likely to quit their jobs. However, evidence suggests that job performance is only very weakly associated with dissatisfaction. Levels of job satisfaction can be raised by paying people fairly, improving the quality of supervision, decentralizing control of organizational power, and assigning people to jobs that match their interests.

4. Describe the concept of organizational commitment, the major consequences of low levels of organizational commitment, and how to overcome them.

Organizational commitment focuses on people's attitudes toward their organizations. There are three major types of organizational commitment. One is continuance commitment—the strength of a person's tendency to continue working for an organization because he or she has to and cannot afford to do otherwise. Another is affective commitment—the strength of a person's tendency to continue working for an organization because he or she agrees with its goals and values and desires to stay with it. A third is normative commitment—commitment to remain in an organization stemming from social obligations to do so. Low levels of organizational commitment have been linked to high levels of absenteeism and voluntary turnover, the unwillingness to share and make sacrifices for the company, and negative personal consequences for employees. However, organizational commitment may be enhanced by enriching jobs, aligning the interests of employees with those of the company, and recruiting and selecting newcomers whose values closely match those of the organization.

5. Distinguish between prejudice and discrimination, and identify various victims of prejudice in organizations.

Prejudice refers to negative attitudes toward members of specific groups, and discrimination refers to treating people differently because of these prejudices. Today's workforce is characterized by high levels of diversity with many groups finding themselves victims of prejudicial attitudes and discriminatory behaviors (based on many different factors, including age, sexual orientation, physical condition, racial or ethnic group membership, gender, and religious beliefs). Although people are becoming more tolerant of individuals from diverse groups, prejudicial attitudes persist.

6. Describe some of the steps being taken by organizations today to manage diversity in the workforce and their effectiveness.

To help tap the rich pool of resources available in today's highly diverse workforce many companies are using diversity management programs—techniques for systematically teaching employees to celebrate the differences between people. Typically, these programs go beyond efforts to recruit and hire women and members of minority groups to creating supportive work environments for them. The most effective programs focus on enhancing awareness of the benefits of a diverse workforce. Although implementing diversity management programs is potentially difficult, experts acknowledge that the benefits, both organizational and personal, are considerable. For example, research has shown that companies whose employees systematically embrace diversity tend to be more profitable than those that allow discrimination to occur.

Questions for Review

1. What are the three main components of attitudes?
2. What is job satisfaction; what are its major causes and the consequences of dissatisfaction?
3. What is organizational commitment; what are its major causes and the consequences of low levels of organizational commitment?
4. What steps can be taken to promote job satisfaction and organizational commitment?
5. What is the difference between prejudice and discrimination?
6. What steps are today's organizations taking to promote diversity, and are these efforts effective?

Experiential Questions

1. Think of a particular job you have enjoyed most. What did you like about it so much? Now, think of a particular job that you enjoyed least. What made you dislike it so much? Did the factors you liked fall into the "motivator" category of two-factor theory? Did the factors you disliked fall into the "hygiene" category of the two-factor theory?
2. Think about the particular organization at which you have worked the longest. What were the main reasons you stayed there? How do these compare to the three forms of organizational commitment described in this chapter?
3. If you have ever participated in a diversity management training program, what effects did it have on you? In what ways, if any, did your attitudes or behavior change? If you have never participated in a diversity management training program, how do you think you would react to being in one? Do you think you would find it enjoyable? Useful? What challenges to effectiveness, if any, do you suspect you might encounter?

Questions to Analyze

1. One of the strategies that has been recommended for enhancing job satisfaction is to make jobs more fun. We all like having fun, of course, but do you really think this matters when it comes to job satisfaction? In other words, is job satisfaction promoted by just having a pleasant, joking atmosphere in the workplace? Or is what really matters making the work itself more interesting and enjoyable to perform? Explain your thoughts on this matter.
2. In today's economy, where replacing employees can be an expensive proposition, it pays to be able to maintain a highly committed workforce. Of the various things that can be done to promote commitment to an organization, which tactics do you believe may be most effective? Explain the basis for your answer.
3. Racial prejudice has been a serious problem in American society for a long time. How do you reconcile this with the fact that diversity management training generally seems to be successful? In other words, do you think diversity training actually changes people's prejudicial attitudes? Or do you think that such programs get people to change their behavior—at least long enough to allow different kinds of people to be accepted? Explain.

INDIVIDUAL EXERCISE

Are You Committed to Your Job?

Questionnaires similar to the one presented here (which is based on established instruments) are used to assess three types of organizational commitment—continuance, affective, and normative. Completing this scale (based on Meyer & Allen, 1991; see Note 41) will give you a good feel for your own level of job commitment and how this important construct is measured.

Directions

In the space to the left of each of the following 12 statements write the one number that reflects the extent to which you agree with it personally. Express your answers using the following scale: 1 = not at all, 2 = slightly, 3 = moderately, 4 = a great deal, 5 = extremely.

_____ 1. At this point, I stay on my job more because I have to than because I want to.
_____ 2. I feel I strongly belong to my organization.
_____ 3. I am reluctant to leave a company once I have been working there.
_____ 4. Leaving my job would entail a great deal of personal sacrifice.
_____ 5. I feel emotionally connected to the company for which I work.
_____ 6. My employer would be very disappointed if I left my job.
_____ 7. I don't have any other choice but to stay on my present job.
_____ 8. I feel like I am part of the family at the company in which I work.
_____ 9. I feel a strong obligation to stay on my job.
_____ 10. My life would be greatly disrupted if I left my present job.
_____ 11. I would be quite pleased to spend the rest of my life working for this organization.
_____ 12. I stay on my job because people would think poorly of me for leaving.

Scoring

1. Add the scores for items 1, 4, 7, and 10. This reflects your degree of *continuance commitment*.
2. Add the scores for items 2, 5, 8, and 11. This reflects your degree of *affective commitment*.
3. Add the scores for items 3, 6, 9, and 12. This reflects your degree of *normative commitment*.

Questions for Discussion

1. Which form of commitment does the scale reveal you have most? Which do you have least? Are these differences great, or are they highly similar?
2. Did the scale tell you something you didn't already know about yourself, or did it merely reinforce your intuitive beliefs about your own organizational commitment?
3. To what extent is your organizational commitment, as reflected by this scale, related to your interest in quitting your job and taking a new position?
4. How do your answers to these questions compare to tose of your classmates? Are your responses similar to theirs or different from them? Why do you think this is?

GROUP EXERCISE

Recognizing Differences in Cultural Values on the Job

One of the major barriers in understanding and appreciating people from other cultures is the fact that they may adopt widely different values—especially when it comes to basic organizational activities, such as hiring. The following exercise (adapted from

Gardenswartz & Rowe, 1994; see Note 99) is designed to make you aware of such differences and to sensitize you to their impact on life in organizations.

Directions

1. Divide the class into groups of approximately 5 to 10 students.
2. Review the values differences noted in the following chart.
3. As a group, identify and discuss specific examples of each of the cultural distinctions noted in the chart based on your personal experiences.
4. As a group, discuss the implications of these values differences. Note, for example, specific problems that are likely to arise as a result of such differences.
5. As a class, review the major implications identified by each group in step 4.

In mainstream American culture . . .	*But in many other cultures . . .*
• People's primary obligation is toward their jobs.	• People's primary obligation is toward their family and friends.
• Employment is "at will"; an employee may be terminated at the discretion of the organization.	• Employment is for life.
• Competition is an accepted way of life.	• Cooperation is considered better because it promotes harmony between people.
• People strive for personal achievement	• Personal ambition is frowned upon; group achievement is highly valued.

Questions for Discussion

1. Was your group or the class as a whole generally sensitive to the differences in values noted in this exercise?
2. What were the major organizational implications of the cultural differences in values identified by the class? What do you think could be done to help people recognize and accept these cultural differences?
3. Did you come away from this exercise with a better understanding of the way cultural differences between people may impact organizational activities?

WEB SURFING EXERCISE

Gripe Sites

You can learn a lot about workers' complaints about their companies by visiting the Web sites at which they post their concerns. Some of the more interesting ones are as follows:

www.walmartyrs.com	Visitors to this Web site are dissatisfied Wal-Mart customers and employees.
www.untied.com	Pilots, flight attendants, and passengers go to this Web site to voice their complaints against United Airlines.
www.stainedapron.com	If you'd like to know what restaurant workers think about each other and their customers, this site is a real eye-opener.
www.netslaves.com	People who work in high-tech fields grouse their long hours in addition to discussing the latest technical gadgets.

Visit these Web sites and then answer the following questions based on what you see. Before you do, it's only fair to caution that these are open to anyone and what you read may be completely untrue, so don't take them as valid representations of the companies depicted. It's also possible that some of the postings may be offensive, so use discretion.

1. At which of these Web sites were employees most upset? How would you characterize the gripes you spotted?
2. In any of these Web sites, did you spot any concerns that appeared consistently, the kind that would warrant your attention as a corporate officer?
3. Taking any two of the complaints voiced, what steps would you recommend as a company official to help turn things around and enhance organizational commitment?

Net-Working for Women

Increasing numbers of women are entering high-tech fields, although these fields still tend to be dominated by men. As a result, women often find it difficult to compare notes with each other about how to get ahead. With this in mind, the following Web sites have come to the rescue:

> www.girlgeeks.com
> www.iwt.org
> www.springboard2000.org
> www.winm.org
> www.witi.com
> www.worldwit.org

After visiting these sites, answer the following questions about them.

1. How would you characterize the general types of advice that are given?
2. Which of these Web sites do you most prefer? Why?
3. Do you believe that these Web sites can be useful?

PRACTICING OB

Improving Attitudes to Reduce Absenteeism

Absenteeism has been so chronically high at a manufacturing plant that on many days there is not enough crew present at the start of a shift to staff all stations of the assembly line. The company is suffering as a result and turns to you for advice. Answer the following questions based on material in this chapter.

1. How can the job be made more interesting so as to encourage the employees to show up for work?
2. What can be done to improve organizational commitment, which also may contribute to the problem of absenteeism?
3. How might prejudice and discrimination contribute to the absenteeism problem? What can be done to reduce them?

CASE IN POINT

Texaco Yesterday Versus Today: Now, Only the Oil Is Crude

The year 1996 was a bleak one for Texaco (now Chevron Texaco Corp.). One fall day while the company was in the midst of defending itself against legal charges of discrimination brought by 1,400 African American employees, a few top executives met to decide how to proceed. Secret tape recordings of that meeting revealed not only that these officials discussed destroying some incriminating documents, but also they freely used racial epithets in the course of doing so. After these tapes were shared with the plaintiffs' attorneys and the *New York Times,* Texaco found itself in the midst of a public relations nightmare. In the days that followed, the company's stock dropped so much that it lost nearly $1 billion in value.

Shortly thereafter, Texaco's chairman and CEO, Peter I. Bijur, settled the lawsuit, paying $140 million in damages and back pay to minority employees and setting aside another $35 million for a task force to monitor the company's treatment of women and minorities for the next five years. In doing so, Texaco's goal, according to Bijur, was to become "a model of workplace opportunity for all men and women." Has Texaco met this goal? Observers note that although Texaco is still not among the most hospitable companies for members of minority groups, it has made considerable strides.

Statistics tell the story. In recent years, over 40 percent of new hires and about a quarter of all newly promoted employees have come from minority ranks. Also, over $1 billion—approximately 15 percent of the company's spending—has been directed at businesses owned by women and members of minority groups. And although 80 percent of the company's top executives are still white men, growing numbers are coming from minority ranks. "Now," Bijur remarks, "we treat all people with the utmost respect—and that is a real achievement."

Because Texaco is under careful scrutiny—both from the courts and from the public—with respect to its treatment of women and minorities, it doesn't have much choice in the matter. Still, the company has shown that it is quite serious. Completely overhauling the way it went about hiring and treating people, Bijur took several steps to show that he would not tolerate disrespect. Rather than simply talking about promoting equality and respect for everyone, he set meaningful goals and timetables to help advance women and minorities. So serious are these goals that a portion of all top executives' and managers' annual evaluations is based on how effectively they meet them. Importantly, the company has prospered financially as it has strived toward these goals.

Clearly, changes have resulted: Corporate attorneys who used to spend time defending against discrimination lawsuits have found that virtually no such complaints have reached their desks in recent years. Even Bari-Ellen Roberts, the woman who initiated the lawsuit against Texaco, is optimistic that the company will continue its efforts to improve the treatment of women and minorities in the years ahead. "Then again," she said, "they had to—things could not remain the same."

Critical Thinking Questions

1. To what extent do you believe that Texaco's actions will be effective in getting its high-ranking employees to feel less prejudice toward members of minority groups?
2. How severely do you believe Texaco's public image was harmed because of this incident? Analogously, do you believe the company's image will be helped because of its new diversity management efforts?
3. What kinds of diversity management efforts do you believe would be most effective at Texaco?

6

Motivation in Organizations

LEARNING OBJECTIVES

After reading this chapter, you should be able to:
1. **Define** motivation and **explain** its importance in the field of organizational behavior.
2. **Describe** need hierarchy theory and what it recommends about improving motivation in organizations.
3. **Identify** and **explain** the conditions through which goal setting can be used to improve job performance.
4. **Describe** distributive justice, procedural justice, and interactional justice, and **explain** how they may be applied to motivating people in organizations.
5. **Describe** expectancy theory and how it may be applied in organizations.
6. **Distinguish** between job enlargement, job enrichment, and the job characteristics model as techniques for motivating employees.

■ PREVIEW CASE
PAULA LAWLOR: NOT YOUR ORDINARY CEO

Helping hospitals maintain patient records and organize documents for accreditation is probably not the most glamorous business, especially when housed in a nondescript facility in King of Prussia, Pennsylvania. Yet, none of the 175 employees of Medi-Health Outsourcing consider their jobs to be boring. Most are so highly charged, in fact, that they hardly can wait to get to work. Strange? Maybe so, but Medi-Health has a secret weapon—CEO Paula Lawlor.

It isn't your ordinary CEO who storms headquarters wearing track pants and running shoes, admonishing everyone to get up and exercise. And it certainly isn't any ordinary CEO who disrupts office routine with sidesplitting personal stories. Then again, there's nothing ordinary about Paula Lawlor. Described by her sisters, both of whom work at the company, as "a tornado," Lawlor is considered charming but demanding. Goof off, and you're out the door, but do well, and you can go very far. Indeed, the sky's the limit for employees of Medi-Health, where salaried managers are encouraged to run their divisions as they see fit, and hourly employees are treated more like independent consultants.

At Medi-Health, nobody has to get bored. All employees are free to move around the company until they find a job that best suits them, no matter what it takes to train them! No one can have any excuse for failing to get their work done. If it means working from home, that's fine, and if it means arranging their schedules around their family obligations, that's acceptable as well. You even can take a three-month leave of absence without risking your job. As chaotic as things seem, there's a method to Lawlor's madness: She doesn't care when or how you work, so long as you get the job done. Employees are free to manage their work and their lives as they see fit without discussion. However, if you fail to meet your goals, you'll have to answer to Lawlor, who can be just as unforgiving about what you don't do as she is accepting of how you do it!

Responsibility is the flip side of flexibility, and both are key to Medi-Health's operations. Some employees have adjusted their schedules to attend their kids' soccer games, even if it means working into the wee hours of the morning. For a while, financial analyst Gabe Urban took off every Friday to train for the Ironman Triathlon, but nobody minded because he got all his work done by Thursday. For most, the target numbers are clear: Meet the required goal—in one department, abstracting 100 medical records per week with 95 percent accuracy—and the rest of the time is yours.

> She doesn't care when or how you work, so long as you get the job done. Employees are free to manage their work and their lives as they see fit without discussion.

At the executive level, each of the four departments is run as a separate business. Each senior manager drafts a mini business plan. Then, with Lawlor's approval, he or she is given a budget to bring it to fruition. How much everyone gets paid depends on the company's performance in satisfying that plan, as well as each individual's success in hitting targets along the way. Because everyone's pay is tied to the company's success, there's a great deal of peer pressure to perform, and everyone pitches in to make things work. Those who don't relish the responsibility tend to leave the company right away. Lawlor admits, "It's a hard place to work because we expect people to manage their lives." But those who welcome the responsibility are given whatever tools they need to succeed—and succeed they do. Not one of the company's top managers has ever left his or her position. With profit consistently running at 15 percent annually, what's working out so well for the employees is also showing up on the company's bottom line.

Paula Lawlor surely knows what it takes to light a fire under her employees. She gives them responsibility over what they do, she holds them to target goals, and she pays them based on how well they perform. But why does doing these things stimulate people into action? In other words, through what psychological mechanisms are people encouraged to work hard? And from a practical perspective, what can we learn from this situation when it comes to motivating the people with whom we work every day? With an eye toward answering these questions, we will examine the process of *motivation* in this chapter.

We will discuss several ways of motivating employees in this chapter—identifying not only what you can do to motivate people but also precisely what makes various motivational techniques successful. In other words, in keeping with the dual orientation of the field of OB, our approach is based on conducting and applying sound scientific research to issues faced by managers attempting to motivate their employees. With this in mind, we are interested in asking both theoretical questions (e.g., "*What* motivates people, and *why*?") and applied questions (e.g., "*How* can this knowledge be put to practical use?"). This dual focus will be apparent in this chapter.

The question of exactly what it takes to motivate workers has received a great deal of attention by both practicing managers and organizational scientists.[1] In addressing this issue, we examine five different approaches. Specifically, we will focus on motivating by (1) meeting basic human needs, (2) setting goals, (3) treating people fairly, (4) enhancing beliefs that desired rewards can be attained, and (5) designing jobs to make them more desirable. Our discussion of each major approach to motivation will focus on what each theory says, the research bearing on it, and its practical implications. We think this orientation will help you develop a solid understanding of the importance of motivation as a topic of interest to organizational scientists and practitioners. However, before turning to these theories and applications, we first must consider a very basic matter—namely, exactly what is meant by the term *motivation*.

motivation
The set of processes that arouse, direct, and maintain human behavior toward attaining some goal.

Although motivation is a broad and complex concept, organizational scientists have agreed on its basic characteristics.[2] We defined **motivation** as the set of processes that arouse, direct, and maintain human behavior toward attaining some goal. The diagram in Figure 6.1 will guide our explanation as we elaborate on this definition.

Components of Motivation

The first part of our definition deals with *arousal*. This has to do with the drive, or energy, behind our actions. For example, people may be guided by their interest in making a good impression on others, doing interesting work, being successful at what they do, and so on. Their interest in satisfying these motives stimulates them to engage in behaviors designed to bring them about.

But what will people do to satisfy their motives? Motivation also is concerned with the choices people make and the *direction* their behavior takes. For example, employees interested in cultivating a favorable impression on their supervisors may do many different things: compliment them on their good work, do special favors for them, work extra hard on an important project, and the like. Each of these options may be recognized as a path toward meeting the person's goal.

The final part of our definition deals with *maintaining* behavior. How long will people persist at attempting to meet their goal? To give up in advance of goal attainment means to not satisfy the need that stimulated the behavior in the first place. Obviously, people who do not persist at meeting their goals (e.g., salespeople who give up before reaching their quotas) cannot be said to be highly motivated.

To summarize, motivation requires all three components: the arousal, direction, and maintenance of goal-directed behavior. An analogy may help to tie these components together. Imagine that you are driving down a road on your way home. The arousal part of motivation is like the energy created by the car's engine. The direction component is like the steering wheel, taking you along your chosen path. Finally, the maintenance aspect of the definition is the persistence that keeps you going until you arrive home, thereby reaching your goal.

FIGURE 6.1

Basic Components of Motivation
Motivation involves the arousal, direction, and maintenance of behavior toward a goal.

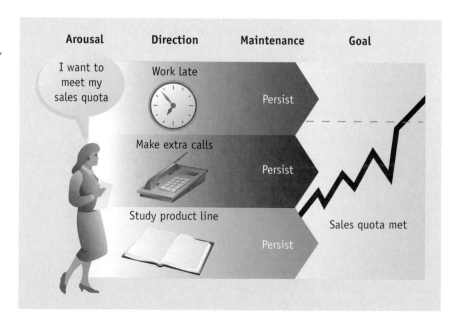

Three Key Points About Motivation

Now that we have defined motivation, it is time to bring up three important points that may change the way you think about motivation on the job.

1. **Motivation and job performance are not synonymous.** Motivation is just one of several possible determinants of job performance. Just because someone performs well at a task does not mean that he or she is highly motivated. This person actually may be very skillful but not be putting forth much effort at all. If you're a mathematical genius, for example, you may breeze through your calculus class without hardly trying. By contrast, someone who performs poorly may be putting forth a great deal of effort but may be falling short of a desired goal because he or she lacks the skill needed to succeed. If you've ever tried to learn a new sport but found that you couldn't get the hang of it no matter how hard you tried, you know what we mean.

2. **Motivation is multifaceted.** By this, we mean that people may have several different motives operating at once. Sometimes, these may conflict. For example, a word processing operator might be motivated to please his boss by being as productive as possible. However, being too productive may antagonize his coworkers, who fear that they're being made to look bad. The result is that the two motives may pull the individual in different directions, and the one that predominates is the one that's stronger in that situation. These examples clearly show that motivation is a complex and important concept in the field of organizational behavior.

3. **People are motivated by more than just money.** Surveys show that most Americans would continue working even if they didn't need the money.[3] Although money certainly is important to people, they are motivated to attain many other goals on the job as well. Because technological advances have taken the drudgery out of many jobs, today's workers are motivated by the prospect of performing jobs that are interesting and challenging—not just jobs that pay well. They also seek jobs that actively involve them in the success of the business and reward them for this (e.g., through stock ownership, bonuses, and the like). Today's workers also expect to be treated well by supervisors who value their employees' opportunities for growth and development and who hold clear and consistent expectations of them (see Figure 6.2).[4] As you will see in the rest of this chapter, the field of OB considers a wide variety of factors that motivate people, including those just described.

FIGURE 6.2

When It Comes to Motivation, Money Isn't Everything
When most of us think of motivation, we think of money. Although money is important, of course, there's far more to motivation. Martin Neath, CEO and founder of Works.com, shown here enjoying a massage, recognizes the importance of providing employees with generous benefits. He also recognizes that such perks, although important, ultimately motivate people less than doing interesting and important work.

Our discussion thus far has indicated that a wide variety of factors are responsible for motivating people on the job. However, we have not yet explained anything about exactly how these factors work in conjunction with each other. The first conceptualization of motivation we will consider—need hierarchy theory—will do just this.

Specifically, these theories explain motivation in terms of the satisfaction of basic human needs. Indeed, organizational scholars have paid a great deal of attention to the idea that people are motivated to use their jobs as mechanisms for satisfying their needs. We will describe two such theories: Maslow's *need hierarchy theory* and Alderfer's *ERG theory.*

Maslow's Need Hierarchy Theory

Probably the best-known conceptualization of human needs in organizations has been proposed by Abraham Maslow.[5] Maslow was a clinical psychologist who introduced a theory of personal adjustment, known as **need hierarchy theory,** based on his observations of patients throughout the years. His premise was that if people grow up in an environment in which their needs are not met, they will be unlikely to function as healthy, well-adjusted individuals. Much of the popularity of Maslow's approach is based on applying the same idea in organizations. That is, unless people get their needs met on they job, they will not function as effectively as possible.

Specifically, Maslow theorized that people have five types of needs and that these are activated in a *hierarchical* manner. This means that the needs are aroused in a specific order from lowest to highest, and that the lowest-order need must be fulfilled before the next highest-order need is triggered, and so on. The five major categories of needs are listed on the left side of Figure 6.3. Please refer to this diagram as a summary of the needs as we describe them here.

Physiological needs. At the bottom of the hierarchy are **physiological needs,** the lowest-order, most basic needs specified by Maslow. These refer to satisfying fundamental biological drives, such as the need for food, air, water, and shelter. To satisfy such needs, organizations must provide employees with a salary that allows them to afford adequate

need hierarchy theory
Maslow's theory specifying that there are five human needs (physiological, safety, social, esteem, and self-actualization) and that these are arranged in such a way that lower, more basic needs must be satisfied before higher-level needs become activated.

physiological needs
The lowest-order, most basic needs specified by Maslow's *need hierarchy theory,* including fundamental biological drives, such as the need for food, air, water, and shelter.

FIGURE 6.3

Need Theories: A Comparison
The five needs identified by Maslow's need hierarchy theory (left) correspond with the three needs of Alderfer's ERG theory (right). Whereas Maslow's theory specifies that these needs are activated in order from the lowest level to the highest level, Alderfer's theory specifies that needs can be activated in any order.

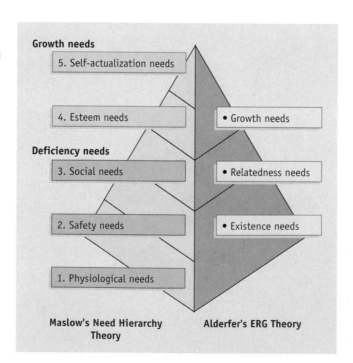

living conditions. Similarly, sufficient opportunities to rest (e.g., coffee breaks) and to engage in physical activity (e.g., fitness and exercise facilities) also are important for people to meet their physiological needs. With increasing frequency, companies are providing exercise and physical fitness programs for their employees to help them stay healthy (see Figure 6.4).[6] The rationale is quite simple: People who are too hungry or too ill to work will hardly be able to make much of a contribution to their companies.

Safety needs. The second level of need in Maslow's hierarchy, **safety needs,** is activated after physiological needs are met. Safety needs refer to the need for a secure environment that is free from threats of physical or psychological harm. Organizations can do many things to help satisfy safety needs. For example, they may provide employees with safety equipment (e.g., hard hats and goggles), life and health insurance plans, and security forces (e.g., police and fire protection). Similarly, jobs that provide tenure (such as teaching) and no-layoff agreements provide a psychological security blanket that helps satisfy safety needs. All of these practices enable people to do their jobs without fear of harm in a safe and secure atmosphere.

Social needs. Maslow's third level of need, **social needs,** is activated after safety needs have been met. Social needs refer to the need to be affiliative—to have friends and to be loved and accepted by other people. To help meet social needs, organizations may encourage participation in social events, such as office picnics or parties. Company bowling or softball leagues, as well as country club memberships, also provide good opportunities for meeting social needs. Not only do such activities help promote physical fitness—helping satisfy physiological needs, as we noted earlier—but they also give employees a chance to socialize and develop friendships.

Taken together as a group, physiological needs, safety needs, and social needs are known as **deficiency needs.** Maslow's idea was that if these needs are not met, an individual will fail to develop into a healthy person—both physically and psychologically. In contrast, the next two highest-order needs, the ones at the top of the hierarchy, are known as **growth needs.** Gratification of these needs is said to help a person grow and develop to his or her fullest potential.

Esteem needs. The fourth level of needs is **esteem needs**—a person's need to develop self-respect and to gain the approval of others. The desire to achieve success, to have prestige, and to be recognized by others falls into this category. Companies do many things to satisfy their employees' esteem needs. They may, for example, have awards banquets to recognize distinguished achievements. Giving monetary bonuses—even small ones—in recognition of employees' suggestions for improvement helps promote

safety needs
In Maslow's *need hierarchy theory,* safety needs include the need for a secure environment and to be free from threats of physical or psychological harm.

social needs
In Maslow's *need hierarchy theory,* the need to be affiliative—that is, to have friends, and to be loved and accepted by other people.

deficiency needs
The group of physiological needs, safety needs, and social needs in Maslow's need hierarchy theory. As these needs are not met, people will fail to develop in a healthy fashion.

growth needs
In Maslow's *need hierarchy theory,* esteem needs and the need for self-actualization, as a group. Gratification of these needs helps a person reach his or her full potential.

esteem needs
In Maslow's *need hierarchy theory,* the need to develop self-respect and to gain the approval of others.

FIGURE 6.4
Working Out: Staying Fit While Having Fun
Will Smith III, CEO of Enscicon, the information technology and engineering consulting firm, believes in having employees work out while on the job. It not only helps them stay fit and healthy, but it also builds camaraderie. At lunchtime in the Denver headquarters, about a third of the staff works out together. Says Smith, "It creates an atmosphere that says, 'Yes, we're working together, but we're also having fun.'"

their esteem. Nonmonetary awards, such as trophies and plaques, provide reminders of an employee's important contributions, continuously fulfilling esteem needs.[7] Including articles in company newsletters describing an employee's success, giving keys to the executive washroom, assigning private parking spaces, and posting signs identifying the "employee of the month" (see Figure 6.5) also are examples of things that can be done to satisfy esteem needs.

Self-actualization needs. Atop Maslow's hierarchy is a need that is aroused only after all the lower-order needs have been met—the need for **self-actualization.** This refers to the need to become all that one is capable of being, to develop one's fullest potential. By working at their maximum creative potential, employees who are self-actualized can be extremely valuable assets to their organizations. Individuals who have self-actualized are working at their peak and represent the most effective use of an organization's human resources.

Research testing Maslow's theory has supported the distinction between deficiency needs and growth needs. Unfortunately, the research has shown that not all people are able to satisfy their higher-order needs on the job. For example, research has found that although lower-level managers are able to satisfy only their deficiency needs on the job, managers from the higher echelons of organizations are able to satisfy both their deficiency and growth needs.[8] In general, Maslow's theory has not received a great deal of support with respect to the specific notions it proposes—namely, the exact needs that exist and the order in which they are activated.[9] Specifically, many researchers have failed to confirm that there are only five basic categories of need and that they are activated in the exact order specified by Maslow.

Alderfer's ERG Theory

In response to these criticisms, an alternative formulation has been proposed by Alderfer.[10] His approach, known as **ERG theory,** is much simpler than Maslow's. Alderfer specifies not only that there are only three types of needs instead of five but also that these are not necessarily activated in any specific order. In fact, Alderfer postulates that any need may be activated at any time. The three needs specified by ERG theory are the needs for existence, relatedness, and growth (ERG). *Existence* needs correspond to Maslow's physiological needs and safety needs. *Relatedness* needs correspond to Maslow's social needs, including the need for meaningful social relationships. Finally, *growth* needs correspond to the esteem needs and self-actualization needs in Maslow's theory—the need

self-actualization
In Maslow's *need hierarchy theory,* the need to discover who we are and to develop ourselves to the fullest potential.

ERG theory
An alternative to Maslow's need hierarchy theory proposed by Alderfer, which asserts that there are three basic human needs: existence, relatedness, and growth.

FIGURE 6.5
Esteem Needs: How *Not* to Satisfy Them
We doubt that this woman's esteem needs are being met, despite the fact that she is "Employee of the Month."
(*Source:* Copyright 2000 by Carol Simpson.)

"As Employee of the Month, I expect you to set an example for the rest of your work team... now go lay yourself off."

for developing one's potential. A summary of Alderfer's ERG theory is shown on the right side of Figure 6.4, along with the corresponding needs proposed by Maslow.

Clearly, ERG theory is much less restrictive than Maslow's need hierarchy theory. Its advantage is that it fits better with research evidence suggesting that, although basic needs exist, they are not exactly as specified by Maslow.[11] Despite the fact that need theories are not in complete agreement about the precise number of needs and the relationships between them, they do agree that satisfying human needs is an important part of motivating behavior on the job.

Managerial Applications of Need Theories

Probably the greatest value of need theories lies in the practical implications they have for management. In particular, the theories are important insofar as they suggest specific things that managers can do to help their subordinates become self-actualized. Because self-actualized employees are likely to work at their maximum creative potential, it makes sense to help people attain this state by helping them meet their needs. With this in mind, it is worthwhile to consider what organizations may do to help satisfy their employees' needs.

Promote a healthy workforce. Some companies are helping satisfy their employees' physiological needs by providing incentives to keep them healthy. For example, Hershey Foods Corporation and Southern California Edison Company, among others, give insurance rebates to employees with healthy lifestyles, while charging extra premiums to those whose habits (e.g., smoking) put them at greater risk for health problems.[12] To the extent that these incentives encourage employees to adopt healthier lifestyles, the likelihood of satisfying their physiological needs is increased.[13]

It is not only employees' physical health but also their mental health that companies are interested in promoting. However, visits to psychotherapists can be very expensive, and mental health professionals are not always available to people in remote locations. To meet this need, the psychological services company, Wilson Banwell, based in Vancouver, British Columbia, Canada, provides a Web-based counseling service, PROACT.[14] For a fee to subscribing companies, Wilson Banwell provides live, online "cybertherapy" sessions with one of the company's 68 staff psychologists. Although it may not be as intimate as face-to-face therapy, patients generally like the service, and their employers welcome the unique opportunities it affords.

Provide financial security. Financial security is an important type of safety need. In this regard, some companies are going beyond the more traditional forms of payroll savings and profit-sharing plans. Notably, Com-Corp Industries (an auto-parts manufacturer based in Cleveland, Ohio) found that its employees had serious financial difficulties when faced with sending their children to college. The company now offers low-interest loans (only 3 percent annually for 10 years) for this purpose.[15]

Financial security is a key aspect of job security, particularly in troubled economic times, when layoffs are inevitable. To help soften the blow of layoffs, more and more organizations, such as AT&T and Wang, are providing **outplacement services** to assist laid-off employees in securing new jobs.[16] Although it is certainly more desirable not to be laid off at all, knowing that such assistance is available, if needed, helps reduce the negative emotional aspects of job insecurity.

outplacement services
Assistance in finding new jobs that companies provide to employees they lay off.

Provide opportunities to socialize. To help satisfy its employees' social needs, IBM holds a "Family Day" picnic each spring near its Armonk, New York, headquarters.[17] Some other companies also have incorporated social activities into the fabric of their culture. For example, Odetics Inc. (the Anaheim, California, manufacturer of intelligent machine systems) not only has its own repertory theater troupe, but it also holds regular "theme" days (e.g., a "sock hop" in the company's cafeteria), and has a standing "fun committee," which organizes such events as a lunch-hour "employee Olympics," complete with goofy games.[18] For the many young employees who work at today's high-tech firms, having fun at work has become a way of life (see Figure 6.6).

FIGURE 6.6

Opportunities to Socialize Are Critical to Motivation

The 420 employees of Ask Jeeves, the Web navigation company in Emeryville, California, are given lots of opportunities to socialize with one another on the job. By playing foosball, one of their favorite pastimes, these employees get good opportunities to satisfy their social needs.

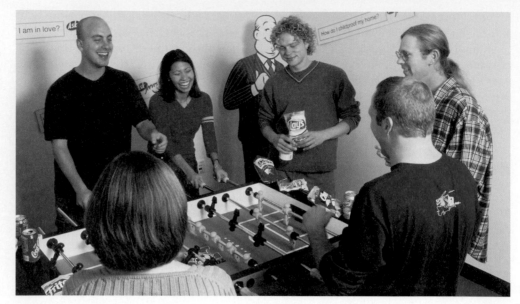

Recognize employees' accomplishments. Recognizing employees' accomplishments is an important way to satisfy their esteem needs. In this regard, GTE Data Services (Temple Terrace, Florida) gives awards to employees who develop ways of improving customer satisfaction or business performance.[19] The big award is a four-day, first-class vacation; $500; a plaque; and recognition in the company magazine. Not all such awards are equally extravagant, however. Companies such as American Airlines, Shell Oil, Campbell Soup Company, AT&T, and each of the big-three automakers (General Motors, Ford, and Chrysler) all offer relatively small nonmonetary gifts (e.g., dinner certificates, VCRs, and computers) to employees in recognition of their accomplishments.[20] (As indicated in the Best Practices section on page 198, some companies make fairly lavish gestures to meet employees' needs.

Whatever form it takes, it is important to caution that awards are effective at enhancing esteem only when they are clearly linked to desired behaviors. Awards that are too general (e.g., a trophy for "best attitude") may not only fail to satisfy esteem needs but also may minimize the impact of awards that are truly deserved.

MOTIVATING BY SETTING GOALS

Just as people are motivated to satisfy their needs on the job, they also are motivated to strive for and to attain goals. In fact, the process of setting goals is one of the most important motivational forces operating on people in organizations.[25] With this in mind, we will describe a prominent theory of **goal setting** and then identify some practical suggestions for setting goals effectively.

goal setting
The process of determining specific levels of performance for workers to attain.

Goal-Setting Theory

Suppose that you are doing a task, such as word processing, when a performance goal is assigned. You are now expected, for example, to enter 70 words per minute (wpm) at the keyboard instead of the 60 wpm you've been doing all along. Would you work hard to meet this goal, or would you simply give up? Some insight into the question of how people respond to assigned goals is provided by a model known as *goal-setting theory*.[26] This theory claims that an assigned goal influences people's beliefs about being able to perform the task in question (i.e., the personality variable of **self-efficacy,** described in Chapter 3) and their personal goals. Both of these factors, in turn, influence performance.

self-efficacy
One's belief about having the capacity to perform a task.

The basic idea behind **goal-setting theory** is that a goal serves as a motivator because it causes people to compare their present capacity to perform with that required to succeed at the goal. To the extent that people believe they will fall short of a goal, they will feel dissatisfied and will work harder to attain it so long as they believe it is possible for them to do so. When they succeed at meeting a goal, they feel competent and successful.[27] Having a goal enhances performance in large part because the goal makes clear exactly what type and level of performance are expected.

The model also claims that assigned goals will lead to the acceptance of those goals as personal goals. In other words, they will be accepted as one's own. This is the idea of **goal commitment**—the extent to which people invest themselves in meeting a goal.[28] Indeed, it has been shown that people will become more committed to a goal to the extent that they desire to attain that goal and believe they have a reasonable chance of doing so.[29] Likewise, the more strongly people believe they are capable of meeting a goal, the more strongly they will accept it as their own. By contrast, workers who perceive themselves as being physically incapable of meeting performance goals, for example, are generally not committed to meeting them and do not strive to do so.[30]

Finally, the model claims that beliefs about both self-efficacy and goal commitment influence task performance. This makes sense insofar as people are willing to exert greater effort when they believe they will succeed than when they believe their efforts will be in vain.[31] Moreover, goals that are not personally accepted will have little capacity to guide behavior. In fact, research has shown that the more strongly people are committed to meeting goals, the better they will perform.[32] In general, this model of goal setting has been supported by several studies, suggesting that is a valuable source of insight into how the goal-setting process works (for a summary, see Figure 6.7).[33]

goal-setting theory
The theory according to which a goal serves as a motivator because it causes people to compare their present capacity to perform with that required to succeed at the goal.

goal commitment
The degree to which people accept and strive to attain goals.

Managers' Guidelines for Setting Effective Performance Goals

Because researchers have been involved actively in studying the goal-setting process for many years, it is possible to summarize their findings in the form of principles. These represent practical suggestions that managers can use to enhance motivation.

Assign specific goals. Probably the best-established finding of research on goal setting is that *people perform at higher levels when asked to meet a specific high-performance goal than when simply asked to "do their best," or when no goal at all is assigned.*[34] People tend to find specific goals quite challenging, and they are motivated to try to meet them—not only to fulfill management's expectations but also to convince themselves that they have performed well.

FIGURE 6.7

A Cognitive Summary of the Goal-Setting Process
When people are challenged to meet higher goals, several things happen. First, they assess their desire to attain the goal as well as their chances of attaining the goal. Together, these judgments affect their *goal commitment*. Second, they assess the extent to which meeting the goal will enhance their beliefs in their own *self-efficacy*. When levels of goal commitment and self-efficacy are high, people are motivated to perform at the goal level.

BEST PRACTICES
MEETING NEEDS IN HIGH STYLE

Traditionally, someone who gets a new job receives not only a salary but also a standard set of fringe benefits, such as health insurance, life insurance, a paid vacation, and a retirement plan. Today, however, these basic benefits are often not enough to bring job prospects through the door. The incentives that motivate today's employees are far more varied—and, in many cases, truly lavish.[21]

Suppose, for example, you work at the Framingham, Massachusetts, corporate headquarters of the office supply chain, Staples, and that you have children who need to be cared for while you are at work. No problem. You simply drop them off at the company's brand-new, $1.4 million, 8,000–square foot child care center near your office. Although there is a great need for

on-site child care facilities, only 11 percent of today's companies, like Staples, offer them. This benefit makes it possible for Staples employees to concentrate on their work without having to worry about who's taking care of their children.

If you work at Staples, you also have available to you a wonderful concierge service, which runs all kinds of errands for busy employees (e.g., picking up dry cleaning, washing their cars), making their lives far easier. Staples isn't alone in offering concierge services. In fact, several companies have come into being in the past few years that offer concierge services to organizations who seek them for their employees. For example, a San Francisco–based firm, LesConcierges, provides this service to employees of several well-known companies, including America Online and its sister

A classic study conducted at an Oklahoma lumber camp provides a particularly dramatic demonstration of this principle.[35] The participants in this research were lumber camp crews who hauled logs from forests to their company's nearby sawmill. Over a three-month period before the study began, it was found that the crew loaded trucks to only about 60 percent of their legal capacity, wasting trips that cost the company money. Then a specific goal was set, challenging the loggers to load the trucks to 94 percent of their capacity before returning to the mill. How effective was this goal in raising performance? The results, summarized in Figure 6.8, show that the goal was extremely effective. In fact, not only was the specific goal effective in raising performance to the goal level in just a few weeks, but the effects were long-lasting as well. In fact, the loggers were found to sustain this level of performance as long as seven years later! The resulting savings for the company were considerable.

This is just one of many studies that clearly demonstrate the effectiveness of setting specific, challenging performance goals. Other research has found that specific goals also are helpful in bringing about other desirable organizational goals, such as reducing absenteeism and industrial accidents.[36] Naturally, to reap such beneficial effects, goals must not only be highly specific but challenging as well.

Assign difficult, but acceptable performance goals. The goal set at the logging camp was successful not only because it was specific, but also because it pushed crew members to a higher standard. Obviously, a goal that is too easy to attain will *not* bring about the desired increments in performance. For example, it you already type at 70 wpm, a goal of 60 wpm—although specific—would probably *lower* your performance. The key point is that *a goal must be difficult as well as specific for it to raise performance.* At the same time, however, people will work hard to reach challenging goals so long as these goals are within the limits of their capability. As goals become too difficult, performance suffers because people reject the goals as unrealistic and unattainable.[37]

For example, you may work much harder as a student in a class that challenges your ability than in one that is very easy. At the same time, you probably would give up trying if the only way of passing was to get perfect scores on all exams—a standard you would company, CompuServe. A Boston-based concierge service, Circles, provides a wide variety of services for its clients, including the 1,700 North American employees of the anesthesia supply company, Datex-Ohmeda, who appreciate the time the service saves them on such mundane matters as making dentist appointments, getting the car washed, and finding household help.[22]

Some companies offer even more lavish benefits. For example, to attract employees to its out-of-the-way location in rural Wisconsin, Quad/Graphics, the printing company, offers its employees rental apartments in its new $5 million complex. During its annual slow period, Rhino Foods (in Burlington, Vermont) helps its employees find jobs at other local businesses. Getting holidays off isn't so special; everyone gets them, right? Well, they might not be exactly the ones that you want to celebrate. This isn't a problem for employees of Marquardt & Roche, the Stamford, Connecticut, marketing firm. This firm allows its employees to select any 11 out of 24 possible holidays.

In an exceptionally generous move, the investment bank John Nuveen & Co. pays the college tuition for the children of employees who have been with the company for at least five years. Less extravagant but quite convenient, Honeywell employees have access to an on-site beauty salon and dry-cleaning facilities.[23] Some companies are offering such benefits as pet insurance, auto financing, home security systems, prepaid legal services, and even personal loans to their employees.

But what do most employees want? A recent survey found that 64 percent wanted discounted or free home computers, 44 percent wanted discounted or free home Internet access, 37 percent wanted spa or health club memberships, 31 percent wanted free mobile phone or wireless access, and the same number wanted car access.[24] Clearly, the days of finding so-called "standard" fringe benefits are over. What passes for standard today is anybody's guess.

reject as being unacceptable. In short, specific goals are most effective if they are set neither too low nor too high.

The same phenomenon occurs in organizations. For example, Bell Canada's telephone operators are required to handle calls within 23 seconds, and FedEx's customer service agents are expected to answer customers' questions within 140 seconds.[38] Although both goals were initially considered difficult when they were imposed, the employees of both companies eventually met—or exceeded—these goals and enjoyed the satisfaction of knowing they succeeded at these tasks. At a General Electric manufacturing plant, specific goals were set for productivity and cost reduction. Those goals that were perceived as challenging but possible led to improved performance, whereas

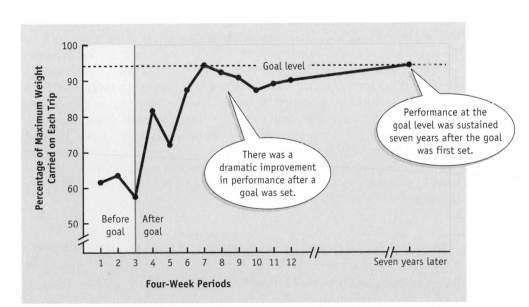

FIGURE 6.8

Goal Setting: Some Impressive Effects
The performance of loggers loading timber onto trucks markedly improved after a specific, difficult goal was set. The percentage of the maximum possible weight loaded onto the trucks rose from approximately 60 percent before any goal was set to approximately 94 percent—the goal level—after the goal was set. Performance remained at this level as long as seven years.
(*Source:* Adapted from Latham & Baldes, 1975; see Note 35.)

those thought to be unattainable led to decreased performance.[39] How, then, should goals be set in a manner that strengthens employees' commitment to them?

One obvious way of enhancing goal acceptance is to *involve employees in the goal-setting process*. Research on workers' participation in goal setting has demonstrated that people better accept goals that they have been involved in setting than goals that have been assigned by their supervisors—and they work harder as a result.[40] In other words, participation in the goal-setting process tends to enhance goal commitment. Not only does participation help workers to better understand and appreciate goals they had a hand in setting, but it also helps ensure that the goals set are not unreasonable.

Provide feedback concerning goal attainment. The final principle of goal setting appears to be glaringly obvious, although in practice it is often not followed: *Feedback helps people attain their performance goals.* Just as golfers interested in improving their swings need feedback about where their balls are going, so do workers need feedback about how closely they are approaching their performance goals in order to meet them.

The importance of using feedback in conjunction with goal setting has been demonstrated in a study of people in a vital but underinvestigated profession—pizza delivery drivers.[41] These individuals have to deliver their customers' pizzas quickly, but of course, they must do so safely and in compliance with all traffic laws. All too often, however, in the interest of keeping their pizzas hot, some delivery people's driving styles are even hotter (and saucier). To speed up delivery, for example, some have been known to fail to come to complete stops at intersections.

With an eye toward curbing this behavior, officials of pizza shops in two different towns participated in a study in which their delivery people's driving behavior was systematically observed over a nine-month period. Trained observers, hidden from view, recorded various aspects of the delivery people's driving behavior during prime-time hours—particularly the percentage of time they came to complete stops at intersections. Over a six-week period, drivers from both locations were found to come to complete stops, on average, just under half the time. Because this was unacceptable, the drivers in one location, the experimental group, were asked to come to a complete stop 75 percent of the time. And, over a four-week period, they were given regular feedback on how successful they were in meeting this goal. Drivers in the control group were not asked to meet any goals and were not given any feedback on their driving. Following this feedback period, drivers in the experimental group were asked to maintain the 75 percent goal but stopped getting feedback. Observations of their driving behavior, and that of control group drivers, were continued during this six-month period.

How did the drivers do? The results of the study, summarized in Figure 6.9, show that goal setting in conjunction with feedback was highly successful. Specifically, it led drivers to come very close to the assigned goal of coming to a complete stop at intersections three-quarters of the time. However, once feedback was withdrawn, drivers returned to stopping only half the time—as often as they did before the study began (and as often as drivers in the control group, who received neither goals nor feedback). These findings clearly demonstrate the importance of accompanying specific, difficult goals with clear feedback about the extent to which those goals are being met. Setting goals without providing feedback with respect to meeting those goals effectively forces workers to do their jobs blindly. Providing feedback, however, shines a spotlight on task performance that is essential to succeeding.

In sum, goal setting is a very effective tool managers can use to motivate people. Setting a specific, acceptably difficult goal and providing feedback about progress toward that goal greatly enhance job performance.

MOTIVATING BY BEING FAIR: ORGANIZATIONAL JUSTICE

The theories we've described thus far are based on completely individual processes—the activation of needs and the responses to goals. The next approach to motivation we

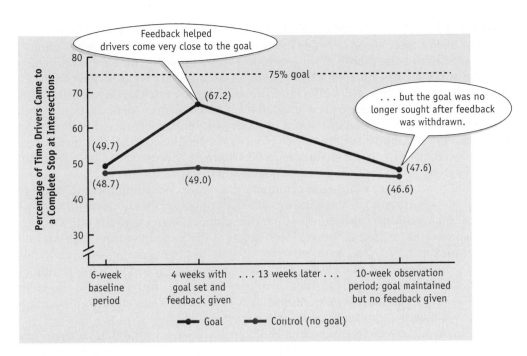

FIGURE 6.9

Feedback: An Essential Element of Goal Setting
Pizza delivery drivers came very close to reaching a goal—coming to a complete stop at intersections 75 percent of the time—during the period in which they were given regular feedback on goal performance. Several months later, however, after feedback was no longer given, their performance returned to previous levels. (*Source:* Based on data reported by Ludwig & Geller, 1997; see Note 41.)

will consider, **organizational justice,** is also an individual-based theory but one that adds a social component.[42] Specifically, various conceptualizations of organizational justice view motivation from the perspective of the *social comparisons* people make—that is, what people see when they compare themselves to others and prevailing standards.[43] We will describe three major approaches to organizational justice—*distributive justice,* which focuses on the way organizational resources are distributed, *procedural justice,* which focuses on the processes used to make those resource-allocation decisions, and *interactional justice,* which focuses on the quality of the interpersonal treatment accorded people (see Figure 6.10).[44] After describing these approaches to organizational justice, we will summarize their implications for motivating people on the job.

Distributive Justice: Equity Theory

Matters of **distributive justice** concern people's perceptions of the fairness of the distribution of resources between people. The major approach to distributive justice, **equity theory,** proposes that individuals are motivated to maintain fair, or *equitable,* relationships between themselves and others with respect to the distribution of reward and to

organizational justice
People's perceptions of fairness in organizations, consisting of perceptions of how decisions are made regarding the distribution of outcomes (*procedural justice*) and the perceived fairness of those outcomes themselves (as studied in *equity theory*).

distributive justice
The perceived fairness of the way rewards are distributed among people.

equity theory
The theory stating that people strive to maintain ratios of their own outcomes (rewards) to their own inputs (contributions) that are equal to the outcome/input ratios of others with whom they compare themselves.

FIGURE 6.10

Three Types of Organizational Justice
People's perceptions of fairness in organizations (known as *organizational justice*) fall into three categories. *Distributive justice* concerns people's perceptions of how fairly rewards are distributed. *Procedural justice* concerns people's perceptions of the fairness of the procedures used to determine those rewards. *Interactional justice* focuses on people's perceptions of the fairness of the interpersonal encounters they have with others.

Organizational Justice

Distributive Justice	Procedural Justice	Interactional Justice
Perceived fairness of outcomes received	Perceived fairness of the procedures used to determine outcomes	Perceived fairness of the interpersonal treatment received from others

avoid those relationships that are unfair, or *inequitable*.[45] The ways in which this is done has been a topic of considerable interest in the field of organizational behavior.

Specifically, equity theory proposes that people comparing themselves to others focus on two variables, *outcomes* and *inputs*.[46] **Outcomes** are what we get out of our jobs, including pay, fringe benefits, and prestige. **Inputs** refer to the contributions made, such as the amount of time worked, the amount of effort expended, the number of units produced, and the qualifications brought to the job. Equity theory is concerned with outcomes and inputs as they are *perceived* by the people involved, and are not necessarily based on any objective standards. Not surprisingly, therefore, people sometimes disagree about what constitutes equitable treatment on the job.

Equity theory states that people compare their outcomes and inputs to those of others and judge the equitableness of these relationships in the form of a ratio. Specifically, they compare the ratios of their own outcomes/inputs to the ratios of others' outcomes/inputs. These "others" who serve as the basis of comparison may be other employees in a work group, other employees in the organization, individuals working in the same field, or even the employees themselves at earlier points in time—in short, almost anyone against whom employees compare themselves. As shown in Figure 6.11, these comparisons can result in any of three different states: *overpayment inequity, underpayment inequity,* or *equitable payment.*

To illustrate these concepts, let's consider an example. Imagine that Jack and Ray work alongside each other on an assembly line doing the same job. Both men have equal amounts of experience, training, and education and work equally long and hard at their jobs—in other words, their inputs are equivalent. But suppose Jack is paid a salary of $500 per week whereas Ray is paid only $350 per week: In this case, Jack's ratio

outcomes
The rewards employees receive from their jobs, such as salary and recognition.

inputs
People's contributions to their jobs, such as their experience, qualifications, or the amount of time worked.

FIGURE 6.11

Equity Theory: An Overview
To judge equity or inequity, people compare the ratios of their own outcomes to inputs with the corresponding ratios of others (or of themselves at earlier points in time). The resulting states—*overpayment inequity, underpayment inequity,* and *equitable payment*—are summarized here, along with their associated emotional responses.

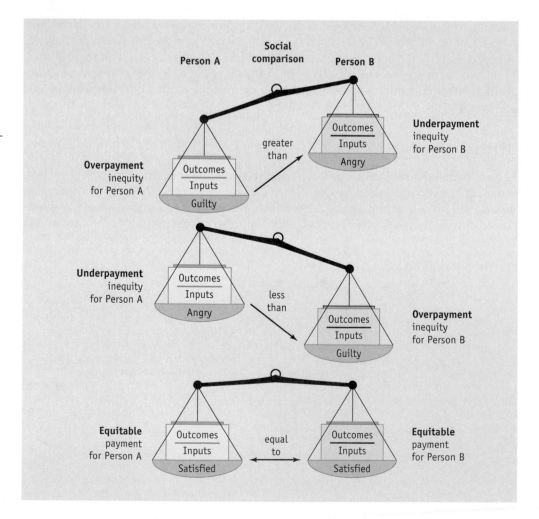

of outcomes/inputs is higher than Ray's, creating a state of **overpayment inequity** for Jack and **underpayment inequity** for Ray (since the ratio of his outcome/input is lower). According to equity theory, Jack, realizing that he is paid more than an equally qualified person doing the same work, will feel *guilty* in response to his overpayment. By contrast, Ray, realizing that he is paid less than an equally qualified person for doing the same work, will feel *angry* in response to his underpayment. Feeling guilty or angry is a negative emotional state that people are motivated to change. Specifically, they will seek to create a state of **equitable payment** in which their outcome/input ratios are equal, leading them to feel *satisfied*.

How can people change inequitable states to equitable ones? Equity theory suggests several possible courses of action (see Table 6.1). In general, people who are underpaid either may lower their inputs or raise their outcomes. Either action would effectively bring the underpaid individual's outcome/input ratio into line with that of the comparison person. In our example, the underpaid Ray might lower his inputs by slacking off, arriving at work late, leaving early, taking longer breaks, doing less work or lower-quality work—or, in an extreme case, quitting his job. He also may attempt to raise his outcomes by asking for a raise or even taking home company property, such as tools or office supplies. By contrast, the overpaid person, Jack, may do the opposite—raise his inputs or lower his outcomes. For example, he might put forth much more effort, work longer hours, and try to make a greater contribution to the company. He also might lower his outcomes by working through a paid vacation or not taking advantage of fringe benefits the company offers. These are all specific *behavioral* reactions to inequitable conditions—that is, things people *do* in attempting to change inequitable states to equitable ones.

As you might imagine, people may be unwilling to do some of the things necessary to respond behaviorally to inequities. In particular, they may be unwilling to restrict their productivity (in fear of getting caught "goofing off") or may be uncomfortable asking their boss for a raise. As a result, they may resort to resolving the inequity not by changing their behavior, but by changing the way they think about the situation. Because equity theory deals with perceptions of fairness or unfairness, it is reasonable to expect that inequitable states may be redressed merely by altering one's thinking about the circumstances. For example, underpaid people may rationalize that others' inputs are really higher than their own (e.g., "I suppose she really *is* more qualified than I am"), thereby convincing themselves that others' higher outcomes are justified. Similarly, overpaid people may convince themselves that they really *are* better and really do deserve their relatively higher pay. So, by changing the way they see things, people can come to perceive inequitable situations as equitable, thereby effectively reducing their inequity distress.[47]

overpayment inequity
The condition resulting in feelings of guilt, in which the ratio of one's outcomes/inputs is more than the corresponding ratio of another person with whom that person compares himself or herself.

underpayment inequity
The condition resulting in feelings of anger, in which the ratio of one's outcomes/inputs is less than the corresponding ratio of another person with whom that person compares himself or herself.

equitable payment
The state in which one person's outcome/input ratio is equivalent to that of another person with whom the person compares himself or herself.

TABLE 6.1   POSSIBLE REACTIONS TO INEQUITY: A SUMMARY

People can respond to overpayment and underpayment inequities in behavioral and/or psychological ways. A few of these are summarized here. These reactions help change the perceived inequities into a state of perceived equity.

	TYPE OF REACTION	
TYPE OF INEQUITY	BEHAVIORAL (WHAT YOU CAN DO IS . . .)	PSYCHOLOGICAL (WHAT YOU CAN THINK IS . . .)
Overpayment inequity	Raise your inputs (e.g., work harder) or lower your outcomes (e.g., work through a paid vacation).	Convince yourself that your outcomes are deserved based on your inputs (e.g., rationalize that you work harder than others and so you deserve more pay).
Underpayment inequity	Lower your inputs (e.g., reduce effort) or raise your outcomes (e.g., get raise in pay).	Convince yourself that others' inputs are really higher than your own (e.g., rationalize that the comparison worker is really more qualified and so deserves higher outcomes).

There is a great deal of evidence to suggest that people are motivated to redress inequities at work and that they respond much as equity theory suggests. For example, research has shown that professional basketball players who are underpaid (i.e., ones who are paid less than others who perform as well or better) score fewer points than those who are equitably paid.[48] That is, they lower their inputs. Research also has shown that people who have their pay cut tend to steal from their employers much more than those who receive their regular pay.[49] From the perspective of equity theory, these individuals may be seen as raising their outcomes. Indeed, it is not unusual for people to retaliate against their employers for treating them unfairly.[50]

Procedural Justice: Making Decisions Fairly

procedural justice

Perceptions of the fairness of the procedures used to determine outcomes.

The idea of *procedural justice* originally came from the legal arena, where it long was understood that for the outcome of a trial to be fair, the procedures used in that trial (e.g., rules regarding the nature of evidence) must be fair.[51] More recently, OB specialists recognized that this same basic idea applies to decisions made on the job, as well.[52] Hence, we refer to **procedural justice** as the perceived fairness of the processes by which organizational decisions are made. People in organizations are greatly concerned about making decisions fairly and are motivated to get others to accept their decisions as fair. The reason is simple: Both individual employees and entire organizations benefit when it is believed that the organization follows fair procedures.

In examining procedural justice, we are interested in determining how decisions have to be made for them to be considered fair. (Remember, we are *not* talking about *what* those decisions are but, rather, *how* they are made!) Research has revealed several things that can be done to make organizational decisions seem fair. Among these are the following:

1. *Give people a say in how decisions are made.* It has been well established that *voice*—that is, a say in decision-making procedures—is key to procedural justice. For example, people believe their performance appraisals are made more fairly when they are given an opportunity to provide information regarding their performance than when no such input is solicited.[53]
2. *Provide an opportunity for errors to be corrected.* Just as fairness demands that court decisions can be appealed when they are suspect, so too should organizational decisions be open to revision. In fact, for drug-screening procedures to be considered fair, the people tested have to be given an opportunity to request a retest.[54] (For another example, see Figure 6.12.)

FIGURE 6.12

Enhancing Procedural Justice by Correcting Errors: An Example
For the game of football to be as fair as possible, it's essential that officials make proper rulings about plays on the field. With this in mind, National Football League officers have initiated an "instant replay rule," which permits officials on the field to review plays in question and to correct any errors in judgment that might have led to inappropriate calls. Although the rule is controversial in many respects, most agree that it contributes to the overall procedural justice of the game.

3. *Apply rules and policies consistently.* Suppose an organization has a policy regarding how vacation time is to be selected: People with greatest seniority get to pick first, leaving remaining times to more junior staff members. Although this policy may be fair on its own, the organization wouldn't be fair if it applied this policy to some people but not to others. Clearly, consistency is key to establishing procedural justice.

4. *Make decisions in an unbiased manner.* For an organizational decision to be considered procedurally fair, it is essential for the decision maker to be unbiased. Suppose, for example, a human resources manager holds prejudicial attitudes against members of a certain racial group, leading him or her to systematically reject potential hires belonging to that group (we discussed such biases in Chapter 5). We would say that procedurally fair decisions could not be made in this case.[55]

Interactional Justice

When making judgments about fairness, people take into account not only the outcomes received and the procedures used, but also the quality of the interpersonal treatment they receive at the hands of decision makers. Judgments of this type are known as **interactional justice.**

Two major factors contribute to the interpersonal justice. These are *informational justification* (the thoroughness of the information received about a decision) and *social sensitivity* (the amount of dignity and respect demonstrated in the course of presenting an undesirable outcome, such as a pay cut or the loss of a job). In recent years, it has been demonstrated repeatedly that people respond much more favorably to negative outcomes when these are presented in a thorough and informative manner with a great deal of interpersonal sensitivity than when these are presented in a less informative and more insensitive manner.[56] By "more favorably," we mean a wide variety of things. For example, it has been found that high levels of interactional justice facilitate acceptance of smoking bans among smokers and even extreme outcomes such as pay cuts and layoffs. Although people might not like these things, they are more likely to accept them if they are presented in an interpersonally fair manner—that is, by adhering to interactional justice.

interactional justice
The perceived fairness of the interpersonal treatment used to determine organizational outcomes.

Organizational Justice: Some Motivational Tips for Managers

Organizational justice has some important implications for ways of motivating people. We will highlight several of these here.

Avoid underpayment. Companies that attempt to save money by reducing employees' salaries may find that employees respond in many different ways to even the score. For example, they may steal, or they may shave a few minutes off their workdays or otherwise withhold production.

In extreme cases, employees express their feelings of extreme underpayment inequity by going on strike. This is exactly what happened in August 1997, when 185,000 members of the Teamsters Union went on strike against UPS, the world's largest package distribution company. Their claim was that the company hired lots of part-time workers, who were paid less than full-time workers doing the same exact jobs. After a 16-day strike that cost UPS millions of dollars in lost revenue and that crippled package shipments throughout the world, a settlement was reached that the Teamsters believed would result in more equitable treatment for their members. This included limiting the use of part-timers and increasing hourly wages by $3.10 for full-timers and $4.10 for part-timers over five years. This is only one example of employees going on strike when they believe they are underpaid. For another, see Figure 6.13.

Over the past few years, a particularly unsettling form of institutionalizing underpayment has materialized in the form of **two-tier wage structures**—payment systems in which newer employees are paid less than those hired to do the same work at an earlier point in time. Not surprisingly, such systems are considered to be highly unfair, particu-

two-tier wage structures
Payment systems in which newer employees are paid less than employees hired at earlier times to do the same work.

FIGURE 6.13
Striking in Response to Inequitable Treatment
In the spring of 2000, members of 14 labor unions went on strike against General Electric, claiming that the average $12,000 annual pension paid to retirees severely underrepresents what they deserve and what the company's pension fund can afford to pay. The signs carried by these angry GE workers in Ohio reflect the feelings of injustice they experienced.

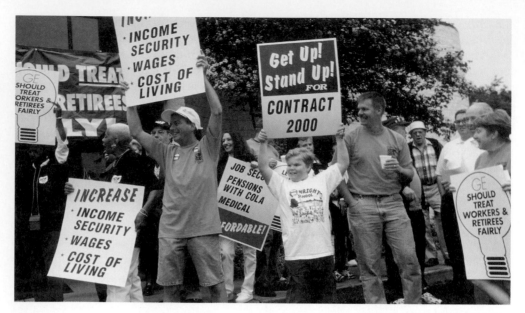

larly by those in the lower tier.[57] When such a plan was instituted at the Giant Food supermarket chain a few years ago, two-thirds of the lower-tier employees quit their jobs in the first three months. "It stinks," said one clerk at a Giant store in Los Angeles. "They're paying us lower wages for the same work."[58] Not surprisingly, proposals to introduce two-tier wage systems have met with considerable resistance among employees and, when applicable, the unions representing them.

Avoid overpayment. You may think that because overpaid employees work hard to deserve their pay, it would be a useful motivational technique to pay people more than they merit. There are several reasons why this would not work. First, the increases in performance shown in response to overpayment inequity tend to be only temporary. As time goes on, people begin to believe that they actually deserve the higher pay they're getting and bring their work level down to normal. A second reason why it is unwise to overpay employees is that when you overpay one employee, you are underpaying all the others. When the majority of the employees feel underpaid, they will lower their performance, resulting in a net *decrease* in productivity—and widespread dissatisfaction. Hence, the conclusion is clear: *Managers should strive to treat all employees equitably.*

We realize, of course, that this may be more easily said than done. Part of the difficulty resides in the fact that feelings of equity and inequity are based on perceptions, and these aren't always easy to control. One approach that may help is to *be open and honest about outcomes and inputs.* People tend to overestimate how much their superiors are paid and, therefore, tend to feel that their own pay is not as high as it should be.[59] However, if information about pay is shared, inequitable feelings may not result.

Give people a voice in decisions affecting them. People are likely to believe that decisions have been made fairly to the extent that they have had a chance to influence those decisions—that is, they are given a "say in the matter." As a simple example, people consider the results of elections to be fair so long as all those who are eligible were given an opportunity to participate in the process (whether or not they chose to do so). When people are denied a voice that they believe they should have, they respond negatively—even if the resulting decision is the same as it would have been if they did participate.

As a case in point, consider the work slowdown among New York City taxicab drivers that caused serious traffic problems (more serious than usual!) one week in 1998. The drivers were protesting the mayor's decision to impose certain rules on the drivers, which they resented. Interestingly, the drivers did not object to the rules themselves—in fact, most gladly accepted them. Rather, they were upset about the fact that the mayor imposed these rules on them without consulting them in the matter.

Explain outcomes thoroughly using a socially sensitive manner. This suggestion follows from research on procedural justice and interactional justice showing that people's assessments of fairness on the job go beyond merely what their outcomes and inputs are and include also their knowledge of *how* these assessments are determined. For example, it has been found that negative outcomes such as layoffs, pay freezes, and even pay cuts can be accepted and recognized as being fair to the extent that people understand the procedures that brought them about. When such procedures appear to be unbiased and carefully enacted, and when the negative outcomes of such procedures are presented in a highly sensitive and caring manner, the sting is taken out of the undesirable outcomes.[60]

Illustrating this point, consider what it's like to have to live through a long pay freeze. Although it's likely to be painful, people may be more accepting of a pay freeze as fair if the procedure used to determine the need for the pay freeze is believed to be thorough and careful—that is, if "a fair explanation" for it can be provided. This was precisely what was found in a recent study of manufacturing workers' reactions to a pay freeze.[61] Specifically, the researchers made comparisons between two groups of workers: those who received a thorough explanation of the procedures necessitating the pay freeze (e.g., information about the organization's economic problems) and those who received no such information. Although all workers were adversely affected by the freeze, those receiving the explanation better accepted it. In particular, the explanation reduced their interest in looking for a new job. These findings suggest that even if managers cannot do anything to eliminate workplace inequities, they may be able to take some of the sting out of them by providing explanations as to why these unfortunate conditions are necessary.

MOTIVATING BY ALTERING EXPECTATIONS

Instead of focusing on individual needs, goals, or social comparisons, **expectancy theory** takes a broader approach; it looks at the role of motivation in the overall work environment. In essence, the theory asserts that people are motivated to work when they expect that they will be able to achieve the things they want from their jobs. Expectancy theory characterizes people as rational beings who think about what they have to do to be rewarded and how much the reward means to them before they perform their jobs. But, as we will see, the theory doesn't only focus on what people think. It also recognizes that these thoughts combine with other aspects of the organizational environment to influence job performance.

Basic Elements of Expectancy Theory

Although several different versions of expectancy theory have been proposed, expectancy theorists agree that motivation is the result of three different types of beliefs that people have.[62] These are **expectancy**—the belief that one's effort will result in performance, **instrumentality**—the belief that one's performance will be rewarded, and **valence**—the perceived value of the rewards to the recipient (see Figure 6.14).

expectancy theory
The theory that asserts that motivation is based on people's beliefs about the probability that effort will lead to performance (*expectancy*), multiplied by the probability that performance will lead to reward (*instrumentality*), multiplied by the perceived value of the reward (*valence*).

expectancy
The belief that one's efforts will positively influence one's performance.

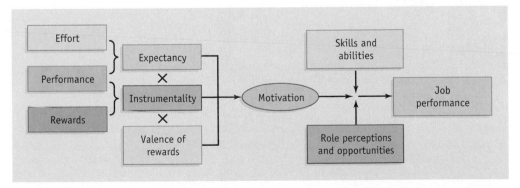

FIGURE 6.14
Expectancy Theory: An Overview
According to *expectancy theory*, motivation is the result of three types of beliefs. These are *expectancy* (the belief that one's effort will influence performance), *instrumentality* (the belief that one will be rewarded for one's performance), and *valence* (the perceived value of the rewards expected). The theory also recognizes that motivation is only one of several factors responsible for job performance.

instrumentality
An individual's beliefs regarding the likelihood of being rewarded in accord with his or her own level of performance.

valence
The value a person places on the rewards he or she expects to receive from an organization.

Expectancy. Sometimes people believe that by putting forth a great deal of effort, they will get a lot accomplished. However, in other cases, people do not expect that their efforts will have much effect on how well they do. For example, an employee operating a faulty piece of equipment may have a very low *expectancy* that his or her efforts will lead to high levels of performance. Naturally, someone working under such conditions probably would not continue to exert much effort.

Instrumentality. Even *if* an employee works hard and performs at a high level, motivation may falter if that performance is not suitably rewarded—that is, if the performance is not perceived as *instrumental* in bringing about the rewards. So, for example, a worker who is extremely productive may be poorly motivated to perform if he or she has already reached the top level of pay given by the company (for more on this, see the OB in a Diverse World section on page 210).

Valence. Finally, even *if* employees believe that hard work will lead to good performance *and* that they will be rewarded according to their performance, they still may be poorly motivated *if* those so-called rewards have a low *valence* to them. In other words, someone who doesn't care about the rewards offered by the organization is not motivated to attain them. As an example, a reward of $100 would not be likely to motivate a multimillionaire, whereas it may be a very desirable reward for someone of more modest means. Only those rewards that have a high positive valence to their recipients will motivate behavior. With this in mind, many of today's companies are going out of their way to motivate employees by giving them the kinds of job perks they most desire (for an example, see Figure 6.15).[65]

Combining all three types of beliefs. Expectancy theory claims that motivation is a multiplicative function of all three components. This means that higher levels of motivation will result when expectancy, instrumentality, and valence are all high than when they are all low. The multiplicative assumption of the theory also implies that if any one of these three components is zero, the overall level of motivation will be zero. So, for example, even if an employee believes that her effort will result in performance that will result in reward, motivation will be zero if the valance of the reward she expects to receive is zero.

Other determinants of job performance. Figure 6.14 also highlights a point we made in our opening remarks about motivation—that motivation is not equivalent to job performance. Expectancy theory recognizes that motivation is one of several important determinants of job performance.

FIGURE 6.15

Valence: Give the People What They Want
In today's highly competitive job market, it's important for employers to go to great lengths to attract and retain the best employees by giving them rewards that they value greatly. It is with this in mind that Etensity, a Web consulting and services firm based in Vienna, Virginia, offers its employees the "Hot Wheels" program, which contributes $400/month to their car payments, enabling them to get their dream cars. According to CEO Peter Noce, "It's showing your employees that you honestly care about them . . . so they're going to stay with you."

For example, the theory assumes that *skills and abilities* also contribute to a person's job performance. It's no secret that some people are better suited to performing their jobs than others by virtue of their unique characteristics and special skills and abilities. For example, a tall, strong, well-coordinated person is likely to make a better professional basketball player than a very short, weak, uncoordinated one—even if the shorter person is highly motivated to succeed.

Expectancy theory also recognizes that job performance will be influenced by people's *role perceptions*—in other words, what they believe is expected of them on the job. To the extent that there are disagreements about what one's job duties are, performance may suffer. For example, an assistant manager who believes her primary job duty is to train new employees may find that her performance is downgraded by a supervisor who believes she should be spending more time doing routine paperwork instead. In this case the person's performance wouldn't suffer as a result of any deficit in motivation but simply because of misunderstandings regarding what the job entails.

Finally, expectancy theory also recognizes the role of *opportunities to perform* one's job. Even the best employees may perform at low levels if their opportunities are limited. For example, a highly motivated salesperson may perform poorly if opportunities are restricted (such as if the territory is having a financial downturn or if the available inventory is limited).

It is important to recognize that expectancy theory views motivation as just one of several determinants of job performance. Motivation, combined with a person's skills and abilities, role perceptions, and opportunities, influences job performance.

Expectancy theory has generated a great deal of research and has been successfully applied to understanding behavior in many different organizational settings.[66] Although the theory has received only mixed support about some of its specific aspects (e.g., the multiplicative assumption), it is still one of the dominant approaches to the study of motivation in organizations. Probably the primary reason for expectancy theory's popularity is the many useful suggestions it makes for practicing managers. We will now describe some of the most essential applications of expectancy theory, giving examples from organizations in which they have been implemented.

Managerial Applications of Expectancy Theory

Expectancy theory is a very practical approach to motivation. In fact, it suggests several important things that can be done to motivate employees.

Clarify people's expectancies that their effort will lead to performance. Motivation may be enhanced by training employees to do their jobs more efficiently, thereby achieving higher levels of performance from their efforts. It also may be possible to enhance effort–performance expectancies by following employees' suggestions about ways to change their jobs. To the extent that employees are aware of problems in their jobs that interfere with their performance, attempting to alleviate these problems may help them perform more effectively. In essence, what we are saying is *make the desired performance attainable.* Good supervisors not only make it clear to people what is expected of them, but they also help them attain that level of performance.

Administer rewards that are positively valent to employees. In other words, the carrot at the end of the stick must be tasty for it to have potential as a motivator. These days, with a highly diverse workforce, it would be misleading to assume that all employees care about having the same rewards. Some might recognize the incentive value of a pay raise, whereas others might prefer additional vacation days, improved insurance benefits, day care, or elder care facilities. With this in mind, many companies have introduced **cafeteria-style benefit plans**—incentive systems allowing employees to select their fringe benefits from a menu of available alternatives.

Given that fringe benefits represent almost 40 percent of payroll costs, more and more companies are recognizing the value of administering them flexibly—about 30 percent in some industries, such as mining, where a particularly diverse workforce drives the

cafeteria-style benefit plans
Incentive systems in which employees have an opportunity to select the fringe benefits they want from a menu of available alternatives.

OB IN A DIVERSE WORLD
WHY DO AMERICANS WORK LONGER HOURS THAN GERMANS?

Over the years, an interesting disparity has emerged between the work habits of Americans and their European counterparts. For example, in 1970, Americans and West Germans worked approximately the same number of hours per year, 1,900. Since that time, however, changes have occurred on both sides of the ocean. Whereas the number of hours worked annually by Americans has risen to about 2,000 (because they now work longer days), the comparable figure for Germans has dropped to about 1,500 (because they now work shorter days, have shorter workweeks, and take more vacation time).[63]

Many have taken this as evidence of cultural differences, arguing that Americans tend to be workaholics who are motivated to work harder than their counterparts in Europe who prefer their leisure time. However, recent research by economists suggests that there's more involved than cultural differences.[64] Simply put, there is a greater pay disparity in the United States than in Germany. In other words, the difference between the

need for diverse compensation options.[67] For example, financial services company Primerica (a member of Citigroup) has had a flexible benefit plan in use since 1978.[68] Southwest Airlines has a modified program in place, in which employees get to select their medical benefits in cafeteria style. Instead of allowing employees to completely customize their benefit package, some companies have made it possible for their employees to pick their perks together as a group. At Powered.com, for example, the workers decided that what they needed was something that made their 20-hour workdays more comfortable. They set up what they call the Web Lounge, a comfortable space where people can hold meetings, watch movies, or do whatever they want.[69] "Democratizing the benefits," says Ian Steyaert, vice president of development, is what it's all about.

Clearly link valued rewards and performance. Unfortunately, not all incentive plans do as good a job as they should in rewarding desired performance. A recent survey found that only 25 percent of employees see a clear link between good job performance and their pay raises. In some professions, the problem is considerable. Take major league baseball, for example. If, as a fan, you ever thought that some players are paid more than they're worth while others are paid less than they're worth, you are not mistaken. Indeed, statistics reveal a very low correlation between how well pitchers pitch (their earned run average) and how much they are paid. Likewise, batters' overall performance (batting average) also is only weakly linked to their pay (for an example, see Figure 6.16).[70]

Obviously many organizations have a long way to go in raising their employees' instrumentality beliefs.[71] In other words, managers should enhance their subordinates' beliefs about instrumentality by specifying exactly what job behaviors will lead to what rewards. How can they do this? To the extent that it is possible for employees to be paid in ways directly linked to their performance—such as through piece-rate incentive systems, sales commission plans, or bonuses—expectancy theory specifies that it would be effective to do so. This is the idea behind **pay-for-performance plans**—pay plans that systematically reward employees in proportion to how well they have done their jobs.[72]

To illustrate the importance of selecting only the most desired performance to reward, let's consider the pay plan IBM uses for its 30,000 sales representatives. Previously, most of the pay these reps received was based on flat salary; their compensation was not linked to how well they did. Now, however, their pay is carefully tied to two factors that are essential to the company's success—profitability and customer sat-

pay-for-performance plan

A payment system in which employees are paid differentially based on the quantity and quality of their performance. Pay-for-performance plans strengthen *instrumentality* beliefs.

highest-paid and lowest-paid workers is considerably greater among Americans, and this creates an incentive for American employees to work harder. After all, the more hours Americans work, the more money they can expect to make. For example, Americans who raise the number of annual hours worked by 10 percent—from 2,000 to 2,200—can expect a 1 percent increase in pay for that year. Although this isn't much, the considerably smaller range in pay among Germans leads them to expect that pay raises will not be forthcoming at all, even if they put in longer hours. Accordingly, there is limited incentive for them to do so. In expectancy theory terms, the instrumentality beliefs of Americans appear to be considerably higher than those of the Germans—that is, Americans expect to receive higher rewards for performing at high levels. This contributes to their high levels of performance.

Interestingly, it's hard to say who's better off. Because the Americans are more productive, they tend to be more highly paid but work more hours than desired. Germans, however, long for the American standard of living but are reluctant to give up their leisure time. Although the free time versus extra income issue is a matter of preference, it's interesting to note how these findings lend support to expectancy theory. It's also noteworthy that these findings support the old saying that "the other man's grass is always greener"—apparently, even if it's on the other side of the Atlantic.

isfaction. So, instead of receiving commissions on the amount of the sale, as so many salespeople do, 60 percent of IBMers' commissions are tied to the company's profit on that sale. As a result, the more the company makes, the more the reps make. And, to make sure that the reps don't push only high-profit items that customers might not need, the remaining 40 percent of their commissions is based on customer satisfaction (assessed in regular surveys). Since introducing this plan in late 1993, IBM has been effective in reversing its unprofitable trend. Although there are certainly many factors responsible for this turnaround, experts are confident that this practice of clearly linking desired performance to individual rewards is a key factor.

Another example comes from Continental Airlines. In 1994, this air carrier was ranked dead last with respect to on-time performance—a problem that was costing the company $6 million per month.[73] To combat this, management started paying bonuses to employees to reward on-time performance: $100 per employee for a top ranking and

FIGURE 6.16

Is Pay Linked to Performance? In Major League Baseball, Not Always
In the 1999 baseball season, Carlos Beltran batted in an extraordinary 108 runs for the Kansas City Royals, but he was paid only baseball's minimum salary of $200,000. Following two more seasons of impressive stats, the slugger signed for $3.5 million for the 2002 season, a figure that is more in line with his performance (at least by the standards of that profession). Had Beltran's pay not been raised, it's unlikely that he would have been motivated to continue performing at such a high level.

$65 per employee for a number-two or number-three ranking. Since initiating this plan, Continental consistently has placed among the industry's on-time leaders, earning each employee some $700 each in one recent year.

Of course, the rewards need not be monetary in nature; even symbolic and verbal forms of recognition for a job well done can be very effective. Some companies help recognize their employees' organizational contributions by acknowledging them on the pages of their corporate newsletter. For example, employees of the large pharmaceutical company Merck enjoyed the recognition they received for developing Proscar (a highly successful drug treatment for prostate enlargement) when they saw their pictures in the company newsletter. This example illustrates the important point that recognizing employees need not be lavish or expensive. It can involve nothing more than a heartfelt "thank you." As Mark Twain put it, "I can live for two months on a good compliment." With this in mind, some companies have taken very creative measures. For some examples, see Table 6.2.[74]

Some companies are so serious about paying employees for their performance that they are giving their employees a small piece of the company in exchange for their contributions—a practice that is sure to link performance with rewards in their minds.[75] One popular form this has taken in many high-tech start-ups is known as **incentive stock option (ISO) plans.** In such plans, a company grants an employee the opportunity to purchase its stock at some future time at a specified price. So, over time, if the value of the company's stock increases, the employee can "exercise the option" by selling the stock at a profit and with certain income tax advantages.[76] Although the exact rules to incentive stock options are complex, the underlying rationale is straightforward: Give employees a stake in the success of the company. So, what's good for the company also is good for the employee. In expectancy theory terms, ISOs may be beneficial insofar as they reward employees when their company does well. And this motivates them to put forth the effort to succeed. (For closer look at some important considerations involving ISOs, see the OB in an E-World section on page 214.)

incentive stock option (ISO) plans
Corporate programs in which a company grants an employee the opportunity to purchase its stock at some future time at a specified price.

MOTIVATING BY STRUCTURING JOBS TO MAKE THEM INTERESTING

The final approach to motivation we will consider is the largest in scope because it is directed at improving the nature of the work performed. The idea behind **job design** is

TABLE 6.2 NONMONETARY RECOGNITION: SOME CREATIVE EXAMPLES FROM SMALL COMPANIES

Recognition can be one of the most effective types of reward, and because it can be so inexpensive, it is popular among small companies. The small companies identified here recognize thier employees in some particularly creative ways. The companies involved also have found these techniques to be useful in attracting new employees.

COMPANY	NATURE OF BUSINESS	FORM OF RECOGNITION
Kendle	Designs clinical tests for drugs	Photos of all 288 employees, posed engaging in their favorite outside activity, line the hallways.
Leonhardt Plating Company	Manufactures steel plating	Employees of the polishing department are allowed to manage themselves.
50 small businesses in the vicinity of the Cincinnati/Northern Kentucky Airport	Miscellaneous	These companies banded together to offer free transportation services to their employees who don't live nearby.
Payne Firm, Inc.	Environmental consulting firm	Set up telecommuting facilities that make it easy for some employees to work while staying at home.

(*Source:* Based on information in Schafer, 1997; see Note 74.)

that motivation can be enhanced by making jobs more appealing to people. As you may recall from Chapter 1, Frederick W. Taylor's principle of *scientific management* attempted to stimulate performance by designing jobs in the most efficient fashion. However, treating people like machines often meant having them engage in repetitive movements that they found highly routine and monotonous. Not surprisingly, people became bored with such jobs and frequently quit.[81] Fortunately, today's organizational scientists have found several ways of designing jobs that can not only be performed very efficiently but that are also highly pleasant and enjoyable.

job design

An approach to motivation suggesting that jobs can be created to enhance people's interest in doing them. (See *job enlargement, job enrichment,* and the *job characteristics model*).

Job Enlargement and Job Enrichment

Imagine that you have a highly routine job, such as tightening the lugs on the left rear wheel of a car as it rolls down the assembly line. Naturally, such a highly repetitive task would be monotonous and not very pleasant. One of the first modern approaches to redesigning jobs suggested that such consequences could be minimized by having people perform an increased number of different tasks all at the same level. This approach is known as **job enlargement.** To enlarge the jobs in our example, workers could be required to tighten the lugs on all four wheels. As a result of such an action, employees have no more responsibility nor use any greater skills but perform a wider variety of different tasks at the same level. Adding tasks in this fashion is said to increase the *horizontal job loading* of the position.

job enlargement

The practice of expanding the content of a job to include more varitey and a greater number of tasks at the same level.

A few years ago, American Greetings Corp., Cleveland, Ohio's greeting card and licensing concern, enlarged some 400 jobs in its creative division.[82] Now, rather than always working exclusively on Christmas cards, for example, employees will be able to move back and forth between different teams, such as those working on birthday ribbons, humorous mugs, and Valentine's Day gift bags. Employees at American Greetings reportedly enjoy the variety, as do those at RJR Nabisco, Corning, and Eastman Kodak, which are other companies that recently have allowed employees to make lateral moves.

Although most reports of the effectiveness of job enlargement have been anecdotal, a few carefully conducted empirical studies also have examined their impact. For example, one group of researchers studied the effects of a job enlargement program instituted at a large financial services company.[83] The unenlarged jobs had different employees perform separate paperwork tasks such as preparing, sorting, coding, and keypunching various forms. By contrast, in the enlarged jobs these various functions were combined into larger jobs performed by the same people. Although it was more difficult and expensive to train people to perform the enlarged jobs than the separate jobs, important benefits resulted. In particular, employees expressed greater job satisfaction and less boredom. And, because one person followed the whole job all the way through, greater opportunities to correct errors existed. Not surprisingly, customers were satisfied with the result.

Unfortunately, in a follow-up investigation of the same company conducted two years later, it was found that not all the beneficial effects continued.[84] Notably, employee satisfaction leveled off and the rate of errors went up, suggesting that as employees got used to their enlarged jobs they found them less interesting and stopped paying attention to all the details. Hence, although job enlargement may help improve job performance, its effects may not be long lasting.

In contrast to job enlargement, **job enrichment** gives employees not only more jobs to do but also more tasks to perform at a higher level of skill and responsibility (see Figure 6.17). Job enrichment gives employees the opportunity to take greater control over how to do their jobs. Because people performing enriched jobs have increased opportunities to work at higher levels, the job enrichment process is said to increase a position's *vertical job loading*.

job enrichment

The practice of giving employees a high degree of control over their work, from planning and organization, through implementing the jobs and evaluating the results.

Although evidence suggests that job enrichment programs also have been successful at other organizations, several factors limit their popularity.[85] Most obvious is the *difficulty of implementation.* To redesign existing facilities so that jobs can be enriched is often prohibitively expensive. The technology needed to perform certain jobs also may make it impractical for them to be redesigned. Another impediment is the *lack of employee acceptance.* Although many relish it, some people do *not* desire the additional responsibility associated with performing enriched jobs. In particular, individuals low in achievement motivation (see Chapter 3) are especially frustrated with enriched jobs.[86] Similarly, people may get used to having to do their jobs in certain ways and not like having to change. In fact, when a group of American auto workers was sent to Sweden to work in a Saab engine assembly plant where jobs were highly enriched, five out of six indicated that they preferred their traditional assembly-line jobs.[87] As one union leader put it, "If you want to enrich the job, enrich the paycheck."[88] Clearly, enriched jobs are not for everyone.

Thus far, we have failed to specify precisely *how* to enrich a job. *What* elements of a job need to be enriched for it to be effective? An attempt to expand the idea of job enrichment, known as the *job characteristics model,* provides an answer to this important question.

The Job Characteristics Model

job characteristics model

An approach to job enrichment that specifies that five core job dimensions (skill variety, task identity, task significance, autonomy, and job feedback) produce critical psychological states that lead to beneficial outcomes for individuals (e.g., high job satisfaction) and the organization (e.g., reduced turnover).

This approach assumes that jobs can be designed to help people get enjoyment out of their jobs and to care about the work they do. The **job characteristics model** identifies how jobs can be designed to help people feel that they are doing meaningful and valuable work. In particular, the model specifies that enriching certain elements of jobs alters people's psychological states in a manner that enhances their work effectiveness.[89] Specifically, the model identifies five *core job dimensions* that help create three *critical psychological states,* leading, in turn, to several beneficial *personal and work outcomes* (see Figure 6.18).

Components of the model. The five critical job dimensions are *skill variety, task identity, task significance, autonomy,* and *feedback.* Let's take a closer look at these.

- *Skill variety* refers to the extent to which a job requires a number of different activities using several of the employee's skills and talents. For example, an office manager with high skill variety may have to perform many different tasks (e.g., do word processing, answer the telephone, greet visitors, and file records).
- *Task identity* refers to the extent to which a job requires completing a whole piece of work from beginning to end. For example, tailors will have high task identity if they

workers. Interestingly, although the chances of making it big in today's dot-com world are quite low, many people still hope to beat the odds. As a result, ISOs remain in widespread use. For example, 88 percent of information technology companies grant stock options to their employees, and the numbers are highest among small firms (those with fewer than 100 employees and revenues less than $50 million).

Today, several career strategists are warning against taking ISOs in lieu of salary.[78] For example, visitors to one high-tech Web site have been warned as follows: "With options, every second you spend at work becomes an investment. And with any investment, one of the hardest decisions is knowing whether or not to cut bait as the stock heads south."[79] Indeed, this is precisely why ISOs are so effective in motivating employees—but, of course, only if they pay off. Because, with increasing frequency, their value cannot be assured, today's high-tech workers are being advised to take cash in hand instead, accepting higher salaries and less generous stock options. In the words of Patrick Neeman, a program manager at Stamps.com, "Stock options only hurt you if you take a drastic pay cut to join a dot-com. Real cash and fewer options is better than a princely stash of options, because potential doesn't pay the rent."[80]

do everything related to making a whole suit (e.g., measuring the client, selecting the fabric, cutting and sewing it, and altering it to fit).

- *Task significance* refers to the degree of impact the job is believed to have on others. For example, medical researchers working on a cure for a deadly disease probably recognize the importance of their work to the world at large. Even more modest contributions to the company can be recognized as being significant to the extent that employees understand the role of their jobs in the overall mission of the organization.

- *Autonomy* refers to the extent to which employees have the freedom and discretion to plan, schedule, and carry out their jobs as desired. For example, a furniture repair person may act highly autonomously by freely scheduling his or her day's work and by freely deciding how to tackle each repair job confronted.

- *Feedback* refers to the extent to which the job allows people to have information about the effectiveness of their performance. For example, telemarketing representatives regularly receive information about how many calls they make per day and the number and values of the sales made.

The model specifies that these various job dimensions have important effects on various critical psychological states. For example, skill variety, task identity, and task significance contribute jointly to a task's *experienced meaningfulness*. A task is considered to be meaningful to the extent that it is experienced as being highly important, valuable, and worthwhile. Jobs that provide a great deal of autonomy are said to make people feel *personally responsible and accountable for their work*. When they are free to decide what to do and how to do it, they feel more responsible for the results, whether good or bad. Finally, effective feedback is said to give employees *knowledge of the results of their work*. When a job is designed to provide people with information about the effects of their actions, they are better able to develop an understanding of how effectively they have performed—and such knowledge improves their effectiveness.

The job characteristics model specifies that the three critical psychological states affect various personal and work outcomes—namely people's feelings of motivation, the quality of work performed, satisfaction with work, absenteeism, and turnover. The higher the experienced meaningfulness of work, responsibility for the work performed, and knowledge of results, the more positive the personal and work benefits will be. When performing jobs that incorporate high levels of the five core job dimensions, peo-

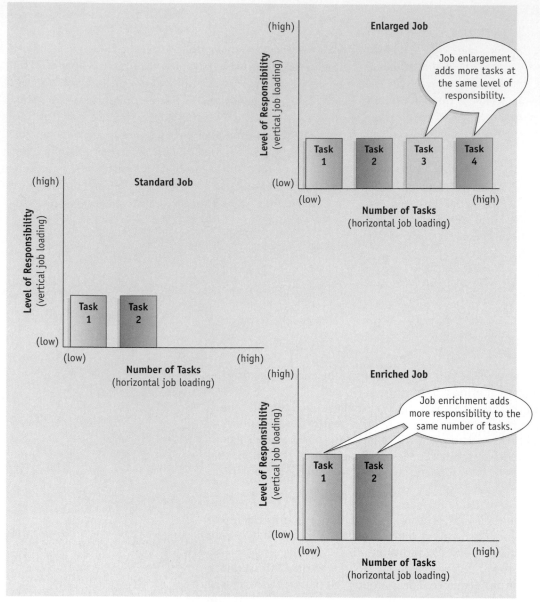

FIGURE 6.17

Job Enlargement and Job Enrichment: A Comparison
Redesigning jobs by increasing the number of tasks performed at the same level (*horizontal job loading*) is referred to as *job enlargement*. Redesigning jobs by increasing the employees' level of responsibility and control (*vertical job loading*) is referred to as *job enrichment*.

ple should feel highly motivated, perform high-quality work, be highly satisfied with their jobs, be absent infrequently, and be unlikely to resign from their jobs.

Does the model apply to everyone? We also should note that the job characteristics model is theorized to be especially effective in describing the behavior of individuals who are high in **growth need strength**—that is, people who have a high need for personal growth and development. People not particularly interested in improving themselves on the job are not expected to experience the theorized psychological reactions to the core job dimensions nor, consequently, to enjoy the beneficial personal and work outcomes predicted by the model.[90] By introducing this variable, the job characteristics model recognizes the important limitation of job enrichment noted earlier—not everyone wants and benefits from enriched jobs.

growth need strength

The personality variable describing the extent to which people have a high need for personal growth and development on the job. The *job characteristics model* best describes people high in growth need strength.

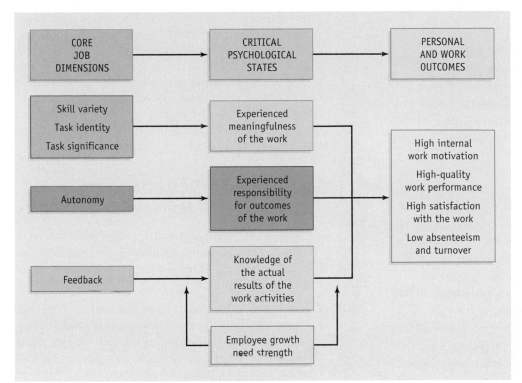

FIGURE 6.18

The Job Characteristics Model: Basic Components
The *job characteristics model* stipulates that certain *core job dimensions* lead to certain *critical psychological states,* which in turn lead to several beneficial *personal and work outcomes.* The model also recognizes that these relationships are strongest among individuals with high levels of *growth need strength.*

Putting it all together. Based on the proposed relationship between the core job dimensions and their associated psychological reactions, the job characteristics model claims that job motivation will be highest when the jobs performed rate highly on the various dimensions. To assess this, a questionnaire known as the *Job Diagnostic Survey* (*JDS*) has been developed to measure the degree to which various job characteristics are present in a particular job.[91] Based on responses to the JDS, we can make predictions about the degree to which a job motivates people who perform it. This is done by using an index known as the **motivating potential score (MPS),** computed as follows:

$$\text{MPS} = \frac{\text{Skill variety} + \text{Task identity} + \text{Task significance}}{3} \times \text{Autonomy} \times \text{Feedback}$$

The MPS is a summary index of a job's potential for motivating people. The higher the score for a given job, the greater the likelihood of experiencing the personal and work outcomes specified by the model. Knowing a job's MPS helps one identify jobs that might benefit by being redesigned.

motivating potential score (MPS)
A mathematical index describing the degree to which a job is designed so as to motivate people, as suggested by the *job characteristics model.* It is computed on the basis of a questionnaire known as the Job Diagnostic Survey (JDS). The higher the MPS, the more the job may stand to benefit from redesign.

Evidence for the model. The job characteristics model has been the focus of many empirical tests, most of which are supportive of many aspects of the model.[92] One study conducted among a group of South African clerical workers found particularly strong support.[93] The jobs of employees in some of the offices in this company were enriched in accordance with techniques specified by the job characteristics model. Specifically, employees performing the enriched jobs were given opportunities to choose the kinds of tasks they perform (high skill variety), to do the entire job (high task identity), to receive instructions regarding how their job fit into the organization as a whole (high task significance), to freely set their own schedules and inspect their own work (high autonomy), and to keep records of their daily productivity (high feedback). Another group of employees, equivalent in all respects except that their jobs were not enriched, served as a control group.

After employees performed the newly designed jobs for six months, comparisons were made between them and their counterparts in the control group. With respect to most of the outcomes specified by the model, individuals performing redesigned jobs showed superior results. Specifically, they reported feeling more internally motivated and

MAKING AUTONOMY WORK

Autonomy is not a panacea. If autonomy *always* were effective in motivating people, all companies would be using it all the time. There are, however, some commonalties among organizations in which autonomy is used effectively. By understanding these, we can recognize ways of using autonomy in an effective manner in our own organizations. That said, we ask: What, exactly, do companies do to make autonomy work?

First, it is necessary to invest a lot of time and effort in making sure that you *hire people who can do their jobs properly* without close supervision. Giving people autonomy without making sure they want it is a sure path to disaster.

Second, once employees are selected who are interested in autonomy (e.g., those who are high in growth need strength), you must *train employees to do their jobs effectively*. After all, they have to know what they're doing very, very well before they're left to do that job on their own.

Third, *make it clear that high-quality performance is demanded*. As you know, some companies are more tolerant of marginal performance—or even average performance—than others. Although no one ever likes to see marginal work, it tends to be accepted without question in some places more than others. However, employees should not be given a great deal of autonomy in any such organization. In fact, in those organizations in which autonomy works effectively, it does so because everyone involved strongly buys into the importance of performing at exceptionally high levels.

In closing, we acknowledge that the three guidelines we have identified here are far easier to describe than to implement. After all, personnel selection is rarely perfect, and people who are wrong for the job sometimes do slip in. By the same token, even the most highly trained people can make poor decisions when left on their own. And, finally, even the strongest organizational norms embracing high-quality work may not always yield beneficial results. Despite these concerns, we believe that the potential benefits associated with giving workers job autonomy make worthwhile any efforts at tackling these challenges head-on.

more satisfied with their jobs. There also were lower rates of absenteeism and turnover among employees performing the enriched jobs. The only outcome predicted by the model that was not found to differ was actual work performance; people performed equally well in enriched and unenriched jobs. Considering the many factors that are responsible for job performance (as discussed in connection with expectancy theory), this finding should not be too surprising.

Techniques for Designing Jobs That Motivate: Some Managerial Guidelines

The job characteristics model specifies several ways in which jobs can be designed to enhance their motivating potential.[94] In Table 6.3 we present these in the form of general principles.

Combine tasks. Instead of having several workers each perform a separate part of a whole job, it would be better to have each person perform the entire job. Doing so helps provide greater skill variety and task identity. For example, Corning Glass Works in Medford, Massachusetts, redesigned jobs so that people who assembled laboratory hot plates put together entire units instead of contributing a single part to the assembly process.[95]

Open feedback channels. Jobs should be designed to give employees as much feedback as possible. The more people know how well they're doing (be it from customers, supervisors, or coworkers), the better equipped they are to take appropriate corrective action (we already noted the importance of feedback in the learning process in Chapter 2). Sometimes cues about job performance can be clearly identified as people perform their jobs (as we noted in conjunction with goal setting). In the best cases, open lines of communication between employees and managers are so strongly incorporated into the corporate culture—as has been reported to exist at Boise Cascade's paper products group—that feedback flows without hesitation.[96]

Establish client relationships. The job characteristics model suggests that jobs should be set up so that the person performing a service (such as an auto mechanic) comes into contact with the recipient of the service (such as the car owner). Jobs designed in this manner will not only help the employee by providing feedback, but also will provide skill variety (e.g., talking to customers in addition to fixing cars) and enhance autonomy (by giving people the freedom to manage their own relationships with clients).

This suggestion has been implemented at Sea-Land Service, the large containerized ocean-shipping company.[97] After this company's mechanics, clerks, and crane operators started meeting with customers, they became much more productive. Having faces to associate with the once abstract jobs they did clearly helped them take the jobs more seriously.

Load jobs vertically. As we described earlier, loading a job vertically involves giving people greater responsibility for their jobs. Taking responsibility and control over performance away from managers and giving it to their subordinates increases the level of

TABLE 6.3 ENRICHING JOBS: SOME SUGGESTIONS FROM THE JOB CHARACTERISTICS MODEL

The job characteristics model specifies several ways jobs can be designed to incorporate the core job dimensions responsible for enhancing motivation and performance. A few are listed here.

PRINCIPLES OF JOB DESIGN	CORE JOB DIMENSIONS INCORPORATED
1. Combine tasks, enabling workers to perform the entire job	Skill variety Task identity
2. Establish client relationships, allowing providers of a service to meet the recipients	Skill variety Autonomy Feedback
3. Load jobs vertically, allowing greater responsibility and control over work	Autonomy
4. Open feedback channels, giving workers knowledge of the results of their work	Feedback

(*Source:* Based on information in Hackman, 1976; see Note 95.)

autonomy the jobs offer these lower-level employees. And, according to a recent poll, autonomy is among the most important things people look for in their jobs—even more important than high pay.[98] In view of this, a growing number of companies are yielding control and giving employees increasing freedom to do their jobs as they wish (within limits, at least).

Consider, for example, Childress Buick, a Phoenix, Arizona, auto dealership. This company suffered serious customer dissatisfaction and employee retention problems before owner Rusty Childress began encouraging his employees to use their own judgment and initiative. Sometimes, previously autocratic managers are shocked when they see how hard people work when they are allowed to make their own decisions. Bob Freese, CEO of Alphatronix Inc., in Research Triangle Park, North Carolina, is among the newly converted. "We let employees tell us when they can accomplish a project and what resources they need," he says. "Virtually always they set higher goals than we would ever set for them."[99] (For suggestions on how, exactly, to make autonomy work, see the How to Do It section on page 218.)

SUMMARY AND REVIEW OF LEARNING OBJECTIVES

1. Define motivation and explain its importance in the field of organizational behavior.

Motivation is concerned with the set of processes that arouse, direct, and maintain behavior toward a goal. It is not equivalent to job performance but is one of several determinants of job performance. Today's work ethic motivate people to seek interesting and challenging jobs instead of just money.

2. Describe need hierarchy theory and what it recommends about improving motivation in organizations.

Maslow's need hierarchy theory postulates that people have five basic needs, activated in a specific order from the most basic, lowest-level need (physiological needs) to the highest-level need (need for self-actualization). Although this theory has not been supported by rigorous research studies, it has been quite useful in suggesting several ways of satisfying employees' needs on the job. A less restrictive conceptualization, Alderfer's ERG theory proposes that people have only three basic needs: existence, relatedness, and growth. Following from these theories, companies are encouraged to do several things to motivate their employees. Notably, they should promote a healthy workforce, provide financial security, provide opportunities to socialize, and recognize employees' accomplishments.

3. Identify and explain the conditions through which goal setting can be used to improve job performance.

Locke and Latham's goal-setting theory claims that an assigned goal influences a person's beliefs about being able to perform a task (referred to as self-efficacy) and his or her personal goals. Both of these factors, in turn, influence performance. Research has shown that people will improve their performance when specific, acceptably difficult goals are set and feedback about task performance is provided. The task of selecting goals that are acceptable to employees is facilitated by allowing employees to participate in the goal-setting process.

4. Describe distributive justice, equity theory, procedural justice, and interactional justice, and explain how they may be applied to motivating people in organizations.

Distributive justice concerns people's perceptions of the fairness of the distribution of rewards. The major theory of distributive justice is equity theory. This theory claims that people desire to attain an equitable balance between the ratios of their work rewards (outcomes) and their job contributions (inputs) and the corresponding ratios of comparison others. Inequitable states of overpayment inequity and underpayment inequity are undesirable, motivating people to try to attain equitable conditions. Responses to inequity may be either behavioral (e.g., raising or lowering one's performance) or psychological (e.g., thinking differently about work contributions). People are concerned not only about establishing equitable relationships but also about procedural justice—that is, having organizational decisions made by way of fair processes (both in structural terms, such as having a voice in decision-making procedures, and interpersonally, such as by being treated with dignity and respect). In addition, people also are concerned about the fairness of the manner in which they are treated by others, known as interactional justice. These concepts (known collectively as theories of organizational justice) suggest that companies should avoid intentionally underpaying or overpaying employees, that managers should follow fair procedures (e.g., ones that are consistent and correctible), and that managers should explain the basis for outcomes in a thorough and socially sensitive manner.

5. Describe expectancy theory and how it may be applied in organizations.

Expectancy theory recognizes that motivation is the product of a person's beliefs about expectancy (effort will lead to performance), instrumentality (performance will result in reward), and valence (the perceived value of the rewards). In conjunction with skills, abilities, role perceptions, and opportunities, motivation contributes to job performance. Expectancy theory suggests that motivation may be enhanced by linking rewards to performance (as in pay-for-performance plans) and by administering rewards that are highly valued (as may be done using cafeteria-style benefit plans).

6. Distinguish between job enlargement, job enrichment, and the job characteristics model as techniques for motivating employees.

An effective organizational-level technique for motivating people is the designing or redesigning of jobs. Job design techniques include job enlargement (performing more tasks at the same level) and job enrichment (giving people greater responsibility and control over their jobs). The job characteristics model identifies the specific job dimensions that should be enriched (skill variety, task identity, task significance, autonomy, and feedback) and relates these to the critical psychological states influenced by including these dimensions on a job. These psychological states will, in turn, lead to certain beneficial outcomes for both individual employees (e.g., job satisfaction) and the organization (e.g., reduced absenteeism and turnover). Jobs may be designed to enhance motivation by combining tasks, opening feedback channels, establishing client relationships, and loading jobs vertically (i.e., enhancing responsibility for one's work).

Questions for Review

1. What are Maslow's five categories of needs, and how might each be satisfied on the job?
2. What rules should be followed when setting goals to motivate workers?
3. What does equity theory say about the role of money as a motivator?
4. How do procedural justice and interactional justice contribute to motivation on the job?
5. What are the basic components of expectancy theory and how are they combined to predict performance?
6. How, specifically, can jobs be designed in an effort to enhance motivation?

Experiential Questions

1. What experiences have you had in setting personal goals (e.g., for saving money, for losing weight, for getting a certain job)? Which rules of goal setting did you follow? Which rules might you have followed to be even more successful?
2. Think of a time in which you felt unfairly treated by your employer or manager. How did it make you feel, and how did you respond as a result? Which particular forms of organizational justice were involved, and how?
3. Think of the job you currently do or one that you have done recently. Describe two specific things that could be done to redesign that job so that employees will be more motivated to perform it.

Questions to Analyze

1. Consider a poor-performing employee who explains to his boss that he is trying very hard. According to expectancy theory, what factors would contribute to such effort? What additional factors, besides motivation, contribute to task performance?
2. Explain the role that money plays as a motivator in all of the theories of motivation presented in this chapter.
3. Imagine that you are devising a policy for determining the order in which vacation times are selected in your department. How could you do so in a manner that the people involved will believe is procedurally fair?

INDIVIDUAL EXERCISE

Do You Receive Fair Interpersonal Treatment on the Job?

A key element of procedural justice focuses on how fairly people believe they are treated by others, including coworkers, bosses, and the company as a whole. The following questionnaire is designed to provide insight into these beliefs.

Directions
Think about what your organization is like most of the time. Then, for each of the 18 items, select *Yes* if the statement describes your organization, *No* if it does not, and *?* if you cannot decide.

In this organization . . .

1. Employees are praised for good work.	Yes	?	No
2. Supervisors yell at employees.	Yes	?	No
3. Supervisors play favorites.	Yes	?	No
4. Employees are trusted.	Yes	?	No
5. Employees' complaints are dealt with effectively.	Yes	?	No
6. Employees are treated like children.	Yes	?	No
7. Employees are treated with respect.	Yes	?	No
8. Employees' questions and problems are responded to quickly.	Yes	?	No
9. Employees are told lies.	Yes	?	No
10. Employees' suggestions are ignored.	Yes	?	No
11. Supervisors swear at employees.	Yes	?	No
12. Employees' hard work is appreciated.	Yes	?	No
13. Supervisors threaten to fire or to lay off employees.	Yes	?	No
14. Employees are treated fairly.	Yes	?	No
15. Coworkers help each other.	Yes	?	No
16. Coworkers argue with each other.	Yes	?	No
17. Coworkers put each other down.	Yes	?	No
18. Coworkers treat each other with respect.	Yes	?	No

(*Source:* Questionnaire copyright © 1997 by Michelle A. Donovan, Fritz Drasgow, and Liberty J. Munson, University of Illinois at Urbana-Champaign.)

Scoring

1. Give yourself one point each time you answer *Yes* to the following questions: 1, 4, 5, 7, 8, 12, 14, 15, and 18.
2. Give yourself one point each time you answer *No* to the following questions: 2, 3, 6, 9, 10, 11, 13, 16, and 17.
3. Add up the number of points that you scored to find your *fair interpersonal treatment score.* Your score may range from 0 to 18, with higher scores representing more positive interpersonal treatment in your organization.

Questions for Discussion

1. What did your score reveal about the degree of interpersonal treatment in your organization? Is this what you would have guessed in advance?
2. Do you think other people in your organization would agree or disagree with how you answered these questions? Why?
3. Is there any one person (e.g., a particular boss) who, in your estimation, is mostly responsible for how you answered the questions? If so, how would you have answered the questions if the organization did not include this individual?
4. What could be done to improve the fairness of the interpersonal treatment you receive in your organization?

GROUP EXERCISE

Does Goal Setting Really Work? Demonstrate It for Yourself

Specific, difficult goals tend to enhance task performance. The following exercise is designed to help you demonstrate this effect for yourself. All you need is a class of students willing to participate and a few simple supplies.

Directions

1. Select a page of text from a book, and make several photocopies. Carefully count the words, and number each word on one of the copies. This will be your score sheet.

2. Find another class of 30 or more students who do not know anything about goal setting. (We do not want their knowledge of the phenomenon to bias the results.) On a random basis, divide the students into three equal-size groups.

3. Ask the students in the first group—the "baseline" group—to copy as much of the text as they can onto another piece of paper, and give them exactly one minute to do so. Direct them to work quickly. Using the score sheet created in step 1, identify the highest number of words copied by any one of the students, and then multiply this number by 2. This will be the specific, difficult goal level.

4. Ask the students in the second group—the "specific goal" group—to copy the number of words on the same printed page for exactly one minute. Tell them to try to reach the specific goal number identified in step 3.

5. Repeat this process with the third group—the "do your best" group—but instead of giving them a specific goal, direct them to "try to do your best at this task."

6. Compute the average number of words copied in the "difficult goal" group and the "do your best" group. Have your instructor compute the appropriate statistical test (a *t*-test, in this case) to determine the statistical significance of this difference in performance levels.

Questions for Discussion

1. Was there a statistically significant difference between the performance levels of the two groups? If so, did students in the "specific goal" group outperform those in the "do your best" group, as expected? What does this reveal about the effectiveness of goal setting?

2. If the predicted findings were not supported, why do you suppose this happened? What was it about the procedure that may have led to this failure? Was the specific goal (i.e., twice the fastest speed in the "baseline" group) too high, thus making the goal unreachable? Alternatively, was it too low, thus making the specific goal too easy?

3. What do you think would happen if the goal was lowered, thus making it easier, or raised, thus making it more difficult?

4. Do you think that providing feedback about goal attainment (e.g., someone counting the number of words copied and calling this out to the performers as they worked) would have helped?

5. For what other kinds of tasks do you believe goal setting may be effective? Specifically, do you believe that goal setting can improve your own performance on something? Explain this possibility.

WEB SURFING EXERCISE

Pay Equity in Sports

Visit the Web site of your favorite professional sports team or other related sites that have information about players' performance and their salaries. Prepare a spreadsheet summarizing (a) how much each player was paid in two recent years and (b) how well that player performed in those same years. (Select a good measure of performance, such as batting average for baseball players or points made for basketball players.) Answer the following questions based on your examination of these data.

1. In general, were players paid in proportion to their performance? In other words, did the better players tend to get higher pay?

2. If some workers were overpaid (i.e., paid a lot considering their performance), did their performance go up the following year? Why might this occur?

3. If some players were underpaid (i.e., paid very little considering their performance), did their performance go down the following year? Why might this occur?

Nonmonetary Rewards

Visit the Web sites of some of your favorite companies and search for the various types of nonmonetary rewards they use. This information may appear in pages headed "Press Releases" or "About the Company."

1. What particularly interesting nonmonetary rewards did you discover?
2. How effective were these rewards in motivating the employees at this company? Why do you think they may have been so effective?
3. How do these nonmonetary rewards compare to those listed in Table 6.2?

PRACTICING OB

Motivating Workers at a Chemical Company

Suppose that you were just hired by executives of a large chemical company to help resolve problems of poor morale that have been plaguing the workforce. Nobody wants to work on their assignments, claiming they don't find the work interesting. Turnover and absenteeism are high, and performance is at an all-time low. Answer the following questions relevant to this situation based on the material in this chapter.

1. After interviewing the workers, suppose you found that they believed that no one cared how well they were doing. What theories could help explain this problem? Applying these approaches, what would you recommend the company do to resolve this situation?
2. Company officials tell you that the employees are well paid, adding to their surprise about the low morale. However, your interviews reveal that the employees themselves feel otherwise. Theoretically, why is this a problem? What could be done to help?
3. "I'm bored with my job," an employee tells you, and you believe he speaks for many within the company. What could be done to make the jobs more interesting to those who perform them? What are the limitations of your plan? Would it work equally well for all employees?

CASE IN POINT

Wal-Mart: Everyday Motivated Employees

When Sam Walton died in 1992, some industry insiders doubted that the Wal-Mart chain that he had founded some 30 years earlier would retain its prominence as a discount retailer. Lost for good, they feared, would be the "magic spark" that Walton used to light fires under the chain's 1.3 million associates. And, as Wal-Mart stock failed to enjoy the same bull-market growth as many other companies in the mid-1990s, the pundits appeared to be correct. Today, however, with stores in all 50 U.S. states and nine other contries, Wal-Mart has rebounded, leading the pack of discount stores with record earnings. In fact, with $218 billion in annual sales and 100 million customers per week, Wal-Mart is the world's largest retailer and was named "Retailer of the Century" by *Discount Store News*.

One key to Wal-Mart's success, many believe, is the way it energizes its sales force. For example, employee meetings at Wal-Mart stores are the same pep rally–type affairs that Walton organized years ago. Cries of "Give me a W, give me an A, give me an L, give me a squiggly. . . ." are led by store managers who whip salesclerks into selling frenzies as they prepare for the day's onslaught of customers. And those clerks know just what their customers want and how many are buying their merchandise. Just to make sure, they are given thorough sales figures to show exactly how their particular store is doing. How much money did they take in compared to the previous day, or week, or year? What items are hot sellers, and what's their markup?

Representatives of the various departments proudly announce the answers but not in the dry tone used at most business meetings. At Wal-Mart, they make it fun for everyone. For example, if you were an employee of the Wal-Mart store in Pasadena, Texas, not too long ago, you could have won a package of Oreo cookies for correctly guessing that the store sold 15,850 packages in the previous four weeks. Granted, the prize does more for the winner's waistline than his or her net worth. However, such events promote camaraderie and a sense of fun that define the working experience at Wal-Mart.

As you might imagine, the sales figures quoted come from the company's computers. What you probably never would have imagined, however, is that Wal-Mart's information technology is so advanced that it provides up-to-the-minute tabs on every sales figure you possibly could imagine throughout the chain. In fact, Wal-Mart spends some $500 million each year on the latest information technology, and it is second only to the U.S. government in the amount of information storage capacity it has at its disposal (a whopping 24 terabytes!). No other retail establishment even comes close.

This technology gives employees complete information on the status of every item Wal-Mart sells. For example, with the stroke of a simple handheld scanning wand over an item's bar code, a store manager can get detailed information about that item's past, present, and projected sales. (Did you know, for example, that Wal-Mart sells a Barbie doll every 20 seconds?) And if a Wal-Mart employee finds a competing store advertising a lower price on any item Wal-Mart sells, his or her store manager can immediately match the price and send the new, lower price to all 2,400 Wal-Mart stores via the company's satellite system. The price reduction is then trumpeted on in-store bulletin boards.

Wal-Mart officials view this whiz-bang technology not only as a useful merchandising tool but also as a high-tech counterpart to the company's other employee-energizing tactics, such as its decidedly low-tech pep rallies. Armed with information on how well they're doing, company officials contend, Wal-Mart employees will be inspired to rise to the occasion to do their very best. And if the company's recent $3 billion profit is any indication, this strategy seems to be working just fine.

Critical Thinking Questions

1. What specific things does Wal-Mart to motivate employees?
2. What do you see as the strengths and limitations of these tactics?
3. How effective do you think these various tactics would be in the job you perform in the company in which you work?

Motivating Employees

One of the keys to motivating employees at SA is making them feel like they own the company. Indeed, by virtue of an employee stock ownership plan, they actually do own a portion of the company. As a result, the employees' rewards rise and fall with the value of the company. Although the financial struggles of dot-coms in recent years has led to a decline in the company's worth, SA employees still maintain strong incentives to work hard on behalf of their organization.

There are several reasons for this. Among them is that the company's human resources manager ensures that SA's core values reflect the values of the employees themselves. As a result, they work hard to attain the same goal—the good of the company. This is made possible by strong efforts to make everyone's job interesting and by giving them the freedom to make their own decisions. With this autonomy comes opportunities to make a difference, a factor that motivates SA employees to give their all. They have a vision—making SA the largest college marketing company in the world—and they are free to do whatever it takes to bring this about. The goals they set are difficult, but they are very effective in helping the company grow.

Questions for Discussion

1. In what ways consistent with job design (e.g., the job characteristics model) are SA officials attempting to boost productivity by making jobs more interesting to employees?
2. What is the company doing to help satisfy the social and physiological needs of employees?
3. In what specific ways are the concepts of instrumentality, expectancy, and valence (from expectancy theory) put into practice at SA?
4. How are the principles of goal setting used at SA, and how else might they be used?

Career Dynamics

■ PREVIEW CASE
FOR TODAY'S M.B.A.'S, JOB CHOICE IS DOT-COMPLICATED

Only a few years ago, the formula used to be simple: Go to a top-tier business school and get on the fast track for a top-tier job in a top-tier company. That's precisely the path Patrick Mullane had in mind when he entered the M.B.A. program at the prestigious Harvard Business School. But, somewhere along the way, he changed his mind. A month from graduating, Andersen Consulting offered him a six-figure starting salary, a $30,000 signing bonus, and agreed to pay back his $50,000 student loan. He turned it down. Although you might think that Mullane is crazy to reject such a lucrative offer, decisions like these are being made all the time. In fact, so many of today's top business students are spurning blue-chip offers that companies such as General Motors, Coca-Cola, and Procter & Gamble are finding it difficult to fill important slots.

> Mullane and those like him are betting on the future of these much smaller firms, hoping to get in on the ground floor, where in just a few years they can be part of something big.

Despite the fact that dot-coms are no longer the path to instant riches that they may have been only a few years ago, many top business school grads still are opting for the lure of working for smaller Internet start-ups rather than traditional positions in the corporate world. As Mullane explains, "I didn't want to miss the next Industrial Revolution. I didn't want to have any regrets." Although the starting pay and bonuses aren't anywhere near as lucrative, Mullane and those like him are betting on the future of these much smaller firms, hoping to get in on the ground floor, where in just a few years they can be part of something big. Then they stand to make more money than they ever could imagine. Meanwhile, for Mullane and many of his classmates, it's not all about money. There's also the matter of lifestyle. The corporate world typically requires lots of time on the road, and an even longer trip up the corporate ladder—even for fast-trackers.

Sharon Goldstein, a graduate of Northwestern University's Kellogg Graduate School of Management, is one of those fast-trackers. Like Mullane, she had offers from major consulting firms but turned them down in favor of a much more modest-paying position in the media systems group of RealNetworks in Seattle. While in school, she spent a summer there as an intern and grew to love the laid-back lifestyle. Believing that the corporate world was too bureaucratic and too confining for her, she is convinced she made the right choice.

So too, is Mullane certain of his decision. At Harvard, he was wooed by many big companies, but like Goldstein, he couldn't imagine carving out a place for himself in the bureaucratic world of corporate America. So, where did he end up? A few of his classmates were writing a business plan for a Web-based business whose mission is to help manufacturers reduce their supply-chain costs. He liked what he saw, and he joined them, beginning his career as director of marketing for the start-up SupplierMarket.com. In exchange for the big bucks he turned down up front, Mullane opted for enough money to sustain his family today, and "as much equity as I could get," in the hope of a huge payoff tomorrow. Although this huge payoff has never materialized, Mullane is pleased to have taken the risk.

Mullane and Goldstein probably would be the first to tell you that they are fortunate to have had the opportunities they turned down. After all, not everyone has a chance at a good position in a prestigious company. Yet, these two young people chose nontraditional paths, opting to invest the early stages of their work lives in positions that could make them wealthy later on. Maybe you can relate to what these individuals have done, or maybe, like many of us, your options are more limited. In either case, like all of us, you will follow a sequence of jobs over your lives known as *careers*.

Thanks to rapidly advancing technology, the shifting economy, and society's broadening views of acceptable career options, the career picture has been changing. Although your father and grandfather may have worked their way up a single corporate ladder during most of their adult lives, this is not the only option for people today. During the course of your working life, for example, you might decide to shift positions or go into an entirely different line of work. Alternatively, you may decide to start your own business, take off a few years, and then do something completely different. These paths, and many others, are all viable options for you, suggesting that careers can be very different.

Despite these differences, all careers share several fundamental characteristics. These are worth knowing because the more we understand about how careers operate, the better equipped we are to take control over our own careers. It is with this in mind that we will examine the topic of *career dynamics* in this chapter.

THE BASIC NATURE OF CAREERS

career dynamics
The wide variety of factors that influence the nature of people's career choices, the directions their careers take, and their ultimate success and satisfaction over the course of their working lives.

By **career dynamics,** we are referring to the wide variety of factors that influence the nature of people's career choices, the directions their careers take, and their ultimate success and satisfaction over the course of their working lives. Before considering these factors later in this chapter, we begin by addressing two very fundamental issues: What is a career, and what general categories of careers are there?

What Is a Career?

Over the course of their lives, most people find themselves in a variety of different jobs in several different organizations. In fact, during the course of his or her working life, the average American holds eight different jobs. In most cases, these positions are interconnected in some systematic way, weaving a path, however twisted and indirect, representing a *career*. Formally, a **career** can be defined as the evolving sequence of work experiences over time.

Given that people often use the terms *job, occupation,* and *career* interchangeably, it makes sense to distinguish among these terms before going any further. Simply put, a **job** is a predetermined set of activities one is expected to perform. An **occupation,** by contrast, is a coherent set of jobs.[1] So, for example, it may be said of the president of the United States that his current job (president) is in keeping with his occupation (politician), which represents a particular stage in his career (during which he held other jobs in this particular occupation). For a summary of the differences among these terms, see Figure 7.1.

Careers mean a great deal to individuals—both financially and psychologically. After all, the career path you take determines a great deal about how much money you will make throughout your life. Historically, some careers are more lucrative than others. For example, the average salary of people in finance, insurance, and real estate is over $55,000 whereas people who work in retail stores make only about $19,000.[2] Of course, money isn't everything; it also matters that you're happy with whatever you do.

This hints at the psychological importance of careers. Our careers can give us a sense of accomplishment and pride, and they also can give meaning to our lives (e.g., such as doctors who feel good about themselves because they save people's lives). Like it or not, your job defines your identity in the eyes of others. After all, when you meet someone at a party, the question often is asked, "What do you do?" Indeed, we define ourselves and others define us by the work we do. Although this may be misleading, of course, the fact that we spend about half our waking hours as adults engaged in work, it is easy to understand why we so often associate people with the career paths they've chosen.

It is not only workers themselves who are concerned about their own individual careers but so too are organizational officials concerned about the courses their employees' careers take. After all, when people are motivated to advance their careers, they can be expected to work hard and become productive employees. For this reason,

career
The evolving sequence of work experiences over time.

job
A predetermined set of activities a worker is expected to perform.

occupation
A coherent set of jobs.

FIGURE 7.1

Distinguishing Among Careers, Occupations, and Jobs
The typical career consists of several occupations (coherent sets of jobs), each of which is composed of a succession of individual jobs (predetermined sets of activities). A hypothetical example is presented here.

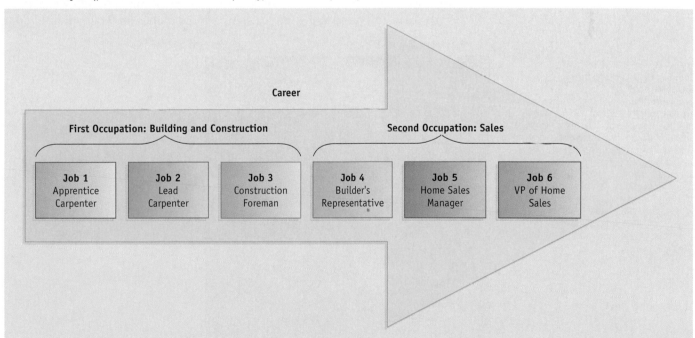

many companies take steps to help employees develop their careers in the direction that's best suited for them.

At the Synovus Financial Group, for example, a financial services and bank credit card processing company in Columbus, Georgia, company officials meet with employees every four months just to check on their satisfaction with their careers and to help them make whatever changes are best for them. If you're asking yourself, "why bother?" Elizabeth R. James could set you straight. Says Synovus's vice chairwoman and "chief people officer" (a position that's been in place since 1995), "We believe in the worth of the individual and we're going to make sure people are growing professionally, financially, personally, and spiritually."[3] And there's no doubt that this strategy is helping the company as well. Indeed, in 2001, Synovus was named Georgia's top-performing public company and in 2002 it was named by *Fortune* magazine as one of the "100 best companies to work for" for the fifth straight year.[4]

Today's Careers Are Not What They Used to Be

It's always useful to get career advice from others, and most friends and relatives are not shy about sharing their opinions. Fortunately, people can tell you lots of things about certain jobs, companies, and entire fields that are useful to know. When considering others' advice, however, you should keep in mind that today's careers are very different from careers just a generation ago. This is something you surely will want to keep in mind when you get advice from others. Let's now consider some of the key characteristics of today's careers and how they are different from the traditional careers of our parents and grandparents.[5]

Lifetime employment is a thing of the past. We remember how our fathers worked in one or two different companies for their whole lives. They started at a position in their late teens or early twenties and stayed there for 40 to 45 years, retiring with a gold watch in hand. That was how things were done: People expected to stay with their companies, and these organizations expected to keep them employed for as long as they wanted. Although this pattern still exists today, it is the exception rather than the rule. It is not unusual for people to hold about a half dozen different occupations during their careers, each with several jobs (see Figure 7.2).

There are several reasons for the shift away from lifetime employment. Briefly, these are as follows:

- *Technological advances.* Developments in technology occur so blindingly fast these days that new jobs are coming into existence and old ones are being phased out all

FIGURE 7.2

Cooking Up a Career—But for How Long?
In an effort to ensure that talented chefs are available to staff its banquet facilities, the Hyatt Corp. invested a quarter of a million dollars in a state-of-the-art kitchen in a Chicago high school, where Sandra Marquez (left) and Diana Villanueva are studying. Although these young women may well begin their careers at a Hyatt property, if they are like most people, they may change occupations a half dozen times throughout their lives and move between jobs even more frequently.

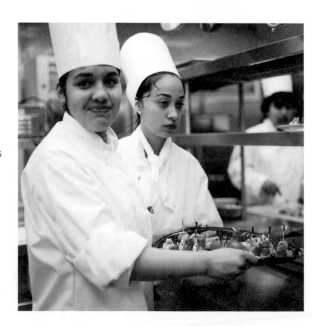

the time. Traditionally, although people's jobs always changed somewhat, the process was slow, and people were able to make the necessary adjustments. Now, they change so quickly that any one individual is unlikely to be ready, willing, or able to stay with a single job for very long—if that job even continues to exist at all.

- *Economic shifts.* Job security is highly unlikely whenever the economy is changing. Hardly a day goes by in which you fail to hear something about mergers and buy-outs (e.g., the merger between Hewlett-Packard and Compaq), restructurings and layoffs (e.g., at closing Kmart stores), and companies that are going out of business entirely (e.g., Enron). When such changes occur, jobs are lost—frequently with little or no notice—making loyalty a thing of the past.
- *Social norms.* Because it's difficult, if not impossible, for companies to be loyal to their employees, it follows that employees have little incentive to refrain from seeking better jobs elsewhere, whenever they may be found. "Job hopping," which once used to be considered an act of disloyalty, is now considered an acceptable way to move on to bigger and better things. In fact, it's often easier for people to advance in their careers by taking new jobs than by remaining at their old ones.

This discussion poses an important practical question: How long should you stay at a job? Occupational experts consider two to three years a good rule of thumb. However, if you are at a rapidly changing dot-com, even shorter times are considered acceptable. Interestingly, whereas staying in a single job for five years or longer used to be taken as a sign of stability, today it sends the message that you might be "stuck" and lack the skills to move on. (As you might imagine, this situation may be very different in other countries. In the following OB in a Diverse World section on page 232, we examine the very different norms with respect to lifetime employment in Japan.)

Careers are boundaryless. Traditionally, career success in the white-collar world meant only one thing—devoting your life to a single company and working your way up the corporate ladder. Although this still goes on today, most people's careers are not so simple. Instead, there is a trend toward what is known as the **boundaryless career**—that is, the tendency for people's careers to cut across various companies and industries. Boundaryless careers are especially popular in high-tech companies, where people frequently move from position to position at a rate that's twice as high as the national average. In fact, in California's Silicon Valley, one employee out of four changes jobs within a year.[7]

Although boundaryless careers are relatively common today, it would be misleading to suggest that all this moving around is considered desirable. In fact, most of today's high-tech job hoppers would prefer to remain with a single employer for most of their careers and to have a series of jobs for four years each.[8] Why, then, does it occur? Several reasons appear to be involved. These are as follows:

- *Downsizing eliminates employment options.* People often change jobs either because their jobs were eliminated or because they believe that they are about to be eliminated. In other words, a career may be boundaryless insofar as it is composed of jobs that are insecure. In other words, many people find that they are no longer working their way up "the corporate ladder" because the ladder is no longer present.
- *Careers progress more quickly outside the organization.* To avoid stagnation, many people are seeking jobs in new organizations or entirely different fields. The more new skills they develop in this manner, the more employable they will be. As a result, people who once were stigmatized as "job hoppers" may now be seen more favorably, as people who have developed important new skills.[9]
- *Changing careers is more socially acceptable than ever.* "Moving up" used to be considered the only acceptable way to go. Today, however, people find lots of social support for making lateral moves, moving up different ladders, or even "downshifting" their careers. In other words, it is considered acceptable for one's career to look more like a web than a ladder.

Career success is defined in many different ways. "Wow, look at that big house and that luxury car; he sure must have a successful career." If this line sounds familiar, it's

boundaryless career
The tendency for people to have careers that cut across various companies and industries.

because it represents the traditional means of defining success—a stable job with a high salary. Although this remains an extremely popular option for many people, this particular way of defining success is not the only way for growing numbers of people. Today, many people prefer to have a more balanced lifestyle than the hectic kind that's usually required to make a lot of money. Many are being true to themselves, recognizing that they value making a difference in the community, preferring, for example, to spend time helping their church or taking a job teaching first grade instead of focusing all their energy on pushing harder for extra dollars. These days, it's all about options. If you want to work the long hours needed to get a high-paying corporate job, you still can do so. However, if you prefer to live a more modest lifestyle, with time to spend with your family, it's considered perfectly acceptable to go that route as well.

Where, when, and for whom you work are not necessarily fixed. Going into the office at 8:00 in the morning and leaving at 5:00 in the afternoon is a cherished tradition. Lots of people do it all the time. However, as we noted in Chapter 1, growing numbers of people are telecommuting. They are "going to work" by staying at home or clicking away on their computers while on a boat or at a cabin in the woods.

Also as we described in Chapter 1, growing numbers of people are working flexible hours. Some work a core of fixed hours and can choose when else during the day to work. Other people are working four 10-hour days instead of five 8-hour days. A very few people even have jobs in which they don't have any specified hours to work at all. Instead, they are responsible for meeting certain objectives, no matter how much time, or how little time, it may take.

Finally, recall as well from Chapter 1 that many people are deciding not to work full time at all and are considered to be in the *contingent workforce*. These are individuals who work on specific projects for companies on an as-needed basis.[10] Although such individuals generally enjoy the freedom and flexibility of being a *permanent temp,* they also face several challenges. For a summary of the pros and cons, see Table 7.1.

resources down the drain, as in the U.S. system, where employees, once let go, may never return. In addition, Japan has laws preventing companies from advertising for labor and from hiring their competitors' employees. Therefore, the lifetime employment policy assures that training increases the value of employees to their organization and not to competitors who may steal them away.

■ With laws against hiring each others' employees, Japanese companies are assured former employees will not take R&D secrets to competitors. Because they have little fear of losing the fruits of their R&D activities to other companies, Japanese firms spend more time on these vital activities—and with excellent results.

In addition to benefiting the employees and the companies involved, lifetime employment also offers advantages to Japanese society at large. By keeping employees on their payrolls even during recessions, downswings in the business cycle are dampened. Most employees still have their jobs (if not their bonuses, too), so they can purchase goods and services, preventing the snowball effect that deepens and prolongs recession in other countries.

In sum, the Japanese system of lifetime employment persists because it works. Could the same system be adopted in other countries, such as the United States? Perhaps, but doing so would require extensive changes in existing labor laws, involving restrictions on stealing employees from other companies as well as stiff penalties for firing them. Adoption of such laws is unlikely in the United States, where the freedom to release employees as needed (known as the *employment-at-will* doctrine) is accepted. So, for now, Japan probably will remain relatively unique in the commitment to lifetime employment offered by many of its leading organizations.

Types of Careers

Although everyone's career is unique, scientists who have studied careers have observed that there are some general patterns or categories into which the vast majority of careers fall.[11] Specifically, four different types of careers have been identified, and we now will describe each of them (for a summary, see Figure 7.3).

Steady-state careers. Mike's father owns an auto-repair shop, Walton's Garage. When Mike was a young boy, he used to hang out at the shop after school, and he became interested in that line of work. After getting a technical degree from the local community college, Mike took over the family business. For all his working life, some 40 years, he ran Walton's Garage and fixed cars. Over the years, Mike had several opportunities to

TABLE 7.1 BEING A PERMANENT TEMP: PROS AND CONS

Whether by choice or by happenstance, many people today are forsaking regular full-time employment with a company in favor of having a series of temporary positions. To consider whether being a permanent temp is right for you, consider the following pros and cons.

PROS	CONS
Temporary jobs frequently offer flexible hours.	Health care insurance benefits are rarely provided, and these are expensive to purchase privately.
Greater earnings potential by working for several different companies.	Financial insecurity; temps cannot count on a regular paycheck.
Because temps are not around too long, they avoid the stress of office politics.	Unstable conditions; temps must start over with each new assignment.

(*Source:* Based on information in Damico, 2002; see Note 10.)

FIGURE 7.3

Four Major Types of Careers
Scientists have found it useful to distinguish among four different types of careers—*steady-state careers, linear careers, spiral careers,* and *transitory careers*—each of which is depicted here.

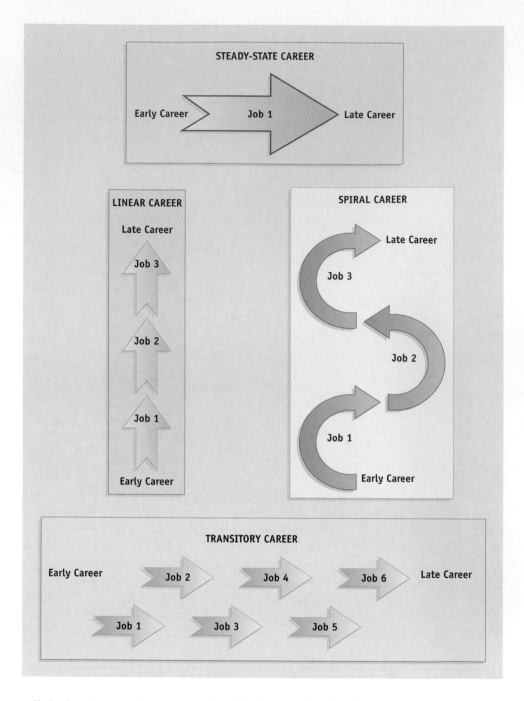

steady-state career

The type of career, characterized by a lifetime of employment in a single job.

sell the business and do something else, but he didn't. When it came time for him to retire, he simply handed over the family business to his own son.

Mike made a career choice that led him to a lifetime commitment to a single job, or what is called a **steady-state career.** People who have steady-state careers are generally very satisfied with what they are doing. Also, because they work at their jobs for so long, they tend to become highly skilled experts at what they do. After all, for Mike to have stuck it out in the garage as long as he did, he must like what he does and be pretty good at it, as well.

Linear careers. Janice always loved tinkering with computers, even as a young girl. Nobody was surprised, therefore, when she did an internship at a software development firm before getting a bachelor's degree in computer science. After graduating, she took an entry-level position at a Silicon Valley start-up, where she did lots of different jobs and got great experience. After about four years, it became clear that the company wasn't going anywhere (except out of business, perhaps), so she moved on to a much larger company, where she took a position in which she helped develop and test new wireless products. Her assignments were small, at first, but after a few years of proving herself, Janice found herself taking on larger and larger projects, until eventually, she became a vice president of technology for the company. It was a dream job for Janice, but she wanted still more. At about the same time, the company decided to invest more of its resources in manufacturing and marketing, and to outsource research and product development. So, Janice sold her stock in the company, and started her own firm— not a competitor, but a lab that specialized in developing new wireless technology for her old employer, and lots of other companies as well.

Janice had what's known as a **linear career.** That is, she stuck with a certain field and worked her way up the occupational ladder. Sometimes, she stayed at a single company, but at other times, she changed jobs. In all cases, however, she took on greater challenges. Linear careers are rather traditional paths. For many years, working one's way "up the occupational ladder" until "you made it" was considered the true sign of career success. Indeed, although achieving increasingly higher levels of success in a single line of work is a considerable accomplishment, it is no longer regarded as the only acceptable option for people today.

Spiral careers. John always loved science, especially physics, so he kept going to school and getting higher degrees. Before he knew it, he had a Ph.D. and found that he enjoyed studying thermal dynamics. Fortunately, a local aeronautics lab was looking for someone in that area to conduct research, and they were impressed with John's accomplishments so they hired him. Working there was satisfying for John for a few years, but research wasn't his passion. Then, one day, he was asked to give a talk about his work to a group of students at a small college nearby. John became hooked on teaching and soon took a job teaching physics courses at that same school. The pay wasn't great and the hours were long, but John enjoyed explaining physical principles in simple ways, and he proved to be pretty good at it. The students loved him—in part because he made complex ideas more understandable than the textbook and far more fun, too. "If you don't like the textbook," he soon reasoned, "write one yourself." And that he did. Now, John has moved on to his third career—this time as an author of textbooks.

Over his working life, John has moved between three jobs—first, he was a laboratory scientist; second, he was a professor; and third, he was an author. These jobs are very different from one another, and each requires different skills. However, John pieced them together such that each position built on the previous one. He did exciting new and different things with each career move, but they all drew on his interest in physics. In other words, he had what's called a **spiral career**—the kind of career in which people evolve through a series of occupations, each of which requires new skills and builds on existing knowledge and skills. People who have spiral careers are not "job hoppers" who move from one post to another. Rather, they are constantly growing and improving as they explore different facets of the same profession (physics, in John's case). Typically, people in spiral careers spend about 7 to 10 years in each position, enabling them to become pretty good at what they do before moving on.

Transitory careers. After high school, Cheryl worked as a waitress while she tried to find a job as an actress. The tips were good, but after it became clear that Hollywood wasn't going to come calling, she took a job at an art gallery. She wasn't especially interested in art, but she had a friend who worked there, who helped her get the job. A few months later, she got bored and took a part-time job at a bookstore. To help make ends meet, she started a dog-walking and pet-sitting business for her neighbors—all while taking a few college classes at night. Although we could say more about the other jobs Cheryl had, you probably get the picture: She continuously moves from job to job, with little connection between them. In other words, Cheryl has what is known as a **transitory career.** People in transitory careers move between many different unrelated positions, spending about one to four years in each.

Although it may be tempting to dismiss Cheryl on the grounds that she is "trying to find herself," it would be unfair to assume that she is in any way inept or incompetent. In fact, many people in transitory careers are those who have not been fortunate

linear career
The type of career in which someone stays in a certain field and works his or her way up the occupational ladder from low-level jobs to high-level jobs.

spiral career
The type of career in which people evolve through a series of occupations, each of which requires new skills and builds on existing knowledge and skills.

transitory career
The type of career in which someone moves between many different unrelated positions, spending about one to four years in each.

enough to discover the kind of work that allows them to derive satisfaction. In fact, many of the most successful people in the business world have been "late bloomers," who drifted between jobs until they found their calling. For example, before Ray Croc founded McDonald's at age 52, he worked such jobs as being an ambulance driver, a piano player, and a paper cup salesman.[12] Obviously, to say that he was anything other than a huge success, despite his transitory career, would be very misleading.

Of course, it also is important to acknowledge that some people simply do not find work the major source of fulfillment in their lives. Such individuals may elect to "make a career out of their hobbies," so to speak, preferring to devote their energies and talents to their avocations instead of their vocations. Perhaps you know someone who's a talented musician, but who moves from one low-level "day job" to the next, so as to have time to play local gigs at night. Although such an individual may have a transitory career during the daytime, it's quite possible that he or she is moving along in a very linear fashion once the sun goes down. Even if the hobby brings personal satisfaction instead of occupational recognition, it clearly would be unfair to think any less of such an individual.

Career Stages

At the risk of oversimplification, it's clear that many people's lives progress in systematic fashion: school, then marriage, children, and before you know it, grandchildren. Within each of these stages, there are unique issues with which we must deal (e.g., learning to read and write, finding a mate, figuring out the mysteries of effective parenting, and so on). In similar fashion, many people's careers also follow several distinct stages of development, and within each stage a host of special issues and challenges may arise.

Specifically, organizational scientists have noted that careers progress between five distinct stages.[13] These are as follows:

- *Preparation for work.* Acquiring various skills, learning about various career options, and determining what career you want to pursue.
- *Organizational entry.* Finding out about specific jobs and getting your foot in the door.
- *Early career.* Establishing yourself in a specific job and then achieving success at it.
- *Middle career.* Figuring out how to continue to be productive after you've been working for over 20 years.
- *Late career.* Keeping from becoming obsolete and planning for retirement.

In Figure 7.4 we summarize these five stages and identify the decades of our lives within which they tend to be associated.

We realize, of course, that not everybody's life follows the same path. People go to school for different amounts of time; some never marry, whereas others marry several times; and various people have different size families, if any at all. What's more, people who go to school, marry, and have families don't always do these things following the same order. Analogously, not everyone's career progresses smoothly along the five steps outlined. After all, people who have spiral careers and transitory careers often have to start the organizational entry process all over again each time they take a new position. However, these five stages do a good job of identifying the chronology through which people in linear careers experience certain milestones. Even if someone's particular career does not develop in this straightforward order, at some point he or she still may expect to confront many of the same challenges and opportunities associated with each step.

Throughout the rest of this chapter we will describe the various issues faced by people at different career stages. We will present these in chronological order, beginning with issues that are likely to be of concern to you as you get started in your career (confronted in the preparation for work stage, the organizational entry stage, and the early career stage), followed by issues that arise in careers that have matured (confronted in the middle career stage and the late career stage). Finally, at the end of this chapter we will describe some important challenges and personal strategies we all must consider to be successful at whatever careers we choose.

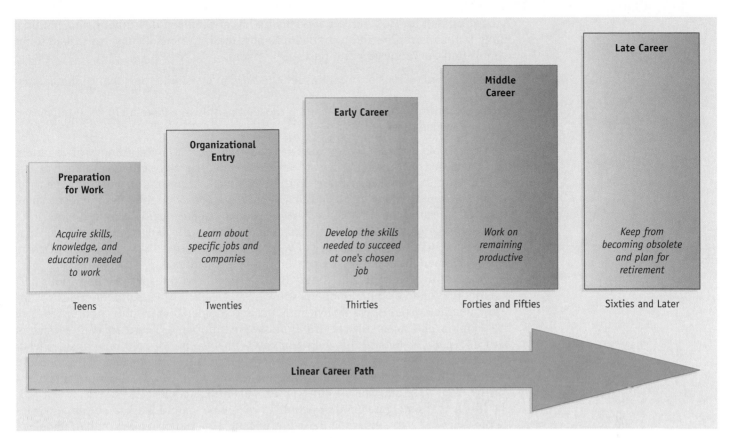

FIGURE 7.4
The Five Stages of Career Development
Careers generally develop in five stages, each of which occurs at different ages and is associated with different issues.

MAKING CAREER CHOICES

"What do you want to be when you grow up?" This is a question you probably heard many times as you were growing up (if not later in life, too!). As children, we learn about different careers, based mostly on the people with whom we come into contact in real life (e.g., teachers and doctors) and on television (e.g., athletes). This continues into our adult years as well, although as adults we come into contact with a broader range of professions and we have had experiences with some.

In this section of the chapter we will discuss three major factors that determine people's career choices. The first is how well a particular job matches an individual's skills, interests, and values—the concept of *person–job fit*, which we described in Chapter 3. Generally speaking, the more closely the jobs that people select match their personalities, the more satisfied they tend to be on those jobs.[14] However, this is only part of the story. It matters not only how well people fit the demands of a specific job but also how well that specific job compares to *self-concepts*—that is, their images of who they are. This is the second determinant of career choice we will consider. Finally, we will consider a very important determinant of career choice—job opportunities. Obviously, regardless of how well suited a person is for a certain job, it doesn't matter much if such positions are difficult to find.

Holland's Theory of Vocational Choice

Why is it that you may decide to become a lawyer whereas your sister is interested in being a doctor, a police officer, a musician, or a chef—anything other than a lawyer?

According to John Holland, a scientist who has specialized in studying occupational choice, the answer lies in an individual's personality.[15] Specifically, his research has established two important findings:

- People from various occupations tend to have many similar personality characteristics.
- People whose characteristics match those of people in a given field are predisposed to succeed in that field.

So, for example, assume for argument's sake that successful lawyers tend to have certain characteristics in common: They are very inquisitive, detail oriented, and analytical—all characteristics that help them do their jobs well. According to *Holland's theory of vocational choice,* you would be attracted to the field of law to the extent that you share many of the same characteristics. In other words, because being a lawyer "suits you," and you "have what it takes" to succeed at that field, you are likely to select that occupation. In essence, **Holland's theory of vocational choice** says that people will perform best at occupations that match their traits and personalities.

As you might imagine, the theory is quite specific with respect to the various personality types and occupational types involved. Specifically, Holland identifies six different characteristics of work environments and the personality traits and interests of the people who are most successful in those environments. These are summarized in Figure 7.5. As you look at this diagram, you probably cannot help but consider what particular type best describes you. It is important to be very cognizant of this because the more closely your personality type matches the work you do, the more successful you are likely to be and the less stress you are likely to encounter.[16]

It's clear from Figure 7.5 that people in each type should work in certain environments, but what happens when these don't occur? Holland has noted that for people of each type there are second-best matches, third-best matches, and some jobs that constitute the worst possible match of all. These are summarized in Figure 7.6, known as **Holland's hexagon.** Interpreting this diagram is straightforward. The position of each Holland type around the hexagon indicates those occupations for which people are best suited and worst suited, based on their personality types. The closer a job environment comes to the associated personality type on this diagram, the more effective the person will be.

So, for example, someone with an enterprising personality type is expected to be most successful when working in an occupation that permits enterprising qualities to come out (e.g., a sales job). However, neither people nor jobs fit perfectly into only a single category. As such, fairly good matches may occur in cases in which people in a certain category perform work in environments that favor adjacent types. So, for example, an enterprising person may perform reasonably well at jobs in social environments or in conventional environments, each of which is adjacent to the enterprising type in the hexagon. By the same token, poorer matches, such as with environments favoring artistic or realistic people, which are two steps away, are likely to be quite problematic for enterprising individuals. And, finally, we have the point along the hexagon that lies directly opposite—in the case of the enterprising type, it's the investigative environment. These represent the poorest matches. So, for example, we would expect people who do well in enterprising occupations (such as salesperson) to do poorly in occupations (such as scientist) that require the more analytical talents of the investigative type.

Holland's model has been used widely by *vocational counselors,* professionals specializing in helping people find the kind of work that best suits them. The rationale is straightforward. People taking various vocational tests can determine how closely their traits and personality characteristics match those of people in various occupational groups. Then, using Holland's hexagon, people are encouraged to seek work in fields whose job incumbents tend to have those various qualities, and to avoid work in fields whose job incumbents have qualities that lie opposite their own along the hexagon. The happiest and most successful workers tend to be those for whom there is a close fit between their personality and their work environment. According to Holland, and supported by research, this is the key to successful career development.[17]

Holland's theory of vocational choice

A theory that claims that people will perform best at occupations that match their traits and personalities.

Holland's hexagon

A conceptualization specifying the occupations for which people are best suited based on which of six personality types most closely describes them.

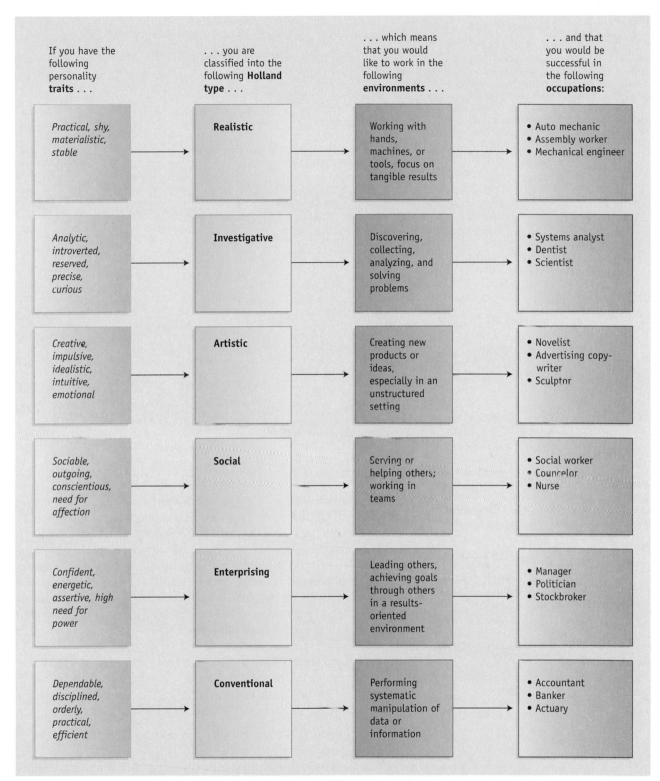

FIGURE 7.5
Holland's Theory of Vocational Choice: An Overview
Holland's theory of vocational choice specifies that people are most satisfied with occupations that match their personalities. People are classified into any of six distinct personality types, each of which is associated with a particular work environment that best suits them. These pairings and the occupations that most closely match them are summarized here.

FIGURE 7.6

Holland's Hexagon
The diagram known as *Holland's hexagon* summarizes the relationship between each of the six personality and work environment types. According to Holland's theory of vocational choice, the closer these are, the more satisfied one will be with one's occupational choice. Occupations with demands opposite each personality type (shown here with dashed lines) identify those for which people are most poorly suited.

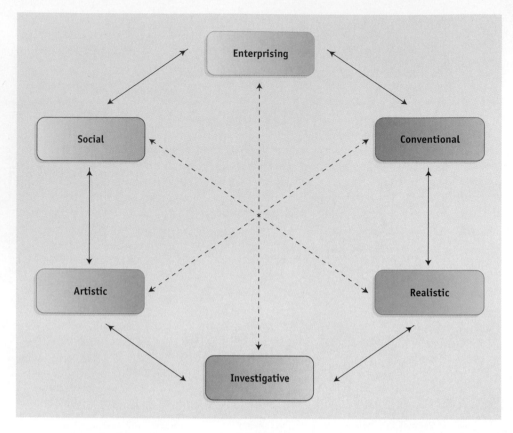

Career Anchors

Thus far, we've considered the extent to which a person's occupation matches his or her personality. However, another very important consideration when it comes to selecting careers has to do with the extent to which various jobs are in keeping with our images of ourselves. For example, suppose you think of yourself as a creative kind of person, someone who likes to build or produce new things on your own. Because of this, based on your experiences and knowledge, you may find yourself moving in directions that bring out your creative side. So, instead of managing a restaurant, for example, you might come to think of yourself as a chef and be motivated to develop a new set of skills. In other words, these beliefs about yourself "anchor" your choice of careers—and, as such, they are known as *career anchors.*

Formally defined, a **career anchor** is a person's occupational self-concept, based on his or her self-perceived talents, abilities, values, needs, and motives.[18] As people spend time working, they gradually develop career anchors. Scientists studying careers have identified five major career anchors.[19] These are as follows:

- *Technical or functional*—concentration on jobs focusing on specific content areas (e.g., auto mechanics, graphic arts)
- *Managerial competence*—focus on jobs that allow for analyzing business problems and dealing with people
- *Security and stability*—attraction to jobs that are likely to continue into the future (e.g., the military)
- *Creativity or entrepreneurship*—primary interest in starting new companies from visions of unique products or services but not necessarily running them
- *Autonomy and independence*—attraction to jobs that allow for freedom from constraints and to work at one's own pace (e.g., novelists and creative artists)

Despite the fact that people have many interests and abilities, not all of these guide them toward careers. Instead, people regularly are attracted to careers that are in keep-

career anchor
A person's occupational self-concept that is based on his or her self-perceived talents, abilities, values, needs, and motives.

ing with their particular career anchors. Scientists have used various questionnaires to assess people's career anchors. One of these, known as the Career Orientation Inventory, is regularly used by vocational counselors for purposes of helping people decide the kind of occupations to which they are best suited.

Job Opportunities

Let's face it: No matter how much you think you would like to be a shepherd, and how good a job a you think you might do roaming through the pasture and tending the flock, job opportunities for shepherds are not exactly what they were in biblical days. Fortunately, most people tend to be highly rational when it comes to making career choices, favoring occupations in which opportunities are most likely to exist and avoiding positions in which opportunities are declining. For a summary of recent projections of job growth and decline by the U.S. Department of Labor, see Figure 7.7.[20] As you look at these statistics, it's interesting to note that most of the growth is expected to come in computer-related occupations despite the collapse of many small technologically oriented companies in recent years. Apparently, although many firms are struggling for dominance in high-tech fields, that area is still expected to grow through 2010—and job opportunities along with it.

Because openings in many high-tech jobs are expected to grow in the years ahead, these positions tend to capture people's attention when considering occupations they might want to enter. Not surprisingly, they also capture the attention of people administering vocational programs in high schools, technical schools, and colleges. To be popular with prospective students, these programs offer training in areas where the jobs are likely to be. The availability of such training opportunities also attracts people to the kind of jobs that require this training, creating the cycle shown in Figure 7.8.

ORGANIZATIONAL SOCIALIZATION: LEARNING THE ROPES

It's your first day on the job. After years of training and experience, you have all the skills needed to succeed, but you still have a lot to learn. Some things may be minor, such as finding out where to find the coffee machine or the water fountain. Others may be more critical, such as policies regarding the treatment of customers or informal standards about how hard to work. The process through which people move from outsiders to effective, participating members of their organizations is referred to as **organizational socialization.** In this section of the chapter, we will describe this process and the ways organizations go about making the socialization process effective. As you might imagine, people do not become fully socialized members of their organizations instantly or even after a few weeks. Rather, organizational socialization is a gradual process that occurs in three discrete stages over a matter of years (for a summary, see Figure 7.9).[21]

organizational socialization
The process through which people move from outsiders to effective, participating members of their organizations.

Anticipatory Socialization: Avoiding Entry Shock with Realistic Job Previews

The first stage, **anticipatory socialization,** is concerned with "getting in." This involves learning about an organization from the outside, before one may even consider becoming a part of it. If this sounds strange, just ask yourself if there is a specific organization in which you would be interested in working someday. What makes you attracted to it? If you can answer this question even tentatively, it's clear that you know something about an organization even before you begin working there.

How do such expectations develop? First, as friends or relatives who work in an organization share their experiences with you, you may develop an image of the company. Second, there also are formal sources, such as professional journals, magazine and newspaper articles, and corporate annual reports. These also provide information that may help cultivate an impression of what it would be like to work in a certain orga-

anticipatory socialization
The first stage of socialization, concerned with learning about an organization before working there.

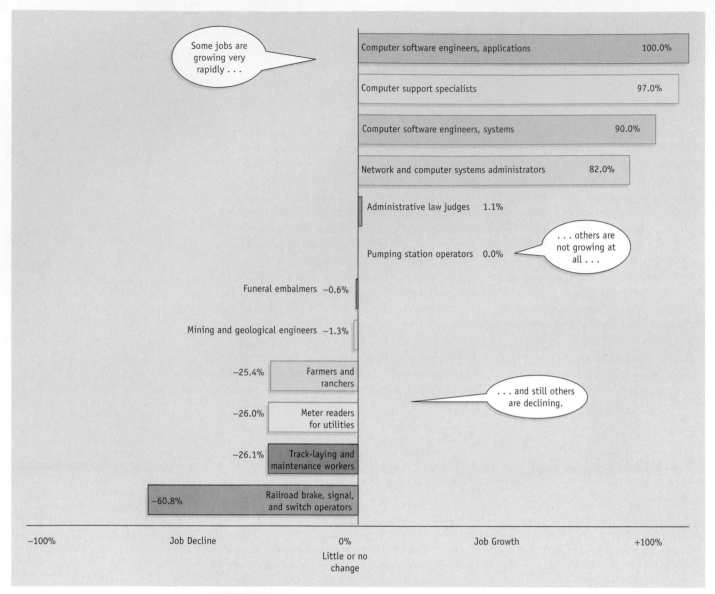

FIGURE 7.7

Occupational Outlook for This Decade: Where Jobs Will—and Will Not—Be Found
Economists from the Bureau of Labor Statistics have compiled statistics regarding the fastest-growing occupations in the United States for the period from 2000 to 2010. Here, we identify four jobs that are expected to show the most growth, four expected to show the greatest decline, and four expected to have little or no changes. As shown here, technical jobs in the computer field look like they will provide the most opportunities for job hunters in the near future.
(*Source:* Based on data reported by Hecker, 2001; see Note 20.)

nization. Unfortunately, both formal and informal sources of information may be biased. For example, you may hear your acquaintances talk about their jobs only when they have negative things to say. Likewise, press reports about organizations often are reserved for sensationalistic accounts of either extremely positive news (e.g., record-breaking earnings) or negative news (e.g., illegal activities). Thus, although we often rely on secondhand information from personal contacts and the popular press as bases for our judgments about organizations, it is important to keep in mind that the information they provide may be questionable.

The most direct way to learn about an organization is to get the information "straight from the horse's mouth," so to speak—that is, by listening to corporate recruiters. Sometimes, however, these individuals paint overly rosy pictures of their organizations. In response to intense competition for the best job candidates, they may

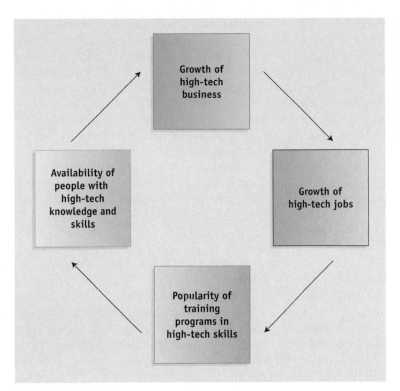

FIGURE 7.8

The Cyclical Nature of Job Growth, Training Opportunities, and Skilled Labor
As summarized here, the growth of high-tech companies leads to high-tech jobs, which leads to high-tech training, which leads to more people with high-tech skills, which further supports the growth of more high-tech jobs.

describe their companies in glowing terms, glossing over internal problems and emphasizing the positive aspects. As a result, potential employees often receive unrealistically positive impressions of what it would be like to work in those organizations. Then, when new employees actually arrive on the job and find their expectations are unmet, strong feelings of disappointment, confusion, and disillusionment may result—what is referred to as **entry shock.** In fact, the less employees' job expectations are met, the less satisfied and committed they are, and the more likely they are to think about quitting and to actually do so.

With this in mind, the trick for corporate recruiters is not to give job candidates unrealistically positive descriptions, but rather, highly accurate descriptions—both positive and negative—of the jobs they will perform and the organizations they will enter. Such descriptions are called **realistic job previews.**[22] Research has shown that people exposed to realistic job previews later report higher satisfaction and show lower turnover than those who receive glowing but often unrealistic information about the companies in question.[23] By making their expectations more realistic, employees are less likely to

entry shock
The disillusionment, disappointment, and confusion that result when new employees' job expectations are unmet.

realistic job preview
The practice of giving prospective employees both positive and negative information about the jobs they are considering and the organizations they will enter.

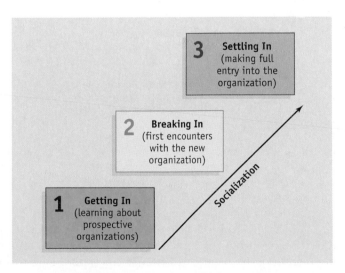

FIGURE 7.9

The Three Stages of Organizational Socialization
Organizational socialization generally follows the three stages summarized here: *getting in, breaking in,* and *settling in.*

resign when they confront negative conditions (see Figure 7.10). For this reason, it makes sense for recruiters to not only inform prospective employees about the many benefits of working for their companies (as they are already prone to do) but also to supplement this information with realistic accounts of what life will be like in the organization.[24]

Several companies have been doing just this. For example, recruiters at AT&T have used realistic job previews to recruit operators and customer service representatives, and at NBD Bank they have been used to recruit tellers. Using realistic job previews also has been found to increase the amount of time cooperative extension service field agents stay on their jobs.[25] In probably the largest-scale example, realistic job previews are used in the process of recruiting men and women for all branches of the Canadian Armed Forces. Clearly, these organizations have a great deal of confidence in realistic job previews as a tool for avoiding entry shock and avoiding problems associated with turnover.

The Encounter Stage

encounter stage
The second stage of organizational socialization, faced as newcomers to an organization learn their new duties and the organization's ways of operating.

The second stage of organizational socialization, the **encounter stage,** begins when individuals actually assume their new duties. During this stage, they face several key challenges. First, of course, they must master the skills required by their new jobs. Second, they must become oriented to the practices and procedures of the new organization—that is, the way things are done there. Third, new members of an organization must establish good social relations with others. They must get to know these people and gain their acceptance. Only when they do can they become effectively functioning members of the work team.

corporate orientation programs
Formal sessions designed to teach new employees about their organizations.

It is during the encounter stage that formal **corporate orientation programs** are conducted. These are formal sessions designed to teach new employees about their organizations.[26] This includes not only the ways they operate but also information about their histories, missions, and traditions. Such programs are considered a vital part of employee training insofar as they help new employees fit in and understand what their organization is all about. Although much of what is covered in such sessions may be picked up informally over time, formal orientation programs are highly efficient ways of indoctrinating new employees and introducing them to company officials. Of course, such efforts are merely supplements to the informal socialization between coworkers that may be expected to go on continuously.

The Metamorphosis Stage

metamorphosis stage
The third stage of organizational socialization, in which a person becomes a full-fledged member of the organization (e.g., after having completed a training program for new recruits).

The third stage of organizational socialization, the **metamorphosis stage,** occurs as the individual enters an organization and attains full member status. Just as a caterpillar

FIGURE 7.10
Realistic Job Previews: How They Work
As summarized here, people receiving realistic job previews before being hired tend to have reasonable expectations about the jobs they will be doing. As a result, when they encounter negative experiences once on the job, they will be more likely to remain than those who did not receive realistic job previews.

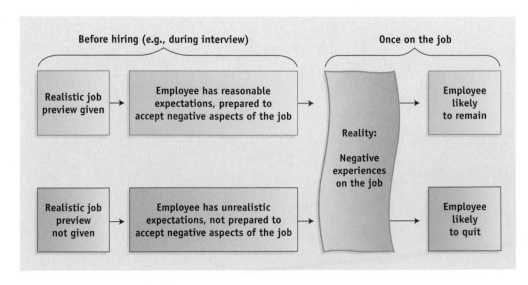

undergoes a metamorphosis when it becomes a butterfly, so too does a trainee develop fully when he or she eventually becomes a full-fledged member of the organization. Sometimes this entry is marked by a formal event, such as a dinner, reception, or graduation ceremony. The ceremony in which cadets graduate from a police academy is a good example insofar as it marks their transition from student to police officer. At this time, we can expect one's title to change from a temporary one, such as trainee or apprentice, to a permanent one, such as associate or partner. In other cases, especially when training has been short or informal, full acceptance into the work group may not be marked by any specific ceremony at all. Instead, it may be acknowledged by informal actions, such as being invited to lunch by one's new coworkers.

Whatever form it takes, the metamorphosis phase of socialization marks important shifts both for individuals and for organizations. Employees now make permanent adjustments to their jobs (e.g., they resolve conflicting demands between their jobs and their personal lives). And organizations begin treating them as if they will be long-term members of their work teams.

MENTORING: SOCIALIZING PEOPLE INDIVIDUALLY

Some of the most effective forms of socialization involve the one-on-one contact between senior and junior people. For example, at Fu Associates Ltd. (a computer consulting firm in Arlington, Virginia) all new employees start out working directly with a midlevel manager who shows them the ropes. After a few months, Ed Fu, the owner and senior systems analyst, selects a few of the more promising new employees to work with him on important projects. This is an example of mentoring—the process by which a more experienced employee, known as a mentor, advises, counsels, and otherwise enhances the professional development of a new employee, known as a protégé. If you've ever had an older, more experienced employee take you under his or her wing and guide you, then you probably already know how valuable mentoring can be. Indeed, mentoring is strongly associated with career success: The more mentoring people receive, the more promotions and pay raises they subsequently receive during their careers.[27]

Development of the Mentoring Process

As you might expect, mentor–protégé relationships do not develop in a haphazard fashion. Rather, they follow certain regular patterns. Notably, mentors are usually older than their protégés (by about 8 to 15 years). They also tend to be individuals with considerable power and status in their companies. As a result, they can assist rising young stars without themselves feeling threatened. On some occasions, mentor–protégé relationships are initiated by the mentor, who recognizes something impressive about the junior person. However, it also is possible for junior employees to approach prospective mentors about the possibility of entering into a mentoring relationship. Regardless of who initiates the relationship, for it to succeed, both parties must enter into it willingly—and, of course, the organization must be supportive of this association.

Some organizations so strongly believe in the benefits of mentoring that they are unwilling to leave the process to chance and formally encourage or even require mentoring in corporate-wide programs. For example, at Colgate-Palmolive, all new white-collar employees are assigned higher-ranking employees who serve as mentors. Other companies make mentoring more of a group process. For example, at the Hosiery Division of Sara Lee Corporation (which makes L'eggs pantyhose), a "women's information network" was formed in which groups of lower-ranking female employees meet regularly with higher-ranking female employees to discuss career-path opportunities. These are only two examples of a wide variety of mentoring programs in use today.

Despite their different formats, most mentor–protégé relationships pass through several distinct phases. The first, known as *initiation,* lasts from six months to a year, and represents a period during which the relationship gets started and takes on impor-

mentoring
The process by which a more experienced employee (see *mentor*) advises, counsels, and otherwise enhances the professional development of a new employee (see *protégé*).

mentor
A more experienced employee who guides a newer employee (see *protégé*) in learning about the job and organization.

protégé
An inexperienced employee who receives assistance from a more experienced employee in learning about a new job and/or organization (see *mentor*).

tance for both parties. The second phase, known as *cultivation,* may last from two to five years. During this time, the bond between mentor and protégé deepens, and the young individual may make rapid career strides because of the skilled assistance he or she is receiving.

The third stage, *separation,* begins when the protégé feels it is time to assert independence and strikes out on his or her own, or when there is some externally produced change in their roles (e.g., the protégé is promoted, or the mentor is transferred). Separation also can occur if the mentor feels unable to continue providing support and guidance to the protégé (e.g., if the mentor becomes ill). As you might imagine, this phase can be quite stressful if the mentor resents the protégé's growing independence, or if the protégé feels that the mentor has withdrawn support prematurely.

If this separation is successful, the relationship may enter its final stage, termed *redefinition.* Here, both parties perceive their bond primarily as one of friendship. They come to treat one another as equals, and the roles of mentor and protégé fade away completely. However, the mentor may continue to take pride in the accomplishments of his or her former protégé. Likewise, the protégé may continue to feel a debt of gratitude toward the former mentor. Although there is bound to be variation in the way mentor–protégé relationships actually develop, these four phases accurately depict the way in which these important relationships generally unfold (see the summary in Figure 7.11).

Benefits and Costs of Mentoring

Mentoring is generally a very beneficial process for all involved. However, it can have certain costs associated with it. To fully understand the mentoring process, we now discuss these benefits and costs.

Mentors, protégés, and their organizations come out ahead. Mentors do many important things for their protégés.[28] For example, they provide much needed emotional sup-

FIGURE 7.11

Mentoring: A Four-Stage Process
Relationships between mentors and their protégés tend to develop following the four stages summarized here.

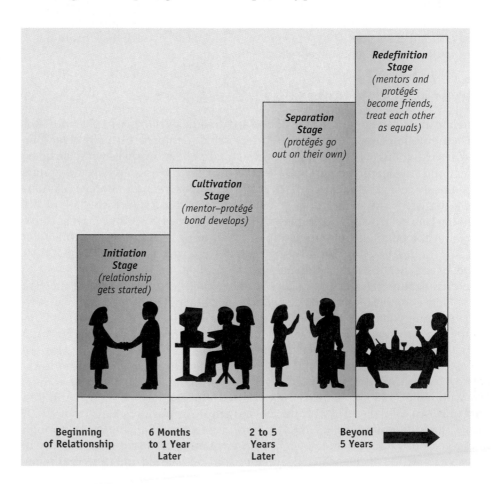

Initiation Stage (relationship gets started)

Cultivation Stage (mentor–protégé bond develops)

Separation Stage (protégés go out on their own)

Redefinition Stage (mentors and protégés become friends, treat each other as equals)

Beginning of Relationship

6 Months to 1 Year Later

2 to 5 Years Later

Beyond 5 Years

port and confidence. For those who are just starting out and are likely to be insecure about their abilities, this can be a big help. Mentors also help pave the way for their protégés' job success, such as by nominating them for promotions and by providing opportunities for them to demonstrate their competence. They also suggest useful strategies for achieving work objectives—especially ones that protégés might not generate for themselves. In doing all these things, they help bring the protégé to the attention of top management—a necessary first step for advancement. Finally, mentors often protect their protégés from the repercussions of errors and help them avoid situations that may be risky for their careers.

As you might suspect from these benefits, organizations generally come out ahead when their employees engage in mentoring. At Scotiabank, for example, mentoring was used to reduce the time required for newly minted M.B.A.'s to become loan officers. This was necessary because these recent grads maintained traditional, not particularly service-oriented, beliefs about banking that were holding them back. Through Scotiabank's Competency-Based Mentoring Program, however, branch managers reinforced what these new employees learned about service in their training programs. As a result, training time was reduced from a full year to nine months, allowing the bank to get these new employees fully functioning that much sooner.

"True mentoring is a process by which you buy into another's dream," according to Ben Borne, a human resources consultant. "It is a dynamic partnering that benefits all the participants."[29] The main benefits to protégés, of course, are the various types of career support just described. Still, Borne is correct in implying that mentor–protégé relationships may benefit the mentor as well. Indeed, it would be misleading to depict mentors as totally selfless benefactors who seek nothing in return for their guidance.

Often, people become mentors because they are so very appreciative of having received such help earlier in their careers. For example, Borne recalls how senior managers at Motorola and Kaiser Aluminum helped him get started some 35 years ago. Knowing what it's like to have people pay attention to you, he is pleased to be in the position to offer help to junior colleagues who now need his assistance. In other words, mentors may reap psychological benefits from feeling needed and a sense of accomplishment in helping the younger generation.

However, gratification is not the only source of benefit for mentors. In exchange for their guidance, mentors often expect certain things from their protégés. First, they expect their protégés to work hard at the tasks assigned to them, which makes for a highly productive employee. Second, mentors often expect protégés to be loyal supporters within their organization. (After all, they are now members of the mentor's team!) Third, mentors may gain recognition from others in the company for their work in helping nurture young talent and can feel proud of their protégés' successes.

Mentoring can be risky. This discussion of benefits is not meant to imply that mentor–protégé relationships are totally without costs. Indeed, there are several potential risks. For example, protégés may find that their own success hinges on the success of their mentor. If the mentor should happen to be a falling star in the company and suffers setbacks, the protégé's own career may be in jeopardy. Likewise, because the protégé's behavior reflects on the mentor, any failures on the part of the protégé may harm the mentor's reputation. In addition, there's always the risk that a mentor's advice might not be as good as it should be. This can be problematic regardless of whether the protégé follows the bad advice (and receives a negative outcome) or does not follow it (and risks insulting the mentor). To the extent that the mentor and protégé blame each other for the poor result, their relationship is likely to develop an uncomfortable level of conflict.

Finally, there's always a risk that protégés will become so highly dependent on their mentors that they will become slow to develop as self-reliant individuals. Similarly, it's possible for mentors to grow overly reliant on their protégés for help, delegating too many responsibilities that they should be discharging themselves. It is, of course, one thing to guide others and quite another to take advantage of them by having them do too much of your work. In conclusion, although mentoring offers many possible rewards to mentors, protégés, and their companies, it is wise to keep in mind the poten-

TABLE 7.2 TEN TIPS FOR SUCCESSFUL MENTORING

The long-term success of mentoring can be enhanced by adhering to the suggestions identified here. Both mentors and protégés should familiarize themselves with these guidelines before entering into a relationship.

MENTORS SHOULD . . .

1. Be responsible *to* protégés, not *for* them.

2. Make the mentoring relationship fun and enjoyable.

3. Recognize that their involvement with their protégé extends beyond the workday.

4. Listen carefully to their protégés.

5. Openly acknowledge their failures as well as their successes.

6. Protect their protégés and expect their protégés to protect them.

7. Give their protégés not only directions but also options.

8. Recognize and encourage their protégés' small successes and accomplishments.

9. Encourage independent thinking among their protégés.

10. Focus not only on job skills but also on ethical values.

(*Source:* Based on suggestions by Wickman & Sjodin, 1997; see Note 30.)

tial problems of such relationships as well. In view of the rewards and costs of mentoring, it makes sense to consider ways of making the mentoring experience successful for all involved. For some useful suggestions in this regard, see Table 7.2.[30] (To get a better sense of the benefits and costs of mentoring, perform the Group Exercise on page 267.)

Mentoring Members of Diverse Groups

When you think of a mentor, the image probably comes to mind of an older, white male executive helping a younger male manager work his way up the corporate ladder by introducing him to the most influential people in the organization. Typically, these are men who wield most of the power in the organization—what is known as the **old boys network.** By definition, any old *boy* network is sexist. Not surprisingly, because women frequently are left out, they generally have more limited access to suitable mentors than men have.[31]

Likewise, mentoring often fails to occur among members of minority groups who are not well represented in their companies. After all, insofar as people tend to be more comfortable with others who are similar to themselves, members of minority groups often tend to be denied informal mentoring opportunities simply because there are few others like them in the organization. This is problematic given that people who don't have mentors face a barrier to success in the corporate world. And, insofar as affirmative action programs and diversity management programs (reviewed in Chapter 5) demand giving opportunities to women and minorities, providing mentors is essential. Fortunately, several companies have developed formal programs that bring together mentors and protégés from diverse groups. For some examples, see Table 7.3. Not only have such programs helped minority group members get the mentoring they need to succeed, they also have been quite effective in promoting diversity in the workplace (see Chapter 5).

old boys network
An informal collection of men who wield power within an organization.

CHALLENGES IN ESTABLISHED CAREERS

Although getting started in one's career can be very difficult, so too do people face considerable challenges once they've been working for a while. We will describe three such

TABLE 7.3   MENTORING DIVERSE GROUPS: WHAT SOME COMPANIES ARE DOING

Many of today's companies have taken successful steps to ensure that women and members of minority groups are receiving proper mentoring. Some of these practices and the resulting benefits are summarized here.

COMPANY	MENTORING ACTIVITY	RESULT
Chubb & Son (insurance)	In its Sponsorship Program, women managers are assigned to higher-ranking female protégés.	Over half of the women were promoted within two years.
Dow Jones	"Quad Squads" of high-level mentors are grouped with three others, including a white male, a woman of any race, and a minority group member of either gender.	More members of minority groups are finding mentors than ever before, and racial tensions are minimal
DuPont	Protégés are paired with mentors of different races so as to broaden each individual's exposure to new ideas and ways of looking at things.	The proportion of minorities in top management positions has risen from 10 percent to 30 percent, even as the overall number of management jobs has dropped.

challenges: the career plateau, making career changes, and planning for succession and retirement.

Confronting the Career Plateau

If early career issues pertain to people in their twenties and thirties, then middle career issues apply to the 40-something crowd. This is sometimes a difficult period in which people look down the road and realize that they never may fulfill their career aspirations. As you might imagine, this can be problematic for both employees and their organizations. Fortunately, however, as we will describe, something can be done to help.

The nature of the career plateau. The point at which one's career has peaked and is unlikely to develop further is known as a **career plateau.** One way to identify a career plateau is by noting how long someone has been in his or her current position. Employees who have been in a particular post for five or more years would be considered immobile and to have reached a career plateau. Another popular approach for identifying a career plateau is subjective in nature. People may be considered to have plateaued whenever they no longer expect to move on to higher-status positions. Using either definition, about one employee in four is considered to have reached a career plateau.[32]

Although it is tempting to assume that employees whose careers have plateaued are no longer motivated or effective at their current jobs, this isn't always so. In fact, some people are quite satisfied to remain at their present jobs for a long time, finding it more relaxing and a source of contentment to be a "solid citizen" of the company instead of being one of its "fast-trackers" or "high fliers." Of course, career plateauing can be a serious source of dissatisfaction for individuals who believe that the only path to contentment is via upward movement in the company. This is more likely to be the case among managers than for employees holding other jobs given that people in managerial positions tend to define their success in terms of upward advancement.

Today, as companies are reducing the sizes of their staffs and competition for good jobs becomes intense, more people than ever are reaching career plateaus earlier than expected. Faced with poor chances for promotion and few alternatives for employment, they may feel unmotivated and simply stick with their jobs until they retire from them. If you think this picture is depressing, imagine how serious the problem becomes when companies are faced with large cohorts of midcareer employees who are unmotivated because their careers have plateaued. Surely, a workforce composed of people who are merely "going through the motions" will be neither productive nor satisfied.

career plateau
The point at which one's career has peaked and is unlikely to develop further.

career development interventions
Systematic efforts to help manage people's careers while simultaneously helping the organizations in which they work.

Career development interventions. To avoid the problems associated with career plateaus and other career-related issues, such as finding the right job or adjusting to new jobs, organizations have been relying on **career development interventions.** These are systematic efforts to help manage people's careers while simultaneously helping the organizations in which they work.

The career development interventions used in several companies are quite interesting. For example, at Chevron, employees are counseled to seek outside hobbies during periods in which their jobs offer little gratification. Some are encouraged to make lateral moves within the company in order to keep their work lives stimulating. Not only have Chevron employees done this, but so too have thousands of employees at General Motors, where the white-collar workforce has been reduced dramatically over the last few years. In fact, it has been reported that GM has spent some $10 million per year helping employees whose careers have reached plateaus find appropriate new positions within the company.

Much of what goes on in career development interventions involves helping employees assess the skills and interests they have so that they may be placed into positions for which they are well suited. Some companies, such as Hewlett-Packard and Lawrence Livermore Laboratories, provide *self-assessment exercises* for this purpose. Others, such as Coca-Cola and Disneyland, rely on *individualized counseling sessions* in which employees meet with trained professionals. Still others, including AT&T, IBM, Ford, Shell Oil, and Kodak, take it a step further, offering *organizational assessment programs* through which employees are systematically tested to discover their profiles of skills and interests. (For an overview of what such tests look like and a chance to examine your own career aspirations, see the Individual Exercise on page 266.)

At the very least, companies such as CBS, Merck, Aetna, and General Electric all provide services, such as job posting systems and career resource centers, through which employees can learn about new career options within their companies. And, when companies find that they must reduce the size of their workforces, terminated employees at Exxon, Mutual of New York, General Electric, and other companies receive the services of **outplacement programs.** These generally include assistance in developing the skills needed to find new jobs (such as networking, interviewing skills, résumé writing, and the like). Despite these various differences, it is safe to characterize the vast majority of career development interventions as following the six steps listed in Figure 7.12.

outplacement programs
Systematic efforts to find new jobs for employees who are laid off.

Making Career Changes

Changing jobs or even entire occupations is quite common today. In fact, most new graduates with M.B.A. degrees expect to stay at their first jobs for no more than four years.[34] It is easy to understand that, as we begin our careers, we may find that a particular job may not be as desirable as expected and then move on. Similarly, we may find that it is difficult or impossible to gain entry into some professions. (If you have ever tried to become a professional actor, you probably know only too well what we mean!) The result, in either case, is the same: You pursue a different job. Traditionally, people were far more likely to change jobs early in their careers, when career expectations are just forming and life responsibilities make it easier to be mobile (e.g., no spouse, no children). However, people today are not unwilling to seek new jobs. In fact, it's not at all unusual for people to start their careers anew, going to school later in life and seeking training to help them. In other words, although changing jobs may be easier earlier in life, people today are impatient with careers that lead them nowhere or that fail to fulfill them personally or financially. For this reason, we're finding people making career changes throughout their working lives (see Figure 7.13).

About 45 percent of all U.S. workers say that they would make major career changes if they could, and each year 10 percent (approximately 10 million workers) actually do make major career changes. And, of those who made such career changes in recent years, 53 percent did so voluntarily, with the majority of these reporting that their

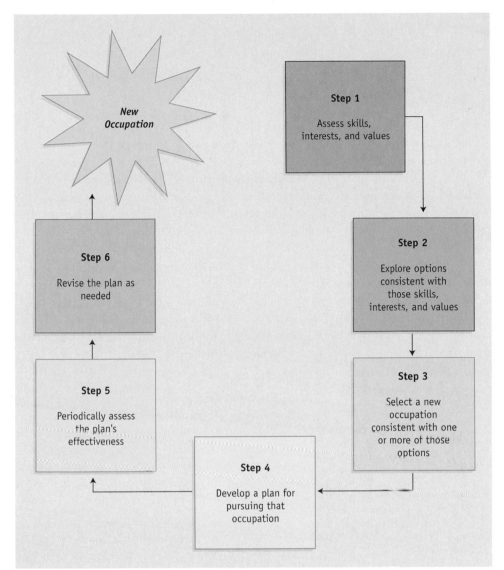

FIGURE 7.12
Career Development Interventions: Step by Step
Although each specific career development intervention may be unique in various ways, most involve the six steps summarized here.

New Occupation

Step 1
Assess skills, interests, and values

Step 2
Explore options consistent with those skills, interests, and values

Step 3
Select a new occupation consistent with one or more of those options

Step 4
Develop a plan for pursuing that occupation

Step 5
Periodically assess the plan's effectiveness

Step 6
Revise the plan as needed

FIGURE 7.13
Out with the New, In with the Old
Nathan Myhrvold long was considered one of Microsoft's most creative minds. Having reached the vaulted position of chief technology officer and working directly with Bill Gates after 14 years at Microsoft, Myhrvold decided he was ready for a change. He wanted to do something completely different. So, along with one of his former Microsoft colleagues, Myhrvold founded and now heads Intellectual Ventures, a private entrepreneurial investment company in the Seattle area. Today, instead of developing the latest technology, he is more likely to be finding sources of funding for archeologists seeking to dig up dinosaur fossils.

OB IN AN E-WORLD
MAKING CONNECTIONS IN CYBERSPACE: ONLINE NETWORKING

There can be no mistaking the importance of networking when it comes to advancing your career. After all, by establishing networks (connections with others who know you) you get to know others in your field who recognize your expertise and who can provide assistance in finding a new job. For example, you rely on your "connections" to provide information about where the jobs are, to get "the inside scoop" on what a particular company is like, and if they know you well enough, to "put in a good word" on your behalf.

Developing connections with people inside your company is not difficult. In fact, as social beings, the process of making connections with others comes naturally to most of us. However, the most highly effective networking goes considerably beyond the bounds of your own office. You are expanding your networks when you meet other people at social events and at professional meetings in your field. But this is just the beginning. Today, one of the most effective ways to expand your professional network is by making connections online. As the name implies, **online networking** involves making and developing business contacts via e-mail. Because the potential benefits of online networking are considerable, it pays to learn how to do it effectively—especially since very few of us have done it, and even fewer have done it effectively.

One popular way of engaging in online networking is by participating in online discussions or chat rooms organized by various professional groups. For example, discussion groups have been used widely by various professional groups interested in communicating about shared interests (e.g., the National Association of Health Underwriters; www.nahu.org), groups promoting various social causes (e.g., preserving the natural environment; www.onenw.org), and groups serving the needs of people in certain groups (e.g., women; www.womens net.org). Getting involved in such online discussions is an excellent way to meet people with similar interests. Of course, simply logging on and participating is only the beginning. To be an effective online networker there are several rules of "netiquette" (i.e., Net etiquette) that should be followed carefully.[33] Some of the key ones are as follows:

- *Demonstrate that you care about others and are willing to help them.* After all, people are more likely to help you if you have helped them. Often this simply takes the form of expressing interest in what someone else is doing or passing along information that may be of use to that individual.

---

online networking
The process of establishing potentially helpful business contacts via e-mail.

incomes went up.[35] People who make major career changes do so for a variety of reasons. The major ones are that they recognize that:

- They either don't like or can't succeed at their chosen profession.
- Prospects are poor for future employment in their present occupation.
- Their needs or interests have shifted, requiring a life change.

The traditional way of making a major career change is by starting completely anew. You may, for example, quit your present job, return to school for new training, and then begin starting over in your new career. People do this all the time. If you've done it, or if you know anyone who has, you probably know how very difficult it can be, both emotionally (because you're making a lot of changes at once) and financially (because you're likely to be without an income for a while and then to have a lower income). For example, suppose that Michelle is a lawyer who specializes in computers. But she is unhappy and looking to make a brand new start by becoming, say, a business teacher. The hard way of doing this would be for Michelle to give up her job and go back to college, where she studies both education and business. Then, after graduating and receiving her teaching credentials, she can look for a new job. Although this would take Michelle to that new place she desires, this way of making the change would be very disruptive.

So, how can Michelle go about making a major career change in such a way that minimizes the disruption in her life? Career experts advise making the changes in two steps:

- *Develop your online network while you're still employed.* By the time you're out of a job, it's going to be difficult to both develop and then call on your online contacts for help. Even if you're not looking for a job, online contacts can help you stay current and improve your standing in the professional community. By the way, it's not too early to build network contacts while you're still a student. In fact, several of our own students have benefited by finding jobs because of contacts they made through us.

- *Seek quality instead of quantity.* In other words, it's more useful to develop good relationships with a few people than many relationships that aren't as close. After all, it's the people with whom you have the closest contacts who are most likely to help you. How many is enough? Although there's no clear answer to this question, you can consider yourself very fortunate if you regularly keep in touch with a dozen people via e-mail.

- *Share personal interests with your professional contacts.* People often are drawn together via common interests, whether these are shared in person or online. By sharing such information with others, you are creating potential network opportunities by throwing out something onto which people can grab. Indeed, many a good job lead has followed from conversations about favorite golf courses, favorite restaurants, or any shared interest.

- *Get involved in professional associations.* Some of the most widely networked people are those who are active in commu-nity and professional groups. These are not only excellent ways to find others with common interests but also a useful way for people to get to know you.

- *Be careful what you say; the Net remembers.* If you don't get along with someone in person, in time either or both of you might forget your differences of opinion. E-mails, especially those shared in open communications between participants in an online chat room or a bulletin board, can be retrieved easily by lots of people. As a result, your words linger for a long time and are out there for everyone to see. So, unless you're very careful, a misplaced word or two can cause problems down the line. Remember, because you're not there in person to neutralize any derogatory remark with your facial expressions or the tone of your voice, it's important to be extremely polite when communicating with others online.

In closing, we acknowledge that many of these suggestions may be considered common sense. Unfortunately, however, they are not common practice. Many people fail to use their online networks to their advantage. Still others make mistakes that can backfire (e.g., showing disinterest in others or being impolite), leading others to say unflattering things about them. In conclusion, online networking can be a valuable tool if used appropriately. If followed carefully, these suggestions promise to improve the quality of your online networking and, hence, your career.

first changing either your occupation or your field of expertise, and then changing the other.[36] In our example Michelle has a present occupation (lawyer) and desires a new one (teacher). She also has a present field, computers, and desires a new one, business. Using the two-step method, she first may change her field, such as by expanding her practice into business law. Then, after getting established in her new field, Michelle should consider changing occupations, such as by teaching a class or two during the evenings at a local community college. After a while, she might want to take on more teaching responsibilities and limit the size of her legal practice, until eventually she is teaching business on a full-time basis (see Figure 7.14). It also would be possible for Michelle to first change her occupation (e.g., by teaching law) and then her field (shifting from law to business). Either way, there you have it—from computer lawyer to business teacher in two steps. Again, although this transition might not be easy for Michelle, it certainly is a lot more feasible than attempting to change both occupation and field at once.

Planning for Succession and Retirement

When we speak of the late career stage, the image probably comes to mind of the faithful employee retiring after some 40 years of employment with the same company, proudly showing off the gold watch he just received to an audience of adoring soon-to-

FIGURE 7.14

Making Career Changes: A Two-Step Process
Career experts advise that the most effective way to make a major career change is by changing your occupation and your field in two separate steps, as illustrated here.
(*Source:* Based on suggestions by Bolles, 2002; see Note 35.)

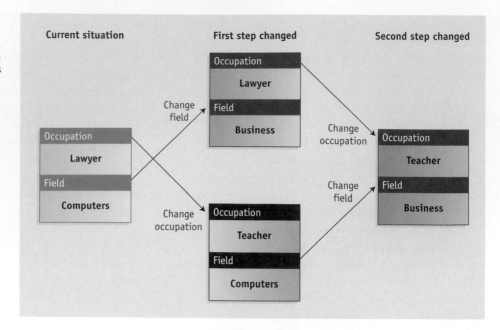

be-former coworkers. Indeed, preparation for retirement is an important issue faced during one's sixties. Psychologically, there is a reorientation from being directed in one's life by work activities to an increased focus on leisure-time activities.

Retirement. The phase of people's lives in which they reach the end of their careers and stop working for their primary income is known as **retirement.** It's important to recognize that retirement does not necessarily imply inactivity, but rather, a different kind of activity.[38] Many retired people lead very active lives, such as by working part time, engaging in volunteer work, spending time engaged in leisure pursuits, or some combination of these activities. Generous pension plans, coupled with more sophisticated investments and a generally good economy have made it possible for many people to retire earlier than ever. This, coupled with the fact that advances in health care enable people to live longer, makes it not unusual for people to spend 20 years or more in retirement.

People retire for either voluntary or involuntary reasons (see Figure 7.15). Sometimes people retire earlier than they originally planned—that is, involuntarily—because they fear that their jobs may be eliminated or because they are in ill health. In other words, like turnover and absenteeism, sometimes retirement is a form of withdrawal (see Chapter 5).[39] Fortunately, in most cases, retirement occurs voluntarily, with employees leaving their companies on good terms and happily moving on to the next stage of their lives. Research has shown that the underlying reason why people retire makes a difference in how their retirement goes.[40] Those who retire for work-related or health-related reasons tend to be less satisfied with their retirement than those who retire as planned by personal choice.

Preparing for retirement also involves careful planning to meet the special challenges faced by retired workers, including adjustment to reduced earnings. Fortunately, it has been shown that through careful planning people can greatly enjoy the new era

retirement
The phase of people's lives in which they reach the end of their careers and stop working for their primary income.

HOW TO DO IT

TIPS ON FINDING A NEW JOB

Changing your career means finding a new job. And, these days, it's harder than ever to find a good job. Companies are not hiring as many people as they used to—if they're even hiring at all. So, for every job that gets posted, there are lots of prospective candidates. According to employment expert Richard N. Bolles, here are some things you can do to help put the odds in your favor.[37]

1. Don't limit your job search to only large companies. Companies with 20 employees or less account for two-thirds of all new jobs.

2. Make sure you learn all you can about a company before interviewing there. Do your homework by reading about the company online and at the library, and by talking with friends.

3. During an interview, be careful about time. Take between 20 seconds and 2 minutes to answer each question asked.

4. Present yourself not as someone who's desperate for work but rather as "a resource person," someone who can help the company in different ways.

5. Immediately following an interview, write and mail a brief thank-you note to the people who interviewed you. Doing this will show that you are thoughtful and considerate.

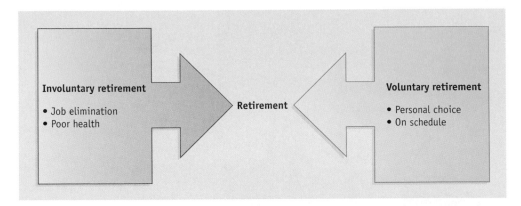

Involuntary retirement
• Job elimination
• Poor health

Retirement

Voluntary retirement
• Personal choice
• On schedule

of their lives that begins when their working lives end. To help ensure that this occurs, many companies are offering intensive counseling services to their employees to prepare them for retirement. For example, employees of the Walt Disney Company and their spouses are invited to seminars in which their incomes and financial needs are carefully investigated before it's time to retire. As a result, when the day comes that they are given a gold watch, employees will not have to hock it to pay their bills.

Today, rather than retiring from work altogether, many people in their sixties are opting for brand-new careers (see Figure 7.16). In fact, only about 37 percent of recent retirees expect to never return to work. The rest plan on staying active by working at least part time.[41] Apparently, the image of retirees spending their golden years leisurely golfing and playing with their grandkids is fading fast. Speaking of golf, many professional golfers who find that aging makes it hard for them to compete against the likes of Tiger Woods no longer have to retire from the game. Instead, they are discovering second careers by competing in the Senior PGA tour, where at age 50, they once again can rise to the top of their game.[42] Although precious few of us have the luxury of making a living by playing golf, many companies also are finding it beneficial to hire semiretired executives as consultants. Instead of putting these talented, experienced people out to pasture, so to speak, they are taking full advantage of the expertise they can bring to the job—especially as mentors to young employees.[43]

Succession planning. Before people retire—whether to a world of leisure or to an entirely new career—high-level executives typically assist their companies in preparing for the void created by their departure. This process is known as **succession planning**— the systematic attempt to identify possible holders of particular positions ahead of time

succession planning
The systematic attempt to identify possible holders of particular positions ahead of time in preparation for an executive's departure.

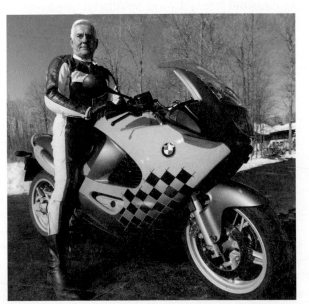

FIGURE 7.16
Some People Just Cannot Stay Retired for Long
After successfully leading Chrysler Corp. through a major turnaround, Robert Lutz retired as that company's CEO. Although he enjoyed riding around on his motorcycle for a while, at age 68, he eventually got bored. Missing the challenge of tending to a troubled company, Lutz became CEO of Exide Technologies, the car-battery maker, where he is once again lending his skills to helping another struggling company. Although Lutz says that he'll retire when he reaches 70, he also says, "Why should I stop?"

FIGURE 7.17

Succession Planning at American Express

In April 2001, after seven successful years as CEO of American Express Co., Harvey Golub (right) retired and passed his position along to the company's president and chief operating officer, Kenneth I. Chenault. Recognizing the importance of succession planning at the upper echelons of this big company, Golub personally selected Chenault as his successor and carefully groomed him for the post.

short-term successors

Individuals who are considered suitable candidates, at least temporarily, to fill the position of someone who leaves his or her job unexpectedly.

in preparation for their departure.[44] After spending years building a successful business, it is unlikely that the owner would feel comfortable retiring without taking steps to preserve what has been done and to ensure that the company is left in good hands. People generally also want to pass the baton to another whose goals and values match their own. And, of course, careful planning of this nature is in the best interest of the company as well. One way of identifying successors, particularly for top executives, is by having the retiring individual identify and develop a successor (over a course of years, if possible).[45] Mentoring at this level not only assures the retiring executive that he or she will have a successor qualified to fill the post but also helps to prepare the successor for the job and ease his or her transition within the organization (see Figure 7.17).

Formal succession-planning efforts are more likely to occur in large organizations than small ones. Large firms generally have formal plans on record, specifying exactly who will move into certain positions once they are vacated. These typically include frequently updated information on the specific skills and qualifications of the individuals involved. Many succession plans identify **short-term successors,** individuals who are suitable candidates, at least temporarily, to fill a post vacated unexpectedly (e.g., through termination, resignation, or death).[46] This is not to say that leaders of small companies are unconcerned about succession. Indeed, their small size makes it crucial to consider how jobs will be filled in the event of an emergency. However, leaders of small companies are more likely to discuss these things privately than to have a formal plan specifying succession in any systematic fashion.

PERSONAL CHALLENGES AND STRATEGIES FOR CAREER MANAGEMENT

Almost all of us care greatly about becoming successful in our careers, and most of us expect to attain some measure of success. In fact, a recent survey by the firm Ernst & Young found that over 70 percent of M.B.A.s and undergraduates expect to become millionaires—and over half expect to retire in their fifties.[47] With this in mind, we had better get right down to several important considerations for having a successful career.

Job Rotation

Because jobs are always changing, it makes sense to not only stay current but also to be able to perform a variety of different jobs. Doing so not only can help alleviate stress (see Chapter 4) and promote job satisfaction (see Chapter 5), but learning to perform a variety of different jobs also can be a good career move. After all, the more skills you have, the more valuable you are to your present employer. With this in mind, many companies are engaging in **job rotation**—the practice of transferring employees laterally between different jobs in an organization. The best-performing employees in their companies (i.e., those who receive the highest salaries and who are promoted most rapidly) tend to experience job rotation relatively early in their careers.[48] Not surprisingly, people who rotate through a succession of jobs find this a valuable experience. It not only keeps life at work interesting, but it also helps enhance career advancement—either at their current employer or at another.

Job rotation can be so very beneficial that Blockbuster has put into place a systematic program designed to place entry-level employees interested in corporate finance into a succession of positions designed to give them valuable experiences. Known as BLAST (Blockbuster Leadership and Skills Training), the two-year program provides an opportunity for new employees to gain experience in finance and accounting by rotating them through a comprehensive series of assignments within the company's finance and accounting departments (see Figure 7.18). Specifically, the BLAST program involves four six-month rotations selected from among such departments as corporate accounting, financial reporting, treasury, business partnerships, strategic planning, and international finance.

Entrepreneurship: Should You Start Your Own Business?

You all know the legendary story of Bill Gates, who, with partner Paul Allen, dropped out of Harvard to found Microsoft and made it one of the world's most successful companies. But you probably never heard of Robert F. Young, who in only four years made his company, Red Hat, one of today's fastest-growing software companies (on the strength of its Linux operating system), increasing his net worth some $2 billion in the process. You also probably never heard of Alain Rossmann, although if you have ever used an Internet browser in a wireless phone, chances are good that you used a product developed by the wildly successful company he founded, Phone.com.[49] Like Gates, Young and Rossmann are people who started their own companies—individuals known as **entrepreneurs.**

Today, growing numbers of people are turning away from the corporate world, opting instead to start their own businesses. In fact, in the United States, 30 percent of the population is involved in a start-up company, and 5.51 percent have invested in one—

job rotation
The practice of transferring employees laterally between different jobs in an organization.

entrepreneurs
Individuals who start their own businesses.

FIGURE 7.18

Job Rotation at Blockbuster
Blockbuster is so serious about developing the careers of its corporate-level employees that it has implemented a systematic program to rotate them through a succession of positions.

FIGURE 7.19

Two Under-40 Entrepreneurs
Adam and Eric Henegan founded Giant
Step in the 1990s and grew it into one of
the most successful e-business consultation services. When the company joined
forces with Novo in 2001, the brothers
moved on. But, like so many other young
entrepreneurs, they're likely to start
another business.

making it the leading nation in terms of the number of entrepreneurs.[50] So commonplace is the entrepreneurship movement, in fact, that two-thirds of teenagers report
being interested in starting a business of their own someday.[51]

Given its popularity, it probably comes as no surprise that people today consider
entrepreneurship as a viable career option. This is especially the case among adults
under the age of 40 (see Figure 7.19). The general reasons for this boil down to the fact
that young entrepreneurs are prepared to ride the wave of technology, have cheap capital available to them, and have boundless optimism.[52] Furthermore, entrepreneurship
is looked upon very favorably today. Although not too long ago someone starting his or
her own business was considered by some to be "a greedy businessperson," in recent
years entrepreneurship has become legitimized. In fact, most colleges and universities
have classes on the topic—and very popular ones, at that. For a more detailed look at
some of the forces that keep young entrepreneurs going today, see Table 7.4.

Despite these considerations, it is important to note that success as an entrepreneur cannot be assured. In fact, many of today's once thriving Internet start-up compa-

TABLE 7.4 WHY ARE YOUNG ENTREPRENEURS SO PREVALENT TODAY?

**Several recent trends in business and technology have made entrepreneurship a very popular and viable
option among today's young people.**

1. Young people are more *tech savvy* than the generation ahead of them. In fact, many of today's entrepreneurs grew up in an era in which they never knew life without computers.

2. The *Internet* makes it easy for entrepreneurs to gain access to new markets and permits sophisticated
   research to be conducted inexpensively.

3. Because many companies are *downsizing,* security in the corporate world cannot be assured, reducing
   people's interest in scaling the corporate ladder.

4. Small businesses have opportunities because many larger companies are *outsourcing* specialized services.

5. *Entrepreneurship programs* have become commonplace in both undergraduate- and graduate-level business
   programs, thereby giving today's students the basic skills needed to become entrepreneurs.

6. The fact that many start-ups become successful has attracted *venture capitalists* to finance start-up companies, making them viable.

(*Source:* Based on suggestions by Rosenberg, 1999; see Note 52.)

nies have disappeared. Clearly, to start a company is one thing, but to make it successful is quite another. In fact, the statistics are sobering: About 60 percent of all businesses fail within the first two years.[53] A survey of entrepreneurs indicated that 32 percent say they failed because they were undercapitalized (i.e., they didn't begin with enough money to develop the business properly). The other major reasons for failure noted are a slow economy (30 percent), creditor problems (8 percent), slow receivables (8 percent), and tax problems (6 percent).[54]

Even if your company can make a go of it, it's important to note that an entrepreneur's life is not always as glamorous as one hears. In fact, it can be rather difficult. Typically, founders of companies work longer and harder than they ever worked before—often giving up much of their personal time in the process.[55] Furthermore, they usually find that they do not make any money for the first few years, making it difficult for them to stay afloat personally. Thus, although stories abound of people who made it big on a shoestring—even from their college dormitory rooms (as was Michael Dell's case, the founder of Dell Computers)—adding to the allure of entrepreneurship, it is important to note that entrepreneurs face a long, difficult challenge ahead of them.[56] (Fortunately, services exist to help budding entrepreneurs become successful. For a close-up look at one such approach, see the Best Practices section on page 260.)

Starting a Home-Based Business

When British colonists first settled in what became the United States, local business consisted largely of trading with the merchant ships that came to port. Most of the goods they traded, such as clothing woven from local fibers, were made in their homes (which, by the way, is how the term *cottage industry* came into being). After a while, as the industrial revolution took hold, businesses outgrew homes and moved into factories. Now, some 300 years later, the modern industrial revolution has brought so many sophisticated technological advances into the home (e.g., computers with broadband connections) that it is possible to do a great deal of productive work without ever leaving your living room. And, with traffic congestion high and air quality low, growing numbers of people are finding little incentive to work anywhere else.

A wide variety of businesses can be based at home. Some, such as small, family-owned farms and bed-and-breakfast inns, are home-based businesses by their very nature. So, too, it is natural for writers and fine artists to work from home, as well as many music teachers. And, with growing popularity, home is the preferred base of operations for many people who run desktop publishing businesses and consultants of various types. If you tried running an auto-repair shop in your garage, however, your neighbors might complain and you might find yourself running into problems with the local zoning board. And, of course, there are some professions that cannot be accommodated at home no matter how hard you try. Airline pilots and police officers, for example, have to perform their jobs in many different locations.

What we're seeing today is somewhat unique: Many people who formerly worked outside the home now are deciding to stay at home and have their own businesses. Many people who run Internet-based businesses, for example, do so out of their homes. This may involve designing Web sites or operating a small e-commerce business. Even before the Internet, it was not unusual for people to run small mail-order businesses out of their homes. Many of the people who run small businesses out of their homes do so because they find it more appealing than having to confront the office politics of the corporate world.

Home-based businesses are not without their own challenges.[61] Some of the most important ones are as follows:

- The average American home-based worker earns only 70 percent as much as he or she would make outside the home.
- Many people decide to work at home so that they can have a better balance between work and family. However, when you have a home-based business, you're always "at work." Consequently, your family or your business often gets shortchanged.

BEST PRACTICES
HELPING ENTREPRENEURS MAKE IT B.I.G.

■ Shop Well With You, was the idea of Emily Spivak—a nonprofit company that provides a free personalized shopping service for women with cancer, who have a difficult time finding clothes that look and fit good.[57]

■ Jessica's Wonders, founded by Jessica Nam, is a bakery that makes and sells delicious confections, such as her own secret recipe, Kelli Belli Jelli Banana Bread.[58]

Although these two businesses are very different, they share something in common: Both were started by young people who had ideas and were launched with the help of New York City's

Business Incubation Group (better known as B.I.G.). Founded by Steve Massarsky, a former entertainment lawyer (who represented such bands as Aeorsmith, Cindi Lauper, and the Psychedelic Furs), B.I.G. is what's known as a **business incubator**—a kind of business that provides support for new, entrepreneurial companies, to launch them and help them grow.[59] B.I.G. works by providing expert guidance to people who have promising ideas for new businesses. It assigns an experienced mentor to a new entrepreneur to help "hatch" his or her project. This individual provides intellectual guidance and support, as well as assistance in finding financial backing (either through B.I.G.'s own network of "angels" or through outside contacts). As he did in the music business, Massarsky still sees him-

---

business incubator

A kind of business that provides support for new, entrepreneurial companies, to launch them and help them grow.

■ In most cases, there is a limit to how large home-based businesses can become (see Figure 7.20). Of course, a few make it so big that they quickly outgrow their original quarters. For example, Michael Dell started Dell Computers by assembling computers from standard components working out of his dormitory room at the University of Texas.

FIGURE 7.20

Home-Based Businesses Often Have Growing Pains

Although many people find it desirable to run a business from their home, there is a limit to how much any home-based business can grow.

(*Source:* Sidney Harris, www.sciencecartoonsplus.com)

"YES, THE BUSINESS HAS BECOME BIGGER, BUT FRED STILL LIKES TO WORK AT HOME."

self as managing talent (albeit now without a lot of the temperamental issues).

B.I.G.'s success is based on the idea that it's easier to find money than help. Indeed, every month billions of dollars are poured into companies that are little more than an idea. To ensure that any financial investments pay off, B.I.G. carefully screens prospective clients and matches them with great care to experienced businesspeople who are ready, willing, and able to help. Experts agree that to be successful, entrepreneurs must surround themselves with trusted advisors and mentors who can help them navigate around the many inevitable challenges faced by a new business. This is critical. In fact, according to the National Business Incubation Association, four out of five new businesses fail. However, four out of five new businesses that receive incubation and mentoring succeed in the marketplace.

Frequently, entrepreneurs become so immersed in their ideas that an innovative and objective source can be invaluable. In Jessica Nam's case, it was Massarsky himself. Although he recognized that Jessica was an excellent baker, her most unique talents, he realized, were in marketing. Not only could she describe her products so vividly that it made your mouth water, but she also had the personality and drive to sell them—even if it meant dressing up in a banana suit. So, they decided to hire a professional bakery to manufacture the products and to put Jessica herself out front to represent the brand.[60]

Just a few years ago, Jessica was making cookies in her dorm room at Brown University and selling them one by one. Today, her products are sold throughout New England (with plans to go national very soon), and she's president and CEO of Jessica's, Inc. Steve Massarsky is secretary and chairman of the company. She never could have done it without the B.I.G. help she got from him.

The Glass Ceiling: A Career Challenge for Women

There can be no doubt that women and men have very different job experiences and that, despite their prevalence in the workplace, women still continue to face discrimination in the workplace. For example, although increased training, work experience, and education benefit both men and women, they have less beneficial impact on women.[62] Also, as we described in Chapter 5, women continue to find it difficult to advance into the highest ranks of organizations. According to the U.S. Department of Labor, although women hold 45 percent of all managerial jobs at large companies, only 6 of the 1,000 largest companies are run by women. Clearly, there's a barrier that's keeping women from reaching the highest organizational levels, and this is known as the *glass ceiling*. In Chapter 5, we depicted the glass ceiling as an invisible barrier that prevents qualified individuals from advancing in their organizations (see Figure 7.21).[63]

Beyond any conscious efforts by male executives to keep women from their domain, the glass ceiling often takes subtle forms. For example, women may receive fewer opportunities to develop their skills and competencies—opportunities that would prepare them for top-level jobs. Women also report fewer chances than men to take part in projects that increase their visibility or widen the scope of their responsibilities. In short, women are not given work assignments that teach them new skills while permitting them an opportunity to demonstrate their competence.[64] In addition, women report encountering more obstacles overall in their jobs: They note that it is harder to find personal support, they often are left out of important networks, and they must fight hard to be recognized for doing excellent work.[65]

Fortunately, the glass ceiling appears to be cracking in places. A study comparing the outcomes and experiences of female and male executives in one large company found that, although men generally supervised more people, women and men were generally equivalent with respect to salary, bonuses, and development opportunities.[66] Because this research examined only a single organization, we cannot determine the extent to which these findings represent a general trend or are merely descriptive of the particular company studied. Still, they offer some basis for encouragement.

FIGURE 7.21

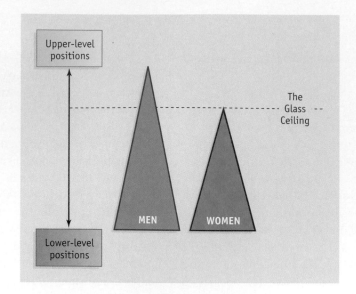

Given that the glass ceiling still seems to exist, it is worthwhile to consider what women can do to help break down occupational barriers entirely. Some suggestions in this regard are as follows:

- *Be yourself.* Traditionally, many women thought that becoming as successful as a man meant adopting the management style of men. However, there isn't any good reason to do so. Many top female executives have been successful by using their own "feminine style." In general, women tend to be warmer and more gracious than men and have more highly developed social skills. This more interpersonally approachable style tends to work very well, so don't consider changing it.
- *Develop your own networks and support groups.* Earlier we described the importance of mentoring in career success. However, women tend to shy away from mentoring more often than men, fearing the negative consequences of a protégé who fails.[67] As such, it is important for women who want to achieve success to go out of their way to establish a broad base of contacts (both inside and outside the company) that can provide good career advice and even open some doors. Cracking the glass ceiling requires the leverage of others.
- *Consider all job options—even those that are traditionally male.* Although it is strictly illegal in the United States to discriminate on the basis of gender, many people continue to think in terms of "men's jobs" (e.g., welder) and "women's jobs" (e.g., obstetrics nurse). Limiting your own thinking in this way may strengthen those stereotypes, making it difficult to crack the glass ceiling. The key is to consider all job options for which you are suited, regardless of their traditional sex types. Doing this is a useful step toward cracking the glass ceiling.

Dealing with the Dual Career

It's no secret that today's families are quite different from those of just one generation ago.[68] Slightly over 30 years ago, the typical nuclear family consisted of a husband who worked outside the home, a wife working as a homemaker, and two children. Today, however, this configuration exists in less than 4 percent of all American households. In fact, in well over half of all American families both individuals are employed. These are known as **dual-career couples.** In addition, about twice as many children are currently being raised in single-parent families (mostly mothers) compared to 1970, and two-thirds of these single parents work outside the home.

As you might imagine, these changing demographics have had considerable impact on the nature of people's careers, and organizational scientists have been highly involved in studying them. When both members of married couples work outside the

dual-career couples
Married couples in which both partners are employed.

home, it becomes particularly challenging to be able to balance the demands of one's job (e.g., to work late to meet special projects) with the demands of one's family life (e.g., quality time with the children). Often this involves what has been referred to as a **dual-career conflict**—a situation in which the career demands on one member of a couple are incompatible with the career demands on the other member of the couple. Research has shown that dual-career conflicts are major sources of stress that can have a profound negative impact on people's satisfaction with both their work lives and their family lives, increasing depression and lowering overall life satisfaction.[69]

In view of the changing nature of the workplace and the adjustments that people must make, many companies are making special efforts to resolve some of the problems of dual-career conflicts. We already summarized some of these key practices in Chapter 1, in conjunction with our discussion of flexibility in the workplace and *employee support policies*. These include various *flextime* programs, where employees get to select the hours they work; *job sharing*, in which two or more employees assume the responsibilities of a single position; and *child care* and *elder care* facilities, in which provisions are made for others to help care for the children or elderly relatives of employees while they are at work. Sometimes, however, such arrangements do not go quite far enough, leading people in dual-career situations to take more extreme measures.

For example, growing numbers of people in dual-career couples are avoiding potential conflicts by taking *career breaks*. A **career break** is the practice in which an employee leaves and subsequently reenters a job following an agreed-upon period of absence. Although the benefits to employees are clear—having a job waiting when ready to return to work—many employers are reluctant to go along with this practice. However, those that do recognize that it's sometimes more efficient to let employees take off for extended periods of time (e.g., a year)—particularly when they have scarce skills—than to have to bear the considerable costs of recruiting and training replacements. However, with rapid advances in technology, it's not always the case that someone who leaves his or her job for any length of time will be able to stay sufficiently up to date on job skills to be an asset to the company upon reentering the workforce.[70] Still, as we discussed in Chapter 4, several companies are finding that it's beneficial to encourage employees to take time off the job, known as a **sabbatical,** to allow them to recharge and come back fresh, avoiding potential stress-related problems and illnesses.

Today, instead of hoping their employers will let them take a sabbatical, some of the most in-demand workers (especially well-regarded employees in high-tech fields) are simply resigning their jobs, taking off however much time they want, and then taking new jobs when they're ready to resume work—a practice known as **dropping out.** This particular way of dealing with dual careers is limited, of course, to those who can afford to go without bringing in a salary and to those who expect to find new jobs.[71] Although most career experts have long advised against having a gap in your résumé, many of today's most talented workers are in such great demand that they can get away with it. In fact, the mere decision to drop out is taken by many as a sign of a person's success. Although the job market for high-tech workers is nowhere near as hot as it was just a few years ago, many workers are dropping out anyway. This is because their former start-up firms have now matured to the point where they feel they can leave without creating serious problems, and because they have worked so hard over the past few years that they now feel it's necessary to drop out to avoid burnout and to enjoy the fruits of their labor.

For a growing number of dropouts, the preferred course of action is not returning to a job at another company, but rather, abandoning traditional jobs and starting their own small businesses. In recent years, such individuals have been referred to as **corporate refugees.** As we noted, it is quite difficult to begin new business ventures. However, corporate refugees generally are not looking for an easy way out. Instead, they seek to regain the challenges left behind in their corporate jobs and to find a more fulfilling existence. Moreover, many are looking to keep the size of the business sufficiently manageable to be able to allow them to spend time with their families.

dual-career conflict
A situation in which the career demands on one member of a couple are incompatible with the career demands on the other member of a couple.

career break
The practice in which an employee leaves and then subsequently reenters a job following an agreed-upon period of absence.

sabbatical
Time taken off the job, typically for purposes of recharging, coming back fresh, and avoiding potential stress-related problems.

dropping out
The practice of resigning from a job for a long period of time and then taking another job at another time.

corporate refugees
People who leave corporate jobs so they can start their own small businesses.

Hiring a Career Coach

career coach

An expert hired for purposes of helping someone accomplish his or her career objectives.

Not everyone is fortunate enough to have a mentor—especially top executives who have few others available to guide them. However, such individuals are not necessarily without the help they need to improve their lives at work and at home. They can—and in increasing numbers often do—hire *career coaches*. According to the Internal Coach Federation, which boasts 10,000 coaches working worldwide, a **career coach** is an expert hired for purposes of helping someone accomplish his or her career objectives.[72]

Career coaches are personal consultants, sounding boards, and therapists all rolled into one. People who don't know how to handle a delicate situation at work or who are experiencing very stressful situations (see Chapter 4) simply can pick up their phones and find their coaches at the other end ready, willing, and able to lend a hand. Many employees find this highly personal service preferable to, say, confiding in a mentor, who may not know what to do, or a superior to whom people would prefer to keep their vulnerabilities confidential. Most coaching services today are provided via either telephone or online connections; few coaches actually meet face to face with their clients.[73]

This form of coaching was pioneered in the 1980s by Thomas J. Leonard, a Seattle-based financial planner who discovered that his clients wanted to talk more about life issues than tax and investment advice.[74] Soon, Leonard gave up his financial planning practice and began what he calls a "life planning" service, which his clients referred to as coaching. There was so much demand for his services that in 1992 Leonard began a formal program for training other coaches known as Coach University. Although coaching services are not inexpensive (they range in price from $600 to $2,000 per month for three or four 30- to 60-minute phone calls), many executives have benefited so much from these services that they more than pay for themselves. Because of this, several large companies, such as IBM, Kodak, and Goldman Sachs, have brought coaches aboard to help their employees become more productive. For example, at AT&T, executive coach Cheryl Weir inspired managers to shoot for and to attain such high goals that the company's investment in coaching services was recovered in only one week.

SUMMARY AND REVIEW OF LEARNING OBJECTIVES

1. Define career and distinguish among the various types of careers that exist.
A career is the evolving sequence of work experiences over time. There are four major types of careers. Steady-state careers are those in which people keep only one (or very few) job throughout their working lives. Linear careers are those in which people continuously work their way up the occupational hierarchy in a succession of related jobs. Spiral careers are those in which people continue working their way up the occupational hierarchy but do so by moving into related occupations. Transitory careers are marked by a succession of unrelated jobs that fail to show upward movement in an organizational hierarchy.

2. Describe the three major considerations in making career choices.
Career choices are made by taking into account three major considerations. The first is the extent to which the particular skills and characteristics required for success in an occupation match one's own. These are specified by Holland's theory of occupational choice. A second consideration has to do with the extent to which various jobs are in keeping with our self-images, referred to as career anchors. A third consideration has to do with job opportunities. Choices are restricted by the availability of jobs, of course, but also people tend to seek positions in fields that show the greatest potential for growth.

3. Describe the process of organizational socialization, including the stages by which it occurs.

Organizational socialization is the process through which people become participating members of their organizations. During the earliest stage, anticipatory socialization, people consider what it would be like to become a member of an organization. To help avoid disappointments and subsequent turnover, it helps for corporate recruiters to provide realistic job previews—accurate descriptions of both the negative and positive aspects of a job likely to be encountered. Once people enter the organization, the encounter stage, they are likely to be exposed to corporate orientation programs designed to systematically socialize them with respect to the operations of the organizations as well as its history and traditions. Finally, in the metamorphosis stage, new employees become full-fledged members of the organization, a passage sometimes marked by formal ceremonies.

4. Define mentoring and describe the processes through which mentorship develops.

Mentoring is a special one-on-one form of socialization. It involves a mentor, a generally older, more experienced person, who counsels and advises a younger, less experienced person, a protégé. Relationships between mentors and their protégés offer benefits to both parties, although they have potential costs as well. Such relationships pass through regular stages during which mentors and protégés work closely together and then begin to separate, as the protégé goes off on his or her own. Several of today's companies have been helping women and members of minority groups gain from mentoring experiences.

5. Identify and describe the special challenges likely to be confronted in established careers.

People in established careers are likely to face three major challenges. First, there is the career plateau—the point at which further upward changes in one's career have stopped. Career plateaus can be overcome by career development interventions, which help people find new ways of making work more stimulating. Second, people in established careers find it challenging to make career changes. One effective way of doing so is by changing one's occupation and field of specialization in two steps instead of one. Third, people in established careers often are concerned about retirement, the phase of life in which they stop working full time for their primary incomes. This requires adjustments to new life activities and a new financial situation. Among these concerns is succession planning, the process through which high-level executives consider possible replacements when they retire.

6. Explain various personal challenges and strategies for managing your own career.

In attempting to manage your career effectively, it is useful to follow several strategies. First, it is advisable to get experience performing a wide variety of different jobs, a practice known as job rotation. Second, instead of working for a company, many people are choosing to start their own businesses by becoming entrepreneurs. Fueled by their knowledge of technology, the availability of cheap capital, and boundless optimism, many young people are drawn in this direction. For many of the same reasons, growing numbers of people are starting small, home-based businesses. For women, effective career management often involves attempting to overcome the attitudinal barriers against them in the workplace—that is, cracking the glass ceiling. Maintaining a career is challenging for today's dual-career couples—those in which both adult members of most households work outside the home. Many such individuals are balancing their personal demands with their work demands by taking advantage of employee support policies that provide flexibility in scheduling or by taking time off work in the form of career breaks and sabbaticals or by dropping out. In recent years, employees who have questions about their careers and their lives have turned to career coaches for help. These professionals, hired either individually or by companies for their employees, are providing useful guidance to people in today's complex world.

4. During the interview, one of you should ask questions and the other partner should take careful notes on how the person answers each of the following questions:
   a. Were you ever someone's mentor on the job? (If yes, go to b, c, d, and e.)
   b. What exactly did you do to help this individual?
   c. Did this relationship develop informally or was it part of a formal program?
   d. What were the major benefits that you got out of the experience?
   e. What were the major problems, if any, that you experienced in this relationship?
   f. Were you ever someone's protégé on the job? (If yes, go to g, h, i, and j.)
   g. How exactly did this individual help you?
   h. Did this relationship develop informally or was it part of a formal program?
   i. What were the major benefits that you got out of the experience?
   j. What were the major problems, if any, that you experienced in this relationship?
5. As a team, repeat this process with another interviewee. This time, reverse roles as questioner and note-taker.
6. Compare each team's results with the entire class.

Questions for Discussion

1. What were the major benefits that people reported about being a mentor?
2. What were the major problems that people reported about being a mentor? In your opinion, how might these be overcome?
3. What were the major benefits that people reported about being a protégé?
4. What were the major problems that people reported about being a protégé? In your opinion, how might these be overcome?

WEB SURFING EXERCISE

Searching for Jobs Online

Currently, online job databases are very popular. Every day, they are used to bring together thousands of employers with prospective employees. There are many such online services, with some of the largest and most popular being:

www.careerbuilder.com	www.careermosaic.com
www.headenter.com	www.joboccupations.com
www.careerpath.com	www.hotjobs.com
www.jobs.com	www.monster.com

Go to any three of these Web sites, examine them carefully, and then answer the following questions based on what you find.

1. In what kinds of jobs does each site specialize?
2. How do these various services differ from one another?
3. As illustrated by these sites, what do you believe to be the greatest advantages and the greatest disadvantages of online job searches?

Jobs for New College Grads

Many major job sites have special sections on internships and jobs for new college graduates. Some of the top ones are as follows:

www.campuscareercenter.com	www.collegegrad.com
www.drake.edu/career	www.jobdirect.com
www.jobtrack.com	www.studyweb.com

Go to any three of these Web sites, examine them carefully, and then answer the following questions based on what you find.

1. In what ways are each of these sites similar to and different from one another?

2. Compared to job seekers with more experience, do you think it is more useful or less useful for recent college graduates to search for jobs on the Web? Explain your answer.
3. Which one of these sites would be of greatest interest to you in looking for a job? Why?

PRACTICING OB

The Trash Man Never Showed Up

You are the vice president of human resources for Rubbish World, a private trash removal service located in a large metropolitan area. Customers have been complaining that their trash isn't always been picked up on time. After investigating the matter, the dispatcher discovered that quite a few drivers have been taking time off their routes to run personal errands. The offending parties were disciplined, even dismissed, yet the practice persists. You and other company officials are concerned because you don't want the problem to continue with the new employees you hire. At a high-level meeting you are asked to provide advice on this matter.

1. How might you use realistic job previews to help select new employees who would not be predisposed to goofing off in this fashion?
2. What would you do to socialize prospective employees about the company's values? Do you think a corporate orientation program would help? If so, what should it emphasize? How about mentors? Would they be effective in this case? Why or why not?
3. After interviewing some employees, you learn that dual-career conflicts lay at the root of the problem. In view of this, what steps can the company take to help alleviate such conflicts?

CASE IN POINT

Toal's Career Takes Its Toll

It's a crisp fall morning in 2001, and Chris Toal is working out furiously in a gym near his office in Burlington, Massachusetts. Some of this energy, no doubt, stems from his nervousness. Now a middle manager in his midfifties, Toal finds himself in a scary situation: The e-commerce service company for which he worked for only two years, Open Market, was being acquired by a similar firm, Devine. Would this mean that he'd be losing his job? Or might it bring greater opportunities for growth and development—which, at his age, weren't his top priorities. These were the questions that laid heavily on his mind that morning. Born just before the baby boom generation, Toal never could have envisioned that at his age he'd be worried about such things. Rather, he had expected to be able to slow down, spend more time with his family, and enjoy life more as he coasted into retirement. But this was not to be.

After several years as a high school teacher, he decided to make what appeared to be a big career change: He would go to law school. After graduating, he worked for a law firm in a poor Boston neighborhood but was tired of being poor himself, so he decided to opt for a more lucrative position at LTX, a high-tech start-up firm. Just as things began moving along nicely, LTX started downsizing to remain competitive. This sent Toal scrambling along a treadmill of positions at the company—searching for shelter in any job that looked like it might survive the cuts. He moved from manufacturing to purchasing to sales administration, but eventually the inevitable happened, and Toal got the axe.

At age 50, this sent Toal back into the job market but with only limited computer skills under his belt. Remaining in Massachusetts, he went to Proteon, a network services firm, but lasted only a few years there. Again, he was the victim of downsizing. Finally, this led him to Open Market, where he is now, although nobody knows for how long. Toal is one of the oldest employees at Open Market, and he has had to learn many new computer-related skills just to stay afloat. Sadly, he now realizes that his age and experience do not give him the advantages they once conferred such as the respect of his younger colleagues and a high level of job security. On the contrary, as he sees it, his age has become a liability instead of an asset. "The younger folks don't come to you as a mentor or experienced person," he observes. "You are all competing for jobs and the future and success." His boss is considerably younger and often kids him about his rather shaky computer skills as well as the fact that he is just about the only one who wears a necktie to the office. To compensate, he typically works 12- to 15-hour days.

Every few weeks Toal gets together with a group of other 50-something employees to bemoan how they have suffered because of changes in the workplace. "I feel like I've peaked in my career, but I don't think I've peaked as a human being," Toal sighs. Then, somewhat wistfully, he adds, "Things are not what any of us anticipated—that with natural talent, hard work, and good values there would come some sense of stability. In fact, there is no security and no stability." We wish you good luck, Mr. Toal. You'll need it.

Critical Thinking Questions

1. What steps could Chris Toal have taken early on to avoid the problem he's having now?
2. What advice would you now give Toal about the best thing to do for his career?
3. In what ways do you think Toal stands to benefit from his casual get-togethers with the other people his age?

Group Processes and Work Teams

8

■ PREVIEW CASE
PEOPLE POWER AT CONSOLIDATED DIESEL

Whitakers, North Carolina, is a small town with a very large building—the 1.2 million-square-foot factory operated by Consolidated Diesel Company. As out of scale as the facility is with its surrounding rural community, what's going on inside is equally out of scale with the world of manufacturing. A brand-new diesel engine for a tractor, truck, combine, or bus rolls off the assembly line amazingly fast—every 72 seconds. Unlike other factories, where layoffs are common and turnover is high, Consolidated Diesel has never had a layoff, and the annual turnover rate is under 2 percent. Also unique is the fact that managers are responsible for four times as many employees as those in the average factory—100, as opposed to 25, saving Consolidated Diesel an estimated $1 million per year. As if all this is not special enough, the injury rate at the plant is only about one-fifth of the national average.

Obviously, something special is going on at this factory, but what? Anyone at the plant will tell you that the answer lies in the fact that employees work together in teams. What's more, they've been working this way since 1980, when the factory opened its doors. Exactly how they do this is based on several key practices. Possibly the most important thing the company does is give teams total responsibility over everything they do. Team members not only routinely solve their own problems, but they also are

> Possibly the most important thing the company does is give teams total responsibility over everything they do. Team members not only routinely solve their own problems, but they also are responsible for making all their own decisions.

271

responsible for making all their own decisions. They even are responsible for hiring (and, when necessary, firing) their own members. The decisions they make are the ones they live by.

The company's second key to success involves extensively cross-training everyone. Consolidated Diesel's employees know how to do many different jobs. One day someone may be operating a machine and the next day he may be making quality inspections. The idea is that people who know how to do someone else's job have respect for what that person is doing, and this breeds a sense of cooperation.

Third, Consolidated Diesel executives listen to their employees and enlist their help in finding ways to improve plant operations. Recently, for example, a third-shift skeleton crew was added to help meet the growing demand for engines. Overtime costs grew but performance remained flat. After teams got involved, a better solution was found. When flexible schedules were developed, shifts soon returned to eight-hour days and Saturday work was eliminated. As general manager Jim Lyone explains, "Sometimes, the fact that it's the team's plan and not a plan dictated by management means everything. The team will make it work."

All of these practices are effective because none of the employees believe that the company is out to hurt them. Instead, they feel that the company treats them fairly. The good and the bad are distributed equally. For example, either everyone gets a bonus, or nobody gets one. The burden of working the night shift is shared equally as well. Entire teams move from working days to working nights every two weeks.

The interesting thing about Consolidated Diesel's operations is that everyone has grown to expect superior results. Mediocrity is not tolerated. The expectations are considerable, but for the most part they have been self-imposed. Everyone expects a great deal from everyone else, and delivering it is the general rule.

O bviously, many things about working life at Consolidated Diesel are very special and amazingly effective. Although this company may be extreme in many ways, elements of what it does may be seen in factories and offices everywhere. Indeed, *work teams* are extremely popular today in all kinds of organizations—and, in view of Consolidated Diesel's experiences, there's little wonder why. In the second half of this chapter we will take a close-up look at the nature of teams in the modern workplace. Acknowledging that they don't always operate as successfully as they do at Consolidated Diesel, we will describe the general effectiveness of teams and outline steps that can be taken to make teams as productive as possible.

To help you understand the underlying factors that contribute to team success and failure, we first must turn attention to the basic nature of *groups* in general. As you know, a great deal of the work performed in organizations is done by people working together in groups. In view of this, it makes sense to understand the types of groups that exist and the variables governing the interrelationships between them and individuals—commonly referred to as *group dynamics*. **Group dynamics** focuses on the nature of groups—the variables governing their formation and development, their structure, and their interrelationships with individuals, other groups, and the organizations within which they exist.[1] Because groups exist in all types of social settings, the study of group dynamics has a long history in the social sciences, including OB.[2]

In the first half of this chapter we will draw on this work. Specifically, we will describe the nature of groups by defining what groups are, identifying various types of groups and why they form, explaining the various stages through which groups develop, and describing the dynamics of the way groups are structured. Following this, we will shift our attention to how effectively groups operate. Specifically, we will describe how people are affected by the presence of others, how the cultural makeup of

group dynamics
The social science field focusing on the nature of groups—the factors governing their formation and development, the elements of their structure, and their interrelationships with individuals, other groups, and organizations.

a group affects performance, and the tendency for people to withhold their individual performance under certain conditions.

GROUPS AT WORK: THEIR BASIC NATURE

To understand the dynamics of groups and their influence on individual and organizational functioning, we must begin by raising some basic questions—namely, what is a group, what types of groups exist, why do people join groups, how do groups come into being, and how are groups structured? We will now address these questions.

What Is a Group? A Working Definition

Imagine three people waiting in line at the cashier's stand at a supermarket. Now, compare them to the board of directors of a large corporation. Which collection would you consider to be a "group"? Although in our everyday language we may refer to the people waiting in line as a group, they clearly are not a group in the same sense as the members of the board. Obviously, a group is more than simply a collection of people. But what exactly is it that makes a group a group?

Social scientists have formally defined a **group** as a collection of two or more interacting individuals with a stable pattern of relationships between them who share common goals and who perceive themselves as being a group.[3] To help us examine this definition more closely, we summarize the four key characteristics of groups in Figure 8.1.

Social interaction. One of the most obvious characteristics of groups is that they are composed of *two or more people in social interaction*. In other words, the members of a group must have some influence on each other. The interaction between the parties may be either verbal (such as sharing strategies for a corporate takeover) or nonverbal (such as exchanging smiles in the hallway), but the parties must have some impact on each other to be considered a group.

Stability. Groups also must possess a *stable structure*. Although groups can change—and often do—there must be some stable relationships that keep group members together and functioning as a unit. A collection of individuals that constantly changes (e.g., the people inside an office waiting room at any given time) cannot be thought of as a group. To be a group, a greater level of stability would be required.

group
A collection of two or more interacting individuals who maintain stable patterns of relationships, share common goals, and perceive themselves as being a group.

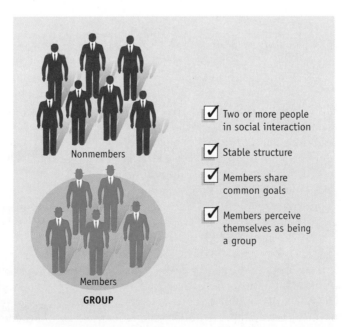

Nonmembers

☑ Two or more people in social interaction

☑ Stable structure

☑ Members share common goals

☑ Members perceive themselves as being a group

Members

GROUP

FIGURE 8.1
A Group: Its Defining Characteristics
To be a group, four different criteria must be met: (1) there must be two or more people in social interaction, (2) they must have a stable group structure, (3) they must share common goals, and (4) the individuals must perceive themselves as being a group.

Common interests or goals. A third characteristic of groups is that their *members share common interests or goals.* For example, members of a stamp collecting club constitute a group that is sustained by the mutual interest of members. Some groups form because members with common interests help each other achieve a mutual goal. For example, the owners and employees of a sporting goods shop constitute a group formed around a common interest in athletic equipment and the common goal of making money.

Recognition as being a group. Finally, to be a group, the individuals involved must *perceive themselves as a group.* Groups are composed of people who recognize each other as a member of their group and can distinguish these individuals from nonmembers. The members of a corporate finance committee or a chess club, for example, know who is in their group and who is not. In contrast, shoppers in a checkout line probably don't think of each other as being members of a group. Although they stand physically close to each other and may have passing conversations, they have little in common (except, perhaps, a shared interest in reaching the end of the line) and fail to identify themselves with the others in the line.

By defining groups in terms of these four characteristics, we have identified a group as a very special collection of individuals (see Figure 8.2). As we shall see, these characteristics are responsible for the important effects groups have on organizational behavior. To better understand these effects, we will now review the wide variety of groups that operate within organizations.

Types of Groups

What do the following have in common: a military combat unit, three couples getting together for dinner, the board of directors of a large corporation, and the three-person cockpit crew of a commercial airliner? As you probably guessed, the answer is that they are all groups. But, of course, they are very different kinds of groups, ones people join for different reasons.

Formal and informal groups. The most basic way of identifying types of groups is to distinguish between *formal groups* and *informal groups* (see Figure 8.3). **Formal groups** are created by the organization and are intentionally designed to direct members toward some important organizational goal. One type of formal group is referred to as a **command group**—a group determined by the connections between individuals who are a formal part of the organization (i.e., those who legitimately can give orders to others). For example, a command group may be formed by the vice president of marketing

formal groups

Groups that are created by the organization, intentionally designed to direct its members toward some organizational goal.

command group

A group determined by the connections between individuals who are a formal part of the organization (i.e., those who legitimately can give orders to others).

FIGURE 8.2

Is This a Group?
A collection of people waiting in a super-market checkout line is *not* considered a group. Although the people may talk to one another and share the goal of want-ing to leave the store, they are not con-sidered a group because different people are always entering and leaving the line and because the shoppers are unlikely to think of themselves as belonging to a group.

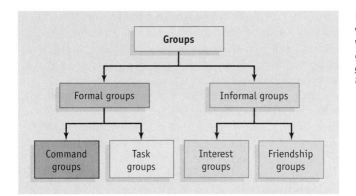

FIGURE 8.3
Varieties of Groups in Organizations
Within organizations one may find formal groups (such as *command groups* and *task groups*) and informal groups (such as *interest groups* and *friendship groups*).

who gathers together the regional marketing directors from around the country to hear their ideas about a new national advertising campaign. The point is that command groups are determined by the organization's rules regarding who reports to whom and usually consist of a supervisor and his or her subordinates.

A formal organizational group also may be formed around some specific task. Such a group is referred to as a **task group.** Unlike command groups, a task group may be composed of individuals with some special interest or expertise in a specific area regardless of their positions in the organizational hierarchy. For example, a company may have a committee on equal employment opportunities whose members monitor the fair hiring practices of the organization. It may be composed of personnel specialists, corporate vice presidents, and workers from the shop floor. Whether they are permanent committees, known as **standing committees,** or temporary ones formed for special purposes (such as a committee formed to recommend solutions to a parking problem), known as **ad hoc committees or task forces,** task groups are common in organizations.

As you know, not all groups found in organizations are as formal as those we've identified. Many groups are informal in nature. **Informal groups** develop naturally among an organization's personnel without any direction from the management of the organization within which they operate. One key factor in the formation of informal groups is a common interest shared by its members. For example, a group of employees who band together to seek union representation or who march together to protest their company's pollution of the environment may be called an **interest group.** The common goal sought by members of an interest group may unite workers at many different organizational levels. The key factor is that membership in an interest group is voluntary—it is not created by the organization but encouraged by an expression of common interests.

Of course, sometimes the interests that bind individuals together are far more diffuse. Groups may develop out of a common interest in participating in sports, or going to the movies, or just getting together to talk. These kinds of informal groups are known as **friendship groups.** A group of coworkers who hang out together during lunch may also bowl or play cards together after work. Friendship groups extend beyond the workplace because they provide opportunities for satisfying the social needs of workers that are so important to their motivation and well-being (see Chapter 6).

Informal work groups are an important part of life in organizations. Although they develop without direct encouragement from management, friendships often originate out of formal organizational contact. For example, three employees working alongside each other on an assembly line may get to talking and discover their mutual interest in basketball and decide to get together to shoot a few hoops after work. As we will see, such friendships can bind people together, helping them cooperate with each other, and have beneficial effects on organizational functioning.

Why Do People Join Groups?

We have already noted that people often join groups to satisfy their mutual interests and goals. To the extent that getting together with others allows us to achieve ends that

task group
A formal organizational group formed around some specific task.

standing committees
Committees that are permanent, existing over time.

ad hoc committee
A temporary committee formed for a special purpose.

task force
See *ad hoc committee.*

informal groups
Groups that develop naturally among people, without any direction from the organization within which they operate.

interest groups
A group of employees who come together to satisfy a common interest.

friendship groups
Informal groups that develop because their members are friends, often seeing each other outside of the organization.

would not be possible alone, forming groups makes a great deal of sense. In fact, organizations can be thought of as collections of groups that are focused toward achieving the mutual goal of achieving success for the company. But this is not the only motivation that people have for joining groups. There are also several additional reasons (see summary in Figure 8.4).

Not only do groups form for purposes of mutually achieving goals, they also frequently form for purposes of seeking protection from other groups. If you've ever heard the phrase "there's safety in numbers," you are probably already aware that people join groups because they seek the security of group membership. Historically, for example, trade unions, such as the AFL/CIO, the UAW, and the Teamsters, have been formed by labor for purposes of seeking protection against abuses by management. Similarly, professional associations, such as the American Medical Association and the American Bar Association, were created, in large part, for purposes of protecting people in their respective fields against undesirable governmental legislation.

This is not to say that groups are always designed to promote some instrumental good; indeed, they also exist because they appeal to a basic psychological need to be social. As we already discussed in the context of Maslow's need hierarchy theory (in Chapter 6), people are social animals; they have a basic need to interact with others. Groups provide good opportunities for friendships to develop and, hence, for social needs to be fulfilled.

Also as suggested by Maslow, people have a basic desire for their self-esteem to be fulfilled. Group memberships can be a very effective way of nurturing self-esteem. For example, if a group to which one belongs is successful (such as a sales group that meets its quota), the self-esteem of all members (and supporters) may be boosted. Similarly, election to membership in an exclusive group (e.g., a national honor society) surely will raise one's self-esteem.

As we have shown, people are attracted to groups for many different reasons. Despite the fact that people may have different motivations for forming groups, it is

FIGURE 8.4

Why Do People Join Groups?
People join groups for many different reasons. Four of the most important reasons are identified and explained here.

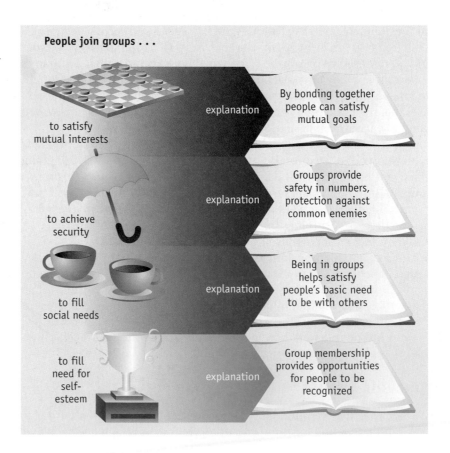

People join groups . . .

to satisfy mutual interests → explanation → By bonding together people can satisfy mutual goals

to achieve security → explanation → Groups provide safety in numbers, protection against common enemies

to fill social needs → explanation → Being in groups helps satisfy people's basic need to be with others

to fill need for self-esteem → explanation → Group membership provides opportunities for people to be recognized interesting to note that once formed, groups develop in remarkably similar ways. We will now turn our attention to this issue.

How Groups Are Formed

Social scientists have long been interested in the question of how people form groups. Although we cannot predict with perfect certainty exactly how all groups will form, two systematic models of group development appear to be most descriptive—the *five-stage model* and the *punctuated-equilibrium model*.

The five-stage model. Just as infants develop in certain ways during their first months of life, groups also show relatively stable signs of maturation and development.[4] One popular theory, the **five-stage model,** identifies five distinct stages through which groups develop.[5] As we describe these next, you may want to review our summary of the five stages shown in Figure 8.5.

five-stage model
The conceptualization claiming that groups develop in five stages—forming, storming, norming, performing, and adjourning.

1. The first stage of group development is known as *forming*. During this stage of group development, the members get acquainted with each other. They establish the ground rules by trying to find out what behaviors are acceptable with respect to both the job (how productive they are expected to be) and interpersonal relations (who's really in charge). During the forming stage, people tend to be a bit confused and uncertain about how to act in the group and how beneficial it will be to become a member of the group. Once the individuals come to think of themselves as members of a group, the forming stage is complete.

2. The second stage of group development is referred to as *storming*. As the name implies, this stage is characterized by a high degree of conflict within the group. Members often resist the control of the group's leaders and show hostility toward each other. If these conflicts are not resolved and group members withdraw, the group may disband. However, as conflicts are resolved and the group's leadership is accepted, the storming stage is complete.

3. The third stage of group development is known as *norming*. During this stage, the group becomes more cohesive, and identification as a member of the group becomes greater. Close relationships develop, shared feelings become common, and a keen interest in finding mutually agreeable solutions develops. Feelings of camaraderie and shared responsibility for the group's activities are heightened. The

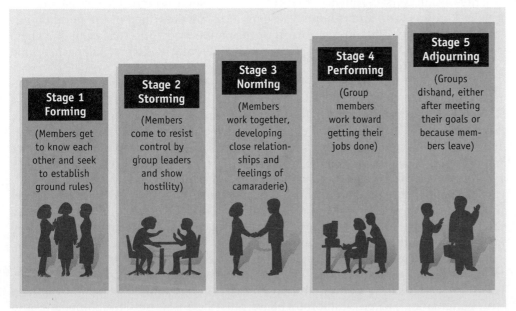

FIGURE 8.5
The Five-Stage Model of Group Development
In general, groups develop according to the five stages summarized here.
(*Source:* Based on information in Tuckman & Jensen, 1977; see Note 5.)

Stage 1 Forming
(Members get to know each other and seek to establish ground rules)

Stage 2 Storming
(Members come to resist control by group leaders and show hostility)

Stage 3 Norming
(Members work together, developing close relationships and feelings of camaraderie)

Stage 4 Performing
(Group members work toward getting their jobs done)

Stage 5 Adjourning
(Groups disband, either after meeting their goals or because members leave)

norming stage is complete when the members of the group accept a common set of expectations that constitutes an acceptable way of doing things.

4. The fourth stage is known as *performing*. During this stage, questions about group relationships and leadership have been resolved and the group is ready to work. Having fully developed, the group may now devote its energy to getting the job done—the group's good relations and acceptance of the leadership help the group perform well.

5. Recognizing that not all groups last forever, the final stage is known as *adjourning*. Groups may cease to exist because they have met their goals and are no longer needed (such as an ad hoc group created to raise money for a charity project), in which case the end is abrupt. Other groups may adjourn gradually, as the group disintegrates, either because members leave or because the norms that have developed are no longer effective for the group.

To illustrate these various stages, imagine that you have just joined several of your colleagues on your company's newly created budget committee. At first, you and your associates feel each other out: You watch to see who comes up with the best ideas, whose suggestions are most widely accepted, who seems to take charge, and the like (the forming stage). Then, as members struggle to gain influence over others, you may see a battle over control of the committee (the storming stage). Soon, this will be resolved, and an accepted leader will emerge. At this stage, the group members will become highly cooperative, working together in harmony and doing things together, such as going out to lunch as a group (the norming stage). Now it becomes possible for committee members to work together at doing their best and giving it their all (the performing stage). Then, once the budget is created and approved, the group's task is over and it is disbanded (the adjourning stage).

It is important to keep in mind that groups can be in any one stage of development at any given time. Moreover, the amount of time a group may spend in any given stage is highly variable. In fact, some groups may fail long before they have had a chance to work together. Research has revealed that the boundaries between the various stages may not be distinct and that several stages may be combined, especially as deadline pressures force groups to take action.[6] It is best, then, to think of this five-stage model as a general framework of group formation. Although many of the stages may be followed, the dynamic nature of groups makes it unlikely that they will progress through the various stages in a completely predictable order.

The punctuated-equilibrium model. Not all scientists agree that groups develop in the order identified in the five-stage model. In fact, it has been argued that, although there may not be a universal sequence of stages, there are some remarkable consistencies in the ways groups form and change. These patterns are described in the **punctuated-equilibrium model.** This approach to group formation recognizes that group members working to meet a deadline approach their task differently in the first half of their time together than in the second half.[7]

During the first half of the time, *phase 1,* groups define their task, setting a mission that is unlikely to change until the second half of the group's life. Even if group members have new ideas, these are generally not acted on. Interestingly, as soon as groups reach the midpoints of their lives (whether this is just a few hours or several months), something curious happens. Almost as if an alarm goes off, at the midpoint of their lives groups experience a sort of "midlife crisis," that is, a time when they recognize that they are going to have to change the way they operate if they are going to meet their goals. This begins *phase 2* of their existence—a time when groups drop old ways of thinking and adopt new perspectives. Groups then carry out these missions until they reach the end of phase 2, when they show bursts of activity needed to complete their work. For a summary of these processes, see Figure 8.6.

The idea is straightforward: Groups develop inertia, which keeps them going (i.e., an "equilibrium") until the halfway point, when they realize that deadlines loom large. This stimulates them to confront important issues and to initiate changes, beginning (i.e., "punctuating") a new equilibrium phase. This phase lasts until the group kicks into

punctuated-equilibrium model
The conceptualization of group development claiming that groups generally plan their activities during the first half of their time together, and then revise and implement their plans in the second half.

FIGURE 8.6
The Punctuated-Equilibrium Model
According to the *punctuated-equilibrium model,* groups go through two stages marked by the midpoint of the group's time together. The first half is a period of equilibrium, in which the group makes plans, but accomplishes little. During the second half, group members make changes that lead them to accomplish the group's task as the deadline approaches. (*Source:* Based on suggestions by Gersick, 1989; see Note 7.)

a final push just before the deadline. To illustrate the punctuated-equilibrium model, consider what might happen in a group of people working to elect a political candidate. When the group first meets in January, the members get to know each other and plan their campaign strategy. They figure out what they have to do in the 10 months that follow to get their candidate into office, and they spring into action. Then, by the following May or June, something happens: It becomes clear that there are problems, and the original plan needs to be changed. People working on the campaign begin taking critical looks at what they've been doing and take active steps to change things. This would continue through October. Then, in the weeks or days right before the November election, the group will meet for a long time and make its final push.

Although the punctuated-equilibrium model is relatively new, studies suggest that it does a good job of describing how groups develop.[8] We think it will make great sense to you if you compare it to your own experience working with others in groups (e.g., on class projects).

THE STRUCTURAL DYNAMICS OF WORK GROUPS

As noted earlier, one of the key characteristics of a group is its stable structure. When social scientists use the term **group structure,** they are referring to the interrelationships between the individuals constituting a group, the characteristics that make group functioning orderly and predictable. In this section, we will describe four different aspects of group structure: the various parts played by group members (*roles*), the rules and expectations that develop within groups (*norms*), the prestige of group membership (*status*), and the members' sense of belonging (*cohesiveness*).

group structure
The pattern of interrelationships between the individuals constituting a group; the guidelines of group behavior that make group functioning orderly and predictable.

Roles: The Hats We Wear

One of the primary structural elements of groups is members' tendencies to play one or more specific roles in group interaction. Social scientists use the term *role* in much the same way as a director of a play would refer to the character who plays a part. Indeed, the part one plays in the overall group structure is what we mean by a role. More formally, we may define a **role** as the typical behaviors that characterize a person in a social context.[9]

role
The typical behavior that characterizes a person in a specific social context.

In organizations, many roles are assigned by virtue of an individual's position within an organization. For example, a boss may be expected to give orders, and a teacher may be expected to lecture and to give exams. These are behaviors expected of the individual in that role. The person holding the role is known as the **role incumbent,** and the behaviors expected of that person are known as **role expectations.** The person holding the office of the president of the United States (the role incumbent) has certain role expectations simply because he or she currently has that post. When a new president takes office, that person assumes the same role and has the same formal powers as the previous president. This is the case although the new president may have very different ideas about key issues facing the nation.

role incumbent
A person holding a particular role.

role expectations
The behaviors expected of someone in a particular role.

role ambiguity
Confusion arising from not knowing what one is expected to do as the holder of a role.

role differentiation
The tendency for various specialized roles to emerge as groups develop.

task-oriented role
The activities of an individual in a group who, more than anyone else, helps the group reach its goal.

socioemotional role
The activities of an individual in a group who is supportive and nurturant of other group members, and who helps them feel good.

relations-oriented role
See *socioemotional role*.

self-oriented role
The activities of an individual in a group who focuses on his or her own good, often at the expense of others.

norms
Generally agreed on informal rules that guide group members' behavior.

The role incumbent's recognition of the expectations of his or her role helps avoid the social disorganization that surely would result if clear role expectations did not exist. Sometimes, however, workers may be confused about the things that are expected of them on the job, such as their level of authority or their responsibility. Such **role ambiguity,** as it is called, is typically experienced by new members of organizations who have not had much of a chance to "learn the ropes" and often results in job dissatisfaction, a lack of commitment to the organization, and an interest in leaving the job.[10]

As work groups and social groups develop, the various group members come to play different roles in the social structure—a process referred to as **role differentiation.** The emergence of different roles in groups is a naturally occurring process. Think of committees to which you have belonged. Was there someone who joked and made people feel better and another member who worked hard to get the group to focus on the issue at hand? These examples of differentiated roles are typical of role behaviors that emerge in groups. Organizations, for example, often have their "office comedian" who makes everyone laugh, or the "company gossip" who shares others' secrets, or the "grand old man" who tells newcomers the stories about the company's "good old days."

Scientists have noted that roles tend to be differentiated in some standard ways. For example, in any group there tends to be one person who, more than anyone else, helps the group reach its goal.[11] Such a person is said to play the **task-oriented role.** In addition, another group member may emerge who is quite supportive and nurturant, someone who makes everyone else feel good. Such a person is said to play a **socioemotional role** (also known as a **relations-oriented role**). Still others may be recognized for the things they do for themselves, often at the expense of the group—individuals recognized for playing a **self-oriented role.** Many specific role behaviors can fall into one or another of these categories. For a listing of some of the most common forms that these three types of roles may take, see Table 8.1.

Norms: A Group's Unspoken Rules

One feature of groups that enhances their orderly functioning is the existence of group norms. **Norms** may be defined as generally agreed upon informal rules that guide group members' behavior.[12] They represent shared ways of viewing the world. Norms differ from organizational rules in that they are not formal and written. In fact, group mem-

TABLE 8.1   SOME ROLES COMMONLY PLAYED BY GROUP MEMBERS

Organizational roles may be differentiated into task-oriented, relations-oriented (or socioemotional), and self-oriented roles—each of which has several subroles. A number of these are shown here.

TASK-ORIENTED ROLES	RELATIONS-ORIENTED ROLES	SELF-ORIENTED ROLES
Initiator-contributors *Recommend new solutions to group problems*	Harmonizers *Mediate group conflicts*	Blockers *Act stubborn and resistant to the group*
Information seekers *Attempt to obtain the necessary facts*	Compromisers *Shift own opinions to create group harmony*	Recognition seekers *Call attention to their own achievements*
Opinion givers *Share own opinions with others*	Encouragers *Praise and encourage others*	Dominators *Assert authority by manipulating the group*
Energizers *Stimulate the group into action whenever interest drops*	Expediters *Suggest ways the group can operate more smoothly*	Avoiders *Maintain distance, isolate themselves from fellow group members*

(*Source:* Based on Benne & Sheats, 1948; see Note 11.)

bers may not even be aware of the subtle group norms that exist and regulate their behavior. Yet, they have profound effects on behavior. Norms regulate the behavior of groups in important ways, such as by fostering workers' honesty and loyalty to the company, establishing appropriate ways to dress, and dictating when it is acceptable to be late for or absent from work.

If you recall the pressures placed on you by your peers as you grew up to dress or wear your hair in certain styles, you are well aware of the profound normative pressures exerted by groups. Some norms, known as **prescriptive norms,** dictate the behaviors that should be performed. Other norms, known as **proscriptive norms,** dictate specific behaviors that should be avoided (see Figure 8.7). For example, groups may develop prescriptive norms to follow their leader or to help a group member who needs assistance. They may also develop proscriptive norms to avoid absences or to refrain from telling each other's secrets to the boss.

Sometimes the pressure to conform to norms is subtle, as in the dirty looks given a manager by his peers for going to lunch with one of the assembly-line workers. At other times normative pressures may be quite severe, such as when one production worker sabotages another's work because he is performing at too high a level and making his coworkers look bad. Although our examples emphasize the underlying social dynamics responsible for how groups develop norms, this is only one reason. There are, in fact, several factors responsible for the formation of norms.[13] For a summary of these, see Table 8.2.

Status: The Prestige of Group Membership

Have you ever been attracted to a group because of the prestige accorded its members? You may have wanted to join a certain fraternity or sorority because it is highly regarded by others on campus. No doubt, members of championship-winning football teams proudly sport their Super Bowl rings to identify themselves as members of that highly regarded team. Clearly, one potential reward of group membership is enjoying the status associated with being in that group. Even within social groups, different members are accorded different levels of prestige. Fraternity and sorority officers and committee chairpersons, for example, may be recognized as more important members of their respective groups. This is the idea behind **status**—the relative social position or rank given to groups or group members by others.[14]

Within most organizations, status may be recognized as both formal and informal in nature. **Formal status** refers to attempts to differentiate between the degrees of formal authority given employees by an organization. This is typically accomplished

prescriptive norms
Expectations within groups regarding what is supposed to be done.

proscriptive norms
Expectations within groups regarding behaviors in which members are not supposed to engage.

status
The relative prestige, social position, or rank given to groups or individuals by others.

formal status
The prestige one has by virtue of his or her official position in an organization.

"Yes, Ted, on this team we take off our jackets, but we don't loosen our ties."

FIGURE 8.7
Norms Dictate What to Do and Not to Do
Norms are informal rules about behaviors that are considered acceptable and unacceptable in groups. As illustrated here, it is not unusual for norms to be communicated explicitly in an effort to get others to conform to them.
(©The New Yorker Collection 1991. William Hamilton from cartoonbank.com. All rights reserved.)

TABLE 8.2   NORMS: HOW DO THEY DEVELOP?

This table summarizes four ways in which group norms can develop.

BASIS OF NORM DEVELOPMENT	EXAMPLE
1. Precedents set over time	Seating location of each group member around a table
2. Carryovers from other situations	Professional standards of conduct
3. Explicit statements from others	Working a certain way because you are told "that's how we do it around here"
4. Critical events in group history	After the organization suffers a loss due to one person's divulging company secrets, a norm develops to maintain secrecy

(*Source:* Based on Feldman, 1984; see Note 15.)

status symbols

Objects reflecting the position of any individual within an organization's hierarchy of power.

through the use of **status symbols**—objects reflecting the position of an individual within an organization's hierarchy. Some examples of status symbols include job titles (e.g., director); perquisites, or perks (e.g., a reserved parking space); the opportunity to do desirable and highly regarded work (e.g., serving on important committees); and luxurious working conditions (e.g., a large, private office that is lavishly decorated) (see Figure 8.8).[15]

Status symbols help groups in many ways.[16] For one, such symbols remind organizational members of their relative roles, thereby reducing uncertainty and providing stability to the social order (e.g., your small desk reminds you of your lower organizational rank). In addition, they provide assurance of the various rewards available to those who perform at a superior level (e.g., "maybe one day I'll have a reserved parking spot"). They also provide a sense of identification by reminding members of the group's values (e.g., a gang's jacket may remind its wearer of his expected loyalty and boldness). It is, therefore, not surprising that organizations do much to reinforce formal status through the use of status symbols.

informal status

The prestige accorded individuals with certain characteristics that are not formally recognized by the organization.

Symbols of **informal status** within organizations are also widespread. These refer to the prestige accorded individuals with certain characteristics that are not formally recognized by the organization. For example, employees who are older and more experienced may be perceived as higher in status by their coworkers. Those who have certain special skills (such as the home-run hitters on a baseball team) also may be regarded as

FIGURE 8.8

Working Conditions: A Symbol of Organizational Status
A large, elegantly decorated office is a sure symbol of the occupant's high status within his or her organization.

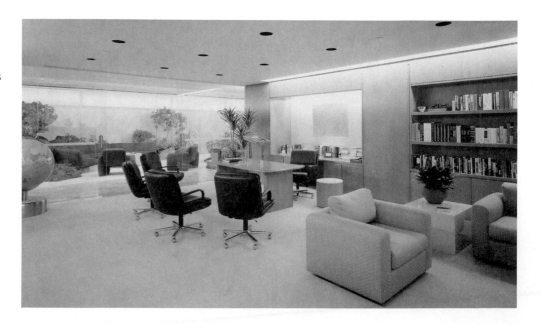

having higher status than others. In some organizations, the lower value placed on the work of women and members of minority groups by some individuals also can be considered an example of informal status in operation.[17]

One of the best-established findings in the study of group dynamics is that higher-status people tend to be more influential than lower-status people. This phenomenon may be seen in a classic study of decision making in three-man bomber crews.[18] After the crews had difficulty solving a problem, the experimenter planted clues to the solution with either a low-status group member (the tail gunner) or a high-status group member (the pilot). It was found that the solutions offered by the pilots were far more likely to be adopted than the same solutions presented by the tail gunners. Apparently, the higher status accorded the pilots (because they tended to be more experienced and hold higher military ranks) was responsible for the greater influence they wielded.

Cohesiveness: Getting the Team Spirit

One obvious determinant of any group's structure is its **cohesiveness**—the strength of group members' desires to remain part of their groups. Highly cohesive work groups are ones in which the members are attracted to one another, accept the group's goals, and help work toward meeting them. In very uncohesive groups, the members dislike each other and may even work at cross-purposes.[19] In essence, cohesiveness refers to a *we-feeling*, an *esprit de corps*, a sense of belonging to a group.

Several important factors have been shown to influence the extent to which group members tend to "stick together." One such factor involves the severity of initiation into the group. Research has shown that the greater the difficulty people overcome to become a member of a group, the more cohesive the group will be.[20] To understand this, consider how highly cohesive certain groups may be that you have worked hard to join. Was it particularly difficult to "make the cut" on your sports team? The rigorous requirements for gaining entry into elite groups, such as the most prestigious medical schools and military training schools, may well be responsible for the high degree of camaraderie found in such groups. Having "passed the test" tends to keep individuals together and separates them from those who are unwilling or unable to "pay the price" of admission.

Group cohesion also tends to be strengthened under conditions of high external threat or competition. When workers face a "common enemy," they tend to draw together (see Figure 8.9). Such cohesion not only makes workers feel safer and better protected but also aids them by encouraging them to work closely together and coordi-

cohesiveness
The strength of group members' desires to remain a part of the group.

FIGURE 8.9
Confronting Common Enemies Breeds Group Cohesiveness
Groups become highly cohesive as they work together to ward off common enemies. This applies not only to military groups, such as these American soldiers fighting in Afghanistan, but also to groups in business organizations whose members face less physical (but equally hostile) battles with their own enemies.

nate their efforts toward the common enemy. Under such conditions, petty disagreements that may have caused dissension within groups tend to be put aside so that a coordinated attack on the enemy can be mobilized.

Research also has shown that the cohesiveness of groups is established by several additional factors.[21] For one, cohesiveness generally tends to be greater the more time group members spend together. Obviously, limited interaction cannot help but interfere with opportunities to develop bonds between group members. Similarly, cohesiveness tends to be greater in smaller groups. Generally speaking, groups that are too large make it difficult for members to interact and, therefore, for cohesiveness to reach a high level. Finally, because "nothing succeeds like success," groups with a history of success tend to be highly cohesive. It is often said that "everyone loves a winner," and the success of a group tends to help unite its members as they rally around their success. For this reason, employees tend to be loyal to successful companies.

Thus far, our discussion has implied that cohesiveness is a positive thing. Indeed, it can be. For example, people are known to enjoy belonging to highly cohesive groups. Members of closely knit work groups participate more fully in their group's activities, more readily accept their group's goals, and are absent from their jobs less often than members of less cohesive groups.[22] Not surprisingly, cohesive groups tend to work together quite well, are sometimes exceptionally productive, and have low levels of voluntary turnover.[23]

However, highly cohesive groups also can be problematic. For example, if a highly cohesive group's goals are contrary to the organization's goals, that group is in a position to inflict a great deal of harm to an organization by working against its interests.[24] Highly cohesive group members who conspire to sabotage their employers are a good example. With this in mind, it's important to recognize that when it comes to performance, group cohesiveness is a double-edged sword: Its effects can be both helpful and harmful.

INDIVIDUAL PERFORMANCE IN GROUPS

Now that we have reviewed the basic nature of groups, we will turn to an aspect of group dynamics most relevant to the field of organizational behavior—the effects of groups on individual performance. Specifically, we will take a look at two different issues in this connection: how people's work performance is affected by the presence of others and how performance is affected by group size.

Social Facilitation: Working in the Presence of Others

Imagine that you have been studying drama for five years and you are now ready for your first acting audition in front of some Hollywood producers. You have been rehearsing diligently for several months, getting ready for the part. Now you are no longer alone at home with your script in front of you. Your name is announced, and silence fills the auditorium as you walk to the front of the stage. How will you perform now that you are in front of an audience? Will you freeze, forgetting the lines you studied so intensely when you practiced alone? Or will the audience spur you on to your best performance yet? In other words, what impact will the presence of the audience have on your behavior?

After studying this question for a century, using a wide variety of tasks and situations, social scientists found that the answer to this question is not straightforward.[25] Sometimes people were found to perform better in the presence of others than when alone, and sometimes they were found to perform better alone than in the presence of others. This tendency for the presence of others to enhance an individual's performance at times and to impair it at other times is known as **social facilitation.** (Although the word *facilitation* implies improvements in task performance, scientists use the term *social facilitation* to refer to both performance improvements and decrements stem-

social facilitation
The tendency for the presence of others sometimes to enhance an individual's performance and at other times to impair it.

ming from the presence of others.) What accounts for these seemingly contradictory findings?

Explaining social facilitation. Many scientists believe the matter boils down to several basic psychological processes.[26] First, social facilitation is the result of the heightened emotional arousal (e.g., feelings of tension and excitement) people experience when in the presence of others. (Wouldn't you feel more tension playing the piano in front of an audience than alone?) Second, when people are aroused, they tend to perform the most dominant response—their most likely behavior in that setting. (Returning the smile of a smiling coworker may be considered an example of a dominant act; it is a very well learned act to smile at another who smiles at you.) If someone is performing a very well learned act, the dominant response would be a correct one (such as speaking the right lines during your fiftieth performance). However, if the behavior in question is relatively novel or newly learned, the dominant response would likely be incorrect (such as speaking incorrect lines during an audition).

Together, these ideas are known as the **drive theory of social facilitation.**[27] According to this theory, the presence of others increases arousal, which increases the tendency to perform the most dominant responses. If these responses are correct, the resulting performance will be enhanced; if they are incorrect, the performance will be impaired. Based on these processes, performance may either be helped (if the task is well learned) or hindered (if the task is not well learned). (For a summary of this process, see Figure 8.10.)

Research has shown considerable support for this theory: People perform better on tasks in the presence of others if that task is very well learned, but poorer if it is not well learned. Although there are several good explanations for this effect, a key one is based on the idea of **evaluation apprehension**—the fear of being evaluated or judged by another person.[28] Indeed, people may be aroused by performing a task in the presence of others because of their concern over what those others might think of them. For example, lower-level employees may suffer evaluation apprehension when they are worried about what their supervisor thinks of their work. Similarly, in the example that opened this section of the chapter, you may face evaluation apprehension in your big acting audition. After all, how well you are received by the producers will go a long way in determining the success of your career. If you know your part well, you probably will perform better in this situation than when rehearsing alone. But, if you're new to the part and can't quite get the hang of it, fear of what important others will think of you will probably lead you to blow this big opportunity.

drive theory of social facilitation
The theory according to which the presence of others increases arousal, which increases people's tendencies to perform the dominant response. If that response is well learned, performance will improve. But, if it is novel, performance will be impaired.

evaluation apprehension
The fear of being evaluated or judged by another person.

FIGURE 8.10

Social Facilitation: A Drive Theory Approach
The *drive theory of social facilitation* states that the presence of others is arousing. This, in turn, enhances the tendency to perform the most dominant (i.e., strongest) responses. If these are correct (such as if the task is well learned), performance will be improved, but if these are incorrect (such as if the task is novel), performance will suffer.

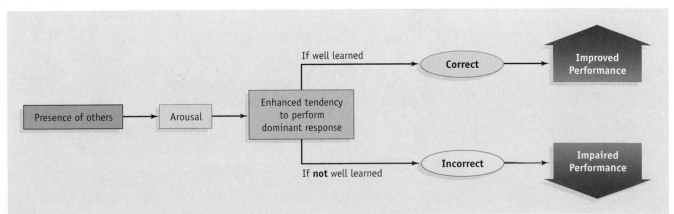

Social facilitation via an "electronic presence": Computerized performance monitoring.
If you've ever read George Orwell's classic book, *1984*, you will recall "Big Brother," the all-knowing power that monitored people's every move. As often occurs, the science fiction of one era eventually becomes scientific fact in another. And, in the case of "Big Brother," in the workplace, at least, Orwell wasn't many years off in his predictions. The use of computers to monitor work performance today is becoming increasingly common. **Computerized performance monitoring** already is used widely in the insurance, banking, communications, and transportation industries, and it promises to become even more prevalent in tomorrow's organizations.[29] In view of this, it is important to learn about the effects of monitoring on people's job performance.

One way of understanding how computerized monitoring may influence performance is by extending our thinking about social facilitation. After all, instead of having an individual who is physically present to watch, this technique is akin to doing the same thing indirectly, by computer—an "electronic presence." Imagine, for example, that you are entering data into a computer terminal. You can be monitored in a directly physical way by an individual looking over your shoulder, or indirectly, by someone checking a computerized record of the speed and accuracy of your every keystroke. If the task being performed is a complex one, social facilitation research suggests that the physical presence of an observer would lead to reduced performance. But would the same thing occur when there is only an electronic presence?

Research provides an answer. In one particular study, college students were asked to solve complex anagram puzzles (unscrambling letters to form words) by entering their responses into a computer terminal.[30] The conditions under which they performed this task were varied systematically by the researchers in several different ways. One group of participants (the "control" condition) performed the task without anyone observing them work in any form. A second group (the "person-monitored" condition) was monitored by stationing two female observers immediately behind them as they performed their task in front of the computer. Finally, a third group of subjects (the "computer-monitoring" condition) was told that their performance would be monitored by people who could see their work on another computer to which theirs was connected on a network. (To make this convincing, participants were shown the other computer equipment.) Participants performed the task for 10 minutes, after which the researchers counted the number of anagrams solved correctly by people in each condition. A summary of these findings is shown in Figure 8.11.

As these data show, people performed worse when others were physically observing them (person-monitored group) than when they performed the task alone (control group). This finding is in keeping with research and theory on social facilitation, according to which performance on complex tasks is expected to suffer when in the presence of others. Even more interesting is the finding that performance also suffered when it was monitored by computer—that is, even when participants in the study didn't have

computerized performance monitoring
The process of using computers to monitor job performance.

FIGURE 8.11
Computer Monitoring: Evidence of Its Counterproductive Effects
Participants in a recent study performed complex tasks either alone, or while being monitored by a computer or by two other people who were physically present. Consistent with other research on *social facilitation*, people performed the complex task worse in the presence of others than alone. They also performed more poorly when they were monitored by the "electronic presence" of a computer.
(*Source:* Based on data reported by Aiello & Svec, 1993; see Note 30.)

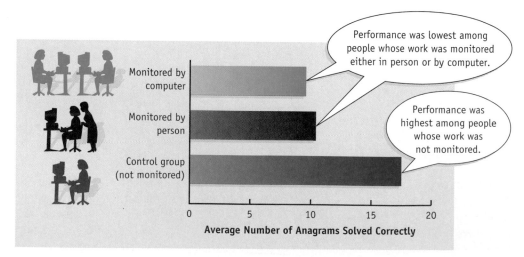

others looking over their shoulders. Apparently, performance can suffer even when the presence of another, although imperceptible, is believed to exist.

These findings support the idea that social facilitation may be due to people's concerns about being evaluated negatively by another—that is, evaluation apprehension. In the case of the task at hand, participants in the study knew that their performance could be just as easily evaluated by watching a remote computer as by watching them directly. Accordingly, opportunities for evaluation existed in both conditions, possibly accounting for the apprehension that led to the performance decrements found.

There is a very important applied implication of these results—namely, the act of monitoring job performance to keep levels high actually may backfire. That is, instead of causing people to improve their performance (for fear of being caught doing poorly), monitoring might actually interfere with performance (in part because employees believe that it is unfair for them to be monitored).[31] Because participants in the study we just described performed their tasks for only brief periods of time, we cannot tell whether people would eventually get used to the monitoring and improve their performance over time. However, until further research addresses this question, we must issue the following caution: Using computers to monitor work performance might impair the very performance that monitoring is intended to improve. "Big Brother" just might be defeating his own purposes.

Social Loafing: "Free Riding" When Working with Others

Have you ever worked with several others helping a friend move into a new apartment, each carrying and transporting part of the load from the old place to the new one? Or how about sitting around a table with others stuffing political campaign letters into envelopes and addressing them to potential donors? Although these tasks may seem quite different, they actually share an important common characteristic: Performing each requires only a single individual, but several people's work can be pooled to yield greater outcomes. Insofar as each person's contributions can be added together with another's, such tasks have been referred to as **additive tasks.**[32]

If you've ever performed additive tasks, such as the ones described here, there's a good chance that you found yourself working not quite as hard as you would have if you did them alone. Does this sound familiar to you? Indeed, a considerable amount of research has found that when several people combine their efforts on additive tasks, each individual contributes less than he or she would when performing the same task alone.[33] As suggested by the old saying "Many hands make light the work," a group of people would be expected to be more productive than any one individual. However, when several people combine their efforts on additive tasks, each individual's contribution tends to be less. Thus, five people working together raking leaves will *not* be five times more productive than a single individual working alone; there are always some who go along for a "free ride." In fact, the more individuals who are contributing to an additive task, the less each individual's contribution tends to be—a phenomenon known as **social loafing.**[34]

This effect was first noted almost 70 years ago by a German scientist who compared the amount of force exerted by different-sized groups of people pulling on a rope.[35] Specifically, he found that one person pulling on a rope alone exerted an average of 63 kilograms of force. However, in groups of three, the per-person force dropped to 53 kilograms, and in groups of eight it was reduced to only 31 kilograms per person—less than half the effort exerted by people working alone! Social loafing effects of this type have been observed in many different studies conducted in recent years.[36] The general form of the social loafing effect is portrayed in Figure 8.12.

The phenomenon of social loafing has been explained by **social impact theory.**[37] According to this theory, the impact of any social force acting on a group is divided equally among its members. The larger the size of the group, the less the impact of the force on any one member. As a result, the more people who might contribute to a group's product, the less pressure each person faces to perform well—that is, the responsibility for doing the job is diffused over more people. As a result, each group member feels less responsible for behaving appropriately, and social loafing occurs.

additive tasks
Types of group tasks in which the coordinated efforts of several people are added together to form the group's product.

social loafing
The tendency for group members to exert less individual effort on an additive task as the size of the group increases.

social impact th
The theory that
terms of the di
doing what i
a group (se
size of a
influenc
the gr

FIGURE 8.12

Social Loafing: Its General Form
According to the social loafing effect, when individuals work together on an additive task, the more people contributing to the group's task, the less effort each individual exerts.

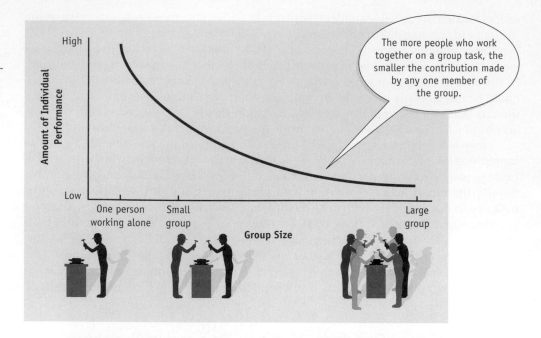

individualistic cultures

National groups whose members place a high value on individual accomplishments and personal success.

collectivistic cultures

National groups whose members place a high value on shared responsibility and the collective good of all.

Is social loafing a universal phenomenon? A simple way of understanding social loafing is that it occurs because people are more interested in themselves (getting the most for themselves while doing the least) than their fellow group members (who are forced to do their work for them). That this phenomenon occurs in the United States should not be particularly surprising in view of the tendency for American culture to be highly individualistic. In **individualistic cultures** people highly value individual accomplishments and personal success.

However, in other countries, such as Israel and the People's Republic of China, people place a high value on shared responsibility and the collective good of all. Such nations are referred to has having **collectivistic cultures.** In such cultures, people working in groups would not be expected to engage in social loafing because doing so would have them fail in their social responsibility to the group (a responsibility that does not prevail in individualistic cultures). In fact, to the extent that people in collectivistic cultures are strongly motivated to help their fellow group members, they would be expected to be *more* productive in groups than alone. That is, not only wouldn't they loaf, but they would work especially hard!

These ideas were tested in an interesting experiment.[38] In this research managers from the United States, Israel, and the People's Republic of China were each asked to complete an "in-basket" exercise. This task simulated the daily activities of managers in all three countries, such as writing memos, filling out forms, and rating job applicants. They were asked to perform this task as well as they could for a period of one hour under one of two different conditions: either *alone* or as part of a *group* of ten. Research participants who worked alone were asked to write their names on each item they completed and to turn it in. In the group condition participants were told that their group's overall performance would be assessed at the end of the performance period. Fellow group members were not physically present but were described as being highly similar to themselves with respect to their family and religious backgrounds as well as their interests. (The researchers reasoned that groups of this type would be ones whose members people would be especially reluctant to let down by loafing.) To compare the various groups, each participant's in-basket exercises were scored by converting the responses to standardized performance scores. Did social loafing occur, and, if so, in which countries? The results are summarized in Figure 8.13.

These data clearly show that social loafing occurred in the United States. That is, individual performance was significantly lower among people working in groups than those working alone. However, the opposite was found in each of the two highly collec-

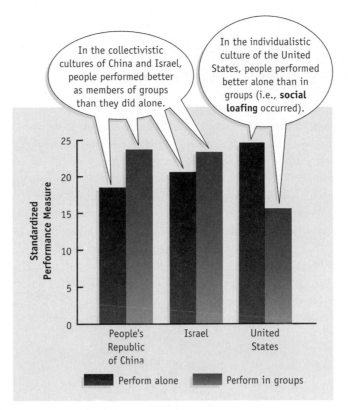

FIGURE 8.13
Social Loafing: Not Exactly a Universal Phenomenon
Researchers compared the performance of people from the United States, Israel, and the People's Republic of China who worked alone in groups on a managerial task. Although individual performance alone was lower than performance as part of a group in the United States (i.e., *social loafing* occurred), the opposite was found in China and Israel. Compared to the more *individualistic* nature of American culture, the highly *collectivistic* nature of Chinese and Israeli cultures discouraged people in these nations from letting down their fellow group members.
(*Source:* Based on data reported by Earley, 1993; see Note 33.)

tivistic cultures, the People's Republic of China and Israel. In both these countries, individuals performed at higher levels when working in groups than when working alone. In these nations, people not only failed to loaf in groups but they also worked *harder* than they did alone. Because they strongly identified with their groups and were concerned about the welfare of group members, members of collectivistic cultures placed their group's interests ahead of their own. (It is important to note that these findings only occurred when people believed that they had strong ties to the members of their groups.)

This research suggests that culture plays an important part in determining people's tendencies to engage in social loafing. Although it is tempting to think of social loafing as an inevitable aspect of human nature, it appears that the phenomenon is not as universal as you might think. Instead, loafing appears to be a manifestation of cultural values: Among cultural groups in which individualism is stressed, individual interests guide performance, but among groups in which collectivism is stressed, group interests guide performance.

Suggestions for overcoming social loafing. Obviously, the tendency for people to reduce their effort when working with others could be a serious problem in organizations. Fortunately, research has shown that there are several ways in which social loafing can be overcome.

1. *Make each performer identifiable.* Social loafing may occur when people feel they can get away with "taking it easy," namely, under conditions in which each individual's contributions cannot be determined. A variety of studies on the practice of *public posting* support this idea.[39] This research has found that when each individual's contribution to a task is displayed where it can be seen by others (e.g., weekly sales figures posted on a chart), people are less likely to slack off than when only overall group (or company-wide) performance is made available. In other words, the more one's individual contribution to a group effort is highlighted, the more pressure each person feels to make a group contribution. Thus, social loafing can be overcome if one's contributions to an additive task are identified: Potential loafers are not likely to loaf if they fear getting caught.

2. *Make work tasks more important and interesting.* Research has revealed that people are unlikely to go along for a free ride when the task they are performing is believed to be vital to the organization.[40] For example, research has found that the less meaningful salespeople believe their jobs are, the more they engage in social loafing—especially when they think their supervisors know little about how well they are working.[41] To help in this regard, corporate officials should deliberately attempt to make jobs more intrinsically interesting to employees. To the extent that jobs are interesting, people may be less likely to loaf.

3. *Reward individuals for contributing to their group's performance.* That is, encourage individuals' interest in their group's performance.[42] Doing this (e.g., giving all salespeople in a territory a bonus if they jointly exceed their sales goal) may help employees focus more on collective concerns and less on individualistic concerns, increasing their obligations to their fellow group members. This is important, of course, in that the success of an organization is more likely to be influenced by the collective efforts of groups than by the individual contributions of any one member.

4. *Use punishment threats.* To the extent that performance decrements may be controlled by threatening to punish the individuals who are slacking off, loafing may be reduced. This effect was demonstrated in a experiment involving members of high school swim teams who swam either alone or in relay races during practice sessions.[43] In some conditions, the coach threatened the team by telling them that everyone would have to swim "penalty laps" if anyone on the team failed to meet a specified difficult time for swimming 100 yards freestyle. In a control group, no punishment threats were issued. How did the punishment threats influence task performance? The researchers found that people swam faster alone than as part of relay teams when no punishment was threatened, thereby confirming the social loafing effect. However, when punishment threats were made, group performance increased, thereby eliminating the social loafing effect.

Together, these findings suggest that social loafing is a potent force—and one that can be a serious threat to organizational performance. But it can be controlled in several ways that counteract the desire to loaf, such as by making loafing socially embarasked to analyze business cases (a task with which these management students were familiar). The groups worked on four occasions scheduled one month apart. Their case analyses were then scored (using several different predetermined criteria) by experts who did not know which groups were diverse and which were homogeneous.

How did following these two different recipes for group composition influence task performance? The results showed that the answer depends on the amount of time the group spent together. At first, the homogeneous group did considerably better than the diverse group. Then, during the second session, these differences grew smaller. By the third session, the differences almost completely disappeared, and by the fourth session they did disappear (in fact, the diverse group even did slightly better than the homogeneous group). Although all groups improved their performance over time, as you would expect, the initial

advantage of homogeneous groups was only a temporary condition found in newly created groups. As group members had more experiences working with each other, the differences among them became less of a source of interference.

Because research on the effects of racial and ethnic group composition on task performance is just beginning, we do not yet know if these same results would hold for different kinds of tasks. We also don't know whether diverse groups eventually would perform even better than homogeneous ones. In fact, on tasks in which differing perspectives might help a group do its job, diverse groups may be expected to have an edge over homogeneous ones. Although several key questions about the effects of diversity on group performance remain unanswered, the importance of this factor as a variable in group performance is clearly established.

rassing or harmful to other individual interests. (As we have been describing, social loafing is based on the size of the group. However, how effectively groups perform depends not only on the number of members present but also who they are. For a look at the impact of the racial diversity of groups on task performance, see the OB in a Diverse World section above.)

TEAMS: SPECIAL KINDS OF GROUPS

If you think about some of the groups we've described thus far in this chapter, such as the ones in use at Consolidated Diesel (described in our Preview Case on page 271) and the hypothetical budget committee (described in conjunction with the five-stage model on page 277), you'll quickly recognize that they are somehow different. Although each is composed of several individuals working together toward common goals, the connections between the employees at Consolidated Diesel appear to be much deeper in scope. Although the budget committee members may be interested in what they're doing, the group members at Consolidated Diesel seem more highly committed to their work and are more highly involved in the way their jobs are done. This is not to say that there is necessarily anything wrong with the corporate budget committee; in fact, it would appear to be a rather typical group. The groups at Consolidated Diesel, however, are examples of special kinds of groups known as *teams*.

Defining Teams and Distinguishing Teams from Groups

A **team** may be defined as a group whose members have complementary skills and are committed to a common purpose or set of performance goals for which they hold themselves mutually accountable.[45] At this point, it probably is not entirely clear to you exactly how a team is different from an ordinary group. This confusion probably stems in part from the fact that people often refer to their groups as teams, although they are

team
A group whose members have complementary skills and are committed to a common purpose or set of performance goals for which they hold themselves mutually accountable.

really not teams.[46] Yet, there are several important distinctions between them (see Figure 8.14).

- In groups, performance typically depends on the work of individual members. The performance of a team, however, depends on both individual contributions and *collective work products*—the joint outcome of team members working in concert.

- Typically, members of groups pool their resources to attain a goal, although it is individual performance that is taken into consideration when it comes to issuing rewards. Members of groups usually do not take responsibility for any results other than their own. By contrast, teams focus on both individual and *mutual accountability*—that is, they work together to produce an outcome (e.g., a product, service, or decision) that represents their joint contributions, and each team member shares responsibility for that outcome. The key difference is this: In groups, the supervisor holds individual members accountable for their work, whereas in teams, members hold themselves accountable.

- Whereas group members may share a common interest in attaining a goal, team members also share a *common commitment to purpose.* Moreover, these purposes typically are concerned with winning in some way, such as being first or best at something. For example, a work team in a manufacturing plant of a financially troubled company may be highly committed to making the company the top one in its industry. Another team, one in a public high school, may be committed to preparing all its graduates for the challenges of the world better than any other school in the district. Team members focusing jointly on such lofty purposes, in conjunction with specific performance goals, become heavily invested in its activities. In fact, teams are said to establish "ownership" of their purposes and usually spend a great deal of time establishing their purpose. Like groups, teams use goals to monitor their progress. Teams, however, also have a broader purpose that supplies a source of meaning and emotional energy to the activities performed.

- Teams differ from groups with respect to the nature of their connections to management. Work groups are typically required to be responsive to demands regularly placed on them by management. By contrast, once management establishes the mission for a team and sets the challenge for it to achieve, it typically gives the team enough flexibility to do its job without any further interference. In other words, teams are to varying degrees *self-managing*—that is, they are to some extent free to set their own goals, timing, and the approach that they wish to take, usually without management interference. Thus, many teams are described as being *autonomous* or *semiautonomous* in nature. This is not to say that teams are completely independent of corporate management and supervision. They still must be responsive to

FIGURE 8.14

Groups vs. Teams: A Comparison
Groups may be distinguished from teams in terms of the various characteristics summarized here.

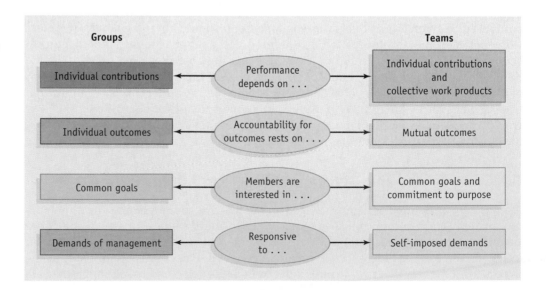

demands from higher levels (often higher-level teams, known as *top-management teams*).

Teams are getting so much attention in the workplace these days that you'd almost think they are the latest management fad. But, they are not. In fact, teams have been around for several decades—and they are here to stay. This does not mean that the nature of teams hasn't changed considerably over the years. Indeed, what constituted teams a quarter century ago is very different from teams today. During the 1980s, most so-called teams were merely work groups that made an effort to have high levels of camaraderie. Although they were concerned about enhancing good feelings, there was still an individual leader in place and individual accomplishments were valued. As summarized in Figure 8.15, things are different today. Contemporary teams are a special way of configuring work groups so as to enhance productivity. Camaraderie is still important, of course, but today the emphasis is on team performance.

Types of Teams

In view of their widespread popularity, it should not be surprising to learn that there are many different kinds of teams. To help make sense out of these, scientists have categorized teams into several different commonly found types that vary along five major dimensions (see Figure 8.16 on page 295).[50]

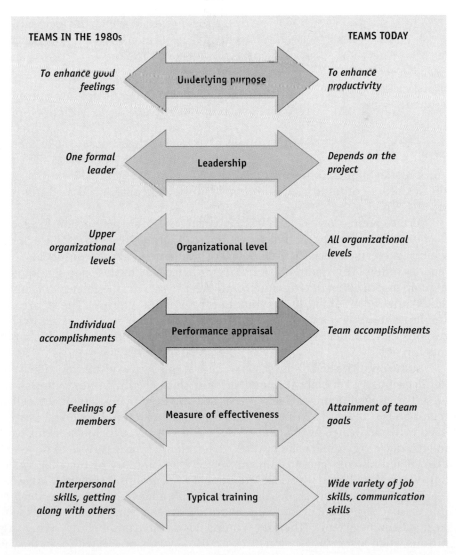

FIGURE 8.15

Work Teams: Then and Now
Although work teams are not new, their basic orientation has changed over the years. As shown here, the primary emphasis on promoting good feelings that prevailed in teams of the 1980s is supplemented today by an emphasis on achieving high levels of performance.

LEARNING FROM HIGH-PERFORMANCE TEAMS

Clearly, teams are very special entities. However, some teams go so far beyond the ordinary characteristics of teams that they are known as **high-performance teams.** These are teams whose members are deeply committed to one another's personal growth and success.[47] Consolidated Diesel may be considered an example. Such teams are referred to as high-performance teams because they perform at much higher levels than ordinary teams (whose members lack this additional commitment to others' growth and success).[48]

Members of the best performing teams show exceptionally high levels of mutual care, trust, and respect for each other. How do they get that way? Although creating high performance teams can be very challenging, research suggests that there are several characteristics that must be emulated for high performance teams to exist.[49] These are as follows.

1. *Empower people to make decisions.* In the best-performing work teams, people are free to make their own decisions without checking with others.
2. *Share responsibility.* It's not only an individual manager who is responsible for what happens but also everyone on the team shares the responsibility.
3. *Have a common sense of purpose.* Everyone on the team must be pulling in the same direction; all members agree on what they are trying to accomplish.
4. *Focus on the task at hand.* Successful teams care about results and members coordinate their individual talents to achieve them.

Purpose or mission. The first dimension has to do with a team's major *purpose or mission.* In this regard, some teams—known as **work teams**—are primarily concerned with the work done by the organization, such as developing and manufacturing new products, providing services for customers, and so on. Their principle focus is on using the organization's resources to effectively create its results (be they goods or services). (The teams at Consolidated Diesel, described in our Preview Case, are of this type.) Other teams—known as **improvement teams**—are primarily oriented toward the mission of increasing the effectiveness of the processes that are used by the organization. For example, Texas Instruments has relied on teams to help improve the quality of operations at its plant in Malaysia.[51]

Time. A second dimension has to do with *time.* Specifically, some teams are only *temporary* and are established for a specific project with a finite life. For example, a team set up to develop a new product would be considered temporary. As soon as its job is done, it disbands. However, other kinds of teams are *permanent* and stay intact as long as the organization is operating. For example, teams focusing on providing effective customer service tend to be permanent parts of many organizations.

Degree of autonomy. A third distinction has to do with the degree to which teams operate autonomously.[52] This reflects the extent to which employees are responsible for making their own decisions (as opposed to having their bosses make them) and the degree to which they (as opposed to their bosses) are accountable for their own work outcomes. As shown in Figure 8.17, various points along the resulting continuum of autonomy can be conceptualized as different types of groups.

At the extreme low end of the scale (where bosses are responsible for decisions and accountable for work outcomes), we find standard *work groups.* These are groups in which leaders make decisions on behalf of group members, whose job it is to follow the leader's orders. This traditional kind of group has become less popular in recent years, as more organizations have granted employees higher degrees of responsibility for decisions and accountability for outcomes to work groups. These are known as **semiautonomous work groups**—work groups in which employees get to share in the responsibility for decisions with their bosses and are jointly accountable for their work outcomes.

At the opposite end of the scale, we find employees who are free to make their own key decisions and who are accountable for them. Such groups are commonly referred to as **self-managed teams** (also known as **self-directed teams**). Typically, self-managed teams consist of small numbers of employees, often around 10, who take on duties that used to be performed by their supervisors. This is likely to include making work assignments, deciding on the pace of work, determining how quality is to be assessed, and even deciding who gets to join the team.[53] A summary of the major distinctions between self-managed teams and traditional work groups is shown in Table 8.3.[54]

Self-managed work teams are growing in popularity. In fact, it has been estimated that close to 50 percent of companies have at least one team in place that is self-directed to at least some extent.[55] The list of companies using teams includes many large corporations, such as Xerox, Hewlett-Packard, Honeywell, and PepsiCo. In fact, Procter &

high-performance teams
Teams whose members are deeply committed to one another's personal growth and success.

work teams
Teams whose members are concerned primarily with using the organization's resources to effectively create its results.

improvement teams
Teams whose members are oriented primarily toward the mission of increasing the effectiveness of the processes used by the organization.

semiautonomous work groups
Work groups in which employees and their bosses get to share in the responsibility for decisions with and are jointly accountable for their work outcomes.

self-managed teams
Teams whose members are permitted to make key decisions about how their work is done.

self-directed teams
See *self-managed teams.*

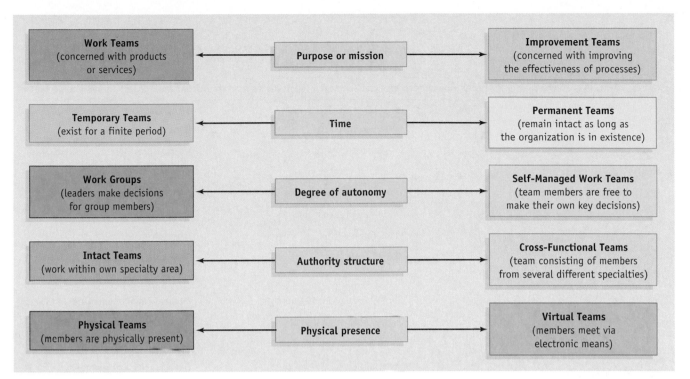

FIGURE 8.16

Types of Teams

The teams found in organizations may be distinguished from each other with respect to the five major dimensions identified here

(*Source:* Based on suggestions by Mohrman, 1993; see Note 50.)

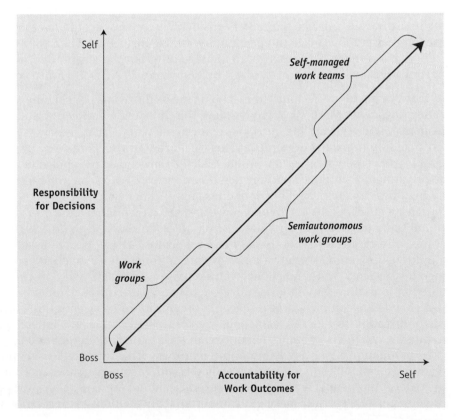

FIGURE 8.17

A Continuum of Autonomy

In *work groups,* bosses have responsibility over decisions and are accountable for work outcomes. The workers themselves have very little autonomy. By contrast, in *self-managed work teams,* the workers themselves have responsibility over decisions and are accountable for work outcomes. They are highly autonomous. Semiautonomous work groups are positioned between these two extremes.

TABLE 8.3 SELF-MANAGED TEAMS VS. TRADITIONAL WORK GROUPS: A COMPARISON

As summarized here, self-managed teams differ from traditional work groups in many important ways.

SELF-MANAGED TEAMS	TRADITIONAL WORK GROUPS
Customer driven	Management driven
Multiskilled workforce	Workforce of isolated specialists
Few job descriptions	Many job descriptions
Information shared widely	Information limited
Few levels of management	Many levels of management
Whole-business focus	Function/department focus
Shared goals	Segregated goals
Seemingly chaotic	Seemingly organized
Purpose achievement emphasis	Problem-solving emphasis
High worker commitment	High management commitment
Continuous improvements	Incremental improvements
Self-controlled	Management controlled
Values/principle based	Policy/procedure based

(*Source:* From K. Fisher, *Leading Self-Directed Work Teams,* © 1993. New York: McGraw-Hill. Reprinted with permission of the McGraw-Hill Companies.)

Gamble, Cummins Engine, and General Motors have used self-managed work teams for over 30 years.[56] (For a close-up look at another company's particularly successful self-directed work teams, see the Best Practices section on page 298.) All self-managed work teams are not alike. In fact, they differ considerably with respect to what exact aspects of the job they get to manage (for a summary, see Figure 8.18).[57] When you consider that different self-managed teams get to manage different aspects of their operations, it becomes clear why we depict the degree of autonomy in Figure 8.17 on a continuum.

Authority structure. The fourth dimension reflects the team's connection to the organization's overall *authority structure*—that is, the connection between various formal job responsibilities. In some organizations teams remain *intact* with respect to their organizational functions. For example, at Ralston-Purina projects are structured such that people work together on certain products all the time and do not apply their specialty to a wide range of products. Within such organizations, teams can operate without the ambiguities created by straying from one's area of expertise.

However, with growing frequency, we are seeing teams that cross over various functional units (e.g., marketing, finance, human resources, and so on). Such teams are commonly referred to as **cross-functional teams.** These are teams composed of employees at identical organizational levels, but from different specialty areas, to work together on a task. Cross-functional teams represent an effective way of bringing people together from throughout the organization to cooperate with each other on the diverse tasks needed to complete large projects. In organizations using cross-functional teams, the boundaries between all teams must be considered permeable. Indeed, people are frequently members of more than one team—a situation often required for organizations to function effectively. For example, members of an organization's manufacturing team must carefully coordinate their activities with members of its marketing team. To the extent that people are involved in several different kinds of teams, they may gain broader perspectives and make more important contributions to their various teams.

cross-functional teams
Teams represented by people from different specialty areas within organizations.

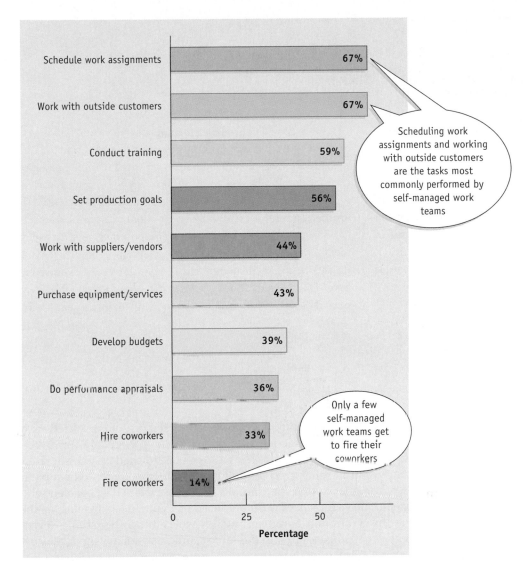

FIGURE 8.18
Self-Managed Work Teams: What Do They Manage?
As shown here, all self-managed work teams are not alike. Whereas the vast majority are able to schedule their own work assignments and to work with outside customers, far fewer are able to fire coworkers.
(*Source*: Training, 1996; see Note 57.)

For over a decade, many automobile manufacturers—including the major American and Japanese companies—have relied on cross-functional teams to create and manufacture new models. As a case in point, the successful Neon was completely created by cross-functional teams of experts from throughout Chrysler (now, Daimler–Chrysler). Similarly, in the aircraft industry, Boeing created cross-functional teams that designed and manufactured its latest aircraft, the 777. In both cases, the use of teams has been credited with both the record speed with which the products came to market and their exceptional quality. As you might imagine, cross-functional teams are difficult to manage. It takes time for specialists in different areas to learn to communicate with each other and to coordinate their efforts. It also takes time to develop the mutual trust and acceptance that are required for people to work closely with each other. However, in view of the great successes of cross-functional teams, the effort required to make them work out appears to be worthwhile. (For another example, see Figure 8.19.)

Physical presence. The teams we have been describing thus far may be considered *physical teams* insofar as they involve people who physically meet to work together. Although teams have operated this way for many years and will continue to do so, technology has made it possible for teams to exist without ever having their members physically meet. Teams of this sort are known as **virtual teams**—teams that operate across space, time, and organizational boundaries, communicating with each other only through electronic technology.[61]

virtual teams

Teams that operate across space, time, and organizational boundaries, communicating with each other only through electronic technology.

BEST PRACTICES
SEI INVESTMENTS: WHERE TOTAL TEAMWORK RULES

SEI Investments in Oaks, Pennsylvania, is a leading global provider of asset management and investment technology solutions. The company processes over $1.5 trillion of investment transactions daily, administering $257 billion in assets, and managing $77 billion in assets for wealthy investors in 11 countries.[58] Despite what you might think about the starched-collar formality normally found in the world of high finance, SEI does not fit this stereotype. In fact, it doesn't even come close. The people who work at SEI don't wear suits and they don't have secretaries. In fact, they don't even have offices.

What they do have is self-managed work teams—about 140 of them. And teams are the only unit of operation found at SEI.[59] If you're looking for some hierarchy reflected in an organization chart, forget it. There is none. All the work to be done is divided up among various teams ranging in size from 2 to 30. Some teams are permanent, serving important clients or major markets. Others, however, are temporary—composed of people coming together as needed to do a job or to solve a problem. Then, when finished, the team disbands. According to Al West, SEI's chairman and CEO (titles he holds for legal reasons), "People figure out what they're good at, and that shapes what their roles are. There's

Sometimes virtual teams form quite unintentionally, such as when valued team members begin telecommuting (the practice of working from home but communicating via e-mail, which we described in Chapter 1). They also may be formed very deliberately, such as when it is important to bring together on a project the most talented people in the world.[62] Sun Microsystems did this, for example, when it developed a new electronic customer order system. The virtual team was composed of 15 engineers from three different companies in three different countries.[63] They worked together over a seven-month period without ever being together in the same room. Instead, intranets, teleconferencing, conference calls, and e-mails were used to bring the members together.

Today, virtual teams are possible because technology allows them to exist. To the extent that computer-based technology makes possible communication over long dis-

FIGURE 8.19

An Amazing Exhibition from a Cross-Functional Team
The Journey Zone, a multimedia exhibition inside Britain's Millennium Dome, the world's largest domed building, was designed by a 350-person cross-functional team consisting of graphic artists, architects, historians, and computer engineers working for Imagination, Ltd. According to the company's director of marketing and strategic planning Ralph Ardill, "When you sit in on our creative meetings, you don't know the writer from the multimedia person from the architect. Our approach involves relationships, camaraderie, and working things through." Working in teams, he admits can be more challenging than hiring a bunch of outside experts, "But when it clicks," he adds, "the result is a seamless experience."

not one leader. Different people lead during different parts of the process."

To keep things fluid, there are no walls in SEI's facility. Desks are on wheels, allowing them to be easily repositioned as needed to serve team members. In fact, access to electricity, phone lines, and Internet access is through colorful cables that dangle from the ceiling so that physical barriers cannot keep team members from accessing the resources needed to get down to work. In keeping with this ready physical access to others is an absence of power differences that separate people in traditional organizations. At SEI, if you want something done, you have to persuade someone to join your team. And, if you have a good project idea and can sell others on it, they flock to your team. Have a poor idea and it probably will die off from lack of support. For those who thrive on the traditional structure of the

investment world, SEI is no place to work. Not surprisingly, the company has to search very carefully to find new recruits who are receptive to its highly fluid culture. Without a bureaucracy to provide resources and a hierarchy to issue commands, life at SEI isn't for everybody.

However, the numbers suggest that what SEI is doing is working just fine. In fact, its 2002 revenues, some $159 million, held steady despite declines in the stock market. CEO Al West revels in not only this shining economic picture but also in the way people work at SEI. Compared to when the company operated more like a traditional investment firm, in the 1980s, he describes his current job as being "a lot more fun." This is reflected in the fact that in 2001 and 2002, SEI was named among the "100 Best Companies to Work For" by *Fortune* magazine.[60]

---

tances, the fact that the team members are far away from each other becomes less important. This is known as the **law of telecosm**—the idea that as computer networks expand, distances become irrelevant.[64] In today's global economy, it is safe to say that virtual teams are not only possible, but they also are a clear necessity.

law of telecosm
The idea that as computer networks expand, distances become irrelevant.

Creating Teams: A Four-Stage Process

As you might imagine, assembling a team is no easy task. Doing so requires not only having the right combination of skilled people but also having individuals who are willing to work together with others as a team. Designing a work team is a project that, when done effectively, involves four distinct stages.[65] Making an effort to carefully follow these steps is a useful way of giving groups a head start on the road to success.

Stage 1: Prework. Before teams are created, a decision has to be made about whether or not a team should be formed—a stage known as *prework*. One of the most important objectives of this phase is to determine whether a team should be created. A manager may decide to have several individuals working alone answer to him, or a team may be created if it is believed that it may develop the most creative and insightful ways to get things done. In considering this, it is important to note exactly what work needs to be done. The team's objectives must be established, and an inventory of the skills needed to do the job should be made. In addition, decisions should be made in advance about what authority the team should have. It may just be advisory to the manager, or it may be given full responsibility and authority for executing its task (i.e., self-regulating).

Stage 2: Creating performance conditions. Building on the prework, organizational officials must ensure that the team has the proper resources needed to carry out its work. This involves both material resources (e.g., tools, equipment, and money), human resources (e.g., the appropriate blend of skilled professionals), and support from the organization (e.g., willingness to let the team do its own work as it sees fit). Unless managers help create the proper conditions for team success, they are contributing to its failure.

Stage 3: Forming and building the team. Three things may be done to help a team get off to a good start. First, managers should form boundaries—clearly establish who is and who is not a member of the team. Some teams fail simply because membership in it is left unclear. Reducing such ambiguity can help avoid confusion and frustration. Second, members must accept the team's overall mission and purpose. Unless they do, failure is inevitable. Third, organizational officials should clarify the team's mission and responsibilities—make perfectly clear exactly what it is expected to do (but not necessarily *how* to do it). Will team members be responsible for monitoring and planning their own work? If so, such expectations should be spelled out explicitly.

Stage 4: Providing ongoing assistance. Finally, once a team is functioning, supervisors may be needed to help the team to eliminate problems and perform even better. For example, disruptive team members may be either counseled or replaced. Similarly, material resources may have to be replenished or upgraded. Although it may be unwise for a manager to intervene in the successful affairs of a team that has taken on its own life, it also may be unwise to neglect opportunities to help a team do even better.

As you ponder these suggestions, you will doubtlessly recognize the considerable managerial skill and hard work required to create and manage teams effectively. However, as managers learn these skills, and as individuals gain successful experiences as members of effective work teams, the deliberate steps outlined earlier may become second nature to all concerned. In the words of one expert, "When that stage is reached, the considerable investment required to learn how to use work teams well can pay substantial dividends—in work effectiveness and in the quality of the experience of both managers and [team] members."[66]

EFFECTIVE TEAM PERFORMANCE

In recent years, the popular press has been filled with impressive claims about the success of teams in improving quality, customer service, productivity, and the bottom line.[67] For a sampling of the findings cited, see Table 8.4.[68]

Clearly, we are led to believe that teams in general can produce very impressive results. However, it is important to consider whether or not such claims are valid. In this section we will examine evidence bearing on this question. Then we will focus on some of the obstacles to team success and some of the things that can be done to help promote highly successful teams.

How Successful Are Teams? A Look at the Evidence

Now that you understand the basic nature of teams, you are prepared to consider a key question: How successful are teams in organizations? The most direct way to learn about companies' experiences with work teams is to survey the officials of organizations that use them. One large-scale study did precisely this.[69] The sample consisted of several hundred of the 1,000 largest companies in the United States. About 47 percent used some work teams, although these were typically in place in only a few selected sites as opposed to the entire organization. Where they were used, however, they were generally highly regarded. Moreover, teams were viewed as becoming increasingly popular over time.

Case studies. These optimistic results are further supported by in-depth case studies of numerous teams in many different organizations.[70] Research of this type, although difficult to quantify and to compare across companies, provides some interesting insight into what makes teams successful and why.

Consider, for example, the work teams used in General Motors' battery plant in Fitzgerald, Georgia. The 320 employees at this facility operate in various teams, including managers working together in *support teams*, middle-level employees (such as foremen and technicians) working in *coordination teams*, and *employee teams*, natural work units of 3 to 19 members performing specific tasks. Although the teams work closely together, coordinating their activities, they function almost as separate businesses. Because employees must perform many different tasks in their team, they are not paid

TABLE 8.4 A SUMMARY OF TEAM SUCCESS STORIES

Here are just a few of the organizational successes touted in support of teams.

ORGANIZATION	RESULTS
P&G manufacturing	30–50% lower manufacturing cost.
Federal Express	Cut service glitches (incorrect bills and lost packages) by 13% in one year.
Shenandoah Life Insurance	Case handling time went from 27 to 2 days. Service complaints "practically eliminated."
Sherwin-Williams Richmond	Costs 45% lower. Returned goods down 75%.
Tektronix Portables	Moved from least profitable to most profitable division within two years.
Rohm and Haas Knoxville	Productivity up 60%.
Tavistock coal mine	Output 25% higher with lower costs than on a comparison face. Accidents, sickness, and absenteeism cut 50%.
Westinghouse Airdrie	Reduced cycle time from 17 weeks to 1 week.
AT&T Credit Corp.	Teams process 800 lease applications/day vs. 400/day under old system. Growing at 40–50% compound annual rate.
General Electrical Salisbury	Productivity improved 250%.
Aid Association for Lutherans (AAL)	Raised productivity by 20% and cut case processing time by 75%.
Cummins Engine Jamestown	Met $8,000 price of Japanese competitor for an engine expected to sell for $12,000.
Xerox	Teams at least 30% more productive than conventional operations.
Best Foods Little Rock	Highest-quality products at lowest costs of any Best Foods plant.
Volvo Kalmar	Production costs 25% less than Volvo's conventional plants.
Ford Hermosillo	In first year of operation, lower defect rate than in most Japanese automakers.
Weyerhauser Manitowoc	Output increased 33%. Profits doubled.
Northern Telecom Harrisburg	Profits doubled.
General Mills	Productivity 40% higher than traditional factories.
Honeywell Chandler	Output increased 280%. Quality stepped up from 82% to 99.5%.
American Transtech	Reduced costs and processing time by 50%.

(*Source:* From K. Fisher, *Leading Self-Directed Work Teams,* © 1993. New York: McGraw-Hill. Reprinted with permission of the McGraw-Hill Companies.)

based on their positions, but for their knowledge and competence. In fact, the highest-paid employees are individuals who have demonstrated their competence (usually by highly demanding tests) on all the jobs performed in at least two different teams. This is GM's way of rewarding people for broadening their perspectives, appreciating "the other guy's problems." By many measures, the Fitzgerald plant has been very effective. Its production costs are lower than comparable units in traditionally run plants. Employee satisfaction surveys also reveal that job satisfaction at this plant is among the highest found at any General Motors facility.

Teams also have been successful in service businesses. For example, consider IDS, the financial services subsidiary of American Express. In response to rapid growth, IDS officials realized that their operations were becoming highly inefficient, leading them to create several teams to work on reorganizing the company's operations. Like many companies, the move to teams wasn't well accepted by all employees. Particularly resistant were individuals who, before teams, had high-status jobs with high pay to match. Naturally, they resented becoming co-equals with others when teams were formed. Still, these employees—and all others, for that matter—soon benefited from the company's improved operations. Accuracy in the processing of paperwork (e.g., orders to buy or to sell stock) rose from 70 percent before teams were created to over 99 percent afterward. With the help of employee teams, IDS's operations became so highly efficient that response time improved by 96 percent, from several minutes to only a few seconds. These cases are two examples of very different companies that used teams in different ways but with something in common—high levels of success (although not without some difficulties). And there are many more.[71]

Empirical studies. Although case studies report successful experiences with teams, they are not entirely objective. After all, companies may be unwilling to broadcast their failures to the world. This is not to say that case studies cannot be trusted. Indeed, when the information is gathered by outside researchers (such as those on which we have reported here), the stories they tell about how teams are used, and the results of using them, can be quite revealing.[72] Still, there is a need for completely objective, empirical studies of team effectiveness.

Research objectively assessing the effectiveness of work teams has been performed in recent years. In one such investigation comparisons were made between various aspects of work performance and attitudes of two groups of employees at a railroad car repair facility in Australia: those who were assembled into teams who could freely decide how to do their jobs, and those whose work was structured in the more traditional, nonautonomous fashion.[73] After the work teams had been in place for several months, it was found that they had significantly fewer accidents as well as lower rates of absenteeism and turnover.

Not all empirical studies, however, paint such an optimistic picture of the benefits of work teams. For example, in one study examining work teams in an English manufacturing plant it was found that employees were more satisfied with their jobs in teams than those who worked in conventional arrangements (in which individuals took orders from a supervisor) but they were individually no more productive.[74] However, because the use of teams made it possible for the organization to eliminate several supervisory positions, the company became more profitable.

What's the conclusion? Are teams effective? Taken together, research suggests that teams are well received. Most people enjoy working in teams, at least after they have adjusted to them (which can take some work). Certainly, teams help enhance commitment among employees, and as we described in Chapter 5, there are benefits to be derived from this (e.g., reduced absenteeism and turnover). From an organizational perspective, teams appear to be an effective way of eliminating layers of management, thereby allowing more to be done by fewer people, which also can be a valuable money-saving contribution. All of these benefits are tangible. However, it is important to keep in mind that teams are not always responsible for making individuals and organizations more productive. Cases of companies becoming wildly successful after adopting teams, although compelling, cannot always be generalized to all teams in all situations.

Potential Obstacles to Success: Why Some Teams Fail

Although we have reported many success stories about teams, we also have hinted at several possible problems and difficulties in implementing them. After all, working in a team demands a great deal, and not everyone may be ready for them. Fortunately, we can learn from these experiences. Analyses of failed attempts at introducing teams into the workplace suggest several obstacles to team success—pitfalls that can be avoided if you know about them.[75]

First, some teams fail because their members are *unwilling to cooperate with each other*. This is what happened a few years ago at Dow Chemical Company's plastics group in Midland, Michigan, where a team was put into place to create a new plastic resin.[76]

Some members (those in the research field) wanted to spend several months developing and testing new options, whereas others (those on the manufacturing end) wanted to slightly alter existing products and start up production right away. Neither side budged, and the project eventually stalled. By contrast, when team members share a common vision and are committed to attaining it, they are generally very cooperative with each other, leading to success.

A second reason why some teams are not effective is that they *fail to receive support from management.* Consider, for example, the experience at the Lenexa, Kansas, plant of the Puritan-Bennett Corporation, a manufacturer of respiratory equipment.[77] After seven years of working to develop improved software for its respirators, product development teams have not gotten the job done, despite the fact that the industry average for such tasks is only three years. According to Roger J. Dolida, the company's director of research and development, the problem is that management never made the project a priority and refused to free up another key person needed to do the job. As he put it, "If top management doesn't buy into the idea . . . teams can go nowhere."[78]

A third obstacle to group success, and a relatively common one, is that *some managers are unwilling to relinquish control.* Good supervisors work their way up from the plant floor by giving orders and having them followed. However, team leaders have to build consensus and must allow team members to make decisions together. As you might expect, letting go of control isn't always easy for some to do. This problem emerged at Bausch & Lomb's sunglasses plant in Rochester, New York.[79] In 1989 some 1,400 employees were put into 38 teams. By 1992 about half the supervisors had not adjusted to the change, despite receiving thorough training in how to work as part of a team. They argued bitterly with team members whenever their ideas were not accepted by the team, and eventually they were reassigned. An even tougher approach was taken at the Shelby Die Casting Company, a metal-casting firm in Shelby, Mississippi.[80] When its former supervisors refused to cooperate as co-equals in their teams, the company eliminated their jobs and let the workers run their own teams. The result: The company saved $250,000 in annual wages, productivity jumped 50 percent, and company profits almost doubled. The message sent by both companies is clear: Those who cannot adjust to teamwork are unwelcome.

Fourth, teams might fail not only because their members do not cooperate with each other but also because they *fail to cooperate with other teams.* This problem occurred in General Electric's medical systems division when it assigned two teams of engineers, one in Waukesha, Wisconsin, and another in Hino, Japan, the task of creating software for two new ultrasound devices.[81] Shortly, teams pushed features that made their products popular only in their own countries and duplicated each other's efforts. When teams met, language and cultural barriers separated them, further distancing the teams from each other. Without close cooperation between teams (as well as within them!), organizations are not likely to reap the benefits they hoped for when creating teams in the first place.[82]

HOW TO DEVELOP SUCCESSFUL TEAMS

Making teams work effectively is no easy task. Success is not automatic. Rather, teams need to be carefully nurtured and maintained for them to accomplish their missions.[83] As one expert expressed it, "Teams are the Ferraris of work design. They're high performance but high maintenance and expensive."[84] What, then, could be done to help make teams as effective as possible? Based on analyses of successful teams, several keys to success may be identified.[85]

Provide Training in Team Skills

To be effective, team members must have the right blend of skills needed for the team to contribute to the group's mission. Rather than simply putting teams together and hoping they will work, many companies are taking proactive steps to ensure that team members will get along and perform as they should. Formal efforts directed toward making teams effective are referred to as **team building.** Team building is usually used when established teams are showing signs of trouble, such as when members lose sight of their objectives and when turnover is high. Workers having high degrees of freedom and anonymity require a depth of skills and knowledge that surpasses that of people performing narrower, traditional jobs. For this reason, successful teams are those in which investments are made in developing the skills of team members and leaders. In the words of one expert, "Good team members are trained, not born."[86]

Illustrating this maxim is Development Dimensions International, a printing and distribution facility for a human resource company, located in Pittsburgh, Pennsylvania. This small company has each of its 70 employees spend some 200 hours in training (in such areas as interaction skills, customer service skills, and various technical areas) during their first year—even more for new leaders. Then, after this initial period, all employees receive a variety of training on an ongoing basis.

Key areas of team training. Two areas of emphasis are essential to the success of any team training effort—training in being a team member and training in self-management.

- *Being a team member.* Linda Godwin, a mission specialist at NASA's Johnson Space Center in Houston, likens team success to the kind of interpersonal harmony that must exist within space shuttle crews. "We have to be willing to compromise and to make decisions that benefit everyone as a whole," says Godwin, a veteran of two successful shuttle missions.[87] In this regard, there are several key interpersonal skills in which training is most useful, and these are summarized in Table 8.5
- *Self-management.* For teams to operate effectively, members must be able to manage themselves. However, most employees are used to being told what to do and don't know how to manage their own behavior. Specifically, this involves the various skills summarized in Figure 8.20.[88]

Team-training exercises. Typically, team building involves having team members participate in several different exercises designed to help employees learn how to function effectively as team members. Among the most widely used are the following.[89]

- *Role-definition exercises.* Are team members doing what others expect them to be doing? Teams whose members answer "no" are destined for trouble. To avoid such problems, some team-building exercises ask members to describe their own roles

TABLE 8.5   INTERPERSONAL SKILLS REQUIRED BY TEAM MEMBERS

Experts have advocated that team members be trained in the various interpersonal skills summarized here (many of which are described elsewhere in this book).

SKILL	DESCRIPTION
Advocating	Ways of persuading others to accept one's point of view (see Chapter 12)
Inquiring	Listening effectively to others and drawing information out of them (see Chapter 9)
Tension management	Managing the tension that stems from conflict with others (see Chapter 11)
Sharing responsibility	Learning to align personal and team objectives (see Chapter 6)
Leadership	Understanding one's role in guiding the team to success (see Chapter 13)
Valuing diversity	Acceptance—and taking advantage—of differences between members (see Chapter 5)
Self-awareness	Willingness to criticize others constructively and to accept constructive criticism from others (see Chapters 9 and 11)

(*Source:* Based on information in S. Caudron, "Teamwork Takes Work," *Personnel Journal,* 1994.)

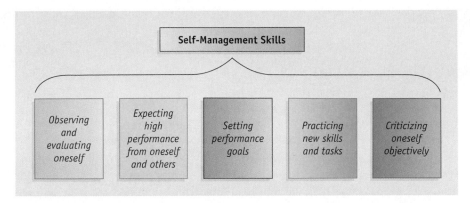

and the roles of others on their team. Members then systematically discuss these perceptions and highlight areas of disagreement so these can be worked on.

- *Goal-setting exercises.* As we described in Chapter 6, successful performance is enhanced by the setting of goals. As a team-building strategy, team members meet to clarify the various goals toward which they are working and to identify ways they can help achieve them.

- *Problem-solving exercises.* Building successful teams requires ensuring that members are able to work together at solving important problems. To help in this regard, some team-building sessions require members to get together to systematically identify and discuss ways of solving problems more effectively.

- *Interpersonal-process exercises.* Some of the most popular team-building exercises involve activities that attempt to build trust and to open communication among members. After all, those members who harbor hostility toward each other or who have hidden agendas are unlikely to work together well. There is usually a fun aspect to interpersonal-process training. Black & Decker, for example, had members of its design team participate in a Spider Web activity requiring members to crawl through a large web of woven rope suspended between two trees without touching the rope. The underlying idea is that by helping each other through these exercises, team members can develop more positive relationships and learn how to influence each other's potential back on the job. In doing this, companies have used such diverse activities as trekking in the wilderness, going through obstacle courses, and having paintball wars. For a close-up example of one extreme form of building teams through interpersonal processes, see the OB in an E-World section on page 306.

Is team building effective? Although these various meetings and physical exercises may be fun, we must ask if they have any value. In other words, are they worth the time and money invested in them? The answer is *only sometimes.* For team-building exercises to be effective, they must be applied correctly. Too often, exercises are used without first thoroughly analyzing precisely what the team needs. When it comes to team building, one size does not fit all! Another problem is that team-building exercises often are used as a one-time panacea. For them to be most effective, however, team-building exercises should be repeated regularly to keep the team in tip-top shape or, at least, at the very first sign of problems. And then, when on the job, everyone should be reminded of the lessons learned off-site.

Compensate Team Performance

Because the United States and Canada are highly individualistic cultures, most North American workers are used to highly individualistic compensation systems—ones that recognize individual performance. However, when it comes to teams, it is also very important to recognize group performance. Teams are no places for hot shots who want to make their individual marks—rather, teams require "team players." And the more organizations reward employees for their teams' successes, the more strongly team spirit will be reinforced. Several companies in which teams are widely used—including the Hannaford Brothers retail food distribution company in New York; Board na Mona, a peat-extraction company in Ireland; and Westinghouse's defense and commercial electronics plant in Texas—rely on *gain-sharing plans* to reward teams. These plans reward team members for reaching company-wide performance goals, allowing them to share in the company's profits.

In view of the importance of team members having a variety of different skills, many companies, including Milwaukee Insurance, Colgate-Palmolive, and Sterling Winthrop, have taken to paying employees for their demonstrated skills as opposed to their job performance. Such a system is known as *skill-based pay* (Chapter 5). A highly innovative skill-based pay system has been in use at Tennessee Eastman. This company's "pay-for-applied-skills-and-knowledge" plan—or *PASK*, as it is known—requires employees to demonstrate their skills in several key areas, including technical skills and interpersonal skills. The pay scale is carefully linked to the number of skills acquired and the level of proficiency attained. By encouraging the development of vital skills in this manner, the company is ensuring that it has the resources for its teams to function effectively.

Provide Support

For teams to survive, let alone thrive, it is essential for them to receive unqualified support from top management. In the absence of such support, the system may falter. In addition to support from managers, it is essential that the basis for the movement to teams be fully understood and accepted by the individuals who are involved. Unless employees can understand fully the importance of cooperating with each other, problems are likely to result. By contrast, when team members share a common vision and are committed to attaining it, they are generally very cooperative with one another, leading to success. For example, members of Hallmark's new-product development team (consisting of artists, designers, printers, and financial experts) work carefully together, contributing to the company's dominance in the greeting cards market.

skeptical about whether the "touchy-feely" trip would be anything more than a fun adventure. The first three days were just plain scary, but on the fourth, the team faced a "sink-or-swim" challenge. Amidst what the guide called particularly "flippy" rapids, the raft rose straight up into the air and plummeted from a height of a story and a half, dumping everyone into the water. Fortunately, everyone came out okay—even better than okay, as they learned how to help each other confront a force bigger than themselves.

The real challenge began immediately after the adventure, as Altrec.com's senior management team put its words into practice. Two particular strategies emerged. First, team members realized there was tension due to the fact that nobody knew exactly what a particular employee was supposed to be doing. Because this individual happened to be close friends with Morford, everyone just sidestepped the issue and resentment

grew. During the trip, everyone agreed on a way to tackle the problem, and a plan was put in place to address it. Second, the team developed a strategy for development in four key areas: communication, feedback, decision making, and respect. After seeing his team in action, Morford, who welcomed a return to the dry and safe harbor of his office back in Bellevue, learned an important lesson himself: He had assembled a group of aggressive decision makers, and his job was to leverage, but not cripple, that strength.

Although everyone claims to have enjoyed the adventure, back at the office, team members are no more than cautiously optimistic about what the future holds for the company and the extent to which their river trip helped at all. If, after six months, the individuals begin working together as a team, none of the skeptical engineers is likely to bad-mouth the "touchy-feely" experience they had on—and in—the Salmon River.

Similarly, by forming teams with highly cooperative members from different fields, Thermos was able to launch its highly successful electric grill. Also, for many years, Volvo has operated profitably because of the considerable support its work teams receive from company management (see Figure 8.21).

Communicate the Urgency of the Team's Mission

Team members are prone to rally around challenges that compel them to meet high-performance standards. As a result, the urgency of meeting those standards should be

FIGURE 8.21

Management Support: A Key to Team Success
These five employees of Volvo's Torslanda plant in Göteborg, Sweden, shown here on break, comprise one of many teams that are free to make many decisions with respect to assembling automobiles. The company's strong support for work teams has contributed to its success over the years.

expressed. For example, a few years ago, employees at Ampex Corporation (a manufacturer of videotape equipment for the broadcasting industry) worked hard to make their teams successful when they recognized the changes necessitated by the shift to digital technology. Unless the company met these challenges, the plug surely would be pulled. Realizing that the company's very existence was at stake, work teams fast-forwarded Ampex into a position of prominence in its industry by ramping up development of digital recording technology.

Promote Cooperation Within and Between Teams

Team success requires not only cooperation within teams, but between teams as well. As one expert put it, "Time and time again, teams fall short of their promise because companies don't know how to make them work together with other teams. If you don't get your teams into the right constellations, the whole organization can stall."[91]

Boeing successfully avoided such problems in the course of developing its 777 passenger jet—a project involving some 200 teams. As you might imagine, on such a large project, coordination of effort between teams is essential. To help, regular meetings were held between various team leaders who disseminated information to members. And team members could go wherever needed within the organization to get the information required to succeed. As one Boeing employee, a team leader, put it, "I can go to the chief engineer. Before, it was unusual just to see the chief engineer."[92] Just as importantly, if after getting the information they need, team members find problems, they are empowered to take action without getting management's approval. According to Boeing engineer, Henry Shomber, "We have the no-messenger rule. Team members must make decisions on the spot. They can't run back to their functions [department heads] for permission."[93]

Select Team Members Based on Their Skills or Potential Skills

Insofar as the success of teams demands that they work together closely on a wide variety of tasks, it is essential for them to have a complementary set of skills. This includes not only job skills but also interpersonal skills (especially since getting along with teammates is very important). With this in mind, at Ampex (noted above) three-person subsets of teams are used to select their own new members insofar as they have the best idea about what skills are needed and who would best fit into the teams. It is also frequently important for teams to project future skills that may be needed and to train team members in these skills. With this in mind, work teams at Colgate-Palmolive Company's liquid detergents plant in Cambridge, Ohio, initially received 120 hours of training in such skills as quality management, problem solving, and team interaction and, subsequently, received advanced training in all these areas.

In an effort to keep team members' skills fresh, it is important to confront members with new facts regularly. Fresh approaches are likely to be prompted by fresh information, and introducing new facts may present the kind of challenges that teams need to stay innovative. For example, when information about pending cutbacks in defense spending was introduced to teams at Florida's Harris Corporation (an electronics manufacturer), new technologies were developed that positioned the company to land large contracts in nonmilitary government organizations—including a $1.7 billion contract to upgrade the FAA's air traffic control system.

A Cautionary Note: Developing Successful Teams Requires Patience

It is important to caution that, although these suggestions are important, they alone do not ensure the success of work teams. Many other factors, such as the economy, the existence of competitors, and the company's financial picture, also are important determinants of organizational success. Still, the fact that these practices are followed in many highly successful teams certainly makes them worthy of consideration.

However, developing effective teams is difficult, and the path to success is riddled with obstacles. It is also time consuming. According to management expert Peter Drucker, "You can't rush teams. It takes five years just to learn to build a team and decide what kind you want."[94] And it may take most organizations over a decade to make a complete transition to teams. Clearly, teams are not an overnight route to success. But with patience and careful attention to the suggestions outlined in this chapter, teams have ushered many companies into extraordinary gains in productivity. For this reason, they must be considered a viable option for organizing people.

SUMMARY AND REVIEW OF LEARNING OBJECTIVES

1. Define what is meant by a group and identify different types of groups operating within organizations.

A group is a collection of two or more interacting individuals with a stable pattern of relationships between them who share common goals and who perceive themselves as being a group. Within organizations, there are two major classes of groups—formal groups (which include command groups and task groups) and informal groups (which include interest groups and friendship groups).

2. Describe the importance of norms, roles, status, and cohesiveness within organizations.

Norms are generally agreed upon informal rules. Roles are the typical pattern of behavior in a social context. Status refers to the prestige accorded group members. Cohesiveness describes the pressures faced by group members to remain in their groups. Together, these factors determine the dynamics of people working in groups.

3. Explain how individual performance in groups is affected by the presence of others (social facilitation), the cultural diversity of group membership, and the number of others with whom one is working (social loafing).

Individual productivity is influenced by the presence of other group members. Sometimes a person's performance improves in the presence of others (when the job he or she is doing is well learned), and sometimes performance declines in the presence of others (when the job is novel). This phenomenon is known as social facilitation. Not only is performance influenced by the presence of others but also by the group's racial/ethnic diversity. Performance in diverse groups is initially worse than performance in homogeneous groups, although these differences disappear with repeated involvement with the group. On additive tasks (i.e., ones in which each member's individual contributions are combined), social loafing occurs. According to this phenomenon, the more people who work on a task, the less each group member contributes to it.

4. Define what teams are and describe the various types of teams that exist in organizations.

Teams are special kinds of groups—ones whose members focus on collective rather than individual work products, are mutually accountable to each other, share a common commitment to purpose, and are usually self-managing. Teams differ with respect to several dimensions: their purpose or mission (work teams versus improvement teams), time (temporary teams or permanent teams), degree of autonomy (work groups, semiautonomous work groups, or self-managed teams), authority structure (intact teams versus cross-functional teams), and physical presence (physical teams versus virtual teams).

5. Understand the evidence regarding the effectiveness of teams in organizations.
Comprehensive case studies also have found organizational productivity gains (e.g., increased outcome, improved quality, lowered costs) resulting from the use of teams. However, more objective empirical studies have found that, although employees are generally more satisfied in teams than working under traditional management, they tend to be no more productive at the individual level.

6. Explain the factors responsible for the failure of some teams to operate as effectively as possible and identify steps that can be taken to build successful teams.
Despite some evidence of team successes, some teams fail. This is often because team members are unwilling to cooperate with each other, they fail to receive support from management, some managers are unwilling to relinquish control, and some teams fail to coordinate their efforts effectively with other teams. With some effort, teams can yield exceptionally high levels of performance. To build successful teams, it helps to do the following: provide training in team skills, compensate team performance, provide managerial support, promote employee support, promote cooperation within and between teams, and select team members based on their skills or potential skills.

POINTS TO PONDER

Questions for Review

1. What is a group and how do groups form?
2. How do norms, roles, status, and cohesiveness influence the operation of groups?
3. How do the phenomena of social facilitation and social loafing influence the performance of individuals in group settings?
4. What are teams and how do they differ from groups?
5. What does the evidence reveal about the effectiveness of work teams?
6. What are the major obstacles to team success and how can they be overcome?

Experiential Questions

1. Think of a group in which you have been working. How do the *five-stage model* and the *punctuated-equilibrium model* apply to this experience?
2. Describe an incident of *social loafing* in which you may have been involved (e.g., a class project). What might be done to overcome this effect?
3. How have your own experiences in work teams compared to those described in this chapter? Based on what you read, what could be done to make your own team experiences more successful?

Questions to Analyze

1. Imagine that you are about to go on stage to give a solo piano recital. How would the phenomenon of social facilitation account for your performance?
2. Based on the evidence regarding the effectiveness of teams, would you say that the popularity of teams today is well founded?
3. Think of any professional sports team, such as a professional baseball, football, or basketball team. In what ways do they fit the description of teams used in this chapter? In what ways do they *not* fit the description of teams used in this chapter?

INDIVIDUAL EXERCISE

Are You a Team Player?

Let's face it, some people find it easier to work in teams than others. Are you already a "team player," or have you not yet developed the skills needed to work effectively with others in teams? Knowing where you stand along this dimension may come in handy when it comes to considering a new job or planning your next work assignment. The following questionnaire will give you insight into this question.

Directions

1. Read each of the following statements and carefully consider whether or not it accurately describes you on the job most of the time.
2. Then, on the line next to each statement, write "yes" if the statement describes you most of the time, or "no" if it does not describe you most of the time. If you are uncertain, write a question mark ("?").
3. Do your best to respond to all items as honestly as possible.

Most of the time, on the job, I . . .

_____ 1. demonstrate high ethical standards.
_____ 2. deliver on promises I make.
_____ 3. take initiative, doing what's needed without being told.
_____ 4. follow the norms and standards of the groups in which I work.
_____ 5. put team goals ahead of my own.
_____ 6. accurately describe my team to others in the organization.
_____ 7. pitch in to help others learn new skills.
_____ 8. do at least my share of the work.
_____ 9. coordinate the work I do with others.
_____ 10. try to attend all meetings and arrive on time for them.
_____ 11. come to meetings prepared to participate.
_____ 12. stay focused on the agenda during team meetings.
_____ 13. share with others new knowledge I may have about the job.
_____ 14. encourage others to raise questions about the way things are.
_____ 15. affirm positive things about others' ideas before noting concerns.
_____ 16. listen to others without interrupting them.
_____ 17. ask questions to others to make certain I understand them.
_____ 18. make sure I attend to a speaker's nonverbal messages.
_____ 19. praise others who have performed well.
_____ 20. give constructive, nonjudgmental feedback to others.
_____ 21. receive constructive feedback without acting defensively.
_____ 22. communicate ideas without threats or ridicule.
_____ 23. explain the reasoning behind my opinions.
_____ 24. demonstrate my willingness to change my opinions.
_____ 25. speak up when I disagree with others.
_____ 26. show disagreement in a tactful, polite manner.
_____ 27. discuss possible areas of agreement with others with whom I am in conflict.

Source: Based on material appearing in L. C. McDermott, N. Brawley, and W. W. Waite, *World Class Teams* (New York: John Wiley & Sons, 1998).

Scoring

1. Count the number of times you responded by saying "yes."
2. Then count the number of times you responded by saying "no."

3. Add these two numbers together.
4. To compute your *team player score,* divide the number of times you say yes (step 1) by the total (step 3). Then multiply by 100. Your score will be between 0 and 100. Higher scores reflect greater readiness for working in teams.

Questions for Discussion

1. What was your score, and how did it compare to those of others in your class?
2. What underlying criteria of team success are assessed by this questionnaire?
3. What does this questionnaire reveal about the ways in which you are best equipped to work in teams?
4. What does this questionnaire reveal about the ways in which you are most deficient when it comes to working in teams? What do you think you could do to improve your readiness for working in teams?

GROUP EXERCISE

Demonstrating the Social Loafing Effect

The social loafing effect is quite strong and is likely to occur in many different situations in which people make individual contributions to an additive group task. This exercise is designed to demonstrate the effect firsthand in your own class.

Directions

1. Divide the class into groups of different sizes. Between five and ten people should work alone. In addition, there should be a group of two, a group of three, a group of four, and so on, until all members of the class have been assigned to a group. (If the class is small, assign students to groups of vastly different sizes, such as two, seven, and fifteen.) Form the groups by putting together at tables people from the same group.
2. Each person should be given a page or two from a telephone directory and a stack of index cards. Then have the individuals and the members of each group perform the same additive task—copying entries from the telephone directory onto index cards. Allow exactly 10 minutes for the task to be performed, and encourage everyone to work as hard as they can.
3. After the time is up, count the number of entries copied.
4. For each group, and for all the individuals, compute the average per-person performance by dividing the total number of entries copied by the number of people in the group.
5. At the board, the instructor should graph the results. Along the vertical axis show the average number of entries copied per person. Along the horizontal axis show the size of the work groups—one, two, three, four, and so on. The graph should look like the one in Figure 8.12.

Questions for Discussion

1. Was the social loafing effect demonstrated? What is the basis for this conclusion?
2. If the social loafing effect was not found, why do you think this occurred? Do you think it might have been due to the possibility that your familiarity with the effect led you to avoid it? Test this possibility by replicating the exercise using people who do not know about the phenomenon (e.g., another class) and then compare the results.
3. If the social loafing effect was found, how strong was it? What could have been done to strengthen it?

WEB SURFING EXERCISE

Tools for Virtual Teams

Virtual teams are likely to include members from all over the company, and in some cases even outside the company (e.g., suppliers and customers). Although they may never meet in the same place at the same time, they can draw on the Web for tools to help them work together in an effective manner. Among companies providing services in this regard are the following:

Agillion	www.agillion.com
GroupVine	www.groupvine.com
Intranets.com	www.intranets.com
ScheduleOnline	www.scheduleonline.com
TeamWave	www.teamwave.com

Visit these Web sites and answer the following questions based on what you find.

1. What particular service does each company provide?
2. What do you perceive as the strengths and weaknesses of each service?
3. What does each service cost?

Team Training

Given the popularity of work teams in today's workplace, it is not particularly surprising that many companies have sprung up that provide training assistance to companies that want to improve (or to introduce) teams. Among these are the following:

Experience Based Learning, Inc.	www.ebl.org
Team Training Solutions	www.teamtrainingsolutions.com
Applied Knowledge Group	www.akgroup.com

Visit these Web sites and answer the following questions based on what you find.

1. In what kinds of services do these companies specialize?
2. What forms of training do these companies provide?
3. What specific emphasis, if any, do these companies provide on creating virtual teams?

PRACTICING OB

Gearing Up for Self-Managed Teams

Officials of a large manufacturing company are concerned about the stagnant productivity they've seen in the past year. Although sales have been good, employees in the company's manufacturing plant are having a hard time keeping up with demand. Right now, they are working on an assembly line, requiring each individual to perform only one or two highly specific tasks. To remedy the situation, they are considering moving to self-managed teams. You have been asked to give your advice on this matter.

1. Do you think teams would be effective in this situation? Why or why not?
2. What potential problems do you think would be associated with the move to teams, and how might these be overcome?
3. What advice would you give to help the teams work as effectively as possible?

CASE IN POINT

A Team Approach to Selling at Cutler-Hammer

Cutler-Hammer is one of the world's leading suppliers of electrical control products and power distribution equipment. Whether it's a circuit breaker for your home or apartment building or a power transformer for the factory in which you work, this Pittsburgh-based division of Cleveland's Eaton Corp. is sure to make it.

For many years, Cutler-Hammer sales reps worked in a very traditional manner. They took orders from customers, who relied on their knowledge of the company's products to sell them what they needed. This worked fine until a few years ago, when the company's product line grew so dramatically in size and complexity that sales reps found it impossible to keep up. As a result, they sold whatever products they happened to know, whether or not these were the best choices. But this wasn't the only problem. Although some reps worked hard to land multimillion-dollar contracts, some associates just goofed off and lived off the fat of their colleagues' successes, contributing little of their own. Naturally, there was considerable resentment; and, as you might imagine, customers were not being well served.

Recognizing that this was a formula for failure, Bruce Broussard, a manager from Cutler-Hammer's commercial division, introduced a team-selling approach. Instead of having a sales force of reps struggling to stay abreast of the latest product developments, Broussard composed sales teams—referred to as "pods"—whose individual members specialized in a particular product or service. Today, when a customer has a problem, a rep can call on the person in his or her pod who has the appropriate expertise to solve it. As a result, Cutler-Hammer sales reps now think of themselves as selling solutions rather than products—and their customers appreciate it.

Not surprisingly, this idea met with a great deal of resistance at first. Getting members of the sales force to accept it took a great deal of training. After all, most sales reps grew up believing that they will be called on to know everything there is to know about their company's products, and they expect to be rewarded for doing so. As a result, learning to pass a potential account over to someone who was better equipped to service it didn't come easily.

But, given the positive impact of this plan, it appears that the effort needed to bring it about was well worthwhile. In fact, the changes have been dramatic. The company now maintains a book of testimonials from satisfied customers—currently numbering 150 and growing. Not so long ago, any such book would have been empty. To the delight of company officials, this high level of customer satisfaction is reflected in the bottom line. In a recent period in which the market grew only 4 to 7 percent a year, Cutler-Hammer had sustained growth of 18 percent.

It wasn't only the company whose bottom line benefited but also the bank accounts of individual sales reps, too. Although reps may lose by passing along an individual account to a colleague in their pod, they more than make up for it by servicing other accounts with which they have greater technical expertise. And there's no fear of someone goofing off under this system: Anyone suspected of doing so is certain not to get any referrals from colleagues. Any Cutler-Hammer reps who were reluctant to give up the old ways now take one look at their paychecks and find themselves among the most ardent supporters of the company's team-based sales approach.

Critical Thinking Questions

1. Would you say that there was a "social loafing" problem at Cutler-Hammer before teams were introduced? Why or why not?
2. What challenges had to be overcome for teams to operate effectively at Cutler-Hammer?
3. What lessons can be learned from what happened at Cutler-Hammer to help make teams more effective in the company in which you work?

Work Groups

Working together in teams is a key part of life at SA. There is a top management team, teams within departments, and teams within divisions. Each team meets regularly and is self-managed. Some teams are composed of representatives of various divisions—such as those devoted to philanthropy, quality of life, and cutting costs. As in many teams, conflict within teams at SA is inevitable, and employees receive extensive training on how to minimize and resolve those conflicts.

The practice of working in teams came into use at SA when it had only 70–100 employees. Today, however, because the company is considerably larger and because its employees work in several different locations, the task of coordinating members within teams is more challenging. There also is considerable difficulty coordinating the efforts of different teams, enabling them to work together. Not surprisingly, not all work groups at SA are organized as teams. Some are traditionally managed and hierarchical in nature. In these groups, employees work to meet the goals assigned to them by a group leader—a higher-level boss who gives orders, and to whom they must answer on a regular basis.

Questions for Discussion

1. Of the various types of teams identified in the text, which ones appear to be in place at SA?
2. Based on the material in the text, what are some of the major reasons why the work teams at SA might be expected to succeed? Also, why might they fail?
3. What concrete steps can be taken to improve the chances of success of the work teams?
4. Because many of SA's employees work in different locations, how might they benefit from the use of virtual teams?

Communication in Organizations

LEARNING OBJECTIVES

After reading this chapter, you should be able to:
1. Describe the process of communication and its role in organizations.
2. Identify various forms of verbal media used in organizations, and explain which ones are most appropriate for communicating messages of different types.
3. Explain how style of dress and the use of time and space are used to communicate nonverbally in organizations.
4. Describe various types of individual differences with respect to how people communicate with each other.
5. Describe the formal and informal forces that are responsible for communication in organizations.
6. Explain the various things you can do to improve your effectiveness as a communicator in organizations.

■ PREVIEW CASE
US WEST: INFORMATION SHARING IN REAL TIME

If we are living in the information age, then surely US West's network-reliability operations center in Littleton, Colorado, is ground zero. Admittedly, the huge, beige, corrugated-metal building doesn't look like much from the outside, but inside it's a different story. With massive display panels positioned at one end of the cavernous facility facing banks of computer terminals, it looks a lot like *Star Trek*'s legendary *USS Enterprise*. And, with crowds of people checking out the rows of names and numbers on the screens, you'd think you were in the operations room of a Las Vegas sports-betting parlor.

In reality, however, the scene is neither science fiction nor gambling fancy. Rather, the high-tech displays report the real-time status of telecommunications in a 14-state region. Data on performance of customers' telephone lines are updated every five minutes and reported on eight large display screens. The idea is to provide all employees with critical information needed to help resolve service problems or to avoid them in the first place. This information alerts workers to the nature and location of any outages they spot, allowing them to take appropriate action. Technical managers, seated at the front of the room, diagnose the problem, seeking help from hundreds of technicians seated behind them. These experts range from those who monitor equipment in the field to those who set up lines for new service. When they succeed at what they're doing, problems are resolved so quickly that most customers don't know they ever existed.

One day, for example, the board showed an exceptionally busy pattern of traffic that was threatening to tie up telephone service in a small area. As it worked out, the problem was caused by thousands of people trying to call a merchant who just received a shipment of Beanie Babies. Activity on the trunk line was so great that merchants in neighboring stores couldn't make any outgoing calls—that is, until technicians at the center made appropriate adjustments to the equipment.

Aware that phone service may be affected by more than just a shipment of Beanie Babies, US West also receives continuous feeds from the Weather Channel and CNN. This enables it to take advance precautions when serious weather or major news events threaten to increase phone traffic into or out of its service area. A good example is the tragic 1999 shooting at Columbine High School, just a few miles away. By getting a lead on the breaking story, technicians were able to anticipate the increased phone traffic and make appropriate adjustments so that nobody's service was disrupted.

Sixty-five percent of the outages stem not from bad weather or breaking news but from human error. To avoid these problems, weekly meetings are held in which the previous week's most significant service problems are reviewed to assess how they began and to consider how they may be avoided in the future. Nobody is singled out by name, and no blame is assigned. The emphasis is on recognizing problems so that people can be better trained to anticipate them. And, given US West's outstanding service, it seems to be working quite well.

weekly meetings are held in which the previous week's most significant service problems are reviewed to assess how they began and to consider how they may be avoided in the future.

Beyond the technological marvel that is US West's network-reliability operations center lies a good demonstration of the importance of sharing information in organizations. Instead of having one person gather information on his or her computer terminal who then shares it with others, as is typical in many companies, US West's approach allows all technicians to access the same information at once. This is a good example of efficient *communication*—the processes through which people send information to others and receive information from them. As you might imagine, successful communication is required for organizations to succeed. With this in mind, in this chapter we will explain how the communication process works and ways of fostering communication in organizations.

Not surprisingly, experts consider communication to be a key process underlying all aspects of organizational operations.[1] Contemporary scholars have referred to organizational communication as "the social glue . . . that continues to keep the organization tied together,"[2] and "the essence of organization."[3] Writing many years earlier, well-known management theorist and former New Jersey Bell Telephone president Chester Barnard said, "The structure, extensiveness and scope of the organization are almost entirely determined by communication techniques."[4] This strong statement makes sense once you realize that supervisors spend as much as 80 percent of their time engaging in some form of communication, such as speaking or listening to others, or writing to and reading material from others.[5] And, in today's highly technical world, we count on a wide variety of communication media that have transformed the way people do their jobs (see Figure 9.1).

Given the importance of communication in organizations, we will examine this process closely in this chapter. To begin, we will define the process of communication and characterize its role in organizations. Following this, we will describe the two basic forms of communication: verbal and nonverbal. Then, recognizing that people don't always communicate in the same fashion, we will examine several key individual differences with respect to communication—differences in personal style, gender differences, and cross-cultural differences. We will then distinguish between two major types of communication in which we all engage—formal communication and informal communication. Finally, we will conclude this chapter by offering a series of concrete suggestions regarding how to become a better communicator yourself. After all, learning

FIGURE 9.1

Technology Has Transformed Communication
Although the scene depicted here may be a bit extreme, there can be no doubt that advances in technology have changed the way in which people communicate with one another on the job. This topic is of considerable interest to scientists and practitioners in the field of OB.
(*Source:* Mike Smith. Reprinted by permission of United Features Syndicate, Inc.)

about the importance of organizational communication will get you to appreciate the importance of developing your own communication skills.

COMMUNICATION: ITS BASIC NATURE

Before we can fully appreciate the process of organizational communication, we need to address some basic issues. To begin, we will formally define what we mean by communication and then elaborate on the process by which it occurs. Following this, we will describe the important role that communication plays in organizations.

Communication: A Working Definition and Description of the Process

What do the following situations have in common? The district manager posts a notice stating that smoking is prohibited on company property. An executive prepares a report about the financial status of a potential corporate takeover prospect. A taxi dispatcher directs Cab 54 to pick up a fare at 1065 Cherry Drive. A foreman smiles at one of his subordinates and pats him on the back in recognition of a job well done. The answer, if you haven't already guessed it, is that each of these incidents involves some form of *communication*. Although you probably already have a good idea of what communication entails, we can better understand communication in organizations by defining it precisely and describing the nature of the communication process.

With this in mind, we define **communication** as the process by which a person, group, or organization (the *sender*) transmits some type of information (the *message*) to another person, group, or organization (the *receiver*). To clarify this definition and to further elaborate on how the process works, we have summarized it in Figure 9.2. You may find it helpful to follow along with this diagram as we review the various steps.

Encoding. The communication process begins when one party has an idea that it wishes to transmit to another (either party may be an individual, a group, or an entire organization). It is the sender's mission to transform the idea into a form that can be sent to and understood by the receiver. This is what happens in the process of **encoding**—translating an idea into a form, such as written or spoken language, that can be recognized by a receiver. We encode information when we select the words we use to

communication
The process by which a person, group, or organization (the sender) transmits some type of information (the message) to another person, group, or organization (the receiver).

encoding
The process by which an idea is transformed so that it can be transmitted to, and recognized by, a receiver (e.g., a written or spoken message).

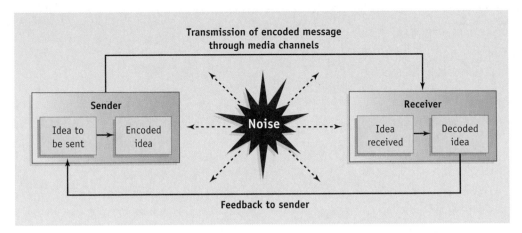

FIGURE 9.2
The Communication Process
Communication generally follows the steps outlined here. Senders *encode* messages and *transmit* them via one or more communication channels to *receivers,* who then *decode* them. The process continues as the original receiver sends *feedback* to the original sender. Factors distorting or limiting the flow information, known as *noise,* may enter into the process at any point.

write a letter or speak to someone in person. This process is critical if we are to clearly communicate our ideas. Unfortunately, people are far from perfect when it comes to encoding their ideas (although, as we will note later, this skill can be improved).

Channels of communication. After a message is encoded, it is ready to be transmitted over one or more **channels of communication** to reach the desired receiver—that is, the pathways along which information travels. Telephone lines, radio and television signals, fiber-optic cables, mail routes, and even the airwaves that carry the vibrations of our voices all represent potential channels of communication. Of course, the form of encoding largely determines the way information may be transmitted. Visual information—such as pictures and written words—may be mailed, delivered in person by a courier, shipped by an express delivery service, or sent electronically via modems, fax machines, and satellite dishes. Oral information may be transmitted over the telephone, via radio and television waves, and of course the old-fashioned way, in person. Whatever channel is used, the goal is the same: to send the encoded message accurately to a desired receiver.

channels of communication
The pathways over which messages are transmitted (e.g., telephone lines, mail, etc.).

Decoding. Once a message is received, the recipient must begin the process of **decoding**—converting the message back into the sender's original ideas. This can involve many different subprocesses, such as comprehending spoken and written words, interpreting facial expressions, and the like. To the extent that the sender's message is accurately decoded by the receiver, the ideas understood will be the ones intended. Of course, our ability to comprehend and interpret information received from others may be imperfect (e.g., restricted by unclear messages or by our own language skills). Thus, as in the case of encoding, limitations in our ability to decode information represent another potential weakness in the communication process but, as we will describe later in this chapter, one that can be developed.

decoding
The process by which a receiver of messages transforms them back into the sender's ideas.

Feedback. Finally, once a message has been decoded, the process can continue with the receiver transmitting a new message back to the original sender. This part of the process is known as **feedback**—knowledge about the impact of messages on receivers. Receiving feedback allows senders to determine whether their messages have been understood properly. At the same time, giving feedback can help convince receivers that the sender really cares about what he or she has to say. Once received, feedback can trigger another idea from the sender, and another cycle of transferring information may begin. For this reason, we have characterized the process of communication summarized in Figure 9.2 as continuous.

feedback
Knowledge about the impact of messages on receivers.

Noise. Despite the apparent simplicity of the communication process, it rarely operates as flawlessly as we have described it here. As we will see, there are many potential barriers to effective communication. The name given to factors that distort the clarity of a message is **noise.** As we have shown in Figure 9.2, noise can occur at any point along the communication process. For example, messages that are poorly encoded (e.g., writ-

noise
Factors capable of distorting the clarity of messages at any point during the communication process.

OB IN AN E-WORLD
THE SPAM PROBLEM: COSTLIER THAN YOU MAY THINK

If you use e-mail, as most of us do, chances are good that you've received unsolicited messages known as **spam** (technically referred to as *unsolicited commercial e-mail,* or UCE). Such messages send unwanted and sometimes objectionable material into our e-mailboxes. Many of these are solicitations to participate in contests or to purchase merchandise. Although most are legitimate, some are scams. Regardless, most of us find them unwanted intrusions—truly the cyber equivalent of "junk mail."

A recent survey of 13,000 e-mail users found that over 90 percent receive spam at least once a week, and almost 50 percent get spammed six or more times per week.[6] This same survey (which included individuals using a wide variety of the most popular Internet service providers, ISPs) found that over 40 percent are displeased with the time it takes to handle spam, 30 percent consider spam a significant invasion of privacy, and 15 percent find it offensive. In fact, a quarter of those surveyed expressed willingness to pay an extra fee for a spam-filter service.

If you're thinking, "what's the big deal?" and that it's easy enough to delete such messages, you're missing the big picture. To you as an individual the lost time and productivity may be minimal, but if you consider the cumulative effect on an entire organization, the impact of spam can be dramatic. Computer Mail Services, a company that sells spam-filtering software, includes a calculator on its Web site (www.cmsconnect.com/Marketing/spamcalc.htm) that allows you to compute the companywide cost of spam. For example, suppose your company has 100 employees with e-mail, each of whom works 230 days per year and gets paid $25 per hour. If each of these individuals receives only five spam e-mails per day and spends only 5 seconds reading each one, almost $4,000 in salary is wasted and over 10 days of productivity are lost each year.

spam
Unsolicited commercial e-mail.

ten in an unclear way) or poorly decoded (e.g., not comprehended) or channels of communication that are too full of static (e.g., receivers' attentions are diverted from the message) may reduce communication's effectiveness. These factors and others (e.g., time pressure, organizational politics) may contribute to the distortion of information transmitted from one party to another and add to the complexity of the communication process. As you continue reading this chapter, you will come to appreciate many of the factors that make the process of organizational communication so very complex and important. (For a look at one particular form of noise that has come to people's attention in recent years, see the OB in an E-World section above.)

The Fundamental Role of Communication in Organizations

When you think about people in organizations communicating with each other, what image comes to mind? A typical picture might involve one person telling another what to do. Indeed, one key purpose of organizational communication is to *direct action*, that is, to get others to behave in a desired fashion. However, communication in organizations often involves not only single efforts but also concerted action. Thus, for an organization to function, individuals and groups must coordinate carefully their efforts and activities.[9] The waiter must take the customer's order and pass it along to the chef. The market researcher must collect information about consumers' needs and share it with the people in charge of manufacturing and advertising. Communication is the key to these attempts at coordination. Without it, people would not know what to do, and organizations would not be able to function effectively—if at all. In other words, it may be said that another key function of communication in organizations is to *achieve coordinated action.*

According to the SpamCon Foundation, a public-interest group dedicated to stopping spamming, the public at large pays the cost for spam. For example, from $2 to $3 of an individual's monthly Internet bills is due to spam. In fact, spam consumes so much time on e-mail servers (e.g., from 5 percent to 30 percent on AOL) that substantial increases in the fees charged by ISPs are passed on to consumers.[7] Even more than the financial costs, another public-interest group, the Center for Democracy and Technology, fears that the greatest dangers of spam come in the form of soiling the reputation of e-mail and discouraging people from using it, thereby reducing its effectiveness as a communications medium.[8]

As an individual there are several things you can do to stop spam. The SpamCon Foundation recommends the following:

- *Contact the sender.* Ask why you received the message and ask to be delisted.
- *Report the spam to agencies that maintain statistics.* You can send complaints to the U.S. Federal Trade Commission (usce@ftc.gov) or report your situation to the Spam Recycling Center (spamrecycle@chooseyourmail.com), which keeps statistics for informational purposes.
- *Report fraudulent or illegal content to appropriate authorities.* It is illegal to advertise goods or services fraudulently or that are in violation of laws. Your local law enforcement agencies should be contacted.
- *Tell your ISP.* Although most ISPs will tell you that the spam you receive is not their fault, they will want to know about how various spam attacks are affecting their system. About 7 percent of people who switch ISPs do so because they receive too much spam, so complaining cannot hurt.
- *Contact the sender's ISP.* All ISPs forbid members from sending spam. After enough complaints, a sender of spam might lose connectivity privileges.
- *Demand restitution from the spammer.* Although your legal rights vary considerably, spammers will be inclined to take notice if you demand repayment for the time and resources lost by virtue of their activities.

This function is served by the systematic sharing of information. Indeed, *information*—whether it's data about a product's sales performance, directions to a customer's residence, or instructions on how to perform a task—is the core of all organizational activities. It would be misleading, however, to imply that communication involves only the sharing of facts and data. There is also an *interpersonal* facet of organizational communication, a focus on the social relations between people.[10] For example, communication also is highly involved in such important objectives as *developing friendships* and *building trust and acceptance*. As you know, what you say and how you say it can have profound effects on the extent to which others like you. To the extent that people are interested in creating a pleasant interpersonal atmosphere in the workplace, they must be highly concerned about communication.

Now that we have established the role of communication in organizations, we will continue by examining two important forms of communication in the next two sections—verbal communication (involving the use of words) and nonverbal communication (the process of communicating without words).

VERBAL COMMUNICATION: SHARING MESSAGES WITH WORDS

Because you are reading this book, we know you are familiar with **verbal communication**—the process of using words to transmit and receive ideas. Whether it's a face-to-face chat with a coworker, a phone call from a supplier, an e-mail message from the boss, or a memo from company headquarters, people in today's organizations use many different communications media. When we speak of verbal media, we are referring to com-

verbal communication
The transmission of messages using words, either written or spoken.

munication involving the use of words. These words may be transmitted either orally or in written form. As we will see, both play an important role in organizations.

Traditional Verbal Media Vary in Richness

traditional verbal media
Forms of communication that do not depend on the use of computers.

Traditional verbal media are forms of communication that are not dependent on the use of computers, such as face-to-face conversations, letters, and telephone conversations. These various forms of communication can be distinguished with respect to their capacity to convey information (see Figure 9.3).[11]

Some verbal media, such as *face-to-face discussions* are considered especially *rich* insofar as they not only provide vast amounts of information but also are highly personal in nature and provide opportunities for immediate feedback. A bit less rich are other interactive media that are not face to face, such as the *telephone*. However, not all business communication requires a two-way flow of information. For example, toward the *lean* end of the continuum are personal but static media, such as *memos* (written messages used for communication within an organization) and *letters* (written messages used for external communication).[12] This includes one-way communications sent either physically (e.g., letter) or electronically (e.g., fax or e-mail). Finally, at the most lean end of the continuum are highly impersonal, static media, such as *flyers* and *bulletins*, written information that is targeted broadly and not aimed at any specific individual.

newsletters
Regularly published internal documents describing information of interest to employees regarding an array of business and nonbusiness issues affecting them.

Two types of written media deserve special mention because of the important role they play in organizations—*newsletters* and *employee handbooks*. Although they are impersonal and aimed at a general audience, **newsletters** serve important functions in organizations. Newsletters are regularly published internal documents describing information of interest to employees regarding an array of business and nonbusiness issues affecting them.[13] Approximately one-third of companies rely on newsletters, typically as a way of supplementing other means of communicating important information, such as group meetings.[14]

employee handbook
A document describing to employees basic information about a company; a general reference regarding a company's background, the nature of its business, and its rules.

Another important internal publication used in organizations is the **employee handbook**—a document describing to employees basic information about the company. It is a general reference regarding the company's background, the nature of its business, and its rules.[15] Specifically, the major purposes of employee handbooks are (1) to explain key aspects of the company's policies, (2) to clarify the expectations of the company and employees toward each other, and (3) to express the company's philosophy.[16] Handbooks are more popular today than ever before. This is not only because clarifying company policies may help prevent lawsuits but also because corporate officials are recognizing

FIGURE 9.3

A Continuum of Traditional Verbal Communication Media
Traditional verbal communication media may be characterized along a continuum ranging from highly rich, interactive media, such as face-to-face discussions, to lean, static media, such as bulletins. (*Source:* Based on material in Lengel & Daft, 1988; see Note 11.)

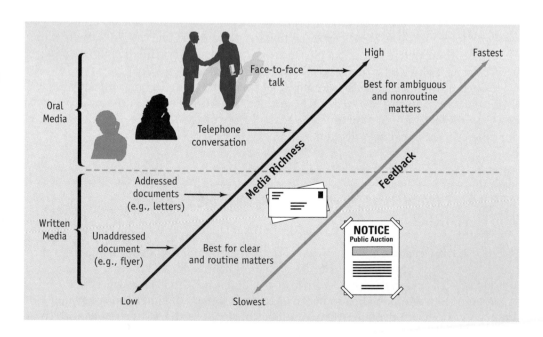

that explicit statements about what their company stands for is an effective means of socializing new employees (see Chapter 7) and promoting the company's values.

Computer-Mediated Communication

To this point, we have been discussing traditional, low-tech forms of verbal communication. However, a great deal of communication that takes place in organizations occurs online through e-mail, chat rooms, instant messaging, and videoconferences. These are considered forms of **computer-mediated communication** insofar as they depend on the use of computers.

E-mail. By far, the most popular form of computer-mediated communication is **electronic mail (e-mail).** In fact, according to a recent survey, e-mail is the most used communications tool in the United States and Canada, with 97 percent of workers using it daily.[17] And, although usage is less widespread in other countries, it is gaining fast. E-mail has become such a popular means of communication, in fact, that as of 2002 e-mail has surpassed print advertising as the most widely used form of direct marketing.[18] The main reason for e-mail's popularity is the freedom it provides people to send and receive messages quickly and efficiently anytime of day or night and to organize and store them as well.

E-mail is the preferred means of communicating facts, such as information needed to coordinate effort between individuals and work groups. Brief, factual messages (e.g., about schedule changes) and announcements (e.g., about forthcoming events) also are popular uses of e-mail. E-mail has made it easier to break down status barriers between people that often present obstacles to sharing ideas. For example, whereas one may find it difficult to get an in-person appointment with the head of a company, it's just as simple to send an e-mail message to that individual as it is to reach anyone else, effectively altering the flow of information within an organization.[19] Not surprisingly, many top executives are relying on e-mail as an effective means of reaching out to everyone in the company.

However, because it is written, e-mail messages lack the warmth and subtlety of in-person communication or even telephone communication. Communicating emotions is difficult when using e-mail, even when using *emoticons* (those popular smiley faces we described in Chapter 4). The emotional meaning of our messages is not only difficult to express but easily misinterpreted. As such, e-mail is an outstanding medium for some, but not all, messages that need to be communicated in organizations.

Instant messaging. A variation of e-mail that has become very popular in recent years is known as **instant messaging.** Services of this type (such as those offered by AOL and MSN) allow people who are online to share messages with one another instantaneously, without having to go through an e-mail program. Sending an instant message opens up a small onscreen window into which each party can type messages for the other to read. This makes it possible to exchange notes in real time, as well as to share Web links and files of all types. Although e-mail is quite fast, sometimes even the rapid response of e-mail is not fast enough given that it requires checking for incoming messages and then having to click through a few steps to read, reply, and send the e-mail. This accounts for the popularity of instant messaging. In fact, AOL alone reports having over 100 million users.

Although intended originally for home users, instant messaging has become a popular communications medium for business. According to a major marketing research firm, 29 percent of U.S.-based companies currently were using instant messaging on an official basis as of spring 2002 and 11 percent indicated that they will be using it shortly.[20] However, a total of 84 percent of those surveyed are using this technology whether or not it is officially sanctioned by the company. Employees are using instant messaging primarily as a way to communicate quickly and inexpensively with employees in remote locations.

Video-mediated communication. A particularly promising trend for enhancing communication efficiency is **video-mediated communication (VMC).**[21] Simply put, these

computer-mediated communication
Forms of communication that depend on the use of computers.

electronic mail (e-mail)
A system whereby people use personal computer terminals to send and receive messages between each other.

instant messaging
A form of e-mail that allows people who are online to share messages with one another instantaneously.

video-mediated communication (VMC)
Conferences in which people can hear and see each other using computers.

OB IN A DIVERSE WORLD
"HOLA AND HELLO": WELCOME TO STARMEDIA'S TRILINGUAL WEBCAST

From his New York office, CEO Fernando Espuelas runs StarMedia Network, one of the largest Internet portals for Spanish- and Portuguese-speaking people throughout the world. Despite the company's reliance on cutting-edge technology, his most serious problems usually aren't technical in nature. Rather, with offices in 11 different countries, his greatest challenge is finding a way to communicate effectively with his 750 employees.

Phone, fax, and e-mail work just fine for routine communication. But, when it comes to communicating crucial information about the company's mission or important new initiatives, nothing can beat an in-person meeting between all the staffers and Espuelas himself. Because vast distances make this impractical, however, StarMedia relies on the next best thing—holding Webcasts on the company's intranet. At least every three months everyone gathers in their local conference room

are ways of simultaneously transmitting audio and video between two or more computers. Companies use this technique as an inexpensive way of linking employees in distant locations to allow them to have *cybermeetings*. Not only is this much less expensive than air travel, both with respect to money and time, but it also allows for meetings to be scheduled at the last minute. Boeing, for example, uses VMC to connect the employees in the company's Seattle headquarters with others in satellite locations.[22] (For a close-up example of another company that uses this technology, see the OB in a Diverse World section above.)

Although meeting others via computer makes it impossible to experience the human touch associated with actually being there, VMC is considered much more effective than other more traditional forms of linking people in distant locations—such as phone, e-mail, and fax. In fact, there are several situations under which VMC is preferable to these other communications media.[23] This is the case, for example, when visual information needs to be shared with several people at once, especially when the information involved is stored on computers.

Speech technology. You may have inexpensive voice recognition software installed on your computer. If so, you speak into a microphone and what you say (or something kind of like it) appears on the screen. What you may not know is that companies all over the world are using advanced speech recognition technology to do their jobs more effectively. Today's most sophisticated devices are far more accurate than what we use on our own computers. For example, if you receive a collect call placed through AT&T, you are asked if you will accept the charges. A computer interprets your "yes" or "no" response, saving the company $100 million a year on wages it would have paid to operators.[24]

Experts tell us that this is only the beginning. Companies already use voice recognition technology to dial telephones, to allow customers to find telephone numbers, and to help them browse the Internet. And, from the rapidly growing advances in this area, there is much more to come. Perhaps, in not too many years, you'll be able to ask this book to read itself to you, and it will. Of course, the prospect of getting the book's ideas into your head directly may be a few more years down the line.

Matching the Medium to the Message

What types of communication are most effective under various circumstances? In general, *communication is most effective when it uses multiple channels, such as using both* equipped with monitors and speakers. StarMedia's chief of staff, Gally Bar-on, thinks of these as "virtual gatherings" and coordinates them to communicate vital news, strategic goals, and quarterly reports.

Although it would be far easier to "slice and dice" the information, presenting a little at a time to different groups, Bar-on acknowledges that doing so would eliminate one of the most important benefits—getting to see the highly enthusiastic Espuela in action. This is important to the employees, who frequently say, "We want Fernando." They want to know what he's thinking, and the two-way Webcast allows them to find out by asking him questions directly.

Communicating with the employees isn't straightforward, even with the Webcast, because StarMedia's employees speak three different languages, Spanish, Portugese, and English. Fortunately, so does Espuelas. Although the trilingual sessions take extra time to complete, everyone appreciates his efforts to address them in their own language—despite the good-natured teasing he sometimes gets about his accent. To ensure that nothing important is lost in the translation, meetings at each location are followed up with a recap in the workers' native language. StarMedia keeps its workforce together using advanced technology, but with a human touch. And, given the company's success, that seems to make all the difference.

oral and written messages.[25] Apparently, oral messages are useful in getting people's immediate attention, and the follow-up written portion helps make the message more permanent, something that can be referred to in the future. Oral messages also have the benefit of allowing for immediate two-way communication between parties, whereas written messages frequently are only one-way or take too long for a response.

Not surprisingly, two-way communications (e.g., face-to-face discussions, telephone conversations) are more commonly used in organizations than one-way communications (e.g., memos). For example, in a study of civilian employees of a U.S. Navy agency, approximately 83 percent of the communications taking place used two-way media.[26] In fact, 55 percent of all communications were individual face-to-face interactions. One-way, written communications tended to be reserved for more formal, official messages that needed to be referred to in the future at the receiver's convenience (e.g., official announcements about position openings). Apparently, both written and spoken communications have their place in organizational communication. The trick to any communication medium is not only when to use it but also how to use it wisely.[27] For some valuable suggestions in this regard, see Table 9.1.

In essence, a medium's effectiveness depends on how appropriate it is for the kind of message being sent. Specifically, research has shown that oral media (e.g., telephone conversations, face-to-face meetings) are more effective than written media (e.g., notes, memos) when messages are ambiguous (requiring a great deal of assistance in interpreting them). However, written media are more effective when messages are clear.[28] Not surprisingly, managers who match the type of communications media they use to the kind of message they are sending are considered to perform their jobs more effectively than those who are not as "media sensitive."

NONVERBAL COMMUNICATION: COMMUNICATING WITHOUT WORDS

As you surely know from experience, many of the messages we share with others come not from words but from nonverbal cues. This form of communication, known as **nonverbal communication,** refers to communicating without the use of words. The gestures we make, the distance we keep from others, and our use of eye contact, for example, speak volumes about our relationships with others. As you might imagine,

nonverbal communication
The transmission of messages without the use of words (e.g., by gestures, the use of space).

TABLE 9.1 GUIDELINES FOR PROPERLY USING POPULAR COMMUNICATION MEDIA

The most widely used communication media are e-mail, fax, postal mail, telephone, and of course, face-to-face discussions. Each of these can be very useful if a few simple rules are followed, such as those summarized here.

MEDIUM	BEST USE	RULES FOR USE
E-mail	Sending key information, confirming and documenting facts and appointments	■ Keep messages brief. ■ Words stay forever, so don't be sarcastic or insulting. ■ Don't ignore conventional rules of grammar.
Fax	Sending complete documents requiring a signature, drafts for approval, or notes to someone who doesn't have e-mail	■ Phone ahead to announce that your fax is forthcoming. ■ Follow up faxes with a quick phone call or e-mail to confirm receipt. ■ Avoid sending personal or confidential information that might be seen by others.
Postal mail	Sending long and complicated material or short thank-you notes	■ Verify spelling and grammar. ■ Summarize key points at the beginning. ■ Avoid long sections; break up with bullet points.
Telephone	Communicating information in which emotion must be conveyed (if face-to-face discussions are not possible)	■ Stay focused; avoid multitasking while on the phone. ■ Make appointments to have important phone calls ("phone dates"). ■ Let the other person finish speaking before talking.
Face-to-face	Communicating highly sensitive and delicate information	■ Keep discussions brief and focused on the issues. ■ Make sure personal discussions cannot be overheard. ■ Plan for meetings and arrive prepared to discuss the topic.

(*Source:* Based on information in Gantenbein, 2002; see Note 27.)

however, precisely *what* these nonverbal cues communicate often varies from country to country (see Figure 9.4).[29] Despite the possibility of cultural differences, some of the most prevalent nonverbal communication cues in organizations come from three sources: how people dress, the way they use time, and the manner in which they use space. As we will see, although nonverbal cues may communicate many different things, one message they seem to send loud and clear has to do with one's status in an organization (a topic discussed in more detail in Chapter 8).

Style of Dress: Communicating by Appearance

If you have ever heard the expression "clothes make the man (or woman)," you probably are already aware of the importance of mode of dress as a communication vehicle. This is especially the case in organizations where, as self-styled "wardrobe engineer" John T. Malloy reminds us, the clothing we wear communicates a great deal about us as employees.[30]

However, as we discussed in Chapter 2, precisely what our wardrobe communicates about us may not be as simple as suggested in any "dress for success" guide. Although we cannot make up for the absence of critical job skills simply by donning "the right"

When a person from the United States does this	it means . . .	BUT	When the same thing is done by a person from	it means . . .
stands close to another while talking	the speaker is considered pushy		Italy	the speaker is behaving normally
looks away from another	the speaker is shy		Japan	the speaker is showing deference to authority
extends the palm of her hand	the speaker is greeting the other party by offering a handshake		Greece	the speaker is insulting the other party
joins the index finger and thumb to form an "O"	"okay"		Tunisia	"I'll kill you"

FIGURE 9.4

Beware of Nonverbal Miscommunication in Different Countries
Successfully conducting business in another country involves learning not only that country's spoken language but its nonverbal mannerisms as well. As suggested here, even the best-intentioned communicators run the risk of sending the wrong message—some of which can be quite serious.
(*Source:* Based on information in Barnum & Wolniansky, 1989; see Note 29.)

clothing, people who are qualified for jobs communicate certain things about themselves by the way they dress. For example, a recent study has shown that women working in a variety of different jobs dress in intentionally different ways so as to differentiate their status in the organization.[31] Generally speaking, higher-status people are less likely to dress in a casual fashion.

This trend is rapidly changing, however. In fact, these days, the preferred style of dress is likely to be *business casual*. A recent survey revealed that casual dress is the standard at over one-third of the fastest-growing privately held companies in the United States.[32] Moreover, the hanging up of the pinstriped suit, starched white shirt, and "power tie," long considered the uniform of choice among business leaders, and the donning of more comfortable business clothing appears to be not just an American trend but also a worldwide one.[33] Although there is no objective evidence that employees are any more or less productive when dressing in standard business attire than when dressing more casually, it is clear that the trend toward casualization is highly regarded by employees (not to mention the manufacturers of casual clothing that have cashed in on the trend), who take it as sign of an organization's interest in treating its employees well.[34]

Time: The Waiting Game

Another important mechanism of nonverbal communication in organizations is the use of time. Have you ever waited in the outer office of a doctor or dentist? Surely you have—after all, they have special "waiting rooms" just for this purpose! Why do you have to wait for such people? Mainly because they have special skills that create high demands for their services. As a result, their time is organized in a manner that is most efficient for them—by keeping others lined up to see them at their convenience.[35]

Medical professionals are not the only ones who make people wait to see them. Individuals in high-status positions in many different organizations communicate the idea that their time is more valuable than others' (and, therefore, that they hold higher-status positions) by making others wait to see them. This is a very subtle but important form of nonverbal communication. Typically, the longer you have to wait to see someone, the higher the organizational status that person has attained.[36] In fact, waiting too long to see a low-status person may be taken as a sure sign of disrespect.

The Use of Space: What Does It Say About You?

Like clothing and time, space is another important communication vehicle. Research has shown that one's organizational status is communicated by the amount of space at one's disposal. Generally speaking, the more space one commands, the more powerful one is likely to be in an organization. For example, higher-status life insurance underwriters in one organization were found to have larger desks and larger offices than lower-status underwriter trainees.[37]

Not only does the amount of space communicate organizational status, but also the way that space is arranged. For example, among faculty members at a small college, senior professors were more likely to arrange their offices so as to separate themselves from visitors with their desks, whereas junior professors were less likely to impose such physical barriers.[38] These various office arrangements systematically communicated different things about the occupants. Specifically, professors who did not distance themselves from their students by use of their desks were seen as more open and unbiased in their dealing with students than those who used their desks as a physical barrier.

The use of space appears to have symbolic value in communicating something about group interaction. Consider, for example, who usually sits at the head of a rectangular table. In most cases, it is the group leader. It is, in fact, traditional for leaders to do so. But at the same time studies have shown that people emerging as the leaders of groups tend to be ones who just happened to be sitting at the table heads.[39] Apparently, *where* a person sits influences the available communication possibilities. Sitting at the head of a rectangular table enables a person to see everyone else and to be seen by them (see Figure 9.5). That leaders tend to emerge from such positions is, therefore, not surprising.

It is not only individuals who communicate something about themselves by the use of space but organizations as well.[40] For example, according to John Sculley, former president of PepsiCo, his company's world headquarters were designed to communicate to visitors that they were seeing "the most important company in the world."[41] Similarly, by adding a second office tower to its company headquarters in Cincinnati, Procter & Gamble was said to be attempting to create a gateway-like complex that communicated the company's connection to the community.[42] As these examples suggest,

FIGURE 9.5

The Head of the Table: A Good Location for Communication
In part because of the ease with which they can see others and be seen by them, people who sit at the heads of rectangular tables enjoy effective communication with others seated at the sides.

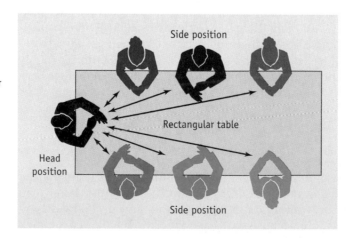

Side position

Rectangular table

Head position

Side position

organizations as well as individuals use space to communicate certain aspects of their identities.

In concluding this section, we note that the nonverbal mechanisms we have presented here, as important as they are, represent only a single channel of communication. Both verbal and nonverbal channels are important sources of information used in conjunction with each other in the process of communication. Thus, although we isolated the various forms of communication for purposes of presenting them to you, it is important to realize that they operate together, complementing each other in complex ways in actual practice.

INDIVIDUAL DIFFERENCES IN COMMUNICATION

As you know from experience, different people tend to communicate in different ways. Two people saying the same thing might do so very differently and communicate their messages in ways that may have different effects on you. In other words, there seem to be individual differences in the way people communicate. Scientists have verified that such differences are indeed real. We now will examine key individual differences in communication—differences based on personal style, gender, and nationality.

Personal Communication Style

Steve and Charlie are two supervisors who are approached by a subordinate, Greg, to discuss the possibility of receiving a salary increase. They both think that Greg is not deserving of the raise he requests. However, Steve and Charlie each go about communicating their feelings quite differently. Steve couldn't have been more direct. "I'll be frank," he said, "Greg, a raise is out of the question." Charlie's approach was far more analytical: "Well, Greg, let's look at the big picture. I see here in your file that we just gave you a raise two months ago and that you're not scheduled for another salary review for four months. Let me share with you some of the numbers and thoroughly explain why the company will have to stick with that schedule. . . ."

Although the message was the same in both cases, Steve and Charlie presented it quite differently. In other words, they appear to differ with respect to their **personal communication style**—the consistent ways people go about communicating with others. As you might imagine, some personal communication styles may be more effective than others—particularly depending on the people involved and the situation they are in. Communication style is learned, and so it can change. But, before we can consider changing how we communicate, we must first recognize the style we use. With this in mind, communication experts have identified six major communication styles, one of which is likely to describe most people (for a summary, see Figure 9.6).[43]

personal communication style
The consistent ways people go about communicating with others (e.g., the *Noble,* the *Socratic,* the *Reflective,* the *Magistrate,* the *Candidate,* and the *Senator*).

- *The Noble.* Such individuals tend to not filter what they are thinking, but come right out and say what's on their minds (like Steve in our example). Nobles use few words to get their messages across. They cut right to the bottom line.
- *The Socratic.* These are people who believe in carefully discussing things before making decisions. Socratics enjoy the process of arguing their points and are not afraid to engage in long-winded discussions. They have a penchant for details and often "talk in footnotes."
- *The Reflective.* These individuals are concerned with the interpersonal aspects of communication. They do not wish to offend others, and they are great listeners. Reflectives would sooner say nothing, or tell you what you want to hear (even if it's a "little white lie") than say something that might cause conflict.
- *The Magistrate.* A magistrate is a person whose style is a mix of part Noble and part Socratic. Magistrates tell you exactly what they think and make their cases in great detail (such as Charlie in our example). These individuals often have an air of superiority about them as they tend to dominate the discussion.

FIGURE 9.6

Personal Communication Styles: A Summary
People tend to communicate using one of six different *personal communication styles*. These styles and their interrelationships are summarized here.
(*Source:* Based on suggestions by McCallister, 1994; see Note 43.)

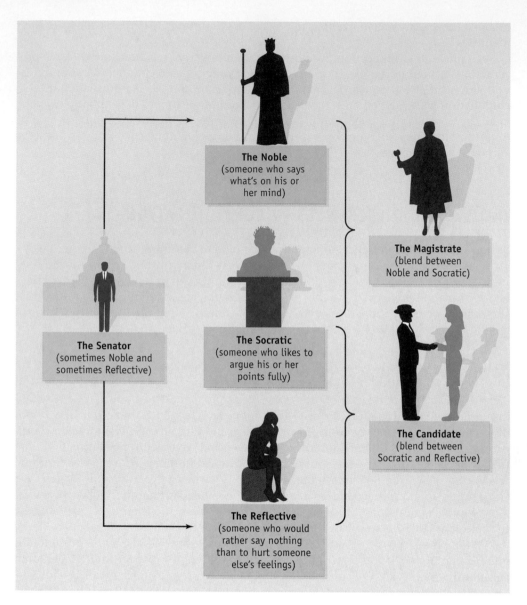

■ *The Candidate.* Such individuals have a style that is a mix between Socratics and Reflectives. As such, they tend to be warm and supportive while also being analytical and chatty. They base their interactions on a great deal of information and do so in a very likable manner.

■ *The Senator.* A Senator is an individual who has developed both the Noble style *and* the Reflective style. They do not mix the two styles. Rather, they move back and forth between the two of them as needed.

It is important to keep in mind that we all have the potential to use any of these styles.[44] However, we generally tend to rely on one style more than any other. Each has its strengths and weaknesses, and no one style is better than another. They are simply different. Effective communication begins with understanding your own style (which you can assess in the Individual Exercise on page 353) and that used by others. Then, when you first meet another, it is advisable to attempt to match that person's style. This is because people generally expect others to communicate in the same manner as they do. However, the better we get to know and accept another's communication style, the better we come to accept how it blends with our own. In either case, the advice is the same: Recognizing and responding to communication styles can enhance the extent to which people are able to communicate effectively with one another.

Gender Differences in Communication: Do Women and Men Communicate Differently?

Infuriated and frustrated, Kimberly stormed out of Mike's office. "I explained the problem I was having with the freelancers," she grumbled, "but he just doesn't listen!" If this situation sounds at all familiar to you, chances are good that you are already aware of the communication barriers that often exist between women and men. Recently, Deborah Tannen, a sociolinguist, has explained that men and women frequently miscommunicate with each other because they have learned different ways of using language.[45] In general, what appears "natural" to women doesn't come easily to men, and vice versa (see Figure 9.7).

When it comes to communication, the basic difference between women and men, Tannen argues, is that men emphasize and reinforce their status when they talk, whereas women downplay their status. Rather, women focus on creating positive social connections between themselves and others. Thus, whereas men tend to say "I," women tend to say "we." Similarly, whereas men try to exude confidence and boast, thinking of questions as signs of weakness, women tend to downplay their confidence (even when they are sure they are correct) and are not afraid to ask questions. (What comes to mind here is the stereotypical image of the couple that gets hopelessly lost because the man overrules the woman's pleas to ask for directions.)

This difference in style between women and men explains why they respond differently to problems. Whereas women tend to listen and lend social support, men tend to take control by offering advice. When men do this, they are asserting their power, contributing to a communication barrier between the sexes. Not surprisingly, whereas men may complain that women are "too emotional," women may complain that men "do not listen." Similarly, men tend to be much more direct and confrontative than women. Although a man might come right out and say, "I think your sales figures are inaccurate," a woman might ask, "Have you verified your sales figures by comparing them to this morning's daily report?" A man may consider this approach to be sneaky, whereas a woman may believe it to be kinder and gentler than a more direct statement. Likewise, women may interpret a man's directness as unsympathetic.

The implications of this set of differences come to the surface once we point out another of Tannen's findings: People in powerful positions tend to reward people whose linguistic styles match their own.[46] As a result, in most organizations, where men tend to be in charge, the contributions of women are often downplayed because the things they say tend to be misinterpreted. The woman who politely defers to a dominant male speaker at a meeting may come across (to men, at least) as being passive. As a result, her

FIGURE 9.7

Men and Women Have Different Communication Styles
Whereas men generally seek to reinforce their status when they communicate (saying "I"), women are more interested in creating positive social connections between themselves and others (saying "we"). Too often this leads to miscommunication between the sexes.

contributions may never come to the table. However, the woman who breaks from this pattern and interjects her ideas may come across (again, to men) as being pushy and aggressive. And here, too, her contributions may be discounted. In both cases, the communication barrier has caused a situation in which organizations are not only breeding conflict, but they also are not taking advantage of the skills and abilities of their female employees.

The solution, although not easy, lies in appreciating and accepting the different styles that people have. As Tannen put it, "Talk is the lifeblood of managerial work, and understanding that different people have different ways of saying what they mean will make it possible to take advantage of the talents of people with a broad range of linguistic styles."[47]

Cross-Cultural Differences in Communication

In Chapter 1 we noted that the phenomenon of globalization presents many challenges. Clearly, one of the most immediate challenges has to do with communication. When people speak different languages, it makes sense that communication between them may be imperfect.

Part of the problem is that different words may mean different things to different people.[48] For example, as hard as it might be for people from countries with long-standing capitalist economies to realize, Russians have difficulty understanding words such as *efficiency* and *free market,* which have no direct translation in their own language. People who have never known a free-market economy while they were growing up certainly may find it difficult to grasp the concept. It is, therefore, not surprising to find that communication barriers have been found to exist among American executives who are attempting to conduct business in Russia.[49]

Another factor that makes cross-cultural communication difficult is that different cultures sometimes have very different norms about using certain words. Take the simple word *no,* for example. Although the term exists in the Japanese language, the Japanese people are reluctant to say "no" directly to someone because doing so is considered insulting. For this reason, they often rely on other ways of saying no that can be quite difficult for foreigners to understand (see Table 9.2).[50] As such, it frequently is considered wise for foreign visitors to other countries to learn not only the language of that country but the customs about using language as well.

In addition to different vocabularies, cross-cultural communication also is made difficult by the fact that in different languages even the same word can mean different things. Just imagine, for example, how confused an American executive might become when she speaks to her counterpart in Israel, where the same Hebrew word, *shalom,* means both "hello" and "good-bye" (as well as "peace"). Confusion is bound to arise. The same may be said for cultural differences in the tone of speech used in different settings. Whereas Americans might feel free to say the word *you* in both formal and informal situations, the French have different words in each (*tu* for informal speech, and *vous* for formal speech). To confuse these may be tantamount to misinterpreting the nature of the social setting, a potentially costly blunder—and all because of a failure to recognize the subtleties of cross-cultural communication. (What can be done to eliminate blunders likely to be caused by the barriers inherent in cross-cultural communication? In the OB in a Diverse World section on page 334 we outline several key suggestions.)

FORMAL AND INFORMAL COMMUNICATION IN ORGANIZATIONS

Think of the broad range of messages that may be communicated to you in the course of a workday. For example, among many other things, your boss may ask you to complete an important sales report, another manager from across the hall may hand you a

TABLE 9.2   HOW TO SAY NO IN JAPAN

Although most Americans are not reluctant to come out directly and say "no" when necessary, doing so is frowned on by Japanese culture. As such, the Japanese rely on the following more indirect ways of communicating "no."

Saying "no" in a highly vague and roundabout manner

Saying "yes or no" in an ambiguous fashion

Being silent and not saying anything at all

Asking questions that change the topic

Responding in a highly tangential manner

Leaving the room

Making a polite excuse

Saying, "yes, but . . . "

Delaying the answer, such as by promising a future letter

(*Source:* Based on information in Hodgson, Sango, & Graham, 2000; see Note 50.)

memo regarding the status of a new project, you may read an e-mail message from a coworker regarding who won the office football pool, and the custodian may tell you a joke. From just these few examples, it's easy to distinguish between two basic types of communication that occur in organizations: **formal communication**—the sharing of messages regarding the official work of the organization, and **informal communication**—the sharing of unofficial messages, ones that go beyond the organization's formal activities. Because both formal and informal communication is so widespread in organizations, we will describe both in this section of the chapter.

Formal Communication: Up, Down, and Across the Organizational Chart

Although the basic process of communication described thus far is similar in many different contexts, a unique feature of organizations has a profound impact on the communication process—namely, their *structure*. Organizations are often set up in ways that dictate who may and may not communicate with whom. Given this, we may ask: How is the communication process affected by the structure of an organization?

Organizational structure influences communication. **Organizational structure** refers to the formally prescribed pattern of interrelationships existing between the various units of an organization (a topic to which we will return in Chapter 15). An organization's structure may be described using a diagram known as an **organizational chart.** An organizational chart showing the structure of part of a fictitious organization is shown in Figure 9.8. Such a diagram provides a graphic representation of an organization's structure. It may be likened to an x-ray showing the organization's skeleton, an outline of the planned, formal connections between its various units.[52]

Note the various boxes in the diagram and the lines connecting them. Each box represents a person performing a specific job. The diagram shows the titles of the individuals performing the various jobs and the formally prescribed pattern of communication between them. These are relatively fixed and defined. Each individual is responsible for performing a specified job. Should the people working in the organization leave their jobs, they must be replaced if their jobs are to be done. The key point is that the formal structure of an organization does not change just because the personnel changes.

formal communication
The sharing of messages regarding the official work of the organization.

informal communication
The sharing of unofficial messages, ones that go beyond the organization's formal activities.

organizational structure
The formally prescribed pattern of interrelationships existing between the various units of an organization.

organizational chart
A diagram showing the formal structure of an organization, indicating who is to communicate with whom.

The lines connecting the boxes in the organizational chart are lines of *authority* showing who must answer to whom. Each person is responsible to (or answers to) the person at the next higher level to which he or she is connected. At the same time, people are also responsible for (or give orders to) those who are immediately below them. The boxes and lines form a sort of blueprint of an organization showing not only what people have to do but also with whom they have to communicate for the organization to operate properly.

As you might imagine, the nature and form of communication vary greatly as a function of people's relative positions within an organization. Even a quick look at an organizational chart reveals that information may flow up (from lower to higher levels), down (from higher to lower levels), or horizontally (between people at the same level). However, as summarized in Figure 9.8, different types of information typically travel in different directions within a hierarchy.

FIGURE 9.8

The Organizational Chart: An Organization's Formal Communication Network

An organizational chart, such as this simple one, shows the formally prescribed patterns of communication in an organization. Different types of messages typically flow upward, downward, and horizontally throughout organizations.

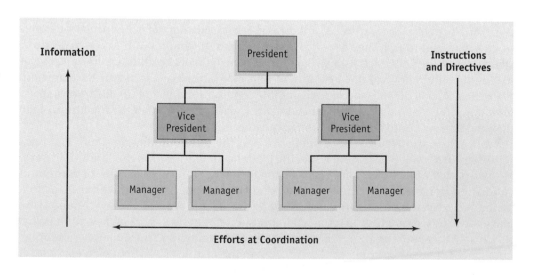

2. *Do not jump to conclusions.* When we perceive various situations, we tend to assume that our judgments are correct. However, experts caution that when it comes to cross-national settings, we should consider our judgments more as educated guesses than as certain conclusions. If you think that something is correct (such as your interpretation of the lazy workers in the preceding example), it is best to compare these to the judgments of experts in the local culture than to assume you are correct. By confirming the accuracy of your judgments misinterpretation is less likely.

3. *Assume that people are different from yourself.* Most of us tend to assume that others are similar to ourselves until we learn otherwise. However, such an assumption is likely to lead us down the wrong track. And seasoned international managers know this. They take the opposite stance, assuming that others are different until proven otherwise. Because

they "know that they don't know," they are less likely to be surprised by differences they don't expect but that are inevitable.

4. *Take the other person's perspective.* Try to see the situation through the eyes of your foreign colleague. Consider this individual's values and experiences, and ask yourself how he or she might view things differently. To the extent that you can effectively switch roles, you will be able to avoid the narrow-mindedness ("cultural myopia") with which we all tend to make decisions.

Although these measures may be more easily said than done, with a little practice they can be mastered. Given that such practices are key to the success of international managers, the effort involved in doing so would appear to be well worthwhile.

Downward communication. Suppose that you are a supervisor. What types of messages would you send to your subordinates? Typically, *downward communication* consists of instructions, directions, and orders—messages telling subordinates what they should be doing.[53] We also would expect to find feedback on past performance flowing in a downward direction (such as when managers tell subordinates how well they have been working). A sales manager, for example, might direct members of her sales force to promote a certain product and may then congratulate them for being successful.

Downward communication flows from one level to the next lowest one, slowly trickling down to the bottom. As a message passes through various levels, it often becomes less accurate (especially if the information is spoken). Thus, it is not surprising to find that the most effective downward communication techniques are ones directly aimed at those who are most affected by the messages—namely, small group meetings and organizational publications targeting specific groups.[54] Not suprisingly, such methods are being used very successfully in many companies.

Upward communication. Information flowing from lower levels to higher levels within an organization, such as from a subordinate to her supervisor, is referred to as *upward communication.* Messages flowing in this direction tend to contain the information managers need to do their jobs, such as data required for decision making and the status of various projects. In short, upward communication is designed to keep managers aware of what is going on. Among the various types of information flowing upward are suggestions for improvement, status reports, reactions to work-related issues, and new ideas.

Upward communication is not simply the reverse of downward communication. The difference in status between the communicating parties makes for some important distinctions. For example, it has been established that upward communication occurs much less frequently than downward communication. In fact, one classic study found that 70 percent of assembly-line workers initiated communication with their supervisors less than once a month.[57] Further research has found that managers direct less than 15 percent of their total communication to their superiors.[58] And, when people do

COMMUNICATING THE ULTIMATE ORGANIZATIONAL BAD NEWS: "YOU'RE FIRED!"

Although no one likes to have to "drop the ax" on an employee, doing so is an inevitable part of any manager's job. Not only is the task unpleasant, but if done incorrectly, the results also can prove quite costly. This is because terminated employees might sue their former employers on the grounds of wrongful termination and because the morale of the employees who remain in the company might suffer if the termination of one of their colleagues is handled poorly. Fortunately, several things can be done to minimize these problems.[55]

1. *Document and maintain written records of performance problems.* Employers should maintain careful written logs documenting problems, goals for improvement, and a reasonable timetable for meeting these goals, and employees should be asked to sign all such documents. This will help employers defend themselves among employees who file suit against them, and it also may discourage employees from thinking about suing in the first place.

2. *Give fair notice.* If an employee is doing something illegal or something that endangers others in the workplace, it is advisable to fire that person on the spot. In less extreme cases, however, firing without notice only adds insult to injury—and these injured feelings may stimulate aggrieved employees to visit their attorney.

3. *Clearly but briefly explain the termination decision.* Too often, when people are fired they claim that they had no idea why it happened.[56] Supervisors should explain the problems in clear terms. Then, after explaining the decision and emphasizing that it is final, they should move on to practical matters like severance pay and the continuance of health care insurance.

4. *Be sympathetic to the fired worker's feelings.* When one loses a job, the resulting feelings of uncertainty—both personal and financial—are quite unsettling. This is bad enough, so don't make the situation worse by being insensitive and uncaring. Compassion is just what is needed at such a time.

5. *Do the job in person.* However tempting it may be to fire someone in writing (by e-mail or in a written letter) or by leaving a voice-mail message, don't do it. As obviously insensitive as this may be, believe it or not, this has been done!

6. *Reassure the surviving employees.* When someone gets fired, the word tends to spread quickly, and the surviving employees cannot help but wonder what the future holds for them. To the extent that uncertainty may breed distrust and spin off rumors, it is wise for supervisors to provide appropriate reassurances about the future.

Although firing someone is never easy, following these six suggestions can make the task much less distasteful for all concerned. Implementing them also can make the termination process less expensive for the company and less emotionally draining for the ex-employee.

communicate upward, their conversations tend to be shorter than discussions with their peers.[59]

Perhaps more important, upward communication often tends to suffer from serious inaccuracies. For example, subordinates frequently feel they must highlight their accomplishments and downplay their mistakes if they are to be looked on favorably.[60] Similarly, some individuals fear that they will be rebuked by their supervisors if they anticipate that their remarks will be perceived as threatening.[61] As a result, many people frequently avoid communicating bad news to their supervisors or simply "pass the buck" for doing so to someone else.[62] This general reluctance to transmit bad news is referred to as the **MUM effect**.[63] As you might imagine, because superiors rely on information when making decisions, keeping silent about important news, even if it's bad, may be one of the worst things a subordinate can do. As one executive put it, "All of us have our share of bonehead ideas. Having someone tell you it's a bonehead idea before you do something about it is really a great blessing."[64]

Horizontal communication. Finally, we note the nature of *horizontal communication* within organizations. Messages that flow laterally (at the same organizational level) are characterized by efforts at coordination (attempts to work together). Consider, for example, how a vice president of marketing would have to coordinate her efforts to initiate an advertising campaign for a new product with information from the vice president of production about when the first products will be coming off the assembly line.

Unlike vertical communication, in which the parties are at different status levels, horizontal communication involves people at the same level and, therefore, tends to be easier and friendlier. Communication between peers also tends to be more casual and occurs more quickly because fewer social barriers exist between the parties. Note, however, that even horizontal communication can be problematic. For example, people in different departments may feel that they are competing against each other for valued organizational resources and may show resentment toward each other, thereby substituting an antagonistic, competitive orientation for the friendlier, cooperative one needed to get things done.[65]

Informal Communication Networks: Behind the Organizational Chart

Think about the people with whom you communicate during the course of an average day. Friends, family members, classmates, and colleagues at work are among those with whom you may have informal communication, information shared without any formally imposed obligations or restrictions. It's easy to recognize how widespread our informal networks can be. You know someone who knows someone else, who knows your best friend—and before long, your informal networks become very far-reaching.

Informal communication networks, in part because they are so widespread, constitute an important avenue by which information flows in organizations.[66] In fact, middle managers ranked informal networks as better sources of organizational information than formal networks.[67] Therefore, if an organization's formal communication represents its skeleton, its informal communication constitutes its central nervous system.[68]

Organizations' hidden pathways. It is easy to imagine how important the flow of informal information may be within organizations. People transmit information to those with whom they come into contact, thereby providing conduits through which messages can travel. We also tend to communicate most with those who are similar to ourselves on such key variables as age and time working on the job.[69] Because we are more comfortable with similar people than with dissimilar ones, we tend to spend more time with them and, of course, communicate with them more often. As a result, many informal gender-segregated networks tend to form in organizations—what, among men, has been referred to the *old boys network* (see Chapter 7).

To the extent that these associations may isolate people from others in power who may be different from themselves, this practice is limiting.[70] At the same time, however, exposure to similar others with whom people feel comfortable provides valuable sources of information. For example, many African American business leaders have formed informal networks with others of the same race so as to help them share ways of succeeding in a business world in which they constitute an ethnic minority—alliances that have been helpful to the careers of many.[71] This informal observation is in keeping with scientific evidence showing that the more involved people are in their organizations' communication networks, the more powerful and influential they become.[72]

The idea that people are connected informally also has been used to explain a very important organizational phenomenon—turnover. Do people resign from their jobs in ways that are random and unrelated to each other? Research suggests that they do not but, rather, that turnover is related to the informal communication patterns between people.[73] In fact, voluntary turnover (employees freely electing to resign their jobs) occurs in a kind of **snowball effect.** A snowball does not accumulate snowflakes randomly but collects those that are in its path. Analogously, patterns of voluntary turnover are not independently distributed within a work group, but are the result of people's influences on each other. Thus, predicting which people will resign from their jobs may be based, in large part, on knowledge of the informal communication patterns within work groups. A person who leaves his or her job for a better one in another organization is likely to be an individual who knows someone who has already done so. For a suggestion regarding how this may operate, see Figure 9.9.

Unlike formal communication networks, informal communication networks are composed of individuals at different organizational levels. In such informal groups, people can tell anyone whatever they wish. For example, jokes and funny stories tend to cross organizational boundaries and are freely shared by people in both the managerial and nonmanagerial ranks of organizations.[74] On the other hand, it would be quite unlikely—indeed, considered "out of line"—for a lower-level employee to communicate something to an upper-level employee about how to do the job. What flows within the pathways of informal communication is informal information, messages not necessarily related to individuals' work.

The grapevine and the rumor mill. When anyone can tell something informal to anyone else, it results in a very rapid flow of information along what is commonly referred to as the **grapevine**—the pathways along which unofficial, informal information travels. In contrast to a formal organizational message, which might take several days to reach its desired audience, information traveling along the organizational grapevine tends to flow very rapidly, often within hours. This is not only because informal communication can cross formal organizational boundaries (e.g., you might be able to tell a good joke to

MUM effect
The reluctance to transmit bad news, shown either by not transmitting the message at all or by delegating the task to someone else.

snowball effect
The tendency for people to share informal information with others with whom they come into contact.

grapevine
An organization's informal channels of communication, based mainly on friendship or acquaintance.

FIGURE 9.9

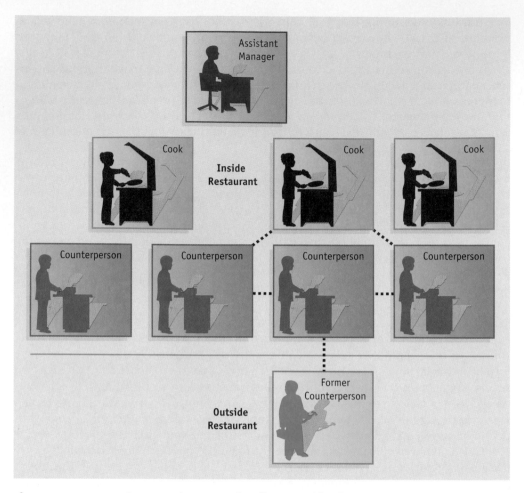

Informal Communication Networks: A Predictor of Turnover Patterns
The informal networks of communication between people (shown in dotted lines) provide channels through which messages about better job opportunities may be communicated. Patterns of voluntary turnover have been linked to the existence of such informal networks.
(*Source:* Based on suggestions by Krackhardt & Porter, 1986; see Note 73.)

almost anyone, not just your boss or subordinates with whom you are required to communicate) but also because informal information tends to be communicated orally.

As we noted earlier, oral messages are communicated faster than written ones, but become increasingly inaccurate as they flow from person to person. Because of the confusion grapevines may cause, some people have sought to eliminate them, but they are not necessarily bad. Informally socializing with our coworkers can help make work groups more cohesive and also may provide excellent opportunities for desired human contact, keeping the work environment stimulating. Grapevines must be considered an inevitable fact of life in organizations.[75] Interestingly, the vast majority of organizations do little or nothing to counter the spread of rumors within its walls.[76]

It is interesting to note that most of the information communicated along the grapevine is accurate. In fact, one study found that 82 percent of the information communicated along a particular company's organizational grapevine on a single occasion was accurate.[77] The problem with interpreting this figure is that the inaccurate portions of some messages may alter their overall meaning. If, for example, a story is going around that someone got passed by for promotion over a lower-ranking employee, it may cause quite a bit of dissension in the workplace. However, suppose everything is true except that the person turned down the promotion because it involved relocating. This important fact completely alters the situation. Only one fact needs to be inaccurate for the accuracy of the entire communication to suffer.

This problem of inaccuracy is clearly responsible for giving the grapevine such a bad reputation. In extreme cases, information may be transmitted that is almost totally without any basis in fact and usually unverifiable. Such messages are know as **rumors.** Typically, rumors are based on speculation, an overactive imagination, and wishful thinking rather than on objective facts. Rumors race like wildfire through organizations because the information they present is so interesting and ambiguous. The ambiguity leaves it open to embellishment as it passes orally from one person to the next. Before

rumors
Information with little basis in fact, often transmitted through informal channels (see *grapevine*).

you know it, almost everyone in the organization has heard the rumor, and its inaccurate message becomes taken as fact ("It must be true, everyone knows it"). Hence, even if there was, at one point, some truth to a rumor, the message quickly becomes untrue.

If you've ever been the victim of a personal rumor, then you know how difficult they can be to crush and how profound their effects can be. This is especially so when organizations are the victims of rumors. For example, rumors about the possibility of corporate takeovers may not only influence the value of a company's stock but also threaten its employees' feelings of job security. Sometimes rumors about company products can be very costly. Some examples:

■ A rumor about the use of worms in McDonald's hamburgers circulated in the Chicago area in the late 1970s. Although the rumor was completely untrue, sales dropped as much as 30 percent in some restaurants.[78]

■ In June 1993, stories appeared in the press stating that people across the United States found syringes in cans of Pepsi-Cola. Although the stories proved to be completely without fact, the hoax cost Pepsi a great deal in terms of investigative and advertising expenses—not to mention, lost business.[79]

■ The consumer-products giant Procter & Gamble (P&G) has been subject to consistent, nagging rumors linking it to Satanism.[80] Since 1980, rumors have swirled that the company's moon-and-stars trademark was linked to witchcraft. Although the company has emphatically denied the rumor and has won court judgments against various individuals spreading rumors, the rumors have persisted.

What can be done to counter the effects of rumors? Although this is a difficult question to answer, evidence suggests that directly refuting a rumor may not always counter its effects. Although Pepsi officials denied the reports about their tainted product, the rumor was not only implausible but also was disproved quickly by independent investigators from the Food and Drug Administration. Sometimes, however, as the P&G rumor illustrates, rumors are more difficult to disprove and do not die quickly. In such cases, directly refuting the rumors only fuels the fire. When you directly refute a rumor (e.g., "I didn't do it"), you actually may help spread it among those who have not already heard about it ("Oh, I didn't know people thought that") and strengthen it among those who have already heard it ("If it weren't true, they wouldn't be protesting so much"). In the case of P&G, the problem is compounded by the allegation that some parties may be making a concerted effort to keep the rumor alive. In such cases, directing the public's attention away from the rumor may help minimize its adverse impact. For example, the company can focus its advertising on other positive things the public knows about it. In research studying the McDonald's rumor, for example, it was found that reminding people of other things they thought about McDonald's (e.g., that it is a clean, family-oriented place) helped counter the negative effects of the rumor.[81]

If you should ever become the victim of a rumor, try immediately to refute it with indisputable facts if you can. But, if it lingers on, try directing people's attention to other positive things they already believe about you. Although rumors may be impossible to stop, with some effort their effects can be effectively managed.

Communicating Inside Versus Outside the Organization

All corporate communication can be distinguished with respect to whether it is aimed at other people within the organization (e.g., fellow employees) or outside the organization (e.g., the general public).[82] Do executives say different kinds of things when aiming their remarks inside versus outside the company?

Research suggests that they do.[83] Illustrating this, consider a study in which scientists analyzed the comments made by CEOs of 10 forest products companies appearing in their letters to shareholders (external communications) over the 10-year period from 1979 to 1988. They also examined various planning documents (internal communications) for these same companies during this period. Instead of looking at exactly what was said, they categorized these communications with respect to how they were

FIGURE 9.10

Internal vs. External Communications: Is There a Difference?
Research has shown that executives tend to communicate differently when sending messages inside and outside their organizations. Internal communications tend to focus on threats more than opportunities, whereas external communications tend to focus on opportunities more than threats. (*Source:* Based on suggestions by Fiol, 1995; see Note 83.)

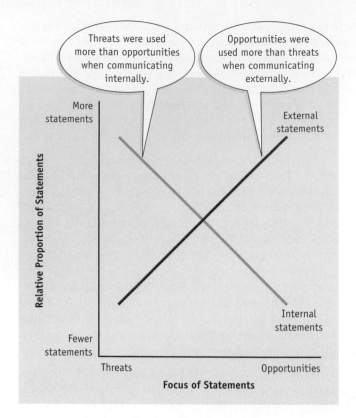

framed. Specifically, they considered whether the statements focused on threats the company faced (e.g., the rising cost of materials) or on opportunities (e.g., growth in the housing market).

The results were quite interesting. In general, because the industry improved during the period studied, the proportion of documents framed in terms of threat dropped. However, the mention of threat was not equally likely to occur in both internal and external statements. For each year studied, a greater proportion of internal documents than external documents referred to threats. Likewise, with only few exceptions, a greater proportion of internal documents than external documents focused on opportunities. (For a summary of these results, see Figure 9.10.)

These findings suggest that executives were attempting to present their companies in a positive light to the public (by focusing on opportunities) but were more willing to address threats internally. They may well have been thinking that whereas it is important to not frighten the investing public, it is also important to keep employees appraised of any and all threats the company faces so that it can take proper steps to defend itself.

strategic communication
The practice of presenting information about the company to broad, external audiences, such as the press.

This is the idea behind what is called **strategic communication**—the practice of presenting information about the company to broad, external audiences, such as the press. The more effectively companies manage this process, the better they will be received by the general public, yielding considerable benefits, such as enhanced customer loyalty and increased sales. Given the importance of clearly and appropriately managing a corporate image through strategic communication, public relations firms are often hired to do the work.

IMPROVING YOUR COMMUNICATION SKILLS

Throughout this chapter we have noted the central role of communication in organizational functioning. Given this, it is easy to understand how any efforts at improving the communication process in organizations may have highly desirable payoffs for organizations as well as for the individuals and groups working in them. Several steps can be taken to obtain the benefits of effective communication.[84] In this final section, we will describe some of these techniques, including measures that can be taken by individuals, as well as tactics for improving communication that involve entire organizations.

Use Simple, Clear Language

Have you ever driven your "previously owned motor vehicle" up to an "ethyl-dispensing device" and been greeted by a "petroleum transfer engineer" who filled your "fuel containment module"? Or perhaps you've gone to a "home improvement center" looking for a "manually powered impact device." In either case, we wouldn't blame you if you went to another "operating entity" that had a better "customer interface capacity." You've certainly already encountered enough business double-talk without getting any more from us. Fortunately, our point can be stated simply: Using needlessly formal language imposes a serious barrier to communication.

Recognize that all organizations, fields, social groups, and professions have their **jargon**—their own specialized language. Your own college or university may have a "quad," or, as a student, you may have a "roomie" who wants to go "Greek" and is interested in "rushing." These are examples of a college student's jargon. No doubt, you've encountered a lot of language in this book that may have at first sounded strange to you. Our point is that the use of jargon is inevitable when people within the same field or social groups communicate with each other.

Some degree of highly specialized language may help communication by providing an easy way for people in the same fields to share complex ideas. Jargon also allows professionals to identify unknown others as people in their field because they "speak the same language." For example, management professors would describe this book as dealing with the field of *OB*, a term that would have a very different meaning to medical doctors (for whom it refers to the field of obstetrics). Obviously, within professions, jargon helps communication, but it can lead to confusion when used outside the groups within which it has meaning.

In addition to avoiding jargon, the clearest communicators also keep language short, simple, and to the point. Hence, it is wise to adopt the **K.I.S.S. principle** when communicating— that is, keep it short and simple.[85] People are better able to understand messages that do not overwhelm them with too much information at once than those that present more than they can absorb. A wise communicator is sensitive to this and knows how to monitor his or her audience for signs of overloading audience members' circuits with too much information. Again, although you may know what you are talking about, you may not be able to get your ideas across to others unless you package them in doses small and simple enough to be understood. When this is done effectively, even the most complex ideas can be clearly communicated.[86] (You certainly wouldn't want a professor to write an ambiguous message when he or she sends out a letter of recommendation for you.[87] For an example of serious ambiguities that may appear in such important documents, see Table 9.3.)

jargon
The specialized language used by a particular group (e.g., people within a profession).

K.I.S.S. principle
A basic principle of communication advising that messages should be as short and simple as possible (an abbreviation for keep it short and simple).

Become an Active, Attentive Listener

Just as it is important to make your ideas understandable to others (i.e., sending messages), it is equally important to work at being a good listener (i.e., receiving messages). Although people do a great deal of listening, they pay attention to and comprehend only a small percentage of the information directed at them.[88]

Most of us usually think of listening as a passive process of taking in information sent by others, but when done correctly the process of listening is much more active.[89] For example, good listeners ask questions if they don't understand something, and they nod or otherwise signal when they understand. Such cues provide critical feedback to communicators about the extent to which they are coming across to you. As a listener, you can help the communication process by letting the sender know if and how his or

TABLE 9.3   THE NOT-SO-FAVORABLE RECOMMENDATION

Sometimes ambiguities in the way letters of recommendation are written disguise truly negative opinions in a highly positive manner. Examples of such statements are shown here. You may need to read these twice to see exactly what the problem is.

TO DESCRIBE SOMEONE WHO IS . . .	YOU MIGHT SAY . . .
Extremely inept	"I most enthusiastically recommend this candidate with no qualifications whatsoever."
Not particularly industrious	"In my opinion you will be very fortunate to get this person to work for you."
Not worthy of further consideration	"I would urge you to waste no time in making this candidate an offer of employment."
Lacking in credentials	"All in all, I cannot say enough good things about this candidate or recommend him too highly."
An ex-employee whom you do not miss	"I am pleased to say that this candidate is a former colleague of mine."
So unproductive as to be worthless	"I can assure you that no person would be better for this job."

(*Source:* Robert J. Thornton, *Lexicon of Intentionally Ambiguous Recommendations (L.I.A.R.),* 2nd edition, 1998, Almus Publications, Central Point, Oregon. Used with permission from the author.)

her messages are coming across to you. *Asking questions* and *putting the speaker's ideas into your own words* are helpful ways of ensuring you are taking in all the information presented.

It also is very useful to avoid distractions in the environment and to concentrate on what the other person is saying. When listening to others, *avoid jumping to conclusions or evaluating their remarks.* It is important to completely take in what is being said before you respond. Simply dismissing someone because you don't like what is being said is much too easy. Doing so, of course, poses a formidable barrier to effective communication.

Being a good listener also involves making sure you are aware of others' main points. What is the speaker trying to say? *Make sure you understand another's ideas before you formulate your reply.* Too many of us interrupt speakers with our own ideas before we have fully heard theirs. If this sounds like something you do, rest assured that it is not only quite common, but also correctable.

Although it requires some effort, incorporating these suggestions into your own listening habits cannot help but make you a better listener. Indeed, many organizations have sought to help their employees in this way. For example, the corporate giant Unisys has for some time systematically trained thousands of its employees in effective listening skills (using seminars and self-training cassettes). Clearly, Unisys is among those companies acknowledging the importance of good listening skills in promoting effective organizational communication.

HURIER model

The conceptualization that describes effective listening as made up of the following six components: hearing, understanding, remembering, interpreting, evaluating, and responding.

The development of listening skills requires identifying the individual elements of listening, the separate skills that contribute to listening effectiveness. These may be clustered into six groups known as the **HURIER model.**[90] The term *HURIER* is an acronym composed of the initials of the words reflecting the component skills of effective listening: hearing, understanding, remembering, interpreting, evaluating, and responding. (For a summary of these individual skills, see Figure 9.11.) Although it might seem easy to do the six things needed to be a good listener, we are not all as good as we think we are in this capacity, suggesting that listening might not be as easy as it seems.

Management consultant Nancy K. Austin would agree and explains that when you invite people to talk to you about their problems on the job, you're implicitly making a promise to listen to them.[91] Of course, when you do, you may feel hostile and defensive

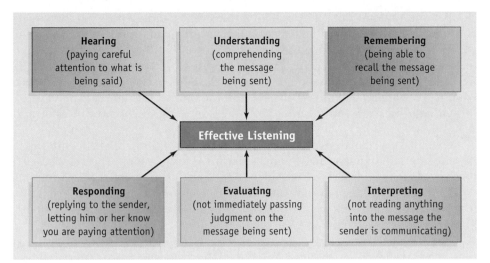

FIGURE 9.11
The HURIER Model: Components of Effective Listening
Research has shown that the six skills identified here—hearing, understanding, remembering, interpreting, evaluating, and responding—contribute greatly to the effectiveness of listening.
(*Source:* Based on suggestions by Brownell, 1985; see Note 90.)

toward the speaker and become more interested in speaking up and setting the record straight if you don't like what you hear. This is the challenge of listening. Good listeners should resist this temptation and pay careful attention to the speaker. When they cannot do so, they should admit the problem and reschedule another opportunity to get together.

Austin also advises people to "be an equal opportunity listener," that is, to pay attention not only to those whose high status commands our attention but also to anyone at any level, and to make time to hear them all in a democratic fashion. The idea is not only that people at any job level might have something to say but also that they may feel good about you as a manager for having shown consideration to them. Austin notes that by listening to an employee, you are saying, "You are smart and have important things to say; you are worth my time."[92] Such a message is critical to establishing the kind of open, two-way communication essential for top management.

Research has confirmed the importance of listening as a management skill. In fact, it has shown that the better a person is as a listener, the more likely he or she is to rapidly rise up the organizational hierarchy[93] and to perform well as a manager.[94] Apparently, good listening skills are an important aspect of one's ability to succeed as a manager. Unfortunately, however, most people tend to think of themselves as being much better listeners than others think they are.[95] Such overconfidence in one's own listening ability can be a barrier to seeking training in listening skills inasmuch as people who believe they are already good listeners may have little motivation to seek training in this important skill. However, when managers actually do complete formal training programs to enhance their listening skills, it generally pays off quite well. (To get some practice in this important management skill, complete the Group Exercise at the end of this chapter on page 354.)

Gauge the Flow of Information: Avoiding Overload

Imagine a busy manager surrounded by a tall stack of papers with a telephone receiver in each ear and a crowd of people gathered around waiting to talk to her. Obviously, the many demands put on this person can slow down the system and make its operation less effective. When any part of a communication network becomes bogged down with more information than it can handle effectively, a condition of **overload** is said to exist. Consider, for example, the bottleneck in the flow of routine financial information that might result when the members of the accounting department of an organization are tied up preparing corporate tax returns. Naturally, such a state poses a serious threat to effective organizational communication. And it's only getting worse. Because today's managers face more information overload than ever before, they tend to ignore a great deal of the information they need to do their jobs. Fortunately, however, several concrete steps can be taken to manage information more effectively.

overload
The condition in which a unit of an organization becomes overburdened with too much incoming information.

For one, organizations may employ *gatekeepers,* people whose jobs require them to control the flow of information to potentially overloaded units. For example, administrative assistants are responsible for making sure that busy executives are not overloaded by the demands of other people or groups. Newspaper editors and television news directors also may be thought of as gatekeepers because such individuals decide what news will and will not be shared with the public. It is an essential part of these individuals' jobs to avoid overloading others by gauging the flow of information to them.

Overload also can be avoided through *queuing.* This term refers to lining up incoming information so that it can be managed in an orderly fashion. The practices of "stacking" jets as they approach a busy airport and making customers take a number (i.e., defining their position in the line) at a busy deli counter are designed to avoid the chaos that otherwise may result when too many demands are made on the system at once. For a summary of these techniques, see Figure 9.12.

When systems are overloaded, *distortion* and *omission* are likely to result. That is, messages may be either changed or left out when they are passed from one organizational unit to the next. If you've ever played the parlor game "telephone" (in which one person whispers a message to another, who passes it on to another, and so on until it reaches the last person), you likely have experienced—or contributed to—the ways messages get distorted and omitted. When you consider the important messages that often are communicated in organizations, these problems can be very serious. They also tend to be quite extreme. A dramatic demonstration of this was reported in a study tracing the flow of downward communication in more than 100 organizations. The researchers found that messages communicated downward over five levels lost approximately 80 percent of their original information by the time they reached their destination at the lowest level of the organizational hierarchy.[96] Obviously, something needs to be done.

One strategy that has proven effective in avoiding the problems of distortion and omission is *redundancy.* Making messages redundant involves transmitting them again, often in another form or via another channel. For example, in attempting to communicate an important message to her subordinates, a manager may tell them the message and then follow it up with a written memo. In fact, managers frequently encourage this practice.[97]

Another practice that can help avoid distortion and omission is *verification.* This refers to making sure messages have been received accurately. Pilots use verification when they repeat the messages given them by air traffic controllers (see Figure 9.13). Doing so assures both parties that the messages the pilots heard were the actual mes-

FIGURE 9.12

Overload: A Problem That Can Be Solved
Overload, receiving too many messages at once, can interfere seriously with organizational functioning. This problem can be minimized by using *gatekeepers* (individuals who control the flow of information) and *queuing* (lining up incoming information so that it arrives in an orderly fashion).

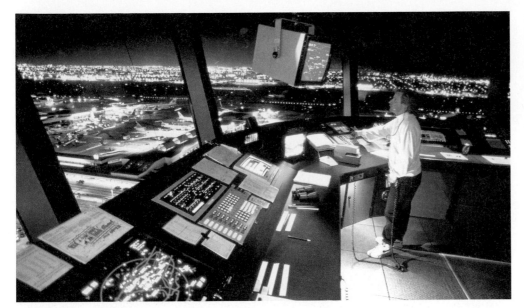

FIGURE 9.13
Verifying Information: Critical in Some Jobs
The accuracy of communication cannot be taken for granted in some jobs. Among air traffic controllers, for example, verifying messages from airline pilots is a standard procedure used to ensure that they correctly heard the message sent. This practice helps avoid potentially catastrophic errors resulting from miscommunication.

sages the controllers sent. Given how busy pilots may be during takeoffs and landings and the interference inherent in radio transmissions, coupled with the vital importance of the messages themselves, the practice of verifying messages is a wise safety measure. The practice not only is used in airline communication systems but may be used by individual communicators as well. Active listeners may wish to verify that they correctly understood a speaker and do so by paraphrasing the speaker's remarks within a question, asking "If I understood, you were saying. . . ."

Give and Receive Feedback: Opening Channels of Communication

To operate effectively, organizations must be able to communicate accurately with those who keep them running—their employees. Unfortunately, the vast majority of employees believe that the feedback between themselves and their organizations is not as good as it should be.[98] For various reasons, people often are unwilling or unable to communicate their ideas to top management. Part of the problem is the lack of available channels for upward communication and people's reluctance to use whatever ones exist. How, then, can organizations obtain information from their employees and improve the upward flow of communication? Several approaches have been used widely.

360-degree feedback. As we discussed in Chapter 2, *360-degree feedback* is a technique in which people at all organizational levels give feedback to others at different levels and receive feedback from them, as well as outsiders (e.g., customers and suppliers). This technique has been used successfully in such companies as Alcoa, BellSouth, General Mills, Hewlett-Packard (HP), Merck, Motorola, and 3M.

Suggestion systems. Too often, employees' good ideas about how to improve organizational functioning fail to work their way up the organizational chart because the people with the ideas do not know how to reach the people who can implement them. Even worse, they may feel they will not be listened to even if they can reach the right person. **Suggestion systems** are procedures designed to help avoid these problems, by providing a formal mechanism through which employees can present their ideas to the company. Research has found that about 15 percent of employees use their companies' suggestion boxes and that about 25 percent of the suggestions made are implemented.[99] Employees are usually rewarded for their successful suggestions, either with a flat monetary reward or some percentage of the money saved by implementing the suggestion.

suggestion systems
Procedures that provide formal mechanisms to employees for presenting their ideas to the company.

corporate hotlines

Telephone lines staffed by experts ready to answer employees' questions, listen to their comments, and the like.

Corporate hotlines. Growing numbers of companies are using **corporate hotlines**—telephone lines staffed by experts ready to answer employees' questions, listen to their comments, and the like.[100] A good example of this is the hotline that HP and Compaq set up in 2002 when these companies merged. As thousands of stockholders and employees sought information about what the merger would mean for them, the hotline proved to be a useful means of sharing needed information.

In general, by providing personnel with easy access to information, companies benefit in several ways. Doing so not only shows employees that the company cares about them, but it also encourages them to address their concerns before the issues become more serious. In addition, by keeping track of the kinds of questions and concerns voiced, top management is given invaluable insight into ways of improving organizational conditions. These days, inasmuch as 40 percent of calls to hotlines are made after regular working hours or on weekends, companies are finding it difficult to staff their own hotlines. As a result, some organizations have begun to outsource their hotline services. In fact, several companies—such as Pinkerton Services Group, the largest supplier of outsourced, hotlines—have emerged in response to this need.[101]

Informal meetings. Many companies have found it useful to hold informal meetings between employees at a wide variety of corporate levels as a means of facilitating communication. Sometimes called *"brown bag" meetings* or *"skip level" meetings,* such sessions are designed to facilitate communication between people who don't usually get together because they work at different organizational levels.[102] Brown bag meetings are informal get-togethers over breakfast or lunch (brought in from home in a brown bag, hence, the term) at which people discuss what's going on in the company. The informal nature of the meetings is designed to encourage the open sharing of ideas (eating a sandwich out of a bag is a status equalizer!).

Skip level meetings do essentially the same thing. These are gatherings of employees with corporate superiors who are more than one level higher than themselves in the organizational hierarchy. The idea is that new lines of communication can be established by bringing together people who are two or more levels apart because these individuals usually don't come into contact with each other (see Figure 9.14).

Employee surveys. Many companies attempt to gather feedback from employees systematically by giving them questionnaires referred to as *employee surveys.* Often, these are used to collect information about employees' attitudes and opinions about key areas of organizational operations. Surveys administered at regular intervals may be useful for spotting changes in attitudes as they occur. Such surveys tend to be quite effective when their results are shared with employees, especially when the feedback is

FIGURE 9.14

At Kellogg, Communication Is "Gr-r-reat"

As CEO of the breakfast cereal giant, Kellogg Co., Carlos M. Gutierrez recognizes that in a highly competitive market, ideas for new products are vital to the company's success. Until recently, these could come only from the head of research and development. Today, Gutierrez gladly meets with any employee of the company's Institute for Food & Nutritional Research who wants to share ideas—even Tony the Tiger.

used as the basis for changing the way things are done. Some managers even go so far as to ask their employees to rate them on a "report card."[103]

The various techniques we have described here are among those most commonly used to gather feedback. However, for a close-up look at another effective but highly unorthodox approach, see the Best Practices section on page 348.

Be a Supportive Communicator: Enhancing Relationships

To be an effective communicator, you must be supportive of others. By **supportive communication** we are referring to any communication that is accurate and honest and that builds and enhances relationships instead of jeopardizing them.

Simply put, how you act toward another influences the nature of your relationship with that person and affects the quality of communication, which may influence various work-related attitudes (see Chapter 5) and job performance. Suppose, for example, that you send someone a very abrasive, insensitive message. That person is likely to become distant and distrustful, believing that you are uncaring. This, in turn, will lead the attacked person to become defensive, spending more time and energy constructing a good defense rather than listening carefully to your message. And, of course, a message that is not carefully attended to will not be comprehended, leading to problematic job performance.

This discussion leads us to a very important question: What can you do to become a supportive communicator? Several tried-and-true tactics can be identified.[105]

Focus on the problem, not the person. Referring to an individual's characteristics (e.g., saying "you are lazy") is likely to make that person defensive (e.g., thinking, "no, I'm not"). However, focusing on the problem itself (e.g., saying "we lost the account") is likely to move the conversation toward a solution (e.g., asking "what can we do about it?"). Communication tends to be far more supportive when it focuses on the problem and possible solutions than on one person's beliefs about the characteristics of another that caused it.

Honestly say what you mean. Too often, people avoid difficult matters by disguising their true feelings. Instead of saying that everything's fine when it clearly isn't, for example, it helps to make it clear how you feel. Don't be afraid of saying, "I'm upset by what you did," if that's how you really feel.

Own up to your decisions. Don't hesitate to make it clear exactly what you did and how you feel. It's far more supportive, for example, to explain to someone precisely why you voted to deny his or her request than to hide behind a general statement, such as "the committee saw problems in your proposal." If you were on the committee, speak for yourself.

Use validating language. Of course, when you do speak your mind, always avoid language that arouses negative feelings about one's self-worth, such as "what can you expect from a lawyer?" Statements of this type use what is referred to as **invalidating language.**[106] It's far more effective to state your point in a way that makes people feel recognized and accepted for who they are—that is, to use **validating language.** For example, you might say, "I'm not sure I agree, but I'm interested in hearing your side." Although you might disagree with the speaker, this is a far more supportive approach.

Strive to keep the conversation going. Saying something like, "that's nice, let me tell you about my problems" is a real conversation-stopper. By deflecting the speaker's concerns to your own, you are not being at all supportive. It's far more supportive to probe for additional information (e.g., by saying "tell me about it") or by reflecting back what you think the speaker said (e.g., "If I heard you correctly, you feel . . .").

Another trick for helping conversations move along is to use **conjunctive statements**—comments that connect what you will be saying to the speaker's remarks, instead of **disjunctive statements**—comments that are disconnected from the speaker's remarks. So, for example, it's better to say something like, "On that same topic, I think . . . ," as opposed to saying something on a completely different subject. Doing so is sure to end the conversation.

supportive communication
Any communication that is accurate and honest and that builds and enhances relationships instead of jeopardizing them.

invalidating language
Language that arouses negative feelings about one's self-worth.

validating language
Language that makes people feel recognized and accepted for who they are.

conjunctive statements
Statements that keep conversations going by connecting one speaker's remarks to another's.

disjunctive statements
Statements that are disconnected from a previous statement, tending to bring conversations to a close.

Use Inspirational Communication Tactics

The most effective leaders know how to inspire others when they communicate with them. To become an effective leader or even a more effective employee, it helps to consider several key ways of inspiring others when communicating with them.[107]

Project confidence and power with emotion-provoking words. The most persuasive communicators attempt to inspire others by sprinkling their speech with words that provoke emotion. For example, it helps to use phrases such as "bonding with customers" instead of the more benign "being friendly." Effective communicators also use words in ways that highlight their power in an organization. For some linguistic tips in this regard, see Table 9.4.[108]

Be credible. Communicators are most effective when they are perceived to be credible. Such perceptions are enhanced when one is considered trustworthy, intelligent, and knowledgeable. Bill Joy of Sun Microsystems (considered "the Thomas Edison of the Internet"), for example, has considerable credibility in the computer business because he is regarded as highly intelligent. At the very least, credibility is enhanced by backing up your claims with clear data. People might not believe you unless you support your ideas with objective information.

Pitch your message to the listener. The most effective communicators go out of their way to send messages that are of interest to listeners. Assume that people will pay greatest attention when they are interested in answering the question "how is what you are saying important to me?" People will attend most carefully to messages that have value to them. Jürgen Schempp, CEO of Daimler–Chrysler, appeared to have this rule in mind when he explained how his plan for organizing the company into three divisions would result in higher salaries and bonuses for employees as well as greater autonomy.

Cut through the clutter. People are so busy these days that they easily become distracted by the many messages that come across their desks (see Figure 9.15 on page 350).[109] The most effective communicators attempt to cut through the clutter by making their messages interesting, important, and special. Dull and inspiring messages are likely to get lost in the shuffle.

scheduled a presentation at Coca-Cola but left the presentation materials behind.

So many people learned so many things about ways to mess things up—and how to avoid them—that the "Mistake of the Month" soon became a feature of staff meetings at Delahaye. It works like this. At each monthly staff meeting, a half-hour is devoted to identifying and discussing everyone's mistakes. Each is written on a board, and everyone gets to vote on two categories of mistakes—the one from which they learned the most and the one from which they learned the least. The person whose mistake is identified as helping the most is awarded a highly coveted downtown parking space for the next month. The person from whose mistake people learned the least is required to speak at the next meeting about what he or she is doing to ensure that it will never happen again. The time spent on this exercise is considered a wise investment insofar as it allows all employees to learn from everyone else's mistakes.

During the program's first 10 years, more than 2,000 mistakes have been identified—but few ever have been repeated, creating a positive effect on the company's work. Paine also notes that the program helps her identify steps she needs to take to improve things at Delahaye. She also notes that sharing mistakes has been "a bonding ritual," adding, "once you go through it, you're a member of the club."

Avoid "junk words" that dilute your message. Nobody likes to listen to people who constantly use phrases such as, "like," "know what I mean?" and "you know." Such phrases send the message that the speaker is ill-prepared to express himself or herself clearly and precisely. Because many of us use such phrases in our everyday language, it helps to practice by tape-recording what you are going to say so you can keep track of the number of times you say these things. Make a conscious effort to stop saying these words, and use your tape-recordings to monitor your progress.

TABLE 9.4   HOW TO PROJECT CONFIDENCE WITH YOUR WORDS

The most powerful and confident people tend to follow certain linguistic conventions. By emulating the way they speak, you, too, can enhance the confidence you project. Here are some guidelines.

RULE	EXPLANATION OR EXAMPLE
Always know exactly what you want.	The more committed you are to achieving a certain end, the more clearly and powerfully you will be able to sell your idea.
Use the pronoun *I*, unless you are a part of a team.	This allows you to take individual credit for your ideas.
Downplay uncertainty.	If you are unsure of your opinion, make a broad but positive statement, such as "I am confident this new accounting procedure will make things more efficient."
Ask very few questions.	You may come across as being weak or unknowledgeable if you have to ask what something means or what's going on.
Don't display disappointment when your ideas are challenged.	It is better to act as though opposition is expected and to explain your viewpoint.
Make bold statements.	Be bold about ideas but avoid attacking anyone personally.

(*Source:* Based on suggestions by Tannen, 1998; see Note 108.)

FIGURE 9.15

We All Are Bombarded by Messages
The average U.S. office worker receives 189 messages per day—that's over 23 per hour. As summarized here, they come in many different forms.
(*Source:* Wurman, 2000; see Note 109.)

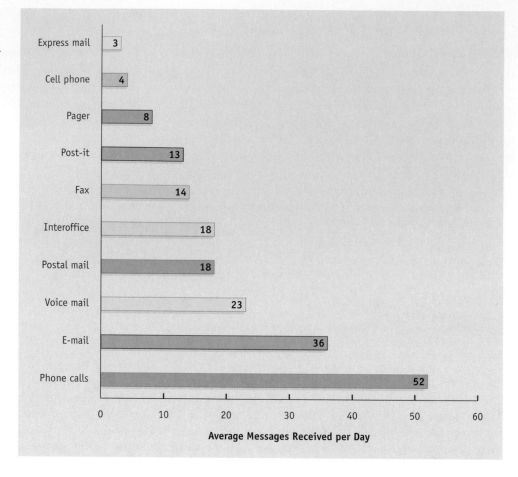

Average Messages Received per Day

Message type	Value
Express mail	3
Cell phone	4
Pager	8
Post-it	13
Fax	14
Interoffice	18
Postal mail	18
Voice mail	23
E-mail	36
Phone calls	52

Use front-loaded messages. The most effective communicators come right out and say what they mean. They don't beat around the bush, and they don't embed their most important message in a long speech or letter. Instead, they begin by making the point they are attempting to communicate and then use the remainder of the message to illustrate it and flesh out the details.

We realize that these tips for inspiring people when communicating with them might be difficult to follow. Some even may run counter to communication patterns you have established over the years (especially given that most of us are rather timid when it comes to communicating). Then again, most of us probably inspire others very little when we communicate with them. If you have aspirations for a career as a politician or a business leader, you will need to turn this around. In doing so, we're sure you'll find these suggestions to be extremely worthwhile.

SUMMARY AND REVIEW OF LEARNING OBJECTIVES

1. Describe the process of communication and its role in organizations.
The process of communication occurs when a sender of information encodes a message and transmits it over communication channels to a receiver, who decodes it and then sends feedback. Factors interfering with these processes are known as noise. Communication is used in organizations not only to direct individual action but also to achieve coordinated action. Although the heart of communication is information, communication also is used to develop friendships and to build interpersonal trust and acceptance in organizations.

2. Identify various forms of verbal media used in organizations, and explain which ones are most appropriate for communicating messages of different types.

Communication in both oral and written forms is commonly used in organizations. Verbal media range from those that are rich (highly personal and provide opportunities for immediate feedback), such as face-to-face discussions, to those that are lean (impersonal and one-way), such as flyers. Rich forms of communication are best for communicating ambiguous and nonroutine matters, whereas leaner forms of communication are adequate for more routine matters.

3. Explain how style of dress and the use of time and space are used to communicate nonverbally in organizations.

People tend to have greater self-confidence when they dress appropriately for the jobs they perform, although there are widespread differences in what constitutes appropriate dress (e.g., business casual dress is rapidly becoming the new standard). People communicate their higher organizational status by requiring lower-ranking individuals to spend more time waiting for them. Status also is communicated nonverbally by the use of space: Higher-status people tend to sit at the heads of rectangular tables.

4. Describe various types of individual differences with respect to how people communicate with each other.

People tend to have different personal communication styles. Six such styles have been identified: the Noble, the Socratic, the Reflective, the Magistrate, the Candidate, and the Senator. Interpersonal communication is enhanced when people's styles match or when one person anticipates another's style. There also are gender differences in communication. Whereas men tend to communicate with the intent of emphasizing their status, women tend to focus on making positive social connections. Such differences frequently lead to miscommunication between men and women. Cross-cultural communication is hampered by the fact that people from different cultures frequently misunderstand each other's intentions. This may stem from different vocabularies and subtle differences in the meanings of words that may not be understood outside the culture.

5. Describe the formal and informal forces that are responsible for communication in organizations.

Communication is influenced by organizational structure, the formally prescribed pattern of interrelationships between people in organizations. Structure dictates who must communicate with whom (as reflected in an organizational chart, a diagram outlining these reporting relationships) and the form that communication takes. Orders flow down an organizational hierarchy, and information flows upward. However, the upward flow of information is often distorted insofar as people are reluctant to share bad news with their superiors. Attempts at coordination characterize horizontal communication, messages between organizational members at the same level. Information flows rapidly along informal communication networks. These informal connections between people are responsible for spreading information very rapidly because they transcend formal organizational boundaries. Informal pathways known as the grapevine are often responsible for the rapid transmission of partially inaccurate information known as rumors. Rumors may be costly to organizations as well as individuals. Fortunately, there are several ways they can be combated.

6. Explain the various things you can do to improve your effectiveness as a communicator in organizations.

There are several things you can do to become a better communicator. First, keep your messages brief and clear and avoid using jargon when communicating with those who may not be familiar with specialized terms. Second, improve your listening skills, learning to listen actively (thinking about and questioning the speaker) and attentively (without distraction). Third, you can minimize the problem of overload by using gatekeepers (individuals who control the flow of information to others) or by queuing (the orderly lining up of incoming information). And you can minimize the problems of distortion and omission of messages by making messages redundant and by encouraging their verification. Fourth, you can improve communication at the organizational level by using techniques that open upward channels of communication to employee feedback (e.g., suggestion systems, corporate hot lines, and employee surveys). Fifth, you should attempt to be a supportive communicator—someone who makes an effort to enhance his or her relationships with others. You do so by focusing attention on the problem instead of the person, honestly saying what you mean, owning up to your own decisions, using validating language, and striving to keep the conversation going. Sixth, you can improve your effectiveness as a communicator by taking advantage of technology, such as by using video-mediated communication and speech recognition technology.

POINTS TO PONDER

Questions for Review

1. What are the various steps in the communication process?
2. What types of verbal media are best suited to various situations?
3. What kinds of things do people communicate about themselves nonverbally, and how can these be improved upon?
4. What are the various communication styles that people possess?
5. What can be done to improve the quality of formal and informal communication in organizations?
6. What steps can be taken to improve the quality of communication in organizations?

Experiential Questions

1. Think of an instance in which you had to transmit bad news to another person (e.g., firing, unwanted transfer). Were you reluctant to share this information (as per the MUM effect)? How did you respond in this situation?
2. Think of an instance in which you used a particular communication medium (e.g., e-mail) in a manner that proved to be ineffective. What occurred? In retrospect, what could you have done to avoid the problems you encountered?
3. Do you regard yourself as a good listener? What might you do to improve your skills as a listener?

Questions to Analyze

1. What particular communication problem do you believe occurs most frequently in organizations? Why is this so? What would you recommend to combat this particular problem?
2. In your opinion, how vital a factor is communication style when it comes to causing communication problems? Do communication style differences really matter? If not, why not? If so, how can they be overcome?
3. In what ways has rapidly advancing technology helped communication in organizations and in what ways has it been a hindrance? Explain your answer.

INDIVIDUAL EXERCISE

Assessing Your Personal Communication Style

When you read about the six different personal communication styles on pages 329–330, did you have some idea of which one you tend to use? The following test, based on questions similar to those used by scientists to test communication style (McCallister, 1994; see Note 43), will give you a good idea of your own personal communication style.

Directions

Read all 18 of the following statements. For each one, think of how you *actually* communicate (and not what you think you should do). If you believe that the statement describes how you usually communicate, mark a "Y" for "yes." If you believe the statement does not describe how you usually communicate, mark an "N" for "no."

_____ 1. When I talk to others, I tend to be direct and straightforward.
_____ 2. I am a "tell it like it is" kind of person.
_____ 3. I freely share my opinions with others.
_____ 4. I usually say the first thing that comes to my mind.
_____ 5. I tend to get impatient when others speak.
_____ 6. I tend to avoid long, detailed discussions.
_____ 7. I very much enjoy chatting with other people.
_____ 8. I tend to give very long, exact directions to others.
_____ 9. I am sometimes accused of being redundant.
_____ 10. I am prone to explain things by using anecdotes and examples.
_____ 11. I enjoy arguing and debating things with others.
_____ 12. I have seen people "tune me out" when I speak.
_____ 13. People tend to tell me their problems.
_____ 14. I tend to ignore people who seem angry.
_____ 15. I tend to be soft-spoken.
_____ 16. I may tell another person that I agree with him or her, even if I do not.
_____ 17. People tend to interrupt me when I am speaking to them.
_____ 18. I tend to be polite and supportive when I talk to people.

Scoring

1. Add the number of "Y's" in response to items 1 through 6. This is your Noble score.
2. Add the number of "Y's" in response to items 7 through 12. This is your Socratic score.
3. Add the number of "Y's" in response to items 13 through 18. This is your Reflective score.
4. To determine your style, compare your scores to each other.
   a. If your Noble score is higher than the other two, you are a Noble. If your Socratic score is higher than the other two, you are a Socratic. If your Reflective score is much higher than the other two, you are a Reflective. These are the three dominant styles.
   b. If your Noble and Socratic scores are close to each other but far from your Reflective score, you are a Magistrate. If your Socratic and Reflective scores are close to each other but far from your Noble score, you are a Candidate. If your Noble and Reflective scores are close to each other but far from your Socratic score, you are a Senator.
   c. If all three of your scores are very close to each other, you might not be aware of how you communicate. Retake the test, concentrating on what you actually do instead of what you think you should do.

Questions for Discussion

1. What style did the test reveal that you have? How did this compare to the style you thought you had before you took the test?
2. Based on the descriptions of the personal communication styles in the text, were you able to guess in advance which test items were indicative of which styles? What additional items may be added to the test to assess each style?
3. How effective do you think you would be in altering your communication style to match the style of another?

GROUP EXERCISE

Sharpening Your Listening Skills

Are you a good listener, a *really* good listener—one who understands exactly what someone else is saying to you? Most of us tend to think that we are much better than we really are when it comes to this important skill. After all, we've been listening to others our whole lives. And, with that much practice, we must certainly be okay. To gain some insight into your own listening skills, try the following group exercise.

Directions

1. Divide the class into pairs of people who do not already know each other. Arrange the chairs so that the people within each pair are facing one another but are separated from the other pairs.
2. Within each pair, one person should be selected as the speaker and the other as the listener. The speaker should tell the listener about a specific incident on the job in which he or she was somehow harmed (e.g., disappointed by not getting a raise, being embarrassed by another, losing a battle with a coworker, getting fired, etc.), and how he or she felt about it. The total discussion should last about 10 to 15 minutes.
3. Listeners should carefully attempt to follow the suggestions for good listening summarized in Figure 9.11. To help, the instructor should discuss these with the class.
4. After the conversations are over, review the suggestions with your partner. Discuss which ones the listener followed and which ones were ignored. Try to be as open and honest as possible about assessing your own and the other's strengths and weaknesses. Speakers should consider the extent to which they felt the listeners were really paying attention to them.
5. Repeat steps 2 through 4 but change roles. Speakers now become listeners, and listeners now become speakers.
6. As a class, share your experiences as speakers and listeners.

Questions for Discussion

1. What did this exercise teach you about your own skills as a listener? Are you as good as you thought? Do you think you can improve?
2. Was there general agreement or disagreement about each listener's strengths and weaknesses? Explain.
3. After the discussion about the first listener's effectiveness, you might expect the second listener to do a better job. Was this the case in your own group or throughout the class?
4. Which particular listening skills were easiest and most difficult to put into practice? Are there certain conditions under which good listening skills may be difficult to implement?
5. Do you think you will learn something from this exercise that will get you to improve your listening skills in other situations? If so, what? If not, why not?

WEB SURFING EXERCISE

High-Tech Jargon

Although jargon is used in all fields, it seems that computer-related jargon (i.e., *techno-speak*) is more widespread than most. Not only is it used by lots of people, but much of it has worked its way into everyday language—sometimes causing confusion. These terms, plus lots more, may be found online in the *New Hacker's Dictionary,* at www.tuxedo.org/~esr/jargon/jargon.html#The%20Jargon%20Lexicon. Answer the following questions based on what you find at this site.

1. Searching through the dictionary, what interesting and potentially useful terms have you found that you never used before (but that you might want to start using now)?
2. Look up a few computer-related terms you already know and compare their stated definitions to the meanings you attach to these terms. Have you been using the terms correctly? What alternate meanings do these terms have?
3. In your opinion, what is it about this particular field that lends itself to developing and sustaining so much jargon?

Finding Rumors

In your favorite search engine (e.g., Google, Lycos, etc.) type the word *rumors.* Skip over the links containing rumors about celebrities and follow the links to at least two sites containing stories about various corporate rumors. Examine the content carefully and answer the following questions based on what you find.

1. What rumors did you find and where did you find them? Do you believe that these are credible sources of information?
2. Have you heard about these rumors before, or were they new to you? In what ways have the rumors influenced your feelings about the company?
3. What efforts were reported to neutralize or overcome the rumors if false?

PRACTICING OB

Keeping the Peace

The employees in a company's phone center are not paying any attention to new procedures for taking orders from clients. They are following the old procedures, which they prefer, and avoiding the changes that they dislike. What's more, they are spending so much time bickering with one another that overall productivity has been suffering. You are called in to handle this situation.

1. How might differences in personal communication styles lie at the heart of this situation? What can be done about this?
2. Might gender differences and cultural differences have some impact on the problem?
3. What can be done to make the employees better listeners and more supportive of each other? How do you think these measures would help address the problem?

CASE IN POINT

Physician Sales & Service: Where Keeping Up with Policies Is More Fun Than Any Policy Manual

At most large companies, the challenge of getting things done uniformly at different facilities is met in straightforward fashion. You have rules, regulations, and procedures, so you write a policy manual. Then you toss it at your managers as rules to live by. All too often, they toss it right back—back to the forsaken recesses of a file drawer, that is. Acknowledging how useless that practice can be, the founders of Physician Sales & Service (PSS) have taken an alternative approach to corporate communication—one that's lots more fun. They don't write down much. In fact, people in the various branches—86 in the United States and several more in Europe—are asked to read only the first memo sent to them from the corporate office each month. But, when company officials do share important information in writing, they don't count on any boring policy manuals. For example, when company lawyers insisted that PSS have a written nondiscrimination policy, they created a poster using cartoon characters to explain the policy and hung one in each facility. And, when company founder Patrick Kelly wanted to get across the company's top 20 core values, he printed them on wallet-size cards for all employees to carry.

None of these tactics should be taken to suggest that Kelly and his associates don't get involved in branch operations. Far from it. As Kelly explained it, "We certainly want uniformity from one branch to another. PSS's reputation rests on delivering world-class service to its customers, and we have developed systems and methods to ensure that customers get that service. We have our business model, and we don't really want local-branch leaders experimenting with business models of their own."

So, how does PSS maintain uniformity without a policy manual? It uses a 100-point checklist known as the Blue Ribbon book by which employees are expected to guide their operations. For example: Are trucks clean? Are there refreshments for guests? Are truck maintenance logs properly maintained? And is there a "Wall of Fame" celebrating employee accomplishments? To ensure that these standards and the 96 remaining ones are met, Kelly or another company official makes unannounced visits to each branch twice a year for a "Blue Ribbon Tour." But, in true PSS style, these are no military-type inspections. Rather, they become fun events in which employees start hooting and hollering as they run around emptying wastebaskets and checking restrooms for toilet paper.

By marking "pass" or "fail" on each of the 100 standards, each branch can score up to 100 points. Not only does the highest-scoring branch earn bragging rights inside the company, but each employee gets a bonus as well. These range from $3,000 per employee of the top-scoring branch to $500 per employee of the tenth highest-scoring branch—funds that come from the operating profits of all the other branches. If a branch performs poorly, no one gets in trouble. Instead, as Kelly figures, they have plenty of incentive to do better next time. The Blue Ribbon Tour keeps employees following company standards far more stringently than you may expect from a more standard policy manual.

What makes this practice so impressive is that PSS is a large and incredibly efficient company. Based in Jacksonville, Florida, PSS has grown into the United States' largest provider of medical supplies to the physician market. With 50 PSS service centers distributing medical supplies to roughly 92,000 offices in all 50 states, the company is able to process and deliver any order within approximately three hours.

Critical Thinking Questions

1. What is it about the approach taken at PSS that makes it so successful? Do you think this approach would be as effective in an organization in which you work? Why or why not?
2. What place, if any, do you believe formal policy manuals have in an organization? Explain where they may be most useful.
3. How might the various techniques for improving organizational communication described in this chapter be used to communicate organizational policies at PSS?

Decision Making in Organizations

10

LEARNING OBJECTIVES

After reading this chapter, you should be able to:

1. **Identify** the steps in the analytical model of decision making and distinguish between the various types of decisions that people make.
2. **Describe** different individual decision styles and the various organizational and cultural factors that influence the decision-making process.
3. **Distinguish** among three approaches to how decisions are made: the rational-economic model, the administrative model, and image theory.
4. **Identify** the various factors that lead people to make imperfect decisions.
5. **Compare** the conditions under which groups make more superior decisions than individuals and when individuals make more superior decisions than groups.
6. **Describe** various traditional techniques and high-tech techniques that can be used to enhance the quality of individual decisions and group decisions.

■ PREVIEW CASE
THE ENRON–ARTHUR ANDERSEN SCANDAL: DECISION MAKING GONE AWRY

In July 1985, the Houston Natural Gas Company merged with InterNorth to form Enron. In the years that followed, shrewd financial dealings led the fledgling enterprise to become one of the world's richest and most powerful companies, eventually reaching number five on the *Fortune* 500. Or so it seemed. That was until December 2, 2001, when the company filed for Chapter 11 bankruptcy protection—just days after announcing a $1.2 billion loss.

As the story unfolded, it became clear that the demise of Enron was no ordinary business failure. Rather, Enron's collapse was the inevitable result of a complex web of lies, deceit, and unethical decisions by company officials that led to the ongoing illusion that Enron was in excellent financial condition when the truth was quite the opposite. By way of some questionable accounting practices, actual losses were reported as profits (a jump of 37.6 percent in 2001 alone) in deals alleged to have put some $30 million in the pocket of Enron CEO Kenneth Lay. Despite Lay's obvious windfall, the company's collapse led to the loss of jobs and vaporized the pension savings of some 4,000 company employees. It also sent reverberations through the stock market amid fears that there may be "other Enrons out there."

> Enron's collapse was the inevitable result of a complex web of lies, deceit, and unethical decisions by company officials

In January 2002, the U.S. Justice Department launched an investigation of Enron that painted a picture of ongoing blatant financial mismanagement and greed that spread beyond Enron to its accounting firm, the then highly regarded firm of Arthur Andersen. As soon as it became apparent that it was going to be investigated by the Securities and Exchange Commission, Andersen officials allegedly ordered employees to destroy thousands of documents that could connect it to the questionable business practices of its client. Indicted by a federal grand jury, Andersen was cited with undermining the justice system by destroying "tons" of paperwork and by attempting to purge electronic data, even working around-the-clock to do it.

Andersen spokespersons have claimed that these actions were not directed by high-ranking officials, nor did they conform to company policy. Rather, they say that these acts stemmed from poor decisions by a few rogue employees in the Houston office, who subsequently were fired, including a partner in the firm, David Duncan, who is alleged to have spearheaded the destruction operations. Although the truth may never be known, it's clear that Andersen suffered greatly from its association with Enron. Not wanting to be linked to an accounting firm whose ethics may be questioned, major clients such as Delta Airlines and FedEx fired Andersen, leading the company to falter. In the fallout, as many as 7,000 Andersen employees have lost their jobs and the company's German operations have been purchased by competitor Ernst & Young.

Few cases in the annals of business have been as serious and as broad-reaching as the tales of corruption at Enron and its beleaguered accounting firm, Arthur Andersen, that unfolded on the pages of the business press in 2002. The resulting changes in accounting practices and government regulation of business are sure to be monumental. Yet, at the heart of all this lies a process that is very fundamental to human beings and of considerable concern to the field of OB—the making of *decisions*. Whether guided by greed or power, some Enron officials decided to engage in business practices that were intentionally misleading. Then, guided by the desire to protect its client, Andersen officials made decisions to cover up Enron's misdeeds. When viewed from this perspective, it's clear that understanding how people come to make decisions can be quite important.

Although the decisions you make as an individual may be less monumental than those associated with the Enron scandal, they are very important to you. For example, personal decisions about what college to go to, what classes to take, and what company to work for can have a major impact on the direction your life takes. If you think about the difficulties involved in making decisions in your own life, you surely can appreciate how complicated—and important—the process of decision making can be in organizations, where the stakes are often considerable and the impact is widespread. In both cases, however, the essential nature of **decision making** is identical. It may be defined as the process of making choices from among several alternatives.

It is safe to say that decision making is one of the most important—if not *the* most important—of all managerial activities.[1] Management theorists and researchers agree that decision making represents one of the most common and most crucial work roles of executives. Every day, people in organizations make decisions about a wide variety of topics ranging from the mundane to the monumental.[2] Understanding how these decisions are made, and how they can be improved, is an important goal of the field of organizational behavior.

This chapter will examine theories, research, and practical managerial techniques concerned with decision making in organizations both by individuals and groups. Beginning with individuals, we will review various perspectives on how people go about making decisions. We then will identify factors that may adversely affect the quality of individual decisions and ways of combating them—that is, techniques for improving the quality of decisions. Then we will shift our focus to group decisions, focusing on the conditions under which individuals and groups are each better suited to making decisions. Finally, we will describe some of the factors that make group decisions imperfect

decision making
The process of making choices from among several alternatives.

and various techniques that can be used to improve the quality of group decisions. But, first, we will begin by examining the general nature of the decision-making process and the wide variety of decisions made in organizations.

THE NATURE OF DECISION MAKING

We begin by examining the basic nature of the decision-making process itself. With this in mind, we will present a model describing the general steps by which decisions are made. We then will consider the idea that all people don't make decisions in exactly the same manner. Specifically, we will discuss individual differences and cultural differences in the ways people go about making decisions.

A General, Analytical Model of the Decision-Making Process

Traditionally, scientists have found it useful to conceptualize the process of decision making as a series of analytical steps that groups or individuals take to solve problems.[3] This is accomplished by the **analytical model of the decision-making process,** which can help us understand the complex nature of organizational decision making (see Figure 10.1).[4] This approach highlights two important aspects of decision making: **formulation**, the process of understanding a problem and making a decision about it, and **implementation,** the process of carrying out the decision made.[5] As we present this model, keep in mind that all decisions might not fully conform to the neat, eight-step pattern described (e.g., steps may be skipped and/or combined).[6] However, for the purpose of pointing out the general way the decision-making process operates, the model is quite useful.

1. The first step is *problem identification*. To decide how to solve a problem, one must first recognize and identify the problem. For example, an executive may identify as a problem the fact that the company cannot meet its payroll obligations. This step isn't always as easy as it sounds. In fact, research has shown that people often dis-

analytical model of the decision-making process

An eight-step approach to organizational decision making that focuses on both the formulation of problems and the implementation of solutions.

formulation

The process of understanding a problem and making a decision about it.

implementation

The process of carrying out a decision.

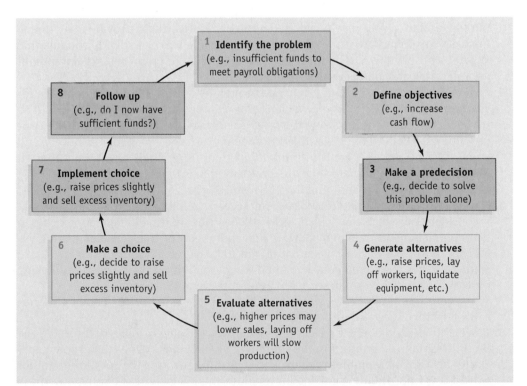

FIGURE 10.1
Overview of the Decision-Making Process
The analytical model of the decision-making process describes most decisions as following the eight steps shown here. Note how each step may be applied to a hypothetical organizational problem (in this example, not having sufficient funds to meet payroll obligations).
(*Source:* Based on information in Wedley & Field, 1984; see Note 4.)

tort, omit, ignore, and/or discount information around them that provides important cues regarding the existence of problems.[7] You may recall from our discussion of the social perception process (see Chapter 2) that people do not always accurately perceive social situations. It is easy to imagine that someone may fail to recognize a problem if doing so makes him or her uncomfortable. Denying a problem may be the first impediment on the road to solving it!

2. After a problem is identified, the next step is to *define the objectives to be met in solving the problem.* It is important to conceive of problems in such a way that possible solutions can be identified. The problem identified in our example may be defined as not having enough money, or in business terms, "inadequate cash flow." By looking at the problem in this way, the objective is clear: increase available cash reserves. Any possible solution to the problem should be evaluated relative to this objective. A good solution is one that meets it.

3. The third step in the decision-making process is to *make a predecision.* A **predecision** is a decision about how to make a decision. By assessing the type of problem in question and other aspects of the situation, managers may opt to make a decision themselves, delegate the decision to another, or have a group make the decision. Decisions about how to make a decision should be based on research that tells us about the nature of the decisions made under different circumstances, much of which we will review later in this chapter.

predecision
A decision about what process to follow in making a decision.

For many years, managers have been relying on their own intuition or empirically based information about organizational behavior (contained in books like this) for the guidance needed to make predecisions. Recently, however, computer programs have been developed summarizing much of this information in a form that gives managers ready access to a wealth of social science information that may help them decide how to make decisions.[8] Such **decision support systems (DSS)**, as they are called, can only be as good as the social science information that goes into developing them. Research has shown that DSS techniques are effective in helping people make decisions about solving problems.[9] The use of decision-making technology leads to outcomes that are higher in quantity and better in quality than those made in the absence of such techniques.[10] (For an example of DSS in use in a particularly vital application, see the Best Practices section on page 362.)

decision support systems (DSS)
Computer programs in which information about organizational behavior is presented to decision makers in a manner that helps them structure their responses to decisions.

4. The fourth step in the process is *alternative generation,* the stage in which possible solutions to the problem are identified. In attempting to come up with solutions, people tend to rely on previously used approaches that might provide ready-made answers for them.[13] In our example, some possible ways of solving the revenue shortage problem would be to reduce the workforce, sell unnecessary equipment and material, and increase sales.

5. Because all these possibilities may not be equally feasible, the fifth step calls for *evaluating alternative solutions.* Which solution is considered best? What would be the most effective way of raising the revenue needed to meet the payroll? The various alternatives need to be identified. Some may be more effective than others, and some may be more difficult to implement than others. For example, although increasing sales would help solve the problem, that is much easier said than done. It is a solution, but not an immediately practical one.

6. Next, in the sixth step, *a choice is made.* After several alternatives are evaluated, one that is considered acceptable is chosen. As we will describe shortly, different approaches to decision making offer different views of how thoroughly people consider alternatives and how optimal their chosen alternatives are. Choosing which course of action to take is the step that most often comes to mind when we think about the decision-making process. However, as you can see, it is only one of several key steps.

7. The seventh step calls for *implementation of the chosen alternative.* That is, the chosen alternative is carried out.

8. The eighth and final step is *follow-up.* Monitoring the effectiveness of the decisions put into action is important to the success of organizations. Does the problem still exist? Have any new problems been caused by implementing the solution? In other words, it is important to seek feedback about the effectiveness of any attempted

solution. For this reason, the decision-making process shown in Figure 10.1 is presented as circular in nature. If the solution works, the problem may be considered solved. If not, a new solution will have to be attempted.

It is important to reiterate that the analytical model we have been describing is a very general model of the decision-making process. Although it may not be followed exactly as specified in all circumstances, it paints a good picture of the general nature of a complex set of operations.

The Broad Spectrum of Organizational Decisions

As you might imagine, because the process of decision making is so fundamental to organizations, decisions themselves tend to be of many different kinds. Understanding the wide variety of decisions that are made in organizations is an important first step toward understanding the nature of the decision-making process. With this in mind, we will distinguish among decisions in three important ways: how routine they are, how much risk is involved, and who in the organization gets to make them.

Programmed versus nonprogrammed decisions. Think of a decision that is made repeatedly according to a preestablished set of alternatives. For example, a word processing operator may decide to make a backup copy of the day's work on disk, or a manager of a fast-food restaurant may decide to order hamburger buns as the supply starts to get low. Decisions such as these are known as **programmed decisions**—routine decisions, made by lower-level personnel, that rely on predetermined courses of action.

By contrast, we may identify **nonprogrammed decisions**—ones for which there are no ready-made solutions. The decision maker confronts a unique situation in which the solutions are novel. A research scientist attempting to find a cure for a rare disease faces a problem that is poorly structured. Unlike the restaurant manager, whose course of action is clear when the supply of buns runs low, the scientist in this example must rely on creativity rather than preexisting answers to solve the problem at hand.

The differences between programmed and nonprogrammed decisions can be described with respect to three important questions. First, *what type of tasks are involved?* Programmed decisions are made on tasks that are common and routine, whereas nonprogrammed decisions are made on unique and novel tasks. Second, *how much reliance is there on organizational policies?* In making programmed decisions, the decision maker can count on guidance from statements of organizational policy and procedure. However, nonprogrammed decisions require the use of creative solutions that are implemented for the first time; past solutions may provide little guidance. Finally, *who makes the decisions?* Not surprisingly, nonprogrammed decisions typically are made by upper-level organizational personnel, whereas the more routine, well-structured decisions are usually relegated to lower-level personnel.[14] For a summary of these three distinctions between programmed and nonprogrammed decisions, see Table 10.1.

Certain types of nonprogrammed decisions are known as **strategic decisions.**[15] These decisions are typically made by coalitions of high-level executives and have important long-term implications for the organization. Strategic decisions reflect a consistent pattern for directing the organization in some specified fashion—that is, according to an underlying organizational philosophy or mission. For example, an organization may make a strategic decision to grow at a specified yearly rate or to be guided by a certain code of corporate ethics. Both of these decisions are likely to be considered "strategic" because they guide the future direction of the organization. Some excellent examples of highly successful strategic decisions made in business settings may be found in Table 10.2.[16]

Certain versus uncertain decisions. Just think of how easy it would be to make decisions if we knew what the future had in store. Making the best investments in the stock market would simply be a matter of looking up the changes in tomorrow's newspaper. Of course, we never know exactly what the future holds, but we can be more certain at some times than others. Certainty about the factors on which decisions are made is highly desired in organizational decision making.

programmed decisions
Highly routine decisions made by lower-level personnel following preestablished organizational routines and procedures.

nonprogrammed decisions
Decisions made about a highly novel problem for which there is no prespecified course of action.

strategic decisions
Nonprogrammed decisions typically made by high-level executives regarding the direction their organization should take to achieve its mission.

BEST PRACTICES
NAVAL OFFICERS USE DECISION SUPPORT SYSTEMS TO MAKE COMBAT DECISIONS

The phrase "don't fire until you see the whites of their eyes" may have provided useful guidance to soldiers fighting in the U.S. Revolutionary War, but today, as you might imagine, the guidelines used as the basis for making decisions about military engagements rely on more advanced technology. In particular, sophisticated decision support systems have been developed to assist combat officers in deciding precisely what actions to take in combat situations. In the U.S. Navy, for example, a program known as Tactical Decision Making Under Stress (TADMUS) was initiated in response to the accidental shooting down of an Iranian civilian aircraft by the USS *Vincennes* in 1988.[11]

Although the technology on which it is based may be sophisticated, the basic idea underlying the Navy's DSS is straightforward: to summarize incoming information and to present it in a format that helps officers take appropriate action. Suppose, for example, an unknown object is spotted in the skies. Based on key variables, such as where it came from, its size, and how fast it's moving, among several others, computers help identify the

Degrees of certainty and uncertainty are expressed as statements of *risk*. All organizational decisions involve some degree of risk—ranging from complete certainty (no risk) to complete uncertainty, "a stab in the dark" (high risk). To make the best possible decisions in organizations, people seek to "manage" the risks they take—that is, minimizing the riskiness of a decision by gaining access to information relevant to the decision.[17]

What makes an outcome risky or not is the *probability* of obtaining the desired outcome. Decision makers attempt to obtain information about the probabilities, or odds, of certain events occurring given that other events have occurred. For example, a financial analyst may report that a certain stock has risen 80 percent of the time that the prime rate has dropped, or a meteorologist may report that the precipitation probability is 50 percent (i.e., in the past, it rained or snowed half the time certain atmospheric conditions existed). These data may be considered reports of *objective probabilities* because they are based on concrete, verifiable data (for another example, see Figure 10.2). Many decisions also are based on *subjective probabilities*—personal beliefs or

TABLE 10.1 PROGRAMMED AND NONPROGRAMMED DECISIONS: A COMPARISON

The two major types of organizational decisions—programmed decisions and nonprogrammed decisions—differ regarding the types of tasks on which they are made, the degree to which solutions may be found in existing organizational policies, and the typical decision-making unit.

VARIABLE	TYPE OF DECISION	
	PROGRAMMED DECISIONS	NONPROGRAMMED DECISIONS
Type of task	Simple, routine	Complex, creative
Reliance on organizational policies	Considerable guidance from past decisions	No guidance from past decisions
Typical decision maker	Lower-level workers (usually alone)	Upper-level supervisors (usually in groups)

degree of threat faced and recommend appropriate action (ranging from issuing a warning to shooting it down). Officers can then use this information as the basis for making an appropriate military decision.

Research using experienced military personnel in simulated combat situations has found that the decision support systems were helpful in three key ways.[12] Specifically, TADMUS had the following effects:

- It helped officers identify possible enemy targets earlier and more accurately.
- It significantly increased the amount of time available to military officers who needed to make vital decisions.

- It helped military personnel track suspicious targets without having to ask as many questions to check with each other about what they thought they saw.

Given these benefits, it is not surprising that the military personnel involved in the study became strong advocates of the DSS. They especially liked the fact that the system didn't make crucial military decisions for them but, rather, that it gave them the information they needed to make these decisions themselves. In other words, the computers did not replace the military experts. Instead, they summarized incoming information in a way that helped personnel make better decisions. And this, after all, is precisely what decision support systems are all about.

TABLE 10.2 STRATEGIC DECISIONS: SOME HIGHLY SUCCESSFUL EXAMPLES

Decisions that guide the future directions of organizations are known as *strategic decisions*. Some of the best-known and most successful strategic decisions are shown here.

COMPANY	DECISION MADE
Toyota	In the aftermath of World War II, the company decided to emphasize high-quality manufacturing techniques.
Coca-Cola	During World War II, the company developed brand loyalty by selling bottles of Coke to members of the armed services.
IBM	In 1924, founder Thomas Watson, Sr. changed the company's name from the Computing-Tabulating-Recording Company to International Business Machines although it had no international operations at the time, boldly declaring its ambitions.
Microsoft	In 1981, Bill Gates decided to license MS-DOS to IBM, which relinquished control of the operating system for all non-IBM personal computers.
Apple	Steve Jobs decided to build his company around sales of a simple computer that could be used by individuals.
Sears	In 1905, the company decided on a way to bring its products to a wider audience by introducing a mail-order catalog.
Johnson & Johnson	In 1982, the company pulled all bottles of Tylenol capsules off store shelves after a few capsules were found to be poisoned.
Sony	In 1980, the company introduced the Walkman after officials noticed that young people like to have music with them wherever they go.
Hewlett-Packard	In 1979, the company decided to exploit an engineer's observation that metal heated in a certain way tended to splatter, resulting in the development of the ink-jet printer.

(*Source:* Based on material in Crainer, 1998; see Note 16.)

FIGURE 10.2

Relying on Objective Probabilities
Many of the decisions that restaurant managers are required to make during the course of a day are based on objective probabilities. For example, records of past sales patterns (e.g., the average number of guests who visit at any given time of day and what they order) make it possible for them to make better judgments regarding which menu items to have prepared in advance and how many staff members to schedule on each shift.

hunches about what will happen. For example, a gambler who bets on a horse because it has a name similar to one of his children's or a person who suspects it's going to rain because he just washed his car is basing these judgments on subjective probabilities.

Obviously, uncertainty is an undesirable characteristic in decision-making situations. We may view much of what decision makers do in organizations as attempting to reduce uncertainty (i.e., putting the odds in their favor) so they can make better decisions. How do organizations respond when faced with highly uncertain conditions, when they don't know what the future holds for them? Studies have shown that decision uncertainty can be reduced by *establishing linkages with other organizations.* The more an organization knows about what another organization will do, the greater certainty it will have in making decisions.[18] This is part of a general tendency for organizational decision makers to respond to uncertainty by reducing the unpredictability of other organizations in their business environments. Those outside organizations with which managers have the greatest contact are most likely to be the ones with whom they establish the closest connections.[19]

In general, what reduces uncertainty in decision-making situations? The answer is *information.* Knowledge about the past and the present can be used to help make projections about the future. A modern executive's access to the data needed to make important decisions may be as close as the nearest computer terminal. Indeed, computer technology has aided greatly managers' ability to make decisions quickly, using the most accurate and thorough information available.[20] A variety of online information services are designed to provide organizational decision makers with the latest information relevant to the decisions they are making.

Of course, not all information needed to make decisions comes from computers. Many managerial decisions also are based on the decision maker's past experiences and intuition.[21] This is not to say that top managers rely on subjective information in making decisions (although they might), but that their history of past decisions—both successes and failures—is often given great weight in the decision-making process. In other words, when it comes to making decisions, people often rely on what has worked for them in the past. Part of the reason this strategy is often successful is because experienced decision makers tend to make better use of information relevant to the decisions they are making.[22] Individuals who have expertise in certain subjects know what information is most relevant and also how to interpret it to make the best decisions. It is, therefore, not surprising that people seek experienced professionals, such as doctors and lawyers who are seasoned veterans in their fields, when it comes to making important decisions. With high levels of expertise comes information relevant to assessing the riskiness of decision alternatives and how to reduce it. (Another way of reducing the riskiness of a decision relies on advanced technology. For a look at how this is done in a particular retail store, see the OB in an E-World section on page 366.)

Top-down versus empowered decisions. Traditionally, in organizations the job of making all but the most menial decisions belonged to managers. In fact, organizational scientist Herbert Simon, who won a Nobel prize for his work on the economics of decision making, has gone so far as to describe decision making as synonymous with managing.[24] Subordinates collected information and gave it to superiors, who used it to make decisions. This approach, known as **top-down decision making,** puts decision-making power in the hands of managers, leaving lower-level workers little or no opportunities to make decisions. If this sounds familiar to you, it is because it has been the way most organizations have operated for a long time.

Today, however, a new approach has come into vogue that is in many ways exactly the opposite. The idea of **empowered decision making** allows employees to make the decisions required to do their jobs without first seeking supervisory approval. As the name implies, it gives them the power to decide what they need to do in order to do their jobs effectively. The rationale for this philosophy of decision making is that the people who do the jobs know what's best, so having someone else make the decision may not make the most sense. In addition, when people are empowered to make their own decisions they are more likely to accept the consequences of those decisions. If the decision was a good one, they can feel good about it. If not, then they have learned a valuable lesson for the next time. In either case, people are more committed to courses of action based on decisions they have made themselves than ones based on decisions that others have made. And such commitment can be important to keeping the organization functioning effectively.

Many different companies today are empowering their employees to make a wide variety of decisions. As an example, the Ritz-Carlton hotel chain has empowered each of its employees to spend up to $2,000 of the company's money per day to fix whatever they find that needs to be repaired. No longer would a chambermaid who finds a broken lamp in one of the guest rooms need to fill out a form that gets passed from one person to the next. He or she is empowered to get the right person to get the job done right away. It is not only individual employees who might be empowered but work teams as well. For example, employees at the Chesapeake Packaging Company's box plant in Baltimore, Maryland are organized into eight separate internal companies.[25] Each such unit is empowered to make its own decisions about key issues, be it ordering, purchasing new equipment, or measuring their own work. Indeed, the concept of self-managed work teams discussed in Chapter 8 involves systematically empowering several individuals working together with the tools needed to make the most effective decisions possible.

top-down decision making
The practice of vesting decision-making power in the hands of superiors as opposed to lower-level employees.

empowered decision making
The practice of vesting power for making decisions in the hands of employees themselves.

FACTORS AFFECTING DECISIONS IN ORGANIZATIONS

Given how fundamental the decision-making process is in organizations, it makes sense that it is influenced by a wide variety of factors. In fact, as we will see, organizational decisions are affected by all three levels studied in the field of OB—individuals, groups, and organizations—as well as by an even broader consideration, national culture. We will consider each of these factors here.

Decision Style: Individual Differences in Decision Making

Do all individuals go about making decisions the same way, or are there differences in the general approaches people take? In general, research has shown that there are meaningful differences between people with respect to their orientation toward decisions—that is, their **decision style.**

decision style
Differences between people with respect to their orientations toward decisions.

OB IN AN E-WORLD
ADAPTIVE AGENTS AS DECISION AIDS

To make good decisions, it helps to know in advance how things will work out. With this in mind, scientists are developing sophisticated computer models that capture the rules of complex human behavior. The so-called **adaptive agents** created by engineers and consultants at PricewaterhouseCoopers are software-based "people" programmed to behave in the same ways as human beings.[23] Their goal is ambitious: to be able to mimic what people will do in certain situations, thereby allowing managers to see the impact of their decisions without ever making them in the real world.

This would be the ultimate way of reducing the uncertainty of decisions. Although even the most sophisticated computer programs cannot predict the future perfectly, they will be able to provide extremely useful information to decision makers about likely outcomes. Although this technology is in its infancy, several companies that are optimistic about how it will facilitate complex decision making have invested in its development, hoping to bring this technology to fruition. For example, Macy's is relying on using the technology to help it determine the number of salespeople to schedule in each store department and where to locate service desks and cash registers within stores. They also want to know how

adaptive agents
Sophisticated computer models that capture the rules of complex human behavior.

decision-style model
The conceptualization according to which people use one of four predominant decision styles: *directive, analytical, conceptual,* and *behavioral.*

Whereas some people are concerned primarily with achieving success at any cost, others are more concerned about the effects of their decisions on others. Furthermore, some individuals tend to be more logical and analytical in their approach to problems, whereas others are more intuitive and creative. Clearly, important differences exist in the approaches decision makers take to problems. The **decision-style model** identifies four major decision styles (see summary in Figure 10.3).[26]

1. The *directive style* is characterized by people who prefer simple, clear solutions to problems. Individuals with this style tend to make decisions rapidly because they

FIGURE 10.3
Decision-Style Model: A Summary
According to the decision-style model, people may be characterized as adhering to one of the four decision styles summarized here.
(*Source:* Based on information in Rowe, Boulgaides, & McGrath, 1984; see Note 26.)

Decision Styles

Directive	Analytical	Conceptual	Behavioral
• Prefer simple, clear solutions • Make decisions rapidly • Do not consider many alternatives • Rely on existing rules	• Prefer complex problems • Carefully analyze alternatives • Enjoy solving problems • Willing to use innovative methods	• Socially oriented • Humanistic and artistic approach • Solve problems creatively • Enjoy new ideas	• Concern for their organization • Interest in helping others • Open to suggestions • Rely on meetings

a sales associate's age, gender, and length of service will influence sales by consumers. US West also has expressed interest in the technology, hoping to be able to predict how both competitors and customers will respond to different pricing and promotion plans.

As useful as this technology is, scientists freely admit that they have a long way to go before it's perfected. Still, it already has seen some successes. For example, the group at PricewaterhouseCoopers has developed 40,000 adaptive agents for a major entertainment company. Cloned from a survey of actual moviegoers, programming these agents has made it possible to forecast first-week box-office receipts 30 percent more accurately than using traditional methods.

The real benefit from creating adaptive agents comes from the fact that you can simulate in just a few minutes what it otherwise would take entire days or weeks to find out. And, of course, mistakes have no cost because you're playing "what-if" games with a simulated public. Those of you who have crashed airplanes while playing with flight simulation programs surely can appreciate the safety of using simulated decisions. At the same time, just as what you learn about real flying using a flight simulator can be invaluable, so too can what you learn about the behavior of real people when using simulated ones.

As promising as this technology may be, experts caution that it's only as good as the assumptions built into it (which, of course, require considerable research in organizational behavior). And, although it could be useful as a decision aid, it certainly won't be replacing actual human decision makers anytime soon.

use little information and do not consider many alternatives. They tend to rely on existing rules to make their decisions and aggressively use their status to achieve results.

2. By contrast, individuals with the *analytical style* tend to be more willing to consider complex solutions based on ambiguous information. People with this style tend to analyze their decisions carefully using as much data as possible. Such individuals tend to enjoy solving problems. They want the best possible answers and are willing to use innovative methods to achieve them.

3. Compared to the directive and analytical styles, people with the *conceptual style* tend to be more socially oriented in their approach to problems. Their approach is humanistic and artistic. Such individuals tend to consider many broad alternatives when dealing with problems and to solve them creatively. They have a strong future orientation and enjoy initiating new ideas.

4. Individuals with the *behavioral style* may be characterized as having a deep concern for the organizations in which they work and the personal development of their coworkers. They are highly supportive of others and very concerned about others' achievements, frequently helping them meet their goals. Such individuals tend to be open to suggestions from others and, therefore, tend to rely on meetings for making decisions.

It is important to point out that although most managers may have one dominant style, they use many different styles. In fact, those who can shift between styles—that is, those who are most flexible in their approach to decision making—have highly complex, individualistic styles of their own. Despite this, people's dominant style reveals a great deal about the way they tend to make decisions. Not surprisingly, conflicts often occur between individuals with different styles. For example, a manager with a highly directive style may have a hard time accepting the slow, deliberate actions of a subordinate with an analytical style.

Researchers have argued that being aware of people's decision styles is a potentially useful way of understanding social interactions in organizations. With this in mind, scientists have developed an instrument known as the *decision-style inventory,* a questionnaire designed to reveal the relative strength of people's decision styles.[27] The higher an individual scores with respect to a given decision style, the more likely that style is to dominate his or her decision making. (To give you a feel for how the various decision styles are measured, and your own decision style, see the Individual Exercise on pages 398–399.)

Research using the decision-style inventory has revealed some interesting findings. For example, when the inventory was given to a sample of corporate presidents, their scores on each of the four categories were found to be approximately equal. Apparently, they had no one dominant style but were able to switch back and forth between categories with ease. Further research has shown that different groups tend to have, on average, different styles that dominate their decision making. For example, military leaders tend to have high conceptual-style scores. They were not the highly domineering individuals that stereotypes suggest. Rather, they were highly conceptual and people oriented in their approach. Such findings paint a far more humanistic and less authoritarian picture of military officers than many would guess.

In conclusion, research on decision styles suggests that people tend to take very different approaches to the decisions they make. Their personalities, coupled with their interpersonal skills, lead them to approach decisions in consistently different ways— that is, using different decision styles. Although research on decision styles is relatively new, it is already clear that understanding such stylistic differences is a key factor in appreciating potential conflicts likely to arise between decision makers.

Group Influences: A Matter of Trade-Offs

As you might imagine, groups influence organizational decisions in a wide variety of ways, potentially positive and negative. We say "potentially" because the wide variety of factors influencing organizational decisions makes it difficult to predict whether anticipated benefits or problems actually will occur. Still, it is useful to understand some of the major forces that have the potential to affect the way groups make decisions in organizations.

Potential benefits of decision-making groups. There is little doubt that much can be gained by using decision-making groups. Several potential advantages of this approach may be identified. First, bringing people together may increase the amount of knowledge and information available for making good decisions. In other words, there may be a *pooling of resources*. A related benefit is that in decision-making groups there can be a *specialization of labor*. With enough people around to share the workload, individuals can perform only those tasks at which they are best, thereby potentially improving the quality of the group's efforts.

Another benefit is that group decisions are likely to enjoy *greater acceptance* than individual decisions. People involved in making decisions may be expected to understand those decisions better and be more committed to carrying them out than decisions made by someone else.[28]

Potential problems of decision-making groups. Of course, there also are some problems associated with using decision-making groups. One obvious drawback is that groups are likely to *waste time*. The time spent socializing before getting down to business may be a drain on the group and be very costly to organizations.

Another possible problem is that potential disagreement over important matters may breed ill will and *group conflict*. Although constructive disagreement sometimes can lead to better group outcomes, highly disruptive conflict may interfere with group decisions (see Chapter 11). Indeed, with corporate power and personal pride at stake, it is not at all surprising to find that lack of agreement can cause bad feelings to develop between group members.

Finally, we may expect groups to be ineffective sometimes because of members' *intimidation by group leaders*. A group composed of several "yes" men or women trying to please a dominant leader tends to discourage open and honest discussion of solutions. In view of these problems, it is easy to understand the old adage, "A camel is a horse put together by a committee."

Groupthink: Too much cohesiveness can be a dangerous thing. As we described in Chapter 8, sometimes members of groups become so concerned about not "rocking the boat" that they are reluctant to challenge the group's decisions. When this happens, group members tend to isolate themselves from outside information, and the process of critical thinking deteriorates. This phenomenon is referred to as **groupthink**.[29]

To illustrate the phenomenon of groupthink, consider the tragic decision to launch the space shuttle *Challenger* in January 1986. Analyses of conversations between key personnel suggested that NASA officials made the decision to launch the shuttle under freezing conditions while ignoring admonitions from engineers that this may be unsafe.[30] Because NASA had such a successful history, the decision makers operated with a sense of invulnerability. They also worked so closely together and were under such intense pressure to launch the shuttle without further delay that they all collectively went along with the launch decision, creating the illusion of unanimous agreement. For a more precise description of groupthink and a practical guide to recognizing its symptoms, see Figure 10.4.

Groupthink doesn't occur only in governmental decision making, as you might imagine, but in the private sector as well (although, in such cases, the failures may be less well publicized). For example, analyses of the business policies of large corporations such as British Airlines, Lockheed, and Chrysler have suggested that it was the failure of top-management teams to respond to changing market conditions that at one time led these firms to the brink of disaster.[31] The problem is that members of very cohesive groups may have considerable confidence in their group's decisions, making them unlikely to raise doubts about these actions (i.e., "the group seems to know what it's doing"). As a result, they may suspend their own critical thinking in favor of conforming to the group. When group members become fiercely loyal to each other, they may ignore potentially useful information from other sources that challenges the group's decisions. The result of this process is that the group's decisions may be completely uninformed, irrational, or even immoral.[32] (Fortunately, several concrete steps can be taken to avoid groupthink. For some suggestions, see the How to Do It section on page 370.)

groupthink
The tendency for members of highly cohesive groups to so strongly conform to group pressures regarding a certain decision that they fail to think critically, rejecting the potentially correcting influences of outsiders.

Organizational Barriers to Effective Decisions

Thus far we have emphasized the human cognitive shortcomings and biases that limit effective decision making. However, we must not ignore several important organizational factors that also interfere with rational decisions. Indeed, the situations faced by many organizational decision makers cannot help but interfere with their capacity to make decisions.

One obvious factor is *time constraints*. Many important organizational decisions are made under severe time pressure. Under such circumstances, it is often impossible

FIGURE 10.4

Groupthink: An Overview
Groupthink occurs when highly cohesive conditions in groups discourage members from challenging their group's overall decision. Poor-quality decisions result.

STRATEGIES FOR AVOIDING GROUPTHINK

Because scientists have such a good feel for why groupthink occurs, it is possible to identify several tactics aimed at weakening the dynamics that make it occur. With this in mind, here are several tried-and-true techniques.

1. *Promote open inquiry.* Remember, groupthink arises in response to group members' reluctance to "rock the boat." Group leaders should encourage members to be skeptical of all solutions and to avoid reaching premature agreements. It sometimes helps to play the role of *devil's advocate,* that is, to intentionally find fault with a proposed solution.[33] Research has shown that when this is done, groups make higher quality decisions.[34] In fact, some corporate executives use exercises in which conflict is intentionally generated just so the negative aspects of a decision can be identified before it's too late.[35] This is not to say that leaders should be argumentative. Rather, raising a nonthreatening question to force both sides of an issue can be very helpful in improving the quality of decisions.

2. *Use subgroups.* Because the decisions made by any one group may be the result of groupthink, basing decisions on the recommendations of two groups is a useful check. If the two groups disagree, a discussion of their differences is likely to raise important issues. However, if the two groups agree, you can be relatively confident that their conclusions are not *both* the result of groupthink.

3. *Admit shortcomings.* When groupthink occurs, group members feel very confident that they are doing the right thing. Such feelings of perfection discourage people from considering opposing information. However, if group members acknowledge some of the flaws and limitations of their decisions, they may be more open to corrective influences. Keep in mind that no decision is perfect. Asking others to point out their misgivings about a group's decisions may help avoid the illusion of perfection that contributes to groupthink.

4. *Hold second-chance meetings.* Before implementing a decision, it is a good idea to hold a *second-chance meeting* during which group members are asked to express any doubts and propose any new ideas they may have. Alfred P. Sloan, former head of General Motors, is known to have postponed acting on important matters until any group disagreement was resolved.[36] As people get tired of working on problems, they may hastily reach agreement on a solution. Second-chance meetings can be useful devices for seeing if a solution still seems good even after "sleeping on it."

Given the extremely adverse effects groupthink can have on organizations, practicing managers would be wise to put these simple suggestions into action. The alternative—facing the consequences of groupthink—clearly suggests the need for serious consideration of this issue.

for exhaustive decision making to occur. This is particularly the case when organizations face crisis situations requiring immediate decisions. Under such conditions, when decision makers feel "rushed into" taking action, they frequently restrict their search for information and consideration of alternatives that may otherwise help them make effective decisions.[37]

The quality of many organizational decisions also may be limited by *political "face-saving" pressure.* In other words, decision makers may make decisions that help them look good to others, although the resulting decisions might not be in the best interest of their organizations. Imagine, for example, how an employee might distort the available information needed to make a decision if the correct decision would jeopardize his job. Unfortunately, such misuses of information to support desired decisions are all too common.

A study on the topic of political face-saving found that a group of businesspeople working on a group decision-making problem opted for an adequate—although less than optimal—decision rather than risk generating serious conflicts with their fellow group members.[38] In an actual case, a proponent of medical inoculation for the flu was so interested in advancing his pro-inoculation position that he proceeded with the inoculation program although there was only a 2 percent chance of an epidemic.[39] Apparently, people often make the decisions they need to make to cultivate the best impressions although these may not be the best ones for their organizations.

Cultural Differences in Decision Making

People are people, and the process of decision making is essentially the same all over the world—right? Not exactly. Even if people were to follow the same basic steps when making decisions, there exist widespread differences in the *way* people from various cultures may go about doing so.[40] Because we tend to take for granted the way we do things in our own country, especially such basic tasks as making decisions, some of these differences may seem quite surprising.

For example, suppose you are managing a large construction project when you discover that one of your most important suppliers will be several months late in delivering the necessary materials. What would you do? You're probably thinking, "This is a silly question; I'd simply try to get another supplier." If you're from the United States, this is probably just what you'd do. But if you're from Thailand, Indonesia, or Malaysia, chances are good that you'd simply accept the situation as fate and allow the project to be delayed (see Figure 10.5). In other words, to the American, Canadian, or Western European manager, the situation

FIGURE 10.5
Culture's Influence on Decision Making
These businessmen from Kuala Lumpur, Malaysia are likely to make different decisions than their counterparts in Western cultures (e.g., the United States, Canada, or Great Britain) even when confronted with the same information. This reflects the fact that cultural differences influence the way people think about various problems and their willingness to consider various courses of action.

may be perceived as a problem in need of a decision, whereas no such problem would be recognized by Thai, Indonesian, or Malaysian managers. Thus, as basic as it seems that decision making begins with recognizing that a problem exists, it is important to note that not all people are likely to perceive the same situations as problems.

Cultures also differ with respect to the nature of the decision-making unit they typically employ. In the United States, for example, where people tend to be highly individualistic, individual decisions are commonly made. However, in more collectivist cultures, such as Japan, it would be considered inconceivable for someone to make a decision without first gaining the acceptance of his or her immediate colleagues.

Similarly, there exist cultural differences with respect to *who* is expected to make decisions. In Sweden, for example, it is traditional for employees at all levels to be involved in the decisions affecting them. This is so much the case, in fact, that Swedes may totally ignore an organizational hierarchy and contact whomever is needed to make a decision, however high-ranking that individual may be. However, in India, where autocratic decision, making is expected, it would be considered a sign of weakness for a manager to consult a subordinate about a decision.

Another cultural difference in decision making has to do with the amount of time taken to make a decision. For example, in the United States, one mark of a good decision maker is that he or she is "decisive," willing to take on an important decision and make it without delay. However, in some other cultures, time urgency is downplayed. In Egypt, for example, the more important the matter, the more time the decision maker is expected to take in reaching a decision. Throughout the Middle East, reaching a decision quickly would be perceived as overly hasty.

As these examples illustrate, there exist some interesting differences in the ways people from various countries go about formulating and implementing decisions. Understanding such differences is an important first step toward developing appropriate strategies for conducting business at a global level.[41]

Time Pressure: Making Decisions in Emergencies

An unavoidable fact of life in contemporary organizations is that people often have only limited amounts of time to make important decisions. The rapid pace with which businesses operate these days results in severe pressures to make decisions almost immediately. Among firefighters, emergency room doctors, and fighter pilots, it's clear that time is of the essence. But even those of us who toil in less dramatic settings also face the need to make good decisions quickly. The practice of thoroughly collecting information, carefully analyzing it, and then leisurely reviewing the alternatives is a luxury few modern decision makers can afford. In a recent survey, 77 percent of a broad cross section of managers polled felt that the number of decisions they were required to make each day has increased, and 43 percent reported that the time they can devote to making decisions has decreased.[42] Often the result is that bad—and inevitably, costly—decisions are made.

Highly experienced experts, psychologists tell us, are able to make good decisions quickly because they draw on a wealth of experiences collected over the years.[43] Whereas novices are very deliberate in their decision making, considering one option at a time, experts are able to make decisions quickly because they are able to assess the situations they face and compare them to experiences they have had earlier in their careers. They know what matters, what to look for, and what pitfalls to avoid. What is so often considered "gut instinct" is really nothing more than the wealth of accumulated experiences. The more experiences a person has from which to draw, the more effectively he or she can "size up" a situation and take appropriate action.

"Fine, but I'm not yet an expert," you may be thinking, "so what can I do to make good decisions under pressure?" The answer lies in emulating some of the things that experts do.[44] These are as follows:

1. *Recognize your prime objectives.* Many organizations have cardinal rules by which they must live. Relying on these can help you make decisions quickly. Take the job of a newspaper editor, for example. The news has to get out quickly, but it also has to be right. With this in mind, editors at the *Washington Post* follow a "when in doubt, leave it out" policy. According to Mary Hadar, an assistant managing editor, "With that firmly in mind, my decision to run or not run a story becomes much easier."

2. *Rely on experts.* Although you might not be an expert, chances are good that your organization has an expert available to you to whom you can look for decisions. Tina Carlstrom is an institutional sales trader for Merrill Lynch. She's worked for eight years on the New York trading floor, where quick decisions often can mean the difference between making and losing millions of dollars. What does she do when a buying opportunity comes along for a company she doesn't know well? The key, she says, is knowing where to turn for quick answers. Fortunately, the large brokerage firm has experts on staff on whom she can rely for the information she needs to make quick decisions.

3. *Anticipate crises.* If you want to avoid crisis situations, anticipate them in advance. This way, should they occur, you already have an idea of how to respond. In other words, if you don't have the luxury of having experienced a situation from which you were able to learn, it's a good idea to anticipate and prepare for those situations in advance. For example, psychologists tell us that you can prepare for situations by rehearsing in advance.[45] Imagine, for example, that you are a manager who has never had an encounter with a hostile employee. By practicing how to respond should you ever have to deal with a hostile employee, it becomes easier for you to jump into action if you ever confront one.

4. *Learn from mistakes.* The one thing on which you can count for sure is making mistakes. We all make mistakes at one time or another (often, far too many). Although they are inevitable, mistakes should not be dismissed. Rather, it's essential to learn from them. One thing that makes experts so effective is that they have made many mistakes from which they have learned valuable lessons. The key is to think of each poor decision you make as training for the next time.

Commercial airline pilots used to be taught to respond to crisis situations by following a "STAR" approach—stop, think, analyze, respond. We now know better. Whether you are a pilot, a professor, or a president, you will have to make split-second decisions at one time or another, and these cannot be made in such a deliberate fashion. By following the suggestions we've outlined here, you will be better prepared to face whatever quick decisions you have to make.

HOW ARE INDIVIDUAL DECISIONS MADE?

Now that we have identified the types of decisions people make in organizations, we are prepared to consider the matter of how people go about making them. Perhaps you are thinking, "What do you mean? You just think things over and do what you think is best." Although this may be true, you will see that there's a lot more to decision making than meets the eye. In fact, scientists have considered several different approaches to how individuals make decisions. Here we will review three of the most important ones.

The Rational-Economic Model: In Search of the Ideal Decision

We all like to think that we are "rational" people who make the best possible decisions. But what exactly does it mean to make a *rational* decision? Organizational scientists view **rational decisions** as ones that maximize the attainment of goals, whether they are the goals of a person, a group, or an entire organization.[46] What would be the most rational way for an individual to go about making a decision? Economists interested in predicting market conditions and prices have relied on a **rational-economic model** of decision making, which assumes that decisions are optimal in every way. An economically rational decision maker will attempt to maximize his or her profits by systematically searching for the *optimal* solution to a problem. For this to occur, the decision maker must have complete and perfect information and be able to process all this information in an accurate and unbiased fashion.[47]

In many respects, rational-economic decisions follow the same steps outlined in the analytical model of decision making presented earlier (see Figure 10.1). However, what makes the rational-economic approach special is that it calls for the decision maker to recognize *all* alternative courses of action (step 4) and to accurately and completely evaluate each one (step 5). It views decision makers as attempting to make *optimal* decisions.

Of course, the rational-economic approach to decision making does not fully appreciate the fallibility of the human decision maker. Based on the assumption that people have access to complete and perfect information and use it to make perfect decisions, the model can be considered a *normative* (also called *prescriptive*) approach—one that describes how decision makers ideally ought to behave so as to make the best possible decisions. It does not describe how decision makers actually behave in most circumstances. This task is undertaken by the next major approach to individual decision making, the *administrative model.*

The Administrative Model: The Limits of Human Rationality

As you know from your own experience, people generally do not act in a completely rational-economic manner. To illustrate this point, consider how a personnel department might select a new receptionist. After several applicants are interviewed, the personnel manager might choose the best candidate seen so far and stop interviewing. Had the manager been following a rational-economic model, he or she would have had to interview all possible candidates before deciding on the best one. However, by ending the search after finding a candidate who was good enough to do the job, the manager is using a much simpler approach.

The process used in this example characterizes an approach to decision making known as the **administrative model.**[48] This conceptualization recognizes that decision makers may have a limited view of the problems confronting them. The number of solutions that can be recognized or implemented is limited by the capabilities of the decision maker and the available resources of the organization. Also, decision makers do not have perfect information about the consequences of their decisions, so they cannot tell which one is best.

How are decisions made according to the administrative model? Instead of considering all possible solutions, decision makers consider solutions as they become avail-

rational decisions
Decisions that maximize the chance of attaining an individual's, group's, or organization's goals.

rational-economic model
The model of decision making according to which decision makers consider all possible alternatives to problems before selecting the optimal solution.

administrative model
A model of decision making that recognizes the *bounded rationality* that limits the making of optimally rational-economic decisions.

able. Then they decide on the first alternative that meets their criteria for acceptability. Thus, the decision maker selects a solution that may be just good enough, although not optimal. Such decisions are referred to as **satisficing decisions.** Of course, a satisficing decision is much easier to make than an optimal decision. In most decision-making situations, satisficing decisions are acceptable and are more likely to be made than optimal ones.[49] The following analogy is used to compare the two types of decisions: *Making an optimal decision is like searching a haystack for the sharpest needle, but making a satisficing decision is like searching a haystack for a needle just sharp enough with which to sew.*

As we have noted, it is often impractical for people to make completely optimal, rational decisions. The administrative model recognizes the **bounded rationality** under which most organizational decision makers must operate. The idea is that people lack the cognitive skills required to formulate and solve highly complex business problems in a completely objective, rational way.[50] In addition, decision makers limit their actions to those that fall within the bounds of current moral and ethical standards—that is, they use **bounded discretion.**[51] So, although engaging in illegal activities, such as stealing, may optimize an organization's profits (at least in the short run), ethical considerations strongly discourage such actions.

It should not be surprising that the administrative model does a better job than the rational-economic model of describing how decision makers actually behave. The approach is said to be *descriptive* (also called *proscriptive*) in nature. This interest in examining the actual, imperfect behavior of decision makers, rather than specifying the ideal, economically rational behaviors that decision makers ought to engage in, lies at the heart of the distinction between the administrative and rational-economic models. Our point is not that decision makers do not want to behave rationally but that restrictions posed by the innate capabilities of the decision makers preclude making "perfect" decisions.

Image Theory: An Intuitive Approach to Decision Making

If you think about it, you'll probably realize that some, but certainly not all, decisions are made following the logical steps of the analytical model of decision making. Consider Elizabeth Barrett Browning's poetic question, "How do I love thee? Let me count the ways."[52] It's unlikely that anyone would ultimately answer the question by carefully counting what one loves about another (although many such characteristics can be enumerated). Instead, a more intuitive-based decision making is likely, not only for matters of the heart but for a variety of important organizational decisions as well.[53]

The point is that selecting the best alternative by weighing all the options is not always a major concern when making a decision. People also consider how various decision alternatives fit with their personal standards as well as their personal goals and plans. The best decision for one person might not be the best for someone else. In other words, people may make decisions in a more automatic, *intuitive* fashion than is traditionally recognized. Representative of this approach is **image theory.**[54] This approach to decision making is summarized in Figure 10.6.

Image theory deals primarily with decisions about adopting a certain course of action (e.g., should the company develop a new product line?) or changing a current course of action (e.g., should the company drop a present product line?). According to the theory, people make adoption decisions on the basis of a simple two-step process. The first step is the *compatibility test,* a comparison of the degree to which a particular course of action is consistent with various images—particularly individual principles, current goals, and plans for the future. If any lack of compatibility exists with respect to these considerations, a rejection decision is made. If the compatibility test is passed, then the *profitability test* is carried out. That is, people consider the extent to which using various alternatives best fits their values, goals, and plans. The decision is then made to accept the best candidate. These tests are used within a certain *decision frame*—that is, with consideration of meaningful information about the decision con-

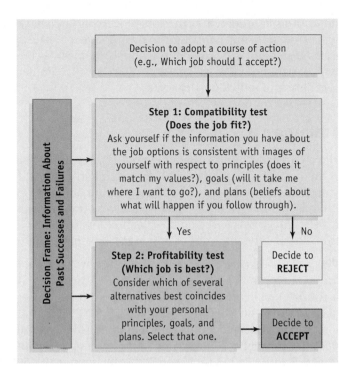

FIGURE 10.6
Image Theory: An Overview and Example
According to image theory, decisions are made in a relatively automatic, intuitive fashion following the two steps outlined here.
(*Source:* Adapted from Beach & Mitchell, 1990; see Note 54.)

Decision to adopt a course of action (e.g., Which job should I accept?)

Decision Frame: Information About Past Successes and Failures

Step 1: Compatibility test (Does the job fit?)
Ask yourself if the information you have about the job options is consistent with images of yourself with respect to principles (does it match my values?), goals (will it take me where I want to go?), and plans (beliefs about what will happen if you follow through).

Yes / No

Step 2: Profitability test (Which job is best?)
Consider which of several alternatives best coincides with your personal principles, goals, and plans. Select that one.

Decide to **REJECT**

Decide to **ACCEPT**

text (such as past experiences). The basic idea is that we learn from the past and are guided by it when making decisions. The example shown in Figure 10.6 highlights this contemporary approach to decision making.

According to image theory, the decision-making process is very rapid and simple. The theory suggests that people do not ponder and labor over decisions, but make them using an intuitive process with minimal cognitive processing. If you've ever found yourself saying that something "seemed like the right thing to do" or that something "doesn't feel right," you're probably well aware of the kind of intuitive thinking that goes on in a great deal of decision making. Recent research suggests that when it comes to making relatively simple decisions, people tend to behave as suggested by image theory.[55] For example, it has been found that people decide against various options when past evidence suggests that these decisions may be incompatible with their images of the future.[56]

To summarize, we have described three major approaches to decision making. The rational-economic approach represents the ideal way optimal decisions are made. However, the administrative model and image theory represent ways that people actually go about making decisions. Both approaches have received support, and neither should be seen as a replacement for the other. Instead, several different processes may be involved in decision making. Not all decision making is carried out the same way: Sometimes decision making might be analytical, and sometimes it might be more intuitive. Modern organizational behavior scholars recognize the value of both approaches. Something both approaches have in common is that they recognize the fallibility of the human decision maker. With this in mind, we will now turn our attention to the imperfect nature of individual decisions.

IMPERFECTIONS IN INDIVIDUAL DECISIONS

Let's face it, as a whole, people are less than perfect when it comes to making decisions. Mistakes are made all the time. Obviously, people have limited capacities to process information accurately and thoroughly like a computer. For example, we often focus on irrelevant information in making decisions.[57] We also fail to use all the information made available to us, in part because we may forget some of it.[58] Beyond these general limitations in human information-processing capacity, we may note several systematic biases—factors that contribute to the imperfect nature of people's decisions. These variables reside not only within individuals themselves but also the organizations within which we operate. We will now examine several major factors contributing to the imperfect nature of individual decisions.

Framing Effects

Have you ever found yourself changing your mind about something because of *how* someone explained it to you? If so, you might have said something such as, "Now that you put it that way, I agree." This may sound familiar to you because it describes a well-established decision-making bias known as **framing**—the tendency for people to make different decisions based on how the problem is presented to them. Scientists have identified three different forms of framing effects that occur when people make decisions.[59]

Risky choice frames. For many years, scientists have noted that when problems are framed in a manner that emphasizes the positive gains to be received, people tend to shy away from taking risks and go for the sure thing (i.e., decision makers are said to be *risk averse*). However, when problems are framed in a manner that emphasizes the potential losses to be suffered, people are more willing to take risks so as to avoid those losses (i.e., decision makers are said to make *risk-seeking* decisions).[60] This is known as the **risky choice framing effect.** To illustrate this phenomenon consider the following example:

> The government is preparing to combat a rare disease expected to take 600 lives. Two alternative programs to combat the disease have been proposed, each of which, scientists believe, will have certain consequences. *Program A* will save 200 people if adopted. *Program B* has a one-third chance of saving all 600 people, but a two-thirds chance of saving no one. Which program do you prefer?

When such a problem was presented to people, 72 percent expressed a preference for Program A and 28 percent for Program B. In other words, they preferred the "sure thing" of saving 200 people over the one-third possibility of saving them all. However, a curious thing happened when the description of the programs was framed in negative terms. Specifically:

> *Program C* was described as allowing 400 people to die if adopted. *Program D* was described as allowing a one-third probability that no one would die, and a two-thirds probability that all 600 would die. Now, which program would you prefer?

Compare these four programs. Program C is just another way of stating the outcomes of Program A, and Program D is just another way of stating the outcomes of Program B. However, Programs C and D are framed in negative terms, which led to opposite preferences: 22 percent favored Program C and 78 percent favored Program D. In other words, people tended to avoid risk when the problem was framed in terms of "lives saved" (i.e., in positive terms) but to seek risk when the problem was framed in terms of "lives lost" (i.e., in negative terms). This classic effect has been replicated in several studies.[61]

Attribute framing. Risky choice frames involve making decisions about which course of action is preferred. However, the same basic idea applies to situations not involving risk but involving evaluations. Suppose, for example, you're walking down the meat aisle of your local supermarket when you spot a package of ground beef labeled "75% lean." Of course, if the same package were to say "25% fat," you would know exactly the same thing. However, you probably wouldn't perceive that to be the case. In fact, consumer marketing research has shown that people rated the same sample of ground beef as being better tasting and less greasy when it was framed with respect to a positive attribute (i.e., 75% lean) than when it was framed with respect to a negative attribute (i.e., 25% fat).[62]

Although this example is easy to relate to, its generalizability goes way beyond product evaluation situations. In fact, the **attribute framing effect** occurs in a wide vari-

framing
The tendency for people to make different decisions based on how the problem is presented to them.

risky choice framing effect
The tendency for people to avoid risks when situations are presented in a way that emphasizes positive gains and to take risks when situations are presented in a way that emphasizes potential losses that may be suffered.

attribute framing effect
The tendency for people to evaluate a characteristic more positively when it is presented in positive terms than when it is presented in negative terms.

ety of organizational settings. In other words, people evaluate the same characteristic more positively when it is described in positive terms than when it is described in negative terms. Take performance evaluation, for example. In this context, people whose performance is framed in positive terms (e.g., percentage of shots made by a basketball player) tend to be evaluated more positively than those whose identical performance is framed in negative terms (e.g., percentage of shots missed by that same basketball player).[63]

Goal framing. A third type of framing, goal framing, focuses on an important question: When attempting to persuade someone to do something, is it more effective to focus on the positive consequences of doing it or the negative consequences of not doing it? For example, suppose you are attempting to get women to engage in self-examination of their breasts to check for signs of cancer. You may frame the desired behavior in positive terms:

> "Research shows that women who *do* breast self-examinations have an *increased* chance of finding a tumor in the early, more treatable stages of the disease."

Or you may frame it in negative terms:

> "Research shows that women who *do not* do breast self-examinations have a *decreased* chance of finding a tumor in the early, more treatable stages of the disease."

Which approach is more effective? Research has shown that women are more likely to engage in breast self-examination when presented with the consequences of not doing it rather than the benefits of doing it.[64] This is an example of the **goal framing effect** in action. According to this phenomenon, people are more strongly persuaded by the negatively framed information than by the positively framed information.

A general note about framing. The three kinds of framing we have described here, although similar in several key ways, are also quite different. Specifically they focus on different types of behavior: preferences for risk in the case of *risky choice framing*, evaluations of characteristics in the case of *attribute framing*, and taking behavioral action in the case of *goal framing*. For a summary of these three effects, see Figure 10.7.

Scientists believe that framing effects are due to the tendency for people to perceive equivalent situations framed differently as not really equivalent.[65] In other words, focusing on the glass as "half full" leads people to think about it differently than when it is presented as being "half empty," although they might recognize intellectually that the two are really the same. Such findings illustrate our point that people are not completely rational decision makers, but are systematically biased by the cognitive distortions created by simple differences in the way situations are framed.

goal framing effect
The tendency for people to be more strongly persuaded by information that is framed in negative terms than information that is framed in positive terms.

FIGURE 10.7
Framing Effects: A Summary of Three Types
Information presented (i.e., framed) negatively is perceived differently than the same information presented positively. This takes the three different forms summarized here—*risky choice framing*, *attribute framing*, and *goal framing*. (*Source*: Based on suggestions by Levin et al., 1998; see Note 59.)

Type of Framing	Negative Frame		Positive Frame
Risky choice framing	Avoid losses (lives lost)		Experience gains (lives saved)
		Likelihood of taking risks	
	less likely ←		→ more likely
Attribute framing	Negative qualities (25% fat)		Positive qualities (75% lean)
		Evaluation	
	negative ←		→ positive
Goal framing	Suffer loss (no breast exam → decreased chance of finding early tumor)		Experience gain (breast exam → increased chance of finding early tumor)
		Likelihood of performing exam	
	more likely ←		→ less likely

Reliance on Heuristics

heuristics

Simple decision rules (rules of thumb) used to make quick decisions about complex problems. (See *availability heuristic* and *representativeness heuristic*.)

availability heuristic

The tendency for people to base their judgments on information that is readily available to them although it may be potentially inaccurate, thereby adversely affecting decision quality.

representativeness heuristic

The tendency to perceive others in stereotypical ways if they appear to be typical representatives of the category to which they belong.

Framing effects are not the only cognitive biases to which decision makers are subjected. It also has been established that people often attempt to simplify the complex decisions they face by using **heuristics**—simple rules of thumb that guide them through a complex array of decision alternatives.[66] Although heuristics are potentially useful to decision makers, they represent potential impediments to decision making. Two very common types of heuristics may be identified.

The availability heuristic. The **availability heuristic** refers to the tendency for people to base their judgments on information that is readily available to them—even though it might not be accurate. Suppose, for example, that an executive needs to know the percentage of entering college freshmen who go on to graduate. There is not enough time to gather the appropriate statistics, so she bases her judgments on her own recollections of when she was a college student. If the percentage she recalls graduating, based on her own experiences, is higher or lower than the usual number, her estimate will be off accordingly. In other words, basing judgments solely on information that is conveniently available increases the possibility of making inaccurate decisions. Yet, the availability heuristic is often used when making decisions.[67]

The representativeness heuristic. The **representativeness heuristic** refers to the tendency to perceive others in stereotypical ways if they appear to be typical representatives of the category to which they belong. For example, suppose you believe that accountants are bright, mild-mannered individuals, whereas salespeople are less intelligent but much more extroverted. Furthermore, imagine that there are twice as many salespeople as accountants at a party. You meet someone at the party who is bright and mild-mannered. Although mathematically the odds are two-to-one that this person is a salesperson rather than an accountant, you are likely to guess that the individual is an accountant because she possesses the traits you associate with accountants. In other words, you believe this person to be representative of accountants in general—so much so that you would knowingly go against the mathematical odds in making your judgment. Research consistently has found that people tend to make this type of error in judgment, thereby providing good support for the existence of the representativeness heuristic.[68]

The helpful side of heuristics. It is important to note that heuristics do not *always* deteriorate the quality of decisions made. In fact, they can be quite helpful. People often use rules of thumb to help simplify the complex decisions they face. For example, management scientists employ many useful heuristics to aid decisions regarding such matters as where to locate warehouses or how to compose an investment portfolio.[69] We also use heuristics in our everyday lives, such as when we play chess ("control the center of the board") or blackjack ("hit on 16, stick on 17").

However, the representativeness heuristic and the availability heuristic may be recognized as impediments to superior decisions because they discourage people from collecting and processing as much information as they should. Making judgments on the basis of only readily available information or on stereotypical beliefs, although making things simple for the decision maker, does so at the potentially high cost of poor decisions. Thus, these systematic biases represent potentially serious impediments to individual decision making.

THE INHERENTLY BIASED NATURE OF INDIVIDUAL DECISIONS

As individuals, we make imperfect decisions not only because of our overreliance on heuristics but also because of certain inherent biases we bring to the various decision-making situations we face. Among the several biases people have when making decisions, four have received special attention by OB scientists—the *bias toward implicit favorites,* the *hindsight bias,* the *person sensitivity bias,* and the *escalation of commitment bias.*

Bias Toward Implicit Favorites

Don was about to receive his M.B.A. This was going to be his big chance to move to San Francisco, the city by the bay. Don had long dreamed of living there, and his first "real" job, he hoped, was going to be his ticket. As the corporate recruiters made their annual migration to campus, Don eagerly signed up for several interviews. One of the first was Baxter, Marsh, and Hidalgo, a medium-size consulting firm in San Francisco. The salary was right and the people seemed pleasant, a combination that excited Don very much. Apparently the interest was mutual; soon Don was offered a position.

Does the story end here? Not quite. It was only March, and Don felt he shouldn't jump at the first job to come along, even though he really wanted it. So, to do "the sensible thing," he signed up for more interviews. Shortly thereafter, Sping and Feu, a local firm, made Don a more attractive offer. Not only was the salary higher but also there was every indication that the job promised a much brighter future than the one in San Francisco.

What would he do? Actually, Don didn't consider it much of a dilemma. After thinking it over, he came to the conclusion that the work at Sping and Feu was much too low level—not enough exciting clients to challenge him. And the starting salary wasn't really all *that* much better than it was at Baxter, Marsh, and Hidalgo. The day after graduation, Don was packing for his new office overlooking the Golden Gate Bridge.

Do you think the way Don made his decision was atypical? He seemed to have his mind made up in advance about the job in San Francisco and didn't really give the other one a chance. Research suggests that people make decisions in this way all the time. That is, people tend to pick an **implicit favorite** option (i.e., a preferred alternative) very early in the decision-making process.[70] Then, the other options they consider subsequently are not given serious consideration. Rather, the other options are merely used to convince themselves that the implicit favorite is indeed the best choice. An alternative considered for this purpose is known as a **confirmation candidate.** It is not unusual to find that people psychologically distort their beliefs about confirmation candidates so as to justify selecting their implicit favorites. Don did this when he convinced himself that the job offered by the local firm really wasn't as good as it seemed.

Research has shown that people make decisions very early in the decision process. For example, in one study of the job recruitment process, investigators found that they could predict 87 percent of the jobs that students would take as early as two months before the students acknowledged that they actually had made a decision.[71] Apparently, people's decisions are biased by the tendency for them to not consider all the relevant information available to them. In fact, they tend to bias their judgments of the strengths and weaknesses of various alternatives so as to make them fit their already-made decision, their implicit favorite.[72] This phenomenon clearly suggests that people not only fail to consider all possible alternatives when making decisions but also that they even fail to consider all readily available alternatives. Instead, they tend to make up their minds very early and convince themselves that they are right. As you might imagine, this bias toward implicit favorites is likely to severely limit the quality of decisions that are made.

implicit favorite
One's preferred decision alternative, selected even before all options have been considered.

confirmation candidate
A decision alternative considered only for purposes of convincing onself of the wisdom of selecting the *implicit favorite.*

Hindsight Bias

"Hindsight is 20-20" is a phrase commonly heard. It means that when we look back on decisions that already were made, we know better what we should have done. Indeed, research has revealed that this phenomenon is quite pervasive. For example, studies have shown that people tend to distort the way they see things so as to conform to what they already know about the past. This effect, known as the **hindsight bias,** refers to the

hindsight bias
The tendency for people to perceive outcomes as more inevitable after they have occurred (i.e., in hindsight) than they did before they occurred (i.e., in foresight).

tendency for people to perceive outcomes as more inevitable after they occurred (i.e., in hindsight) than they did before they occurred (i.e., in foresight). Hindsight bias occurs when people believe that they could have predicted past events better than they actually did—that is, when they say they "knew it all along."

The hindsight bias occurs because people feel good about being able to judge things accurately. As such, we may expect that people will be more willing to say that they expected events from the past to have occurred whenever these are positive about themselves or their work team but not when these events are negative. After all, we look good when we can take credit for predicting successes, but we look bad when we anticipated negative outcomes without doing anything to stop them. Indeed, recent research has shown precisely this.[73] This qualification of the hindsight bias may have important effects on the way people make decisions (see Figure 10.8).

Let's consider an example. During the 1970s, a group of public utilities known as the Washington Public Power Supply System (WPPSS) made plans to build seven nuclear power plants in an effort to meet the need for energy, estimated as growing by 7 percent each year. Through the early 1980s, 27,000 investors bought bonds to support this project. As things worked out, however, consumers found ways to conserve energy as energy prices rose, resulting in far smaller increases in energy demands than anticipated. As a result, only one of the seven planned power plants was ever completed, and in 1983, the WPPSS defaulted on bonds valued at $2.25 billion. When investors sued, they claimed that the WPPSS "should have known" that the demand for energy was going to change, thereby precluding the need for the power plants. In other words, they were biased such that they saw the decision to invest in ways that made themselves look good and the WPSS look bad. Likewise, officials from the WPPSS claimed that they had no way of anticipating the changes the future was going to bring, therefore justifying their decision to raise money and build power plants as a wise one.

Person Sensitivity Bias

When President George W. Bush first took office in January 2001, it followed a highly controversial election that some don't believe he won fairly and squarely. Many disapproved of his foreign policy, claiming that he was ill-suited to the position. Then, only eight months later, following the terrorist attacks on New York and Washington, DC, President Bush unified the country with impassioned speeches that sent his approval ratings into the stratosphere. His stance with respect to foreign policy was now widely

FIGURE 10.8

Hindsight Bias: An Example
These doctors from the Family Medical Center in Bakersfield, California, are meeting to make important decisions about medical procedures to be followed at their facility. In keeping with hindsight bias, when reviewing cases that had positive outcomes, they are likely to claim that they "knew it all along." However, they are unlikely to acknowledge that they were able to predict the outcomes of cases having negative results.

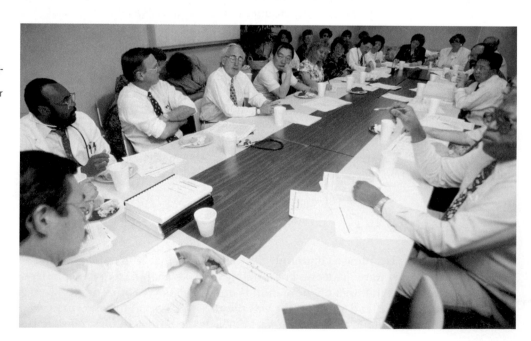

praised. This mini history lesson nicely illustrates an interesting aspect of human nature (beyond the fickle nature of politics, that is): When things are going poorly, nobody likes you, but when things are going well, everyone's your friend. Scientists refer to this as **person sensitivity bias.** Formally, this refers to the tendency for people to blame others too much when things are going poorly and to give them too much credit when things are going well.

Evidence for the person sensitivity bias has been reported in an interesting experiment that was conducted recently.[74] Participants in the study were people asked to judge the performance of either individuals who staffed an assembly line or machines that performed the same assembly task. The people or the machines also were described either as exceeding the company standards or not meeting them. When people were said to be responsible for exceeding the standards, they were perceived more positively than machines that also exceeded the standard. However, when the standards were not met, participants judged other people more harshly than the machines (see Figure 10.9). These findings are in keeping with both the positive and negative aspects of the person sensitivity bias.

The person sensitivity bias is important insofar as it suggests that the decisions we make about others are not likely to be completely objective. As people, we need to understand others (as we emphasized in Chapter 2), and it makes things easier for us if we keep our perceptions consistent: What's good is very good; what's bad is very bad. With such a bias underlying our judgments of others, it's little wonder that the decisions we make about them may be highly imperfect. After all, to the extent that effective decisions rely on accurate information, biases such as the person sensitivity bias predispose us to perceive others in less than objective ways.

Escalation of Commitment Bias

Because decisions are made all the time in organizations, some of these inevitably will be unsuccessful. What would you say is the rational thing to do when a poor decision has been made? Obviously, the ineffective action should be stopped or reversed. In other words, it would make sense to "cut your losses and run." However, people don't always respond in this manner. In fact, it is not unusual to find that ineffective decisions are sometimes followed up with still further ineffective decisions.

Imagine, for example, that you have invested money in a company, but the company appears to be failing. Rather than lose your initial investment, you may invest still more money in the hope of salvaging your first investment. The more you invest, the more you may be tempted to protect those earlier investments by making later investments. That is to say, people sometimes may be found "throwing good money after bad" because they have "too much invested to quit." This is known as the **escalation of commitment phenomenon**—the tendency for people to continue to support previously unsuccessful courses of action because they have sunk costs invested in them.[75]

person sensitivity bias
The tendency for people to give others too little credit when things are going poorly and too much credit when things are going well.

escalation of commitment phenomenon
The tendency for individuals to continue to support previously unsuccessful courses of action.

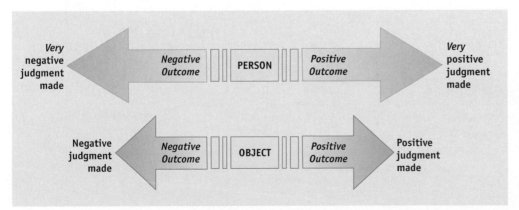

FIGURE 10.9
Person Sensitivity Bias: An Overview
According to the person sensitivity bias, we are likely to blame people too much when things are going poorly and to give them too much credit when things are going well. Accordingly, the same positive decision outcomes are perceived as being more positive when caused by people than by objects, such as machines. Likewise, equally negative decision outcomes are perceived as being more negative when caused by people than by objects.
(*Source:* Based on suggestions by Moon & Conlon, 2002; see Note 74.)

Although this might not seem like a rational thing to do, this strategy is frequently followed. For example, Motorola has invested over $1.3 billion in its Iridium Satellite System, a network of 66 low-orbiting communication satellites that make it possible to make wireless telephone calls from anywhere on earth. In recent years, however, it has become clear that the system has serious technical limitations. Moreover, the service has failed to attract as many subscribers as expected. And now Motorola is beginning to face competition from other major companies. Instead of accepting its losses and walking away from the project, Motorola officials are investing still more in the Iridium project, hoping that each successive dollar invested will be the one needed to turn the project around to make it profitable.[76]

Why do people do this? If you think about it, you may realize that the failure to back your own previous courses of action in an organization would be taken as an admission of failure—a politically difficult act to face in an organization. In other words, people may be very concerned about "saving face"—looking good in the eyes of others and oneself.[77] Researchers have recognized that this tendency for *self-justification* is primarily responsible for people's inclination to protect their beliefs about themselves as rational, competent decision makers by convincing themselves and others that they made the right decision all along and are willing to back it up.[78] Although there are other possible reasons for the escalation of commitment phenomenon, research supports the self-justification explanation.[79] For a summary of the escalation of commitment phenomenon, see Figure 10.10.

Researchers have noted several conditions under which people will refrain from escalating their commitment to a failing course of action.[80] Notably, it has been found that people will stop making failing investments under conditions in which the *available funds for making further investments are limited* and when the *threat of failure is overwhelmingly obvious.*[81] For example, when the Long Island Lighting Company decided in 1989 to abandon plans to operate a nuclear power plant in Shoreham, New York, it was in the face of 23 years' worth of intense political and financial pressure (a strong antinuclear movement and billions of dollars of cost overruns).[82]

It also has been found that people will refrain from escalating commitment when they can *diffuse their responsibility for the earlier failing actions.* That is, the more people feel they are just one of several individuals responsible for a failing course of action, the less likely they are to commit to further failing actions.[83] In other words, the less one is responsible for an earlier failure, the less one may be motivated to justify those earlier failures by making further investments in them.

FIGURE 10.10

Escalation of Commitment: An Overview

According to the escalation of commitment phenomenon, people who have repeatedly made poor decisions continue to support those failing courses of action to justify their earlier decisions. Under some conditions, however, as summarized here, this effect will not occur.

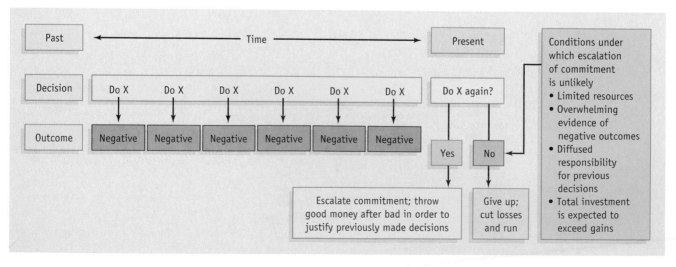

Third, escalation of commitment toward a losing course of action will be low in organizations in which the people who have made ineffective decisions have left and are replaced by others who are not linked to those decisions. In other words, *turnover* lessens an organization's commitment to a losing course of action. Illustrating this, recent research has shown that although some banks continue to make bad (i.e., uncollectible) loans to customers to whom they have loaned money in the past, this is less likely to occur in banks whose top executives (individuals who are considered responsible for those loans) have left their posts.[84]

Finally, it has been found that people are unwilling to escalate commitment to a course of action when it is made clear that the *total amount invested exceeds the amount expected to be gained.*[85] Although people may wish to invest in projects that enable them to recoup their initial investments, there is little reason for them to do so when it is obvious that doing so will be a losing proposition. Under such conditions, it is difficult to justify doing so, even if one "hopes against hope" that it will work out. Indeed, research has shown that decision makers do indeed refrain from escalating commitment to decisions when it is made clear that the overall benefit to be gained is less than the overall costs to be borne.[86] This finding was more apparent among students with accounting backgrounds than those without such backgrounds, presumably because their training predisposed them to be more sensitive to these issues.

To conclude, the escalation of commitment phenomenon represents a type of irrational decision making that has the potential to occur. However, whether or not it does occur will depend on the various circumstances that decision makers confront.

GROUP DECISIONS: DO TOO MANY COOKS SPOIL THE BROTH?

Decision-making groups are a well-established fact of modern organizational life. Groups such as committees, study teams, task forces, or review panels often are charged with the responsibility for making important business decisions.[87] They are so common, in fact, that it has been said that some administrators spend as much as 80 percent of their time in committee meetings.[88]

In view of this, it is important to ask how well groups do at making decisions compared to individuals. Given the several advantages and disadvantages of having groups make decisions we described earlier, this question is particularly important. Specifically, we may ask: Under what conditions might individuals or groups be expected to make superior decisions? Fortunately, research provides us with some concrete answers.[89]

When Are Groups Superior to Individuals?

Whether groups will do better than individuals or worse than individuals depends on the nature of the task. Specifically, any advantages that groups may have over individuals will depend on how complex or simple the task is.

Complex decision tasks. Imagine a situation in which an important decision has to be made about a complex problem—such as whether one company should merge with another. This is not the kind of problem about which any one individual working alone would be able to make a good decision. After all, its highly complex nature may overwhelm even an expert, thereby setting the stage for a group to do a better job. Naturally, groups may excel in such situations.

However, this doesn't happen automatically. In fact, for groups to outperform individuals, several conditions must exist. First, we must consider who is in the group. Successful groups tend to be composed of *heterogeneous group members with complementary skills.* So, for example, a group composed of lawyers, accountants, real estate agents, and other experts may make much better decisions on the merger problem than would a group composed of specialists in only one field. Indeed, research has shown that the diversity of opinions offered by group members is one of the major advantages of using groups to make decisions.[90]

As you might imagine, it is not enough simply to have skills. For a group to be successful, its members also must be able to communicate their ideas to each other freely—in an open, nonhostile manner. Conditions under which one individual (or group) intimidates another from contributing his or her expertise easily can negate any potential gain associated with composing groups of heterogeneous experts. After all, *having* expertise and being able to make a contribution by *using* that expertise are two different things. Indeed, research has shown that only when the contributions of the most qualified group members are given the greatest weight does the group derive any benefit from that member's presence.[91] Thus, *for groups to be superior to individuals, they must be composed of a heterogeneous collection of experts with complementary skills who can freely and openly contribute to their group's product.*

Simple decision tasks. In contrast to complex decision tasks, imagine a situation in which a judgment is required on a simple problem with a readily verifiable answer. For example, make believe that you are asked to translate a phrase from a relatively obscure language into English.

Groups might do better than individuals on such a task because the odds are increased that someone in the group knows the language and can perform the translation for the group. However, there is no reason to expect that even a large group will be able to perform such a task better than a single individual who has the required expertise. In fact, an expert working alone may do even better than a group. This is because an expert individual performing a simple task may be distracted by others and suffer from having to convince them of the correctness of his or her solution. For this reason, exceptional individuals tend to outperform entire committees on simple tasks.[92] In such cases, for groups to benefit from a pooling of resources, there must be some resources to pool. The pooling of ignorance does not help.

In sum, the question, "Are two heads better than one?" can be answered this way: *On simple tasks, two heads may be better than one if at least one of those heads has in it enough of what it takes to succeed.* Thus, whether groups perform better than individuals depends on the nature of the task performed and the expertise of the people involved. We have summarized some of these key considerations in Figure 10.11.

FIGURE 10.11

When Are Group Decisions Superior to Individual Decisions?
When performing complex problems, groups are superior to individuals if certain conditions prevail (e.g., when members have heterogeneous and complementary skills, when they can freely share ideas, and when their good ideas are accepted by others). However, when performing simple problems, groups perform only as well as the best individual group member—and then, only if that person has the correct answer and if that answer is accepted by others in the group.

When Are Individuals Superior to Groups?

As we have described thus far, groups may be expected to perform better than the average or even the exceptional individual under certain conditions. However, there also are conditions under which individuals are superior to groups.

Most of the problems faced by organizations require a great deal of creative thinking. For example, a company deciding how to use a newly developed adhesive in its consumer products is facing decisions on a poorly structured task. Although you would expect that the complexity of such creative problems would give groups a natural advantage, this is not the case. In fact, research has shown that *on poorly structured, creative tasks, individuals perform better than groups.*[93]

An approach to solving creative problems commonly used by groups is **brainstorming.** This technique was developed by an advertising executive as a tool for coming up with creative, new ideas.[94] The members of brainstorming groups are encouraged to present their ideas in an uncritical way and to discuss freely and openly all ideas on the floor. Specifically, members of brainstorming groups are required to follow four main rules:

brainstorming
A technique designed to foster group productivity by encouraging interacting group members to express their ideas in a noncritical fashion.

1. Avoid criticizing others' ideas.
2. Share even far-out suggestions.
3. Offer as many comments as possible.
4. Build on others' ideas to create your own.

Does brainstorming improve the quality of creative decisions? To answer this question, researchers compared the effectiveness of individuals and brainstorming groups working on creative problems.[95] Specifically, participants were given 35 minutes to consider the consequences of situations such as "What if everybody went blind?" or "What if everybody grew an extra thumb on each hand?" Clearly, the novel nature of such problems requires a great deal of creativity. Comparisons were made of the number of solutions generated by groups of four or seven people and a like number of individuals working on the same problems alone. The results were clear: Individuals were significantly more productive than groups.

In summary, groups perform worse than individuals when working on creative tasks. A great part of the problem is that some individuals feel inhibited by the presence of others even though one rule of brainstorming is that even far-out ideas may be shared. To the extent that people wish to avoid feeling foolish as a result of saying silly things, their creativity may be inhibited when in groups. Similarly, groups may inhibit creativity by slowing down the process of bringing ideas to fruition. Yet, many creative professionals strongly believe in the power of brainstorming.[96] For some suggestions on how to reap the benefits of brainstorming, see Table 10.3.

TRADITIONAL TECHNIQUES FOR IMPROVING THE EFFECTIVENESS OF DECISIONS

As we have made clear in this chapter, certain advantages can be gained from sometimes using individuals and sometimes using groups to make decisions. A decision-making technique that combines the best features of groups and individuals, while minimizing the disadvantages, would be ideal. Several techniques designed to realize the "best of both worlds" have been widely used in organizations. These include techniques that involve the structuring of group discussions in special ways. An even more basic approach to improving the effectiveness of group decisions involves training decision makers in ways of avoiding some of the pitfalls of group decision making. We will begin this section of the chapter with a discussion of this training approach to improving group decisions and then go on to consider various ways of creating specially structured groups.

TABLE 10.3   TIPS FOR USING BRAINSTORMING SUCCESSFULLY

The rules of brainstorming are simple enough, but doing it effectively is not as easy as it seems. Many brainstorming sessions fail because people don't fully appreciate the finer points of how to conduct them. Following these guidelines will help make your own brainstorming sessions more effective.

SUGGESTION	EXPLANATION
Brainstorm frequently, at least once per month.	Practice makes perfect. The more frequently people engage in brainstorming, the more comfortable they are with it—hence, the more effective it becomes.
Keep brainstorming sessions brief, less than an hour in length.	Brainstorming effectively can be very exhausting, so limit the time dedicated to it. After about an hour, people become too inefficient to make it worthwhile to continue.
Focus on the problem at hand.	The best brainstorming sessions begin with a clear statement of the problem at hand. These shouldn't be too broad or too narrow.
Don't forget to "build" and "jump."	The best ideas to result from brainstorming sessions are those that build on other ideas. Everyone should be strongly encouraged to jump from one idea to another as they build on the earlier one.
Prepare for the session.	Brainstorming is much more effective when people prepare in advance by reading up on the topic than when they come in "cold."
Don't limit yourself to words—use props.	Some of the most effective brainstorming sessions result when people introduce objects to help model their ideas.

(*Source:* Based on suggestions by Kelley, 2001; see Note 96.)

Techniques for Improving Individual Decision Making

One of the oldest ways of improving the quality of individual decisions is by training people in specific techniques they can use to avoid some of the pitfalls inherent in decision making. Some of the most widely used techniques involve training people to improve group performance and also training them to avoid ethical pitfalls.

Training individuals to improve group performance. Earlier in this chapter we noted that how well groups solve problems depends in part on the composition of those groups. If at least one group member is capable of coming up with a solution, groups may benefit by that individual's expertise. Based on this reasoning, it follows that the more qualified individual group members are to solve problems, the better their groups as a whole will perform. What, then, might individuals do to improve the nature of the decisions they make?

Researchers looking into this question have found that people tend to make four types of mistakes when attempting to make creative decisions and that they make better decisions when trained to avoid these errors.[97] Specifically, these are as follows:

1. *Hypervigilance.* The state of **hypervigilance** involves frantically searching for quick solutions to problems, going from one idea to another out of a sense of desperation that one idea isn't working and that another needs to be considered before time runs out. A poor, "last chance" solution may be adopted to relieve anxiety. This problem may be avoided by keeping in mind that it is best to stick with one suggestion and work it out thoroughly and reassuring the person solving the problem that his or her level of skill and education is adequate to perform the task at hand. In other words, a little reassurance may go a long way toward keeping individuals on the right track and avoiding the problem of hypervigilance.
2. *Unconflicted adherence.* Many decision makers make the mistake of sticking to the first idea that comes into their heads without more deeply evaluating the conse-

hypervigilance
The state in which an individual frantically searches for quick solutions to problems and goes from one idea to another out of a sense of desperation that one idea isn't working and that another needs to be considered before time runs out.

quences, a mistake known as **unconflicted adherence.** As a result, such people are unlikely to become aware of any problems associated with their ideas or to consider other possibilities. To avoid *unconflicted adherence,* decision makers are urged (1) to think about the difficulties associated with their ideas, (2) to force themselves to consider different ideas, and (3) to consider the special and unique characteristics of the problem they are facing and avoid carrying over assumptions from previous problems.

3. *Unconflicted change.* Sometimes people are very quick to change their minds and adopt the first new idea to come along—a problem known as **unconflicted change.** To avoid unconflicted change, decision makers are encouraged to ask themselves about (1) the risks and problems of adopting that solution, (2) the good points of the first idea, and (3) the relative strengths and weaknesses of both ideas.

4. *Defensive avoidance.* Too often, decision makers fail to solve problems effectively because they go out of their way to avoid working on the task at hand. This is known as **defensive avoidance.** People can do three things to minimize this problem. First, they should attempt to *avoid procrastination.* Don't put off the problem indefinitely just because you cannot come up with a solution right away. Continue to budget some of your time on even the most frustrating problems. Second, *avoid disowning responsibility.* It is easy to minimize the importance of a problem by saying "It doesn't matter, so who cares?" Avoid giving up so soon. Finally, *don't ignore potentially corrective information.* It is tempting to put your nagging doubts about the quality of a solution to rest in order to be finished with it. Good decision makers would not do so. Rather, they use their doubts to test and potentially improve the quality of their ideas.

It is encouraging to note that people make better-quality decisions just by merely considering these four pitfalls. How well groups perform depends to a great extent on the problem-solving skills of the individual group members. And attempting to avoid the four major pitfalls described here appears to be an effective method of improving individual decision-making skills—and, hence, the quality of group decisions.

Making ethical decisions. Although the suggestions we just outlined may help individuals come up with decisions that are improved in many key ways, they may not help people make decisions that are any more ethical. And this is an important consideration, too. After all, considering the Enron–Arthur Andersen scandal in our Case in Point (pages 357–358), it's easy to see that people often have difficulty judging what's right and behaving accordingly. Unfortunately, as we will describe in Chapter 11, stealing in the workplace has become far more commonplace than we would like.[98] However, the pursuit of quality in organizations demands that everyone adheres to the highest moral standards.

The problem with this ideal is that even those of us who subscribe to high moral values sometimes are tempted to behave unethically. If you're thinking, "other people act unethically, but not me," then ask yourself: Have you ever taken home small articles of company property (e.g., pencils, tape) for personal use? Or have you ever made personal copies on the company copier, or fudged a little on your expense account?

If the answer is yes, you may be saying, "Sure, but companies *expect* employees to do these things." And, besides, everyone does it. Although this may be true, we cannot ignore the fact that people often attempt to justify their actions by rationalizing that they are not really unethical. This is especially the case when someone does something that may be seen as unethical, except for the fact that the others with whom we work convince us that it's really okay. This kind of rationalization makes it possible for us to talk ourselves into making unethical decisions, thinking that they are really not so bad. To avoid such situations—and thereby to improve ethical decision making—it may be useful to run your contemplated decisions through an ethics test.[99] To do so, ask yourself the following questions.

1. *Does it violate the obvious "shall nots"?* Although many people realize that "thou shall not lie, or cheat, or steal," they do it anyway. So, instead of thinking of a way

unconflicted adherence
The tendency for decision makers to stick to the first idea that comes to their minds without more deeply evaluating the consequences.

unconflicted change
The tendency for people to quickly change their minds and to adopt the first new idea to come along.

defensive avoidance
The tendency for decision makers to fail to solve problems because they go out of their way to avoid working on the problem at hand.

OB IN A DIVERSE WORLD
ARE U.S. BUSINESSES OVERLY CONCERNED ABOUT ETHICAL DECISIONS?

As we have chronicled in Chapter 1, today's economy is truly global in nature. Indeed, manufacturing, marketing, and financial operations tend to be similar across the industrialized regions of the world. Interestingly, however, there do not appear to be equally similar norms regarding what constitutes ethical and unethical behavior. Rather, ethical standards vary widely across capitalist nations. And, in this connection, Americans appear to be more concerned about ethics than their counterparts in other countries—too much so, according to some.

Any American business leader would have little difficulty identifying instances in which a business leader has made an unethical decision. In fact, incidents of corporate officers and prominent businesspeople in the United States who have behaved unethically (e.g., by embezzling funds, by offering bribes, or by fixing elections), and who have been jailed or fined for doing so, are part of ethical folklore. However, such incidents are more likely to be ignored by executives in other countries. By the same token, Americans also are more likely than their foreign counterparts to pay attention to the social responsibility of organizations (e.g., concern about the environment, treatment of employees, animal testing) and to boycott those companies whose actions they find ethically questionable. Although it may be tempting for proud Americans to point to these things as evidence of their own high moral standards, it is important to note that throughout the world they are taken as signs that Americans' ethical concerns are overblown.[100]

In many highly industrialized nations throughout the world, the same acts that Americans generally regard as unethical are widely accepted business practices. For example, in Germany, insider trading isn't considered so bad, and tax evasion is not only accepted but also it is revered as "a gentleman's sport."[101]

around such prohibitions (e.g., by convincing yourself that "it's acceptable in this situation"), avoid violating these well-established societal rules altogether.

2. *Will anyone get hurt?* Philosophers consider an action to be ethical to the extent that it brings the greatest good to the greatest number. Thus, if someone may be harmed in any way as a result of your actions, you should probably rethink your decision; it's probably unethical.

3. *How would you feel if your decision was reported on the front page of your newspaper?* If your decision is really ethical, you wouldn't have any reason to worry about having it made public. (In fact, you'd probably be pleased to receive the publicity.) However, if you find yourself uneasy about answering this question affirmatively, the decision you are contemplating may be unethical.

4. *What if you did it 100 times?* Sometimes an unethical action doesn't seem so bad because it's done only once. In such a case, the damage might not be so bad, although the action still might not be ethical. However, if the act you're contemplating appears to be more wrong if it were done 100 times, then it's probably also wrong the first time.

5. *How would you feel if someone did it to you?* If something you are thinking of doing to another really is ethical, you would probably find it acceptable if your situations were reversed. Thus, if you have any doubts as to how you'd feel being the person affected by your decision, you may wish to reconsider.

6. *What's your gut feeling?* Sometimes things just look bad—probably because they *are*. If your actions are unethical, you probably can tell by listening to that little voice inside your head. The trick is to listen to *that* voice and to silence the one that tells you to do otherwise.

Admittedly, considering these questions will not transform a devil into an angel. Moreover, they are far easier said than done. Still, they may be useful for judging how

And in Japan, under-the-table favors are so much a part of the culture, that people who grant them do not think of themselves as doing anything wrong.[102] Many European businesspeople are amused by the attention American companies pay to ethics training and codes of ethics, leading some to refer to the United States as an "unusually moralizing society," urging it to "lighten up a little." And in Japan, putting up with the policies of many U.S. companies to not accept gifts is considered one of the idio-syncrasies of dealing with Americans.[103]

Rather than drawing conclusions about whether or not the American approach is appropriate, it makes more sense to ask *why* the differences exist. To a great extent, the answer seems to be based on the distinction between "us" and "them." Specifically, American society places a great deal of emphasis on treating everyone in an arm's-distance manner; fairness is done when everyone is given an equal chance of success. People in Europe and Japan, however, place less emphasis on giving every-one an equal opportunity. (In fact, the phrases "equal opportu-nity" and "level playing field" are difficult to translate into Japanese.) Instead, people from Europe (especially southern

Europe) and Japan pay more attention to fulfilling their obliga-tions to those individuals and institutions with whom they have developed long-term relationships. To individuals from these countries, behaving ethically involves arriving at decisions that reflect shared values of the company and that reaffirm one's obligations to those values.

Despite these long-standing cultural differences, it is begin-ning to look like things may be changing, and that American eth-ical values are being adopted in businesses throughout the world. In Europe, for example, we see this in the strengthening of environmental regulations and in the recent enactment of legis-lation banning sexual harassment. People convicted of insider trading also are now serving time in jail. Although the growing global economy and the growth of multinational corporations are surely responsible for this trend, it is interesting to consider what may happen to distinctive national differences in ethical values as time goes on. Will societies change to match businesses' adaptation to American standards, or will these new business standards wither to the extent that they are inconsistent with national norms? Only time will tell.

ethical the decisions are that you may be contemplating. Your answers to these six ques-tions may help you avoid rationalizing that unethical acts are really ethical. And once we recognize that the decisions we are thinking of making may not be ethical, we are well on the way to behaving in an ethical fashion. (One factor that may influence peo-ple's perceptions of the ethical appropriateness of a decision is national culture. Indeed, people from different nations may have different views about ethical and unethical business decisions. For a look at the implications of this, see the OB in a Diverse World section above.)

Techniques for Enhancing Group Decisions

Just as there are various things individuals can do to improve decision making, so too are there steps that groups can take to enhance the quality of their decisions. The basic idea underlying these techniques is identical: Structure the group experience so as to enable the many benefits of groups to occur without also experiencing the weaknesses.

The Delphi technique: Decisions by expert consensus. According to Greek mythology, people interested in seeing what fate the future held for them could seek the counsel of the Delphic oracle, the ultimate authority on things to come. Today's organizational decision makers sometimes consult experts to help them make the best decisions as well. A technique developed by the Rand Corporation, known as the **Delphi technique,** represents a systematic way of collecting and organizing the opinions of several experts into a single decision.[104] For a summary of the steps in this process, see Figure 10.12.

The Delphi process starts by enlisting the cooperation of experts and presenting the problem to them, usually in a letter or an e-mail message. Each expert then proposes what he or she believes is the most appropriate solution. The group leader compiles all

Delphi technique

A method of improving group decisions using the opinions of experts, which are solicited by mail and then compiled. The expert consensus of opinions is used to make a decision.

FIGURE 10.12

The Delphi Technique
The Delphi technique allows decisions to be made by several experts while avoiding many of the pitfalls of face-to-face group interaction. Its general steps are outlined here.

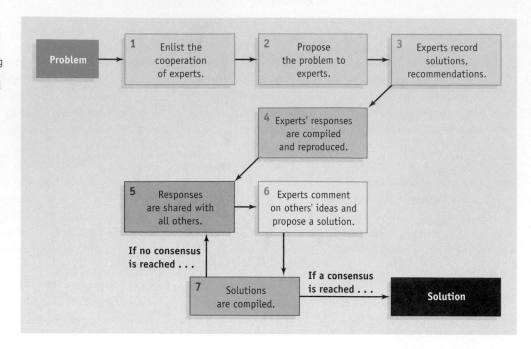

of these individual responses and reproduces them so they can be shared with all the other experts in a second mailing. At this point, each expert comments on the others' ideas and proposes another solution. These individual solutions are returned to the leader, who compiles them and looks for a consensus of opinions. If a consensus is reached, the decision is made. If not, the process of sharing reactions with others is repeated until a consensus is eventually obtained.

The obvious advantage of using the Delphi technique to make decisions is that it allows the collection of expert judgments without the great costs and logistical difficulties of bringing many experts together for a face-to-face meeting. However, the technique is not without limitations. As you might imagine, the Delphi process can be very time consuming. Sending out letters or e-mail messages, waiting for everyone to respond, transcribing and disseminating the responses, and repeating the process until a consensus is reached can take quite a long time. Experts have estimated that before the advent of e-mail the minimum time required to use the Delphi technique would be more than 44 days. In one case, the process took five months to complete.[105] With today's widespread use of e-mail, the Delphi approach can be sped up considerably, but it is still slow. Obviously, the Delphi approach is not appropriate for making decisions in crisis situations, or whenever time is of the essence. However, the approach has been successfully employed to make decisions requiring systematic input from several parties such as, what items to put on a conference agenda and what the potential impact of implementing new land-use policies would be.[106]

The nominal group technique: A structured group meeting. When there are only a few hours available to make a decision, group discussion sessions can be held in which members interact with each other in an orderly, focused fashion aimed at solving problems. The **nominal group technique (NGT)** brings together a small number of individuals (usually about seven to ten) who systematically offer their individual solutions to a problem and share their personal reactions to others' solutions.[107] The technique is referred to as nominal because the individuals involved form a group in name only. The participants do not attempt to agree as a group on any solution, but rather, vote on all the solutions proposed. For a summary of this process, see Figure 10.13.

As shown in Figure 10.13, the nominal group process begins by gathering the group members together around a table and identifying the problem at hand. Then each member writes down his or her solutions. Next, one at a time, each member presents his or her solutions to the group and the leader writes these down on a chart. This process continues until all the ideas have been expressed. Following this, each solution

nominal group technique (NGT)
A technique for improving group decisions in which small groups of individuals systematically present and discuss their ideas before privately voting on their preferred solution. The most preferred solution is accepted as the group's decision.

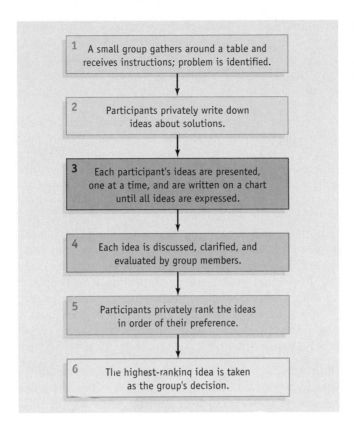

FIGURE 10.13
The Nominal Group Technique
The nominal group technique structures face-to-face group meetings in such a way that the open expression and evaluation of ideas is encouraged. It follows the six steps summarized here.

1 A small group gathers around a table and receives instructions; problem is identified.

2 Participants privately write down ideas about solutions.

3 Each participant's ideas are presented, one at a time, and are written on a chart until all ideas are expressed.

4 Each idea is discussed, clarified, and evaluated by group members.

5 Participants privately rank the ideas in order of their preference.

6 The highest-ranking idea is taken as the group's decision.

is discussed, clarified, and evaluated by the group members. Each member is given a chance to voice his or her reactions to each idea. After all the ideas have been evaluated, the group members privately rank-order their preferred solutions. The idea that receives the highest rank is taken as the group's decision.

The NGT has several advantages and disadvantages.[108] We have already noted that it can be used to arrive at group decisions in only a few hours. This can be useful for many types of decisions—but, of course, not for urgent decisions that have to be made on the spot (see Figure 10.14). The benefit of the technique is that it discourages any pressure to conform to the wishes of a high-status group member because all ideas are

"Under new business: Peterson, at Hammond Point Beach, reports that a person in the water is flailing about and calling for help. Peterson wants to know what action, if any, he should take."

FIGURE 10.14

Nominal Groups: Good, but Not Always Fast Enough
The nominal group technique is an effective way to make group decisions because it systematically assesses people's opinions about key issues. However, because it can take several hours to complete, it is inappropriate whenever decisions need to be made on the spot, such as in emergency situations.

evaluated and the preferences are expressed in private balloting. The technique must be considered limited, however, in that it requires the use of a trained group leader. In addition, using NGT successfully requires that only one narrowly defined problem be considered at a time. So, for very complex problems, many NGT sessions would have to be run—and only *if* the problem under consideration can be broken down into smaller parts.

It is important to consider the relative effectiveness of nominal groups and Delphi groups over face-to-face interacting groups. In general, research has shown the superiority of these special approaches to decision making in many ways on a variety of decision problems.[109] Overall, members of nominal groups tend to be the most satisfied with their work and make the best-quality judgments. In addition, both nominal groups and Delphi groups are much more productive than interacting groups.

As we noted earlier, however, there is a potential benefit to be derived from face-to-face interaction that cannot be realized in nominal and Delphi groups—that is, acceptance of the decision. Groups are likely to accept their decisions and to be committed to them if members have been actively involved in making them. Thus, the more detached and impersonal atmosphere of nominal and Delphi groups sometimes makes their members less likely to accept their groups' decisions. We may conclude, then, that there is no one best type of group used to make decisions. Which type is most appropriate depends on the trade-offs decision makers are willing to make in terms of speed, quality, and commitment.[110]

The stepladder technique: Systematically incorporating new members. Another way of structuring group interaction is known as the **stepladder technique**.[111] This approach minimizes the tendency for group members to be unwilling to present their ideas by adding new members to a group one at a time and requiring each to present his or her ideas independently to a group that already has discussed the problem at hand. To begin, each of two people works on a problem independently and then come together to present their ideas and discuss solutions jointly. While the two-person group is working, a third person working alone also considers the problem. Then this individual presents his or her ideas to the group and joins in a three-person discussion of a possible solution. During this period a fourth person works on the problem alone and then presents his or her ideas to the group and joins into a four-person group discussion. After each new person has been added to the group, the entire group works together at finding a solution. (For a summary of the steps in this technique, see Figure 10.15.)

In following this procedure, it is important for all individuals to be given enough time to work on the problem before they join the group. Then each person must be given enough time to present thoroughly his or her ideas to the group. Groups then must have sufficient time to discuss the problem at hand and reach a preliminary deci-

stepladder technique

A technique for improving the quality of group decisions that minimizes the tendency for group members to be unwilling to present their ideas by adding new members to a group one at a time and requiring each to present his or her ideas independently to a group that already has discussed the problem at hand.

FIGURE 10.15

The Stepladder Technique

By systematically adding new individuals into decision-making groups, the stepladder technique helps to increase the quality of the decisions made.
(*Source:* Adapted from Rogelberg & O'Connor, 1998; see Note 111.)

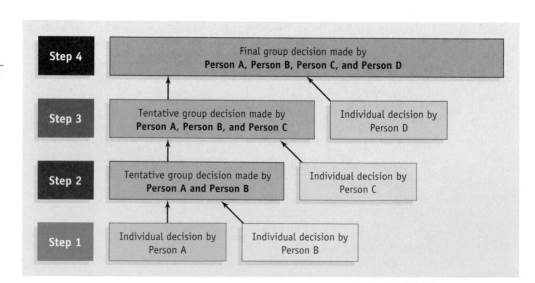

sion before the next person is added. The final decision is made only after all individuals have been added to the group.

The rationale underlying this procedure is that by forcing each person to present independent ideas without knowing how the group has decided, the new person will not be influenced by the group, and the group is required to consider a constant infusion of new ideas. If this is so, then groups solving problems using the stepladder technique would be expected to make better decisions than conventional groups meeting all at once to discuss the same problem. Research has found that this is exactly what happens. Moreover, members of stepladder groups reported feeling more positive about their group experiences than their counterparts in conventional groups. Although the stepladder technique is new, evidence suggests that it holds a great deal of promise as a way of enhancing the decision-making capacity of groups.

COMPUTER-BASED APPROACHES TO PROMOTING EFFECTIVE DECISIONS

Now that we have reviewed traditional, low-tech techniques for improving decision-making effectiveness, we will move on to examining several new, technology-based approaches that have been used in recent years. Given the widespread use of computers in the workplace, it probably comes as no surprise that attempts have been made to put computers to use in improving the quality of group decisions. For the most part, these techniques are not especially sophisticated and make good use of widely available and inexpensive computer technology. As a result, they stand to be widely used to the extent that they are effective. With this in mind, we will examine three such techniques: *electronic meetings, computer-assisted communication,* and *group decision support systems.*

Electronic Meetings

Although nominal groups traditionally meet in face-to-face settings, advances in modern technology enable them to be formed even when members are in distant locations. Specifically, **electronic meetings,** as they are known, involve holding teleconferences in which individuals in different locations participate in group conferences by means of telephone lines or direct satellite transmissions.[112] The messages may be sent either via characters on a computer monitor or images viewed during a teleconference. Despite their high-tech look, electronic meetings are really just nominal groups meeting in a manner that approximates face-to-face contact. And, for the most part, they have proven to be equally effective.

Insofar as electronic meetings allow for groups to assemble more conveniently than face-to-face meetings, they are growing in popularity. Presently, such companies as GE Appliances, US West, Marriott Corp., and Sun Microsystems (see Figure 10.16) have relied on electronic meetings, and growing numbers of companies are using them all the time.

electronic meetings
The practice of bringing individuals from different locations together for a meeting via telephone or satellite transmissions, either on television monitors or via shared space on a computer screen.

Computer-Assisted Communication

Another way of leveraging technology to facilitate group decision making involves using **computer-assisted communication**—that is, the sharing of information, such as text messages and data relevant to the decision, over computer networks. The underlying idea of computer-assisted communication is that on-screen messages provide an effective means of sending some forms of information that can help groups make better decisions. But does it really work? In other words, does being able to communicate with other team members via computer help teams make more effective decisions than they would make without computer assistance?

computer-assisted communication
The sharing of information, such as text messages and data relevant to the decision, over computer networks.

FIGURE 10.16

An Electronic Meeting in Progress
Using a teleconference to connect them to research and development scientists in Australia, these computer engineers at Sun Microsystems' headquarters in Palo Alto, California, are making important decisions regarding a new version of the company's Java programming language. Like many other companies today, Sun Microsystems relies on using electronic meetings to facilitate decision making by calling on experts wherever in the world they may be located.

Research suggests that the answer is "only sometimes."[113] Recently, a study was conducted that compared the effectiveness of three-person groups whose members were allowed only to speak to each other (the talk-only condition) with other three-person groups whose members also were allowed to send text messages to one another over a computer network (the computer-assisted communication condition). Participants were asked to perform a task that simulated the kind of decisions made in a military "command and control" situation. This involved assessing the threat risk of aircraft spotted on a computer screen (based on such information as speed and size) after they were trained to perform this task. The teams' decisions were scored on the basis of accuracy and then were compared to one another.

The results, summarized in Figure 10.17, revealed that the effectiveness of the teams' decisions depended on another variable. Specifically, teams using the computer-assisted communication made better decisions than teams using verbal communica-

FIGURE 10.17

Computer-Assisted Communication Improves Decision Making Among People Who Are Open to Experience
Computer-assisted communication involves the sharing of information (e.g., text messages and data relevant to them) over computer networks. Research simulating a military decision-making situation has shown that the effectiveness of this technique depends on people's openness to experience. As summarized here, computer-assisted communication improved the decision-making performance of three-person teams only when they were composed of individuals who scored highly on a personality test measuring openness to experience. However, individuals who were not open to experience were not helped by computer-assisted communication.
(*Source:* Based on data reported by Colquitt et al., 2002; see Note 113.)

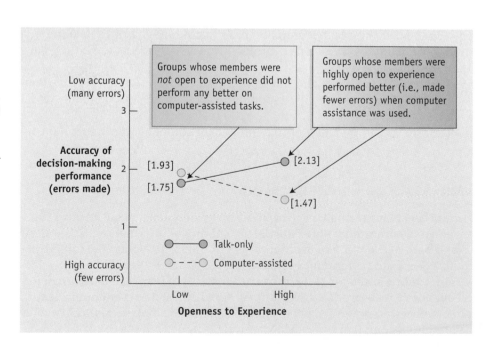

tion only when they were composed of individuals whose scores on a personality test indicated that they were highly open to experience. People scoring high on **openness to experience** tend to have intellectual curiosity, value learning, have an active imagination, and are intrigued by artistic endeavors. By contrast, people scoring low on this measure tend to be exactly the opposite. Apparently, because computer-assisted communication was new to many of the participants, its effectiveness was limited to those who were most accepting of the new technology and who possessed the creativity to use the technology in an efficient manner. These individuals reaped the benefits associated with the computer assistance. However, those who were less open to experience failed to perform better when using computer-assisted communication—actually, they performed slightly worse. Apparently, the computer-assisted communication was not much "assistance" to them, after all.

Because it provides a useful means of exchanging crucial information, one might be inclined to assume that computer-assisted communication is an effective way to improve group decision quality. And, because it can be adopted readily and inexpensively, some may be tempted to put it into practice. However, given that it appears not to be effective for everyone, implementing computer-assisted communications on a widespread basis would be unwise—at least, it may be premature. Perhaps, after such systems are in use for a while and people come to be familiar with them, even those who are not open to experiences will find them acceptable. Furthermore, training on how to integrate computer-assisted communication with more traditional forms also could compensate for any lack of openness. For the moment, however, officials implementing computer-assisted communication systems would be wise to proceed with caution.

Group Decision Support Systems

Another approach to using technology to improve the effectiveness of decisions that has received attention in recent years is known as **group decision support systems (GDSS).** These are interactive computer-based systems that combine communication, computer, and decision technologies to improve the effectiveness of group problem-solving meetings. They often involve having people type their ideas into a computer program and discuss these ideas anonymously with others in chat rooms. A record of these discussions is then left for all to examine as needed. Their underlying rationale is straightforward: The quality of group decisions stands to be improved insofar as this process removes some of the impediments to decision making. In this sense, just as decision support systems, described earlier (see page 360), can be used to identify effective ways of making decisions, so too can group decision support systems.

One of the reasons why face-to-face groups sometimes make poor decisions is that group members do not always share information they have available to them that might help the group. As we discussed earlier, in connection with the phenomenon of groupthink, this may occur because people sometimes censor unpopular ideas voluntarily, even if these are good ideas that can improve the quality of group decisions. This is where GDSS can be useful. Groups using GDSS may avoid this problem insofar as the anonymous recording of ideas makes people less reluctant to share them and makes it easier than ever to have access to them. In this manner, some of the most potent impediments to group decision quality can be eliminated. Recent research has found that this is, in fact, exactly what happens in groups using GDSS. An experiment was conducted comparing the effectiveness of groups of managers asked to solve simulated management problems in face-to-face groups and using GDSS.[114] As expected, the results showed that, compared to face-to-face groups, groups using GDSS not only shared considerably more information, but they also made far better decisions as a result.

For now, it seems that group decision support systems appear to be quite effective. However, because they are very new, we don't yet know all the conditions under which they will continue to be successful. As OB researchers conduct further research on this topic, we surely will learn more about this promising technique in the future.

openness to experience
A personality variable reflecting the degree to which individuals have intellectual curiosity, value learning, have an active imagination, and are intrigued by artistic endeavors.

group decision support systems (GDSS)
Interactive computer-based systems that combine communication, computer, and decision technologies to improve the effectiveness of group problem-solving meetings.

1. Identify the steps in the analytical model of decision making and distinguish between the various types of decisions that people make.

According to the analytical model of decision making, the making of decisions is a multistep process through which (1) a problem is identified, (2) solution objectives are defined, (3) a predecision is made (i.e., a decision about how to make a decision), (4) alternatives are generated, (5) these alternatives are evaluated, (6) an alternative is chosen, (7) that alternative is implemented, and then (8) a follow-up evaluation occurs to determine if the problem still exists. Decisions made in organizations can be characterized as being either programmed, routine decisions made according to preexisting guidelines or nonprogrammed decisions requiring novel and creative solutions. Decisions also differ with respect to the amount of risk involved, ranging from those in which the decision outcomes are relatively certain to those in which the outcomes are highly uncertain. Uncertain situations are expressed as statements of probability based on either objective or subjective information. Decisions also differ with respect to whether they are made by high-level organizational officials (top-down decisions) or by employees themselves (empowered decisions).

2. Describe different individual decision styles and the various organizational and cultural factors that influence the decision-making process.

There are individual differences in the way people make decisions. Generally, people demonstrate one of four dominant decision styles: directive (preference for simple, clear solutions), analytical (willingness to consider complex situations based on ambiguous information), conceptual (a humanistic and artistic orientation), or behavioral (a concern for the organization). Within organizations, decision quality may be adversely affected by severe time constraints and by political face-saving pressures. Decisions made in organizations also are affected by the national culture in which the organization exists. For example, Americans are more likely to confront problems as decisions that need to be made, whereas people from Thailand are more likely to accept these problems as they are. Also, whereas Americans make decisions in a highly individualistic way (by looking out for themselves), Asians are more likely to make decisions in a collective manner (by taking into account the group or organization).

3. Distinguish among three approaches to how decisions are made: the rational-economic model, the administrative model, and image theory.

The rational-economic model characterizes decision makers as thoroughly searching through perfect information to make an optimal decision. This is a normative approach, in that it describes how decision makers ideally ought to behave to make the best possible decisions. In contrast, the administrative model is a descriptive approach, which describes how decision makers actually behave. It recognizes that limitations imposed by people's ability to process the information needed to make complex decisions (bounded rationality and bounded discretion) restrict decision makers to making satisficing decisions—solutions that are not optimal but are good enough. An alternative approach, image theory, recognizes that decisions are made in an automatic, intuitive fashion. It claims that people will adopt a course of action that best fits their individual principles, current goals, and plans for the future.

4. Identify the various factors that lead people to make imperfect decisions.

People make imperfect decisions due to cognitive biases. One such bias, framing, refers to the tendency for people to make different decisions based on how a problem is presented. For example, when a problem is presented in a way that emphasizes positive gains to be received, people tend to make conservative, risk-averse decisions, whereas when the same problem is presented in a way that emphasizes potential losses to be suffered, people tend to make riskier decisions. Simple rules of thumb, known as heuristics, also may bias decisions. For example, according to the availability heuristic, people base their judgments on information readily available to them, and according to the representativeness heuristic, people are perceived in stereotypical ways if they appear to be representatives of the categories to which they belong. People also are biased toward implicit favorites, alternatives they prefer in advance of considering all the options. Other alternatives, confirmation candidates, are considered for purposes of convincing oneself that one's implicit favorite is the best alternative. Decisions also are biased because of the tendency to believe that we were far better at judging past events than we actually were (known as the hindsight bias) and the tendency for people to give too little credit to others when things are going poorly and too much credit when things are going well (known as the person sensitivity bias). Finally, decisions are biased insofar as people tend to escalate commitment to unsuccessful courses of action because they have sunk costs invested in them. This occurs in large part because people need to justify their previous actions and wish to avoid having to admit that their initial decision was a mistake.

5. Compare the conditions under which groups make more superior decisions than individuals and when individuals make more superior decisions than groups.

Groups make more superior decisions than individuals when these are composed of a heterogeneous mix of experts who possess complementary skills. However, groups may not be any better than the best member of the group when performing a task that has a simple, verifiable answer. Individuals make more superior decisions than face-to-face brainstorming groups on creative problems. However, when brainstorming is done electronically—that is, by using computer terminals to send messages—the quality of decisions tends to improve.

6. Describe various traditional techniques and high-tech techniques that can be used to enhance the quality of individual decisions and group decisions.

Decision quality may be enhanced in several different ways. First, the quality of individual decisions has been shown to improve following individual training in problem-solving skills. Training in ethics also can help people make more ethical decisions. Group decisions may be improved in three ways. First, in the Delphi technique, the judgments of experts are systematically gathered and used to form a single joint decision. Second, in the nominal group technique, group meetings are structured so as to elicit and evaluate systematically the opinions of all members. Third, in the stepladder technique, new individuals are added to decision-making groups one at a time, requiring the presentation and discussion of new ideas. Contemporary techniques also employ the use of computers as aids in decision making. One of these is known as electronic meetings. These are computer networks that bring individuals from different locations together for a meeting via telephone or satellite transmissions, either on television monitors or via shared space on a computer screen. Another computer-based approach is computer-assisted communication—the sharing of information, such as text messages and data relevant to the decision, over computer networks. Finally, computers have been used to facilitate decision making by way of group decision support systems. These are interactive computer-based systems that combine communication, computer, and decision technologies to improve the effectiveness of group problem-solving meetings.

POINTS TO PONDER

Questions for Review

1. What are the general steps in the decision-making process, and how can different types of organizational decisions be characterized?

2. How do individual decision style, group influences, and organizational influences affect decision making in organizations?

3. What are the major differences between the rational-economic model, the administrative model, and the image theory approach to individual decision making?

4. Explain how each of the following factors contributes to the imperfect nature of decisions: framing effects, reliance on heuristics, decision biases, and the tendency to escalate commitment to a losing course of action.

5. When it comes to making decisions, under what conditions are individuals superior to groups and under what conditions are groups superior to individuals?

6. What traditional techniques and computer-based techniques can be used to improve the quality of decisions made by groups or individuals?

Experiential Questions

1. Think of any decision you recently made. Would you characterize it as programmed or nonprogrammed? Highly certain or highly uncertain? Top-down or empowered? Explain your answers.

2. Identify ways in which various decisions you have made were biased by framing, heuristics, the use of implicit favorites, and the escalation of commitment.

3. Think of various decision-making groups in which you may have participated over the years. Do you think that groupthink was involved in these situations? What signs were evident?

Questions to Analyze

1. Imagine that you are a manager facing the problem of not attracting enough high-quality personnel to your organization. Would you attempt to solve this problem alone or by committee? Explain your reasoning.

2. Suppose you were on a committee charged with making an important decision and that committee was composed of people from various nations. How do you think this might make a difference in the way the group operates?

3. Argue pro or con: "All people make decisions in the same manner."

DEVELOPING OB SKILLS

INDIVIDUAL EXERCISE

What Is Your Personal Decision Style?

As you read about the various personal decision styles, did you put yourself into any one of the categories? To get a feel for what the *Decision-Style Inventory* reveals about your personal decision style, complete this exercise. It is based on questions similar to those appearing in the actual instrument (see Rowe, Boulgaides, & McGrath, 1984; see Note 26).

Directions

For each of the following questions, select the one alternative that best describes how you see yourself in your typical work situation.

1. When performing my job, I usually look for:
   a. practical results
   b. the best solutions to problems
   c. new ideas or approaches
   d. pleasant working conditions

2. When faced with a problem, I usually:
   a. use approaches that have worked in the past
   b. analyze it carefully
   c. try to find a creative approach
   d. rely on my feelings
3. When making plans, I usually emphasize:
   a. the problems I currently face
   b. attaining objectives
   c. future goals
   d. developing my career
4. The kind of information I usually prefer to use is:
   a. specific facts
   b. complete and accurate data
   c. broad information covering many options
   d. data that are limited and simple to understand
5. Whenever I am uncertain about what to do, I:
   a. rely on my intuition
   b. look for facts
   c. try to find a compromise
   d. wait and decide later
6. The people with whom I work best are usually:
   a. ambitious and full of energy
   b. self-confident
   c. open-minded
   d. trusting and polite
7. The decisions I make are usually:
   a. direct and realistic
   b. abstract or systematic
   c. broad and flexible
   d. sensitive to others' needs

Scoring

1. For each *a* you select, give yourself a point in the *directive* category.
2. For each *b* you select, give yourself a point in the *analytical* category.
3. For each *c* you select, give yourself a point in the *conceptual* category.
4. For each *d* you select, give yourself a point in the *behavioral* category.

The points reflect the relative strength of your preferences for each decision style.

Questions for Discussion

1. What style did the test reveal that you have? How did this compare to the style you thought you had before you took the test?
2. Based on the descriptions of the personal decision styles in the text, were you able to guess in advance which test items were indicative of which styles?
3. What additional items may be added to the test to assess each style?

GROUP EXERCISE

Running a Nominal Group: Try It Yourself

A great deal can be learned about nominal groups by running one—or, at least, participating in one—yourself. Doing so will not only help illustrate the procedure but also demonstrate how effectively it works.

Directions

1. Select a topic suitable for discussion in a nominal group composed of students in your class. It should be a topic that is narrowly defined and on which people have many different opinions (these work best in nominal groups). Some possible examples include:
   - What should your school's student leaders be doing for you?
   - What can be done to improve the quality of instruction in your institution?
   - What can be done to improve the quality of jobs your school's students receive when graduating?

2. Divide the class into groups of approximately 10 members each. Arrange each group in a circle or around a table, if possible. In each group, select one person to serve as the group facilitator.

3. Following the steps outlined in Figure 10.13, facilitators should guide their groups in discussions regarding the focal question identified previously in step 1. Allow approximately 45 minutes to 1 hour to complete this process.

4. If time allows, select a different focal question and a different group leader, and repeat the procedure.

Questions for Discussion

1. Collectively, how did the group answer the question? Do you believe that this answer accurately reflected the feelings of the group?

2. How did the various groups' answers compare? Were they similar or different? Why?

3. What were the major problems, if any, associated with the nominal group experience? For example, were there any group members who were reluctant to wait their turns before speaking up?

4. How do you think your group experiences would have differed had you used a totally unstructured, traditional face-to-face group instead of a nominal group?

WEB SURFING EXERCISE

Decision Skills Training

In recent years, several commercial enterprises and nonprofit organizations have been created that offer services designed to help people become better decision makers. Using your favorite search engine, enter search terms such as "decision skills," "empowered decision making," or "decision training." Examine the sites that emerge from this search and answer the following questions based on what you find.

1. In what ways do these services differ from one another? Specifically, what services are being offered and to what groups?

2. How effective do you think these services may be?

3. Under what circumstances, if any, might you envision yourself using such services?

Decision Support Systems

Most companies that offer decision support systems (DSS) describe their products and services online. To get a feel for these, enter the search term "decision support systems" in your favorite search engine. Examine the sites that emerge from this search and answer the following questions based on what you find.

1. With respect to what types of decisions are DSS available? How do these differ from one another?

2. Besides software-based solutions, what other types of decision support services are available?

3. For what types of situations might you be interested in using DSS in your own work?

The Disruptive Manager

A large product-distribution company is having a problem during its group meetings: One department manager is constantly disrupting the meetings while trying to get his ideas across. He has so consistently intimidated his coworkers that they are reluctant to speak up. As a result, their ideas are not coming across.

1. Explain what steps might be taken to avoid this problem.
2. What is your rationale for this advice?
3. What are the advantages and disadvantages of the tactic you identify?

CASE IN POINT

Keeping the New Orleans Saints Marching Down the Field

Bruce Lemmerman spends 363 days per year preparing for important decisions that have to be made in just a few minutes during the other two days. As director of college scouting for the New Orleans Saints, he visits colleges and universities throughout the United States in search of football players who are good enough to be selected for the "Big Show" (slang for the National Football League) during the NFL's two-day college draft each April.

The key to Lemmerman's mission is gathering all pertinent information so that it can be called up when Saints officials need to make decisions about which prospects to select as their draft choices. With this in mind, Lemmerman is almost always on the road, going to as many as 70 schools in four months. While there, he closely watches players during games or in practice sessions—live from the sidelines when he can but at least on videotape. He also talks to coaches and trainers, getting their slant on each athlete's strengths and weaknesses.

He routinely gathers detailed information on a player's physical qualities, such as his height, weight, speed, percentage of body fat, and height of vertical leap, but that's not all. Lemmerman also pays close attention to personal qualities and intangible characteristics, such as a player's "football intelligence," his work ethic, his competitiveness, and his workout habits during the off-season.

Traditionally, the records were written by hand and kept in folders, resulting in disarray. Player profiles were kept in blue folders in the team's conference room, medical evaluations were in the trainer's office, and scouting reports were someplace else. Getting all the critical information on a player was a hopelessly difficult task—and it was only made worse by the fact that until Lemmerman joined the Saints in 1994, much of the recruiting was outsourced. His first mission was to assist in developing a database so that anyone in the front office could access whatever information was needed at any time.

Acknowledging that such a system is only as good as the data entered into it, Lemmerman spends a great deal of time entering information about players into his notebook computer. But he can't run up and down the sidelines while typing notes into the computer. Neither is a handheld computer practical because the screen is too small. So Lemmerman prefers doing things the old-fashioned way—he takes notes on paper forms attached to a clipboard while speaking his impressions into a microcassette recorder. Then, either while on the plane or back at the hotel, he enters all of this information into the notebook computer and transmits it back to the main computer on his desktop in New Orleans.

As tedious as this process may be, Lemmerman realizes that it's necessary to enable the team to make the best possible recruiting decisions. As he puts it, "Imagine it's the fourth quarter and you're tired. You want to quit, but you suck it up and play anyway. At times like that it's easy to be less sharp and to take shortcuts." However, knowing that there are multimillion-dollar decisions at stake, Lemmerman does his part for the team by keeping the recruiting records in impeccable form.

Critical Thinking Questions

1. As an individual who is potentially overwhelmed by statistics and observations about individual players, how do you think Lemmerman's own decision processes may be biased?
2. In what ways do you think that the quality of the decisions made by officials from the New Orleans Saints is helped or harmed by the practice of making draft decisions as a group?
3. In what ways do you think that escalation of commitment may be involved in the decisions Lemmerman makes for the team?

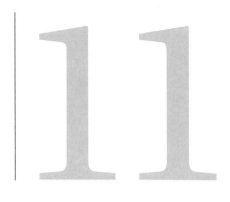

Interpersonal Behavior: Working with and Against Others

LEARNING OBJECTIVES

After reading this chapter, you should be able to:
1. Describe two types of psychological contracts in work relationships and the types of trust associated with each.
2. Describe organizational citizenship behavior and ways in which it may be promoted.
3. Identify ways in which cooperation can be promoted in the workplace.
4. Describe the causes and effects of conflict in organizations.
5. Describe the techniques that can be used to manage conflict in organizations.
6. Identify two forms of deviant organizational behavior and how to minimize their occurrence.

■ PREVIEW CASE
A VENTI CUP OF TRUST BREWS AT STARBUCKS

Think of sipping coffee at a cafe and the name Starbucks is likely to come to mind. With some 5,000 shops throughout the world, and several new stores opening each day, it's difficult to think otherwise. As chairman and CEO of Starbucks Coffee, that suits Howard Schultz just fine. There can be no doubt that with revenues approaching $3 billion and a considerable lead over the competition in the coffeehouse business, Schultz sits atop a successful coffee empire. But Schultz will be the first to tell you that Starbucks is less about numbers than it is about people. In fact, Schultz claims that the company's success stems in large part from the way it treats its employees.

When Schultz was a young boy growing up in the housing projects of Brooklyn, New York, he saw his father move through a succession of poorly paying blue-collar jobs that offered virtually no benefits, dashing any hopes he ever had of achieving financial stability for his family. These bitter memories inspired Schultz to treat his own employees far better. Indeed, people who work at Starbucks acknowledge that it is like no other place they've ever worked before. At Starbucks, employees refer to each other as "partners," which they are: Each receives up to 14 percent of his or her base pay in stock options

> **People who work at Starbucks acknowledge that it is like no other place they've ever worked before.**

each year—even those who work part time. They also receive comprehensive medical, dental, and vision insurance, as well as a generous retirement plan. It's no wonder that Starbucks' turnover rate, under 60 percent, is four to five times lower than the national average for similar businesses—a whopping 250 percent. Although shareholders were at first skeptical about Schultz's apparent generosity, they soon realized that the low turnover rates helped the company save far more than it spent. Investing in people paid off on the bottom line.

With figures like these to support his case, Schultz claims that being benevolent is not so much an added cost as it is a way of building people's emotional ties to the company, enriching their lives as well as the company's profitability. At the core of Schultz's approach lies his belief in the importance of trust. To help promote trust, Schultz regularly meets with his partners, allowing them to understand each other better, and to give them a sense of his vision for the company. In too many companies, Schultz observes, nothing of this nature goes on: "One of the outgrowths of the last 10 to 15 years in business is that there has been a fracturing of trust between senior management and rank-and-file employees. You have to change that," he adds, "but it can't be in words; it has to be in everyday actions. . . . Once you break that trust, the ability to inspire people is over."

In sharing the company's success with those who have helped create it, most of the 40,000 people who work at Starbucks likely would agree that Schultz practices what he preaches. They also would have to acknowledge that Schultz epitomizes the first guiding principle in his company's mission statement: "to provide a great work environment and to treat each other with respect and dignity." Few would argue with him when he says, "I take these kinds of issues very, very seriously," adding, "the ability to get people to think passionately and do things as if it were their own business can only be achieved when they are truly part of the business." And, at Starbucks, that sentiment amounts to far more than just a hill of beans.

T he lesson we can learn from the way Howard Schultz treats his "partners" at Starbucks is important: Respecting the welfare of others, being trustworthy, and promoting harmony are key ingredients to a successful workplace. As you know, however, not all executives follow this lead. Although there are times when people do help each other, they sometimes work at cross-purposes or even go out of their way to purposely harm one another. It is these processes of working with others and against them that are the focus of this chapter on **interpersonal behavior** at work. Specifically, we will summarize a wide array of interpersonal behaviors that occur in the workplace and describe how they influence the way people work and how they feel about their jobs and organizations.

Figure 11.1 identifies the major forms of interpersonal behavior in the workplace reviewed in this chapter. This diagram organizes interpersonal behaviors along a continuum ranging from those that involve working with others, shown on the left, to those that involve working against others, shown on the right. This forms a useful roadmap of how we will proceed in this chapter. Beginning on the left, we first will examine *prosocial behavior*—the tendency for people to help others on the job, sometimes even when there doesn't appear to be anything in it for them. Following this, we will discuss situations in which people help each other and receive help from them—that is, the tendency to *cooperate.* In the world of business, as you know, people and entire companies don't always work with each other, they also *compete* against each other—that is, as one tries to win, it forces the other to lose. Under such circumstances, it is not unusual for *conflict* to emerge, breeding ill-will. And, when taken to the extreme, this results in *deviant* behavior—extreme acts such as stealing from the company or even harming another person. Before examining these various forms of behavior, we will begin by

interpersonal behavior
A variety of behaviors involving the ways in which people work with and against one another.

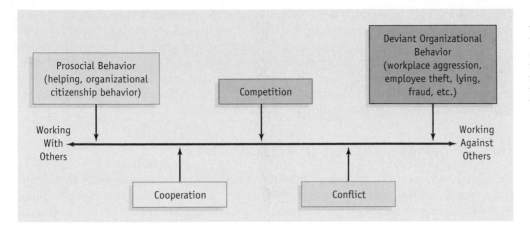

FIGURE 11.1

Varieties of Interpersonal Behavior
The five types of interpersonal behavior observed in organizations and presented in this chapter can be summarized as falling along a continuum ranging from those involving working with other people to those involving working against them.

describing some of the basic dynamics that guide all forms of interpersonal behavior in the workplace.

THE DYNAMICS OF INTERPERSONAL RELATIONSHIPS

To understand interpersonal behavior in organizations we must have an understanding of the basic building blocks of social relationships in general. What factors influence the kinds of relationships people develop between them? Although the answer to this question is more complicated than we can address here, we can identify two important factors—*psychological contracts* and *trust*.

Psychological Contracts: Our Expectations of Others

Whenever people have relationships with others, they are bound to have certain expectations about what things will be like in that relationship. Leave a phone message for a friend, for example, and you expect him or her to return your call. Put in a fair day's work for your boss, and you expect to get paid in return. These examples illustrate what is known as the **psychological contract**—a person's beliefs about what is expected of another in a relationship.[1]

Although these are not legal contracts, they guide what we expect of others in much the same way. However, unlike legal contracts, in which the terms are made explicit, psychological contracts are perceptual in nature. Not surprisingly, there may be differences of opinion regarding psychological contracts: What one person expects may not be exactly what the other expects. As you know from experience, such perceptual disagreements often make interpersonal relationships challenging.

As you might imagine, the nature of the psychological contracts we have with others depends on the kind of relationships we have with them.[2] This is particularly clear in the workplace. Suppose, for example, that you are a temporary employee working in the order-fulfillment department of a large retail e-business during the busy holiday period. You know that your relationship with your employer will have a definite ending and that it is based on a clearly defined set of economic terms. You go to work each day as scheduled, you do your job as directed, you get your paycheck, and at the end of the season, it's over. In this case, you would be said to have a **transactional contract** with your employer.[3] This relationship is characterized by an exclusively economic focus, a brief time span, an unchanging nature, and a narrow and well-defined scope.

By contrast, other relationships between employers and employees are much closer psychologically and far more complex in nature. In fact, they operate more like marriages—long term in scope, ever changing, and not clearly defined. For example, if you have worked 20 years for the same boss in the same company, chances are good that your relationship is based not only on money but on friendship as well. You expect that

psychological contract
A person's beliefs about what is expected of another in a relationship.

transactional contract
A type of psychological contract in which the parties have a brief and narrowly defined relationship that is primarily economic in focus.

relational contract
A type of psychological contract in which the parties have a long-term and widely defined relationship with a vast focus.

trust
A person's degree of confidence in the words and actions of another.

calculus-based trust
A form of trust based on deterrence, whenever people believe that another will behave as promised out of fear of getting punished for doing otherwise.

relationship to last well into the future, and you recognize that it may change over the years. In addition, your relationship with your boss has likely become quite complex and involves aspects of your lives that go beyond those of worker and supervisor. Such relationships are based on **relational contracts.** Compared to the transactional contracts that short-term employees are likely to have with their supervisors, long-term employees are likely to have relational contracts. For a summary of the defining characteristics of transactional and relational contracts, see Figure 11.2.

The Importance of Trust in Relationships

One thing that makes relationships based on transactional contracts so different from those based on relational contracts is the degree to which the parties trust each other. By **trust,** we are referring to a person's degree of confidence in the words and actions of another.[4] Suppose, for example, that your supervisor, the local sales manager, will be talking to his own boss, the district sales manager, about getting you transferred to a desirable new territory. You are counting on your boss to come through for you because he says he will. To the extent you believe that he will make a strong case on your behalf, you trust him. However, if you believe that his recommendation will not be too enthusiastic, or that he will not recommend you at all, you will trust him less.

Two major types of trust. These examples illustrate two different types of trust, each of which is linked to different kinds of relationships we have with others (see Figure 11.3). The first is known as **calculus-based trust,** a kind of trust based on deterrence.[5] Calculus-based trust exists whenever people believe that another person will behave as promised out of fear of getting punished for doing otherwise. We trust our employers to withhold the proper amount of taxes from our paychecks, for example, insofar as they risk fines and penalties from government agencies for failing to do so. People develop calculus-based trust slowly and incrementally: Each time they behave as promised, they build up the level of trust others have for them. This kind of trust is characteristic of professional relationships—the very kind in which people develop transactional contracts.

FIGURE 11.2

Two Kinds of Psychological Contracts: A Comparison
Psychological contracts may be considered either transactional or relational. The characteristics of each type are summarized here.
(*Source:* Based on suggestions by Rousseau, 2001; see Note 2.)

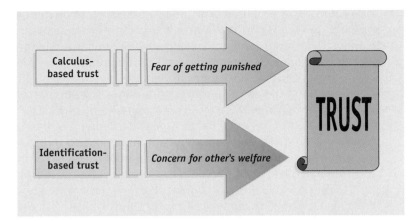

FIGURE 11.3
Trust: Two Basic Types
Trust can take either of two different forms. *Calculus-based trust* is based on the belief that someone will behave as promised out of fear of getting punished for doing otherwise. *Identification-based trust* is based on the belief that someone will act in a manner consistent with one's wants and desires.

A second kind of trust, known as **identification-based trust,** is based on accepting and understanding the other person's wants and desires. Identification-based trust occurs when people know and understand each other so well that they are willing to allow that individual to act on his or her behalf. For example, you might allow your spouse or a very good friend to select furniture for your house based on the belief that his or her judgment will be much like yours and that this person would not make any decisions of which you would disapprove. In short, you trust this person. The example we described earlier in which you allow your boss to discuss your transfer with a higher-ranking official also illustrates identification-based trust. As you might imagine, identification-based trust is likely to be found in very close relationships, be they personal or professional in nature—those based on relational contracts.

identification-based trust
A form of trust based on accepting the wants and desires of another person.

How does trust develop? Even when people first meet, chances are good that they already have some level of trust or distrust in each other. What is responsible for this? In other words, what factors are responsible for the development of trust? Scientists have identified two important factors.

First, as you may already know from experience, some people tend to be more trusting than others. Indeed, the predisposition to be trusting of others is a personality variable (see Chapter 3). You probably know some people at the extremes in this regard: Whereas some individuals are cynical and hardly ever trust anyone, there are still others who are overly trusting of people even when not warranted, to the point of being gullible.

Second, as you know, people develop reputations for being trustworthy or not trustworthy. That is, you may have learned by dealing with others directly that they will let you down and are not to be trusted. Importantly, based on their reputations, we also may judge someone to be trustworthy or untrustworthy even if we have never met that person. Because violating one's trust is such an affront, we are all very sensitive to this, making such information likely to be passed along to others—either by way of offering praise about never having been let down, or by way of warning about the likelihood of getting let down (e.g., "Don't trust him!").

How to promote trust in working relationships. Obviously, it is important to be thought of as being a trustworthy individual. The success of your relationships with others depends on it. That said, the question arises as to what we can do to get others to trust us. Clearly, the key is to not let others down. But this is easier said than done. Fortunately, there are specific things we all can do to build others' trust in us. These are as follows:

1. *Always meet deadlines.* If you promise to get something done on time, it is essential to meet that deadline. Although one or two incidents of lateness may be overlooked, people who are chronically late in meeting deadlines rapidly gain a reputation for being untrustworthy. When others believe that you will not meet important deadlines, they are likely to overlook you when it comes to getting any important, career-building assignments.

2. *Follow through as promised.* It is not only important to do things on time but also to perform those tasks in the manner in which others expect them to be done. Suppose, for example, that the manager of your department often gives you incomplete sales figures to use in preparing important reports for which you are responsible. Your manager's inconsistency in behaving as promised will lead you to be distrusting of him. And as this individual develops a reputation within the company for not being trustworthy, he may come across some serious barriers to promotion.

3. *Spend time sharing personal values and goals.* Remember that identification-based trust requires a keen understanding and appreciation of others. And getting this understanding requires spending time together discussing common interests, common objectives, and the like. If you think about it, this is the key to Howard Schultz's success (as described in our Preview Case on pages 403–404). By taking time to get to know his employees and by sharing ideas with each other, they get to know what he is like. And this is key to developing trust.

PROSOCIAL BEHAVIOR: HELPING OTHERS

prosocial behavior
Acts that benefit others.

At Starbucks, Howard Schultz goes out of his way to help his employees. Not only is he polite and attentive, as you might imagine, but he also does things to help his "partners" get ahead in life. Indeed, helping others is essential to making work not only a pleasant experience but also a productive one for both individuals and their organizations. Scientists refer to such acts that benefit others as **prosocial behavior.** We will now discuss two important forms of prosocial behavior.

Organizational Citizenship Behavior: Above and Beyond Job Requirements

Imagine the following scene. It's coming up on 5:00 P.M. and you're wrapping up your work for the day. You're anxiously looking forward to getting home and relaxing. While this is going on, the scene is quite different at the next cubicle. One of your colleagues has been working feverishly to complete an important report but appears to have hit a snag. She now has little hope of getting the report on the boss's desk before he leaves for the day—that is, without your help. Pitching in to help your colleague is something you don't have to do. After all, there's nothing in your formal job description that makes it necessary for you to do so. What's more, you're quite weary after your own long day's work. However, when you see the bind your colleague is in, you put aside your own feelings and offer to stay and help her out.

organizational citizenship behavior (OCB)

An informal form of behavior in which people go beyond what is formally expected of them to contribute to the well-being of their organization and those in it.

In this case, although you're probably not going to win any medals for your generosity, you are being helpful, and you have gone "above and beyond the call of duty." Actions such as these, which exceed the formal requirements of one's job, are known as **organizational citizenship behavior** (or **OCB,** for short).[6] It is easy to imagine how such behaviors, although informal and sometimes minor in nature, play a very important role when it comes to the smooth functioning of organizations. The example we just gave of volunteering to help one of your coworkers is just one of five different forms that OCB can take (see Figure 11.4).[7] For a summary of all five, including examples of each, see Table 11.1.

Why does OCB occur? As you know, people sometimes are selfish and do not engage in OCB. What, then, lies behind the tendency to be a good organizational citizen? Although there are several factors involved, evidence strongly suggests that people's beliefs that they are being treated fairly by their organization (especially their immediate supervisors) is a critical factor. The more people believe they are treated fairly by the organization, the more they trust its management, and the more willing they are to go the extra mile to help out when needed. By contrast, those who feel that their organizations are taking advantage of them are untrusting and not at all likely to engage in OCB.

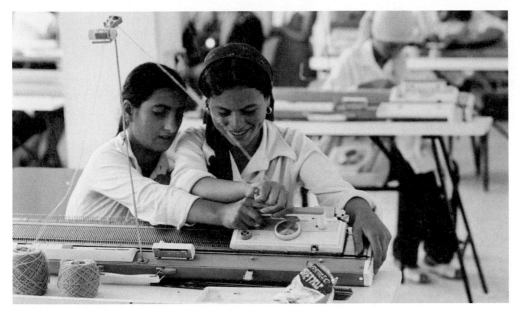

Does OCB really matter? As you might imagine, the effects of OCB are difficult to assess because OCB is generally not included as part of any standard performance measures that a company gathers about its employees. However, OCB does have important effects on organizational functioning. Specifically, people's willingness to engage in various types of OCB corresponds to such work-related measures as job satisfaction and organizational commitment, which, as described in Chapter 5, are related to organizational functioning in a number of complex ways.[8] In addition, being a good organizational citizen can have important effects on recruiting efforts. After all, the more positive statements current employees make about the companies where they are employed, the

TABLE 11.1 ORGANIZATIONAL CITIZENSHIP BEHAVIOR: SPECIFIC FORMS AND EXAMPLES

Organizational citizenship behavior (OCB) can take many different forms, most of which fall into the five major categories shown here.

FORM OF OCB	EXAMPLES
Altruism	■ Helping a coworker with a project
	■ Switching vacation dates with another person
	■ Volunteering
Conscientiousness	■ Never missing a day of work
	■ Coming to work early if needed
	■ Not spending time on personal calls
Civic virtue	■ Attending voluntary meetings and functions
	■ Reading memos; keeping up with new information
Sportsmanship	■ Making do without complaint ("Grin and bear it!")
	■ Not finding fault with the organization
Courtesy	■ "Turning the other cheek" to avoid problems
	■ Not "blowing up" when provoked

more effectively those companies will be able to recruit the best new employees.[9] In conclusion, although the effects of OCB may be indirect and difficult to measure, they can be very profound.

Tips for promoting OCB. Given the importance of OCB, it makes sense to highlight some specific ways of bringing it about. Several potentially useful suggestions may be made.

1. *Go out of your way to help others.* The more you help your colleagues, the more likely they will be to help you. Soon, before you know it, with everyone helping everyone else, prosocial behavior will become the norm—that is, a widely accepted practice in the company.

2. *Be an example of conscientiousness.* Employees are inclined to model the citizenship behavior of their supervisors. If, as a manager, you set a good example by coming to work on time and not making personal phone calls, your subordinates may be expected to follow your lead. Although it might not be this easy, at least, you have some credibility when you do insist that your subordinates refrain from these forms of poor citizenship.

3. *Make voluntary functions fun.* It only makes sense that employees will not be motivated to attend voluntary meetings or corporate functions of one kind or another (e.g., picnics, award banquets) unless these are enjoyable. People are more likely to show the good citizenship associated with attending corporate functions when the company makes it worthwhile for them to do so. After all, the more desirable it is for someone to be prosocial, the more likely that individual will be a good organizational citizen.

4. *Demonstrate courtesy and good sportsmanship.* When something goes wrong, don't complain, but "grin and bear it." Someone who "blows up" at the slightest provocation is not only a poor organizational citizen but also is one who may discourage good citizenship among others.

Although these suggestions all seem like common sense, they certainly are not common practice. Even if you have only limited work experience, you probably can tell a few tales about one or more individuals who behaved in just the opposite manner—people who always complain and never pitch in to make things better. Keeping in mind just how unpleasant these people made life in your organization may be just the incentive you need to follow these guidelines. Doing so will keep you from becoming a bad organizational citizen yourself—and from encouraging others to follow suit.

Whistle-Blowing: Helping Through Dissent

Sometimes employees face situations in which they recognize that their organization is behaving in an improper fashion. To right the wrong, they reveal the improper or illegal practice to someone who may be able to correct it—an action known as **whistle-blowing.**[10] Formally, whistle-blowing is the disclosure by employees of illegal, immoral, or illegitimate practices by employers to people or organizations able to take action.

Is whistle-blowing a prosocial action? From the point of view of society, it usually is.[11] In many instances, the actions of whistle-blowers can protect the health, safety, or security of the general public. Consider, for example, the well-known case of Erin Brokovich, depicted in the 2000 film that bears her name (see Figure 11.5). While working as a clerk at a small law firm, Brokovich noticed some irregularities in the use of chemicals by the large California utility company, Pacific Gas & Electric (PG&E). This led her to dig deeper, eventually learning that the company admitted to using a chemical, which it claimed to be safe, although insiders knew that it really was deadly. Over many years, she got the facts and worked within her firm to build a case on behalf of over 600 families who lost loved ones due to PG&E's actions. This resulted in the largest settlement ever paid in a direct-action lawsuit in U.S. history—$333 million.

Although most whistle-blowing cases are far less inspirational and smaller in magnitude, they tend to have the same type of "David versus Goliath" theme to them. Also,

whistle-blowing
The disclosure by employees of illegal, immoral, or illegitimate practices by employers to people or organizations able to take action.

FIGURE 11.5
The "Real" Erin Brokovich: Whistle-Blower
Made famous by an Academy Award–winning film that told her tale (albeit with a bit of Hollywood elaboration), Erin Brokovich is one of several people who have gone public with claims that companies have committed some wrongdoing. This particular whistle-blower alleged that the large utility company, PG&E, was exposing some California residents to a deadly chemical.

as in the Brokovich case, claims based on environmental abuse have been common. During the past two decades, the health care industry has become so plagued with fraud (e.g., billing government agencies for services not performed or inflating bills) that it has become a breeding ground for whistle-blowers. However, as you can see from the summary of some actual cases of whistle-blowing shown in Table 11.2, whistle-blowers are active in many different areas.[12]

TABLE 11.2   WHISTLE-BLOWING: SOME EXAMPLES

As the following examples illustrate, employees blow the whistle on many different types of organizations accused of committing a wide range of questionable activities.

WHISTLE-BLOWER	INCIDENT
Coleen Rowley	This special agent wrote a letter to the FBI director (with copies to two key members of Congress) about the bureau's failure to take action that could have prevented the terrorist attacks of September 11, 2001.
Sherron Watkins	In 2001, she notified the press about her letter to her boss at Enron identifying the company's fictitious accounting practices.
Paul van Buitenen	Went public in 1999 with claims of fraud and corruption within the European Commission.
An unnamed U.S. customs inspector	Alerted Congress of security problems at the Miami airport in 1995 after management took no action.
Tonya Atchinson	This former internal auditor at Columbia-HCA Healthcare Corp. charged the company with illegal Medicare billing.
Daniel Shannon	An in-house attorney for Intelligent Electronics protested the company's alleged misuse of marketing funds from computer manufacturers.
Robert Young	This agent for Prudential Insurance Co. in New Jersey accused company agents of encouraging customers to needlessly sell some policies and buy more expensive ones, boosting their commissions.
Bill Bush	This manager at the National Aeronautics and Space Administration (NASA) went public with the administration's policy of discouraging the promotion of employees older than 54 years of age.

(*Sources:* See Note 12.)

As you might imagine, blowing the whistle on one's employer is likely to be a very costly act for employees, as they often find themselves facing a long, uphill battle attempting to prove the wrongdoing. They also frequently face ostracism and losing their jobs in response to their disloyalty. For example, five agents from State Farm Insurance were fired recently after they accused the company of various consumer abuses.[13] Although various laws prevent employers from firing people directly because they blew the whistle, organizations frequently find alternative official grounds for dismissing "troublemakers."[14] It is not surprising, therefore, that six senior employees of the company that runs the 900-mile Trans-Alaskan pipeline chose to remain anonymous when voicing their complaints about safety violations to BP Amoco.[15] It is interesting to note that, although whistle-blowing often involves considerable personal cost, the importance of the action motivates some people to go through with it.

COOPERATION: PROVIDING MUTUAL ASSISTANCE

cooperation

A pattern of behavior in which assistance is mutual and two or more individuals, groups, or organizations work together toward shared goals for their mutual benefit.

Thus far, our discussion has focused on one person's giving help to another. However, it is probably even more common in organizations to find situations in which assistance is mutual, with two or more individuals, teams, or organizations working together toward some common goal. Such efforts are known as acts of *cooperation*. Formally, **cooperation** is a pattern of behavior in which assistance is mutual and two or more individuals, groups, or organizations work together toward shared goals for their mutual benefit. Cooperation is a common form of coordination in work settings largely because, by cooperating, the individuals or groups involved can accomplish more than by working alone.

Pure Competition Occurs Rarely

Given the obvious benefits of cooperation, an interesting question arises: If cooperation is so useful, then why does it sometimes fail to occur? In other words, why do people

FIGURE 11.6

Cooperation vs. Competition: A Comparison

When *cooperating* with one another, people contribute to attaining the same goal that they share. However, when *competing* against one another, people attempt to attain the same goal, which only one can have.

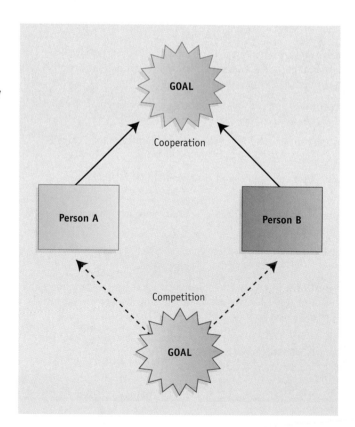

with similar goals sometimes keep from joining forces? Although there may be many different possibilities, the answer in many situations is simply that cooperation cannot occur because the goals sought by the individuals or groups involved are incompatible—that is, they cannot be shared. For example, two people going after the same job cannot both get it. Likewise, when two companies court the same merger candidate, only one can be victorious. This describes a type of behavior known as **competition**—the pattern of behavior in which each person, group, or organization seeks to maximize its own gains, often at the expense of others. For a comparison between cooperation and competition, see Figure 11.6.

Think about what happens when two teams play baseball against one another. Naturally, we find cooperation occurring within each team as players work together to defeat the other team (e.g., by coordinating their efforts on a double-play or by hitting a sacrifice fly) and competition between the teams as each strives to be the winner (e.g., scoring more runs than the other team). However, things are not that simple. After all, even within professional sports teams, players sometimes compete against one another, such as for various forms of recognition (batting records, most-valuable-player status, and, of course, salary). To make professional football more even, prohibiting rich teams from always buying the best players, teams face "salary caps," which restrict the total amount of its payroll. Under such conditions, the more one team member gets paid, the less others can be paid. This also adds to competition within a team. At the same time, most competitive situations involve some degree of cooperation. After all, teams wouldn't be able to play and races wouldn't be able to be won if the parties didn't cooperate with one another on playing by the rules. What we are saying here is that most situations are such that neither cooperation nor competition is involved exclusively. Rather, most social situations are considered **mixed-motive situations** because they combine both cooperative and competitive interests in varying degrees.

BEING AN EFFECTIVE WHISTLE-BLOWER

Although you probably think it will never happen to you, it's possible that one day you will find yourself working for a company that is doing something you consider to be immoral, unethical, or illegal. Should that day come, it's likely that you will be torn between ignoring the matter so as to avoid jeopardizing your career and "doing the right thing" by blowing the whistle. Fortunately, you don't have to choose between these options. There are several things you can do to blow the whistle while also safeguarding your career.

1. *Document your claims.* Before you claim that some wrongdoing has occurred, you better be able to back it up with very clear evidence. Making unsubstantiated claims will surely brand you a "troublemaker," putting your career at risk.

2. *Keep things inside the company before going public.* Rather than risking embarrassment by going public with something that's not really wrong, it's best to begin asking questions about possible wrongdoings within the company. Start with your immediate supervisor and work your way up the corporate hierarchy as needed until someone will listen and take action. Only then, if nothing happens, should you consider announcing your concerns to parties outside the company.

3. *Talk to a lawyer.* Many U.S. states and several countries have laws on the books that protect whistle-blowers. However, because these laws vary greatly, it's best to consult an attorney to determine how you may or may not be protected by law after you have blown the whistle.

4. *Plan for the worst.* Regardless of what the law says and how your moral compass guides you, it's likely that you will face a long and difficult battle when blowing the whistle on a powerful company. The wrongdoers are unlikely to go down without a fight, and they will try to take you with them when they fall. Therefore, you should prepare yourself financially and emotionally for the future.

If these suggestions get you to rethink your plans for whistle-blowing, they have served their purpose. Being a whistle-blower can be very trying, so you surely will want to consider all the consequences before picking up that whistle and moving it anywhere near your lips.

Determinants of Cooperation

Many factors determine whether individuals choose to cooperate with others in situations involving mixed motives. However, three appear to be most important—the tendency toward *reciprocity, personal orientation,* and *organizational reward systems.*

The reciprocity principle. We all know that "the golden rule" admonishes us to do unto others as we would have them do unto us. However, this doesn't describe exactly the way people behave. Instead of treating others as they would like to be treated, most people tend to treat others the way they have been treated in the past by them. In short, we are more inclined to follow a different principle: "an eye for an eye and a tooth for a tooth." Social scientists refer to this as the principle of **reciprocity**—the tendency to treat others as others have treated us.

competition
A pattern of behavior in which each person, group, or organization seeks to maximize its own gains, often at the expense of others.

mixed-motive situations
Contexts in which people are interested in both competition and cooperation to varying degrees.

To a great extent, the principle of reciprocity describes the way people behave when cooperating with others.[16] The key task in establishing cooperation in organizations is straightforward: getting it started. Once individuals or teams have begun to cooperate, the process may be largely self-sustaining. That is, one unit's cooperation encourages cooperation among the others. To encourage cooperation, therefore, managers should attempt to get the process underway.

Personal orientation. As you know from experience, some people tend to be more cooperative, by nature, than others. In contrast, other people tend to be far more competitive—interested in doing better than others in one way or another. Not surprisingly, scientists have found that people can be reliably classified into four different categories in terms of their natural predispositions toward working with or against others.[17] These are as follows:

competitors
People whose primary motive is doing better than others, besting them in open competition.

- **Competitors**—People whose primary motive is doing better than others, besting them in open competition.
- **Individualists**—People who care almost exclusively about maximizing their own gain and don't care whether others do better or worse than themselves.
- **Cooperators**—People who are concerned with maximizing joint outcomes, getting as much as possible for their team.
- **Equalizers**—People who are interested primarily in minimizing the differences between themselves and others.

individualists
People who care almost exclusively about maximizing their own gain and don't care whether others do better or worse than themselves.

cooperators
People who are concerned with maximizing joint outcomes and getting as much as possible for their team.

equalizers
People who are primarily interested in minimizing the differences between themselves and others.

Although there are individual differences, men as a whole tend to favor a competitive orientation, attempting to exploit others around them. By contrast, women tend to favor a cooperative orientation, preferring to work with other people rather than against them, and they also tend to develop friendly ties with others.[18] Still, it would be a mistake for managers to assume that men and women automatically fall into certain categories. Instead, it is widely recommended that managers take the time to get to know their individual workers' personal orientations and then match these to the kinds of tasks to which they may be best suited. For example, competitors may be effective in negotiation situations whereas cooperators may be most effective in teamwork situations. (To get a sense of which category best describes you, complete the Individual Exercise on page 432.)

Organizational reward systems. It is not only differences between people that lead them to behave cooperatively but differences in the nature of organizational reward systems as well. Despite good intentions, companies all too often create reward systems that lead their employees to compete against each other. This would be the case, for example, in a company in which various divisions sell products that compete with each other. Sales representatives who receive commissions for selling their division's products have little incentive to help the company by attempting to sell another division's products. In other words, the company's reward system discourages cooperative behavior.

team-based rewards
Organizational reward systems in which at least a portion of an individual's compensation is based on the performance of his or her work team.

With an eye toward eliminating such problems and fostering cooperation, many of today's companies are adopting **team-based rewards**.[19] These are organizational reward systems in which at least a portion of an individual's compensation is based on the performance of his or her work team (see Chapter 8). The rationale behind these incentive systems is straightforward (and follows from the principle of reinforcement described in Chapter 2): People who are rewarded for contributing to their group's performance will focus their energies on group performance. In other words, they will cooperate with each other. Although there are many difficult challenges associated with setting up team-based reward programs that are manageable (e.g., based on measurable rewards that really matter) and that people find acceptable (e.g., ones that are administered fairly), companies that have met these challenges have reaped benefits in terms of increased job satisfaction and productivity.

Cooperation Between Organizations

In business, competition is the natural order of things. Take the motorcycle business, for example. In recent years, several start-up companies, such as Victory and Excelsior-

Henderson, have made high-quality motorcycles that compete very favorably with "cruisers" from the legendary Harley-Davidson.[20] They are trying to attract customers by offering more bike for the money, while Harley fans continue to be attracted to something less tangible—that company's reputation. Although only time will tell the outcome of this competition, it is clear that no matter what happens, there will always be companies competing against other companies. Yet, this does not mean that companies do not find it beneficial to cooperate with one another by coordinating their efforts. This takes several forms.

Partnering with suppliers. Years ago, companies used to think of suppliers (other companies from whom they purchase goods and services) as more or less disposable. They'd select the best one and ignore the others. Today, however, companies are far more likely to work closely with their suppliers to ensure that they can provide the high-quality products that are desired. That is, they are inclined to coordinate their efforts with suppliers. Kontron, for example, is a German company that provides data to Microsoft about the effectiveness of its new operating systems. Rather than being forced to guess what Microsoft wants, Kontron officials work in close harmony with Microsoft engineers to provide the kind of information that is most useful to them. Many auto companies also have developed close, cooperative relationships with their suppliers, ensuring a constant flow of high-quality components required to stay competitive (see Figure 11.7).

Promoting business growth. In the business world, sometimes 1 + 1 equals not 2, but 3—or even more. In other words, when companies merge, they combine so many assets that the resulting new company stands to be even bigger and better than the individual companies from which it was composed. A company with strength in one particular market may merge with another company with a presence in another market to gain strength. For example, in 2002, Hewlett-Packard, a leader in computer printers, joined forces with Compaq, a leader in personal and business microcomputers, to form a new company that stood to enjoy more dominance in the rapidly changing computer market than either could achieve alone. In other words, by cooperating with each other, the newly formed company was so much stronger that it stood a better chance of surviving the rapid changes that make survival in the computer business so challenging.

Responding to external threats. In wartime, nations seek allies to be able to gain strength in battle. Likewise, companies facing threatening conditions often find it use-

FIGURE 11.7
Cooperative Partnering in Action
Cooperation between companies must be at high levels when one company provides critical supplies to another involved in the assembly process. This woman works at New Sabina Industries, a company that makes instrument clusters for Honda automobiles. By carefully coordinating its assembly processes with Honda's needs, both companies benefit.

ful to join forces by cooperating with one another against external forces. This was the case some 30 years ago when the three large American auto manufacturers (Chrysler, Ford, and General Motors) faced such strong competition from Japanese automakers that their very survival was in question. Although these companies were traditionally highly competitive toward each other, in the face of the strong foreign threat, they knew they had to join forces in several important ways. They did this by lobbying the government to impose quotas on imports that would allow them the opportunity to compete. They also did this by joining forces on research efforts that showed them how to produce safer and more comfortable cars at lower cost. Any one of the big three companies might have done this, but the success of such measures was due to the fact that all three coordinated their efforts.

CONFLICT: THE INEVITABLE RESULT OF INCOMPATIBLE INTERESTS

conflict
A process in which one party perceives that another party has taken or will take actions that are incompatible with one's own interests.

If we conceive of prosocial behavior and cooperation as being at one end of a continuum (such as in Figure 11.1), then it makes sense to conceive of *conflict* as approaching the other end. In the context of organizations, **conflict** may be defined as a process in which one party perceives that another party has taken or will take actions that are incompatible with one's own interests.

As you might imagine, conflict occurs quite commonly in organizations. In fact, about 20 percent of managers' time is spent dealing with conflict and its effects.[21] Considering this, it makes sense to examine the causes and consequences of conflict and ways to effectively manage conflict that occurs in the workplace.

Causes of Conflict

The conflicts we face in organizations may be viewed as stemming from a variety of causes, including both our interactions with other people and the organization itself. Some of the most important sources of organizational conflict are as follows.

Perceptual distortion. As we described in Chapter 2, people tend to be biased in the way they perceive the world. In general, we tend to see situations in ways that favor ourselves. Of course, this type of distortion can lead us to be very "myopic" when it comes to recognizing another's position on a matter of disagreement. And this can interfere greatly with what it takes to resolve conflict. Specifically, several kinds of perceptual errors come into play that may serve as sources of conflict. We describe these in Table 11.3.

Grudges. All too often, conflict is caused when people who have lost face in dealing with someone attempt to "get even" with that person by planning some form of revenge. Employees involved in this kind of activity are not only going out of their way to harm one of their coworkers, but also, by holding a grudge, they are wasting energy that could be devoted to more productive organizational endeavors.

Distrust. The more strongly people suspect that some other individual or group is out to get them, the more likely they are to have a relationship with that person or group that is riddled with conflict. In general, companies that are considered great places in which to work are characterized by high levels of trust between people at all levels.

Competition over scarce resources. Because organizations never have unlimited resources (such as space, money, equipment, or personnel), it is inevitable that conflicts will arise over the distribution of those resources. This occurs in large part because of a self-serving tendency in people's perceptions (see Chapter 2), that is, the tendency for people to overestimate their own contributions to their organizations. Believing that we made greater contributions leads us to feel more deserving

TABLE 11.3 PERCEPTUAL ERRORS RESPONSIBLE FOR CONFLICT

People in conflict with others tend to misperceive the differences between themselves in ways that tend to make that conflict worse. Some of the most serious perceptual errors of this type are described here.

PERCEPTUAL ERROR	DESCRIPTION
Naïve realism	People tend to perceive their own views about things as being objective and as reflecting reality whereas others' views are believed to more biased. This leads people to magnify whatever differences between them they may encounter.
Incompatibility error	Conflicting parties tend to assume that their interests are entirely incompatible. In reality, there is likely to be agreement on some issues.
Fixed-sum error	Each side to a conflict tends to assume that the other party places the same importance on every issue as it does. However, it is quite possible that the issues that matter most to one side matter less to the other.
Transparency overestimation	Conflicting parties often assume that what they want is perfectly apparent to the other side, whereas in reality it may not be so clear.

of resources than others. Inevitably, conflict results when others do not see things this same way.

Destructive criticism. Communicating negative feedback in organizations is inevitable. All too often, however, this process arouses unnecessary conflict. The problem is that some people make the mistake of using **destructive criticism**—that is, negative feedback that angers the recipient instead of helping him or her do a better job. The most effective managers attempt to avoid conflict by using constructive criticism instead. For some important comparisons between these two forms of criticism, see Table 11.4.

destructive criticism
Negative feedback that angers the recipient instead of helping him or her do a better job

TABLE 11.4 CONSTRUCTIVE VERSUS DESTRUCTIVE CRITICISM: A COMPARISON

The factors listed here distinguish constructive criticism (negative feedback that may be accepted by the recipient to improve his or her performance) from destructive criticism (negative feedback likely to be rejected by the recipient and unlikely to improve his or her performance).

CONSTRUCTIVE CRITICISM	DESTRUCTIVE CRITICISM
Considerate—protects the recipient's self-esteem	Inconsiderate—harsh, sarcastic, biting
Does not contain threats	Contains threats
Timely—occurs as soon as possible after the substandard performance	Not timely—occurs after an inappropriate delay
Does not attribute poor performance to internal causes	Attributes poor performance to internal causes (e.g., lack of effort, motivation, ability)
Specific—focuses on aspects of performance that were inadequate	General—a sweeping condemnation of performance
Focuses on performance, not on the recipient	Focuses on the recipient—his or her personal characteristics
Motivated by desire to help the recipient improve	Motivated by anger, desire to assert dominance over the recipient, desire for revenge
Offers concrete suggestions for improvement	Offers no concrete suggestions for improvement

Consequences of Conflict: Both Negative and Positive

The word *conflict* doubtlessly brings to mind negative images—thoughts of anger and confrontation. Indeed, there is no denying the many negative effects of conflict. But, as you will see, conflict has a positive side as well. With this in mind, we now will identify the many consequences of conflict in organizations, both positive and negative.

Negative consequences of conflict. The major problem with conflict, as you know from experience, is that it yields strong negative emotions. However, these emotional reactions mark only the beginning of a chain of reactions that can have harmful effects in organizations.

The negative reactions, besides being quite stressful, are problematic in that they may divert people's attention from the task at hand. For example, people who are focused on getting even with a coworker and making him look bad in front of others are unlikely to be attending to the most important aspect of their jobs. In particular, communication between individuals or teams may be so adversely affected that any coordination of effort between them is compromised. Not surprisingly, such lowered coordination tends to lead to decrements in organizational functioning. In short, organizational conflict has costly effects on organizational performance.[22] For some helpful suggestions on how to avoid many of these problems, see Table 11.5.

Positive consequences of conflict. Have you ever worked on a team project and found that you disagreed with someone on a key matter? If so, how did you react? Chances are good that you fell short of sabotaging that person's work or acting aggressively. In fact, the conflict may have even brought the two of you to the table to have a productive discussion about the matter at hand. As a result of this discussion you may have even improved relations between the two of you and the quality of the decisions that resulted from your joint efforts. If you can relate to this scenario, then you already recognize an important fact about organizational conflict—that some of its effects are positive.

Specifically, organizational conflict can be the source of several benefits. Among these are the following:

- Conflict may improve the quality of organizational decisions (as in the foregoing example).
- Conflict may bring out into the open problems that have been previously ignored.

TABLE 11.5   HOW TO MANAGE CONFLICT EFFECTIVELY

Although conflict is inevitable, there are concrete steps that managers can take to avoid the negative consequences that result from conflict between people in the workplace.

- Agree on a process for making decisions *before* a conflict arises. This way, when a conflict needs to be addressed, everyone knows how it is going to be handled.
- Make sure everyone knows his or her specific areas of responsibility, authority, and accountability. Clarifying these things avoids potential conflicts when people either avoid their responsibilities or overstep their authority.
- Recognize conflicts stemming from faulty organizational systems, such as a pay system that rewards one department at the expense of another. In such cases, work to change the system rather than training employees.
- Recognize the emotional reactions to conflict. Conflicts will not go away until people's hurt feelings are addressed.
- Consider how to avoid problems rather than assigning blame for them. Questions such as "Why did you do that?" only make things worse. It is better to ask, "How can we make things better?"
- Conflicts will not go away by making believe they don't exist; doing so only will make them worse. Avoid the temptation to not speak to the other party and discuss your misunderstanding thoroughly.

(*Source:* Based on suggestions by Bragg, 1999; see Note 22.)

- Conflict may motivate people to appreciate each others' positions more fully.
- Conflict may encourage people to consider new ideas, thereby facilitating change.

In view of these positive effects of conflict, the key is to make sure that more of these benefits occur, as opposed to costs. It is with this goal in mind that managers work so diligently to effectively manage organizational conflict. We will now examine some of the ways they go about doing this.

MANAGING ORGANIZATIONAL CONFLICT

Given that conflict has both benefits and costs, the key task facing organizations, then, is to manage that conflict so as to minimize those costs and maximize those benefits. Typically, this involves finding a solution that is acceptable to all the parties involved. This process is known as *bargaining* (or *negotiation*). Formally, we may define **bargaining** (or **negotiation**) as the process by which two or more parties in dispute with one another exchange offers, counteroffers, and concessions in an attempt to find a mutually acceptable agreement.

Negotiating Win-Win Solutions

As you might imagine, bargaining does not work when the parties rigidly adhere to their positions without budging—that is, when they "stick to their guns." For bargaining to be effective, the parties involved must be willing to adjust their stances on the issues at hand. And, for the people involved to be willing to make such adjustments, they must believe that they have found an acceptable outcome—one that allows them to claim victory in the negotiation process. For bargaining to be most effective in reducing conflict, this must be the case for all sides. That is, outcomes must be found for all sides that allow them to believe that they have "won" the negotiation process—results known as **win-win solutions.** In win-win solutions, both parties get what they want, precisely as the name implies. Of course, getting each side to feel successful can take some effort. Fortunately, previous research and practice in organizations lead to several useful suggestions for finding win-win solutions. These are as follows:

1. *Avoid making unreasonable offers.* Imagine that a friend of yours is selling a used car with an asking price of $10,000—the car's established "book value." If you were to attempt to "lowball" the seller by offering only $1,000, your bad-faith offer might end the negotiations right there. A serious buyer would offer a more reasonable price, say $9,000—one that would allow both the buyer and the seller to come out ahead in the deal. In short, extreme offers tend to anger one's opponents, sometimes ending the negotiation process on a sour note, allowing none of the parties to get what they want.
2. *Seek the common ground.* All too often, people in conflict with others assume that their interests and those of the other party are completely incompatible. When this occurs, they tend to overlook the fact that they actually might have several areas of interest in common (see Figure 11.8). When parties focus on the areas of agreement between them, it helps bring them together on the areas of disagreement. So, for example, in negotiating the deal for purchasing the used car, you might establish the fact that you agree to the selling price of $9,000. This verifies that the interests of the buyer and the seller are not completely incompatible, thereby encouraging them to find a solution to the area in which they disagree, such as a payment schedule. By contrast, if either party believed that they were completely far apart on all aspects of the deal, they would be less likely to negotiate a win-win solution.
3. *Uncover the "real" issues.* Frequently, people focus on the conflicts between them in only a single area although they may have multiple conflicts between them—some of which are hidden. Suppose, for example, that your friend is being extremely stubborn when it comes to negotiating the price of the used car. He's sticking firmly to

bargaining
The process by which two or more parties in dispute with one another exchange offers, counteroffers, and concessions in an attempt to find a mutually acceptable agreement.

negotiation
See *bargaining*.

win-win solutions
Resolutions to conflicts in which both parties get what they want.

"*Look, everyone here loves vanilla, right? So let's start there.*"

his asking price, refusing to budge despite your reasonable offer, possibly adding to the conflict between you. However, it may be the case that there are other issues involved. For example, he may be trying to "get even" with you for harming him several years ago. In other words, what may appear to be a simple conflict between two people may actually have multiple sources. Finding long-lasting solutions requires identifying all the important issues—even the hidden ones—and bringing them to the table.

4. *Broaden the scope of issues considered.* Sometimes parties bargaining with each other have several issues on the table. When this occurs, it is often useful to consider the various issues together as a total package. (This is the idea behind what is known as integrative agreements, a conflict management technique we examine more closely in the Best Practices section on page 422.) Labor unions often do this in negotiating contracts with company management whenever they give in on one issue in exchange for compensation on another issue. So, for example, in return for not freezing wages, a company may agree to concede to the union's other interests, such as gaining representation on key corporate committees. In other words, compared to bargaining over single issues (e.g., the price of the used car), when the parties get to bargaining across a wide array of issues, it often is easier to find solutions that are acceptable to all sides.

Alternative Dispute Resolution

When a customer canceled a $60,000 wedding reception, Anthy Capetola, a caterer from Long Island, New York, was able to fill that time slot with an event bringing in only half as much.[23] Although Capetola was harmed by the customer's actions, as you might imagine, that customer was unwilling to cough up the lost revenue. Many business owners in Capetola's shoes would seek restitution by taking the customer to court, resulting in a delay of many months, or even years, and a huge bill for litigation—not to mention, lots of adverse publicity. Fortunately, in their contract, Capetola and the customer agreed to settle any future disagreements using what is known as **alternative dispute resolution (ADR).** This refers to a set of procedures in which disputing parties work together with a neutral party who helps them settle their disagreements out of court.[24] There are two popular forms of ADR—*mediation* and *arbitration* (see Figure 11.9).

Mediation. The process of **mediation** involves having a neutral party (the *mediator*) work together with both sides to reach a settlement. Typically, mediators meet together

alternative dispute resolution (ADR)

A set of procedures, such as *mediation* and *arbitration,* in which disputing parties work together with a neutral party who helps them settle their disagreements out of court.

mediation

The process in which a neutral party (known as a *mediator*) works together with two or more parties to reach a settlement to their conflict.

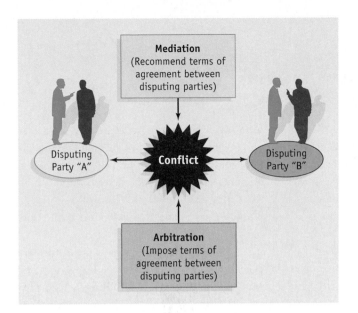

FIGURE 11.9
Mediation vs. Arbitration: A Summary
Mediation and *arbitration* are both popular techniques for resolving conflicts. Third parties known as *arbitrators* can impose terms of agreement between the disputants, whereas *mediators* can merely recommend such terms.

and separately with each side and try to find a common ground that will satisfy everyone's concerns. Mediators do not consider who's wrong and who's right, but set the stage for finding a resolution. They have no formal power and cannot impose any agreements. Instead, they seek to clarify the issues involved and to enhance communication between the parties. Mediators sometimes offer specific recommendations for compromise or integrative solutions, but in other cases they merely guide the parties toward developing such solutions themselves. Their role is primarily that of a facilitator—that is, someone who helps the two sides toward agreements that each will find acceptable. Because it requires voluntary compliance by the disputing parties, mediation often proves to be ineffective. Indeed, when the mediation process fails, it simply underscores the depth of the differences between the two sides.

Arbitration. As you might imagine, for mediation to work, the two sides must be willing to communicate with each other. When this doesn't happen, ADR may take the form of **arbitration.** This is a process in which a third party (the *arbitrator*) has the power to impose, or at least to recommend, the terms of an agreement between two parties.[25] Four types of arbitration are most common. These are as follows:

arbitration
A process in which a third party (known as an *arbitrator*) has the power to impose, or at least to recommend, the terms of an agreement between two or more conflicting parties.

- *Binding arbitration.* The two sides agree in advance to accept the terms set by the arbitrator, whatever they may be.
- *Voluntary arbitration.* The two sides retain the freedom to reject the recommended agreement.
- *Conventional arbitration.* The arbitrator can offer any package of terms he or she wishes.
- *Final-offer arbitration.* The arbitrator chooses between final offers made by the disputing parties themselves.

ADR today. ADR is very popular these days because it helps disputants reach agreements rapidly (often in a matter of a day or two, compared to months or years for court trials) and inexpensively (usually for just a few thousand dollars split between the parties, compared to astronomical sums for attorney fees). Moreover, it keeps people who otherwise might end up in court out of the public eye, which could be damaging to their reputations—even the party in whose favor the judgment goes. Because it is low key and nonconfrontational, mediation is particularly valuable in cases in which the parties have an ongoing relationship (business or personal) that they do not want to go sour.[26] After all, the mediation process brings the parties together, helping them see each other's side—something that is usually lost for sure in the heat of a courtroom battle.

BEST PRACTICES
INTEGRATIVE AGREEMENTS AS SOLUTIONS TO ORGANIZATIONAL CONFLICTS

Typically, we think of win-win solutions as compromises, such as when buyers and sellers "split the difference" between them in the course of negotiating the sale price of an item. However, this is only one way of finding an acceptable outcome for each party. In fact, sometimes splitting an outcome down the middle can result in an unsatisfactory result for both parties.

Suppose, for example, that two chefs each need five oranges to prepare their recipes but a total of only six oranges is available. Splitting the difference by giving each three oranges would satisfy neither chef. However, a solution may be reached by having the two chefs talk to one another about what they really need. Through this process we may discover that one chef needs the pulp of five oranges to make juice whereas the other chef needs the rind of five oranges to make marmalade. This makes it possible for both chefs to get what they need.

This example illustrates what is known as an **integrative agreement**. This is a type of solution to a conflict situation in which the parties consider joint benefits that go beyond a simple

---

integrative agreement
A type of solution to a conflict situation in which the parties consider joint benefits that go beyond a simple compromise.

Not surprisingly, the popularity of ADR these days has led to the development of several companies specializing in rendering mediation and arbitration services. The largest of these, the American Arbitration Association, boasts offices in half the U.S. states, with a caseload pushing 80,000 cases per year. It maintains a file of some 18,000 arbitrators and mediators (typically lawyers, businesspeople, and former judges), enabling them to find a neutral party who is experienced in just about any kind of dispute that people are likely to have. (Although our discussion of conflict resolution thus far has ignored the matter of culture, it is important to note that people from different countries favor different approaches to managing the conflicts that confront them. For a look at recent evidence bearing on this, see the OB in a Diverse World section on page 424.)

DEVIANT ORGANIZATIONAL BEHAVIOR

In recent years, TV news reports have aired an alarming number of accounts of disgruntled employees who have returned to their past places of employment to exact revenge on their former bosses by holding them at gunpoint—and, tragically, sometimes pulling the trigger. This scenario became so prominent among employees of the U.S. Postal Service in the late 1990s that the phrase "going postal" entered into our everyday language to describe this form of violence—clearly the most negative end of the continuum of positive to negative behaviors we have been describing in this chapter.

Although acts of physical violence have been the subject of news stories, they represent just one very extreme form of what OB scientists call **deviant organizational behavior.**[29] This refers to actions on the part of employees that intentionally violate the norms of organizations and/or the formal rules of society, resulting in negative consequences. *Workplace aggression,* which we have been describing, is only one extreme example of deviant organizational behavior. Another form that is less extreme and more common is known as **incivility,** which refers to a lack of regard for others, denying them the respect they are due. Yes, simply being rude to one of your coworkers is a type of deviant behavior. OB scientists are interested in reducing deviant organizational behavior because it can be a very disruptive and costly problem in terms of both the financial toll it takes on the company and the emotional toll it takes on employees.

---

deviant organizational behavior
Actions on the part of employees that intentionally violate the norms of organizations and/or the formal rules of society, resulting in negative consequences.

incivility
Demonstrating a lack of regard for others and denying them the respect they are due.

compromise. Some specific techniques for reaching integrative solutions are as follows:

- *Broadening the pie.* Additional resources are made available, enabling each party to get what it needs. For example, a budget officer might find additional funds to support worthy projects proposed by two teams of engineers.
- *Nonspecific compensation.* One side gets what it wants and the other side is compensated on an unrelated issue. For example, a regional supervisor may give a restaurant manager a raise but require him or her to work a split shift.
- *Logrolling.* Each party makes concessions on low-priority issues in exchange for concessions on more important issues. For example, union representatives may agree to smaller-

than-desired wage increases in exchange for greater job security for their members.

- *Cost cutting.* One party gets what it wants, but the costs to the other party are reduced or eliminated. For example, a company department may be required to allocate some of its employees to work on a special project, but during this time its performance goals will be lowered to compensate for the reduced resources.

Despite their differences, when you consider these techniques carefully, you will recognize that they all share something in common—a way that allows each of two conflicting parties to achieve what they want. This is precisely what integrative agreements are all about.

With examples ranging from rudeness to murder, it's an understatement to say that deviant organizational behavior is enormously broad in scope! Fortunately, scientists have devised a useful way of categorizing workplace deviance in a manner that helps us understand the various forms it takes.

Varieties of Deviant Behavior

The wide variety of behaviors that may be considered deviant can be categorized along two dimensions (see Figure 11.10).[30] First, deviant behavior may be distinguished in terms of the seriousness of its consequences. At the most serious extreme (shown on the

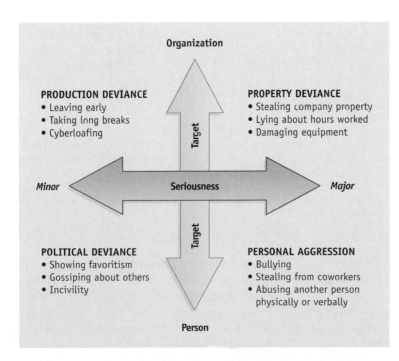

FIGURE 11.10

Dimensions and Categories of Deviant Organizational Behavior
Research has shown that deviant organizational behavior falls along the two dimensions shown here: seriousness (major or minor) and target (person or organization). Combining these two dimensions results in the four categories of behavior identified here, along with examples of each.
(*Source:* Based on findings reported by Robinson & Bennett, 1995; see Note 30.)

right side of the diagram), we may find employees physically attacking and harming their past or present coworkers. Fortunately, physical violence doesn't occur all that often. Far more commonplace are acts that, although also considered deviant, are far less extreme (shown on the left side of the diagram), such as spreading malicious gossip about others, lying about your work, blaming others falsely, and the like. Scientists also categorize deviant organizational behavior with respect to the intended target. In this regard, we may distinguish between deviant acts designed to harm other individuals, such as one's bosses or coworkers (e.g., verbally abusing a coworker), and deviant acts designed to harm the organization itself (e.g., sabotaging company equipment). By combining these two dimensions, we get the four categories of deviant behavior shown in Figure 11.10.

Looking through Figure 11.10, you will find a broad variety of deviant behaviors ranging from some very benign acts directed at the company, such as taking long breaks, to very extreme acts aimed at other individuals, such as physical abuse. Among these various forms of deviant organizational behavior is one that is relatively new because it is made possible by the availability of modern information technology—*cyberloafing*. For a closer look at this particular form of deviant organizational behavior, see the OB in an E-World section on page 426.

To give you a better feel for the nature of deviant organizational behavior, we now will take a closer look at two of the most prominent and widely studied forms of workplace deviance—*workplace aggression* and *employee theft*.

Workplace Aggression: Physical or Verbal Abuse and Bullying

Approximately 1.5 million Americans annually become victims of violence while on the job, costing some $4.2 billion.[33] Despite all the publicity given to workers going berserk and shooting up their offices, the good news is that such extreme acts of violence in the workplace occur very rarely. For example, only about 800 people are murdered at work each year in the United States (and even more in some other countries), and most of these crimes are committed by outsiders, such as customers.[34]

The study's findings underscore the role of national culture in implementing ways to resolve conflicts. Different strategies were favored by people from different cultures. Specifically, three sets of findings were noteworthy.

First, participants from the United States and Germany were significantly more likely to use the interests strategy than were participants from Japan. This is in keeping with the tendency for Americans and Germans to be more highly individualistic in their orientation to life—that is, to be focused on the contributions of individuals over groups as a whole.

Second, participants from Germany were more inclined to use the regulations strategy than those from the United States or Japan. Insofar as rules and procedures are expected to be universally applied in German culture but less so elsewhere, this finding was expected.

Third, and finally, it was found that appeals to social power, such as by finding a solution suggested by a high-ranking official, occurred far more commonly in Japan than in either the United States or Germany. This finding also was expected insofar as Japanese culture is strongly characterized by a willingness to defer to high-status others. Among the Germans and the Americans, the willingness to defer to others of higher power was considerably lower.

Although this study compared only three different countries and is based on a simulated conflict rather than a real one, it provides compelling evidence that culture makes a big difference in terms of how people go about resolving conflicts. As OB researchers begin to focus attention on this issue, it appears that we will learn still more about the effects of national culture on conflict resolution tactics in the years to come.[28]

Despite their low occurrence, it is important to acknowledge such violent acts because they represent the visible "tip of the iceberg" of more prevalent forms of physical and verbal aggression that do occur. For example, even when guns are not involved, fistfights have been known to break out in offices and factories. Still, deviant acts of the physical variety occur far less frequently than verbal forms of aggression, such as threatening physical harm or by degrading or humiliating someone. If you've ever suffered verbal humiliation from another, you probably know only too well that such "sticks and stones," as the saying goes, can indeed be very harmful (see Figure 11.11). Collectively, such acts of verbal and physical abuse are referred to as **workplace aggression.**[35]

Who engages in workplace aggression? Recently, a study was conducted in which employees were asked to report on the extent to which they behaved aggressively at

workplace aggression
Acts of verbal and physical abuse toward others in organizations, ranging from mild to severe.

FIGURE 11.11
Verbal Abuse: A Potent Source of Workplace Aggression
A great deal of the aggressive behavior that occurs in the workplace is not physical, but verbal in nature. If you've ever been a victim of verbal abuse on the job, you know that the resulting stress and harm to self-esteem can be devastating.

OB IN AN E-WORLD
CYBERLOAFING: DEVIANT BEHAVIOR GOES HIGH TECH

The advent of Internet technology has brought with it increased efficiency in accessing information and communicating with others—both of which are vital objectives. However, it also has created new ways for employees to loaf or "goof off." Although workers have devised ways to slack off ever since people have been employed, access to the Internet and e-mail has provided tempting and more insidious opportunities than ever before. Employees who use their company's e-mail and/or Internet facilities for personal use are considered to be engaged in **cyberloafing**.[31]

In the United States, 40 million people have Internet and/or e-mail access at work and use it regularly. They are referred to as online workers. However, further statistics reveal that much of what online workers are doing while online is not work related. For example:

- According to an MSNBC survey, one-fifth of all people who have visited pornographic Web sites have done so while on the job.
- One-third of workers surveyed by the Society of Financial Service Professionals reported playing computer games while at work.
- Eighty-three percent of employers surveyed by the Privacy Foundation indicated that their employees were using e-mail for personal purposes.

These and other forms of cyberloafing are costing U.S. organizations, both private and public, untold millions of dollars a year. In fact, just one $40,000/year employee can cost his or her employer as much as $5,000 annually by playing around on the Internet for one hour a day.

cyberloafing
The practice of using a company's e-mail and/or Internet facilities for personal use.

work.[36] These individuals also completed various personality measures. Interestingly, the individuals who were most inclined to behave aggressively possessed characteristics that were associated with aggression. These were as follows:

- *High trait anger*—the tendency to respond to situations in a predominantly angry manner.
- *Positive attitude toward revenge*—the belief that it is justifiable to get back at others who have caused one harm.
- *Past experience with aggression*—a history that involves exposure to aggressive behavior.

These results are important insofar as they suggest that some people are predisposed to behave more aggressively than others. In the future, as OB scientists come to understand this profile more fully, we will have a good chance of developing methods for screening those individuals who are most likely to behave aggressively on the job and keeping them out of the workplace altogether.

workplace bullying
The repeated mistreatment of an individual at work in a manner that endangers his or her physical or mental health.

Workplace bullying. In recent years, OB specialists have become aware of a particularly widespread form of aggressive behavior known as **workplace bullying**.[37] This refers to the repeated mistreatment of an individual at work in a manner that endangers his or her physical or mental health.[38] Workplace bullying occurs by virtue of things people do intentionally to bring harm (e.g., chastising another) as well as things they don't do (e.g., withholding valuable information and training). Unlike harassment based on race or gender, bullying is not strictly illegal (unless, of course, it results in harm), and it is quite widespread. According to a recent survey, one in six workers in the United States has been the victim of bullying in the past year.[39] Typically, bullies tend to be bosses (81 percent) who are abusing their power. Interestingly, bullies are equally likely to be women or men, but the vast majority of the targets of bullying tend to be women (especially

Executives are implicitly aware of this problem, and over three-quarters believe that some type of online monitoring and filtering efforts are needed. Recent polls found, however, that only about a third of online workers are monitored, and most of this monitoring is highly sporadic. In fact, only 38 percent acknowledge monitoring the online work of employees who already have been suspected of cyberloafing. Bottom line: Cyberloafing is a costly problem about which perilously little is being done.

Although various software products make it possible to monitor employees (Baltimore MIMEsweeper and Websense being the most widely used), and such products are growing in popularity, this technology is not a panacea. Although some problems are technical in nature, the most notable ones are social-psychological. Specifically, employees believe that being monitored constitutes an invasion of their privacy and reject the practice as being unfair.

Recent decisions in federal courts are in agreement. In September 2001, for example, the 27-judge Judicial Conference of the United States repealed a proposed monitoring policy for their own employees that they feared would violate employees' constitutional rights to privacy. Speaking for the group, federal appeals court judge Alex Kozinski objected to the policy's assertion that "court employees should have no expectation of privacy at any time while at work." The resulting policy permitted virtually no monitoring of employees' e-mail and only highly limited monitoring of their Internet use.

Where we stand now is quite interesting: Although cyberloafing is admittedly a widespread and costly problem, efforts aimed at addressing it that involve employee monitoring are not well accepted (or even legally permissible, in some cases). Clearly, the key is to find additional ways of discouraging people from cyberloafing. Admittedly, given the ancient problem of "goofing off" coupled with the vast opportunities to goof off provided by Internet access, cyberloafing looks like it's going to be problem that stays around for years to come. Fortunately, organizational behavior specialists are now beginning to study this phenomenon, which hopefully will provide some helpful suggestions in the years to come.[32]

when the bullies are themselves women).[40] For a summary of the various forms of workplace bullying that exist, see Table 11.6.

The interesting thing about bullying is that it tends to repeat itself, thereby escalating its effects. For example, a bully's target is likely to complain to a higher-ranking organizational official. Typically, most higher-level managers will take some form of action (e.g., admonishing the bully) but will still leave the bully in place to strike again. This time, however, the bully is likely not only to strike again, but also to retaliate with vengeance. Often, this results in high levels of fear that paralyze the workplace, causing people to seek new jobs and exposing employers to litigation. Part of the difficulty in dealing with this problem is that bullies often are so highly effective that they bring other employees into their webs, getting them either to join in on the abuse or to agree to keep silent about it. Soon, what appears to be the inappropriate behavior of a lone individual mushrooms into a serious problem for the entire organization.

Today's workplace bully is not simply a grown-up version of the same person as the schoolyard bully who threatened to beat you up after school back in second grade. Rather, workplace bullies are best understood from the same perspective as those who perpetrate domestic violence—they are individuals whose needs to control others are so extreme as to require psychological counseling. As you might imagine, the workplace bully, once rooted out, should be dealt with in a swift and effective manner. This might result in a leave of absence during which professional help is provided—or, in many cases, termination.

As you might imagine, of course, this is far easier said than done. After all, few among us would be willing to admit that we have a bully working in our midst, causing us to take only mild action, which, as we noted, can only make things worse. As in so many cases, the best offense here is likely to be "a good defense," that is, to be on the lookout for bullies and to step in before they can get a foothold into the organization.

TABLE 11.6   FORMS OF WORKPLACE BULLYING

Workplace bullying takes a variety of forms. Some of the most prevalent are summarized here.

CATEGORY	DESCRIPTION
Constant Critic	■ Uses insulting and belittling comments, engages in name-calling ■ Constantly harangues the victim about his or her incompetence ■ Makes aggressive eye contact
Two-Headed Snake	■ Denies victims the resources needed to work ■ Demands that coworkers provide damning evidence against the victim ■ Assigns meaningless work as punishment
Gatekeeper	■ Isolates the victim; ignoring him or her with "the silent treatment" ■ Deliberately cuts the target out of the communication loop but expects the victim to have the missing information
Screaming Mimi	■ Yells, screams, and curses ■ Makes loud, angry outbursts and tantrums ■ Intimidates by slamming things and throwing objects

(*Source:* Based on information in Namie & Namie, 2000; see Note 40.)

Although bullies are far too common in organizations, they still represent an extreme. Even the average worker who is not a bully, or a "hothead" with a "short fuse" who is prone to "explode," may, if provoked, react strongly to adverse situations he or she has experienced. Frequent mergers and acquisitions make working conditions uncertain for lots of people, causing almost anyone to behave aggressively from time to time.

Tips for avoiding workplace aggression. To keep such incidents from intensifying, it is important to recognize several things that managers can do to minimize the occurrence of aggression in the workplace. Here are three such tips.

1. *Establish clear disciplinary procedures.* It is not unusual for people to curb aggressive reactions in organizations that have clearly understood disciplinary procedures in place. Such programs send strong messages that inappropriate behavior will not be tolerated and that it will be punished if it occurs. Such deterrents go a long way toward many forms of workplace aggression.[41]

2. *Treat people with dignity and respect.* Managers who belittle their subordinates and who fail to show them the dignity and respect they deserve unknowingly may be promoting aggressive behavior. In some cases, this takes the form of people suing their former employers on the grounds of wrongful termination. Individuals who file such lawsuits are striking back at their former employers, attempting to get even with them for harming them. Recent research has shown that the more unfairly people believe they have been treated on the job (i.e., the less dignity and respect they have been shown), the more likely they are to file lawsuits against their former employers.[42] Obviously, this provides a strong lesson to managers about the importance of treating people fairly, something that is easily under their control.

3. *Train managers in ways to recognize and avoid aggression.* Although we all recognize aggressive behavior when it occurs, too few of us know how to recognize potentially dangerous situations before they become serious. Managers should be trained in techniques for recognizing threats and be familiar with ways to defuse those threats. Probably the most significant tip in this regard is to take all threats seriously. Never assume that someone is merely making a joke. Talking calmly and rationally to someone who appears to be troubled can go a long way toward avoiding a potentially explosive situation.

Employee Theft

Retail stores are very concerned with problems of shoplifting, as you know. What you might not know, however, is that companies lose more money and goods from their own employees than from customers. Although estimates of costs of employee theft are quite varied, it is clear that the figures are staggering. For some recent figures on the costs and scope of employee theft in several types of organizations, see Table 11.7.[43]

To fully understand these statistics, it is important to consider an important fact: Almost everyone takes home some company property for personal purposes, but we are unlikely to consider this as theft. You may say, "they expect it." Whether or not this is true, the taking of company property for nonbusiness uses constitutes **employee theft.** After all, who among us hasn't taken home a few pens or paper clips from the office at one time or another? Although these acts may seem innocent and innocuous enough, petty theft is so common that cumulatively it costs companies far more than the few acts of grand theft that grab newspaper headlines.[44]

employee theft
The taking of company property for personal use.

Why do employees steal? It's hardly surprising that many employees steal because they are troubled in some way (e.g., they are in serious debt or have a narcotics or gambling habit). Although this is undoubtedly true in some cases, it doesn't account for everyone.

Lots of people steal for a very simple reason—because they see their coworkers doing it. To the extent that everyone around you is taking home tools, office supplies, and even petty cash, it seems to be not so inappropriate. After all, we rationalize, "everyone is doing it" and "the company expects us to do it." Although this doesn't make it right, of course, and it clearly costs the company money, people are quick to convince themselves that petty theft is "no big deal" and not worth worrying about.

Similarly, many employees engage in theft because in some companies not stealing goes against the norms of the work group.[45] Unspoken rules go a long way toward determining how people behave on the job (as we discussed in Chapter 8), and in some companies, an employee has to steal to feel accepted and to belong.

Finally, employees also frequently engage in theft because they want to "even the score" with employers whom they believe have mistreated them. In fact, people who believe they have been underpaid frequently steal from their employers because in so doing they are righting a wrong by taking what they should have had all along (this is in keeping with our discussion of equity theory in Chapter 6).

Tips for reducing employee theft. Although you see security cameras just about everywhere, it's clear that they are not completely effective.[46] After all, many people keep on stealing. As a practicing manager, there are several things you can do to help chip away at the problem. Although you won't be able to stop theft completely, it's encouraging to know that you can make a difference by following these practical suggestions.

TABLE 11.7 EMPLOYEE THEFT: SOME FACTS AND FIGURES

The following statistics will give you a sense of the scope and serious nature of employee theft today.

- In the restaurant business, theft by employees costs between $15 billion and $25 billion per year.
- Although fewer consumers are stealing wireless phone service than ever before, there has been a significant rise in theft of service by employees of wireless companies.
- Most employees dislike the use of video surveillance cameras at work. At a Virginia restaurant, seven cashiers resigned the day before they believed closed-circuit surveillance cameras were going to be installed.
- Fraud cost American businesses about $400 billion a year.
- The average convenience store loses $20,000 per year due to employee theft.
- In Asian retail businesses, about 3 percent of the staff steals every day and 8 percent steals every week.
- Breaches of computer security are on the rise, but most of the people who break into corporate or government computers illegally are current employees rather than outsiders.

(*Sources:* See Note 43.)

1. *Involve employees in the creation of a theft policy.* It is not always clear what constitutes theft. Does your company prohibit the use of personal phone calls or using the copy machine for personal purposes? If so, violating these policies constitutes theft of company resources, although chances are good that few will think of them as such. The trick is to develop very clear policies about employee theft and to involve employees in the process of doing so. The more involved they are, the more they will "buy into" the policies and follow them. Once such policies are developed, of course, it is critical to articulate them carefully in a formal document (such as a policy manual or code of ethics) and to carefully train all employees in them.

2. *Communicate the costs of stealing.* Chances are good that someone in the accounting department of any company has a good idea of how much the company is losing each year due to employee theft. To the extent that this information is shared with other employees, along with a clear indication of how it costs them personally (e.g., through smaller raises and bonuses), many employees will think twice before they take company property for personal use.

3. *Treat people fairly.* Many employees who steal from their employers are doing so because they are trying to strike back at employers whom they believe have treated them unfairly in the past. Indeed, as we explained in Chapter 6, underpaid employees may steal company property in an effort to take for themselves what they are not being given by their company.

4. *Be a good role model.* One of the most effective things managers can do to discourage theft is to not engage in theft themselves. After all, to the extent that employees see their managers making personal phone calls, padding their expense accounts, or taking home office supplies, they are left with the message that doing these kinds of things is perfectly acceptable. When it comes to discouraging employee theft, "walking the talk" is very important.

SUMMARY AND REVIEW OF LEARNING OBJECTIVES

1. Describe two types of psychological contracts in work relationships and the types of trust associated with each.
One type of psychological contract is the transactional contract. It is characteristic of relationships that have an exclusively economic focus, last for a brief period of time, are unchanging in nature, and have a narrow, well-defined scope. Calculus-based trust—trust based on deterrence—is associated with transactional contracts. A second type of contract is the relational contract. Such contracts are based on friendship and exist in relationships in which the parties take a long-term perspective. Such relationships are characterized by identification-based trust—that is, trust based on accepting and understanding one another.

2. Describe organizational citizenship behavior and ways in which it may be promoted.
Organizational citizenship behavior consists of acts that go above and beyond one's formal job requirements in helping one's organization or fellow employees. It can be promoted by going out of the way to help others, being an example of conscientiousness, making voluntary functions fun, and demonstrating courtesy and good sportsmanship.

3. Identify ways in which cooperation can be promoted in the workplace.
Although by nature some people are more cooperative than others, interpersonal cooperation may be promoted by following the reciprocity principle and by adopting reward systems (e.g., team-based pay) that encourage cooperation with others.

4. Describe the causes and effects of conflict in organizations.
Conflict is caused by a wide variety of factors, including grudges, malevolent attributions, destructive criticism, distrust, and competition over scarce resources. Conflict

can be not only a source of negative emotions, but it also can lead to a lack of coordination, which can make performance suffer in organizations. But conflict also can have beneficial effects. These include bringing out into the open problems that have been previously ignored, motivating people to appreciate each others' positions more fully, and encouraging people to consider new ideas.

5. Describe the techniques that can be used to manage conflict in organizations.
Conflict can be managed effectively by encouraging the conflicting parties to negotiate win-win solutions between them. These may include integrative agreements, in which solutions are sought that go beyond simple compromise. Alternative dispute resolution techniques are widely used to resolve conflicts today. The most popular of these are mediation (in which a neutral third party works with the conflicting parties to find a mutually satisfying solution to the conflict) and arbitration (in which a neutral third party proposes solutions for conflicting parties).

6. Identify two forms of deviant organizational behavior and how to minimize their occurrence.
Workplace aggression is one form of deviant organizational behavior. It can be minimized by establishing clear disciplinary procedures, by treating people fairly, and by training managers in ways to recognize and avoid aggression. Employee theft is another form of deviant organizational behavior. It can be reduced by involving employees in the creation of a theft policy, by communicating the costs of stealing, and by having managers be good role models by not stealing themselves.

POINTS TO PONDER

Questions for Review

1. What are psychological contracts and what role do they play in developing trusting relationships in organizations?
2. In what ways do good organizational citizens and whistle-blowers contribute to the well-being of the organizations in which they work?
3. What are the major determinants of cooperation between individuals and between organizations?
4. What are the major causes and consequences of organizational conflict?
5. In what ways can organizational conflict be managed effectively?
6. What are the major types of deviant organizational behavior and what can be done to minimize their occurrence?

Experiential Questions

1. Think of individuals whom you trust and those whom you don't trust. In what key ways do your relationships with these people differ?
2. What are the major sources of conflict operating within the company at which you are employed? How do you think these conflicts may be resolved?
3. What specific forms of deviant organizational behavior have you ever observed? Why do you think these occurred?

Questions to Analyze

1. Do you agree or disagree with the following statement? People are inherently good but are forced into behaving in negative ways by virtue of compelling forces they encounter within their organizations.
2. What would you say are the major barriers to interpersonal cooperation within the workplace?
3. We hear a lot about deviant organizational behavior in the popular press. Do you think it is becoming more prevalent in society or is it just more likely to be reported?

INDIVIDUAL EXERCISE

Assessing Your Personal Orientation Toward Others

On page 414 you read descriptions of four different personal orientations toward others—*competitors, individualists, cooperators,* and *equalizers.* As you read these, you probably developed some ideas as to which orientation best described you. This exercise is designed to help you find out.

Directions

Use the following scale to indicate how well each of the following statements describes you.

1 = Does not describe me at all/never
2 = Describes me somewhat/some of the time
3 = Describes me moderately/half of the time
4 = Describes me greatly/much of the time
5 = Describes me perfectly/all of the time

_____ 1. I don't care how much money one of my coworkers earns, so long as I make as much as I can.
_____ 2. When playing a game with a close friend, I always try to keep the score close.
_____ 3. So long as I do better than the next guy, I'm happy.
_____ 4. I will gladly give up something for myself if it can help my team get ahead.
_____ 5. It's important to me to be the best in the class, even if I'm not doing my personal best.
_____ 6. I feel badly if I do too much better than my friends on a class assignment.
_____ 7. I want to get an A in this class regardless of what grade others might get.
_____ 8. I enjoy it when the people in my work team all pitch in together to beat other teams.

Scoring

Insert the numbers corresponding to your answers to each of the questions in the spaces corresponding to those questions. Then add the numbers in each column (these can range from 2 to 10). The higher your score, the more accurately the personal orientation heading that column describes you.

Competitor	Individualist	Cooperator	Equalizer
3. _____	1. _____	4. _____	2. _____
5. _____	7. _____	8. _____	11. _____
Total = _____	Total = _____	Total = _____	Total = _____

Questions for Discussion

1. What did this exercise reveal about you?
2. Were you surprised at what you learned, or was it something you already knew?
3. Do you tend to maintain the same orientation most of the time or are there occasions in which you change from one orientation to another? What do you think this means?

GROUP EXERCISE

Negotiating the Price of a Used Car

This exercise is designed to help you put into practice some of the skills associated with being a good negotiator. In completing this exercise, follow the steps for negotiating a win-win solution found on pages 419–420.

Steps

1. Find a thorough description of a recent-model used car in a newspaper or online.
2. Divide the class into groups of six. Within each group, assign three students to the role of buyer and three to the role of seller.
3. Each group of buyers and sellers should meet in advance to plan their strategies. Buyers should plan on getting the lowest possible price; sellers should seek the highest possible price.
4. Buyers and sellers should meet to negotiate the price of the car within the period of time specified by the instructor. Feel free to meet within your groups at any time to evaluate your strategy.
5. Write down the final agreed-upon price and any conditions that may be attached to it.

Questions for Discussion

1. Did you reach an agreement? If so, how easy or difficult was this process?
2. Which side do you think "won" the negotiation? What might have changed the outcome?
3. How might the negotiation process or the outcome have been different had this been a real situation?

WEB SURFING EXERCISE

Arbitration

Each of the following Web sites contains useful information about arbitration. Visit each one and answer the following questions based on what you found.

www.nasdar.com	This is the site of NASD Dispute Resolution, the largest arbitration forum. It lists arbitration rules and filing costs and helps you find an appropriate arbitrator.
www.nyse.com/arbitration	If you need to file an arbitration claim at the New York Stock Exchange, this is the place to go.
www.piaba.org.	At this site you will find lists of attorneys who specialize in arbitration disputes.

1. In what types of issues do these arbitration experts specialize?
2. What are the general backgrounds of the people who provide arbitration services?
3. Based on what you found at these sites, what do you believe are the strengths and weaknesses of the arbitration process?

Deviant Behavior

Because so much attention has been paid by the press to various forms of deviant workplace behavior (e.g., employee theft, workplace aggression), it is not surprising that many organizational consultants and companies specializing in managerial training have become interested in this topic. Several of these have developed programs focusing on ways to predict, detect, and prevent various forms of deviance. To get a feel for these efforts, enter keywords such as "workplace aggression" and "employee theft" into your favorite search engine and answer the following questions based on what you find when visiting the Web sites that are identified.

1. What are the major areas of emphasis in training programs designed to curtail deviant behavior in the workplace?
2. In what ways do the various programs differ from one another?
3. To what extent would you characterize the emphasis of these programs as being on predicting deviance in advance as opposed to handling it once it occurs?

PRACTICING OB

Unhealthy Conflict in an Office

Although you work in a relatively small office of a mortgage title company, life on the job has become tumultuous. Not only are people always at each others' backs but also sometimes they get downright hostile. You've witnessed lots of name-calling and even some people sabotaging others' work. Nobody is immune. Even those who have not been involved are suffering the consequences—getting sick over the stress that's always in the air—and good employees are resigning. Answer the following questions using the material in this chapter.

1. What possible causes of the problem would you consider, and why?
2. Assuming that these causes are real, what advice would you offer about how to eliminate the problem?
3. What steps would you advise taking to help reduce the negative effects of stress that are likely to arise in this workplace?

CASE IN POINT

The True Story of George, the "Paraillegal"

A few years ago George worked as a paralegal for a personal injury law firm. It was not exceptionally challenging work, and his pay, only $7.00/hour, reflected it. His job was to handle the paperwork for all aspects of cases from intake through litigation. He would, for example, get police reports, contact witnesses, and write to insurance companies demanding money for pain and suffering on behalf of clients. In short, he did all the leg-work for the lawyers.

Although George had lots of autonomy when it came to how to do the job (perhaps, too much, as you will see), he faced considerable pressure because the caseload was enormous. The small firm (consisting of one boss, three attorneys, and 10 paralegals) advertised heavily on television, giving the firm over a thousand clients at any given time. Putting lots of pressure on George and the other paralegals, it was the firm's practice to lead all clients to believe they stood an excellent chance of collecting damages. The hungrier they became, the more pressure they applied, making the job very demanding. Turnover was very high, but George stuck it out for two and a half years. It wasn't because he was so loyal. Rather, he found a way to work only 5 hours a day but make $2,500 a month (which is quite impressive at only $7/hour).

Apparently, this particular paralegal was more of a "paraillegal," shall we say. Some cases dragged so slowly that after several years, clients eventually gave up, forgot, moved on, or for one reason or another simply did nothing. At any given time, these "missing-in-action" cases needed to be settled by the insurance companies, and so they were. However, without actual clients clamoring for checks, payment went to the doctors and lawyers who worked on the cases, and the paralegals kept the rest. This involved forging the client's name to settle the case, but nobody ever asked any questions. The case was settled, and everyone was happy.

Did George feel guilty about what he did? Not in the slightest. In his own words, "We felt that we had a right to the money. This guy [the boss] was underpaying us, and I really felt that he owed me." If clients reemerged and asked about their settlements, as some did, they simply were paid off. After all, the firm couldn't afford the bad publicity associated with letting the truth come out.

Critical Thinking Questions

1. Do you think George really would have refrained from defrauding the insurance companies if he were more highly paid? In other words, do you think his justification for stealing is ingenuine?
2. How would you have behaved in George's situation?
3. In what ways might the jobs of the paralegals be changed so as to avoid this kind of situation?

12

Influence, Power, and Politics in Organizations

■ PREVIEW CASE
THE MAN WHO SWALLOWED CHRYSLER

In many ways, Jurgen E. Schrempp, the head of Daimler-Chrysler, is the prototypic German executive: tall and elegant, dressed in Euro-style clothes and sporting sleek frameless eyeglasses, he looks every inch a Teutonic leader. And his reputation in Germany matches this image: He is often described as Germany's Rambo or sometimes as Neutron Jurgen, after General Electric's former CEO, Jack Welch (Neutron Jack), whose restructuring of *that* giant company eliminated entire labor forces but left their factories standing (as a neutron bomb would do). Like Welch, Schrempp drastically reengineered his own company, Daimler-Benz,

> Like most highly successful people, he knows how to get his way and has lots of techniques for assuring that he does.

before undertaking the gargantuan task of swallowing Chrysler, the third largest auto manufacturer in the United States. He radically restructured Daimler-Benz, dissolving entire divisions and cutting tens of thousands of jobs; and he showed his strong disdain for corporate bureaucracies, reducing the administrative staff at the company's headquarters from 1,200 to 300.

Schrempp clearly knows about power—how to get it and how to use it. But even this powerful CEO recognizes that power has its limits. In describing the merger between Daimler-Benz and Chrysler, for instance, he frequently notes that combining the two cultures will take years—and is *not* a task that can be accomplished through executive decrees. Rather, it will be a slow process in which top people at the two companies get to know—and trust—each other.

Schrempp, who is known as one of the most ruthless and ambitious businessmen in Europe, also can be charming when the need arises. He recognizes the importance of being persuasive, not just commanding. And he also understands the auto business from the ground up. In fact, Schrempp spent years as an apprentice mechanic at Daimler-Benz and is one of the few executives in the industry who can actually repair his company's products. This earns him the respect of production-line people and engineers, who recognize that he knows their products in a way few other executives do.

It was this expertise, perhaps, that allowed him to pull the company's new A-Class car (sold in Europe) from production when it performed poorly in a crucial "Moose test," in which it is driven at about 45 miles per hour without braking, swerving hard to the right or left (as a driver would have to do if a moose jumped in front of the car). The decision turned out to be a brilliant one, and the redesigned A-Class car far surpassed its competitors in terms of safety and performance. So yes, Jurgen Schrempp is tough, but at the same time he understands how to get things done and how to do so without relying solely on raw power. Like most highly successful people, he knows how to get his way and has lots of techniques for assuring that he does.

F ew individuals in the business world are as powerful as Jurgen Schrempp—after all, he heads one of the largest manufacturing companies on the face of the globe. But his career illustrates a very basic fact: In the business world, as in every other setting, people often attempt to influence the actions of others—people with whom they work or live or people they meet during the course of their daily lives. This process is visible in situations ranging from the mundane—for instance, when the manager of a convenience store asks a part-time employee to work extra hours—to the exceptional, as when a CEO like Jurgen Schrempp seeks to convince his counterpart in another giant corporation that a merger would be beneficial to both companies.

Efforts to induce others to behave in some desired way are known as *social influence* and are truly a part of everyday life in all organizations. But how, precisely, do people try to get others to do what they want—to act as they wish? They do so in many different ways. One of these involves the use of *power,* the formal capacity of one or more persons (or organizations) to exert influence over one or more people—to tell them, more or less, what to do. Certainly, Jurgen Schrempp used his power as CEO in restructuring Daimler-Benz. But, just as obviously, he had no direct power over Robert J. Eaton, CEO of Chrysler. Getting Eaton to do what Schrempp desired (merging Chrysler into Daimler-Benz) required the use of other techniques such as persuasion or offering various financial inducements. As we'll soon see, people (and organizations) use a very wide range of strategies for exerting influence over others when they lack formal power over them.

What about the motives behind influence attempts? These, too, can vary greatly. When Jurgen Schrempp sought to promote a merger between Chrysler and Daimler-Benz, he did so because he believed, sincerely, that this would be in the best interests of both companies. Sometimes, though, individuals attempt to influence others strictly for personal gain, even if doing so runs counter to the best interests of their organization. Such efforts in which influence is used for strictly selfish means are known as *organizational politics.* As you probably know from experience, this type of influence is all too common in many organizations, and it can exert powerful effects on individuals' careers and even on the success of entire organizations.[1]

In this chapter, we'll examine the nature of these three processes—influence, power, and politics—and their impact on important outcomes, both for individuals and organizations. We'll start by distinguishing carefully and more fully these three concepts. They all center around the theme of changing others' actions, but as we have already noted, they involve contrasting tactics, goals, and motives. After that initial discussion, we'll focus on each of these processes in more detail. With respect to influence, we'll consider a wide range of tactics used by individuals and groups in work settings to change others' behavior. Turning to power, we'll focus on two key issues: how it is gained, both by individuals and by organizational subunits, and how it is used. Finally, with respect to organizational politics, we'll examine the political mechanisms used by individuals to promote their selfish goals as well as the ethical issues raised by these tactics.

SOCIAL INFLUENCE: A BASIC ORGANIZATIONAL PROCESS

Imagine that you are a supervisor heading a group of a dozen staff members working on an important new project for your company. Tomorrow you're scheduled to make a big presentation to company officials, but the report isn't quite ready. If only several staff members would work a few hours extra, the job could be done on time. There's a problem, however. This evening the people in your department are planning on going out together, so nobody wants to work late. If anything, they'd prefer to leave early. What can you do to persuade some of your staff to work late and complete the job? In other words, how will you attempt to influence their behavior?

Managers confront situations like this one nearly every day: They want to change others' behavior, and this requires them to select various techniques for reaching this goal. In this section, we'll examine some strategies that are often used for exerting social influence in organizations. Before turning to that interesting task, though, we'll first focus on the important differences between social influence, power, and politics.

Social Influence, Power, and Politics: Their Basic Nature

Let's return to our example, but this time we'll take the perspective of one of the employees. You know of your boss's predicament, but you don't want to work overtime. You've been looking forward to a night out, and you don't want anything to ruin it. At the same time, you don't want to risk angering the boss by rejecting his or her request. After all, you generally try hard to be a good citizen. What do you do? Thinking about it, you come up with a simple solution: If the boss doesn't see you, he or she will approach someone else, and you'll be spared the discomfort of having to deal with the problem. So, when you see the boss approaching your desk from across the office, you turn away to avoid making eye contact and walk briskly to the restroom to avoid the request you are sure she or he soon will make.

social influence

Attempts to affect another in a desired fashion, whether or not these are successful.

Can we say that the boss influenced you in this situation? After all, you used your stealth and cunning to avoid the situation. Despite this, the answer is "yes," the boss has, in fact, influenced you. The definition of social influence suggests why this is so. In concrete terms, **social influence** refers to *attempts* to affect another in a desired fashion, whether or not these are successful. In fact, it may be said that we have influenced someone to the extent that our behavior has had an effect—even if unintended—on that person (see Figure 12.1). In terms of our example, we have to say that the boss clearly *did* have an effect on you. After all, you avoided speaking with her or him. So although the boss did not affect your behavior as desired (by getting you to work overtime), your boss *did* influence you in this way.

If influence involves attempts to affect other persons, then where do power and politics fit into the picture? As shown in Figure 12.1, these processes are somewhat narrower in scope. *Power* refers to the potential to successfully influence another. It is the capacity to change the behavior or attitudes of another in a desired fashion.[2] In contrast with social influence, power refers to the *capacity* to have a desired effect on others. As we will see in the next section, there are several different bases of power. In general, these stem from two sources—one's personal characteristics and one's organizational position. For now, assume that the boss has power over you by virtue of access to considerable resources that enable him or her to reward you with raises (in exchange for being cooperative) or to punish you by not supporting your promotion (if you refrain from pitching in). These represent the formal actions the supervisor can take to attempt to influence you successfully. That is, they are the sources of her or his power.

FIGURE 12.1
Social Influence, Power, and Politics: How They Are Related
When we do something that has had an effect on someone else, whether or not it is the effect we desire, we have exerted *social influence* over that person. Our capacity to exert influence over another is known as *power*. Unofficial uses of power to enhance or protect our self-interest, usually at the expense of organizational goals, are known as *organizational politics*.

Often, when people exercise power, they take into account their own individual interests. For example, the supervisor in our example may be motivated by an interest in promoting—or at least in saving—his or her own career by making sure that the report gets done on time. This is not to say that the boss also might not recognize the value of the report to the company. It's just that the boss's actions are motivated primarily by his or her own selfish concerns.

Such actions—ones taken to further personal, selfish goals—lie at the heart of *organizational politics.* This term refers to unauthorized uses of power that enhance or protect one's own personal interests, usually at the expense of organizational goals.[3] It is the opposite of what is expected—using power to enhance organizational goals. If this kind of behavior sounds quite negative, that's because it is. In fact, organizational politics is technically illegitimate in both its means and ends, and not surprisingly, it is often a source of conflict. Later in this chapter we will describe many types of political actions and ways in which people can use their power to promote their personal interests in organizations. Now, however, we will take a closer look at the process of social influence.

Tactics of Social Influence: Getting to "Yes"

It is widely acknowledged that successful managers are those who are adept at influencing others.[4] But how do they do so? And how do *you* attempt to influence others—get them to do what you want them to do? In recent years, researchers have identified several techniques that people use to influence each other in organizations.[5] The most common ones are these:[6]

- *Rational persuasion.* Using logical arguments and facts to persuade another that a desired result will occur.
- *Inspirational appeal.* Arousing enthusiasm by appealing to one's values and ideals.
- *Consultation.* Asking for participation in decision making or planning a change.
- *Ingratiation.* Getting someone to do what you want by putting that person in a good mood or getting him or her to like you.
- *Exchange.* Promising some benefits in exchange for complying with a request.
- *Personal appeal.* Appealing to feelings of loyalty and friendship before making a request.
- *Coalition building.* Persuading by seeking the assistance of others or by noting the support of others.
- *Legitimating.* Pointing out one's authority to make a request or verifying that it is consistent with prevailing organizational policies and practices.
- *Pressure.* Seeking compliance by using demands, threats, or intimidation.

OB IN AN E-WORLD
DOWNLOAD TIME: IS IT ALWAYS A NEGATIVE FOR COMPANIES DOING E-BUSINESS?

If you ever shop online, you certainly have had the experience of finding a company selling something you want but then sitting there for what seems like an eternity while information about the products you are seeking load—slowly!—on your screen. If you are like many people, after a while you get tired of waiting and click to another location. In short, because of excessive *download time*, you are lost as a customer and aren't even there to be persuaded by the company's Web page.

In the past, it was suggested that ever-increasing bandwidth would soon solve this problem: Pages would load so quickly that download time would become unimportant. But even today, only about 10 percent of Web users in the United States, and a much lower figure elsewhere, use high-bandwidth Internet providers.[10] This means that a large majority are still waiting—patiently or impatiently—while pages load through their modems.

But how long is too long? Recent research suggests that the answer is, "It depends," and what it depends on, to an important extent, is the culture in which people live. Around the world, countries can be divided into two major groups with respect to how they view time. Countries such as the United States and

When are these various tactics used? Not surprisingly, research findings indicate that they are used differently depending on whether one is attempting to influence another who is at a higher, lower, or equivalent organizational level as oneself (see Figure 12.2).[7] For example, leaders often use inspirational appeal to influence their subordinates (see Chapter 13). However, subordinates are unlikely to use these techniques when attempting to influence their bosses. Instead, they are likely to rely on consultation or ingratiation when attempting to appeal to their bosses. Finally, when attempting to influence peers, both exchange and personal appeal were among the most popularly used techniques.

Consultative techniques (ones that involve trying to persuade others directly) are generally viewed as more appropriate than coercive techniques (ones that involve pressuring others or "cutting the ground from under them").[8] Accordingly, the most popular

FIGURE 12.2

Social Influence Depends on Organizational Level
Because of their different organizational levels, the manager and the subordinate shown here are likely to use different tactics when attempting to influence each other.

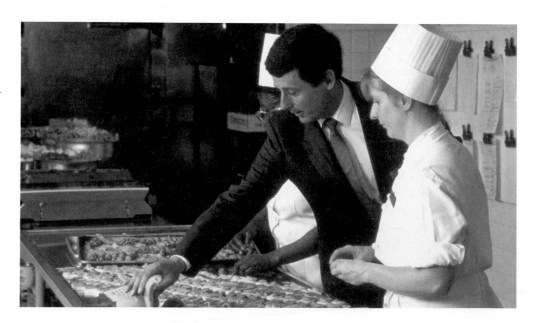

ones in Northern Europe (e.g., Britain, Germany, Finland) are described as being *monochromic* in their sense of time. In these cultures, people feel that being on time is important, that events should begin and end at the scheduled times, and that people should do one activity at a time—hence, the existence of daily calendars and scheduling programs. In other countries— ones described as *polychromic*—the sense of time is very different. In these countries (e.g., in South America and Asia), people feel that is not very important to be on time and that it is perfectly fine to work on several activities at once—hold a meeting, read, eat, and so on. Download time seems to have sharply different effects in these two cultural groups. As you can probably guess, lengthy download time is viewed as unacceptable in monochromic cultures but as more acceptable in polychromic cultures. Why? Perhaps because in polychromic cultures, peo-ple waiting for downloads to complete do other things—they read, talk to friends, or whatever. So the time passes quickly and they are not upset by it. In monochromic cultures, in contrast, people sit in front of their screens, becoming more and impatient.[11]

The moral of these findings is clear: If you are doing business in monochromic cultures, download is indeed crucial. You should design your pages to load quickly without much delay (more than 15 seconds seems to be "too long" in such cultures). In contrast, if your markets are in polychromic cultures, download time is less crucial, and you can design more complex and slower-loading Web pages. In both cases, the purpose is to persuade customers to buy your products, but how you should go about this varies in terms of the cultures in which you do business.

techniques to influence people at all levels are consultation, inspirational appeal, and rational persuasion.[9] Each one of these techniques involves getting someone else to accept a request as being highly desirable, and each is socially acceptable for influencing people at all levels. It is, therefore, not surprising that people who use these techniques are believed to be highly effective in carrying out their responsibilities.

In contrast, the less desirable forms of influence, such as pressure and legitimating, are not used as frequently. In fact, pressure, when it is used, is more likely to be relied on as a follow-up technique than as a tool for one's initial influence attempt—and then only for subordinates. It is important to note that some techniques such as ingratiation, coalition building, personal appeal, and exchange are more likely to be used in combination with other techniques than to be used alone.

Techniques like persuasion are not used only by individuals. In fact, efforts at persuasion are the foundation of the field of marketing. And as described in the OB in an E-World section above, efforts at persuasion certainly are present on the Web.

Other Tactics of Influence

Although the tactics described earlier are certainly important ones, they are far from the entire picture. Additional research offers important insights into the nature of influence. This work has focused on one aspect of social influence that is truly central to organizational behavior: *compliance*—getting others to say "yes" to specific requests. In order to reach this goal, we rely on a wide range of tactics. But all of these, it appears, rest on a small number of basic principles.[12] Among these, the ones most relevant to organizational behavior are described below:

- *Friendship/Liking:* The more we like other persons or feel friendship for them, the more likely we are to comply with their requests or to accept other forms of influence from them.
- *Commitment/Consistency:* Individuals wish to be consistent in their beliefs and actions. Thus, once they have adopted a position or committed themselves to a

course of action, they experience strong pressure to comply with requests that are consistent with these initial commitments; in fact, they may find it virtually impossible to refuse such requests because doing so would force them to reject or disown actions or beliefs they previously adopted.

- *Scarcity:* In general, opportunities, objects, or outcomes are valued in inverse proportion to their scarcity. Thus, requests that emphasize scarcity or the fact that some object, opportunity, or outcome will soon no longer be available are difficult to resist.
- *Reciprocity:* Individuals generally experience powerful pressures to reciprocate benefits they have received from others. As a result, requests that activate this principle are more likely to be accepted than requests that do not.

These basic principles appear to underlie many tactics of influence. For example, *ingratiation* and *impression management* are closely related to the principle of liking/friendship. The basic idea is simple: First, get others to like you and then, once they do, ask them to do what you want.

The principle of commitment/consistency has been found to play an important role in several common and often highly successful tactics for gaining compliance including (1) *the foot in the door*—starting with a small request and, once this is accepted, escalating to a larger one; and (2) the *lowball*—attempting to change a deal or agreement by making it less attractive to the target person after it is negotiated. This latter tactic is often used by salespersons and goes something like this. An attractive deal is offered to a customer. Once the customer accepts, the salesperson indicates that the sales manager or someone else has rejected the arrangement and offers one less desirable to the customer. Rationally, people should walk away from such changes but often they don't: They feel committed to their initial decision, so they accept the less attractive deal.

Turning to the principle of scarcity, such tactics as *playing hard to get* and *the fast-approaching-deadline technique* are widely used in the world of business (see Figure 12.3). Job applicants who mention that they are under consideration for other positions or are very satisfied with their current position are using the hard-to-get tactic to manipulate important organizational outcomes in their favor. Similarly, salespersons who suggest that various products are in short supply or that a price cannot be guaranteed beyond a specific date are using tactics related to the principle of scarcity and to the fast-approaching-deadline technique.

Finally, the principle of reciprocity is related to a tactic of influence known as the *door-in-the-face* tactic. In this strategy, individuals start with a request that is very large and certain to be rejected. Then they "scale down" their request to a more acceptable one, thus putting the target person under considerable pressure to reciprocate this concession. In fact, their concession is not a real one, but the tactic often works. Here's an example: A venture capitalist demands 90 percent of the equity in a company from an entrepreneur. The entrepreneur refuses, and then the venture capitalist "backs down" to "only" 80 percent—the figure he really wanted all along. The entrepreneur is relieved and agrees. The result: The entrepreneur surrenders more equity than would have been the case if the venture capitalist did not use the door-in-the-face tactic skillfully.

HOW TO DO IT

PROTECTING YOURSELF FROM UNWANTED INFLUENCE

On the job, we are constantly bombarded by people who are attempting to change our attitudes or behavior in some manner. However, we need not be helpless against them. There are several steps you can take to protect yourself when you do not wish to be influenced.

1. *Recognize influence tactics.* Merely being familiar with various influence tactics can be helpful. So, if you are on the lookout for the tactics described in this chapter, you stand a chance of being immune from them.

2. *Always question motives.* Ask yourself *why* someone else is trying to influence you. If you believe the person's motives are appropriate, you may decide to accept his or her influence attempt. But, if you suspect that there may be something inappropriate with that person's motive, you may reject his or her influence.

3. *Question influence from illegitimate sources.* Some people in your organization—primarily your boss and team members—have a legitimate right to influence you. Generally, you should succumb to their influence. However, you should be on guard against being influenced by others who have no such legitimate authority.

4. *View attempts at persuasion as assaults on your personal freedom.* When someone is attempting to influence you, remind yourself that you are in charge of your own life. You can decide to accept another's ideas and views, or to reject them. Although you might face considerable pressure and consequences, ultimately, the choice is always yours.

Following the steps outlined here can help reduce the impact of even strong and well-executed influence attempts. The decision to reject another's influence might be difficult to make freely, but you may have more freedom than you think.

FIGURE 12.3
Fast-Approaching-Deadline Technique
When stores place signs like this one in their windows, they may be using the "fast-approaching-deadline" technique to influence customers. This technique is based on the principle of *scarcity*—it seeks to boost the value of products (or even people) by suggesting that they are scarce or hard to obtain.

This is only a small sampling of the many strategies people use to gain compliance—to induce others to say "yes" to their requests. (See Figure 12.4 for yet another illustration of the fact that such tactics do not always produce their intended effects!) Although procedures for exerting influence over others are often effective, you *can* protect yourself against them. For some suggestions, see the How to Do It section on page 442.

INDIVIDUAL POWER: A BASIS FOR INFLUENCE

Power, as we noted earlier, involves the potential to influence others successfully—both the things they do and the ways they feel about something. In this section, we will focus on the individual bases of power—factors that give people the capacity to influence others successfully.

power
The potential to influence others successfully.

It is an inevitable fact of organizational life that some individuals can boast a greater capacity to influence the people around them than others. In other words, power is definitely *not* distributed equally in most organizations. Why is this so? What sources of power do people have at their disposal? We will consider several specific bases of power falling into two major categories—ones deriving mainly from the positions individuals occupy in their organizations and ones deriving mainly from personal characteristics.

Position Power: Influence That Comes with the Office

A great deal of the power people have in organizations comes from the specific jobs or titles they hold. In other words, they are able to influence others because of the formal

FIGURE 12.4
Social Influence: It Takes Many Forms
As this cartoon suggests, social influence can be exerted in many different ways! (*Source:* United Features Syndicate, August 19, 1996.)

position power
Power based on one's formal position in an organization.

legitimate power
The individual power base derived from one's position in an organizational hierarchy; the accepted authority of one's position.

reward power
The individual power base derived from an individual's capacity to administer valued rewards to others.

coercive power
The individual power base derived from the capacity to administer punishment to others.

power associated with their jobs. This is known as **position power.** For example, there are certain powers that the president of the United States has simply because he holds office (e.g., signing bills into law, making treaties, etc.). These formal powers remain vested in the position and are available to anyone who holds it. When the president's term is up, these powers transfer to the new office holder. There are four bases of position power: *legitimate power, reward power, coercive power,* and *information power.* For a summary of these, see the left part of Figure 12.5.

Legitimate power. The power that people have because others recognize and accept their authority is known as **legitimate power.** As an example, students recognize that their instructors have the authority to make class policies and to determine grades, giving them legitimate power over the class.

It is important to note that legitimate power covers a relatively narrow range of influence and that it may be inappropriate to overstep these bounds. For example, whereas a boss may require her secretary to type and fax a company document, it would be an abuse of power to ask that secretary to type her son's homework assignment. This is not to say that the secretary might not take on the task as a favor, but doing so would *not* be the direct result of the boss's formal authority. Legitimate power applies only to the range of behaviors that is recognized and accepted as appropriate by the parties and institution involved.

Reward power. Associated with holding certain jobs comes the power to control the rewards others receive—that is, **reward power.** For example, instructors have reward power over students because they may reward them with high grades and glowing letters of recommendation. In the case of managers, the rewards available may be either tangible, such as raises and promotions, or intangible, such as praise and recognition. In both cases, access to these desired outcomes gives power to the individuals who control them.

Coercive power. In contrast, power also results from the capacity to control punishments—that is, **coercive power.** Although most managers do not like using the threat of punishments, it is a fact of organizational life that many people rely on coercive power. If any boss has ever directly told you, "do what I say, or else," or even implied it, you are probably all too familiar with coercive power. Often, people have power simply because

FIGURE 12.5

Types of Individual Power: A Summary
Individual power consists of two major types—*position power* (stemming from one's formal organizational role) and *personal power* (stemming from one's personal characteristics). Four specific types of power fall under each category.

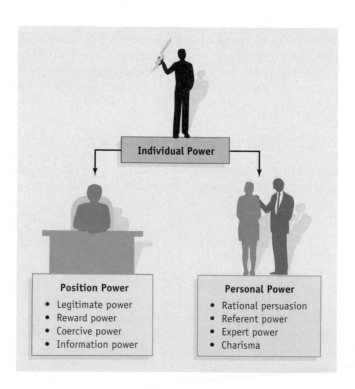

Individual Power

Position Power
- Legitimate power
- Reward power
- Coercive power
- Information power

Personal Power
- Rational persuasion
- Referent power
- Expert power
- Charisma

others know that they have the opportunity to punish them, even if the threat of doing so is not made explicit. For example, in the military, when your commanding officer asks you to do something, you may comply because that request can turn into an order with severe consequences for not going along. In private organizations, implied threats of demotions, suspensions without pay, and assignments to undesirable duties may enhance the coercive power of many managers.

Information power. The fourth source of power available to people by virtue of their positions is based on the data and other knowledge—known as **information power.** Traditionally, people in top positions have available to them unique sources of information that are not available to others (e.g., knowledge of company performance, market trends, etc.). As they say, "knowledge is power," and such information greatly contributes to the power of people in many jobs. Although information power still exists, it is becoming a less potent source of influence in many of today's organizations. The reason is that technology has made it possible for more information to be available to more people than ever before. As a result, information in many companies is no longer the unique property of a few people holding special positions.

information power
The extent to which a supervisor provides a subordinate with the information needed to do the job.

Personal Power: Influence That Comes from the Individual

So far, all the sources of influence we've discussed have been based on an individual's position in an organization. However, this is not the only way people are able to influence others. As summarized on the right side of Figure 12.5, power can also derive from an individual's own unique qualities or characteristics. This is known as **personal power.** There are four sources of personal power: *rational persuasion, referent power, expert power,* and *charisma.*

personal power
The power that one derives because of his or her individual qualities or characteristics.

Rational persuasion. In the early 1990s Apple Computer's former chairman John Scully didn't like what he saw when he looked into the future. Apple was doing well, but computer sales threatened to flatten out in the years ahead. The future of the company, he envisioned, involved applying Apple's user-friendly digital technology in new areas. Integrating telephones, computers, televisions, and entertainment systems was the key. So, Scully's first task was to get Apple's Chief Operating Officer Michael H. Spindler and the board of directors to share his dream. After drawing on all his knowledge of the computer business and carefully studying what needed to be done to make the dream a reality, using **rational persuasion** Scully thoroughly explained his plan for changing Apple from a single-product company with a straightforward distribution system to a multi-product, multibusiness conglomerate. Spindler and the board were convinced, and Apple's new strategy was launched. (As we know, however, this strategy failed. With the introduction of the iMac computer in 1998, Apple returned to its core business—selling only simple, easy-to-use computers.)

rational persuasion
Using logical arguments and factual evidence to convince others that an idea is acceptable.

Expert power. Scully's ideas were accepted partly because he argued persuasively for them but also for another reason: He had considerable expertise in the business. In other words, he possessed a high degree of **expert power.** In a similar manner, the conductor of a symphony orchestra or band has expert power; the musicians follow this person's directions and lead because the conductor is a recognized expert in the field. Once experts have proven themselves, their power over others can be considerable. After all, people will respect and want to follow those in the know.

Should a supervisor's expertise be shown to be lacking, any power he or she may have based on that expertise is threatened. Because no one is expected to be an expert on everything, this is not necessarily a serious problem. The supervisor can simply admit his or her shortcomings and seek guidance from others. Problems do develop, however, when someone in a position of power has not yet developed a level of expertise that is acknowledged and respected by lower-ranking persons (especially when these individuals believe they are more expert!). In short, people who have not demonstrated their expertise clearly lack an important source of power. In contrast, those

expert power
The individual power base derived from an individual's recognized superior skills and abilities in a certain area.

BEST PRACTICES
JOE TORRE: THE YANKEES' POWER HITTER WITHOUT A BAT

Arguably, few baseball teams have been as successful as the New York Yankees, and even fewer Yankee managers have been as successful as Joe Torre in leading this storied franchise to success. In his first six years as manager (1996 through 2001), Torre led the Yankees to five World Series appearances and four victories. Regarded by experts to be "a master manager in the clubhouse," it's clear that Torre has incredible power over his team.[14] And, given that Yankee players have had more than their share of disharmony and problems with substance abuse in recent years, the fact that Torre has been so successful in getting through to his players—and leading them to remarkable success on the field—makes his record that much more remarkable. As such, it is worthwhile to take a few choice tips from Torre's playbook about how to use power.

- *Talk to players one-on-one.* Many coaches like to gather members of their teams around them and make them listen to motivational speeches. Instead of doing this, Torre builds power by developing close relationships with his players—an objective he achieves by holding one-on-one meetings with them. In these sessions, he not only monitors what's on his players' minds, but also gets them to think about things from his perspective.

whose expertise is highly regarded are among the most powerful individuals in their organizations.

Referent power. Another source of personal power centers around the extent to which individuals are liked or respected by others. Such respect may stem, in part, from expertise, but it can also derive from other sources, too—personable likableness, a good reputation, high social skills.[13] Individuals who are liked and respected by others can get them to alter their actions through their **referent power.** Senior managers who possess desirable qualities and good reputations may find that they have referent power over younger managers who identify with them and wish to emulate them.

Charisma. Some people are liked so much by others that they are said to have the quality of **charisma**—an engaging and magnetic personality. What makes such individuals so influential? There appear to be several factors involved. First, highly charismatic people have definite visions of the future of their organizations and how to get there. The late Mary Kay Ash, the founder of Mary Kay Cosmetics, is widely regarded to be such a visionary. Second, people with charisma tend to be excellent communicators. They tend to rely on colorful language and exciting metaphors to excite the crowd. They also supplement their words with emotionally expressive and animated gestures. Third, charismatic individuals inspire trust. Their integrity is never challenged and is a source of their strength. President Franklin D. Roosevelt has been so described by many historians as a charismatic leader (we will discuss charismatic leaders more thoroughly in Chapter 13). Fourth, people with charisma make others feel good about themselves. They are receptive to others' feelings and acknowledge them readily. "Congratulations on a job well done" is a phrase that may flow freely from a charismatic individual.

To summarize, people may influence others because of the jobs or positions they hold, their individual characteristics, or both. When you consider these factors, it's not difficult to understand why large differences exist in most organizations with respect to personal power: Some have it, and some do not. For a look at the way one highly successful manager of a baseball team uses power, see the Best Practices Section above.

referent power
The individual power base derived from the degree to which one is liked and admired by others.

charisma
An attitude of enthusiasm and optimism that is contagious; an aura of leadership.

- *Build intensity in moderation.* Although some coaches like to whip their team members into a frenzy, Torre has found that he can be far more influential by keeping players' emotional levels down. Making players too emotional, he has found, interferes with their ability to concentrate on what they're doing on the field.
- *Make everyone feel important.* A key source of Torre's power over his players comes from their recognition of his respect for their talent and ability. Torre makes everyone feel important—even players who are only rarely used. Reinforcing Torre's philosophy, utility player Luis Sojo hit the game-winning home run in the final game of the 2000 World Series.
- *Remain loyal to players in slumps.* In baseball, batting slumps (i.e., long periods without hits) are inevitable—and as a long-time player himself, Torre knows it. What's more, his players know that as a former player (playing catcher, first-base, and third-base from 1960 through 1977) he can appreciate it. Rather than rejecting a player suffering from a slump by making him feel bad about himself, Torre kicks into action as an expert, teaching the player how to get out of his slump.
- *Be a buffer from the administration.* Yankee players appreciate the fact that Torre bears the brunt of owner George Steinbrenner's impatience, thereby protecting them from his sometimes erratic ways. In so doing, Torre enables players to concentrate on the game of baseball without getting involved in front office politics.

Although you might not be a manager of a major league sports team, we think that there's lots to be learned from the way Joe Torre uses power. If emulating his ways leads you to experience the same degree of success that Torre has enjoyed with the Yankees, you surely will be doing extremely well.

Power: How Is It Used?

What bases of power do you use? Chances are good that you don't rely on just one but use several, including different types of power on different occasions. Not surprisingly, researchers in the field of OB have found that the various power bases are closely related to each other in how they are used.[15]

For example, the more someone uses coercive power, the less that person is liked and, hence, the lower his or her referent power tends to be. Similarly, managers who have expert power also are likely to have legitimate power because people accept their expertise as a basis for having power over them. In addition, the higher someone's organizational position, the more legitimate power that person has, which in turn, is usually accompanied by greater opportunities to use reward and coercion.[16] Clearly, then, the various bases of power should not be thought of as completely separate and distinct from each other. They are often used together in varying combinations.

What bases of power do people prefer to use? Although the answer is complex, research has shown that people most prefer using expert power and least prefer using coercive power.[17] These findings are limited to the power bases we've identified thus far. However, when we broaden the question and ask people to report exactly what sources of power they have on their jobs, a fascinating picture emerges. Figure 12.6 presents the results of a survey in which 216 CEOs of American corporations were asked to rank-order the importance of a series of specific sources of power.[18] The numbers reflect the percentage of executives who included that source of power among their top three choices. These findings indicate not only that top executives rely on a broad range of powers but also that they base these powers on support from people located in a host of other places throughout their organizations.

Although many different forms of power tend to be used to influence subordinates, research has shown that expert power is the preferred form to influence peers and superiors.[19] After all, it is almost always appropriate to try to get others to go along with you if you justify your attempt on the basis of your expertise. In contrast, coercive tactics tend to be frowned upon in general and are especially inappropriate when one is attempting to influence a higher-ranking person.[20] Influencing superiors is tricky

FIGURE 12.6

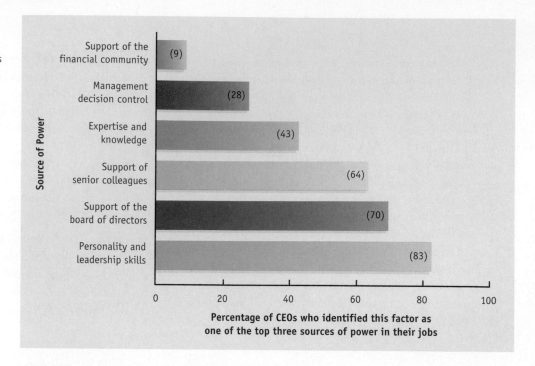

American CEOs: What Are Their Power Bases?
A survey of more than 200 American CEOs revealed that they obtained their power primarily by cultivating the support of others at different levels throughout the organization.
(*Source:* Based on data appearing in Stewart, 1999; see Note 18.)

because of the *counterpower* they have. When attempting to influence another who is believed to have no power at his or her disposal, one doesn't have to worry about fear of retaliation. When dealing with an individual with considerably greater power, however, one can do little other than simply comply with that more powerful person.

The situation is complicated, however, by the fact that one party may have higher power on one dimension, and another party may have higher power on another dimension. Consider, for example, the case of secretaries who have acquired power because they have been with their companies for many years. They know the ropes and can get things done for you if they want, or they can get you hopelessly bogged down in red tape. Their expert knowledge gives them a great sense of power over others. Although they may lack the legitimate power of their executive bosses, secretaries' expertise can be a valuable source of counterpower over those with more formal power. (To see how scientists measure different types of power and to make some preliminary judgments about the types of power your own supervisor uses, see the Individual Exercise on pages 465–466.)

Empowerment: The Shifting Bases of Power in Today's Organizations

A phenomenon is occurring in a growing number of today's organizations: Power is shifting out of the offices of managers and into the hands of employees themselves. Many of today's employees are not being "managed" in the traditional, authoritarian styles that have been used by managers of generations past. Instead, power is shifting down the ladder to teams of workers allowed to make decisions themselves. Survey findings tell the story clearly: When asked about how much power they currently had compared to 10 years ago, only 19 percent of CEOs surveyed said they now had more power. Thirty-six percent indicated that they had the same amount of power. However, the largest group, 42 percent, indicated that they had less power.[21] These figures are in keeping with the idea of **empowerment**—a process in which employees are given increasing amounts of autonomy and discretion in connection with their work.[22]

empowerment
The process in which employees are given increasing amounts of autonomy and discretion in connection with their work.

As you might imagine, empowerment is not just a simple yes-or-no option, but a matter of degree (see Figure 12.7).[23] At one end of the scale are jobs, such as working on assembly lines, in which workers have virtually no power to determine how to do their work. At the opposite end are jobs in which employees have complete control over what they do and how they do it. We see this at companies using self-managed work teams, as described

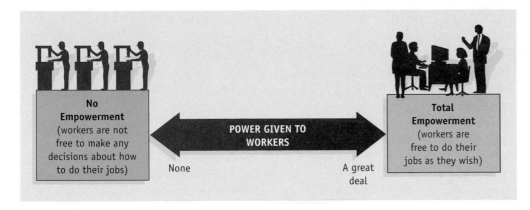

FIGURE 12.7
The Empowerment Continuum: Relinquishing Control Is a Matter of Degree
As shown here, empowering subordinate workers may take several different forms, ranging from giving workers complete power to determine how to do their jobs to giving them no power at all.

in Chapter 8. For example, at Chapparel Steel managers are free to hire, train, and use new employees however they think best.[24] At W. L. Gore, the empowerment philosophy is so strongly entrenched that employees work without any fixed, assigned sets of responsibilities.[25] Between these two extremes are companies whose employees have some degree of responsibility for their work and have a voice in important decisions but are not completely free to work however they see fit. A growing number of companies fall into this category, including the General Motors Saturn plant in Spring Hill, Tennessee.[26]

When employees are empowered, their supervisors are less likely to be "bosses" who push people around (using coercive power) and more likely to serve as teachers or "facilitators" who guide their teams by using their knowledge and experience (i.e., their expert power). In the words of John Ring, the director of Okidata (the Tokyo-based maker of printers and other office tools), "to influence people you have to prove you're right."[27]

Whereas traditional managers tell people what to do and how and when to do it, supervisors of empowered workers are more inclined to ask questions to get people to solve problems and to allow them to make decisions on their own. And in some cases, they may even get to evaluate their bosses. This is precisely what happens at Superior Bank FSB, where employees complete an "Improve Your Boss" assessment tool. When she received the ratings provided by the people in her department, Sonia Russomanno learned that she had earned a "B." Her reaction? Relief that it wasn't worse! But she was disappointed, too. "I'm not as wonderful as I thought I was," she remarked. But she learned a lot, too. "I thought I was awesome at the vision thing," says Russomanno. And although she thought, prior to the review by her staff, that rewarding employees was one of her strengths, their ratings painted a different picture. So Russomanno vowed to improve—just as her employees often did after receiving their own yearly performance reviews.[28]

If the practices we've been describing here don't square with your experiences, don't be surprised. Because most managers are afraid of relinquishing control, the empowered employee is still in the minority in the vast majority of today's organizations.[29] However, experts predict a change in that direction is coming fast.[30] If this prediction is correct, as we believe it is, we can look forward to significant changes in the way people will use power in organizations in the years ahead.

Employees' Reactions to Empowerment: Always Positive?

If empowerment is indeed a growing trend in today's organizations, an important question follows: How do employees react to it? Growing evidence suggests that, in general, they respond very favorably.[31] For instance, consider Xerox. Since February 1992, a corporate reorganization plan at Xerox has encouraged employees to take greater responsibility over their work. Nowhere in the company has this plan been more completely implemented than in its sprawling distribution center outside Atlanta. The head of that facility considers the 24 hourly-paid union workers as managers and treats them as such. They are free to take responsibility for their own jobs and to solve problems as they see fit. And that's just what they've done. For example, employees have found ways to save the company money on trash removal (by recycling) and in shipping costs (by

OB IN A DIVERSE WORLD
EMPOWERMENT IN LOW POWER DISTANCE AND HIGH POWER DISTANCE CULTURES

Cultures differ greatly, and one of the ways in which they vary involves the extent to which inequalities among people associated with hierarchies are seen as appropriate. In high power distance cultures ("vertical" societies), such differences are viewed as natural and acceptable and people are comfortable with hierarchical distinctions.[36] In low power distance cultures ("horizontal" societies), by contrast, differences in power are viewed as less acceptable and people feel uncomfortable with distinctions based on position or rank. Examples of high power distance cultures include India and Japan, whereas examples of low power distance cultures are the United States and Mexico.

How will people in these two kinds of cultures react to empowerment? Presumably, people in low power distance cultures will react more favorably. After all, empowerment tends to reduce distinctions based on hierarchies so that managers and their subordinates are on a more equal footing, and this would be consistent with the basic values of a low power distance culture. In contrast, people in high power distance cultures might find empowerment somewhat disturbing: They are comfortable with

using lighter weight pallets). They even have reorganized warehousing procedures such that 99.9 percent of orders now ship on time. Absenteeism is almost nonexistent and productivity is up dramatically. Xerox officials are now studying the Atlanta facility in the hope of duplicating its success elsewhere in the company.[32]

Another example of the benefits of empowerment is provided by Omni Hotels. This company implemented a program called the Power of One in June 1990 to help combat exceptionally high employee turnover and low levels of satisfaction among guests. This involved training all employees to make independent decisions that benefit guests—even if it meant bending the rules. Frontline employees also were empowered to listen to angry customers and to give them whatever they wanted (within reason, of course).[33] Within the first month, customer satisfaction surged 16 percent, and after the first year, turnover was reduced to 42 percent from 65 percent before the plan was introduced. The hotel chain has enjoyed higher profits ever since. In fact, it placed among the top three upscale domestic hotel chains in a recent J.D. Power and Associates survey.[34]

These and many other similar success stories indicate that empowerment does indeed often confer important benefits both on employees and their organizations.[35] And these beneficial effects have occurred in companies where tall hierarchies of power tend to prevail. If empowerment strategies can be implemented successfully in such organizations, they should be even easier to introduce in "flatter" ones, where people have less formally defined powers. Clearly, leaders of organizations of all sizes have good reason to consider the benefits that may result from granting power to their employees. (Do employees all over the world react in the same way to empowerment? The answer seems to be "no." For information on this interesting fact, see the OB in a Diverse World section above.)

GROUP OR SUBUNIT POWER: STRUCTURAL DETERMINANTS

So far, we have examined the uses of power by individuals. However, in organizations, it is not only people acting alone who wield power, but also groups.[38] Traditionally, organizations are divided into subunits that are given responsibility for different functions such as finance, human resource management, marketing, and research and develop-differences based on hierarchies and might be somewhat uncomfortable with the blurring of such differences produced by empowerment.

In fact, recent research findings confirm these predictions. In one intriguing project, a team of researchers asked employees of a multinational corporation to indicate the extent to which empowerment was occurring in their company and to rate their satisfaction with their work, their supervisors, and their coworkers.[37] These measures were collected in four different countries: the United States, Poland, Mexico, and India. The first three are relatively low in power distance, whereas the fourth (India) is relatively high. As predicted, there was a positive relationship between empowerment and job satisfaction in the United States, Poland, and Mexico but a negative relationship between these factors in India. In other words, in the United States, Poland, and Mexico, the greater was employees' empowerment, the greater was their job satisfaction. In India, however, the reverse was true.

These findings indicate that although empowerment is often a positive development in organizations, this is not always so. In fact, in cultures where people are used to distinctions based on hierarchies, employees may find empowerment a strange concept because it is inconsistent with traditional cultural values. Once again, then, we come face-to-face with a basic fact of organizational life: To succeed, management practices must be adapted to take account of cultural differences. Failing to do so runs the real risk of accepting a "one-practice-fits-all" mentality, and that, in turn, is bound to fail.

ment (we will describe these arrangements more fully in Chapter 15). The formal departments devoted to these various organizational activities often must direct the actions of other groups, and this, in turn, requires them to have power. What are the sources of such power? By what means do formal organizational groups successfully control the activities of other groups? Two conceptual approaches have been proposed to answer these questions—the *resource-dependency model* and the *strategic contingencies model,* and we'll consider each here.

The Resource-Dependency Model: Controlling Critical Resources

It is not difficult to think of an organization as a complex set of subunits that are constantly exchanging resources with each other. By this, we mean that formal organizational departments may be both giving to and receiving from other departments such valued commodities as money, personnel, equipment, supplies, and information. These critical resources are necessary for the successful operation of organizations.

Various subunits often depend on others for such resources. To illustrate this point, imagine a large organization that develops, produces, and sells its products. The sales department provides financial resources that enable the research and development department to create new products. Of course, it cannot do so effectively without information from the marketing department about what consumers are interested in buying and how much they would be willing to pay. The production department has to do its part by manufacturing the goods on time, but only if the purchasing department can supply the needed raw materials—and at a price the finance department accepts as permitting the company to turn a profit.

It is easy to see how the various organizational subunits are involved in a complex set of interrelationships. To the extent that one subunit controls the resources on which another subunit depends, it may be said to have power over it. After all, controlling resources allows groups to influence successfully the actions of other groups. Subunits that control more resources than others may be considered more powerful in the organization. Indeed, such imbalances, or *asymmetries,* in the pattern of resource dependencies occur normally in organizations. The more one group depends on another for needed resources, the less power it has (see Figure 12.8).

FIGURE 12.8

**The Resource-Dependency Model:
An Example**
The *resource-dependency model* of organizational power explains that subunits acquire power when they control critical resources needed by other subunits. In this example, the accounting department would be considered more powerful than either the production department or the marketing department because it controls more important resources.

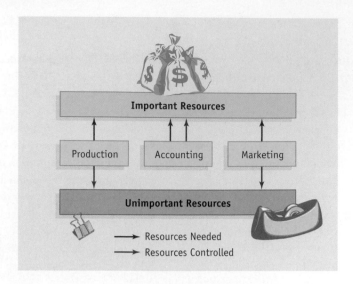

resource-dependency model
The view that power resides within subunits that are able to control the greatest share of valued organizational resources.

The **resource-dependency model** proposes that a subunit's power is based on the degree to which it controls the resources required by other subunits.[39] Thus, although all subunits may contribute something to an organization, the most powerful ones are those that contribute the most important resources. Controlling the resources other departments need puts a subunit in a better position to bargain for the resources it, in turn, requires.

To illustrate this point, let's consider a classic study of differences between power wielded by departments in a large university.[40] Within a university, the various academic departments may be very unequal with respect to the power they possess. For example, compared to others, some may have more students, be more prestigious in their national reputation, receive greater grant support, and have more representatives on important university committees. As such, they would be expected to have greater control over valued resources. This was found to be the case within the large state university examined in this study. Specifically, the more powerful departments proved to be those that were most successful in gaining scarce and valued resources from the university (e.g., funds for graduate student fellowships, faculty research grants, and summer faculty fellowships). As a result, they became even more powerful, suggesting that within organizations the rich subunits do indeed tend to get richer.

A question that follows from this conclusion is: How do various organizational subunits come to be more powerful to begin with? That is, why might certain departments come to control the most resources when an organization is newly formed? Insight into this question is provided by a fascinating study of the semiconductor industry in California.[41] Using personal interviews, market research data, and archival records, it was found that two main factors account for how much power an organizational subunit has: (1) the period within which the company was founded, and (2) the background of the entrepreneur starting the company. For example, because research and development functions were critical among the earliest semiconductor firms (founded from 1958 to 1966, when semiconductors were new), this department had the most power among the oldest firms. In short, the importance of each area of corporate activity at the time the company started operations determined the relative power of that area years later (in 1985, when the study was conducted).

It also was found that the most powerful organizational subunits tended to be those that represented the founder's area of expertise. Thus, for example, the marketing and sales departments of companies founded by experts in marketing and sales tended to have the greatest amounts of power. This research provides an important missing link in our understanding of the attainment of subunit power within organizations. The tendency for the greatest corporate power to reside in areas of the founder's expertise applies to companies throughout the world. As one case in point, Mr. Ibuka, the founder of Sony (then Tokyo Telecommunications Laboratory), was an engineer—a very powerful functional area in that company to this day.

The resource-dependency model suggests that a key determinant of subunit power is the control of valued resources. However, as we will now see, it is not only control over resources that determines organizational power but also control over the activities of other subunits.

The Strategic Contingencies Model: Power Through Dependence

In many companies, the accounting department has the responsibility of approving or disapproving funds requested by various departments. To the extent that it has this power, its actions greatly affect the activities of other units, which depend on its decisions. Specifically, other departments' operations are *contingent* on what the accounting department does. To the extent that a department is able to control the relative power of various organizational subunits by virtue of its actions, it is said to have control over *strategic contingencies*. For example, if the accounting department consistently approved the budget requests of the production department but rejected the budget requests of the marketing department, it would be making the production department more powerful.

Where do the strategic contingencies lie within organizations? In a classic study researchers found out that power was distributed differently (i.e., across various departments) in different industries.[42] They found that within successful firms, strategic contingencies are controlled by the departments that are most important for organizational success. For example, within a food-processing industry, where it was critical for new products to be developed and sold, successful firms had strategic contingencies controlled by the sales and research departments. In the container manufacturing field, where the timely delivery of high-quality goods is a critical determinant of organizational success, successful firms placed most of the decision-making power in the sales and production departments. Thus, successful firms focused the control over strategic contingencies within the subunits most responsible for their organization's success.

What factors give subunits control over strategic contingencies? The **strategic contingencies model** suggests that several are crucial; these are summarized in Figure 12.9.[43] First, power may be enhanced by subunits that have the *capacity to reduce the levels of uncertainty faced by others*. Any department that can shed light on the uncertain situations organizations may face (e.g., those regarding future markets, government regulation, availability of needed supplies, financial security, etc.) can be expected to wield the most organizational power. Accordingly, the balance of power within organizations may be expected to change as organizational conditions change.

Consider, for example, changes that have taken place over the years in public utility companies. When public utilities first began, the engineers tended to wield the most power. But now that these companies have matured and face problems of litigation and

strategic contingencies model
A view explaining power in terms of a subunit's capacity to control the activities of other subunits. A subunit's power is enhanced when (1) it can reduce the level of uncertainty experienced by other subunits, (2) it occupies a central position in the organization, and (3) its activities are highly indispensable to the organization.

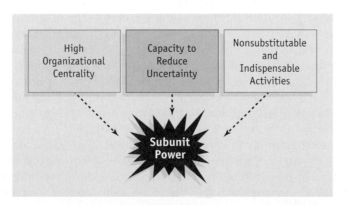

FIGURE 12.9
Strategic Contingencies Model: Identifying Sources of Subunit Power
The *strategic contingencies model* explains intraorganizational power in terms of the capacity of some subunits to control the actions of others. Subunit power may be enhanced by the factors shown here.

governmental regulation (particularly over nuclear power), the power has shifted to lawyers.[44] A similar shift toward the power of the legal department has occurred in recent years in the area of human resource management, where a complex set of laws and governmental regulations has created a great deal of uncertainty for organizations. Powerful subunits are those that can help reduce organizational uncertainty.

Second, subunits control power to the extent that they possess a *high degree of centrality in the organization.* Some organizational subunits perform functions that are more central and others more peripheral. For example, some departments—such as accounting—may have to be consulted by most others before any action can be taken, giving them a central position in their organizations. Centrality also is high when a unit's duties have an immediate effect on an organization. For example, the immediate effects would be much more dramatic on an auto manufacturer if the production lines stopped than if market research activities ceased. The central connection of some departments to organizational success dictates the power they wield.

Third, a subunit controls power when its *activities are nonsubstitutable and indispensable.* If any group can perform a certain function, subunits responsible for controlling that function may not be particularly powerful. In a hospital, for example, personnel on surgical teams are certainly more indispensable than personnel in the maintenance department because fewer individuals have the skills needed to perform their unit's duties. Whenever a department easily can replace its employees with others from either within or outside it, that department tends to wield very little organizational power.

The strategic contingencies model has been tested and supported in many organizational studies.[45] For example, an investigation conducted in several companies found that a subunit's power within an organization was higher when it could reduce uncertainty, when it occupied a central place in the work flow, and when it performed functions that other subunits could not perform.[46] The strategic contingencies model should be considered a valuable source of information about the factors influencing the power of subunits within organizations.

ORGANIZATIONAL POLITICS: POWER IN ACTION

organizational politics

Actions by individuals that are directed toward the goal of furthering their own self-interest without regard for the well-being of others or their organizations.

When individuals working in a wide range of industries and companies are asked to list the key problems they face at work, they mention a wide range of difficulties. Near the top of most lists, though, is **organizational politics.** Although different people mean slightly different things when they use this phrase, it is generally used in OB to refer to actions by individuals that are directed toward the goal of furthering their own self-interest without regard for the well-being of others or their organizations. You probably have encountered many instances of organizational politics yourself—situations in which individuals with whom you worked took actions not officially approved by your organization designed to attain their personal goals.[47] For example, a colleague may put his name on someone else's report or develop close friendships with others who are in a position to help him get a promotion.

If this sounds to you like something that is a bit selfish and appears to be an abuse of organizational power, you are correct. Organizational politics *does* involve placing one's self-interests above the interests of the organization. Indeed, this element of using power to foster one's own interests distinguishes organizational politics from uses of power that are approved and accepted by organizations.[48]

Not surprisingly, many people in the business world condemn organizational politics and those who engage in it. For example, as the outspoken billionaire and former presidential candidate H. Ross Perot put it, "I don't want any corporate politicians . . . some guy that wants to move ahead at the expense of others."[49] Also, in recent years, growing numbers of people have found organizational politics so intolerable that they have left the corporate world altogether, venturing out on their own (see Figure 12.10).

In this discussion of organizational politics, we'll first consider the antecedents of such behavior—why it occurs. Next we'll describe some of the important forms it takes;

FIGURE 12.10

Organizational Politics Made Him Leave the Corporate World
Working out of his home in suburban Washington, DC, Lak Vohra publishes the *Party Digest,* a monthly letter about business and social networking events. The self-proclaimed "party guru" left the corporate world, complaining how very miserable he felt because of organizational politics. Mr. Vohra is just one of a growing number of people who are becoming their own bosses because they find organizational politics intolerable.

finally, we'll examine its effects. In the next section, we'll consider some of the complex ethical issues it raises.

The Antecedents of Politics: Why and When It Occurs

If you have worked in several different organizations, you probably realize that although politics occurs almost everywhere, the amount of such activity varies greatly. In some settings, people seem to spend a large proportion of their time engaging in organizational politics, whereas in others such actions are less frequent or less pervasive. This raises an important question: What factors encourage—or discourage—such behavior? Research findings suggest that both personal and organizational variables play a role.

Personal and organizational variables. Turning first to personal factors, it appears that people high in Machiavellianism, a personality factor we discussed in Chapter 3, are more likely to engage in such behavior than persons low in Machiavellianism.[50] Given that high Machiavellians believe that it is acceptable to use others for their personal needs, this is hardly surprising. Other research indicates that *self-monitoring* (which we also discussed in Chapter 3) also may be related to organizational politics: People high on this dimension, who are sometimes described as "social chameleons" (those who do whatever it takes to get others to like them), are more likely to engage in politics than persons low in self-monitoring (those who tend to behave in much the same way across a wide range of situations).[51] Finally, it has been found that people who engage in organizational politics seem to show several skills or traits that equip them for this role: They often are described as being socially adept, popular, extroverted, self-confident, aggressive, ambitious, devious, intelligent, and articulate. No wonder they often succeed in their efforts to get ahead, no matter what.[52]

Turning next to organizational factors, it appears that to the extent certain conditions exist in an organization, political behavior is likely to occur. Specifically, to the extent that goals and roles are ambiguous, the organization has a history or climate of political activity, and resources are scarce, political behavior is likely to occur.[53] Furthermore, to the extent that an organization is highly centralized (with decision making and power concentrated in the hands of a small number of individuals or units) and different individuals or units in the organization have conflicting interests or goals, political behavior also is likely to occur. Figure 12.11 provides a summary of the factors that have been found to facilitate the occurrence of organizational politics.

Politics in human resource management. Another important finding concerning organizational politics is that it often occurs in connection with key human resource man-

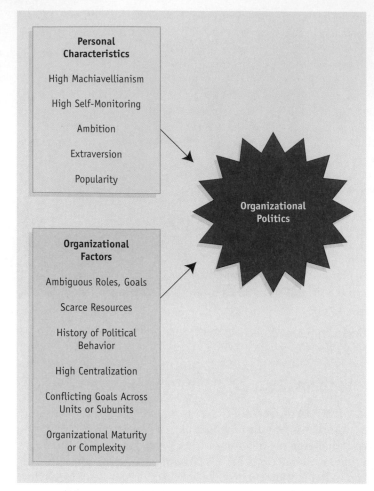

Personal Characteristics

High Machiavellianism

High Self-Monitoring

Ambition

Extraversion

Popularity

Organizational Factors

Ambiguous Roles, Goals

Scarce Resources

History of Political Behavior

High Centralization

Conflicting Goals Across Units or Subunits

Organizational Maturity or Complexity

Organizational Politics

agement activities such as performance appraisal, personnel selection, and compensation decisions.[54] Given that there is often a certain amount of ambiguity associated with evaluating another's performance, this leaves lots of room for individuals to cultivate certain images as they perform this task. As a result, performance ratings sometimes are more a reflection of the rater's interest in promoting a certain image of himself or herself than in accurately evaluating another's behavior.[55] Similarly, when making personnel decisions, people are at least as much concerned about the implications of their hires for their own ideal careers (e.g., will this person support me or make me look bad?) as they are concerned about doing what's best for the organization.[56]

Finally, pay raise decisions have been shown to be politically motivated, as well. Specifically, researchers conducting a management simulation exercise found that managers gave the highest raises to individuals who threatened to complain if they didn't get a substantial raise, particularly if it were known that these people had political connections within the organization.[57] Taken together, these findings suggest that the very nature of human resource management activities in organizations makes them prime candidates for activities within which organizational politics is likely to be activated.

Politics and the organizational life span. The occurrence of political behavior also varies with an organization's stage of development.[58] When an organization is new, it may have little or no structure and is often guided by the philosophy of the founder. During this stage, the entrepreneur gains political power by presenting his or her ideas as rational to the employees, who accept this person's image of the corporate mission. The founder usually has complete access to information and makes decisions based on his or her own values. Explaining these decisions to subordinates is a way of inculcating these values to others in the organization and thereby exercising power over them. Political activity is not particularly likely during this stage.

As organizations mature and become more complex, however, they tend to departmentalize, creating conditions in which the vested interests of different groups are likely to come into conflict. Political means may be used to gain an advantage in such a situation. And later, when organizations begin to decline, subunits may be quite insecure and the need for political action may be great as people and groups compete for the power to control (and perhaps turn around) the organization. A period of decline reflects a time of great uncertainty and is, thus, a period in which political activity is likely to be quite intense. For example, researchers found that staff members employed in California school districts experiencing decline tended to have more intense competitive interactions and were at odds with each other more than members of similar organizations during periods of growth.[59] Clearly, the use of political practices in organizations is likely to be affected by its degree of maturity.

Political Tactics: What Forms Do They Take?

Now that we've addressed the question of why and when political behaviors occur, let's consider a closely related issue: What specific forms do they take? In other words, what do people do to promote their own selfish ends by influencing others? Many strategies exist, but among the most important are the following.[60]

1. *Gaining control over and selective use of information.* Information is the lifeblood of organizations. Therefore, controlling information and determining who knows what is one of the most important ways of exercising power in organizations. Although outright lying and falsifying information are relatively rare (in part because of the consequences of getting caught), there are other ways of controlling information to enhance one's organizational position. For example, you might (1) withhold information that makes you look bad (e.g., negative sales information), (2) avoid contact with those who may ask for information you would prefer not to disclose, (3) be very selective in the information you disclose, or (4) overwhelm others with information that may not be completely relevant. These are all ways of controlling the nature and degree of information people have at their disposal. Such information control can be critical.

   An analysis of the organizational restructuring of AT&T's Phone Stores in the 1980s revealed that control was transferred through the effective manipulation, distortion, and creation of information.[61] A vice president's secret plan to feed incomplete and inaccurate information to the CEO was responsible for that vice president's winning control over the stores.

2. *Cultivating a favorable impression.* People interested in enhancing their organizational control commonly engage in some degree of image building—attempts to enhance the goodness of their impressions on others. Such efforts may take many forms, such as (1) "dressing for success," (2) associating oneself with the successful accomplishments of others (or, in extreme cases, taking credit for others' successes), or (3) simply calling attention to one's own successes and positive characteristics.[62]

3. *Building powerful coalitions.* To successfully influence people, it is often useful to gain the support of others within the organization. Managers may, for example, lobby for their ideas before they officially present them at meetings, ensuring that others are committed to them in advance and thereby avoiding the embarrassment of public rejection. Sometimes, of course, it's difficult even to get an audience with high-ranking organizational officials so as to make your argument. Not letting this become a barrier, a particularly ingenious up-and-coming executive at Lotus Development Co. admits to having rehearsed an "elevator speech" so that he'd have a chance to present his point to the company president should he happen to run into him in the elevator.[63]

4. *Blaming and attacking others.* One of the most popular tactics of organizational politics involves blaming and attacking others when bad things happen. A commonly used political tactic is finding a **scapegoat**, a person who is made to take the blame for someone else's failure or wrongdoing. A supervisor, for example, may

scapegoat
Someone who is made to take the blame for someone else's failure or wrongdoing.

explain that the failure of a sales plan she designed was based on the serious mistakes of one of her subordinates—even if this is not entirely true. Explaining that "it's his fault" (i.e., making another "take the fall" for an undesirable event) gets the real culprit "off the hook" for it.

Finding a scapegoat can allow the politically astute individual to avoid (or at least minimize) association with the negative situation. For example, research has found when corporate performance drops, powerful chief executives often resort to placing the blame on a lower-ranking individual, protecting themselves from getting fired while their subordinate gets the ax.[64]

5. *Associating with powerful others.* One of the most direct ways to gain power is by connecting oneself with more powerful others. There are several ways to accomplish this. For example, a lower-power person may become more powerful if she has a very powerful mentor, a more powerful and better-established person who can look out for and protect her interests (see Chapter 7).

People also may align themselves with more powerful others by giving them "positive strokes" in the hope of getting these more powerful individuals to like them and help them—the process to which we earlier referred as *ingratiation*.[65] Agreeing with someone more powerful may be an effective way of getting that person to consider you an ally. Such an alliance, of course, may prove indispensable when you are looking for support within an organization. To summarize, having a powerful mentor, forming coalitions, and using ingratiation are all potentially effective ways of gaining power by aligning oneself with others.

6. *Creating obligations and using reciprocity.* Still another way to gain power is to gather a lot of obligations—IOUs from others that will be paid back with interest. People who are adept at using this tactic do favors for others in their organization—favors that cost them relatively little. Later, they attempt to wring major benefits from such obligations. "I helped you," they suggest, "now it's your turn." In a way, this is like the *door-in-the-face technique* people use to get target persons to say "yes." They do relatively little for others but expect a lot in return.

Organizational Politics: Its Effects

Political behavior is selfish by definition. So when people engage in such actions and do so effectively, one result is that they personally benefit: They get the promotions, raises, or power that they are seeking. The effects on other persons and the organization itself, however, can be far more negative (see Figure 12.12). Research findings indicate that the greater the frequency of politics in an organization, the lower are job satisfaction and organizational commitment among its employees.[66] Similarly, the greater the incidence of political behavior, the stronger the intention of employees to leave (voluntary turnover).[67] As discussed in Chapter 5, job satisfaction, commitment, and turnover are all important factors in an organization's performance, so to the extent these are affected by political behavior, important consequences may result.

Importantly, the greater the incidence of politics in an organization, the lower the perceived levels of organizational support reported by employees.[68] Because feelings of support often play a role in individuals' work motivation, the belief that such support is lacking, too, can have strongly negative effects. In sum, although organizational politics may benefit those who are adept at such behavior, its occurrence tends to undermine employees' satisfaction with and commitment to their organizations. And in extreme cases, many individuals—often the best employees—may choose to leave rather than put up with an environment in which politics is widespread.

Interestingly, not everyone reacts to organizational politics in the same way. Research findings confirm what common sense suggests: Some people are bothered by politics more than others. For instance, people low in *conscientiousness*—one of the "Big Five" dimensions of personality we examined in Chapter 3—are more strongly affected in terms of reduced on-the-job performance than persons high in conscientiousness.[69] This is because people high in conscientiousness are reliable, responsible,

FIGURE 12.12
Adverse Effects of Organizational Politics
When the level of political behavior is high in an organization, job satisfaction and organizational commitment may suffer—with the result that good people decide to leave and seek employment elsewhere. Clearly, this is a very negative effect of organizational politics.

and persistent, so they have the tenacity and diligence to get things done even in an environment that is highly political. In contrast, people who are low in conscientiousness lack these characteristics, and so they are more easily distracted or discouraged by politics. In a sense, therefore, political antics are most harmful to the "weakest links" in an organization—those employees who are not top performers anyway.

THE ETHICS OF ORGANIZATIONAL POLITICS

Probably one of the most important effects of organizational power is that it invites corruption. Indeed, the more power an individual has at his or her disposal, the more tempted that person is to use that power toward some immoral or unethical purpose.[70] Obviously, then, the potential is quite real for powerful individuals and organizations to abuse their power and to behave unethically. Because such behaviors are negatively regarded, the most politically astute individuals—including politicians, themselves—often attempt to present themselves as being highly ethical.

Unfortunately, the potential to behave unethically is often very real and, judging from many recent events, difficult to resist. Consider, for example, how greed overtook concerns about the well-being of employees and investors in recent years among top officials of such once-esteemed companies as Enron, Arthur Andersen, GlobalCrossing, WorldCom, and Adelphia Communications who have been alleged to engage in questionable accounting practices for their own personal benefit.[71]

Companies that dump dangerous waste into our rivers and oceans also appear to favor their own interests over public safety and welfare. For example, as you may know, General Electric Corporation was ordered by the Environmental Protection Agency to dredge PCBs from the Hudson River—an operation that ultimately may cost the company billions of dollars. GE had knowingly dumped many tons of this highly dangerous chemical into the river in past decades. As a result of this contamination, it is still not safe to eat fish from the Hudson decades after the dumping ceased (see Figure 12.13).

Given the scope of the problems associated with unethical organizational behaviors, we will focus on the ethical aspects of politics in this final section.[72]

What, If Anything, Is Unethical About Organizational Politics?

A few years ago, over 1,000 professionals in the field of human resources management were surveyed concerning their feelings about the ethics of various managerial practices.[73]

FIGURE 12.13

Environmental Pollution: One Manifestation of Corporate Greed
In an effort to boost its "bottom line" thereby helping executives look good, General Electric allegedly dumped a dangerous chemical (PCB) into the Hudson River for decades. As a result, it is unsafe to eat fish caught in the river. Recently, the Environmental Protection Agency ordered GE to dredge the river to remove these chemicals. The cost? More than a billion dollars.

Interestingly, among the ethical situations considered most serious were several practices that dealt with political activities reflecting an abuse of power. These included practices such as "making personnel decisions based on favoritism instead of job performance" and "basing differences in pay on friendship." In fact, these were the two most frequently cited types of unethical situations faced by human resources managers (with almost 31 percent of the sample indicating that each of these was among *the* most serious violations).

Another type of unethical political behavior (indicated as being most serious by over 23 percent of the sample) was "making arrangements with vendors or consulting agencies leading to personal gain." As shown in Figure 12.14, these actions are in addition to various other types of unethical behavior that represent bias but that are not so clearly self-serving as to constitute political acts.

Given that so many critical ethics violations appear to be politically motivated, self-serving actions, it is not surprising that these happened to be the very behaviors that managers had the greatest difficulty addressing. In fact, only about half of the managers surveyed reported having any success in minimizing a problem such as hiring based on favoritism. The very fact that such behaviors benefit oneself makes them difficult to eliminate. In contrast, it is easier to combat unethical behaviors based on insensitivity (e.g., lack of attention to privacy) because these serve no beneficial functions for the person doing the violating.

Managers tend to be relatively unaware of the political biases underlying their unethical actions, however. Instead, they attribute their actions to the attitudes and behaviors of senior management. Specifically, whereas only 10 percent of the participants attributed unethical behaviors to political pressures, 56 percent attributed unethical behaviors to the attitudes and behaviors of senior management. They blamed top management most frequently for instances of unethical behavior, but they also recognized that top management of organizations tends to be committed to ethical conduct. Despite such commitment, company officials tend to overlook the capacity of human resources managers to help promote their company's ethical values. Too often, they tend to concentrate on using human resources managers for maintaining up-to-date legal information about personnel matters.

But ethics goes well beyond mere compliance with the law. And, society expects companies to go well beyond the ethical minimums. For these reasons—not to mention the long-term success of companies themselves—it is essential for human resource officials to help institute policies that encourage basing personnel-related decisions on job performance instead of favoritism.[74] In view of the potential problems that may arise in organizations in which the amount of political activity is high, it is necessary to consider ways of curbing such behavior.[75] For a look at several ways of doing so, see Table 12.1.

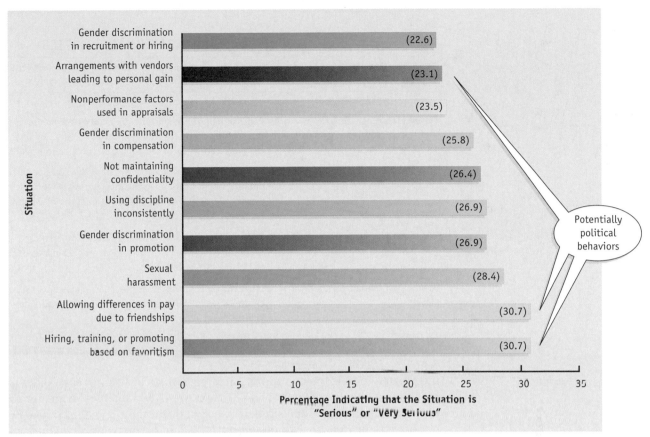

FIGURE 12.14

Political Antics Top the "Most Unethical List"

Among the most widely reported sources of unethical behaviors noted in a survey of human resources managers are those dealing with an especially inappropriate form of political behavior—favoritism.
(*Source:* Based on data reported by the Commerce Clearing House, 1991; see Note 73.)

Assessing the Ethics of Political Behavior

Although there are no clear-cut ways to identify whether a certain organizational action is ethical, we can offer some useful guidelines.[76] For a summary of the central questions associated with assessing the ethics of political behavior, see Figure 12.15.

Are only selfish interests promoted? As a first consideration, we may ask: Will the political tactics promote purely selfish interests, or will they also help meet organizational goals? If only one's personal, selfish interests are nurtured by a political action, it may be considered unethical. Usually, political activity fails to benefit organizational goals, but not always. Suppose, for example, that a group of top corporate executives is consistently making bad decisions that are leading the organization down the road to ruin. Would it be unethical in such a case to use political tactics to try to remove the power holders from their positions? Probably not. In fact, political actions designed to benefit the organization as a whole (as long as they are legal) may be justified as appropriate and highly ethical. After all, they are in the best interest of the entire organization.

Are privacy rights respected? A second question in considering the ethics of organizational politics is: Does the political activity respect the rights of the individuals affected? Generally speaking, actions that violate basic human rights are, of course, considered unethical. For example, dirty political tricks that rely on espionage techniques (such as wiretapping) are not only illegal but also unethical in that they violate the affected individual's *right to privacy.*

However, as you may know, police agencies sometimes are permitted by law to use methods that violate privacy rights (e.g., wiretapping) under circumstances in which

TABLE 12.1 HOW TO COMBAT ORGANIZATIONAL POLITICS

Abolishing organizational politics completely may be impossible but managers can limit its effects. Some of the most successful tactics are summarized here.

SUGGESTION	DESCRIPTION
Clarify job expectations	Political behavior is nurtured by highly ambiguous conditions. To the extent managers help reduce uncertainty (e.g., by giving precise work assignments), they can minimize the likelihood of political behavior.
Open the communication process	People have difficulty fostering their own goals at the expense of organizational goals when the communication process is open to scrutiny. It is hard to "get away with anything" when the system is open for all to examine.
Be a good role model	Employees model the behavior of higher-ranking officials. Accordingly, an openly political manager may encourage subordinates to behave in the same way.
Do not turn a blind eye to game players	Immediately confront an employee who attempts to take credit for another's work. Managers who do not do so send a message that this kind of behavior is acceptable.

the greater good of the community at large is at stake. It is not easy, of course, to weigh the relative benefits of an individual's right to privacy against the greater societal good. Indeed, making such decisions involves a potential misuse of power in itself. It is because of this that society often entrusts such decisions to high courts charged with the responsibility for considering both individual rights and the rights and benefits of the community at large.

Is it fair? There is also a third consideration in assessing the ethics of political action: Does the activity conform to standards of equity and justice; is it fair (see Chapter 6)? Any political behavior that unfairly benefits one party over another may be considered unethical. Paying one person more than another similarly qualified person is one exam-

FIGURE 12.15
Guidelines for Determining Ethical Action
Although assessing the ethicality of a behavior is a complex matter, answers to the three questions shown here can provide a good indication. This flowchart shows the path that must be taken to achieve ethical action.
(*Source:* Based on suggestions by Velasquez, Moberg, & Cavanaugh, 1983; see Note 76.)

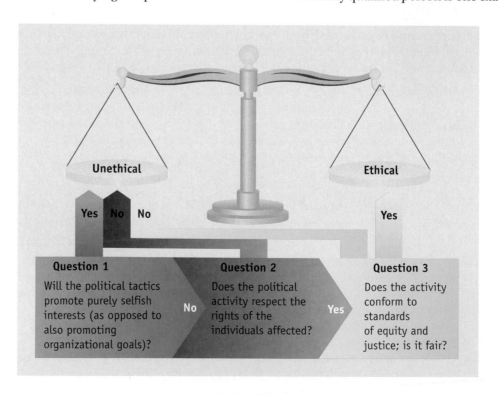

ple. Standards regarding the fair treatment of individuals are often unclear. Not surprisingly, more powerful individuals often use their power to convince others (and themselves!) that they are taking action in the name of justice. That is, they seek to implement seemingly fair rules that benefit themselves at the expense of others.[77] This, of course, represents an abuse of power.

However, we sometimes must consider instances in which violating standards of justice may be considered appropriate. For example, it has been found that managers sometimes give poorly performing employees higher pay than they deserve in the hope of stimulating them to work at higher levels.[78] Although the principle of equity (see Chapter 6) is violated in this case (people should be paid in proportion to their job contributions), the manager may argue that the employee and the organization benefit as a result. Of course, the result may be considered unfair to the other individuals who are not so generously treated. Obviously, we cannot settle this complex issue here. Our point is that, although ethical behavior involves adhering to standards of justice, there may be instances in which violations of these standards may be considered ethically acceptable.

As you probably can tell by now, most matters involving the resolution of moral and ethical issues are quite complex. Each time a political strategy is considered, its potential effects should be evaluated in terms of the questions outlined here. If the practice appears to be ethical based on these considerations, it may be acceptable in that situation. If ethical questions arise, however, alternative actions should be considered.

SUMMARY AND REVIEW OF LEARNING OBJECTIVES

1. Define the concepts of social influence, power, and organizational politics.
When someone attempts to affect another in a desired fashion, that person is said to be using social influence. The concept of power refers to the capacity to change the behavior or attitudes of others in a desired manner. Behaving in a manner that is not officially approved by an organization to meet one's own goals by influencing others is known as organizational politics.

2. Describe the major varieties of social influence that exist.
Social influence may take the forms of rational persuasion, inspirational appeal, consultation, ingratiation, exchange, personal appeal, coalition building, legitimating, and pressure. Other techniques derive from basic principles governing human relations (e.g., reciprocity, commitment, liking) and range from ingratiation through playing hard to get and the door-in-the-face technique.

3. Identify the major types of individual power in organizations.
One major type of power, position power, resides within one's formal organizational position. It includes (1) reward power; (2) coercive power, the capacity to control valued rewards and punishments, respectively; (3), legitimate power, the recognized authority that an individual has by virtue of his or her organizational position; and (4) information power, the power that stems from having special data and knowledge. Another major type of power, personal power, resides within an individual's own unique qualities or characteristics. It includes (1) rational persuasion, using logical arguments and factual evidence to convince others that an idea is acceptable; (2) expert power, the power an individual has because he or she is recognized as having some superior knowledge, skill, or expertise; (3) referent power, influence based on the fact that an individual is admired by others; and (4) charisma, having an engaging and magnetic personality.

4. Describe the two major approaches to the development of subunit power in organizations (the resource-dependency model and the strategic contingencies model).
The resource-dependency model asserts that power resides within the subunits that control the greatest share of valued organizational resources. The strategic contingen-

The Smith Brothers: A Low-Key Approach to Gaining—and Keeping—Organizational Power

Two brothers who are both CEOs of major companies? That's certainly a rarity in the modern world of business. But it is exactly the situation for the Smith brothers, John and Michael. John is chairman of General Motors (GM), while his brother Mike is the retired CEO of Hughes Electronics, Corp., a leading telecommunication and satellite company that is owned by GM. So both are powerful persons, indeed. But how, you may be wondering, did they both acquire so much power—and such a high level of success? People who know them well note that, even as children, they showed tremendous interest in business. Sally Mahoney, who knew the Smith brothers and their parents, recalls that as children they loved to play board games, especially Monopoly. "I can just remember them stacking up those hotels and houses. Money was always very interesting to them," she notes. And the Smiths themselves were aware of this interest from childhood on. "We like business. We grew up in a business-oriented family," Michael Smith says.

Although they attended different schools, the Smith brothers were both described by people who knew them as bright, hardworking, and unassuming. "Ego doesn't show," says M. Hoglund, a retired GM executive who worked with both brothers. "They are great guys to work around and as a result generate a lot of loyalty." David Cole, director of the University of Michigan's Center for the Study of Automotive Transportation, says "Jack will wander down the halls, his head down, trying to be obscure, where the king would be looking around for recognition."

And their orientation toward their organizations rather than their own careers certainly seems to have played an important role in their rise to power. Both Smith brothers are true team players, with genuine concern for the people with whom they work as well as for their companies. As we noted earlier, most top executives strongly prefer to gather power from their personal characteristics—their charisma, expertise, personality—rather than from their position. The Smith brothers seem to understand this lesson very well and have converted it into highly successful careers.

Critical Thinking Questions

1. What bases of personal power contribute to the Smith brothers' success?
2. What specific characteristics do you believe contributed to the Smith brothers' outstanding careers?
3. If we studied the Smith brothers' family background closely, do you think we could identify specific factors (e.g., in the way their parents raised them) that played a role in their successful rise to corporate power?

Leadership in Organizations

■ PREVIEW CASE
URBAN BOX OFFICE LOSES ITS LEADER, THEN THE BUSINESS

The sad truth is that sometimes you don't know how important a leader is to an organization until he or she isn't around anymore. That's precisely the lesson the 300 employees of Urban Box Office learned when its CEO, George Jackson, died at age 42, two weeks after suffering a stroke in February 2000.

Jackson was CEO of Motown Records until 1998, when he joined his longtime friends Adam Kidron and Frank Cooper in starting an Internet business to serve the interests of millions of lovers of hip-hop music. Because Urban Box Office was just getting off the ground when Jackson passed away, it was uncertain if the company could continue in his absence. After all, Jackson not only had a keen vision of what the company should be, but he also had important qualities that kept the enterprise going: Jackson was able to get people to buy into his dream, and he was able to keep them focused on doing whatever was necessary to stay on task. However, Kidron and Cooper pressed on without their esteemed leader and vowed to keep the business going—something that they would not have done had Jackson died even six months earlier.

> Jackson was able to get people to buy into his dream, and he was able to keep them focused on doing whatever was necessary to stay on task.

In fact, after Jackson's passing, Urban Box Office launched several new Web sites, including IndiePlanet, a site designed to help independent designers of film, music, and fashion sell their works online. This was in keeping with one of Jackson's goals for his enterprise: using the Internet to promote groups that traditionally had not benefited from the boom in Web technology. Still, there was no doubt that Jackson's absence was felt every day. Without him at the helm, everyone had to work much harder to keep the business afloat. Poignantly, Kidron even said that he sometimes found himself dialing Jackson's number in search of advice, forgetting that he no longer could be reached.

Unfortunately, investors failed to share Kidron and Cooper's optimism about being able to keep Urban Box Office afloat. Financing dried up, and on November 2, 2000, Urban Box Office declared bankruptcy, logging off for good.

Although the demise of Urban Box Office was not directly attributed to the passing of George Jackson, those in the know would tell you otherwise. His magnetism and vision kept everyone optimistic about Urban Box Office. Because the business was still in its infancy, it depended on Jackson's magic to keep the music rolling. So when he died, investors feared that the business would no longer be viable, leading them to back out of their commitments. If you're thinking to yourself, "But he's just one person in an entire business," you are underestimating the importance of having a strong leader at the helm—especially when the business is new. In fact, if you gathered a group of top executives and asked them to identify the single most important determinant of organizational success, most would likely reply "effective leadership." Indeed, it is widely believed in the world of business that *leadership* is the key ingredient in the recipe for corporate achievement. And this view is by no means restricted to business organizations. As you know, leadership also is important when it comes to politics, sports, and many other activities.[1]

Is this view justified? Do leaders really play crucial roles in shaping the fortunes of organizations? A century of research on this topic suggests that they do. Effective leadership is indeed a key determinant of organizational success.[2] Given its importance, you may not be surprised to learn that leadership has been one of the most widely studied concepts in the social sciences.[3] In view of this, we will devote this chapter to describing various approaches to the study of leadership as well as their implications for managerial practice.

To make the task of summarizing this wealth of information manageable, we will proceed as follows. First, we will consider some basic points about leadership—what it is and why being a leader is not necessarily synonymous with being a manager. Then we will examine views of leadership, focusing on the traits of leaders, followed by another view that focuses on leaders' behaviors. Next, we will examine several major theories of leadership that focus on the relationship between leaders and their followers. Finally, we will review several contrasting theories dealing with the conditions under which leaders are effective or ineffective in their important role.

THE NATURE OF LEADERSHIP

In a sense, leadership resembles love: It is something most people believe they can recognize but often find difficult to define. What, precisely, is it? And how does being a leader differ from being a manager? We will now focus on these questions.

Leadership: A Working Definition

Imagine that you have accepted a new job and entered a new work group. How would you recognize its leader? One possibility, of course, is through the formal titles and assigned roles each person in the group holds. In short, the individual designated as department head or project manager would be the one you would identify as the group's leader.

Now imagine that during several staff meetings, you noticed that this person was really not the most influential. Although she or he held the formal authority, these meetings were actually dominated by another person, who, ostensibly, was the top person's subordinate. What would you conclude about leadership in this case? Probably that the real leader of the group was the person who actually ran things—not the one with the formal title and the apparent authority.

In many cases, of course, the disparity we have just described does not exist. The individual possessing the greatest amount of formal authority also is the most influential. In some situations, however, this is not so. And in such cases, we typically identify the person who actually exercises the most influence over the group as its **leader.** These facts point to the following working definition of leadership that is accepted by many experts on this topic: **Leadership** is the process whereby one individual influences other group members toward the attainment of defined group or organizational goals.[4] For a summary of some of the key characteristics of the leadership process, see Figure 13.1.

Leadership involves noncoercive influence. According to this definition, leadership is primarily a process involving influence—one in which a leader changes the actions or attitudes of several group members or subordinates. As we saw in Chapter 12, many techniques for exerting such influence exist, ranging from relatively coercive ones, wherein the recipient has little choice but to do what is requested, to relatively noncoercive ones, wherein the recipient can choose to accept or reject the influence offered. In general, leadership refers to the use of noncoercive influence techniques. This characteristic distinguishes a leader from a *dictator.* Whereas dictators gets others to do what they want by using physical coercion or by threats of physical force, leaders do not.[5]

As Mao Zedong (founder of the People's Republic of China) put it, "Power grows out of the barrel of a gun." This may be true with respect to the power of dictators but *not true* regarding the power of leaders. Our point is that leadership rests, at least in part, on positive feelings between leaders and their subordinates. In other words, subordinates accept influence from leaders because they respect, like, or admire them—not simply because they hold positions of formal authority.[6]

Leadership influence is goal directed. The definition we just presented also suggests that leadership involves the exercise of influence for a purpose—to attain defined group or organizational goals. In other words, leaders focus on changing those actions or attitudes of their subordinates that are related to specific goals. They are far less concerned with altering followers' actions or attitudes that are irrelevant to such goals.

Leadership requires followers. Finally, note that our definition, by emphasizing the central role of influence, implies that leadership is really something of a two-way street. Although leaders do indeed influence subordinates in various ways, leaders also are influenced by their subordinates. In fact, it may be said that leadership exists only in relation to followers. After all, one cannot lead without followers!

Leaders Versus Managers: A Key Distinction—At Least in Theory

In everyday speech, the terms *leader* and *manager* tend to be used interchangeably. Although we understand the temptation to do so, the two terms are not identical and need to be clearly distinguished. In essence, the primary function of a *leader* is to estab-

leader
An individual within a group or an organization who wields the most influence over others.

leadership
The process whereby one individual influences other group members toward the attainment of defined group or organizational goals.

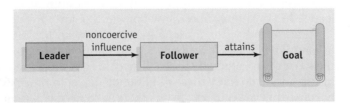

FIGURE 13.1
The Leadership Process: A Summary
Leadership is a process in which one person, a *leader,* influences a *follower* in a noncoercive manner to attain a goal.

FIGURE 13.2

Leaders and Managers: Distinguishing Their Roles
Leaders primarily are responsible for establishing an organizational mission, whereas *managers* primarily are responsible for implementing that mission through others. The intermediate steps— formulating a strategy for the mission and increasing people's commitment toward it—tend to be performed by either leaders or managers. It is these overlapping functions that make the distinction between leaders and managers blurred in actual practice.

lish the fundamental purpose or mission of the organization and the strategy for attaining it. By contrast, the job of a *manager* is to implement that vision.

Essentially, the manager's job is to put into practice a means for achieving the vision created by the leader. Thus, whereas management is about coping with complexity, leadership is about coping with change. Specifically, managers create plans and monitor results relative to those plans. However, leaders establish direction by creating a vision of the future. Effective leaders then get people to buy into their vision and to go along with it.[7]

Although these differences are simple to articulate and to comprehend, the distinction between establishing a mission and implementing it is often blurred in practice (see Figure 13.2). This is so because many leaders, such as top corporate executives, frequently are called on not only to create a vision and to formulate a strategy for implementing it, but also to play a role in increasing people's commitment toward that vision and plan. By contrast, managers are charged with responsibility for implementing organizational strategy through others. At the same time, they also frequently are involved in helping to formulate strategy and in increasing people's commitment and effort toward implementing that plan.

In other words, there are several overlapping roles played by leaders and managers in actual practice—a fact that makes it difficult to distinguish between them. However, some managers are considered leaders, whereas others are not. Similarly, some leaders take on more of a management role than others. Thus, although the differences are not always obvious, they are real. For this reason, we will distinguish carefully between leaders and managers throughout this chapter.

THE TRAIT APPROACH TO LEADERSHIP: HAVING THE RIGHT STUFF

At one time or another, most people have daydreams about being a leader. They fantasize about taking charge of large groups and being viewed with great awe and respect. Despite the prevalence of such daydreams, however, relatively few individuals convert them into reality by becoming leaders. Furthermore, among those who do make it to leadership positions, only a small proportion are considered effective in this role.

This fact raises an intriguing question: What sets effective leaders apart from most others? Why, in short, do some people, but not others, become effective leaders? One of the most widely studied approaches to this question suggests that effective leadership is based on the characteristics that people have. In other words, people become leaders because they are different from others in some special ways.[8]

The Great Person Theory

Are some people born to lead? Common sense suggests that this is so. Great leaders of the past such as Alexander the Great, Queen Elizabeth I, and Abraham Lincoln do seem to differ from ordinary human beings in several respects. The same applies to contemporary leaders as well, such as General Colin Powell, U.S. President George W. Bush, and retired astronaut-U.S. Senator John Glenn. No matter what you may feel about these individuals, you'd have to agree that they all possess high levels of ambition coupled with clear visions of precisely where they want to go. To a lesser degree, even leaders lacking in such history-shaping fame seem different from their followers.

Top executives, some politicians, and even sports heroes or heroines often seem to possess an aura that sets them apart from others. Contemporary theorists have expressed this idea as follows.

> It is unequivocally clear that *leaders are not like other people.* Leaders do not have to be great men or women by being intellectual geniuses or omniscient prophets to succeed, but they do need to have the "right stuff" and this stuff is not equally present in all people. Leadership is a demanding, unrelenting job with enormous pressures and grave responsibilities. It would be a profound disservice to leaders to suggest that they are ordinary people who happened to be in the right place at the right time. . . . In the realm of leadership (and in every other realm), the individual does matter.[9]

This orientation expresses an approach to the study of leadership known as the **great person theory.** According to this orientation, great leaders possess key traits that set them apart from most other human beings. Furthermore, the theory contends that these traits remain stable over time and across different groups.[10] Thus, it suggests that all great leaders share these characteristics regardless of when and where they lived or the precise role in history they fulfilled.

great person theory
The view that leaders possess special traits that set them apart from others and that these traits are responsible for their assuming positions of power and authority.

What Are the Characteristics of Great Leaders?

What are these characteristics? In other words, in precisely what measurable ways do successful leaders differ from other people in general? Researchers have identified several such characteristics, and these are listed in Table 13.1.[11] You will readily recognize and understand most of these characteristics (drive, honesty and integrity, self-confidence) and require no elaboration. However, we will explain several that are not quite as obvious.[12]

TABLE 13.1 CHARACTERISTICS OF SUCCESSFUL LEADERS

Successful leaders possess many of the traits listed here.

TRAIT OR CHARACTERISTIC	DESCRIPTION
Drive	Desire for achievement, ambition, high energy, tenacity, and initiative.
Honesty and integrity	Trustworthy, reliable, and open.
Leadership motivation	Desire to influence others to reach shared goals.
Self-confidence	Trust in own abilities.
Cognitive ability	Intelligence; ability to integrate and interpret large amounts of information.
Knowledge of the business	Knowledge of industry and relevant technical matters.
Creativity	Capacity to come up with original ideas.
Flexibility	Ability to adapt to needs of followers and the situation.

leadership motivation
The desire to influence others, especially toward the attainment of shared goals.

personalized power motivation
The wish to dominate others, reflected by an excessive concern with status.

socialized power motivation
The desire to cooperate with others, to develop networks and coalitions.

Leadership motivation: The desire to lead. First, consider what has been termed **leadership motivation.** This refers to leaders' desire to influence others and, in essence, to lead.[13] Such motivation, however, can take two distinct forms. On the one hand, it may cause leaders to seek power as an end in itself. Leaders who demonstrate such **personalized power motivation** wish to dominate others, and their desire to do so is often reflected in an excessive concern with status. In contrast, leadership motivation can cause leaders to seek power as a means to achieve desired, shared goals. Leaders who evidence such **socialized power motivation** cooperate with others, develop networks and coalitions, and generally work with subordinates rather than try to dominate or control them. Needless to say, this type of leadership motivation is usually far more adaptive for organizations than personalized power motivation.

Flexibility. Another special characteristic of effective leaders is flexibility. This refers to the ability of leaders to recognize what actions are required in a given situation and then to act accordingly. Evidence suggests that the most effective leaders are not prone to behave in the same ways all the time, but are adaptive—matching their style to the needs of followers and the demands of the situations they face.[14]

Multiple domains of intelligence. Scientists have acknowledged that leaders have to "be smart" in a variety of different ways. In other words, they have to demonstrate what is known as **multiple domains of intelligence.**[15] Specifically, leaders have to be intelligent in three special ways.

multiple domains of intelligence
Intelligence as measured in several different ways, such as cognitive intelligence (traditional measures of the ability to integrate and interpret information), emotional intelligence (the ability to be sensitive to one's own and others' emotions), and cultural intelligence (awareness of cultural differences between people).

- *Cognitive intelligence.* Of course, leaders must be capable of integrating and interpreting large amounts of information. However, mental genius does not seem to be necessary for leadership. Although the best leaders are surely smart, they tend not to be geniuses.[16] Moreover, research has shown that for people to become leaders, it's important for them to appear to be smart.[17] After all, people are unlikely to accept leaders whose intellectual competence is questionable (see Chapter 3).
- *Emotional intelligence.* In Chapters 3 and 4 we described *emotional intelligence,* which refers to people's abilities to be sensitive to their own and others' emotions. As you might imagine, successful leaders must have high levels of emotional intelligence. Indeed, effective leaders are keenly aware of people's emotional states and demonstrate the ability to connect with others.[18]

cultural intelligence
A person's sensitivity to the fact that leaders operate differently in different cultures.

- *Cultural intelligence.* Most of the research on leadership has focused on Americans working in companies based in the Unites States. However, the behavior of leaders is likely to be influenced by the cultures within which they operate, requiring different approaches to leadership in different countries. Sensitivity to this fact has been referred to as **cultural intelligence.**[19] In today's global economy, cultural intelligence is more important than ever. In the words of C. R. "Dick" Shoemate, chairman and CEO of Bestfoods, "It takes a special kind of leadership to deal with the differences of a multicountry, multicultural organization such as ours."[20] Not surprisingly, most of the companies on *Fortune* magazine's list of "Global Most Admired Companies" (such as General Electric, BASF, Berkshire Hathaway, and SBC Communications) pay considerable attention to training leaders to deal with the realities of the global economy.[21] For some guidelines on doing this, see the How To Do It section on page 475.

LEADERSHIP BEHAVIOR: WHAT DO LEADERS DO?

autocratic leadership style
A style of leadership in which the leader makes all decisions unilaterally.

participative leadership style
A style of leadership in which the leader permits subordinates to take part in decision making and also gives them a considerable degree of autonomy in completing routine work activities.

The trait approach to leadership we just reviewed focuses on the appealing idea that various traits distinguish effective leaders from others. In short, it focuses on *who leaders are.* As plausible as this approach may be, it also makes sense to consider the idea that leaders may be distinctive with respect to the way they behave. In other words, we can supplement our focus on leadership traits with attention to leadership behavior—that is, examining *what leaders do.*

This leadership approach is appealing because it offers an optimistic view of the leadership process. After all, although we may not all be born with "the right stuff," we certainly can at least strive to do "the right things," that is, to do what it takes to become a successful leader. The general question underlying the behavior approach is quite simple: What do leaders do that make them effective as leaders? As we will describe here, there are several good answers to this question.

Participative Versus Autocratic Leadership Behaviors

When it comes to describing the behavior of leaders, a key variable involves how much influence they allow subordinates to have over the decisions that are made. As we will see, there are two ways of describing these behaviors.

The autocratic-delegation continuum model. Think about the different bosses you have had in your life or career. Can you remember one who wanted to control virtually everything—someone who made all the decisions, told people precisely what to do, and wanted, quite literally, to run the entire show? Such a person is said to have an **autocratic leadership style.** In contrast, can you recall a boss or supervisor who allowed employees to make their own decisions? This individual would be described as relying on *delegation.*

You probably also know supervisors who have acted in ways that fall between these extremes—that is, bosses who invited your input before making decisions, were open to suggestions, and who allowed you to carry out various tasks in your own way. These individuals may be said to have a **participative leadership style.**[24] More precisely, they may be *consulting* with you or involving you in a *joint decision* of some sort. In either case, you were more involved than you would have been in the case of an autocratic leader but less involved than you would have been in the case of a leader who delegated all responsibility to you. (For a summary of this **autocratic-delegation continuum model,** see Figure 13.3.)

Although the autocratic-delegation continuum model does a reasonable job of describing the role of the leader in organizational decision making, it is regarded as overly simplistic. In fact, upon more carefully studying the way leaders make decisions, researchers have observed that describing a leader's participation in decision making involves two separate dimensions.[25]

The two-dimensional model of subordinate participation. Acknowledging the need for a more sophisticated approach, scientists have proposed the **two-dimensional model of subordinate participation.** As the name implies, it describes subordinates' participation in decisions in terms of two dimensions.

Reminiscent of the autocratic-delegation continuum model, the first dimension characterizes the extent to which leaders permit subordinates to take part in decisions; this is the *autocratic-democratic* dimension. The autocratic extreme is marked by no participation whereas the democratic extreme is marked by high participation. The second dimension involves the extent to which leaders direct the activities of subordinates and tell them how to carry out their jobs; this is the *permissive-directive* dimension. The permissive extreme is marked by not telling subordinates how to do their jobs, whereas the directive extreme is marked by considerable attempts to tell subordinates how to do their jobs. Combining these two variables yields the four possible patterns described in Table 13.2. These are:

BOOSTING CULTURAL INTELLIGENCE

Companies use a variety of approaches when it comes to training global leaders in ways of boosting their cultural intelligence. Some of the most widely used methods follow.

1. In-house *leadership seminars* (focusing on many of the concepts in this chapter) that traditionally have been used to train lenders continue to be popular. However, these are being supplemented by carefully customized programs that prepare leaders for global assignments.

2. Companies are intensely *coaching* individuals who take on overseas assignments and are carefully planning a succession of career assignments to prepare leaders for global business. For example, the pharmaceuticals giant Pfizer systematically assigns key managers and potential leaders to project teams that will give them overseas experience. Just as the company takes a long-term perspective on developing its products, Pfizer also "takes a long-term view of developing people," says Chick Dombeck, vice president of human resources.[22]

3. Like other companies, American Express relies extensively on individual coaching but also incorporates *international assignments* in its strategy for developing leaders. According to Linda Mllndek, vice president of worldwide operations, American Express's goal is "to ensure our people have the required capabilities to lead the company to future success."[23]

There can be no doubt that when it comes to developing leaders, today's companies are paying careful attention to the global world in which they do business. And training them to operate effectively in this world by enhancing their cultural intelligence is an important part of the process.

autocratic-delegation continuum model

An approach to leadership describing the ways in which leaders allocate influence to subordinates. This ranges from controlling everything (*autocratic*) to allowing others to make decisions for themselves (*delegating*). Between these extremes are more participative forms of leadership—*consulting* and *making joint decisions.*

two-dimensional model of subordinate participation

An approach to leadership that describes the nature of the influence leaders give followers. It distinguishes between leaders who are *directive* or *permissive* toward subordinates and the extent to which they are *participative* or *autocratic* in their decision making. Individual leaders may be classified into four types in terms of where they fall when these two dimensions are combined.

FIGURE 13.3

The Autocratic-Delegation Continuum Model
Traditionally, the amount of influence leaders give followers has been summarized as a continuum ranging from *autocratic* behavior (no influence) to *delegation* behavior (high influence). *Consultation* and *joint decisions* are intermediate forms of *participation* in decision making.
(*Source:* Based on suggestions by Yukl, 2002; see Note 1.)

- *directive autocrat*
- *permissive autocrat*
- *directive democrat*
- *permissive democrat*

Although any attempt to divide human beings into discrete categories raises thorny issues, these patterns do seem to make good sense. Many leaders adopt a style that fits, at least roughly, within one of these categories.

Given that leaders differ along these two dimensions and can, as a result, be classified as falling into one of the preceding four patterns, do any of them have a clear-cut edge? In short, is one pattern superior to the others in many, if not most, situations? Existing evidence suggests that this is doubtful. All four styles seem to involve a mixed pattern of advantages and disadvantages. Moreover—and this is the crucial point—the relative success of each depends heavily on conditions existing within a given organization and its specific stage of development.

To illustrate this point, consider a leader who is a *directive autocrat*. Such a person makes decisions without consulting subordinates and supervises subordinates' work activities very closely. It is tempting to view such a pattern as undesirable insofar as it runs counter to the value of personal freedom. However, this approach may actually be highly successful in some settings—such as when employees are inexperienced or underqualified for their jobs, or when subordinates adopt an adversarial stance toward management and must be closely supervised. As you might imagine, such individuals tend to be unpopular.

In contrast, consider the case of the *permissive autocrat*—a leader who combines permissive supervision with an autocratic style of making decisions. This pattern may be useful in dealing with employees who have a high level of technical skill and who want to be left alone to manage their own jobs (e.g., scientists, engineers, computer programmers) but who have little desire to participate in routine decision making. The remaining two patterns (*directive democrat* and *permissive democrat*) are also most suited to specific organizational conditions. The key task for leaders, then, is to match

TABLE 13.2 THE TWO-DIMENSIONAL MODEL OF SUBORDINATE PARTICIPATION

Leaders can be described as having different styles based on how they involve subordinates in making decisions about how to do their jobs. Four distinct styles are summarized here.

ARE SUBORDINATES TOLD EXACTLY HOW TO DO THEIR JOBS?	ARE SUBORDINATES PERMITTED TO PARTICIPATE IN MAKING DECISIONS?	
	YES (*DEMOCRATIC*)	NO (*AUTOCRATIC*)
Yes (*directive*)	**Directive democrat** (*makes decisions participatively; closely supervises subordinates*)	**Directive autocrat** (*makes decisions unilaterally; closely supervises subordinates*)
No (*permissive*)	**Permissive democrat** (*makes decisions participatively; gives subordinates latitude in carrying out their work*)	**Permissive autocrat** (*makes decisions unilaterally; gives subordinates latitude in carrying out their work*)

(*Source:* Based on suggestions by Muczyk & Reimann, 1987; see Note 25.)

their own style to the needs of their organization and to change as these needs shift and evolve.

What happens when leaders in organizations lack such flexibility? Actual events in one now defunct company—People Express Airlines—are instructive.[26] Don Burr, the founder and CEO, had a very clear managerial style: He was a highly permissive democrat. He involved employees in many aspects of decision making and emphasized autonomy in work activities. Indeed, he felt that everyone at People Express should be viewed as a "manager." This style worked well while the company was young, but as it grew and increased in complexity in the mid-1980s, such practices created mounting difficulties. New employees were not necessarily as committed as older ones, so permissive supervision was ineffective with them. And, as decisions increased in both complexity and number, a participative approach became less appropriate. Unfortunately, top management was reluctant to alter its style; after all, it seemed to have been instrumental in the company's early success. This poor match between the style of top leaders and changing external conditions seems to have contributed (along with many other factors, of course) to People Express's ultimate demise.

To conclude, no single leadership style is best under all conditions and in all situations. However, recognizing the importance of differences in this respect can be a constructive first step toward assuring that the style most suited to a given set of conditions is, in fact, adopted.

Person-Oriented Versus Production-Oriented Leaders

Think again about all the bosses you have had in your career. Now divide these into two categories—those who were relatively effective and those who were relatively ineffective. How do the two groups differ? If you think about this issue carefully, your answers are likely to take one of two forms. First, you might reply, "My most effective bosses helped me get the job done. They gave me advice, answered my questions, and let me know exactly what was expected of me. My most ineffective bosses didn't do this." Second, you might answer, "My most effective bosses seemed to care about me as a person. They were friendly, listened to me when I had problems or questions, and seemed to help me toward my personal goals. My ineffective bosses didn't do this."

A large body of research, much of it conducted in the 1950s at the University of Michigan[27] and at the Ohio State University[28] suggests that leaders differ greatly along these dimensions. Those at the high end of the first dimension, known as **initiating structure** (or **production oriented leadership**), are concerned mainly with production and focus primarily on getting the job done. They engage in actions such as organizing work, inducing subordinates to follow rules, setting goals, and making leader and subordinate roles explicit. In contrast, other leaders are lower on this dimension and show less tendency to engage in these actions.

Leaders at the high end of the second dimension, known as **consideration** (or **person oriented leadership**), are primarily concerned with establishing good relations with their subordinates and being liked by them. They engage in actions such as doing favors for subordinates, explaining things to them, and taking steps to assure their welfare. Others, in contrast, are low on this dimension and don't really care much about how they get along with their subordinates.

At first glance, you might assume that initiating structure and consideration are linked such that people high on one of these dimensions are automatically low on the other. In fact, this is *not* the case. The two dimensions actually seem to be largely independent.[29] Thus, a leader may be high on both concern with production and concern for people, high on one of these dimensions and low on the other, moderate on one and high on the other, and so on (see Figure 13.4).

Is any one of these possible patterns best? Careful study indicates that this is a complex issue; production-oriented and people-oriented leadership behaviors both offer a mixed pattern of advantages and disadvantages. With respect to showing consideration (high concern with people and human relations), the major benefits are improved

initiating structure
Activities by a leader designed to enhance productivity or task performance. Leaders who focus primarily on these goals are described as demonstrating a task-oriented style.

production oriented leadership
See *initiating structure*.

consideration
Actions by a leader that demonstrate concern with the welfare of subordinates and establish positive relations with them. Leaders who focus primarily on this task are often described as demonstrating a person-oriented style.

person oriented leadership
See *consideration*.

FIGURE 13.4
**Two Basic Dimensions
of Leader Behavior**
Leaders' behavior can vary from low to
high with respect to *consideration* (person
orientation) and *initiating structure* (task
orientation). Patterns of leader behavior
produced by variations along these two
dimensions are illustrated here.

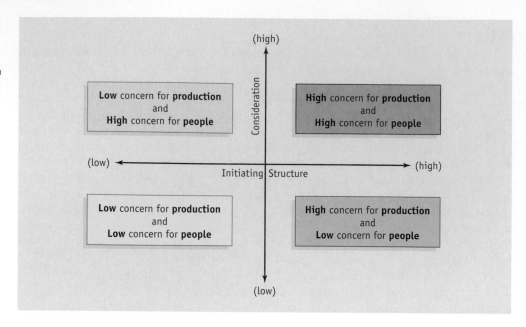

group atmosphere and morale.[30] However, since leaders high on this dimension are reluctant to act in a directive manner toward subordinates and often shy away from presenting them with negative feedback, productivity sometimes suffers. Regarding initiating structure (high concern with production), efficiency and performance are indeed sometimes enhanced by this leadership style. If leaders focus entirely on production, however, employees soon may conclude that no one cares about them or their welfare. Then work-related attitudes such as job satisfaction and organizational commitment may suffer.

Having said all this and pointing out the complexities, we add that one specific pattern may indeed have an edge in many settings. This is a pattern in which leaders demonstrate high concern with both people *and* production.[31] Indeed, research has shown that high amounts of concern with people (showing consideration) and concern with productivity (initiating structure) are not incompatible. Rather, skillful leaders can combine both of these orientations into their overall styles to produce favorable results. Thus, although no one leadership style is best, leaders who combine these two concerns may often have an important edge over leaders who show only one or the other. In the words of U.S. Army Lieutenant General William G. Pagonis:

> To lead successfully, a person must demonstrate . . . expertise and empathy. In my experience, both of these traits can be deliberately and systematically cultivated; this personal development is the first important building block of leadership.[32]

Developing Successful Leadership Behavior: Grid Training

grid training
A multi-step process designed to cultivate two important leadership skills—concern for people and concern for production.

How can one go about developing these two forms of leadership behavior—demonstrating concern for production and concern for people? A technique known as **grid training** proposes a multistep process designed to cultivate these two important skills.[33]

The initial step consists of a *grid seminar*—a session in which an organization's leaders (who have been previously trained in the appropriate theory and skills) help organization members analyze their own leadership styles. This is done using a specially designed questionnaire that allows leaders to determine how they stand with respect to their *concern for production* and their *concern for people*. Each participant's approach on each dimension is scored using a number ranging from 1 (low) to 9 (high).

Leaders who score low on both concern for production and concern for people are scored 1,1—evidence of *impoverished management*. A leader who is highly concerned about production but shows little interest in people, the *task management* style, scores

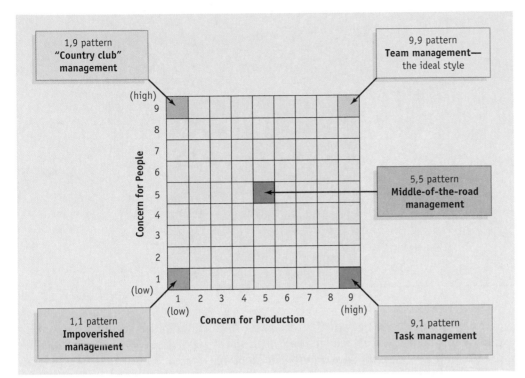

FIGURE 13.5
The Managerial Grid®
A leader's standing on two basic dimensions, concern for production and concern for people, can be illustrated by means of a diagram such as this, known as the *managerial grid®*. In *grid training*, people are trained to be effective leaders by demonstrating high amounts of both dimensions.
(*Source:* Based on dimensions by Blake & Mouton, 1969; see Note 33.)

9,1. In contrast, ones who show the opposite pattern—high concern with people but little concern with production—are described as having a *country club* style of management; they are scored 1,9. Leaders scoring moderately on both dimensions, the 5,5 pattern, are said to follow a *middle-of-the-road* style. Finally, there are individuals who are highly concerned with both production and people, those scoring 9,9. This is the most desirable pattern, representing what is known as *team management*. These various patterns are represented in a diagram like that shown in Figure 13.5, known as the *managerial grid®*.

After a leader's position along the grid is determined, training begins to improve concern over production (planning skills) and concern over people (communication skills) to reach the ideal 9,9 state. This consists of organization-wide training aimed at helping leaders interact more effectively with others. Then training is expanded to reducing conflict between groups that work with each other. Additional training includes efforts to identify the extent to which the organization is meeting its strategic goals and then comparing this performance to an ideal. Next, plans are made to meet these goals, and these plans are implemented in the organization. Finally, progress toward the goals is continuously assessed, and problem areas are identified.

Grid training is widely considered an effective way of improving the leadership behavior of people in organizations. Indeed, the grid approach has been used to train hundreds of thousands of people in developing the two key forms of leadership behavior.

LEADERS AND FOLLOWERS

Thus far throughout this chapter, we have focused on leaders—their traits and their behaviors. Followers, by and large, have been ignored. But, in a crucial sense, followers are the essence of leadership. Without them, there really is no such thing as leadership (see Figure 13.6). As one expert put it, "Without followers leaders cannot lead. . . . Without followers, even John Wayne becomes a solitary hero, or, given the right script, a comic figure, posturing on an empty stage."[34]

The importance of followers and the complex, reciprocal relationship between leaders and followers are widely recognized by organizational researchers. Indeed,

"My platform can be summarized in a single word: Leadership!"

major theories of leadership, such as those we will consider in this section note—either explicitly or implicitly—that leadership is really a two-way street. We will now consider three such approaches: the *leader–member exchange model*, the practice of *team leadership*, and the *attribution approach* to leadership.

The Leader–Member Exchange (LMX) Model: The Importance of Being in the "In-Group"

Do leaders treat all their subordinates in the same manner? Informal observation suggests that, clearly, they do not. Yet, many theories of leadership ignore this fact. They discuss leadership behavior in terms that suggest similar actions toward all subordinates. The importance of potential differences in this respect is brought into sharp focus by the **leader–member exchange (LMX) model.**[35]

leader–member exchange (LMX) model

A theory suggesting that leaders form different relations with various subordinates and that their nature can exert strong effects on subordinates' performance and satisfaction.

This theory suggests that, for various reasons, leaders form different kinds of relationships with various groups of subordinates. One group, referred to as the *in-group*, is favored by the leader. Members of in-groups receive considerably more attention from the leader and larger shares of the resources they have to offer (such as time and recognition). By contrast, other subordinates fall into the *out-group*. These individuals are disfavored by leaders. As such, they receive fewer valued resources from their leaders.

Leaders distinguish between in-group and out-group members very early in their relationships with them—and on the basis of surprisingly little information. Sometimes perceived similarity with respect to personal characteristics, such as age, gender, or personality, is sufficient to categorize followers into a leader's in-group.[36] Similarly, a particular follower may be granted in-group status if the leader believes that person to be especially competent at performing his or her job.[37]

Research has supported the idea that leaders favor members of their in-groups. For example, one study found that supervisors inflated the ratings they gave poorly performing employees when these individuals were members of the in-group but not when they were members of the out-group.[38] Given the favoritism shown toward in-group members, it follows that such individuals would perform their jobs better and would hold more positive attitudes toward their jobs than members of out-groups. In general, research has supported this prediction. For example, it has been found that in-group members are more satisfied with their jobs and more effectively perform them than out-group members.[39] In-group members also are less likely to resign from their jobs than out-group members.[40] And, as you might imagine, members of in-groups tend to

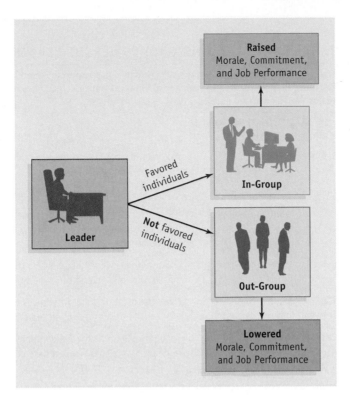

FIGURE 13.7
The LMX Model: A Summary
According to the *leader–member exchange (LMX) model,* leaders distinguish between groups they favor (*in-groups*) and those they do not favor (*out-groups*). Members of in-groups generally enjoy higher levels of morale and commitment, and perform their jobs better than members of out-groups.

receive more mentoring from their superiors than do members of out-groups, thereby helping them become more successful in their careers (for a summary, see Figure 13.7).[41]

Together, these studies provide good support for the LMX model. Such findings suggest that attention to the relations between leaders and their followers can be very useful. The nature of such relationships strongly affects the morale, commitment, and performance of employees. Helping leaders to improve such relations, therefore, can be extremely valuable in several respects.

The Challenge of Leading Work Teams

Traditionally, leaders make strategic decisions on behalf of followers, who are responsible for carrying them out. In many of today's organizations, however, where *teams* predominate (see Chapter 8), leaders are called on to provide special resources to team members, who are empowered to implement their own missions in their own ways. Instead of "calling the shots," team leaders help subordinates take responsibility for their own work. As such, they are very different from the traditional "command and control" leadership role we have been discussing.[42] As Table 13.3 suggests, leading teams is clearly very different from leading groups in the traditional manner.

The role of leaders in self-managed work teams. When most people think of leaders, they tend to think of individuals who make strategic decisions on behalf of followers, who are responsible for carrying them out. In many of today's organizations, however, where the movement toward *self-managed teams* predominates, it is unlikely that leaders are responsible for getting others to implement their orders to help fulfill their visions. Instead, team leaders may be called on to provide special resources to groups empowered to implement their own missions in their own ways. They don't call all the shots, but help subordinates take responsibility for their own work.

Given the special role of team leaders, we will identify a few key guidelines that should be followed to achieve success as a team leader.[43]

TABLE 13.3   LEADING GROUPS VERSUS LEADING TEAMS

The popularity of teams in today's organizations has important implications for how leaders go about fulfilling their roles. Some of the key differences between leading traditional work groups and leading teams are summarized here.

IN TRADITIONAL WORK GROUPS, LEADERS . . .	BUT, IN TEAMS, LEADERS . . .
Tell people what to do.	Ask people what they think and share responsibility for organizing and doing the work.
Take all the credit.	Share the limelight with all their teammates.
Focus on training employees.	Concentrate on expanding their team's capabilities by functioning primarily as coaches who build confidence in team members, cultivating their untapped potential.
Relate to others individually.	Create a team identity by helping the team set goals, helping members meet them, and celebrating when they have been met.
Work at reducing conflict between individuals.	Make the most of team differences by building respect for diverse points of view and ensuring that all team members' views are expressed.
Respond to change reactively.	Recognize that change is inevitable and foresee it, better preparing the organization to make appropriate adaptations.

1. Instead of directing people, *team leaders work at building trust and inspiring teamwork.* One way this can be done is by encouraging interaction between all members of the team as well as between the team and its customers and suppliers. Another key ingredient is taking initiative to make things better. Instead of taking a reactive, "if it ain't broke, don't fix it" approach, teams may be led to success by individuals who set a good example for improving the quality of their team's efforts.
2. Rather than focusing simply on training individuals, effective *team leaders concentrate on expanding team capabilities.* In this connection, team leaders function primarily as coaches, helping team members by providing all members with the skills needed to perform the task, removing barriers that might interfere with task success, and finding the necessary resources required to get the job done. Likewise, team leaders work at building the confidence of team members, cultivating their untapped potential.
3. Instead of managing one-on-one, *team leaders attempt to create a team identity.* In other words, leaders must help teams understand their missions and recognize what they're doing to help fulfill it. In this connection, team leaders may help the group set goals—pointing out ways they may adjust their performance when they do not meet them, and planning celebrations when team goals are attained.
4. Although traditional leaders have worked at preventing conflict between individuals, *team leaders are encouraged to make the most of team differences.* Without doubt, it is a considerable challenge to meld a diverse group of individuals into a highly committed and productive team, but doing so is important. This can be done by building respect for diverse points of view, making sure that all team members are encouraged to present their views, and respecting these ideas once they are expressed.
5. Unlike traditional leaders who simply respond to change reactively, team leaders should *foresee and influence change.* To the extent that leaders recognize that change is inevitable (a point we will emphasize in Chapter 16), they may be better prepared to make the various adaptations required. Effective team leaders continuously scan the business environment for clues as to changes that appear to be forthcoming and help teams decide how to implement them.

In conclusion, leading teams is a far cry from leading individuals in the traditional directive (or even a participative) manner. The special nature of teams makes the leader's job very different. Although appreciating these differences is easy, making the appropriate adjustments may be extremely challenging—especially for individuals who are well practiced in the ways of traditional leadership. However, given the prevalence of teams in today's work environment, the importance of making the adjustments cannot be overstated. Leading new teams using old methods is a surefire formula for failure.

Grassroots leadership. A good example of team leadership may be found in a most unlikely place—aboard a U.S. Navy warship. For 20 months, D. Michael Abrashoff was commander of the USS *Benfold*, one of the U.S. Navy's most modern, technologically advanced, and lethal warships (see Figure 13.8). Although you'd surely think that Commander Abrashoff ran this $1 billion floating computerized arsenal in the strict, top-down manner of most military companies, you couldn't be farther off.[44] In fact, he actually relied on a **grassroots leadership** approach in which the traditional management hierarchy is turned upside down. Aboard the *Benfold*, it's the 300 sailors who are really in charge. The commander expressed it as follows.

> In most organizations today, ideas still come from the top. Soon after arriving at this command, I realized that the young folks on this ship are smart and talented. And I realized that my job was to listen aggressively—to pick up all of the ideas that they had for improving how we operate. The most important thing that a captain can do is to see the ship from the eyes of the crew.[45]

Abrashoff's approach to commanding the ship was highly personalized. Like all good team leaders do, he met face-to-face with each of the crew members in an attempt to understand their personal and professional goals. Moreover, he made decisions that paved the way for the sailors under his command to spend more time on mission-critical tasks and less time on unpleasant chores. No longer did they have to sand off rust and repaint the ship. Abrashoff arranged for an outside firm to replace rusting bolts with stainless steel hardware and to apply a special rust-inhibiting finish to the ship's surfaces. This not only relieved the sailors from having to perform tedious, demoralizing chores, but also freed them to spend more time on their true purpose—preparing for combat.

Grassroots leadership has been an unqualified success aboard the *Benfold*. During his command, the ship became recognized as the best in the Pacific Fleet and was rec-

grassroots leadership
An approach to leadership that turns the traditional management hierarchy upside down by empowering people to make their own decisions.

FIGURE 13.8
The USS *Benfold*: Grassroots Leadership at Sea
Gunner's Mate 1st Class Joe Brown, shown here looking through the scope of a 25-mm chain gun, and other sailors aboard the USS *Benfold*, operate as a team and are empowered to make many decisions themselves. This *grassroots leadership* approach is quite different from the traditional top-down approaches to leadership found in most civilian organizations and almost all other military groups.

ognized as the most combat-ready ship in the entire U.S. Navy. In addition, the crew became so efficient that it was able to return a third of the budget allocated for maintenance. Finally, and perhaps most impressively, literally all of the career sailors aboard the *Benfold* reenlisted for a second tour of duty, enabling the Navy to get the most from its highly trained personnel.

It is not only aboard the USS *Benfold* where one can see grassroots leadership at work. The same basic approach also has been used very successfully at Royal Dutch Shell—which, like the U.S. Navy, is an organization with a strong tradition of top-down leadership.[46] The success of grassroots leadership in such rigid and traditional organizations is a good indication that this approach may have considerable value in a wide variety of organizations—even those whose leaders may be expected to be reluctant to give up some of their power.

The Attribution Approach: Leaders' Explanations of Followers' Behavior

As we have just noted, leaders' relationships with individual subordinates play an important role in determining the performance and satisfaction of these individuals. One specific aspect of such exchanges serves as the focus of another contemporary perspective on leadership—the **attribution approach**.[47] This theory emphasizes the role of leaders' attributions concerning the causes behind followers' behavior—especially the causes of their job performance (see Chapter 2).

Leaders observe the performance of their followers and then attempt to understand why this behavior met, exceeded, or failed to meet their expectations. Because poor performance often poses greater difficulties than effective performance, leaders are more likely to engage in a careful attributional analysis when confronted with the former. When they do, they examine the three kinds of information described in Chapter 2 (consensus, consistency, and distinctiveness), and on the basis of such information form an initial judgment as to whether followers' performance stemmed from internal causes (e.g., low effort, commitment, or ability) or external causes (factors beyond their control, such as faulty equipment, unrealistic deadlines, or illness). Then, on the basis of such attributions, they formulate specific plans designed to change the present situation and perhaps improve followers' performance. Attribution theory suggests that such actions are determined, at least in part, by leaders' explanations of followers' behavior. For example, if they perceive poor performance as stemming from a lack of required materials or equipment, they may focus on providing such items. If, instead, they perceive poor performance as stemming mainly from a lack of effort, they may reprimand, transfer, or terminate the person involved (for a summary example, see Figure 13.9).

Evidence supporting these predictions has been reported in several studies.[48] In one investigation, for example, researchers presented nursing supervisors with brief accounts of errors committed by nurses.[49] The incidents suggested that the errors stemmed either from internal causes (lack of effort or ability) or from external causes (e.g., an overdemanding work environment). After reading about the incidents, supervisors indicated what kind of action they would be likely to take in each situation. Results showed that they were more likely to direct corrective action toward the nurses (e.g., showing them how to do something) when they perceived the errors as stemming from internal causes but more likely to direct action toward the environment (e.g., changing schedules or improving facilities) when they perceived the errors as stemming from external factors.

Thus far, we have discussed the attributions leaders make about followers' behavior. However, followers also make attributions about their leaders' behavior. In fact, recent research suggests that this takes a particularly interesting form: Followers tend to rally around their leaders in times of crisis, what is known as the **rally 'round the flag effect.** In other words, they make positive attributions about their leaders when they appear to be working to keep things together during a crisis situation. Probably the most poignant recent example of this is the dramatic boost in popularity experienced by U.S. President

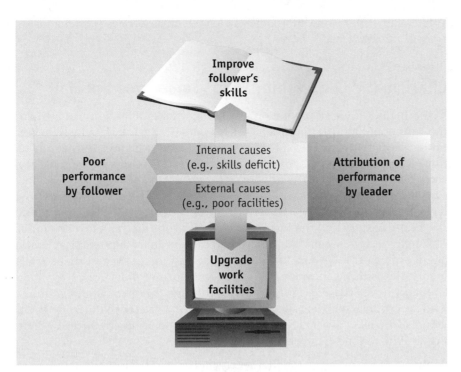

FIGURE 13.9
Leaders' Attributions of Followers'
Poor Performance
The way leaders respond to their followers depends on the attributions leaders make regarding the causes of followers' performance. In this example, attributions made about the causes of a subordinate's poor performance direct a leader to take very different courses of action.

George W. Bush following the terrorist attacks of September 11, 2001. The American public put aside its political differences (which were considerable given the vagaries of the 2000 presidential election) and supported the president during this crisis. Interestingly, this is not the only time this has happened. A team of researchers recently analyzed all the militarized disputes that occurred between 1933 and 1992. They found that support for the president grew in all instances, especially during large-scale wars.[50]

Although comparable evidence has not been collected in the case of business organizations, anecdotal evidence suggests that a similar effect occurs there as well—although it takes a slightly different form. Specifically, many employees tend to stick by CEOs who are engaged in efforts to help their companies when they face a crisis (such as when Microsoft had to defend itself against antitrust charges). However, when CEOs are perceived to be the cause of the problem (as in the case of Enron) or when the consequences appear to be so dire as to threaten the existence of the company, loyalty may not be found. Rather, the most qualified employees may "abandon ship," seeking employment elsewhere, before it's too late.

In summary, the attribution approach suggests that the attitudes and behaviors of leaders and followers often reflect the attributions they make about one another's behavior. From this perspective, then, leadership lies as much in the perceptions of the people who exercise such influence as in the perceptions of those who confer the right to wield it over them.

CHANGE-ORIENTED LEADERSHIP: FUTURE VISIONS

For organizations to thrive—let alone survive—they must be led by individuals who have a strong commitment to change. As such, leaders must have clear visions about what the future holds. The world's top leaders tend to agree. In a large-scale survey of CEOs from 20 different countries, having "a strong sense of vision" was identified by 98 percent as the most important characteristic for a CEO to have. Not surprisingly, companies with the most visionary leaders tend to outperform those with less visionary leaders in all important financial respects.

Having said this, the question arises about what precisely is involved in giving leaders the capacity to envision the most effective changes for the future. Answers are provided by two interesting approaches to leadership known as *charismatic leadership* and *transformational leadership*.

Charismatic Leadership: That "Something Special"

In the 1970s, Chrysler Corporation was being written off as terminal by many analysts of the automobile industry. Lee Iacocca, Chrysler's CEO, however, refused to accept this economic verdict. Instead, he launched a campaign to win government loan guarantees for Chrysler, paving the way for the company's survival. By setting an example of personal sacrifice—taking only $1 as salary for one year during Chrysler's crisis—Iacocca rallied Chrysler's tens of thousands of employees to unheard of levels of effort and, thus, saved the day. Chrysler not only paid back all its loans ahead of schedule, but also it is now thriving.

World history and the history of organizations are replete with similar examples. Through the ages, some leaders have had extraordinary success in generating profound changes in their followers. Indeed, it is not extreme to suggest that some such people (e.g., Microsoft co-founder Bill Gates and former New York City Mayor Rudolph Giuliani) have changed entire societies through their words and actions. Individuals who accomplish such feats have been referred to as **charismatic leaders.** These are individuals who exert especially powerful effects on followers by virtue of their commanding confidence and clearly articulated visions.

charismatic leaders

Leaders who exert especially powerful effects on followers by virtue of their commanding confidence and clearly articulated visions.

Qualities of charismatic leaders. Researchers have found that charismatic leaders tend to be special in a number of important ways. Specifically, several factors differentiate charismatic leaders from noncharismatic leaders. These are as follows:

- *Self-confidence:* Charismatic leaders are highly confident in their ability and judgment. Others readily become aware of this. For example, John Bryan, CEO of Sara Lee, is both extremely knowledgeable and widely regarded as such by his employees.
- *A vision:* A leader is said to have vision to the extent that he or she proposes a state of affairs that improves on the status quo. He or she also must be able to articulate that vision clearly and show willingness to make sacrifices to make it come true. This is precisely what Lee Iacocca did when he took the $1 salary during Chrysler's troubled period. For some further examples of visions stated by some well-known charismatic leaders, see Table 13.4.
- *Extraordinary behavior:* Charismatic leaders are frequently unconventional. Their quirky ways, when successful, elicit admiration. For example, much of the success of Southwest Airlines is attributed to the zany antics of its CEO, Herb Kelleher, who has been known to dress in funny costumes aboard planes.
- *Recognized as change agents:* The status quo is the enemy of charismatic leaders. They make things happen. This can be said about the late Roberto Goizueta, who made Coca-Cola one of the most admired—and profitable—companies in America.
- *Environmental sensitivity:* Charismatic leaders are highly realistic about the constraints imposed on them and the resources needed to change things. Consequently, they know what they can and cannot do.

Reactions to charismatic leaders. At first glance, it is tempting to assume that charismatic leaders are special merely because of the traits they possess. However, it also makes sense to look at charismatic leadership as involving a special relationship between leaders and their followers. That is to say, leaders are considered charismatic by virtue of their effects on followers. Such reactions include:

- Levels of performance beyond those that normally would be expected.[51]
- High levels of devotion, loyalty, and reverence toward the leader.[52]
- Enthusiasm for and excitement about the leader and his or her ideas.[53]

In short, charismatic leadership involves a special kind of leader–follower relationship, in which the leader can, in the words of one author, "make ordinary people do extraordinary things in the face of adversity."[54]

TABLE 13.4 SOME FAMOUS CHARISMATIC LEADERS AND THEIR VISIONS

One quality that makes charismatic leaders so effective is that they share clear visions for their organizations and then help to pave the way toward attaining them. The visions of a few well-known charismatic leaders are paraphrased here.

CHARISMATIC LEADER	COMPANY	VISION
Steven Jobs	Apple Computer	To make computing simple and available to everyone.
Charles Schwab	Charles Schwab	To provide high-quality financial services to people at reasonable prices.
Herb Kelleher	Southwest Airlines	To provide excellent service and great value to the flying public.
Mary Kay Ash	Mary Kay Cosmetics	To enhance the self-esteem of women by building their financial independence while providing quality cosmetics.
Rupert Murdoch	News Corporation	To provide accurate access to news for people throughout the world.
Walt Disney	Walt Disney Co.	To provide wholesome, high-quality entertainment to families throughout the world.

The effects of charismatic leadership—both good and bad. As you might imagine, charismatic leaders have dramatic effects on the behavior of their followers. Because these leaders are perceived as being so heroic, followers are very pleased with them—satisfaction that generalizes to perceptions of the job itself. In short, people enjoy working for charismatic leaders and do well under their guidance. On a larger scale, research has found that U.S. presidents believed to be highly charismatic (as suggested by biographical accounts of their personalities and their reactions to world crises) received higher ratings by historians of their effectiveness as president.[55] In short, evidence suggests that charismatic leadership can have some very beneficial effects.

It is important to caution, however, that being charismatic does not necessarily imply being virtuous. In fact, throughout history, many of the most vicious dictators (Adolph Hitler and Osama Bin Laden, among them) were able to rise to power because of the considerable charisma they had. Indeed, it was their clear visions of different worlds, misguided though they may have been, that led them to have such profound effects on their followers.

Are charismatic leaders always needed? It is important to note that there may not always be a place for charismatic leaders in organizations. They tend to be needed most under circumstances in which there is some crisis.[56] For example, charismatic leaders tend to emerge under wartime conditions, such as when U.S. General Norman Schwartzkopf expressed a vision of victory over Iraq and led his troops to victory in 1991's Operation Desert Storm. A crisis, such as the Great Depression, led to the election of President Franklin D. Roosevelt, the individual who would lead the United States out of the Great Depression. And, as noted earlier, the economic crisis at Chrysler during the 1970s led to the emergence of Lee Iacocca, the man who saved the company.

By the same token, it is easy to imagine that under everyday conditions, leaders who approach others with such overwhelming levels of arrogance and self-confidence that they ignore others may be more of a liability than an asset. Such was the case, for example, at Borland International, the large database software provider.[57] When the company faced financial crises in the late 1980s, charismatic president and CEO Philippe R. Kahn was most helpful in turning things around. Interestingly, however, as the company emerged from crisis, Kahn's "barbarian" approach to leadership only interfered with the company's operations. Likewise, several of the most famous political leaders were not charismatic at all. Take Benjamin Franklin, for example. For all his accomplishments as an inventor (of bifocals, among other things) and his stature in American history (he cowrote and signed both the Declaration of Independence and the U.S. Constitution), Franklin was not at all charismatic. Instead, he took a very functional, problem-centered approach known as **pragmatic leadership.**[58] This is a type of leadership based on methodically developing solutions to problems and working them through in a thorough manner. Clearly, although being charismatic may be useful in some situations, it is not a necessary requirement for leadership success.

pragmatic leadership
A type of leadership based on methodically developing solutions to problems and working them through in a thorough manner.

The liabilities of being a charismatic leader. In closing, we should point out a particularly interesting thing about charismatic leaders: People's reactions to them tend to be highly polarized. That is, people either love them (as is the case most of the time) or hate them. With this in mind, it is not surprising that some of the world's most charismatic leaders, such as John F. Kennedy, Martin Luther King, and Israeli leader Itzak Rabin, have fallen victim to assassination. Less visionary leaders certainly would have done little to inspire would-be assassins from attempting to leave their marks on the world in such clearly inappropriate ways.

Transformational Leadership: Beyond Charisma

If you're thinking that charismatic leaders are really something special, we're inclined to agree. But being charismatic is only the beginning when it comes to doing what it takes to get followers to be their most effective. Theorists have recognized that although charisma is important, the most successful leaders also do things that revitalize and transform their organizations. Accordingly, their orientation is referred to as **transformational leadership.**

transformational leadership
Leadership in which leaders use their charisma to transform and revitalize their organizations.

Characteristics of transformational leaders. Transformational leaders may be described in terms of several characteristics. First, as we said, they have *charisma*. That is, they provide a strong vision and a sense of mission for the company. As one leadership theorist put it, "If you as a leader can make an appealing dream seem like tomorrow's reality, your subordinates will freely choose to follow you."[59] Consider, for example, the great visions expressed by the highly charismatic leaders, Dr. Martin Luther King, Jr., when he shared his vision of world peace in his "I have a dream" speech, and President John F. Kennedy when he shared his vision of landing a man on the moon and returning him safely to earth before 1970.

But charisma alone is insufficient for changing the way an organization operates. For this to occur, transformational leaders also must provide the following:

- *Intellectual stimulation:* Transformational leaders help their followers recognize problems and ways of solving them.
- *Individualized consideration:* Transformational leaders give their followers the support, encouragement, and attention they need to perform their jobs well.
- *Inspirational motivation:* Transformational leaders clearly communicate the importance of the company's mission and rely on symbols (e.g., pins and slogans) to help focus their efforts.

As you might imagine, transformational leaders arouse strong emotions. They also help transform their followers by teaching them, often by serving as mentors.[60] In so doing, transformational leaders seek to elevate followers to do their own thing. By contrast, charismatic leaders may keep their followers weak and highly dependent on them. A charismatic leader may be the whole show, whereas a transformational leader does a good job of inspiring change in the whole organization. Many celebrities, be they musicians, actors, or athletes, tend to be highly charismatic, but they do not necessarily have any transformational effects on their followers. As such, although some people may idolize certain rock stars and dress like them, these musicians' charisma is unlikely to stimulate their fans into making sacrifices that revitalize the world. (This is not to say, however, that some rock stars—such as Sting and Bono, for example—may attempt to use their charisma to call their fans' attention to various social causes.) When you think of it this way, it's easy to see how charisma is just a part of transformational leadership.

Profile of a transformational leader. Jack Welch, the past chairman and CEO of General Electric (GE), is a good example of a transformational leader. Under Welch's leadership, GE underwent a series of changes with respect to the way it does business.[61] At the individual level, GE has abandoned its highly bureaucratic ways and now does a better job of listening to its employees. Not surprisingly, GE has consistently ranked among the most admired companies in its industry in *Fortune* magazine's annual survey of corporate reputations—including a number-one ranking in 2002 and several previous years![62]

In the 1980s, Welch bought and sold many businesses for GE, using as his guideline the fact that GE would only keep a company if it placed either number one or number two in market share. If this meant closing plants, selling assets, and laying off personnel, he did it, and got others to follow suit. Not surprisingly, he earned the nickname "Neutron Jack." Did Welch transform and revitalize GE? Having added $52 billion of value to the company, there can be no doubt about it.[63] Jack Welch is not the only transformational leader we can identify; for another example, see Figure 13.10.

Measuring transformational leadership and its effects. Scientists measure transformational leadership by using a questionnaire known as the Multifactor Leadership Questionnaire (MLQ). In completing this instrument, subordinates answer a series of questions in which they describe the behavior of their superiors. It consists of items tapping the four aspects of transformational leadership described previously. So, for example, agreeing with an item, such as "Because my leader makes things better, I am proud to be associated with him or her," is taken as an indication of the leader's transformational ways. The more subordinates agree with such statements as they describe the leader in question, the more highly that leader is scored as being transformational. Using this questionnaire, scientists have found that transformational leaders tend to be very effective in making their organizations highly successful.

Research has shown managers at FedEx who are rated by their subordinates as being highly transformational tend to be higher performers and are recognized by their superiors as being highly promotable.[64] These and other studies suggest that the benefits of being a transformational leader may be considerable.

With this in mind, it certainly would be useful to consider ways in which people might go about developing ways of transforming their organizations through their leadership. We have summarized several key guidelines in Table 13.5. Although you may find it easier to understand than to carry out some of these suggestions, the evidence regarding the effectiveness of transformational leadership suggests that the effort it takes to follow them may be worthwhile.

FIGURE 13.10

Estée Lauder: A Transformational Leader
It's safe to say that Estée Lauder (born Josephine Esther Mentzer on July 1, 1908) has transformed the cosmetic business. After all, the lines she developed and acquired over a half-century now account for over 45 percent of the cosmetics market in U.S. department stores—three times as much as the company's closest competitor. When founding Estée Lauder Cosmetics in 1946, her mesmerizing ways were influential in getting counter space in some of the most exclusive department stores.

TABLE 13.5 GUIDELINES FOR BECOMING A TRANSFORMATIONAL LEADER

Being a transformational leader is not easy. However, by following these suggestions, leaders may transform and revitalize their organizations.

SUGGESTION	EXPLANATION
Develop a vision that is both clear and highly appealing to followers.	A clear vision guides followers toward achieving organizational goals and makes them feel good about doing so.
Articulate a strategy for bringing your vision to life.	Don't present an elaborate plan. Rather, state the best path toward achieving the mission.
State your vision clearly and promote it to others.	Visions must not only be clear but made compelling, such as by using anecdotes.
Show confidence and optimism about your vision.	If a leader lacks confidence about success, followers will not try very hard to achieve that vision.
Express confidence in followers' capacity to carry out the strategy.	Followers must believe they can implement a leader's vision. Leaders should build followers' self-confidence.
Build confidence by recognizing small accomplishments toward the goal.	If a group experiences early success, it will be motivated to continue working hard. (This is based on the concept of positive reinforcement described in Chapter 2.)
Celebrate successes and accomplishments.	Formal or informal ceremonies are useful for celebrating success, thereby building optimism and commitment.
Take dramatic action to symbolize key organizational values.	Visions are reinforced by things leaders do to symbolize them. For example, one leader demonstrated concern for quality by destroying work that was not up to standards.
Set an example; actions speak louder than words.	Leaders serve as role models. If they want followers to make sacrifices, for example, they should do so themselves.

(*Source:* Based on suggestions by Yukl, 2002; see Note 1.)

CONTINGENCY THEORIES OF LEADER EFFECTIVENESS

contingency theories of leader effectiveness

Any of several theories that recognize that certain styles of leadership are more effective in some situations than others.

That leadership is a complex process should be obvious by now. It involves intricate social relationships and is affected by a wide range of factors. Given all these complications, you may wonder why so many researchers focus so much of their time and energy on attempting to understand all of its intricacies. The answer, of course, is that effective leadership is an essential ingredient in organizational success. With effective leadership organizations can grow, prosper, and compete. Without it, many simply cannot survive. Recognition of this basic point lies behind several modern theories of leadership collectively referred to as **contingency theories of leader effectiveness.**

As soon will be clear, these theories differ sharply in their content, terminology, and scope. Yet, all are linked by two common themes. First, all adopt a *contingency approach*—they recognize that there is no single preferred style of leadership and that the key task of organizational behavior researchers is determining which leadership styles will prove most effective under which specific conditions. Second, all are concerned with the issue of *leader effectiveness.* They seek to identify the conditions and factors that determine whether, and to what degree, leaders will enhance the performance and satisfaction of their subordinates. Several theories fall into this category.[65] Among these are five that we will describe here: *LPC contingency theory, situational leadership theory, path-goal theory, normative decision theory,* and the *substitutes for leadership* framework.

LPC Contingency Theory: Matching Leaders and Tasks

Earlier, we explained that the behaviors associated with effective leadership fall into two major categories—concern for people and concern for production. Both types of behavior contribute to a leader's success. However, a more refined look at this issue leads us to ask exactly when each type of behavior works best. That is, under what conditions are leaders more successful when they demonstrate a concern for people compared to a concern for production?

The basics of the theory. This question is addressed by a widely studied approach to leadership known as **LPC contingency theory.** The contingency aspect of the theory is reflected by the assumption that a leader's contribution to successful performance by his or her group is determined both by the leader's own traits and by various features of the situation. Different levels of leader effectiveness occur under different combinations of conditions. To fully understand leader effectiveness, both types of factors must be considered.

According to the theory, *esteem (liking) for least preferred coworker* (**LPC** for short) is the most important personal characteristic. This refers to a leader's tendency to evaluate in a favorable or unfavorable manner the person with whom she or he has found it most difficult to work. Leaders who perceive this person in negative terms (low LPC leaders) are primarily concerned with attaining successful task performance. In contrast, those who perceive their least preferred coworker in a positive light (high LPC leaders) are mainly concerned with establishing good relations with subordinates. A questionnaire is used to measure one's LPC score. It is important to note that the theory views LPC as being fixed—that is, an aspect of an individual's leadership style that cannot be changed. As we will explain later, this has important implications for applying the theory to improve a leader's effectiveness.

Which type of leader—one low in LPC or one high in LPC—is more effective? As suggested by the word *contingency* in the name, the answer is: "It depends." And what it depends on is the degree to which the situation is favorable to the leader—that is, how much it allows the leader to have control over subordinates. This, in turn, is determined largely by three factors:

1. The nature of the *leader's relations with group members* (the extent to which he or she enjoys their support and loyalty).
2. The *degree of structure* in the task being performed (the extent to which task goals and subordinates' roles are clearly defined).
3. The leader's *position power* (as described in Chapter 12, his or her formal capacity to influence subordinates successfully).

Combining these three factors, the leader's situational control can range from very high (positive relations with group members, a highly structured task, and high position power) to very low (negative relations, an unstructured task, and low position power).

What types of leaders are most effective under these various conditions? According to the theory, low LPC leaders (ones who are task oriented) are superior to high LPC leaders (ones who are relations oriented) when situational control is either very low or very high. In contrast, high LPC leaders have an edge when situational control falls within the moderate range (refer to Figure 13.11).

The rationale for these predictions is quite reasonable. Under conditions of low situational control, groups need considerable guidance to accomplish their tasks. Without such direction, nothing would get done. For example, imagine a military combat group led by an unpopular platoon leader. Any chance of effectiveness this person has would result from paying careful attention to the task at hand rather than hoping to establish better relations with the group. (In fact, in the Army, it is often said that a leader in an emergency is better off giving wrong orders than no orders whatsoever.) Since low LPC leaders are more likely to provide structure than high LPC leaders, they usually will be superior in such cases.

LPC contingency theory
A theory suggesting that leader effectiveness is determined both by characteristics of leaders (their *LPC* scores) and by the level of situational control they are able to exert over subordinates.

LPC
Short for "esteem for least preferred coworker," a personality variable distinguishing individuals with respect to their concern for people (high LPC) and their concern for production (low LPC).

FIGURE 13.11

LPC Contingency Theory: An Overview

LPC contingency theory predicts that low LPC leaders (ones who are primarily task oriented) will be more effective than high LPC leaders (ones who are primarily people oriented) when situational control is either very low or very high. However, the opposite is true when situational control is moderate.

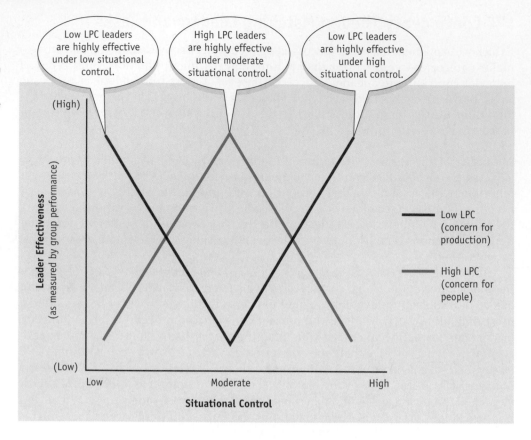

Similarly, low LPC leaders also are superior under conditions that offer the leader a high degree of situational control. Indeed, when leaders are liked, their power is not challenged, and when the demands of the task make it clear what a leader should be doing, it is perfectly acceptable for them to focus on the task at hand. Subordinates expect their leaders to exercise control under such conditions and accept it when they do so. And this leads to task success. For example, an airline pilot leading a cockpit crew is expected to take charge and to not seek the consensus of others as she guides the plane onto the runway for a landing. Surely, she would be less effective if she didn't take charge but simply asked the copilot what he thought she should do.

Things are different, however, when situations offer leaders moderate situational control. Consider, for example, a situation in which a leader's relations with subordinates are good, but the task is unstructured, and the leader's power is somewhat restricted. This generally is the case within a research and development team attempting to find creative new uses for a company's products. Here, it clearly would be inappropriate for a low LPC leader to impose directives. Rather, a highly nurturant leader who is considerate of the feelings of others would likely be most effective—that is, a high LPC leader (see Figure 13.12).

Applying LPC contingency theory. Practitioners have found LPC contingency theory to be quite useful when it comes to suggesting ways of enhancing leaders' effectiveness. Because the theory assumes that certain kinds of leaders are most effective under certain kinds of situations and that leadership style is fixed, the best way to enhance effectiveness is to fit the right kind of leaders to the situations they face.

This involves completing questionnaires that can be used to assess both the LPC score of the leader and the amount of situational control he or she faces in the situation. Then, using these indexes, a match can be made such that leaders are put into the situations that best suit their leadership styles—a technique known as **leader match.** This approach also focuses on ways of changing the situational control variables—leader–member relations, task structure, and leader position power—when it is impractical to change leaders. For example, a high LPC leader may be moved to a job in which

leader match

The practice of matching leaders (based on their LPC scores) to the groups whose situations best match those in which they are expected to be most effective according to LPC contingency theory.

FIGURE 13.12

Matching Leadership Style to the Situation

LPC contingency theory recognizes that the most appropriate leadership style depends on the situation leaders are confronting. The aircraft cockpit crew (pictured left) may be most effective when its leader, the pilot, uses a highly directive (low LPC) style. So, too, would a military troop in a difficult battle situation (pictured center) perform best when its commanding officer adopts a low LPC style. However, a research and development team (pictured right) would perform poorly if its leader behaved this same way. In that setting, a less directive (high LPC) style would be more effective.

situational control is either extremely high or extremely low. Alternatively, we may attempt to change the situation, such as by altering relations between leaders and group members, or raising or lowering his or her position power, so as to increase or decrease the amount of situational control encountered.

Several companies, including Sears, have used the leader match approach with some success. In fact, several studies have found that the approach is effective—on at least some occasions—in improving group effectiveness.

Situational Leadership Theory: Adjusting Leadership Style to the Situation

Another theory of leadership, **situational leadership theory,** is considered a contingency theory because it focuses on the best leadership style for a given situation. Specifically, the scientists who developed the theory argue that leaders are effective when they select the right leadership style for the situation they face.[66] Specifically, this depends on the *maturity* of followers—that is, their readiness to take responsibility for their own behavior. This, in turn, is based on two variables with which we are already familiar: (1) *task behavior* (the degree to which followers have the appropriate job knowledge and skills—that is, their need for guidance and direction), and (2) *relationship behavior* (the degree to which followers are willing to work without taking direction from others—that is, their need for emotional support).

As shown in Figure 13.13, by combining high and low levels of these independent dimensions, four different types of situations are identified (denoted by "S" in the diagram), each of which is associated with a leadership style that is most effective.

■ *Lower-right corner of Figure 13.13 (S1):* situations in which followers need a great deal of direction from their leaders but don't need much emotional support from them. The practice of *telling* followers what to do is most useful in such situations. That is, giving followers specific instructions and closely supervising their work may be the best approach.

■ *Upper-right corner of Figure 13.13 (S2):* situations in which followers still lack the skill to be able to succeed, although in this case, they require more emotional support. Under these conditions, *selling* works best (i.e., they need to be "sold" on what to do). Being very directive may make up for followers' lack of ability, whereas being very supportive will help get them to go along with what the leader is asking of them.

situational leadership theory

A theory suggesting that the most effective style of leadership—delegating, participating, selling, or telling—depends on the extent to which followers require guidance, direction, and emotional support.

FIGURE 13.13

Situational Leadership Theory: Its Basic Dimensions
Situational leadership theory specifies that the most appropriate leadership style depends on the amount of emotional support followers require in conjunction with the amount of guidance they require to do their jobs.
(*Source:* Adapted from Hersey & Blanchard, 1986; see Note 66.)

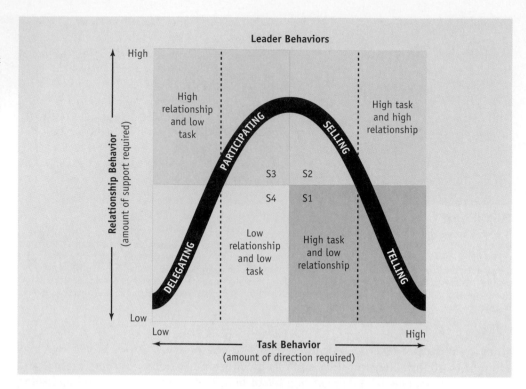

- *Upper-left corner of Figure 13.13 (S3):* conditions in which followers need very little guidance with respect to how to do their jobs but considerable emotional handholding and support to motivate them. That is, low levels of task behavior but high levels of relationship (supportive) behavior are required. A *participating* style of leadership works well in such situations because it allows followers to share their expertise while enhancing their desire to perform.
- *Lower-left corner of Figure 13.13 (S4):* situations in which followers are both willing and able to do what is asked of them. In other words, low levels of task behavior and low levels of relationship behavior are required. Under such conditions, *delegating* is the best way to treat followers—that is, turning over to them the responsibility for making and implementing their own decisions.

According to this situational leadership theory, leaders must be able (1) to diagnose the situations they face, (2) to identify the appropriate behavioral style, and then (3) to implement that response. Because the situations leaders face may change all the time, leaders must constantly reassess them, paying special attention to their followers' needs for guidance and emotional support. To the extent that they do so, they are likely to be effective.

Specialized training in these skills has been found to be quite useful. In fact, the approach has been widely used to train leaders in such corporate giants as Xerox, Mobil Oil, and Caterpillar, as well as the U.S. military services. (Which style of leadership are you most prone to follow in your treatment of others? To give you some insight into this question, complete the Individual Exercise on pages 509–510.)

Path-Goal Theory: Leaders as Guides to Valued Goals

Suppose you conducted an informal survey in which you asked 100 people to indicate what they expect from their leaders. What kind of answers would you receive? Although they would vary greatly, one common theme you might uncover would be, "I expect my leader to *help*—to assist me in reaching goals I feel are important." This basic idea plays a central role in **path-goal theory** of leadership.[67]

In general terms, this theory contends that subordinates will react favorably to a leader only to the extent that they perceive this person as helping them progress toward

path-goal theory
A theory of leadership suggesting that subordinates will be motivated by a leader only to the extent they perceive this individual as helping them to attain valued goals.

various goals by clarifying actual paths to such rewards. That is, effective leaders clarify for followers what they need to do to get from where they are to where they should be, and help them do so. More specifically, the theory contends that actions by a leader that clarify the nature of tasks and that reduce or eliminate obstacles will increase perceptions on the part of subordinates that working hard will lead to good performance and that good performance, in turn, will be recognized and rewarded. (This is in keeping with expectancy theory, as described in Chapter 6.) Under such conditions, the theory suggests, job satisfaction, motivation, and actual performance will all be enhanced.

How, precisely, can leaders best accomplish these tasks? The answer, as in other contingency views of leadership, is: "It depends." (In fact, that's how you can tell it is a contingency theory.) And what it depends on is a complex interaction between key aspects of *leader behavior* and certain *contingency* factors. With respect to leader behavior, path-goal theory suggests that leaders can adopt four basic styles:

- *Instrumental (directive):* An approach focused on providing specific guidance and establishing work schedules and rules.
- *Supportive:* A style focused on establishing good relations with subordinates and satisfying their needs.
- *Participative:* A pattern in which the leader consults with subordinates, permitting them to participate in decisions.
- *Achievement oriented:* An approach in which the leader sets challenging goals and seeks improvements in performance.

According to the theory, these styles are not mutually exclusive; in fact, the same leader can adopt them at different times and in different situations. Indeed, showing such flexibility is one important aspect of an effective leader. (Recognizing that it is important to adopt these styles, many of today's leaders have adopted an approach to leadership known as *coaching*. (We will describe the practice of *executive coaching* in more detail on page 504. Meanwhile, for a closer look at the coaching orientation to leadership, see the Best Practices section on page 490.)

Which of these contrasting styles is best for maximizing subordinates' satisfaction and motivation? The answer depends on two contingency factors. First, the style of choice is strongly affected by several *characteristics of subordinates*. For example, if followers are high in ability, an instrumental style of leadership may be unnecessary; instead, a less structured, supportive approach may be preferable. On the other hand, if subordinates are low in ability, the opposite may be true; people with poor ability need considerable guidance to help them attain their goals. Similarly, people high in need for affiliation (that is, those desiring close, friendly ties with others) may strongly prefer a supportive or participative style of leadership. By contrast, those high in the need for achievement may strongly prefer an achievement-oriented leader.

Second, the most effective leadership style also depends on several *aspects of the work environment*. For example, path-goal theory predicts that when tasks are unstructured and nonroutine, an instrumental approach by the leader may be best insofar as much clarification and guidance are needed. However, when tasks are structured and highly routine, such leadership may get in the way of good performance and may be resented by subordinates who think the leader is engaging in unnecessary meddling. (See Figure 13.14 for an overview of all these aspects of path-goal theory.)

Path-goal theory has been subjected to empirical testing in several studies.[72] In general, results have been consistent with major predictions derived from the theory, although not uniformly so. Thus, at present, path-goal theory appears to be another framework offering valuable insights into leadership and the many factors that determine the degree to which individual leaders are successful in this role.

Normative Decision Theory: The Right Time for Employee Participation

As we discussed in Chapter 10, making decisions is one of the major tasks performed by leaders. Indeed, to some, a defining characteristic of leadership positions is that they are making decisions. Each pattern offers its own mixture of benefits and costs. For example, decisions reached through participative means stand a better chance of gaining support and acceptance among subordinates. However, such decisions require a great deal of time—often more time than a leader or organization can afford. Similarly, decisions reached autocratically (by the leader alone) can be made more rapidly and efficiently. But such an approach can generate resentment among followers and encounter difficulties with respect to actual implementation. A major task faced by leaders is selecting the specific decision-making approach that will maximize potential benefits but minimize potential costs. How can this be done?

According to the theory, leaders should attempt to select the best approach (or at least eliminate ones that are not useful) by answering several basic questions about the situation. These relate primarily to the *quality of the decision*—the extent to which it will affect important group processes such as communication or production—and to *acceptance of the decision* regarding the degree of commitment among subordinates needed for its implementation. For example, with respect to decision quality, a leader should ask questions such as: Is a high-quality decision required? Do I have enough information to make such a decision? Is the problem well structured? With respect to decision acceptance, he or she should ask: Is it crucial for effective implementation that subordinates accept the decision? Do subordinates share the organizational goals that will be reached through solution of this problem?

Normative decision theory claims that answering such questions and applying specific rules, such as those shown in Table 13.7, eliminate some of the potential approaches to reaching a given decision. Those that remain constitute a feasible set that can potentially be used to reach the necessary decision.

To simplify this process, theorists recommend using a decision tree such as the one shown in Figure 13.15. To apply this diagram, a leader begins on the left side and responds, in turn, to the questions listed under each letter (A, B, C, and so on). As the leader replies to each question, the set of feasible approaches narrows. For example, imagine that the leader's answers are as follows:

TABLE 13.7 DECISION RULES IN NORMATIVE DECISION THEORY

By applying the rules shown here, leaders can eliminate decision-making strategies that are likely to prove ineffective in a given situation and select those likely to be most effective.

RULES DESIGNED TO PROTECT DECISION QUALITY		RULES DESIGNED TO PROTECT DECISION ACCEPTANCE	
■ Leader Information Rule	If the quality of the decision is important and you do not have enough information or expertise to solve the problem alone, eliminate an autocratic style.	■ Acceptance Rule	If acceptance by subordinates is crucial for effective implementation, eliminate the autocratic styles.
■ Goal Congruence Rule	If the quality of the decision is important and subordinates are not likely to make the right decision, rule out the highly participative style.	■ Conflict Rule	If acceptance by subordinates is crucial for effective implementation and they hold conflicting opinions over the means of achieving some objective, eliminate autocratic styles.
■ Unstructured Problem Rule	If the quality of the decision is important but you lack sufficient information and expertise and the problem is unstructured, eliminate the autocratic leadership styles.	■ Fairness Rule	If the quality of the decision is unimportant but acceptance is important, use the most participatory style.
		■ Acceptance Priority Rule	If acceptance is critical and not certain to result from autocratic decisions and subordinates are not motivated to achieve the organization's goals, use a highly participative style.

do? Cha
in the fo

■ Anal
   ing y
■ Crea
   opm
■ Enco
   how

Coachi
recently
organiz

FIGURE
Path-Goal
According
among em
them read
employee:
tion. Such
encourage
sistent wi
of subordi
rience) an
ment (e.g
being per

- Question A: Yes—a high-quality decision is needed.
- Question B: No—the leader does not have sufficient information to make a high-quality decision alone.
- Question C: No—the problem is not structured.
- Question D: Yes—acceptance by subordinates is crucial to implementation.
- Question E: No—if the leader makes the decision alone, it may not be accepted by subordinates.
- Question F: No—subordinates do not share organizational goals.
- Question G: Yes—conflict among subordinates is likely to result from the decision.

As you can see, these replies lead to the conclusion that only one decision-making approach is feasible: full participation by subordinates. (The path leading to this conclusion is shown in the broken orange line in Figure 13.15.) Of course, different answers to any of the seven key questions would have led to different conclusions.

FIGURE 13.15
Normative Decision Theory: An Example
By answering the questions listed here and tracing a path through this decision tree, leaders can identify the most effective approaches to making decisions in a specific situation. Note: The path suggested by the answers to questions A through G (see above) is shown by the broken orange line.
(*Source:* Based on suggestions by Vroom & Yetton, 1973; see Note 73.)

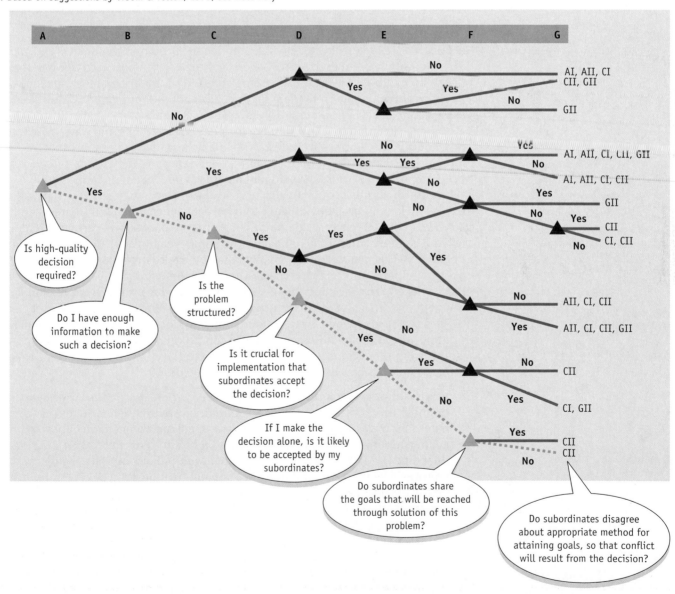

The normative decision model is highly appealing because it takes full account of the importance of subordinates' participation in decisions and offers leaders clear guidance for choosing among various methods for reaching decisions. As with any theory, though, the key question remains: Is it valid? Are its suggestions concerning the most effective style of decision making under various conditions really accurate? The results of several studies designed to test the model have been encouraging.

The latest version of the theory is more complex: Instead of seven contingency questions there are twelve, and instead of answering questions with a simple "yes" or "no," there are now five response options. This revised model is so highly complex that a computer program is used instead of a decision tree to help find the most appropriate leadership style. Preliminary evidence suggests that the resulting theory is more valid than the original, although it is far too complex to present here.

Whether we're talking about the more sophisticated version or the original version of normative decision theory, it is clear that this formulation makes an important contribution to our understanding of leadership. Insofar as there is widespread current interest in allowing subordinates to participate in decision making, normative decision theory is useful in giving leaders clear guidance as to when such a move may be expected to improve task performance.

Substitutes for Leadership: When Leaders Are Superfluous

Throughout this chapter, we have emphasized that leaders are important. Their style, actions, and degree of effectiveness all exert major effects on subordinates and, ultimately, on organizations. In many cases, this is certainly true. Yet, almost everyone has observed or been part of groups in which the designated leaders actually had little influence—groups in which these people were mere figureheads with little impact on subordinates. One explanation for such situations involves the characteristics of the leaders in question: They are simply weak and unsuited for their jobs. Another, and in some ways more intriguing, possibility is that in certain contexts, other factors actually may substitute for a leader's influence, making it superfluous, or neutralize the effects of the leader's influence. This has been proposed in what is known as the **substitutes for leadership** framework.[74]

According to this conceptualization, leadership may be irrelevant because various factors make it impossible for leaders to have any effect on subordinates—that is, they *neutralize* the effects of leadership. For example, people who are indifferent to the rewards a leader controls are unlikely to be influenced by them. The leader's influence is negated by this factor. Leadership also may be irrelevant because conditions make a leader's influence unnecessary. That is, various factors *substitute for* leadership. For example, leadership may be superfluous when individuals have a highly professional orientation and find their work to be intrinsically satisfying. When the leader's impact is either neutralized or substituted for by various conditions, his or her impact is limited, at best.

Specifically, many different variables can produce such effects. Thus, we may ask: Under what conditions are leaders expected to have limited impact on task performance? The answers fall into three different categories.

- Leadership may be unnecessary because of various *individual characteristics*. For example, a high level of knowledge, commitment, or experience on the part of subordinates may make it unnecessary for anyone to tell them what to do or how to proceed.
- Leadership may be unnecessary because *jobs may be structured in ways that make direction and influence from a leader redundant.* For example, highly routine jobs require little direction, and jobs that are highly interesting also require little in the way of outside leadership stimulation.
- Various *characteristics of organizations* may make leadership unnecessary. For example, various work norms and strong feelings of cohesion among employees may directly affect job performance and render the presence of a leader unnecessary. Similarly, the technology associated with certain jobs may determine the decisions and actions of people performing them and leave little room for input from a leader. (At the same time, advances in information technology have changed the nature of

leadership in today's fast-paced world. For a close-up look at this phenomenon, see the OB in an E-World section on page 502.)

Evidence for these assertions has been obtained in several studies.[79] For example, researchers examined the work performance and attitudes of a broad sample of workers who completed scales measuring their perceptions of the extent to which various leadership behaviors and substitutes for leadership were exhibited on their jobs.[80] Consistent with the conceptualization, it was found that job performance and attitudes were more strongly associated with the various substitutes than with the leadership behaviors themselves.

If leaders are superfluous in many situations, why has this fact often been overlooked? One possibility is that people have a strong tendency to *romanticize* leadership—that is, to perceive it as more important and more closely linked to performance in many contexts than it actually is.[81] Researchers testing this possibility presented M.B.A. students with detailed financial information about an imaginary firm, including a paragraph describing the firm's key operating strengths. The content of this paragraph was varied, so that four different groups of subjects received four different versions. These paragraphs attributed the firm's performance either to its leaders, the quality of its employees, changing patterns of consumer needs and preferences, or federal regulatory policies, respectively.

After reading one of these paragraphs and examining other general information about the firm, subjects rated two aspects of its overall performance—profitability and risk. It was reasoned that because of the tendency to overestimate the importance of leadership, subjects would rate the firm more favorably when its performance was attributed to its leaders than when it was attributed to any of the other factors. As you can see in Figure 13.16, this was precisely what occurred. The imaginary company was rated as higher in profitability and lower in risk when subjects had read the leadership-based paragraph than when they had read any of the others.

These findings, plus others, help explain why leaders are often viewed as important and necessary even when, to a large degree, they are superfluous. Note that this in no

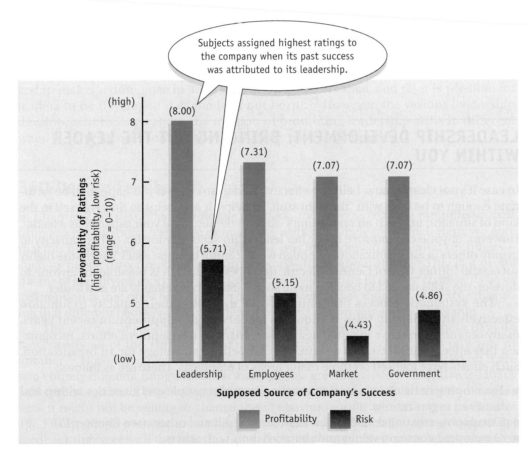

Subjects assigned highest ratings to the company when its past success was attributed to its leadership.

FIGURE 13.16

Overestimating the Importance of Leadership: Research Evidence
People who received information suggesting that an imaginary company's past success was attributable to its leaders rated the company more favorably (higher in profitability, lower in risk) than those who received information suggesting that the identical record resulted from other causes. These findings suggest that people *romanticize* leadership, overestimating its impact in many situations.
(*Source:* Based on data reported by Meindl & Ehrlich, 1987; see Note 81.)

In some organizations, being assigned a coach is seen as a remedial measure, a sign of weakness. In such cases, any benefits of coaching may be minimized because leaders fail to get involved in the process out of embarrassment. For this reason, organizations that use coaches are advised to provide these services to an entire executive group, thereby removing any stigma associated with coaching and putting all leaders on an equal footing. Research has found that executive coaching is particularly effective when it is used following a formal training program. In fact, the customized, one-on-one coaching provided after a standardized training program has been found to increase leaders' productivity by as much as 88 percent.[90]

Mentoring

In Chapter 5 we discussed how minority group members stand to benefit by having relationships with *mentors*, more senior associates who help show them the ropes. Again, in Chapter 7, we described the formal process of mentoring, in which employees receive help, either formally or informally, from more experienced colleagues in the organization as a means of helping them develop their careers. (Mentors also may come from outside the organization, but such relationships are more likely to take the form of coaching.) Although mentoring is unlikely to include a formal assessment of a leader's strengths and limitations, it is inclined to be focused on personal and professional support. Recent research shows that officials from a wide array of organizations consider mentoring one of the most effective forms of leadership development they have in place.[91]

A potential problem with mentoring (as we noted in Chapter 7) is that protégés may become so highly connected to their mentors that they fail to think independently. When this occurs, what a protégé does is precisely what the mentor would have done. Although this can be beneficial, it is also potentially quite limiting, leading to a narrowness of thought. This problem is especially likely to occur in the case of executive coaching because protégés making important decisions may fear straying from the tried-and-true solutions of their mentors. As a result, the organization is denied any fresh new perspective that the less seasoned executive might be able to provide. Clearly, although mentoring can be a beneficial leadership development technique, it is not without limitations.

Job Assignments

When it comes to leadership, the phrase "experience is the best teacher" seems to hold true. Indeed, one of the most effective ways of training leaders is by assigning them to positions that promise to give them needed experience.

With this in mind, several companies intentionally assign personnel to other countries so they can broaden their experiences. For example, the Coca-Cola Company recently transferred over 300 professional and managerial employees from the United States to facilities in other countries for one year in an effort to develop their skills before returning them home to assume new positions of leadership. Gillette International does the same thing on a regular basis, assigning prospective leaders to positions at foreign affiliates for periods of one to three years. In many ways, this may be thought of as developing baseball players by sending them to the minor leagues. Likewise, teams from the National Football League are able to develop their players by sending them to compete in NFL Europe teams.

For job assignments to serve their developmental function, it is necessary for the newly assigned positions to provide the kind of opportunities that make learning possible. Ideally, the new positions are ones that give newly developing leaders opportunities to try out different approaches to leadership so they can see what works for them. In other words, they should have the latitude to try different approaches, even if they fail. It is important to keep in mind that the purpose of the job assignment is to facilitate learning, in which case failure is inevitable. However, should an emphasis be placed on job performance instead, it's unlikely that the new assignment will have the intended benefits and is destined to be looked upon unfavorably.

Action Learning

Traditionally, much of the learning that takes place when people learn to lead occurs in the classroom. The problem with this approach, however, is that shortly after the formal training sessions are over, people revert back to their old ways, resulting in little if any developmental progress. To combat this problem, many organizations have been turning to **action learning,** which is a continuous process of learning and reflection that is supported by colleagues and that emphasizes getting things done.[92] The underlying assumption of action learning is that leaders develop most effectively when they are working on real organizational problems.[93]

Citibank used action learning to help develop its leaders, who were having difficulty thinking about problems from a broad perspective.[94] Specifically, the following steps were taken.

1. The issues to be worked on were selected by heads of business units. These had to be ones that affected total Citibank performance.
2. Participants were selected from throughout the world based on a thorough review of their talents.
3. A three-day orientation session was held off-site in which team-building skills were practiced (as discussed in Chapter 8).
4. For two to three weeks, data were collected about effective banking practices from both inside and outside Citibank.
5. These findings were analyzed systematically and from them, recommendations were developed.
6. Findings were presented to area heads and the CEO in 90-minute meetings.
7. A one-day debriefing session was held with a coach. These sessions focused on the recommendations, team processes, and individual development opportunities.
8. One to two weeks later, senior managers followed up and made decisions regarding the various recommendations.

Although the business imperatives that drive action learning are often different, this basic process is generally quite similar. Action learning has been used not only at Citibank, but also at such organizations as General Electric (to develop new markets), ARAMARK (to promote cross-cultural opportunities), Shell Oil (to alter perceptions of the company's financial strength), and even the U.S. Army (to share lessons from battlefield experiences).[95] Because action learning is a general idea that takes different forms in different organizations, its effectiveness has been difficult to assess. However, available research generally confirms the effectiveness of training leaders by using the kind of active approaches described here instead of more passive, classroom training (see also our discussion of the factors that make training effective in Chapter 2).

action learning
A leadership development technique involving a continuous process of learning and reflection that is supported by colleagues and that emphasizes getting things done.

SUMMARY AND REVIEW OF LEARNING OBJECTIVES

1. Describe the trait approach to leadership and identify the characteristics that distinguish successful leaders from ordinary people.
The trait approach to leadership, referred to as the great person theory, claims that successful leaders have characteristics that set them apart from other people. Such individuals tend to be higher in leadership motivation (i.e., the desire to be a leader), drive, honesty, self-confidence, and several other traits. Successful leaders also tend to have multiple sources of intelligence (e.g., cognitive intelligence, emotional intelligence, and cultural intelligence) and demonstrate high amounts of flexibility—that is, the ability to adapt their style to the followers' needs and to the requirements of specific situations.

2. Distinguish between the two basic forms of leader behavior: person-oriented behavior and production-oriented behavior, explaining, how grid training helps develop them.

Leaders differ with respect to the extent to which they focus on efforts to attain successful task performance—known as initiating structure (or being task oriented)—and their concern with maintaining favorable personal relations with subordinates—known as consideration (or being person oriented). Grid training is a systematic way of training managers to raise their concern for people as well as their concern for production (by training them in communication skills and planning skills).

3. Explain what the leader–member exchange (LMX) model and the attributional approach to leadership say about the relationships between leaders and followers.

The leader–member exchange (LMX) model specifies that leaders favor members of some groups, referred to as *in-groups,* more than others that are referred to as *out-groups.* As a result, in-groups tend to perform better than out-groups. The relationship between leaders and followers is also the focus of the attributional approach to leadership. This approach focuses on leaders' assessments of the underlying causes of followers' performance. Specifically, when leaders perceive that their subordinates' poor performance is caused by internal factors, they react by helping him or her to improve. However, when poor performance is attributed to external sources; leaders direct their attention toward changing aspects of the work environment believed to be responsible for the poor performance.

4. Describe the nature of charismatic leadership and how it compares to transformational leadership.

Charismatic leaders exert profound effects on the beliefs, perceptions, and actions of their followers. Such individuals have a special relationship with their followers in which they inspire exceptionally high levels of performance, loyalty, and enthusiasm. Charismatic leaders tend to have high amounts of self-confidence, present a clearly articulated vision, behave in extraordinary ways, are recognized as change agents, and are sensitive to the environmental constraints they face. In addition to being charismatic, transformational leaders also do things that transform and revitalize their organizations. They provide intellectual stimulation, individualized consideration, and inspirational motivation. Transformational leaders tend to be very effective.

5. Summarize what LPC contingency theory and situational leadership theory say about the connection between leadership style and situational variables.

LPC contingency theory suggests that a leader's characteristics in conjunction with various situational factors determine his or her group's effectiveness. Task-oriented leaders (termed low LPC leaders) are more effective than people-oriented leaders (termed high LPC leaders) under conditions in which the leader has either high or low control over the group in question. In contrast, people-oriented leaders are more effective under conditions in which the leader has moderate control. The situational leadership theory suggests that the most effective style of leadership—delegating, participating, selling, or telling—depends on the extent to which followers require guidance, direction, and emotional support. Effective leaders are required to diagnose the situations they face and implement the appropriate behavioral style for that situation.

6. Describe various techniques used to develop leadership in organizations.

One popular technique of leadership development, 360-degree feedback, involves giving people multiple sources of feedback about their strengths and weaknesses. Networking, another technique, is aimed at helping leaders learn to whom they should turn for information, both inside and outside their organization. Executive coaching is a one-on-one experience in which a leader is given an integrative assessment of his or her strengths and weaknesses. Leadership development also involves giving people special job assignments that allow them to develop new skills. Finally, action learning is a leadership development technique in which people get to learn by experiencing real organizational problems.

Questions for Review

1. What is the difference between leadership and management? And what are the characteristics that distinguish successful leaders from ordinary managers?
2. What is the difference between person-oriented leadership and production-oriented leadership?
3. How are the relationships between leaders and followers explained by the LMX model and the attribution approach to leadership? Also, what assumptions must be made about the relationships between leaders and followers when leading work teams?
4. What makes charismatic leaders and transformational leaders so special in organizations?
5. What are the basic assumptions of contingency theories of leadership? What particular theories fall into this category?
6. What is meant by "leadership development," and what techniques are used to bring it about?

Experiential Questions

1. Do you know anyone whom you consider to be a charismatic leader or a transformational leader? If so, what is this person like? What has this individual done that suggests that he or she is so special?
2. Think about the leaders of teams in which you have worked and how they compare to the leaders of other groups that do not operate as teams. In what ways do these leaders behave similarly or differently?
3. Have you ever participated in a leadership development program? If so, what exactly was done? In what ways was the program effective or ineffective?

Questions to Analyze

1. As we noted, the lines between leading and managing sometimes are blurred in practice. What factors (e.g., technology, the economy, etc.) do you believe are responsible for making this distinction so vague?
2. As technology advances further in the years to come, how do you think the nature of leadership in work organizations is likely to change?
3. What techniques of leadership development do you believe would be most effective in the company in which you work? Also, what do you see as the major impediments to the effectiveness of leadership development?

DEVELOPING OB SKILLS

INDIVIDUAL EXERCISE

Determining Your Leadership Style

As noted on pages 493–494, *situational leadership theory* identifies four basic leadership styles. To be able to identify and enact the most appropriate style of leadership in any given situation, it is first useful to understand the style to which you are most predisposed. This exercise will help you gain such insight into your own leadership style.

Directions

Following are eight hypothetical situations in which you have to make a decision affecting you and members of your work group. For each, indicate which of the following actions you are most likely to take by writing the letter corresponding to that action in the space provided.

3. Do you think that these conditions might exist in his company? If not, how might they be created?

Chan Suh: Not Your Typical Advertising Executive—Yet

You see them all the time when you visit Web sites—those flashy banner ads beckoning for your attention with catchy text and animated graphics. Although you probably never think much about how they get there, that's the main thought running through Chan Suh's head these days. Suh, a 40-year-old Korean native who moved to New York with his mother in 1976, is the founder and CEO of Agency.com, one of the largest interactive, online ad agencies around these days.

Although interactive advertising comprises only about 1 percent of the $200 billion advertising market, its potential is enormous. In 1998 alone, the four-year-old Agency.com quadrupled in size as sales zoomed from $18 million to $80 million. Its client list, including 3M, DIRECTV, Gucci, Land Rover, Saab, the Olive Garden, and Visa, would be the envy of any of the traditional Big Six advertising agencies. Unlike these firms, however, Agency.com is not populated by slick executives in tailored suits luxuriating in the wood-paneled suites of New York City high-rises. Instead, Agency.com's casually attired, body-pierced twenty-somethings work in a poorly ventilated room over the loading dock in Manhattan's Time-Life building.

Suh considers himself fortunate to have not only the 600 talented people who make up the company but also the space itself—his major first business asset. Although bankers just laughed at his business plan in 1995, Suh was determined to launch his agency. So, cashing in on the goodwill he developed with his former employer, Time-Life (for whom he earlier developed *Vibe* online before venturing out on his own), Suh struck a deal in which he got the space in exchange for completing several projects. One of these was the highly regarded Web site for the 1995 *Sports Illustrated* swimsuit edition video. On the strength of his successful experiences with Time, Suh was able to attract more blue-chip clients, for whom he struck gold. The Web site Agency.com developed for MetLife, for example, grew in popularity from 300,000 hits in 1996 to over 4 million hits in 1997. This Web site was only one of over two dozen for which the company won awards for various clients in 1998 (including a prestigious Clio for Pacific Bell). In 2001 alone, Agency.com won 15 prestigious awards for its various Web designs.

For Agency.com to continue to grow—or even to survive the inevitable shakeout that's forthcoming in the interactive advertising business—Suh realizes that his company will have to double in the coming months. And with offices now extending beyond New York—including Boston, Chicago, Dallas, San Francisco, London, Amsterdam, Paris, and his native home, Seoul, Korea—the company's reach has broadened dramatically. Importantly, as clients grow more sophisticated, they are moving from being knocked out by the novel, whiz-bang technology to the stage where they now are demanding results—a return on their advertising investments. Suh knows that this will keep him busy hiring the most talented and creative people he can find—individuals who share his vision for taking technology to places where no advertising agency has ever been before.

It's having a vision and chasing it that keeps Chan Suh navigating these uncharted waters. After all, only a true visionary and pioneer would say, "We love the fact that we get to invent the future while we live in it." If Suh's vision even comes close to being as accurate as it has been, there's every indication that he easily will reach the goal of making Agency.com a $1 billion company. Based on recent figures, he appears to be well on his way.

Critical Thinking Questions

1. What special qualities make Chan Suh so effective as a leader?
2. Would you say that Chan Suh is a charismatic leader or a transformational leader?
3. What challenges do you believe Agency.com is likely to face in the next few years?

Organizational Culture, Creativity, and Innovation

14

LEARNING OBJECTIVES

After reading this chapter, you should be able to:
1. Define organizational culture and identify the various functions it serves in organizations.
2. Describe the four types of organizational culture identified by the double S cube.
3. Identify the factors responsible for creating and transmitting organizational culture and for getting it to change.
4. Define creativity and describe the basic components of individual and team creativity.
5. Describe various approaches to promoting creativity in organizations.
6. Identify the basic components of innovation and the various stages of the innovation process.

■ PREVIEW CASE
SULLIVAN PARK: WHERE CORNING INVENTS THE FUTURE

To look at Corning, Inc.'s seven-building Sullivan Park complex nestled atop a hill in upstate New York, you'd never imagine that inside 1,200 scientists and technicians work at what they immodestly regard as "inventing the future." It's not Corning's freezer-to-oven-to-table Pyrex cookware that occupies these experts, but the development of optical fiber—tiny threads of pulled glass the width of a human hair and clearer than the air around you. These strands are woven into cables through which 400 billion pulses of light pass per second, enabling millions of telephone conversations and Internet transmissions to be carried over long distances with perfect clarity.

> They don't simply *want* to come up with exciting new ideas, they *must* do so to keep the company alive.

   Although Corning is the dominant manufacturer of products such as optical fiber and LCD computer screens, don't expect to see the company pursuing these lines in the years to come. The explanation rests in Corning's fundamental business strategy, which accounts for why the 150-year-old company is constantly inventing the future. Corning scientists invent special glass-based materials along with ways of producing them. Other companies then copy what Corning has done and put it out of that particular business, leaving Corning to reinvent itself. For example, along with Thomas Edison, Corning developed the first mass-produced glass lightbulb, although it is no longer in that business. This philosophy is passed down from one generation of Corning scientists to the next, making it part of corporate culture: They don't simply *want* to come up with exciting new ideas, they *must* do so to keep the company alive.

Making this possible, as you might imagine, requires people who are incredibly creative. Indeed, creativity is the keystone of Corning's culture; the company attracts scientists who relish working on new ideas and it gives them the materials and equipment needed to turn this into reality. What drives the scientists at Corning is not that their inventions stand to make lots of money for the company (although they do!), but that they stand to revolutionize the world. To accomplish this, the scientists are given considerable leeway to champion their ideas. Although they generally are free to work on projects of their own choosing (even if it takes two decades, as in the case of optical fiber), Corning scientists ultimately must have a commercially viable product to show for their time. Helping keep the company's future alive, almost 80 percent of Corning's sales currently come from products that are under four years old.

Profits from these sales are essential given that they generate the funds needed to make future research and development efforts possible. And indeed, Corning has been profitable. The company's annual sales have been around $5 billion in recent years and are projected to rise at a staggering 30 percent a year—figures suggesting that Corning's approach to developing innovative new products is paying off handsomely.

T here can be no doubt that the scientists and technicians who work at the Sullivan Park laboratory bring an enormous amount of *creativity* and talent to the process of developing products from glass. At the same time, it is not only their creativity as individuals that makes Corning so successful, but also the company's commitment to *innovation*. To be sure, there is something special about Corning that makes its scientists willing to develop important new products. This special something is not a chemical concoction developed in the Sullivan Park labs, but the product of effective management. That is, the scientists are treated in ways that make them want to succeed and that enable them to do so—and, quite regularly, at that. In this way, Corning is certainly unique.

If you have worked in several different organizations, it's probably been your experience that each is unique in one way or another. Even organizations concerned with the same activities or that provide similar products or services can be very different from one another. For example, in the world of retailing, Wal-Mart employees long have been encouraged to be agents for the customer, focusing on service and satisfaction.[1] By contrast, over the years, employees of Sears Roebuck & Co. allegedly have been pressured into meeting sales quotas and pushing customers to make unnecessary purchases.[2] Both are national chains selling a large variety of goods. Somehow these similar businesses have taken very different approaches to customer service. Why is this so? To a great extent, the answer rests in the shared beliefs, expectations, and core values of people in the organization—what is known as *organizational culture*.[3] Once established, these beliefs, expectations, and values tend to be relatively stable and exert strong influences on organizations and those working in them.

Among these influences lies a particularly important one—an organization's tendency toward *creativity* and *innovation*. As you know, some people regularly take novel, ingenious, and cutting-edge approaches to the problems they face. Likewise, some organizations—Corning, for example—are far more innovative than others. It's unlikely that people in one organization, by chance alone, will just happen to be more creative than people in another. Indeed, companies such as 3M, BMW, Gillette, and Rubbermaid go out of their way to breed the kind of cultures in which creativity and innovation flourish (see Figure 14.1).[4]

What makes these companies—and others like them—the kinds of places where people routinely do the nonroutine? This question, concerning the culture of creativity and innovation, is the focus of this chapter. We will begin by describing the basic nature of organizational culture, including the role it plays in organizations. Then we will describe the processes through which organizational culture is formed and maintained.

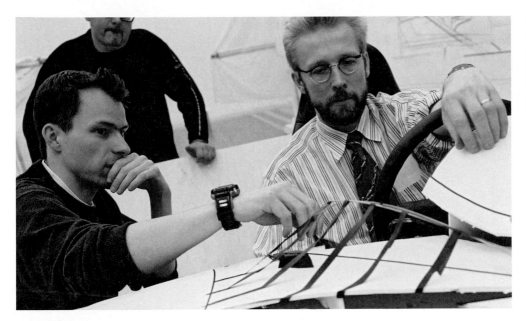

FIGURE 14.1
BMW: A Driving Passion for Creativity
Automotive designers at BMW's research and development campus in Munich, Germany, strive to create cars they regard to be "moving works of art." To help accomplish this mission, Chris Bangle, BMW's global chief of design, shields his creative team from any unproductive comments of others that might be made.

Following this, we will review the effects of organizational culture on individual and organizational functioning, examining when and how culture is subject to change. This discussion will prepare us for understanding the nature of creativity and innovation in organizations, the major topic covered in the second half of this chapter. Our focus will move from consideration of what makes individuals and teams creative to how this creativity can be harnessed to implement innovative ideas in organizations.

THE BASIC NATURE OF ORGANIZATIONAL CULTURE

To fully appreciate organizational culture we have to understand its basic nature. With this in mind, we now will examine three key aspects of culture: (1) its basic characteristics, (2) whether there is generally only one or more than one culture within organizations, and (3) the role that culture plays in organizational functioning.

Organizational Culture: A Definition and Core Characteristics

Although we have been talking about organizational culture in general terms thus far, a specific definition is now in order. Accordingly, we define **organizational culture** as a cognitive framework consisting of attitudes, values, behavioral norms, and expectations shared by organization members.[5] At the root of any organization's culture is a set of core characteristics that is valued collectively by members of an organization (see Table 14.1).[6]

organizational culture
A cognitive framework consisting of attitudes, values, behavioral norms, and expectations shared by organization members.

TABLE 14.1 CORE ORGANIZATIONAL VALUES REFLECTED IN CULTURE

Organizations may be distinguished by their basic values, such as the fundamental ones summarized here.

- Sensitivity to the needs of customers and employees.
- Interest in having employees generate new ideas.
- Willingness to take risks.
- The value placed on people.
- Openness of available communication options.
- Friendliness and congeniality of the employees toward one another.

(*Source:* Based on suggestions by Martin, 1996; see Note 6.)

OB IN AN E-WORLD
TODAY, HIGH-TECH START-UPS FILL THE SPIRIT RATHER THAN THE BANK ACCOUNT

Only a few years ago, the most talented computer programmers, analysts, and executives were lured to jobs in high-tech start-up companies by lavish signing bonuses, such as BMWs, and the promise of stock options that would allow them to get rich quick. Today, however, the party's over. The dreams of overnight wealth that once made positions at dot-com companies so appealing at the end of the twentieth century have faded now that many such enterprises have gone bust. High-tech start-ups are still around, to be sure, but the culture of excess that once prevailed in such firms has given way to one that is, shall we say, far more basic.

To attract and retain the best brains in the business, today's high-tech firms continue to be nontraditional in their culture, but in ways that are decidedly holistic and nurturing of the human spirit—a far cry from the expensive trips and lavish lunches that once prevailed. Cultures that promote the freedom to nurture one's soul are far more typical in today's high-tech firms. For example, at Ninth House Network, a San Francisco–based firm specializing in interactive online training in business

Sensitivity to the needs of customers and employees. Years ago, the culture at UPS was relatively rigid and inflexible with respect to customer needs. They operated however they thought best and forced customers to adjust to their ways. Today, however, a new culture is in place in which customer service and satisfaction are highly valued. UPS now strives to suit the needs of its customers; the culture is such that changes are driven by opportunities to better serve customers.[7]

Interest in having employees generate new ideas. Walt Disney Co. employees—or, "cast members," as they are called—undergo lengthy orientation programs to ensure that they know exactly what to say and how to behave toward guests.[8] For the most part, their behavior is scripted. By contrast, people working at MCI are encouraged to be unique and to bring fresh ideas to their work. In fact, company founder Bill McGowan is so adamant about this that procedure manuals are nowhere to be found at MCI.[9]

Willingness to take risks. At some companies, such as the Bank of America, the culture is very conservative, and employees make only the safest investments. In contrast, buyers at The Limited are discouraged from making too many "safe" choices. Taking risks in the purchasing of fashion merchandise is valued.[10]

The value placed on people. Some companies consider their employees as valuable only insofar as they contribute to production, much as they view machinery. Such organizations, where people do not feel valued, are considered to have **toxic organizational cultures.** A recent survey found that 48 percent of people believe they work in toxic cultures.[11] Organizations with toxic cultures tend to lose good employees and struggle to be profitable as a result. By contrast, organizations that treat people well—said to have **healthy organizational cultures**—tend to have very low turnover and generally thrive.[12] Examples of companies with healthy cultures include Enterprise Rent-A-Car, the Men's Wearhouse, and the Container Store (see Figure 14.2).[13]

Openness of available communication options. In some companies such as Yahoo!, the popular Internet media company, employees are expected to make decisions freely and to communicate with whoever is needed to get the job done—even if it means going directly to CEO Timothy A. Koogle.[14] At IBM, however, the tradition has been to work

toxic organizational cultures
Organizational cultures in which people feel that they are not valued (opposite of healthy organizational cultures).

healthy organizational cultures
Organizational cultures in which people feel that they are valued (opposite of toxic organizational cultures).

skills, employees are permitted to bring their dogs to work. In fact, a recent survey found that dogs have their day in as many as 8 percent of today's dot-com companies—at least so long as they remain well behaved.[18] When not playing with their dogs, Ninth House employees also are free to seek refuge in an incense-filled, candlelit room. Although unorthodox, the idea is that this provides a place to where employees can escape when they yearn to get out of their cubicles and think about things.

In addition to Zen-like experiences, companies like Google, the highly regarded Internet search engine, have found it useful to promote a caring culture by having employees break bread together—literally. Google's director of technology, Craig Silverstein, regularly rides around the company's Mountain View, California, headquarters on a motorized scooter delivering loaves of his homemade bread to his coworkers. The culture is free, and this keeps channels of communication far more open than is typical at traditional companies with more formal cultures. Officials, such as Chairman and CEO Eric E. Schmidt, are convinced that Google's culture is responsible for its many accolades, including a 2001 Webby Award for best practices.

The key to the success of good-for-the-soul corporate cultures, according to Mark Goldstein, CEO of BlueLight.com, the online arm of Kmart, is that they help employees reach their creative potential by celebrating their individualism and helping them connect with themselves. And, in an environment in which 28 percent of Silicon Valley workers plan to move on to a new company next year, having an appealing culture is an essential ingredient in the recipe for retaining the best and the brightest.[19]

within the proper communication channels and to vest power in the hands of only a few key individuals, although this has been changing in recent years.[15]

Friendliness and congeniality of the employees toward one another. At some companies, such as Nokia Corp., the employees tend to get along well. Friendships tend to run deep, and employees see each other outside of work.[16] At the toy maker, Mattel, however, the culture is far more cutthroat and competitive.[17] As we chronicle in the OB in an E-World section above, having a highly collegial culture helps many high-tech companies retain their employees.

FIGURE 14.2

The Container Store: A Healthy Organizational Culture
Considered one of the best companies to work for in the United States by *Fortune* magazine, employees of the Container Store enjoy a healthy organizational culture. The vast majority are so enthusiastic about how strongly people care about each other that they recommend the company as a place for their friends to work. Trust in management, pride in work, and friendly relations contribute to the Container Store's healthy culture.

Cultures Within Organizations: One or Many?

Our discussion thus far has implied that each organization has only a single, uniform culture—one set of shared values, beliefs, and expectations. In fact, this is rarely the case. Instead, organizations, particularly large ones, typically have *several* cultures operating within them.

People generally have attitudes and values that are more in common with others in their own fields or work units than they do with those in other fields or other parts of the organization. These various groups may be said to have several different **subcultures**—cultures existing within parts of organizations rather than entirely throughout them. These typically are distinguished with respect to either functional differences (i.e., the type of work done) or geographic distances (i.e., the physical separation between people). Indeed, research suggests that several subcultures based on occupational, professional, or functional divisions usually exist within any large organization.

This is not to say, however, that there also may not be a **dominant culture,** a distinctive, overarching "personality" of an organization—the kind of culture to which we have been referring. An organization's dominant culture reflects its core values, dominant perceptions that are generally shared throughout the organization. Typically, members of subcultures, who generally share additional sets of values, also accept the core values of their organizations as a whole. Thus, subcultures should not be thought of as a bunch of totally separate cultures but, rather, as "mini" cultures operating within a larger, dominant culture.

The Role of Culture in Organizations

As you read about the various cultural values that make organizations special, it probably strikes you that culture is an intangible force—albeit, one with far-reaching consequences. Indeed, culture plays several important roles in organizations.

Culture provides a sense of identity. The more clearly an organization's shared perceptions and values are defined, the more strongly people can associate with their organization's mission and feel a vital part of it. For example, employees at Southwest Airlines feel special because of their company's emphasis on having fun and joking around on the job, a widespread practice initiated by founder Herb Kelleher.[20] Southwest's employees feel strongly associated with the company—that they belong there. As a result, they only infrequently resign to take other positions in the airline industry.

Culture generates commitment to the organization's mission. Sometimes it's difficult for people to go beyond thinking of their own interests (i.e, how will this affect me?). When there is a strong, overarching culture, however, people feel that they are part of that larger, well-defined whole and are involved in the entire organization's work. Bigger than any one individual's interests, culture reminds people of what their organization is all about.

Culture clarifies and reinforces standards of behavior. Culture guides employees' words and deeds, making it clear what they should do or say in a given situation, which is especially useful to newcomers. In this sense, culture provides stability to behavior, both with respect to what an individual might do at different times and also what different individuals may do at the same time. For example, in a company with a culture that strongly supports customer satisfaction, employees will have clear guidance as to how they are expected to behave: doing whatever it takes to please the customer. By serving these three important roles, it is clear that culture is an important force influencing behavior in organizations (for a summary, see Figure 14.3).

IDENTIFYING ORGANIZATIONAL CULTURES: THE DOUBLE S CUBE

As you might imagine, the culture of any organization can be described in many ways. To understand and to compare organizational cultures, however, it helps to have a sys-

subcultures
Cultures existing within parts of organizations rather than entirely throughout them.

dominant culture
The distinctive, overarching "personality" of an organization.

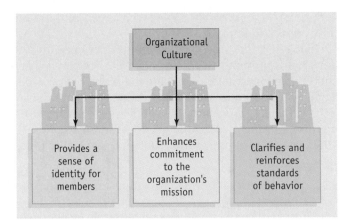

FIGURE 14.3
**The Basic Functions
of Organizational Culture**
Organizational culture serves the three
major functions summarized here.

tematic way to organize them. Recently, scientists have developed a very useful system for doing this.[21] We will describe this system here.

Two Underlying Dimensions of Organizational Culture

The system for categorizing varieties of organizational culture is known as the **double S cube**, and it is summarized in Figure 14.4. The name comes from the fact that the approach characterizes organizational culture along two independent dimensions, both of which begin with the letter *s*—*sociability* and *solidarity*.

By combining high and low amounts of these two dimensions, four basic types of organizational culture can be identified, as indicated by the large square (containing the four smaller squares) at the front of the diagram. Then, recognizing that each of the four resulting types of organizational culture has both positive and negative qualities, a third dimension is added, extending the square into a cube. We will now describe the two basic dimensions on which the four types of culture are based.

The sociability dimension. The first dimension, **sociability,** is as it sounds—a measure of the friendliness of members of the organization. Among the first things a new employee notices about a company is its degree of sociability. Some are very friendly and have people who always socialize and go out together (high sociability). Others, by

double S cube
A system of categorizing four types of organizational culture by combining two dimensions—*sociability* and *solidarity*. Each of the four resulting cultural types—*networked culture, mercenary culture, fragmented culture,* and *communal culture*—can be both positive and negative in nature.

sociability
A dimension of the *double S cube* characterized by the degree of friendliness typically found among members of an organization.

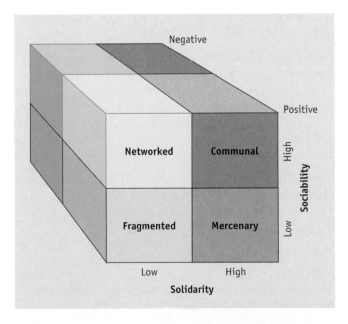

FIGURE 14.4
The Double S Cube
According to the *double S cube* of organizational culture, four types of organizational culture may be identified by combining two key dimensions—*sociability* and *solidarity*. Each of the four types of culture has both positive and negative aspects associated with it.
(*Source:* "Double S Cube" from *The character of a corporation* by Rob Goffee and Gareth Jones. Copyright © 1998 by Rob Goffee and Gareth Jones. Reproduced by permission of HarperCollins Publishers, Inc.)

contrast, are composed of people who largely refrain from socializing and stick to themselves (low sociability).

Sociability has both a positive side and a negative side. On the positive side, sociability helps promote creativity because it encourages people to work together in teams and to share information, making them open to new ideas.[22] On the negative side, high degrees of sociability can cause workers to form informal cliques that can become so influential as to subvert the usual decision-making process. In keeping with this idea, members of highly sociable groups may be reluctant to disagree and criticize each other, possibly leading to the problem of groupthink (described in Chapter 10).

solidarity
A dimension of the *double S cube* characterized by the degree to which people in an organization share a common understanding of the tasks and goals about which they are working.

The solidarity dimension. The second dimension of organizational culture, **solidarity**, focuses on the extent to which coworkers share a common understanding of their organization's tasks and goals. Police officers in pursuit of a criminal and surgeons at an operating table have a high degree of solidarity because they tend to stick together in a highly focused way to accomplish an agreed-upon goal. Many times, however, people work together on tasks but share little common focus. Such a low-solidarity group may be seen whenever a committee is composed of individuals who have little interest in working on the topic at hand.

It's easy to imagine how high degrees of solidarity can be beneficial when it comes to getting an important job done. The police officers who come to each other's aid and the members of the surgical team who coordinate their efforts are capable of accomplishing a great deal because of their solidarity. At the same time, however, high solidarity can be painful to anyone who is not part of the team. Just imagine, for example, how difficult things might be for a rookie police officer on a squad of veterans who all work together like the gears of a finely tuned clock. The newcomer might feel excluded and wonder if he or she will ever "fit in."

Four Organizational Cultures

By combining high and low levels of both sociability and solidarity, we can identify four basic types of organizational culture.[23] Each of these is identified in Figure 14.4, and we also describe them here.

networked culture
In the *double S cube,* this type of organizational culture is characterized by high levels of sociability and low levels of solidarity.

Networked culture. Starting in the upper-left corner of Figure 14.4, we find the **networked culture.** This type of organizational culture is characterized by high levels of sociability and low levels of solidarity. Networked cultures are extremely friendly and lighthearted in style. People tend to keep their doors open, talk about business in a casual, informal manner, and spend a great deal of time socializing—and without getting into trouble because of it. In networked cultures, people generally get to know each other quickly and feel that they are part of the group.

mercenary culture
In the *double S cube,* this type of organizational culture is characterized by a low degree of sociability and a high degree of solidarity.

Mercenary culture. At the opposite extreme, in the lower-right corner of Figure 14.4 is the **mercenary culture.** This organizational culture is characterized by a low degree of sociability and a high degree of solidarity. Mercenary cultures involve people who are highly focused on pulling together to get the job done. Communication tends to be swift, direct, and handled in a no-nonsense way. A businesslike manner predominates, and idle chatter is not tolerated because it is considered a waste of time. Winning is considered everything, and people are encouraged to put in whatever time is necessary to make that happen.

fragmented culture
In the *double S cube,* this type of organizational culture is characterized by a low degree of sociability and a low degree of solidarity.

Fragmented culture. In the lower-left corner of Figure 14.4 is the **fragmented culture.** This organizational culture is characterized by low solidarity and low sociability. People working in fragmented cultures are likely to have little contact with their associates, and in many cases, they may not even know each other. Although employees will talk to others when it is considered necessary or useful to do so, people generally leave each other alone. In fact, people will go to the office only when they feel it is absolutely necessary; absence is common. Not surprisingly, members of fragmented cultures do not identify with the organization in which they work. Instead, they tend to identify with the profession of which they are a part.

FIGURE 14.5
Communal Cultures Predominate Among Internet Start-Ups
Howard Gordon (left) and Steve Stanford created Icebox.com to bring together accomplished writers and producers to do the TV shows they always wanted to do and to broadcast them online. Their mission is to allow talented people to roll up their sleeves and to enjoy the creative process without having to worry about corporate middlemen. In this Internet start-up, as in many others, a highly communal culture prevails.

Communal culture. Finally, in the upper-right corner of Figure 14.4, we find the **communal culture.** This is characterized by both high sociability and high solidarity. Members of communal cultures are very friendly to each other and get along well, both personally and professionally. Communal cultures widely exist within many high-tech companies, particularly Internet start-ups (see Figure 14.5). Because individuals in such organizations tend to share so many things, it's often difficult to determine who is assigned to a particular office. Communication flows very easily—across people at all levels of the organization and in all formats. Everyone is so friendly that the distinction between work and nonwork is often blurred in practice. Employees strongly identify with communal organizations. They wear the company logo, they live the company credo, and they staunchly support the organization when talking about it to outsiders.

communal culture
In the *double S cube,* this type of organizational culture is characterized by both a high degree of sociability and a high degree of solidarity.

Interpreting Organizational Culture

To assess systematically people's perceptions of their organization's culture using the double S cube, large numbers of employees complete a questionnaire containing questions used to assess sociability and solidarity similar to the ones shown in Table 14.2. Items such as these may be helpful in identifying which type of culture people believe their organization possesses, but it is important to keep three key points in mind once you have this information.

1. *Companies contain not one, but several cultures.* As we said earlier, an organization may have one dominant culture and several distinct subcultures. Any one individual completing a questionnaire can tell you only about his or her personal experiences, which are likely to be limited.
2. *Organizational cultures tend to change over time.* A new company is likely to be small and friendly—that is, communal—but, as it goes through various ups and downs, its culture may be expected to change as well. In other words, organizational culture is not fixed, but fluid. This may be likened to a family. If you consider how the dynamics of your family may have changed over the years (as relationships change and as people and conditions change, such as when new children are born or when older ones leave the house), you can appreciate how the culture of an organization also is likely to change.
3. *No one culture is necessarily better or worse than any other.* Is any one culture better than another? The answer is "no." As we said earlier, all cultures have both positive and negative sides. Interestingly, some organizations are successful even when they have particular cultures that may be completely inappropriate in other companies.

TABLE 14.2 ASSESSING ORGANIZATIONAL CULTURE

Questions similar to these are used to assess the *sociability* and the *solidarity* dimensions of organizational culture. Responses take the form of indicating (on a scale ranging from 1 to 5) the extent to which the respondent agrees with each statement, with higher scores reflecting greater agreement.

The more you agree with these statements, the higher is your score with respect to . . .

SOCIABILITY	SOLIDARITY
■ Where I work, the people like each other a great deal.	■ The people in my company know their goals very clearly.
■ In my company, people generally get along very well.	■ At work, we give and get very strong guidelines about what to do.
■ At work, we do small favors for each other.	■ If someone performs poorly, we deal with it at once.
■ On the job, we make friends just because we want to; there is no other agenda.	■ Where I work, being successful is the most important thing.
■ We look out for each other on the job.	■ Every project we start, we also complete; nothing is left hanging.

(*Source:* Based on material in Goffee and Jones, 1998; see Note 21.)

The trick is to not strive for any one particular form of culture, but rather, whatever culture is right for the specific conditions.

Clearly, identifying organizational culture is just the beginning. Interpreting what it really means for an organization to have a certain culture is important as well.

CREATING AND SUSTAINING ORGANIZATIONAL CULTURE

Now that we have described the basic nature of organizational culture, we will consider two additional important issues: how culture is initially created, and how it is sustained—that is, what keeps it going once it is created.

How Is Organizational Culture Created?

Why do many individuals within an organization share basic attitudes, values, and expectations? Several factors contribute to this state of affairs and, hence, to the emergence of organizational culture.

Company founders. Organizational culture may be traced, at least in part, to the founders of the company.[24] These individuals often possess dynamic personalities, strong values, and a clear vision of how the organization should operate. Since they are on the scene first and play a key role in hiring initial staff, their attitudes and values are readily transmitted to new employees. As a result, their views become the accepted ones in the organization and persist as long as the founders are on the scene.

For example, the culture at Microsoft calls for working exceptionally long hours, in large part because that's what co-founder Bill Gates always has done. Sometimes, founders' values can continue to drive an organization's culture even after that individual is no longer alive. For example, the late Ray Kroc founded the McDonald's restaurant chain on the values of good food at a good value served in clean, family-oriented surroundings—key cultural values that persist today. Likewise, Walt Disney's wholesome family values are still cherished at the company that bears his name—in large part because employees ask themselves, "What would Walt think?" (see Figure 14.6).[25] These individuals' values continue to permeate their entire companies and are central parts of their dominant cultures.

FIGURE 14.6
**Walt Disney: A Founder
with a Powerful Impact**
Despite Walt Disney's death and his company's acquisition of the media giant Capitol Cities/ABC, the culture of the company that bears his name continues to reflect the founder's commitment to wholesome family entertainment.

Experience with the environment. Organizational culture often develops out of an organization's experience with the external environment. Every organization must find a niche for itself in its industry and in the marketplace. For example, consumer electronics companies, such as Sony, have found that being first on the market with cutting-edge, technologically advanced products is their unique market niche.[26] Not surprisingly, the cultures of these organizations embrace innovation and commitment to high quality.

Contact with others. Organizational culture also develops out of contact between groups of individuals within an organization who come to share interpretations of events and actions in the organization. For example, a few years ago, after the American Red Cross discovered that some of its blood supply was tainted, a vast army of officials rallied to solve the problem and to put procedures in place that would prevent it from reoccurring.[27] As Red Cross employees and volunteers discuss this incident, they assign similar meaning to what happened, perceiving the organization in a similar manner, thereby reinforcing its culture.

Tools for Transmitting Culture

How are cultural values transmitted between people? In other words, how do employees come to learn about their organization's culture? Several key mechanisms are involved, including *symbols, slogans, stories, jargon, ceremonies,* and *statements of principle.*

Symbols: Objects that say more than meets the eye. Organizations often rely on **symbols**—material objects that connote meanings that extend beyond their intrinsic content. For example, some companies use impressive buildings to convey their strength and importance, signifying that they are large, stable places. Indeed, research has found that the way an organization is furnished provides useful insight into its culture.[28] For example, firms in which there are lots of plants and flower arrangements are believed to have friendly, person-oriented cultures, whereas those in which waiting areas are adorned with awards and trophies are believed to be highly interested in achieving success. These findings suggest that material symbols are potent tools for sending messages about organizational culture. (To demonstrate this phenomenon for yourself, try the Group Exercise on page 544.)

Slogans: Phrases that capture organizational culture. When you think of the catchy phrases that companies use to call attention to their products and services, you may dismiss them as being merely advertising tools. It should be noted, however, that slogans also communicate important aspects of an organization's culture, both to the public at large and to the company's own employees. For some examples of such slogans and what they communicate about organizational culture, see Table 14.3. As you peruse

symbols
Material objects that connote meanings that extend beyond their intrinsic content.

TABLE 14.3 FAMOUS SLOGANS THAT REFLECT ORGANIZATIONAL CULTURE

Many companies rely on catchy slogans not only to promote their products but also to help communicate their organizational culture, both to customers and to their own employees. Some particularly well-known examples are listed here.

COMPANY/PRODUCT	SLOGAN	MESSAGE
Ace Hardware Stores	"Ace is the place with the helpful hardware man."	We are committed to helping our customers.
Allstate Insurance	"You're in good hands with Allstate."	We are there for our clients when they need us.
American Express Card	"Don't leave home without it."	We provide an essential service to travelers.
Borden's	"If it's Borden's it's got to be good."	We produce and sell only the purest dairy products.
Campbell's Soups	"Soup is good food."	Ours is a wholesome food product.
Dial Soap	"Aren't you glad you use Dial? Don't you wish everybody did?"	Using our product can spare you some social embarrassment.
Ford Motor Company	"Quality is job 1."	Producing high-quality products is our top priority.
General Electric	"Progress is our most important product."	We strive to be innovative.
Lay's Potato Chips	"Bet you can't eat just one."	We make chips that are too good to stop eating.

this list, you will see that slogans help convey important information about an organization's culture, such as what the company stands for and what it values.

Stories: "In the old days, we used to . . . ". Organizations also transmit information about culture by virtue of the *stories* that are told in them, both formally and informally. Stories illustrate key aspects of an organization's culture and telling them can effectively introduce or reaffirm those values to employees.[29] It is important to note that stories need not involve some great event, such as someone who saved the company with a single wise decision, but may be small tales that become legends because they so effectively communicate a message. An example may be found in our Preview Case. As one generation of Corning scientists tells the next about how the company once developed electric lightbulbs but now no longer makes them, the point is reinforced that the company specializes in developing innovative new products. Another example may be found at Nike, where employees are told tales about how the company was founded in an effort to help athletes (for some examples of these stories, see Table 14.4).[30]

Jargon: The special language that defines a culture. Even without telling stories, the everyday language used in companies helps sustain culture. For example, the slang or *jargon* that is used in a company or in a field helps people define their identities as members of that group (see Chapter 8). Illustrating this, for many years employees at IBM referred to disk drives as *hard files* and circuit boards as *planar boards*, terms that defined the insulated nature of their culture.[31] Today's jargon continues to predominate in the high-tech world. For example, within the information technology (IT) community, the term *geek keys* is used to refer to a loose deck of electronically encoded pass cards that are used to gain access to restricted areas, and *egosurfing* refers to the practice of feeding one's own name to search engines and visiting the resulting hits.[32] Over time, as departments, organizations, or professional groups develop unique language, their terms, although strange to newcomers, serve as a common factor that brings together individuals belonging to a corporate culture or subculture.

TABLE 14.4 THE NIKE STORY: JUST TELLING IT—AND KEEPING IT ALIVE

New employees at Nike are told stories that transmit the company's underlying cultural values. The themes of some of the most important Nike stories are summarized here along with several of the ways the company helps keep its heritage alive.

NEW EMPLOYEES ARE TOLD THE FOLLOWING STORIES . . .

- Founder Phil Knight was a middle-distance runner who started the business by selling shoes out of his car.
- Knight's running coach and company co-founder, Bill Bowerman, developed the famous "waffle sole" by pouring rubber into the family waffle iron.
- The late Steve Prefontaine, coached by Bowerman, battled to make running a professional sport and was committed to helping athletes.

TO ENSURE THAT THESE TALES OF NIKE'S HERITAGE ARE KEPT ALIVE, THE COMPANY . . .

- Takes new hires to the track where Bowerman coached and the site of Prefontaine's fatal car crash.
- Has created a "heritage wall" in its Eugene, Oregon, store.
- Requires salespeople to tell the Nike story to employees of the retail stores that sell its products.

(*Source:* Based on information in Ransdell, 2000; see Note 30.)

Ceremonies: Special events that commemorate corporate values. Organizations also do a great deal to sustain their cultures by conducting various types of *ceremonies*. Indeed, ceremonies may be seen as celebrations of an organization's basic values and assumptions. Just as a wedding ceremony symbolizes a couple's mutual commitment and a presidential inauguration ceremony marks the beginning of a new presidential term, various organizational ceremonies also celebrate some important accomplishment (see Figure 14.7). For example, one accounting firm celebrated its move to much better facilities by throwing a party, a celebration signifying that it "has arrived" or "made it to the

"J.D. always considered dance a neglected element in corporate culture."

FIGURE 14.7

Ceremonies: Important Tools for Transmitting Organizational Culture
Although few companies are likely to rely on dance to communicate their corporate culture, ceremonies of other types are widely used for this purpose.
(*Source:* Copyright 2000 by Patrick Hardin for the Harvard Business Review.)

big time." Such ceremonies convey meaning to people inside and outside the organization. As one expert put it, "Ceremonies are to the culture what the movie is to the script . . . values that are difficult to express in any other way."[33]

Statements of principle: Defining culture in writing. Organizational culture also may be transmitted directly using written **statements of principle.** Some organizations have explicitly written their principles for all to see. For example, Forrest Mars, the founder of the candy company M&M Mars developed his "Five Principles of Mars," which still guide his company today: quality (everyone is responsible for maintaining quality), responsibility (all employees are responsible for their own actions and decisions), mutuality (creating a situation in which everyone can win), efficiency (most of the company's 41 factories operate continuously), and freedom (giving employees opportunities to shape their futures).[34]

Some companies have chosen to make explicit the moral aspects of their cultures by publishing **codes of ethics**—explicit statements of a company's ethical values (see Chapter 1). According to Hershey Foods' chief executive officer, Richard Zimmerman, this is an effective device: "[O]ften, an individual joins a firm without recognizing the type of environment in which he will place himself and his career. The loud and clear enunciation of a company's code of conduct . . . [allows] that employee to determine whether or not he fits that particular culture."[35]

statements of principle

Explicitly written statements describing the principle beliefs that guide an organization. Such documents can help reinforce an organization's culture.

codes of ethics

Documents in which explicit statements are made that express a company's ethical values.

ORGANIZATIONAL CULTURE: ITS CONSEQUENCES AND CAPACITY TO CHANGE

By now, you probably are convinced that organizational culture can play an important role in the functioning of organizations. To make this point explicit, we now will examine the various ways in which organizational culture has been found to affect organizations and the behavior of individuals in them. Because some of these effects might be undesirable, sometimes officials are interested in changing their organizations' cultures. Accordingly, we also will consider why and how organizational culture might be changed.

The Effects of Organizational Culture

Organizational culture exerts many influences on individuals and organizational processes—some dramatic and others more subtle. Culture generates strong pressures on people to go along, to think and act in ways consistent with the existing culture. An organization's culture strongly can affect everything from the way employees dress (e.g., the white shirts traditionally worn by male employees of IBM) and the amount of time allowed to elapse before meetings begin, to the speed with which people are promoted.

Researchers have established a link between culture and performance, especially when that culture is strong—that is, when its basic elements are widely accepted.[36] This is the case at the consumer products company Alberto-Culver, known for such brands as Alberto VO-5 shampoo, Mrs. Dash seasonings, and the Sally Beauty Company chain of stores. In the early 1990s turnover was high and sales were flat, leading Carol Lavin Bernick, president of Alberto-Culver North America (see Figure 14.8), to take steps to humanize the company's cold and indifferent culture.[37] Employees were kept in the dark about company operations, and even the most productive people were dissatisfied.

Realizing that things had to change, throughout the 1990s Bernick took several steps to alter the company's culture. Her key moves were as follows.

- 1993: A program was launched in which certain individuals called "growth development leaders" (GDLs) were honored by being selected to mentor a dozen or so other employees in such matters as the company's family-friendly benefit policies and career development.
- 1995: Bernick attempted "to open" the culture by giving detailed annual speeches on "the state of the company."

FIGURE 14.8

Carol Lavin Bernick: Mastermind of Alberto-Culver's New Organizational Culture
As president of Alberto-Culver North America, headquartered in Melrose Park, Illinois, Carol Lavin Bernick developed several successful initiatives to change corporate culture from one that kept employees in the dark to one that made them active partners in the company's activities.

- 1997: The first "Business Builders Awards" were given to individuals and teams who went beyond their job requirements in ways that had a great impact on the company's growth and profitability.
- 1998: Brief statements describing how each employee contributes to the company's profitability, called "individual economic values" (IEVs), were developed to help employees recognize precisely how their work helps the business.
- 1998: A list of 10 core cultural values was formalized (honesty, ownership, trust, customer orientation, commitment, fun, innovation, risk taking, speed and urgency, and teamwork), which employees are expected to be able to recite by heart.

As summarized in Figure 14.9, these efforts to transform the culture at Alberto-Culver North America had beneficial effects on the bottom line. From 1994 through

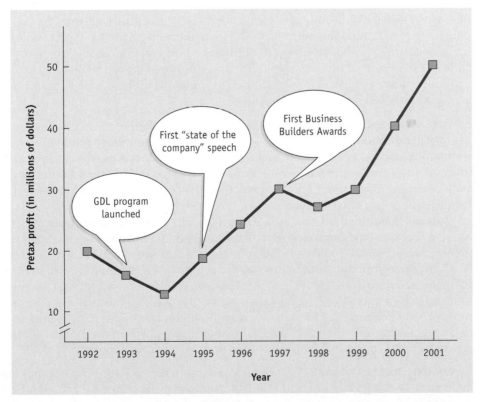

FIGURE 14.9

Cultural Changes Boost Profits at Alberto-Culver
During the 1990s, attempts to improve corporate culture have led to sizable gains in Alberto-Culver's pretax profitability. The various milestones in this effort are identified here.
(*Source:* Adapted from Bernick, 2001; see Note 37.)

2001, sales increased 83 percent and pretax profit jumped 336 percent. As importantly, Bernick attributes changes in the corporate culture as responsible for dramatic reductions in turnover and newfound ease in acquiring other companies. In fact, the founder of one recently purchased company agreed to the acquisition not because Alberto-Culver was the highest bidder but because he had a good feeling about its culture.

Why and How Does Organizational Culture Change?

Our earlier comments about the relative stability of organizational culture may have left you wondering why and how culture ever changes. In other words, why isn't it simply passed down from one generation of organizational members to the next in a totally static manner? The answer lies in the fact that the world in which all organizations operate constantly changes (see Chapter 16). External events such as shifts in market conditions, new technology, altered government policies, and many other factors change over time, necessitating changes in an organization's mode of doing business and, hence, in its culture.

Composition of the workforce. Over time, the people entering an organization may differ in important ways from those already in it, and these differences may impinge on the existing culture of the organization. For example, people from different ethnic or cultural backgrounds may have contrasting views about various aspects of behavior at work. For example, they may hold dissimilar views about style of dress, the importance of being on time (or even what constitutes "on-time" behavior), the level of deference one should show to higher-status people, and even what foods should be served in the company cafeteria. In other words, as people with different backgrounds and values enter the workplace, changes in organizational culture may be expected to follow suit.

Mergers and acquisitions. Another, and even more dramatic, source of cultural change is *mergers* and *acquisitions*, events in which one organization purchases or otherwise absorbs another.[38] When this occurs, there is likely to be a careful analysis of the financial and material assets of the acquired organization. However, it is rare that any consideration is given to the acquired organization's culture. This is unfortunate, insofar as there have been several cases in which the merger of two organizations with incompatible cultures has led to serious problems referred to as **culture clashes.** As you might imagine, life in companies with incompatible cultures tends to be conflict-ridden and highly disruptive, often resulting in arguments and considerable uncertainty about what to do. In some cases, organizations have even been known to disband because of extreme culture clashes. For several good examples of culture clashes resulting from mergers and acquisitions, see Table 14.5.[39]

Planned organizational change. Our earlier discussion of Alberto-Culver illustrated that a company deliberately can decide to change its culture in a specific effort to solve problems. Cultural change also may result from the conscious decisions to alter the internal structure or the basic operations of an organization (see Chapter 16). Once such decisions are reached, many practices in the company that both reflect and contribute to its culture may change.

A good example of this can be seen at IBM.[40] In response to staggering losses IBM realized that one of its problems was that it was heavily bureaucratic, making it difficult for lower-level people to make on-the-spot decisions. As a result, IBM changed the nature of its corporate structure from one in which there was a steep hierarchy with many layers of management to a "delayered" one with far fewer managers (we will discuss this topic more fully in Chapter 15). As you might imagine, the newly "rightsized" IBM developed a new corporate culture. Once known for having a highly rigid, autocratic culture in which decision making was centralized in the hands of just a few, the reorganized company is now much more open and democratic in its approach than ever before.[41]

Responding to the Internet. There can be no doubt that the Internet is a major influence on organizational culture these days. Compared to traditional brick-and-mortar

culture clashes
Problems resulting from attempts to merge two or more organizational cultures that are incompatible.

TABLE 14.5   ORGANIZATIONAL CULTURE CLASHES: THREE EXAMPLES

Three major examples of culture clashes in the past few decades are summarized here, along with the cast of characters. As you read about these, think about what it must have been like to work in these companies at the time the clashes were occurring.

ORIGINAL COMPANY AND CEO AT TIME OF MERGER	ORIGINAL COMPANY AND CEO AT TIME OF MERGER	NEW COMPANY (MERGER DATE) AND ORIGINAL OFFICERS	NATURE OF CULTURE CONFLICT
Chrysler *Robert J. Eaton, CEO*	**Daimler-Benz** *Jüergen E. Schrempp, CEO*	**Daimler-Chrysler (1998)** *Robert J. Eaton and Jüergen E. Schrempp, co-CEOs*	The so-called "merger of equals" was decidedly unequal. Executives' lifestyles were in sharp contrast. Those who came from Chrysler traveled together to meetings in minivans and flew economy class. However, Daimler-Benz officials arrived in chauffer-driven Mercedes-Benz sedans and flew first class. While spending six months working this out, executives ignored important corporate problems. Sales have slumped and many officials have left the company. In 2001, Chrysler laid off a quarter of its employees.
RJ Reynolds *Tylee Wilson, CEO*	**Nabisco** *Ross Johnson, CEO*	**RJR Nabisco (1988)** *Ross Johnson, CEO*	Nabisco executives had a fast-paced lifestyle, with perks such as corporate jets, penthouse apartments, and lavish parties. RJ Reynolds was characterized by a strong work ethic, much less autonomy for employees, and a deep commitment to its local community. A bitter feud erupted and Johnson fired RJ Reynolds executives.
HFS (franchising company) *Henry Silverman, CEO*	**CUC International (membership-club company)** *Walter Forbes, CEO*	**Cendant (1997)** *Henry Silverman, CEO; and Walter Forbes, chairman of the board*	Silverman was a control freak who insisted on seeing and knowing everything. However, Forbes saw himself as a visionary and left the details to others. Power clashes grew, eventually leading someone to blow the whistle on CUC officials for creating phony profits. The resulting scandal harmed the company greatly.

(Source: Based on information from APPENDICUL CIH II In IIvt 20.)

businesses, in which things move slowly and people look at change skeptically, the culture of Internet businesses is agile, fast-paced, and receptive to new solutions.[42] Information sharing is key, as such organizations not only accept, but embrace the expansion of communication networks and business relationships across organizational boundaries. When traditional businesses expand into e-commerce (in which case, they sometimes are referred to as "click-and-mortar businesses"), changes in their organizational cultures follow suit. We see this, for example, at the investment firm Merrill Lynch, which launched a Web site for trading stock in an effort to compete with brokerage firms such as E*Trade, which do business only online. The organizational culture at this venerable, traditional firm has become far more fast-paced ever since it adapted to the Internet economy.

To conclude, it is clear that although organizational culture is generally stable, it is not immutable. In fact, culture often evolves in response to outside forces (e.g., changes in workforce composition and information technology) as well as to deliberate attempts to change the design of organizations (e.g., through mergers and corporate restructuring). An important aspect of culture that organizations frequently strive to change is the degree to which it approaches problems in creative and innovative ways. With this in mind, we now will turn attention to the topics of *creativity* and *innovation* in organizations.

CREATIVITY IN INDIVIDUALS AND TEAMS

Although you probably have no difficulty recognizing creativity when you see it, defining creativity can be a bit more challenging. Scientists define **creativity** as the process by which individuals or teams produce novel and useful ideas.[43] With this definition to guide us, we will explain how the process of creativity operates. Specifically, we begin by

creativity
The process by which individuals or teams produce novel and useful ideas.

describing the components of individual and team creativity and then outline several steps you can take to enhance your own creativity.

Components of Individual and Team Creativity

Creativity in individuals and teams is composed of three basic components—*domain-relevant skills*, *creativity-relevant skills*, and *intrinsic task motivation*.

Domain-relevant skills. Whether it's the manual dexterity required to play the piano or to use a computer keyboard or the sense of rhythm and knowledge of music needed to conduct an orchestra, specific skills and abilities are necessary to perform these tasks. In fact, as we described in Chapter 3, any task you might undertake requires certain talents, knowledge, or skills. These skills and abilities that we already have constitute the raw materials needed for creativity to occur. After all, without the capacity to perform a certain task at even a basic level, one has no hope of demonstrating creativity on that task. For example, before he can even begin to create stunning automotive stunts, a stunt driver must have the basic skills of dexterity and eye–hand coordination required to drive a car.

Creativity-relevant skills. Beyond the basic skills, being creative also requires additional skills—special abilities that help people approach the things they do in novel ways. Specifically, when fostering creativity, it helps to do the following.

- *Break mental sets and take new perspectives.* Creativity is enhanced when people do not limit themselves to old ways of doing things. Restricting oneself to the past can inhibit creativity. Take a fresh look at even the most familiar things. This involves what is known as **divergent thinking**—the process of reframing familiar problems in unique ways. Divergent thinking often is promoted by asking people to identify as many unusual uses for common objects as possible (see Figure 14.10).
- *Understand complexities.* Instead of making things overly simplistic, don't be afraid to consider complex ways in which ideas may be interrelated.
- *Keep options open and avoid premature judgments.* Creative people are willing to consider all options. To do so, they consider all the angles and avoid reaching conclusions prematurely. People are particularly good at this when they are new to an organization and, therefore, don't know enough to accept everything the way it is. With this in mind, some companies actually prefer hiring executives from outside their own industries.
- *Follow creativity heuristics.* People sometimes follow certain strategies, known as **creativity heuristics,** to help them come up with creative new ideas. These are rules

divergent thinking
The process of reframing familiar problems in unique ways.

creativity heuristics
Rules that people follow to help them approach tasks in novel ways.

FIGURE 14.10
Nike Shox: A Product of Divergent Thinking
At Nike, the idea for the spring-loaded athletic shoe, Shox, shown here being tested, was a product of divergent thinking. Members of the design team drew their inspiration from an automobile's shock absorbers.

that people follow to help them approach tasks in novel ways. They may involve such techniques as considering the counterintuitive and using analogies.

- *Use productive forgetting.* Sometimes our creativity is inhibited by becoming fixated on certain ideas that we just cannot seem to get out of our heads. With this in mind, it helps to practice **productive forgetting**—the ability to abandon unproductive ideas and temporarily put aside stubborn problems until new approaches can be considered.

productive forgetting
The ability to abandon unproductive ideas and temporarily put aside stubborn problems until new approaches can be considered.

To help individuals and groups become more creative, many organizations are inviting employees to participate in training exercises designed to promote some of these skills. Although not assessed scientifically, many companies have reported successes using these techniques to boost creativity in the workplace.[44]

Intrinsic task motivation. The first two components of creativity, domain-relevant skills and creativity-relevant skills, focus on what people are *capable* of doing. However, the third component, intrinsic task motivation, refers to what people are *willing* to do. The idea is simple: For someone to be creative, he or she must be interested in performing the task in question. In other words, there must be a high degree of **intrinsic task motivation**—the motivation to do work because it is interesting, engaging, or challenging in a positive way. (This is the same basic idea behind the job design approach to motivation described in Chapter 6.) Someone who has the capacity to be creative but who isn't motivated to do what it takes to produce creative outcomes certainly wouldn't be considered creative. People are most likely to be highly creative when they are passionate about their work.[45]

intrinsic task motivation
The motivation to do work because it is interesting, engaging, or challenging in a positive way.

Intrinsic task motivation tends to be high under several conditions. For example, when an individual has a *personal interest* in the task at hand, he or she will be motivated to perform it—and may go on to do so creatively. However, anyone who doesn't find a task interesting surely isn't going to perform it long enough to demonstrate any signs of creativity. Likewise, task motivation will be high whenever an individual perceives that he or she has internal reasons to be performing that task (e.g., because they think it's fun). People who come to believe that they are performing a task for some external reason—such as high pay or pressure from a boss—are unlikely to find the work inherently interesting, in and of itself, and are unlikely to show much creativity when performing it.

Putting it all together. As you might imagine, the components of creativity are important insofar as they can be used to paint a picture of when people will be creative. In this connection, scientists claim that people will be at their most creative when they have high amounts of all three of these components (see Figure 14.11).

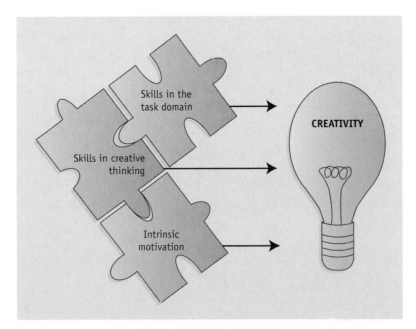

FIGURE 14.11
Components of Creativity
Scientists claim that people will be at their most creative when they exhibit high levels of the three factors shown here.
(*Source:* Adapted from Amabile, 1988; see Note 43.)

Specifically, it has been claimed that there is a multiplicative relationship between these three components of creativity. Thus, if any one component is low, the overall level of creativity will be low. In fact, people will not be creative at all if any one of these components is at zero (i.e., if it is missing completely). After all, you would be unlikely to be creative at a job if you didn't have the skills needed to do it, regardless of how motivated you were to be creative and how well practiced you were at coming up with new ideas. Likewise, creativity would be expected to be nonexistent if either creativity-relevant skills or motivation were zero. The practical implications are clear: To be as creative as possible, people must strive toward attaining high levels of all three components of creativity.

A Model of the Creative Process

Although it isn't always obvious to us how people come up with creative ideas, scientists have developed a model that outlines the various stages of the creative process.[46] Specifically, this model, summarized in Figure 14.12, specifies that the process of creativity occurs in the following four stages.

1. *Prepare to be creative.* Although we often believe that our most creative ideas come "out of thin air," people are at their most creative when they have made suitable preparations. This involves gathering the appropriate information and concentrating on the problem.
2. *Allow ideas to incubate.* Because ideas take time to develop, creativity can be enhanced by putting the problem out of our conscious minds and allowing it to incubate. If you've ever been successful at coming up with a fresh approach to a problem by putting it aside and working on something else, you know what we are describing. The phrase "sleep on it" captures this stage of the process.
3. *Document insight.* At some point during the first two stages, you are likely to come up with a unique idea. However, that idea may be lost if it is not documented. With this in mind, many people carry small voice recorders that allow them to capture their ideas before they become lost in the maze of other ideas. Likewise, writers

FIGURE 14.12

Steps in the Creative Process
Scientists have proposed that the creative process follows the four steps outlined here.
(*Source:* Kabanoff & Rossiter, 1994; see Note 46.)

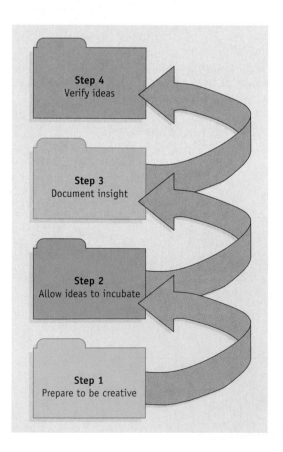

Step 4
Verify ideas

Step 3
Document insight

Step 2
Allow ideas to incubate

Step 1
Prepare to be creative

keep diaries, artists keep sketch pads, and song writers keep tape recorders handy to capture ideas whenever inspiration strikes.

4. *Verify ideas.* Coming up with an idea is one thing but verifying that it's any good is quite another. Assessing the usefulness of an idea requires consciously thinking about it and verifying it, such as by seeing what others have to say about it. In other words, you want to see if those ideas that came to you in a moment of inspiration in the middle of the night are any good in the morning light.

Knowing about the creative process is particularly useful insofar as it can be applied to promoting individual and team productivity. I will now turn to the process of doing so.

PROMOTING CREATIVITY IN ORGANIZATIONS

Highly creative people are an asset to any organization. But what exactly do organizations do to promote creativity within their ranks? In general terms, the answer lies in things that we can do as individuals and that organizations can do as a whole. Specifically, three major approaches may be identified.

Training People to Be Creative

It is true that some people, by nature, are more creative than others. Such individuals are inclined to approach various situations in new ways and tend not to be bogged down by previous ways of doing things.[47] However, there are skills that anyone can develop to become more creative. Generally, training people to become more creative involves three steps.[48]

Encourage openness to new ideas. Many good ideas go undeveloped because they are not in keeping with the current way of doing things. Becoming more creative requires allowing oneself to be open to new ideas or, as it is often described, *thinking outside the box.* Some companies do this by sending their employees on *thinking expeditions* — trips specifically designed to put people in challenging situations in an effort to help them think differently and become more creative. According to the CEO of a company that specializes in running such expeditions for clients, these trips "push people out of their 'stupid zone'—a place of mental and physical normalcy—so that they can start to think differently," adding, "it's an accelerated unlearning experience."[49]

Take the time to understand the problem. Meaningful ideas rarely come to those who don't fully understand the problem at hand. Only when time is taken to understand the many different facets of the issue can people be equipped to develop creative solutions. Consider, for example, BrightHouse, the 17-employee Atlanta-based company that specializes in developing new ideas for its clients (e.g., Coca-Cola, Home Depot, and Georgia-Pacific).[50] For a fee of $500,000, the entire staff devotes a full 10 weeks to the issues their clients have in mind. Recently, for example, BrightHouse was called upon to find ways to improve billboard advertising at Turner Field, the home of baseball's Atlanta Braves.

Develop divergent thinking. As we noted earlier, divergent thinking involves taking new approaches to old problems. Teaching people various tactics for divergent thinking allows problems to incubate, setting the stage for creative new ideas to develop. One popular way of developing divergent thinking is known as **morphology.** A *morphological analysis* of a problem involves identifying its basic elements and combining them in systematically different ways. (For an example of this approach, and for a chance to practice it yourself, see the Individual Exercise on page 543.)

morphology
An approach to analyzing problems in which basic elements are combined in systematically different ways.

Developing Creative Work Environments

Thus far, we have identified ways of making people more creative as individuals. In conjunction with these approaches, it also is useful for organizations to take concrete steps to change work environments in ways that bring out people's creativity.[51] Several such approaches may be identified.[52]

Provide autonomy. It has been established that people are especially creative when they are given the freedom to control their own behavior—that is, when they have *autonomy* (see Chapter 6) and are *empowered* to make decisions (see Chapter 12). At the Japanese video game manufacturer Nintendo, for example, creativity is so important that no one considers it odd when designers leave work to go see a movie or a play.

Allow ideas to cross-pollinate. People who work on just one project run the risk of getting stale, whereas those who work on several are likely to come into contact with different people and have a chance of applying an idea they picked up on one project to another project. This is done all the time at IDEO, the company described in this chapter's Case in Point (see page 545). For example, in coming up with an idea about how to develop a more comfortable handle for a scooter, designers might use ideas they picked up while working on a project involving the design of a more comfortable computer mouse. Because of the upheaval that is bound to result when companies are downsizing, ideas are unlikely to cross-pollinate. It is, therefore, not surprising that creativity tends to be considerably lower at such times.[53]

Make jobs intrinsically interesting. Research has shown that people are inclined to be creative when they are intrinsically interested in the work they do. After all, nobody will want to invest the effort it takes to be creative at a task that is uninteresting. With this in mind, creativity can be promoted by enhancing the degree to which tasks are intrinsically interesting to people. The essence of the idea is to turn work into play by making it interesting.

This approach is used routinely at Play, a marketing agency in Richmond, Virginia. Instead of coming up with ideas by sitting in boring meetings, staff members are encouraged to play. For example, to aid the process of coming up with a new marketing campaign for the Weather Channel, employees spent time in a corner office developing costumes for superheroes. According to co-founder Andy Stefanovich, the idea is simple: "When you turn work into a place that encourages people to be themselves, have fun, and take risks, you fuel and unleash their creativity. The best ideas come from playful minds. And the way to tap into that playfulness is to play—together."[54] For some specific suggestions on how to do this, see the How to Do It section.

Set your own creative goals. Being free to do as you wish does not necessarily imply goofing off. In fact, the freedom to make your own decisions pays off most handsomely when people set their own creative goals. For example, the famous inventor Thomas A. Edison set the goal of having a minor invention every 10 days and a major invention every six months. This kept Edison focused on being creative—and, with over 1,000 patents in his name, he clearly did an outstanding job of meeting his goals. We are not talking about strict external pressure to be creative, which rarely results in anything positive. However, creativity is aided when people strive to meet difficult goals for achieving creativity (recall our discussion of goal setting in Chapter 6).[55]

Support creativity at high organizational levels. Nobody in an organization is going to go out of his or her way to be creative if it is not welcomed by the bosses. Supervisors, team leaders, and top executives

HOW TO DO IT

BOOSTING CREATIVITY BY MAKING JOBS INTRINSICALLY INTERESTING

Several specific features of the work environment can boost a job's intrinsic interest and, hence, the degree to which people are likely to demonstrate creativity. To do this effectively, it helps to design jobs in the following ways.

1. *Make tasks challenging.* People are likely to be creative at tasks they find interesting because they are required to work hard at them.

2. *Encourage subordinates.* Workers are likely to work creatively when they believe their immediate supervisor or the organization as a whole encourages their efforts.

3. *Provide work group support.* Creativity is likely to be enhanced when the people in one's work group are encouraged to share ideas and have the skills required to perform their jobs effectively.

4. *Remove organizational impediments.* People are likely to be creative when key organizational impediments are eliminated, such as political problems, negative criticism of new ideas, and pressure to maintain the status quo.

must encourage employees to take risks if they are to have any chance of being creative. At the same time, this involves accepting any failures that result. This idea is embraced by Livio D. DeSimone, CEO of 3M, one of the most innovative companies in the world. "Failure is not fatal," he says, adding, "Innovations are simply chance breakthroughs. And when you take a chance, there is always the possibility of a failure."[56]

Have fun! For people to be motivated to be creative, it helps to have an incentive, and one of the most potent incentives is fun. Indeed, people strive to be creative when they can have fun along the way. It is with this in mind that many companies encourage creative thinking by providing employees with opportunities to have fun on the job. This is especially so at today's high-tech firms, where creativity is essential and where long hours at the office are typical. With this in mind, companies have created opportunities for their employees to do everything from playing Nerf basketball to having paintball contests and hula contests.[57] Should a company have difficulty finding a way to bring fun to the workplace, the widely regarded Second City Communications comedy troop sells a service in which it brings humor to the workplace (see Figure 14.13).[58]

Promote diversity. When companies are staffed by people from diverse ethnic and cultural groups, they are bound to think differently about the situations they face. And, as we noted earlier, divergent thinking is a key element of creativity. Therefore, companies with ethnically diverse workforces are inclined to have cultures that allow creativity to flourish. In fact, some high-tech experts attribute the highly creative ideas emanating from California's Silicon Valley to the fact that over one-third of its resident engineers and scientists come from countries outside the United States.[59] (For more on the connection between national culture and creativity, see the OB in a Diverse World section on pages 536–537.)

Many of today's most successful multinational corporations acknowledge that the adjustments they have made in the course of getting different kinds of people to work together in harmony has had a beneficial if sometimes unintended by-product—namely, boosting creativity. Although having a diverse population does not ensure creativity, to be sure, it is safe to say that *not* having one surely can limit creativity. Today's multinational corporations are unwilling to be denied this benefit. It is not surprising, therefore, that Edgar van Ommen, managing director of Sony's corporate office in Berlin, follows what he calls the "principle of the United Nations" when it comes to recruiting—hiring the best people in the world regardless of their nationality.[60]

FIGURE 14.13
Promoting Funny Business
In an effort to stimulate creativity, players from Second City Communications are being called on to help companies develop a "corporate sense of humor." The idea is that massaging the skills it takes to be funny (which are often overlooked in the usual course of business) can free people to think differently about things.

OB IN A DIVERSE WORLD
WHERE IN THE WORLD IS ENTREPRENEURIAL CREATIVITY PROMOTED?

To be a successful entrepreneur, it helps to live someplace where the culture supports entrepreneurial activity and where people value creative thinking and innovation. Not only is entrepreneurship likely to thrive under such conditions, but the reverse is especially true: The entrepreneurial spirit is likely to be snuffed out whenever creativity and innovation are frowned upon. This applies not only to differences in organizational cultures but also to national cultures as well. With this in mind, it is interesting to consider the possibility that various countries differ with respect to how strongly their cultures support creativity and innovation.[61]

In a recent study, scientists administered a questionnaire to people from Spain, Norway, Sweden, Germany, Italy, and the United States to assess citizens' perceptions of (1) their society's admiration for people who start their own businesses, (2) the extent to which they believe that innovative and creative thinking is good, and (3) the belief that starting one's own business is a valued career option.[62]

The results were striking: People from the United States scored considerably higher than their counterparts in the European countries included in the study. That is, Americans, as a whole, believed their country was more supportive of entrepre-

THE PROCESS OF INNOVATION

Having examined the process of individual and team creativity, we will extend our analyses to situations in which people implement their creative skills for the sake of improving the organization. This is the process of *innovation* to which we referred earlier. Specifically, **innovation** may be defined as the successful implementation of creative ideas within an organization. As you might imagine, some companies are more innovative than others (see Table 14.6).[63] To understand this process we will review the various stages through which innovation progresses. Before doing this, however, we first identify the various components of innovation.

innovation
The successful implementation of creative ideas within an organization.

Components of Innovation: Basic Building Blocks

Earlier, we depicted individual creativity as being composed of three components—motivation, resources, and skills. As it works out, these same components are involved in organizational innovation as well, albeit in somewhat different ways.

Motivation to innovate. Just as individual creativity requires that people are motivated to do what it takes to be creative, organizational innovation requires that organizations have the kind of cultures that encourage innovation. When top executives fail to promote a vision of innovation and accept the status quo, change is unlikely. However, at companies such as Microsoft, where leaders (including co-founder, Bill Gates) envision innovation as being part of the natural order of things, it is not surprising that innovative efforts constantly are underway.

Resources to innovate. Again, a parallel to individual creativity is in order. Just as people must have certain basic skills to be creative, so too must organizations possess certain basic resources that make innovation possible. For example, to be innovative, at the very least, organizations must have what it takes in terms of human and financial resources. After all, unless the necessary skilled people and deep pockets are available to do what it takes to innovate, stagnation is likely to result.

Innovation management. Finally, just as individuals must hone special skills needed to be creative, so too must organizations develop special ways of managing people to encourneurial activity and the creativity and innovativeness required to make that activity successful than did people from Sweden, Norway, Spain, Italy, or Germany. Furthermore, the Europeans all scored remarkably similarly to each other.

Although these findings are interesting, three important points should be taken into account when interpreting them. First, considerations in addition to the value placed on creativity also are likely to make a difference. In fact, the same study found that knowledge of how to finance, structure, and manage new businesses and the extent to which the government provides helpful support along the way also were important considerations. Along these dimensions, people from the two Scandinavian countries (Norway and Sweden) ranked highly along with the Americans.

Second, these findings do *not* mean that American entrepreneurs are destined to be more successful than their European counterparts. Clearly, many different factors are involved in determining the ultimate success of any entrepreneurial venture. Still, the findings reveal that when it comes to nurturing the creative activities that promote entrepreneurial activity, Americans appear to have the edge.

Finally, it is important to recognize that the study considered only a small number of countries. To the extent that entrepreneurs come from all over the world, it would be interesting to extend these findings to people from places such as Asia, Latin America, Africa, and the Middle East.

age innovation—that is, *skills in innovation management*. Most notable in this regard is the matter of *balance*. Specifically, managers help promote innovation when they show balance with respect to three key matters: goals, reward systems, and time pressure.

- Organizational innovation is promoted when *goals* are carefully linked to the corporate mission. However, they should not be so specific as to tie the hands of those who put them into practice. Innovation is unlikely when such restrictions are imposed.

TABLE 14.6 THE MOST INNOVATIVE COMPANIES OF THE TWENTIETH CENTURY

An effective measure of an organization's innovativeness is the number of U.S. patents it holds. Based on this, the following companies may be considered the most innovative companies of the twentieth century.

RANK	COMPANY	NUMBER OF PATENTS
1	General Electric Co.	50,837
2	IBM Corp.	32,498
3	Westinghouse Electric Corp.	28,005
4	AT&T Corp.	24,578
5	General Motors Corp.	23,948
6	E. I. Du Pont de Nemours & Co.	23,559
7	Hitachi, Ltd.	19,645
8	Eastman Kodak Co.	19,576
9	Canon Kabushiki Kaisha	18,876
10	United States Navy	17,805

(*Source:* MicroPatent, 2001; see Note 63.)

- *Reward systems* should generously and fairly recognize one's contributions, but they should not be so specific as to connect literally every move to a bonus or some type of monetary reward. To do so discourages people from taking the kinds of risks that make innovation possible.
- Innovation management requires carefully balancing the *time pressures* under which employees are placed. If pressures are too great, people may be unimaginative and offer routine solutions. By the same token, if pressure is too weak, employees may have no sense of time urgency and believe that the project is too unimportant to warrant any creative attention on their part.

Stages of the Organizational Innovation Process

Any CEO who snaps her fingers one day and expects her troops to be innovative on command surely will be in for disappointment. Innovation does not happen all at once. Rather, innovation occurs gradually through a series of stages. Specifically, scientists have identified five specific stages through which the process of organizational innovation progresses.[64] We now describe each of these (see the summary in Figure 14.14).

Stage 1: Setting the agenda. The first stage of the process of innovation begins by setting the agenda for innovation. This involves creating a **mission statement**—a document describing an organization's overall direction and general goals. The component of innovation that is most involved here is motivation. After all, the highest-ranking officials of the organization must be highly committed to innovation before they will initiate a push toward it.

Stage 2: Setting the stage. Once an organization's mission has been established, it is prepared to set the stage for innovation. This may involve narrowing down certain broad goals into more specific tasks and gathering the resources required to meet them. It also may involve assessing the environment, both outside and inside the organization, searching for anything that either may support or inhibit later efforts to "break the rules" by being creative. Effectively setting the stage for innovation requires using the skills necessary for innovation management as well as fully using the organization's human and financial resources.

mission statement
A document describing an organization's overall direction and general goals.

FIGURE 14.14
The Process of Innovation
The innovation process consists of the various components and follows the steps shown here.
(*Source:* Adapted from Amabile, 1988; see Note 43.)

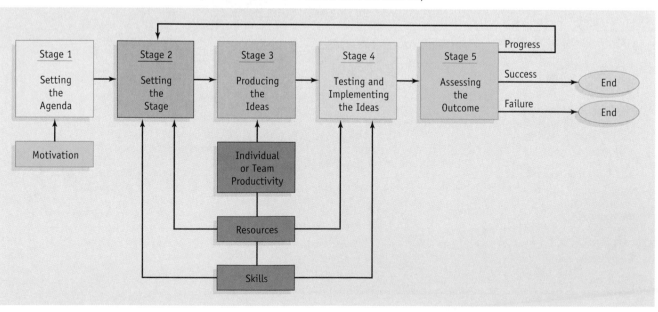

Stage 3: Producing the ideas. This stage of the process involves coming up with new ideas and testing them. It is in this third stage that individual and team creativity enters the picture. As a result, all of the components of individual creativity mentioned earlier are involved. What's more, these may combine in important ways with various organizational factors. For example, an individual who has the skills and motivation to be highly creative might find his motivation waning as he attempts to introduce novel ideas in an organization that is not committed to innovation and that fails to make the necessary resources available. In contrast, the highly innovative nature of an organization may bring out the more creative side of an individual who otherwise may not have been especially creative.

Stage 4: Testing and implementing the ideas. This is the stage in which implementation occurs. Now, after an initial group of individuals has developed an idea, other parts of the organization get involved. For example, a prototype product may be developed and tested, and market research may be conducted. In short, input from the many functional areas of the organization is provided. As you might imagine, resources in the task domain are important at this stage. After all, unless adequate amounts of money, personnel, material systems, and information are provided, the idea will be unlikely to survive.

Interestingly, even a good idea and plentiful resources are not enough to bring innovation to life. Skills in innovation management are critical because for good ideas to survive it is necessary for them to be "nourished" and supported throughout the organization. Even the best ideas may be "killed off" if people in some parts of the organization are not supportive. For some remarkable examples of this, see Table 14.7.[65] When you see all the great ideas that didn't quite make it at first, you realize that you are in excellent company if your own ideas are rejected.

Stage 5: Outcome assessment. The final stage of the process involves assessing the new idea. What happens to that idea depends on the results of the assessment. Three outcomes are possible. If the resulting idea (e.g., a certain product or service) has been a total success, it will be accepted and carried out in the future. This ends the process. Likewise, the process is over if the idea has been a complete failure. In this case, there is no good reason to continue. However, if the new idea shows promise and makes some progress toward the organization's objectives but still has problems, the process is likely to start all over again at stage 2.

TABLE 14.7   IS YOUR INNOVATIVE IDEA REJECTED? IF SO, YOU'RE IN GOOD COMPANY

Some of the best, most innovative ideas were rejected at first because one or more powerful people failed to see their merit. When you look at these examples, you can imagine how bad these individuals must have felt about "the one that got away."

PRODUCT	REJECTION STORY
Star Wars	Turned down by 12 Hollywood studios before finally being accepted
Photocopying process	Rejected as a viable technology by IBM, GM, and DuPont
Velcro	Victor Kiam (of Remington Razor fame) turned down the patent for $25,000
Transistor radio	In the 1950s, Sony's founder, Akio Morita, was unsuccessful in marketing this idea
The Beatles	Turned down by Decca Records in 1962 because it was believed that "groups with guitars were on the way out"
Movies with soundtracks	In 1927, Harry Warner, president of Warner Brothers, said "nobody wanted to hear actors talk"

(*Source:* Based on information reported by Ricchiuto, 1997; see Note 65.)

BEST PRACTICES
HOW EFFECTIVE COMPANIES INSPIRE INNOVATION

The noted organizational consultant Gary Hamel believes that top management plays an important role when it comes to inspiring innovation in their companies. Radical innovation, he argues, "is no longer an option for big companies—it's the imperative," adding, that top management's job is "to build an organization that can continually spawn cool new business concepts."[66] Hamel identifies several ways in which today's most effective companies are doing this.[67] Some of these are as follows.

Set very high expectations. In Chapter 6 we emphasized that people strive to meet performance goals. When employees are confronted with goals they find to be especially challenging—but still not impossible, of course—they are forced to consider highly novel ways of bringing them about. At GE Capital, for example, executives are expected to grow annual earnings by at least 20

percent. This leads them to consider more creative approaches and to develop more innovative products than they would if they were required to meet a more modest goal, such as the more typical 5 percent.

Listen to new voices. If you ask questions of the same old people, you get the same old answers. But if you seek the opinions of outsiders free from industry prejudices, they are less likely to say "you can't do it." Indeed, Jeff Bezos was not a retailing mogul when he started Amazon.com, and neither was Ted Turner a seasoned broadcast journalist when he founded CNN. With this in mind, many of today's most innovative companies are doing things like seeking out the revolutionaries in the company, those whose voices are getting muffled by the hierarchy. They also are paying special attention to newcomers to the company, especially the youngest people. Again, GE Capital provides a good

Although this five-stage process does not account for all innovations you may find in organizations, this general model does a good job of identifying the major steps through which most innovations go as they travel along their path from a specific organizational need to a product or service that meets that need. (For some further suggestions on how to promote innovation in an organization, see the Best Practices section that appears above.)

SUMMARY AND REVIEW OF LEARNING OBJECTIVES

1. Define organizational culture and identify the various functions it serves in organizations.

Organizational culture is a cognitive framework consisting of attitudes, values, behavioral norms, and expectations shared by organization members. Culture plays three major roles in organizations: It provides a sense of identity for its members, it generates commitment to the organization's mission, and it also serves to clarify and reinforce standards of behavior.

2. Describe the four types of organizational culture identified by the double S cube.

The double S cube identifies four different types of organizational culture created by combining high and low levels of two variables—solidarity (the extent to which people focus together on the job) and sociability (the extent to which people get along with each other personally). Networked culture exists when solidarity is low and sociability is high. Mercenary culture exists when solidarity is high and sociability is low. Fragmented culture exists when both sociability and solidarity are low. Communal culture exists example: Seeking a youthful perspective, management teams at this well-established financial services firm are all under 30 years old.

Create opportunities for talented employees. It is widely believed that the best people always are interested in the best opportunities within a company. The most effective organizations capitalize on this by allowing employees to move to other jobs within the company that they find more exciting. At GE, for example, rather than risking an exodus of talented people from the company, employees are permitted to move to any new opportunity within the company that interests them. To make this as appealing as possible, GE employees have "portable titles"—that is, they get to take their titles with them—eliminating one of the most frequent reasons why employees hesitate to shift positions.

Reward innovation. GE also does something else that has proven to be very effective: They pay people like entrepreneurs. If employees come up with an innovative idea that proves to be suc-

cessful, they are given a share of the profits that result from its implementation. This provides a valuable incentive for employees to take the risks needed to be highly innovative.

Identify a cause. Most think of Charles Schwab as a well-established, rather traditional investment firm. Although in many ways it is, that's not how president and co-CEO David Pottruck prefers to think of it. Rather, Pottruck envisions Charles Schwab's mission in far loftier terms—as guardians of its customers' financial dreams. By sharing this vision, Pottruck has gotten his employees to recognize that they are doing something important, contributing to a cause that will make a difference in people's lives. It was such thinking that inspired Schwab employees to take innovative steps, such as offering its services online and at a sizable discount.

If you are thinking that implementing these guidelines is akin to being innovative about innovation, we are inclined to agree. Indeed, although these suggestions may be challenging to adopt, their considerable impact makes it unwise to ignore them.

when both sociability and solidarity are high. Each of these four cultures can have both positive and negative characteristics.

3. Identify the factors responsible for creating and transmitting organizational culture and for getting it to change.

Organizational culture generates strong pressures on people to go along, to think, and to act in ways consistent with the existing culture. Culture has effects on organizational performance only when culture is strong. Subtle nuances of organizational culture have little or no effects on organizational performance. Although organizational culture tends to be stable, it is subject to change. Among the factors most responsible for changing organizational culture are the composition of the workforce, mergers and acquisitions, and planned organizational change.

4. Define creativity and describe the basic components of individual and team creativity.

Creativity is the process by which individuals or small groups produce novel and useful ideas. Creativity in organizations is based on three fundamental components: domain-relevant skills (basic knowledge needed to perform the task at hand), creativity-relevant skills (special abilities needed to generate creative new ideas), and intrinsic task motivation (people's willingness to perform creative acts).

5. Describe various approaches to promoting creativity in organizations.

Creativity in organizations may be promoted by training people to be creative, by encouraging openness to new ideas (e.g., "thinking outside the box"), by taking the time to understand the problem at hand, and by developing divergent thinking (e.g., using morphology). It also may be accomplished by developing creative work environments. These are ones in which autonomy is provided, ideas are permitted to cross-pollinate, jobs are made intrinsically interesting, creative goals are set, creativity is supported within the organization, people have fun, and in which diversity is promoted.

6. Identify the basic components of innovation and the various stages of the innovation process.
Innovation refers to the implementation of creative ideas within organizations. Innovation is composed of three components that are analogous to the three components of creativity. These are motivation to innovate, resources to innovate, and innovation management. These components are used in a process that generally proceeds in five stages: setting the agenda, setting the stage, producing the ideas, testing and implementing the ideas, and assessing the outcome.

POINTS TO PONDER

Questions for Review

1. What is organizational culture, what role does it play in organizations, and how is it created?
2. How does organizational culture influence individuals and organizations, and what makes organizational culture change?
3. What are the three components of individual and team creativity, and what can be done to promote creativity in individuals, work teams, and the whole work environment?
4. What are the basic components of innovation and the stages through which the process of innovation progresses?

Experiential Questions

1. Think of an organization in which you have worked. In what ways was its culture transmitted to the people who worked in it and those who remained outside, such as the public?
2. Have you ever worked for an organization whose culture is in need of change? If so, what was the problem? What could have been done to change the culture? What obstacles would have had to be overcome for the changes to be effective?
3. Do you think of yourself as a creative person? What could you do to become more creative when it comes to the work you do?
4. Have you ever worked for a highly innovative company? If so, what was done that made it so innovative? If not, what could have been done to make it more innovative?

Questions to Analyze

1. Organizational culture is a "mushy" concept. You can't quite see it, yet you know it's there. What indications are there that organizational culture really does exist?
2. Think of an organization in which you have worked. Was its culture predominantly communal, mercenary, fragmented, or networked? Was this an effective culture given the nature of the people who were employed there and the type of work done?
3. Think of an instance in which you were especially creative. Did it involve a task at which you were particularly skillful and that you found interesting (e.g., composing music)? Also, did you use any of the creativity-relevant skills identified here (e.g., divergent thinking, productive forgetting)? In retrospect, what additional skills might you have used to be even more creative in that situation?

INDIVIDUAL EXERCISE

Morphology in Action: Using an Idea Box

One day, the marketing director of a company that makes laundry hampers was tinkering with ways of boosting sales in a stagnant, mature market. To trigger his imagination, he thought explicitly about something that most of us take for granted—the basic parameters of laundry hampers. Specifically, he noted that they differed in four basic ways: the materials of which they were made, their shape, their finish, and how they are positioned. For each of these dimensions, he identified five different answers, resulting in the following chart, known as an *idea box*.

IMPROVED DESIGN FOR LAUNDRY HAMPER

	MATERIAL	SHAPE	FINISH	POSITION
1	Wicker	Square	Painted	Sits on Floor
2	Plastic	Cylindrical	Painted	On Ceiling
3	Paper	Rectangle	Clear	On Wall
4	Metal	Hexagonal	Luminous	Chute to Basement
5	Net Material	Cube	Neon	On Door

(*Source*: Reprinted with permission from *Thinkertoys* by Michael Michalko. Ten Speed Press, Berkeley, California.)

Then, by randomly combining one item from each column—net material, cylindrical shape, painted finish, and positioning on a door—he came up with a completely new idea. It was a laundry hamper made to look like a basketball net: about a yard of netting attached to a cylindrical hoop, hung from a backboard attached to the back of a door.

With some quick math, you can see that this particular idea box generates 3,125 different combinations. Given that this is a far greater number of ideas than you could probably generate without the aid of the idea box, it makes sense to practice generating idea boxes for situations you face in which creative new solutions are required. Nurture your own creativity by following the directions given here.

Directions

To generate an idea box, do the following.

1. *Specify the challenge you are facing.* Although you may not be interested in developing exciting new laundry baskets, you must start at the same point indicated in our example—that is, by identifying exactly what you are attempting to do.
2. *Select the parameters of your challenge.* Material, shape, finish, and position were the parameters of the laundry basket problem. What are yours? To help determine if the parameter you are considering is important enough to add, ask yourself if the challenge would still exist without that parameter.
3. *List variations.* Our example shows five variations of each parameter, but feel free to list as many key ones as you can. After all, as your idea box grows larger, it gets increasingly difficult to spot new ideas. (For example, if your idea box had 10 parameters, each of which contained 10 variations, you'd face 10 billion potential combinations to consider—hardly a practical task!)
4. *Try different combinations.* After your idea box is completed, work your way through the box to find some of the most promising combinations. Begin by exam-

ining the entire box, and then eventually limit yourself to the most promising combinations.

Questions for Discussion

1. Have you ever used the idea box, or something similar to it, before now? If so, how effectively has it worked?
2. For what kinds of challenges is the idea box most useful and least useful?
3. It has been said that generating an idea box is similar to writing a poem. How is this so?

GROUP EXERCISE

What Does Your Workspace Say About Your Organizational Culture?

Newcomers' impressions of an organization's culture depend greatly on the visual images of the organization that they first see. Even without knowing anything about an organization, just seeing the workplace sends a message, intentional or unintentional, regarding what that organization is like. The following exercise is designed to demonstrate this phenomenon.

Directions

1. Each member of the class should take several photographs of his or her workplace and select the three that best capture, in his or her own mind, the essence of what that organization is like.
2. One member of the class should identify the company depicted in his or her photos, describe the type of work it does, and present the photos to the rest of the class.
3. Members of the class should then rate the organization shown in the photos using the following dimensions. Circle the number that comes closest to your feelings about the company shown.

```
unfamiliar     : 1 : 2 : 3 : 4 : 5 : 6 : 7 : familiar
unsuccessful   : 1 : 2 : 3 : 4 : 5 : 6 : 7 : successful
unfriendly     : 1 : 2 : 3 : 4 : 5 : 6 : 7 : friendly
unproductive   : 1 : 2 : 3 : 4 : 5 : 6 : 7 : productive
not innovative : 1 : 2 : 3 : 4 : 5 : 6 : 7 : innovative
uncaring       : 1 : 2 : 3 : 4 : 5 : 6 : 7 : caring
conservative   : 1 : 2 : 3 : 4 : 5 : 6 : 7 : risky
closed         : 1 : 2 : 3 : 4 : 5 : 6 : 7 : open
```

4. Take turns sharing your individual reactions to each set of photos. Compare the responses of the student whose company pictures were examined with those of the students who were seeing the photos for the first time.
5. Repeat this process using the photos of other students' organizations.

Questions for Discussion

1. For each set of photos examined, how close did the descriptions of members of the class come to the photographers' assessments of their own companies? In other words, how well did the photos capture the culture of the organization as perceived by an "insider"?
2. As a whole, were people more accurate in assessing the culture of companies with which they were already familiar than those they didn't already know? If so, why do you think this occurred?
3. Was there more agreement regarding the cultures of organizations in some types of industries (e.g., manufacturing) than in others (e.g., service)? If so, why do you think this occurred?

WEB SURFING EXERCISE

Organizational Culture

Go to the Web site of any large company and search for information about its organizational culture. You should be able to find such information by typing "culture" in the site's search engine. Alternatively, you may find statements describing aspects of corporate culture in pages dedicated to "corporate philosophy," "mission statement," "our people," "about the company," or similar pages.

1. Write a brief description of that company's culture based on the information you find.
2. Based on the culture described, do you think you'd like to work for this company? Why or why not?
3. How does the culture about which you read compare to what you knew about the company in advance? In what ways was this culture similar to and different from your expectations?

Creativity

Type the keyword "creativity" in the entry box of your favorite search engine. Examining the entries that appear, look for sites that offer resources designed to promote creativity or innovation. Go to one of these sites and read about the resources that are available.

1. Write a brief description of the specific techniques that are identified.
2. How do these techniques compare to those described in this text?
3. Which of the techniques described do you think would be most effective? Describe why you think so.

PRACTICING OB

Stimulating a Creative Culture

The president of your organization, a small manufacturing company, has been complaining that sales are stagnant. A key problem, you discover, is that the market for the products your firm makes is fully developed—and frankly, the products themselves are not very exciting. No one seems to care about doing anything innovative. Instead, the employees seem more interested in doing things the way they have always done them.

1. What factors do you suspect are responsible for the way the culture in this organization has developed over the years?
2. What do you recommend should be done to enhance the creativity of this company's employees?
3. What could be done to help make the company's products more innovative?

CASE IN POINT

IDEO: Where Silliness Is Taken Seriously

Although you probably never heard of IDEO, you most certainly are familiar with the products it has designed, including the optical computer mouse (for Apple Computer), the stand-up toothpaste tube for Procter & Gamble's Crest, and 3Com's sleek Palm V personal digital assistant. IDEO's team of product design specialists even created the 25-foot robotic whale used in the movie, "Free Willy." Although we take such products for granted, coming up with them, as you might imagine, requires incredibly creative people. CEO and founder David Kelley knows that maintaining IDEO's status as the largest product design firm in the United States requires keeping ideas flowing from his 350-person staff, which is something he doesn't take for granted.

The key to nurturing creativity at IDEO is having fun—not just telling a few jokes, but playing games and acting goofy. Having fun for the sake of nurturing creativity permeates the atmosphere at IDEO. For example, when employees are not playing miniature golf or tossing Nerf balls in the corridors, they may be found racing desk chairs on the streets outside the company's Palo Alto, California, headquarters. According to Jim Hackett, the CEO of Steelcase (which bought an equity stake in IDEO after being impressed with its operations), this way of operating "appeals to the childlike aspirations of all of us to be continually creative," adding that at IDEO, "work doesn't look like work."

Although Kelly's approach is unconventional, there is a method to his madness. By creating an atmosphere in which people are encouraged to play and have fun, he believes that the barriers that keep people from sharing ideas with each other will be broken down. In other words, if you're willing to throw a Nerf ball at your boss, you also might be willing to toss a few crazy ideas across the table. In Kelly's own words, "You can be playful when everybody feels they're just as important as the next person." Given the company's phenomenal success at coming up with innovative new product designs, his approach seems to be working.

As its clients noticed IDEO's innovative—and highly effective—way of nurturing creativity, they soon became interested not only in *what* the firm designs but in *how* it goes about doing so. After several such inquiries, Kelly decided to diversify IDEO's services by teaching its customers its own special recipe for creativity. In fact, with clients such as NEC, Kodak, Canon McDonald's, and Samsung, creativity training now accounts for a quarter of IDEO's revenues. Acknowledging the adage that *genius is 99 percent perspiration and 1 percent inspiration,* Dennis Boyle, one of IDEO's trainers, says, "Most companies have that 99 percent. It's that 1 percent that's really hard, and that's why our clients are asking us to work with their people and not just their products."

Critical Thinking Questions

1. How successful do you think IDEO will be in teaching its special recipe for creativity to other companies? What barriers to success do you expect it will face as it attempts to do so?
2. Do you think the people who work at IDEO are naturally creative or that the environment brings out whatever creativity they may have—or both? Explain.
3. Do you think you would like to work at a highly innovative company such as IDEO? Why or why not? If so, what pressures do you think you would face?

Organizational Structure and Design

15

■ PREVIEW CASE
VF CORP. SEWS TOGETHER ITS OPERATIONS

Although you may never have heard of VF Corp., you probably are quite familiar with its products, including jeans (with such brands as Lee, Wrangler, Britannica, and Rustler) and underwear (Vanity Fair and Vassarette), as well as Healtex clothing for children, and Jantzen bathing suits. In fact, VF is currently the world's largest apparel company. For over a century, Greensboro, North Carolina–based VF did just fine. Although the company wasn't falling apart at the seams, in recent years, sales have been flat and expenses have been rising.

Among other problems, officials realized that the apparel company had grown to be incredibly inefficient. Each of the 17 brands, for example, operated independently, with their own purchasing, manufacturing, and marketing. Making matters worse, each brand had its own computer system that was incompatible with the others. But lack of coordination at VF went beyond the realm of computers. People in the various divisions never consulted with one another before ordering raw materials—and worse, the various brands competed for the same customers. According to a high-ranking company official at VF, "We had all the disadvantages of a small company and none of the advantages of a big one."

> According to a high-ranking company official at VF, "We had all the disadvantages of a small company and none of the advantages of a big one."

When Mackey McDonald became VF's new CEO, he developed a four-pronged plan for stitching things together. First, he combined the 17 different brands into five units—jeanswear, intimates, playwear, knitwear, and international operations and marketing. Second, he relocated the company from its Wyomissing, Pennsylvania, headquarters to a new facility in Greensboro, North Carolina, which was closer to most of VF's factories. Third, he worked out a unified system for developing products, planning the manufacturing process, and distributing merchandise. At the core of McDonald's plan was a secret weapon—a highly sophisticated new information technology center, called VF Services, which interconnected the various units in a centralized computer network. The idea was not only to organize work more efficiently but also to do so in a manner that maximized sales. Ultimately, the system McDonald envisioned would be so sophisticated in its understanding of consumer purchase patterns that it would have precisely the right items on the right store shelves at the very time consumers wanted to buy them.

McDonald's plan cost the company over $100 million—mostly from the complete overhaul and installation of an integrated computer system—and cut into the company's operating expenses. However, preliminary information shows that the plan seems to be working: On-floor inventory has been reduced 11 percent and product turnover has increased 15 percent. In other words, the merchandise is moving. Will it work in the end? McDonald is optimistic, noting, "Our people designed the products and the process. That's why I think we can have success."

V F Corp. made several drastic changes to the way its various work functions are organized: Among other things, it rearranged 17 units into five, and trimmed 17 separate systems for planning, developing, manufacturing, and distributing merchandise to a single unified plan. Although this approach seems to be working thus far, we have said nothing in this book about the fundamental question underlying McDonald's actions: How should companies organize themselves into separate units to be most effective? This question is a venerable one in the field of business—and, as we shall explain, a very important one.

OB researchers and theorists have provided considerable insight into this matter by studying what is called *organizational structure*—the way individuals and groups are arranged with respect to the tasks they perform—and *organizational design*—the process of coordinating these structural elements in the most effective manner. As you probably suspect, finding the best way to structure and design organizations is not a simple matter. However, insofar as understanding the structure and design of organizations is essential to fully appreciating their functioning, organizational scientists have devoted considerable energy to this topic. We will highlight these efforts in this chapter.

To begin, we will describe the basic building blocks of organizations, which can be identified by the *organizational chart*, a useful pictorial way of depicting key features of organizational structure. Following this, we will examine how these structural elements can be most effectively combined into productive organizational designs. Finally, we will discuss the role of technology as a cause—and a consequence—of organizational design. In so doing, we will be describing the role of the environment on organizational design.

ORGANIZATIONAL STRUCTURE: THE BASIC DIMENSIONS OF ORGANIZATIONS

Think about how a simple house is constructed. It is composed of a wooden frame positioned atop a concrete slab covered by a roof and siding materials. Within this basic structure are separate systems operating to provide electricity, water, and services (e.g., telephone, satellite, cable). Similarly, the structure of the human body is composed of a skeleton surrounded by various systems of organs, muscles, and tissues serving bodily functions such as respiration, digestion, and the like. Although you may not have thought about it much, we can also identify the structure of an organization in a similar fashion.

Consider, for example, the college or university you attend. It probably is composed of various groupings of people and departments working together to serve special functions. Individuals and groups are dedicated to tasks such as teaching, providing financial services, maintaining the physical facilities, and so on. Of course, within each group, even more distinctions can be found between the jobs people perform. For example, it's unlikely that the instructor for your organizational behavior course is also teaching seventeenth-century French literature. You also can distinguish between the various tasks and functions people perform in other organizations. In other words, an organization is not a haphazard collection of people, but a meaningful combination of groups and individuals working together purposefully to meet the goals of the organization.[1] The term **organizational structure** refers to the formal configuration between individuals and groups with respect to the allocation of tasks, responsibilities, and authority within organizations.[2]

Strictly speaking, one cannot see the structure of an organization; it is an abstract concept. However, the connections between various clusters of functions of which an organization is composed can be represented in the form of a diagram known as an **organizational chart.** In other words, an organizational chart can be considered a representation of an organization's internal structure. As you might imagine, organizational charts may be recognized as useful tools for avoiding confusion within organizations regarding how various tasks or functions are interrelated (see Figure 15.1). With this in mind, we will now turn our attention to the five basic dimensions of organizational structure that can be revealed by organizational charts.

Organizational charts provide information about the various tasks performed within an organization and the formal interconnections between them. For example, look at the chart depicting part of a hypothetical manufacturing organization shown in Figure 15.2. Each box represents a specific job, and the lines connecting them reflect the formally prescribed *reporting relationships* between the individuals performing those jobs. In other words, as we noted in Chapter 9, an organizational chart reveals "who answers to whom." As we will see in this chapter, organizational charts also reveal a great deal more.

organizational structure
The formal configuration between individuals and groups with respect to the allocation of tasks, responsibilities, and authorities within organizations.

organizational chart
A diagram representing the connections between the various departments within an organization; a graphic representation of organizational design.

"Just how long has there been a maraschino cherry at the top of the organizational chart?"

FIGURE 15.1
Organizational Charts Reveal a Great Deal
Although we suspect that this particular revelation is totally unique, it's true that organizational charts reveal a great deal about organizations. They provide a guide to an organization's structure, indicating the formal reporting relationships between individuals at different organizational levels.

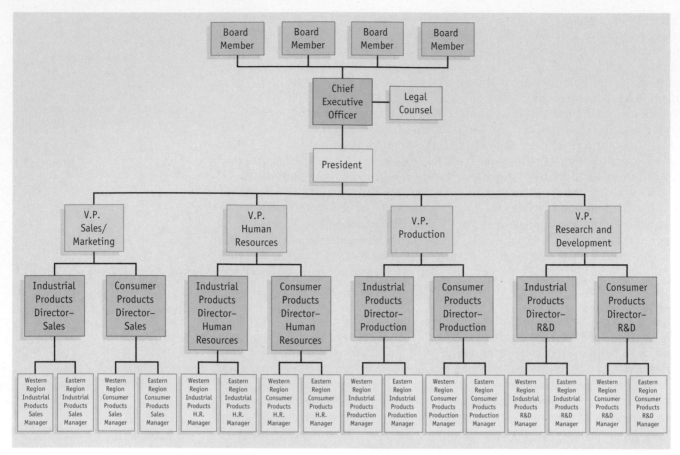

FIGURE 15.2
Organizational Chart of a Hypothetical Manufacturing Firm
An organizational chart, such as this one, identifies pictorially the various functions performed within an organization and the lines of authority between people performing those functions.

Hierarchy of Authority: Up and Down the Organizational Ladder

hierarchy of authority

A configuration of the reporting relationships within organizations, that is, who reports to whom.

In particular, the organizational chart also provides information about who reports to whom—what is known as the **hierarchy of authority.** The diagram reveals which particular lower-level employees are required to report to which particular individuals immediately above them in the organizational hierarchy. In our hypothetical example in Figure 15.2, the various regional salespeople (at the bottom of the hierarchy and the bottom of the diagram) report to their respective regional sales directors, who report to the vice president of sales, who report to the president, who reports to the chief executive officer, who reports to the members of the board of directors. As we trace these reporting relationships, we work our way up the organization's hierarchy. In this case, the organization has six levels. Organizations may have many levels, in which case their structure is considered *tall,* or only a few, in which case their structure is considered *flat.*

In recent years, a great deal has appeared in the news about organizations restructuring their workforces by flattening them out.[3] This is what is taking place as companies "downsize," "rightsize," "delayer," or "retrench" by eliminating entire layers of organizational structure (we will return to this topic again in Chapter 16).[4] Job losses due to restructuring have hit particularly hard at the middle levels of organizations (see Figure 15.3). In keeping with the trend toward getting work done through teams (see Chapter 8), tall organizational hierarchies become unnecessary. The underlying assumption is that fewer layers reduce waste and enable people to make better decisions (by moving them closer to the problems at hand), thereby leading to greater profitability.

550 PART VI: ORGANIZATIONAL PROCESSES

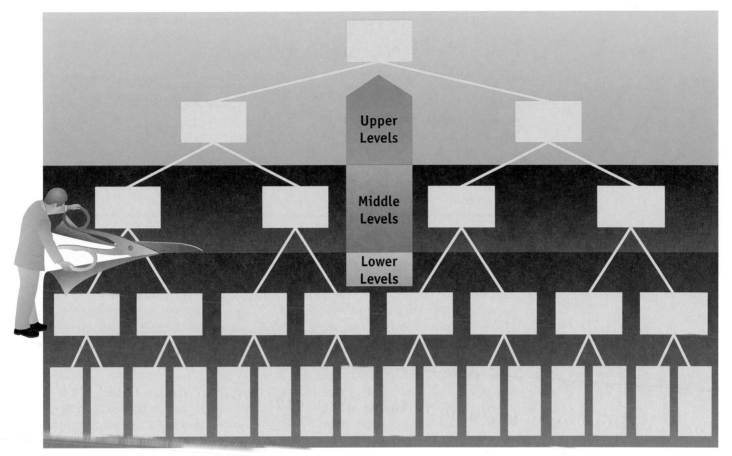

FIGURE 15.3
The Flattening of Organizational Hierarchies: A Modern Trend
As today's organizations restructure, the middle layers of organizational hierarchies tend to get removed. The result is a flatter organizational structure, which puts managers closer to the issues about which they have to make decisions.

Division of Labor: Carving Up the Jobs

The standard organizational chart makes clear that the many tasks to be performed within an organization are divided into specialized jobs, a process known as the **division of labor.** The more that tasks are divided into separate jobs, the more those jobs are *specialized* and the narrower the range of activities that job incumbents are required to perform. In theory, the fewer tasks a person performs, the better he or she may be expected to perform them, freeing others to perform the tasks they perform best. Taken together, an entire organization is composed of people performing a collection of specialized jobs. This is probably the most obvious feature of an organization that can be observed from its organizational chart.

When you might imagine, the degree to which employees perform specialized jobs is likely to depend on the size of the organization. The larger the organization, the more the opportunities for specialization are likely to exist. For example, an individual working in a large advertising agency may get to specialize in a highly narrow field, such as writing jingles for radio and TV spots for automobiles. By contrast, someone working at a much smaller agency may be required to do all writing of print and broadcast ads in addition to helping out with the artwork and meeting with the clients. Obviously, the larger company might be expected to reap the benefits of efficiently using the talents of employees (a natural result of an extensive division of labor).

When companies downsize, many managerial jobs often become less specialized. For example, at General Electric, quite a few middle-management positions have been eliminated in recent years. As a consequence, the remaining managers must perform a wider variety of jobs, making their own jobs less specialized.[5] You can see this relationship in our summary in Table 15.1.

division of labor
The process of dividing the many tasks performed within an organization into specialized jobs.

TABLE 15.1   DIVISION OF LABOR: A SUMMARY

Low and high levels of division of labor can be characterized regarding the dimensions shown here.

DIMENSION	DIVISION OF LABOR	
	LOW	HIGH
Degree of specialization	General tasks	Highly specialized tasks
Typical organizational size	Small	Large
Economic efficiency	Inefficient	Highly efficient

Span of Control: Breadth of Responsibility

Over how many individuals should a manager have responsibility? The earliest management theorists and practitioners alike (even the Roman legions) addressed this question.[6] When you look at an organizational chart, the number of people formally required to report to each individual manager is immediately clear. This number constitutes what is known as a manager's **span of control.** Those responsible for many individuals are said to have a *wide* span of control, whereas those responsible for fewer are said to have a *narrow* span of control. In our organizational chart (Figure 15.2), the CEO is responsible for only the actions of the president, giving this individual a narrower span of control than the president himself or herself, who has a span of control of five individuals.

Sometimes, when an organization's leaders are concerned that they do not have enough control over lower-level employees, they restructure their organizations so that managers have responsibility over smaller numbers of subordinates. This is the case at Canada's largest bank, Royal Bank, where a team of top managers recently recommended that area managers reduce the number of branches under their control to between seven and twelve.[7]

When a manager's span of control is wide, the organization itself tends to have a flat hierarchy. In contrast, when a manager's span of control is narrow, the organization itself tends to have a tall hierarchy. This is demonstrated in Figure 15.4. The diagram at the top shows a *tall* organization—one in which there are many layers in the hierarchy, and the span of control is relatively narrow (i.e., the number of people supervised is low). By contrast, the diagram at the bottom of Figure 15.4 shows a *flat* organization—one in which there are only a few levels in the hierarchy, and the span of control is relatively wide. Note that both organizations depicted here have the same number of positions (31), but these are arranged differently.

The organizational chart may not reflect perfectly a manager's actual span of control. Other factors not immediately forthcoming from the chart itself may be involved. For example, managers may have additional responsibilities that do not appear on the chart—notably, assignments on various committees. Moreover, some subordinates (e.g., new people to the job) might require more attention than others. Also, the degree of supervisory control needed may increase (e.g., when jobs change) or decrease (e.g., when subordinates become more proficient).

It is not readily possible to specify the "ideal" span of control that should be sought. Instead, it makes better sense to consider what form of organization is best suited to various purposes. For example, because supervisors in a military unit must have tight control over subordinates and get them to respond quickly and precisely, a narrow span of control is likely to be effective. As a result, military organizations tend to be extremely tall. In contrast, people working in a research and development lab must have an open exchange of ideas and typically require little managerial guidance to be successful. Not surprisingly, units of this type tend to have very flat structures.

span of control

The number of subordinates in an organization who are supervised by an individual manager.

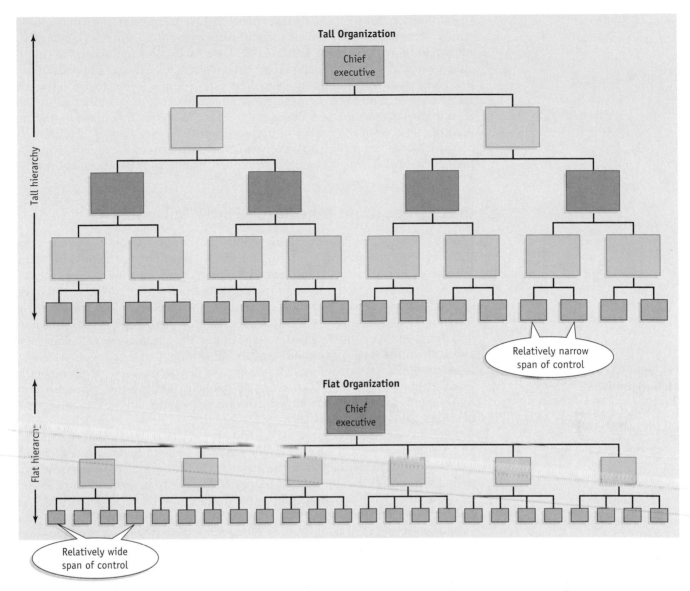

FIGURE 15.4

Tall vs. Flat Organizations: A Comparison
In *tall* organizations, the hierarchy has many layers and managers have a narrow span of control (i.e., they are responsible for few subordinates). However, in *flat* organizations, the hierarchy has few layers and managers have a wide span of control (i.e., they are responsible for many subordinates). Each of the organizations depicted here have 31 members, although each one is structured differently.

Line Versus Staff Positions: Decision Makers Versus Advisors

The organizational chart shown in Figure 15.2 reveals an additional distinction between *line positions* and *staff positions* that deserves to be highlighted. People occupying **line positions** (e.g., the various vice presidents and managers) have decision-making power. However, the individual shown in the dotted box—the legal counsel—cannot make decisions, but provides advice and recommendations to be used by the line managers. Such an individual is said to have a **staff position.**

For example, a corporate attorney may help management officials decide whether a certain product name can be used without infringing on copyright restrictions. In many of today's organizations, human resources managers also may be seen as occupying staff positions because they provide specialized services regarding testing and interviewing procedures as well as information about the latest laws on personnel discrimination. However, the ultimate decisions on personnel selection might be made by more senior managers in specialized areas—that is, staff managers.

line positions

Positions in organizations in which people can make decisions related to doing its basic work.

staff positions

Positions in organizations in which people make recommendations to others but who are not themselves involved in making decisions concerning the organization's day-to-day operations.

Differences between line and staff personnel are not unusual. Such differences may be conflict–arousing or even may be used to create intentional sources of conflict. For example, when Harold Green was the CEO of ITT, staff specialists in the areas of planning and strategy regularly were brought in from headquarters to challenge the decisions made by line managers in an attempt to "keep them on their toes."[8] Sociologists have noted that staff managers tend to be younger, better educated, and more committed to their fields than to the organizations employing them.[9] Line managers might feel more committed not only because of the greater opportunities they have to exercise decisions, but also because they are more likely to perceive themselves as part of a company than as an independent specialist (whose identity lies primarily within his or her specialty area).

Decentralization: Delegating Power Downward

During the first half of the twentieth century, as companies grew larger and larger, they shifted power and authority into the hands of a few upper-echelon administrators—executives whose decisions influenced the many people below them in the organizational hierarchy. In fact, it was during the 1920s that Alfred P. Sloan, Jr., then the president of General Motors, introduced the notion of a "central office," the place where a few individuals made policy decisions for the entire company.[10] As part of Sloan's plan, decisions regarding the day-to-day operation of the company were pushed lower and lower down the organizational hierarchy, allowing those individuals who were most affected to make the decisions. This process of delegating power from higher to lower levels within organizations is known as **decentralization.** It is the opposite, of course, of *centralization,* the tendency for just a few powerful individuals or groups to hold most of the decision-making power.

Recent years have seen a marked trend toward increasingly greater decentralization. As a result, organizational charts might show fewer staff positions, as decision-making authority is pushed farther down the hierarchy. Many organizations have moved toward decentralization to promote managerial efficiency and to improve employee satisfaction (the result of giving people greater opportunities to take responsibility for their own actions, which we discussed in Chapters 5 and 6). Indeed, recent research has shown that employees regard their companies as being more fair to the extent that they are decentralized.[11] In recent years, thousands of staff jobs have been eliminated at many companies as they have become decentralized.[12]

Decentralization is not always an ideal step for organizations to take. In fact, for some types of jobs, it actually may be a serious hindrance to productivity. Consider production-oriented positions, such as assembly-line jobs. In a classic study, researchers found that decentralization improved the performance on some jobs—notably, the work of employees in a research lab—but interfered with the performance of people performing more routine, assembly-line jobs.[13] These findings make sense once you consider that people working in research and development positions are likely to enjoy the autonomy to make decisions that decentralization allows, whereas people working on production jobs are likely to be less interested in taking responsibility for decisions and may enjoy not having to take such responsibility (this is in keeping with our discussion of job satisfaction in Chapter 5). With this in mind, many of today's companies heavily involved in research and development, including parts of Intel Corporation, Philips Electronics, and Lucent Technology, have shifted to more decentralized designs.[14]

In contrast, under some conditions, such as when only a few individuals are in a position to judge what's best for the company, highly centralized authority makes the most sense. For example, during the recession of the 1990s, Delta Airlines' then-CEO Ronald W. Allen used to personally approve every expenditure over $5,000 (except jet fuel).[15] By so doing, he was able to very carefully monitor the company's expenses and keep it afloat during difficult times. To conclude, although the potential exists to derive considerable benefits from decentralization, it should be avoided under certain conditions (see the summary in Table 15.2).

decentralization

The extent to which authority and decision making are spread throughout all levels of an organization rather than being reserved exclusively for top management (centralization).

TABLE 15.2   DECENTRALIZATION: BENEFITS WHEN LOW AND WHEN HIGH

Various benefits are associated with low decentralization (high centralization) and high decentralization (low centralization) within organizations.

LOW DECENTRALIZATION (HIGH CENTRALIZATION)	HIGH DECENTRALIZATION (LOW CENTRALIZATION)
■ Eliminates the additional responsibility not desired by people performing routine jobs	■ Can eliminate levels of management, making a leaner organization
■ Permits crucial decisions to be made by individuals who have the "big picture"	■ Promotes greater opportunities for decisions to be made by people closest to problems

The five elements of structure described thus far—hierarchy of authority, division of labor, span of control, line versus staff positions, and decentralization—are the building blocks of organizational structure. They represent key dimensions along which organizations differ.

DEPARTMENTALIZATION: WAYS OF STRUCTURING ORGANIZATIONS

Thus far, we have been talking about "the" organizational chart of an organization. Typically, such charts, like the one shown in Figure 15.2, divide the organization according to the various functions performed. However, as we will explain in this section, this is only one option. Organizations can be divided not only by function but also by product or market, or by a special blend of function and product or market known as the *matrix* form. We now will take a closer look at these various ways of breaking up organizations into coherent units—that is, the process of **departmentalization**.

departmentalization
The process of breaking up organizations into coherent units.

Functional Organizations: Departmentalization by Task

Because it is the form organizations usually take when they are first created and because it is how we usually think of organizations, the **functional organization** can be considered the most basic approach to departmentalization. Essentially, functional organizations departmentalize individuals according to the nature of the functions they perform, with people who perform similar functions assigned to the same department. For example, a manufacturing company might consist of separate departments devoted to basic functions such as production, sales, research and development, and accounting (see Figure 15.5).

functional organization
The type of departmentalization based on the activities or functions performed (e.g., sales, finance).

Naturally, as organizations grow and become more complex, additional departments are added or deleted as the need arises. As certain functions become centralized, resources can be saved by avoiding duplication of effort, resulting in a higher level of efficiency. Not only does this form of organizational structure take advantage of economies of scale (by allowing employees performing the same jobs to share facilities and not duplicating functions), but also it allows individuals to specialize, thereby performing only those tasks at which they are most expert. The result is a highly skilled workforce, which is a direct benefit to the organization.

Partly offsetting these advantages, however, are several potential limitations. The most important of these stems from the fact that functional organizational structures encourage separate units to develop their own narrow perspectives and to lose sight of overall organizational goals. For example, in a manufacturing company, an engineer

FIGURE 15.5
Functional Organization of a Hypothetical Manufacturing Firm
Functional organizations are ones in which departments are formed on the basis of common functions performed. In the hypothetical manufacturing firm shown in this simplified organization chart, four typical functional departments are identified. In specific organizations, the actual functions may differ.

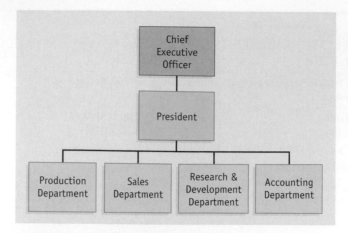

might see the company's problems in terms of the reliability of its products and lose sight of other key considerations, such as market trends, overseas competition, and so on. Such narrow-mindedness is the inevitable result of functional specialization—the downside of people seeing the company's operations through a narrow lens.

A related problem is that functional structures discourage innovation because they channel individual efforts toward narrow, functional areas and do not encourage coordination and cross-fertilization of ideas between areas. As a result, functional organizations are slow to respond to the challenges and opportunities they face from the environment (such as the need for new products and services). In summary, although functional organizations are certainly logical in nature and have proven useful in many contexts, they are by no means the perfect way to departmentalize people in organizations.

Product Organizations: Departmentalization by Type of Output

Organizations—at least successful ones—do not stand still; they constantly change in size and scope. As they develop new products and seek new customers, they might find that a functional structure doesn't work as well as it once did. Manufacturing a wide range of products using a variety of different methods, for example, might put a strain on a manufacturing division of a functional organization. Similarly, keeping track of the varied tax requirements for different types of business (e.g., restaurants, farms, real estate, manufacturing) might pose quite a challenge for a single financial division of a company. In response to such strains, a product organization might be created. This type of departmentalization creates self-contained divisions, each of which is responsible for everything to do with a certain product or group of products. An organization structured this way is known as a **product organization.** (For a look at the structure of a product organization, see Figure 15.6.)

product organization
The type of departmentalization based on the products (or product lines) produced.

When organizations are departmentalized by products, separate divisions are established, each of which is devoted to a certain product or group of products. Each unit contains all the resources needed to develop, manufacture, and sell its products. The organization is composed of separate divisions, operating independently, the heads of which report to top management. Although some functions might be centralized within the parent company (e.g., human resource management or legal staff), on a day-to-day basis each division operates autonomously as a separate company or, as accountants call them, *cost centers* of their own. A good example is the separate divisions of General Motors devoted to manufacturing different brands of cars and trucks (e.g., Chevrolet, Buick, Saturn, GMC Trucks, Pontiac, and Cadillac). There also are still more divisions that are responsible for manufacturing and selling locomotives, refrigerators, and auto parts. Because GE relies on a product organization, the managers of each division can devote their energies to their one particular business (see Figure 15.7).

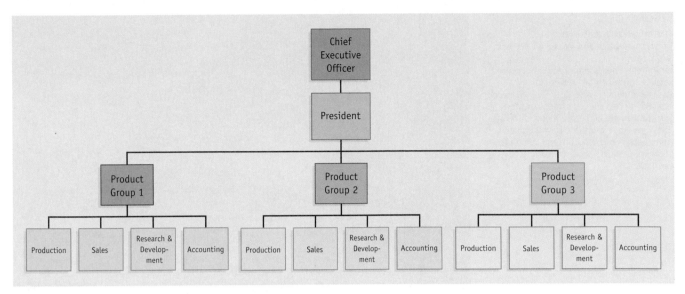

FIGURE 15.6

A Product Organization
In a *product organization,* separate units are established to handle different products or product lines. Each of these divisions contains all of the departments necessary for operating as an independent unit.

This is not to say that product organizations do not have limitations. Indeed, they have several drawbacks. The most obvious of these is the loss of economies of scale stemming from the duplication of various departments within operating units. For example, if each unit carries out its own research and development functions, the need for costly equipment, facilities, and personnel may be multiplied. Another problem associated with product designs involves the organization's ability to attract and retain talented employees. Since each department within operating units is necessarily smaller than a single combined one would be, opportunities for advancement and career development may suffer. This, in turn, may pose a serious problem with respect to the long-term retention of talented employees. Finally, problems of coordination across product lines may arise. In fact, in extreme cases, actions taken by one operating division may have adverse effects on the outcomes of one or more others.

A clear example of such problems was provided by Hewlett-Packard, a major U.S. manufacturer of printers and scientific test equipment (see Figure 15.8). During most of

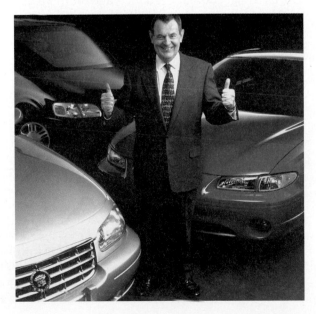

FIGURE 15.7

General Motors: An Example of a Product Organization
Jack Smith, CEO of General Motors, is shown here along with a Chevrolet, a Pontiac, and a Cadillac cars representing three of the company's separate divisions, each of which is dedicated to designing, manufacturing, and selling a separate line of vehicles. Because the company is organized with respect to different product lines, GE is considered an example of a product organization.

FIGURE 15.8
The New Hewlett-Packard:
Departmentalization Based on Market
Segment
Rather than being organized around products as it used to be, after acquiring
Compaq Computers Hewlett-Packard experienced success by departmentalizing
around market segments. Today, different
divisions are responsible for consumer
items (such as computers and printers),
business products, and scientific test
equipment.

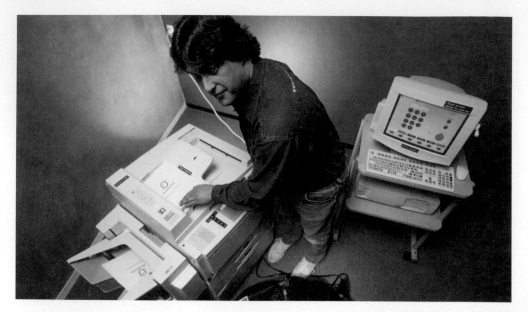

its history, Hewlett-Packard adopted a product design. It consisted of scores of small, largely autonomous divisions, each concerned with producing (and selling) certain products. As it grew in size and complexity, eventually acquiring Compaq Computers, the company found itself in an increasingly untenable situation in which sales represen-tatives from different divisions sometimes attempted to sell different lines of equipment, often to be used for the same basic purposes, to the same customers! To deal with such problems, top management at Hewlett-Packard decided to restructure the company into sectors based largely on the markets they served (such as business customers, and scien-tific and manufacturing customers). In short, Hewlett-Packard switched from a fairly tra-ditional product organization to an internal structure driven by market considerations.[16]

The Hewlett-Packard example points out a particular variation on the basic theme of market departmentalization. Self-contained operating units can also be established on the basis of specific geographic regions or territories and even on the basis of cus-tomers rather than different products. So, for example, a large retail chain might develop separate divisions for different regions of the country (e.g., Macy's-New York and Macy's-California) or for different customer bases (e.g., Bloomingdales by Mail and Bloomingdales Retail). Similarly, a large record company (itself likely a division of a larger entertainment company) may establish independent divisions (each with its own labels) to sign, develop, produce, and promote recordings of interest to people in differ-ent markets (e.g., children, classical, Latin, pop). For example, Sony owns Columbia records, which operates many smaller labels (e.g., So So Def, which specializes in rap music). Departmentalizing in this fashion is like having separate companies within a large company. In this manner, the company can give artists the attention they would expect from a smaller company and the specialization and economies of scale they would expect from a large company. Regardless of the exact basis for departmentaliz-ing—be it product, region, market, or customer group—the basic rationale remains the same: Divide the organization's operations in a way that enhances efficiency.

Matrix Organizations: Departmentalization by Both Function and Product

When the aerospace industry was first developing, the U.S. government demanded that a single manager in each company be assigned to each of its projects so that it was immediately clear who was responsible for the progress of each project. In response to this requirement, TRW established a "project leader" for each project, someone who shared authority with the leaders of the existing functional departments.[18] This tempo-rary arrangement later evolved into what is called a **matrix organization,** the type of

matrix organization
The type of departmentalization in which a product or project form is superimposed on a functional form.

organization in which an employee is required to report to both a functional (or division) manager and the manager of a specific project (or product). In essence, they developed a complex type of organizational structure that combines both the function and product forms of departmentalization.[19] Recently, matrix organizational forms have been used in many organizations, such as Citibank and Liberty Mutual Insurance.[20] To better understand matrix organizations, let's take a closer look at the organizational chart shown in Figure 15.9.

Employees in matrix organizations have two bosses (or, more technically, they are under *dual authority*). One line of authority, shown by the vertical axes in Figure 15.9, is *functional,* managed by vice presidents in charge of various functional areas. The other, shown by the horizontal axes, is *product* (or it may be a specific project or temporary business), managed by specific individuals in charge of certain products (or projects).

In matrix designs, there are three major roles. First, there is the *top leader*—the individual who has authority over both lines (the one based on function and the one based on product or project). It is this individual's task to enhance coordination between functional and product managers and to maintain an appropriate balance of power between them. Second, there are the *matrix bosses*—people who head functional departments or specific projects. Because neither functional managers nor project managers have complete authority over subordinates, they must work together to assure that their efforts mesh rather than conflict. In addition, they must agree on issues such as promotions and raises for specific people working under their joint authority. Finally, there are *two boss managers*—people who must report to both product and functional managers and who attempt to balance the demands of each.

Not all organizations using the matrix structure do so on a permanent basis. Several partial, or temporary, types of matrix design have been identified.[21] First, the *temporary overlay* is a form of matrix structure in which projects are crossed with functions on a special, short-term basis. This is in contrast to a *permanent overlay*, in which project teams are kept going after each project is completed. Finally, there are *mature matrix organizations*, those in which both the functional lines and the product lines are permanent and equally strong within the organization.

With a matrix organization that has been in effect for over 30 years, Dow Corning is an example of a mature matrix organization.[22] At this company, each functional representative reports to the leaders of his or her own department, while also contributing to the design and operation of the particular product line for which he or she is responsible. Because people working in this fashion have two bosses, they must have sufficient freedom to attain their objectives. As you might imagine, a fair amount of coordination, flexibility, openness, and trust is essential for such a design to work, suggesting that not everyone adapts well to such a system.

Organizations are most likely to adopt matrix designs when they confront certain conditions. These include a complex and uncertain environment (one with frequent changes) and the need for economies of scale in the use of internal resources. Specifically, a matrix approach often is adopted by medium-size organizations with several product lines that do not possess sufficient resources to establish fully self-

DESIGNING HIGH-TECH ORGANIZATIONS WITH FLEXIBILITY IN MIND

Most of what we have said about designing organizations is based on traditional technology. However, because today's high-tech world is so fast paced, it is essential for today's well-designed high-tech firm to be designed with one key factor in mind: *flexibility*. This is accomplished in several ways.[17]

1. High-tech firms should be extremely flat and have *little or no vertical hierarchy*. Because their world moves so rapidly, there is no time for the slow responses associated with seeking decisions from higher up.

2. In high-tech firms *organizational designs must be permitted to change frequently*. A design that worked when a company was small and made only a few products might be less effective after it has grown. As a case in point consider ROLM, the telecommunications company that operated as an independent company from 1969 to 1984, when it was acquired by IBM. During this 15-year period, the company grew so fast that it was forced to have four different organizational designs.

3. *The distinction between line and staff functions should be blurred.* Thus, instead of having some specialists who merely advise others (the traditional staff function) and others who have the power to make decisions based on that advice (the traditional line function), the use of teams in many high-tech work groups is putting decision-making power into the hands of those individuals who need to take action.

4. Instead of dividing jobs into specific predetermined roles and formal hierarchical relationships, high-tech firms should *rely on informal networks and relationships*. Continuous changes make institutionalized roles and positions impractical. Instead, informal groupings of people based on the knowledge and skills they bring to the task at hand determine how people work together and what they do.

FIGURE 15.9

A Typical Matrix Organization
In a *matrix organization,* a product structure is superimposed on a basic functional structure. This results in a dual system of authority in which some employees report to two bosses—a project (or product) manager and a functional (departmental) manager.

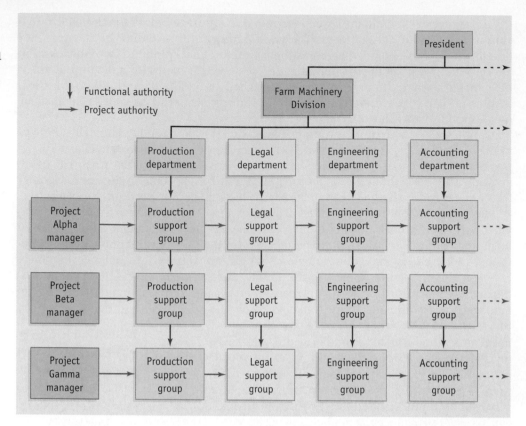

contained operating units. Under such conditions, a matrix design provides a useful compromise. Some companies that have adopted this structure, at least on a trial basis, and only in some parts of the company, are TRW Systems Group, Liberty Mutual Insurance, and Citibank.[23]

Key advantages offered by matrix designs already have been suggested by our discussion so far.[24] First, they permit flexible use of an organization's human resources. Individuals within functional departments can be assigned to specific products or projects as the need arises and then return to their regular duties when this task is completed. Second, matrix designs offer medium-size organizations an efficient means of responding quickly to a changing, unstable environment. Third, such designs often enhance communication among managers; indeed, they literally force matrix bosses to discuss and agree on many matters.

Disadvantages of such designs include the frustration and stress faced by two-boss employees in reporting to two different supervisors, the danger that one of the two authority systems (functional or product) will overwhelm the other, and the consistently high levels of cooperation required from the people involved for the organization to succeed.[25] In situations in which organizations must stretch their financial and human resources to meet challenges from the external environment or take advantage of new opportunities, however, matrix designs often play a useful role.

ORGANIZATIONAL DESIGN: COORDINATING THE STRUCTURAL ELEMENTS OF ORGANIZATIONS

We began the first major section of this chapter by likening the structure of an organization to the structure of a house. Now, we are prepared to extend that analogy for purposes of introducing the concept of *organizational design.* Just as a house is designed in a particular fashion by combining its structural elements in various ways, so too can an organization be designed by combining its basic elements in certain ways. Accordingly, **organizational design** refers to the process of coordinating the structural elements of organizations in the most appropriate manner.

organizational design
The process of coordinating the structural elements of an organization in the most appropriate manner.

As you might imagine, this is no easy task. Although we might describe some options that sound neat and rational on the next few pages, in reality this is hardly ever the case. Even the most precisely designed organizations will face the need to change at one time or another, adjusting to the realities of technological changes, political pressures, accidents, and so on. Organizational designs also might be changed purposely in an attempt to improve operating efficiency, such as the promise by some recent U.S. presidents to streamline the huge federal bureaucracy. Our point is simple: Because organizations operate within a changing world, their own designs must be capable of changing as well. Those organizations that are either poorly designed or inflexible cannot survive. If you consider the large number of banks and airlines that have gone out of business in the last few years because of their inability to deal with rapid changes brought about by deregulation and a shifting economy, you'll get a good idea of the ultimate consequences of ineffective organizational design. (In Chapter 16 we will discuss in detail this matter of the need for organizations to adapt to change. Meanwhile, for an example of a contemporary approach to organizational design that is sensitive to the need for rapid change, see the Best Practices section on page 562.)

Classical and Neoclassical Approaches: The Quest for the One Best Design

The earliest theorists interested in organizational design did not operate out of awareness of the point we just made regarding the need for organizations to be flexible. Instead, they approached the task of designing organizations as a search for "the one best way." Although today we are more attuned to the need to adapt organizational designs to various environmental and social conditions, theorists in the early and middle part of the twentieth century sought to establish the ideal form for all organizations under all conditions—the universal design.

In Chapter 1, we described the efforts of organizational scholars such as Max Weber, Frederick Taylor, and Henri Fayol. These theorists believed that effective organizations were ones that had a formal hierarchy, a clear set of rules, specialization of labor, highly routine tasks, and a highly impersonal working environment. You may recall that Weber referred to this organizational form as a *bureaucracy*. This **classical organizational theory** has fallen into disfavor because it is insensitive to human needs and is not suited to a changing environment. Unfortunately, the "ideal" form of an organization, according to Weber, did not take into account the realities of the world within which it operates. Apparently, what is ideal is not necessarily what is realistic.

classical organizational theory
The approach that assumes that there is a single best way to design organizations.

In response to these conditions, and with inspiration from the Hawthorne studies, the classical approach to the bureaucratic model gave way to more of a human relations orientation. Organizational scholars such as McGregor, Argyris, and Likert attempted to improve on the classical model—which is why their approach is labeled **neoclassical organizational theory**—by arguing that not only economic effectiveness, but also employee satisfaction, should be goals of an industrial organization.

neoclassical organizational theory
An attempt to improve on the classical organizational theory that argues that not only economic effectiveness, but also employee satisfaction, should be goals of an industrial organization.

Specifically, Douglas McGregor was an organizational theorist who objected to the rigid hierarchy imposed by Weber's bureaucratic form because it was based on negative assumptions about people—primarily that they lacked ambition and wouldn't work unless coerced (the *Theory X* approach discussed in Chapter 1).[29] In contrast, McGregor argued that people desire to achieve success by working and that they seek satisfaction by behaving responsibly (the *Theory Y* approach). Another neoclassical theorist, Chris Argyris, expressed similar ideas.[30] Specifically, he argued that managerial domination of organizations blocks basic human needs to express oneself and to successfully accomplish tasks. Such dissatisfaction, he argued, would encourage turnover and lead to poor performance. (Today, of course, as we described in Chapter 5, the relationship between job satisfaction and performance is known to be far more complex.)

Another neoclassical theorist, Rensis Likert, shared these perspectives, arguing that organizational performance is enhanced not by rigidly controlling people's actions, but by actively promoting their feelings of self-worth and their importance to the organiza-

If the experts are right, we are in store for a new way of structuring work in tomorrow's organizations—one that means more than just tinkering with the boxes on an organization chart. It's called the **horizontal organization**—an approach advocated by many organizational experts and touted by consultants from the firm McKinsey & Co. as "the first real, fundamentally different, robust alternative" to the functional organization.[26]

The essence of the idea is simple. Instead of organizing jobs in the traditional, vertical fashion, by having a long chain of groups or individuals perform parts of a task (e.g., one group that sells the advertising job, another that plans the ad campaign, and yet another that produces the ads), horizontal organizations have flattened hierarchies. That is, they arrange autonomous

work teams (see Chapter 8) in parallel, each performing many different steps in the process (e.g., members of an advertising team may bring different skills and expertise to a single team responsible for all aspects of advertising). Essentially, organizations are structured around *processes* instead of tasks. Performance objectives are based on customers' needs, such as lowered cost or improved service. Once the core processes that meet these needs (e.g., order generation, new-product development) have been identified, they become the company's major components—instead of the traditional departments such as sales or manufacturing.

According to consultant Michael Hammer, "In the future, executive positions will not be defined in terms of collections of people, like head of the sales department, but in terms of

---

horizontal organization

The practice of structuring organizations by processes performed, using autonomous work teams in flattened hierarchies.

tion.[31] An effective organization, Likert proposed, was one in which individuals would have a great opportunity to participate in making organizational decisions—what he called a *Systems 4 organization*. Doing this, he claimed, would enhance employees' personal sense of worth, motivating them to succeed. Likert called the opposite type of organization *System 1*, the traditional form in which organizational power is distributed in the hands of a few top managers who tell lower-ranking people what to do. (*System 2* and *System 3* are intermediate forms between the System 1 and System 4 extremes.)

The organizational design implications of these neoclassical approaches are clear. In contrast to the classical approach, calling for organizations to be designed with a rigid, tall hierarchy, with a narrow span of control (allowing managers to maintain close supervision over their subordinates), the neoclassical approach argues for designing organizations with flat hierarchical structures (minimizing managerial control over subordinates) and a high degree of decentralization (encouraging employees to make their own decisions). (For a summary of these differences, see Figure 15.10.) Indeed, such design features may well serve the underlying neoclassical philosophy.

Like the classical approach, the neoclassical approach also may be faulted on the grounds that it is promoted as "the one best approach" to organizational design. Although the benefits of flat, decentralized designs may be many, to claim that this represents the universal, ideal form for all organizations would be naive. In response to this criticism, more contemporary approaches to organizational design have given up on finding the one best way to design organizations in favor of finding designs that are most appropriate to various circumstances and contexts within which organizations operate.

---

contingency approach to organizational design

The contemporary approach that recognizes that no one approach to organizational design is best, but that the best design is the one that best fits with the existing environmental conditions.

The Contingency Approach: Design According to Environmental Conditions

The idea that the best design for an organization depends on the nature of the environment in which the organization is operating lies at the heart of the modern, **contingency** processes, like senior-VP-of-getting-stuff-to-customers, which is sales, shipping, billing. You'll no longer have a box on an organization chart. You'll own part of a process map."[27] Envision it as a whole company lying on its side and organized by process. An ardent believer in this approach, Lawrence Bossidy, CEO of Allied-Signal, says, "Every business has maybe six basic processes. We'll organize around them. The people who run them will be the leaders of the business."[28] In an industrial company, for example, these processes might include areas such as new-product development, flow of materials, and the order-delivery-billing cycle. Individuals will constantly move into and out of various teams as needed, drawing from a directory of broadly skilled in-house corporate experts available to lend their expertise.

The horizontal organization is already a reality in at least parts of several of today's organizations, including AT&T (network systems division), Eastman Chemical, Hallmark Cards, and Xerox. Consider, for example, General Electric's factory in Bayamón, Puerto Rico. The 172 hourly workers, 15 salaried "advi-sors," plus a single manager manufacture "arresters" (surge protectors that guard power stations from lightning). That's the entire workforce; there are no support staff and no supervisors—only about half as many people as you'd find in a conventional factory. Bayamón employees are formed into separate teams of approximately 10 widely skilled members who "own" such parts of the work as shipping and receiving, assembly, and so on. The teams do whatever is needed to get the job done; the advisors get involved only when needed.

Although carefully controlled studies have yet to assess the impact of this approach, those who have used it are convinced of its effectiveness. One top McKinsey consultant, for example, claims that this new approach to organizational design can help companies cut their costs by at least a third. Some of their clients, they boast, have done even better. Will the horizontal organization replace the traditional pyramid of the hierarchical organization? Only time will tell. Meanwhile, those who have turned to horizontal organizational structures appear to be glad they did.

approach to organizational design. We use the term "contingency" here in a manner similar to the way we used it in our discussion of leadership in Chapter 13. But rather than considering the best approach to leadership for a given situation, we are considering the best way to design an organization given the environment within which the organization functions.

The external environment and its connection to organizational design. It is widely assumed that the most appropriate type of organizational design depends on the organization's *external environment*. In general, the external environment is the sum of all the forces impinging on an organization with which it must deal effectively if it is to survive.[32] These forces include general work conditions, such as the economy, geography,

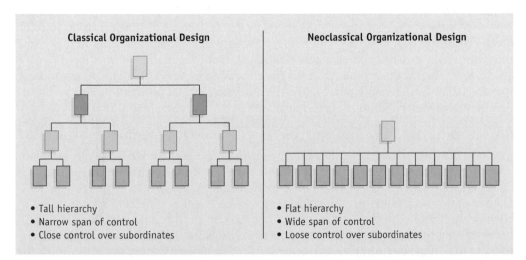

Classical Organizational Design

- Tall hierarchy
- Narrow span of control
- Close control over subordinates

Neoclassical Organizational Design

- Flat hierarchy
- Wide span of control
- Loose control over subordinates

FIGURE 15.10

Classical vs. Neoclassical Designs: A Summary

The classical approach to designing organizations assumed that managers needed to have close control over their subordinates. As such, it called for designing organizations with tall hierarchies and a narrow span of control. In contrast, the neoclassical approach to designing organizations assumed that managers did not have to carefully monitor their subordinates. As such, it called for designing organizations with flat hierarchies and a wide span of control.

and national resources, as well as the specific task environment within the company—notably, its competitors, customers, workforce, and suppliers.

Let's consider some examples. Banks operate within an environment that is highly influenced by the general economic environment (e.g., interest rates and government regulations) as well as a task environment sensitive to other banks' products (e.g., types of accounts) and services (e.g., service hours, access to account information via the Internet and/or by telephone), the needs of the customer base (e.g., direct deposit for customers), the availability of trained personnel (e.g., individuals suitable for entry-level positions), as well as the existence of suppliers providing goods and services (e.g., automated teller equipment, surveillance equipment, computer workstations) necessary to deliver requisite services. Analogous examples can be found in other industries as well. For example, think about the environmental forces faced by the airlines (e.g., growing needs for security), the computer industry (e.g., faster microprocessors), and automobile manufacturers (e.g., zero-percent financing). It's easy to recognize the features of their environments that must be taken into account when considering how organizations in these industries could be designed.

Although many features of the environment may be taken into account when considering how an organization should be designed, a classic investigation provides some useful guidance.[33] The scientists conducting this study interviewed people in 20 industrial organizations in the United Kingdom to determine the relationship between managerial activities and the external environment. In so doing, they distinguished between organizations that operated in highly *stable,* unchanging environments and those that operated in highly *unstable,* turbulent environments. For example, a rayon company in their sample operated in a highly stable environment: The environmental demands were predictable, people performed the same jobs in the same ways for a long time, and the organization had clearly defined lines of authority that helped get the job done. In contrast, a new electronics development company in their sample operated in a highly turbulent environment. Conditions changed on a daily basis, jobs were not well defined, and no clear organizational structure existed.

The researchers noted that many of the organizations studied tended to be described in ways that were appropriate for their environments. For example, when the environment is stable, people can do the same tasks repeatedly, allowing them to perform highly specialized jobs. However, in turbulent environments, many different jobs may have to be performed, and such specialization should not be designed into the jobs. Clearly, a strong link exists between the stability of the work environment and the proper organizational form. The researchers concluded that two different approaches to management existed and that these are largely based on the degree of stability within the external environment. These two approaches are known as **mechanistic organizations** and **organic organizations.**

Mechanistic versus organic organizations: Designs for stable versus turbulent conditions. If you've ever worked at a McDonald's, you probably know how highly standardized each step of the most basic operations must be.[34] Boxes of fries are to be stored 2 inches from the wall in stacks 1 inch apart. Making those fries is another matter—one that requires 19 distinct steps, each clearly laid out in a training film shown to new employees. The process is the same, whether it's done in Moscow, Idaho, or in Moscow, Russia. This is an example of a highly mechanistic task. Organizations can be highly mechanistic when conditions don't change. Although the fast-food industry has changed a great deal in recent years (with the introduction of new, healthier menu items, competitive pricing, and the like), the making of fries at McDonald's has not changed. If the environment doesn't change, a highly mechanistic organizational form can be very efficient.

An environment is considered stable whenever there is little or no unexpected change in product, market demands, or technology. Have you ever seen an old-fashioned-looking bottle of E. E. Dickinson's witch hazel, a topical astringent used to cleanse the skin in the area of a wound? Since the company has been making the product following the same distillation process since 1866, it is certainly operating in a relatively stable manufacturing environment.[35] As we described earlier, stability affords the

mechanistic organization
An internal organizational structure in which people perform specialized jobs, many rigid rules are imposed, and authority is vested in a few top-ranking officials.

organic organization
An internal organizational structure in which jobs tend to be very general, there are few rules, and decisions can be made by lower-level employees.

luxury of high employee specialization. Without change, people easily can specialize. However, when change is inevitable, specialization is impractical.

Mechanistic organizations can be characterized in several additional ways (for a summary, see Table 15.3). Not only do mechanistic organizations allow for a high degree of specialization, but they also impose many rules. Authority is vested in a few people located at the top of a hierarchy who give direct orders to their subordinates. Mechanistic organizational designs tend to be most effective under conditions in which the external environment is stable and unchanging.

Now, think about high-technology industries, such as those dedicated to computers, aerospace products, and biotechnology. Their environmental conditions are likely to be changing all the time. These industries are so prone to change that as soon as a new way of operating could be introduced into one of them, it would have to be altered. It isn't only technology, however, that makes an environment turbulent. Turbulence also can be high in industries in which adherence to rapidly changing regulations is essential. For example, times were turbulent in the hospital industry when new Medicaid legislation was passed, and times were turbulent in the nuclear power industry when governmental regulations dictated the introduction of many new standards that had to be followed. In the aftermath of the September 11, 2001 terrorist attacks, the airline industry has faced highly turbulent times due to lower demands for seats and the need to adopt new security regulations. Unfortunately, financial difficulties in the airplane industry in 2002 suggest that they are not adapting as well as desired.

The pure organic form of organization may be characterized in several different ways (see Table 15.3). The degree of job specialization possible is very low; instead, a broad knowledge of many different jobs is required. Very little authority is exercised from the top. Rather, self-control is expected, and an emphasis is placed on coordination between peers. As a result, decisions tend to be made in a highly democratic, participative manner. It is important to note that the mechanistic and organic types of organizational structure described here are ideal forms. The mechanistic–organic distinction should be thought of as opposite poles along a continuum rather than as completely distinct options for organization. In other words, organizations can be relatively organic or relatively mechanistic compared to others although they may not be located at either extreme.

Finally, research shows that organizational effectiveness is related to the degree to which an organization's structure (mechanistic or organic) is matched to its environment (stable or turbulent). In a classic study, researchers evaluated four departments in a large company—two of which manufactured containers (a relatively stable environment) and two of which dealt with communications research (a highly unstable environment).[36] One department in each pair was evaluated as being more effective than the other. It was found that for the container manufacturing departments, the more effective unit was the one structured in a highly mechanistic form (roles and duties

TABLE 15.3   MECHANISTIC VERSUS ORGANIC DESIGNS: A SUMMARY

Mechanistic and organic designs differ along several key dimensions identified here. These represent extremes; organizations can be relatively organic, relatively mechanistic, or somewhere in between.

| DIMENSION | STRUCTURE | |
	MECHANISTIC	ORGANIC
Stability	Change unlikely	Change likely
Specialization	Many specialists	Many generalists
Formal rules	Rigid rules	Considerable flexibility
Authority	Centralized in few top people	Decentralized, diffused throughout the organization

were clearly defined). In contrast, the more effective communications research department was structured in a highly organic fashion (roles and duties were vague). Additionally, the other, less effective departments were structured in the opposite manner (i.e., the less effective manufacturing department was organically structured, and the less effective research department was mechanistically structured) (see Figure 15.11).

Taken together, the results made it clear that departments were most effective when their organizational structures fit their environments. This notion of determining which design is best under certain conditions lies at the heart of the modern orientation—the contingency approach—to organizational structure. Rather than specifying *which* structure is best, the contingency approach specifies *when* each type of organizational design is more effective.

Mintzberg's Framework: Five Organizational Forms

Although the distinction between mechanistic and organic designs is important, it is not terribly specific with respect to exactly how organizations should be designed. Filling this void, however, is the work of contemporary organizational theorist, Henry Mintzberg.[37] Specifically, Mintzberg claims that organizations are composed of five basic elements, or groups of individuals, any of which may predominate in an organization. The one that predominates will determine the most effective design in that situation. The five basic elements are:

- The **operating core:** employees who perform the basic work related to the organization's product or service. Examples include teachers (in schools) and chefs and waiters (in restaurants).
- The **strategic apex:** top-level executives responsible for running the entire organization. Examples include the entrepreneur who runs her own small business and the general manager of an automobile dealership.
- The **middle line:** managers who transfer information between the strategic apex and the operating core. Examples include middle managers, such as regional sales managers (who connect top executives with the sales force) and the chair of an academic department in a college or university (an intermediary between the dean and the faculty).
- The **technostructure:** those specialists responsible for standardizing various aspects of an organization's activities. Examples include accountants, auditors, and computer systems analysts.

operating core
Employees who perform the basic work related to an organization's product or service.

strategic apex
Top-level executives responsible for running an entire organization.

middle line
Managers who transfer information between higher and lower levels of the organizational hierarchy.

technostructure
Organizational specialists responsible for standardizing various aspects of an organization's activities.

FIGURE 15.11

Matching Organizational Design and Industry: The Key to Effectiveness
In a classic study, researchers evaluated the performance of four departments in a large company. The most effective units were ones in which the way the group was structured (mechanistic or organic) matched the most appropriate form for the type of task performed (i.e., organic for research work, and mechanistic for manufacturing work).
(*Source:* Based on suggestions by Morse & Lorsch, 1970; see Note 36.)

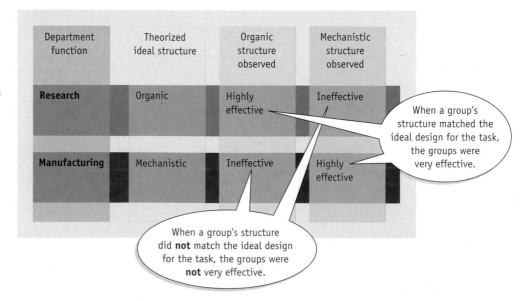

- The **support staff:** individuals who provide indirect support services to the organization. Examples include consultants on technical matters and corporate attorneys.

support staff

Individuals who provide indirect support services to an organization.

What organizational designs best fit under conditions in which each of these five groups dominate? Mintzberg has identified five specific designs: *simple structure, machine bureaucracy, professional bureaucracy,* the *divisionalized structure,* and the *adhocracy* (see summary in Table 15.4).

Simple structure. Imagine that you open up an antique shop and hire a few people to help you out around the store. You have a small, informal organization in which there is a single individual with the ultimate power. There is little in the way of specialization or formalization, and the overall structure is organic in nature. The hierarchy is quite flat, and all decision-making power is vested in a single individual—you. An organization so described, simple in nature, with the power residing at the strategic apex, is referred to by Mintzberg as having a **simple structure.** As you might imagine, organizations with simple structure can respond quickly to the environment and be very flexible. For example, the chef-owner of a small, independent restaurant can change the menu to suit the changing tastes of customers whenever needed, without first consulting anyone else. The downside of this, however, is that the success or failure of the entire enterprise is dependent on the wisdom and health of the individual in charge. Not surprisingly, organizations with simple structure are risky ventures.

simple structure

An organization characterized as being small and informal, with a single powerful individual, often the founding entrepreneur, who is in charge of everything.

Machine bureaucracy. If you've ever worked for your state department of motor vehicles, you probably found it to be a very large place, with numerous rules and procedures for employees to follow. The work is highly specialized (e.g., one person gives the vision tests and another completes the registration forms), and decision making is concentrated at the top (e.g., you need to get permission from your supervisor to do anything other than exactly what's expected). This type of work environment is highly stable and does not have to change. An organization so characterized, where power resides with the technostructure, is referred to as a **machine bureaucracy.** Although machine bureaucracies can be highly efficient at performing standardized tasks, they tend to be dehumanizing and very boring for the employees.

machine bureaucracy

An organizational form in which work is highly specialized, decision making is concentrated at the top, and the work environment is not prone to change (e.g., a government office).

Professional bureaucracy. Suppose you are a doctor working at a large city hospital. You are a highly trained specialist with considerable expertise in your field. You don't need to check with anyone else before authorizing a certain medical test or treatment for your patient; you make the decisions as they are needed, when they are needed. At the same time, the environment is highly formal (e.g., there are lots of rules and regulations for you to follow). Of course, you do not work alone; you also require the services of other highly qualified professionals such as nurses and laboratory technicians. Organizations

---

TABLE 15.4 MINTZBERG'S FIVE ORGANIZATIONAL FORMS: A SUMMARY

Mintzberg has identified five distinct organizational designs, each of which is likely to occur in organizations in which certain groups are in power.

DESIGN	DESCRIPTION	DOMINANT GROUP	EXAMPLE
Simple structure	Simple, informal, authority centralized in a single person	Strategic apex	Small, entrepreneurial business
Machine bureaucracy	Highly complex, formal environment with clear lines of authority	Technostructure	Government office
Professional bureaucracy	Complex, decision-making authority is vested in professionals	Operating core	University
Divisionalized structure	Large, formal organizations with several separate divisions	Middle line	Multidivisional business, such as General Motors
Adhocracy	Simple, informal, with decentralized authority	Support staff	Software development firm

(*Source:* Based on suggestions by Mintzberg, 1983; see Note 37.)

professional bureaucracy

Organizations (e.g., hospitals and universities) in which there are lots of rules to follow, but employees are highly skilled and free to make decisions on their own.

divisional structure

The form used by many large organizations, in which separate autonomous units are created to deal with entire product lines, freeing top management to focus on large-scale, strategic decisions.

adhocracy

A highly informal, organic organization in which specialists work in teams, coordinating with each other on various projects (e.g., many software development companies).

of this type, including universities, libraries, and consulting firms as well as hospitals, maintain power with the operating core and are called **professional bureaucracies.** Such organizations can be highly effective because they allow employees to practice those skills for which they are best qualified. However, sometimes specialists become so overly narrow that they fail to see the "big picture," leading to errors and potential conflict between employees.

Divisional structure. When you think of large organizations, such as General Motors, DuPont, Xerox, and IBM, the image that comes to mind is probably closest to what Mintzberg describes as **divisional structure.** Such organizations consist of a set of autonomous units coordinated by a central headquarters (i.e., they rely on departmental structure based on products, as described on pages 556–558). In such organizations, because the divisions are autonomous (e.g., a General Motors employee at Buick does not have to consult with another at Chevrolet to do his or her job), division managers (the *middle line* part of Mintzberg's basic elements) have considerable control. Such designs preclude the need for top-level executives to think about the day-to-day operations of their companies and free them to concentrate on larger-scale, strategic decisions. At the same time, companies organized into separate divisions frequently tend to have high duplication of effort (e.g., separate order processing units for each division). Having operated as separate divisions for the past 80 years, General Motors is considered the classic example of divisional structure.[38] Although the company has undergone many changes during this time, including the addition of the Saturn Division and the elimination of the Oldsmobile Division, it has maintained its divisional structure.

Adhocracy. After graduating from college, where you spent years learning how to program computers, you take a job at a small software company. Compared to your friends who found positions at large accounting firms, your professional life is much less formal. You work as a member of a team developing a new time-management software product. There are no rules, and schedules are made to be broken. You all work together, and although there is someone who is "officially" in charge, you'd never know it. Using Mintzberg's framework, you work for an **adhocracy**—an organization in which power resides with the support staff. Essentially, this is the epitome of the organic structure identified earlier. Specialists coordinate with each other not because of their shared functions (e.g., accounting, manufacturing) but as members of teams working on specific projects.

The primary benefit of the adhocracy is that it fosters innovation. Some large companies, such as Johnson & Johnson (J&J), nest within their formal divisional structure units that operate as adhocracies. In the case of J&J, it's the New Products Division, a unit that has been churning out an average of 40 products per year during recent years.[39] As in the case of all other designs there are disadvantages. In this case, the most serious limitations are their high levels of inefficiency (they are the opposite of machine bureaucracies in this regard) and the greatest potential for disruptive conflict.

The Boundaryless Organization: A New Corporate Architecture

You hear it all the time: Someone is asked to do something but responds defiantly, saying, "It's not my job." As uncooperative as this may seem, such a comment may make a great deal of sense when it comes to the traditional kind of organizational structures we've been describing—ones with layers of carefully connected boxes neatly stacked atop each other in hierarchical fashion. The advantage of these types of organizations is that they clearly define the roles of managers and employees. Everyone knows precisely what he or she is supposed to do. The problem with such arrangements, however, is that they are inflexible. As a result, they do not lend themselves to the rapidly changing conditions in which today's organizations operate. Not surprisingly, the traditional boundaries that once separated organizations into separate departments are now blurred in actual practice in many organizations.[40]

This movement toward eliminating the boundaries that once carefully delineated organizational functions began with Jack Welch, a former CEO of General Electric, who proposed the **boundaryless organization.** This is an organization in which chains of command are eliminated, spans of control are unlimited, and rigid departments give way to empowered teams (see Figure 15.12). Replacing rigid distinctions between people are fluid, intentionally ambiguous, and ill-defined roles. Welch's vision was that GE would operate like a family grocery store (albeit a $60 billion store)—one in which the barriers within the company that separate employees from each other and that separate the company from its customers and suppliers would be eliminated.[41] The idea is that such barriers inhibit creativity, waste time, smother dreams, and generally slow things down. In a speech given on April 24, 1990, Welch referred to organizational boundaries as "speed bumps that slow down the enterprise."[42] Although GE never quite became the completely boundaryless organization Welch envisioned, it has made significant strides toward breaking down boundaries.

So, too, have other organizations. As an example, consider the way Chrysler went about making its successful small car, the Neon.[43] In 1990 Robert P. Marcell, head of Chrysler's small-car engineering group, assembled a team of 600 engineers, 289 suppliers, and busses full of blue-collar workers. Together they developed the inexpensive new car in a speedy 42 months, and on budget at $1.3 billion. Instead of working sequentially using separate specialists in design, manufacturing, and marketing, as typically occurs, members of Marcell's team worked concurrently on several tasks. People from different areas, such as engineering, marketing, purchasing, and finance worked together with assembly-line workers, suppliers, and consumers to coordinate their efforts. In other words, the traditional boundaries that separate people (both inside and outside the organization) were eliminated. As a result, the team was able to work quickly and unhindered by the usual restrictions imposed by their traditionally narrow roles.

For boundaryless organizations to function effectively, they must meet many of the same requirements as successful teams (see Chapter 8). For example, there must be high levels of trust between all parties concerned. Also, everyone involved must have such high levels of skill that they can operate without much, if any, managerial guidance. Insofar as the elimination of boundaries weakens traditional managerial power bases, some executives may find it difficult to give up their authority, leading to political behavior (see Chapter 12). However, to the extent that the elimination of boundaries leverages the talents of all employees, such limitations are worth striving to overcome.

The boundaryless organizations we have been describing involve breaking down both internal and external barriers. As a result, they sometimes are referred to as *barrier-free organizations.* However, there are variations of the boundaryless organization involving only the elimination of external boundaries.[44] These are known as

boundaryless organization

An organization in which chains of command are eliminated, spans of control are unlimited, and rigid departments give way to empowered teams.

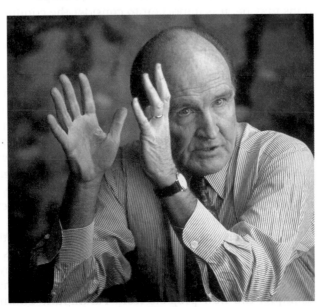

FIGURE 15.12

Jack Welch: Making General Electric a Boundaryless Organization
Although it's difficult to envision one of the world's largest organizations operating without a rigid structure, that's just what former CEO Jack Welch (who retired in 2002) proposed for GE. His concept of the *boundaryless organization* entails eliminating rigid departments and having people work together in fluid teams. Although the company hasn't achieved this state entirely, the elimination of boundaries has been credited with much of GE's recent successes.

cles have engines containing Autolite spark plugs, separate companies that are owned by their respective parent companies. In this manner, conglomerates can benefit by providing a network of organizations that are dependent on each other for products and services, thereby creating considerable advantages.

Strategic Alliances: Joining Forces for Mutual Benefit

strategic alliance

A type of interorganizational design in which two or more separate companies combine forces to develop and operate a specific business. (See *mutual service consortia, joint ventures,* and *value-chain partnerships.*)

A **strategic alliance** is a type of organizational design in which two or more separate firms join their competitive capabilities to operate a specific business. The goal of a strategic alliance is to provide benefits to each individual organization that could not be attained if they operated separately. They are low-risk ways of diversifying (adding new business operations) and entering new markets. Some companies, such as GE and Ford, have strategic alliances with many others. Although some alliances last only a short time, others have remained in existence for well over 30 years and still are going strong.[56] For a good example of a strategic alliance, see Figure 15.14.

The continuum of alliances. A study of 37 strategic alliances from throughout the world identified three types of cooperative arrangements between organizations.[57] These may be arranged along a continuum from those alliances that are weak and distant, at one end, to those that are strong and close, at the other end. As shown in Figure 15.15, at the weak end of the continuum are strategic alliances known as **mutual service consortia.** These are arrangements between two similar companies from the same or similar industries to pool their resources to receive a benefit that would be too difficult or expensive for either to obtain alone. Often, the focus is some high-tech capacity, such as an expensive piece of diagnostic equipment that might be shared by two or more local hospitals (e.g., a magnetic resonance imaging, or MRI unit).

mutual service consortia

A type of strategic alliance in which two similar companies from the same or similar industries pool their resources to receive a benefit that would be too difficult or expensive for either to obtain alone.

value-chain partnerships

Strategic alliances between companies in different industries that have complementary capabilities.

At the opposite end of the scale are the strongest and closest type of collaborations, referred to as **value-chain partnerships.** These are alliances between companies in different industries that have complementary capabilities. Customer–supplier relationships are a prime example. In such arrangements one company buys necessary goods and services from another so that it can do business. Because each company greatly depends on the other, each party's commitment to their mutual relationship is high. As noted earlier, Toyota has a network of 230 suppliers with whom it regularly does business. The relationships between Toyota and these various companies represent value-chain partnerships.

joint ventures

Strategic alliances in which several companies work together to fulfill opportunities that require the capabilities of one another.

Between these two extremes are **joint ventures,** which are arrangements in which companies work together to fulfill opportunities that require the capabilities of one

FIGURE 15.14

Toys "R" Us and Amazon.com: A Strategic Alliance That Works
In 2000, Amazon.com and Toys "R" Us joined forces to create the largest alliance between consumer e-commerce businesses. This alliance has been successful because it capitalizes on the strengths of each company, pooling the toy expertise and name recognition of Toys "R" Us with the highly efficient e-commerce capacity of Amazon.com. Toysrus.com CEO John Barbour (left) and Amazon.com Toys General Manager Harrison Miller (right) carefully structured a relationship between their respective companies that now benefits both.

FIGURE 15.15

Strategic Alliances: A Continuum of Interorganizational Relationships
The three types of strategic alliances identified here may be distinguished with respect to their location along a continuum ranging from weak and distant to strong and close.
(*Source:* Based on suggestions by Kanter, 1994; see Note 56.)

another. For example, two companies might enter into a joint venture if one has a valuable technology and the other has the marketing knowledge to help transform that technology into a viable commercial product.

In recent years, as information technology has flourished, many Internet-based organizations have developed joint ventures with newly forming companies (referred to as *start-ups*). Their mission is to facilitate the flow of knowledge and talent across companies in a manner that boosts their joint technical and marketing competence. This special kind of joint venture is known as a **networked incubator**.[58] These are partnerships between established companies (often Internet-based firms), which provide valued resources and experience, and start-ups, which are able to develop and market products quickly. When properly designed, networked incubators combined the best of both worlds—the scale and scope of large, established companies and the entrepreneurial spirit of small firms.

As an example, consider Hotbank, a company known as an **incubator** because it specializes in starting up new businesses. Hotbank is managed by another company, Softbank Venture Capital (SBVC), which leases the office space, funds the projects, and provides the basic services needed to run a business (recruiting, public relations, accounting, and so on). SBVC provides the services needed to develop business ideas identified by Hotbank. For example, Hotbank's first company was Model E, a firm specializing in build-to-order vehicles and a Web-based comprehensive service packet (e.g., registration, insurance, financing). It was able to get off the ground because of the business ingenuity of Hotbank and the resources of SBVC. Because networked incubators are a new form of business relationship, it is too soon to tell how successful they will prove to be. However, if early reports provide any indication, it looks like they will be quite successful.

An alternative to the joint venture. Although forming joint ventures with other companies is a popular way for companies to grow in new directions, it is not the only way. An alternative that has been popular in many companies has been to create a **spinoff**—that is, an entirely new company that is separate from the original parent organization, one with its own identity, a new board of directors, and a different management team. The idea is that instead of looking around for a suitable partner, a rich and powerful company can create its own partner.

Consider, for example, the development of Expedia, Microsoft's online travel service. In 1996, Expedia was launched as just another Microsoft product.[59] As it became more successful, Expedia was set up as a separate operating unit. Then, in November 1999, Expedia was "spun off" into a separate publicly traded company (i.e., it can be purchased by anyone on the stock market). This raised $84 million for Microsoft, and because the company retains 85 percent of Expedia's stock it promises to make even more money in the future. Despite the highly competitive market within which it operates, Expedia has been flourishing, enjoying record profits in 2002. This is in large part because it was the offspring of a wealthy and successful parent (which gave Expedia a

networked incubator

Partnerships between established companies (often Internet-based firms), which provide valued resources and experience, with start-ups, which are able to develop and market products quickly.

incubator

A company that specializes in starting up new businesses.

spinoff

An entirely new company that is separate from the original parent organization, one with its own identity, a new board of directors, and a different management team.

OB IN A DIVERSE WORLD
JOINT VENTURES IN CHINA: BEWARE OF OBSTACLES

With an enormous market that is opening its doors to Western capitalism, it's not surprising that the idea of forming joint ventures with Chinese companies is very appealing to organizations in other parts of the world. Some companies, such as Johnson & Johnson, have enjoyed considerable success in its joint ventures with Chinese firms. Most others, however, are finding it difficult to make these relationships work.[65]

Consider, for example, the experiences of a U.S.-based household-products company that formed a joint venture with Shanghai Jawa Corporation, China's largest cosmetics manufacturer. The U.S. company was looking for help introducing its products into the large Chinese market by tapping into Jahwa's distribution system. It also was hoping to find what the Chinese call *guanxi,* the social and political connections required to become successful in China (see Chapter 12). Jahwa officials were looking for help in upgrading technology and boosting capacity to compete in the international marketplace. Unfortunately, the two companies had serious disagreements over directions and resources that paralyzed them, resulting in a failed deal. Making matters worse, joint ventures are difficult to dissolve in Chinese culture because the relationship between the two companies is based on trust. Walking away from such relationships comes at a considerable loss of face (i.e., loss of esteem in the eyes of others).

Several factors make the prospects of forming joint ventures with Chinese firms difficult, at best. To begin with, there is the obvious matter of cultural differences. Compared to Western countries, Chinese culture and traditions are profoundly different. In particular, its social, governmental, and economic systems are far more complex. Compared to Western companies, for example, Chinese companies are more likely to become lax after achieving success, and they are less likely to consider strategies that take a long-term approach. If this were the only

head start) and also because it was allowed to develop on its own as needed, without too much "parental supervision," so to speak. Further extending the parent–child metaphor, the spinoff company is forever associated with the parent company, providing services to it and getting help from it. However, it also is free to develop other business relationships that stand to strengthen it further.

Strategic alliances in the global economy. Strategic alliances with companies in nations with transforming economies (such as China and the countries of eastern Europe) provide good opportunities for those nations' economies to develop. Given the rapid move toward globalization of the economy, we may expect to see many companies seeking strategic alliances in the future as a means of gaining or maintaining a competitive advantage. Frequently, companies form strategic alliances with foreign firms to gain entry into that country's market.[60] Such arrangements also may allow for an exchange of technology and manufacturing services. For example, Korea's Daewoo receives technical information and is paid to manufacture automobiles for companies with which it has entered into alliances, such as General Motors, as well as Germany's Opel, and Japan's Isuzu and Nissan.[61] Some companies, such as the telecommunications giant MCI, are actively involved in several strategic alliances, including one in Canada and several in New Zealand.[62]

In addition to the financial incentives (circumventing trade and tariff restrictions) and marketing benefits (access to internal markets) associated with strategic alliances, direct managerial benefits also are associated with extending one company's organizational chart into another's. These benefits primarily come from improved technology and greater economies of scale (e.g., sharing functional operations across organizations). For these benefits to be derived, a high degree of coordination and fit must exist between the parties, each delivering on its promise to the other. Finally, it is noteworthy challenge, however, it most likely would be overcome. After all, executives interested in conducting business in various countries have been successful in learning all about the cultural ways of their hosts (see Chapter 2).[66] In China, however, there are several more unique problems.

First, is the fact that the Chinese market is becoming extremely competitive as many companies are attempting to be the first to introduce their products to the vast Chinese population. Competition has become so fierce in some industries (e.g., construction, pharmaceuticals, and electronics), in fact, that companies have been aggressively pursuing market share, even if it has meant lowering prices so much that they were selling at a loss. This is a game that very few companies can afford to play for very long.

A second unique problem associated with forming joint ventures with Chinese companies is that very few have presence throughout the country. Most operate either regionally or locally. This is a vestige of the country's planned economic system, in effect until 1979, which required companies to operate in very narrow market niches. Because only the earliest companies to form joint ventures with Chinese companies (e.g., Coca-Cola Co.) managed to make contact with the few that operate nationally, it is very difficult for today's foreign companies to find a suitable partner.

A third unique problem has to do with government intervention. Although governments are involved in one way or another in businesses in all countries, their connection to Chinese businesses runs deep—so much so, in fact, that many companies are actually owned, in part, by government agencies. What makes this particularly frustrating is that different governmental rules operate in different territories. As a case in point, consider the difficulties that companies such as AT&T, NEC, and Siemens have been having in establishing telephone service through their various Chinese partners. The problem resides in the fact that Shanghai Bell has a Chinese partner, which just happens to be the Ministry of Post and Telecommunication, the government agency that controls communications. To say that Shanghai Bell has a distinct advantage, as a result, probably comes as no surprise.

In view of these considerations, experts advise companies seeking joint ventures with Chinese firms to consider all their options carefully. The benefits that stand to be received from an enormous market may never be realized because several important obstacles stand in the way.

that strategic alliances with companies in nations with transforming economies provide good opportunities for those nations' economies to develop.[63] Given the rapid move toward globalization of the economy, we may expect to see many companies seeking strategic alliances in the future as a means for gaining or maintaining a competitive advantage.[64] (For a close-up look at this process in operation in China, see the OB in a Diverse World section above.)

Strategic alliances can help minority-owned businesses. Although members of minority groups represent about 28 percent of the U.S. population, they control only 12 percent of the nation's businesses. In an effort to bring parity to this situation by boosting the number of minority-owned businesses, the U.S. government requires companies to meet specified targets for conducting business with minority-owned companies. The underlying rationale is that this practice is good for business. Jethro Joseph, Daimler–Chrysler's head of special supplier relations, offers a simple explanation: "If we buy from minority suppliers, they will hire minority employees, who will have the wherewithal to buy our products. We look at it as a never-ending wheel."[67] To get this wheel moving, many large companies are finding it useful to form alliances with minority-owned companies, creating relationships from which both parties can benefit. For a sample of some of these alliances, see Table 15.5.

Are strategic alliances successful? As our descriptions of the various types of alliances illustrate, there are clear benefits to be derived from forming alliances. These primarily come in the form of improved technology, widened markets, and greater economies of scale (e.g., sharing functional operations across organizations). However, for these benefits to be realized, a high degree of coordination and fit must exist between the parties, each delivering on its promise to the other.

TABLE 15.5   ALLIANCES INVOLVING MINORITY-OWNED BUSINESSES

In recent years, many large companies have found it useful to enter into strategic alliances with small, minority-owned companies. Other companies have served as "matchmakers," bringing together firms with one or more minority group owners. Here are a few examples.

LARGE COMPANY	INVOLVEMENT WITH SMALL, MINORITY-OWNED COMPANY
Bank of America	Bank of America wanted to do business with R. J. Leeper, a black entrepreneur in the construction business. However, because he lacked experience, Bank of America helped him learn the business by getting him a job at a successful construction company and paying half his salary while he worked there. Leeper now has his own construction company, R. J. Leeper Construction, which is a supplier to Bank of America.
Procter & Gamble	Procter & Gamble purchases plastic bottles for Sunny Delight from a company that it helped create—a joint venture between Plastitec and minority-owned Madras Packaging.
Daimler–Chrysler	Daimler–Chrysler helped International Paper, one of its suppliers, form a joint venture with a black entrepreneur, Carlton Highsmith. His company, Specialized Packaging Group, now produces packaging for automotive parts made by Daimler–Chrysler.
Ford Motor Company	Ford Motor Company officials wanted to buy conveyor systems from one of three minority-owned companies (Devon Contracting Services, Scion, and Gala & Associates), but they were too small. Ford helped these three firms merge, forming Tri-Tec, the larger and more stable company from which Ford now buys conveyor systems.
Johnson Controls	Johnson Controls purchases interior car parts from TKA Plastics. This company was the result of a partnership between two parties that Johnson Controls brought together: Del-Met, an injection molding company, and Michael Cherry, a black entrepreneur.

(*Source:* Based on information in Weisul, 2001; see Note 67.)

As you might imagine, not all strategic alliances are successful. Often, culture clashes are to blame (see Chapter 14). For example, AT&T and Olivetti tried unsuccessfully to work together on manufacturing personal computers. Strong differences in management styles and organizational culture were cited as causes. Similarly, a planned alliance between Raytheon and Lexitron, a small word processing company, failed because of clashes between the rigid culture of the much larger Raytheon and the more entrepreneurial style of the smaller Lexitron. Clearly, for strategic alliances to work, the companies must not only be able to offer each other something important, but they also must be able to work together to make it happen.

SUMMARY AND REVIEW OF LEARNING OBJECTIVES

1. Describe what is meant by organizational structure and how it is revealed by an organizational chart.

The formal configuration between individuals and groups with respect to the allocation of tasks, responsibilities, and authority within organizations is known as organizational structure. It is an abstract concept that can be represented by an organizational chart, a diagram indicating the relationships between the various units (individuals or departments) in an organization.

2. Explain the basic characteristics of organizational structure revealed in an organizational chart (hierarchy of authority, division of labor, span of control, line versus staff, and decentralization).

Organizational charts depict five different elemental building blocks of organizational structure. These are hierarchy of authority (a summary of reporting relationships), division of labor (the degree to which jobs are specialized), span of control (the number of individuals over which a manager has responsibility), line versus staff positions (jobs permitting direct decision-making power versus jobs in which advise is given), and decentralization (the degree to which decisions can be made by lower-ranking employees as opposed to a few higher-ranking individuals).

3. Describe different approaches to departmentalization—functional organizations, product organizations, matrix organizations, and boundaryless organizations.

Within organizations, groups of people can be combined into departments in various ways. The most popular approach is the functional organization, organizations created by combining people in terms of the common functions they perform (e.g., sales, manufacturing). An alternative approach is to departmentalize people by virtue of the specific products for which they are responsible, known as the product organization. Another form of departmentalization combines both of these approaches into a single form known as the matrix organization. In such organizations, people have at least two bosses; they are responsible to a superior in charge of the various functions and a superior in charge of the specific product. Employees also may have to answer to high-ranking people responsible for the entire organization, the top leader. Following the lead of General Electric, many of today's companies are moving toward boundaryless organizations (ones in which chains of command are eliminated, spans of control are unlimited, and rigid departments give way to empowered teams). These eliminate all internal boundaries (such as those between employees) and external boundaries (such as those between the company and its suppliers).

4. Distinguish between classical and neoclassical approaches to organizational design and between mechanistic organizations and organic organizations, as described by the contingency approach to organizational design.

Organizational design is the process of coordinating the structural elements of organizations in the most appropriate way. Classical organizational theories (such as Weber's notion of bureaucracy) claim that a universally best way to design organizations exists, an approach based on high efficiency. Neoclassical organizational theories (such as those advanced by McGregor, Argyris, and Likert) also believe that there is one best way to design organizations. Their approach, however, emphasizes the need to pay attention to basic human needs to succeed and express oneself. The contingency approach to organizational design is predicated on the belief that the most appropriate way to design organizations depends on the external environments within which they operate. Specifically, a key factor has to do with the degree to which the organization is subject to change: A stable environment is one in which business conditions do not change, whereas a turbulent environment is one in which conditions change rapidly. When conditions are stable, a mechanistic organization is effective. This is one in which people perform specialized jobs, many rigid rules are imposed, and authority is vested in a few top-ranking officials. However, when conditions are turbulent, an organic organization is effective. This is one in which jobs tend to be very general, there are few rules, and decisions can be made by low-level employees.

5. Describe the five organizational forms identified by Mintzberg: simple structure, machine bureaucracy, professional bureaucracy, divisional structure, and adhocracy.

Five specific organizational forms have been identified by Mintzberg. Organizations with simple structure are small and informal and have a single powerful individual, often the founding entrepreneur, who is in charge of everything (e.g., a small retail store owned by a sole proprietor). In a machine bureaucracy work is highly specialized, decision making is concentrated at the top, and the work environment is not prone to change (e.g., a government office). In professional bureaucracies, such as hospitals and universities, there are lots of rules to follow, but employees are highly skilled and free to make decisions on their own. Divisional structure characterizes many large organizations (such as General Motors) in which separate autonomous units are created to deal with entire product lines, freeing top management to focus on larger-scale, strategic decisions. Finally, the adhocracy is a highly informal, organic organization in which specialists work in teams, coordinating with each other on various projects (e.g., many software development companies).

6. Characterize two forms of intraorganizational design—conglomerates and strategic alliances.

Some organizational designs represent ways of combining more than one organization. Such interorganizational designs include the conglomerate (large corporations that diversify by getting involved in unrelated businesses) and the strategic alliance (organizations combining forces to operate a specific business). There are three major types of strategic alliances: mutual service consortia, joint ventures, and value-chain partnerships.

POINTS TO PONDER

Questions for Review

1. What are the fundamental dimensions of organizations that are described by organizational structure?
2. What are the major ways that traditionally have been used to organize departments in organizations?
3. What are the major differences among classical, neoclassical, and contingency approaches to organizational design?
4. What are the five organizational forms identified by Mintzberg?
5. What is meant by the "boundaryless organization" and what forms does it take?
6. What are the major types of interorganizational designe, in which two or more organizations can coordinate their efforts?

Experiential Questions

1. Think of the organization in which you currently work—specifically, the work group or department with which you are most closely affiliated. How would you characterize this unit with respect to division of labor, span of control, and centralization?
2. Based on your own experiences, do you think that traditional, hierarchical organizations are giving way to less well-structured, boundaryless forms of organization? In other words, do you see this trend in your own organizational life?
3. Have you ever worked for a company that was involved in a strategic alliance of some kind? How about a virtual organization? If so, how was the experience different than working for a traditional company?

Questions to Analyze

1. How have advances in information technology changed the way organizations are structured and designed today?
2. For what types of business endeavors do you think virtual organizations are particularly well suited, and for what type do you believe they should be avoided?
3. Much has been said about the successes of networked incubators. However, they can have problems. What do you believe are the most important limitations of this form of organizational design?

INDIVIDUAL EXERCISE

Which Do You Prefer—Mechanistic or Organic Organizations?

Because mechanistic and organic organizations are so different, it is reasonable to expect that people will tend to prefer one of these organizational forms over the other. This questionnaire is designed to help you identify your own preferences (and, in so doing, to help you learn about the different forms themselves).

Directions

Each of the following questions deals with your preferences for various conditions that may exist where you work. Answer each one by checking the one alternative that best describes your feelings.

1. When I have a job-related decision to make, I usually prefer to:
   _____ a. make the decision myself.
   _____ b. have my boss make it for me.
2. I usually find myself more interested in performing:
   _____ a. a highly narrow, specialized task.
   _____ b. many different types of tasks.
3. I prefer to work in places in which working conditions:
   _____ a. change a great deal.
   _____ b. generally remain the same.
4. When a lot of rules are imposed on me, I generally feel:
   _____ a. very comfortable.
   _____ b. very uncomfortable.
5. I believe that governmental regulation of industry is:
   _____ a. usually best for all.
   _____ b. rarely good for anyone.

Scoring

1. Give yourself 1 point each time you answered as follows: 1 = b; 2 = a; 3 = b; 4 = a; 5 = a. This score is your preference for *mechanistic organizations*.
2. Subtract this score from 5. This score is your preference for *organic organizations*.
3. Interpret your scores as follows: Higher scores (closer to 5) reflect stronger preferences, and lower scores (closer to 0) reflect weaker preferences.

Questions for Discussion

1. How did you score? That is, which organizational form did you prefer?
2. Think back over the jobs you've had. Have these been in organizations that were mechanistic or organic?
3. Do you think you performed better in organizations whose designs matched your preferences than those in which there was a mismatch?
4. Do you think you were more committed to organizations whose designs matched your preferences than those in which there was a mismatch?

GROUP EXERCISE

Comparing Span of Control in Organizational Charts

One of the easiest things to determine about a company by looking at its organizational chart is its span of control. This exercise will allow you to learn about, and compare span of control within companies in your area.

Directions

1. Divide the class into four equal size groups.
2. Assign one of the following industry types to each group: (a) manufacturing companies, (b) financial institutions, (c) public utilities, and (d) charities.
3. Within the industry assigned to each group, identify one company per student. Also, consider larger organizations inasmuch as these are more likely to have formal organization charts. For example, if there are five students in the "financial institutions" group, name five different banks or savings and loan institutions.
4. Each student should search the Internet for a copy of the organizational chart for the company assigned to him or her in step 3.
5. Meet as a group to discuss the spans of control of the organizations in your sample.
6. Gather as a class to compare the findings of the various groups.

Questions for Discussion

1. How easy or difficult was it to find organizational charts on the Internet?
2. Did you find that there were differences with respect to span of control?
3. Were spans of control different at different organizational levels? If so, how? Were these differences the same for all industry groups?
4. In what ways did spans of control differ for the various industry groups? Were the spans broader for some industries and narrower in others? How do you explain these differences? Do these differences make sense to you?

WEB SURFING EXERCISE

Virtual Organizations

Because of their growing popularity, virtual organizations are a topic of a considerable amount of research. Much of this work is summarized in VoNet, the Virtual Organizations Network (www.virtual-organization.net/). Visit this Web site and answer the following questions based on what you find.

1. What kinds of issues are addressed by the articles published in the *Electronic Journal of Organizational Virtualness?*
2. What types of resources does the network offer its members?
3. To what particular groups is the network most likely to appeal?

Incubators

The success of many start-ups can be traced to the use of *incubators,* companies specifically designed to help start new businesses. These often bring together two different kinds of companies, such as a group of entrepreneurs who have exciting new ideas, and a group of seasoned veterans who can provide valuable expertise, advice, funding, and other services. The growing popularity of incubators has led to a proliferation of organizations designed to provide information about them. Some examples include:

The National Business Incubation Association	www.nbia.org
The International Business Incubator	www.ibi-sv.org
The Texas Business Incubator Association	www.tbia.org

Visit these Web sites and answer the following questions based on what you find.

1. What kinds of services do these organizations provide?
2. How might these organizations be useful to entrepreneurs?
3. Besides entrepreneurs, who else might benefit by the services provided by these organizations?

CASE IN POINT

Ameritech and Random House Join Forces on Emerging Technology

In view of the uncertainties involved, no one company can expect to have control over all the technologies needed to deliver multimedia entertainment to the home market. Of all the emerging key players, however, Ameritech appears to have a head start. After all, given that its parent is **SBC,** it has considerable wire and fiber networks throughout the Midwest. But it's clear that Ameritech cannot blaze the path itself. There are just too many undeveloped technologies and too many unanswered questions about market interests for any one company, even Ameritech, to go it alone.

It is with this in mind that Ameritech's leaders have positioned its technological skills and considerable assets alongside those of other companies with complementary skills. One such alliance has been formed with Random House, the giant publisher of books and magazines. But why, you ask, would Ameritech join forces with a publisher when another high-tech company would make more sense? The answer is simple: The capacity to deliver multimedia information to the home is of limited use unless there is some desired content involved. That's where Random House comes in. As the owner of the *New Yorker* magazine and various travel guides (including Fodor's and the Arthur Frommer series), Random House brings some highly regarded content to the table.

As of this writing, you cannot yet receive Random House's content through Ameritech's networks in your home. However, the two firms already have formed a company called Worldview Systems, which publishes an electronic monthly current-events database of travel information sold primarily to travel agents. It consists of information about 170 international destinations that agents can access online and through toll-free telephone number.

Ameritech's vice president of development, Thomas Thornton, is optimistic that his company can take the lead in opening up this service to the consumer market. The key to doing so, he notes, is not only in advancing technology to the point where a viable product emerges but also in management's ultimate commitment to the project. Although this is always the case with any new direction an organization takes, there's something special about this case. Senior managers, he cautions, must be willing to "move fast investing, but be patient in waiting for returns." Not all companies are in a position to do this.

Two things are certain. First, to at least some extent, Ameritech will be involved in advancing this technology and then marketing it. Second, Ameritech will not, and cannot, be alone in bringing it to fruition. Experts estimate that hundreds, if not thousands, of companies are, or will be, joining forces to capitalize on this emerging technology. Ameritech is clearly just one tile in the emerging multimedia mosaic. With the help of Random House, Ameritech just might find its way.

Questions for Discussion

1. What potential problems do you suspect will be inclined to emerge as Ameritech and Random House join forces?
2. In what ways are the images of each company likely to change as a result of their association with each other?
3. Besides entering into this joint venture, what else might these companies do to develop in these new directions?

VIDEO CASE

Organizational Structure

When it first started, SA was run very informally. In fact, it didn't have an organizational chart for the first 4 years. Then, once a formal structure was put into place, it changed very rapidly—every 3 to 6 months. SA's first structure was functional, but it then moved to a structure differentiated by the three key markets served—student services, university services, and corporate partners. In addition, there also are support services (e.g., information technology) that cut across all these departments.

Over the years, SA has grown into a company that recognizes differences in hierarchy, but is still relatively flat (in other words, the hierarchy is compressed). Individuals are assigned to the various departments based on their skills. So, for example, the executives from newly acquired companies, mostly entrepreneurs, are put in charge of business development, whereas others with expertise in operational areas are assigned to more everyday functions. This represents only the company's formal structure. Executives at SA also recognize that a great deal of the work is conducted informally—in ways that are not indicated by the organizational chart.

Questions for Discussion

1. Given that the organizational structure at SA is relatively flat, how would you expect the span of control to be affected?
2. What are the advantages and disadvantages of the particular way in which SA is designed?
3. What would be the major advantages, if any, of redesigning SA as a boundaryless organization or a modular organization?
4. Organizations often enter into strategic alliances with other organizations to help them grow. How might this be done in the case of SA?

16

Managing Organizational Change: Strategic Planning and Organizational Development

LEARNING OBJECTIVES

After reading this chapter, you should be able to:

1. **Characterize** the prevalence of the change process in organizations.
2. **Understand** what, exactly, is changed when organizational change comes about, and the forces responsible for unplanned organizational change.
3. **Describe** what is meant by strategic planning and explain the types of strategic changes that organizations make.
4. **Identify** the 10 steps in the strategic planning process.
5. **Explain** why people are resistant to organizational change and how this resistance may be overcome.
6. **Identify** and describe the major organizational development techniques that are used today.

■ PREVIEW CASE
MAKING CHANGE AT THE U.S. MINT

When Philip Diehl became director of the United States Mint in September 1994, he found it to be the stereotype of an old government agency—inefficient, slow, and without a clue about the standards of performance required for success in the private sector. Today, however, the U.S. Mint makes money by making money. It sells the services of its heralded

> "If the Mint were a company," Diehl told his colleagues at a meeting, "a bunch of you would be millionaires."

police force to other government agencies, and it sells collectable coins to the public, including the popular 50 State Quarters Program. It even has a full-featured Web site where visitors can share their ideas on the design of coins and purchase such items as commemorative coins, jewelry, and gifts of all types. So successful is the Mint that it has grown to a *Fortune* 500–sized manufacturing and international marketing company with 2,200 employees and over $1 billion in annual revenue. "If the Mint were a company," Diehl told his colleagues at a meeting, "a bunch of you would be millionaires."

During his six years at the Mint, Diehl has made big changes, "but they've been made incrementally," he cautions, adding, "You do big things by doing lots of small things." Diehl's first order of business involved improving the Mint's relationships with its customers. Until he came along, the Mint treated its customers awfully. Orders were held an average of two months until customers' checks cleared before shipping them. Irate customers called, but often no one answered the phone. Not only wasn't there any sense of urgency about the problem, but many sensed that there wasn't even a problem at all.

To find out exactly what customers thought of the Mint and how to improve services, Diehl decided to administer a questionnaire. He found, however, that the Office of Management and Budget actively discouraged government agencies from spending money on surveys. So, if the Mint couldn't conduct a survey, Diehl decided to do his own survey. He went to coin conventions where he spoke to hobbyists and writers from coin collecting magazines, listening carefully to what they had to say. Two problems immediately came to his attention: orders took too long to be filled, and the Mint held onto its customers' up-front payments too long.

To tackle these problems, Diehl assembled a task force, which made some progress, but more was needed. So, he went public with a new customer-service agenda. To the media, he announced that the Mint would process 95 percent of its orders within six weeks. Although this goal was modest, it was a reasonable beginning. Soon, employees felt a sense of urgency, leading them to feel accountable to customers. As this goal was approached, Diehl tightened the standard to 95 percent in four weeks, ratcheting it up still further with each successive improvement in performance. Today, 95 percent of the products are delivered within two weeks, and many are shipped in only one week.

Soon, Mint employees developed a new sense of pride and excitement in their work, and customers became more enthusiastic about the Mint's products. Calls to the customer service center that used to be answered in 2 minutes, if at all, are now being answered in only 17.5 seconds. Similarly, returns or credits that used to take a month to process are now being handled in only three days. So improved are the Mint's services that it has received the highest scores of any government agency in a national poll. Its customer satisfaction scores are tied with the venerable H. J. Heinz and rank second only to Mercedes-Benz.

There can be no doubt that Diehl has supervised a dramatic change in the Mint's operations, helping it attain "mint condition" as a service provider. Of course, it's not only the Mint that has seen dramatic changes over the years. Just think about how the menus of fast-food restaurants have become more diversified, many offices are "going paperless," and banks are merging into "megafinancial institutions."

If you think of the many changes in the ways businesses operate that we've seen in recent years, it's clear that change has become the rule rather than the exception. Acknowledging just the tip of the iceberg, commerce over the Internet now occurs regularly, and small companies in most businesses—especially auto manufacturers and banks—have been consolidating at a breathtaking rate. Change in the world of business is inevitable: As some companies grow, still others fail to stay afloat (see Figure 16.1).

It is an understatement to say that the impact of *organizational change* can be found everywhere. **Organizational change** refers to planned or unplanned transformations in an organization's structure, technology, and/or people. To understand this important process, we will examine it from several key perspectives in this chapter. To begin, we will describe the nature of the process of change, describing forces that require organizations to change. Then, we will shift our focus to changes that are more deliberate, describing what is known as *strategic planning*. This involves deliberately making radical changes in the way the organization operates.

organizational change
Planned or unplanned transformations in an organization's structure, technology, and/or people.

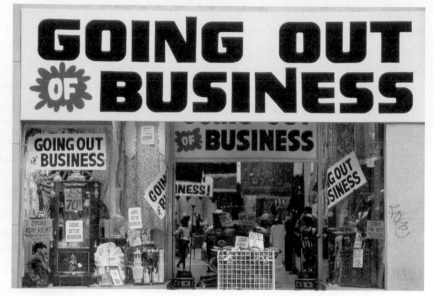

FIGURE 16.1

Change: Signs of the Times
Organizational change frequently is reflected by the signs we see posted outside of business establishments every day. Signs indicating growth and decline are most common.

As you might imagine, most people have difficulty accepting that they may have to work with a new group of people or change the jobs they do. After all, if you're used to working a certain way, a sudden change can be very unsettling. In other words, as we will describe, there are various reasons why people are resistant to change. Fortunately, such resistance can be overcome. With this in mind, social scientists have developed various methods, known collectively as *organizational development* techniques, that are designed to implement needed organizational change in a manner that both is acceptable to employees and enhances the effectiveness of the organizations involved. We will close this chapter with a discussion of these techniques.

THE PREVALENCE OF CHANGE IN ORGANIZATIONS

A century ago, advances in machine technology made farming so highly efficient that fewer hands were needed to plant and reap the harvest. Displaced laborers fled to nearby cities, seeking jobs in newly opened factories, opportunities created by some of the same technologies that sent them from the farm. The economy shifted from agrarian to manufacturing, and the *industrial revolution* was under way. With it, came dramatic shifts in where people lived, how they worked, how they spent their leisure time, how much money they made, and how they spent it.

Today's business analysts claim that we currently are experiencing *another* industrial revolution—one driven by a new wave of economic and technological forces centered on the use of computers and the Internet. As one observer put it, "This workplace revolution . . . may be remembered as a historic event, the Western equivalent of the collapse of communism."[1]

The Message Is Clear: Change or Disappear!

The business landscape is not the same as it was just a few years ago. Take the auto industry, for example. Within the past decade, Volvo merged with Ford, Chrysler merged with Daimler-Benz (the manufacturer of the Mercedes-Benz), and the Volkswagen Beetle has reemerged. In banking, things are even more extreme. Almost every small bank has been gobbled up by a large bank in recent years—and the largest ones have been joining forces. No industry, no organization is immune; change is everywhere.

Even leaders of different industries have been merging to create megacorporations. The 2000 merger of media giant, Time Warner and Internet giant, AOL is a prime example (see Figure 16.2).[2] The handwriting on the wall is clear: The world is changing, and those companies that fail to change when required find themselves out of business as a result.[3] Actually, research has shown that support for organizational change among senior managers is a characteristic that distinguishes the most successful organizations (where such support occurred 94 percent of the time) from other organizations (where it occurred only 76 percent of the time).[4]

This is important because business failure is the rule rather than the exception: Fully 62 percent of new ventures fail to last as long as five years, and only 2 percent make it as long as 50 years.[5] In view of this, it is particularly impressive that some American companies have beaten the odds—so soundly, in fact, that they have remained in business for well over 200 years (see Table 16.1 for a summary of these "corporate Methuselahs").[6] As you might imagine, these companies have undergone *many* changes during their years of existence. For example, the United States' oldest company, J. E. Rhoads & Sons, now makes conveyer belts, although it originally started out in 1702 making buggy whips. Another company, Dexter, in Windsor Locks, Connecticut, began in 1767 as a grist mill. As you might imagine, it is no longer involved in grinding grain. Instead, the company now makes adhesives and coatings for aircraft. Earlier, it manufactured specialty papers for stationery and for tea bags. Obviously, this company is very willing to change. According to Dexter spokesperson Ellen Cook, "We have no traditions, whatsoever. None."[7]

First-order change. As you might imagine, the changes that organizations make differ in scope; some are only minor, whereas others are major. Change that is continuous in nature and involves no major shifts in the way an organization operates is known as **first-order-change.** Changes of this type are apparent in the very deliberate, incremental changes that Toyota has been making in continuously improving the efficiency of its production process.[8] Similarly, a restaurant may be seen as making first-order changes as it gradually adds new items to its menu and gauges their success before completely revamping its basic concept.

Second-order change. As you might imagine, however, other types of organizational change are far more complex. **Second-order change** is the term used to refer to more radical change, major shifts involving many different levels of the organization and many different aspects of business.[9] Citing only some of the most publicized examples of second-order change from recent years, General Electric, AlliedSignal, Ameritech, and Tenneco have radically altered the ways they operate, their culture, the technology they use, their structure, and the nature of their relations with employees.[10]

first-order change

Change that is continuous in nature and involves no major shifts in the way an organization operates.

second-order change

Radical change; major shifts involving many different levels of the organization and many different aspects of business.

FIGURE 16.2

The Biggest Deal Ever
Gerald M. Levin (left) from Time Warner and Stephen M. Case from AOL are celebrating the announcement of the merger of their companies in January 2000. Although AOL had only one-fifth the revenue and 15 percent of the workforce of Time Warner, the Internet giant's stock was worth twice that of the venerable publishing and entertainment giant. This enabled AOL to acquire Time Warner at a hefty $183 billion, making it the largest business deal ever.

TABLE 16.1 THE 10 OLDEST COMPANIES IN AMERICA

Very few companies continue to exist as long as the ones shown here. As you might expect, all have undergone considerable changes in their 200 to 300 years.

RANK	YEAR FOUNDED	NAME	CURRENT BUSINESS
1	1702	J. E. Rhoads & Sons	Conveyer belts
2	1717	Covenant Life Insurance	Insurance
3	1752	Philadelphia Contributorship	Insurance
4	1767	Dexter	Adhesives and coatings
5	1784	D. Landreth Seed	Seeds
6	1784	Bank of New York	Banking
7	1784	Mutual Assurance	Insurance
8	1784	Bank of Boston	Banking
9	1789	George R. Ruhl & Sons	Bakery supplies
10	1790	Burns & Russell	Building materials

(*Source:* Reprinted from the July 26, 1993 issue of *FORTUNE* by special permission; copyright 1993, Time Inc.)

Change Is a Global Phenomenon

Interestingly, the forces for organizational change are not isolated to the United States; they appear to be global in nature. To illustrate this point, consider the findings of a survey of 12,000 managers in 25 different countries conducted a few years ago.[11] When asked to identify the changes they've experienced in the past two years, respondents reported that major restructurings, mergers, divestitures and acquisitions, reductions in employment, and international expansion had occurred in their organizations.

Figure 16.3 shows the percentage reporting each of these activities in six selected nations. Although some forms of change were more common in some countries than others, organizations in all countries were actively involved in each of these change efforts. This evidence suggests that organizational change is occurring throughout the world. Although different forces may be shaping change at different rates in different places, the conclusion is apparent: Change is a universal fact of life for organizations.

THE NATURE OF THE CHANGE PROCESS

Given that change occurs so commonly, it is important to understand the basic nature of the change process. With this in mind, we will turn our attention to two key questions: (1) What, exactly, is changed when organizational change occurs? (2) What forces are responsible for unplanned organizational change?

Targets: What Is Changed?

Imagine that you are an engineer responsible for overseeing the maintenance of a large office building. The property manager has noted a dramatic increase in the use of heat in the building, causing operating costs to skyrocket. In other words, a need for change exists—specifically, a reduction in the building's heat usage. You cannot get the power company to lower its rates, so you recognize that you must bring about changes in the use of heat. But how?

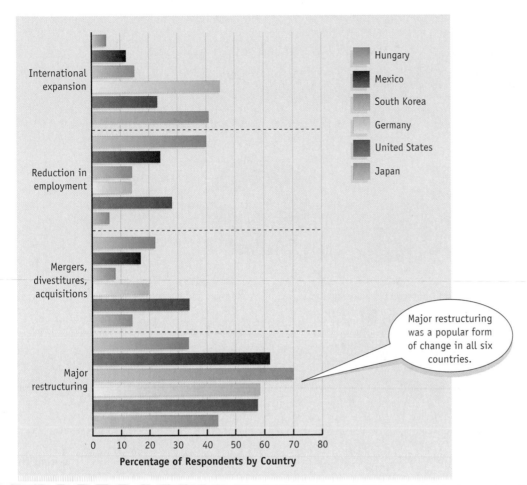

FIGURE 16.3

Organizational Change: An International Phenomenon
A large cross-national survey found that various forms of organizational change are reported to occur throughout the world. Shown here are the percentages of respondents in six countries indicating that each of four different forms of change occurred in organizations within their country in the past two years. Major restructuring was found to be the most widely encountered form of change in most countries.
(*Source:* Based on data reported by Kanter, 1991; see Note 11.)

One possibility is to rearrange job responsibilities so that only maintenance personnel are permitted to adjust the thermostats. Another option is to put timers on all thermostats so that the building temperature is automatically lowered during periods of nonuse. Finally, you consider the idea of putting stickers next to the thermostats, requesting that occupants do not adjust them. These three options are good examples of the three potential targets of organizational change that we will consider—changes in *organizational structure, technology,* and *people* (see Figure 16.4).

Changes in organizational structure. In Chapter 15 we described the key characteristics of organizational structure. Here, we note that altering the structure of an organization may be a reasonable way of responding to a need for change. In our example, a structural solution to the heat-regulation problem came in the form of reassigning job responsibilities. Indeed, modifying rules, responsibilities, and procedures may be an effective way to manage change. Changing the responsibility for temperature regulation from a highly decentralized system (whereby anyone can make adjustments) to a centralized one (in which only maintenance personnel may do so) is one way of implementing organizational change in response to a problem. This particular structural solution called for changing the power structure (i.e., who is in charge of a particular task).

Different types of structural changes may take other forms. For example, changes may be made in an organization's span of control, altering the number of employees for which supervisors are responsible. Structural changes also may take the form of revising the basis for creating departments—such as from product-based departments to functional departments. Other structural changes may be much simpler, such as clarifying someone's job description or the written policies and procedures followed.

Changes in technology. In our example, we noted that one possible solution would be to use thermostats that automatically reduce the building's temperature while it is not

FIGURE 16.4
Organizational Change Targets:
Structure, Technology, People
To create change in organizations, one
can rely on altering organizational structure, technology, and/or people. Changes
in any one of these areas may necessitate
changes in the others.

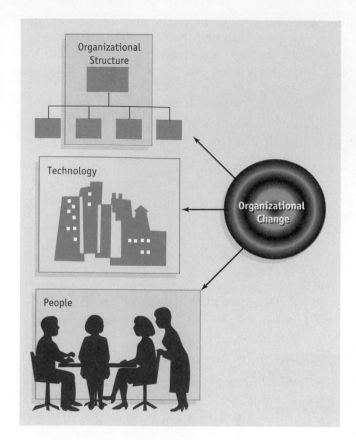

in use. This is an example of a technological approach to the need to conserve heat in
the building. Placement of regulating devices on the thermostats that would thwart
attempts to raise the temperature also would be possible. The thermostats also could be
encased in a locked box or simply removed altogether. A new, modern, energy-efficient
furnace could be installed in the building. All of these suggestions represent technological approaches to the need for change.

Changes in people. You've probably seen stickers next to light switches in hotels asking
guests to turn off the lights when not in use. These are similar to the suggestion in our
opening example of affixing signs near thermostats asking occupants to refrain from
adjusting the thermostats. Such efforts represent attempts to respond to the needed
organizational change by altering the way people behave. The basic assumption is that
the effectiveness of organizations is greatly dependent on the behavior of the people
working within them.

As you might imagine, the process of changing people is not easy—indeed, it lies at
the core of most of the topics discussed in this book. However, theorists have identified
three basic steps that summarize what's involved in the process of changing people.

The first step is known as *unfreezing*. This refers to the process of recognizing that
the current state of affairs is undesirable and in need of change. Realizing that change is
needed may be the result of some serious organizational crisis or threat (e.g., a serious
financial loss, a strike, or a major lawsuit) or simply becoming aware that current conditions are unacceptable (e.g., antiquated equipment, inadequately trained employees).

In recent years, some executives have gotten employees to accept the need to
change while things are still good by creating a sense of urgency. They introduce the
idea that there is an impending crisis although conditions are, in fact, currently acceptable—an approach referred to as **doomsday management.** This process effectively
unfreezes people, stimulating change before it's too late to do any good.

After unfreezing, *changing* may occur. This step occurs when some planned
attempt is made to create a more desirable state for the organization and its members.
Change attempts may be quite ambitious (e.g., an organization-wide restructuring) or

doomsday management

The practice of introducing change by
suggesting that an impending crisis is
likely.

only minor (e.g., a change in a training program). (A thorough discussion of such planned change techniques will be presented in the next major part of this chapter.)

Finally, *refreezing* occurs when the changes made are incorporated into the employees' thinking and the organization's operations (e.g., mechanisms for rewarding behaviors that maintain the changes are put in place). Hence, the new attitudes and behaviors become a new, enduring aspect of the organizational system.

Forces Behind Unplanned Organizational Change

As technology and markets change, organizations face a formidable challenge to adapt. Indeed, organizations also must be responsive to changes that are unplanned. Such forces include changes in the demographic composition of the workforce, performance gaps, government regulation, and international competition. The term **unplanned change** refers to shifts in organizational activities due to forces that are external in nature, those beyond an organization's control.

unplanned change
Shifts in organizational activities due to forces that are external in nature, those beyond an organization's control.

Shifting employee demographics. It is easy to see how, even within your own lifetime, the composition of the workforce has changed. As noted in Chapters 1 and 5, the American workforce is now more highly diverse than ever. To people concerned with the long-term operation of organizations, these are not simply curious sociological trends, but shifting conditions that force organizations to change.

For example, questions regarding how many people will be working, what skills they will bring to their jobs, and what new influences they will bring to the workplace are of key interest to human resources managers. In the words of Frank Doyle, corporate vice president for external and industrial relations at General Electric, the impending changes in workforce demographics "will turn the professional human-resources world upside down."[12]

Performance gaps. If you've ever heard the phrase "If it's not broken, don't fix it," you already have a good feel for one of the most potent sources of unplanned changes in organizations—*performance gaps*. A product line that isn't moving, a vanishing profit margin, a level of sales that isn't up to corporate expectations—these are examples of gaps between real and expected levels of organizational performance.

Few things force change more than sudden and unexpected information about poor performance. Organizations usually stay with a winning course of action and change in response to failure. Indeed, a performance gap is one of the key factors providing an impetus for organizational innovation. Those organizations that are best prepared to mobilize change in response to unexpected downturns are expected to be the ones that succeed.

Government regulation. Some of the most commonly witnessed unplanned organizational changes come from government regulations. In the late 1980s, for example, restaurant owners in the United States had to alter the way they report the income of waiters and waitresses to the federal government for purposes of collecting income taxes. More recently, the U.S. federal government has been involved in both imposing and eliminating regulations in industries such as commercial airlines (e.g., mandating inspection schedules but no longer controlling fares) and banking (e.g., restricting the amount of time checks can be held before clearing but no longer regulating interest rates). Such activities have greatly influenced the way business is conducted in these industries.

If you want to know more, just ask Microsoft's CEO, Steve Ballmer, and founder, Bill Gates, about the U.S. government's influence on their company (see Figure 16.5). For three years, the U.S. government pursued an antitrust case against Microsoft, alleging that the company has a monopoly on fundamental aspects of the personal computer business. Although the case has been settled, it's clear that the government's intervention has had a chilling effect on the company and it surely will force changes in the computer industry.

Global competition. It happens every day—someone builds a better mousetrap or, at least, a cheaper one. As a result, companies often must fight to maintain their shares of

FIGURE 16.5

Governmental Intervention: A Force for Change
On November 2, 2001, Microsoft reached a settlement with the U.S. Justice Department, which charged that the company monopolized certain aspects of the personal computer business. Company founder and chief software architect Bill Gates (right) watches as CEO Steve Ballmer announces the terms of the settlement at a press conference. For a five-year period, Microsoft faces restrictions on how it develops and licenses software and how it communicates the inner workings of its software with partners and competitors.

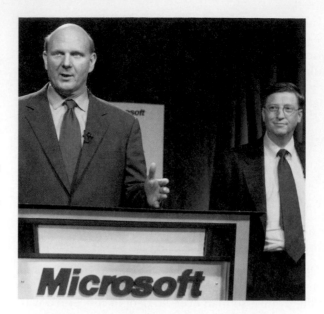

the market, advertise more effectively, and produce goods less expensively. This kind of economic competition not only forces organizations to change but also demands that they change effectively if they are to survive.

Although competition always has been crucial to organizational success, today competition comes from all over the world. As it has become increasingly less expensive to transport materials around the world, the industrialized nations have found themselves competing with each other for shares of the marketplace in nations all over the world. This extensive globalization of the economy presents a strong need to change and to be innovative. For example, consider how the large American automobile manufacturers suffered by being unprepared to meet the world's growing demand for small, high-quality cars—products their Japanese competitors were only too glad to supply to an eager marketplace. With this rapidly changing growth in globalization, one thing is certain: Only the most adaptive organizations can survive.

Changing economic conditions. The constantly changing economy has been very challenging for organizations in recent years. A recession in the early 1990s required laying off workers. The U.S. Bureau of Labor Statistics reported that from 1979 through 1995, some 43 million jobs were lost in the United States, affecting one-third of all households.[13] The number of job reductions reached a peak in 1992 and then leveled off. By the late 1990s, things had changed. Many organizations realized that they cut their workforces too deeply and struggled to rehire many of the workers they once released. The economy was strong and unemployment was at an exceptionally low level, causing a monstrous labor crunch that led some prospective employees to be offered generous salaries and benefits.

Today, in the early 2000s, the economy has adjusted downward once again, and job losses have been mounting throughout the world. In just the last week of May 2002 alone, the following layoffs were announced: 22,000 at Deutsche Telekom, 7,000 at Siemens, 3,500 at Nortel Networks, 2,000 at Verizon, 2,000 at IBM, and 1,000 at Barclay's.[14] Sometimes, cutbacks are necessary because of seasonal fluctuations in the business cycle (see Figure 16.6). However, sometimes they occur as a result of unforeseen situations. For example, the terrorist attacks of September 11, 2001, forced hundreds of companies to scale back in an effort to cut costs amid one of the biggest shocks to the economy in history. Not surprisingly, the biggest losers were in travel-related businesses, including the aerospace industry (e.g., 30,000 jobs lost at Boeing), the airlines (e.g., 20,000 jobs lost at United), hotels (e.g., 3,000 jobs lost at the MGM Mirage in Las Vegas). Fortunately, the economy has been rebounding. Still, our point is nicely made by these statistics: Economic conditions are a major source of unplanned organizational change.

"I'm afraid that due to a change in seasons we're going to be forced to make some cutbacks."

Advances in technology. As you know, advances in technology have produced changes in the way organizations operate. Senior scientists and engineers, for example, probably can tell you how their work was altered drastically in the mid-1970s, when their ubiquitous plastic slide rules gave way to powerful pocket calculators. Things changed again only a decade later, when calculators were supplanted by powerful desktop microcomputers, which have revolutionized the way documents are prepared, transmitted, and filed in an office.

Today, powerful handheld devices make portable, wireless communication a reality, further changing the way work is done. Companies that once may have thought of jumping on the technology bandwagon to gain an advantage over their competitors quickly found out that doing so wasn't an option needed to get ahead but, rather, a requirement just to stay in the game. In the late 1990s, technology made it possible for people to develop new, Web-based businesses with only limited start-up capital. Businesses started by *Internet entrepreneurs* became commonplace although they were unheard of only a few years earlier. Today, reality has set in, turning the boom in many high-tech businesses to bust. Although the Internet is no longer seen as a path to instant riches, it is clear that Internet technology has transformed the way many people work. (For a summary of ways in which computer technology has changed the way we work, see Table 16.2.)

STRATEGIC PLANNING: DELIBERATE CHANGE

Thus far, we have been describing unplanned organizational change. However, not all changes that organizations make fall into this category. Indeed, organizations also make changes that are very carefully planned and deliberate. This is the idea of **strategic planning,** which we define as the process of formulating, implementing, and evaluating decisions that enable an organization to achieve its objectives.[15]

strategic planning
The process of formulating, implementing, and evaluating decisions that enable an organization to achieve its objectives.

Basic Assumptions About Strategic Planning

To clearly understand the nature of strategic plans used in organizations today, it is important to highlight three fundamental assumptions about them.[16]

Strategic planning is deliberate. When organizations make strategic plans, they make conscious decisions to change fundamental aspects of themselves. These changes tend to be radical (e.g., changing the nature of the business) as opposed to

TABLE 16.2   HOW HAS COMPUTER TECHNOLOGY CHANGED THE WAY WE WORK?

Advances in computer technology have revolutionized many of the ways we work. Some key ways in which this has been occurring are summarized here.

AREA OF CHANGE	OLD WAY	NEW TECHNOLOGY EXAMPLES
Use of machines	Materials were moved by hand, with the aid of mechanical devices (e.g., pulleys and chains).	*Automation* is prevalent—the process of using machines to perform tasks that otherwise might be done by people. For example, computer-controlled machines manipulate materials and perform complex functions, a process known as *industrial robotics (IR)*.
Work by employees with disabilities	People with various physical or mental disabilities either were relegated to the most simple jobs, or they didn't work at all.	*Assistive technology* is widespread—devices and other solutions that help individuals with physical or mental problems perform the various actions needed to do their jobs. For example, *telephone handset amplifiers* make it possible for people with hearing impediments to use the telephone and *voice recognition systems* read to people with visual impairments.
Monitoring employees	Supervisors used to physically enter the offices of employees at work and observe them from afar.	*Computerized performance monitoring* systems are in widespread use, which allow supervisors to access their subordinates' computers for purposes of assessing how well they are performing their jobs.
Customer service	Individual service providers did things to help employees, customizing goods and services as time and skill allowed.	*Personalized service* is likely to take the form of greeting visitors to one's Web page with information customized to match the goods and services in which they expressed interest in their last visit (e.g., Amazon.com does this).
Environmental friendliness	Products at the end of their lives were buried in landfills, often polluting the earth.	*Design for disassembly (DFD)* is the process of designing and building products so that their parts can be reused several times and then disposed of at the end of the product's life without harming the environment.

minor (e.g., changing the color of the office walls) in nature.[17] These may be inspired by any of several factors, such as the presence of new competitors, new technologies, and the like.

Strategic planning occurs when current objectives no longer can be met. For the most part, when a company's present strategy is bringing about the desired results, change is unlikely to occur. However, when it becomes clear that the current objectives no longer can be met, new strategies are formulated to turn things around.

New organizational objectives require new strategic plans. Whenever a company takes steps to move in a completely new direction, it establishes new objectives, and a strategic plan is designed to meet them. Acknowledging that the various parts of an organization are all interdependent, the new strategic plan is likely to involve all functions and levels of the organization. Moreover, the plan will require adequate resources from throughout the organization to bring it to fruition.

To illustrate how these assumptions come to life, we now will describe some examples of the kinds of things about which companies tend to make strategic plans for change.

About What Do Companies Make Strategic Plans?

As you might imagine, organizations can make strategic plans to change just about anything. However, most of the strategic planning we see these days involves changing either (a) a company's products and services or (b) its organizational structure.

Products and services. Imagine that you and a friend have a small janitorial business. The two of you divide the duties, each doing some cleaning, buying supplies, and performing some administrative work. Before long, the business grows and you expand, adding new employees, and you really start "cleaning up." Many of your commercial clients express interest in window cleaning, and so you and your partner think it over and decide to expand into the window-cleaning business as well. This decision to take on a new direction to the business, to add a new, specialized service, will require a fair amount of organizational change. Not only will new equipment and supplies be needed, but also new personnel will have to be hired and trained, new insurance will have to be purchased, and new accounts will have to be secured. In short, you made a strategic decision to change the company's line of services, and this necessitates organizational change.

Real companies make these kinds of changes all the time. For example, in 1989 Federal Express (now FedEx) sought to expand its package delivery service, formerly limited exclusively to North America, to international markets. Although the company initially faced difficult challenges in its attempt to expand its service market beyond its traditional boundaries, FedEx's international services are now performing well (for another example, see Figure 16.7).

Organizational structure. But it is not only changes in products and services about which companies make strategic plans. They also make strategic plans to change the structure of the organization itself. For example, consider the decision by PepsiCo to reorganize its structure.[18] For many years, PepsiCo had a separate international food service division, which included the operation of 62 foreign locations of the company's Pizza Hut and Taco Bell restaurants. Then, in 1990, because of the great profit potential of these foreign restaurants, PepsiCo officials decided to reorganize, putting these restaurants directly under the control of the same executives responsible for the successful national operations of Pizza Hut, Kentucky Fried Chicken, and Taco Bell. However, in 1997, PepsiCo made another strategic decision—this time, it was to get out of the restaurant business entirely. That's when it spun off these three restaurants to form a separate company, TRICON Global Restaurants.

In recent years, many organizations that struggled to stay competitive responded by reducing the size and basic configurations of their organizational charts. The process of reducing the number of employees needed to operate effectively is known as **downsizing.** Earlier, we mentioned that layoffs are a common response to economic downturns. However, downsizing is likely to involve more than just laying off people in a move to save money. It is directed at adjusting the number of employees needed to work in newly designed organizations (which is why it also has been called **rightsizing**).

downsizing
The process of systematically reducing the number of employees required to operate effectively.

rightsizing
See *downsizing*.

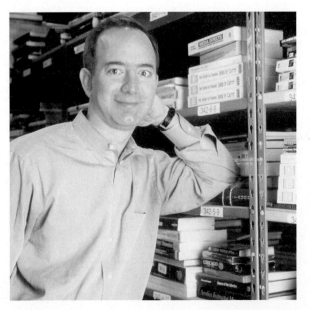

FIGURE 16.7

Amazon.com Made a Strategic Decision to Broaden Its Product Line
When Jeff Bezos founded Amazon.com and opened its virtual doors in July 1995, the company's strategic plan was to use the Internet to transform book buying into a fast and easy shopping experience. Recognizing that it had the online infrastructure and warehousing facilities in place to sell more than books, it soon broadened its strategic plan to sell even more products. Today Amazon.com sells books, CDs, videos, DVDs, toys and games, electronics, kitchenware, and computers and also offers free services such as electronic greeting cards and online auctions. The effectiveness of this growth strategy remains to be seen.

outsourcing
The practice of eliminating parts of organizations that focus on noncore sectors of the business and hiring outside firms to perform these functions instead.

Another way organizations are restructuring is by completely eliminating parts of themselves that focus on noncore sectors of the business and hiring outside firms to perform these functions instead—a practice known as **outsourcing.** For example, companies such as ServiceMaster, which provides janitorial services, and ADP, which provides payroll processing services, make it possible for organizations to concentrate on the business functions most central to their mission, thereby freeing them from these peripheral support functions.

Some critics fear that outsourcing represents a "hollowing out" of companies—a reduction of functions that weakens organizations by making them more dependent on others. Others counter that outsourcing makes sense when the work that is outsourced is not highly critical to competitive success (e.g., janitorial services), or when it is so highly critical that the only way to succeed requires outside assistance. If you think that outsourcing is an unusual occurrence, guess again. One industry analyst has estimated that 30 percent of the largest American industrial firms outsource over half their manufacturing (you may recall the examples of this we identified in Chapter 15).

The 10 Steps of the Strategic Planning Process

The process of strategic planning typically follows 10 ordered steps, which we now will describe.[19] Although these steps are not immutable and are not always followed in perfect order, they do a reasonably good job of describing the way companies go about planning change strategically. As we describe these, you may find it useful to follow along with the summary of steps appearing in Figure 16.8.

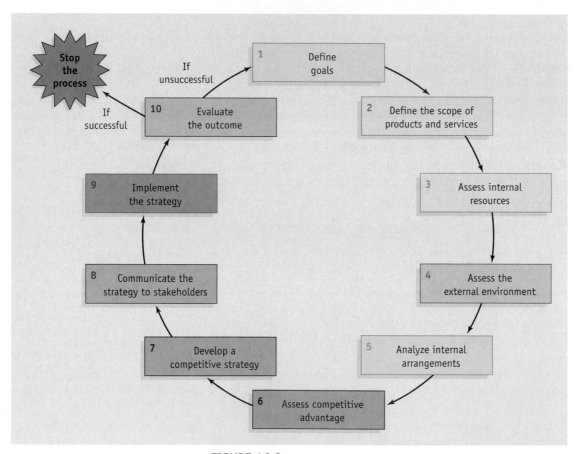

FIGURE 16.8
Strategic Planning: A 10-Step Process
Strategic planning—the process of formulating, implementing, and evaluating decisions that enable an organization to achieve its objectives—generally follows the 10 steps summarized here.
(*Source:* Based on suggestions by Christensen, 1994; see Note 19.)

Define goals. A strategic plan must begin with a stated goal. Typically, goals involve a company's market (e.g., to gain a certain position in the product market) and/or its financial standing (e.g., to achieve a certain profit level). Organizational goals also involve society (e.g., to benefit certain groups or the environment) or organizational culture (e.g., to make the workplace pleasant).

It is important to note that a company's overall goals must be translated into corresponding goals to be achieved by the various organizational units. For example, suppose a company wants to change its position in the market from a manufacturer of wholesale machinery to a manufacturer of consumer products. It identifies as its goal reaching 10 percent of the market within the first two years. This strategic goal must then be translated into goals for the various departments. For example, the marketing department must have goals with respect to reaching certain consumers in its advertising. Likewise, the production department must have certain goals about being able to manufacture certain numbers of products within a specific period of time.

Define the scope of products or services. For a strategic plan to be effective, company officials must clearly define their organization's *scope*—that is, the businesses in which it already operates and the new ones in which it aims to participate. If scope is defined too narrowly, the company will overlook opportunities; if scope is defined too broadly, it will dilute its effectiveness.

The matter of defining scope involves answering questions about what business a company is in and what business it could be in. For example, Beech-Nut, long known for its infant food, faced a challenge created by lowered birthrates, which decreased the size of its market. That's when someone recognized that the company's scope could be broadened to include the elderly—another group that had difficulty digesting hard food. Broadening its scope in this manner was a key part of the company's strategic plan for success.[20]

Assess internal resources. The question with respect to internal resources is: What resources does the company have available to plan and implement its strategy? The resources in question involve funds (e.g., money to make purchases), physical assets (e.g., required space), and human assets (e.g., knowledge and skills of the workforce). In this regard, it helps to have in place a complete system for knowledge management (see Chapter 2).

Assess the external environment. As we have said throughout this book, organizations do not operate in a vacuum. Rather, they function within environments that influence their capacity to operate and to grow as desired. The extent to which the environment either aids or hinders a company's growth (or even its existence) depends on several key factors. Specifically, a company has an advantage over its competitors with respect to resources when (a) its resources cannot be easily imitated by others, (b) its resources will not depreciate anytime soon, and when (c) competitors do not have resources that are any better.[21]

Analyze internal arrangements. By "internal arrangements," we are referring to the nature of the organization itself as identified by the characteristics described in this book. For example, are the employees paid in a way that motivates them to strive for corporate goals (Chapter 6)? Also, does the culture of the organization encourage people to be innovative and to make changes—or does it encourage them to be stagnant (see Chapter 14)? Furthermore, do people communicate with each other clearly enough (Chapter 9), and do they get along well enough with each other (Chapter 11) to accomplish their goals? These and other basic questions about the organization itself must be answered to formulate an effective strategic plan. After all, unless the organization is operating properly in these key respects, even the best strategic plans may not pan out.

Assess competitive advantage. One company is said to have a competitive advantage over another to the extent that customers perceive its products or services as being superior to the products or services of that other company. Superiority may be assessed in terms of such factors as quality, price, breadth of product line, reliability of performance, styling, service, and company image. A company is considered to have an advantage over its competitors to the extent that customers perceive it as offering higher quality at an equal or lower price.

Develop a competitive strategy. A competitive strategy is the means by which an organization achieves its goal. Based on a careful assessment of the company's standing on the factors described previously (e.g., the company's available resources, its competitive advantage, etc.), a decision is made about how to go about achieving its goal. Although there are many possible strategies, some of the most popular ones used by today's organizations are summarized in Table 16.3.

stakeholder

Any individual or group in whose interest an organization is run.

Communicate the strategy to stakeholders. The term **stakeholder** is used to describe an individual or group in whose interest an organization is run. In other words, these are individuals who have a special stake, or claim, on the company. The most important stakeholders include employees at all levels, boards of governors, and stockholders. It is essential to clearly communicate a firm's strategy to stakeholders so that they can contribute to its success, either actively (e.g., employees who pitch in to help meet goals) or passively (e.g., investors who pour money into the company to help meet goals). Without the stakeholders fully understanding and accepting a firm's strategy, it is unlikely to receive the full support it needs to meet its goals.

Implement the strategy. Once a strategy has been formulated and communicated, the time is ready for it to be implemented. When this occurs, there is likely to be some upheaval as people scramble to adjust to new ways of doing things. As we will describe later, people tend to be reluctant to make changes in the way they work. However, as we also will describe later, several steps can be taken to ensure that the people who are responsible for making the changes come about will embrace them rather than reject them.

Evaluate the outcome. Finally, after a strategy has been implemented, it is crucial to determine if the goals have been met. If so, then new goals may be sought. If not, then different goals may be defined or different strategies may be followed so as to achieve success next time. (The process of strategic planning we have been describing here may strike you as perfectly rational—so much so, in fact, that you may expect it to be universal. However, as we describe in the OB in a Diverse World section on page 602, this is not the case.)

TABLE 16.3   VARIETIES OF COMPETITIVE STRATEGIES

Some of the most popular competitive strategies used by today's organizations are summarized here.

STRATEGY	DESCRIPTION
Market-share increasing strategies	Developing a broader share of an existing market, such as by widening the range of products, or by forming a joint venture (see Chapter 15) with another company that already has a presence in the market of interest
Profit strategies	Attempting to derive more profit from existing businesses, such as by training employees to work more efficiently or salespeople to sell more effectively
Market concentration strategies	Withdrawing from markets where the company is less effective and, instead, concentrating resources in markets where the company is likely to be more effective
Turnaround strategies	Attempting to reverse a decline in business by moving to a new product line or by radically restructuring operations
Exit strategies	Withdrawing from a market, such as by liquidating assets

RESISTANCE TO CHANGE: MAINTAINING THE STATUS QUO

Even if people are unhappy with the current state of affairs confronting them in organizations, they may be afraid that any changes will be potentially disruptive and only will make things worse. Indeed, fear of new conditions is quite real and it creates unwillingness to accept change. For this reason, they may react to organizational change quite negatively. Then again, if the process is managed effectively, people may respond to change in a very enthusiastic manner. Scientists have summarized the nature of people's reactions to organizational change as falling along a continuum ranging from acceptance, through indifference and passive resistance, to active resistance.[26] For a summary of the various forms these reactions may take, see Figure 16.9.

As you might imagine, for organizations to make the changes needed to remain competitive—let alone, to survive—they must tackle the problem of resistance to change head on. With this in mind, we will discuss the issue of readiness for change and examine both the individual and organizational barriers to change. Then, we will conclude this section of the chapter by identifying specific steps that can be taken to overcome resistance to change.

Individual Barriers to Change

Organizational scientists have recognized that *resistance to change* stems from both individual and organizational variables. **Resistance to change** refers to the tendency for organizational employees to be unwilling to go along with changes either because of individual fears of the unknown or organizational impediments. Here, we will describe several key factors that are known to make people resistant to change in organizations.[27] Then, in the following section, we will describe various organizational barriers to change.

- *Economic insecurity.* Because any changes on the job have the potential to threaten one's livelihood—by either loss of job or reduced pay—some resistance to change is inevitable.

resistance to change
The tendency for employees to be unwilling to go along with organizational changes, either because of individual fears of the unknown, or organizational impediments.

FIGURE 16.9

A Continuum of Reactions to Organizational Change
People's reactions to organizational change can range from acceptance (left) to active resistance (right). Some of the specific forms these reactions might take are indicated here.
(*Source:* Based on suggestions by Goldstein, 2001; Judson, 2001; see Note 26.)

- *Fear of the unknown.* Employees derive a sense of security from doing things the same way, knowing who their coworkers will be, and to whom they're supposed to answer from day to day. Disrupting these well-established, comfortable patterns creates unfamiliar conditions, a state of affairs that often is rejected.
- *Threats to social relationships.* As people continue to work within organizations, they form strong bonds with their coworkers. Many organizational changes (e.g., the reassignment of job responsibilities) threaten the integrity of friendship groups that provide valuable social rewards.
- *Habit.* Jobs that are well learned and that become habitual are easy to perform. The prospect of changing the way jobs are done challenges people to develop new job skills. Doing this is clearly more difficult than continuing to perform the job as it was originally learned.
- *Failure to recognize need for change.* Unless employees recognize and fully appreciate the need for change in their organizations, any vested interests they may have in keeping things the same may overpower their willingness to accept change.

Organizational Barriers to Change

Resistance to organizational change also stems from conditions associated with organizations themselves.[28] Several such factors may be identified.

Structural inertia. Organizations are designed to promote stability. To the extent that employees are carefully selected and trained to perform certain jobs and are rewarded for doing them well, the forces acting on individuals to perform in certain ways are very powerfully determined—that is, jobs have **structural inertia.** Thus, because jobs are designed to have stability, it is often difficult to overcome the resistance created by the forces that create stability.

Work group inertia. Inertia to continue performing jobs in a specified way comes not only from the jobs themselves but also from the social groups within which people work—*work group inertia.* Because of the development of strong social norms within

structural inertia
The organizational forces acting on employees, encouraging them to perform their jobs in certain ways (e.g., training, reward systems), thereby making them resistant to change.

nation, almost nothing is ever said about being competitive. Rather, the good work of the company is likely to be stressed in formal company publications. Ironically, however, Japanese companies tend to be fierce competitors in the international market. Thus, although competitive values may not be expressed in Japan (where, as a result, they are not likely to appear in any strategic plans), they certainly exist.

Our discussion of strategic planning is based on the idea that *radical change is not only possible but also desirable.* Again, we use Southeast Asian culture as a counterexample. In Vietnam and Thailand, for example, experts caution that radical change is doomed to fail. Instead, minor incremental adjustments to ways of operating are advised.[24]

Finally, in the United States, strategic decisions tend to be made primarily in the *interest of stockholders.* In fact, it is often said that the mission of a company is to raise stockholder value. Outside the United States, the interests of other parties are given more weight. For example, in Germany and France, the interests of the employees tend to be accorded far greater importance in the planning process. And, in Japan, companies are considered to belong to a variety of parties, with employees being given precedence over all others.[25]

In conclusion, it is clear that the values underlying the strategic planning process tend to prevail in the United States but are not equally prevalent elsewhere throughout the world. As a result, it appears questionable whether the strategic planning process we've described here would work—or that it is even worth attempting—outside the United States.

groups (see Chapter 8), potent pressures exist to perform jobs in certain ways. Introducing change disrupts these established normative expectations, leading to formidable resistance.

Threats to existing balance of power. If changes are made with respect to who's in charge, a shift in the balance of power between individuals and organizational subunits is likely to occur. Those units that now control the resources, have the expertise, and wield the power, may fear losing their advantageous positions resulting from any organizational change.

Previously unsuccessful change efforts. Anyone who has lived through a past disaster understandably may be reluctant to endure another attempt at the same thing. Similarly, groups or entire organizations that have been unsuccessful in introducing change in the past may be cautious about accepting further attempts at introducing change into the system.

An example. For two decades, General Electric (GE) has been undergoing a series of widespread changes in its basic strategy, organizational structure, and relationships with employees. In this process, it has experienced several of the barriers just identified. For example, GE managers had mastered a set of bureaucratic traditions that kept their habits strong and their inertia moving straight ahead. The prospect of doing things differently was scary for those who were so strongly entrenched in doing things the "GE way." In particular, the company's interest in globalizing triggered many fears of the unknown.

Resistance to change at GE also was strong because it threatened to strip power from those units that traditionally possessed most of it (e.g., the Power Systems and Lighting division). Changes also were highly disruptive to GE's "social architecture"; friendship groups were broken up and scattered throughout the company. In all, GE has been a living example of many different barriers to change all rolled into a single company.

Readiness for Change: When Will Organizational Change Occur?

As you might imagine, there are times when organizations are likely to change, and times during which change is less likely. In general, change is likely to occur when the people involved believe that the benefits associated with making a change outweigh the costs.[29] The factors contributing to the benefits of making a change are as follows.

- the amount of dissatisfaction with current conditions
- the availability of a desirable alternative
- the existence of a plan for achieving that alternative

Theorists consider that these three factors combine multiplicatively to determine the benefits of making a change (see Figure 16.10). Thus, if any one of these factors is zero, the benefits of making a change, and the likelihood of change itself, will be zero. If you think about it, this makes sense. After all, people are unlikely to initiate change if they are not at all dissatisfied, or if they don't have any desirable alternative in mind (or any way of attaining that alternative, if they do have one in mind). Of course, for change to occur, the expected benefits must outweigh the likely costs involved (e.g., disruption, uncertainties).

How Can Resistance to Organizational Change Be Overcome?

Because organizational change is inevitable, managers should be sensitive to the barriers to change so that resistance can be overcome. This, of course, is easier said than done. However, several useful approaches have been suggested, and the key ones are summarized here.[30]

1. *Shape political dynamics.* For change to be accepted, it often is useful (if not absolutely necessary) to win the support of the most powerful and influential individuals in the company. Doing so builds a critical internal mass of support for change. Demonstrating clearly that key organizational leaders endorse the change is an effective way to get others to go along with it—either because they share the leader's vision or because they fear the leader's retaliation. Either way, their support will facilitate acceptance of change.

2. *Identify and neutralize change resisters.* An important way of supporting change initiatives involves neutralizing those who resist change. Often, change is resisted because people say things publicly that express their fears of change, but organizational officials fail to respond. An offhand remark about change that expresses concerns and fears about impending change can be contagious, sending fear into the workplace. Not saying anything to counter such statements is to tacitly support that concern. As such, it is important for people promoting organizational change to identify and neutralize those who resist change. Several statements reflecting a fear of change and ways of responding to them are identified in Table 16.4.[31]

3. *Educate the workforce.* Sometimes people are reluctant to change because they fear what the future has in store for them. Fears about economic security, for example,

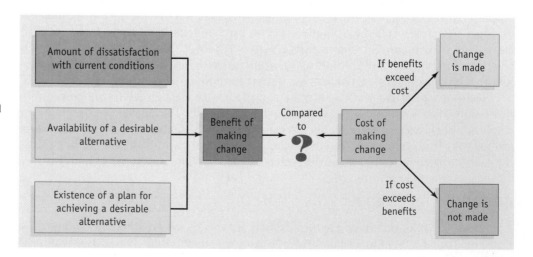

FIGURE 16.10

Organizational Change: When Will It Occur?
Whether or not an organizational change will be made depends on people's beliefs regarding the relative benefits and costs of making the change. The benefits are reflected by three considerations reviewed here.
(*Source:* Based on suggestions by Beer, 1980; see Note 29.)

TABLE 16.4 IDENTIFYING AND RESPONDING TO PEOPLE WHO RESIST CHANGE

It generally is not difficult to identify employees who are most resistant to change. The things they say give them away. Unless such statements are immediately countered, they run the risk of spreading resistance further throughout the company. Here are some statements that reflect an underlying resistance to change and some guidelines for responding to them.

WHEN THEY SAY . . .	YOU SHOULD COUNTER BY SAYING . . .
That seems risky.	Yes, but the risk is worth taking. After all, it is even riskier to do nothing.
Let's get back to basics.	The world has changed so much that what once seemed appropriate because it was "basic" no longer works today.
It worked in the past.	Maybe so, but as conditions have changed, there is reason to consider a new approach.
Things are okay as they are.	Possibly, but unless we take action, things are unlikely to be okay in the future.
I don't see any threat.	There's always a threat. Just because you don't see any compelling threat doesn't mean that one doesn't exist.
That's not our core competence.	Just because a particular area used to be an organization's core competence doesn't mean that it should stay that way.
The numbers don't work.	In the new Internet-based economy, new rules of accounting may be considered.
Once we start down that road, we can never go back.	Don't be afraid of relinquishing control. Anything that doesn't work can be stopped.
There will be unforeseen consequences.	This is always the case. In fact, that is precisely why it is necessary to consider making changes.

(*Source:* Based on suggestions by Reich, 2000; see Note 3.)

may be put to rest by a few reassuring words from powerholders. As part of educating employees about what organizational changes may mean for them, top management must show a considerable amount of emotional sensitivity. Doing so makes it possible for the people affected by change to help make it work. Some companies have found that simply answering the question, "what's in it for me?" can help allay a lot of fears.

4. *Involve employees in the change efforts.* It is well established that people who participate in making a decision tend to be more committed to the outcomes of the decision than are those who are not involved. Accordingly, employees who are involved in responding to unplanned change or who are made part of the team charged with planning a needed organizational change may be expected to have very little resistance to change. Organizational changes that are "sprung" on the workforce with little or no warning might be expected to encounter resistance simply as a knee-jerk reaction until employees have a chance to assess how the change affects them. In contrast, employees who are involved in the change process are better able to understand the need for change and are, therefore, less likely to resist it. Says Duane Hartley, general manager of Hewlett-Packard's microwave instruments division, "I don't think people really enjoy change, but if they can participate in it and understand it, it can become a positive [experience] for them."[32]

5. *Reward constructive behaviors.* One rather obvious and quite successful mechanism for facilitating organizational change is rewarding people for behaving in the desired fashion. Changing organizational operations may necessitate changing the kinds of behaviors that need to be rewarded by the organization. This is especially

critical when an organization is in the transition period of introducing the change. For example, employees who are required to learn to use new equipment should be praised for their successful efforts. Feedback on how well they are doing not only provides a great deal of useful assurance to uncertain employees but also also helps shape the desired behavior.

6. *Create a "learning organization."* Although all organizations change, whether they want to or not, some do so more effectively than others. Those organizations that have developed the capacity to adapt and change continuously are known as *learning organizations.*[33] In a **learning organization**, people set aside old ways of thinking, freely share ideas with others, form a vision of the organization, and work together on a plan for achieving that vision. Examples of learning organizations include Ford, General Electric, Wal-Mart, Xerox, and Motorola (see Figure 16.11).

learning organization
An organization that is successful at acquiring, cultivating, and applying knowledge that can be used to help it adapt to changes.

As you might imagine, becoming a learning organization is no simple feat. In fact, it involves implementing many of the principles of organizational behavior described in this book. Specifically, for a firm to become a continual learner, management must take the following steps.

- *Establish commitment to change.* Unless all employees clearly see that top management is strongly committed to changing and improving the organization, they will be unlikely to make the changes necessary to bring about improvements.

- *Adopt an informal organizational structure.* Change is more readily accepted when organizational structures (described in Chapter 15) are flat, cross-functional teams are created (see Chapter 8), and the formal boundaries between people are eliminated (as in boundaryless organizations, described in Chapter 15).

- *Develop an open organizational culture.* As we described in Chapter 14, managers play a key role in forming organizational culture. To effectively adapt to changes in their environments, organizations should have cultures that embrace risk taking, openness, and growth. Companies whose leaders are reluctant to confront the risk of failure are ones that will be unlikely to grow and develop.

7. *Take the situation into account.* Although the suggestions we have identified thus far may be very useful, they fail to take into account the nature of the situation in which change efforts are to be undertaken. Should changes be imposed on employees or should personnel be involved in the process of designing the change efforts? Organizational scientists have determined that precisely how one should approach the change process depends on the nature of the situation that is being faced.[34] Some strategies for ways to overcome resistance to change in various situations are summarized in Table 16.5.

FIGURE 16.11

Motorola: A Learning Organization
This woman works at a Motorola factory in Penong, Malaysia, which makes two-way radios and cell phones. Her company has been actively engaged in becoming a learning organization, one in which people set aside old ways of thinking in an effort to make continuous changes that help the business.

TABLE 16.5 SITUATION-BASED STRATEGIES FOR OVERCOMING RESISTANCE TO CHANGE

An effective way to approaching how to overcome resistance to change is to consider the nature of the situation in which change is required and to respond accordingly. Some important ways of overcoming resistance to change in various situations are summarized here.

IN SITUATIONS IN WHICH . . .	RESISTANCE TO CHANGE SHOULD BE OVERCOME BY . . .	THIS IS EFFECTIVE BECAUSE . . .
Information is lacking or is inaccurate	Educating employees and communicating with them	Employees can help make the changes once they appreciate their importance
Management doesn't know what type of change is best	Involving employees in the process of making the change	Employees' commitment to change will be enhanced
Employees are concerned about losses resulting from change	Negotiating an agreement about other aspects of work	It finds a way for employees to win, thereby offsetting their losses
Changes are vital and must be made immediately	Imposing the required changes	Time is of the essence; explanations can follow

(*Source*: Based on suggestions by Kotter, 1995; Kotter & Schlesinger, 1979; see Note 34.)

Although these six suggestions may be easier to state than to implement, efforts at following them will be well rewarded. Given the many forces that make employees resistant to change, managers should keep these guidelines in mind.

ORGANIZATIONAL DEVELOPMENT INTERVENTIONS: IMPLEMENTING PLANNED CHANGE

Now that we have shed some light on the basic issues surrounding organizational change, we are ready to look at planned ways of implementing it—collectively known as techniques of **organizational development (OD)**. Formally, we may define organizational development as a set of social science techniques designed to plan and implement change in work settings for purposes of enhancing the personal development of individuals and improving the effectiveness of organizational functioning. By planning organization-wide changes involving people, OD seeks to enhance organizational performance by improving the quality of the work environment and the attitudes and well-being of employees.

Over the years, many different strategies for implementing planned organizational change (referred to as *OD interventions*) have been used by specialists (referred to as *OD practitioners*) attempting to improve organizational functioning.[36] All the major methods of organizational development attempt to produce some kind of change in individual employees, work groups, and/or entire organizations. This is the goal of the four OD interventions we will review here.

organizational development (OD)
A set of social science techniques designed to plan change in organizational work settings for purposes of enhancing the personal development of individuals and improving the effectiveness of organizational functioning.

Management by Objectives: Clarifying Organizational Goals

In Chapter 6 we discussed the motivational benefits of setting specific goals. As you might imagine, not only individuals but also entire organizations stand to benefit from setting specific goals. For example, an organization may strive to "raise production" and "improve the quality" of its manufactured goods. These goals, well intentioned though they may be, may not be as useful to an organization as more specific ones, such as "increase production of widgets by 15 percent" or "lower the failure rate of widgets by 25 percent." After all, as the old saying goes, "It's usually easier to get somewhere if you know where you're going." Peter Drucker, consulting for General Electric during the early 1950s, was well aware of this idea and is credited with promoting the

management by objectives (MBO)
The technique by which managers and their subordinates work together to set and then meet organizational goals.

MAKING CHANGES STICK: TIPS FROM THREE ESTABLISHED ORGANIZATIONS

If you want to understand change, it makes sense to look at successful organizations that have been around for a while. After all, to have made it for 100 years, an organization must be managing change quite effectively. This clearly applies to three of the world's largest organizations—Sears, Royal Dutch Shell, and the United States Army. By analyzing what they have done to manage change effectively, it's possible to identify several practices that are worth emulating.[35]

1. *Fully incorporate employees into challenges faced by the organization.* This means more than simply involving employees in the organization's operations, but also actively engaging employees at all levels in the problems it faces. Officials from Shell Malaysia long had been unsuccessful in getting employees to work together to beat the competition. They were far too complacent, and the competition was rapidly gaining market share. In response to this, Shell officials called together all 260 managers for a 2½-day session in which the problem of the rapidly encroaching competition was put before them. They emerged from this marathon session with a firm plan that was put into place. Back on the job, regular follow-up meetings were held to make sure the plan was implemented. Finally, because the employees bought into the problem and met the challenge themselves, Shell was successful in changing the way it operated.

2. *Lead in a way that stresses the urgency of change.* It's not unusual for company officials to get in a rut, becoming lazy and complacent about the way they operate—even if it's necessary to take decisive action. This is *almost* what happened to Sears a few years ago. The retailing giant was losing customers rapidly as officers sat by merely lowering sales goals. That's when CEO Arthur Martinez lit a fire under everyone by stressing the importance of turning things around—or else! He generated a sense of urgency by setting very challenging goals (e.g., quadrupling market share and increasing customer satisfaction by 15 percent). Although Martinez didn't have all the answers to Sears's problems, he provided something even more important—straightforward, honest talk about the company's problems, creating a sense of urgency that got everyone moving in the right direction.

3. *Create relentless discomfort with the status quo.* Following military maneuvers, the U.S. Army thoroughly debriefs all participants in what is called an "After Action Review." In these sessions, careful feedback is given about what soldiers did well, and where they would stand to improve. By focusing in a relentless, detailed manner on work that needs to be done, officers eventually get soldiers to internalize the need for excellence. Soldiers return to their home bases asking themselves how they can do something better (faster, cheaper, or more accurately) of if there is a new and better approach that could be taken. In short, the status quo is the enemy; current performance levels are never accepted. Things always can be better. Army brass liken this commitment to continuous improvement to painting a bridge: The job is never over.

Although these are rather extreme measures and are not always easy to implement, they certainly warrant careful consideration. After all, they have worked well for some of the most successful organizations in the world.

benefits of specifying clear organizational goals—a technique known as **management by objectives (MBO).**

The MBO process, summarized in Figure 16.12, consists of three basic steps. First, goals are selected that employees will try to attain to best serve the needs of the organization. The goals should be selected by managers and their subordinates together. The goals must be set mutually by all those involved, not simply imposed. Furthermore, these goals should be directly measurable and have some time frame attached to them. Goals that cannot be measured (e.g., "make the company better") or that have no time limits are useless. It also is crucial that managers and their subordinates work together to plan ways of attaining the goals they have selected—developing what is known as an *action plan.*

Once goals are set and action plans have been developed, the second step calls for *implementation*—carrying out the plan and regularly assessing its progress. Is the plan working? Are the goals being approximated? Are there any problems being encountered in attempting to meet the goals? Such questions need to be considered while implementing an action plan. If the plan is failing, a midcourse correction may be in order—changing the plan, the way it's carried out, or even the goal itself. Finally, after monitoring progress toward the goal, the third step may be instituted: *evaluation*—assessing goal attainment. Were the organization's goals reached? If so, what new goals should be set to improve things still further? If not, what new plans can be initiated to help meet the goals? Because the ultimate assessment of the extent to which goals are met helps determine the selection of new goals, MBO is a continuous process.

MBO represents a potentially effective source of planning and implementing strategic change for organizations. Individual efforts designed to meet organizational goals get the individual employee and the organization itself working together toward common ends. Hence, systemwide change results. Of course, for MBO to work, everyone involved has to buy into it. Because MBO programs typically require a great deal of participation by lower-level employees, top managers must be willing to accept and support the cooperation and involvement of all.

Making MBO work also requires a great deal of time—anywhere from three to five years. Hence, MBO may be inappropriate in organizations that do not have the time to commit to making it work. Despite these considerations, MBO has become one of the most widely used techniques for affecting organizational change in recent years. It not only is used on an ad hoc basis by many organizations but it also constitutes an ingrained element of the organizational culture in certain companies, such as Hewlett-Packard and IBM.

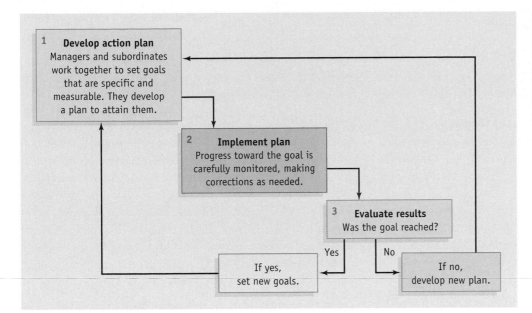

FIGURE 16.12
Management by Objectives: Developing Organizations Through Goal Setting
The organizational development technique of *management by objectives* requires managers and their subordinates to work together on setting and trying to achieve important organizational goals. The basic steps of the process are outlined here.

Survey Feedback: Inducing Change by Sharing Information

For effective organizational change to occur, employees must understand the organization's current strengths and weaknesses. That's the underlying rationale behind the **survey feedback** method. This technique follows the three steps summarized in Figure 16.13. First, data are collected that provide information about matters of general concern to employees, such as organizational climate, leadership style, and job satisfaction. This may take the form of intensive interviews or structured questionnaires, or both. Because it is important that this information be as unbiased as possible, employees providing feedback should be assured that their responses will be kept confidential. For this reason, this process often is conducted by outside consultants.

The second step calls for reporting the information obtained back to the employees during small group meetings. Typically, this consists of summarizing the average scores on the attitudes assessed in the survey. Profiles are created of feelings about the organization, its leadership, the work done, and related topics. Discussions also focus on why the scores are as they are, and what problems are revealed by the feedback.

The third and final step involves analyzing problems dealing with communication, decision making, and other organizational processes to make plans for dealing with them. Such discussions are usually most effective when they are carefully documented and a specific plan of implementation is made with someone put in charge of carrying it out.

Survey feedback is a widely used organizational development technique. This is not surprising in view of the advantages it offers. It is efficient, allowing a great deal of information to be collected relatively quickly. Also, it is very flexible and can be tailored to the needs of different organizations facing a variety of problems. However, the technique can be no better than the quality of the questionnaire used—it must measure the things that really matter to employees. Of course, to derive the maximum benefit from survey

survey feedback

An OD technique in which questionnaires and interviews are used to collect information about issues of concern to an organization. This information is shared with employees and is used as the basis for planning organizational change.

FIGURE 16.13
Survey Feedback: An Overview
The *survey feedback* technique or organizational development follows the three steps outlined here: collecting data, giving feedback, and developing action plans.

Collect data
Employees complete surveys to provide information about problems in their organization.

Give feedback
Feelings about the organization are summarized and shared with all employees.

Develop action plans
Through group discussions, specific plans for overcoming problems are identified and developed.

OB IN AN E-WORLD
USING ONLINE COMPETITIVE INTELLIGENCE FOR ORGANIZATIONAL CHANGE

Only about 10 percent of American companies do it, and the other 90 percent probably should. What, you ask? The answer is **competitive intelligence (CI)**—the process of gathering information about one's competitors that can be used as the basis for planning organizational change. CI is a search for clues about what one's competitor is actually doing or considering doing and staying ahead of the competition by using this information as part of the strategic planning process. To stay competitive, some of the biggest companies—especially those in rapidly changing, high-tech fields, such as General Electric, Motorola, Microsoft, Hewlett-Packard, IBM, AT&T, and Intel—engage in CI all the time. In fact, Gary Costley, former president of Kellogg Co. North America, says that managers who don't engage in CI are "incompetent" insofar as it is "irresponsible to not understand your competitors."[37]

It's important not to dismiss CI on the grounds that it is unethical. CI is not industrial espionage (which involves illegally spying on competitors), and it is completely legal. CI efforts usually involve gathering readily available information, such as that contained in public records. In fact, it has been said that 90 percent of what a company needs to make critical decisions and to understand its market and its competitors is available in public data.[38] For example, publicly traded companies are required to disclose information on their finances, inventories, and compliance with various legal regulations. Documents containing this information are available to anyone online, and growing numbers of competitors are availing themselves of them. One set of experts put it as such:

> By using the Internet, a company can monitor (manually or by using intelligent agents) the presence, posture, products, and pieces of other players in its industry. It can track the views of customers and seek out new ideas and expertise internationally. It can also draw upon files and databases from government agencies, foundations, universities, and research centers to broaden its thinking and help it be aware of the needs of the marketplace.[39]

---

competitive intelligence (CI)

The process of gathering information about one's competitors that can be used as the basis for planning organizational change.

feedback, it must have the support of top management. The plans developed by the small discussion groups must be capable of being implemented with the full approval of the organization. When these conditions are met, survey feedback can be a very effective OD technique. (The basic idea behind survey feedback is that employees receive information that guides them through the process of making changes. However, another source of information that may be used for this purpose comes from finding out what competitors are doing. For a closer look at this practice, see the OB in an E-World section above.)

Appreciative Inquiry

Although survey feedback and MBO are highly regarded OD techniques, they focus on deficiencies, such as negative feedback and unmet goals. A new approach to organizational development known as *appreciative inquiry* helps organizations break out of this focus on negative dynamics by focusing on the positive and the possible.[44] Specifically; **appreciative inquiry** is an OD intervention that focuses attention away from an organization's shortcomings and toward its capabilities and its potential. It is based on the assumption that members of organizations already know the problems they face and that they stand to benefit more by focusing on what is possible.

As currently practiced, the process of appreciative inquiry follows four straightforward steps. These are as follows.[45]

appreciative inquiry

An OD intervention that focuses attention away from an organization's shortcomings and toward its capabilities and its potential; based on the assumption that members of organizations already know the problems they face and that they stand to benefit more by focusing on what is possible.

1. *Discovery.* The discovery step involves identifying the positive aspects of the organization, the best of "what is." This frequently is accomplished by documenting the positive reactions of customers or people from other organizations.

Valuable CI information may be obtained online from a variety of sources. These include conference speakers, patent holders, former employees, technical recruiters, authors, and reporters. Companies also find it useful to post queries on bulletin boards and to join discussion groups.[40] Research has found that the more a company uses the Internet, the better quality competitive intelligence information it is able to collect. And, as the quality of competitive intelligence information improves, so too does a firm's capacity to make strategic decisions.[41] After all, companies that have competitive information not only recognize the need for change but also find it possible to make the kinds of changes that are necessary to succeed. Not surprisingly, companies that have advanced systems in place to monitor their competitors' activities are more profitable than those that do not have such systems.[42]

Procter & Gamble (P&G), the large consumer products company, is one of the leading users of CI techniques.[43] Recently, the company found it necessary to change its organizational structure and business processes in a way that made it possible for it to compete more effectively by bringing new products to market faster than the competition. With this in mind, P&G focused its CI efforts beyond its traditional focus, identifying the strengths and weaknesses of competing products. To bring about the desired changes P&G is now using the Internet to gather information about new ways of doing business that are being developed in the various markets in which it intends to be operating. P&G also is doing a much better job of sharing the information it gets with departments within the company that stand to benefit from it (recall our discussion of knowledge management in Chapter 2). Managers at P&G explain how everyone at the company can benefit from using CI. They emphasize that CI is everyone's job, and they show employees how to gather and share whatever such information they may come across—even, accidentally.

There's no mistaking the fact that competitive intelligence has become an important source of profit for many companies. As just one example, Robert Flynn, the former CEO of the NutraSweet division of Monsanto, has claimed that CI was worth some $50 million to his company (in terms of revenues gained and revenues not lost to competitors). With figures like these, it's easy to make the case that companies cannot afford *not* to make CI an important part of their strategic change plans.

2. *Dreaming.* Through the process of discovering the organization's strengths, it is possible to begin dreaming by envisioning "what might be." By discussing their visions of a theoretically ideal organization, employees are free to reveal their thoughts about how good their own organization can be.

3. *Designing.* The designing stage involves having a dialogue in which participants discuss their ideas about "what should be." The underlying idea is that by listening to others in a highly receptive manner, it is possible to understand others' ideas and to come to a common understanding of what the future should look like.

4. *Delivering.* After having jointly discussed the ideal state of affairs, members of the organization are ready to begin instituting a plan for delivering their ideas. This involves establishing specific objectives and directions regarding "what will be."

Because appreciative inquiry is an emerging approach to OD, it has not been widely used. However, those organizations in which it has been used have been quite pleased with the results.[46]

Action Labs

Bringing about change in organizations is generally a very slow process. At a typical large company, it involves painstakingly analyzing and planning ideas and then rolling out only small changes in a deliberate sequence. However, in today's rapidly moving world, this pace is likely to be far too slow. To accelerate the change process a technique known as the *action lab* has been introduced in recent years. The action lab is meant to be a "greenhouse" in which change can be created by insulating a group of decision makers from daily operations and getting them to focus on a business problem.

action lab

An OD intervention in which teams of participants work off-site to develop and implement new ways of solving organizational problems by focusing on the ineffectiveness of current methods.

Specifically, an **action lab** is an OD intervention in which teams of participants work off-site to develop and implement new ways of solving organizational problems by focusing on the ineffectiveness of current methods.[47]

One of the unique features of action labs is that the participants are in contact with one another for such extended periods of time (e.g., every day for four weeks) that they eventually find it impossible to cling to their established ways. For example, in one particular action lab team, participants faced a frustrating few days in which bold proposals were constantly being shot down. Inevitably, an executive in the team would find some flaw and the idea was dropped in an attempt to avoid conflict. Soon, members of the team realized that despite the aim of treating everyone as equals, they inevitably retreated to the safety of the company's established practice of pleasing the bosses. Eventually, the lab participants figured out that the very forces that were blocking changes in the company were present within the lab. They were more concerned with avoiding conflict than with getting new ideas out into the open. Only once this insight occurred was the way paved for the team to develop innovative new ideas.

Let's consider an example of how an action lab helped facilitate change in an organization. A few years ago, the Cummins Engine Company used an action lab consisting of several teams that focused on ways in which the company could regain its former leadership in the diesel engine manufacturing business. One of these teams included union stewards, manufacturing supervisors, and plant managers.[48] Carefully analyzing the situation, they discovered that customers were turning to competitors because they offered less expensive products. Cummins's long-time strategy was to attract customers by emphasizing "lifetime customer value," that is, by getting them to realize that the high quality of their engines made them less expensive over the product's lifetime. This image served the company well, but it didn't compensate for the competitors' lower initial prices, causing sales to slip.

Analyzing the problem, the team figured out that Cummins had to reduce prices by 20 percent to remain competitive. The barrier was the long-standing practice of manufacturing all components in-house to assure the highest quality standards. The lab team realized that this cherished practice had to be abandoned. Within one month's time, the team established strategic alliances (see Chapter 15) with various suppliers that could manufacture the parts less expensively. Cummins would assemble the final products and be the "quality watchdog" for the overall manufacturing process.

Although this process has been in place for only a few years, it seems to be very successful thus far. Quality has been high and Cummins is on its way to regaining its leadership in the diesel engine business. Similarly encouraging results have been reported at Royal Dutch Shell and British Gas, which also have used action labs to introduce timely solutions to problems.

Quality of Work Life Programs: Humanizing the Workplace

When you think of work, do you think of drudgery? Although many people believe these two terms go together naturally, it has grown increasingly popular to systematically improve the quality of life experienced on the job. As more people demand satisfying and personally fulfilling places to work, OD practitioners have attempted systematically to create work situations that enhance employees' motivation, satisfaction, and commitment—factors that may contribute to high levels of organizational performance. Such efforts are known collectively as **quality of work life** (**QWL**) programs. Specifically, such programs are ways of increasing organizational output and improving quality by involving employees in the decisions that affect them on their jobs. Typically, QWL programs support highly democratic treatment of employees at all levels and encourage their participation in decision making. Although many approaches to improving the quality of work life exist, they all share a common goal: humanizing the workplace.

quality of work life (QWL)

An OD technique designed to improve organizational functioning by humanizing the workplace, making it more democratic, and involving employees in decision making.

work restructuring

The process of changing the way jobs are done to make them more interesting to workers.

One popular approach to improving the quality of work life involves **work restructuring**—the process of changing the way jobs are done to make them more interesting to workers. We already discussed several such approaches to redesigning jobs—including *job enlargement, job enrichment,* and the *job characteristics model*—in our discussion of motivation in Chapter 6. Not surprisingly, these same techniques also are considered effective ways of improving the quality of work life for employees.

Another approach to improving the quality of work life is **quality circles (QCs).** These are small groups of volunteers (usually around 10) who meet regularly (usually weekly) to identify and solve problems related to the quality of the work they perform and the conditions under which people do their jobs. An organization may have several QCs operating at once, each dealing with a particular work area about which it has the most expertise. To help them work effectively, the members of the circle usually receive some form of training in problem solving. Large companies such as Westinghouse, Hewlett-Packard, and Eastman Kodak, to name only a few, have included QCs as part of their QWL efforts. QCs have dealt with issues such as how to reduce vandalism, how to create safer and more comfortable working environments, and how to improve product quality. Research has shown that although quality circles are very effective at bringing about short-term improvements in quality of work life (i.e., those lasting up to 18 months), they are less effective at creating more permanent changes.

As you might imagine, a variety of benefits (even if short term) might result from QWL programs. These fall into three major categories. The most direct benefit is usually increased job satisfaction, organizational commitment, and reduced turnover among the workforce. A second benefit is increased productivity. Related to these first two benefits is a third—namely, increased organizational effectiveness (e.g., profitability, goal attainment). Many companies, such as Ford, General Electric, and AT&T, have active QWL programs and are reportedly quite pleased with their results.

Achieving these benefits is not automatic, however. Two major potential pitfalls must be avoided for QWL programs to be implemented successfully. First, both *management and labor must cooperate in designing the program.* Should any one side believe that the program is really just a method of gaining an advantage over the other, it is doomed to fail. Second, the *plans agreed to by all concerned parties must be fully implemented.* It is too easy for action plans developed in QWL groups to be forgotten amid the hectic pace of daily activities. It is the responsibility of employees at all levels—from the highest executive to the lowest-level laborer—to follow through on their parts of the plan.

quality circles (QCs)
An approach to improving the quality of work life, in which small groups of volunteers meet regularly to identify and solve problems related to the work they perform and the conditions under which they work.

CRITICAL QUESTIONS ABOUT ORGANIZATIONAL DEVELOPMENT

Our discussion of organizational development would be incomplete without addressing three very important questions—do the techniques work, are they culture bound, and are they ethical?

The Effectiveness of Organizational Development: Does It Really Work?

Thus far, we have described some of the major techniques used by OD practitioners to improve organizational functioning. As is probably clear, carrying out these techniques requires a considerable amount of time, money, and effort. Accordingly, it is appropriate to ask if this investment is worthwhile. In other words, does OD really work? Given the popularity of OD in organizations, this question is very important. Most of the studies bearing on the answer show the effects of the various interventions to be beneficial—mostly in the area of improving organizational functioning.[49]

We hasten to add that any conclusions about the effectiveness of OD should be qualified in several important ways. First, OD interventions tend to be more effective among blue-collar employees than among white-collar employees. Second, the beneficial effects of OD can be enhanced by using a combination of several techniques (e.g.,

BEST PRACTICES
SIMULATING ORGANIZATIONAL CHANGE

Toronto's Optus Corp. has a problem: It's growing too fast for its own good. In just its first 13 months, the company, which designs custom documents for financial-services companies, such as Aetna and Citibank, has boosted its employee base 500 percent and has acquired a new company every three months. Revenues jumped from $40 million in 1999 to $100 million (Canadian) in 2000. Although many executives would be envious of such a "problem," such dramatic growth has taken its toll on company officials, who wonder how they ever will be able to catch up with the deadlines without slowing down the company's growth.

To help, Chief Operating Officer John Hantho decided that the members of his senior executive team should cross the Sahara Desert—virtually, that is.[50] And so they did. With help from two facilitators from InCourage, a Canadian multimedia company, the 10-person team worked its way through *Shifting Sands,* an exercise that helps groups prepare for organizational change. The simulation consists of a full-day multimedia recreation of an actual 1977 expedition across the 1,000-mile-wide Sahara Desert. At various points along the journey, the team is challenged to make decisions that either will help them make it further across the desert or bury them in the sand. The trip across the various microclimates, ecosystems, and cultures is a metaphor for the changes confronting Optus.

As the journey begins, the travelers bid goodbye to the lives they knew in the civilized world, prompting one of the facilita-

four or more together) instead of any single one. Finally, the effectiveness of OD techniques depends on the degree of support they receive from top management: The more programs are supported from the top, the more successful they tend to be.

Despite the importance of attempting to evaluate the effectiveness of OD interventions, a great many of them go unevaluated. Although there are undoubtedly many reasons for this, one key factor is the difficulty of assessing change. Because many factors can cause people to behave differently in organizations and because such behaviors may be difficult to measure, many OD practitioners avoid the problem of measuring change altogether. In a related vein, political pressures to justify OD programs also may discourage some OD professionals from honestly and accurately assessing their effectiveness. After all, in doing so, one runs the risk of scientifically demonstrating one's wasted time and money. (With an eye toward assessing the effectiveness of change efforts before they are implemented, growing numbers of organizations are turning to simulations. For a closer look at how organizational change is simulated, see the Best Practices section above.)

We may conclude that despite some limitations, organizational development is an approach that shows considerable promise in its ability to benefit organizations and the individuals working within them.

Is Organizational Development Dependent on National Culture?

For organizational development to be effective, people must be willing to share their ideas candidly with others, they must be willing to accept uncertainty, and they must be willing to show concern for others, especially members of their own teams. However, not all people are willing to do these things; this pattern better characterizes the people from some countries than others. For example, this profile perfectly describes people from Scandinavian countries, suggesting that OD may be most effective in such nations. However, people from Latin American nations are much the opposite, suggesting that OD interventions will be less successful when conducted there.[51] For a sum-tors to ask what people are willing to give up as their old company evolves into something entirely new. The response that emerged from the ensuing discussion was that employees of the various companies acquired by Optus had to give up their identities and think of themselves as being part of Optus. To do this without completely giving up their previous identities, the team came up with the idea of developing a Hall of Fame, where names of the acquired companies could be put to rest in an honorable fashion.

Further into the trip, the group saw a slide showing a two-track road that ended abruptly with nothing but desert sand beyond it. This was Optus—moving into an unknown world without signs to point the way. Slowing down to get their bearing made sense, but competing in the rapidly changing marketplace didn't allow them to do so. Metaphorically, they were stuck in the sand, spinning their wheels but getting nowhere. Eventually, the team found a solution: Keep the sales reps from making unrealistic promises to clients, allowing them to take on new business without getting further behind and angering clients with unfulfilled promises.

Optus officials are convinced that the simulation helped the company in two key ways. First, the simulation provided a mechanism that allowed members of the executive team to stand back and gain perspective from daily job pressures, allowing them to identify problems and ways of solving them. By testing their ideas in the simulated desert environment, they came away from the exercise with a good idea of what would work back in the office. Second, the simulation helped by building camaraderie in the executive suite, allowing the team members to reconnect. In the simulation's terms, they could recalibrate their compasses before heading into the next leg of their journey.

mary of the extent to which the basic assumptions of OD fit with the cultural styles of people from various nations, see Figure 16.14.

Although the predominant cultural values of people from the United States and Canada place them in the middle region of Figure 16.14, this is not to say that OD is doomed to be ineffective in North American companies. Not all OD techniques are alike with respect to their underlying cultural values.[52] For example, MBO has become a very popular OD technique in the United States in large part because it promotes the American values of willingness to take risks and working aggressively at attaining high performance. However, because MBO also encourages superiors and subordinates to negotiate freely with each other, the technique has been generally unsuccessful in France, where others' higher levels of authority are well accepted.[53] Similarly, OD generally is unsuccessful in the southeast Asian nation of Brunei, where the prevailing cultural value is such that problems are unlikely to be confronted openly.[54]

These examples illustrate a key point: The effectiveness of OD techniques will depend, in part, on the extent to which the values of the technique match the underlying values of the national culture in which it is employed. As such, OD practitioners

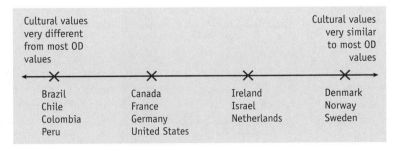

FIGURE 16.14

Organizational Development: Its Fit with National Values
Organizational development (OD) techniques tend to be more successful when the underlying values of the technique match the cultural values of the nations in which they are used. General OD values tend to conform more to the cultural norms of some nations, shown on the right (where OD is more likely to be accepted) than others, shown on the left (where OD is less likely to be accepted). (*Source:* Based on suggestions by Jaeger, 1986; see Note 51.)

must fully appreciate the cultural norms of the nations in which they are operating. Failure to do so not only may make OD interventions unsuccessful, but they even may have unintended negative consequences.

Is Organizational Development Inherently Unethical?

By its very nature, OD applies powerful social science techniques in an attempt to change attitudes and behavior. From the perspective of a manager attempting to accomplish various goals, such tools are immediately recognized as very useful. However, if you think about it from the perspective of the individual being affected, several ethical issues arise (for a summary of these, see Figure 16.15).[55]

For example, it has been argued that OD techniques impose the values of the organization on the individual without taking the individual's own attitudes into account. OD is a very one-sided approach, some claim, reflecting the imposition of the more powerful organization on the less powerful individual. A related issue is that the OD process does not provide any free choice on the part of the employees. As a result, it may be seen as *coercive* and *manipulative*. When faced with a "do it, or else" situation, employees tend to have little free choice and are forced to allow themselves to be manipulated, a potentially degrading prospect.

Another issue is that the unequal power relationship between the organization and its employees makes it possible for the true intent of OD techniques to be misrepresented. As an example, imagine that an MBO technique is presented to employees as a means of allowing greater organizational participation, whereas in reality it is used as a technique for holding individuals responsible for their poor performance and punishing them as a result. Although such an event might not happen, the potential for abuse of this type does exist, and the potential to misuse the technique—even if not originally intended—might later prove to be too great a temptation.

Despite these considerations, many professionals do *not* agree that OD is inherently unethical. Such a claim, it has been countered, is to say that the practice of management is itself unethical. After all, the very act of going to work for an organization requires one to submit to the organization's values and the overall values of society at large. One cannot help but face life situations in which others' values are imposed. This is not to say that organizations have the right to impose patently unethical values on people for the purpose of making a profit (e.g., stealing from customers). Indeed,

FIGURE 16.15

The Ethics of OD: Summary of the Debate
Some have claimed that OD is an inherently unethical practice, whereas others have countered that it is not. The arguments for each side are summarized here.

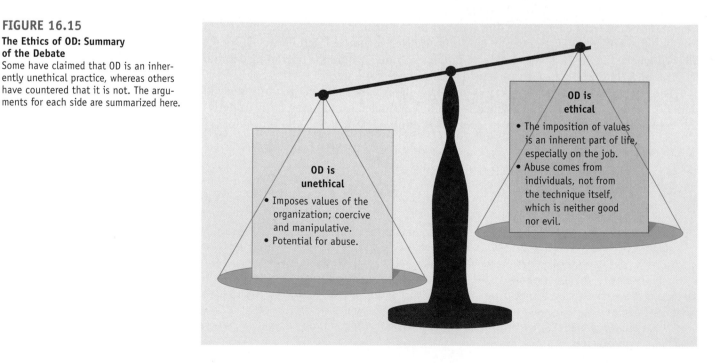

OD is unethical
- Imposes values of the organization; coercive and manipulative.
- Potential for abuse.

OD is ethical
- The imposition of values is an inherent part of life, especially on the job.
- Abuse comes from individuals, not from the technique itself, which is neither good nor evil.

because they have the potential to abuse their power (such as in the preceding MBO example), organizations have a special obligation to refrain from doing so.

Although abuses of organizational power sometimes do occur, OD itself is not necessarily the culprit. Indeed, like any other tool (even a gun!), OD is not inherently good or evil. Instead, *whether the tool is used for good or evil will depend on the individual using it*. With this in mind, the ethical use of OD interventions will require that they be supervised by professionals in an organization that places a high value on ethics. To the extent that top management officials embrace ethical values and behave ethically themselves, norms for behaving ethically are likely to develop in organizations. When an organization has a strong ethical culture, it is unlikely that OD practitioners would even think of misusing their power to harm individuals. The need to develop such a culture has been recognized as a way for organizations to take not only moral leadership in their communities, but financial leadership as well.

SUMMARY AND REVIEW OF LEARNING OBJECTIVES

1. Characterize the prevalence of the change process in organizations.
Organizational change is very prevalent and is occurring at a rapid pace. Almost all organizations are changing in one way or another in order to survive. Inevitably, those that fail to adapt fail to survive. Research has shown that the tendency for organizational change to occur is not limited to organizations in North America. Change is occurring rapidly in organizations of all nations throughout the world.

2. Understand what, exactly, is changed when organizational change comes about and the forces responsible for unplanned organizational change.
The process of organizational change involves some combination of changing organizational structure, technology, and people. Unplanned change occurs in organizations due to shifting employee demographics, performance gaps, governmental regulation, economic competition in the global arena, and advances in technology.

3. Describe what is meant by strategic planning and explain the types of strategic changes that organizations make.
Strategic planning is the process of formulating, implementing, and evaluating decisions that enable an organization to achieve its objectives. Typically, strategic plans are made about changing either a company's products and services or its organizational structure.

4. Identify the 10 steps in the strategic planning process.
The strategic planning process follows 10 steps: (1) define goals, (2) define the scope of products or services, (3) assess internal resources, (4) assess the external environment, (5) analyze internal arrangements, (6) assess competitive advantage, (7) develop a competitive strategy, (8) communicate the strategy to stakeholders, (9) implement the strategy, and (10) evaluate the outcome.

5. Explain why people are resistant to organizational change and how this resistance may be overcome.
In general, people are resistant to change because of individual factors (e.g., economic insecurity, fear of the unknown) and organizational factors (e.g., the stability of work groups, threats to the existing balance of power). However, resistance to change can be overcome in several ways, including shaping political dynamics, educating the workforce about the effects of the changes and involving employees in the change process, involving employees in change efforts, rewarding constructive behaviors, and creating a learning organization.

6. Identify and describe the major organizational development techniques that are used today.

Survey feedback uses questionnaires and/or interviews as the basis for identifying organizational problems, which are then addressed in planning sessions. Team building involves using work groups to diagnose and develop specific plans for solving problems with respect to their functioning as a work unit. Quality of work life programs attempt to humanize the workplace by involving employees in the decisions affecting them (e.g., through quality circle meetings) and by restructuring the jobs themselves. Finally, management by objectives focuses on attempts by managers and their subordinates to work together at setting important organizational goals and developing a plan to help meet them. The rationale underlying all of these techniques is that they may enhance organizational functioning by involving employees in identifying and solving organizational problems.

POINTS TO PONDER

Questions for Review

1. Some changes in organizations are unplanned, whereas others are the result of strategic plans. Give examples of each of these varieties of change and explain their implications for organizational functioning.
2. Under what conditions will people be most willing to make changes in organizations? Explain your answer and give an example.
3. What is meant by strategic planning and what are the steps in the strategic planning process?
4. What are the major techniques of organizational development?
5. Overall, how effective is organizational development in improving organizational functioning? With respect to what factors does it work or not work?
6. Argue for or against the following statement: "Organizational development is inherently unethical and should not be used."

Experiential Questions

1. Think about the one job in a company with which you are most familiar (e.g., because either you, a friend, or a family member have held it). How has the nature of this job changed over the years? What is done differently, and why? In what ways has technology been involved? To what extent do you believe that the company benefited from these changes?
2. Think back to one particular change that was made in the organization in which you work. What concerns did you have about it? Were you resistant to this change? If so, what, if anything, did management do to allay your fears? What might they have done?
3. Have you ever participated in some type of organizational development effort? If so, what was done? How did you feel about the program? Do you believe the effort was effective?

Questions to Analyze

1. Suppose you are having difficulty managing a small group of subordinates who work in an office 1,000 miles away from your home base. What kinds of changes in structure, technology, and people can be implemented to more closely supervise these distant employees?
2. Suppose that you are a top executive of a large organization about to undertake an ambitious restructuring involving massive changes in job responsibilities for most employees. Explain why people might be resistant to such changes and what steps could be taken to overcome this resistance.

3. Imagine that you are a manager facing the problem of not attracting enough high-quality personnel to your organization. Would you attempt to solve this problem alone or by committee? Explain your reasoning.

DEVELOPING OB SKILLS

INDIVIDUAL EXERCISE

Developing a Strategic Plan

Developing a strategic plan is not an easy matter. In fact, doing it right requires a great deal of information and a great deal of practice. This exercise will give you a feel for some of the challenges involved in developing such a plan.

Directions

1. Suppose that you are the president of a small software development firm that has for years sold a utility that has added functionality to the operating system used in most computers. Now you suddenly face a serious problem: Microsoft has changed its operating system such that your product no longer serves any purpose.
2. Using the 10 steps outlined in Figure 16.8 (page 598), develop a strategic plan to keep your company alive. Make any assumptions you need to develop your plan, but state these in the process of describing it.

Questions for Discussion

1. How easy or difficult was it for you to develop this strategic plan? What would have made the process easier or more effective?
2. Which of the 10 steps would you imagine is easiest to implement? Which do you think would be most challenging?
3. Would you use competitive intelligence in the course of implementing your plan? If so, how?
4. What special challenges, if any, would the employees of your company face as they attempted to implement this plan? How would you attempt to overcome these challenges?

GROUP EXERCISE

Recognizing Impediments to Change and How to Overcome Them

To confront the reality of organizational change, one of the most fundamental steps involves recognizing the barriers to change. Then, once these impediments have been identified, consideration can be given to ways of overcoming them. This exercise is designed to help you practice thinking along these lines while working in groups.

Directions

1. Divide the class into groups of approximately six and gather each group around a circle.
2. Each group should consider each of the following situations.
   - *Situation A:* A highly sophisticated e-mail system is being introduced at a large university. It will replace the practice of transmitting memos on paper.
   - *Situation B:* A very popular employee who's been with the company for many years is retiring. He will be replaced by a completely new employee from the outside.
3. For each situation, discuss three major impediments to change.

4. Identify a way of overcoming each of these impediments.
5. Someone from the group should record the answers and present them to the class for a discussion session.

Questions for Discussion

1. For each of the situations, were the impediments to change similar or different?
2. Were the ways of overcoming the impediments similar or different?
3. How might the nature of the situation confronted dictate the types of change barriers confronted and the ease with which these may be overcome?

WEB SURFING EXERCISE

Organizational Learning

The topic of organizational learning is a popular one today because organizations are finding it more important than ever to make effective changes in the way they operate. In support of this interest, several societies and journals have been developed. Among these are the following:

The Society for Organizational Learning	www.sol-ne.org/
Stanford Learning Organization Web (SLOW)	www.stanford.edu/group/SLOW/
Emerald Insight	www.emeraldinsight.com/tlo.htm

Visit these Web sites and answer the following questions based on what you find.

1. What products and services do these groups provide?
2. In what ways do these groups help promote organizational learning?
3. What kinds of articles are published in the *SoL Journal on Knowledge, Learning, and Change*, and in *The Learning Organization, An International Journal?*

Competitive Intelligence

Boasting clients from over half the *Fortune* 500 companies, Fuld & Company is the leading consulting firm specializing in competitive intelligence. At its impressive Web site is a page called the "Internet Intelligence Index," which contains links to over 600 Web sites that can provide valuable competitive intelligence information. It may be found at www.fuld.com/i3/index.html/. Visit this Web site and answer the following questions based on what you find.

1. What kinds of general business resources are available online?
2. What kinds of industry-specific and international sources are available that provide competitive intelligence information?
3. How might the information found at these sites be used for organizational development purposes?

PRACTICING OB

Concern About an Impending Merger

Your company is exploring the idea of merging with a competitor. This has aroused a great deal of concern in the workplace, as people begin to fear the security of their jobs may be in jeopardy. This, in turn, has been disrupting the flow of work. Productivity is slowing down as people are taking off to find new jobs. Meanwhile, profitability is sagging badly, which threatens to adversely affect the merger deal.

1. Does it make sense to expect the employees to have these fears? Why or why not?
2. Describe the steps you can take to help allay these fears and to return work back to normal. How effective do you think these steps may be?
3. If a merger were to occur, how might you use an organizational development technique to help smooth the transition?

GM Is Driven to Change—And the Chevrolet SSR Is the Vehicle

Let's face it, when it comes to designing the latest, trendy automobiles, the car enthusiast is unlikely to think of General Motors (GM). The world's largest automaker (and the third largest company of any kind) makes lots of respectable vehicles and several truly outstanding ones, but rarely anything as interesting as the Volkswagen Beetle, the Audi TT, or Chrysler's Prowler, Viper, or PT Cruiser.

The problem, according to John Taylor, is that GM is entrenched in established ways of doing things and has been afraid of taking bold design initiatives. As director of the company's Advanced Portfolio Exploration Group (APEX), Taylor and his team of 40 designers, analysts, and engineers are responsible for developing bold new vehicles. Appearing first as concept cars, test vehicles that help attract attention for design features at automobile shows, APEX's projects are aimed squarely at appealing to younger buyers. In the past decade, GM's sales in the United States dropped 18 percent, in large part because its vehicles failed to appeal to this market.

Bill Ochalek, a manager at APEX, dubbed the company's problem the "16 Mile Road mentality," referring to the name of the street that runs through APEX headquarters in the Detroit suburb of Warren, Michigan. "There's this idea that the world runs right around our technical center, that Warren is at the center of the universe," he says, adding, "Being alone is not a good thing in our environment. It's too easy to talk yourself into the brilliance of your ideas." And, because just about everyone at APEX thinks alike, it is insulated from forces that dictate change.

To counter this problem of insularity, Olachek arranged to get his team out of APEX's sprawling Technical Center and into the world. They visited car dealerships, companies in other industries, and went to trade conferences in other fields, such as consumer electronics shows and toy fairs. Among the most important things they learned was that unlike other businesses, GM was overly concerned with avoiding mistakes. By contrast, in the pharmaceuticals industry, only one drug in 5,000 is likely to become successful. At GM, however, people were discouraged from trying anything new because it meant making mistakes. However, Taylor acknowledges that making mistakes and learning from them is exactly what it takes to develop new automotive products. He knew that this would be a tough sell to management but that doing so "was imperative if we were going to create a fear-free, risk-taking workplace. Because if you're frightened of making a mistake, you won't make a thing." And this has proven to be precisely GM's problem in recent years. In fact, the tendency to avoid change and "play things safe" is widely acknowledged to be the main factor that led to the demise of GM's venerable Oldsmobile division in 2002.

If the look of some of the vehicles rolling out of APEX are any indication, change has been coming at a fast and furious pace. The best evidence of GM's new approach to design comes in the form of the 2003 Chevrolet SSR. Part hot rod and part open-air sports car, the SSR, with it's retractable roof and zippy V-8 engine is a head turner. It clearly represents a change for GM in terms of design. Surely, GM officials also are hoping that it will represent a change on the company's bottom line.

Critical Thinking Questions

1. What were the major barriers to change at GM?
2. How were these barriers overcome?
3. What problems are likely to be encountered with respect to sustaining these changes?

Organizational Change

To say that change is a way of life at SA is surely an understatement. At first, the company was small, servicing only 5,000 students, but today, that number has swelled to over two million. To accommodate this growth, the original employees who once worked with only a handful of colleagues, now find themselves working among some 500 associates. As you might expect, today's much larger company has a more formal culture. People who once worked shoulder-to-shoulder with the CEO now hardly ever see him. What's more, the broad-based work that many of the company's original employees once did is now likely to be far more specialized and narrow in scope.

Much of the company's growth has come from mergers and acquisitions—a total of 11 in 10 years. As new companies are acquired, they have to be absorbed into the overall culture of the company, but are in many cases allowed to function autonomously, operating as they did before. As a result, considerable adjustments are required for all.

Change also is inevitable because of the rapidly advancing nature of technology and of the marketplace within which SA operates. Not only are personal computers commonplace, but also, the high school and college students SA serves are generally highly knowledgeable about computers, helping the company reach out to them more efficiently than ever.

Questions for Discussion

1. Of the several forces responsible for change identified in the text, which ones appear to be operating at SA? Give examples.
2. What are SA's strategic plans for the future, and what are the implications of putting them into practice?
3. What barriers to change are likely to exist at SA, and how might they be overcome?
4. Identify a particular organizational development technique that might be used successfully at SA. Why do you think it would work in this case?

Theory and Research: Tools for Learning About Behavior in Organizations

In Chapter 1, we noted that organizational behavior is a science, and as such, it relies on the scientific method to draw conclusions about behavior in organizations. As in the case of other scientific fields, OB uses the tools of science to achieve its goals. In this case, those goals are learning about organizations and the behavior of people working in them. With this in mind, it is useful to understand the basic tools scientists use to learn about behavior in organizations. In this Appendix we will briefly describe some of these techniques. Our goal here is not to make you an expert in scientific methodology, but rather to give you a solid understanding of the techniques you will be encountering in the field of OB.

ISN'T IT ALL JUST COMMON SENSE?

Although you may yet not be a top executive of a large business firm with decades of experience in the work world, you doubtlessly know *something* about the behavior of people on the job. After all, you probably learned quite a bit from whatever jobs you have had and from talking to other people about their experiences. This isn't surprising, given that we all can observe a great deal about people's behavior in organizational settings just by paying casual attention. So, whether you're the CEO of a *Fortune* 500 firm or a part-time pizza delivery driver, chances are good that you already have a few ideas about how people behave on the job. Besides, there probably are some things about behavior in organizations that you take for granted.

For example, would you say that happier employees tend to be more productive? If you're like most people, you probably would say "yes, of course." It's logical, right? Well, despite what you may believe, this generally is *not* true. In fact, as discussed in Chapter 5, people who are satisfied with their jobs are generally no more productive than those who are dissatisfied with their jobs. This contradiction of common sense is not an isolated example. This book is full of examples of phenomena studied in the field of OB that you might find surprising. To see how good you may be at predicting human behavior in organizations, complete the Group Exercise appearing at the end of Chapter 1 (see page 34), if you haven't done so already. If you don't do very well, don't despair. It's just our way of demonstrating that there's more to understanding the complexities of behavior in organizations than meets the eye.

So, if we can't trust our common sense, then on what can we rely? This is where the scientific method enters the picture. Although social science research is far from perfect, the techniques used to study behavior in organizations can tell us a great deal. Naturally, not everything scientific research reveals contradicts common sense. In fact, a considerable amount of research confirms things we already believe to be true. If this occurs, is the research useless? The answer is emphatically *no!* After all, scientific evidence often provides a great deal of insight into the subtle conditions under which various events occur. Such complexities would not have been apparent from only casual, unsystematic observation and common sense. In other words, the field of OB is based solidly on carefully conducted and logically analyzed research. Although common sense may provide a useful starting point for getting us to think about behavior in organizations, there's no substitute for scientific research when it comes to really understanding what happens and why. And, promoting this understanding is one of the major goals of the field of OB

Now that you understand the important role of the scientific method in the field of OB, you are prepared to appreciate the specific approaches used to conduct scientific research in this field. We will begin our presentation of these techniques with a discussion of one of the best-accepted sources of ideas for OB research—*theory*.

THEORY: AN INDISPENSABLE GUIDE TO ORGANIZATIONAL RESEARCH

What image comes to mind when you think of a scientist at work? Someone wearing a white lab coat surrounded by microscopes and test tubes busily at work testing theories? Although OB scientists typically don't wear lab coats or use microscopes and test tubes, it *is* true that they make use of theories. This is the case despite the fact that OB is, in part, an applied science. Simply because a field is characterized as being "theoretical" does not imply that it is impractical and out of touch with reality. To the contrary, a theory is simply a way of describing the relationship between concepts. Thus, theories help, not hinder, our understanding of practical situations. In fact, the better the research and theories we have available to us, the more effectively we can solve practical organizational problems.

What Is a Theory and Why Are Theories Important?

theory
A set of statements about the interrelationships between concepts that allows us to predict and explain various processes and events.

Formally, we define a **theory** as a set of statements about the interrelationships between concepts that allow us to predict and explain various processes and events. As you might imagine, such statements may be of interest to both practitioners and scientists alike. We're certain that as you read this book you will come to appreciate the valuable role that theories play when it comes to understanding behavior in organizations—and putting that knowledge to practical use.

To demonstrate the value of theory in OB, let's consider an example based on a phenomenon described in more detail in Chapter 6—the effects of task goals on performance. Imagine observing that word processing operators type faster when they are given a specific goal (e.g., 75 words per minute) than when they are told to try to do their best. Imagine also observing that salespeople make more sales when they are given quotas than when they are not given any quotas. By itself, these are useful observations insofar as they allow us to predict what will happen when goals are introduced. In addition, it suggests a way to change conditions so as to improve performance among people in these groups. These two accomplishments—*prediction* and *control*—are major goals of science.

Yet, there's something missing—namely, knowing that specific goals improve performance fails to tell us anything about *why* this is so. What is going on here? After all, this was observed in two different settings and with two different groups of people. Why is it that people are so productive in response to specific goals? This is where theory enters the picture. In contrast to some fields, such as physics and chemistry, in which theories often take the form of mathematical equations, theories in OB generally involve verbal assumptions. For example, in the present case, it might be theorized as follows:

- When people are given specific goals, they know exactly what's expected of them.
- When people know what's expected of them, they are motivated to work hard to find ways to succeed.
- When people work hard to succeed, they perform at high levels.

This simple theory, like all others, consists of two basic elements: *concepts* (in this case goals and motives) and *assertions about how they are related.*

Developing and Testing Theories

In science, the formation of a theory is only the beginning of a sequence of events followed to understand behavior. Once a theory is proposed, it is used to introduce **hypotheses**—logically derived statements that follow from a theory. In our example, it may be hypothesized that specific goals only will improve performance when they are not so difficult that they cannot be attained. Next, such predictions need to be tested in actual research to see if they are confirmed. If research confirms our hypotheses, we can be more confident about the accuracy of the theory. However, if it is not confirmed after several well-conducted studies are done, our confidence in the theory is weakened. When this happens, it's time to revise the theory and to generate new, testable hypotheses from it. As you might imagine, given the complexities of human behavior in organizations, theories are rarely—if ever—fully confirmed. In fact, many of the field's most popular and useful theories are constantly being refined and tested. We have summarized the cyclical nature of the scientific endeavor in Figure A.1.

hypotheses
Logically derived, testable statements about the relationships between variables that follow from a theory.

It probably will come as no surprise to you to learn that the process of theory development and testing we have been describing is very laborious. In view of this, why do scientists bother to constantly fine-tune their theories? The answer lies in the very useful purposes that theories serve. Specifically, theories serve three important functions—organizing, summarizing, and guiding. First, given the complexities of human behavior, theories provide a way of *organizing* large amounts of data into meaningful propositions. In other words, they help us combine information so diverse that it might be difficult to grasp without the help of a theory. Second, theories help us to *summarize* this knowledge by making it possible to make sense out of bits and pieces of information that otherwise would be difficult—if not impossible—to understand. Third, and finally, theories provide an important *guiding* function. That is, they help scientists identify important areas of needed research that would not have been apparent without theories to guide their thinking.

FIGURE A.1

Theory Testing: The Research Process
Once a theory is formulated, research is conducted to test hypotheses derived from it. If these hypotheses are confirmed, confidence in the theory is increased. If these hypotheses are disconfirmed, confidence in the theory is diminished. At this point, the theory either is modified and retested, or it is rejected completely.

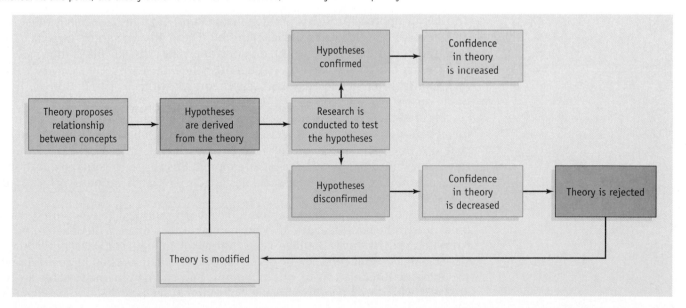

As you read this text you will come across many different theories attempting to explain various aspects of behavior in organizations. When you do, we think you will appreciate the useful organizing, summarizing, and guiding roles theories play—in short, how they help provide meaningful explanations of behavior. In all cases, the usefulness of any theory is based on the extent to which it can be confirmed or disconfirmed. In other words, theories must be *testable*. A theory that cannot be tested serves no real purpose to scientists. Once it's tested, a theory—or, at least part of it—must be confirmed if it is to be considered an accurate account of human behavior. And, of course, that's what the field of OB is all about.

How are theories tested? The answer is: By conducting *research*. Unless we do research, we cannot test theories, and unless we test theories, we are greatly limited in what we can learn about behavior in organizations.[1] This is why research is such a major concern of specialists in OB. So, in order for you to fully appreciate the field of OB, it's critical for you to understand something about the research techniques it uses—that is, how we come to know about the behavior of people at work. As a result, throughout this book, we not only explain *what* is known about OB but also *how* that knowledge was derived. We are confident that the better you understand OB's "tools of the trade," the more you will come to appreciate its value as a field. With this in mind, we now will describe some of the major research techniques used to learn about organizational behavior.

SURVEY RESEARCH: THE CORRELATIONAL METHOD

surveys
Questionnaires in which people are asked to report how they feel about various aspects of themselves, others, their jobs, and organizations.

The most popular approach to conducting research in OB involves giving people questionnaires in which they are asked to report how they feel about various aspects of themselves, other individuals (e.g., coworkers, superiors), their jobs, and/or their organizations. Such questionnaires, also known as **surveys,** make it possible for organizational scientists to delve into a broad range of issues. This research technique is so very popular because it is applicable to studying a wide variety of topics. After all, you can learn a great deal about how people feel by asking them a systematic series of carefully worded questions. Moreover, questionnaires are relatively easy to administer (be it by mail, phone, or in person), and—as we will note shortly—they are readily quantifiable and lend themselves to powerful statistical analyses. These features make survey research a very appealing option to OB scientists. Not surprisingly, we describe quite a few survey studies throughout this text.

Conducting Surveys

The survey approach consists of three major steps. First, the researcher must identify the variables in which he or she is interested. These may be various aspects of people (e.g., their attitudes toward work), organizations (e.g., the pay plans they use), or the environment in general (e.g., how competitive the industry is). They may be suggested from many different sources, such as a theory, previous research, or even hunches based on casual observations.

Second, these variables are measured as precisely as possible. As you might imagine, it isn't always easy to tap precisely into people's feelings about things (especially if they are uncertain about those feelings or reluctant to share them). As a result, researchers must pay a great deal of attention to the way they word the questions they use. For some examples of questions designed to measure various work-related attitudes, see Table A.1.

Finally, after the variables of interest have been identified and measured, scientists must determine how—if at all—they are related to each other. With this in mind, scientists analyze their survey findings using a variety of different statistical procedures.

Scientists conducting survey research typically are interested in determining how variables are interrelated—or, put differently, how changes in one variable are associated with changes in another variable. For example, let's say that a researcher is inter-

TABLE A.1 SURVEY QUESTIONS DESIGNED TO MEASURE WORK ATTITUDES

Items such as these might be used to measure attitudes toward various aspects of work. People completing the survey are asked to circle the number that corresponds to the point along the scale that best reflects their feelings about the attitude in question.

Overall, how fairly are you paid?

Not at all fairly 1 2 3 4 5 6 7 Extremely fairly

Imagine that one of your colleagues needs to stay late to complete an important project. How likely or unlikely would you be to volunteer to help that person, even if you would not receive any special recognition for your efforts?

Not at all likely 1 2 3 4 5 6 7 Extremely likely

How interested are you in quitting your present job?

Not at all interested 1 2 3 4 5 6 7 Extremely interested

ested in learning the relationship between how fairly people believe they are paid and various work-related attitudes, such as their willingness to help their coworkers, and their interest in quitting. Based on various theories and previous research, a researcher may suspect that the more people believe they are unfairly paid, the less likely they will be to help their coworkers and the more likely they will be to desire new jobs. These predictions constitute the researcher's *hypothesis*—which, as we explained earlier, is the untested prediction based on theory that the researcher wishes to investigate. After devising an appropriate questionnaire measuring these variables, the researcher would have to administer it to a large number of people so that the hypothesis can be tested.

Today, the practice of conducting surveys online has become very popular.[2] **Online surveys present questions to people either via e-mail or using a Web site, which they** then complete and return to administrators using the same electronic means. Many employees enjoy taking surveys online because modern software programs have made them highly user friendly, and in some cases, fun to complete (see the samples in Figure A.2). Many employers and researchers also prefer them to paper-and-pencil questionnaires because they are easier to administer and because they also can provide an instant summary and analysis of responses that would have taken many hours to enter into a statistical analysis program by hand.

> **online surveys**
> Questionnaires presented to people either via e-mail or using a Web site, which they then complete and return to administrators using the same electronic means.

This is not to say that online surveys are perfect, by any means. The greatest problem with them is that they cannot always be used because access to online networks is not universal. Thus, any survey results coming from people who complete questionnaires online may not be generalizable to those who either do not have access to computers or who avoid completing online questionnaires because they are uncomfortable working at computers. In short, online surveys should be considered a useful addition to the choices available to researchers interested in administering questionnaires but not yet a replacement for more traditional, low-tech options. Until this turns around, you might want to keep that pencil handy.

Analyzing Survey Results: Using Correlations

Once the data are collected (from either paper-and-pencil surveys or online surveys), the investigator must statistically analyze them so as to compare the results to the hypothesis. Generally speaking, researchers are interested in seeing how the variables of interest are related to each other—that is, if there exists a meaningful **correlation** between them. Variables are correlated to the extent that the level of one variable is associated with the level of another variable.

> **correlation**
> The extent to which two variables are related to each other.

Suppose a researcher obtains results like those shown in the left side of Figure A.2. In this case, the more fairly employees believe they are paid, the more willing they are to

FIGURE A.2

Online Questionnaires: Two Examples
Employee satisfaction questionnaires (left) and self-assessment questionnaires (right) are among the many different kinds of surveys that can be presented via e-mail or on Web pages using the "Form Caster" program by Quask. Companies such as GE Medical Systems, Lockheed Martin, and Procter & Gamble have benefited from using this technique. (*Source:* Used with permission of Qask.com.)

help their coworkers. In other words, the variables are related to each other such that the more one variable increases, the more the other variable also increases. Any variables described in this way are said to have a **positive correlation.**

Now imagine what will be found when the researcher compares the sample's perceptions of pay fairness with their interest in quitting their jobs. If the experimenter's hypothesis is correct, the results will look like those shown on the right side of Figure A.3. In other words, the more people believe their pay is fair, the less interested they are in looking for a new job. Any such case—in which the more one variable increases, the more another decreases—is said to have a **negative correlation.**

OB scientists are not only interested in the direction of the relationship between variables—that is, whether the association is positive or negative—but also in how

positive correlation

A relationship between two variables such that more of one variable is associated with more of the other.

negative correlation

A relationship between two variables such that more of one variable is associated with less of the other.

FIGURE A.3

Positive and Negative Correlations: What They Mean
Positive correlations (left) exist when more of one variable is associated with more of another. Negative correlations (right) exist when more of one variable is associated with less of another.

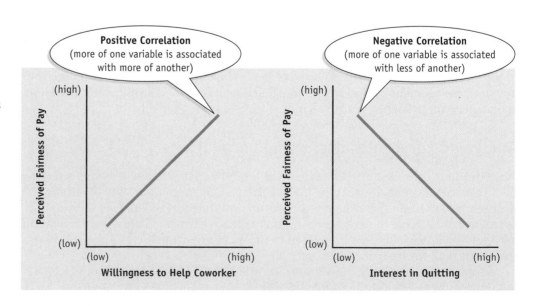

strong that relationship is. To gauge this, researchers rely on a statistic known as the **correlation coefficient.** This is a number between –1.00 and +1.00 used to express the strength of the relationship between the variables studied. The closer this number is to 1.00 (either –1.00 or +1.00), the stronger the relationship is—that is, the more closely the variables are related to each other. However, the closer the correlation coefficient is to 0, the weaker the relationship between the variables—that is, the less strongly they are associated.

So, when interpreting a correlation coefficient, there are two things to keep in mind: its *sign* (in keeping with algebraic traditions, positive correlations are usually expressed without any sign), and its *absolute value* (i.e., the size of the number without respect to its sign). For example, a correlation coefficient of –.92 reflects a much stronger relationship between variables than one of .22. The minus sign simply reveals that the relationship between the variables being described is negative (more of one variable is associated with less of another variable). The fact that the absolute value of this correlation coefficient is greater tells us that the relationship between the variables is stronger.

When variables are strongly correlated, scientists can make more accurate predictions about how they are related to each other. So, using our example of a negative correlation between perceptions of pay fairness and intent to quit, we may expect that in general those who believe they are unfairly paid will be more likely to quit their jobs than those who believe they are fairly paid. If the correlation coefficient were high, say over –.80, we would be more confident that this would occur than if the correlation were low, say under –.20. In fact, as correlation coefficients approach 0, it's impossible to make any accurate predictions whatsoever. In such a case, knowing one variable would not allow us to predict anything about the other. As you might imagine, organizational scientists are extremely interested in discovering the relationships between variables and rely on correlation coefficients to tell them a great deal.

Although the examples we've been using involve the relationship between only two variables at a time, organizational researchers usually are interested in the interrelationships between many different variables at once. For example, an employee's intent to quit may be related to several variables besides the perceived fairness of one's pay—such as satisfaction with the job itself or liking for one's immediate supervisor. Researchers may make predictions using several different variables at once using a technique known as **multiple regression.** Using this approach, researchers may be able to tell the extent to which each of several different variables contributes to predicting the behavior in question. In our example, they would be able to learn the degree to which the several variables studied, together and individually, are related to the intent to quit one's job. Given the complex nature of human behavior on the job and the wide range of variables likely to influence it, it should not be surprising to learn that OB researchers use the multiple regression technique a great deal in their work.

An Important Limitation of Correlations

Despite the fact that the analysis of surveys using correlational techniques such as multiple regression can be so very valuable, conclusions drawn from correlations are limited in a very important way. Namely, *correlations do not reveal anything about causation.* In other words, although correlations tell us about how variables are related to each other, they don't provide any insight into their cause-and-effect relationships.

So, in our example, although we may learn that the less employees feel they are fairly paid the more interested they are in quitting, we cannot tell *why* this is the case. In other words, we cannot tell whether or not employees want to quit *because* they believe they are unfairly paid. Might this be the case? Yes, but it also might be the case that people who believe they are unfairly paid tend to dislike the work they do, and it is this that encourages them to find a new job. Another possibility is that people believe they are unfairly paid because their supervisors are too demanding—and it is this that raises their interest in quitting (see Figure A.4). Our point is simple: Although all these possibilities are reasonable, knowing only that variables are correlated does *not* permit us to

correlation coefficient
A statistical index indicating the nature and extent to which two variables are related to each other.

multiple regression
A statistical technique through which it is possible to determine the extent to which each of several different variables contributes to predicting another variable (typically, where the variable being predicted is the behavior in question).

FIGURE A.4

Correlations: What They *Don't* Reveal About Causation

Even if a strong negative correlation exists between pay fairness and the desire to leave one's job, we cannot tell why this relationship exists. This correlation does *not* show that unfairness causes people to leave. As shown here, there are several possible underlying causes that are not identified by knowledge of the correlation alone.

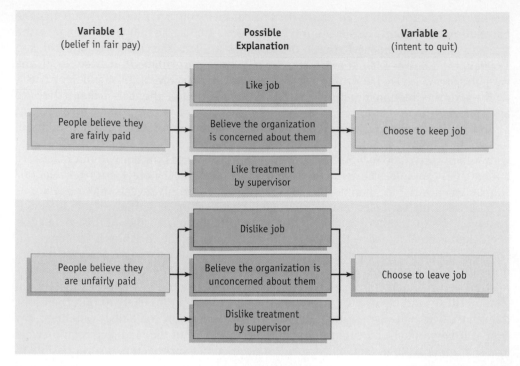

determine what causes what. Because it is important for researchers to establish the causal relationships between the variables they study, OB researchers frequently turn to another technique that *does* permit such conclusions to be drawn—the experiment.

EXPERIMENTAL RESEARCH: THE LOGIC OF CAUSE AND EFFECT

experimental method

A research technique through which it is possible to determine cause-and-effect relationships between the variables of interest—that is, the extent to which one variable causes another.

Because both scientists and practitioners not only want to know the degree to which variables are related but also how much one variable causes another, the **experimental method** also is used in OB. The more we know about the causal connections between variables, the better we can explain the underlying causes of behavior—and this, after all, is one of the major goals of OB.

A Hypothetical Experiment

To illustrate how experiments work, let's consider an example. Suppose we're interested in determining the effects of social density (the number of people per unit of space) on the job performance of clerical employees—that is, the degree to which the crowdedness of working conditions in an office influences how accurately word processing operators do their jobs.

Although this topic might be studied in many different ways, imagine that we do the following. First, we select at random a large group of word processing operators working in a variety of different organizations—the participants in our study. Then we prepare a specially designed office, the setting for the experiment. Throughout the study, we would keep the design of the office and all the working conditions (e.g., temperature, light, and noise levels) identical with one exception—we would systematically vary the number of people working in the office at any given time.

For example, we could have one condition—the "high density" condition—in which 50 people are put into a 500-square-foot room at once (allowing 10 square feet per person). In another condition—the "low density" condition—we could put 5 people into a 500-square-foot room at once (allowing 100 square feet per person). Finally, we can have a "moderate density" condition in which we put 25 people into a 500-square-foot room (allowing 20 square feet per person).

Suppose we have several hundred people participating in the study and that we assign them at random to each of these three conditions. Each word processing operator is then given the same passage of text to type over two hours. After this period, the typists are dismissed, and the researcher counts the number of words accurately typed by each person, noting any possible differences in averages between performance in the various conditions. Suppose we obtain the results summarized in Figure A.5.

Experimental Logic

Let's analyze what was done in this simple hypothetical experiment to help explain the basic elements of the experimental method and its underlying logic. First, recall that we selected participants from the population of interest and assigned them to conditions on a *random* basis. This means that each of the participants had an equal chance of being assigned to any one of the three conditions. This is critical because it is possible that differences between conditions could result from having many very good word processing operators in one condition and many unproductive ones in another. So, to safeguard against this possibility, it is important to assign people to conditions at random. When this is done, we can assume that the effects of any possible differences between people would equalize over conditions.

Thus, by assigning people to conditions at random, we can be assured that there will be just as many fast operators and slow operators in each. As a result, there is no reason to believe that any differences in productivity that may be noted between conditions can be attributed to systematic differences in the skills of the participants. Given "the luck of the draw," such differences can be discounted, thereby enhancing our confidence that differences are solely the result of the social density of the rooms. This is the logic behind random assignment. Although it is not always feasible to use random assignment when conducting experiments in organizations, it is highly desirable whenever possible.

Recall that word processing operators were assigned to conditions that differed with respect to only the variable of interest—in this case, social density. We can say that the experimenter *manipulated* this aspect of the work environment, systematically changing it from condition to condition. A variable altered in this way is called an **independent variable.** An independent variable is a variable that is systematically manipulated by the experimenter so as to determine its effects on the behavior of inter-

independent variable
The variable in an experiment that is systematically manipulated to determine its effects on the behavior of interest.

FIGURE A.5
Example of Simple Experimental Results
In our example, word processing operators are put into rooms that differ with respect to only one variable—social density (i.e., the number of people per unit of space). The hypothetical results summarized here show that people perform best under conditions of lowest density and worst under conditions of highest density.

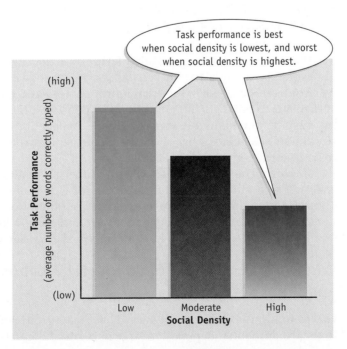

Task performance is best when social density is lowest, and worst when social density is highest.

est. In our example, the independent variable is social density. Specifically, it may be said to have three different *levels*—that is, degrees of the independent variable: high, moderate, and low.

The variable that is measured, the one influenced by the independent variable, is known as the **dependent variable.** A dependent variable is the behavior of interest that is being measured—the behavior that is dependent upon the independent variable. In this case, the dependent variable is word processing performance (measured in terms of the quantity of words accurately typed). Besides studying this, we could have studied other dependent variables, such as satisfaction with the work, or the perceived level of stress encountered. In fact, it would be quite likely for OB researchers to study several dependent variables in one experiment.

By the same token, researchers also frequently consider the effects of several different independent variables in a given experiment. The matter of which particular independent variables and dependent variables are being studied is one of the most important questions researchers have to consider. Often, they base these decisions on suggestions from previous research (other experiments suggesting that certain variables are important) and existing theory (conceptualizations suggesting that certain variables may be important).

Generally speaking, the basic logic behind the experimental method is quite simple. In fact, it involves only two major steps. First, some variable of interest (the independent variable) must be systematically varied. Second, the effects, if any, of such variations must be measured. The underlying idea is that if the independent variable does indeed influence behavior, then people exposed to different amounts of it should behave differently. In our example, we can be certain that social density caused differences in processing performance because when all other factors were held constant, different amounts of density led to different levels of performance. Although our experiment is fabricated, it follows the same basic logic of all experiments—namely, it is designed to reveal the effects of the independent variables on the dependent variables. And, when independent variables and dependent variables are chosen wisely, experiments can reveal a great deal about organizational behavior.

Drawing Valid Conclusions from Experiments

For the conclusions of experiments to be valid it is critical for them to hold constant all factors other than the independent variable. Then, if there are differences in the dependent variable, we can assume that they are the result of the effects of the independent variable. By assigning participants to conditions at random we already took an important step to ensure that one key factor—differences in the ability levels of the participants—would be equalized.

But, as you might imagine, other factors also may affect the results. For example, it also would be essential to hold constant environmental conditions that might influence word processing speed. In this case, more people would generate more heat, so to make sure that the results are influenced only by density—and not by heat—it would be necessary to air condition the work room so as to keep it the same temperature under all conditions at all times. This, of course, would generate noise, which further would have to be taken into account.

If you think about it, our simple experiment is really not that simple at all—especially if it is conducted with all the care needed to permit valid conclusions to be drawn. Thus, experiments require all experimental conditions to be kept identical with respect to all variables except the independent variable so that its effects can be determined unambiguously. As you might imagine, this is often easier said than done.

Where Are Experiments Conducted? Laboratory and Field Settings

How simple it is to control the effects of extraneous variables (i.e., factors not of interest to the experimenter) depends, in large part, on where the experiment is conducted. In

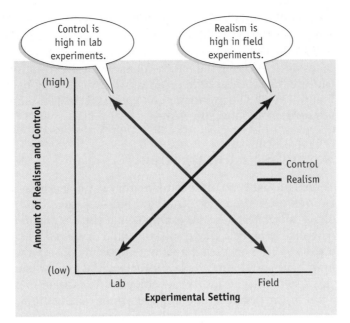

Trade-Offs Between Lab and Field Experiments
Researchers in OB may conduct experiments in laboratory or field settings, each of which has advantages and disadvantages. Generally, the lab offers more control but less realism, whereas the field offers less control but more realism.

the field of OB, there are generally two options available: Experiments can be conducted in naturalistic organizational settings referred to as the *field* or in settings specially created for the study itself, referred to as the *laboratory* (or *lab* for short). As summarized in Figure A.6, there are trade-offs involved with conducting research in each setting.

The study in our example was a lab experiment. It was conducted in carefully controlled conditions specially created for the research. The great amount of control possible in such settings improves the chances of creating the conditions needed to allow valid conclusions to be drawn from experiments. At the same time, however, lab studies suffer from a lack of realism. Although the working conditions can be controlled carefully, they may be relatively unrealistic, not carefully simulating the conditions found in actual organizations. As a result, it may be difficult to generalize the findings of lab studies to settings outside the lab, such as the workplace.

However, if we conducted our study in actual organizations, there would be many unknowns, many uncontrollable factors at work. To conduct such a study, we would have to distinguish between those who worked in offices differing with respect to social density and later compare people's performance. If we did this, we would be sure that the conditions studied were realistic. However, there would be so little control over the setting that many different factors could be operating. For example, because people would not be assigned to conditions at random, it might be the case that people work in those settings they most desire. Furthermore, there would be no control over such factors as distractions and differences in environmental conditions (e.g., noise and temperature).

In short, field experiments, although strong in realism, are weak with respect to the level of control they provide. By contrast, lab experiments permit a great deal of control but tend to be unrealistic. In view of these complementary strengths and weaknesses, it should be clear that experiments should be conducted in *both* types of settings. As researchers do so, our confidence can be increased that valid conclusions will be drawn about behavior in organizations.

QUALITATIVE RESEARCH METHODS

In contrast to the highly empirical approaches to research we have been describing thus far, we also should note that OB researchers sometimes use a less empirical approach. After all, probably the most obvious ways to learn about behavior in organizations is to observe it firsthand and to describe it after it occurs. Organizational scientists have a long tradition of studying behavior using these nonempirical, descriptive techniques, relying on what is known as **qualitative research.**[3] The qualitative approach to research relies on preserving the natural qualities of the situation being studied, attempting to capture the richness of the context while disturbing naturalistic conditions only minimally, if at all. The two major qualitative methods used by OB scientists are *naturalistic observation* and the *case method*.

Naturalistic Observation

There's probably no more fundamental way of learning about how people act in organizations than simply to observe them—a research technique known as **naturalistic observation.** Suppose, for example, that you wanted to learn how employees behave in response to layoffs. One thing you could do would be to visit an organization in which layoffs will be occurring and systematically observe what the employees do and say both before and after the layoffs occur. Making comparisons of this type may provide very useful insights into what's going on. As a variation of this technique, you could take a job in the organization and make your observations as an insider actually working there—giving you a perspective you might not otherwise gain. This technique, often used by anthropologists, is known as **participant observation.**

It's not too difficult to think of the advantages and disadvantages of observational research. It's major advantage is that it can be used without disrupting normal routines, allowing behavior to be studied in its natural state. Moreover, almost anyone—including people already working in the host organization—can be trained to use it.

Observational research also suffers from several important limitations. First, the potential for subjectivity among researchers is considerable. Even among the most diligent of researchers, it's inevitable that different people will make different observations of the same events. Second, being involved in the daily functioning of an organization will make it difficult for observers to be impartial. Researchers interpreting organizational events may be subject to bias due to their feelings about the people involved. Finally, because most of what goes on in an organization is fairly dull and routine, it's very easy for researchers to place a great deal of emphasis on unusual or unexpected events, possibly leading to inaccurate conclusions.

Given these limitations, most OB scientists consider observational research to be more useful as a starting point for providing basic insight into behavior than as a tool for acquiring definitive knowledge about behavior.

The Case Method

Suppose that we conducted our hypothetical study of reactions to layoffs differently. Instead of observing behavior directly, we might fully describe the company's history leading up to the event and some statistics summarizing its aftermath (e.g., how long people were unemployed, how the company was restructured after downsizing, and the like). We might even include some interviews with people affected by the event and quote them directly. The approach we are describing here is known as the **case method.** More often than not, the rationale behind the case method is *not* to teach us about a specific organization per se but to learn what happened in that organization as a means of providing cues as to what may be going on in other organizations.

The case method is similar to naturalistic observation in that it relies on descriptive accounts of events. However, it is different in that it often involves using post hoc accounts of events from those involved as opposed to firsthand observations by scientists.

As you might imagine, a great deal can be learned by detailed accounts of events in organizations summarized in the form of written cases. Especially when these cases are supplemented by careful interviews (in which case the method would be considered quantitative rather than qualitative in nature) cases can paint a particularly detailed picture of events as they unfolded in a particular organization.

qualitative research
A nonempirical type of research that relies on preserving the natural qualities of the situation being studied.

naturalistic observation
A qualitative research technique in which people are systematically observed in situations of interest to the researcher.

participant observation
A qualitative research technique in which people systematically make observations of what goes on in a setting by becoming an insider, part of that setting itself.

case method
A research technique in which a particular organization is thoroughly described and analyzed for purposes of understanding what went on in that setting.

Of course, to the extent that the organization studied is unique, it may be not be possible to generalize what is learned to other organizations. To get around this limitation, some researchers have recommended that multiple, as opposed to single, cases should be used to test theories.[4] Another problem with the case method—a limitation it shares with naturalistic observation—is that the potential for bias is relatively high. As a result, many scientists believe that although the case method may serve as a valuable source of hypotheses about behavior on the job, testing those hypotheses requires more rigorous research methods.[5] As such, it is not surprising that questionnaires and experiments are used more frequently than case studies in today's scientifically-oriented field of OB.

CHAPTER 1

Preview Case Sources

Griffith, V. (2000 third quarter). The people factor in post-merger integration. *Strategy & Business*, issue 20, pp. 82–90. Koberstein, W. (2000). The mergers, miracles, madness, or mahem? *Pharmaceutical Executive, 20*(3), 48–68. Langreth, R. (1999, December 20). Monsanto merger is just latest of bold moves by Pharmacia CEO, *Wall Street Journal*, pp. 1, 3. Miner, J. B. (2002). *Organizational behavior*. New York: Oxford University Press.

Chapter Notes

1. Greenberg, J. (Ed.), (2003). *Organizational behavior: The state of the science* (second edition). Mahwah, NJ: Erlbaum.

2. Risher, H. (1999). *Aligning pay and results*. New York: AMACOM.

3. Judge, T. A., & Church, A. H. (2000). Job satisfaction: Research and practice. In C. A. Cooper & E. A. Locke (Eds.), *Industrial and organizational psychology: Linking theory to practice* (pp. 166–198). Malden, MA: Blackwell.

4. Hackman, J. R., Wageman, R., Ruddy, T. M., & Ray, C. L. (2000). Team effectiveness in theory and in practice. In C. A. Cooper & E. A. Locke (Eds.), *Industrial and organizational psychology: Linking theory to practice* (pp. 109–129). Malden, MA: Blackwell.

5. Greenberg, J. (2001). Promote procedural justice to enhance acceptance of work outcomes. In E. A. Locke (Ed.), *A handbook of principles of organizational behavior*. (pp. 181–195). Malden, MA: Blackwell.

6. Benavides, F. G., Benach, J., Diez-Roux, A. V., & Roman, C. (2000). How do types of employment relate to health indicators? Findings from the Second European Survey on working conditions. *Journal of Epidemiology & Community Health, 54,* 494–501. Roberts, S. (2000, June 26). Integrating EAPs, work/life programs holds advantages. *Business Insurance, 34*(36), 3, 18–19. Vahtera, J., Kivimaeki, M., Pentti, J., & Theorell, T. (2000). Effect of change on the psychosocial work environment on sickness absence: A seven year follow up of initially healthy employees. *Journal of Epidemiology and Community Health, 54,* 484–493.

7. The Corporate Research Foundation UK. (2000). *Britain's best employers: A guide to the 100 most attractive companies to work for.* New York: McGraw-Hill.

8. Bollinger, D. (1996). *Aiming higher: 25 stories of how companies prosper by combining sound management and social vision.* New York: AMACOM.

9. Katz, D., & Kahn, R. (1978). *The social psychology of organizations.* New York: Wiley.

10. Warner, M. (1994). Organizational behavior revisited. *Human Relations, 47,* 1151–1166.

11. Kennedy, C. (1991). *Instant management.* New York: William Morrow and Company.

12. Drucker, P. F. (1974). *Management: Tasks, responsibilities, practices.* New York: Harper & Row.

13. Mayo, E. (1933). *The human problems of an industrial civilization.* London: Macmillan.

14. Crainer, S. (2000). *The management century.* San Francisco: Jossey-Bass.

15. Roethlisberger, F. J., & Dickson, W. J. (1939). *Management and the worker.* Cambridge, MA: Harvard University Press.

16. Weber, M. (1921). *Theory of social and economic organization* (A. M. Henderson & T. Parsons, Trans.), London: Oxford University Press.

17. Colvin, G. (2000, March 6). Managing in the info era. *Fortune,* pp. F6–F9 (quote, p. F9).

18. Gardner, B., & Moore, G. (1945). *Human relations in industry.* Homewood, IL: Irwin.

19. See Note 18.

20. Gordon, R. A., & Howell, J. E. (1959). *Higher education for business.* New York: Columbia University Press.

21. See Note 17.

22. Collins, J. (2000, August 28). Don't rewrite the rules of the road. *BusinessWeek,* pp. 206–208.

23. Cascio, W. E. (1995). Whither industrial and organizational in a changing world of work? *American Psychologist, 50,* 928–939 (quote, p. 928).

24. Lodge, G. C. (1995). *Managing globalization in the age of interdependence.* San Francisco: Pfeifer.

25. Solomon, K. (2001, February). Iceland breaks adoption record. *M-business,* pp. 44–46.

26. Ronen, S. (1986). *Comparative multinational management.* New York: Wiley.

27. Ogbonna, E. (1993). Managing organizational culture: Fantasy or reality? *Human Resource Management Journal, 3*(2), 42–54.

28. DeCieri, H., & Dowling, P. J. (1995). Cross-cultural issues in organizational behavior. In C. L. Cooper & D. M. Rousseau (Eds.), *Trends in organizational behavior* (Vol. 2, pp. 127–145). New York: John Wiley & Sons.

29. Hesketh, B., & Bochner, S. (1994). Technological change in a multicultural context: Implications for training and career planning. In H. C. Triandis, M. D. Dunnette, & L. Hough (Eds.), *Handbook of industrial and organizational psychology* (Vol. 4, pp. 190–240). Palo Alto, CA: Consulting Psychologists Press.

30. Janssens, M. (1995). Intercultural interaction: A burden on international managers? *Journal of Organizational Behavior, 16,* 155–167.

31. See Note 30.

32. Lerman, R. I., & Schmidt, S. R. (2002). *An overview of economic, social, and demographic trends affecting the labor market.* Report to the Urban Institute for U.S. Department of Labor (at www.dol.gov).

33. See Note 32.

34. Mason, J. C. (1993, July). Working in the family way. *HRMagazine,* pp. 25–28.

35. Lewis, S. C. (2002). *Elder care in occupational therapy.* Thorofare, NJ: Slack. Shellenbarger, S. (1994, February 16). The aging of America is making "elder care" a big workplace issue. *Wall Street Journal,* p. A1.

36. Fenn, D. (1993, July) Bottoms up. *Inc.,* pp. 57–60.

37. Martinez, M. N. (1993). Family support makes business sense. *HRMagazine,* pp. 38–43.

38. Meier, L., & Meagher, L. (1993, September). Teaming up to manage. *Working Woman,* pp. 31–32, 108.

39. Mason, J. C. (1993, July). Working in the family way. *HRMagazine,* pp. 25–28.

40. See Note 39.

41. See Note 39.

42. See Note 38.

43. Zachary, G. P. (2003). *The diversity advantage.* Boulder, CO: Westview Press. Carnevale, A. P., & Stone, S. C. (1995). *The American mosaic: An in-depth report on the future of diversity at work.* New York: McGraw-Hill.

44. See Note 43.

45. It all depends where you sit. (2000, August 14). *BusinessWeek,* Frontier Section, p. F8.

46. Zuboff, S. (1988). *In the age of the smart machine.* New York: Basic Books.

47. Bridges, W. (1994). *Job shift: How to prosper in a workplace without jobs.* Reading, MA: Addison-Wesley.

48. See Note 47.

49. Nyran, F. J. (2002). *Truth and trust: The first two victims of downsizing.* Athabasca, AB, Canada: Athabasca University Press. Tomasko, R. M. (1990). *Downsizing: Reshaping the corporation for the future.* New York: AMACOM.

50. Hendricks, C. F. (1992). *The rightsizing remedy.* Homewood, IL: Business One Irwin.

51. Displaced workers summary. (2002, January). Bureau of Labor Statistics (at www.bls.gov/news.release/disp.nr0htm).

52. McGinn, D., & Naughton, K. (2001, February 5). How safe is your job? *Newsweek,* pp. 36–43.

53. Tomasko, R. M. (1993). *Rethinking the corporation,* New York: AMACOM.

54. Bettis, R. A., Bradley, S. P., & Hamel, G. (1992). Outsourcing and industrial decline. *Academy of Management Review, 6,* 7–22.

55. Haapaniemi, P. (1993, Winter). Taking care of business. *Solutions,* pp. 6–8, 10–13.

56. See Note 55.

57. Stewart, T. A. (1993, December 13). Welcome to the revolution. *Fortune,* pp. 66–68, 70, 72, 76, 78.

58. Byrne, J. A., Brandt, R., & Port, O. (1993, February 8). The virtual corporation: The company of the future will be the ultimate in adaptability. *BusinessWeek,* pp. 98–102.

59. Davidow, W. H., & Malone, M. S. (1992). *The virtual corporation.* New York: HarperBusiness.

60. See Note 59 (quote, p. 99).

61. See Note 59.

62. International Telework Association and Council. (2001, October 23). News release: Number of teleworkers increases by 17 percent. www.telecommute.org/twa/twa2001/newsrelease.htm.

63. Zbar, J. D. (2002). *Teleworking and telecommuting.* Deerfield Beach, FL: Made E-Z Products. Kugelmass, J. (1995). *Telecommuting: A manager's guide to flexible work arrangements.* New York: Lexington Books.

64. DuBrin, A. J. (1994). *Contemporary applied management: Skills for managers* (4th ed.). Burr Ridge, IL: Irwin.

65. Mariani, M. (2000, Fall). Telecommuters. *Occupational Outlook Quarterly,* pp. 10–17.

66. Cohen, A. R., & Gadon, H. (1980). *Alternative work schedules.* Reading, MA: Addison-Wesley.

67. Galen, M., Palmer, A. T., Cuneo, A., & Maremont, M. (1993, June 28). Work & family. *BusinessWeek,* pp. 80–84, 86, 88.

68. Fierman, J. (1994, January 24). The contingency workforce. *Fortune,* pp. 30–34, 36.

69. Bureau of Labor Statistics (2001, May 24). Employed contingent and noncontingent workers by occupation and industry. www.bls.gov/news.release/conemp.t04.htm.

70. Aley, J. (1995, September 18). Where the jobs are. *Fortune,* pp. 53–54, 56.

71. Raeburn, P. (2000, March 6). The perils of part-time for professionals. *BusinessWeek,* p. 125.

72. See Note 71.

73. Olmsted, B., & Smith, S. (1994). *Creating a flexible workplace* (2nd ed.). New York: AMACOM.

74. Meier, L., & Meagher, L. (1993, September). Teaming up to manage. *Working Woman,* pp. 31–32, 108.

75. See Note 74.

76. Walton, M. (1990). *The Demming management method at work.* New York: Perigee.

77. Hart, C. W. L. & Bogan, C. E. (1992). *The Baldrige.* New York: McGraw-Hill.

78. Hodgetts, R. M. (1993). *Blueprints for continuous improvement: Lessons from the Baldrige winners.* New York: AMACOM.

79. Boyett, J. H., Schwartz, S., Osterwise, L., & Bauer, R. (1993). *The quality journey: How winning the Baldrige sparked the remaking of IBM.* New York: Dutton.

80. Zellner, W., & Forest, S. A. (2001, December 17). The fall of Enron. *BusinessWeek,* pp. 30–34, 36.

81. DeGeorge, R. T. (2003). *The ethics of information technology and business.* Oxford, England: Blackwell. Ferrell, O. C., & Fraedrich, J. (1994). *Business ethics: Ethical decision making and cases* (2nd ed.). Boston: Houghton Mifflin.

82. Byrnes, N., Byrne, J. A., Edwards, C., Lee, L., Holmes, S., & Muller, J. (2002, September 23). The good CEO. *BusinessWeek,* pp. 80–86, 88. Henderson, V. E. (1992). *What's ethical in business?* New York: McGraw-Hill.

83. MAALA Business for Social Responsibility. (2002). Corporate social responsibility. Tel Aviv, Israel: Author (also at www.maala.com.). Verschoor, C. C. (1998). A study of the link between a corporation's financial performance and its commitment to ethics. *Journal of Business Ethics, 17,* 1509–1516. Embley, L. L. (1993). *Doing well while doing good.* Englewood Cliffs, NJ: Prentice Hall.

84. Singer, A. (2002). Coors Brewing Company's ethics code training. *Ethikos,16*(2), 4–5,11. Manley, W. W., II. (1991). *Executive's handbook of model business conduct codes.* Englewood Cliffs, NJ: Prentice Hall.

85. Treviño, L. K., & Nelson, K. A. (1999). *Managing business ethics* (2nd ed.). New York: Wiley.

86. DuBrin, A. J. (1994). *Contemporary applied management: Skills for managers* (4th ed.). Burr Ridge, IL: Irwin.

Case in Point Source

Yates, R. E. (1998). *The Kikkoman chronicles.* New York: McGraw-Hill.

CHAPTER 2

Preview Case Sources

Balu, R. (1999, December). Whirlpool gets real with customers. *Fast Company,* pp. 7, 76.

Chapter Notes

1. Lee, Y., McCauley, C. R., & Draguns, J. (1998). *Personality and person perception across cultures.* Mahwah, NJ: Lawrence Erlbaum Associates. Kenny, D. A. (1994). *Interpersonal perception.* New York: Guilford.

2. Ashforth, B. E., & Mael, F. (1989). Social identity theory and the organization. *Academy of Management Review, 14,* 20–29.

3. La Tendresse, D. (2000). Social identity and intergroup relations within the hospital. *Journal of Social Distress and the Homeless, 9,* 51–69.

4. Cialdini, R. B., Borden, R. J., Thorne, A., Walker, M. R., Freeman, S., & Sloan, L. R. (1999). Basking in reflected glory: Three (football) field studies. In R. F. Baumeister (Ed.), *The self in social psychology* (pp. 436–445). Philadelphia: Psychology Press/Talor & Francis.

5. Weiner, B. (1995). *Judgments of responsibility.* New York: Guilford.

6. Jones, E. E., & McGillis, D. (1976). Correspondent inferences and the attribution cube: A comparative reappraisal. In J. H. Harvey, W. J. Ickes, & R. F. Kidd (Eds.), *New directions in attribution research* (Vol. 1, pp. 389–420). Hillsdale, NJ: Lawrence Erlbaum Associates.

7. Kelley, H. H. (1972). Attribution in social interaction (pp. 1–26). In E. E. Jones, D. E. Kanous, H. H. Kelley, R. E. Nisbett, S. Valins, & B. Weiner (Eds.), *Attribution: Perceiving the causes of behavior.* Morristown, NJ: General Learning Press.

8. Srull, T. K., & Wyer, R. S. (1988). *Advances in social cognition.* Hillsdale, NJ: Lawrence Erlbaum Associates.

9. Extra pounds, slimmer wages. (2001, January 15). *BusinessWeek,* p. 28.

10. Burger, J. M. (1991). Changes in attribution errors over time: The ephemeral fundamental attribution error. *Social Cognition, 9,* 182–193.

11. Murphy, K. R., Jako, R. A., & Anhalt, R. L. (1993). Nature and consequences of halo error: A critical analysis. *Journal of Applied Psychology, 78,* 218–225.

12. Pulakos, E. D., & Wexley, K. N. (1983). The relationship among perceptual similarity, sex, and performance ratings in manager–subordinate dyads. *Academy of Management Journal, 26,* 129–139.

13. Turban, D. B., & Jones, A. P. (1988). Supervisor–subordinate similarity: Types, effects, and mechanisms. *Journal of Applied Psychology, 73,* 228–234.

14. Dearborn, D. C., & Simon, H. A. (1958). Selective perception: A note on the departmental identification of executives. *Sociometry, 21,* 140–144.

15. Waller, M. J., Huber, G. P., & Glick, W. H. (1995). Functional background as a determinant of executives' selective perception. *Academy of Management Journal, 38,* 943–974.

16. Dougherty, T. W., Turban, D. B., & Callender, J. C. (1994). Confirming first impressions in the employment interview: A field study of interviewer behavior. *Journal of Applied Psychology, 79,* 659–665.

17. Eden, D. (2003). Self-fulfilling prophecies in organizations. In J. Greenberg (Ed.), *Organizational behavior: The state of the science* (2nd ed.). Mahwah, NJ: Lawrence Erlbaum Associates. Eden, D., & Shani, A. B. (1982). Pygmalion goes to boot camp: Expectancy, leadership, and trainee per-

formance. *Journal of Applied Psychology, 67,* 194–199.

18. Oz, S., & Eden, D. (1994). Restraining the Golem: Boosting performance by changing the interpretation of low scores. *Journal of Applied Psychology, 79,* 744–754.

19. Davidson, O. B., & Eden, D. (2000). Remedial self-fulfilling prophecy: Two field experiments to prevent Golem effects among disadvantaged women. *Journal of Applied Psychology, 85,* 386–398.

20. Eden, D. (1997). Leadership and expectations: Pygmalion effects and other self-fulfilling prophecies in organizations. In R. Vecchio (Ed.), *Leadership: Understanding the dynamics of power and influence in organizations* (pp. 177–193). Notre Dame, IN: University of Notre Dame Press.

21. Bethune, G. (1999). *From worst to first: Behind the scenes of Continental's remarkable comeback.* New York: John Wiley & Sons.

22. Mohrman, A. M., Jr., Resnick-West, S. M., & Lawler, E. E., III. (1989). *Designing performance appraisal systems.* San Francisco: Jossey-Bass.

23. Ilgen, D. R., Major, D. A., & Tower, S. L. (1994). The cognitive revolution in organizational behavior (pp. 1–22). In J. Greenberg (Ed.), *Organizational behavior: The state of the science.* Hillsdale, NJ: Lawrence Erlbaum Associates.

24. Hogan, E. A. (1987). Effects of prior expectations on performance ratings: A longitudinal study. *Academy of Management Journal, 30,* 354–368.

25. Wayne, S. J., & Liden, R. C. (1995). Effects of impression management on performance ratings: A longitudinal study. *Academy of Management Journal, 38,* 232–260.

26. Harris, P. R., & Moran, R. T. (1991). *Managing cultural differences* (3rd ed.). Houston: Gulf Publishing.

27. Lewis, R. D. (2000). *When cultures collide.* Naperville, CA: Nicholas Brealey.

28. Morrison, T., Conaway, W. A., & Douress, J. J. (2001). *Dun & Bradstreet's guide to doing business around the world.* Paramus, NJ: Prentice Hall.

29. Hodgson, J. D., Sano, Y., & Graham, J. L. (2001). *Doing business with the new Japan.* Lanham, MD: Rowman & Littlefield.

30. Rosenfeld, P., Giacalone, R. A., & Riordan, C. A. (2002). *Impression management: Building and enhancing reputations at work.* London: Thompson Learning.

31. Giacalone, R. A., & Rosenfeld, P. (1989). *Impression management in the organization.* Hillsdale, NJ: Lawrence Erlbaum Associates.

32. Stevens, C. K., & Kristof, A. L. (1995). Making the right impression: A field study of applicant impression management during job interviews. *Journal of Applied Psychology, 80,* 587–606.

33. Garbett, T. (1988). *How to build a corporation's identity and project its image.* Lexington, MA: Lexington Books.

34. Gatewood, R. D., Gowan, M. A., & Lautenschlager, G. J. (1993). Corporate image, recruitment image, and initial job choice decisions. *Academy of Management Journal, 36,* 414–427.

35. America's most admired companies. (2002, February 20). *Fortune,* Internet site: www.fortune.com.

36. Bongiorno, L. (1995, April 10). The duller the better: For 1994's annual reports, modesty is a virtue. *BusinessWeek,* p. 44.

37. Wick, C. W., & Leon, L. S. (1993). *The learning edge: How smart managers and smart companies stay ahead.* New York: McGraw-Hill.

38. Atkinson, R. C., Herrnstein, R. J., Lindzey, G., & Luce, R. D. (Eds.). (1988). *Steven's handbook of experimental psychology* (2nd ed.) (Vol. 1, pp. 218–266). New York: Wiley.

39. Skinner, B. F. (1969). *Contingencies of reinforcement.* New York: Appleton-Century-Crofts.

40. Scott, W. E., & Podsakoff, P. M. (1985). *Behavioral principles in the practice of management.* New York: Wiley.

41. Bandura, A. (1986). *Social foundations of thought and action.* Englewood Cliffs, NJ: Prentice Hall.

42. Harrison, J. K. (1992). Individual and combined effects of behavior modeling and the cultural assimilator in cross-cultural management training. *Journal of Applied Psychology, 77,* 962–972.

43. Goldstein, I. L. (1991). Training in work organizations. In M. D. Dunnette & L. M. Hough (Eds.), *Handbook of industrial and organizational psychology* (2nd ed.) (Vol. 2, pp. 507–620). Palo Alto, CA: Consulting Psychologists Press.

44. Schnake, M. E. (1986). Vicarious punishment in a work setting. *Journal of Applied Psychology, 71,* 343–345.

45. Lake, D. (2000, October). On-the-Web training. *Grok,* p. 128.

46. Del Valle, C. (1993, April 26). From high schools to high skills. *BusinessWeek,* pp. 110, 112.

47. Francesco, A. M., & Gold, B. A. (1998). *International organizational behavior.* Upper Saddle River, NJ: Prentice Hall.

48. Gist, M. E., Stevens, C. K., & Bavetta, A. G. (1991). Effects of self-efficacy and post-training intervention on the acquisition and maintenance of complex interpersonal skills. *Personnel Psychology, 44,* 837–861.

49. O'Reilly, B. (1993, April 5). How execs learn now. *Fortune,* pp. 52–54, 58.

50. Jarvis, P. (2000). *Universities, corporate universities, and the higher learning industries.* London: Kogan Page. Meister, J. C. (1998). *Corporate universities.* New York: McGraw-Hill.

51. Corporate Alma Maters (2000, November–December). *Across the Board,* p. 5.

52. See Note 45.

53. Rendon, J. (2000, October). Learning potential. *Grok,* pp. 58–60.

54. LeBeau, C. (2000, October). The e-training evolution. *Grok,* pp. 128–134.

55. See Note 54 (quote, p. 130).

56. Muoio, A. (2000, October). Cisco's quick study. *Fast Company,* pp. 287–290, 292, 294–295.

57. Argyris, C. (1991, May–June). Teaching smart people how to learn. *Harvard Business Review, 69*(3), 99–109.

58. Driskell, J. E., Cooper, C., & Moran, A. (1994). Does mental practice enhance performance? *Journal of Applied Psychology, 79,* 481–492.

59. Tracey, B. J., Tannenbaum, S. I., & Kavanaugh, M. J. (1995). Applying trained skills on the job: The importance of the work environment. *Journal of Applied Psychology, 80,* 239–252.

60. Tannenbaum, S. I., & Yukl, G. A. (1992). Training and development in work organizations. *Annual Review of Psychology, 43,* 399–441.

61. Hoffman, R. (1995, April). Ten reasons you should be using 360-feedback. *HRMagazine,* pp. 82–85.

62. Edwards, M. R., & Ewen, A. J. (1996). *360° feedback: The powerful new model for employee assessment and performance improvement.* New York: AMACOM.

63. Tornow, W. W., & London, M. (1998). *Maximizing the value of 360-degree feedback.* San Francisco: Jossey-Bass.

64. Lepsinger, R., & Lucia, A. D. (1997). *The art and science of 360-degree feedback.* San Francisco: Jossey-Bass.

65. Flannery, T. P., Hofrichter, D. A., & Platten, P. E. (1996). *People, performance, and pay.* New York: Free Press.

66. Hills, F., Bergmann, T., & Scarpello, V. (1994). *Compensation decision making.* New York: Dryden.

67. Denton, D. K. (1992, September). Multi-skilled teams replace old work systems. *HRMagazine,* pp. 55–56.

68. Gross, S. E. (1995). *Compensation for teams.* New York: AMACOM.

69. Gross, S. E. (1996, November–December). When jobs become team roles, what do you pay for? *Compensation and Benefits Review,* pp. 48–51.

70. Novak, C. J. (1997, April). Proceed with caution when paying teams. *HRMagazine,* pp. 73–78.

71. Sulzer-Azaroff, B. (2000). Of eagles and worms: changing behavior in a complex world. *Journal of Organizational Behavior Management, 20,* 139–164. Miller, L. (1978). *Behavior management.* New York: Wiley.

72. Frederiksen, L. W. (1982). *Handbook of organizational behavior management.* New York: Wiley.

73. Beyer, J., & Trice, H. M. (1984). A field study of the use and perceived effects of discipline in controlling work performance. *Academy of Management Journal, 27,* 743–754.

74. Trahan, W. A., & Steiner, D. D. (1994). Factors affecting supervisors' use of disciplinary actions following poor performance. *Journal of Organizational Behavior, 15,* 129–139.

75. Oberle, R. J. (1978). Administering disciplinary actions, *Personnel Journal, 18*(3), 30–33.

76. Arvey, R. D., & Jones, A. P. (1985). The use of discipline in organizational settings: A framework for future research. In L. L. Cummings & B. M. Staw (Eds.), *Research in organizational behavior* (Vol. 7, pp. 367–408). Greenwich, CT: JAI Press.

77. Kiechell, W., III. (1990, May 7). How to discipline in the modern age. *Fortune,* pp. 179–180 (quote, p. 180).

78. Arvey, R. E., & Icancevich, J. M. (1980). Punishment in organizations: A review, propositions, and research suggestions. *Academy of Management Review, 5,* 123–132.

79. Gross, N. (2001, August 28). Mining a company's mother lode of talent. *BusinessWeek*, pp. 135, 137. Wah, L. (1999, April). Behind the buzz. *Management Review*, pp. 17–26.

80. McCune, J. C. (1999, April). Thirst for knowledge. *Management Review*, pp. 10–12.

81. Ewing, J. (2001, March 19). Sharing the wealth. *BusinessWeek e.biz*, pp. EB 36–38, 40.

82. Pfeffer, J., & Sutton, R. I. (2000). *The knowing–doing gap: How smart companies turn knowledge into action*. Boston: Harvard Business School Press.

Case in Point Sources

Safeway workers frowning upon service-with-a-smile policy (1998, September 3). *Columbus Dispatch*, p. C1. Kornheiser, T. (1998, September 13). Unsafe way? *Washington Post*, p. F1.

CHAPTER 3

Preview Case Sources

Sharp, R. (2001, June 4). The life of the party. *BusinessWeek e.biz*. pp. EB29–EB32.

Chapter Notes

1. Judge, T. A., Bono, J. E., Iles, R., & Gerhardt, M. W. (2002). Personality and leadership: A qualitative and quantitative review. *Journal of Applied Psychology, 87*, 765–780. Carver, C. S., & Scheier, M. F. (1992). *Perspectives on personality* (2nd ed.). Boston: Allyn & Bacon.

2. Steel, R. P., & Rentsch, J. R. (1997). The dispositional model of job attitudes revisited: Findings of a 10-year study. *Journal of Applied Psychology, 82*, 873–879.

3. Mischel, W. (1985, August). *Personality: Lost or found? Identifying when individual differences make a difference*. Paper presented at the meeting of the American Psychological Association, Los Angeles.

4. George, J. M., & Zhou, J. (2001). When openness to experience and conscientiousness are related to creative behavior: An interactional approach. *Journal of Applied Psychology, 86*, 513–524.

5. Osipow, S. H. (1990). Convergence in theories of career choice and development: Review and prospect. *Journal of Vocational Behavior, 36*, 122–131.

6. Caldwell, D. F., & O'Reilly, C. A., III (1990). Measuring person–job fit with a profile-comparison process. *Journal of Applied Psychology, 75*, 648–657.

7. Kanfer, R. (1992). Work motivation: New directions in theory and research. In C. L. Cooper & I. T. Robsertson (Eds.), *International review of industrial and organizational psychology* (Vol. 7, pp. 1–53). New York: Wiley.

8. Allport, G. W., & Odbert, H. S. (1936). Trait names: A psycholexical study. *Psychological Monographs, 47*, 211–214.

9. Costa, P. T., & McCrae, R. R. (1992). *The NEO-PI Personality Inventory*. Odessa, FL: Psychological Assessment Resources.

10. Salgado, J. F. (1997). The five-factor model of personality and job performance in the European community. *Journal of Applied Psychology, 82*, 30–43.

11. Hurtz, G. M., & Donovan, J. J. (2000). Personality and job performance: The big five revisited. *Journal of Applied Psychology, 85*, 869–879.

12. Mount, M. K., Barrick, M. R. (1995). The Big Five personality dimensions: Implications for resaerch and practice in human resources management. In K. M. Rowland & G. Ferris (Eds.), *Research in personnel and human resources management* (Vol. 13, pp. 153–200). Greenwich, CT: JAI Press.

13. Barrick, M. R., Stewart, G. L., Neubert, M. J., & Mount, M. K. (1998). Relating member ability and personality to work-team processes and team effectiveness. *Journal of Applied Psychology, 83*, 377–391.

14. Smith, D. B., Hanges, P. J., & Dickson, M. W. (2001). Personnel selection and the five-factor model: Reexamining the effects of applicant's frame of reference. *Journal of Applied Psychology, 86*, 304–315.

15. George, J. M., & Zhou, J. (2001). When openness to experience and conscientiousness are related to creative behavior: An interactional approach. *Journal of Applied Psychology, 86*, 513–524.

16. George, J. M., & Breief, A. P. (1992). Feeling good—doing good: A conceptual analysis of the mood at work-organizational spontaneity relationships. *Psychological Bulletin, 112*, 310–329.

17. Barsade, S. G., Brief, A. P., & Spataro, S. E. (2003). In J. Greenberg (Ed.), *Organizational behavior: The state of the science* (2nd ed.). Mahwah, NJ: Lawrence Erlbaum Associates. Isen, A. M., & Baron, R. A. (1992). Positive affect as a factor in organizational behavior. In B. M. Staw & L. L. Cummings (Eds.), *Research in organizational behavior* (Vol. 13, pp. 1–54). Greenwich, CT: JAI Press.

18. Staw, B. M., & Barsade, S. G. (1993). Affect and managerial performance: A test of the sadder-but-wiser vs. happier-and-smarter hypotheses. *Administrative Science Quarterly, 38*, 304–331.

19. George, J. M. (1990). Personality, affect, and behavior in groups. *Journal of Applied Psychology, 75*, 107–116.

20. Douglas, S. C., & Martinko, M. J. (2001). Exploring the role of individual differences in the prediction of workplace aggression. *Journal of Applied Psychology, 86*, 547–559.

21. Aquino, K., Grover, S. L., Bradfield, M. & Allen, D. G. (1999). The effects of negative affectivity, hierarchical status, and self-determination on workplace victimization. *Academy of Management Journal, 42*, 260–272.

22. Maurer, T. J., & Pierce, H. R. (1998). A comparison of Likert scale and traditional measures of self-efficacy. *Journal of Applied Psychology, 83*, 324–329.

23. Wood, R., Bandura, A., & Bailey, T. (1990). Mechanisms governing organizational performance in complex decision-making environments. *Organizational Behavior and Human Decision Processes, 46*, 181–201.

24. Kanger, R., & Kanfer, F. H. (1991). Goals and self-regulation: Applications of theory to work settings. *Advances in Motivation and Achievement, 7*, 287–326.

25. Bandura, A. (1997). *Self-efficacy: The exercise of control*. New York: W. H. Freeman.

26. Judge, T. A., & Bono, J. E. (2001). Relationship of core evaluation traits—self-esteem, generalized self-efficacy, locus of control and emotional stability—with job satisfaction and job performance: A meta-analysis. *Journal of Applied Psychology, 86*, 80–92. Judge, T. A., Locke, E. A., & Durham, C. C. (1997). The dispositional caues of job satisfaction: A core evaluations approach. *Research in Organizational Behavior, 19*, 151–188.

27. Chen, G., Gully, S. M., Whiteman, J. A., & Kilcullen, R. N. (2000). Examination of relationships among trait-like individual differences, state-like individual differences, and learning performance. *Journal of Applied Psychology, 85*, 835–847.

28. Gist, M. E., & Mitchell, T. R. (1992). Self-efficacy: A theoretical analysis of its determinants and malleability. *Academy of Management Review, 17*, 183–211.

29. Mitchell, T. E., Hopper, H., Daniels, D., George-Falvy, J., & James, L. R. (1994). Predicting self-efficacy and performance during skill acquisition. *Journal of Applied Psychology, 79*, 506–507.

30. Judge, T. A., Locke, E. A., Durham, C. C., & Kluger, A. N. (1998). Dispositional effects on job and life satisfaction: The role of core evaluations. *Journal of Applied Psychology, 83*, 17–34.

31. Baron, R. A. (in press). Organizational behavior and entrepreneurship. In B. M. Staw & R. Kramer (Eds.), *Research in organizational behavior*. Greenwich, CT: JAI Press.

32. Markman, G. D., Koen, P. A., & Baron, R. A. (2002). *Individual differences and resource attainment among teams of corporate entprenreurs*. Unpublished manuscript.

33. Eden, D., & Aviram, A. (1993). Self-efficacy training to speed reemployment: Helping people to help themselves. *Journal of Applied Psychology, 78*, 352–360.

34. Snyder, M. (1987). *Public appearance/private realities: The psychology self-monitoring*. San Francisco: Freeman.

35. Caldwell, D. F., & O'Reilly, C. A., III (1982). Boundary spanning and individual performance: The impact of self-monitoring. *Journal of Applied Psychology, 67*, 124–127.

36. Kilduff, M., & Day, D. V. (1994). Do chameleons get ahead? The effects of self-monitoring on managerial careers. *Academy of Management Journal, 37*, 1047–1060.

37. Rosenbaum, J. E. (1979). Tournament mobility: Career patterns in a corporation. *Administrative Science Quarterly, 24*, 220–241.

38. Sellers, P. (1996). What exactly is charisma? *Fortune*, January 15, pp. 68–72, 74–75.

39. Friedman, H. S., & Miller-Herringer, T. (1991). Nonverbal display of emotion in public and private: Self-monitoring, personality, and expressive cues. *Journal of Personality and Social Psychology, 62*, 766–775,

40. Jamieson, D. W., Lydon, J. E., & Zanna, M. P. (1987). Attitude and activity preference similarity: Different bases of interpersonal attraction for low and high self-monitors. *Journal of Personality and Social Psychology, 53*, 1052–1060.

41. Christie, R., & Geis, F. L. (1970). *Studies in Machiavellianism*. New York: Academic Press.

42. McHoskey, J. W., Worzel, W., & Szyarto, C. (1998). Machiavellianism and psychopathy. *Journal of Personality and Social Psychology, 74,* 192–210.

43. See Note 45.

44. Wilson, D. S., Near, D., & Miller, R. R. (1997). Machiavellianism: A synthesis of the evolutionary and psychological literatures. *Psychological Bulletin, 119,* 285–299.

45. Schultz, C. J., II. (1993). Situational and dispositional predictors of performance: A test of the hypothesized Machiavellianism × structure interaction among sales persons. *Journal of Applied Social Psychology, 23,* 478–498.

46. Friedman, M., & Rosenman, R. H. (1974). *Type A behavior and your heart.* New York: Knopf.

47. Lee, C., Ashford, S. J., & Jamieson, L. F. (1993). The effects of Type A behavior dimensions and optimism on coping strategy, health, and performance. *Journal of Organizational Behavior, 14,* 143–157.

48. Schauabroeck, J., Ganster, D. C., & Kemmerer, B. E. (1994). Job complexity, "Type A" behavior, and cardiovascular disorder: A prospective study. *Academy of Management Journal, 37,* 426–439.

49. Glass, D. C. (1977). *Behavior patterns, stress, and coronary disease.* Hillsdale, NJ: Lawrence Erlbaum Associates.

50. Holmes, D. S., McGilley, B. M., & Houston, B. K. (1984). Task-related arousal of Type A and Type B persons: Level of challenge and response specificity. *Journal of Personality and Social Psychology, 46,* 1322–1327.

51. Jamal, M., & Baba, V. V. (1991). Type A behavior, its prevalence and consequences among women nurses: An empirical examination. *Human Relations, 44,* 1213–1228.

52. Lee, M., & Kanungo, R. (1984). *Management of work and personal life.* New York: Praeger.

53. Berman, M., Gladue, B., & Taylor, S. (1993). The effects of hormones, Type A behavior pattern and provocation on aggression in men. *Motivation and Emotion, 17,* 125–138.

54. Baron, R. A. (1989). Personality and organizational conflict: Effects of the Type A behavior pattern and self-monitoring. *Organizational Behavior and Human Decisions Processes, 44,* 281–297.

55. McClelland, D. C. (1985). *Human motivation.* Glenview, IL: Scott, Foresman.

56. McClelland, D. C. (1977). Entrepreneurship and management in the years ahead. In C. A. Bramletter (Ed.), *The individual and the future of organizations* (pp. 12–29). Atlanta, GA: Georgia State University.

57. Miller, D., & Droge, C. (1986). Psychological and traditional determinants of structure. *Administrative Science Quarterly, 31,* 539–560.

58. Turban, D. B., & Keon, T. L. (1993). Organizational attractiveness: An interactionist perspective. *Journal of Applied Psychology, 78,* 184–193.

59. Dweck, C. S. (1999). *Self-theories: Their role in motivation, personality, and development.* Philadelphia: Psychology Press.

60. VandeWalle, D. (1997). Development and validation of a work domain goal orientation instrument. *Educational and Psychological Measurement, 8a,* 995–1015.

61. Chen, G., Gully, S. M., Whiteman, J. A., & Kilcullen, R. N. (2000). Examination of relationships among trait-like individual differences, state-like individual differences, and learning performance. *Journal of Applied Psychology, 85,* 835–847.

62. VandeWalle, D., Cron, W. K., & Slocum, J. W., Jr. (2001). The role of goal orientation following performance feedback. *Journal of Applied Psychology 86,* 629–640.

63. McClelland, D. C. (1961). *The achieving society.* Princeton, NJ: Van Nostrand.

64. Lynn, R. (1991). *The secret of the miracle economy.* London: SAU.

65. Furnham, A., Kirkcaldy, B. D., & Lynn, R. (1994). National attitudes to competitiveness, money, and work among young people: First, second, and third world differences. *Human Relations, 47,* 119–132.

66. Guthrie, J. P., Ash, R. A., & Bandapudi, V. (1995). Additional validity evidence for a measure of *morningness. Journal of Applied Psychology, 80,* 186–190.

67. Fierman, J. (1995, August 21). It's 2 A.M., let's go to work. *Fortune,* pp. 82–86.

68. Totterdell, P., Spelten, E., Smith, L., Barton, J., & Folkard, S. (1995). Recovery from work shifts: How long does it take? *Journal of Applied Psychology, 80,* 43–57.

69. See Note 57.

70. Wallace, B. (1993). Day persons, night persons, and variability in hypnotic susceptibility. *Journal of Personality and Social Psychology, 64,* 827–833.

71. Eysenk, M. W. (1994). *Individual differences.* Hillsdale, NJ: Erlbaum

72. Neisser, U., Boodoo, G., Bouchard, T. J., Jr., Bykin, A. W., Brody, N., Ceci, S. J., Halpen, D. F., Loehlin, J. C., Perloff, R., Sternberg, R. J., & Urbina, S. (1996). Intelligence: Knowns and unknowns. *American Psychologist, 51,* 77–101.

73. Sternberg, R. J. (1986). *Intelligence applied.* New York: Harcourt Brace Jovanovich.

74. Sternberg, J. (in press). Successful intelligence as a basis for entrepreneurship. *Journal of Business Venturing.*

75. Sternberg, R. J., Wagner, R. K., Williams, W. M., & Horvath, J. A. (1995). Testing common sense. *American Psychologist, 50,* 912–927.

76. See Note 70.

77. Goleman, D. (1997). *Emotional intelligence.* New York: Bantam; Goleman, D. (1998). *Working with emotional intelligence.* New York: Bantam.

78. See Note 64.

79. Baron, R. A., & Markman, G. (in press). Beyond social capital: The role of entrepreneurs' social competence in their financial success. *Journal of Business Venturing.*

80. Weber, T. E. (2001). After terror attacks, companies rethink role of face-to-face. *Wall Street Journal,* September 24, 2001, p. B-1.

81. Baron, R. A., & Markman, G. D. (2000). Beyond social capital. *Academy of Management Executive, 14,* 106–116.

82. Sternberg, R. (in press). Successful intelligence. *Journal of Business Venturing.*

83. See Note 81.

84. Reed, T. E., & Jensen, A. R. (in press). Conduction velocity in a brain nerve pathway of normal adults correlates with intelligence level. *Intelligence.*

85. Holweijn, M., & Lotens, W. A. (1992). The influence of backpack design on physical performance. *Ergonomics, 35,* 149–157.

86. Bloswick, D. S., Gerber, A., Sebesta, D., Johnson, S., & Mecham, W. (1994). Effect of mailbag design on musculoskeletal fatigue and metabolic load. *Human Factors, 36,* 210–218.

Case in Point Sources
Various press releases, Rensselaer Polytechnic Institute, October and November, 2000.

CHAPTER 4

Preview Case Sources
Solomon, S. D. (2000, October 11). Fit to be (re)tired. *Inc. 500,* pp. 177–178. Solomon, S. D. (1999, October 12). Fit to be tired. *Inc. 500,* pp. 89–90, 92, 95, 98. Tape Resources Web site: www.taperesources.com.

Chapter Notes
1. Kanfer, R., & Klimoski, R. J. (2002). Affect and work: Looking back into the future. In R. G. Lord, R. J. Klimoski, & R. Kanfer (Eds.), *Emotions in the workplace: Understanding the structure and role of emotions in organizational behavior.* San Francisco: Jossey-Bass.

2. Weiss, H. M., & Cropanzano, R. (1996). Affective events theory: A theoretical discussion of the structure, causes, and consequences of affective experiences at work. In B. M. Staw & L. L. Cummings (Eds.), *Research in organizational behavior* (Vol. 18, pp. 1–74). Greenwich, CT: JAI Press.

3. Ekman, P., Friesen, W. V., & Ancoli, S. (2001). Facial signs of emotional experience. In W. G. Parrott (Ed.), *Emotions in social psychology* (pp. 255–264). Philadelphia, PA: Psychology Press.

4. Nakamura, N. (2000). Facial expression and communication of emotion: An analysis of display rules and a model of facial expression of emotion. *Japanese Psychological Review, 43,* 307–319.

5. Walther, J. B., & Addario, K. P. (2001). The impacts of emoticons on message interpretation in computer-mediated communication. *Social Science Computer Review, 19,* 324–347.

6. Wolf, A. (2000). Emotional expression online: Gender differences in emoticon use. *CyberPsychology & Behavior, 3,* 827–833.

7. George, J. M., & Brief, A. P. (1996). Motivational agendas in the workplace: The effects of feelings on focus of attention and work motivation. In B. M. Staw & L. L. Cummings (Eds.), *Research in organizational behavior* (Vol. 18, pp. 75–109). Greenwich, CT: JAI Press.

8. Freiberg, K., Freiberg, J., & Peters, T. (1998). *Nuts!: Southwest Airlines crazy recipe for business and personal success.* New York: Bantam Doubleday. Cohen, B., Greenfield, J., & Mann, M. (1998). *Ben & Jerry's double dip: How to run a values-led business and make money, too.* New York: Fireside.

9. Barsade, S. G., Brief, A. P., & Spataro, S. E. (2003). The affective revolution in organizational behavior: The emergence of a paradigm. In J. Greenberg (Ed.), *Organizational behavior: The state of the science* (2nd ed.). Mahwah, NJ: Lawrence Erlbaum Associates.

10. Clore, G. L., Schwartz, N., & Conway, M. (1994). Affective causes and consequences of social information processing. In R. S. Wyer, Jr., & T. K. Srull (Eds.), *Handbook of social cognition* (Vol. 1, pp. 323–417). Hillsdale, NJ: Lawrence Erlbaum Associates.

11. Brief, A. P., Butcher, A. B., & Roberson, L. (1995). Cookies, disposition, and job attitudes: The effects of positive mood-inducing agents and negative affectivity on job satisfaction in a field experiment. *Organizational Behavior and Human Decision Processes, 62,* 55–62.

12. Goleman, D. (1998). *Working with emotional intelligence.* New York: Bantam.

13. Morris, J. A., & Feldman, D. C. (1997). Managing emotions in the workplace. *Journal of Managerial Issues, 9,* 257–274.

14. Culture training key to city's success (2002, February 11). sportsillustrated.cnn.com/olympics/2002/.

15. Dutton, J. E., Frost, P. J., Workline, M. C., Lilius, J. M., & Kanov, J. M. (2002, January). Leading in times of trauma. *Harvard Business Review,* pp. 54–61.

16. Hyman, S. E. (2002, February). Managing emotional fallout. *Harvard Business Review,* pp. 55–60.

17. Northwestern National Life Insurance Company. (1999). *Employee burnout: America's newest epidemic.* Minneapolis, MN: Author.

18. Quick, J. C., Murphy, L. R., & Hurrell, J. J., Jr. (1992). *Stress and well-being at work.* Washington, DC: American Psychological Association.

19. Selye, H. (1976). *Stress in health and disease.* Boston: Butterworths.

20. Kane, K. (1997, October–November). Can you perform under pressure? *Fast Company,* pp. 54, 56. Enhanced Performance Web site: www.enhanced-performance.com.

21. Stress at work (1997, April 15). *Wall Street Journal,* p. A12.

22. Heller, R., & Hindle, T. (1998). *Essential manager's manual.* New York: DK Publishing.

23. Fenn, D. (1999, November). Domestic policy. *Inc.,* pp. 38–42, 44–45. Hammonds, K. H., & Palmer, A. T. (1998, September 21). The daddy trap. *BusinessWeek,* pp. 56–58, 60, 62, 64.

24. McGrath, J. E. (1976). Stress and behavior in organizations. In M. D. Dunnette (Ed.), *Handbook of industrial and organizational psychology* (pp. 1351–1398). Chicago: Rand McNally.

25. Shedroff, N. (2000, November 28). Forms of information anxiety. *Business 2.0,* p. 220.

26. Stephens, C., & Long, N. (2000). Communication with police supervisors and peers as a buffer of work-related traumatic stress. *Journal of Organizational Behavior, 21,* 407–424.

27. Beehr, T. A., Jex, S. M., Stacy, B. A., & Murray, M. A. (2000). Work stressors and coworker support as predictors of individual strain and job performance. *Journal of Organizational Behavior, 21,* 391–405.

28. Treharne, G. J., Lyons, A. C., & Tupling, R. E. (2001). The effects of optimism, pessimism, social support, and mood on the lagged relationship between stress and symptoms. *Current Research in Social Psychology, 7*(5), 60–81.

29. Fisher, A. B. (1993, August 23). Sexual harassment: What to do. *Fortune,* pp. 84–86, 88.

30. Kolbert, E. (1991, October 10). Sexual harassment at work is pervasive. *New York Times,* pp. A1, A17.

31. Sullivan, S. E., & Bhagat, R. S. (1992). Organizational stress, job satisfaction, and job performance: Where do we go from here? *Journal of Management, 18,* 353–374.

32. Nieman, C. (1999, July–August). How much is enough? *Fast Company,* pp. 108–116. Wah, L. (2000, January). The emotional tightrope. *Management Review,* pp. 38–43.

33. Motowidlo, S. J., Packard, J. S., & Manning, M. R. (1986). Occupational stress: Its causes and consequences for job performance. *Journal of Applied Psychology, 71,* 618–629.

34. The list: Desk rage. *BusinessWeek* (2000, November 27), p. 12.

35. Bakker, A. B., Schaufeli, W. B., Sixma, H. J., Bosveld, W., & Van Dierendonck, D. (2000). Patient demands, lack of reciprocity, and burnout: A five-year longitudinal study among general practitioners. *Journal of Organizational Behavior, 21,* 425–441.

36. Frese, M. (1985). Stress at work and psychosomatic complaints: A causal interpretation. *Journal of Applied Psychology, 70,* 314–328. Quick, J. C., & Quick, J. D. (1984). *Organizational stress and preventive management.* New York: McGraw-Hill.

37. Trocki, K. F., & Orioli, E. M. (1994). Gender differences in stress symptoms, stress-producing contexts, and coping strategies. In G. P. Keita & J. J. Hurrell, Jr. (Eds.), *Job stress in a changing workforce* (pp. 7–22). Washington, DC: American Psychological Association.

38. Latack, J. C., & Havlovic, S. J. (1992). Coping with job stress: A conceptual evaluation framework for coping measures. *Journal of Organizational Behavior, 13,* 479–508.

39. Wah, L. (2000, January). The emotional tightrope. *Management Review,* pp. 38–43.

40. See Note 39.

41. See Note 39.

42. See Note 35.

43. Singer, T. (2000, October 17). The balance of power. *Inc. 500,* pp. 105–108, 110.

44. Harling, L. (2000, December 12). High-tech insomnia. *Business 2.0,* pp. 254–256.

45. American Academy of Sleep Medicine. (2002). *Sleep and health.* Rochester, MN: Author.

Case in Point Source

Ehrenfeld, T. (2000, July 3). The parent trap. *The Industry Standard,* pp. 222–223, 225.

CHAPTER 5

Preview Case Source

Garsten, E. (2002, January 13). Awareness of Islam aim of diversity effort at Ford. *Chicago Tribune,* p. S8.

Chapter Notes

1. Quarstein, V. A., McAfee, R. B., & Glassman, M. (1992). The situational occurrences theory of job satisfaction. *Human Relations, 45,* 859–873.

2. Hulin, C. L. (1991). Adaptation, persistence, and commitment in organizations. In M. D. Dunnette & L. M. Hough (Eds.), *Handbook of industrial and organizational psychology* (2nd ed.) (Vol. 2, pp. 445–506). Palo Alto, CA: Consulting Psychologists Press.

3. Stone, E. F., Stone, D. L., & Dipboye, R. L. (1991). Stigmas in organizations: Race, handicaps, and physical unattractiveness. In K. Kelley (Ed.), *Issues, theory, and research in industrial/organizational psychology* (pp. 385–457). Amsterdam: Elsevier Science Publishers.

4. McGuire, W. J. (1985). Attitudes and attitude change. In G. Lindzey & E. Aronson (Eds.), *Handbook of social psychology* (3rd ed.) (Vol. 2, pp. 233–346). New York: Random House.

5. Locke, E. A. (1976). The nature and causes of job satisfaction. In M. D. Dunnette (Ed.), *Handbook of industrial and organizational psychology* (pp. 1297–1350). Chicago: Rand McNally.

6. Thornburg, L. (1992, July). When violence hits business. *HRMagazine,* pp. 40–45.

7. Boyle, M. (2001, February 19). Nothing is rotten in Denmark. *Fortune,* p. 242.

8. Koretz, G. (2000, November 13). Yes, workers are grumpier: Job satisfaction is falling sharply. *BusinessWeek,* p. 42.

9. The Gallop Organization and Carlson Marketing Group. (2002). American Workforce Study. From the Internet at www.gallop.com.

10. Weaver, C. N. (1980). Job satisfaction in the United States in the 1970s. *Journal of Applied Psychology, 65,* 364–367.

11. Eichar, D. M., Brady, E. M., & Fortinsky, R. H. (1991). The job satisfaction of older workers. *Journal of Organizational Behavior, 12,* 609–620.

12. Bedian, A. G., Ferris, G. R., & Kacmar, K. M. (1992). Age, tenure, and job satisfaction: A tale of two perspectives. *Journal of Vocational Behavior, 40,* 33–48.

13. Lambert, S. L. (1991). The combined effect of job and family characteristics on the job satisfaction, job involvement, and intrinsic motivation of men and women workers. *Journal of Organizational Behavior, 12,* 341–363.

14. Staw, B. M., & Ross, J. (1985). Stability in the midst of change: A dispositional approach to job attitudes. *Journal of Applied Psychology, 70,* 55–77.

15. Agho, A. O., Price, J. L., & Mueller, C. W. (1992). Discriminant validity of measures of job satisfaction, positive affectivity and negative affectivity. *Journal of Occupational and Organizational Psychology, 65,* 185–196.

16. Smith, P. C., Kendall, L. M., & Hulin, C. L. (1969). *The measurement of satisfaction in work and retirement.* Chicago: Rand McNally.

17. Kinicki, A. J., McKee-Ryan, F. M., Schriescheim, C. A., & Carson K. P. (2002). *Journal of Applied Psychology, 87,* 14–32. Stanton, J. M., Sinar, E. F., Balzer, W. K., Julian, A. L., Thorensen, P., Aziz, S., Fisher,

G. G., & Smith, P. C. (2002). Development of a compact measure of job satisfaction: The abridged Job Descriptive Index. *Educational and Psychological Measurement, 62,* 173–91.

18. Weiss, D. J., Dawis, R. V., England, G. W., & Loftquist, L. H. (1967). *Manual for the Minnesota Satisfaction Questionnaire* (Minnesota Studies on Vocational Rehabilitation, Vol. 22). Minneapolis, MN: Industrial Relations Center, Work Adjustment Project, University of Minnesota.

19. Heneman, H. G., III., & Schwab, D. P. (1985). Pay satisfaction: Its multidimensional nature and measurement. *International Journal of Psychology, 20,* 129–141.

20. Judge, T. A., & Welbourne, T. M. (1994). A confirmatory investigation of the dimensionality of the Pay Satisfaction Questionnaire. *Journal of Applied Psychology, 79,* 461–466.

21. Sutton, R. I., & Callahan, A. L. (1987). The stigma of bankruptcy: Spoiled organizational image and its management. *Academy of Management Journal, 30,* 405–436.

22. Herzberg, F. (1966). *Work and the nature of man.* Cleveland: World.

23. Machungaws, P. D., & Schmitt, N. (1983). Work motivation in a developing country. *Journal of Applied Psychology, 68,* 31–42.

24. Landy, F. J. (1985). *Psychology of work behavior* (3rd ed.). Homewood, IL: Dorsey.

25. Magnet, M. (1993, May 3). Good news for the service economy. *Fortune,* pp. 45–50, 52.

26. Sundstrom, E. (1986). *Workplaces.* New York: Cambridge University Press.

27. Locke, E. A. (1984). Job satisfaction. In M. Gruenberg & T. Wall (Eds.), *Social psychology and organizational behavior* (pp. 93–117). London: Wiley.

28. McFarlin, D. B., & Rice, R. W. (1992). The role of facet importance as a moderator in job satisfaction processes. *Journal of Organizational Behavior, 13,* 41–54.

29. Dalton, D. R., & Todor, W. D. (1993). Turnover, transfer, absenteeism: An interdependent perspective. *Journal of Management, 19,* 193–219.

30. Porter, L. W., & Steers, R. M. (1973). Organizational work and personal factors in employee turnover and absenteeism. *Psychological Bulletin, 80,* 151–176.

31. Tett, R. P., & Meyer, J. P. (1993). Job satisfaction, organizational commitment, turnover intention, and turnover: Path analyses based on meta-analytic findings. *Personnel Psychology, 46,* 259–293.

32. Mitchell, T. R., & Lee, T. W. (2001). The unfolding model of voluntary turnover and job embeddedness: Foundations for a comprehensive theory of attachment. In B. M. Staw & R. I. Sutton (Eds.), *Research in organizational behavior* (Vol. 23, pp. 189–246). Oxford, UK: Elsevier.

33. Lee, T. W., Mitchell, T. R., Holtom, B. C., McDaniel, L., & Hill, J. W. (1999). Theoretical development and extension of the unfolding model of voluntary turnover. *Academy of Management Journal, 42,* 450–462.

34. Bad bossing costs you and your company. (2000, October). *Working Woman,* p. 56.

35. Armour, S. (1998, November 6). Workplace absenteeism soars 25%, costs millions. *USA Today,* p. 1A.

36. Iaffaldano, M. T., & Murchinsky, P. M. (1985). Job satisfaction and job performance: A meta-analysis. *Psychological Bulletin, 97,* 251–273.

37. Porter, L. W., & Lawler, E. E., III. (1968), *Managerial attitudes and performance.* Homewood, IL: Dorsey Press.

38. Boyle, M. (2001, July 23). Beware the killjoy. *Fortune,* pp. 265–266, 268. Lieberman, V. (2000, October). The rules of fun. *Across the Board,* p. 62. Weinstein, M. (1996). *Managing to have fun.* New York: Fireside. Hemsath, D., & Yerkes, L., (1997). *301 ways to have fun at work.* San Francisco: Berrett-Koehler.

39. Rochman, B. (2001, July). OK, so you don't have to be a complete SOB. *E-Company,* pp. 56–57.

40. Heffner, T. S., & Rentsch, J. R. (2001). Organizational commitment and social interaction: A multiple constituencies approach. *Journal of Vocational Behavior, 59,* 471–490.

41. Meyer, J. P., & Allen, N. J. (1997). *Commitment in the workplace: Theory, research, and application.* Thousand Oaks, CA: Sage.

42. Gautam, T., van Dick, R., & Wagner, U. (2001). Organizational commitment in Asia. *Asian Journal of Social Psychology, 4,* 239–248. Kibeom, L., Allen, N. J., Meyer, J. P., & Rhee, K. (2001). The three-component model of organizational commitment: An application to South Korea. *Applied Psychology: An International Review, 50,* 596–614.

43. Carsten, J. M., & Spector, P. E. (1987). Unemployment, job satisfaction, and employee turnover: A meta-analytic test of the Murchinsky model. *Journal of Applied Psychology, 72,* 374–381.

44. O'Reilly, B. (1994, June 13). The new deal: What companies and employees owe each other. *Fortune,* pp. 44–47, 50, 52 (quote, p. 45).

45. Loyalty in numbers (Data from Fortune Personnel Consultants). (2000, November 6). *BusinessWeek,* p. F6. The big picture: Job-hopping (Data from Lee Hecht Harrison). (2001, September 10). *BusinessWeek,* p. 16. Alexander, M. (2000, November 6). Smart and loyal (Data from AON Consulting's Loyalty Institute). *The Industry Standard,* p. 258. Der Hovanesian, M. (2001, August 13). When loyalty erodes, so do profits. *BusinessWeek,* p. 8.

46. Lee, T. W., Ashford, S. J., Walsh, J. P., & Mowday, R. T. (1992). Commitment propensity, organizational commitment, and voluntary turnover: A longitudinal study of organizational entry processes. *Journal of Management, 18,* 15–32.

47. Johns, G., & Xie, J. L. (1998). Perceptions of absence from work: People's Republic of China versus Canada. *Journal of Applied Psychology, 83,* 515–530.

48. Bond, M. H. (1986). *The psychology of the Chinese people.* New York: Oxford University Press.

49. See note 39.

50. Van Dyne, L., & Ang, S. (1998). Organizational citizenship behavior of contingent workers in Singapore. *Academy of Management Journal, 41,* 692–703.

51. Rosen, R. H. (1991). *The healthy company.* Los Angeles: Jeremy P. Tarcher (quote, pp. 71–72).

52. Simons, J. (2001, April 2). Stop moaning about gripe sites and log on. *Fortune,* pp. 181–182.

53. Rosner, B. (2001). *Working wounded.* New York: Warner Books.

54. Stephan, W. G. (1985). Intergroup relations. In G. Lindzey & E. Aronson (Eds.), *Handbook of social psychology* (3rd ed.) (Vol. 2, pp. 599–658). New York: Random House.

55. Fernandez, J. P., & Barr, M. (1993). *The diversity advantage.* New York: Lexington Books.

56. Laroche, L. (2002). *Managing cultural diversity in technical professions.* Woburn, MA: Butterworth-Heinemann. Malone, M. S. (1993, July 18). Translating diversity into high-tech gains. *New York Times,* p. B2.

57. Yang, C. (1993, June 21). In any language, it's unfair: More immigrants are bringing bias charges against employers. *BusinessWeek,* pp. 110–112.

58. Hawkins, C. (1993, June 28). Denny's: The stain that isn't coming out: Can a pact with the NAACP help it overcome charges of bias? *BusinessWeek,* pp. 98–99.

59. Mason, J. C. (1993, July). Knocking on the glass ceiling. *Management Review,* p. 5.

60. Solomon, C. M. (1992, July). Keeping hate out of the workplace. *Personnel Journal,* pp. 30–36.

61. Ornstein, S. L., & Sankowsky, D. (1994). Overcoming stereotyping and prejudice: A framework and suggestions for learning from groupist comments in the classroom. *Journal of Management Education, 18,* 80–90.

62. Gregory, R. F. (2001). *Age discrimination in the American workplace: Old at a young age.* New Brunswick, NJ: Rutgers University Press.

63. Raines, C. (1997). *Beyond generation X. A practical guide for managers.* Menlo Park, CA: Crisp.

64. Magill, B. G. (1999). *Workplace accommodations under the ADA.* Washington, DC: Thompson Publishing Group.

65. Koretz, G. (2000, November 6). How to enable the disabled. *BusinessWeek,* p. 38.

66. Kahn, J. (2001, June 11). A mini-Y2K for the Web. *Fortune,* p. 46. Kanter, L., & McCann, J. (2000, September 11). OK, back to work. *BusinessWeek,* p. F16.

67. Enabling those with disabilities. (2000, March 6). *BusinessWeek,* p. 8.

68. Morris, K. (1998, November 23). You've come a short way, baby. *BusinessWeek,* pp. 82–83, 86, 88.

69. Steinberg, R., & Shapiro, S. (1982). Sex differences in personality traits of female and male master of business administration students. *Journal of Applied Psychology, 67,* 306–310.

70. Lavelle, L. (2001, April 23). For female CEOs, it's stingy at the top. *BusinessWeek,* pp. 70–72.

71. Catalyst (2002). *The glass ceiling in 2000.* New York: Author (from the World Wide Web: www.catalystwomen.org/press/factslabor00.html). Bureau of Labor Statistics, 1999; Catalyst, 1999 Census of Women

Corporate Officers and Top Earners; 1999 Census of Women Board Directors of the *Fortune* 1000.

72. Brown, E. (2000, August 14). Breaking the wineglass ceiling. *Fortune,* pp. 222–232.
73. The list: Women's work. (2000, October 9). *BusinessWeek,* p. 14.
74. Hereck, G. M. (1998). *Stigma and sexual orientation: Understanding prejudice against lesbians, gay men, and bisexuals.* Newbury Park, CA: Sage.
75. Martinez, M. N. (1993, June). Recognizing sexual orientation is fair and not costly. *HRMagazine,* pp. 66–68, 70–72 (quote, p. 68).
76. Fernandez, J. P., & Barr, M. (1993). *The diversity advantage.* New York: Lexington Books.
77. Arndt, W. (2001, July 30). Racism in the workplace. *BusinessWeek,* pp. 64–67.
78. Yang, C. (1993, June 21). In any language, it's unfair: More immigrants are bringing bias charges against employers. *BusinessWeek,* pp. 110–112 (quote, p. 111).
79. Tannenbaum Center for Religious Understanding. (2001). *Survey on religious bias in the workplace.* New York: Author.
80. Pew Research Center for the People and the Press. (2001). *Americans improve their view of Muslims.* Washington, DC: Author. Online at www.people-press.org/.
81. Carnevale, A. P., & Stone, S. C. (1995). *The American mosaic.* New York: McGraw-Hill.
82. Towers Perrin. (1992). *Workforce 2000 today.* New York: Author.
83. See Note 82 (quote, p. 1).
84. See Note 82.
85. Kravitz, D. A., & Klineberg, S. L. (2000). Reactions to two versions of affirmative action among whites, blacks, and Hispanics. *Journal of Applied Psychology, 85,* 597–611.
86. Polus, S. (1996). Ten myths about affirmative action. *Journal of Social Issues, 52,* 25–31.
87. Thomas, R. R., Jr. (1992). Managing diversity: A conceptual framework. In S. E. Jackson (Ed.), *Diversity in the workplace* (pp. 305–317). New York: Guilford Press.
88. Kahn, J. (2001, July 9). Diversity trumps the downturn. *Fortune,* pp. 66–72 (quote, p. 70).
89. Murray, K. (1993, August 1). The unfortunate side effects of "diversity training." *New York Times,* pp. E1, E3.
90. Gottfredson, L. S. (1992). Dilemmas in developing diversity programs. In S. E. Jackson (Ed.), *Diversity in the workplace* (pp. 279–305). New York: Guilford Press.
91. See Note 70.
92. Urresta, L., & Hickman, J. (1998, August 3). The diversity elite. *Fortune,* pp. 114–116, 118, 120, 122.
93. Johnson, R. S. (1998, August 3). The 50 best companies for blacks and Hispanics. *Fortune,* pp. 94–96, 98, 100–102, 104, 106 (quote, p. 116).
94. See Note 93 (quote, p. 98).
95. See Note 93.
96. Battaglia, B. (1992). Skills for managing multicultural teams. *Cultural Diversity at Work, 4,* 4–12.
97. See Note 96.
98. See Note 96.
99. Gardenswartz, L., & Rowe, A. (1994). *The managing diversity survival guide.* Burr Ridge, IL: Irwin.

100. Rynes, S., & Rosen, B. (1995). A field survey of factors affecting the adoption and perceived success of diversity training. *Personnel Psychology, 48,* 247–270.
101. Wright, P., Ferris, S. P., Hiller, J. S., & Kroll, M. (1995). Competitiveness through management of diversity: Effects of stock price valuation. *Academy of Management Journal, 38,* 272–287.
102. Gingold, D. (2000, July 26). Diversity today. *Fortune,* special section, pp. S1–S23.
103. Finnigan, A. (2001, April). Different strokes. *Working Woman,* pp. 42–64.

Case in Point Sources
Labich, K. (1999, September 6). No more crude at Texaco. *Fortune,* pp. 205–206, 208, 210, 212. Roberts, B., & White, J. E. (1999). *Roberts vs. Texaco: A true story of race and corporate America.* New York: Avon. Statistics appear on the Texaco Web site: www.texaco.com.

CHAPTER 6

Preview Case Sources
Ortega, B. (2000). *In Sam we trust.* New York: Times Books. Palmeri, C. (1997, September 8). Believe in yourself, believe in the merchandise. *Forbes,* pp. 118–119, 122, 124. Internet site: www.wal-mart.com/newsroom. Vance, S. S., & Scott, R. V. (1997). *Wal-Mart: A history of Sam Walton's retail phenomenon.* New York: Twayne.

Chapter Notes
1. Erez, M., & Kleinbeck, U. (2001). *Work motivation in the context of a globalizing economy.* Mahwah, NJ: Lawrence Erlbaum Associates.
2. Blau, G. (1993). Operationalizing direction and level of effort and testing their relationships to individual job performance. *Organizational Behavior and Human Decision Processes, 55,* 152–170.
3. Barendam Research (2002). *Managing job satisfaction* (Special reports Vol. 6). Mercer Island, WA: Author. "Work still a labor of love." (1981, April 20). *The Columbus Dispatch,* p. 1.
4. Schwartz, T. (2000, November). The greatest sources of satisfaction in the workplace are internal and emotional. *Fast Company,* pp. 398–400, 402.
5. Maslow, A. H., Stephens, D. C., & Heil, G. (1998). *Maslow on management.* New York: Wiley.
6. Mudrack, P. E. (1992). 'Work' or 'leisure'? The Protestant work ethic and participation in an employee fitness program. *Journal of Organizational Behavior, 13,* 81–88.
7. Miller, A., & Springen, K. (1988, October 31). Forget cash, give me the TV. *Newsweek,* p. 58.
8. Porter, L. W. (1961). A study of perceived need satisfaction in bottom and middle management jobs. *Journal of Applied Psychology, 45,* 1–10.
9. Wahba, M. A., & Bridwell, L. G. (1976). Maslow reconsidered: A review of research on the need hierarchy theory. *Organizational Behavior and Human Performance, 15,* 212–240.

10. Alderfer, C. P. (1972). *Existence, relatedness, and growth.* New York: Free Press.
11. Salancik, G. R., & Pfeffer, J. (1977). An examination of need-satisfaction models of job satisfaction. *Administrative Science Quarterly, 22,* 427–456.
12. Miller, A., & Bradburn, E. (1991, July 1). Shape up—or else! *Newsweek,* pp. 42–43.
13. Tullly, S. (1995, June 12). America's healthiest companies. *Fortune,* pp. 98–100, 104, 106.
14. McLaughlin, S. (1998). Freudian chip. *Inc. Tech.,* no. 1, p. 18.
15. Cronin, M. P. (1993, September). Easing workers' savings woes. *Inc.,* p. 29.
16. Leana, C. R., & Feldman, D. C. (1992). *Coping with job loss.* New York: Lexington Books.
17. Schwartz, E. L. (1991, June 17). Hot dogs, roller coasters, and complaints. *BusinessWeek,* p. 27.
18. Jaffe, C. A. (1990, January). Management by fun. *Nation's Business,* pp. 58–60.
19. Gunsch, D. (1991). Award programs at work. *Personnel Journal, 23*(4), 85–89.
20. Miller, A., & Springen, K. (1988, October 31). Forget cash, give me the TV. *Newsweek,* p. 58.
21. Boreman, A. M. (1999, October 19). Clean my house, and I'm yours forever. *Inc.,* p. 214. Hickins, M. (1999, April). Creative "get-a-life" benefits. *Management Review,* p. 7. Nelson, B. (1994). *1001 ways to reward employees.* New York: Waterman. Palmer, A. T. (1999, April 26). Who's minding the baby? The company. *BusinessWeek,* p. 32.
22. Dannjauser, C. L. (2000, July–August). The right rewards. *Working Woman,* pp. 40–41.
23. Perky benefits. (2000, November–December). *Across the Board,* p. 94.
24. Perks and priorities. (2001, March 6). *Business 2.0,* p. 33.
25. Wood, R. A., & Locke, E. A. (1990). Goal setting and strategy effects on complex tasks. In B. M. Staw & L. L. Cummings (Eds.), *Research in organizational behavior* (Vol. 12, pp. 73–110). Greenwich, CT: JAI Press.
26. Locke, E. A., & Latham, G. P. (1990). *A theory of goal setting and task performance.* Englewood Cliffs, NJ: Prentice Hall.
27. Mento, A. J., Locke, E. A., & Klein, H. J. (1992). Relationship of goal level to valence and instrumentality. *Journal of Applied Psychology, 77,* 395–406.
28. Wright, P. M., O'Leary-Kelly, A. M., Cortinak, J. M., Klein, H. J., & Hollenbeck, J. R. (1994). On the meaning and measurement of goal commitment. *Journal of Applied Psychology, 79,* 795–803.
29. Klein, H. J. (1991). Further evidence on the relationship between goal setting and expectancy theories. *Organizational Behavior and Human Decision Processes, 49,* 230–257.
30. Harrison, D. A., & Liska, L. Z. (1994). Promoting regular exercise in organizational fitness programs: Health-related differences in motivational building blocks. *Personnel Psychology, 47,* 47–71.
31. Gellatly, I. R., & Meyer, J. P. (1992). The effects of goal difficulty on physiological arousal, cognition, and task performance. *Journal of Applied Psychology, 77,* 696–704.

32. Wright, P. M. (1992). An examination of the relationships among monetary incentives, goal level, goal commitment, and performance. *Journal of Management, 18,* 677–693.

33. Earley, P. C., & Litucy, T. R. (1991). Delineating goal and efficacy effects: A test of three models. *Journal of Applied Psychology, 76,* 81–98.

34. Latham, G. P., & Lee, T. W. (1986). Goal setting. In E. A. Locke (Ed.), *Generalizing from laboratory to field settings* (pp. 100–117). Lexington, MA: Lexington Books.

35. Latham, G., & Baldes, J. (2002). Building a practically useful theory of goal setting and task motivation. *American Psychologist, 57,* 705–717. *Journal of Applied Psychology, 60,* 122–124.

36. Locke, E. A., & Latham, G. P. (1984). *Goal setting: A motivational technique that works!* Englewood Cliffs, NJ: Prentice Hall.

37. Wright, P. M., Hollenbeck, J. R., Wolf, S., & McMahan, G. C. (1995). The effects of varying goal difficulty operationalizations on goal setting outcomes and processes. *Organizational Behavior and Human Decision Processes, 61,* 28–43.

38. Bernstein, A. (1991, April 29). How to motivate workers: Don't watch 'em. *BusinessWeek,* p. 56.

39. Stedry, A. C., & Kay, E. (1964). *The effects of goal difficulty on task performance.* General Electric Company, Behavioral Research Service.

40. Latham, G. P., Erez, M., & Locke, E. A. (1988). Resolving scientific disputes by the joint design of crucial experiments by the antagonists: Application to the Erez-Latham dispute regarding participation in goal setting. *Journal of Applied Psychology, 73,* 753–772.

41. Ludwig, T. D., & Geller, E. S. (1997). Assigned versus participative goal setting and response generalization: Managing injury control among professional pizza deliverers. *Journal of Applied Psychology, 82,* 253–261.

42. Greenberg, J. & Colquitt, J. A. (2003). *Organizational justice: A primer.* Upper Saddle River, NJ: Prentice Hall. Greenberg, J., & Colquitt, J. A. (2003). *Handbook of organizational justice.* Mahwah, NJ: Lawrence Erlbaum Associates.

43. Grienberger, I. V., Rutte, C. G., & Van Kippenberg, A. F. M. (1997). Influence of social comparisons of outcomes and procedures on fairness judgments. *Journal of Applied Psychology, 82,* 913–919.

44. Greenberg, J. (1997). *The quest for justice on the job.* Thousand Oaks, CA: Sage.

45. Greenberg, J. (1987). A taxonomy of organizational justice theories. *Academy of Management Review, 12,* 9–22.

46. Adams, J. S. (1965). Inequity in social exchange. In L. Berkowitz (Ed.), *Advances in experimental social psychology* (Vol. 2, pp. 267–299). New York: Academic Press.

47. Greenberg, J. (1989). Cognitive re-evaluation of outcomes in response to underpayment inequity. *Academy of Management Journal, 32,* 176–184.

48. Harder, J. W. (1992). Play for pay: Effects of inequity in a pay-for-performance con-text. *Administrative Science Quarterly, 37,* 321–336.

49. Greenberg, J. (1990). Employee theft as a reaction to underpayment inequity: The hidden cost of pay cuts. *Journal of Applied Psychology, 75,* 561–658.

50. Skarlicki, D. P., & Folger, R. (1997). Retaliation in the workplace: The roles of distributive, procedural, and interactional justice. *Journal of Applied Psychology, 82,* 436–443.

51. Thibaut, J., & Walker, L. (1975). *Procedural justice: A psychological analysis.* Hillsdale, NJ: Erlbaum.

52. Colquitt, J. A., & Greenberg, J. (2003). Organizational justice: A fair assessment of the state of the literature. In J. Greenberg (Ed.), *Organizational behavior: The state of the science* (2nd ed.). Mahwah, NJ: Lawrence Erlbaum Associates. Cropanzano, R., & Greenberg, J. (1997). Progress in organizational justice: Tunneling through the maze. In C. L. Cooper & I. T. Robertson (Eds.), *International review of industrial and organizational psychology* (Vol. 12, pp. 317–372). New York: Wiley.

53. Greenberg, J. (1986). Determinants of perceived fairness of performance evaluations. *Journal of Applied Psychology, 71,* 340–342.

54. Konovsky, M. A., & Cropanzano, R. (1993). Justice considerations in employee drug testing. In R. Cropanzano (Ed.), *Justice in the workplace* (pp. 171–192). Hillsdale, NJ: Erlbaum.

55. Parker, C. P., Baltes, B. B., & Christiansen, N. D. (1997). Support for affirmative action, justice perceptions, and work attitudes: A study of gender and racial-ethnic group differences. *Journal of Applied Psychology, 82,* 376–389.

56. Brockner, J., & Wiesenfeld, B. M. (1996). An integrative framework for explaining reactions to decisions: The interactive effects of outcomes and procedures. *Psychological Bulletin, 120,* 189–208.

57. Martin, J. E., & Peterson, M. M. (1987). Two-tier wage structures: Implications for equity theory. *Academy of Management Journal, 30,* 297–316.

58. Ross, I. (1985, April 29). Employers win big on the move to two-tier contracts. *Fortune,* pp. 82–92.

59. Lawler, E. E., III. (1967). Secrecy about management compensation: Are there hidden costs? *Organizational Behavior and Human Performance, 2,* 182–189.

60. See Note 59.

61. Schaubroeck, J., May, D. R., & Brown, F. W. (1994). Procedural justice explanations and employee reactions to economic hardship: A field experiment. *Journal of Applied Psychology, 79,* 455–460.

62. Porter, L. W., & Lawler, E. E., III. (1968). *Managerial attitudes and performance.* Homewood, IL: Irwin.

63. Organization for Economic Cooperation & Development. (2002). From the Internet at www.oecd.gov.

64. Koretz, G. (2001, June 11). Why Americans work so hard. *BusinessWeek,* p. 34.

65. Spencer, T. (2000, June 26). Paycheck, health benefits, and a mercedes. *Fortune,* p. 336.

66. Mitchell, T. R. (1983). Expectancy-value models in organizational psychology. In N. Feather (Ed.), *Expectancy, incentive, and action* (pp. 293–314). Hillsdale, NJ: Lawrence Erlbaum Associates.

67. Davis, V. A. (2002). Report of the Wyoming Department of Employment, Research, and Planning. From the Internet at lmi.state.wy.us/1099/t2al.htm.

68. Zippo, M. (1982). Flexible benefits: Just the beginning. *Personnel Journal, 17*(4), 56–58.

69. Wilson, A. (2000, September). Let people pick their perks. *Fast Company,* p. 356.

70. Seligman, D. (1999, November 15). The baseball enigma. *Forbes,* pp. 176, 178.

71. Stern, J. M., & Stewart, G. B., III. (1993, June). Pay for performance: Only the theory is easy. *HRMagazine,* pp. 48–49.

72. Heneman, R. L. (2000). *Business-driven compensation policies.* New York: AMACOM. Schuster, J. R., & Zingheim, P. K. (1992). *The new pay: Linking employee and organizational performance.* New York: Lexington Books.

73. Curry, S. (1997, August 18). Surprise! Money talks loudest. *Fortune,* p. 227.

74. Schafer, S. (1997, August). Battling a labor shortage? It's all in your imagination. *Inc.,* p. 97.

75. Ettore, B. (1998, May). The brave new world of executive compensation. *Management Review,* p. 8.

76. Rodric, S. (2001). *The stock options book.* Oakland, CA: National Center for Employee Ownership.

77. National Center for Employee Ownership Web site www.nceo.org/library/equity.html

78. The boom in employee ownership. (2000, August). *Inc.,* pp. 106–112.

79. The NetSlaves (2000, August 21). Are stock options evil? *Business 2.0:* www.business2.com/articles/web/1,1653,7043,00.html.

80. See Note 79.

81. Griffin, R. W., & McMahan, G. C. (1994). Motivation through job design. In J. Greenberg (Ed.), *Organizational behavior: The state of the science* (pp. 23–44). Hillsdale, NJ: Lawrence Erlbaum Associates.

82. Rigdon, J. E. (1992, May 26). Using lateral moves to spur employees. *Wall Street Journal,* pp. B1, B9.

83. Campion, M. A., & McClelland, C. L. (1991). Interdisciplinary examination of the costs and benefits of enlarged jobs: A job design quasi-experiment. *Journal of Applied Psychology, 76,* 186–198.

84. Campion, M. A., & McClelland, C. L. (1993). Follow-up and extension of the interdisciplinary costs and benefits of enlarged jobs. *Journal of Applied Psychology, 78,* 339–351.

85. Luthans, F., & Reif, W. E. (1974). Job enrichment: Long on theory, short on practice. *Organizational Dynamics, 2*(2), 30–43.

86. Steers, R. M., & Spencer, D. G. (1977). The role of achievement motivation in job design. *Journal of Applied Psychology, 62,* 472–479.

87. Goldman, R. B. (1976). *A work experiment: Six Americans in a Swedish plant.* New York: Ford Foundation.

88. Winpisinger, W. (1973, February). Job satisfaction: A union response. *AFL-CIO American Federationist*, pp. 8–10.
89. Hackman, J. R., & Oldham, G. R. (1980). *Work redesign*. Reading, MA: Addison-Wesley.
90. Graen, G. B., Scandura, T. A., & Graen, M. R. (1986). A field experimental test of the moderating effects of growth need strength on productivity. *Journal of Applied Psychology, 71,* 486–491.
91. Hackman, J. R., & Oldham, G. R. (1976). Motivation through the design of work: Test of a theory. *Organizational Behavior and Human Performance, 16,* 250–279.
92. Johns, G., Xie, J. L., & Fang, Y. (1992). Mediating and moderating effects in job design. *Journal of Management, 18,* 657–676.
93. Orpen, C. (1979). The effects of job enrichment on employee satisfaction, motivation, involvement, and performance: A field experiment. *Human Relations, 32,* 189–217.
94. Ropp, K. (1987, October). Candid conversations. *Personnel Administrator*, p. 49.
95. Hackman, J. R. (1976). Work design. In J. R. Hackman & J. L. Suttle (Eds.), *Improving life at work* (pp. 96–162). Santa Monica, CA: Goodyear.
96. Callari, J. J. (1988, June). You can be a better motivator. *Traffic Management*, pp. 52–56.
97. Magnet, M. (1993, May 3). Good news for the service economy. *Fortune*, pp. 46–50, 52.
98. Finegan, J. (1993, July). People power. *Inc.*, pp. 62–63.
99. See Note 98.

Case in Point Source
Ehrenfeld, T. (1993, July). Cashing in. *Inc.*, pp. 69–70.

CHAPTER 7

Preview Case Source
Morris, B. (1999, August 2). MBAs get .com fever. *Fortune*, pp. 60–66.

Chapter Notes
1. Meager, N. (1995). Occupations. In N. Nicholson (Ed.), *The Blackwell encyclopedic dictionary of organizational behavior* (pp. 352–354). Cambridge, MA: Blackwell.
2. Bureau of Labor Statistics (2002). News release, Table 4: State and industry average annual pay for 1999 and 2000. On the Internet at www.bls.gov/news.release/annpay.t04.htm.
3. Tynor, C. L. (2001, July 9). Labor strategies for new century: Englehard, Synovus point the way. *Investors Business Daily*, pp. 1–2.
4. Van Dusen, C. (2001, May 20). Synovus Financial's "secret weapon" helped by being "recession-resistant." *Atlanta Constitution*, p. C1.
5. McClelland, C. L. (2001). *Changing careers*. New York: Hungry Minds.
6. Fingleton, E. (1995, March 20). Jobs for life: Why Japan won't give them up. *Fortune*, pp. 119–123, 125.
7. Arthur, M. B., & Rousseau, D. M. (1996). *The boundaryless career: A new employ-ment principle for a new organizational era*. New York: Oxford University Press.
8. Schmitt, J. (1998, August 21). High-tech job hopping. *USA Today*, p. B1.
9. Jarman, M. (1998, July 26). Job hopping acceptable. *Arizona Republic*, p. 6.
10. Damico, J. (2002). *How to be a permanent temp*. Franklin Lakes, NJ: Career Press.
11. Driver, M. J. (1994). Careers: A review of personal and organizational research. In C. L. Cooper & I. T. Robertson (Eds.), *Key reviews in managerial psychology: Concepts and research for practice* (pp. 237–269). New York: John Wiley & Sons.
12. Pepin, J. (2002, March). Burger meister: Ray Kroc. Time 100 Polls, on the Internet at www.time.com/time/time100/builder/profile/kroc.html. Love, J. F. (1995). *Grinding it out*. New York: Bantam.
13. Greenhaus, J. H. (1987). *Career management*. New York: Dryden.
14. Meier, S. T. (1991). Vocational behavior, 1988–1990: Vocational choice, decision-making, career development interventions, and assessment. *Journal of Vocational Behavior, 39,* 131–138.
15. Holland, J. (1973). *Making vocational choices: A theory of careers*. Englewood Cliffs, NJ: Prentice Hall. Gottfredson, G. D., & Holland, J. L. (1990). A longitudinal test of the influence of congruence: Job satisfaction, competency utilization, and counterproductive behavior. *Journal of Consulting Psychology, 37,* 389–398.
16. Cluskey, G. R., & Vaux, A. (1997). Vocational misfit: Source of occupational stress among accountants. *Journal of Applied Business Research, 12,* 43–54.
17. Savickas, M. L., & Spokane, A. R. (1999). *Vocational interests: Meaning, measurement, and counseling use*. Palo Alto, CA: Davies Black.
18. Lawrence, B. (1995). Career anchor. In N. Nicholson (Ed.), *The Blackwell encyclopedic dictionary of organizational behavior* (pp. 44–45). Cambridge, MA: Blackwell.
19. Schein, E. H. (1978). *Career dynamics: Matching individual and organizational needs*. Reading, MA: Addison-Wesley.
20. Hecker, D. E. (2001, November). Occupational employment projections to 2010. *Monthly Labor Review*, pp. 57–84.
21. Griffin, A. E. C., Collella, A., & Srikanth, G. (2000). Newcomer and organizational socialization tactics: An interactionist perspective. *Human Resource Management Review, 10,* 453–474.
22. Wanous, J. P., & Coella, A. (1989). Organizational entry research: Current status and future directions. In G. Ferris & K. Rowland (Eds.), *Research in personnel and human resources management* (Vol. 7, pp. 59–120). Greenwich, CT: JAI Press.
23. Buckley, M. R., Fedor, D. B., Veres, J. G., Wiese, D. S., & Carraher, S. M. (1998). Investigating newcomer expectations and job-related outcomes. *Journal of Applied Psychology, 83,* 452–461.
24. Wanous, J. P., Poland, T. D., Premack, S. L., & Davis, K. S. (1992). The effects of met expectations on newcomer attitudes and behaviors: A review and meta-analysis. *Journal of Applied Psychology, 77,* 288–297.
25. Harvey, M. E. (1991). The effects of a realistic job preview on the tenure and satisfaction of cooperative extension service field agents. *Dissertation Abstracts International, 51*(10-A), 3303.
26. Wanous, J. P. (1993). Newcomer orientation programs that facilitate organizational entry. In H. Schuler & J. L. Farr (Eds.), *Personnel selection and assessment: Individual and organizational perspectives* (pp. 125–139). Hillsdale, NJ: Lawrence Erlbaum Associates.
27. Darwin, A. (2000). Critical reflections on mentoring in work settings. *Adult Education Quarterly, 50,* 197–211.
28. Ragubsm, B. R., & Scandura, T. A. (1999). Burden or blessing? Expected costs and benefits of being a mentor. *Journal of Organizational Behavior, 20,* 493–509.
29. Rothman, H. (1993, April). The boss as mentor. *Nation's Business*, pp. 66–67 (quote, p. 66).
30. Clutterbuck, D., & Ragins, B. R. (2002). *Mentoring and diversity: An international perspective*. Burlington, MA: Butterworth-Heinemann. Wickman, F., & Sjodin, T. (1997). *Mentoring*. Chicago: Irwin.
31. Ragins, B. R. (1999). Gender and mentoring relationships: A review and research agenda for the next decade. In G. N. Powell (Ed.), *Handbook of gender and work* (pp. 347–370). Thousand Oaks, CA: Sage.
32. Nicholson, N. (1995). Career plateauing. In N. Nicholson (Ed.), *The Blackwell encyclopedic dictionary of organizational behavior* (pp. 49–50). Cambridge, MA: Blackwell.
33. Dixon, P. (2000). *Job searching online*. Foster City, CA: IDG Books.
34. Branch, S. (1998, March 16). MBAs: What they really want. *Fortune*, p. 167.
35. Bolles, R. N. (2002). *What color is your parachute?* (2002 edition). Berkeley, CA: Ten Speed Press.
36. See Note 35.
37. See Note 35.
38. Hanisch, K. A. (1995). Retirement. In N. Nicholson (Ed.), *The Blackwell encyclopedic dictionary of organizational behavior* (pp. 490–491). Cambridge, MA: Blackwell.
39. Hanisch, K. A., & Hulin, C. L. (1990). Job attitudes and organizational withdrawal: An examination of retirement and other voluntary withdrawal behaviors. *Journal of Vocational Behavior, 37,* 60–78.
40. Hanisch, K. A. (1994). Reasons people retire and their relations to attitudinal and behavioral correlates in retirement. *Journal of Vocational Behavior, 45,* 1–16.
41. Forum for Investor Advice (1999, July 26). Work 'til you drop. *BusinessWeek*, p. 8.
42. Decker, J. P. (1999, November 22). Why pro golfers can't wait to hit the big five-oh. *Fortune*, p. 76.
43. Thornton, E. (1999, August 9). No room at the top. *BusinessWeek*, p. 50.
44. Hirsch, W. (1995). Succession planning. In N. Nicholson (Ed.), *The Blackwell encyclopedic dictionary of organizational behavior* (pp. 544–545). Cambridge, MA: Blackwell.
45. Bianco, A., & Lavelle, L. (2000, December 11). The CEO trap. *BusinessWeek*, pp. 86–92.
46. Rothwell, W. J. (2000). *Effective succession planning: Ensuring leadership continuity and building talent from within*. New York: AMACOM.

47. Poe, R., & Courter, C. L. (1999, November–December). Great expectations. *Across the Board*, p. 7.

48. Campion, M. A., Cheraskin, L., & Stevens, M. J. (1994). Career-related antecedents and outcomes of job rotation. *Academy of Management Journal, 37*, 1518–1542.

49. Anonymous. (2000, January 10). The top entrepreneurs. *BusinessWeek*, pp. 80–82.

50. Global entrepreneurship monitor. (1999, July 19). Startup nation. *BusinessWeek*, p. F4.

51. Berman, D. (1999, December 6). One iota. *BusinessWeek*, p. F8.

52. Rosenberg, H. (1999, March 1). This generation is all business. *BusinessWeek*, pp. ENT4, ENT6, ENT8.

53. Meadors, A. L. (2000). Common reasons for business failure. From the World Wide Web, members.tripod.com/mysec/flag/failure.html.

54. Barker, R. (1999, March 29). Lessons from a survivor. *BusinessWeek*, pp. ENT18–ENT20.

55. Lundstrom, M. (1999, December 20). Mommy, do you love your company more than me? *BusinessWeek*, p. 175.

56. MacLean, R. (1999, October 19). Big manager on campus. *Inc.*, pp. 62–64, 66.

57. Miller, B. (2000, September 14). Following the flock is not her fashion. From the Internet at www.delawareonline.com.

58. Barker, E. (2000, October). Bananas, my brand, and me. *Inc.*, pp. 49–50, 53–54.

59. Valdmaris, T. (2000, June 26). Former rock insider gets ideas rolling. *USA Today*, p. C3.

60. Gatlin, G. (2001, July 4). Stop & Shop takes Jessica's cake. *Boston Herald*, p. C1.

61. See Note 35.

62. Tharenou, P., Latimer, S., & Conroy, D. (1994). How do you make it to the top? An examination of women's and men's managerial advancement. *Academy of Management Journal, 37*, 899–931.

63. U.S. Department of Labor (2002). On the Internet at www.dol.gov.

64. Heilman, M. E. (1995). Sex stereotypes and their effects in the workplace: What we know and what we don't know. *Journal of Social Behavior and Personality, 10*, 3–26.

65. Aluetta, K. (1998, April 20). In the company of women. *The New Yorker*, pp. 71–78.

66. Lyness, K. S., & Thompson, D. E. (1997). Above the glass ceiling? A comparison of matched samples of female and male executives. *Journal of Applied Psychology, 82*, 359–375.

67. Ragins, B. R., & Scandura, T. A. (1997). The way we were: Gender and the termination of mentoring relationships. *Journal of Applied Psychology, 82*, 945–953.

68. Jiping, Z., & Tang, S. (2000). Breadwinner status and gender ideologies of men and women regarding family roles. *Sociological Perspectives, 43*, 29–43.

69. Jackson, A. P., Brown, R. P., & Patterson-Stewart, K. E. (2000). African-Americans in dual-career commuter marriages: An investigation of their experiences. *Family Journal-Counseling & Therapy for Couples & Families, 8*, 22–36.

70. Blyton, P. (1995). Career breaks. In N. Nicholson (Ed.), *The Blackwell encyclopedic dictionary of organizational behavior* (pp. 45–46). Cambridge, MA: Blackwell.

71. Colin, M. (2000, July 10). Give a geek a break. *BusinessWeek*, pp. 102–104.

72. Schatz, R. D. (1999, October 11). Put me in, coach. *BusinessWeek*, p. F48.

73. Harrington, A. (1998, September 28). A sounding board in cyberspace. *Fortune*, pp. 301–302.

74. Morris, B. (2000, February 21). So you're a player. Do you need a coach? *Fortune*, pp. 144–146, 148, 150, 152, 154.

75. Adapted from Morrison, E. K. (1994). *Leadership skills*. Tucson, AZ: Fisher Books.

Case in Point Sources
Open Market has been acquired by Divine. (2001, October 25). From the Internet at www.openmarket.com. Kaufman, J. (1998, May 5). A middle manager, 54, and insecure, struggles to adapt to the times. *Wall Street Journal*, pp. A1, AA6.

CHAPTER 8

Preview Case Sources
Sittenfeld, C. (1999, July–August). Power by the people. *Fast Company*, pp. 178–181, 185–189.

Chapter Notes

1. Turner, M. E. (2000). *Groups at work: Theory and research*. Mahwah, NJ: Lawrence Erlbaum Associates. Cartwright, D., & Zander, A. (1968). Origins of group dynamics. In D. Cartwright & A. Zander (Eds.), *Group dynamics: Research and theory* (pp. 3–21). New York: Harper & Row.

2. Toothman, J. (2000). *Conducting the experiential group: An introduction to group dynamics*. New York: Wiley. Bettenhausen, K. L. (1991). Five years of groups research: What we have learned and what needs to be addressed. *Journal of Management, 17*, 345–381.

3. Forsyth, D. L. (1999). *Group dynamics* (3rd ed.). Belmont, CA: Wadsworth.

4. Long, S. (1984). Early integration in groups: "A group to join and a group to create." *Human Relations, 37*, 311–332.

5. Tuckman, B. W., & Jensen, M. A. (1977). Stages of small group development revisited. *Group and Organization Studies, 2*, 419–427.

6. Gersick, C. J. G. (1988). Time and transition in work teams: Toward a new model of group development. *Academy of Management Journal, 31*, 9–41.

7. Gersick, C. J. G. (1989). Marking time: Predictable transitions in task groups. *Academy of Management Journal, 32*, 274–309.

8. Romanelli, E., & Tushman, M. L. (1994). Organizational transformation as punctuated equilibrium: An empirical test. *Academy of Management Journal, 37*, 1141–1166.

9. Biddle, B. J. (1979). *Role theory: Expectations, identities, and behavior*. New York: Academic Press.

10. Jackson, S. E., & Schuler, R. S. (1985). A meta-analysis and conceptual critique of research on role ambiguity and role conflict in work settings. *Organizational Behavior and Human Decision Processes, 36*, 16–78.

11. Benne, K. D., & Sheats, P. (1948). Functional roles of group members. *Journal of Social Issues, 4*, 41–49.

12. Hackman, J. R. (1992). Group influences on individuals in organizations. In M. D. Dunnette & L. M. Hough (Eds.), *Handbook of industrial and organizational psychology* (2nd ed.) (Vol. 3, pp. 199–268). Palo Alto, CA: Consulting Psychologists Press.

13. Feldman, D. C. (1984). The development and enforcement of group norms. *Academy of Management Review, 9*, 48–53.

14. Wilson, S. (1978). *Informal groups: An introduction*. Englewood Cliffs, NJ: Prentice Hall.

15. Greenberg, J. (1988). Equity and workplace status: A field experiment. *Journal of Applied Psychology, 73*, 606–613.

16. Stryker, S., & Macke, A. S. (1978). Status inconsistency and role conflict. In R. H. Turner, J. Coleman, & R. C. Fox (Eds.), *Annual review of sociology* (Vol. 4, pp. 58–90). Palo Alto, CA: Annual Reviews.

17. Jackson, L. A., & Grabski, S. V. (1988). Perceptions of fair pay and the gender wage gap. *Journal of Applied Social Psychology, 18*, 606–625.

18. Torrance, E. P. (1954). Some consequences of power differences on decision making in permanent and temporary three-man groups. *Research Studies: Washington State College, 22*, 130–140.

19. Hare, A. P. (1976). *Handbook of small group research* (2nd ed.). New York: Free Press.

20. Aronson, E., & Mills, J. (1959). The effects of severity of initiation on liking for a group. *Journal of Abnormal and Social Psychology, 59*, 178–181.

21. See Note 4.

22. Cartwright, D. (1968). The nature of group cohesiveness. In D. Cartwright & A. Zander (Eds.), *Group dynamics: Research and theory* (3rd ed.) (pp. 91–109). New York: Harper & Row.

23. George, J. M., & Bettenhausen, K. (1990). Understanding prosocial behavior, sales performance, and turnover: A group-level analysis in a service context. *Journal of Applied Psychology, 75*, 698–709.

24. Douglas, T. (1983). *Groups: Understanding people gathered together*. New York: Tavistock.

25. Aiello, J. R. & Douthitt, E. A. (2001). Social facilitation from Triplett to electronic performance monitoring. *Group Dynamics, 5*, 163–180.

26. Zajonc, R. B. (1965). Social facilitation. *Science, 149*, 269–274.

27. Zajonc, R. B. (1980). Compresence. In P. B. Paulus (Ed.), *Psychology of group influence* (pp. 35–60). Hillsdale, NJ: Lawrence Erlbaum Associates.

28. Geen, R. B., Thomas, S. L., & Gammill, P. (1988). Effects of evaluation and coaction on state anxiety and anagram performance. *Personality and Individual Differences, 6*, 293–298.

29. Stanton, J. M. (2000). Reactions to employee performance monitoring: Framework, review, and research directions. *Human Performance, 13*, 85–113. Aiello, J. R., & Kolb, K. J. (1995). Electronic

performance monitoring and social context: Impact on productivity and stress. *Journal of Applied Psychology, 80,* 339–353.

30. Aiello, J. R., & Svec, C. M. (1993). Computer monitoring of work performance: Extending the social facilitation framework to electronic presence. *Journal of Applied Social Psychology, 23,* 538–548.

31. Alge, B. J. (2001). Effects of computer surveillance on perceptions of privacy and procedural justice. *Journal of Applied Psychology, 86,* 797–804. Ambrose, M. L. Adler, G. S., & Noel, T. W. (1998). Electronic performance monitoring: A consideration of rights. In M. Schmeinke (Ed.), *Managerial ethics: Moral management of people and processes* (pp. 61–80). Mahwah, NJ: Lawrence Erlbaum Associates.

32. Steiner, I. D. (1972). *Group processes and productivity.* New York: Academic Press.

33. Shepperd, J. A. (1993). Productivity loss in performance groups: A motivation analysis. *Psychological Bulletin, 113,* 68–81.

34. Latané, B., Williams, K., & Harkins, S. (1979). Many hands make light the work: The causes and consequences of social loafing. *Journal of Personality and Social Psychology, 37,* 822–832.

35. Kravitz, D. A., & Martin, B. (1986). Ringelmann rediscovered: The original article. *Journal of Personality and Social Psychology, 50,* 936–941.

36. Karau, S. J., & Williams, K. D. (1993). Social loafing: A meta-analytic review and theoretical integration. *Journal of Personality and Social Psychology, 65,* 681–706.

37. Latané, B., & Nida, S. (1980). Social impact theory and group influence: A social engineering perspective. In P. B. Paulus (Ed.), *Psychology of group influence* (pp. 3–34). Hillsdale, NJ: Lawrence Erlbaum Associates.

38. Earley, P. C. (1993). East meets west meets mideast: Further explorations of collectivistic and individualistic work groups. *Academy of Management Journal, 36,* 319–348.

39. Nordstrom, R., Lorenzi, P., & Hall, R. V. (1990). A review of public posting of performance feedback in work settings. *Journal of Organizational Behavior Management, 11,* 101–123.

40. Bricker, M. A., Harkins, S. G., & Ostrom, T. M. (1986). Effects of personal involvement: Thought-provoking implications for social loafing. *Journal of Personality and Social Psychology, 51,* 763–769.

41. George, J. M. (1992). Extrinsic and intrinsic origins of perceived social loafing in organizations. *Academy of Management Journal, 35,* 191–202.

42. Albanese, R. & Van Fleet, D. D. (1985). Rational behavior in groups: The free-riding tendency. *Academy of Management Review, 10,* 244–255.

43. Miles, J. A., & Greenberg, J. (1993). Using punishment threats to attenuate social loafing effects among swimmers. *Organizational Behavior and Human Decision Processes, 56,* 246–265.

44. Watson, W. E., Kumar, K., & Michaelsen, K. K. (1993). Cultural diversity's impact on interaction process and performance: Comparing homogeneous and diverse task groups. *Academy of Management Journal, 36,* 590–602.

45. Katzenbach, J. R., & Smith, D. K. (1993, March–April). The discipline of teams. *Harvard Business Review, 72*(2), 111–120.

46. Harari, O. (1995, October). The dream team. *Management Review,* pp. 29–31.

47. See Note 46.

48. Katzenbach, J. R. (1998). *Teams at the top.* Boston: Harvard Business School.

49. Herbelin, S. (2000). *Work team coaching.* Riverbank, CA: Riverbank Books. Chang, R. Y. (1999). *Success through teamwork.* San Francisco: Jossey-Bass. Sundstrom, E. (1998). *Supporting work team effectiveness: Best practices for fostering high performance.* San Francisco: Jossey-Bass.

50. Mohrman, S. A. (1993). Integrating roles and structure in the lateral organization. In J. R. Galbraith & E. E. Lawler, III (Eds.), *Organizing for the future* (pp. 109–141). San Francisco: Jossey-Bass.

51. Tuckman, B. W., & Jensen, M. A. (1977). Stages of small group development revisited. *Group and Organization Studies, 2,* 419–427.

52. Ray, D., & Bronstein, H. (1995). *Teaming up.* New York: McGraw-Hill.

53. Wellins, R. S., Byham, & Wilson, J. M. (1991). *Empowered teams.* San Francisco: Jossey-Bass.

54. Moravec, M., Johannessen, O. J., & Hjelmas, T. A. (1997, July–August). Thumbs up for self-managed teams. *Management Review,* pp. 42–47.

55. Fisher, K. (1999). *Leading self-directed work teams.* New York: McGraw-Hill. Manz, C. C., & Sims, H. P., Jr. (1993). *Business without bosses.* New York: John Wiley & Sons.

56. Osburn, J. D., Moran, L., Musselwhite, E., & Zenger, J. H. (1990). *Self-directed work teams.* Burr, Ridge, IL: Irwin.

57. 1996 Industry report: What self-managing teams manage. (1996, October). *Training,* p. 69.

58. From the SEI Investments Web site (2002, May 22): www.Seiic.com/company/news.

59. Kirsner, S. (1998, April–May). "Everyday, it's a new place." *Fast Company,* pp. 130–135.

60. Levering, R. & Moskowitz, M. (2002, February 4). The best companies to work for: The best in the worst of times. *Fortune,* pp. 117–133.

61. Duarte, L. L., & Snyder, N. T. (2000). *Mastering virtual teams.* San Francisco: Jossey-Bass.

62. Coovert, M. D., & Foster, L. L. (2001). *Computer supported cooperative work.* New York: Wiley.

63. Lipnak, J., & Stamps, J. (2000). *Virtual teams* (2nd ed.). New York: Wiley.

64. Gilder, G. (2000). *Telecosm: How infinite bandwidth will revolutionize our world.* New York: Free Press.

65. Hackman, J. R. (1987). The design of work teams. In J. W. Lorsch (Ed.), *Handbook of organizational behavior* (pp. 315–342). Englewood Cliffs, NJ: Prentice Hall.

66. See Note 65 (quote, pp. 338).

67. Sheridan, J. H. (1990, October 15). America's best plants. *IndustryWeek,* pp. 28–64.

68. Fisher, K. (1993). *Leading self-directed work teams.* New York: McGraw-Hill.

69. Lawler, E. E., III., Mohrman, S. A., & Ledford, G. E., Jr. (1992). *Employee involvement and total quality management.* San Francisco: Jossey-Bass.

70. Hackman, J. R. (Ed.) (1990). *Groups that work (and those that don't).* San Francisco: Jossey-Bass.

71. Wellins, R. S. Byham, W. C., & Wilson, J. M. (1991). *Empowered teams.* San Francisco: Jossey-Bass.

72. Blanchard, K. H., & Bowles, S. M. (2001). *High five: The magic of working together.* New York: William Morrow.

73. Pearson, C. A. L. (1992). Autonomous workgroups: An evaluation at an industrial site. *Human Relations, 45,* 905–936.

74. Wall, T. D., Kemp, N. J., Jackson, P. R., & Clegg, C. W. (1986). Outcomes of autonomous workgroups: A long-term field experiment. *Academy of Management Journal, 29,* 280–304.

75. Robbins, H., & Finley, M. (1995). *Why teams don't work.* Princeton, NJ: Peterson's/Pacesetters Books.

76. Stern, A. (1993, July 18). Managing by team is not always as easy as it looks. *New York Times,* p. B14.

77. See Note 76.

78. See Note 76.

79. See Note 76.

80. See Note 76.

81. See Note 76.

82. Maginn, M. D. (1994). *Effective teamwork.* Burr Ridge, IL: Business One Irwin.

83. Salas, E., Edens, E., & Nowers, C. A. (2000). *Improving teamwork in organizations.* Mahwah, NJ: Lawrence Erlbaum Associates.

84. Dumaine, B. (1994, September 5). The trouble with teams. *Fortune,* pp. 86–88, 90, 92 (quote, p. 86).

85. Barner, R. W. (2001). Team troubleshooter. Palo Alto, CA: Davies Black. Maruca, R. F. (2000, November). Unit of one. *Fast Company,* pp. 109–140.

86. Redding, J. C. (2000). *The radical team handbook.* New York: John Wiley & Sons. Caudron, S. (1994, February). Teamwork takes work. *Personnel Journal,* pp. 41–46, 49 (quote, p. 43).

87. Caudron, 1994; see Note 86 (quote, p. 42).

88. Stewart, G. L., & Manz, C. C. (1997). Leadership for self-managing work teams: A typology and integrative model. In. R. P. Vecchio (Ed.), *Leadership: Understanding the dynamics of power and influence in organizations* (pp. 396–410). Notre Dame, IN: University of Notre Dame Press.

89. Sundstrom, E., DeMeuse, K. P., & Futrell, D. (1990). Work teams: Applications and effectiveness. *American Psychologist, 45,* 128–137.

90. Balf, T. (1999, November). Extreme off-site. *Fast Company,* pp. 384–388, 390, 396, 398.

91. See Note 84 (quote, p. 88).

92. See Note 84 (quote, p. 90).

93. See Note 84 (quote, p. 88).

94. Anonymous. (1994, December). The facts of life for teambuilding. *Human Resources Forum,* p. 3.

Case in Point Sources
Cutler-Hammer Web site: www.ch.cutler-hammer.com/. Heibeler, R., Kelley, T. B., & Ketteman, C. (1998). *Best practices.* New York: Simon & Schuster.

CHAPTER 9

Preview Case Sources

Olofson, C. (2000, July). What we have here is no failure to communicate. *Inc.*, p. 76.

Fernando Espuelas's call to arms. (1999, November 8). *The Industry Standard.* www.the-standard.com/article/0,1902,7522,00.html.

@NY Staff. (2000, March 15). Questions for . . . Fernando Espuelas. www.atnewyork.com/people.

Chapter Notes

1. Locker, K. O. (2001). *Business and administrative communication.* Burr Ridge, IL: McGraw-Hill. Fulk, J. (1993). Social construction of communication technology. *Academy of Management Journal, 36,* 921–950.
2. Roberts, K. H. (1984). *Communicating in organizations.* Chicago: Science Research Associates (quote, p. 4).
3. Weick, K. E. (1987). Theorizing about organizational communication. In F. M. Jablin, L. L. Putnam, K. H. Roberts, & L. W. Porter (Eds.), *Handbook of organizational communication* (pp. 97–122). Newbury Park, CA: Sage.
4. Barnard, C. I. (1938). *The functions of the executive.* Cambridge, MA: Harvard University Press.
5. Mintzberg, H. (1973). *The nature of managerial work.* New York: Harper & Row.
6. Pastore, M. (1999, June 14). ISPs blamed for SPAM problem. cyberatlas.internet.com/big_picture/traffic_patterns/article/0,,5931_152131,00.html.
7. SpamCon Foundation: www.spamcon.org/about.
8. Center for Democracy in Technology, Ad Hoc Working Group on Unsolicited Commercial Email, www.cdt.org/spam.
9. Baskin, O. W., & Aronoff, C. E. (1980). *Interpersonal communication in organizations.* Santa Monica, CA: Goodyear.
10. Quinn, R. E., Hildebrandt, H. W., Rogers, P. S., & Thompson, M. P. (1991). A competing values framework for analyzing presentational communication in management contexts. *Journal of Business Communication, 28,* 213–232.
11. Lengel, R. H., & Daft, R. L. (1988). The selection of communication media as an executive skill. *Academy of Management Executive, 2,* 225–232.
12. Yates, J., & Orlikowski, W. J. (1992). Genres of organizational communication: A structurational approach to studying communication and media. *Academy of Management Review, 17,* 291–326.
13. Szwergold, J. (1993, June). Employee newsletters help fill an information gap. *Management Review,* p. 8.
14. Sibson and Company, Inc. (1989). *Compensation planning survey, 1989.* Princeton, NJ: Author.
15. Brady, T. (1993, June). Employee handbooks: Contracts or empty promises? *Management Review,* pp. 33–35.
16. Anonymous. (1993, November). The (handbook) handbook. *Inc.*, pp. 57–64.
17. NUA Internet Surveys (2000, August 8). www.nua.ie/surveys/index.cgi?f=VS&art_id=905355960&rel=true.
18. Gartner Group. (2002, March 19). GartnerG2 says e-mail marketing campaigns threaten traditional direct mail promotions. www3.gartner.com/5_about/press_releases/2002_03/pr20020319b.jsp.
19. Saunders, C. C., Robey, D., & Vavarek, K. A. (1994). The persistence of status differentials in computer conferencing. *Human Communication Research, 20,* 443–372.
20. Osterman Research. (2002, March). Osterman Research survey on instant messaging. www.ostermanresearch.com/results/surveyresults_im0302.htm.
21. Creighton, J. L., & Adams, J. W. R. (1998, January). The cybermeeting's about to begin. *Management Review,* pp. 29–31.
22. Craiger, P., & Weiss, R. J. (1998, June). Traveling in cyberspace: Video-mediated communication. *The Industrial-Organizational Psychologist,* pp. 83–92.
23. Diamond, L., & Roberts, S. (1996). *Effective videoconferencing.* Menlo Park, CA: Crisp.
24. Judge, P. C., & Browder, S. (1998, February 23). Let's talk. *BusinessWeek,* pp. 61–64, 66–68, 72, 74, 76, 76.
25. Level, D. A. (1972). Communication effectiveness: Methods and situation. *Journal of Business Communication, 28,* 11–25.
26. Klauss, R., & Bass, B. M. (1982). *International communication in organizations.* New York: Academic Press.
27. Gantenbein, D. (2000, September). Communicate correctly. *Home Office Computing,* pp. 39–40.
28. Daft, R. L., Lengel, R. H., & Treviño, L. K. (1987). Message equivocality, media selection, and manager performance: Implications for information systems. *MIS Quarterly, 11,* 355–366.
29. Barnum, C., & Wolnainsky, N. (1989, April). Taking cues from body language. *Management Review,* pp. 3–8.
30. Malloy, J. T. (1990). *Dress for success.* New York: Warner Books.
31. Rafaeli, A., Dutton, J., Harquail, C., & Mackie-Lewis, S. (1997). Navigating by attire: The use of dress by female administrative employees. *Academy of Management Journal, 40,* 9–45.
32. Caggiano, C. (1997). Benchmark: Does anyone still wear a power tie? *Inc.*, p. 148.
33. Global businesswear trends. (1997, June). *Casual Clothing in the Workplace News,* pp. 2–4.
34. Malloy, A. (1996, June). Counting the intangibles. *Computerworld,* pp. 31–33.
35. Schwartz, G. (1976). *Queuing and waiting.* Chicago: University of Chicago Press.
36. Greenberg, J. (1989). The organizational waiting game: Time as a status-asserting or status-neutralizing tactic. *Basic and Applied Social Psychology, 10,* 13–26.
37. Greenberg, J. (1988). Equity and workplace status: A field experiment. *Journal of Applied Psychology, 73,* 606–613.
38. Zweigenhaft, R. L. (1976). Personal space in the faculty office: Desk placement and student–faculty interaction. *Journal of Applied Psychology, 61,* 621–632.
39. Greenberg, J. (1976). The role of seating position in group interaction: A review, with applications for group trainers. *Group and Organization Studies, 1,* 310–327.
40. Capowski, G. S. (1993, June). Designing a corporate identity. *Management Review,* pp. 37–40.
41. Scully, J. (1987). *Odyssey: Pepsi to Apple . . . a journey of adventure, ideas, and the future.* New York: Harper & Row.
42. Carstairs, E. (1986, February). No ivory tower for Procter & Gamble. *Corporate Design and Reality,* pp. 24–30.
43. McCallister, L. (1994). *"I wish I'd said that!" How to talk your way out of trouble and into success.* New York: Wiley.
44. See Note 43.
45. Tannen, D. (1995). *Talking 9 to 5.* New York: Avon.
46. Tannen, D. (1995, September–October). The power of talk: Who gets heard and why. *Harvard Business Review,* pp. 137–148.
47. See Note 45 (quote p. 148).
48. Munter, M. (1993, May–June). Cross-cultural communication for managers. *Business Horizons,* pp. 75–76.
49. Mellow, C. (1995, August 17). Russia: Making cash from chaos. *Fortune,* pp. 145–146, 148, 150–151.
50. Hodgson, J. D., Sango, Y., & Graham, J. L. (2000). Doing business with the new Japan. Oxford, England: Rowman & Littlefield. Ueda, K. (1974). Sixteen ways to avoid saying no in Japan. In J. C. Condon & M. Saito (Eds.), *International encounters with Japan* (pp. 185–192). Tokyo: Simul Press.
51. Adler, N. (1991). *International dimensions of organizational behavior* (2nd ed.). Boston: PWS/Kent.
52. Argyris, C. (1974). *Behind the front page: Organizational self-renewal in a metropolitan newspaper.* San Francisco: Jossey-Bass.
53. Hawkins, B. L., & Preston, P. (1981). *Managerial communication.* Santa Monica, CA: Goodyear.
54. Szilagyi, A. (1981). *Management and performance.* Glenview, IL: Scott, Foresman.
55. See Note 54.
56. Coulson, R. (1981). *The termination handbook.* New York: Free Press.
57. Walker, C. R., & Guest, R. H. (1952). *The man on the assembly line.* Cambridge, MA: Harvard University Press.
58. Luthans, F., & Larsen, J. K. (1986). How managers really communicate. *Human Relations, 39,* 161–178.
59. Kirmeyer, S. L., & Lin, T. (1987). Social support: Its relationship to observed communication with peers and superiors. *Academy of Management Journal, 30,* 137–151.
60. Read, W. (1962). Upward communication in industrial hierarchies. *Human Relations, 15,* 3–16.
61. Glauser, M. J. (1984). Upward information flow in organizations: Review and conceptual analysis. *Human Relations, 37,* 613–643.
62. Lee, F. (1993). Being polite and keeping MUM: How bad news is communicated in organizational hierarchies. *Journal of Applied Social Psychology, 23,* 1124–1149.
63. Tesser, A., & Rosen, S. (1975). The reluctance to transmit bad news. In L. Berkowitz (Ed.), *Advances in experimental social psychology* (Vol. 8, pp. 192–232). New York: Academic Press.

64. Kiechel, W., III. (1990, June 18). How to escape the echo chamber. *Fortune*, pp. 121–130 (quote, p. 130).

65. Rogers, E. M., & Rogers, A. (1976). *Communication in organizations*. New York: Free Press.

66. Cheng, E. W., Li, H., Love, P. E. D., & Irani, Z. (2001). Network communication in the construction industry. *Corporate Communications*, 6(2), 61–70.

67. Harcourt, J., Richerson, V., & Waitterk, M. J. (1991). A national study of middle managers' assessment of organization communication quality. *Journal of Business Communication*, 28, 347–365.

68. Krackhardt, D., & Hanson, J. R. (1993, July–August). Informal networks: The company behind the chart. *Harvard Business Review*, pp. 104–111.

69. Zenger, T. R., & Lawrence, B. S. (1989). Organizational demography: The differential effects of age and tenure distributions on technical communication. *Academy of Management Journal*, 32, 353–376.

70. Ibarra, H. (1992). Homophily and differential returns: Sex differences in network structure and access in an advertising firm. *Administrative Science Quarterly*, 37, 422–447.

71. Lesley, E., & Mallory, M. (1993, November 29). Inside the Black business network. *BusinessWeek*, pp. 70–72, 77, 80–81.

72. Brass, D. J. (1985). Men's and women's networks: A study of interaction patterns and influence in an organization. *Academy of Management Journal*, 28, 327–343.

73. Krackhardt, D., & Porter, L. W. (1986). The snowball effect: Turnover embedded in communication networks. *Journal of Applied Psychology*, 71, 50–55.

74. Duncan, J. W. (1984). Perceived humor and social network patterns in a sample of task-oriented groups: A reexamination of prior research. *Human Relations*, 37, 895–907.

75. Baskin, O. W., & Aronoff, C. E. (1989). *Interpersonal communication in organizations*. Santa Monica, CA: Goodyear.

76. Crampton, S., Hodge, J. W., & Mishra, J. M. (1998). The informal communication network: Factors influencing grapevine activity. *Public Personnel Management*, 27, 569–584.

77. Walton, E. (1961). How efficient is the grapevine? *Personnel*, 28, 45–49.

78. Thibaut, A. M., Calder, B. J., & Sternthal, B. (1981). Using information processing theory to design marketing strategies. *Journal of Marketing Research*, 18, 73–79.

79. Lesley, E., & Zinn, L. (1993, July 5). The right moves, baby. *BusinessWeek*, pp. 30–31.

80. Schiller, Z. (1995, September 11). P&G is still having a devil of a time. *BusinessWeek*, p. 46.

81. See Note 80.

82. Kitchen, P. J., & Daly, F. (2002). Internal communication during change management. *Corporate Communications*, 7(1), 46–53.

83. Fiol, C. M. (1995). Corporate communications: Comparing executives' private and public statements. *Academy of Management Journal*, 38, 522–536.

84. Alessanddra, T., & Hunksaker, P. (1993). *Communicating at work*. New York: Fireside.

85. Borman, E. (1982). *Interpersonal communication in the modern organization* (2nd ed.). Englewood Cliffs, NJ: Prentice Hall.

86. Cantoni, C. J. (1993). *Corporate dandelions*. New York: AMACOM.

87. Thornton, R. J. (1987, February 25). I can't recommend the candidate too highly: An ambiguous lexicon for job recommendations. *The Chronicle for Higher Education*, p. 42.

88. Rowe, M. P., & Baker, M. (1984, May–June). Are you hearing enough employee concerns? *Harvard Business Review*, pp. 127–135.

89. Burley-Allen, M. (1982). *Listening: The forgotten skill*. New York: John Wiley & Sons.

90. Brownell, J. (1985). A model for listening instructions: Management applications. *ABCA Bulletin*, 48(3), 31–44.

91. Austin, N. K. (1991, March). Why listening's not as easy as it sounds. *Working Woman*, pp. 46–48.

92. See Note 91.

93. Seyper, B. D., Bostrom, R. N., & Seibert, J. H. (1989). Listening, communication abilities, and success at work. *Journal of Business Communication*, 26, 293–303.

94. Penley, L. E., Alexander, E. R., Jernigan, I. E., & Henwood, C. I. (1991). Communication abilities of managers: The relationship to performance. *Journal of Management*, 17, 57–76.

95. Brownell, J. (1990). Perceptions of effective listeners: A management study. *Journal of Business Communication*, 27, 401–415.

96. Nichols, R. G. (1962, Winter). Listening is good business. *Management of Personnel Quarterly*, p. 4.

97. See Note 21.

98. McCathrin, Z. (1990, Spring). The key to employee communication: Small group meetings. *The Professional Communicator*, pp. 6–7, 10.

99. Vernyi, B. (1987, April 26). Institute aims to boost quality of company suggestion boxes. *Toledo Blade*, p. B2.

100. Taft, W. F. (1985). Bulletin boards, exhibits, hotlines. In C. Reuss & D. Silvis (Eds.), *Inside organizational communication* (2nd ed.) (pp. 183–189). New York: Longman.

101. Walter, K. (1995, September). Ethics hot lines tap into more than wrongdoing. *HRMagazine*, pp. 71–85.

102. See Note 101.

103. Beck, S. M. (1997, September 7). How'm I really doing? No, really. *BusinessWeek*, pp. ENT10–ENT11.

104. Labarre, P. (1998, November). Screw up, and get smart. *Fast Company*, p. 58.

105. Schnake, M. E., Dumler, M. P., Cochran, D. S., & Barnett, T. R. (1990). Effects of differences in superior and subordinate perception of superiors' communication practices. *Journal of Business Communication*, 27, 37–50.

106. Whetten, D. A., & Cameron, K. S. (1995). *Developing management skills* (3rd ed.). New York: HarperCollins.

107. Dubrin, A. J. (2001). *Leadership* (3rd ed.). Boston: Houghton Mifflin.

108. Tannen, D. (1998, February 2). How you speak shows where you rank. *Fortune*, p. 156.

109. Wurman, R. S. (2000). *Understanding*. Newport, RI: TED Conferences.

Case in Point Sources

PSS Web site www.pssd.com/about/about.htm. Kelly, P. (1998, April). Forget policy manuals. *Inc.*, pp. 37–38. Kelly, P. (1998). *Faster company: Building the world's nuttiest, turn-on-a-dime, home-grown, billion dollar business*. New York: John Wiley & Sons.

CHAPTER 10

Preview Case Sources

Driscoll, D. M. (2002, September/October). Enron: A failure of corporate governance. *Ethikos*, 16(2), 9, 12. Teather, D. (2002, January 21). Arthur Andersen pins blame on Enron. From the Internet at www.guardian.co.uk/enron/story/0.11337.636598.00.html. Left, S. (2002, March 27). Ex-Andersen boss was "sacrificial lamb." From the Internet at www.guardian.co.uk/enron/story/0,11337,6749 80,00.html. Enron auditor faces criminal charges. (2002, March 15). From the Internet at news.bbc.co.uk/hi/english/business/newsid_1873000/1873758.stm. Saporito, B. (2002, February 20). How Fastow helped Enron fall. From the Internet at www.time.com/time/business/article/0,8599,201871,00.html.

Chapter Notes

1. Mintzberg, H. J. (1988). *Mintzberg on management: Inside our strange world of organizations*. New York: Free Press.

2. Allison, S. T., Jordan, A. M. R., & Yeatts, C. E. (1992). A cluster-analytic approach toward identifying the structure and content of human decision making. *Human Relations*, 45, 41–72.

3. Harrison, E. F. (1987). *The managerial decision-making process* (3rd ed.). Boston: Houghton Mifflin.

4. Wedley, W. C., & Field, R. H. G. (1984). A predecision support system. *Academy of Management Review*, 9, 696–703.

5. Nutt, P. C. (2002). *Why decisions fail?* San Francisco: Berrett–Kohler. Nutt, P. C. (1993). The formulation process and tactics used in organizational decision making. *Organization Science*, 4, 226–251.

6. Nutt, P. (1984). Types of organizational decision processes. *Administrative Science Quarterly*, 29, 414–450.

7. Cowan, D. A. (1986). Developing a process model of problem recognition. *Academy of Management Review*, 11, 763–776.

8. Dennis, T. L., & Dennis, L. B. (1998). *Microcomputer models for management decision making*. St. Paul, MN: West.

9. Fulk, J., & Boyd, B. (1991). Emerging theories of communication in organizations. *Journal of Management*, 17, 407–446.

10. Sainfort, F. C., Gustafson, D. H., Bosworth, K., & Hawkins, R. P. (1990). Decision support systems effectiveness: Conceptual framework and empirical evaluation. *Organizational Behavior and Human Decision Processes*, 45, 232–252.

11. Collyer, S. C., & Malecki, G. S. (1998). Tactical decision making under stress: History and overview. In J. A. Cannon-Bowers & E. Salas (Eds), *Making decisions under stress: Implications for individual and team training* (pp. 3–15). Washington, DC: American Psychological Association.

12. Morrison, J. G., Kelly, R. T., Moore, R. A., & Hutchins, S. G. (1998). Implications of decision-making research for decision support and displays. In J. A. Cannon-Bowers & E. Salas (Eds.), *Making decisions under stress: Implications for individual and team training* (pp. 375–406). Washington, DC: American Psychological Association.

13. Stevenson, M. K., Busemeyer, J. R., & Naylor, J. C. (1990). Judgment and decision-making theory. In M. D. Dunnette & L. M. Hough (Eds.), *Handbook of industrial and organizational psychology* (2nd ed.) (Vol. 1, pp. 283–374). Palo Alto, CA: Consulting Psychologists Press.

14. See Note 5.

15. Dutta, A. (2001). Business planning for network services: A systems thinking approach. *Information Systems Research, 12,* 260–283. Hill, C. W., & Jones, G. R. (1989). *Strategic management.* Boston: Houghton Mifflin.

16. Crainer, S. (1998, November). The 75 greatest management decisions ever made. *Management Review,* pp. 16–23.

17. Amit, R., & Wernerfelt, B. (1990). Why do firms reduce business risk? *Academy of Management Journal, 33,* 520–533.

18. Provan, K. G. (1982). Interorganizational linkages and influence over decision making. *Academy of Management Journal, 25,* 443–451.

19. Galaskiewicz, J., & Wasserman, S. (1989). Mimetic processes within an interorganizational field: An empirical test. *Administrative Science Quarterly, 34,* 454–479.

20. Parsons, C. K. (1988). Computer technology: Implications for human resources management. In G. R. Ferris & K. M. Rowland (Eds.), *Research in personnel and human resources management* (Vol. 6, pp. 1–36). Greenwich, CT: JAI Press.

21. Simon, H. A. (1987). Making management decisions: The role of intuition and emotion. *Academy of Management Executive, 1,* 57–64.

22. Kirschenbaum, S. S. (1992). Influence of experience on information-gathering strategies. *Journal of Applied Psychology, 77,* 343–352.

23. Sutcliffe, K. M., & McNamara, G. (2001). Controlling decision-making practice in organizations. *Organization Science, 12,* 484–501. Byrne, J. A. (1998, September 21). Virtual management. *BusinessWeek,* pp. 80–82.

24. Simon, H. (1977). *The new science of management decisions* (2nd ed.). Englewood Cliffs, NJ: Prentice Hall.

25. Case, J. (1995). *Open-book management.* New York: HarperBusiness.

26. Rowe, A. J., Boulgaides, J. D., & McGrath, M. R. (1984). *Managerial decision making.* Chicago: Science Research Associates.

27. See Note 12.

28. Murninghan, J. K. (1981). Group decision making: What strategies should you use? *Management Review, 25,* 56–62.

29. Janis, I. L. (1982). *Groupthink: Psychological studies of policy decisions and fiascoes* (2nd ed.). Boston: Houghton Mifflin.

30. Morehead, G., Ference, R., & Neck, C. P. (1991). Group decision fiascoes continue: Space shuttle *Challenger* and a revised groupthink framework. *Human Relations, 44,* 531–550.

31. Eaton, J. (2001). Management communication: The threat of groupthink. *Corporate Communication, 6,* 183–192. Janis, I. L. (1988). *Crucial decisions: Leadership in policy making and crisis management.* New York: Free Press.

32. Morehead, G., & Montanari, J. R. (1986). An empirical investigation of the groupthink phenomenon. *Human Relations, 39,* 391–410.

33. Schweiger, D. M., Sandberg, W. R., & Ragan, J. W. (1986). Group approaches for improving strategic decision making: A comparative analysis of dialectical inquiry, devil's advocacy, and consensus. *Academy of Management Journal, 29,* 51–71.

34. Schweiger, D. M., Sandberg, W. R., & Rechner, P. L. (1989). Experiential effects of dialectical inquiry, devil's advocacy, and consensus approaches to strategic decision making. *Academy of Management Journal, 32,* 745–772.

35. Cosier, R. A., & Schwenk, C. R. (1990). Agreement and thinking alike: Ingredients for poor decisions. *Academy of Management Executive, 4,* 61–74.

36. Sloan, A. P., Jr. (1964). *My years with General Motors.* New York: Doubleday.

37. Tjosvold, D. (1984). Effects of crisis orientation on managers' approach to controversy in decision making. *Academy of Management Journal, 27,* 130–138.

38. Johnson, R. J. (1984). Conflict avoidance through acceptable decisions. *Human Relations, 27,* 71–82.

39. Neustadt, R. E., & Fineberg, H. (1978). *The swine flu affair: Decision making on a slippery disease.* Washington, DC: U.S. Department of Health, Education and Welfare.

40. Adler, N. J. (1991). *International dimensions of organizational behavior.* Boston: PWS-Kent.

41. Roth, K. (1992). Implementing international strategy at the business unit level: The role of managerial decision-making characteristics. *Journal of Management, 18,* 761–789.

42. Hurry up and decide (2001, May 14). *BusinessWeek,* p. 16.

43. Breen, B. (2000, September). What's your intuition? *Fast Company,* pp. 290–294, 296, 298, 300. Klein, G. (1999). *Sources of power.* Cambridge, MA: MIT Press.

44. Wild, R. (2000, September). Think fast! *Working Woman,* pp. 89–90.

45. Mayer, B. S. (2000). *The dynamics of conflict resolution.* San Francisco: Jossey-Bass.

46. Linstone, H. A. (1984). *Multiple perspectives for decision making.* New York: North-Holland.

47. Simon, H. A. (1979). Rational decision making in organizations. *American Economic Review, 69,* 493–513.

48. March, J. G., & Simon, H. A. (1958). *Organizations.* New York: Wiley.

49. See Note 29.

50. Simon, H. A. (1957). *Models of man.* New York: Wiley.

51. Shull, F. A., Delbecq, A. L., & Cummings, L. L. (1970). *Organizational decision making.* New York: McGraw-Hill.

52. Browning, E. B. (1850/1950). *Sonnets from the Portuguese.* New York: Ratchford and Fulton.

53. Mitchell, T. R., & Beach, L. R. (1990). ". . . Do I love thee? Let me count . . ." Toward an understanding of intuitive and automatic decision making. *Organizational Behavior and Human Decision Processes, 47,* 1–20.

54. Beach, L. R., & Mitchell, T. R. (1990). Image theory: A behavioral theory of image making in organizations. In B. Staw and L. L. Cummings (Eds.), *Research in organizational behavior* (Vol. 12, pp. 1–41). Greenwich, CT: JAI Press.

55. Dunegan, K. J. (1995). Image theory: Testing the role of image compatibility in progress decisions. *Organizational Behavior and Human Decision Processes, 62,* 71–86.

56. Dunegan, K. J. (1993). Framing, cognitive modes, and image theory: Toward an understanding of a glass half full. *Journal of Applied Psychology, 78,* 491–503.

57. Gaeth, G. J., & Shanteau, J. (1984). Reducing the influence of irrelevant information on experienced decision makers. *Organizational Behavior and Human Performance, 33,* 263–282.

58. Ginrich, G., & Soli, S. D. (1984). Subjective evaluation and allocation of resources in routine decision making. *Organizational Behavior and Human Performance, 33,* 187–203.

59. Levin, I. P., Schneider, S. L., & Gaeth, G. J. (1998). All frames are not created equal: A typology and critical analysis of framing effects. *Organizational Behavior and Human Decision Processes, 76,* 141–188.

60. Kahneman, D., & Tversky, A. (1984). Choices, values, and frames. *American Psychologist, 39,* 341–350.

61. Highhouse, S., & Yüce, P. (1996). Perspectives, perceptions, and risk-taking behavior. *Organizational Behavior and Human Decision Processes, 65,* 151–167.

62. Levin, I. P., & Gaeth, G. J. (1988). Framing of attribute information before and after consuming the product. *Journal of Consumer Research, 15,* 374–378.

63. Levin, I. P. (1987). Associative effects of information framing. *Bulletin of the Psychonomic Society, 25,* 85–86.

64. Meyerowitz, B. E., & Chaiken, S. (1987). The effects of message framing on breast self-examination attitudes, intentions, and behavior. *Journal of Personality and Social Psychology, 52,* 500–510.

65. Frisch, D. (1993). Reasons for framing effects. *Organizational Behavior and Human Decision Processes, 54,* 391–429.

66. Nisbett, R. E., & Ross, L. (1980). Human inference: Strategies and shortcomings of social judgment. Englewood Cliffs, NJ: Prentice Hall.

67. Maule, A. J., & Hodgkinson, G. (2002). Heuristics, biases and strategic decision making. *Psychologist, 15,* 68–71.

68. Kahneman, D., & Tversky, A. (1973). On the psychology of prediction. *Psychological Review, 80,* 251–273.

69. Gaeth, G. J., & Shanteau, J. (1984). Reducing the influence of irrelevant information on experienced decision makers. *Organizational Behavior and Human Performance, 33,* 187–203.

70. Power, D. J., & Aldag, R. J. (1985). Soelberg's job search and choice model: A clarification, review, and critique. *Academy of Management Review, 10,* 48–58.

71. Soelberg, P. O. (1967). Unprogrammed decision making. *Industrial Management Review, 8,* 11–29.

72. Langer, E., & Schank, R. C. (1994). *Belief, reasoning, and decision making.* Hillsdale, NJ: Lawrence Erlbaum Associates.

73. Loouie, T. A., Curren, M. T., & Harich, K. R. (2000). "I knew we would win:" Hindsight bias for favorable and unfavorable team decision outcomes. *Journal of Applied Psychology, 85,* 264–272.

74. Moon, H., & Conlon, D. E. (2002). From acclaim to blame: Evidence of a person sensitivity decision bias. *Journal of Applied Psychology, 87,* 33–42.

75. Conlon, D. E., & Garland, H. (1993). The role of project completion information in resource allocation decisions. *Academy of Management Journal, 36,* 402–413.

76. Crockett, R. L., & Yang, C. (1999, August 30). Why Motorola should hang up on Iridium. *BusinessWeek,* p. 46.

77. Bobocel, D. R., & Meyer, J. P. (1994). Escalating commitment to a failing course of action: Separating the roles of choice and justification. *Journal of Applied Psychology, 79,* 360–363.

78. Staw, B. M. (1981). The escalation of commitment to a course of action. *Academy of Management Review, 6,* 577–587.

79. Whyte, G. (1993). Escalating commitment in individual and group decision making: A prospect theory approach. *Organizational Behavior and Human Decision Processes, 54,* 430–455.

80. Simonson, I., & Staw, B. M. (1992). Deescalation strategies: A comparison of techniques for reducing commitment to losing courses of action. *Journal of Applied Psychology, 77,* 411–426.

81. Garland, H., & Newport, S. (1991). Effects of absolute and relative sunk costs on the decision to persist with a course of action. *Organizational Behavior and Human Decision Processes, 48,* 55–69.

82. Ross, J., & Staw, B. M. (1993). Organizational escalation and exit: Lessons from the Shoreham nuclear power plant. *Academy of Management Journal, 36,* 701–732.

83. Whyte, G. (1991). Diffusion of responsibility: Effects on the escalation tendency. *Journal of Applied Psychology, 76,* 408–415.

84. Staw, B. M., Barsade, S. G., & Koput, K. W. (1997). Escalation at the credit window: A longitudinal study of bank executives' recognition and write-off of problem loans. *Journal of Applied Psychology, 82,* 130–142.

85. Heath, C. (1995). Escalation and de-escalation of commitment in response to sunk costs: The role of budgeting in mental accounting. *Organizational Behavior and Human Decision Processes, 62,* 38–54.

86. Tan, H., & Yates, J. F. (1995). Sunk cost effects: The influences of instruction and future return estimates. *Organizational Behavior and Human Decision Processes, 63,* 311–319.

87. Davis, J. H. (1992). Introduction to the special issue on group decision making.
Organizational Behavior and Human Decision Processes, 52, 1–2.

88. Delbecq, A. L., Van de Ven, A. H., & Gustafson, D. H. (1975). *Group techniques for program planning.* Glenview, IL: Scott, Foresman.

89. Hill, G. W. (1982). Group versus individual performance: Are $N + 1$ heads better than one? *Psychological Bulletin, 91,* 517–539.

90. Wanous, J. P., & Youtz, M. A. (1986). Solution diversity and the quality of group decisions. *Academy of Management Journal, 29,* 141–159.

91. Yetton, P., & Bottger, P. (1983). The relationships among group size, member ability, social decision schemes, and performance. *Organizational Behavior and Human Performance, 32,* 145–149.

92. See Note 91.

93. See Note 91.

94. Osborn, A. F. (1957). *Applied imagination.* New York: Scribner's.

95. Bouchard, T. J., Jr., Barsaloux, J., & Drauden, G. (1974). Brainstorming procedure, group size, and sex as determinants of the problem-solving effectiveness of groups and individuals. *Journal of Applied Psychology, 59,* 135–138.

96. Kelley, T. (2001, June–July). Reaping the whirlwind. *Context,* pp. 56–58.

97. Bottger, P. C., & Yetton, P. W. (1987). Improving group performance by training in individual problem solving. *Journal of Applied Psychology, 72,* 651–657.

98. Patterson, J., & Kim, P. (1991). *The day America told the truth.* New York: Plume.

99. Dubrin, A. J. (1994). *Contemporary applied management* (4th ed.). Burr Ridge, IL: Irwin.

100. Vogel, D. (1993, November–December). Is U.S. business obsessed with ethics? *Across the Board,* pp. 31–33.

101. Insider trading. (1987, March 23). *BusinessWeek,* p. 66.

102. Nomura Securities. (1991, August 26). *BusinessWeek,* p. 27.

103. Singer, A. W. (1991, September). Ethics: Are standards lower overseas? *Across the Board,* pp. 31–34.

104. Dalkey, N. (1969). *The Delphi method: An experimental study of group decisions.* Santa Monica, CA: Rand Corporation.

105. Van de Ven, A. H., & Delbecq, A. L. (1971). Nominal versus interacting group processes for committee decision-making effectiveness. *Academy of Management Journal, 14,* 203–212.

106. See Note 105.

107. Gustafson, D. H., Shulka, R. K., Delbecq, A., & Walster, W. G. (1973). A comparative study of differences in subjective likelihood estimates made by individuals, interacting groups, Delphi groups, and nominal groups. *Organizational Behavior and Human Performance, 9,* 280–291.

108. Ulshak, F. L., Nathanson, L., & Gillan, P. B. (1981). *Small group problem solving: An aid to organizational effectiveness.* Reading, MA: Addison-Wesley.

109. Willis, R. E. (1979). A simulation of multiple selection using nominal group procedures. *Management Science, 25,* 171–181.

110. Stumpf, S. A., Zand, D. E., & Freedman, R. D. (1979). Designing groups for judgmental decisions. *Academy of Management Review, 4,* 581–600.

111. Rogelberg, S. G., & O'Connor, M. S. (1998). Extending the stepladder technique: An examination of self-paced stepladder groups. *Group Dynamics, 2*(2), 82–91. Rogelberg, S. G., Barnes-Farrell, J. L., & Lowe, C. A. (1992). The stepladder technique: An alternative group structure facilitating effective group decision making. *Journal of Applied Psychology, 77,* 730–737.

112. Harmon, J., Schneer, J. A., & Hoffman, L. R. (1995). Electronic meetings and established decision groups: Audioconferencing effects on performance and structural stability. *Organizational Behavior and Human Decision Processes, 61,* 138–147.

113. Colquitt, J. A., Hollenbeck, J. R., Ilgen, D. R., LePine, J. A., & Sheppard, L. (2002). Computer-assisted communication and team decision-making performance: The moderating effect of openness to experience. *Journal of Applied Psychology, 87,* 402–410.

114. Lam, S. S. K., & Shaubroeck, J. (2000). Improving group decisions by better pooling information: A comparative advantage of group decision support systems. *Journal of Applied Psychology, 85,* 564–573.

Case in Point Source

Esterson, E. (1998). Game plan. *Inc. Tech.,* pp. 43–44.

CHAPTER 11

Preview Case Sources

Data as of May 2002, from the Starbucks Web site: www.starbucks.com. Holmes, S., Bennett, D., Carlisle, K., & Dawson, C. (2002, September 9). *Planet Starbucks. BusinessWeek,* pp. 100–108, 110. Neff, T. J., & Citrin, J. M. (1999). *Lessons from the top.* New York: Currency Doubleday (quotes, pp. 262–264). Strauss, K. (2000, January). Howard Schultz: Starbucks' CEO serves a blend of community, employee commitment. *Nation's Restaurant News,* pp. 162–163. Starbucks Web site: www.starbucks.com/company.

Chapter Notes

1. Robinson, S. L., & Morrison, E. W. (2000). The development of psychological contract breach violation: A longitudinal study. *Journal of Organizational Behavior, 21,* 525–541.

2. Rousseau, D. M. (2001). Schema, promise and mutuality: The building blocks of the psychological contract. *Journal of Occupational and Organizational Psychology, 74,* 511–541. Rousseau, D. M., & Schalk, R. (2000). *Psychological contracts in employment: Cross-national perspectives.* Thousand Oaks, CA: Sage.

3. Rousseau, D. M., & Parks, J. M. (1993). The contracts of individuals and organizations. In L. L. Cummings & B. M. Staw (Eds.), *Research in organizational behavior* (Vol. 15, pp. 1–43). Greenwich, CT: JAI Press. Turnley, W. H., & Feldman, D. C. (2000). Re-examining the effects of psychological contract violations: Unmet expectations and job dissatisfaction as mediators. *Journal of Organizational Behavior, 21,* 25–42.

4. Lewicki, R. J., McAllister, D. J., & Bies, R. J. (1998). Trust and distrust: New relationships and realities. *Academy of Management Review, 23,* 438–458.

5. Lewicki, R. J., & Wiethoff, C. (2000). Trust, trust development, and trust repair. In M. Deutsch & P. T. Coleman (Eds.), *The handbook of conflict resolution* (pp. 86–107). San Francisco: Jossey-Bass.

6. Podsakoff, P. M., MacKenzie, S. B., Paine, J. B., & Bachrach, D. G. (2000). Organizational citizenship behaviors: A critical review of the theoretical and empirical literature and suggestions for future research. *Journal of Management, 26,* 513–563.

7. LePine, J. A., Erez, A., & Johnson, D. E. (2002). The nature and dimensionality of organizational citizenship behavior: A critical review and meta-analysis. *Journal of Applied Psychology, 87,* 52–65.

8. See Note 1.

9. Fomburn, C. J. (1996). *Reputation.* Boston: Harvard Business School Press.

10. Miceli, M., & Near, J. (1992). *Blowing the whistle.* Lexington, MA: New Lexington Press.

11. Miceli, M. P., & Near, J. P. (1997). Whistleblowing as antisocial behavior. In R. A. Giacalone & J. Greenberg (Eds.), *Antisocial behavior in organizations* (pp 130–149). Thousand Oaks, CA: Sage.

12. Fricker, D. G. (2002, March 27). Enron whistle-blower honored in Dearborn. From the Internet: www.freep.com/money/business/htm. Anonymous. (2000, April). Paul van Buitenen: Paying the price of accountability. *Accountancy, 125*(1), 280. Taylor, M. (1999, September 13). Another Columbia suit unsealed. *Modern Healthcare, 29*(37), 10. Ettore, B. (1994, May). Whistleblowers: Who's the real bad guy? *Management Review,* p. 18–23.

13. Gjersten, L. A. (1999). Five State Farm agents fired after accusing company of consumer abuse. *National Underwriter, 103*(51), 1, 23.

14. Martucci, W. C., & Smith, E. W. (2000). Recent state legislative development concerning employment discrimination and whistle-blower protections. *Employment Relations Today, 27*(2), 89–99.

15. Jones, M., & Rowell, A. (1999). Safety whistleblowers intimidated. *Safety and Health Practitioner, 17*(8), 3.

16. Falk, A., Gachter, S., & Kovacs, J. (1999). Intrinsic motivation and extrinsic incentives in a repeated game with incomplete contracts. *Journal of Economic Psychology, 20,* 251–284.

17. Knight, G. P., Dubro, A. F., & Chao, C. (1985). Information processing and the development of cooperative, competitive, and individualistic social values. *Developmental Psychology, 21,* 37–45.

18. Knight, G. P., & Dubro, A. F. (1984). Cooperative, competitive, and individualistic social values: An individualized regression and clustering approach. *Journal of Personality and Social Psychology, 46,* 98–105.

19. DeMatteo, J. S., Eby, L. T., & Sundstrom, E. (1998). Team-based rewards: Current empirical evidence and directions for future research. In B. M. Staw & L. L.

Cummings (Eds.), *Research in organizational behavior* (Vol. 20, pp. 141–183). Greenwich, CT: JAI. Heneman, R. L. (2000). *Business-driven compensation policies.* New York: AMACOM.

20. Teerlink, R., & Ozley, L. (2000). *More than a motorcycle: The leadership journey at Harley-Davidson.* Boston: Harvard Business School Press.

21. Thomas, K. W., & Schmidt, W. H. (1976). A survey of managerial interests with respect to conflict. *Academy of Management Journal, 10,* 315–318.

22. Bragg, T. (1999, October). Ten ways to deal with conflict. *IIE Solutions,* pp. 36–37.

23. Lee, M. (1998, October 12). "See you in court—er, mediation." *BusinessWeek Enterprise,* pp. ENT22, ENT24.

24. Lynch, J. F. (2001). Beyond ADR: A systems approach to conflict management. *Negotiation Journal, 17,* 207–216.

25. Richey, B., Bernardin, J. J., Tyler, C. L., & McKinney, N. (2001). The effect of arbitration program characteristics on applicants' intentions toward potential employees. *Journal of Applied Psychology, 86,* 1006–1013.

26. Bordwin, M. (1999). Do-it-yourself justice. *Management Review,* pp. 56–58.

27. Tinsley, C. H. (2001). How negotiators get to yes: Predicting the constellation of strategies used across cultures to negotiate conflict. *Journal of Applied Psychology, 86,* 583–593.

28. Tinsley, C. H., & Brett, J. M. (2001). Managing workplace conflict in the United States and Hong Kong. *Organizational Behavior and Human Decision Processes, 85,* 360–381.

29. Bennett, R. J., & Robinson, S. L. (2003). The past, present, and future of workplace deviance research. In J. Greenberg (Ed.), *Organizational behavior: The state of the science.* Mahwah, NJ: Lawrence Erlbaum Associates.

30. Robinson, S. L., & Bennett, R. J. (1995). A typology of deviant workplace behaviors: A multidimensional scaling study. *Academy of Management Journal, 38,* 555–572.

31. Bidoli, M., & Eedes, J. (2001, February 16). Big Brother is watching you. Future Company. From the Internet at www.futurecompany.co.za/2001/02/16/covstory.htm.

32. Mastrangelo, P., Everton, W., & Jolton, J. (2001). *Computer misuse in the workplace.* Unpublished manuscript. University of Baltimore. Lim, V. K. G., Loo, G. L., & Teo, T. S. H. (2001, August). *Perceived injustice, neutralization and cyberloafing at the workplace.* Paper presented at the Academy of Management, Washington, DC.

33. See Note 27.

34. National Institute for Occupational Safety and Health, Centers for Disease Control and Prevention. (1993). *Homicide in the workplace.* [Document # 705003]. Atlanta, GA: Author.

35. Jockin, V., Arvey, R. D., & McGue, M. (2001). Perceived victimization moderates self-reports of workplace aggression and conflict. *Journal of Applied Psychology, 86,* 1262–1269.

36. Douglas, S. C., & Martinko, M. J. (2001). Exploring the role of individual differences

in the prediction of workplace aggression. *Journal of Applied Psychology, 86,* 547–559.

37. Varita, M., & Jari, R. (2002). Gender differences in workplace bullying among prison officers. *European Journal of Work and Occupational Psychology, 11,* 113–126.

38. Cowie, H., Naylor, P., Rivers, I., Smith, P. K., & Pereira, B. (2002). Measuring workplace bullying. *Aggression and Violent Behavior, 7,* 33–51.

39. Namie, G. (2000). *U.S. hostile workplace survey, 2000.* Benicia, CA: Campaign Against Workplace Bullying.

40. Namie, G., & Namie, R. (2001). *The bully at work.* Naperville, IL: Sourcebooks.

41. Trevino, L. K., & Weaver, G. R. (1998). Punishment in organizations: Descriptive and normative perspectives. In M. Schminke (Ed.), *Managerial ethics: Moral management of people and processes* (pp. 99–114). Mahwah, NJ: Erlbaum.

42. Lind, E. A., Greenberg, J., Scott, K. S., & Welchans, T. D. (2000). The winding road from employee to complainant: Situational and psychological determinants of wrongful-termination claims. *Administrative Science Quarterly, 45,* 557–590.

43. Kooker, N. R. (2000, May 22). Taking aim at crime—stealing the profits: Tighter controls, higher morale may safeguard bottom line. *Nation's Restaurant News, 34*(21), 114–118. Young, D. (2000, May 1). Inside jobs. *Wireless Review, 17*(9), 14–20. Rosner, B. (1999, October). How do you feel about video surveillance at work? *Workforce, 78*(10), 26–27. Anonymous. (1999, May). As new CCTV system goes live, cashiers quit. *Security, 36*(5), 40. Wells, J. T. (1999, August). A fistful of dollars. *Security Management, 43*(8), 70–75. Vara, B. (1999, June). The "steal trap." *National Petroleum News, 91*(6), 28–31. Wimmer, N. (1999, June). Fingers in the till. *Asian Business, 35*(6), 59–60. Golden, P. (1999, May). Dangers without, dangers within. *Electronic Business, 25*(5), 65–70.

44. Jabbkerm, A. (2000, March 29). Agrium seeks $30 million in damages in embezzlement case. *Chemical Week, 162*(13), 22.

45. Greenberg, J. (1998). The cognitive geometry of employee theft: Negotiating "the line" between taking and stealing. In R. W. Griffin, A. O'Leary-Kelly, & J. M. Collins (Eds.), *Dysfunctional behavior in organizations: Non-violent dysfunctional behavior* (pp. 147–194). Stamford, CT: JAI Press.

46. Greenberg, J. & Tomlinson, E. (in press). The evolution of research methods in employee theft: The DATA Cycle. In R. Griffin & A. O'Leary-Kelly (Eds.), *The dark side of organizational behavior.* San Francisco: Jossey-Bass.

Case in Point Source

Sprouse, M. (1992). *Sabotage in the American workplace.* San Francisco: Pressure Drop Press (quote, p. 58).

CHAPTER 12

Preview Case Sources

Ryback, T. W. (1998, November 16). The man who swallowed Chrysler. *The New Yorker,* pp. 80, 82–89.

Chapter Notes

1. Kacmar, K. M., & Baron, R. A. (1999). *Organizational politics.* In G. R. Ferris (Ed.), *Research in personnel and human resources management* (pp. 1–39). Stamford, CT: JAI Press.

2. Cobb, A. T. (1984). An episodic model of power: Toward an integration of theory and research. *Academy of Management Review, 9,* 482–493.

3. Mayes, B. T., & Allen, R. T. (1977). Toward a definition of organizational politics. *Academy of Management Review, 2,* 672–678.

4. Mintzberg, H. (1983). *Power in and around organizations.* Englewood Cliffs, NJ: Prentice Hall.

5. Schriesheim, C. A., & Hinkin, T. R. (1990). Influence tactics used by subordinates: A theoretical and empirical analysis and refinement of the Kipnis, Schmidt, and Wilkinson subscales. *Journal of Applied Psychology, 75,* 246–257.

6. Yukl, G., & Tracey, J. B. (1992). Consequences of influence tactics used with subordinates, peers, and the boss. *Journal of Applied Psychology, 77,* 525–535.

7. Yukl, G., Falbe, C. M., & Youn, J. Y. (1993). Patterns of influence behavior for managers. *Group & Organization Management, 18,* 5–28.

8. Offermann, L. R. (1990). Power and leadership in organizations. *American Psychologist, 45,* 179–189.

9. Falbe, C. M., & Yukl, G. (1992). Consequences for managers of using single influence tactics and combinations of tactics. *Academy of Management Journal, 35,* 638–652.

10. Rose, G. (2000, June). Download time attitudes in the Arab world and the US: A cross-cultural study in e-comerce. Paper presented at the Global Information Technology Management World Conference, Memphis, Tennessee.

11. Rose, G., Lees, J., & Meuter, M. (in press). A refined view of download time impacts on e-consumer attitudes and patronage intentions toward e-retailers. *International Journal of Media Management.*

12. Cialdini, R. B. (1994). Interpersonal influence. In S. Shavitt & T. C. Brock (Eds.), *Persuasion* (pp. 195–218). Boston: Allyn & Bacon.

13. Baron, R. A., & Markman, G. D. (in press). Beyond social capital: The role of social competence in entrepreneurs' success. *Journal of Business Venturing.*

14. Useem, J. (2001, April 30). A manager for all seasons. *Fortune,* pp. 66–70, 72. Torre, J. (2000). *Joe Torre's ground rules for winners: 12 keys to managing team players, tough bosses, setbacks, and success.* New York: Hyperion.

15. Podsakoff, P. M., & Schriesheim, C. A. (1985). Field studies of French and Raven's bases of power: Critique, re-analysis, and suggestions for future research. *Psychological Bulletin, 97,* 387–413.

16. Huber, V. L. (1981). The sources, uses, and conservation of managerial power. *Personnel, 51*(4), 62–67.

17. Kipnis, D., Schmidt, S. M., Swaffin-Smith, C., & Wilkinson, I. (1984, Winter). Patterns of managerial influence: Shotgun managers, tacticians, and bystanders. *Organizational Dynamics,* pp. 58–67.

18. Stewart, T. (1989, November 6). CEOs see clout shifting. *Fortune,* p. 66.

19. Kahn, R. L., Wolfe, D. M., Quinn, R. P., Snoek, J. D., & Rosenthal, R. A. (1964). *Organizational stress: Studies in role conflict and ambiguity.* New York: Wiley.

20. See Note 13.

21. See Note 17.

22. Arnold, J. A., Arad, S., Rhoades, J. A., & Drasgow, F. (in press). The empowering leadership questionnaire: The construction of a new scale for measuring leader behaviors. *Journal of Organizational Behavior.*

23. Ford, R. C., & Fottler, M. D. (1995). Empowerment: A matter of degree. *Academy of Management Executive, 9,* 21–29.

24. Dumaine, B. (1990, May 7). Who needs a boss? *Fortune,* pp. 52–54, 56, 58, 60.

25. Shipper, F., & Manz, C. C. (1991). Employee self-management without formally designated teams: An alternative road to empowerment. *Organizational Dynamics, 20*(3), 48–61.

26. Sherman, J. (1994). *In the rings of Saturn.* New York: Oxford University Press.

27. Dumaine, B. (1993, February 22). The new non-manager managers. *Fortune,* pp. 80–84.

28. Harrington, A. (2000). Workers of the world, rate your boss! *Fortune,* September 18, 2000, p. 340.

29. DeGus, A. (1997). *The living company.* Boston: Harvard Business School.

30. See Note 26.

31. DuBrin, A. J. (1994). *Contemporary applied management* (4th ed.). Burr Ridge, IL: Irwin.

32. Patalon, W., III. (1992, June 14). Xerox's gateway to the world. *Rochester Democrat and Chronicle,* pp. 1F–2F.

33. Lesser, Y. (1992, May). From the bottom up: A toast to empowerment. *Human Resources Forum,* pp. 1–2.

34. Omni Hotels Web site www.omnihotels.com/pages/common/number.html.

35. Byham, W. C., & Cox, J. (1991). *ZAPP: The lightening of empowerment.* New York: Harmony.

36. Triandis, H. A. (1995). *Individualism and collectivism.* Boulder, CO: Westview Press.

37. Robert, C., Probst, T. M., Martocchio, J. J., Drasgow, F., & Lawler, J. J. (2000). Empowerment and continuous improvement in the United States, Poland, and India: Predicting fit on the basis of the dimensions of power distance and individualism. *Journal of Applied Psychology, 85,* 643–658.

38. Gresov, C., & Stephens, C. (1993). The context of interunit influence attempts. *Administrative Science Quarterly, 38,* 252–276.

39. Pfeffer, J., & Salancik, G. (1978). *The external control of organizations.* New York: Harper & Row.

40. Salancik, G., & Pfeffer, J. (1974). The bases and uses of power in organizational decision-making. *Administrative Science Quarterly, 19,* 453–473.

41. Boeker, W. (1989). The development and institutionalization of subunit power in organizations. *Administrative Science Quarterly, 34,* 388–410.

42. Lawrence, P. R., & Lorsch, J. W. (1967). *Organization and environment.* Cambridge, MA: Harvard University Press.

43. Hickson, D. J., Astley, W. G., Butler, R. J., & Wilson, D. C. (1981). Organization as power. In L. L. Cummings & B. M. Staw (Eds.), *Research in organizational behavior* (Vol. 4, pp. 151–196). Greenwich, CT: JAI Press.

44. Miles, R. H. (1980). *Macro organizational behavior.* Glenview, IL: Scott, Foresman.

45. Saunders, C. S., & Scarmell, R. (1982). Intraorganizational distributions of power: Replication research. *Academy of Management Journal, 25,* 192–200.

46. Hinings, C. R., Hickson, D. J., Pennings, J. M., & Schneck, R. E. (1974). Structural conditions of intraorganizational power. *Academy of Management Journal, 19,* 22–44.

47. Drory, A., & Romm, T. (1990). The definition of organizational politics: A review. *Human Relations, 43,* 1333–1354.

48. Ferris, G. R., & Kacmar, K. M. (1992). Perceptions of organizational politics. *Journal of Management, 18,* 93–136.

49. Rosen, R. H. (1991). *The healthy company.* New York: Jeremy P. Tarcher/Perigree (quote, p. 71).

50. Biberman, G. (1985). Personality and characteristic work attitudes of persons with high, moderate, and low political tendencies. *Psychological Reports, 57,* 1303–1310.

51. Kirchmeyer, C. (1990). A profile of managers active in office politics. *Basic and Applied Social Psychology, 22,* 339–350.

52. Allen, R. W., Madison, D. L., Partaer, L. W., Renwick, P. A., & Mayer, B. T. (1979). Organizational politics: Tatics and characteristics of its actions. *California Management Review, 22,* 77–83.

53. Ferris, G. R., Frink, D. D., GilGalang, M. C., Zhou, J., Kacmar, K. M., & Howard, J. L. (1996). Perceptions of organizational politics: Prediction, stress-related implications, and outcomes. *Human Relations, 49,* 233–266.

54. See Note 38.

55. Wayne, S. J., & Ferris, G. R. (1990). Influence tactics, affect, and exchange quality in supervisor–subordinate interactions. *Journal of Applied Psychology, 75,* 487–499.

56. See Note 43.

57. Bartol, K. M., & Martin, D. C. (1990). When politics pays: Factors influencing managerial compensation decisions. *Personnel Psychology, 43,* 599–614.

58. Gray, B., & Ariss, S. S. (1985). Politics and strategic change across organizational life cycles. *Academy of Management Review, 10,* 707–723.

59. Hannan, M. T., & Freeman, J. H. (1978). Internal politics of growth and decline. In M. W. Meyer (Ed.), *Environment and organizations* (pp. 177–199). San Francisco: Jossey-Bass.

60. Mulder, M., de Jong, R. D., Koppelaar, L., & Verhage, J. (1986). Power, situation, and leaders' effectiveness: An organizational field study. *Journal of Applied Psychology, 71,* 566–570.

61. Feldman, S. P. (1988). Secrecy, information, and politics: An essay in organiza-

tional decision making. *Human Relations, 41*, 73–90.

62. Greenberg, J. (1990). Looking fair vs. being fair: Managing impressions of organizational justice. In B. M. Staw & L. L. Cummings (Eds.), *Research in organizational behavior* (Vol. 12, pp. 131–157). Greenwich, CT: JAI Press.

63. Warshaw, M. (1998, April–May). The good guy's and gal's guide to office politics. *Fast Company*, pp. 156–158, 160, 162, 166, 168, 170, 172, 174, 176, 178.

64. Boeker, W. (1992). Power and managerial dismissal: Scapegoating at the top. *Administrative Science Quarterly, 37*, 400–421.

65. Liden, R. C., & Mitchell, T. R. (1988). Ingratiatory behaviors in organizational settings. *Academy of Management Review, 13*, 572–587.

66. Cropanzno, R. S., Howes, J. C., Grandey, A. A., & Toth, P. (1997). The relationships of organizational politics and support to work behaviors, attitudes, and stress. *Journal of Organizational Behavior, 18*, 159–181.

67. Kacmar, K. M., Bozeman, D. P., Carlson, D., & Anthony, W. P. (in press). A partial test of the perceptions of organizational politics model. *Human Relations*.

68. Randall, M. O., Cropanzano, R., Bormann, C. A., & Birjulin, A. (in press). Organizational politics and organizational support as predictors of work attitudes, job performance, and organizational citizenship behavior. *Journal of Organizational Behavior*.

69. Hochwarter, W. A., Witt, L. A., & Kacmar, K. M. (2000). Perceptions of organizational politics as a moderator of the relationship between conscientiousness and job performance. *Journal of Applied Psychology, 85*, 472–478.

70. Kipnis, D. (1976). *The powerholders*. Chicago: University of Chicago Press.

71. Colvin, G. (2002, September 16). Liar, liar, pants on fire. *Fortune*, pp. 162–164.

72. Gellerman, S. W. (1986, July–August). Why "good" managers make bad ethical choices. *Harvard Business Review*, pp. 85–90.

73. Commerce Clearing House. (1991, June 26). *1991 SHRM/CCH survey*. Chicago: Author.

74. Kumar, P., & Ghadially, R. (1989). Organizational politics and its effects on members of organizations. *Human Relations, 42*, 305–314.

75. Andrews, G. (1994, September). Mistrust, the hidden obstacle to empowerment. *HRMagazine*, pp. 66–68, 70.

76. Velasquez, M., Moberg, D. J., & Cavanaugh, G. F. (1983). Organizational statesmanship and dirty politics: Ethical guidelines for the organizational politician. *Organizational Dynamics, 13*, 65–79.

77. See Note 83.

78. Greenberg, J. (1982). Approaching equity and avoiding inequity in groups and organizations. In J. Greenberg & R. L. Cohen (Eds.), *Equity and justice in social behavior* (pp. 389–435). New York: Academic Press.

Case in Point Source

Blumenstein, R. (1997, October 23). How the Smith boys grew up to be CEOs. *Wall Street Journal*, pp. B1, B12.

CHAPTER 13

Preview Case Sources

Leonard, D. (2000, March 20). Living without a leader. *Fortune*, p. 218. Hammer, B. (2000, November 2). Urban Box Office declares bankruptcy. *The Industry Standard*, p. 15.

Chapter Notes

1. Yukl, G. (2002). *Leadership in organizations* (5th ed.). Upper Saddle River, NJ: Prentice Hall. Lord, R. G. (2001). The nature of organizational leadership: Conclusions and implications. In S. J. Zaccaro & R. J. Klimoski, (Eds.), *The nature of organizational leadership: Understanding the performance imperatives confronting today's leaders* (pp. 413–436). San Francisco: Jossey-Bass. Yukl, G. (2002). *Leadership in organizations* (5th ed.). Upper Saddle River, NJ: Prentice Hall.

2. House, R. J., & Podsakoff, P. M. (1995). Leadership effectiveness: Past perspectives and future directions for research. In J. Greenberg (Ed.), *Organizational behavior: The state of the science* (pp. 45–82). Hillsdale, NJ: Lawrence Erlbaum Associates.

3. Bennis, W. G., & Nanus, B. (1985). *Leaders: The strategies for taking charge*. New York: Harper & Row (quote, p. 4)

4. See Note 1.

5. Locke, E. A. (1991). *The essence of leadership*. New York: Lexington Books.

6. Cialdini, R. B. (1988). *Influence* (2nd ed.). Glenview, IL: Scott, Foresman.

7. Kotter, J. P. (1990). *A force for change: How leadership differs from management*. New York: Free Press.

8. Geier, J. G. (1969). A trait approach to the study of leadership in small groups. *Journal of Communication, 17*, 316–323.

9. Kirkpatrick, S. A., & Locke, E. A. (1991). Leadership: Do traits matter? *Academy of Management Executive, 5*, 48–60 (quote, p. 58).

10. Barker, R. A. (2001). The nature of leadership. *Human Relations, 54*, 469–494.

11. House, R. J., Shane, S. A., & Herold, D. M. (1996). Rumors of the death of dispositional research are vastly exaggerated. *Academy of Management Review, 21*, 203–224.

12. See Note 9.

13. Chan, K-Y., & Drasgow, F. (2001). Toward a theory of individual differences and leadership: Understanding the motivation to lead. *Journal of Applied Psychology, 86*, 481–498.

14. Zaccaro, S. J., Foti, R. J., & Kenny, D. A. (1991). Self-monitoring and trait-based variance in leadership: An investigation of leader flexibility across multiple group situations. *Journal of Applied Psychology, 76*, 308–315.

15. Chemers, M. M. (2001). Efficacy and effectiveness: Integrating models of leadership and intelligence. In R. E. Riggio & S. E. Murphy (Eds.), *Multiple intelligences and leadership* (pp. 139–160). Mahwah, NJ: Lawrence Erlbaum Associates.

16. Lord, R. G., DeVader, C. L., & Alliger, G. M. (1986). A meta-analysis of the relation between personality traits and leadership perceptions: An application of validity generalization procedures. *Journal of Applied Psychology, 61*, 402–410.

17. Rubin, R. S., Bartels, L. L., & Bommer, W. J. (2002). Are leaders smarter or do they just seem that way? Exploring perceived intellectual competence and leadership emergence. *Social Behavior and Personality, 30*, 105–118.

18. Goleman, D., Boyzatis, R., & McKee, A. (2002). *Primal leadership: Realizing the power of emotional intelligence*. Boston: Harvard Business School. George, J. M. (2000). Emotions and leadership: The role of emotional intelligence. *Human Relations, 53*, 1027–1055. Aditya, R., & House, R. J. (2001). Interpersonal acumen and leadership across cultures: Pointers from the GLOBE study. In R. E. Riggio & S. E. Murphy (Eds.), *Multiple intelligences and leadership* (pp. 215–240). Mahwah, NJ: Lawrence Erlbaum Associates. Caurso, D. R., Mayer, J. D., & Salovey, P. (2001). Emotional intelligence and emotional leadership. In R. E. Riggio & S. E. Murphy (Eds.), *Multiple intelligences and leadership* (pp. 55–74). Mahwah, NJ: Lawrence Erlbaum Associates.

19. Offerman, L. R., & Phan, L. U. (2001). Culturally intelligent leadership for a diverse world. In R. E. Riggio & S. E. Murphy (Eds.), *Multiple intelligences and leadership* (pp. 187–214). Mahwah, NJ: Lawrence Erlbaum Associates.

20. Anonymous. (1999, October 11). Molding global leaders. *Fortune*, p. 270.

21. Stein, N. (2000, October 2). Global most admired companies: Measuring people power. *Fortune*, pp. 273–288.

22. See Note 21 (quote, p. 283).

23. See Note 21 (quote, p. 285).

24. Sagie, A., Zaidman, N., Amichai–hamburger, Y., Te'Eni, D., & Schwartz, D. G. (2002). An empirical assessment of the loose-tight leadership model: Quantitative and qualitative analyses. *Journal of Organizational Behavior, 23*, 303–320.

25. Muczyk, J. P., & Reimann, B. C. (1987). The case for directive leadership. *Academy of Management Review, 12*, 637–647.

26. Chen, C. C., & Meindl, J. R. (1991). The construction of leadership images in the popular press: The case of Donald Burr and People Express. *Administrative Science Quarterly, 36*, 521–551.

27. Likert, R. (1961). *New patterns in management*. New York: McGraw-Hill.

28. Stogdill, R. M. (1963). *Manual for the leader behavior description questionnaire, form XII*. Columbus, OH: Ohio State University, Bureau of Business Research.

29. Weissenberg, P., & Kavanagh, M. H. (1972). The independence of initiating structure and consideration: A review of the evidence. *Personnel Psychology, 25*, 119–130.

30. Vroom, V. H. (1976). Leadership. In M. D. Dunnette (Ed.), *Handbook of industrial-organizational psychology* (pp. 1527–1552). Chicago: RandMcNally.

31. See Note 3.

32. Band, W. A. (1994). *Touchstones*. New York: John Wiley & Sons (quote, p. 247).

33. Blake, R. R., & Mouton, J. J. (1969). *Building a dynamic corporation through grid organizational development*. Reading, MA: Addison-Wesley.

34. Lee, C. (1991). Followership: The essence of leadership. *Training, 28,* 27–35 (quote, p. 28).

35. Graen, G. B., & Wakabayashi, M. (1994). Cross-cultural leadership-making: Bridging American and Japanese diversity for team advantage. In H. C. Triandis, M. D. Dunnette, & L. M. Hough (Eds.), *Handbook of industrial and organizational psychology* (2nd ed.) (Vol. 4, pp. 415–466). Palo Alto, CA: Consulting Psychologists Press.

36. Phillips, A. S. & Bedian, A. G. (1994). Leader-follower exchange quality: The role of personal and interpersonal attributes. *Academy of Management Journal, 37,* 990–1001.

37. Dunegan, K. J., Duchon, D., & Uhl-Bien, M. (1992). Examining the link between leader–member exchange and subordinate performance: The role of task analyzability and variety as moderators. *Journal of Management, 18,* 59–76.

38. Duarte, N. T., Goodson, J. R., & Klich, N. R. (1993). How do I like thee? Let me appraise the ways. *Journal of Organizational Behavior, 14,* 239–249.

39. Deluga, R. J., & Perry, J. T. (1991). The relationship of subordinate upward influencing behavior, satisfaction and perceived superior effectiveness with leader–member exchanges. *Journal of Occupational Psychology, 64,* 239–252.

40. Ferris, G. R. (1985). Role of leadership in the employee withdrawal process: A constructive replication. *Journal of Applied Psychology, 70,* 777–781.

41. Scandura, T. A., & Schriesheim, C. A. (1994). Leader–member exchange and supervisor career mentoring as complementary constructs in leadership research. *Academy of Management Journal, 37,* 1588–1602.

42. Sheard, A. G., & Kakabadse, A. P. (2001). Key roles of the leadership landscape. *Journal of Managerial Psychology, 17,* 129–144. Zenger, J. H., Musselwhite, E., Hurson, K., & Perrin, C. (1994). *Leading teams: Mastering the new role.* Homewood, IL: Business One Irwin.

43. Zenger, J. H., Musselwhite, E., Hurson, K., & Perrin, C. (1994). *Leading teams: Mastering the new role.* Homewood, IL: Business One Irwin.

44. LaBarre, P. (1999, April). The agenda—grassroots leadership. *Fast Company,* pp. 115–126.

45. See Note 29 (quote pp. 116, 118).

46. Pascale, R. (1998, *Fast Company,* April–May). Grassroots leadership: Royal Dutch Shell. *Fast Company,* pp. 110–120.

47. Lord, R. G., & Maher, K. (1989). Perceptions in leadership and their implications in organizations. In J. Carroll (Ed.), *Applied social psychology and organizational settings* (Vol. 4, pp. 129–154). Hillsdale, NJ: Erlbaum.

48. Heneman, R. L., Greenberger, D. B., & Anonyuo, C. (1989). Attributions and exchanges: The effects of interpersonal factors on the diagnosis of employee performance. *Academy of Management Journal, 32,* 466–476.

49. Mitchell, T. R., & Wood, R. E. (1980). Supervisors' responses to subordinate poor performance: A test of an attribution model. *Organizational Behavior and Human Performance, 25,* 123–138.

50. Baker, W. D., & O'Neal, J. R. (2001). Patriotism or opinion leadership? The nature and origins of the "rally 'round the flag" effect. *Journal of Conflict Resolution, 45,* 661–687.

51. Bass, B. M. (1985). *Leadership and performance beyond expectations.* New York: Free Press.

52. House, R. J. (1977). A 1976 theory of charismatic leadership. In J. G. Hunt & L. L. Larson (Eds.), *Leadership: The cutting edge* (pp. 189–207). Carbondale, IL: Southern Illinois University Press.

53. See Note 38.

54. Dvir, T., Eden, D., Avolio, B. J., & Shamir, B. (2002). Impact of transformational leadership on follower development and performance: A field experiment. *Academy of Management Journal, 45,* 735–744. Conger, J. A. (1991). Inspiring others: The language of leadership. *Academy of Management Executive, 5,* 31–45.

55. House, R. J., Woycke, J., & Fedor, E. M. (1988). Charismatic and noncharismatic leaders: Differences in behavior and effectiveness. In J. A. Conger & R. N. Kanungo (Eds.), *Charismatic leadership* (pp. 122–144). San Francisco: Jossey-Bass.

56. See Note 1.

57. Zachary, G. P. (1994, June 2). How "barbarian" style of Philippe Kahn led Borland into jeopardy. *Wall Street Journal,* p. A1.

58. Mumford, M. D., & Van Doorn, J. R. (2001). The leadership of pragmatism: Reconsidering Franklin in the age of charisma. *The Leadership Quarterly, 12,* 279–309.

59. See Note 7 (quote, p. 44).

60. See Note 1.

61. Tichy, N. M. (1993). *Control your destiny or someone else will.* New York: Doubleday Currency.

62. Stewart, T. A. (2002, March 2). America's most admired companies. *Fortune,* pp. 70–82.

63. Morris, B. (1995, December 11). The wealth builders. *Fortune,* pp. 80–84, 88, 90, 94.

64. Hater, J. J., & Bass, B. M. (1988). Superiors' evaluations and subordinates perceptions of transformational and transactional leadership. *Journal of Applied Psychology, 73,* 695–702.

65. Fiedler, F. E. (1978). Contingency model and the leadership process. In L. Berkowitz (Ed.), *Advances in experimental social psychology* (Vol. 11, pp. 60–112). New York: Academic Press.

66. Hersey, P., & Blanchard, K. H. (1988). *Management of organizational behavior.* Englewood Cliffs, NJ: Prentice Hall.

67. House, R. J., & Baetz, M. L. (1979). Leadership: Some empirical generalizations and new research directions. In B. M. Staw (Ed.), *Research in organizational behavior* (Vol. 1, pp. 341–424). Greenwich, CT: JAI Press.

68. Whitworth, L., House, H., Sandahl, P., & Kimsey-House, H. (1998). *Co-active coaching: New skills for coaching people toward success in work and life.* Palo Alto, CA: Davies Black.

69. Holtz, L. (1998). *Winning everyday.* New York: HarperBusiness.

70. Wolfe, R. (1998). *The Packer way.* New York: St. Martins.

71. Bradley, Bill. (1998). *Values of the game.* New York: Artisan.

72. Milbank, D. (1990, March 5). Managers are sent to "Charm Schools" to discover how to polish up their acts. *Wall Street Journal,* pp. A14, B3.

73. Vroom, V. H., & Jago, A. G. (1988). *The new leadership: Managing participation in organizations.* Englewood Cliffs, NJ: Prentice Hall. Vroom, V. H., & Yetton, P. W. (1973). *Leadership and decision making.* Pittsburgh: University of Pittsburgh Press.

74. Kerr, S., & Jermier, J. M. (1978). Substitutes for leadership: Their meaning and measurement. *Organizational Behavior and Human Performance, 22,* 375–403.

75. Avolio, B. J., Kahai, S., & Dodge, G. E. (2001). E-leadership: Implications for theory, research, and practice. *Leadership Quarterly, 11,* 615–668. Kissler, G. D. (2001). E-leadership. *Organizational Dynamics, 30,* 121–133. Labarre, P. (1999, June). Unit of one: Leaders.com. *Fast Company,* pp. 95–98, 100, 102, 104, 108, 110, 112.

76. See Note 32 (quote, p. 96).

77. See Note 32 (quote, p. 100).

78. See Note 32 (quote, p. 104).

79. Sheridan, J. E., Vredenburgh, D. J., & Abelson, M. A. (1984). Contextual model of leadership influence in hospital units. *Academy of Management Journal, 27,* 57–78.

80. Podsakoff, P. M., Niehoff, B. P., MacKenzie, S. B., & Williams, M. L. (1993). Do substitutes for leadership really substitute for leadership? An empirical examination of Kerr and Jermier's situational leadership model. *Organizational Behavior and Human Decision Processes, 54,* 1–44.

81. Meindl, J. R., & Ehrlich, S. B. (1987). The romance of leadership and the evaluation of organizational performance. *Academy of Management Journal, 30,* 91–109.

82. Pernick, R. (2001). Creating a leadership development program: Nine essential tasks. *Public Personnel Management, 30,* 429–444.

83. Day, D. V. (2001). Leadership development: A review in context. *Leadership Quarterly, 11,* 581–613.

84. Atwater, L. E., Ostroff, C., Yammarino, F. J., & Fleenor, J. W. (1998). Self-other agreement: Does it really matter? *Personnel Psychology, 51,* 577–598.

85. London, M., & Smither, J. W. (1995). Can multi-source feedback change perceptions of goal accomplishments, self-evaluations, and performance-related outcomes? Theory-based applications and directions for research. *Personnel Psychology, 48,* 803–839.

86. Walker, A. G., & Smither, J. W. (1999). A five-year study of upward feedback: What managers do with their results matters. *Personnel Psychology, 52,* 393–423.

87. Leung, T. K., & Wong, Y. H. (2001). *Guanxi: Relationship marketing in a Chinese context.* Binghamton, NY: Haworth Press. Luo, Y. (2000). *Guanxi and business.* River Edge, NJ: World Scientific Publishing.

88. Balfour, F., & Einhorn, B. (2002, February 4). The end of guanxi capitalism? *BusinessWeek,* pp. 122–123.

89. Wood, E., Whiteley, A., & Zhang, S. (2002). The cross model of guanxi usage in Chinese leadership. *Journal of Management Development, 21,* 263–271.

90. Olivero, G., Bane, D. K., & Kopellman, R. E. (1997). Executive coaching as a transfer of training tool: Effects of productivity in a public agency. *Public Personnel Management, 26,* 461–469.

91. Giber, D., Carter, L., & Goldsmith, M. (1999). *Linkage: Inc.'s best practices in leadership development handbook.* Lexington, MA: Linkage Press.

92. Marquardt, M. J., & Revans, R. (1999). *Action learning in action.* Palo Alto, CA: Davies Black.

93. Pedler, M. (1997). Interpreting action learning. In J. Burgoyne & M. Reynolds (Eds.), *Management learning: Integrating perspectives in theory and practice* (pp. 248–264). London: Sage.

94. Dotlich, D. L., & Noel, J. L. (1998). *Action learning: How the world's top companies are recreating their leaders and themselves.* San Francisco: Jossey-Bass.

95. See Note 83.

Case in Point Sources
Farrell, G. (1998, December). "My mouse is my fist." *Business 2.0,* pp. 72–74, 76, 78, 80, 82, 84. Agency.com Web site: www.agency.com/ourcompany/.

CHAPTER 14

Preview Case Sources
Dyer, D., & Gross, D. (2001). *The generations of Corning. The life and times of a global corporation.* New York: Oxford University Press. Fleishman, C. A. (2000, November). Creative tension. *Fast Company,* pp. 358–366, 370, 372, 374, 376, 378, 382, 384, 386, 388. Graham, M. B. W., & Shuldiner, A. T. (2001). *Corning and the craft of creation.* New York: Oxford University Press.

Chapter Notes
1. Saporito, B. (1992, August 24). A week aboard the Wal-Mart express. *BusinessWeek,* pp. 77–81, 84.

2. Flynn, J., Del Valle, C., & Mitchell, R. (1992, August 3). Did Sears take other customers for a ride? *BusinessWeek,* pp. 24–25.

3. Schneider, B. (1990). *Organizational climate and culture.* San Francisco: Jossey-Bass.

4. Bangle, C. (2001). The ultimate creativity machine: How BMW turns art into profit. *Harvard Business Review, 79*(1), 47–55.

5. Schein, E. H. (1985). *Organizational culture and leadership.* San Francisco: Jossey-Bass.

6. Martin, J. (1996). *Cultures in organizations.* New York: Oxford University Press.

7. Perna, J. (2001, July 15). Reinventing how we do business. *Vital Speeches of the Day, 67*(19), 587–591.

8. The Disney Institute & Eisner, M. D. (2001). *Be our guest: Perfecting the art of customer service.* New York: Hyperion.

9. Lewyn, M. (1993, October 22). Fun: It's fundamental. *BusinessWeek,* p. 197.

10. Nash, G. D. (1992). *A. P. Giannini and the Bank of America.* Norman, OK: University of Oklahoma Press.

11. Anonymous. (1999, April). Toxic shock? *Fast Company,* p. 38.

12. Rosen, R. H., & Berger, L. (1992). *Healthy company: Eight strategies to develop people, productivity, and profits.* New York: Jeremy P. Tarcher.

13. Barry, L. L. (1999). *Discovering the soul of service: Nine drivers of sustainable business success.* New York: Free Press.

14. Vlamis, A., & Smith, B. (2001). *Do you? Business the Yahoo! way.* New York: Capstone.

15. Garr, D. (2000). *IBM redux: Lou Gerstner and the business turnaround of the decade.* New York: HarperCollins.

16. Meridden, T. (2001). *Big shots: Business the Nokia way.* New York: Capstone.

17. Florea, G., & Phinney, G. (2001). *Barbie talks!: An expose of the first talking Barbie doll.* New York: Hyperion.

18. Claymon, D. (2000, September 18). It's a dog's life. *The Industry Standard,* pp. 207, 210, 212.

19. See Note 18.

20. Freiberg, K., Freiberg, J., & Peters, T. (1998). *Nuts!: Southwest Airlines' crazy recipe for business and personal success.* New York: Bantam Doubleday Dell.

21. Goffee, R., & Jones, G. (1998). *The character of a corporation.* New York: HarperBusiness.

22. Amabile, T. (1996). *Creativity in context.* Denver, CO: Westview Press.

23. See Note 21.

24. Boeker, W., & Karichalil, R. (2002). Entrepreneurial transitions: Factors influencing founder departure. *Academy of Management Journal, 45,* 818–826. Martin, J., Sitkin, S. B., & Boehm, M. (1985). Founders and the elusiveness of a cultural legacy. In P. J. Frost, L. F. Moore, M. R. Louis, C. C. Lundberg, & J. Martin (Eds.), *Organizational culture* (pp. 99–124). Beverly Hills, CA: Sage.

25. Dobrzynski, J. H. (1993, April 12). "I'm going to let the problems come to me." *BusinessWeek,* pp. 32–33.

26. Asakura, R. (2000). *Revolutionaries at Sony: The making of the Sony Playstation and the visionaries who conquered the world of video games.* New York: McGraw-Hill.

27. Reitman, J. (1998). *Bad blood: Crisis in the American Red Cross.* New York: Pinnacle Books.

28. Ornstein, S. L. (1986). Organizational symbols: A study of their meanings and influences on perceived psychological climate. *Organizational Behavior and Human Decision Processes, 38,* 207–229.

29. Martin, J. (1982). Stories and scripts in organizational settings. In A. Hastorf & A. Isen (Eds.), *Cognitive social psychology* (pp. 255–306). New York: Elsevier-North Holland.

30. Ransdell, E. (2000, January–February). The Nike story? Just tell it. *Fast Company,* pp. 44, 46.

31. Carroll, P. (1993). *Big blues: The unmaking of IBM.* New York: Crown.

32. Branwyn, G. (1997). *Jargon watch: A pocket dictionary for the jitterati.* San Francisco, CA: Hardwired.

33. Neuhauser, P. C. (1993). *Corporate legends and lore: The power of storytelling as a*

management tool. New York: McGraw-Hill (quote p. 63).

34. Brenner, J. G. (1999). *The emperors of chocolate: Inside the secret world of Hershey and Mars.* New York: Random House.

35. Manley, W. W., II. (1991). *Executive's handbook of model business conduct codes.* Englewood Cliffs, NJ: Prentice Hall (quote, p. 5).

36. Weiner, Y., (1988). Forms of value systems: A focus on organizational effectiveness and cultural change and maintenance. *Academy of Management Review, 13,* 534–545.

37. Bernick, C. L. (2001). When your culture needs a makeover. *Harvard Business Review, 79*(6), 53–56, 58, 60–61.

38. Walter, G. A. (1985). Culture collisions in mergers and acquisitions. In P. J. Frost, L. F. Moore, M. R. Louis, C. C. Lundberg, & J. Martin (Eds.), *Organizational culture* (pp. 301–314). Beverly Hills, CA: Sage.

39. Vlasic, B., & Stertz, B. A. (2001). *Taken for a ride: How Daimler-Benz drove off with Chrysler.* New York: HarperBusiness. Naughton, K. (2000, December 11). A mess of a merger. *Newsweek,* pp. 54–57. Elkind, P. (1998, November 9). A merger made in hell. *Fortune,* pp. 134–138, 140, 142, 144, 146, 149, 150. Burrough, B., & Helyar, J. (1990). *Barbarians at the gate.* New York: HarperCollins. Muller, J. (1999, November 29). Lessons from a casualty of the culture wars. *BusinessWeek,* p. 198. Muller, J. (1999, November 15). The one-year itch at Daimler Chrysler. *BusinessWeek,* p. 42.

40. See Note 31.

41. See Note 40.

42. Fischer, I., & Frontczak, D. (1999, September). Culture club. *Business 2.0,* pp. 196–198.

43. Amabile, T. M. (1988). A model of creativity and innovation in organizations. In B. M. Staw & L. L. Cummings (Eds.), *Research in organizational behavior* (Vol. 10, pp. 123–167). Greenwich, CT: JAI Press.

44. The Drucker Foundation, Hesselbein, F., & Johnston, R. (2002). *On creativity, innovation, and renewal: A leader-to-leader guide.* New York: John Wiley & Sons.

45. Amabile, T. M. (2000). Stimulate creativity by fueling passion. In E. A. Locke (Ed.), *The Blackwell handbook of principles of organizational behavior* (pp. 331–341). Oxford, England: Blackwell.

46. Madjar, N., Oldham, G. R., & Pratt, M. G. (2002). There's no place like home? The contributions of work and nonwork creativity to support employees' creative performance. *Academy of Management Journal, 45,* 757–768. Kabanoff, B., & Rossiter, J. R. (1994). Recent developments in applied creativity. In C. Cooper & I. T. Robertson (Eds.), *International review of industrial and organizational psychology* (Vol. 9, pp. 283–324). London: Wiley.

47. Michalko, M. (1998, May). Thinking like a genius: Eight strategies used by the super-creative, from Aristotle and Einstein and Edison. *The Futurist,* pp. 21–25.

48. Kabanoff, B., & Bottiger, P. (1991). Effectiveness of creativity training and its reaction to selected personality factors. *Journal of Organizational Behavior, 12,* 235–248.

49. Muoio, A. (2000, January–February). Idea summit. *Fast Company*, pp. 151–156, 160, 162, 164 (quote, p. 152).

50. Sittenfeld, C. (1999, July–August). This old house is a home for new ideas. *Fast Company*, pp. 58, 60.

51. Amabile, T. M., Conti, R., Coon, H., Lazenby, J., & Herron, M. (1996). Assessing the work environment for creativity. *Academy of Management Journal, 39*, 1154–1184.

52. Oldham, G. R., & Cummings, A. (1996). Employee creativity: Personal and contextual factors at work. *Academy of Management Journal, 39*, 607–634.

53. Amabile, T. M., & Conti, R. (1999). Changes in the work environment for creativity during downsizing. *Academy of Management Journal, 42*, 630–640.

54. Dahle, C. (2000, January–February). Mind games. *Fast Company*, pp. 169–173, 176, 178–179.

55. Shalley, C. E. (1991). Effects of productivity goals, creativity goals, and personal discretion on individual creativity. *Journal of Applied Psychology, 76*, 179–185.

56. Sutton, R. I., & Hargadon, A. (1996). Brainstorming groups in context: Effectiveness in a product design firm. *Administrative Science Quarterly, 41*, 685–718 (quote, p. 702).

57. Hamilton, J. O. (2000, May 15). Can we stop having fun yet? *BusinessWeek e-biz*, pp. EB-125, EB-128.

58. Buchannan, L. (2000, September). Send in the clowns. *Inc.*, pp. 89–94.

59. Zachary, P. C. (2000, July). Mighty is the mongrel. *Fast Company*, pp. 270–272, 276, 278, 280, 282, 284.

60. Zachary, G. P. (2000). *The global me: New cosmopolitans and the competitive edge.* New York: Public Affairs Books.

61. Casson, M. (1990). *Enterprise and competitiveness.* New York: Oxford University Press.

62. Busentiz, L. W., Gomez, C., & Spencer, J. W. (2000). Country institutional profiles: Unlocking entrepreneurial phenomena. *Academy of Management Journal, 43*, 994–1003.

63. Micropat names the most innovative companies of the 20th century. (2001, January 3). Downloaded from *Tech Mall* on the Intenet at www8.techmall.com/ tech-docs/TS0001036.html.

64. See Note 43.

65. Ricchiuto, J. (1997). *Collaborative creativity.* New York: Oakhill.

66. Hamel, G. (2000, June 21). Re-invent your company. *Fortune*, pp. 99–104, 106, 110, 112, 116, 118 (quote, p. 100).

67. Hamel, G. (2000). *Leading the revolution.* Boston, MA: Harvard Business School Press.

Case in Point Sources
Seriously silly. (1999, September 13). *BusinessWeek*, p. F14. Brown, E. (1999, April 12). A day at Innovation U. *Fortune*, pp. 163–165. Garner, R. (2000, April). Innovation for fun and profit. *Upside*, pp. 88–90, 92, 94, 96. Kelley, T. (2001). *The art of innovation.* New York: Doubleday. Myerson, J. (2001). *IDEO: Masters of innovation.* London: Laurence King Publishing.

CHAPTER 15

Preview Case Sources
Cowen, M. (2001, October 26). Cowen on: Lee jeans. *Campaign*, p. 25. Rosier, B. (2001, March 1). Wrangler and Lee plan European sites' revamp. *Marketing*, p. 11. Brown, E. (1998, December 7). VF Corp. changes its underware. *Fortune*, pp. 115–118. VF Corp. Web site: www.vs.com.

Chapter Notes
1. Miller, D. (1987). The genesis of configuration. *Academy of Management Review, 12*, 686–701.

2. Galbraith, L. R. (1987). Organization design. In J. W. Lorsch (Ed.), *Handbook of organizational behavior* (pp. 343–357). Englewood Cliffs, NJ: Prentice Hall.

3. Hendricks, C. F. (1992). *The rightsizing remedy.* Homewood, IL: Business One Irwin.

4. Swoboda, F. (1990, May 28–June 3). For unions, maybe bitter was better. *Washington Post National Weekly Edition*, p. 20.

5. Speen, K. (1988, September 12). Caught in the middle. *BusinessWeek*, pp. 80–88.

6. Urwick, L. F. (1956). The manager's span of control. *Harvard Business Review, 34*(3), 39–47.

7. Charan, R. (1991, July–August). How networks reshape organizations—for results. *Harvard Business Review*, pp. 10–17.

8. Green, H., & Moscow, A. (1984). *Managing.* New York: Doubleday.

9. Dalton, M. (1950). Conflicts between staff and line managerial officers. *American Sociological Review, 15*, 342–351.

10. Chandler, A. (1962). *Strategy and structure.* Cambridge, MA: MIT Press.

11. Schminke, M., Ambrose, M. L., & Cropanzano, R. S. (2000). The effect of organizational structure on perceptions of procedural fairness. *Journal of Applied Psychology, 85*, 294–304.

12. Navran, F. J. (2002). *Truth and trust: The first two victims of downsizing.* Athabaska, Alberta, Canada: Athabasca University Press. Mitchell, R. (1987, December 14). When Jack Welch takes over: A guide for the newly acquired. *BusinessWeek*, pp. 93–97.

13. Lawrence, P., & Lorsch, J. (1967). *Organization and environment.* Boston: Harvard University.

14. Pitta, J. (1993, April 26). It had to be done and we did it. *Forbes*, pp. 148–152.

15. Dumaine, B. (1990, November 5). How to manage in a recession. *Fortune*, pp. 72–75.

16. Uttal, B. (1985, June 29). Mettle test time for John Young. *Fortune*, pp. 242–244, 248.

17. Bahrami, H. (1992). The emerging flexible organization: Perspectives from Silicon Valley. *California Management Review, 34*(4), 33–52.

18. Mee, J. F. (1964). Matrix organizations. *Business Horizons, 7*(2), 70–72.

19. Bartlett, C. A., & Ghoshal, S. (1990). Matrix management: Not a structure, a frame of mind. *Harvard Business Review, 68*(3), 138–145.

20. Wall, W. C., Jr. (1984). Integrated management in matrix organizations. *IEEE Transactions on Engineering Management, 20*(2), 30–36.

21. Davis, S. M., & Lawrence, P. R. (1977). *Matrix.* Reading, MA: Addison-Wesley.

22. Goggin, W. (1974). How the multidimensional structure works at Dow Corning. *Harvard Business Review, 56*(1), 33–52.

23. See Note 20.

24. Ford, R. C., & Randolph, W. A. (1992). Cross-functional structures: A review and integration of matrix organization and project management. *Journal of Management, 18*, 267–294.

25. See Note 22.

26. Ostroff, F. (1999). *The horizontal organization.* New York: Oxford University Press. Stewart, T. A. (1992, May 18). The search for the organization of tomorrow. *Fortune*, pp. 93–98 (quote p. 93).

27. Byrne, J. A. (1993, December 20). The horizontal corporation. *BusinessWeek*, pp. 76–81 (quote, p. 96).

28. See Note 3 (quote, p. 96).

29. McGregor, D. (1960). *The human side of enterprise.* New York: McGraw-Hill.

30. Argyris, C. (1964). *Integrating the individual and the organization.* New York: Wiley.

31. Likert, R. (1961). *New patterns of management.* New York: McGraw-Hill.

32. Duncan, R. (1979, Winter). What is the right organization structure? *Organizational Dynamics*, pp. 59–69.

33. Burns, T., & Stalker, G. M. (1961). *The management of innovation.* London: Tavistock.

34. Deveney, K. (1986, October 13). Bag those fries, squirt that ketchup, fry that fish. *BusinessWeek*, pp. 57–61.

35. Kerr, P. (1985, May 11). Witch hazel still made the old-fashioned way. *New York Times*, pp. 27–28.

36. Morse, J. J., & Lorsch, J. W. (1970). Beyond Theory Y. *Harvard Business Review, 48*(3), 61–68.

37. Mintzberg, H. (1983). *Structure in fives: Designing effective organizations.* Englewood Cliffs, NJ: Prentice Hall.

38. Livesay, H. C. (1979). *American made: Man who shaped the American economy.* Boston: Little, Brown.

39. See Note 1.

40. Shawney, M., & Parikh, D. (2001, June). Break your boundaries. *Business 2.0*, pp. 198–202, 205, 207.

41. GE: Just your average everyday $60 billion family grocery store. (1994, May 2). *IndustryWeek*, pp. 13–18.

42. Slater, R. (1993). *The new GE.* Homewood, IL: Business One Irwin (quote, p. 257).

43. Woodruff, D., & Miller, K. L. (1993, May 3). Chrysler's Neon: Is this the small car Detroit couldn't build? *BusinessWeek*, pp. 116–126.

44. Dees, G. D., Rasheed, A. M. A., McLaughlin, K. J., & Priem, R. L. (1995). The new corporate architecture. *Academy of Management Executive, 9*, 7–18.

45. See Note 41.

46. Tully, S. (1993, February 3). The modular corporation. *Fortune*, pp. 106–108, 110.

47. Taylor, A. (1990, November 19). Why Toyota keeps getting better and better and better. *Fortune*, pp. 72–79.

48. Byrne, J. (1993, February 8). The virtual corporation. *BusinessWeek*, pp. 99–103.

49. Chesbrough, H. W., & Teece, D. J. (1996, January–February). When is virtual virtuous? Organizing for innovation. *Harvard Business Review, 96*, 65–73.

50. Sherman, S. (1992, September 21). Are strategic alliances working? *Fortune,* pp. 77–78 (quote p. 78).

51. Nathan, R. (1998, July–August). NEC organizing for creativity, nimbleness. *Research Technology Management,* pp. 4–6.

52. Moore, J. F. (1998, Winter). The rise of a new corporate form. *Washington Quarterly,* pp. 167–181.

53. Nakarmi, L., & Einhorn, B. (1993, June 7). Hyundai's gutsy gambit. *BusinessWeek,* p. 48.

54. Gerlach, M. L. (1993). *Alliance capitalism: The social organization of Japanese business.* Berkeley, CA: University of California Press.

55. Miyashita, K., & Russell, D. (1994). *Keiretsu: Inside the Japanese conglomerates.* New York: McGraw-Hill.

56. Kanter, R. M. (1994, July–August). Collaborative advantage: The art of alliances. *Harvard Business Review,* pp. 96–108.

57. See Note 50.

58. Hansen, M. T., & Chesbrough, H. W., Nohria, N., & Sull, D. N. (2000, September October). Networked incubators: Hothouses of new economy. *Harvard Business Review,* pp. 74–84.

59. Albrinck, J., Irwin, G., Neilson, G., & Sasina, D. (2000, third quarter). From bricks to clicks: The four stages of e-volution. *Strategy and Business,* pp. 63–66, 68–72.

60. Fletcher, N. (1988, December 10). U.S., China form joint venture to manufacture helicopters. *Journal of Commerce,* p. 58.

61. Bransi, B. (1987, January 3). South Korea's carmakers count their blessings. *The Economist,* p. 45.

62. Mason, J. C. (1993, May). Strategic alliances: Partnering for success. *Management Review,* pp. 10–15.

63. Newman, W. H. (1992). Focused joint ventures in transforming economies. *The Executive, 6,* 67–75.

64. Lewis, J. (1990). *Partnerships for profit: Structuring and managing strategic alliances.* New York: Free Press.

65. Vanhonacker, W. (1997, March–April). Entering China: An unconventional approach. *Harvard Business Review, 97,* 130–131, 134–136, 138–140.

66. Earley, P. C., & Erez, M. (1997). *The transplanted executive: Why you need to understand how workers in other countries see the world differently.* New York: Oxford University Press.

67. Weisul, K., (2001, March 6). Minority mergers. *BusinessWeek,* Frontier section, pp. F14–F19.

Case in Point Sources
Lubove, S. (1995, July 17). New-tech, old-tech. *Forbes,* pp. 58, 60, 62. Leon, K. M. (1995, April). Online operator, may I help you? *Red Herring,* pp. 108–110.

CHAPTER 16

Preview Case Sources
United States Mint Web site: www.usmint.gov/. Muoio, A. (1999, December). Mint condition. *Fast Company,* pp. 330–332, 335–338, 342, 344, 346, 348.

Chapter Notes

1. Sherman, S. (1993, December 13). How will we live with the tumult? *Fortune,* pp. 123–125.

2. Siklos, R., & Yang, C. (2000, January 24). Welcome to the 21st century. *BusinessWeek,* pp. 336–340, 42, 44.

3. Haveman, H. A. (1992). Between a rock and a hard place: Organizational change and performance under conditions of fundamental environmental transformation. *Administrative Science Quarterly, 37,* 48–75.

4. Smith, D. (1998, May). Invigorating change initiatives. *Management Review,* pp. 45–48.

5. Nystrom, P. C., & Starbuck, W. H. (1984, Spring). To avoid organizational crises, unlearn. *Organizational Dynamics,* pp. 44–60.

6. Reese, J. (1993, July 26). Corporate Methuselahs. *Fortune,* pp. 15–16.

7. See Note 5 (quote, p. 15).

8. Miller, K. L. (1993, May 17). The factory guru tinkering with Toyota. *BusinessWeek,* pp. 95, 97.

9. Levy, A. (1986). Second-order planned change: Definition and conceptualization. *Organizational Dynamics, 16*(1), 4–20.

10. A master class in radical change. (1993, December 13). *Fortune,* pp. 82–84, 88, 90.

11. Kanter, R. M. (1991, May–June). Transcending business boundaries: 12,000 world managers view change. *Harvard Business Review,* pp. 151–164.

12. Stewart, T. A. (1993, December 13). Welcome to the revolution. *Fortune,* pp. 66–68, 70, 72, 76, 78.

13. National Performance Review (1997). *Serving the American public: Best practices in downsizing.* Washington, DC: Author. Also available online at govinfo.library. unt.edu/npr/library/papers/benchmrk/downsize.html.

14. Yahoo News: dailynews.yahoo.com/fc/Business/Downsizing_and_Layoffs.

15. David, F. R. (1993). *Concepts of strategic management.* New York: Macmillan.

16. Mead, R. (1998). *International management* (2nd ed.). Malden, MA: Blackwell.

17. Taylor, B. (1995). The new strategic leadership—driving change, getting results. *Long Range Planning, 28*(5), 71–81.

18. McCarty, M. (1990, October 30). PepsiCo to consolidate its restaurants, combining U.S. and foreign operations. *Wall Street Journal,* p. A4.

19. Christensen, H. K. (1994). Corporate strategy: Managing a set of businesses. In L. Fahley, & R. M. Randall (Eds.), *The portable MBA in strategy* (pp. 53–83). New York: Wiley.

20. Markides, C. (1997, Spring). Strategic innovation. *Sloan Management Review,* pp. 9–23.

21. Collis, D. J., & Montgomery, C. A. (1995, July–August). Competing on resources: Strategy in the 1990s. *Harvard Business Review, 73,* 118–128.

22. Dean, J. W., Jr., & Scharfman, M. (1996). Does decision process matter? A study of strategic decision-making effectiveness. *Academy of Management Journal, 29,* 368–396.

23. Porter, M. (1996, March 14). "It's time to grow up." *Far Eastern Economic Review,* pp. 1–2.

24. Lasserre, P., & Putti, J. (1990). *Business strategy and management: Text and cases for managers in Asia.* Singapore: Institute of Management.

25. Yoshimori, M. (1995). Whose company is it? The concept of the corporation in Japan and the West. *Long Range Planning, 28*(4), 33–34.

26. Goldstein, A. P. (2001). *Reducing resistance: Methods for enhancing openness to change.* Champaign, IL: Research Press. Judson, A. S. (1991). *Changing behavior in organizations: Minimizing resistance to change.* Cambridge, MA: Basil Blackwell.

27. Nadler, D. A. (1987). The effective management of organizational change. In J. W. Lorsch (Ed.), *Handbook of organizational behavior* (pp. 358–369). Englewood Cliffs, NJ: Prentice Hall.

28. Katz, D., & Kahn, R. L. (1978). *The social psychology of organizations* (2nd ed.). New York: Wiley.

29. Beer, M. (1980). *Organizational change and development: A systems view.* Glenview, IL: Scott, Foresman.

30. Nadler, D. A. (1987). The effective management of organizational change. In J. W. Lorsch (Ed.), *Handbook of organizational behavior* (pp. 358–369). Englewood Cliffs, NJ: Prentice Hall.

31. Reich, R. B. (2000, October). Your job is change. *Fast Company,* pp. 140–148, 150, 152, 154, 156, 158.

32. Hucy, J. (1993, April 5). Managing in the midst of chaos. *Fortune,* pp. 38–41, 44, 46, 48.

33. Senge, P. M. (1990). *The fifth discipline.* New York: Doubleday.

34. Blundell, B. Saunders, M. & Bennett, R. (2002). *Learning at work. The learning organization in practice.* London: Kogan Page. Kotter, J. P. (1995, March–April). Leading the change: Why transformation efforts fail. *Harvard Business Review,* pp. 59–67. Kotter, J. P., & Schlesinger, L. A. (1979, March–April). Choosing strategies for change. *Harvard Business Review,* pp. 106–114.

35. Pascale, R., Millemann, M., & Gioja, L. (1997, November–December). Changing the way we change. *Harvard Business Review,* pp. 127–139.

36. Collarelli, S. M. (1998). Psychological interventions in organizations. *American Psychologist, 53,* 1044–1056.

37. Ettorre, B. (1995, October). Managing competitive intelligence. *Management Review,* pp. 15–19.

38. Teo, T. S. H., & Choo, W. Y. (2001). Assessing the impact of using the Internet for competitive intelligence. *Information & Management, 39,* 67–83.

39. See Note 39 (quote, pp. 68–69).

40. Burwell, H., Ernst, C. R., & Sankey, M. (1999). *Online competitive intelligence.* Lanham, MD: Facts on Demand Press.

41. See Note 39.

42. Subramanian, R., & Ishak, S. T. (1998). Computer analysis practices of U.S. companies: An empirical investigation. *Management International Review, 38,* 7–24.

43. Pole, J. G., Madsen, E., & Dishman, P. (2000). Competitive intelligence as a construct for organizational change. *Competitive Intelligence Review, 11,* 25–31.

44. Watkins, J. M., & Mohr, B. J. (2001). *Appreciative inquiry: Change at the speed of imagination.* New York: John Wiley & Sons.

45. Whitney, D., & Sachau, C. (1998, Spring). Appreciative inquiry: An innovative process for organization change. *Employment Relations Today, 25,* pp. 11–21.

46. Bushe, G. R., & Coetzer, G. (1995). Appreciative inquiry as a team-developed intervention: A controlled experiment. *Journal of Applied Behavioral Science, 31,* 13–30.

47. Pascale, R. T., & Miller, A. H. (1999, fourth quarter). The action lab: Creating a greenhouse for organizational change. *Strategy & Business,* pp. 64–72.

48. See Note 38.

49. Porras, J. I., & Robertson, P. J. (1992). Organization development: Theory, practice, and research. In M. D. Dunnette & L. M. Hough (Eds.), *Handbook of industrial and organizational psychology* (2nd ed.), (Vol. 3, pp. 719–822). Palo Alto, CA: Consulting Psychologists Press.

50. Blau, R. (1999, December). The practice of change. *Fast Company,* pp. 408–410, 412–416, 418–423.

51. Jaeger, A. M. (1986). Organizational development and national culture: Where's the fit? *Academy of Management Review, 11,* 178–190.

52. Kedia, B. L., & Bhagat, R. S. (1998). Cultural constraints on transfer of technology across nations: Implications for research in international and comparative management. *Academy of Management Review, 13,* 559–571.

53. Trepo, G. (1973, Autumn). Management style *a la française. European Business, 39,* 71–79.

54. Blunt, P. (1988). Cultural consequences for organization change in a southeast Asian state: Brunei. *Academy of Management Executive, 2,* 235–240.

55. Seabright, M. A., & Moberg, D. J. (1998). Interpersonal manipulation: Its nature and moral limits. In M. Schminke (Ed.), *Managerial ethics* (pp. 153–175). Mahwah, NJ; Lawrence Erlbaum Associates. White, L. P., & Wotten, K. C. (1983). Ethical dilemmas in various stages of organizational development. *Academy of Management Review, 8,* 690–697.

Case in Point Sources

Chevrolet SSR home page: www.chevrolet.com/ssr/home.htm. Muoio, A. (2000, December). GM has a new model for change. *Fast Company,* pp. 62, 64.

A

abilities Mental and physical capacities to perform various tasks. (p. 100)

absence control programs Procedures that give employees flexibility with respect to when they can take time off work. (p. 131)

achievement motivation The strength of an individual's desire to excel—to succeed at difficult tasks and to do them better than other persons. (p. 96)

action lab An OD intervention in which teams of participants work off-site to develop and implement new ways of solving organizational problems by focusing on the ineffectiveness of current methods. (p. 612)

action learning A leadership development technique involving a continuous process of learning and reflection that is supported by colleagues and that emphasizes getting things done. (p. 507)

ad hoc committee A temporary committee formed for a special purpose. (p. 275)

adaptive agents Sophisticated computer models that capture the rules of complex human behavior. (p. 366)

additive tasks Types of group tasks in which the coordinated efforts of several people are added together to form the group's product. (p. 287)

adhocracy A highly informal, organic organization in which specialists work in teams, coordinating with each other on various projects (e.g., many software development companies). (p. 568)

administrative model A model of decision making that recognizes the *bounded rationality* that limits the making of optimally rational-economic decisions. (p. 373)

affective commitment The strength of a person's desire to work for an organization because he or she agrees with its underlying goals and values. (p. 162)

affiliate networks Satellite organizations affiliated with core companies that have helped them develop. (p. 570)

affirmative action laws Legislation designed to give employment opportunities to groups that have been underrepresented in the workforce, such as women and members of minority groups. (p. 175)

alternative dispute resolution (ADR) A set of procedures, such as *mediation* and *arbitration,* in which disputing parties work together with a neutral party who helps them settle their disagreements out of court. (p. 420)

analytical model of the decision-making process An eight-step approach to organizational decision making that focuses on both the formulation of problems and the implementation of solutions. (p. 359)

anticipatory socialization The first stage of socialization, concerned with learning about an organization before working there. (p. 241)

appreciative inquiry An OD intervention that focuses attention away from an organization's shortcomings and toward its capabilities and its potential; based on the assumption that members of organizations already know the problems they face and that they stand to benefit more by focusing on what is possible. (p. 610)

apprenticeship programs Formal training programs involving both on-the-job and classroom training usually over a long period; often used for training people in the skilled trades. (p. 61)

arbitration A process in which a third party (known as an *arbitrator*) has the power to impose, or at least to recommend, the terms of an agreement between two or more conflicting parties. (p. 421)

attitudes Relatively stable clusters of feelings, beliefs, and behavioral intentions toward specific objects, people, or institutions. (p. 148)

attribute framing effect The tendency for people to evaluate a characteristic more positively when it is presented in positive terms than when it is presented in negative terms. (p. 376)

attribution The process through which individuals attempt to determine the causes behind others' behavior. (p. 39)

attribution approach (to leadership) The approach to leadership that focuses on leaders' attributions of followers' performance—that is, their perceptions of its underlying causes. (p. 484)

autocratic leadership style A style of leadership in which the leader makes all decisions unilaterally. (p. 474)

autocratic-delegation continuum model An approach to leadership describing the ways in which leaders allocate influence to subordinates. This ranges from controlling everything (*autocratic*) to allowing others to make decisions for themselves (*delegating*). Between these extremes are more participative forms of leadership—*consulting* and *making joint decisions.* (p. 475)

autonomous change A change in one part of an organization that is made independently of the need for change in another part. (p. 572)

availability heuristic The tendency for people to base their judgments on information that is readily available to them although it may be potentially inaccurate, thereby adversely affecting decision quality. (p. 378)

avoidance See *negative reinforcement.* (p. 57)

awareness-based diversity training A type of diversity management program designed to make people more aware of diversity issues in the workplace and to get them to recognize the underlying assumptions they make about people. (p. 177)

B

baby boom generation The generation of children born in the economic boom period following World War II. (p. 18)

bargaining The process by which two or more parties in dispute with one another exchange offers, counteroffers, and concessions in an attempt to find a mutually acceptable agreement. (p. 419)

behavioral component (of attitudes) Predisposition to behave in a way consistent with our beliefs and feelings about an attitude object. (p. 147)

behavioral sciences Fields such as psychology and sociology that seek knowledge of human behavior and society through the use of the scientific method. (p. 4)

benchmarking The process of comparing one's own products or services with the best from others. (p. 27)

big five dimensions of personality Five basic dimensions of personality that are assumed to underlie many specific traits. (p. 85)

boundaryless career The tendency for people to have careers that cut across various companies and industries. (p. 231)

boundaryless organization An organization in which chains of command are eliminated, spans of control are unlimited, and rigid departments give way to empowered teams. (p. 569)

bounded discretion The tendency to restrict decision alternatives to those that fall within prevailing ethical standards. (p. 374)

bounded rationality The major assumption of the administrative model that organizational, social, and human limitations lead to the making of *satisficing* rather than optimal decisions. (p. 374)

brainstorming A technique designed to foster group productivity by encouraging interacting group members to express their ideas in a noncritical fashion. (p. 385)

bureaucracy An organizational design developed by Max Weber that attempts to make organizations operate efficiently by having a clear hierarchy of authority in which people are required to perform well-defined jobs. (p. 11)

burnout A syndrome of emotional, physical, and mental exhaustion coupled with feelings of low self-esteem or low self-efficacy, resulting from prolonged exposure to intense stress, and the strain reactions following from them. (p. 129)

business incubator A kind of business that provides support for new, entrepreneurial companies, to launch them and help them grow. (p. 260)

C

cafeteria-style benefit plans Incentive systems in which employees have an opportunity to select the fringe benefits they want from a menu of available alternatives. (p. 209)

calculus-based trust A form of trust based on deterrence, whenever people believe that another will behave as promised out of fear of getting punished for doing otherwise. (p. 406)

career The evolving sequence of work experiences over time. (p. 229)

career anchor A person's occupational self-concept that is based on his or her self-perceived talents, abilities, values, needs, and motives. (p. 240)

career break The practice in which an employee leaves and then subsequently reenters a job following an agreed-upon period of absence. (p. 263)

career coach An expert hired for purposes of helping someone accomplish his or her career objectives. (p. 264)

career development interventions Systematic efforts to help manage people's careers while simultaneously helping the organizations in which they work. (p. 250)

career dynamics The wide variety of factors that influence the nature of people's career choices, the directions their careers take, and their ultimate success and satisfaction over the course of their working lives. (p. 228)

career plateau The point at which one's career has peaked and is unlikely to develop further. (p. 249)

case method A research technique in which a particular organization is thoroughly described and analyzed for purposes of understanding what went on in that setting. (p. 634)

channels of communication The pathways over which messages are transmitted (e.g., telephone lines, mail, etc.). (p. 319)

charisma An attitude of enthusiasm and optimism that is contagious; an aura of leadership. (p. 446)

charismatic leaders Leaders who exert especially powerful effects on followers by virtue of their commanding confidence and clearly articulated visions. (p. 486)

chief knowledge officer (CKO) A senior-level executive who is responsible for knowledge management within his or her company. (See *knowledge management*.) (p. 71)

child-care facilities Sites at or near company locations where parents can leave their children while they are working. (p. 18)

classical organizational theory An early approach to the study of management that focused on the most efficient way of structuring organizations. (p. 10)

classical organizational theory The approach that assumes that there is a single best way to design organizations. (p. 561)

classroom training Formal training in which instructors describe various job requirements and provide tips on how to meet them. (p. 61)

code of ethics A document describing what an organization stands for and the general rules of conduct it expects of its employees (e.g., to avoid conflicts of interest, to be honest, etc.). (p. 30)

codes of ethics Documents in which explicit statements are made that express a company's ethical values. (p. 526)

coercive power The individual power base derived from the capacity to administer punishment to others. (p. 444)

cognitive appraisal A judgment about the stressfulness of a situation, based on the extent to which someone perceives a stressor as threatening and capable of coping with its demands. (p. 122)

cognitive component (of attitudes) The things we believe about an attitude object, whether they are true or false. (p. 147)

cognitive intelligence The ability to understand complex ideas, to adapt effectively to the environment, to learn from experience, to engage in various forms of reasoning, and to overcome obstacles by careful thought. (p. 100)

cohesiveness The strength of group members' desires to remain a part of the group. (p. 283)

collectivistic cultures National groups whose members place a high value on shared responsibility and the collective good of all. (p. 288)

command group A group determined by the connections between individuals who are a formal part of the organization (i.e., those who legitimately can give orders to others). (p. 274)

communal culture In the *double S cube*, this type of organizational culture is characterized by both a high degree of sociability and a high degree of solidarity. (p. 521)

communication The process by which a person, group, or organization (the sender) transmits some type of information (the message) to another person, group, or organization (the receiver). (p. 318)

competition A pattern of behavior in which each person, group, or organization seeks to

maximize its own gains, often at the expense of others. (p. 413)

competitive intelligence (CI) The process of gathering information about one's competitors that can be used as the basis for planning organizational change. (p. 610)

competitors People whose primary motive is doing better than others, besting them in open competition. (p. 414)

compressed workweeks The practice of working fewer days each week but longer hours each day (e.g., four 10-hour days). (p. 26)

computer-assisted communication The sharing of information, such as text messages and data relevant to the decision, over computer networks. (p. 393)

computer-mediated communication Forms of communication that depend on the use of computers. (p. 323)

computerized performance monitoring The process of using computers to monitor job performance. (p. 286)

confirmation candidate A decision alternative considered only for purposes of convincing onself of the wisdom of selecting the *implicit favorite*. (p. 379)

conflict A process in which one party perceives that another party has taken or will take actions that are incompatible with one's own interests. (p. 416)

conglomerate A form of organizational diversification in which an organization (usually a very large, multinational one) adds an entirely unrelated business or product to its organizational design. (p. 573)

conjunctive statements Statements that keep conversations going by connecting one speaker's remarks to another's. (p. 347)

consensus In *Kelley's theory of causal attribution,* information regarding the extent to which other people behave in the same manner as the person being judged. (p. 43)

consideration Actions by a leader that demonstrate concern with the welfare of subordinates and establish positive relations with them. Leaders who focus primarily on this task are often described as demonstrating a person-oriented style. (p. 477)

consistency In *Kelley's theory of causal attribution,* information regarding the extent to which the person being judged acts the same way at other times. (p. 43)

contingencies of reinforcement The various relationships between one's behavior and the consequences of that behavior—positive reinforcement, negative reinforcement, punishment, and extinction. (p. 57)

contingency approach A perspective suggesting that organizational behavior is affected by a large number of interacting factors. How someone will behave is said to be contingent upon many different variables at once. (p. 9)

contingency approach to organizational design The contemporary approach that recognizes that no one approach to organizational design is best, but that the best design is the one that best fits with the existing environmental conditions. (p. 562)

contingency theories of leader effectiveness Any of several theories that recognize that certain styles of leadership are more effective in some situations than others. (p. 490)

contingent workforce People hired by organizations temporarily to work as needed for finite periods of time. (p. 25)

continuance commitment The strength of a person's desire to continue working for an organization because he or she needs to do so and cannot afford to leave. (p. 161)

continuous reinforcement A schedule of reinforcement in which all desired behaviors are reinforced. (p. 58)

convergence hypothesis A biased approach to the study of management, which assumes that principles of good management are universal, and that ones that work well in the United States will apply equally well in other nations. (p. 16)

cooperation A pattern of behavior in which assistance is mutual and two or more individuals, groups, or organizations work together toward shared goals for their mutual benefit. (p. 412)

cooperators People who are concerned with maximizing joint outcomes and getting as much as possible for their team. (p. 414)

core competency An organization's key capability, what it does best. (p. 21)

corporate hotlines Telephone lines staffed by experts ready to answer employees' questions, listen to their comments, and the like. (p. 346)

corporate image The impressions that people have of an organization. (p. 53)

corporate orientation programs Formal sessions designed to teach new employees about their organizations. (p. 244)

corporate refugees People who leave corporate jobs so they can start their own small businesses. (p. 263)

corporate social responsibility Business decision making linked to ethical values, compliance with legal requirements, and respect for individuals, the community at large, and the environment. It involves operating a business in a manner that meets or exceeds the ethical, legal, and public expectations that society has of business. (p. 28)

corporate universities Centers devoted to handling a company's training needs on a full-time basis. (p. 62)

correlation The extent to which two variables are related to each other. (p. 627)

correlation coefficient A statistical index indicating the nature and extent to which two variables are related to each other. (p. 629)

correspondent inferences Judgments about people's dispositions, traits, and characteristics, that correspond to what we have observed of their actions. (p. 41)

covictimization The negative psychological impact suffered by individuals who share the same background as direct victims of discrimination. (p. 169)

creativity The process by which individuals or teams produce novel and useful ideas. (p. 529)

creativity heuristics Rules that people follow to help them approach tasks in novel ways. (p. 530)

critical incidents technique A procedure for measuring job satisfaction in which employees describe incidents relating to their work that they find especially satisfying or dissatisfying. (p. 152)

cross-cultural training (CCT) A systematic way of preparing employees to live and work in another country. (p. 61)

cross-functional teams Teams represented by people from different specialty areas within organizations. (p. 296)

cultural intelligence A person's sensitivity to the fact that leaders operate differently in different cultures. (p. 474)

culture The set of values, customs, and beliefs that people have in common with other members of a social unit (e.g., a nation). (p. 14)

culture clashes Problems resulting from attempts to merge two or more organizational cultures that are incompatible. (p. 528)

culture shock The tendency for people to become confused and disoriented as they attempt to adjust to a new culture. (p. 14)

cyberloafing The practice of using a company's e-mail and/or Internet facilities for personal use. (p. 426)

cybertherapy See *e-therapy*. (p. 131)

D

decentralization The extent to which authority and decision making are spread throughout all levels of an organization rather than being reserved exclusively for top management (centralization). (p. 554)

decision making The process of making choices from among several alternatives. (p. 358)

decision style Differences between people with respect to their orientations toward decisions. (p. 365)

decision support systems (DSS) Computer programs in which information about organizational behavior is presented to decision makers in a manner that helps them structure their responses to decisions. (p. 360)

decision-style model The conceptualization according to which people use one of four predominant decision styles: *directive, analytical, conceptual,* and *behavioral*. (p. 366)

decoding The process by which a receiver of messages transforms them back into the sender's ideas. (p. 319)

defensive avoidance The tendency for decision makers to fail to solve problems because they go out of their way to avoid working on the problem at hand. (p. 387)

deficiency needs The group of physiological needs, safety needs, and social needs in Maslow's need hierarchy theory. As these needs are not met, people will fail to develop in a healthy fashion. (p. 193)

Delphi technique A method of improving group decisions using the opinions of experts, which are solicited by mail and then compiled. The expert consensus of opinions is used to make a decision. (p. 389)

departmentalization The process of breaking up organizations into coherent units. (p. 555)

dependent variable The behavior of interest that is being measured in an experiment. (p. 632)

depersonalization A pattern of behavior occurring in burnout marked by becoming cynical toward others, treating others as objects, and holding negative attitudes toward others. (p. 129)

desk rage Lashing out at others in response to stressful encounters on the job. (p. 129)

destructive criticism Negative feedback that angers the recipient instead of helping him or her do a better job. (p. 417)

deviant organizational behavior Actions on the part of employees that intentionally violate the norms of organizations and/or the formal rules of society, resulting in negative consequences. (p. 422)

discipline The process of systematically administering punishment. (p. 67)

discrimination The behavior consistent with a prejudicial attitude; the act of treating someone negatively because of his or her membership in a specific group. (p. 168)

disjunctive statements Statements that are disconnected from a previous statement, tending to bring conversations to a close. (p. 347)

display rules Cultural norms about the appropriate ways to express emotions. (p. 116)

dispositional model of job satisfaction The conceptualization proposing that job satisfaction is a relatively stable disposition of an individual—that is, a characteristic that stays with people across situations. (p. 150)

distinctiveness In *Kelley's theory of causal attribution*, information regarding the extent to which a person behaves in the same manner in other contexts. (p. 43)

distributive justice The perceived fairness of the way rewards are distributed among people. (p. 201)

divergence hypothesis The approach to the study of management that recognizes that knowing how to manage most effectively requires clear understanding of the culture in which people work. (p. 16)

divergent thinking The process of reframing familiar problems in unique ways. (p. 530)

diversity management programs Programs in which employees are taught to celebrate the differences between people and in which organizations create supportive work environments for women and minorities. (p. 176)

division of labor The practice of dividing work into specialized tasks that enable people to specialize in what they do best. (p. 11)

division of labor The process of dividing the many tasks performed within an organization into specialized jobs. (p. 551)

divisional structure The form used by many large organizations, in which separate autonomous units are created to deal with entire product lines, freeing top management to focus on large-scale, strategic decisions. (p. 568)

dominant culture The distinctive, overarching "personality" of an organization. (p. 518)

doomsday management The practice of introducing change by suggesting that an impending crisis is likely. (p. 592)

double S cube A system of categorizing four types of organizational culture by combining two dimensions—*sociability* and *solidarity*. Each of the four resulting cultural types—*networked culture, mercenary culture, fragmented culture*, and *communal culture*—can be both positive and negative in nature. (p. 519)

downsizing The process of adjusting downward the number of employees needed to work in newly designed organizations (also known as *rightsizing*). (p. 20)

downsizing The process of systematically reducing the number of employees required to operate effectively. (p. 597)

drive theory of social facilitation The theory according to which the presence of others increases arousal, which increases people's tendencies to perform the dominant response. If that response is well learned, performance will improve. But, if it is novel, performance will be impaired. (p. 285)

dropping out The practice of resigning from a job for a long period of time and then taking another job at another time. (p. 263)

dual-career conflict A situation in which the career demands on one member of a couple are incompatible with the career demands on the other member of a couple. (p. 263)

dual-career couples Married couples in which both partners are employed. (p. 262)

E

e-therapy The process by which people with psychological problems communicate with trained counselors via e-mail. (p. 131)

e-training Training based on disseminating information online, such as through the Internet or a company's internal intranet. (p. 64)

elder-care facilities Facilities at which employees at work can leave elderly relatives for whom they are responsible (such as parents and grandparents). (p. 18)

electronic mail (e-mail) A system whereby people use personal computer terminals to send and receive messages between each other. (p. 323)

electronic meetings The practice of bringing individuals from different locations together for a meeting via telephone or satellite transmissions, either on television monitors or via shared space on a computer screen. (p. 393)

emoticons Simple graphic representations of facial expressions created by typing characters such as commas, hyphens, and parentheses used to express emotions. (p. 116)

emotional dissonance Inconsistencies between the emotions we feel and the emotions we express. (p. 119)

emotional intelligence (EQ) A cluster of skills relating to the emotional side of life (e.g., the ability to recognize and regulate one's own emotions, to influence those of others, and to self-motivate). (p. 102)

emotional labor The psychological effort involved in holding back one's true emotions. (p. 119)

emotions Overt reactions that express feelings about events. (p. 115)

employee assistance programs (EAPs) Plans that provide employees with assistance for various personal problems (e.g., substance abuse, career planning, and financial and legal problems). (p. 131)

employee handbook A document describing to employees basic information about a company; a general reference regarding a company's background, the nature of its business, and its rules. (p. 322)

employee theft The taking of company property for personal use. (p. 429)

employee withdrawal Actions such as chronic absenteeism and voluntary turnover (i.e., quitting one's job) that enable employees to escape from adverse organization situations. (p. 156)

empowered decision making The practice of vesting power for making decisions in the hands of employees themselves. (p. 365)

empowerment The process in which employees are given increasing amounts of autonomy and discretion in connection with their work. (p. 448)

encoding The process by which an idea is transformed so that it can be transmitted to, and recognized by, a receiver (e.g., a written or spoken message). (p. 318)

encounter stage The second stage of organizational socialization, faced as newcomers to an organization learn their new duties and the organization's ways of operating. (p. 244)

entrepreneurs Individuals who start their own businesses. (p. 257)

entry shock The disillusionment, disappointment, and confusion that result when new employees' job expectations are unmet. (p. 243)

equalizers People who are primarily interested in minimizing the differences between themselves and others. (p. 414)

equitable payment The state in which one person's outcome/input ratio is equivalent to that of another person with whom the person compares himself or herself. (p. 203)

equity theory The theory stating that people strive to maintain ratios of their own outcomes (rewards) to their own inputs (contributions) that are equal to the outcome/input ratios of others with whom they compare themselves. (p. 201)

ERG theory An alternative to Maslow's need hierarchy theory proposed by Alderfer, which asserts that there are three basic human needs: existence, relatedness, and growth. (p. 194)

escalation of commitment phenomenon The tendency for individuals to continue to support previously unsuccessful courses of action. (p. 381)

esteem needs In Maslow's *need hierarchy theory*, the need to develop self-respect and to gain the approval of others. (p. 193)

ethics audit The process of actively investigating and documenting incidents of dubious ethical value within a company. (p. 31)

ethics officers Individuals (usually at the vice presidential level) who oversee the ethics of a company's operations. (p. 30)

evaluation apprehension The fear of being evaluated or judged by another person. (p. 285)

evaluative component (of attitudes) Liking or disliking of any particular person, item, or event. (p. 147)

evening persons Individuals who feel most energetic and alert late in the day. (p. 98)

executive coaching A technique of leadership development that involves custom-tailored, one-on-one learning aimed at improving an individual leader's performance. (p. 504)

executive training programs Sessions in which companies systematically attempt to develop their top leaders, either in specific skills or general managerial skills. (p. 61)

expatriates People who are citizens of one country but who are living and working in another country. (p. 14)

expectancy The belief that one's efforts will positively influence one's performance. (p. 207)

expectancy theory The theory that asserts that motivation is based on people's beliefs about the probability that effort will lead to performance (*expectancy*), multiplied by the probability that performance will lead to reward (*instrumentality*), multiplied by the perceived value of the reward (*valence*). (p. 207)

experimental method A research technique through which it is possible to determine cause-and-effect relationships between the variables of interest—that is, the extent to which one variable causes another. (p. 630)

expert power The individual power base derived from an individual's recognized superior skills and abilities in a certain area. (p. 445)

external causes of behavior Explanations based on situations over which the individual has no control. (p. 42)

extinction The process through which responses that are no longer reinforced tend to gradually diminish in strength. (p. 57)

F

feedback Knowledge about the impact of messages on receivers. (p. 319)

feedback Knowledge of the results of one's behavior. (p. 63)

first-impression error The tendency to base our judgments of others on our earlier impressions of them. (p. 47)

first-order change Change that is continuous in nature and involves no major shifts in the way an organization operates. (p. 589)

five-stage model The conceptualization claiming that groups develop in five stages—forming, storming, norming, performing, and adjourning. (p. 277)

fixed interval schedules Schedules of reinforcement in which a fixed period of time must elapse between the administration of reinforcements. (p. 58)

fixed ratio schedules Schedules of reinforcement in which a fixed number of responses must occur between the administration of reinforcements. (p. 58)

flextime programs Policies that give employees some discretion over when they can arrive and leave work, thereby making it easier to adapt their work schedules to the demands of their personal lives. (p. 25)

formal communication The sharing of messages regarding the official work of the organization. (p. 333)

formal groups Groups that are created by the organization, intentionally designed to direct its members toward some organizational goal. (p. 274)

formal status The prestige one has by virtue of his or her official position in an organization. (p. 281)

formulation The process of understanding a problem and making a decision about it. (p. 359)

fragmented culture In the *double S cube*, this type of organizational culture is characterized by a low degree of sociability and a low degree of solidarity. (p. 520)

framing The tendency for people to make different decisions based on how the problem is presented to them. (p. 376)

friendship groups Informal groups that develop because their members are friends, often seeing each other outside of the organization. (p. 275)

functional organization The type of departmentalization based on the activities or functions performed (e.g., sales, finance). (p. 555)

fundamental attribution error The tendency to attribute others' actions to internal causes (e. g., their traits) while largely ignoring external factors that also may have influenced behavior. (p. 46)

G

general self-efficacy People's overall beliefs about their general capacity to perform tasks successfully. (p. 88)

glass ceiling An invisible barrier to job advancement caused by prejudicial attitudes toward some groups, such as women. (p. 169)

globalization The process of interconnecting the world's people with respect to the cultural, economic, political, technological, and environmental aspects of their lives. (p. 14)

goal commitment The degree to which people accept and strive to attain goals. (p. 197)

goal framing effect The tendency for people to be more strongly persuaded by information that is framed in negative terms than information that is framed in positive terms. (p. 377)

goal setting The process of determining specific levels of performance for workers to attain. (p. 196)

goal-setting theory The theory according to which a goal serves as a motivator because it causes people to compare their present capacity to perform with that required to succeed at the goal. (p. 197)

Golem effect A negative instance of the *self-fulfilling prophecy*, in which people holding low expectations of another tend to lower that individual's performance. (p. 50)

grapevine An organization's informal channels of communication, based mainly on friendship or acquaintance. (p. 337)

grassroots leadership An approach to leadership that turns the traditional management hierarchy upside down by empowering people to make their own decisions. (p. 483)

great person theory The view that leaders possess special traits that set them apart from others and that these traits are responsible for their assuming positions of power and authority. (p. 473)

grid training A multi-step process designed to cultivate two important leadership skills—concern for people and concern for production. (p. 478)

group A collection of two or more interacting individuals who maintain stable patterns of relationships, share common goals, and perceive themselves as being a group. (p. 273)

group decision support systems (GDSS) Interactive computer-based systems that combine communication, computer, and decision technologies to improve the effectiveness of group problem-solving meetings. (p. 395)

group dynamics The social science field focusing on the nature of groups—the factors governing their formation and development, the elements of their structure, and their interrelationships with individuals, other groups, and organizations. (p. 272)

group structure The pattern of interrelationships between the individuals constituting a group; the guidelines of group behavior that make group functioning orderly and predictable. (p. 279)

groupthink The tendency for members of highly cohesive groups to so strongly conform to group pressures regarding a certain decision that they fail to think critically, rejecting the potentially correcting influences of outsiders. (p. 369)

growth need strength The personality variable describing the extent to which people have a high need for personal growth and development on the job. The *job characteristics model* best describes people high in growth need strength. (p. 216)

growth needs In Maslow's *need hierarchy theory*, esteem needs and the need for self-actualization, as a group. Gratification of these needs helps a person reach his or her full potential. (p. 193)

guanxi In China, a person's network of personal and business connections. (p. 504)

H

halo effect The tendency for our overall impressions of others to affect objective evaluations of their specific traits; perceiving high correlations between characteristics that may be unrelated. (p. 46)

Hawthorne studies The earliest systematic research in the field of OB, this work was performed to determine how the design of work environments affected performance. (p. 10)

healthy organizational cultures Organizational cultures in which people feel that they are valued (opposite of toxic organizational cultures). (p. 516)

heuristics Simple decision rules (rules of thumb) used to make quick decisions about complex problems. (See *availability heuristic* and *representativeness heuristic*.) (p. 378)

hierarchy of authority A configuration of the reporting relationships within organizations, that is, who reports to whom. (p. 550)

high-performance teams Teams whose members are deeply committed to one another's personal growth and success. (p. 294)

hindsight bias The tendency for people to perceive outcomes as more inevitable after they have occurred (i.e., in hindsight) than they did before they occurred (i.e., in foresight). (p. 379)

Holland's hexagon A conceptualization specifying the occupations for which people are best suited based on which of six personality types most closely describes them. (p. 238)

Holland's theory of vocational choice A theory that claims that people will perform best at occupations that match their traits and personalities. (p. 238)

horizontal organization The practice of structuring organizations by processes performed, using autonomous work teams in flattened hierarchies. (p. 562)

human relations movement A perspective on organizational behavior that rejects the primarily economic orientation of scientific management and recognizes, instead, the importance of social processes in work settings. (p. 10)

HURIER model The conceptualization that describes effective listening as made up of the following six components: hearing, understanding, remembering, interpreting, evaluating, and responding. (p. 342)

hypervigilance The state in which an individual frantically searches for quick solutions to problems and goes from one idea to another out of a sense of desperation that one idea isn't working and that another needs to be considered before time runs out. (p. 386)

hypotheses Logically derived, testable statements about the relationships between variables that follow from a theory. (p. 625)

I

identification-based trust A form of trust based on accepting the wants and desires of another person. (p. 407)

image theory A theory of decision making that recognizes that decisions are made in an automatic, intuitive fashion based on actions that best fit a person's individual principles, current goals, and plans for the future. (p. 374)

implementation The process of carrying out a decision. (p. 359)

implicit favorite One's preferred decision alternative, selected even before all options have been considered. (p. 379)

impression management Efforts by individuals to improve how they appear to others. (p. 52)

improvement teams Teams whose members are oriented primarily toward the mission of increasing the effectiveness of the processes used by the organization. (p. 294)

incentive stock option (ISO) plans Corporate programs in which a company grants an employee the opportunity to purchase its stock at some future time at a specified price. (p. 212)

incivility Demonstrating a lack of regard for others and denying them the respect they are due. (p. 422)

incubator A company that specializes in starting up new businesses. (p. 575)

independent variable The variable in an experiment that is systematically manipulated to determine its effects on the behavior of interest. (p. 631)

individualistic cultures National groups whose members place a high value on individual accomplishments and personal success. (p. 288)

individualists People who care almost exclusively about maximizing their own gain and don't care whether others do better or worse than themselves. (p. 414)

informal communication The sharing of unofficial messages, ones that go beyond the organization's formal activities. (p. 333)

informal groups Groups that develop naturally among people, without any direction from the organization within which they operate. (p. 275)

informal status The prestige accorded individuals with certain characteristics that are not formally recognized by the organization. (p. 282)

informate The process by which workers manipulate objects by "inserting data" between themselves and those objects. (p. 20)

information anxiety Pressure to store and process a great deal of information in our heads and to keep up constantly with gathering it. (p. 125)

information power The extent to which a supervisor provides a subordinate with the information needed to do the job. (p. 445)

information processing Cognitive effort involving the combination, integration, and use of complex information. (p. 100)

initiating structure Activities by a leader designed to enhance productivity or task performance. Leaders who focus primarily on these goals are described as demonstrating a task-oriented style. (p. 477)

innovation The successful implementation of creative ideas within an organization. (p. 536)

inputs People's contributions to their jobs, such as their experience, qualifications, or the amount of time worked. (p. 202)

insomnia The experience of inadequate and poor-quality sleep. (p. 135)

instant messaging A form of e-mail that allows people who are online to share messages with one another instantaneously. (p. 323)

instrumental conditioning See *operant conditioning*. (p. 56)

instrumentality An individual's beliefs regarding the likelihood of being rewarded in accord with his or her own level of performance. (p. 208)

integrative agreement A type of solution to a conflict situation in which the parties consider joint benefits that go beyond a simple compromise. (p. 422)

intellectual capital Areas of expertise represented by the employees within a company. (p. 70)

interactional justice The perceived fairness of the interpersonal treatment used to determine organizational outcomes. (p. 205)

interactionist perspective The view that behavior is a result of a complex interplay between personality and situational factors. (p. 82)

interest groups A group of employees who come together to satisfy a common interest. (p. 275)

intermittent reinforcement See *partial reinforcement*. (p. 58)

internal causes of behavior Explanations based on actions for which the individual is responsible. (p. 42)

interorganizational designs Organizational designs in which two or more organizations come together. (p. 573)

interpersonal behavior A variety of behaviors involving the ways in which people work with and against one another. (p. 404)

intrinsic task motivation The motivation to do work because it is interesting, engaging, or challenging in a positive way. (p. 531)

invalidating language Language that arouses negative feelings about one's self-worth. (p. 347)

J

jargon The specialized language used by a particular group (e.g., people within a profession). (p. 341)

job A predetermined set of activities a worker is expected to perform. (p. 229)

job characteristics model An approach to job enrichment that specifies that five core job dimensions (skill variety, task identity, task significance, autonomy, and job feedback) produce critical psychological states that lead to beneficial outcomes for individuals (e.g., high job satisfaction) and the organization (e.g., reduced turnover). (p. 214)

Job Descriptive Index (JDI) A rating scale for assessing job satisfaction. Individuals respond to this questionnaire by indicating whether or not various adjectives describe aspects of their work. (p. 151)

job design An approach to motivation suggesting that jobs can be created to enhance people's interest in doing them. (See *job enlargement, job enrichment,* and the *job characteristics model*). (p. 213)

job enlargement The practice of expanding the content of a job to include more variety and a greater number of tasks at the same level. (p. 213)

job enrichment The practice of giving employees a high degree of control over their work, from planning and organization, through implementing the jobs and evaluating the results. (p. 213)

job rotation The practice of transferring employees laterally between different jobs in an organization. (p. 257)

job satisfaction Positive or negative attitudes held by individuals toward their jobs. (p. 148)

job sharing A form of regular part-time work in which pairs of employees assume the duties of a single job, splitting its responsibilities, salary, and benefits in proportion to the time worked. (p. 26)

joint ventures Strategic alliances in which several companies work together to fulfill opportunities that require the capabilities of one another. (p. 574)

K

K.I.S.S. principle A basic principle of communication advising that messages should be as short and simple as possible (an abbreviation for keep it short and simple). (p. 341)

Kelley's theory of causal attribution The approach suggesting that people will believe others' actions to be caused by internal or external factors based on three types of information: *consensus, consistency,* and *distinctiveness*. (p. 43)

knowing–doing gap The tendency for employees to refrain from using the knowledge that's available to them in their company, leading to poor performance. (p. 71)

knowledge management The process of gathering, organizing, and sharing a company's information and knowledge assets. (p. 70)

knowledge managers Individuals who are responsible for organizing the wealth of corporate knowledge represented by its people and ensuring that this information gets used effectively. (p. 71)

L

law of effect The tendency for behaviors leading to desirable consequences to be strengthened and those leading to undesirable consequences to be weakened. (p. 56)

law of telecosm The idea that as computer networks expand, distances become irrelevant. (p. 299)

leader An individual within a group or an organization who wields the most influence over others. (p. 471)

leader match The practice of matching leaders (based on their LPC scores) to the groups whose situations best match those in which they are expected to be most effective according to LPC contingency theory. (p. 492)

leader–member exchange (LMX) model A theory suggesting that leaders form different relations with various subordinates and that their nature can exert strong effects on subordinates' performance and satisfaction. (p. 480)

leadership The process whereby one individual influences other group members toward the attainment of defined group or organizational goals. (p. 471)

leadership development The practice of systematically training people to expand their capacity to function effectively in leadership roles. (p. 502)

leadership motivation The desire to influence others, especially toward the attainment of shared goals. (p. 474)

learning A relatively permanent change in behavior occurring as a result of experience. (p. 55)

learning organization An organization that is successful at acquiring, cultivating, and applying knowledge that can be used to help it adapt to changes. (p. 606)

legitimate power The individual power base derived from one's position in an organizational hierarchy; the accepted authority of one's position. (p. 444)

line positions Positions in organizations in which people can make decisions related to doing its basic work. (p. 553)

linear career The type of career in which someone stays in a certain field and works his or her way up the occupational ladder from low-level jobs to high-level jobs. (p. 235)

LPC Short for "esteem for least preferred coworker," a personality variable distinguishing individuals with respect to their concern for people (high LPC) and their concern for production (low LPC). (p. 491)

LPC contingency theory A theory suggesting that leader effectiveness is determined both by characteristics of leaders (their *LPC* scores) and by the level of situational control they are able to exert over subordinates. (p. 491)

M

Machiavellianism A personality trait involving willingness to manipulate others for one's own purposes. (p. 93)

machine bureaucracy An organizational form in which work is highly specialized, decision making is concentrated at the top, and the work environment is not prone to change (e.g., a government office). (p. 567)

Malcolm Baldrige Quality Award An award given annually to American companies that practice effective quality management and make significant improvements in the quality of their goods and services. (p. 28)

management by objectives (MBO) The technique by which managers and their subordinates work together to set and then meet organizational goals. (p. 607)

matrix organization The type of departmentalization in which a product or project form is superimposed on a functional form. (p. 558)

mechanistic organization An internal organizational structure in which people perform specialized jobs, many rigid rules are imposed, and authority is vested in a few top-ranking officials. (p. 564)

mediation The process in which a neutral party (known as a *mediator*) works together with two or more parties to reach a settlement to their conflict. (p. 420)

meditation The process of learning to clear one's mind of external thoughts, often by repeating a single syllable (known as a *mantra*) over and over again. (p. 135)

mentor A more experienced employee who guides a newer employee (see *protégé*) in learning about the job and organization. (p. 245)

mentoring The process by which a more experienced employee (see *mentor*) advises, counsels, and otherwise enhances the professional development of a new employee (see *protégé*). (p. 245)

mercenary culture In the *double S cube*, this type of organizational culture is characterized by a low degree of sociability and a high degree of solidarity. (p. 520)

metamorphosis stage The third stage of organizational socialization, in which a person becomes a full-fledged member of the organization (e.g., after having completed a training program for new recruits). (p. 244)

middle line Managers who transfer information between higher and lower levels of the organizational hierarchy. (p. 566)

Minnesota Satisfaction Questionnaire (MSQ) A rating scale for assessing job satisfaction in which people indicate the extent to which they are satisfied with various aspects of their jobs. (p. 152)

mission statement A document describing an organization's overall direction and general goals. (p. 538)

mixed-motive situations Contexts in which people are interested in both competition and cooperation to varying degrees. (p. 413)

modeling See *observational learning*. (p. 59)

modular organization An organization that surrounds itself by a network of other organizations to which it regularly outsources noncore functions. (p. 570)

mood An unfocused, relatively mild feeling that exists as background to our daily experiences. (p. 116)

mood congruence The tendency to recall positive things when you are in a good mood and to recall negative things when you are in a bad mood. (p. 118)

morning persons Individuals who feel most energetic and alert early in the day. (p. 98)

morphology An approach to analyzing problems in which basic elements are combined in systematically different ways. (p. 533)

motivating potential score (MPS) A mathematical index describing the degree to which a job is designed so as to motivate people, as suggested by the *job characteristics model*. It is computed on the basis of a questionnaire known as the Job Diagnostic Survey (JDS). The higher the MPS, the more the job may stand to benefit from redesign. (p. 217)

motivation The set of processes that arouse, direct, and maintain human behavior toward attaining some goal. (p. 190)

multinational enterprises (MNEs) Organizations that have significant operations spread throughout various nations but are headquartered in a single country. (p. 14)

multiple domains of intelligence Intelligence as measured in several different ways, such as cognitive intelligence (traditional measures of the ability to integrate and interpret information), emotional intelligence (the ability to be sensitive to one's own and others' emotions), and cultural intelligence (awareness of cultural differences between people). (p. 474)

multiple regression A statistical technique through which it is possible to determine the extent to which each of several different variables contributes to predicting another variable (typically, where the variable being predicted is the behavior in question). (p. 629)

MUM effect The reluctance to transmit bad news, shown either by not transmitting the message at all or by delegating the task to someone else. (p. 337)

mutual service consortia A type of strategic alliance in which two similar companies from the same or similar industries pool their resources to receive a benefit that would be too difficult or expensive for either to obtain alone. (p. 574)

N

naturalistic observation A qualitative research technique in which people are systematically observed in situations of interest to the researcher. (p. 634)

need for achievement See *achievement motivation*. (p. 96)

need hierarchy theory Maslow's theory specifying that there are five human needs (physiological, safety, social, esteem, and self-actualization) and that these are arranged in such a way that lower, more basic needs must be satisfied before higher-level needs become activated. (p. 192)

negative affectivity The tendency to experience negative moods in a wide range of settings and under many different conditions. (p. 87)

negative correlation A relationship between two variables such that more of one variable is associated with less of the other. (p. 628)

negative reinforcement The process by which people learn to perform acts that lead to the removal of undesired events. (p. 57)

negotiation See *bargaining*. (p. 419)

neoclassical organizational theory An attempt to improve on the classical organizational theory that argues that not only economic effectiveness, but also employee satisfaction, should be goals of an industrial organization. (p. 561)

networked culture In the *double S cube*, this type of organizational culture is characterized by high levels of sociability and low levels of solidarity. (p. 520)

networked incubator Partnerships between established companies (often Internet-based firms), which provide valued resources and experience, with start-ups, which are able to develop and market products quickly. (p. 575)

networking A leadership development tool designed to help people make connections to others to whom they can turn for information and problem solving. (p. 504)

newsletters Regularly published internal documents describing information of interest to employees regarding an array of business and nonbusiness issues affecting them. (p. 322)

noise Factors capable of distorting the clarity of messages at any point during the communication process. (p. 319)

nominal group technique (NGT) A technique for improving group decisions in which small groups of individuals systematically present and discuss their ideas before privately voting on their preferred solution. The most preferred solution is accepted as the group's decision. (p. 390)

nonprogrammed decisions Decisions made about a highly novel problem for which there is no prespecified course of action. (p. 361)

nonverbal communication The transmission of messages without the use of words (e.g., by gestures, the use of space). (p. 325)

normative commitment The strength of a person's desire to continue working for an organization because he or she feels obligations from others to remain there. (p. 163)

normative decision theory A theory of leader effectiveness focusing primarily on strategies for choosing the most effective approach to making decisions. (p. 497)

norms Generally agreed on informal rules that guide group members' behavior. (p. 280)

O

objective tests Questionnaires and inventories designed to measure various aspects of personality. (p. 83)

observational learning The form of learning in which people acquire new behaviors by systematically observing the rewards and punishments given to others. (p. 59)

occupation A coherent set of jobs. (p. 229)

old boys network An informal collection of men who wield power within an organization. (p. 248)

online networking The process of establishing potentially helpful business contacts via e-mail. (p. 252)

online surveys Questionnaires presented to people either via e-mail or using a Web site, which they then complete and return to administrators using the same electronic means. (p. 627)

open systems Self-sustaining systems that transform input from the external environment into output, which the system then returns to the environment. (p. 8)

openness to experience A personality variable reflecting the degree to which individuals have intellectual curiosity, value learning, have an active imagination, and are intrigued by artistic endeavors. (p. 395)

operant conditioning The form of learning in which people associate the consequences of their actions with the actions themselves. Behaviors with positive consequences are acquired; behaviors with negative consequences tend to be eliminated. (p. 56)

operating core Employees who perform the basic work related to an organization's product or service. (p. 566)

organic organization An internal organizational structure in which jobs tend to be very general, there are few rules, and decisions can be made by lower-level employees. (p. 564)

organization A structured social system consisting of groups and individuals working together to meet some agreed-upon objectives. (p. 3)

organizational behavior management The practice of altering behavior in organizations by systematically administering rewards. (p. 66)

organizational behavior modification (OB Mod) See *organizational behavior management*. (p. 66)

organizational behavior The field that seeks increased knowledge of all aspects of behavior in organizational settings through the use of the scientific method. (p. 4)

organizational change Planned or unplanned transformations in an organization's structure, technology, and/or people. (p. 587)

organizational chart A diagram representing the connections between the various departments within an organization; a graphic representation of organizational design. (p. 549)

organizational chart A diagram showing the formal structure of an organization, indicating who is to communicate with whom. (p. 333)

organizational citizenship behavior (OCB) An informal form of behavior in which people go beyond what is formally expected of them to contribute to the well-being of their organization and those in it. (p. 408)

organizational commitment The extent to which an individual identifies and is involved with his or her organization and/or is unwilling to leave it. (p. 160)

organizational compassion Steps taken by organizational officials to alleviate the suffering of its employees or others. (p. 120)

organizational culture A cognitive framework consisting of attitudes, values, behavioral norms, and expectations shared by organization members. (p. 515)

organizational design The process of coordinating the structural elements of an organization in the most appropriate manner. (p. 560)

organizational development (OD) A set of social science techniques designed to plan change in organizational work settings for purposes of enhancing the personal development of individuals and improving the effectiveness of organizational functioning. (p. 607)

organizational justice People's perceptions of fairness in organizations, consisting of perceptions of how decisions are made regarding the distribution of outcomes (*procedural justice*) and the perceived fairness of those outcomes themselves (as studied in *equity theory*). (p. 201)

organizational politics Actions by individuals that are directed toward the goal of furthering their own self-interest without regard for the well-being of others or their organizations. (p. 454)

organizational socialization The process through which people move from outsiders to effective, participating members of their organizations. (p. 241)

organizational structure The formal configuration between individuals and groups with respect to the allocation of tasks, responsibilities, and authorities within organizations. (p. 549)

organizational structure The formally prescribed pattern of interrelationships existing between the various units of an organization. (p. 333)

outcomes The rewards employees receive from their jobs, such as salary and recognition. (p. 202)

outplacement programs Systematic efforts to find new jobs for employees who are laid off. (p. 250)

outplacement services Assistance in finding new jobs that companies provide to employees they lay off. (p. 195)

outsourcing The practice of eliminating parts of organizations that focus on noncore sectors of the business and hiring outside firms to perform these functions instead. (p. 598)

outsourcing The process of eliminating those parts of organizations that focus on noncore sectors of the business (i.e., tasks that are peripheral to the organization) and hiring outside firms to perform these functions instead. (p. 21)

overload The condition in which a unit of an organization becomes overburdened with too much incoming information. (p. 343)

overpayment inequity The condition resulting in feelings of guilt, in which the ratio of one's outcomes/inputs is more than the corresponding ratio of another person with whom that person compares himself or herself. (p. 203)

P

partial reinforcement A schedule of reinforcement in which only some desired behaviors are reinforced. Types include fixed interval, variable interval, fixed ratio, and variable ratio. (p. 58)

participant observation A qualitative research technique in which people systematically make observations of what goes on in a setting by becoming an insider, part of that setting itself. (p. 634)

participation Active involvement in the process of learning; more active participation leads to more effective learning. (p. 63)

participative leadership style A style of leadership in which the leader permits subordinates to take part in decision making and also gives them a considerable degree of autonomy in completing routine work activities. (p. 474)

path-goal theory A theory of leadership suggesting that subordinates will be motivated by a leader only to the extent they perceive this individual as helping them to attain valued goals. (p. 494)

Pay Satisfaction Questionnaire (PSQ) A questionnaire designed to assess employees' level of satisfaction with various aspects of their pay (e.g., its overall level, raises, benefits). (p. 152)

pay-for-performance plan A payment system in which employees are paid differentially based on the quantity and quality of their performance. Pay-for-performance plans strengthen *instrumentality* beliefs. (p. 210)

perception The process through which people select, organize, and interpret information. (p. 50)

perceptual biases Predispositions that people have to misperceive others in various ways. Types include the *fundamental attribution error*, the *halo effect*, the *similar-to-me-effect*, the *selective perception*, and *first-impression error*. (p. 46)

performance appraisal The process of evaluating employees on various work-related dimensions. (p. 50)

person oriented leadership See *consideration*. (p. 477)

person sensitivity bias The tendency for people to give others too little credit when things are going poorly and too much credit when things are going well. (p. 381)

person–job fit The extent to which individuals possess the traits and competencies required to perform specific jobs. (p. 83)

personal communication style The consistent ways people go about communicating with others (e.g., the *Noble*, the *Socratic*, the *Reflective*, the *Magistrate*, the *Candidate*, and the *Senator*). (p. 329)

personal identity The characteristics that define a particular individual. (p. 40)

personal power The power that one derives because of his or her individual qualities or characteristics. (p. 445)

personal support policies Widely varied practices that help employees meet the demands of their family lives, freeing them to concentrate on their work. (p. 19)

personality The unique and relatively stable patterns of behavior, thoughts, and emotions shown by individuals. (p. 81)

personalized power motivation The wish to dominate others, reflected by an excessive concern with status. (p. 474)

physical abilities People's capacities to engage in the physical tasks required to perform a job. (p. 105)

physiological needs The lowest-order, most basic needs specified by Maslow's *need hierarchy theory*, including fundamental biological drives, such as the need for food, air, water, and shelter. (p. 192)

position power Power based on one's formal position in an organization. (p. 444)

positive affectivity The tendency to experience positive moods and feelings in a wide range of settings and under many different conditions. (p. 87)

positive correlation A relationship between two variables such that more of one variable is associated with more of the other. (p. 628)

positive reinforcement The process by which people learn to perform behaviors that lead to the presentation of desired outcomes. (p. 56)

power The potential to influence others successfully. (p. 443)

practical intelligence Adeptness at solving the practical problems of everyday life. (p. 101)

pragmatic leadership A type of leadership based on methodically developing solutions to problems and working them through in a thorough manner. (p. 488)

predecision A decision about what process to follow in making a decision. (p. 360)

prejudice Negative attitudes toward the members of specific groups, based solely on the fact that they are members of those groups (e.g., age, race, sexual orientation). (p. 168)

prescriptive norms Expectations within groups regarding what is supposed to be done. (p. 281)

primary prevention A category of stress prevention techniques aimed at eliminating stressors from people's lives. (p. 137)

procedural justice Perceptions of the fairness of the procedures used to determine outcomes. (p. 204)

product organization The type of departmentalization based on the products (or product lines) produced. (p. 556)

production oriented leadership See *initiating structure*. (p. 477)

productive forgetting The ability to abandon unproductive ideas and temporarily put aside stubborn problems until new approaches can be considered. (p. 531)

professional bureaucracy Organizations (e.g., hospitals and universities) in which there are lots of rules to follow, but employees are highly skilled and free to make decisions on their own. (p. 568)

profit-sharing plans Incentive plans in which employees receive bonuses in proportion to the company's profitability. (p. 165)

programmed decisions Highly routine decisions made by lower-level personnel following preestablished organizational routines and procedures. (p. 361)

progressive discipline The practice of gradually increasing the severity of punishments for employees who exhibit unacceptable job behavior. (p. 67)

proscriptive norms Expectations within groups regarding behaviors in which members are not supposed to engage. (p. 281)

prosocial behavior Acts that benefit others. (p. 408)

protégé An inexperienced employee who receives assistance from a more experienced employee in learning about a new job and/or organization (see *mentor*). (p. 245)

psychological contract A person's beliefs about what is expected of another in a relationship. (p. 405)

punctuated-equilibrium model The conceptualization of group development claiming that groups generally plan their activities during the first half of their time together, and then revise and implement their plans in the second half. (p. 278)

punishment Decreasing undesirable behavior by following it with undesirable consequences. (p. 57)

Pygmalion effect A positive instance of the *self-fulfilling prophecy*, in which people holding high expectations of another tend to improve that individual's performance. (p. 48)

Q

qualitative overload The belief that one lacks the required skills or abilities to perform a given job. (p. 125)

qualitative research A nonempirical type of research that relies on preserving the natural qualities of the situation being studied. (p. 634)

qualitative underload The lack of mental stimulation that accompanies many routine, repetitive jobs. (p. 126)

quality circles (QCs) An approach to improving the quality of work life, in which small groups of volunteers meet regularly to identify and solve problems related to the work they perform and the conditions under which they work. (p. 613)

quality control audits Careful examinations of how well a company is meeting its standards. (p. 28)

quality of work life (QWL) An OD technique designed to improve organizational functioning by humanizing the workplace, making it more democratic, and involving employees in decision making. (p. 612)

quantitative overload The belief that one is required to do more work than possibly can be completed in a specific period. (p. 125)

quantitative underload The boredom that results when employees have so little to do that they find themselves sitting around doing nothing much of the time. (p. 126)

R

rally 'round the flag effect The tendency for followers to make positive attributions about their leaders when they appear to be working to keep things together during a crisis situation. (p. 484)

rational decisions Decisions that maximize the chance of attaining an individual's, group's, or organization's goals. (p. 373)

rational persuasion Using logical arguments and factual evidence to convince others that an idea is acceptable. (p. 445)

rational-economic model The model of decision making according to which decision makers consider all possible alternatives to problems before selecting the optimal solution. (p. 373)

realistic job preview The practice of giving prospective employees both positive and negative information about the jobs they are considering and the organizations they will enter. (p. 243)

reciprocity The tendency to treat others as they have treated us. (p. 414)

referent power The individual power base derived from the degree to which one is liked and admired by others. (p. 446)

relational contract A type of psychological contract in which the parties have a long-term and widely defined relationship with a vast focus. (p. 406)

relations-oriented role See *socioemotional role*. (p. 280)

reliability The extent to which a test yields consistent scores on various occasions. (p. 84)

religious intolerance Actions taken against a person or group that follows a different faith (e.g., personal ridicule, vandalism). (p. 173)

repatriation The process of readjusting to one's own culture after spending time away from it. (p. 15)

repetition The process of repeatedly performing a task so that it may be learned. (p. 63)

representativeness heuristic The tendency to perceive others in stereotypical ways if they appear to be typical representatives of the category to which they belong. (p. 378)

resistance to change The tendency for employees to be unwilling to go along with organizational changes, either because of individual fears of the unknown, or organizational impediments. (p. 601)

resource-dependency model The view that power resides within subunits that are able to control the greatest share of valued organizational resources. (p. 452)

retirement The phase of people's lives in which they reach the end of their careers and stop working for their primary income. (p. 254)

reward power The individual power base derived from an individual's capacity to administer valued rewards to others. (p. 444)

rightsizing See *downsizing*. (p. 21)

rightsizing See *downsizing*. (p. 597)

risky choice framing effect The tendency for people to avoid risks when situations are presented in a way that emphasizes positive gains and to take risks when situations are presented in a way that emphasizes potential losses that may be suffered. (p. 376)

role The typical behavior that characterizes a person in a specific social context. (p. 279)

role ambiguity Confusion arising from not knowing what one is expected to do as the holder of a role. (p. 280)

role ambiguity Uncertainty about what one is expected to do on a job. (p. 124)

role conflict Incompatibilities between the various sets of obligations people face. (p. 124)

role differentiation The tendency for various specialized roles to emerge as groups develop. (p. 280)

role expectations The behaviors expected of someone in a particular role. (p. 279)

role incumbent A person holding a particular role. (p. 279)

role juggling The need to switch back and forth between the demands of work and family. (p. 124)

rumors Information with little basis in fact, often transmitted through informal channels (see *grapevine*). (p. 338)

S

sabbatical Time taken off the job, typically for purposes of recharging, coming back fresh, and avoiding potential stress-related problems. (p. 263)

safety needs In Maslow's *need hierarchy theory*, safety needs include the need for a secure environment and to be free from threats of physical or psychological harm. (p. 193)

satisficing decisions Decisions made by selecting the first minimally acceptable alternative as it becomes available. (p. 374)

scapegoat Someone who is made to take the blame for someone else's failure or wrongdoing. (p. 457)

schedules of reinforcement Rules governing the timing and frequency of the administration of reinforcement. (p. 58)

scientific management An early approach to management and organizational behavior emphasizing the importance of designing jobs as efficiently as possible. (p. 10)

second-order change Radical change; major shifts involving many different levels of the organization and many different aspects of business. (p. 589)

secondary prevention A category of stress prevention techniques aimed at minimizing the effects of stress in people's lives. (p. 137)

selective perception The tendency to focus on some aspects of the environment while ignoring others. (p. 47)

self-actualization In Maslow's *need hierarchy theory*, the need to discover who we are and to develop ourselves to the fullest potential. (p. 194)

self-directed teams See *self-managed teams*. (p. 294)

self-efficacy Individuals' beliefs concerning their ability to perform specific tasks successfully. (p. 88)

self-efficacy One's belief about having the capacity to perform a task. (p. 196)

self-fulfilling prophecy The tendency for someone's expectations about another to cause that person to behave in a manner consistent with those expectations. This can be either positive (see the *Pygmalion effect*) or negative (see the *Golem effect*) in nature. (p. 48)

self-managed teams Teams whose members are permitted to make key decisions about how their work is done. (p. 294)

self-monitoring A personality trait involving the extent to which individuals adapt their behavior to the demands of specific situations so as to make good impressions on others. (p. 90)

self-oriented role The activities of an individual in a group who focuses on his or her own good, often at the expense of others. (p. 280)

semiautonomous work groups Work groups in which employees and their bosses get to share in the responsibility for decisions with and are jointly accountable for their work outcomes. (p. 294)

sexual harassment Unwanted contact or communication of a sexual nature, usually against women. (p. 127)

short-term successors Individuals who are considered suitable candidates, at least temporarily, to fill the position of someone who leaves his or her job unexpectedly. (p. 256)

similar-to-me effect The tendency for people to perceive in a positive light others who are believed to be similar to themselves in any of several different ways. (p. 46)

simple structure An organization characterized as being small and informal, with a single powerful individual, often the founding entrepreneur, who is in charge of everything. (p. 567)

situational leadership theory A theory suggesting that the most effective style of leadership—delegating, participating, selling, or telling—depends on the extent to which followers require guidance, direction, and emotional support. (p. 493)

skill-based pay An innovative reward system in which people are paid based on the number of different skills they have learned relevant to performing one or more jobs in the organization. (p. 64)

skills-based diversity training An approach to diversity management that goes beyond *awareness-based diversity training* and is designed to develop people's skills with respect to managing diversity. (p. 179)

snowball effect The tendency for people to share informal information with others with whom they come into contact. (p. 337)

sociability A dimension of the *double S cube* characterized by the degree of friendliness typically found among members of an organization. (p. 519)

social facilitation The tendency for the presence of others sometimes to enhance an individual's performance and at other times to impair it. (p. 284)

social identity Who a person is, as defined in terms of his or her membership in various social groups. (p. 40)

social identity theory A conceptualization recognizing that the way we perceive others and ourselves is based on both our unique characteristics (see *personal identity*) and our membership in various groups (see *social identity*). (p. 40)

social impact theory The theory that explains social loafing in terms of the diffused responsibility for doing what is expected of each member of a group (see *social loafing*). The larger the size of a group, the less each member is influenced by the social forces acting on the group. (p. 287)

social influence Attempts to affect another in a desired fashion, whether or not these are successful. (p. 438)

social loafing The tendency for group members to exert less individual effort on an additive task as the size of the group increases. (p. 287)

social needs In Maslow's *need hierarchy theory*, the need to be affiliative—that is, to have friends, and to be loved and accepted by other people. (p. 193)

social perception The process of combining, integrating, and interpreting information about others to gain an accurate understanding of them. (p. 39)

social support The friendship and support of others, which help minimize reactions to stress. (p. 127)

socialized power motivation The desire to cooperate with others, to develop networks and coalitions. (p. 474)

socioemotional role The activities of an individual in a group who is supportive and nurturant of other group members, and who helps them feel good. (p. 280)

solidarity A dimension of the *double S cube* characterized by the degree to which people in an organization share a common understanding of the tasks and goals about which they are working. (p. 520)

spam Unsolicited commercial e-mail. (p. 320)

span of control The number of subordinates in an organization who are supervised by an individual manager. (p. 552)

spinoff An entirely new company that is separate from the original parent organization, one with its own identity, a new board of directors, and a different management team. (p. 575)

spiral career The type of career in which people evolve through a series of occupations, each of which requires new skills and builds on existing knowledge and skills. (p. 235)

staff positions Positions in organizations in which people make recommendations to others but who are not themselves involved in making decisions concerning the organization's day-to-day operations. (p. 553)

stakeholder Any individual or group in whose interest an organization is run. (p. 600)

standing committees Committees that are permanent, existing over time. (p. 275)

statements of principle Explicitly written statements describing the principle beliefs that guide an organization. Such documents can help reinforce an organization's culture. (p. 526)

status The relative prestige, social position, or rank given to groups or individuals by others. (p. 281)

status symbols Objects reflecting the position of any individual within an organization's hierarchy of power. (p. 282)

steady-state career The type of career, characterized by a lifetime of employment in a single job. (p. 234)

stepladder technique A technique for improving the quality of group decisions that minimizes the tendency for group members to be unwilling to present their ideas by adding new members to a group one at a time and requiring each to present his or her ideas independently to a group that already has discussed the problem at hand. (p. 392)

stereotypes Beliefs that all members of specific groups share similar traits and are prone to behave the same way. (p. 44)

strain Deviations from normal states of human functioning resulting from prolonged exposure to stressful events. (p. 122)

strategic alliance A type of interorganizational design in which two or more separate companies combine forces to develop and operate a specific business. (See *mutual service consortia, joint ventures,* and *value chain partnerships*.) (p. 574)

strategic apex Top-level executives responsible for running an entire organization. (p. 566)

strategic communication The practice of presenting information about the company to broad, external audiences, such as the press. (p. 340)

strategic contingencies model A view explaining power in terms of a subunit's capacity to control the activities of other subunits. A subunit's power is enhanced when (1) it can reduce the level of uncertainty experienced by other subunits, (2) it occupies a central position in the organization, and (3) its activities are highly indispensable to the organization. (p. 453)

strategic decisions Nonprogrammed decisions typically made by high-level executives regarding the direction their organization should take to achieve its mission. (p. 361)

strategic planning The process of formulating, implementing, and evaluating decisions that enable an organization to achieve its objectives. (p. 595)

stress The pattern of emotional states and physiological reactions occurring in response to demands from within or outside an organization. (See *stressor*.) (p. 122)

stress management programs Systematic efforts to train employees in a variety of techniques that they can use to become less adversely affected by stress. (p. 132)

stressor Any demand, either physical or psychological in nature, encountered during the course of living. (p. 122)

structural inertia The organizational forces acting on employees, encouraging them to perform their jobs in certain ways (e.g., training, reward systems), thereby making them resistant to change. (p. 602)

subcultures Cultures existing within parts of organizations rather than entirely throughout them. (p. 518)

substitutes for leadership The view that high levels of skill among subordinates or certain features of technology and organizational structure sometimes serve as substitutes for leaders, rendering their guidance or influence superfluous. (p. 500)

successful intelligence Intelligence that represents a good balance between cognitive intelligence (IQ), practical intelligence, and creative intelligence. (p. 104)

succession planning The systematic attempt to identify possible holders of particular positions ahead of time in preparation for an executive's departure. (p. 255)

suggestion systems Procedures that provide formal mechanisms for employees for presenting their ideas to the company. (p. 345)

support staff Individuals who provide indirect support services to an organization. (p. 567)

supportive communication Any communication that is accurate and honest and that builds and enhances relationships instead of jeopardizing them. (p. 347)

survey feedback An OD technique in which questionnaires and interviews are used to collect information about issues of concern to an organization. This information is shared with employees and is used as the basis for planning organizational change. (p. 609)

surveys Questionnaires in which people are asked to report how they feel about various aspects of themselves, others, their jobs, and organizations. (p. 626)

sweatshops Unsafe and uncomfortable factories where people work long hours for low wages making clothing. (p. 28)

symbols Material objects that connote meanings that extend beyond their intrinsic content. (p. 523)

systemic change A change in one part of an organization that is related to change in other parts of it. (p. 572)

T

tacit knowledge Knowledge about how to get things done. (p. 101)

task force See *ad hoc committee*. (p. 275)

task group A formal organizational group formed around some specific task. (p. 275)

task-oriented role The activities of an individual in a group who, more than anyone else, helps the group reach its goal. (p. 280)

team A group whose members have complementary skills and are committed to a common purpose or set of performance goals for which they hold themselves mutually accountable. (p. 291)

team building Formal efforts directed toward making teams more effective. (p. 304)

team-based rewards Innovative reward systems in which employees are paid on the basis of their team's performance. (p. 65)

team-based rewards Organizational reward systems in which at least a portion of an individual's compensation is based on the performance of his or her work team. (p. 414)

technostructure Organizational specialists responsible for standardizing various aspects of an organization's activities. (p. 566)

telecommuting (teleworking) The practice of using communications technology so as to enable work to be performed from remote locations, such as the home. (p. 22)

tertiary prevention A category of stress prevention techniques aimed at treating stress-related symptoms. (p. 137)

theory A set of statements about the interrelationships between concepts that allows us to predict and explain various processes and events. (p. 624)

Theory X A traditional philosophy of management suggesting that most people are lazy and irresponsible and will work hard only when forced to do so. (p. 6)

Theory Y A philosophy of management suggesting that under the right circumstances people are fully capable of working productively and accepting responsibility for their work. (p. 6)

360-degree feedback The practice of collecting performance feedback from multiple sources at a variety of organizational levels. (p. 63)

time management The practice of taking control over how you spend time. (p. 132)

time-and-motion study A type of applied research designed to classify and streamline the individual movements needed to perform jobs with the intent of finding "the one best way" to perform them. (p. 10)

time-out A brief delay in activities designed to reduce mounting tension. (p. 136)

top-down decision making The practice of vesting decision-making power in the hands of superiors as opposed to lower-level employees. (p. 365)

total quality management (TQM) An organizational strategy of commitment to improving customer satisfaction by developing techniques to carefully manage output quality. (p. 27)

toxic organizational cultures Organizational cultures in which people feel that they are not valued (opposite of healthy organizational cultures). (p. 516)

traditional verbal media Forms of communication that do not depend on the use of computers. (p. 322)

training The process of systematically teaching employees to acquire and improve job-related skills and knowledge. (p. 61)

transactional contract A type of psychological contract in which the parties have a brief and narrowly defined relationship that is primarily economic in focus. (p. 405)

transfer of training The degree to which the skills learned during training sessions may be applied to performance of one's job. (p. 63)

transformational leadership Leadership in which leaders use their charisma to transform and revitalize their organizations. (p. 488)

transitory career The type of career in which someone moves between many different unrelated positions, spending about one to four years in each. (p. 235)

trust A person's degree of confidence in the words and actions of another. (p. 406)

two-dimensional model of subordinate participation An approach to leadership that describes the nature of the influence leaders give followers. It distinguishes between leaders who are *directive* or *permissive* toward subordinates and the extent to which they are *participative* or *autocratic* in their decision making. Individual leaders may be classified into four types in terms of where they fall when these two dimensions are combined. (p. 475)

two-factor theory A theory of job satisfaction suggesting that satisfaction and dissatisfaction stem from different groups of variables (*motivators* and *hygiene factors*, respectively). (p. 153)

two-tier wage structures Payment systems in which newer employees are paid less than employees hired at earlier times to do the same work. (p. 205)

Type A behavior pattern A pattern of behavior involving high levels of competitiveness, time urgency, and irritability. (p. 94)

Type B behavior pattern A pattern of behavior characterized by a casual, laid-back style; the opposite of the Type A behavior pattern. (p. 94)

U

unconflicted adherence The tendency for decision makers to stick to the first idea that comes to their minds without more deeply evaluating the consequences. (p. 387)

unconflicted change The tendency for people to quickly change their minds and to adopt the first new idea to come along. (p. 387)

underpayment inequity The condition resulting in feelings of anger, in which the ratio of one's outcomes/inputs is less than the corresponding ratio of another person with whom that person compares himself or herself. (p. 203)

unfolding model of voluntary turnover A conceptualization that explains the cognitive processes through which people make decisions about quitting or staying on their jobs. (p. 157)

unplanned change Shifts in organizational activities due to forces that are external in nature, those beyond an organization's control. (p. 593)

V

valence The value a person places on the rewards he or she expects to receive from an organization. (p. 208)

validating language Language that makes people feel recognized and accepted for who they are. (p. 347)

validity The extent to which a test actually measures what it claims to measure. (p. 84)

value theory (of job satisfaction) A theory suggesting that job satisfaction depends primarily on the match between the outcomes individuals value in their jobs and their perceptions about the availability of such outcomes. (p. 154)

value-chain partnerships Strategic alliances between companies in different industries that have complementary capabilities. (p. 574)

variable interval schedules Schedules of reinforcement in which a variable period of time (based on some average) must elapse between the administration of reinforcements. (p. 58)

variable ratio schedules Schedules of reinforcement in which a variable number of responses (based on some average) must occur between the administration of reinforcements. (p. 58)

verbal communication The transmission of messages using words, either written or spoken. (p. 321)

video-mediated communication (VMC) Conferences in which people can hear and see each other using computers. (p. 323)

virtual corporation A highly flexible, temporary organization formed by a group of companies that join forces to exploit a specific opportunity. (p. 22)

virtual organization A highly flexible, temporary organization formed by a group of companies that join forces to exploit a specific opportunity. (p. 570)

virtual teams Teams that operate across space, time, and organizational boundaries, communicating with each other only through electronic technology. (p. 297)

voluntary reduced work time (V-time) programs Programs that allow employees to reduce the amount of time they work by a certain amount (typically 10 or 20 percent), with a proportional reduction in pay. (p. 27)

W

wellness programs Company-wide programs in which employees receive training regarding things they can do to promote healthy lifestyles. (p. 131)

whistle-blowing The disclosure by employees of illegal, immoral, or illegitimate practices by employers to people or organizations able to take action. (p. 410)

win-win solutions Resolutions to conflicts in which both parties get what they want. (p. 419)

work restructuring The process of changing the way jobs are done to make them more interesting to workers. (p. 612)

work teams Teams whose members are concerned primarily with using the organization's resources to effectively create its results. (p. 294)

work-related attitudes Attitudes relating to any aspect of work or work settings. (p. 148)

workplace aggression Acts of verbal and physical abuse toward others in organizations, ranging from mild to severe. (p. 425)

workplace bullying The repeated mistreatment of an individual at work in a manner that endangers his or her physical or mental health. (p. 426)

Chapter 1, page 3: Angela Wyant/Deborah Schwartz Reps, page 15: Ki Ho Park/Kistone Photography, page 20: Adam Smith/Getty Images, Inc., page 23: IBM Corporation/Courtesy of International Business Machines Corporation. Unauthorized use not permitted, page 24: Syracuse Newspapers/The Image Works, page 29: AP/Wide World Photos

Chapter 2, page 39: Ken Reid/Getty Images, Inc., page 45: Eyewire/Getty Images/Eyewire, Inc., page 53: Angela Wyant/Getty Images, Inc., page 63: Michael L. Abramson/Timepix, page 72: Donna Terek Photography

Chapter 3, page 82: Ariel Skelley/Corbis/Stock Market, page 84: Roger Ressmeyer/CORBIS, page 87: VCG/Getty Images, Inc., page 89: Mel Yates/Getty Images, Inc., page 106: Steve Chenn Photography/Westlight/CORBIS

Chapter 4, page 118: Mario Tama/Getty Images, Inc., page 110: AP/Wide World Photos, page 125: Etran Kafka

Chapter 5, page 154: AP/Wide World Photos, page 177: John Abbott Photography

Chapter 6, page 191: Robert Baumgardner, page 193: Patricia Barry Levy Photography, page 196: Cindy Charles/Photoedit, page 204: John Sommers/Getty Images, Inc., page 206: Jim Callaway Photography, page 208: Sarah A. Friedman/CORBIS, page 211: AP/Wide World Photos

Chapter 7, page 230: Robert Wright Photography, page 251: John Clark, page 255: Sarah A. Friedman/CORBIS, page 256: Shonna Valeska, page 257: David Young-Wolff/Photo Edit, page 258: Andy Kitchen Photography

Chapter 8, page 274: Ian McKinnell, page 282: Peter Mauss/Esto Photographics, Inc., page 283: Oleg Nikishin/Getty Images, Inc., page 298: Bernstein & Andriulli, Inc., page 307: Macduff Etrerton/CORBIS

Chapter 9, page 331: Spencer Rowell/VCL/Getty Images, Inc., page 345: Chad Slattery/Getty Images, Inc., page 346: Michael L. Abramson Photography

Chapter 10, page 364: AP/Wide World Photos, page 371: Serge Attal/TimePix, page 380: Mark Richards/PhotoEdit, page 391: Cindy Charles/PhotoEdit

Chapter 11, page 409: David Turnley/CORBIS, page 411: Michael Springer/Getty Images, Inc., page 415: New Sabrina Industries, Inc., page 425: Andrew Yates Productions/Getty Images, Inc.

Chapter 12, page 440: Richard Pasley/Stock Boston, page 443: Bonnie Kamin/PhotoEdit, page 455: Douglas Woods Photography, page 459: Steven Peters/Getty Images, Inc., page 460: AP/Wide World Photos

Chapter 13, page 483: Mate 2nd Class Rebecca Kearns/US Navy News Photo, page 489: Norman Parkinsin Limited/Fiona/CORBIS, page 493: Walter Bieri/AFP Photo/CORBIS

Chapter 14, page 515: BMW of North America, LLC, page 517: The Container Store, page 521: Gail Albert Halaban/Corbis/SABA Press Photos, Inc., page 523: CORBIS, page 527: Andy Goodwin/Goodwin Photography, page 530: Chris Chapman Photography, page 535: Jeff Sciortino Photography

Chapter 15, page 557: Steve Liss/TimePix, page 558: Andy Freeberg Photography, page 569: John Abbott Photography, page 574: Rex Rystedt Photography

Chapter 16, page 588: David McNew/Getty Images, Inc., page 589: Peter Blakley/Corbis/SABA Press Photos, Inc., page 594: Anthony Bolante/TimePix, page 597: Paul Souders/Getty Images, Inc., page 606: Shepard Sherbell/Corbis/SABA Press Photos, Inc.

A

ADP, 21
Aetna, 250
Agency.com, 166, 512
Aid Association for Lutherans (AAL), 301
Air Force, U.S., 103, 163
Alberto Culver, 526–28
Alcoa, 345
Allied Plywood Corporation, 165
Allied Signal, 563, 589
Allstate, 178
Alphatronix, Inc., 219
Altrec.com, 306–7
Amazon.com, 597
American Airlines, 196
American Express, 118, 256
American Greetings Corporation, 213
American Red Cross, 523
American Transtech, 301
America Online, 198
Ameritech, 583–84, 589
Ampex Corporation, 308
Andersen Consulting, 227
Anheuser-Busch, 178
AOL, 321, 323, 503, 589
Apple Computer, 62, 363, 445, 487
ARAMARK, 507
Army, U.S., 608
Arrow Electronics, 134
Arthur Andersen, 358, 387
Asahi Bank, 573
AT&T, 19, 64, 173, 181, 195, 244, 250, 264, 324,
    457, 537, 563, 577, 578, 613
Audi, 621
Autobytel.com, 143
Avery Dennison, 55
A.W. Chesterton Co., 65

B

Bain & Co., 92
Baltimore MIMEsweeper, 427
Bank of America, 178, 516, 578
Bank of Boston, 590
Bank of New York, 590
Barclay's, 594
Barnesandnoble.com, 502
BASE Berkshire Hathaway, 474
Bausch & Lomb, 303
Bell Canada, 199
BellSouth, 345
Ben & Jerry's Homemade Ice Cream, 30, 116, 173
Berkeley Systems, 160
Berkshire Hathaway, 55
Best Food, 301
Bestfoods, 474
Beth Israel Medical Center, 173

Blockbuster, 257
Bloomingdales, 558
BlueLight.com, 517
BMW, 514, 515
Body Shop, The, 30
Boeing, 594
Boise Cascade, 218
Borland International, 487
BP Amoco, 412
Breakaway Solutions, 143
BrightHouse, 533
Britannica, 547
British Airlines, 369
British Petroleum (BP), 71
Buckman Labs, 72
Buick, 219, 556
Burmah Castrol, 134–35
Burns & Russell, 590
Business Incubation Group (BIC), 260–61

C

Cadillac, 556
Campbell Soup Company, 196
Canon, 537, 546
Capital One, 160
Caterpillar, 171, 494
CBS, 128, 250
CDW Computer Centers, 160
Cendant, 529
Chapparel Steel, 449
Charles Schwab, 163, 172, 487
Chase Capital, 64
Chesapeake Packaging Company, 365
Chevrolet, 556, 568, 621
Chevron Texaco Corporation, 186–87, 250
Childress Buick, 219
CHP, 90
Chrysler, 27, 196, 255, 297, 369, 416, 437, 486,
    487, 529, 568, 588, 621
Chubb & Son, 249
Circles, 199
Cisco Systems, 64–65, 164
Citibank, 559, 560
Citigroup, 55
Coca-Cola, 159, 177, 227, 250, 363, 486, 533, 577
Colgate-Palmolive, 245, 306, 308
Columbia-HCA Healthcare Corporation, 411
Compaq Computer, 231, 346, 415, 558
CompuServe, 199
Computer Mail Services, 320
Consolidated Diesel, 271–72, 291
Container Store, 516, 517
Continental Airlines, 50, 211–12
Co-operative Bank, The, 29
Corning, Inc., 213, 218, 513–14, 524, 570
Covenant Life Insurance, 590

CUC International, 529
Cummins Engine, 296, 301, 612
Cutler-Hammer, 313–14

D

D. Landreth Seed, 590
Daewoo, 576
Daimler-Benz, 529, 588
Daimler-Chrysler, 181, 348, 436–37, 529, 577, 578
Datex-Ohmeda, 199
Delahaye Medialink, 348–49
Dell Computer, 259, 570
Delta Airlines, 358, 554
Deutsche Telekom, 594
Development Dimensions International, 304
Devine, 269
Dexter, 589, 590
Diamond International, 67
DIRECTV, 512
Disneyland, 250
Dodge, 297
Dow Chemical, 302–3
Dow Corning, 559
Dow Jones, 249
DuPont, 64, 131, 178, 181, 249, 568

E

E. E. Dickinson, 564
Eastman Chemical, 563
Eastman Kodak, 213, 306, 537, 613
Eaton Corporation, 313
eBay, 502
Enron, 28, 120, 231, 358–59, 387, 411, 485
Enterprise Rent-A-Car, 516
Equitable Life Insurance, 132
Ernst & Young, 256, 358
Estée Lauder, 489
Excelsior-Henderson, 414–15
Expedia, 575–76
Exxide Corporation, 255
Exxon, 250

F

Farmitalia, 1
FedEx, 28, 55, 64, 155–56, 178, 301, 358, 489, 597
Fidelity Bank, 64
Florida Power and Light, 64
Ford Motor Company, 27, 145–46, 165, 175, 196,
    250, 301, 416, 459, 573–74, 578, 588, 613

G

Gap, The, 171
Gateway, 570
GE Capital, 540–41
General Dynamics, 55

General Electric (GE), 15, 20, 55, 64, 67, 91, 199, 250, 303, 393, 436, 459, 468, 474, 489, 507, 537, 551, 563, 568–69, 589, 603, 606, 613
General Mills, 67, 301, 345
General Motors Company, 62, 95, 196, 227, 250, 296, 300–301, 416, 449, 537, 554, 556, 557, 568, 573, 576, 621
George R. Ruhl & Sons, 590
Georgia-Pacific, 533
Gillette, 514
Global Learning Systems, 64
GMC, 556
Goldman Sachs, 264
Google, 517
Great Plains Software, 23
Groove Network, 103
GTE Data Services, 196
Gucci, 512

H

Hallmark Cards, 563
Hard Rock Cafe, 135
Harley-Davidson, 415
Harris Corporation, 308
Hershey Foods Corporation, 195, 526
Hewlett-Packard, 164, 231, 250, 294, 345, 363, 415, 554, 558, 605, 608, 613
HFS, 529
Hitachi, 537
Home Depot, 55, 533
Honda, 69
Honeywell, 171, 199, 294, 301
Hong Kong Telecom, 103
Hotbank, 575
Hotlinks, 142
Houston Natural Gas Company, 358
Hughes Aircraft Company, 173, 572
Hughes Electronics Corporation, 468
Hyundai, 573

I

IBM, 22–25, 71, 159, 177, 195, 210–11, 227, 250, 264, 363, 516–17, 528, 537, 573, 608
IDEO, 534, 545–46
IDS, 301–2
InCourage, 614
IndiePlanet, 469–70
Intel Corporation, 55, 554, 573
Intellectual Ventures, 251
Intelligent Electronics, 411
Iridium Satellite System, 382
ITT, 554

J

J.D. Power and Associates, 450
J.E. Rhoads & Sons, 589, 590
Jessica's Inc., 260, 261
John Nuveen & Company, 199
Johnson Controls, 578
Johnson & Johnson, 55, 171, 363, 568

K

Kaiser Aluminum, 247
Kellogg Co., 346
Kendle, 212
Kentucky Fried Chicken, 597
Kikkoman, 35–36
Kmart, 231, 517
Kodak, 250, 546
Kontron, 415

L

Lancaster Laboratories, 18
Landmark Stock Exchange, 68–69
Land Rover, 512
Lawrence Livermore Laboratories, 250

Lee, 547
Lego Systems, 65
Leher McGovern Bovis (LMB), 69
Leonhardt Plating Company, 212
LesConcierges, 198–99
Lexitron, 578
Lexus, 27
Liberty Mutual Insurance, 559, 560
Lockheed, 369
Long Island Lighting Company, 382
Lotus Development Company, 457
LTX, 269
Lucent Technologies, 98, 554

M

Macy's, 120, 366–67, 558
Major League Baseball (MLB), 211
Manistique Papers, 72
Manville Corporation, 459
Marquardt & Roche, 199
Marriott Corporation, 154, 178, 393
Mary Kay Cosmetics, 446, 487
Masimo, 102
Matsushita Group, 14, 573
Mattel, 517
MCA, Inc., 173
McDonald's, 62, 236, 339, 522, 546
MCI, 516, 576
McKinsey & Company, 562
Medi-Health, 188–89
Men's Wearhouse, 516
Mercedes-Benz, 588
Merck, 212, 250, 345
Merrill Lynch, 64, 529
Metropolitan Life Insurance Company, 131, 512
MGM Mirage, 594
Microsoft, 55, 171, 251, 257, 323, 363, 415, 485, 522, 570, 573, 593
Milwaukee Insurance, 306
Mint, U.S., 586–87
M&M Mars, 526
Mobil Oil, 494
Monsanto, 1, 2, 64, 611
Monster.Com, 79–82
Morgan Stanley Dean Witter, 172
Motorola, 62–64, 247, 345, 382, 606
Moviefone, Inc., 503
Mutual Assurance, 590
Mutual of New York, 250

N

Nabisco, 64, 529
Nancy's Quiches, 111–12
NASA (National Aeronautics and Space Administration), 304, 411
NASDAQ, 68
National Basketball Association (NBA), 497
National Football League (NFL), 204, 401–2
Natura Cosmeticos, 29
Navy, U.S., 362–63, 483–84, 537
NBD Bank, 244
NEC, 546, 570, 577
New Jersey Bell Telephone, 317
News Corporation, 487
New York Stock Exchange, 68
New York Yankees, 446–47
Nike, 178, 530, 570
Ninth House Network, 64, 516–17
Nippon Life, 573
Nissan, 27, 576
Nortel Networks, 594
Northern Telecom, 301
Northwestern Mutual Life Insurance Company, 69
NPD Group, 23

O

Odetics, Inc., 195
Okidata, 449
Olive Garden, 512
Olivetti, 578
Omni Hotels, 450
Opel, 576
Open Market, 269, 270
Optus Corporation, 614–15

P

Pace Food, 181
Pacific Enterprises (PE), 178–79
Pacific Gas & Electric (PG&E), 410
Pacific Power and Electric, 160
Pain Webber, 172
Paramount Communications, 570, 572
Patagonia, 3
Payne Firm, Inc., 212
Pella, 27
People Express Airlines, 477
PepsiCo, 294, 328, 597
Pepsi-Cola, 28, 339
Pharmacia AB, 1
Pharmacia Corporation, 1–2
Pharmacia & Upjohn (P&U), 1–2
Philadelphia Contributorship, 590
Philip Morris USA, 92
Philips Electronics, 554
Phone.com, 257
Physician Sales & Service (PSS), 356
Pinkerton Service Group, 346
Pitney Bowes, 181
Pixar Studios, 160
Pizza Hut, 597
Play, 534
Pontiac, 556
Postal Service, U.S., 105–6, 326
Powered.com, 210
Priceline.com, 503
PricewaterhouseCoopers, 366, 367
Prince Corporation, 165
PROACT, 195
Procter & Gamble, 142, 227, 294, 296, 301, 328, 339, 545, 578, 611
Proteon, 269–70
Prudential Insurance Company, 162, 411
Puritan-Bennett Corporation, 303

Q

Quad/Graphics, 199

R

Random House, 583–84
Raytheon, 578
RealNetworks, 228
Red Hat, 257
Reebok, 570
Rhino Foods, 199
Ritz-Carlton, 365
RJReynolds, 529
RJR Nabisco, 213, 529
Rohm and Hass, 301
Royal Bank of Canada, 26
Royal Dutch Shell, 484, 608
Rubbermaid, 514
Rustler, 547
Ryder Truck Company, 163

S

Saab, 214, 512
Safeway, 77–78
Samsung, 546, 573

Sara Lee Corporation, 245, 486
Saturn, 62, 448, 556
SBC Communications, 474
Scient, 143
Scotiabank, 247
Sea-Land Service, 218
Sears, 28, 363, 514, 608
Second City Communications, 535
SEI Investments, 298–99
Senior PGA tour, 255
ServiceMaster, 21, 598
Shanghai Bell, 577
Shanhai Jawa Corporation, 576
Shell Oil, 26, 196, 250
Shenandoah Life Insurance, 301
Sherwin-Williams, 301
ShowWellWithYou, 260
Siemens, 71, 72, 570, 577, 594
Snapple, 160
Softbank Venture Capital, 575
Solectron Corporation, 169
Sony, 363
So So Def, 558
Southern California Edison Company, 195
Southern California Gas Co., 178
Southwest Airlines, 55, 116, 486, 487, 518
Sprint, 62
St. Paul Companies, 55
Stamps.com, 215
Standard Oil, 28
Staples, 198
Starbucks, 29, 403–4
StarMedia Network, 324
State Farm Insurance, 412
Steelcase, 546
Sterling Winthrop, 306
Studio Advantage (SA), 144, 226, 315, 585, 622
Sumitomo Life, 573
Sun Microsystems, 340, 303, 304
Superior Bank FSB, 449

SupplierMarket.com, 228
Synopsys, 156
Synovus Financial Group, 230

T
Taco Bell, 597
TAL, 15
Tape Resources, Inc., 113–14
Tavistock, 301
Tektronix Portables, 301
Tellabs, 181
Tenneco, 589
Tennessee Valley Authority, 62
Texaco, 186–87
Thermos, 307
3Com, 545
3M, 514, 535
Time Warner, 572, 589
TIX, 120
Townsend Agency, 135
Toyota, 27, 363, 570, 589
Toys R Us, 574
Travelers Corporation, The, 131
Traveler's Insurance, 23
TRICON Global Restaurants, 597
Trigon Blue Cross-Blue Shield of Virginia, 65–66
TRW, 558–60

U
Union Pacific Railroad, 131
Unisys, 65
United Technologies, 97
Upjohn Co., 1
UPS, 516
Urban Box Office, 469–70
U.S. Mint, 40–42
US West, 23, 316–17, 393

V
Vanity Fair, 547
Vassarette, 547
Vault.com, 166
Venture Partners, 503
Verizon, 594
VF Corporation, 547–48
Victory, 414
Virgin Group Ltd., 79–80
Visa, 512
Vitro, 570
Volkswagen, 621
Volvo, 301, 307, 588

W
Wal-Mart, 55, 224–25, 514, 606
Walt Disney Company, 159, 255, 487, 516
Warner-Lambert, 64
Washington Public Power Supply System (WPPSS), 380
Weather Channel, 534
Websense, 427
Wendy's, 120
Western Electric, 10
Westinghouse, 64, 301, 537, 613
Weyerhauser, 67, 301
Whirlpool, 37–38
Wilson Barnwell, 195
Wilton Connor Packaging, 19
W.L. Gore, 449
Worldview Systems, 583
World Wide International, 15
Wrangler, 547

X
Xerox, 27, 71, 178, 294, 301, 449–50, 494, 563, 568, 606

Y
Yahoo!, 503, 516

A

Abdalall, Mona, 146
Abeloe, Dave, 3
Alexander the Great, 473
Allen, Paul, 257
Allen, Ronald W., 554
Argyris, Chris, 561
Ash, Mary K., 446, 487
Atchinson, Tonya, 411
Austin, Nancy K., 342–43

B

Ballmer, Steve, 593, 594
Barnard, Dawn-Marie, 114
Barnard, Seph, 113–14
Barnat, Samia, 146
Bethick, Carroll, 526–28
Bethune, Gordon, 50
Bezos, Jeff, 540, 597
Bijur, Peter I., 187
Blacklow, Peter, 80
Borne, Ben, 247
Bossidy, Lawrence, 563
Bowerman, Bill, 525
Boyle, Dennis, 546
Bradley, Bill, 497
Branson, Richard, 79–80
Brokovich, Erin, 410, 411
Broussard, Bruce, 314
Brown, Joe, 483
Bryan, John, 486
Buckeley, Jonathan, 502
Buitenen, Paul van, 411
Burr, Don, 477
Bush, Bill, 411
Bush, George W., 473, 485

C

Calise, Karen, 64
Case, Stephen M., 589
Chambers, John, 164
Chan Suh, 512
Chatter, Mukesh, 98
Chenault, Kenneth I., 256
Cherian, Joy, 173
Childress, Rusty, 219
Christensen, Leif, 72
Cole, David, 468
Cook, Ellen, 589
Cooper, Frank, 470, 471
Costley, Gary, 610
Croc, Ray, 236, 522
Cuban, Mark, 503

D

Dell, Michael, 259, 260
Deming, W. Edwards, 27
DeSimone, Livio D., 535

Diehl, Philip, 586–87
Disney, Walt, 487, 522, 523
Dolida, Roger J., 303
Drucker, Peter, 309, 607–8
Duncan, David, 358

E

Eaton, Robert J., 437
Edison, Thomas, 513
English, Edmond, 120
Espuelas, Fernando, 324

F

Fayol, Henri, 11, 561
Fiorina, Carly, 164
Franklin, Benjamin, 488
Freese, Bob, 219

G

Gadiesh, Orit, 92
Galinsky, Ellen, 19
Garrett, Tim, 69
Gates, Bill, 257, 363, 486, 522, 593, 594
Glenn, John, 473
Godwin, Linda, 304
Goizueta, Roberto, 486
Goldstein, Mark, 517
Goldstein, Sharon, 228
Goleman, Daniel, 102
Golub, Harvey, 256
Green, Harold, 554
Guiang, Cynthia, 135
Guiterrez, Carlos M., 346

H

Hamel, Gary, 540
Hammer, Michael, 562–63
Hantho, John, 614
Hartley, Duane, 605
Hassan, Fred, 1–2
Hitler, Adolph, 487
Hoglund, M., 468
Holtz, Lou, 496
Huxley, Aldous, 91

I

Iacocca, Lee, 486
Ibuka, Masaru, 452–53

J

Jackson, George, 469–70
Jackson, Phil, 497
James, Elizabeth R., 230
Jarecki, Andrew, 503
Jobs, Steven, 487

K

Kahn, Philippe R., 487
Kaplan, Mark, 173

Kelleher, Herb, 486, 487, 518
Kelley, David, 545–46
Kelly, Patrick, 356
Kelly, Tom, 64–65
Kennedy, John F., 488
Kidron, Adam, 470, 471
King, Martin Luther, Jr., 488
Knight, Phil, 525
Koogle, Timothy A., 516
Kozinski, Alex, 427
Kroc, Ray, 236, 522
Kukoc, Toni, 497

L

Lanagdale, Brad, 102
Lawlor, Paula, 188–89
Lay, Ken, 358
Lemmerman, Bruce, 401–2
Lennon, John, 486
Leonard, Thomas J., 364
Levin, Gerald M., 589
Likert, Rensis, 561–62
Lincoln, Abraham, 473
Lloyd, Melissa, 142
Lutz, Robert, 255
Lyone, Jim, 272

M

Mao Zedong, 471
Marcell, Robert P., 569
Marquez, Sandra, 230
Mars, Forrest, 526
Massarsky, Steve, 260–61
Mayo, Elton W., 10
McDonald, Mackey, 548
Mentzer, Josephine E., 489
Morford, Mike, 306–7
Morgan, James, 92
Mueller, Nancy, 111–12
Mullane, Patrick, 227–28
Murdoch, Rupert, 487
Myhrvold, Nathan, 251

N

Nam, Jessica, 260, 261
Napoleon, 486
Neath, Martin, 191

O

Ochalek, Bill, 621
Osborn, Alex, 385
Ozzie, Ray, 102–3

P

Pagonis, William G., 478
Paine, Katie, 348–49
Perot, H. Ross, 454
Pfeiffer, Jeffrey, 71

Pippin, Scottie, 497
Pomerantz, Carrie S., 172
Pottruck, David, 163–64, 541
Powell, Colin, 473
Prefontaine, Steve, 525

Q

Quindlen, Ruthann, 503

R

Rabin, Itzak, 488
Richards, Tuck, 142
Ring, John, 449
Rockefeller, John D., 28
Roosevelt, Franklin D., 446, 487
Rosner, Bob, 167
Rossmann, Alain, 257
Rowley, Coleen, 411
Russomanno, Sonia, 449

S

Savoie, Ernest J., 165
Schmidt, Eric E., 517
Schrempp, Jürgen, 348, 436–37
Schultz, Howard, 403–4
Schwab, Charles, 487

Schwartzkopf, Norman, 487
Scully, John, 328, 445
Shannon, Daniel, 411
Shannon, Kyle, 166–67
Shoemate, C. R., 474
Shomber, Henry, 308
Silverstein, Craig, 517
Simon, Herbert, 365
Skinner, B. F., 56
Sloan, Alfred P., Jr., 554
Smith, Jack, 95, 557
Smith, John, 468
Smith, Michael, 468
Smith, Will, III, 193
Spindler, Michael H., 445
Spivak, Emily, 260
Stefanovich, Andy, 534
Sternberg, Robert, 104
Suh, Chan, 512
Sutton, Robert, 71

T

Taylor, Frederick W., 9–10, 213, 561
Taylor, Jeff, 79–82
Taylor, John, 621
Thomas, Dave, 120

Thornton, Thomas, 583
Toal, Chris, 269–70
Torre, Joe, 446–47

V

van Buitenen, Paul, 411
Villanueva, Diana, 230
Vohra, Lak, 455

W

Walker, Jay, 503
Walton, Sam, 224
Ware, Carl, 177
Watkins, Sherron, 411
Watson, Thomas, Sr., 363
Weber, Max, 561
Weir, Cheryl, 264
Welch, Jack, 436, 489, 502, 568–69
West, Al, 298–99
Whitman, Meg, 502
Wolf, Ron, 496
Woods, Tiger, 255

Y

Yardley-Jones, Tony, 134–35
Young, Robert F., 257, 411

SUBJECT INDEX

A

Abilities, 100, 105–6, 209
See also Intellectual abilities
Absence control programs and reducing stress, 131–32
Absenteeism, 156, 163, 164–65, 450
Abuse, verbal, 425
Academic performance and time of day, 100
Accountability and groups/teams, 292
Achievement motivation, 95–99
Action labs and organizational development, 611–12
Action learning and leadership development, 507
Action plans and organizational development, 608, 609
Adaptability and skills-based diversity training, 179
Adaptive agents and decision-making process, 366–67
Additive group tasks, 287
Adherence and decision-making process, unconflicted, 386–87
Ad hoc committees, 275
Adhocracy and organizational design, 568
Adjourning stage and five-stage model of group development, 278
Administrative model and decision-making process, 373–74
Admired companies, the most, 54, 55
Affective commitment, 162–63
Affectivity, positive/negative, 87–88
Affiliate networks, 570
Affirmative action, 175–76
AFL-CIO, 276
African Americans:
demographics of the workforce, shifting, 17, 18
Texaco, 186–87
weight, stereotypes about, 45
See also Culture, ethnic/national; Diversity; Prejudice; Race/ethnicity/national origin
Age discrimination, 170
Aggression, workplace, 424–28
Agreeableness, 85–87
Aid Association for Lutherans (AAL), 301
Air Force, U.S., 103, 163
Alderfer's ERG theory, 192, 194–95
Alliances, strategic, 574–78
Alternative dispute resolution (ADR), 420–22
Altruism and organizational citizenship behavior, 409
Ambiguity and group processes, role, 280
Ambiguous messages, 341, 342
American Arbitration Association, 422
American Bar Association, 276

American Culinary Federation, 61
American Medical Association (AMA), 276
American Society for Training and Development, 175
Analytical model/style and decision-making process, 359–61, 367
Anchors, career, 240–41
Annual reports, 54–55
Anticipatory socialization, 241–44
Apex and organizational design, strategic, 566
Appraisal, social perception and performance, 50–53
Appraisals, cognitive, 122
Appreciative inquiry and organizational development, 610–11
Apprenticeship programs, 61
Arbitration, 421
Army, U.S., 608
Arousal and motivation, 190
Asian Americans and shifting workforce demographics, 17, 18
See also Culture; Diversity; Prejudice; Race/ethnicity/national origin
Attitudes, 146–48, 181
See also Commitment, organizational; Diversity; Job satisfaction; Prejudice
Attribute framing effect, 376–77
Attribution approach to leadership, 484–85
Attribution process and judging causes of behavior, 39, 41–43
Audits, ethics, 31
Audits, quality control, 28
Australia and teams, 302
Authority:
hierarchy of, 550–51
matrix organizations and dual, 559
teams and structure of, 296–97
See also Power; Structure, organizational
Autocratic leadership, 474, 475–77
Automation, 20
Autonomy:
change, autonomous, 572
creativity, 534
motivation, 215, 218, 219
teams, 292–96
Availability heuristic, 378
Avoidance:
decision-making process and defensive, 387
goal orientation, 97
operant conditioning, 57
Awards to employees, 196
Awareness-based diversity training, 177–79

B

Baby boom generation, 18
Balance and innovation, 537
Bargaining, 419–20, 424–25

Behavior, interpersonal:
conflict
best practices, 422–23
causes of, 416–17
consequences of, 418–19
defining terms, 416
managing, 418, 419–22, 424–25
cooperation
competition *vs.*, 412–14
defining terms, 412
determinants of, 413–14
between organizations, 414–16
personal orientation, 414
reciprocity principle, 413–14
defining terms, 404
deviant organizational behavior
aggression, workplace, 424–28
defining terms, 422
overview, 422
theft, employee, 429–30
varieties of, 423–24
Internet, the, 426–27
organizational culture, 518
overview, 404–5
preview case: Starbucks, 403–4
prosocial behavior
defining terms, 408
organizational citizenship behavior, 408–10
whistle-blowing, 410–13
summary/review of learning objectives, 430–35
varieties of, 405
See also behavior *under* Leadership; Organizational behavior; Organizational culture; Research
Behavioral component of attitudes, 147
Behavioral sciences, 2–4, 6
See also Research
Behavioral style and decision-making process, 367
Benchmarking, 27
Benefits, fringe, 209–10, 212
See also Wages/reward systems
Best practices:
change process, 614–15
communication issues, 348–49
conflict, 422–23
decision making, 362–63
diversity, 178–79
entrepreneurship, 260–61
feedback, 68–69
horizontal organizations, 562–63
innovation, 540–41
leadership, 496–97
needs, motivating by meeting, 198–99
power, 446–47

Best practices: (continued)
  self-efficacy, 90–91
  stress, 134–35
  support policies, employee, 18–19
  teams, 298–99
Biases, perceptual, 46–49
  See also biased nature of individual deci-
     sions *under* Decision making; Social
     perception
Binding arbitration, 421
Blockbuster Leadership and Skills Training
  (BLAST), 257
Boundaryless career, 231
Boundaryless organization, 568–73
Boundary-spanning activities, 91
Bounded discretion/rationality and decision-
  making process, 374
Brainstorming, 385, 386
Brown bag meetings, 346
Brown University, 261
Brunei and organizational development, 615
Buddhists and religious bias, 174
Bullying, workplace, 426–27
Bureaucracy, 11, 561, 567–68
Bureau of Labor Statistics, 25
Burnout and stress, 129–30
BusinessWeek, 171

C

Cafeteria-style benefit plans, 209–10
Calculus-based trust, 406–7
Cambodian-Americans and prejudice, 173
Canada:
  absenteeism, 164–65
  alliances, strategic, 576
  decision making, 370–71
  job previews, armed forces and realistic, 244
Candidate communication style, 330
Career dynamics:
  boundaryless career, 231
  choices, making career
    anchors, career, 240–41
      Holland's theory of occupational choice,
       237–40
    opportunities, job, 241, 242
  contingent workforce, 232–33
  defining terms, 228–30
  established careers, challenges in
    changes, making career, 250–53
    development interventions, 250, 251
    overview, 248–49
    plateau, confronting the career, 249–51
    retirement, 253–55
    succession planning, 255–56
  Internet, the, 227–28, 252–53
  lifetime employment, 230–33
  mentoring
    benefits and costs, 246–48
    defining terms, 245
    development of the process, 245–46
    diverse groups, 248, 249
  preview case: dot.coms *vs.* corporate
    America, 227–28
  socialization, organizational
    anticipatory socialization, 241–44
    encounter stage, 244
    metamorphosis stage, 244–45
  stages, career, 236–37
  successful career, considerations for
    having a
    break, career, 263
    coach, hiring a career, 264
    defining career success, 231–32
    dual-career couples, 262–63
    entrepreneurship, 257–61
    glass ceiling, 260–61

home-based businesses, 259–61
job rotation, 256–57
summary/review of learning objectives,
  264–70
types of careers
  linear, 204–5
  overview, 234
  spiral, 235
  steady-state, 233–34
  transitory, 235–36
Career Orientation Inventory, 241
Case method, 634–35
Causal attribution of responsibility, 42–43
Center for Democracy and Technology, 321
Centralization, 454, 554, 555
CEOs, the power bases of, 447, 448
Ceremonies and transmitting organizational
  culture, 525–26
Certain *vs.* uncertain decisions, 361–62, 364–65
Challenger, 369
Change process:
  autonomous change, 572
  best practices, 614–15
  career dynamics, 250–53
  competition, 593–94, 610–11
  decision-making process, 387, 605
  defining terms, 587
  first-order change, 589
  global phenomenon, 590, 591
  Internet, the, 610–11
  organizational culture, 528–29
  overview, 587–88
  people, changes in, 592–93
  prevalence of change, 588–90
  preview case: US Mint, 586–87
  second-order change, 589
  structure, organizational, 591
  successful companies, 608
  summary/review of learning objectives,
    617–22
  systemic change, 572
  targets: what is changed, 590–93
  technology, 591–92, 595
  unplanned change, 593–96
  See also change-oriented *under* Leadership;
    Design, organizational;
    Organizational development;
    Planning, strategic
Channels of communication, 319
Charisma and personal power, 446
Charismatic leadership as change-oriented
  leadership, 486–88
Charts, organizational, 333–34, 549, 550
Chief executive officers (CEOs), power bases of,
  447, 448
Chief knowledge officer (CKO), 71
Child-care facilities, 18, 263
China, People's Republic of:
  absenteeism, 164–65
  joint ventures, 576–77
  leadership and networking, 504–5
  loafing, social, 288–90
Civic virtue and organizational citizenship
  behavior, 409
Classical organizational theory, 10–11, 561–63
Classroom training, 61
Coach, hiring a career, 264
Coaching as leadership philosophy, 496–97,
  504–6
Coalitions and organization politics, 457
Code of ethics, 30, 526
Coercive power, 444–45
Cognitive appraisal, 122
Cognitive component of attitudes, 147
Cognitive intelligence, 100
  See also Intellectual abilities

Cohesiveness and group processes, 283–84
Collectivistic cultures and social loafing, 288
Collegial organizational culture, 517
Command groups, 274–75
Commerce Clearing House, 177
Commitment, organizational:
  defining terms, 160
  developing, approaches to
    enrichment, job, 164–65
    listening to employees, 166
    profit-sharing plans, 165–66
    recruiting new employees, 166, 167
  escalation of commitment bias and deci-
    sion-making process, 381–83
  goal, 197
  influence, social, 441–42
  summary/review of learning objectives,
    182–84
  teams, 292
  varieties of
    affective, 162–63
    continuance, 161–62
    normative, 162, 163
  why strive for committed workforce, 163–64
Communal organizational culture, 519, 521
Communication issues:
  charisma, 447
  computer-assisted/mediated communica-
    tion, 102–3, 323–24, 393–95
  defining terms, 318
  formal communication, 333–36
  improving communication skills
    best practices, 348–49
    feedback, 345–47
    inspirational tactics, 348–50
    listening, 341–43
    mistakes, dealing with, 348–49
    overload, avoiding, 343–45
    simple/clear language, 341
    supportive communication, 347
  individual differences
    culture, ethnic/national, 332–35
    gender, 331–32
    personal communication styles, 329–30
  informal communication, 333, 336–39
  inside *vs.* outside the organization, 339–40
  Internet, the, 323, 324–25
  nonverbal communication
    defining terms, 325
    dress, style of, 326–27
    guidelines for using popular media, 326
    space, the use of, 328–29
    time, the use of, 327–28
  organizational culture, 516–17
  overview, 317–18
  planning, strategic, 600
  preview case: US West, 316–17
  process, description of, 318–20
  role of communication in organizations,
    320–21
  summary/review of learning objectives,
    350–56, 396–402
  technology, 317, 318, 323–24
  verbal communication
    computer-mediated communication,
      102–3, 323–24
    defining terms, 321
    guidelines for using popular media,
      326
    matching medium to message, 324–25
    traditional media, 322–23
  See also Feedback
Compassion, organizational, 119–21
Compatibility test and decision-making
  process, 374
Competence, social, 104

Competition:
change process, 593–94, 610–11
cooperation vs., 412–14
downsizing, 269
planning, strategic, 599–600
scarce resources and conflict, 416–17
Competitive intelligence (CI), 610–11
Compressed workweeks, 26
Computers:
change process, 596
communication, computer-assisted/
mediated, 102–3, 323–24, 393–95
decision making, 393–95
decision support systems, 360, 362–63
monitoring, 286–87, 427
Conceptual style and decision-making process,
367
Concierge services, motivation and, 198–99
Confidence and improving communication
skills, 348, 349
Confirmation candidate and decision-making
process, 379
Conflict. See under Behavior, interpersonal;
Stress
Conglomerates, 573–74
Conjunctive statements, 347
Conscientiousness:
organizational citizenship behavior, 409
personality, aspect of, 85–87
politics, organizational, 458–59
Consensus/consistency in Kelley's theory of
causal attribution, 43
Consistency and social influence, 441–42
Constructive criticism, 417
Consultation and social influence, 439, 440
Contingencies of reinforcement, 58, 59
Contingency approach, 9, 562–66
See also contingency theories of effective
under Leadership
Contingent workforce, 25–26, 232–33
Continuance commitment, 161–62
Continuous improvement, 91
Continuous reinforcement, 58
Conventional arbitration, 421
Convergence hypothesis, 16
Cooperation. See under Behavior, interpersonal
Core competency, outsourcing and, 21
Corporate image, 53–55
Corporate orientation programs, 244
See also Training
Corporate refugees, 263
Corporate social responsibility (CSR):
comprehensive set of policies, 30
defining terms, 21–22
examples of, exemplary, 29
history of American business, 28
promoting ethical behavior, 30–31
why should companies care about ethical
behavior, 30
Corporate universities, 62
Correlations and survey research, 627–30
Correspondent inferences, 41–42
Corruption, 357–58, 434–35
Counterpower, 448
Country club style of management, 479
Courtesy and organizational citizenship behavior, 409
Covictimization, 169
Creativity:
BMW, 515
culture, ethnic/national, 536–37
individuals and teams
components of team/individual, 530–32
defining terms, 529
model of the creative process, 532–33
skills, domain-/creativity-relevant, 530–31

overview, 514
promoting
environments, developing creative work,
533–35
training, 533
summary/review of learning objectives, 541,
543–46
See also Innovation
Credibility and effective communication, 348
Critical incidents technique for measuring job
satisfaction, 152
Criticism, destructive/constructive, 417
Cross-cultural communication, 332–35
Cross-cultural training (CCT), 61, 62
Cross-functional teams, 296
Cultivation stage in mentoring process, 246
Culture, ethnic/national:
absenteeism, 164–65
communication issues, 332–35
creativity, 536–37
decision making, 370–71, 388–89
emotions, 115–16
empowerment, 450–51
globalization and culture/culture shock, 14–17
intelligence, cultural, 474, 475
Internet, the, 440–41
joint ventures, 576–77
leadership, 504–5
lifetime employment, 232–33
loafing, social, 288
negotiation, 424–25
nonverbal communication, 327
organizational culture, 528, 529
organizational development, 614–16
planning, strategic, 602–3
skills-based diversity training, 179
training, cross-cultural, 61, 62
See also Diversity; Organizational culture;
Prejudice; Race/ethnicity/national
origin
Cyberloafing, 426–27
Cybermeetings, 324
Cybertherapy, 131

D
Decentralization, 554–55
Decision making:
analytical model of, 359–61
approaches to how individuals make decisions
administrative model, 373–74
image theory, 374–75
rational-economic model, 373
STAR approach, 372
best practices, 362–63
biased nature of individual decisions
escalation of commitment bias, 381–83
favorites, implicit, 379
hindsight bias, 379–80
overview, 378–79
person sensitivity bias, 380–81
change process, 387, 605
computer-based approaches, 393–95
culture, ethnic/national, 388–89
defining terms, 358
factors affecting decisions
barriers, organizational, 369–70
culture, ethnic/national, 370–71
group influences, 368–69
style, decision, 365–68
time issues, 369–70, 372–73
groups, 2, 368–69, 383–86, 389–93
imperfections in individual decisions
framing effects, 376–77
heuristics, reliance on, 378
overview, 375–76

improving
computer-based approaches, 393–95
Delphi techniques, 389–90
ethics, 387–89
groups, 389–93
individual decision making, 386–89
nominal group technique, 390–92
overview, 385
stepladder technique, 392–93
training, 386–87
Internet, the, 366–67
justice and employee involvement in, organizational, 206
overview, 358–59
predecision, 360
preview case: Enron-Arthur Andersen scandal, 357–58
spectrum of decisions
certain vs. uncertain decisions, 361–62,
364–65
programmed vs. nonprogrammed decisions, 361–63
top-down vs. empowered decisions, 365
staff vs. line positions, 553–54
unfolding model of voluntary turnover,
157–58
See also Planning, strategic
Decision support systems (DSS), 360, 362–63
Decoding and communication process, 319
Defensive avoidance and decision-making
process, 387
Deficiency needs, 193
Delivering and appreciative inquiry, 611
Delphi techniques and decision-making
process, 389–90
Demographics and unplanned change, workforce, 593
Departmentalization. See under Structure, organizational
Dependent variables, 632
Depersonalization and stress, 129
Depression, The Great, 487
Descriptive approach and decision-making
process, 374
Design, organizational:
boundaryless organization, 568–73
classical and neoclassical approaches,
561–62
contingency approach, 562–66
defining terms, 560
flexibility, 559
interorganizational designs
alliances, strategic, 574–78
conglomerates, 573–74
overview, 572–73
mechanistic vs. organic organization,
564–66
Mintzberg's framework, 566–68
overview, 500–501
See also Organizational development;
Planning, strategic; Structure, organizational
Designing and appreciative inquiry, 611
Desk rage and stress, 129
Destructive criticism, 417
Deviant organizational behavior. See under
Behavior, interpersonal
Dictators and charismatic leadership, 487
Diet and stress reduction, 134
Differentiation and group processes, role, 280
Direct experience and self-efficacy, 88, 89
Direction and motivation, 190
Directive style and decision-making process,
366–67
Disabilities, prejudice and workers with,
170–71

Discipline, 67–70
Discount Store News, 224
Discovery and appreciative inquiry, 610
Discrimination, 168, 169
    See also Prejudice
Disjunctive statements, 347
Dispositional model of job satisfaction, 150–51
Dissonance, emotional, 119
Distinctiveness in Kelley's theory of causal attribution, 43
Distortion and communication process, 344
Distributive justice: equity theory, 201–4
Distrust and conflict, 416
Divergence hypothesis, 16
Divergent thinking, 530, 533
Diversity:
    affirmative action, 175–76
    approaches to positively deal with, two major, 175–77
    best practices, 178–79
    caring about, are companies, 175
    creativity, 535
    group processes, 290–91
    management programs
        awareness-based training, 177–79
        defining terms, 176–77
        pitfalls, avoiding, 180
        skills-based training, 178–79
        success, guidelines for, 180–81
        widespread practices, 177
    mentoring, 248, 249
    organizational behavior, 17–19
    preview case: Terrorist attacks of September 11, 145–46
    work habits of Americans/Europeans, 210–11
    See also Culture, ethnic/national; Prejudice; Race/ethnicity/national origin
Divisional structure and organizational design, 568
Division of labor, 11, 551–52
Domain-relevant skills and creativity, 530
Dominant organizational culture, 518
Doomsday management, 592
Door-in-the face tactic and social influence, 442
Double S cube and identifying organizational culture, 519
Download time, the Internet and, 440–41
Downsizing:
    boundaryless career, 231
    competitive, to remain, 269
    defining terms, 20–21
    economic conditions, changing, 594, 595
    restructuring, work, 597
    stress, 125
Downward communication, 335
Dreaming and appreciative inquiry, 611
Dress, nonverbal communication and style of, 326–27
Dressing for success, 53
Drive theory of social facilitation, 285
Dropping out, 263
Dual authority and matrix organizations, 559
Dual-career couples, 262–63
Dynamic nature of organizations, 8–9

E

Economic conditions and change process, 594, 595, 601, 604–5
Economic growth, achievement motivation and, 98–99
Economic shifts and lifetime employment, 231
Education and overcoming resistance to change, 604–5
Egypt and decision-making process, 371

Elderly, the:
    job satisfaction, 149
    prejudice, 170
    support policies, employee, 18–19, 263
Electronic meeting systems, 102–3, 323–24, 393, 394
E-mail, 320–21, 323, 326
Emergencies and decision-making process, 372–73
Emoticons, 116–17
Emotions:
    culture, ethnic/national, 115–16
    defining terms, 115
    exhaustion, stress and emotional, 129
    inspirational communication tactics, 348
    intelligence, emotional, 102–3, 474
    Internet, the, 116–17
    managing emotions in organizations
        compassion, organizational, 119–21
        emotional dissonance/labor, 118–19
    mentoring, 246–47
    mood, basic nature of, 116–18
    performance, emotions/mood and job, 117–18
    preview case: Tape Resources, Inc., 113–14
    properties, four key, 115
    stability, emotional, 85–87
    summary/review of learning objectives, 138–42
    See also Stress
Employee assistance programs (EAPs), 131, 138
Employee involvement and overcoming resistance to change, 605
Empowerment, 365, 448–50
Encoding and communication process, 318–19
Encounter stage of organizational socialization, 244
Enlargement, job, 213, 216, 613
Enrichment, job, 164–65, 213–14, 216, 613
Entitlements as impression management technique, 54
Entrepreneurship, 89, 227–28, 257–61
Entry shock, 243
Environmental Protection Agency (EPA), 459, 460
Environmental sensitivity and charismatic leaders, 486
Equal Employment Opportunity Commission (EEOC), 173
Equalizers and cooperation, 414
Equitable payment and equity theory, 203
Equity theory, 201–4
ERG theory, Alderfer's, 192, 194–95
Escalation of commitment bias and decision-making process, 381–83
Esteem needs, 193, 196
e-therapy, 131
Ethics:
    decision making, 387–89
    officers, 30
    organizational culture, 526
    organizational development, 616–17
    politics, organizational, 459–63
    See also Corporate social responsibility
Ethnocentric behavior, 16
    See also Culture, ethnic/national; Diversity; Prejudice; Race/ethnicity/national origin
e-training, 64–65
Europeans:
    decision making, 370–71
    work habits of, 210–11
    See also Germany
Evaluation apprehension, 285
Evaluative component of attitudes, 147
Evening/morning persons, 98–100
Exchange and social influence, 439

Excuses as impression management technique, 54
Executive coaching, 504–6
Executive training programs, 61–62
Exercise, 134–35, 193
Existence needs, 194
Expatriates and multinational enterprises, 14
Expectancy theory. *See* expectations, motivating by altering *under* Motivation
Expectations and group processes, role, 279–80
Experimental method. *See* experimental *under* Research
Expert power, 445–46
External causes of behavior, 42–43
External *vs.* internal communication, 339–40
Extinction and operant conditioning, 57
Extraordinary behavior and charismatic leaders, 486
Extraversion-introversion degree, 85–87

F

Face-saving pressure and decision-making process, 370
Face-to-face discussions/meetings, 102–3, 322, 326
Facilitation and group processes, social, 284–87
Facilitation skills and skills-based diversity training, 179
Failure, business, 589
Fairness and ethics of organizational politics, 462–63
    See also Ethics; justice, organizational *under* Motivation
Families & Work Institute, 19
Family, the:
    contingent workforce, 26
    dual-career couples, 262–63
    home-based businesses, 259
    stress, 123–24, 142–43
    support policies, employee, 18–19, 263
Fast-approaching deadline technique and social influence, 442, 443
Favorites and decision-making process, implicit, 379
Faxes, 326
Fear as barrier to change, 602
Feedback:
    best practices, 68–69
    communication skills, improving, 345–47
    criticism, destructive/constructive, 417
    defining terms, 319
    goals, motivating by setting, 200, 201
    job characteristics model, 215, 218
    leadership, 503–4
    organizational development, 609–10
    self-efficacy, 88, 90
    360-degree, 63–64, 68–69, 345, 503–4
    training, 63–64
Field experiments, 633
Final-offer arbitration, 421
Financial security as a safety need, 195
Firing employees, 336
    See also Downsizing
First-impression error, 47–48
First-order change, 589
Five-stage model of group development, 277–78
Fixed interval/ratio schedules of reinforcement, 58
Flat *vs.* tall organizations, 552, 553
Flexibility:
    design, organizational, 559
    diversity training, skills-based, 179
    employees' need for
        compressed workweeks, 26
        contingent workforce, 25–26

flextime programs, 25
hours, different working, 24–25
job sharing, 26–27
overview, 23–24
pets at work, 24
voluntary reduced work time programs, 27
leadership, 473, 474
Fodor's, 583
Ford Foundation, 12
Forgetting and creativity, productive, 531
Formal communication, 333–36
Formal groups, 274–75
Formal status and group processes, 281–82
Forming stage and five-stage model of group development, 277
Fortune magazine, 54, 55, 178, 299
Founders of companies and organizational culture, 522
Fragmented organizational culture, 519, 520
Framing effects and decision-making process, 376–77
France:
    organizational development, 615
    planning, strategic, 603
Friendship:
    group processes, 275
    influence, social, 441
    organizational culture, 517
    planning and resistance to change, strategic, 602
Fun at work:
    creativity, 534, 535
    identifying with the company, employees, 518
    job satisfaction, 159, 160
    motivation, 192
    needs, motivating by meeting, 195–96
Functional organizations, 555–56
Fundamental attribution error, 46

G
Gatekeepers and communication process, 344
Gender:
    bullying, workplace, 426–27
    communication issues, 331–32, 337
    demographics of workforce, shifting, 17
    glass ceiling, 169, 260–61
    job satisfaction, 150
    old-boys network, 248, 337
    prejudice, 171–72
    stress, 132–33
    weight, 45
Germany:
    alliances, strategic, 576
    creativity, 536–37
    ethics and decision-making process, 388–89
    negotiation, 424–25
    planning, strategic, 603
    work habits of America and, comparing, 210–11
Glass ceiling, 169, 260–61
Globalization:
    change process, 590, 591, 593–94
    conglomerates, 573–74
    culture and culture shock, 14–17
    defining terms, 14
    megacorporations, 589
    multinational enterprises, 14
    overview, 13–14
Goal(s):
    feedback, 200, 201
    framing effect, 377
    group processes, 274
    leadership, goal-directed, 471
    orientations, 97–98

planning, strategic, 599
teams, 305
See also goals, motivating by setting *under* Motivation
Golem effect, 49–50
Gordon and Howell Report, 12
Government regulation and unplanned change, 593, 594
Grapevine and communication process, 337–39
Grassroots leadership, 483–84
Graveyard shift, coping with the, 99
Great person theory of leadership, 473
Grid training and leadership, 478–79
Group decision support systems (GDSS), 395
Group processes:
    characteristics of groups, four key, 273–74
    decision making, 2, 368–69, 383–86, 389–93
    defining terms, 272, 273
    development, models of group, 277–79
    diversity, 290–91
    five-stage model of group development, 277–78
    individual performance in groups
        loafing, social, 287–91
        social facilitation, 284–87
    preview case: Consolidated Diesel, 271–72
    punctuated-equilibrium model of group development, 278–79
    structural dynamics of work groups
        cohesiveness, 283–84
        norms, 280–82
        roles, 279–89
        status, 281–83
    summary/review of learning objectives, 309–15
    types of groups
        formal, 274–75
        informal, 275
    why do people join groups, 275–77
    See also group/subunit *under* Power; Teams
Groupthink, 369, 370
Growth needs, 193, 194–95
Growth need strength and job characteristics model, 216
Grudges and conflict, 416

H
Halo effect, 46, 47
Hamburger University, 62
Handbook, employee, 322–23
Harris poll, 171
Harvard Business School, 227
Hawthorne studies, 10
Health issues:
    needs, motivating by meeting, 195
    stress, 130, 131, 134, 145
Healthy organizational culture, 516
Herzberg's two-factor theory on job satisfaction, 153–54
Heuristics:
    creativity, 530–31
    decision making, 378
Hierarchy of authority, 550–51
High-performance teams, 294
Hindsight bias and decision-making process, 379–80
Hindus and religious bias, 174
Hispanic Americans and shifting workforce demographics, 17, 18
    See also Culture; Diversity; Prejudice; Race/ethnicity/national origin
Holland's hexagon, 238, 240
Holland's theory of occupational choice, 237–40
Home-based businesses, 259–61
Homosexuality and prejudice, 172–73

Horizontal communication, 336
Horizontal organizations, 562–63
Hot lines, corporate, 346
Hours, flexibility and different working, 24–25
Hudson River, 459, 460
Human relations movement, 10
Human resources management, politics in, 455–56
HURIER model and communication process, 342–43
Hygiene factors and job satisfaction, 154
Hypervigilance and decision-making process, 386
Hypotheses, 625

I
Iceland and wireless technology, 14–15
Identification, fun at work and company, 581
Identification-based trust, 407
Identity, social, 40–41
    See also Social perception
Image, corporate, 53–55
Image theory and decision-making process, 374–75
Impact theory, social, 287
Implicit favorites and decision-making process, 379
Impression management:
    defining terms, 52
    influence, social, 442
    interview, employee, 52–54
    politics, organizational, 457
    self-monitoring, 90
Improvement teams, 294
Incentive stock option (ISO) plans, 212, 214–15
Incivility, 422
Incubator, 575
Incumbent role, group processes and, 279
Independent variables, 621–22
India and empowerment, 451
Individual differences. *See* Abilities; Intellectual abilities; Personality
Individualists and cooperation, 414
Indonesia and decision-making process, 370–71
Industrialized countries and job satisfaction, 149
Industrial revolution, 588
Inertia, structural/work group, 602–3
Influence, social:
    defining terms, 438
    less desirable forms of, 441
    overview, 437, 438
    popular techniques, 440–41
    power/politics compared to, 439
    preview case: Schrempp, Jürgen E., 436–37
    principles underlying tactics of, 441–43
    protecting yourself from unwanted, 442
    summary/review of learning objectives, 463–67
    tactics of, common, 439
    when are various tactics used, 440
    See also Politics, organizational; Power
Informal communication, 333, 336–39
Informal groups, 275
Informal meetings, 346
Informal status and group processes, 282–83
Informate, 20
Information:
    anxiety, 125
    politics, organizational, 457
    power, 445
    processing, 100–101
    sharing, 316–17. *See also* Communication issues
    technology, 20, 225

Infotech age, 12–13
Ingratiation and social influence/power, 439, 442, 458
Initiation stage in mentoring process, 245–46
Innovation:
    best practices, 540–41
    components of, 536–38
    defining terms, 536
    management, 536–38
    overview, 514
    patents, 537
    preview case: Corning, Inc., 513–14
    rejected ideas, 539
    self-efficacy, 89
    stages of process, 538–40
    summary/review of learning objectives, 542, 545–46
    See also Creativity
Inputs and equity theory, 202
Insomnia, 135–36
Inspirational appeal and social influence, 439
Inspirational communication tactics, 348–50
Instant messaging, 323
Institute for Women's Policy Research, 26
Instrumental conditioning, 56–59
Instrumentality and expectancy theory, 207, 208
Integrative agreement, 422
Intellectual abilities:
    cultural intelligence, 474, 475
    defining terms, 100
    emotional intelligence, 102–3, 474
    information processing, 100–101
    leadership, 474
    number aptitude, 105
    perceptual speed, 105
    practical intelligence, 101–2
    spatial visualization, 105
    successful intelligence, 103–4
    summary/review of learning objectives, 107–12
Intellectual capital, 70
Interactional justice, 205
Interactionist perspective, 82–83, 273
    See also Interpersonal relationships, Behavior, interpersonal
Interests, job satisfaction and matching people to jobs that fit their, 159
Interests and group processes, 274, 275
Intermittent reinforcement, 58
Internal causes of behavior, 42–43
Internal Coach Federation, 264
Internal vs. external communication, 339–40
International Teleworkers Association and Council, 22
Internet, the:
    career dynamics, 227–28, 252–53
    change process, 610–11
    communication issues, 323, 324–25
    culture, ethnic/national, 440–41
    decision making, 366–67
    download time, 440–41
    emotions, 116–17
    incentive stock options, 214–15
    job satisfaction, 166–67
    leadership, 502–3
    loafing, 426–27
    organizational culture, 516–17, 528–29
    spam, 320–21
    stress, 131, 142–43
    teams, 306–7
    telecommuting, 24–25
    training, 64–65
    videoconferencing vs. face-face meetings, 102–3
    virtual organizations, 572–73

Interorganizational designs. See under Design, organizational
Interpersonal relationships:
    change, barriers to, 602
    emotional intelligence, 103
    psychological contracts, 405–6
    self-monitoring, 92
    stress, 123–24
    trust, 406–8
    type A behavior pattern, 95
    See also Behavior, interpersonal
Interviews, impression management and employee, 52–54
Interviews for measuring job satisfaction, 153
Intimidation and decision-making groups, 368
Intranets, 64–65, 324–25
    See also Internet, the
Intrinsic task motivation and creativity, 531
Introversion-extraversion degree, 85–87
Invalidating language, 347
Inventory, decision-style, 367–68
Israel and social loafing, 288–89
Italy and creativity, 536–37

J
Japan:
    communication issues, 333
    conglomerates, 573
    ethics and decision-making process, 389
    lifetime employment, 232–33
    negotiation, 424–25
    performance evaluations, 52–53
    planning, strategic, 602–3
Jargon, improving communication by avoiding, 341
Jargon and transmitting organizational culture, 524–25
Job, definition of, 229
Job assignments and leadership development, 506
Job characteristics model:
    defining terms, 214
    dimensions, five critical job, 214–15, 217
    evidence for the model, 217–18
    growth need strength, 216
    Job Diagnostic Survey, 217
    motivating potential score, 217
    psychological states, three critical, 215–16
    quality of life programs, 613
    techniques for designing jobs that will motivate, 218–19
Job Descriptive Index (JDI), 151–52
Job design:
    See under Motivation; Design, organizational
Job Diagnostic Survey (JDS), 217
Job enlargement, 213, 216, 613
Job enrichment, 164–65, 213–14, 216, 613
Job loss and self-efficacy, 89
Job opportunities, 241, 242
Job previews, realistic, 243–44
Job rotation, 256–57
Job satisfaction:
    defining terms, 148
    dispositional model of, 150–51
    dissatisfaction, consequences of job
        absenteeism, 156
        productivity, 158–59
        turnover, 156–58
    geographic comparisons, 148, 149
    Internet, the, 166–67
    measuring, 151–53
    morale, variety of factors leading to lower, 149, 150
    overview, 148
    promoting, guidelines for, 159–60

    rotation, job, 257
    statistics on, 148–51
    summary/review of learning objectives, 182–86
    theories of
        two-factor theory, 153–54
        value theory, 154–56
    who is satisfied with their job, 149–50
Job sharing, 26–27, 263
Joint ventures, 574–77
Judicial Conference of the United States, 427
Junk words, effective communication and avoiding, 349
Justice. See Corporate social responsibility; Ethics; justice, organizational under Motivation
Justifications as impression management technique, 54

K
Kelley's theory of causal attribution, 43, 44
K.I.S.S. principle and communication process, 341
Knowing-doing gap, 71
Knowledge management, 70–72
Korea and strategic alliances, 576

L
Labor, emotional, 119
Labor, organizational structure and division of, 551–52
Laboratory experiments, 633
Law of effect, 56
Law of telecom, 299
Layoffs and unplanned change, 594, 595
    See also Downsizing
Leader-member exchange (LMX) model, 480–81
Leadership:
    behavior
        developing successful leader, 478–79
        overview, 474–75
        participative vs. autocratic, 475–77
        person-oriented vs. production-oriented leaders, 477–78
    best practices, 496–97
    change-oriented
        charismatic leadership, 486–88
        overview, 485–86
        transformational leadership, 488–90
    characteristics of great leaders, 473–74
    China, People's Republic of, 504–5
    coaching, 496–97, 504–6
    contingency theories of effective
        defining terms, 490
        LPC contingency theory, 491–93
        normative decision theory, 496–500
        overview, 490
        path-goal theory, 494–96
        situational leadership theory, 493–94
    culture, ethnic/national, 504–5
    defining terms, 470–71
    development
        action learning, 507
        executive coaching, 504–6
        feedback, 360-degree, 503–4
        job assignments, 506
        mentoring, 506
        networking, 504–5
        overview, 502
    followers, relationship between leaders and
        attribution approach, 484–85
        grassroots leadership, 483–84
        leader-member exchange model, 480–81
        overview, 471, 479–80
        teams, challenge of leading work, 481–84

Internet, the, 502–3
managers and leaders, distinction between, 471–72
overview, 470
preview case: Urban Box Office, 469–70
substitutes for, 500–502
summary/review of learning objectives, 507–12
trait approach to, 472–74
See also Influence, social; Motivation; Power
Learning:
   applications of learning in organizations
      discipline, 67–70
      knowledge management, 70–72
      organizational behavior modification, 66–67
      reward systems, innovative, 64–66
      training, 61–65
   defining terms, 55–56
   goal orientation, 97–98
   leadership and action, 507
   observational, 59–60
   operant conditioning, 56–59
   summary/review of learning objectives, 73–78
Learning organizations and overcoming resistance to change, 606
Legislation:
   Age Discrimination in Employment Act, 170
   Americans with Disabilities Act (ADA) of 1990, 170
   Federal Clean Air Act of 1990, 22
Legitimate power, 444
Legitimating and social influence, 439
Letters of recommendation, 342
Life span, politics and the organizational, 456–57
Lifetime employment, 230–33
Linear careers, 204–5
Line *vs.* staff positions, 553–54
Linux operating system, 257
Listening:
   commitment, organizational, 166
   improving communication skills, 341–43
Little Engine That Could, The, 98
Loafing, social, 287–91, 426–27
Logic, experimental, 631–32
LPC contingency theory on leader effectiveness, 491–93

M
Machiavellianism, 92–94, 455
Machine bureaucracy and organizational design, 567
Magistrate communication style, 329
Mail, postal, 326
Maintenance and motivation, 190
Maintenance factors and job satisfaction, 154
Malaysia and decision-making process, 370–71
Malcolm Baldrige Quality Award, 28
Management by objectives (MBO), 607–9
Managerial grid and management styles, 479
Managers and leaders, distinction between, 471–72
Maslow's need hierarchy theory, 192–94
Matrix organizations, 558–60
Mature matrix organizations, 559
Mechanistic organization, 564–66
Mediation, 135, 420–21
Megacorporations, 589
Men. *See* Gender
Mentoring and leadership development, 506
   See also mentoring *under* Career dynamics
Mercenary organizational culture, 519, 520
Mergers/acquisitions:
   change process, 588–89

conglomerates, 573–74
organizational culture clashes, 528, 529
Metamorphosis stage of organizational socialization, 244–45
Mexico and empowerment, 451
Middle East and decision-making process, 371
Middle line and organizational design, 566
Middle-of-the-road management style, 479
Minnesota Satisfaction Questionnaire (MSQ), 152
Minorities. *See* Culture, ethnic/national; Diversity; Prejudice; Race/ethnicity/national origin
Mintzberg's organizational design framework, 566–68
Mission statements, 307–8, 538
Mistakes, communication process and dealing with, 348–49
Mixed-motive situations, 413
Modeling, 59–60
Modular organizations, 570
Monitoring, computerized, 286–87, 427
Monitoring, self-, 90–92, 455
Monochromic cultures, 441
Mood states, 87–88, 115, 116–18
   See also Emotions
Morale, variety of factors leading to lower, 149, 150
   See also Job satisfaction
Morning/evening persons, 98–100
Morphology and creativity, 533
Motivating potential score (MPS), 217
Motivation:
   achievement, 95–99
   components of, 190
   creativity and intrinsic task, 531
   defining terms, 190
   emotional intelligence, 103
   expectations, motivating by altering
      applications of expectancy theory, 209–12
      attainable, make desired performance, 209
      basic elements of expectancy theory, 207–9
      cafeteria-style benefit plans, 209–10
      rewards and performance, linking, 210–12, 214–15
   goals, motivating by setting
      commitment, goal, 197
      difficult but acceptable performance goals, 198–200
      feedback, 200, 201
      goal setting theory, 196–97
      managers', guidelines for, 197–200
      specific goals, assigning, 197
   innovation, 536
   job design
      enrichment/enlargement, job, 213–14, 216
      job characteristics model, 214–19
      overview, 212–13
   justice, organizational
      defining terms, 201
      distributive justice: equity theory, 201–4
      interactional justice, 205
      procedural justice, 204–5, 207
      tips for managers, motivational, 205–7
   needs, motivating by meeting
      Alderfer's ERG theory, 192, 194–95
      application of need theories, 195–96
      best practices, 198–99
      Maslow's need hierarchy theory, 192–94
   performance and, distinguishing between, 191
   points about, three key, 191

preview case: Medi-Health, 188–89
summary/review of learning objectives, 219–26
Multidisciplinary roots of organizational behavior, 5, 6
Multifactor Leadership Questionnaire (MLQ), 489
Multinational enterprises (MNEs), 14
Multiple domains of intelligence and leadership, 474
Multiple regression, 629
MUM effect, 336
Muslims and religious bias, 174
Mutual service consortia, 574

N
NASA (National Aeronautics and Space Administration), 304, 369, 411
National Association of Health Underwriters, 252
National Bureau of Economic Research, 45
National Business Incubation Association, 261
Naturalistic observation, 634
Navy, U.S., 362–63, 483–84, 537
Needs, basic human. *See* needs, motivating by meeting *under* Motivation
Negative affectivity, 87–88
Negative correlation, 628
Negative reinforcement, 57
Negative views of employees, 5–6
Negotiation, 419–20, 424–25
Neoclassical organizational theory, 561–63
Networked incubator, 575
Networked organizational culture, 519, 520
Networking as leadership development tool, 504–5
Newsletters, 322
New Yorker, 583
New York Times, 128, 180
New York Yankees, 446–47
New Zealand and strategic alliances, 576
1984 (Orwell), 286
Noble communication style, 329
Noise and communication process, 319–20
Nominal group technique (NGT) and decision-making process, 390–92
Nonverbal communication. *See under* Communication issues
Normative approach and decision-making process, 373, 496–500
Normative commitment, 162, 163
Norming stage and five-stage model of group development, 277–78
Norms and group processes, 280–82
Norms and lifetime employment, social, 231
Northwestern University's Kellogg Graduate School of Management, 228
Norway and creativity, 536–37
Number aptitude, 105

O
Objective tests, 83
Observation, naturalistic/participant, 634
Observational learning, 59–60
Occupation, definition of, 229
Occupational demands and stress, 122–23
Old-boys network, 248, 337
Oldest companies in America, 590
Olympics and emotional dissonance/labor, 119
Omission and communication process, 344
Online networking, 252
   See also Internet, the
Openness to experience, 85–87, 395
Open systems, organizations as, 8–9
Operant conditioning, 56–59

Operating core and organizational design, 566
Operation Desert Storm, 487
Opinion conformity as impression management technique, 54
Opportunities, job, 241, 242
Organic organization, 564–66
Organizational behavior modification (OB Mod), 66–67
Organizational behavior (OB)
  analysis, three levels of, 4–5
  assumptions, field's fundamental, 8–9
  behavioral sciences, 2–4
  classical organizational theory, 10–11
  contingency approach, 9
  defining terms, 3–4
  diversity, response to rise in, 17–19
  dynamic nature of organizations, 8–9
  expectations, response to people's changing
    corporate social responsibility, 28–31
    flexibility, in search of, 23–27
    quality revolution, 27–28
  globalization, response to rise of, 13–17
  history, a capsule
    early days: scientific management and Hawthorne studies, 9–10
    today: the infotech age, 12–13
    twentieth century, late, 12
  importance of knowing about, 6–8
  multidisciplinary in nature, 5, 6
  people-centered orientation, 2
  preview case: Pharmacia Corporation, 1–2
  quality of life, improving effectiveness and, 4
  summary/review of learning objectives, 31–36
  technology, response to, 19–25
  Theory X/Y orientation, 5–7
  See also Behavior, interpersonal; individual subject headings
Organizational charts, 333–34, 549, 550
Organizational citizenship behavior (OCB), 408–10
Organizational commitment. See Commitment, organizational
Organizational culture:
  change, how and why does it, 528–29
  creating, 522–23
  defining terms, 515
  dominant culture, 518
  effects of, 526–28
  healthy, 516
  identifying
    dimensions of, two underlying, 519–20
    overview, 518–19
    questionnaires, assessments using, 521–22
    types of, four, 520–21
  Internet, the, 516–17, 528–29
  overview, 514
  preview case: Corning, Inc., 513–14
  role of culture in organizations, 518
  subcultures, 518
  summary/review of learning objectives, 540–45
  total quality management, 27–28
  toxic, 516
  transmitting, tools for, 523–26
  values reflected in, 515–17
  See also Creativity; Innovation
Organizational design. See Design, organizational
Organizational development (OD):
  action labs, 611–12
  appreciative inquiry, 610–11
  defining terms, 607
  management by objectives, 607–9

quality of work life, 612–13
questions, critical
  culture, dependency on national, 614–16
  effectiveness, 613–14
  ethics, 616–17
survey feedback, 609–10
See also Change process; Design, organizational; Planning, strategic
Organizational justice. See Ethics; justice, organizational under Motivation
Organizational structure. See Structure, organizational
Orientation programs, corporate, 244
  See also Training
Outcomes and equity theory, 202
Outplacement services, 195, 250
Outsourcing, 21–22, 598
Overload and communication process, 343–45
Overload and stress, 124–26
Overpayment inequity and equity theory, 203

P
Partial matrix organizations, 559
Partial reinforcement, 58
Participant observation, 634
Participation and training, 63
Participative leadership, 474, 475–77
Party Digest, 455
Patents, 537
Path-goal theory on leader effectiveness, 494–96
Patience and developing successful teams, 308–9
Pay-for-performance plans, 210–12
  See also Wages/reward systems
Pay Satisfaction Questionnaire (PSQ), 152
PCBs, 459, 460
Perceptions:
  biases, 46–49
  conflict and distorted, 416, 417
  group processes, 274
  See also Social perception
Perceptual speed, 105
Performance:
  change process and gaps in, 593
  computerized performance monitoring, 286–87
  emotions/mood and job, 117–18
  ethics and improved financial, 30
  goal orientation, 97
  Hawthorne studies, 10
  motivation and job, distinguishing, 191
  self-monitoring, 91
  social perception and appraising, 50–53
  stress and task, 128–29
  teams, 294, 414
  See also Motivation; Self-efficacy
Performing stage and five-stage model of group development, 278
Permissive-directive dimension and subordinate participation, 475–77
Personal appeal and social influence, 439
Personal communication styles, 329–30
Personal identity, 40
Personality:
  achievement motivation, 95–99
  affectivity, positive/negative, 87–88
  defining terms, 81
  dimensions of, five big, 85–87
  interactionist perspective, 82–83
  Machiavellianism, 92–94
  measuring, 83–85
  morning/evening persons, 98–100
  overview, 80
  preview case: Monster.Com, 79–80
  role of, 81–83

self, two aspects of the, 88–92
summary/review of learning objectives, 106–12
type A behavior pattern, 94–95
Personalized power motivation, 474
Personal power, 445–46
Personal relationships. See Relationships, interpersonal
Personal support policies, 19
Person-job fit, 83, 237
Person-oriented vs. production-oriented leaders, 477–78
Person sensitivity bias and decision-making process, 380–81
Pets at work, 24
Physical abilities/condition, 105–6, 170–71
Physical exhaustion and stress, 129
Physiological needs, 192–93, 195
Planning, strategic:
  assumptions, basic, 595–96
  culture, ethnic/national, 602–3
  defining terms, 595
  process, ten steps in, 598–600
  products and services, 597, 599
  resistance to change
    defining terms, 601
    individual barriers to change, 601–2
    organizational barriers, 602–3
    overcoming, 604–7
    readiness for change, 603–4
  structure, organizational, 597
  summary/review of learning objectives, 617–20
  what do plans involve, 596–98
  See also Change process; Design, organizational; Organizational development
Plateau, confronting the career, 249–51
Poland and empowerment, 451
Polarization and charismatic leadership, 488
Politics, organizational:
  antecedents of, 455–57
  change, overcoming resistance to, 604
  combating, 462
  defining terms, 439
  effects, their, 458–59
  ethics, 459–63
  face-saving pressure and decision-making process, 370
  influence/power compared to, 439
  overview, 437, 438, 454
  summary/review of learning objectives, 463–67
  tactics, forms of political, 457–58
Polychromic cultures, 441
Pooling resources and decision-making groups, 368
Position power, 443–45
Positive affectivity, 87–88
Positive correlation, 628
Positive reinforcement, 56–57
Postal Service, U.S., 105–6, 326
Power:
  change, resistance to, 603
  decentralization, 554–55
  defining terms, 438
  group/subunit
    overview, 450–51
    resource-dependency model, 451–53
    strategic contingencies model, 453–54
  individual
    empowerment, 448–50
    how it is used, 447–48
    personal power, 445–46
    position power, 443–45
  overview, 437, 438–39
  politics/influence compared to, 439

summary/review of learning objectives, 463–68
See also Influence, social; Leadership; Motivation; Politics, organizational
Practical intelligence, 101–2
Pragmatic leadership, 488
Predecision, 360
Prejudice:
  defining terms, 168
  discrimination and, distinguishing between, 168
  diversity, the reality of, 169
  problems stemming from, 169
  summary/review of learning objectives, 182–87
  types of
    age, 170
    physical condition, 170–71
    race and national origin, 173, 174
    religion, 173–75
    sexual orientation, 172–73
    women, 171–72
Prescriptive approach and decision-making process, 373
Prescriptive norms and group processes, 281
Pressure and social influence, 439
Prevention, primary/secondary/tertiary stress, 137–38
Previews, realistic job, 243–44
Primary stress prevention, 137
Prince, The (Machiavelli), 92–93
Privacy rights and ethics of organizational politics, 461–62
Probabilities, decisions based on objective/subjective, 362, 364
Problem identification and decision-making process, 359–60
Problem-solving and group processes, 305
Procedural justice, 204–5, 207
Production-oriented *vs.* person-oriented leaders, 477–78
Productive forgetting and creativity, 531
Productivity and job dissatisfaction, 158
Product organizations, 556–58
Products and strategic planning, 597, 599
Professional bureaucracy and organizational design, 567–68
Profitability test and decision-making process, 374
Profit-sharing plans, 165–66
Programmed *vs.* nonprogrammed decisions, 361–63
Progressive discipline, 67–69
Proscriptive approach and decision-making process, 374
Proscriptive norms and group processes, 281
Prosocial behavior. *See under* Behavior, interpersonal
Protégé, 245
  See also mentoring *under* Career dynamics
Psychological contracts, 405–6
Psychological impact of prejudice on victims of discrimination, 169
Psychological services to meet physiological needs, 195
Psychological states and job characteristics model, 215–16
Psychopaths, 93
Punctuated-equilibrium model of group development, 278–79
Punishment, 57, 67–70
Pygmalion effect, 48–50

Q

Qualitative overload, 125
Qualitative research. *See* qualitative methods *under* Research

Qualitative underload, 126
Quality circles (QCs), 613
Quality of work life (QWL), 4, 612–13
Quality revolution, 27–28
Quantitative overload, 125
Quantitative underload, 126
Queen Elizabeth I, 473
Questionnaires, 151–52, 521–22
Queuing and communication process, 344

R

Race/ethnicity/national origin:
  alliances, strategic, 577
  communication issues, 324–25
  demographics of the workforce, shifting, 17–18
  job satisfaction, 150
  prejudice, 173, 174
  weight, stereotypes about, 45
  See also Culture, ethnic/national; Diversity; Prejudice
Rally' round the flag effect and leader/follower relationship, 484–85
Rating scales measuring job satisfaction, 151–52
Rational-economic model and decision-making process, 373
Rational persuasion and social influence/power, 439, 445
Realistic job previews, 243–44
Reciprocity and social influence/power, 442, 458
Reciprocity principle and cooperation, 413–14
Recommendation, letters of, 342
Recruitment, employee, 54, 166, 167
Redefinition stage in mentoring process, 246
Redundancy and communication process, 344
Referent power, 446
Reflective communication style, 329
Refreezing and changes in people, 593
Refugees, corporate, 263
Regulation and unplanned change, government, 593, 594
Reinforcement contingencies, 56–59
Relatedness needs, 194
Relational contracts, 406
Relationships. *See* Behavior, interpersonal; Interpersonal relationships
Relations-oriented roles and group processes, 280
Relaxation and stress reduction, 135
Reliability, 83–84
Religion, prejudice based on, 173–75
Repatriation and culture shock, 14, 15
Repetition and training, 63
Repetitive jobs, job satisfaction and avoiding boring, 159
Representativeness heuristic, 378
Reputation, ethics and enhanced corporate, 30
Research:
  experimental
    defining terms, 630
    hypothetical experiment, 630–31
    logic, experimental, 631–32
    valid conclusions, drawing, 632
    variables, independent/dependent, 632
    where are experiments conducted, 632–33
  qualitative methods
    case method, 634–35
    defining terms, 634
    naturalistic observation, 634
    overview, 633–34
  survey
    analyzing results, 627–29
    conducting surveys, 626–27

correlations, limitation of, 629–30
    defining terms, 626
Resource-dependency model of power, 451–53
Resource scarcity and conflict competition, 416–17
Responsibility for others, stress and, 126–27
Restructuring, work, 26, 597, 612–13
  See also Design, organizational; Planning, strategic; Structure, organizational
Retention, ethics and increased employee, 30
Retirement, 253–55
Reward power, 444
Reward systems, learning and innovative, 64–66
  See also Wages/reward systems
Rightsizing. *See* Downsizing
Risky choice framing effect, 376, 377
Roles:
  communication in organizations, role of, 320–21
  culture in organizations, the role of, 518
  expectancy theory, 209
  group processes, 279–89, 304–5
  stress and role conflicts, 124
Rotation, job, 256–57
Rumors, 338–39

S

Sabbaticals, 263
Sacrifices, committed employees making, 163–64
Safety needs, 193, 195
Satisfaction. *See* Job satisfaction
Satisficing decisions, 374
Scapegoating and organization politics, 457–58
Scarce resources and conflict competition, 416–17
Scarcity and social influence, 442
Schedules of reinforcement, 58–59
Scientific management, 2–4, 10, 213
Seating arrangements and nonverbal communication, 328
Secondary stress prevention, 137
Second-order change, 589
Securities and Exchange Commission (SEC), 358
Selective perception, 47
Self-actualization needs, 194
Self-concept, career anchor as person's occupational, 240–41
Self-confidence and charismatic leaders, 486
Self-efficacy:
  achievement motivation, 97
  best practices, 90–91
  components of, three basic, 88
  defining terms, 88
  direct/vicarious experiences and development of, 88, 89
  effects of, 88–89
  entrepreneurship and innovation, 89
  goal-setting theory, 196
Self-esteem nurtured by groups, 276
Self-fulfilling prophecies, 48–50
Selfish interests and ethics of organizational politics, 461
Self-justification and decision-making process, 382
Self-managed teams, 294, 296, 297, 304, 305, 481
Self-monitoring, 90–92, 455
Self-motivation and emotional intelligence, 103
Self-oriented roles and group processes, 280
Self-promotion as impression management technique, 52, 54
Self-talk, reducing stress by avoiding inappropriate, 136
Semiautonomous work teams, 294

Senator communication style, 330
Separation stage in mentoring process, 246
Services and strategic planning, 597, 599
Sex role stereotypes, 171
Sexual harassment, 127–28
Sexual orientation, prejudice based on, 172–73
Sharing, job, 26–27, 263
Short-term successors, 256
Similar-to-me effect, 46
Simple structure and organizational design, 567
Situational constraints, 80
Situational leadership theory, 493–94
Situation-based strategies for overcoming resistance to change, 606–7
Skills:
    creativity, 530
    diversity training, skills-based, 178–79
    expectancy theory, 209
    group processes, 308
    job characteristics model, 214
    pay system, skill-based, 64–65, 306
    See also Abilities; Intellectual abilities
Skip level meetings, 346
Sleep and reducing stress, 135–37
Slogans and transmitting organizational culture, 523–24
Snowball effect and communication process, 337
Sociability dimension of organizational culture, 519–20, 522
Social competence, 104
Social facilitation and group processes, 284–87
Social identity, 40–41
    See also Social perception
Social impact theory, 287
Social influence. See Influence, social; Power
Social interaction and group processes, 273
Socialization, organizational:
    See under Career dynamics
Socialized power motivation, 474
Social loafing, 287–91, 426–27
Social needs, 193, 195–96, 276
Social norms and lifetime employment, 231
Social perception:
    attribution process, 41–43
    defining terms, 38–39
    identities, defining personal, 40–41
    imperfect nature of
        biases, perceptual, 46–49
        self-fulfilling prophecies, 48–50
        stereotypes, 44–46
    organizational applications
        image, corporate, 54–55
        impression management in employee interview, 52–54
        performance appraisal, 50–53
    others like, what are, 39
    preview case: Whirlpool, 37–38
    summary/review of learning objectives, 72–76
Social responsibility. See Corporate social responsibility; Ethics
Social science, organizational behavior as a, 12
Social Security Administration, U.S., 170
Social support, stress and lack of, 127
Society for Human Resource Management, 177
Society of Financial Service Professionals, 426
Socioemotional roles and group processes, 280
Socratic communication style, 329
Solidarity dimension of organizational culture, 520, 522
Space and nonverbal communication, 328–29
Spain and creativity, 536–37
SpamCon Foundation, 321
Spam on the Internet, 320–21

Span of control, 552–53
Spatial visualization, 105
Specialization of labor and decision-making groups, 368
Spinoff, 575–76
Spiral careers, 235
Sports Illustrated, 512
Sportsmanship and organizational citizenship behavior, 409
St. Petersburg Times, 18
Stability, emotional, 85–87
Stability and group processes, 273
Staff vs. line positions, 553–54
Standing committees, 275
STAR approach and decision-making process, 372
Statements of principles and transmitting organizational culture, 526
Status and group processes, 281–83
Steady-state careers, 233–34
Stepladder technique and decision-making process, 392–93
Stereotypes, 44–46
Stories and transmitting organizational culture, 524, 525
Stories as impression management technique, personal, 54
Storming stage and five-stage model of group development, 277
Strategic alliances, 574–78
Strategic communication, 340
Strategic contingencies model of power, 453–54
Strategic decisions, 361, 363
Stress:
    approaches for reducing, three major, 137–38
    causes of
        nonwork and work, conflict between, 123–24
        occupational demands, 122–23
        overload and underload, 124–26
        responsibility for others, 126–27
        role ambiguity/conflict/juggling, 124
        sexual harassment, 127–28
        support, lack of social, 127
    defining terms, 121–22
    effects, major
        burnout, 129–30
        desk rage, 129
        health, 130, 131, 134, 145
        statistics about stress, 128
        task performance, 128–29
    gender differences, 132–33
    preview case: Tape Resources, Inc., 113–14
    reducing
        absence control programs, 131–32
        best practices, 134–35
        diet, healthy, 134
        employee assistance programs, 131
        exercise, 134–35
        individuals managing their own, 132–36
        Internet, the, 131
        management programs, 132
        organizational resources, 131–32, 134
        prevention, primary/secondary/tertiary, 137–38
        reactions, controlling, 136
        relaxation and mediation, 135
        self-talk, avoiding inappropriate, 136
        sleep, 135–37
        time issues, 132–33, 136
        wellness programs, 131
    rotation, job, 256–57
    stressors, 122
    summary/review of learning objectives, 138–44

Tactical Decision Making Under Stress, 362–63
    See also Emotions
Striking in response to inequitable treatment, 205, 206
Structural inertia, 602
Structure, organizational:
    best practices, 562–63
    change process, 591
    charts, organizational, 333–34, 549, 550
    communication issues, 333–36
    decentralization, 554–55
    defining terms, 333, 549
    departmentalization
        functional organizations, 555–56
        matrix organizations, 558–60
        product organizations, 556–58
    division of labor, 551–52
    hierarchy of authority, 550–51
    horizontal organizations, 562–63
    line vs. staff positions, 553–54
    overview, 548
    planning, strategic, 597
    preview case: VF Corporation, 547–48
    span of control, 552–53
    summary/review of learning objectives, 578–84
    See also Design, organizational; Organizational culture; structural dynamics of work groups under Group processes
Subcultures within organizational culture, 518
Subordinate participation, two-dimensional model of, 475–77
Substitutes for leadership framework, 500–502
Success:
    achievement motivation, 96–98
    alliances, strategic, 577–78
    change process, 608
    defined in many different ways, 231–32
    diversity management programs, 180–81
    dressing for, 53
    intelligence, successful, 103–4
    leadership behavior, developing successful, 478–79
    Machiavellianism, 94
    mentoring, 247, 248
    organizational development, 613–14
    self-monitoring, 91–92
    type A/B behavior patterns, 94–95
    See also Organizational development; successful career, considerations for having a under Career dynamics; successful under Teams
Succession planning, 255–56
Suggestion systems, 345
Support, stress and lack of social, 127
Support from management, group processes and, 306–7
Supportive communication, 347
Support policies, employee, 18–19, 263
Support staff and organizational design, 567
Surveys, 346–47, 609–10
    See also under Research
Sweatshops, 28, 29
Sweden:
    creativity, 536–37
    decision-making process, 371
Symbols and transmitting organizational culture, 523
Systemic change, 572

T

Tacit knowledge, 101–2
Tactical Decision Making Under Stress (TAD-MUS), 362–63

Taiwan and modular organizations, 570
Tall *vs.* flat organizations, 552, 553
Task groups, 275
Task identity and job characteristics model, 214–15
Task-oriented roles and group processes, 280
Task performance, stress and, 128–29
Task significance and job characteristics model, 215
Teams:
    authority structure, 296–97
    autonomy, degree of, 292–96
    best practices, 298–99
    change, resistance to, 602–3
    creating, 299–300
    defining terms, 291
    groups and, distinguishing between, 291–93
    high-performance, learning from, 294
    Internet, the, 306–7
    leadership, 481–84
    1980s to today, comparing, 293
    purpose or mission, 294
    successful
        cautionary note: patience required, 308–9
        compensate team performance, 305–6
        cooperation with and between teams, 308
        developing successful teams, keys to, 303–9
        interpersonal skills, 304, 305
        mission, communication about team's, 307–8
        obstacles to success, 302–3
        skills, members selected on basis of, 308
        studies, case/empirical, 300–302
        support from management, 306–7
        team building, 304
        training in team skills, 303–5
    summary/review of learning objectives, 309–15
    time in existence, 294
    types of, 293, 295
    virtual, 297–99
    wages/reward systems, 65–66, 305–6, 414
    See also Group processes
Teamsters, 276
Technology:
    change process, 591–92, 595
    communication issues, 317, 318, 323–24
    Iceland and wireless telecommunications, 14–15
    information, 20, 255
    infotech age, 12–13
    leaner organizations: downsizing/outsourcing, 20–22
    lifetime employment, 230–31
    overview, 19–20
    teams, virtual, 297–99
    telecommuting, 22–25
    virtual organizations, 22, 570, 572–73
    Wal-Mart, 225
    See also Computers; Internet, the
Technostructure and organizational design, 566
Telecommuting, 22–25
Telephones, 326
Temporary employees, permanent, 25–26, 232–33
Temporary matrix organizations, 559
Terrorist attacks of September 11, 14, 120, 145–46, 174, 485, 594
Tertiary stress prevention, 137–38
Thailand and decision-making process, 370–71
Theft, employee, 429–30
Theories and learning about behavior in organizations, 623–26
    See also Research; *individual theories*

Theory X/Y orientation, 5–7, 561
360-degree feedback, 63–64, 68–69, 345, 503–4
Time issues:
    decision making, 369–70, 372–73
    Internet and downloading, 440–41
    nonverbal communication, 327–28
    stress, 132–33, 136
    teams, 294
    time-and-motions studies, 10
Time-outs, 136
Top-down *vs.* empowered decisions, 365
Total quality management (TQM), 27–28
Toxic organizational culture, 516
Training:
    aggression, workplace, 427
    Blockbuster Leadership and Skills Training, 257
    change, overcoming resistance to, 604–5
    coach, career, 264
    creativity, 533
    culture, ethnic/national, 61, 62
    decision making, 386–87
    defining terms, 61
    effective, keys to, 63–64
    expectancy theory, 209
    Internet, the, 64–65
    leadership, 478–79
    orientation programs, corporate, 244
    self-efficacy, 89
    teams, 303–5
    varieties of, 61–63
    See also development *under* Leadership; management programs *under* Diversity
Trait approach to leadership, 472–74
Transactional contracts, 405–6
Trans-Alaskan Pipeline, 412
Transfer of training, 63
Transformational leadership, 488–90
Transition countries and job satisfaction, 149
Transitory careers, 235–36
Trust and interpersonal relationships, 406–8
Turnover, employee, 156–58, 338
Two-factor theory on job satisfaction, 153–54
Two-tier wage structure, 205–6
Two-way communication, 325
Type A/B behavior patterns, 94–95

U
UAW, 276
Unconflicted adherence/change and decision-making process, 386–87
Underload and stress, 126
Underpayment inequity and equity theory, 203
Unemployment and unplanned change, 594
Unfolding model of voluntary turnover, 157–58
Unfreezing and changes in people, 592
Universities, corporate, 62
University of Michigan's Center for Study of Automobile Transportation, 468
Unplanned change, 593–96
Unsolicited commercial e-mail (UCE), 320–21
Upward communication, 335–36
USS Benfold, 483–84
USS Vicennes, 362

V
Valence and expectancy theory, 207, 208
Validating language, 347
Validity, 84, 632
Value-chain partnerships, 574
Values reflected in organizational culture, 515–17

Value theory on job satisfaction, 154–56
Variable interval/ratio schedules of reinforcement, 58
Variables, independent/dependent, 632
Verbal abuse, 425
Verbal communication. *See under* Communication issues
Verification and communication process, 344–45
Vertical job loading, 213, 218–19
Vicarious experience and self-efficacy, 88, 89
Video cases:
    change, organizational, 622
    motivating employees, 226
    stress, 144
    structure, organizational, 585
    teams, 315
Video-mediated communication (VMC), 102–3, 323–24, 393, 394
Virtual organizations, 22, 570, 572–73
Virtual teams, 297–99
Vision and charismatic leaders, 486
Voice recognition technology, 324
Voluntary arbitration, 421
Voluntary reduced work time (V-time) programs, 27

W
Wages/reward systems:
    cafeteria-style benefit plans, 209–10
    change, overcoming resistance to, 605–6
    financial security as a safety need, 195
    incentive stock option plans, 212, 214–15
    innovation, 538
    job satisfaction, 159
    motivation involving things other than money, 191
    organizational justice, 205–6
    pay-for-performance plans, 210–12
    Pay Satisfaction Questionnaire, 152
    profit-sharing plans, 165–66
    skill-based pay system, 64–65, 306
    teams, 65–66, 305–6, 414
    weight, stereotypes about women's, 45
Waste time and decision-making groups, 368
Weight, stereotypes about, 45
Wellness programs and reducing stress, 131
Whistle-blowing, 410–13
White-collar personnel and job satisfaction, 149
White people and weight stereotypes, 45
    See also Culture, ethnic/national; Diversity; Race/ethnicity/national origin
Win-win solutions, 419–20
Wireless telecommunications technology, 14–15
Women, stereotypes about the weight of, 45
    See also Gender
Work attitudes, 148
    See also Diversity; Job satisfaction; Organizational commitment; Prejudice
Workforce demographics and unplanned change, 593
Work habits of Americans/Europeans, 210–11
Work restructuring, 26, 597–98, 612–13
    See also Design, organizational; Planning, strategic; Structure, organizational
Work teams. *See* Teams
Workweeks, compressed, 26
Written messages, 320–21, 323, 325, 326

Z
Zajonc's drive theory of social facilitation, 285